S0-BIH-645

Pro ASP.NET 2.0 in VB 2005

Special Edition

■ ■ ■

Laurence Moroney
and Matthew MacDonald (Ed.)

Apress®

Pro ASP.NET 2.0 in VB 2005, Special Edition

Copyright © 2006 by Laurence Moroney, Matthew MacDonald (Ed.), K. Scott Allen, James Avery, Russ Basiura, Mike Batongbacal, Marco Bellinaso, Matt Butler, Andreas Eide, Daniel Cazzulino, Michael Clark, Richard Conway, Robert Eisenberg, Brady Gaster, James Greenwood, Kevin Hoffman, Erik Johansson, Angelo Kastroulis, Dan Kent, Sitaraman Lakshminarayanan, Don Lee, Christopher Miller, Matt Milner, Jan Narkiewicz, Matt Odhner, Ryan O'Keefe, Andrew Reid, Matthew Reynolds, Enrico Sabbadin, Bill Sempf, Doug Seven, Srinivasa Sivkumar, Thiru Thangarathinam, Doug Thews

All rights reserved. No part of this work may be reproduced or transmitted in any form or by any means, electronic or mechanical, including photocopying, recording, or by any information storage or retrieval system, without the prior written permission of the copyright owner and the publisher.

ISBN-13: 978-1-59059-776-7

ISBN-10: 1-59059-776-1

Library of Congress Cataloging-in-Publication data is available upon request.

Printed and bound in the United States of America 9 8 7 6 5 4 3 2 1

Trademarked names may appear in this book. Rather than use a trademark symbol with every occurrence of a trademarked name, we use the names only in an editorial fashion and to the benefit of the trademark owner, with no intention of infringement of the trademark.

Lead Editor: Ewan Buckingham
Technical Reviewer: Andy Olsen
Editorial Board: Steve Anglin, Ewan Buckingham, Gary Cornell, Jason Gilmore, Jonathan Gennick, Jonathan Hassell, James Huddleston, Chris Mills, Matthew Moodie, Dominic Shakeshaft, Jim Sumser, Keir Thomas, Matt Wade
Production Director and Project Manager: Grace Wong
Copy Edit Manager: Nicole LeClerc
Copy Editor: Kim Wimpsett
Assistant Production Director: Kari Brooks-Copony
Production Editor: Katie Stence
Compositor: Dina Quan
Artist: Kinetic Publishing Services, LLC
Proofreader: Lori Bring
Indexer: Broccoli Information Management
Cover Designer: Kurt Krames
Manufacturing Director: Tom Debolski

Distributed to the book trade worldwide by Springer-Verlag New York, Inc., 233 Spring Street, 6th Floor, New York, NY 10013. Phone 1-800-SPRINGER, fax 201-348-4505, e-mail `orders-ny@springer-sbm.com`, or visit `http://www.springeronline.com`.

For information on translations, please contact Apress directly at 2560 Ninth Street, Suite 219, Berkeley, CA 94710. Phone 510-549-5930, fax 510-549-5939, e-mail `info@apress.com`, or visit `http://www.apress.com`.

The information in this book is distributed on an "as is" basis, without warranty. Although every precaution has been taken in the preparation of this work, neither the author(s) nor Apress shall have any liability to any person or entity with respect to any loss or damage caused or alleged to be caused directly or indirectly by the information contained in this work.

The source code for this book is available to readers at `http://www.apress.com` in the Source Code/Download section. You will need to answer questions pertaining to this book in order to successfully download the code.

I would like to dedicate this book to a few people without whom it never would have been possible.

To Yaacov and Philippe Cohen at Mainsoft, who are remarkable men creating an excellent working environment with God at its center. I appreciate every minute, every conversation, and every e-mail I get from you guys. Thanks!

To my wife, Rebecca, and children, Claudia and Christopher, for their eternal patience and support. Thank you so much!

To the God of Abraham, Isaac, Jacob, and Jesus through whom all things are possible.

—Laurence Moroney

Contents at a Glance

PART 4 ■ ■ ■ Security

PART 5 ■ ■ ■ Advanced User Interface

PART 6 ■ ■ ■ Web Services

PART 7 ■ ■ ■ Client-Side Programming

Contents

PART 3 ■■■ Building ASP.NET Websites

PART 4 ■ ■ ■ Security

About the Author

LAURENCE MORONEY is a technology evangelist, working as a director for Mainsoft, the cross-platform company. A speaker at conferences such as JavaOne, Enterprise Architect Summit, and AjaxWorld, he's also a regular author for DevX (`http://www.devx.com`), The Code Project (`http://www.codeproject.com`), *WebSphere Journal*, *WebLogic Developer's Journal*, and more. He cut his development teeth on security and surveillance systems at casinos, airports, and jails (which are more similar to each other than you may think), and he spent many years working as an enterprise architect in financial, news, and messaging systems and assists companies in making the most of their technology, human, and development assets. Laurence is the author of several books, including *Foundations of Atlas* (Apress, 2006), *Java EE and .NET Interoperability* (Prentice Hall, 2006), and the upcoming *Foundations of WPF* (Apress, 2006). He has recently discovered the joys of fantasy baseball and football, and when not buried in his work or his writing, he can usually be found staring at a spreadsheet trying to figure out the difference between R and RBI.

About the Editor

MATTHEW MACDONALD is an author, educator, and Microsoft MVP. He's a regular contributor to programming journals and the author of more than a dozen books about .NET programming, including *Beginning ASP.NET 2.0 in C# 2005* (Apress, 2006), *Microsoft .NET Distributed Applications* (Microsoft Press, 2003), *ASP.NET: The Complete Reference* (Osborne McGraw-Hill, 2002), and *Programming .NET Web Services* (O'Reilly, 2002). In a dimly remembered past life, he studied English literature and theoretical physics.

About the Technical Reviewer

ANDY OLSEN is a freelance consultant and developer based in the United Kingdom. Andy has been working with Microsoft technologies since about 1990 but considers it to be much more fun these days! He is a regular speaker at conferences in the United Kingdom, Europe, and the United States, and he has also written several courses and white papers for Microsoft. You can contact him at `andyo@olsensoft.com` if you want to discuss .NET, football, or rugby.

Introduction

It's not hard to get developers interested in ASP.NET. Without exaggeration, ASP.NET is the most complete platform for web development that has ever been put together. It far outclasses its predecessor, ASP, which was designed as a quick-and-dirty set of tools for inserting dynamic content into ordinary web pages. By contrast, ASP.NET is a full-blown platform for developing comprehensive, blisteringly fast web applications.

In this book, you'll learn everything you need to master ASP.NET 2.0. If you've programmed with a previous version of ASP.NET, you'll sail through the basics and quickly begin learning about the exciting new features in version 2.0. If you've never programmed with ASP.NET, you'll find that this book provides a well-paced tour that leads through all the fundamentals, along with a backstage pass that lets you see how the ASP.NET internals really work. The only requirement for this book is that you have a solid understanding of the Visual Basic language and the basics of .NET. If you're a seasoned Java or C++ developer but you're new to .NET, you may find it easier to start with a book about .NET fundamentals before you read this one.

ASP.NET from 1.0 to 2.0

As you no doubt already know, ASP.NET is Microsoft's next-generation technology for creating server-side web applications. It's built on the Microsoft .NET Framework, which is a cluster of closely related new technologies that revolutionize everything from database access to distributed applications. ASP.NET is one of the most important components of the .NET Framework—it's the part that enables you to develop high-performance web applications and web services.

ASP.NET 1.0 was a revolution in the web programming world. It was so wildly popular that it was licensed on thousands of commercial web servers through Microsoft's Go-Live license program while it was still a beta product. ASP.NET 1.0 was finally released in early 2002.

ASP.NET 1.1 wasn't as ambitious. Instead, it was just a chance for Microsoft architects to pause and catch their collective breath. The focus in ASP.NET 1.1 wasn't on new features—there weren't any—but on performance tune-ups, security tweaks, and minor bug fixes. New features were quietly shelved and saved for the next major milestone, ASP.NET 2.0. ASP.NET 1.1 was released late in 2003, solidifying ASP.NET as the web development platform of choice for professional developers.

Two long years later, ASP.NET 2.0 finally appeared. Unlike the ASP.NET 1.0 release, ASP.NET 2.0 doesn't represent the start of a new direction in web development. In fact, almost all the underlying architecture that underpins ASP.NET 1.0 remains the same in ASP.NET 2.0. The difference is that ASP.NET 2.0 adds layers of higher-level features to the existing technology. Essentially, after the success of ASP.NET 1.0, Microsoft poured developers, time, and resources into planning and preparing ASP.NET 2.0. Because they no longer needed to rewrite the ASP.NET engine, the ASP.NET team members were free to be innovative with new controls, create better data management solutions, build a role-based security framework, and even make a whole toolkit for creating portal websites. In short, ASP.NET 2.0 gives developers a chance to relax and enjoy a wealth of new frills designed for their favorite platform. In this book, you'll learn how to use, customize, and extend all these features.

Note For an example of ASP.NET's remarkable scalability, consider that MySpace.com recently switched to the ASP.NET platform. (Pages were originally created with ColdFusion, and even though they now run on ASP.NET, many still have the original .cfm extension so as not to break old bookmarks.) At the time of this writing, MySpace.com is the fastest-growing site on the Internet. Each day it registers 260,000 new users, handles 2.3 million concurrent users, and processes 1.5 billion page views.

What Does This Book Cover?

Here is a quick breakdown of what you'll find in this book:

Part 1, "Core Concepts": You'll begin in Chapter 1 with a look at the overall ASP.NET platform, the .NET Framework, and the changes in store for ASP.NET 2.0. In Chapter 2 you'll branch out to learn the tools of the trade—namely, Visual Studio 2005. In Chapters 3, 4, 5, and 6 you'll learn the key parts of the ASP.NET infrastructure, such as the web-page model, application configuration, state management, and caching. As you learn these core concepts, you'll take a low-level look at how ASP.NET processes requests and manages the lifetime of your web applications. You'll even learn how to extend the ASP.NET architecture.

Part 2, "Data Access": This part tackles one of the core problem domains for all software development—accessing and manipulating data. In Chapters 7 and 8 you'll consider the fundamentals of ADO.NET as they apply to web applications and learn how to design data access components. In Chapter 9 and Chapter 10 you'll learn about ASP.NET's set of innovative data-bound controls that let you format and present data without writing pages of code. Chapter 11 branches out into advanced caching strategies that ensure blistering performance. Finally, Chapters 12 and 13 move beyond the world of databases to show you how to work with XML content and handle ordinary file access.

Part 3, "Building ASP.NET Websites": In this part you'll learn about essential techniques and features for managing groups of web pages. You'll start simply with user controls in Chapter 14, which allow you to reuse segments of the user interface. In Chapter 15 you'll consider two new ASP.NET innovations—themes (for styling controls automatically) and master pages (for reusing a layout template across multiple pages). Chapter 16 shows how you can use the new navigation model in ASP.NET 2.0 to let visitors surf from one page to another. Finally, Chapter 17 explores localization, and Chapter 18 describes deployment and the IIS web server software.

Part 4, "Security": In this part you'll look at ASP.NET's rich complement of security features. You'll start with a high-level overview of security concepts in Chapter 19 and then learn the ins and outs of forms authentication (Chapter 20) and the new membership API that works with it (Chapter 21). In Chapter 22 you'll tackle Windows authentication, and in Chapter 23 you'll learn how to restrict authenticated users with sophisticated authorization rules and use role-based security. In Chapter 24 you'll explore the profiles API, which is a new, prebuilt solution for storing user-specific information, and in Chapter 25 you'll go one step further and learn how to protect the data you store in a database as well as the information you send in a URL with encryption. Finally, Chapter 26 shows how you can plug into the ASP.NET security model by designing a custom membership provider.

Part 5, "Advanced User Interface": This part shows how you can extend web pages with advanced techniques. In Chapters 27 and 28 you'll tackle custom controls. In Chapter 29 you'll branch out to use GDI+ for handcrafted graphics. Finally, Chapter 30 explores the ASP.NET 2.0 Web Parts Framework for creating flexible web portals.

Part 6, "Web Services": Web services promise to revolutionize the way functionality is shared across different applications, network environments, and computing platforms. In Chapter 31 you'll start at the beginning; you'll see how to create basic web services and how to use them in ASP.NET web applications, .NET Windows applications, and even legacy ASP applications. In Chapter 32 you'll take a low-level look at the standards that make it all possible and see how they work. In Chapter 33 you'll learn how to use advanced techniques to call web services asynchronously, implement secure services, and start working with newer web service standards using the WSE (Web Services Enhancements) toolkit.

Part 7, "Client-Side Programming": Recently, Ajax and other client-side scripting techniques have allowed programmers to create next-generation web applications that are slicker and more responsive than traditional websites. In this part, you'll learn how to incorporate these techniques into your ASP.NET pages. You'll start with handwritten JavaScript code and the ASP.NET callback feature (in Chapter 34) and then move on to Microsoft's emerging Atlas platform (in Chapter 35), which provides a rich API for accessing Ajax features in ASP.NET applications.

What's New in the Special Edition

When *Pro ASP.NET 2.0 in VB 2005* was first released, it quickly became the reference of choice for professional ASP.NET developers. But the web development world doesn't stand still—since the original publication of *Pro ASP.NET 2.0 in VB 2005*, the landscape has continued to change. Microsoft has released incremental add-ins to Visual Studio (such as Web Application Projects and Web Deployment Projects, both of which are covered in this book) and is hard at work building the infrastructure for the next generation of web applications with its Atlas technology. *Pro ASP.NET 2.0 in VB 2005, Special Edition* addresses these areas and adds new content that's designed to take developers to the cutting edge of ASP.NET development.

Some of the topics that are new to this edition (or greatly expanded) include the following:

- **Ajax techniques**, including a comparison of do-it-yourself callbacks and the ASP.NET client callback feature (in Chapter 34).
- **Atlas**, the new ASP.NET technology that's still under development but is already generating intense excitement among developers. Atlas is a set of client-side libraries and server-side .NET classes that let you use advanced Ajax techniques to create more responsive ASP.NET pages. You can also use Atlas to produce one-of-a-kind client-side effects such as drag-and-drop functionality and automatic completion. You'll get the lowdown in Chapter 35.

We made these changes to ensure that this book continues to be the most comprehensive resource for professional ASP.NET developers.

What's Included on the Bonus CD

This special edition includes a bonus CD with additional content in PDF. This content includes the following:

- A carefully selected sampler of chapters from 18 other *Pro* and *Expert* books from the Apress library, including advanced books about ASP.NET 2.0 and SQL Server 2005. These chapters total more than 1,500 information-rich pages in eBook form, with complementary examples at `http://www.apress.com`.
- Thirty-three complete ASPToday.com articles in eBook form. These articles deal with advanced ASP.NET 2.0 and SQL Server 2005 topics.
- A full selection of our .NET 2.0 road maps that illustrate how you, the reader, can link together Apress books to chart a path for custom learning.

Note The bonus CD doesn't contain the code samples for this book. Instead, these samples are available as a separate download from `http://www.prosetech.com` or `http://www.apress.com`. (See the "Sample Code" section later in this introduction for more information.) By keeping the sample code separate, we ensure that you always get the most up-to-date versions, even as prerelease technologies such as Atlas change.

Who Is This Book For?

This book is intended as a primer for professional developers who have a reasonable knowledge of server-side web development. This book doesn't provide an exhaustive look at every ingredient in the .NET Framework—in fact, such a book would require twice as many pages. Instead, this book aims to provide a lean, intelligent introduction to ASP.NET for professional programmers who don't want to rehash the basics. Along the way, you'll focus on other parts of the .NET Framework that you'll need in order to build professional web applications, including data access and XML. Using these features, you'll be able to create next-generation websites with the best tools on hand today.

This book is also relentlessly practical. You won't just learn about *features*; you'll also learn about the real-world *techniques* that can take your website to the next level. Later chapters are dedicated to cutting-edge topics such as custom controls, dynamic graphics, advanced security, and high-performance data access, all with the goal of giving you everything you need to build professional web applications.

To get the most from this book, you should be familiar with the syntax of the C# language and with object-oriented concepts. You don't need to have experience with a previous version of ASP.NET, because all the fundamentals are covered in this book.

What Do You Need to Use This Book?

The main prerequisite for this book is a computer with Visual Studio 2005. Although you could theoretically write code by hand, the sheer tedium of this and the likelihood of error mean this approach is never used in a professional environment.

Note You can use the scaled-down Visual Studio Web Developer 2005 Express Edition, but you'll run into significant limitations on some of the examples. Most important, you can't use Visual Studio Web Developer 2005 Express Edition to create class libraries, which are an essential part of modern component-oriented design.

Additionally, to run ASP.NET pages, you need Windows 2000 Professional, Windows XP Professional, Windows 2000 Server, or Windows Server 2003. You also need to install IIS (Internet Information Services), the web hosting software that's part of the Windows operating system, if you want to create web services or test deployment strategies.

Finally, this book has several examples that use sample databases that are included with SQL Server to demonstrate data access code, security techniques, and web services. If you use other relational database engines, the same concepts will apply, but you will need to modify the example code.

Customer Support

We always value hearing from our readers, and we want to know what you think about this book—what you liked, what you didn't like, and what you think we can do better next time. You can send your comments by e-mail to `feedback@apress.com`. Please be sure to mention the book title in your message.

Sample Code

To download the sample code, visit `http://www.prosetech.com` or the Source Code/Download section of the Apress site at `http://www.apress.com`. In either case, select this book's title to download the sample code, which is compressed in a single ZIP file. Before you use the code, you'll need to uncompress it using a utility such as WinZip. Code is arranged into separate directories by chapter. Before using the code, refer to the accompanying readme.txt file for information about other prerequisites and considerations.

Errata

We've made every effort to make sure the text and the code contain no errors. However, no one is perfect, and mistakes do occur. If you find an error in the book, such as a spelling mistake or a faulty piece of code, we would be grateful to hear about it. By sending in errata, you may save another reader hours of frustration, and you'll be helping us to provide higher-quality information. Simply e-mail the problem to `support@apress.com`, where your information will be checked and posted on the errata page or used in subsequent editions of the book. You can view errata from the book's detail page.

PART 1

Core Concepts

CHAPTER 1

Introducing ASP.NET

When Microsoft created .NET, it wasn't just dreaming about the future—it was also worrying about the headaches and limitations of the current generation of web development technologies. Before you get started with ASP.NET 2.0, it helps to take a step back and consider these problems. You'll then understand the solution that .NET offers.

In this chapter you'll consider the history of web development leading up to ASP.NET, take a whirlwind tour of the most significant features of .NET, and preview the core changes in ASP.NET 2.0. If you're new to ASP.NET, this chapter will quickly get you up to speed. On the other hand, if you're a seasoned .NET developer, you have two choices. Your first option is to read this chapter for a brisk review of where we are today. Alternatively, you can skip to the section "ASP.NET 2.0: The Story Continues" to preview what ASP.NET 2.0 has in store.

The Evolution of Web Development

More than ten years ago, Tim Berners-Lee performed the first transmission across HTTP (Hypertext Transfer Protocol). Since then, HTTP has become exponentially more popular, expanding beyond a small group of computer-science visionaries to the personal and business sectors. Today, it's almost a household term.

When HTTP was first established, developers faced the challenge of designing applications that could discover and interact with each other. To help meet these challenges, standards such as HTML (Hypertext Markup Language) and XML (Extensible Markup Language) were created. HTML established a simple language that could describe how to display rich documents on virtually any computer platform. XML created a set of rules for building platform-neutral data formats that different applications could use to exchange information. These standards guaranteed that the Web could be used by anyone, located anywhere, using any type of computing system.

At the same time, software vendors faced their own challenges. They needed to develop not only language and programming tools that could integrate with the Web but also entire frameworks that would allow developers to architect, develop, and deploy these applications easily. Major software vendors including IBM, Sun Microsystems, and Microsoft rushed to meet this need with a host of products.

ASP.NET 1.0 opened a new chapter in this ongoing arms race. With .NET, Microsoft created an integrated suite of components that combines the building blocks of the Web—markup languages and HTTP—with proven object-oriented methodology.

The Development World Before ASP.NET

Older technologies for server-based web applications rely on scripting languages or proprietary tagging conventions. Most of these web development models just provide clumsy hooks that allow you to trigger applications or run components on the server. They don't provide a modern, integrated framework for web programming.

Overall, most of the web development frameworks that were created before ASP.NET fall into one of two categories:

- Scripts that are interpreted by a server-side resource
- Separate, tiny applications that are executed by server-side calls

Classic ASP (Active Server Pages, the version of ASP that predates ASP.NET) and ColdFusion fall into the first category. You, the developer, are responsible for creating a script file that contains embedded code. The script file is examined by another component, which alternates between rendering ordinary HTML and executing your embedded code. If you've created ASP applications before, you probably know that scripted applications usually execute at a much slower rate than compiled applications. Additionally, scripted platforms introduce other problems, such as the lack of ability to control security settings and inefficient resource usage.

The second approach—used widely by, for example, Perl over CGI (Common Gateway Interface)—yields an entirely different set of problems. In these frameworks, the web server launches a separate application to handle the client's request. That application executes its code and dynamically creates the HTML that should be sent back to the client. Though these applications execute faster than their scripted counterparts, they tend to require much more memory. The key problem with this sort of approach is that the web server needs to create a separate instance of the application for each client request. This model makes these applications much less scalable in environments with large numbers of simultaneous users, unless you code carefully. This type of application can also be quite difficult to write, debug, and integrate with other components.

ASP.NET is far more than a simple evolution of either type of application. Instead, it breaks the trend with a whole new development model. The difference is that ASP.NET is deeply integrated with its underlying framework. ASP.NET is *not* an extension or modification to the .NET Framework with loosely coupled hooks into the functionality it provides. Instead, ASP.NET is a portion of the .NET Framework that's managed by the .NET runtime. In essence, ASP.NET blurs the line between *application* development and *web* development by extending the tools and technologies previously monopolized by desktop developers into the web development world.

What's Wrong with Classic ASP?

If you've programmed only with classic ASP before, you might wonder why Microsoft changed everything with ASP.NET. Learning a whole new framework isn't trivial, and .NET introduces a slew of concepts and can pose some serious stumbling blocks.

Overall, classic ASP is a solid tool for developing web applications using Microsoft technologies. However, as with most development models, ASP solves some problems but also raises a few of its own. The following sections outline these problems.

Spaghetti Code

If you've created applications with ASP, you've probably seen lengthy pages that contain server-side script code intermingled with HTML. Consider the following example, which fills an HTML drop-down list with the results of a database query to get author details from the Pubs database in SQL Server:

```
<%
  Set dbConn = Server.CreateObject("ADODB.Connection")
  Set rs = Server.CreateObject("ADODB.Recordset")
  dbConn.Open "PROVIDER=SQLOLEDB;DATA SOURCE=(local);
           DATABASE=Pubs;User=sa;Password=sa"
%>

<select name="cboAuthors">
  <%
    rs.Open "SELECT * FROM Authors", dbConn, 3, 3
    Do While Not rs.EOF
  %>
  <option value="<%=rs("au_id")%>"><%=rs("au_lname") & ", " &
    rs("au_fname")%></option>
  <%
    rs.MoveNext
    Loop
  %>
</select>
```

This example needs an unimpressive 16 lines of code to generate one simple HTML control. But what's worse is the way this style of coding diminishes application performance because it mingles HTML and script. When this page is processed by the ASP ISAPI (Internet Server Application Programming Interface) extension that runs on the web server, the scripting engine needs to switch on and off multiple times just to handle this single request. This increases the amount of time needed to process the whole page and send it to the client.

Furthermore, web pages written in this style can easily grow to unmanageable lengths. If you add your own custom COM components to the puzzle (which are needed to supply functionality ASP can't provide) and aren't careful about how you design your application, the management nightmare grows. The bottom line is that no matter what approach you take, ASP code tends to become beastly, long, and incredibly difficult to debug—if you can even get ASP debugging working in your environment at all.

In ASP.NET, these problems don't exist. Web pages are written with traditional object-oriented concepts in mind. Your web pages contain controls that can be programmed against in a way similar to desktop applications. This means you don't need to combine a jumble of HTML markup and inline code. If you opt to use the code-behind approach when creating ASP.NET pages, the code and presentation are actually placed in two different files; simplifies code maintenance and allows you to separate the task of web-page design from the heavy-duty work of web coding.

Script Languages

At the time of its creation, ASP seemed like a perfect solution for desktop developers who were moving to the world of the Web. Rather than requiring programmers to learn a completely new language or methodology, ASP allowed developers to use familiar languages such as VBScript on a server-based programming platform. By leveraging the already-popular COM (Component Object Model) programming model as a backbone, these scripting languages also acted as a convenient vehicle for accessing server components and resources. But even though ASP was easy to understand for developers who were already skilled with scripting languages such as VBScript, this familiarity came with a price.

Performance wasn't the only problem. Every object or variable used in a classic ASP script is created as a *variant* data type. As most Visual Basic programmers know, variant data types are weakly typed. They require larger amounts of memory, are late-bound, and result in slower performance. Additionally, the compiler and development tools can't identify them at design time. This made it all but impossible to create a truly integrated IDE (integrated development environment) that could provide ASP programmers with anything like the powerful debugging, IntelliSense, and error checking found in Visual Basic and Visual C++. And without debugging tools, ASP programmers were hard-pressed to troubleshoot the problems in their scripts.

ASP.NET circumvents all these problems. For starters, ASP.NET web pages (and web services) are executed within the CLR (common language runtime), so they can be authored in any language that has a CLR-compliant compiler. No longer are you limited to using VBScript or JavaScript—instead, you can use modern object-oriented languages such as Visual Basic and C#.

It's also important to note that ASP.NET pages are not interpreted but are instead compiled into *assemblies* (the .NET term for any unit of compiled code). This is one of the most significant enhancements to Microsoft's web development model in ASP.NET 2.0. What actually happens behind the scenes is revolutionary. Even if you create your code in Notepad and copy it directly to a virtual directory on a web server, the application is dynamically compiled as soon as a client accesses it (in previous versions you had to precompile the application into a DLL), and it is cached for future requests. If any of the files are modified after this compilation process, the application is recompiled automatically the next time a client requests it.

The Death of COM

Though Microsoft claims undying support for COM, the technology that underlies the Windows operating system, and almost every application that runs on it, it's obvious that .NET is the start of a new path for modern development. Future versions of the Windows operating system (including the elusive Longhorn) will integrate the .NET Framework more deeply into the operating system kernel, making it the first-class language of all application development. And as COM applications wane in popularity and applications are converted to .NET, classic ASP will become a thing of the past. Even though .NET includes robust support for COM interoperability, the fact remains that classic ASP applications have no real place in a .NET world.

ASP.NET 1.0

Microsoft developers have described ASP.NET as their chance to "hit the reset button" and start from scratch with an entirely new, more modern development model. The traditional concepts involved in creating web applications still hold true in the .NET world. Each web application consists of web pages. You can render rich HTML and even use JavaScript, create components that encapsulate programming logic, and tweak and tune your applications using configuration settings. However, behind the scenes ASP.NET works quite differently than traditional scripting technologies such as classic ASP or PHP (PHP: Hypertext Preprocessor). It's also much more ambitious than JSP (Java Server Pages).

Some of the differences between ASP.NET and earlier web development platforms include the following:

- ASP.NET features a completely object-oriented programming model, which includes an event-driven, control-based architecture that encourages code encapsulation and code reuse.
- ASP.NET gives you the ability to code in any supported .NET language (including Visual Basic, C#, J#, and many other languages that have third-party compilers).
- ASP.NET is also a platform for building *web services,* which are reusable units of code that other applications can call across platform and computer boundaries. You can use a web service to do everything from web-enabling a desktop application to sharing data with a Java client running on Unix.
- ASP.NET is dedicated to high performance. ASP.NET pages and components are compiled on demand instead of being interpreted every time they're used. ASP.NET also includes, in ADO.NET, a fine-tuned data access model and flexible data caching to further boost performance.

These are only a few of the features, which include enhanced state management, practical data binding, dynamic graphics, and a robust security model. You'll look at these improvements in detail in this book and see what ASP.NET 2.0 adds to the picture.

Seven Important Facts About ASP.NET

If you're new to ASP.NET (or you just want to review a few fundamentals), you'll be interested in the following sections. They introduce seven touchstones of .NET development.

Fact 1: ASP.NET Is Integrated with the .NET Framework

The .NET Framework is divided into an almost painstaking collection of functional parts, with a staggering total of more than 7,000 *types* (the .NET term for classes, structures, interfaces, and other core programming ingredients). Before you can program any type of .NET application, you need a basic understanding of those parts—and an understanding of why things are organized the way they are.

The massive collection of functionality that the .NET Framework provides is organized in a way that traditional Windows programmers will see as a happy improvement. Each one of the thousands of data types in the .NET Framework is grouped into a logical, hierarchical container called a *namespace*. Different namespaces provide different features. Taken together, the .NET namespaces offer functionality for nearly every aspect of distributed development from message queuing to security. This massive toolkit is called the *class library*.

Interestingly, the way you use the .NET Framework classes in ASP.NET is the same as the way you use them in any other type of .NET application (including a stand-alone Windows application, a Windows service, a command-line utility, and so on). In other words, .NET gives the same tools to web developers that it gives to rich client developers.

If you've programmed extensively with ASP.NET 1.*x*, you'll find that the same set of classes is available in ASP.NET 2.0. The difference is that ASP.NET 2.0 adds even more classes to the mix, many in entirely new namespaces for features such as configuration, health monitoring, and personalization.

■ Tip One of the best resources for learning about new corners of the .NET Framework is the .NET Framework class library reference, which is part of the MSDN Help library reference. If you have Visual Studio 2005 installed, you can view the MSDN Help library by selecting Start ➤ Programs ➤ Microsoft Visual Studio 2005 ➤ Microsoft Visual Studio 2005 Documentation (the exact shortcut depends on your version of Visual Studio). Once you've loaded the help, you can find class reference information grouped by namespace under the .NET Development ➤ .NET Framework SDK ➤ Class Library Reference node.

Fact 2: ASP.NET Is Compiled, Not Interpreted

One of the major reasons for performance degradation in ASP scripts is that all ASP web-page code uses interpreted scripting languages. This means that when your application is executed, a scripting host on the server machine needs to interpret your code and translate it to lower-level machine code, line by line. This process is notoriously slow.

■ Note In fact, in this case the reputation is a little worse than the reality. Interpreted code is certainly slower than compiled code, but the performance hit isn't so significant that you can't build a professional website using ASP.

ASP.NET applications are always compiled—in fact, it's impossible to execute C# or VB .NET code without it being compiled first.

ASP.NET applications actually go through two stages of compilation. In the first stage, the C# code you write is compiled into an intermediate language called Microsoft Intermediate Language (MSIL) code, or just IL. This first step is the fundamental reason that .NET can be language-interdependent. Essentially, all .NET languages (including C#, Visual Basic, and many more) are compiled into virtually identical IL code. This first compilation step may happen automatically when the page is first requested, or you can perform it in advance (a process known as *precompiling*). The compiled file with IL code is an *assembly*.

The second level of compilation happens just before the page is actually executed. At this point, the IL code is compiled into low-level native machine code. This stage is known as *just-in-time* (JIT) compilation, and it takes place in the same way for all .NET applications (including Windows applications, for example). Figure 1-1 shows this two-step compilation process.

.NET compilation is decoupled into two steps in order to offer developers the most convenience and the best portability. Before a compiler can create low-level machine code, it needs to know what type of operating system and hardware platform the application will run on (for example, 32-bit or 64-bit Windows). By having two compile stages, you can create a compiled assembly with .NET code but still distribute this to more than one platform.

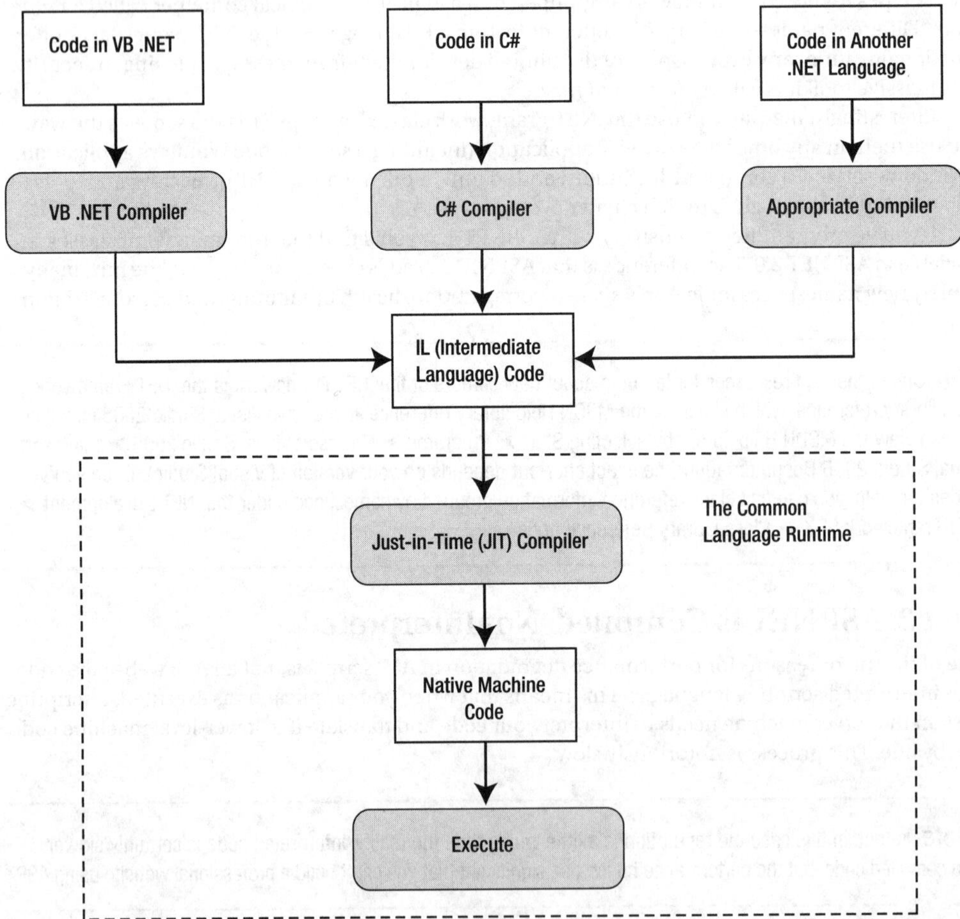

Figure 1-1. *Compilation in an ASP.NET web page*

■ **Note** One day soon, this model may even help business programmers deploy applications to non-Microsoft operating systems such as Linux. This ambitious goal hasn't quite been realized yet, but if you'd like to try the first version of .NET for the Linux platform (complete with a work-in-progress implementation of ASP.NET), visit `http://www.go-mono.com` to download the latest version of this open-source effort.

Of course, JIT compilation probably wouldn't be that useful if it needed to be performed every time a user requested a web page from your site. Fortunately, ASP.NET applications don't need to be compiled every time a web page or web service is requested. Instead, the IL code is created once and regenerated only when the source is modified. Similarly, the native machine code files are cached in a system directory that has a path like c:\[WinDir]\Microsoft.NET\Framework\[Version]\Temporary ASP.NET Files, where [WinDir] in the Windows directory and [Version] is the version number for the currently installed version of the .NET Framework.

■ **Note** Although benchmarks are often controversial, you can find an interesting comparison of Java and ASP.NET at `http://gotdotnet.com/team/compare`. Keep in mind that the real issues limiting performance are usually related to specific bottlenecks, such as disk access, CPU use, network bandwidth, and so on. In many benchmarks, ASP.NET outperforms other solutions because of its support for performance-enhancing platform features such as caching, not because of the speed boost that results from compiled code.

Although the compilation model in ASP.NET 2.0 remains essentially the same, it has one important change. The design tool (Visual Studio 2005) no longer compiles code by default. Instead, your web pages and services are compiled the first time you run them, which improves the debugging experience. To avoid the overhead of first-time compilation when you deploy a finished application (and prevent other people from tampering with your code), you can use a new *precompilation* feature, which is explained in Chapter 18.

Fact 3: ASP.NET Is Multilanguage

Though you'll probably opt to use one language over another when you develop an application, that choice won't determine what you can accomplish with your web applications. That's because no matter what language you use, the code is compiled into IL.

IL is a stepping-stone for every managed application. (A *managed application* is any application that's written for .NET and executes inside the managed environment of the CLR.) In a sense, IL is *the* language of .NET, and it's the only language that the CLR recognizes.

To understand IL, it helps to consider a simple example. Take a look at this example, written in VB .NET:

```
Namespace HelloWorld
    Public Class TestClass
        Private Shared Sub Main(Args() As String)
            Console.WriteLine("Hello World")
        End Sub
    End Class
End Namespace
```

This code shows the most basic application that's possible in .NET—a simple command-line utility that displays a single, predictable message on the console window.

Now look at it from a different perspective. Here's the IL code for the Main method:

```
.method public static void Main() cil managed
{
  .entrypoint
  .custom instance void [mscorlib]System.STAThreadAttribute::.ctor() =
   ( 01 00 00 00 )
  // Code size       14 (0xe)
  .maxstack  8
  IL_0000:  nop
  IL_0001:  ldstr      "Hello World"
  IL_0006:  call       void [mscorlib]System.Console::WriteLine(string)
  IL_000b:  nop
  IL_000c:  nop
  IL_000d:  ret
} // end of method TestClass::Main
```

It's easy enough to look at the IL for any compiled .NET application. You simply need to run the IL Disassembler, which is installed with Visual Studio and the .NET SDK (software development kit). Look for the file ildasm.exe in a directory like c:\Program Files\Microsoft Visual Studio 8\SDK\v2.0\Bin. Once you've loaded the program, use the File ➤ Open command, and select any DLL or EXE that was created with .NET.

If you're patient and a little logical, you can deconstruct the IL code fairly easily and figure out what's happening. The fact that IL is so easy to disassemble can raise privacy and code control issues, but these issues usually aren't of any concern to ASP.NET developers. That's because all ASP.NET code is stored and executed on the server. Because the client never receives the compiled code file, the client has no opportunity to decompile it. If it *is* a concern, consider using an obfuscator that scrambles code to try to make it more difficult to understand. (For example, an obfuscator might rename all variables to have generic, meaningless names such as f__a__234.) Visual Studio includes a scaled-down version of one popular obfuscator, called Dotfuscator.

The following code shows the same console application in C#:

```
namespace HelloWorld
{
    public class TestClass
    {
        private static void Main(string[] args)
        {
            Console.WriteLine("Hello World");
        }
    }
}
```

If you compile this application and look at the IL code, you'll find that every line is semantically equivalent to the IL code generated from the VB .NET version. Although different compilers can sometimes introduce their own optimizations, as a general rule of thumb no .NET language outperforms any other .NET language, because they all share the same common infrastructure. This infrastructure is formalized in the CLS (Common Language Specification), which is described in the "The Common Language Specification" sidebar.

It's important to note that IL was recently adopted as an ANSI (American National Standards Institute) standard. This adoption could quite possibly spur the adoption of other common language frameworks. The Mono project at `http://www.go-mono.com` is an example of one such project.

THE COMMON LANGUAGE SPECIFICATION

The CLS defines the standard properties that all objects must contain in order to communicate with one another in a homogenous environment. To allow this communication, the CLR expects all objects to adhere to a specific set of rules.

The CLS is this set of rules. It defines many laws that all languages must follow, such as types, primitive types, method overloading, and so on. Any compiler that generates IL code to be executed in the CLR must adhere to all rules governed within the CLS. The CLS gives developers, vendors, and software manufacturers the opportunity to work within a common set of specifications for languages, compilers, and data types. As time goes on, you'll see more CLS-compliant languages and compilers emerge, although several are available so far.

Given these criteria, the creation of a language compiler that generates true CLR-compliant code can be complex. Nevertheless, compilers can exist for virtually any language, and chances are that there may eventually be one for just about every language you'd ever want to use. Imagine—mainframe programmers who loved COBOL in its heyday can now use their knowledge base to create web applications!

Fact 4: ASP.NET Runs Inside the Common Language Runtime

Perhaps the most important aspect of ASP.NET to remember is that it runs inside the runtime engine of the CLR. The whole of the .NET Framework—that is, all namespaces, applications, and classes—are referred to as *managed* code. Though a full-blown investigation of the CLR is beyond the scope of this chapter, some of the benefits are as follows:

Automatic memory management and garbage collection: Every time your application creates an instance of a class, the CLR allocates space on the *managed heap* for that object. However, you never need to clear this memory manually. As soon as your reference to an object goes out of scope (or your application ends), the object becomes available for garbage collection. The garbage collector runs periodically inside the CLR, automatically reclaiming unused memory for inaccessible objects. This model saves you from the low-level complexities of C++ memory handling and from the quirkiness of COM reference counting.

Type safety: When you compile an application, .NET adds information to your assembly that indicates details such as the available classes, their members, their data types, and so on. As a result, your compiled code assemblies are completely self-sufficient. Other people can use them without requiring any other support files, and the compiler can verify that every call is valid at runtime. This extra layer of safety completely obliterates low-level errors such as the infamous buffer overflow in C++.

Extensible metadata: The information about classes and members is only one of the types of metadata that .NET stores in a compiled assembly. *Metadata* describes your code and allows you to provide additional information to the runtime or other services. For example, this metadata might tell a debugger how to trace your code, or it might tell Visual Studio how to display a custom control at design time. You could also use metadata to enable other runtime services (such as web methods or COM+ services).

Structured error handling: If you've ever written any moderately useful Visual Basic or VBScript code, you'll most likely be familiar with the limited resources these languages offer for error handling. With structured exception handling, you can organize your error-handling code logically and concisely. You can create separate blocks to deal with different types of errors. You can also nest exception handlers multiple layers deep.

Multithreading: The CLR provides a pool of threads that various classes can use. For example, you can call methods, read files, or communicate with web services asynchronously, without needing to explicitly create new threads.

Figure 1-2 shows a high-level look at the CLR and the .NET Framework.

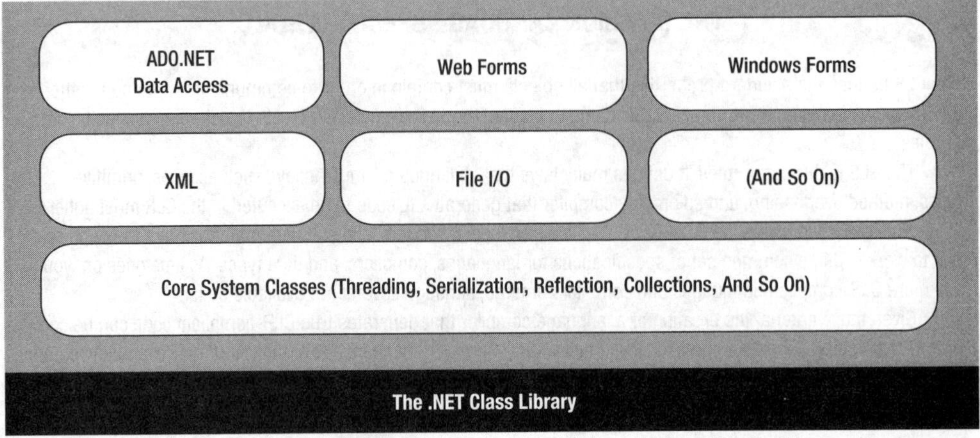

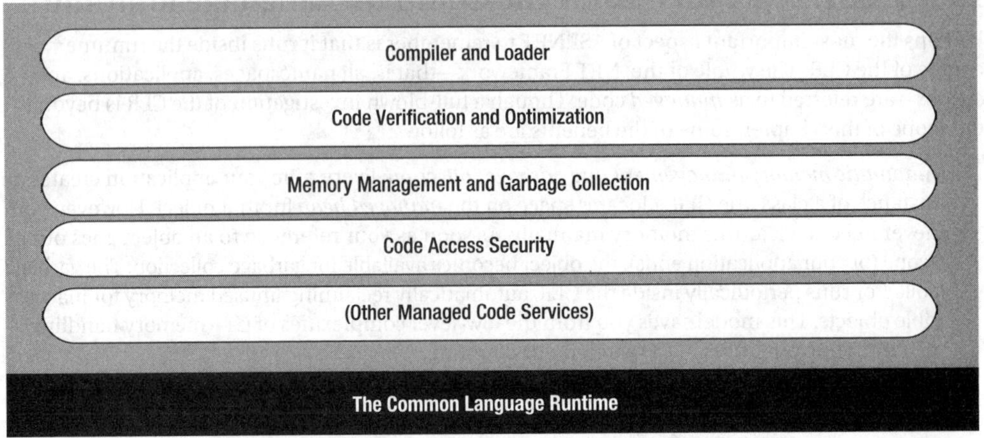

Figure 1-2. *The CLR and .NET Framework*

Fact 5: ASP.NET Is Object-Oriented

ASP provides a relatively lightweight object model, albeit one that is extensible using heavy COM objects. It provides a small set of objects; these objects are really just a thin layer over the raw details of HTTP and HTML. On the other hand, ASP.NET is truly object-oriented. Not only does your code have full access to all objects in the .NET Framework, but you can also exploit all the conventions of an OOP (object-oriented programming) environment, such as encapsulation and inheritance. For example, you can create reusable classes, standardize code with interfaces, and bundle useful functionality in a distributable, compiled component.

One of the best examples of object-oriented thinking in ASP.NET is found in *server-based controls.* Server-based controls are the epitome of encapsulation. Developers can manipulate server controls programmatically using code to customize their appearance, provide data to display, and even react to events. The low-level HTML details are hidden away behind the scenes. Instead of forcing the developer to write raw HTML manually, the control objects render themselves to HTML when the page is finished rendering. In this way, ASP.NET offers server controls as a way to abstract the low-level details of HTML and HTTP programming.

Here's a quick example with a standard HTML text box in an ASP.NET web page:

```
<input type="text" id="myText" runat="server" />
```

With the addition of the runat="server" attribute, this static piece of HTML becomes a fully functional server-side control that you can manipulate in your code. You can now work with server-side events that it generates, set attributes, and bind it to a data source.

For example, you can set the text of this box when the page first loads using the following code:

```
Private Sub Page_Load(ByVal sender As Object, ByVal e As EventArgs) Handles Me.Load
      myText.Value = "Hello World!"
End Sub
```

Technically, this code sets the Value property of an HtmlInputText object. The end result is that a string of text appears in a text box on the HTML page that's rendered and sent to the client.

HTML CONTROLS VS. WEB CONTROLS

When ASP.NET was first created, two schools of thought existed. Some ASP.NET developers were most interested in server-side controls that matched the existing set of HTML controls exactly. This approach allows you to create ASP.NET web-page interfaces in dedicated HTML editors, and it provides a quick migration path for existing ASP pages. However, another set of ASP.NET developers saw the promise of something more—rich server-side controls that didn't just emulate individual HTML tags. These controls might render their interface from dozens of distinct HTML elements while still providing a simple object-based interface to the programmer. Using this model, developers could work with programmable menus, calendars, data lists, and validators.

After some deliberation, Microsoft decided to provide both models. You've already seen an example of HTML server controls, which map directly to the basic set of HTML tags. Along with these are ASP.NET *web controls*, which provide a higher level of abstraction and more functionality. In most cases, you'll use HTML server-side controls for backward compatibility and quick migration and use web controls for new projects.

ASP.NET web control tags always start with the prefix *asp:* followed by the class name. For example, the following snippet creates a text box and a check box:

```
<asp:TextBox ID="myASPText" Text="Hello ASP.NET TextBox" runat="server" />
<asp:CheckBox ID="myASPCheck" Text="My CheckBox" runat="server" />
```

Again, you can interact with these controls in your code, as follows:

```
myASPText.Text = "New text"
myASPCheck.Text = "Check me!"
```

Notice that the Value property you saw with the HTML control has been replaced with a Text property. The HtmlInputText.Value property was named to match the underlying value attribute in the HTML <input> tag. However, web controls don't place the same emphasis on correlating with HTML syntax, so the more descriptive property name Text is used instead.

The ASP.NET family of web controls includes complex rendered controls (such as the Calendar and TreeView), along with more streamlined controls (such as TextBox, Label, and Button), which map closely to existing HTML tags. In the latter case, the HTML server-side control and the ASP.NET web control variants provide similar functionality, although the web controls tend to expose a more standardized, streamlined interface. This makes the web controls easy to learn, and it also means they're a natural fit for Windows developers moving to the world of the Web, because many of the property names are similar to the corresponding Windows controls.

Fact 6: ASP.NET Is Multidevice and Multibrowser

One of the greatest challenges web developers face is the wide variety of browsers they need to support. Different browser brands, versions, and configurations differ in their support of HTML. Web developers need to choose whether they should render their content according to HTML 3.2, HTML 4.0, or something else entirely—such as XHTML 1.0 or even WML (Wireless Markup Language) for mobile devices. This problem, fueled by the various browser companies, has plagued developers since the World Wide Web Consortium proposed the first version of HTML. Life gets even more complicated if you want to use a client-side HTML extension such as JavaScript to create a more dynamic page or provide validation.

ASP.NET addresses this problem in a remarkably intelligent way. Although you can retrieve information about the client browser and its capabilities in an ASP.NET page, ASP.NET actually encourages developers to ignore these considerations and use a rich suite of web server controls. These server controls render their HTML adaptively by taking the client's capabilities into account. One example is ASP.NET's validation controls, which use JavaScript and DHTML (Dynamic HTML) to enhance their behavior if the client supports it. This allows the validation controls to show dynamic error messages without the user needing to send the page back to the server for more processing. These features are optional, but they demonstrate how intelligent controls can make the most of cutting-edge browsers without shutting out other clients. Best of all, you don't need any extra coding work to support both types of client.

■ **Note** Unfortunately, ASP.NET 2.0 still hasn't managed to integrate mobile controls into the picture. As a result, if you want to create web pages for *smart devices* such as mobile phones, PDAs (personal digital assistants), and so on, you need to use a similar but separate toolkit. The architects of ASP.NET originally planned to unify these two models so that the standard set of server controls could render markup using a scaled-down standard such as WML or HDML (Handheld Device Markup Language) instead of HTML. However, this feature was cut late in the beta cycle.

Fact 7: ASP.NET Is Easy to Deploy and Configure

One of the biggest headaches a web developer faces during a development cycle is deploying a completed application to a production server. Not only do the web-page files, databases, and components need to be transferred, but you also need to register components and re-create a slew of configuration settings. ASP.NET simplifies this process considerably.

Every installation of the .NET Framework provides the same core classes. As a result, deploying an ASP.NET application is relatively simple. In most cases, you simply need to copy all the files to a virtual directory on a production server (using an FTP program or even a command-line command like XCOPY). As long as the host machine has the .NET Framework, there are no time-consuming registration steps.

Distributing the components your application uses is just as easy. All you need to do is copy the component assemblies when you deploy your web application. Because all the information about your component is stored directly in the assembly file metadata, there's no need to launch a registration program or modify the Windows registry. As long as you place these components in the correct place (the Bin subdirectory of the web application directory), the ASP.NET engine automatically detects them and makes them available to your web-page code. Try that with a traditional COM component!

Configuration is another challenge with application deployment, particularly if you need to transfer security information such as user accounts and user privileges. ASP.NET makes this deployment process easier by minimizing the dependence on settings in IIS (Internet Information Services). Instead, most ASP.NET settings are stored in a dedicated web.config file. The web.config file is placed in the same directory as your web pages. It contains a hierarchical grouping of application settings stored in an easily readable XML format that you can edit using nothing more than a text editor such as Notepad. When you modify an application setting, ASP.NET notices that change and smoothly restarts the application in a new application domain (keeping the existing application domain alive long enough to finish processing any outstanding requests). The web.config file is never locked, so it can be updated at any time.

ASP.NET 2.0: The Story Continues

When Microsoft released ASP.NET 1.0, even it didn't anticipate how enthusiastically the technology would be adopted. ASP.NET quickly became the standard for developing web applications with Microsoft technologies and a heavy-hitting competitor against all other web development platforms.

■ **Note** Adoption statistics are always contentious, but the highly regarded Internet analysis company Netcraft (`http://www.netcraft.com`) suggests that ASP.NET usage doubled in one year and that it now runs on more web servers than JSP. This survey doesn't weigh the relative size of these websites, but ASP.NET powers the websites for a significant number of Fortune 1000 companies.

It's a testament to the good design of ASP.NET 1.0 and 1.1 that few changes in ASP.NET 2.0 are fixes for existing features. Instead, ASP.NET 2.0 keeps the same underlying plumbing and concentrates on adding new, higher-level features. In other words, ASP.NET 2.0 contains more features, frills, and tools, all of which increase developer productivity. The goal, as stated by the ASP.NET team, is to reduce the number of lines of code you need to write by 70 percent.

■ **Note** In reality, professional web applications probably won't achieve the 70 percent code reduction. However, you'll probably be surprised to find new features that you can drop into your applications with only a few minor tweaks. And unlike many half-baked frills, you won't need to abandon these features and start from scratch to create a real-world application. Instead, you can plug your own modules directly into the existing framework, saving time and improving the flexibility and reusability of the end result.

Officially, ASP.NET 2.0 is backward compatible with ASP.NET 1.0. In reality, 100 percent backward compatibility never exists, because correcting bugs and inconsistencies in the language can change how existing code works. Microsoft maintains a list of the breaking changes (most of which are very obscure) at `http://www.gotdotnet.com/team/changeinfo/Backwards1.1to2.0`. However, you're unlikely to run into a problem when migrating an ASP.NET 1.*x* project to ASP.NET 2.0. It's much more likely that you'll find some cases where the old way of solving a problem still works but ASP.NET 2.0 introduces a much better approach. In these cases, it's up to you whether to defer the change or try to reimplement your web application to take advantage of the new features.

Of course, ASP.NET 2.0 isn't just about adding features. It also streamlines performance and simplifies configuration with a new tool called the WAT (website administration tool). The following sections introduce some of the most important changes in the different parts of the .NET Framework.

Visual Basic 2005

Visual Basic 2005 has several new language features. Some of these are exotic features that only a language aficionado will love, and others are more generally useful. The new features include the following:

Partial classes: Partial classes allow you to split a class into two or more source code files. This feature is primarily useful for hiding messy details you don't need to see. Visual Studio uses partial classes in some project types to tuck automatically generated code out of sight.

Generics: Generics allow you to create classes that are flexible enough to work with different class types but still support strong type checking. For example, you could code a collection class using generics that can store any type of object. When you create an instance of the collection, you "lock it in" to the class of your choice so that it can store only a single type of data. The important part in this example is that the locking happens when you *instantiate* the collection class, not when you code it.

Anonymous methods: Anonymous methods allow you to define a block of code on the fly, inside another method. You can use this technique to quickly hook up an event handler.

The My object: This object encapsulates some of the most common functionality used by developers. It exposes several different objects such as My.Application and My.Computer.

You'll see partial classes in action in Chapter 2, and you'll use generic classes with collections later in this book.

Visual Studio 2005

Microsoft provided two separate design tools for creating web applications with ASP.NET 1.*x*—the full-featured Visual Studio .NET and the free Web Matrix. Professional developers strongly favored Visual Studio .NET, but Web Matrix offered a few innovative features of its own. Because Web Matrix included its own scaled-down web server, programmers could create and test web applications without needing to worry about configuring virtual directories on their computer using IIS.

With .NET 2.0, Web Matrix disappears, but Visual Studio steals some of its best features, including the integrated web server, which lets you get up and running with a test website in no time, without the need for IIS or virtual directories on your development machine.

Another welcome change in Visual Studio 2005 is the support for different coding models. While Visual Studio .NET 2003 locked developers into one approach, Visual Studio 2005 supports a range of different coding models, making it a flexible, all-purpose design tool. That means you can choose to put your HTML tags and event-handling code in the same file, or in separate files, without compromising your ability to use Visual Studio and benefit from helpful features such as IntelliSense. (You'll learn about this distinction in Chapter 2.) You can also use more than one programming language in the same project, mixing C# web pages with VB web pages, or vice versa.

ASP.NET 2.0

For the most part, this book won't distinguish between the features that are new in ASP.NET 2.0 and those that have existed since ASP.NET 1.0. However, in the next few sections you'll tour some of the highlights.

Master Pages

Need to implement a consistent look across multiple pages? With *master pages*, you can define a template and reuse it effortlessly. For example, you could use a template to ensure that every web page in your application has the same header, footer, and navigation controls.

Master pages define specific editable regions, called *content regions*. Each page that uses the master page acquires its layout and its fixed elements automatically and supplies the content for just these regions.

Figure 1-3 shows an example content page at design time. The master page supplies the header and formatting of the outlying page. The content page is limited to inserting additional HTML and web controls in a specific region.

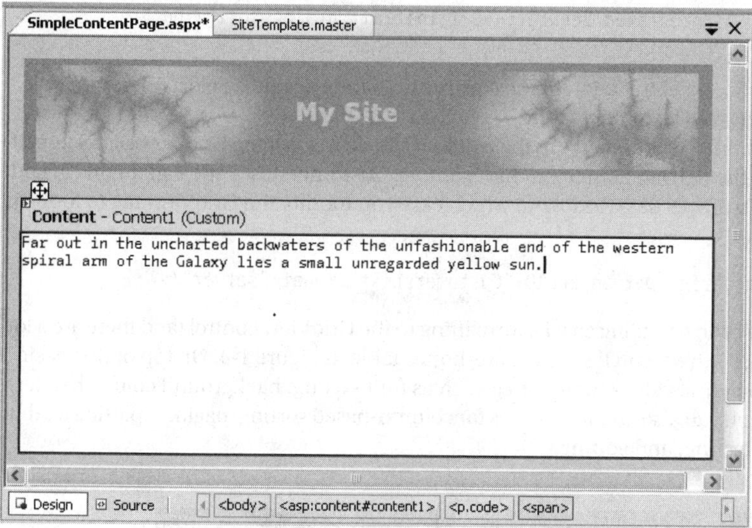

Figure 1-3. *A content page at design time*

On a related note, ASP.NET also adds a new theme feature, which lets you define a standardized set of appearance characteristics for web controls. Once you've defined these formatting presets, you can apply them across your website for a consistent look.

Interestingly, you can set both master and themes pages at runtime. This means you can write code to apply different themes and master pages depending on the type of user or on the user's preferences. In this way, you can use master pages and themes not just to standardize your website but to make it customizable. You'll learn about master pages and themes in Chapter 15.

Data Source Controls

Tired of managing the retrieval, format, and display of your data? With the new data source control model, you can define how your page interacts with a data source *declaratively* in your page, rather than writing the same boilerplate code to access your data objects. Best of all, this feature doesn't force you to abandon good component-based design—you can bind to a custom data component just as easily as you bind directly to the database.

Here's how the new data-binding model works at its simplest. First, drop the GridView onto a page using Visual Studio, or code it by hand using this tag:

```
<asp:GridView id="MyDataGrid" runat="server"/>
```

Next, you need to add the data source, which will fetch the rows you're interested in and make them available to the GridView. This simple example uses the SqlDataSource to connect directly to a SQL Server database, but a professional application will usually use the ObjectDataSource to go through a separate layer of custom components. To create the SqlDataSource tag, you need a few details, including the query used to retrieve the records and the connection string used to access the database. You can walk through this process with a Visual Studio wizard, or you can code it by hand. Either way, you'll end up with something like this (assuming that the SQL Server database you want to connect to is on the current computer and supports Windows authentication):

```
<asp:SqlDataSource ID="CustomersList" Runat="server"
  SelectCommand="SELECT CompanyName, ContactName, ContactTitle, City FROM Customers"
  ConnectionString=
```

```
    "Data Source=127.0.0.1;Integrated Security=SSPI;Initial Catalog=Northwind">
</asp:SqlDataSource>
```

This data source defines a connection to the Northwind database and a Select operation that retrieves all the records in the Customers table.

Finally, you need to bind the data source to the GridView. To do this, set the GridView.DataSourceID property to the name of the SqlDataSource (in this example, CustomersList). You can do this in code or using the Visual Studio properties window, in which case you modify the GridView tag to look like this:

```
<asp:GridView id="MyDataGrid" DataSourceID="CustomersList" runat="server"/>
```

Without writing any code or adding special formatting to the GridView control (and there are a lot of options for doing exactly that), you'll see the bare-bones table in Figure 1-4. On top of this basic representation, you can define values for features such as font styling, background colors, header styles, and much more. You can also enable features for column-based sorting, paging (splitting a table over multiple pages), selecting, and editing.

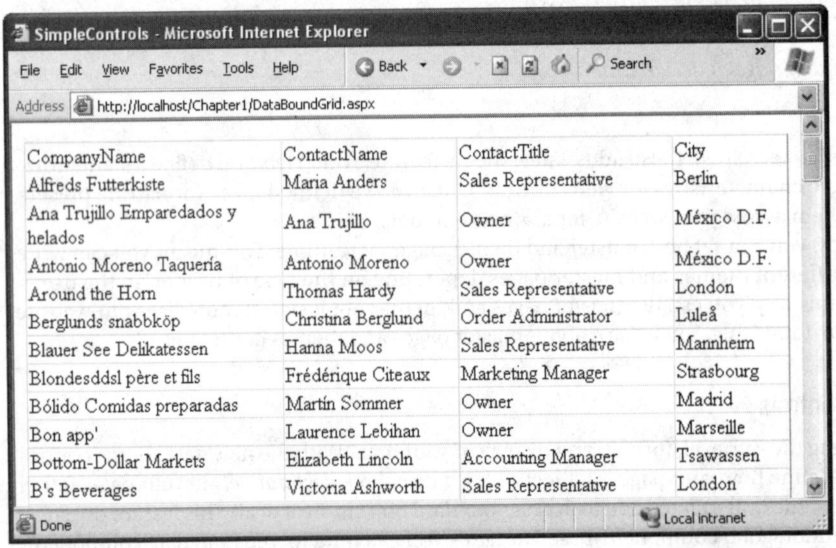

SimpleControls - Microsoft Internet Explorer

File Edit View Favorites Tools Help

Address http://localhost/Chapter1/DataBoundGrid.aspx

CompanyName	ContactName	ContactTitle	City
Alfreds Futterkiste	Maria Anders	Sales Representative	Berlin
Ana Trujillo Emparedados y helados	Ana Trujillo	Owner	México D.F.
Antonio Moreno Taquería	Antonio Moreno	Owner	México D.F.
Around the Horn	Thomas Hardy	Sales Representative	London
Berglunds snabbköp	Christina Berglund	Order Administrator	Luleå
Blauer See Delikatessen	Hanna Moos	Sales Representative	Mannheim
Blondesddsl père et fils	Frédérique Citeaux	Marketing Manager	Strasbourg
Bólido Comidas preparadas	Martín Sommer	Owner	Madrid
Bon app'	Laurence Lebihan	Owner	Marseille
Bottom-Dollar Markets	Elizabeth Lincoln	Accounting Manager	Tsawassen
B's Beverages	Victoria Ashworth	Sales Representative	London

Done Local intranet

Figure 1-4. *A simple data-bound grid*

Along with the GridView, ASP.NET 2.0 also adds other new controls for displaying data, including the DetailsView and FormView controls. Both controls can act as a record browser, showing detailed information for a single record at a time. They also support editing. You'll learn about the new data features throughout Part 2.

Personalization

Most web applications deal extensively with user-specific data. For example, if you're building an e-commerce site, you might need to store and retrieve the current user's address, viewing preferences, shopping basket, and so on. ASP.NET 1.*x* allowed you to cache this information for a short amount of time, but it was still up to you to write this information to a database if you needed it for a longer period of time and then retrieve it later.

ASP.NET 2.0 addresses this limitation with *profile*, an API for dealing with user-specific information that's stored in a database. The idea is that ASP.NET creates a profile object where you can access the user-specific information at any time. Behind the scenes, ASP.NET takes care of the tedious work of retrieving the profile data when it's needed and saving the profile data when it changes.

Most serious developers will quickly realize that the default implementation of profiles is a one-size-fits-all solution that probably won't suit their needs. For example, what if you need to use existing database tables, store encrypted information, or customize how large amounts of data are cached to improve performance? Interestingly, you can customize the profile feature to suit your needs by building your own profile provider. This allows you to use the convenient profile features but still control the low-level details. Of course, the drawback is that you're still responsible for some of the heavy lifting (no more 70 percent code reduction), but you gain the flexibility and consistency of the profile model. You'll learn about profiles in Chapter 24.

Tip Many of the features in ASP.NET 2.0 work through an abstraction called the *provider model*. The beauty of the provider model is that you can use the simple providers to build your page code. If your requirements change, you don't need to change a single page—instead, you simply need to create a custom provider. The provider model is useful enough that a similar organization pattern was used for similar handcrafted solutions in the first edition of this book, before ASP.NET 2.0 appeared.

Security and Membership

One of the most useful features in ASP.NET 1.*x* was forms authentication, a cookie-based system for tracking authenticated users. Although forms authentication worked perfectly well for securing a website, it was still up to each web developer to write the code for authenticating the user in a login page. And forms authentication didn't provide any functionality for user authorization (testing if the current user has a certain set of permissions), which meant developers were forced to add these features from scratch if they were needed.

ASP.NET 2.0 addresses both of these shortcomings by extending forms authentication with new features. First, ASP.NET includes automatic support for tracking user credentials, securely storing passwords, and authenticating users in a login page. You can customize this functionality based on your existing tables, or you can simply point ASP.NET to your database server and let it manage everything. Additionally, ASP.NET includes a handful of new controls for managing security, allowing users to log in, register, and retrieve passwords. You can let these controls work on their own without any custom code, or you can configure them to match your requirements.

Finally, ASP.NET adds support for authorization with a *membership* API. Membership allows you to use role-based authorization. You map your users into different groups (like Guest, Administrator, SalesEmployee) and then you test if a user is a member of the right group before allowing a specific action. Best of all, membership plugs right into the forms-based security infrastructure. You'll learn much more in Part 4.

Rich Controls

All in all, ASP.NET introduces more than 40 controls. Many of these controls support new features, such as the dedicated security controls and web parts controls for portals. You'll also find a handy wizard and MultiView control that allow you to create pages with multiple views. But the two most impressive controls are probably the new TreeView and JavaScript-powered Menu.

The TreeView allows you to show a hierarchical, collapsible tree view of data with extensive customization. Figure 1-5 shows a few of your menu options for outfitting the TreeView with different node pictures.

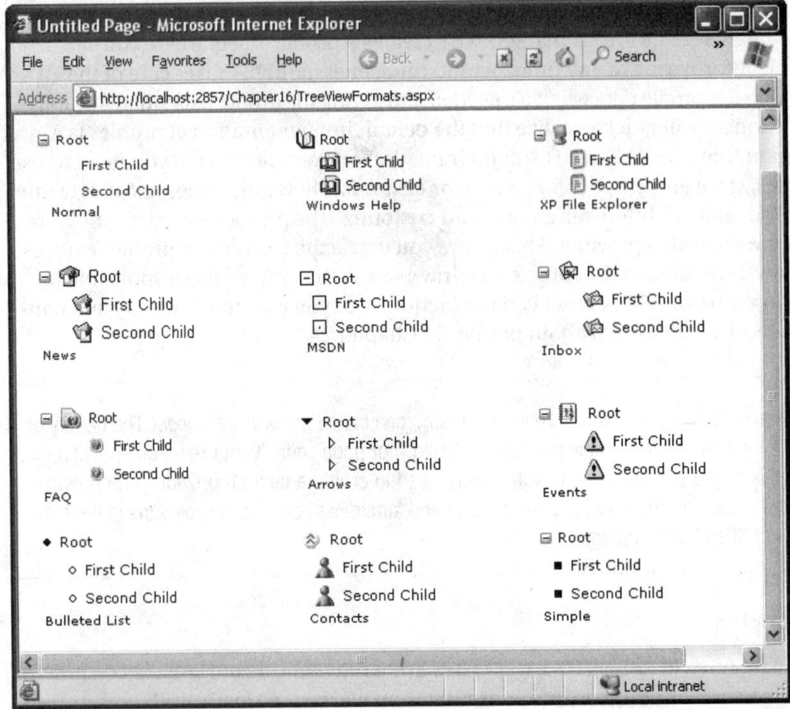

Figure 1-5. *Node styles with the new TreeView control*

The new Menu control also deals with displaying hierarchical data, but it renders itself as a JavaScript-powered fly-out menu. As you move the mouse, the appropriate submenu appears, superimposed over the current page (see Figure 1-6).

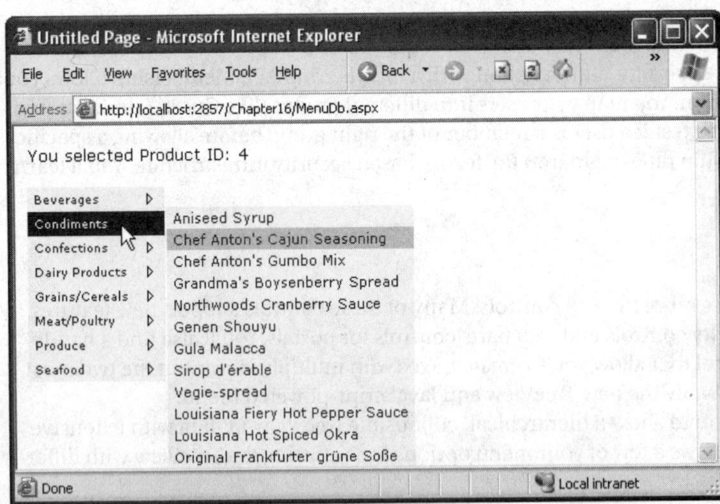

Figure 1-6. *The dynamic Menu control*

Both the TreeView and the Menu are useful for displaying arbitrary data and for showing a navigation tree so that users can surf from one page to another on your website. To make navigation even easier, ASP.NET also adds an optional model for creating site maps that describe your website. Once you create a site map, you can use it with the new navigation seamlessly. Best of all, from that point on you can change the structure of your website or add new pages without needing to modify anything other than a single site-map file. You'll see the navigation controls in action in Chapter 16.

Web Parts

One common type of web application is the *portal*, which centralizes different information using separate panes on a single web page. Although you could create a portal website in ASP.NET 1.*x*, you needed to do it by hand. In ASP.NET 2.0, a new web parts feature makes life dramatically easier with a prebuilt portal framework. And what a model it is—complete with a flow-based layout, configurable views, and even drag-and-drop support. Indeed, if you're planning to create a web portal with these features, it's safe to say that ASP.NET 2.0 will deliver the promised 70 percent code savings. You'll see more of this advanced feature in Chapter 30.

Administration

To configure an application in ASP.NET 1.*x*, you needed to edit a configuration file by hand. Although this process wasn't too difficult, ASP.NET 2.0 streamlines it with a dedicated web administration tool that works through a web-page interface. This tool, called the WAT, is particularly useful if you're also using the personalization and membership features. That's because the WAT gives you a convenient (if slightly sluggish) interface for defining user-specific data, adding users, assigning users to roles, and more. You'll take your first look at the WAT in Chapter 5.

Summary

So far, you've only just scratched the surface of the features and frills that are provided in ASP.NET and the .NET Framework. You've taken a quick look at the high-level concepts you need to understand in order to be a competent ASP.NET programmer. You've also previewed the new features that ASP.NET 2.0 offers. As you continue through this book, you'll learn much more about the innovations and revolutions of ASP.NET 2.0 and the .NET Framework.

CHAPTER 2

Visual Studio 2005

With ASP.NET, you have several choices for developing web applications. If you're inclined (and don't mind the work), you can code every web page and class by hand using a bare-bones text editor. This approach is appealingly straightforward but tedious and error-prone for anything other than a simple page. Professional ASP.NET developers rarely go this route.

Instead, almost all large-scale ASP.NET websites are built using Visual Studio. This professional development tool supports a rich set of design tools, including a legendary set of debugging tools and IntelliSense, which catches errors and offers suggestions as you type. Visual Studio also supports the robust code-behind model, which separates the .NET code you write from the web-page markup tags. To seal the deal, Visual Studio 2005 adds a built-in test web server that makes debugging Web sites easy and relatively hassle-free.

In this chapter, you'll tour the Visual Studio IDE and explore its key features. You'll also learn about the coding model used for ASP.NET 2.0 web pages.

Note Visual Studio 2005 is available in several versions. This chapter assumes you are using the full Visual Studio 2005 Professional or Visual Studio 2005 Team System. If you are using the scaled-down Visual Web Developer 2005 Express Edition, you will lose some features. Most notably, you won't be able to create separate components with class library projects.

VISUAL STUDIO 2005 CHANGES

If you're a seasoned ASP.NET developer, you're most interested in what's new in Visual Studio 2005. Although most of the editing features and debugging tools in Visual Studio 2005 are the same as those in Visual Studio 2003, the underlying model has a few significant changes. Here are the four most significant changes, all of which you'll learn more about in this chapter:

- *Projectless development*: Visual Studio no longer clutters your web projects with extra development files (such as .vbproj and .sln). One obvious benefit of this model is that you can deploy exactly what you develop, without needing to filter out just a subset of the files. However, as you'll see in this chapter, the concept of projectless development is slightly overstated. Visual Studio still stores some information in a solution file (such as breakpoints and build settings), and it quietly stows that file away under a user-specific directory. However, there's a significant difference—these hidden solution files aren't required. Essential details (such as project references) are stored right in the web.config file. You'll learn about projectless development in the "Websites in Visual Studio" section of this chapter.
- *New compilation model*: Visual Studio is no longer responsible for compiling your code. Instead, ASP.NET takes on that responsibility exclusively. This gives Visual Studio more flexible debugging, and it simplifies deployment on different platforms (for example, 32-bit and 64-bit Windows). It also allows you to combine web pages written in C# with web pages written in another .NET language (such as Visual Basic) in the same project.
- *New code model*: The shift in the compilation model also reduces the differences between the code-behind model and the code-inline model of writing web pages, both of which Visual Studio now supports. However, the syntax for code-behind is subtly different from that used for Visual Studio 2003 web pages, and you'll need to perform a one-way conversion operation to edit your web application in Visual Studio 2005. You'll learn about the coding model in "The Coding Model" later in this chapter.
- *Integrated test web server*: If you've programmed with Web Matrix (a scaled-down design tool used with ASP.NET 1.*x*), you'll recognize the new integrated web server, which allows you to run your web pages without setting up virtual directories, deploying your website, or having IIS installed on your development machine.

Along with these changes, a new edition of Visual Studio, called Visual Studio 2005 Team System, adds advanced collaboration and code-versioning support (which is far beyond that available in simpler tools such as Visual SourceSafe). Although Visual Studio Team System isn't discussed in this chapter, you can learn more from `http://lab.msdn.microsoft.com/teamsystem` or *Pro Visual Studio 2005 Team System* (Apress, 2005).

Another interesting new tool is the freely downloadable ASP.NET Development Helper, which gives you the ability to see view state, tracing, and caching information in your web browser. You'll learn about the ASP.NET Development Helper in the later "ASP.NET Development Helper" section.

The .NET Development Model

To create an ASP.NET application in Visual Studio 2005, you need two high-level areas of functionality:

- The compiler, which inspects the developer code and translates it into lower-level code (in this case, IL).
- The IDE, which allows a developer to write code. While not a necessity (you could always use notepad), thanks to the integrated debugging, deployment and code management features, the IDE is an indispensably useful application to have.

The Compiler

.NET separates these two pieces. That way, every language can use the same design tools. The .NET language compilers include the following:

- The Visual Basic compiler (vbc.exe)
- The C# compiler (csc.exe)
- The JScript compiler (jsc.exe)
- The J# compiler (vjc.exe)

■Note For a more-comprehensive list that includes third-party languages, check out `http://www.dotnetpowered.com/languages.aspx`.

If you want to use these compilers manually, you can invoke them from the command line. You'll find all of them in c:\[WinDir]\Microsoft.NET\[Version], where WinDir is the directory of the operating system (like c:\Windows) and Version is the version number of .NET you've installed, like v2.0.50215. However, using the .NET compilers manually is awkward because you need to specify the files you want to compile and the other .NET assemblies they use. You also need to compile your entire application at once or compile each web page separately. To avoid these headaches, most developers rely on ASP.NET's built-in support for compiling pages, or making the most of the precompiling features in Visual Studio 2005.

■Note In ASP.NET 1.*x*, Visual Studio used the precompiled code-behind model and was responsible for compiling all web pages into a single DLL assembly. In Visual Studio 2005, this behavior changes. Now, Visual Studio lets ASP.NET perform the compilation for each page the first time it's requested. This speeds up debugging and allows you to create websites that combine pages written in different languages. The original problems that motivated Visual Studio's precompilation model—optimizing the performance for the first request and reducing the need to deploy source code files—can now be solved using ASP.NET's precompilation features, which you'll learn about in Chapter 18.

The Visual Studio 2005 IDE

For those who are used to the previous version of the Visual Studio IDE, it's an obvious choice to use the new Visual Studio IDE. After all, it offers all the benefits of the previous version but with significant advancements in operability, syntax, and integration with other languages. For those who haven't tried Visual Studio before, the reasons to use Visual Studio may not be immediately obvious. Some of its advantages include the following:

- *WYSIWYG*: Who writes HTML pages by hand? Using Visual Studio, you can tweak and fine-tune even static HTML content, applying fonts and styles.
- *Less code to write*: Most applications require a fair bit of standard boilerplate code, and ASP.NET web pages are no exception. For example, when you add a new control to a web page, you also need to define a variable that allows you to manipulate that control in your code. With Visual Studio, these basic tasks are performed for you. Similar automation is provided for connecting to web services.
- *Intuitive coding style*: By default, Visual Studio formats your code as you type, indenting automatically and using color-coding to distinguish elements such as comments. These minor differences make code much more readable and less prone to error. You can even configure what automatic formatting Visual Studio applies, which is great if you prefer different brace styles (such as K&R style, which always puts the opening brace on the same line as the preceding declaration).

■ Tip To see the formatting options, select Tools ➤ Options, make sure the Show All Settings check box is checked, and then find the Text Editor ➤ C# ➤ Formatting group of settings. You'll see a slew of options that control where curly braces should be placed.

- *An integrated web server*: To host an ASP.NET web application, you need web server software like IIS, which waits for web requests and serves the appropriate pages. Setting up your web server isn't difficult, but it is inconvenient. Thanks to the integrated development web server in Visual Studio, you can run a website directly from the design environment.
- *Multilanguage development*: Visual Studio allows you to code in your language or languages of choice using the same interface (IDE) at all times. Even better, Visual Studio 2005 adds the ability to put web pages coded in C# in the same application as web pages written in Visual Basic. The only limitation is that you can't use more than one language in the same web page (which would create obvious compilation problems).
- *Faster development times*: Many of the features in Visual Studio are geared toward helping you get your work done faster. Convenience features such as powerful search-and-replace and automatic comment and uncomment features, which can temporarily hide a block of code, allow you to work quickly and efficiently.
- *Debugging*: The Visual Studio debugging tools are the best way to track down mysterious errors and diagnose strange behavior. You can execute your code one line at a time, set intelligent breakpoints that you can save for later use, and view current in-memory information at any time.

Visual Studio also has a wealth of features that you won't see in this chapter, including project management, integrated source code control, and a rich extensibility model.

Websites in Visual Studio

When the IDE first loads, it shows an initial start page. You can use various user-specific options from this page and access online information such as recent MSDN articles. But to get right to work, choose File ➤ New Website to create a new ASP.NET application. Visual Studio will then show the New Web Site dialog box (see Figure 2-1). Notice that you *don't* use Visual Studio's File ➤ New Project command. That's because web applications aren't projects, as you'll see later in this chapter.

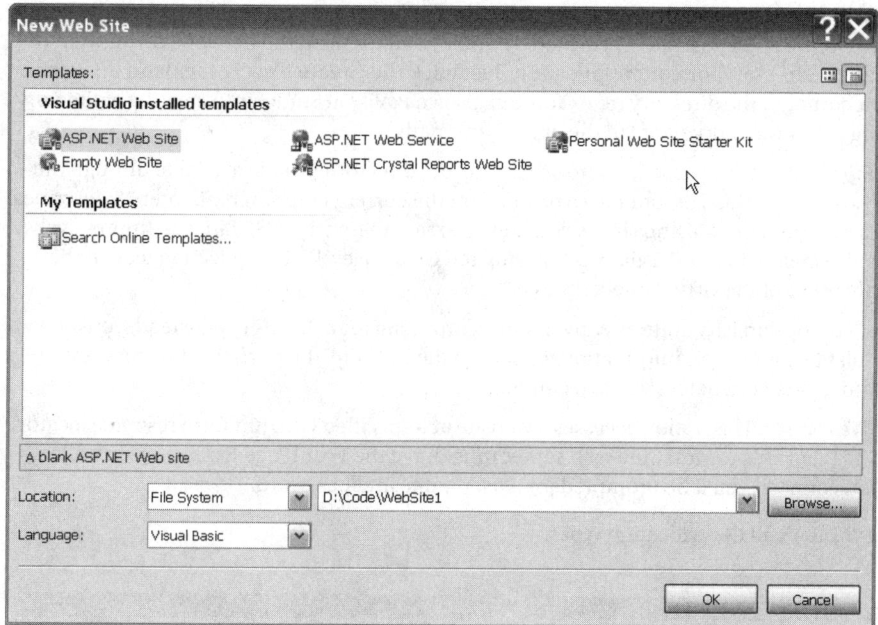

Figure 2-1. *The New Web Site window*

The New Web Site window allows you to specify three details:

Template: The template determines what files your website starts with. Visual Studio supports two types of basic ASP.NET applications: web site applications and web service applications. These applications are actually compiled and executed in the same way. In fact, you can add web pages to a web service application and can add web services to an ordinary web application. The only difference is the files that Visual Studio creates by default. In a web application, you'll start with one sample web page in your project. In a web service application, you'll start with a sample web service. Additionally, Visual Studio includes more sophisticated templates for certain types of sites, and you can even create your own templates (or download third-party offerings).

Location: The location specifies where the website files will be stored. Typically, you'll choose File System and then use a folder on the local computer or a network path. However, you can also edit a website directly over HTTP or FTP (File Transfer Protocol). This is occasionally useful if you want to perform live website edits on a remote web server. However, it also introduces additional overhead. Of course, you should never edit a production web server directly because changes are automatic and irreversible. Instead, limit your changes to test servers.

Language: The language identifies the .NET programming language you'll use to code your website. The language you choose is simply the default language for the project. This means you can explicitly add Visual Basic web pages to a C# website, and vice versa (a feat that wasn't possible with earlier versions of Visual Studio).

Instead of typing the location in hand, you can click the Browse button, which shows the Choose Location dialog box. Along the left side of Choose Location dialog box you'll see four buttons that let you connect to different types of locations:

File System: This is the easiest choice—you simply need to browse through a tree of drives and directories or through the shares provided by other computers on the network. If you want to create a new directory for your application, just click the Create New Folder icon above the top-right corner of the directory tree. (You can also coax Visual Studio into creating a directory by adding a new directory name to the end of your path.)

Local IIS: This choice allows you to browse the virtual directories made available through the IIS web hosting software, assuming it's running on the current computer. Chapter 18 describes virtual directories in detail and shows you how to create them with IIS Manager. Impressively, you can also create them in Visual Studio using the Create New Web Application icon at the top-right corner of the virtual directory tree.

FTP Site: This option isn't quite as convenient as browsing for a directory—instead, you'll need to enter all the connection information, including the FTP site, the port, the directory, a user name, and a password before you can connect.

Remote Web Server: This option accesses a website at a specified URL (uniform resource locator) using HTTP. For this to work, the web server must have the FrontPage Extensions installed. When you connect, you'll be prompted for a user name and password.

Figure 2-2 shows all these location types.

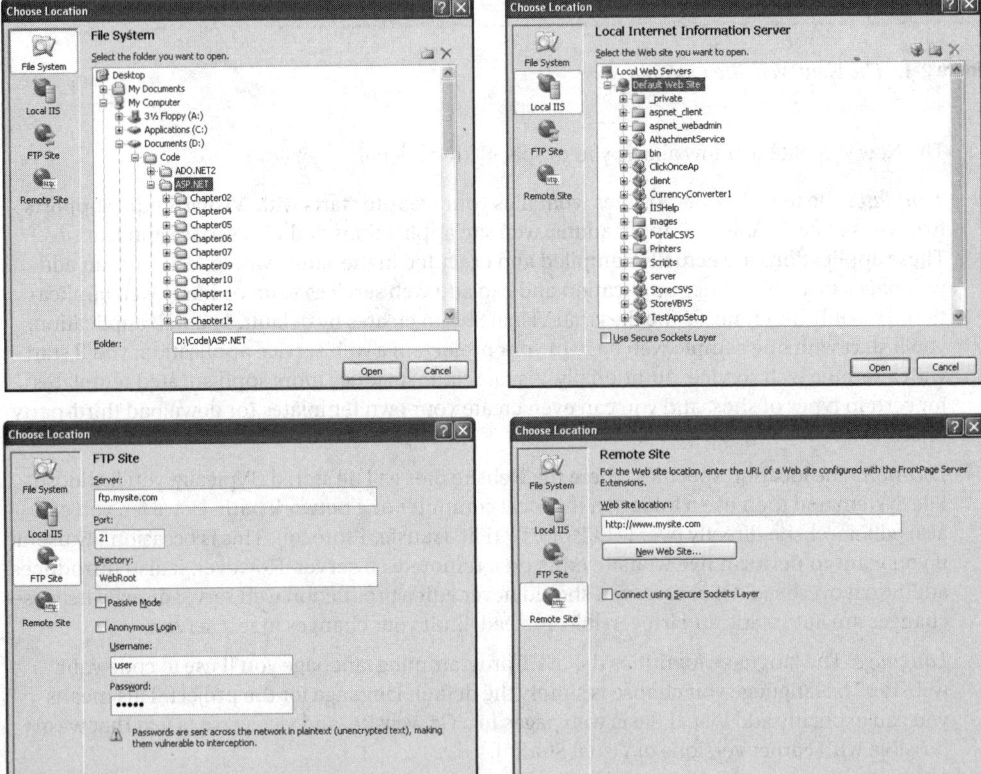

Figure 2-2. *Browsing to a website location*

Once you make your selection and click Open, Visual Studio returns you to the Create New Web Site dialog box. Click OK, and Visual Studio will create the new web application. A new website starts with a Default.aspx start page and its Default.aspx.vb code-behind file.

Projectless Development

In many ways, Visual Studio 2005 web applications are more remarkable for what they *don't* contain than what they do. Unlike previous versions of Visual Studio, Visual Studio 2005 web applications don't include extra files, such as .vbproj project files and .sln solution files. Instead, every file in your web folder automatically is considered part of the web application.

Clearing out this clutter has several benefits:

- It's less work to deploy your website, because you don't need to specifically exclude these files. There's also less duplication of settings, because most of what Visual Studio needs (such as assembly references) is stored in the web.config configuration file.
- Team collaboration is greatly simplified, because different people can work independently on different pages without needing to lock the project files.
- It's easier to author websites with other tools, because no extra project files need to be maintained.
- Files can easily be transferred from one web application to another—all you need to do is copy the file. Do note however, that if it is an .aspx page, you'll likely have to copy the associated code-behind file.

Although this simplifies life dramatically, under the radar there are still the last vestiges of Visual Studio's solution-based system.

When you create a web application, Visual Studio actually creates solution files (.sln and .suo) in a user-specific directory, like c:\Documents and Settings\[UserName]\Visual Studio 2005 \Projects\[ProjectName]. This file provides a few Visual Studio–specific features that aren't directly related to ASP.NET, such as debugging settings. For example, if you add a breakpoint to the code in a web page (as discussed in the "Visual Studio Debugging" section later in this chapter), Visual Studio stores the breakpoint in the .suo file so it's still there when you open the project later. Similarly, Visual Studio tracks the currently open files so it can restore your view when you return to the project. This approach to solution management is fragile—obviously, if you move the project from one location to another, you lose all this information. However, because this information isn't really all that important (think of it as a few project-specific preferences), losing it isn't a serious problem. The overall benefits of a projectless system are worth the trade-off.

Migrating a Visual Studio .NET Project

If you have an existing web application created with Visual Studio .NET 2002 or 2003, you can open the project or solution file using the File ➤ Open Project command. When you do, Visual Studio begins the Conversion Wizard.

The Conversion Wizard is exceedingly simple. It prompts you to choose whether to create a backup and, if so, where it should be placed (see Figure 2-3). If this is your only copy of the application, a backup is a good idea in case some aspects of your application can't be converted successfully. Otherwise, you can skip this option.

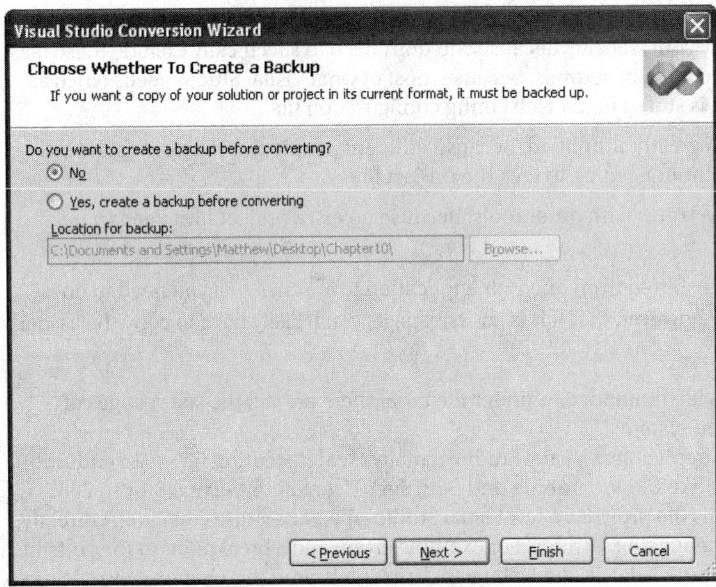

Figure 2-3. *Importing a Visual Studio .NET 2003 project*

When you click Finish, Visual Studio performs an in-place conversion. The conversion tool is fairly aggressive, and it attempts to convert every web page to use Visual Studio's new code-behind model. Any errors and warnings are added to a conversion log, which you can display when the conversion is complete. In a typical website, the conversion operation runs without any errors but generates a long list of warnings. These inform you when Visual Studio removes precompiled files, changes pages to use automatic event wire-up, and modifies the accessibility of event handlers (switching them from Private to Protected). All of these changes are minor modifications designed to apply the new coding model, which is described in the section "The Coding Model" later in this chapter. Figure 2-4 shows a sample log.

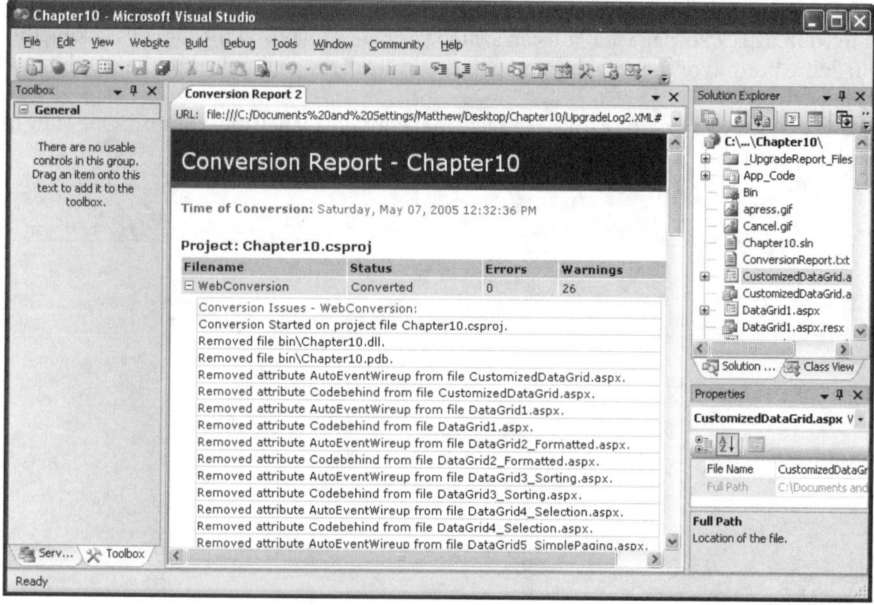

Figure 2-4. *A conversion log with typical warnings*

Visual Studio 2005 doesn't support adding old web pages to a new web application using the Website ➤ Add Existing Item. If you take this step and try to run your web application, you'll receive an error informing you that the Visual Studio .NET 2003 version of the code-behind model is no longer supported. Instead, Visual Studio will recommend you use the Open Project feature to start the Conversion Wizard. However, it's not too difficult to get around this limitation. Simply edit your .aspx page by changing the Codebehind attribute to Src. In other words, this code:

```
<%@ Page language="vb" Codebehind="MyPage.aspx.vb"
    AutoEventWireup="false" Inherits="MyApp.MyPage" %>
```

becomes this:

```
<%@ Page language="vb" Src="MyPage.aspx.vb"
    AutoEventWireup="false" Inherits="MyApp.MyPage" %>
```

This change switches the page so it uses the named code file directly. In most situations, this tactic isn't recommended because it leaves many details of the old coding model intact (such as the way event handlers are wired up), and it won't catch other problems that could thwart conversion. However, it's a good last resort if you want to keep your web page relatively unchanged so that you can bring it back into the Visual Studio .NET 2003 environment later.

Designing a Web Page

To start designing a web page, double-click the web page in the Solution Explorer (start with Default.aspx if you haven't added any pages). A blank page will appear in the designer.

To add controls, choose the control type from the Toolbox on the left. (The controls in the Toolbox are grouped in numerous categories based on their functions, but you'll find basic ingredients in the Standard tab.) Once you've added a control, you can resize it and configure its properties in the

Properties window. Every time you add a web control, Visual Studio automatically adds the corresponding tag to your .aspx web-page file. You can switch your view to look at the tags by clicking the Source button at the bottom of the web designer window. Click Design to revert to the graphical web form designer.

Figure 2-5 shows two views of the same web page that contain a label and a button. One view is in HTML mode, and the other is in design mode.

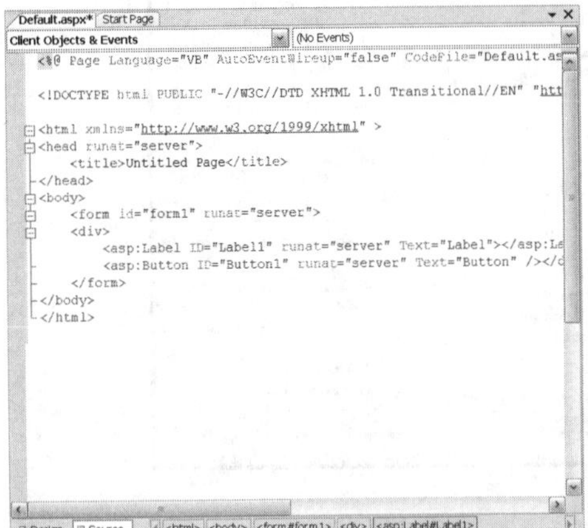
Default.aspx* Start Page
Client Objects & Events
(No Events)
<%@ Page Language="VB" AutoEventWireup="false" CodeFile="Default.as
<!DOCTYPE html PUBLIC "-//W3C//DTD XHTML 1.0 Transitional//EN" "htt
<html xmlns="http://www.w3.org/1999/xhtml" >
<head runat="server">
<title>Untitled Page</title>
</head>
<body>
<form id="form1" runat="server">
<div>
<asp:Label ID="Label1" runat="server" Text="Label"></asp:La
<asp:Button ID="Button1" runat="server" Text="Button" /></d
</form>
</body>
</html>
Design
Source
<html> <body> <form#form1> <div> <asp:Label#Label1>

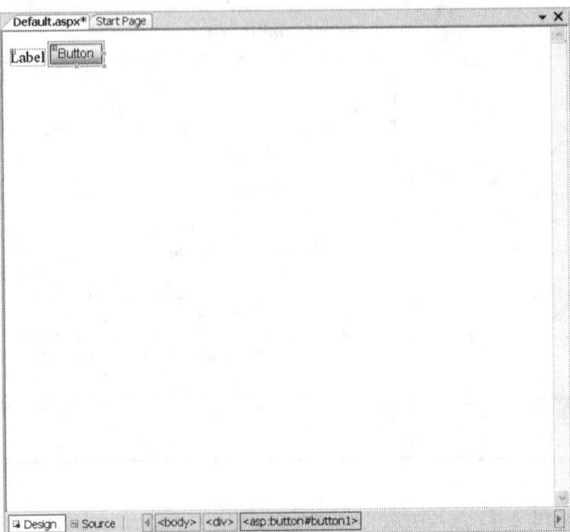
Default.aspx* Start Page
Label
Button
Design
Source
<body> <div> <asp:button#button1>

Figure 2-5. *The two modes for editing web pages*

Using the HTML view, you can manually add attributes or rearrange controls. In fact, Visual Studio even provides limited IntelliSense features that automatically complete opening tags and alert you if you use an invalid tag. Generally, you won't need to use the HTML view in Visual Studio. Instead, you can use the design view and configure controls through the Properties window.

■ **Note** Unlike previous versions, Visual Studio 2005 doesn't tamper with your HTML markup. Instead, it always preserves the indenting you use. You can fine-tune this behavior using the Text Editor ➤ HTML group of settings in the Tools ➤ Options dialog box. For example, one handy option that isn't turned on by default is Format HTML on Paste, which indents arbitrary blocks of markup when you paste them into a page.

To configure a control, click once to select it, or choose it by name in the drop-down list at the top of the Properties window. Then, modify the appropriate properties in the window, such as Text, ID, and ForeColor. These settings are automatically translated to the corresponding ASP.NET control tag attributes and define the initial appearance of your control. Visual Studio even provides special "choosers" (technically known as UITypeEditors) that allow you to select extended properties. For example, you can select a color from a drop-down list that shows you the color, and you can configure the font from a standard font selection dialog box.

To position a control on the page, you need to use all the usual tricks of HTML, such as paragraphs, line breaks, and tables. Unlike previous versions, Visual Studio 2005 doesn't support a grid-layout mode for absolute positioning with CSS (Cascading Style Sheets). Instead, it encourages you to use the more flexible flow-layout mode, where content can grow and shrink dynamically without creating a problem. However, there is a way to get back to the grid-layout behavior. All you need to do is add an inline CSS style for your control that specifies absolute positioning. (This style will already exist in any pages you've created with a previous version of Visual Studio .NET in grid-layout mode.) Here's an example:

```
<asp:Button id="cmd" style="POSITION: absolute; left: 100px; top: 50px;"
 runat="server" ... />
```

Once you've made this change, you're free to drag the button around the window at will. Of course, you shouldn't go this route just because it seems closer to the Windows GUI (graphical user interface) model. Few great web pages rely on absolute positioning, because it's just too awkward and browser-dependent.

Smart Tags

Another timesaving feature that's new in Visual Studio 2005 is the *smart tag*; smart tags make it easier to configure complex controls. Smart tags aren't offered for all controls, but they are used for rich controls such as the GridView, TreeView, and Calendar.

You'll know a smart tag is available if, when you select a control, you see a small arrow in the top-right corner. If you click this arrow, a window will appear with links that trigger other, higher-level tasks. For example, Figure 2-6 shows how you can use this technique to access Calendar autoformatting. (Smart tags can include many more features, but the Calendar smart tag provides only a single link.)

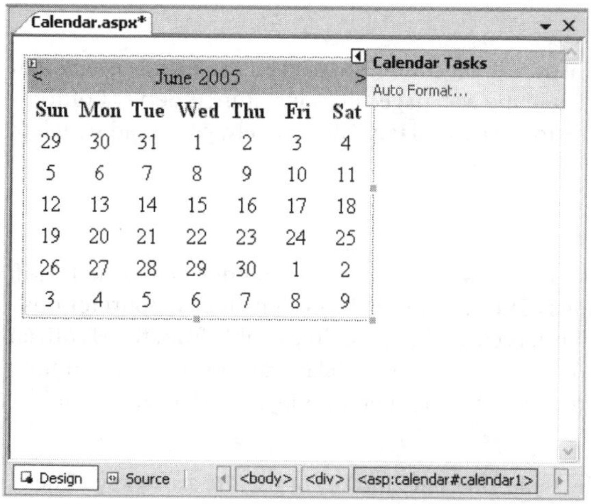

Figure 2-6. *A smart tag for the Calendar control*

Static HTML Tags

Along with full-fledged web controls, you can also add ordinary HTML tags. You simply drag these from the HTML tab of the Toolbox.

For example, you might want to create a simple <div> tag to group some web controls with a border. Visual Studio provides a valuable style builder for formatting any static HTML element with CSS style properties. To test it, add the Div from the HTML section of the Toolbox, which appears on your page as a panel. Then right-click the panel, and choose Style. The Style Builder dialog box (shown in Figure 2-7) will appear, with options for configuring the colors, font, layout, and border for the element. As you configure these properties, the web page's HTML will be updated to reflect your settings.

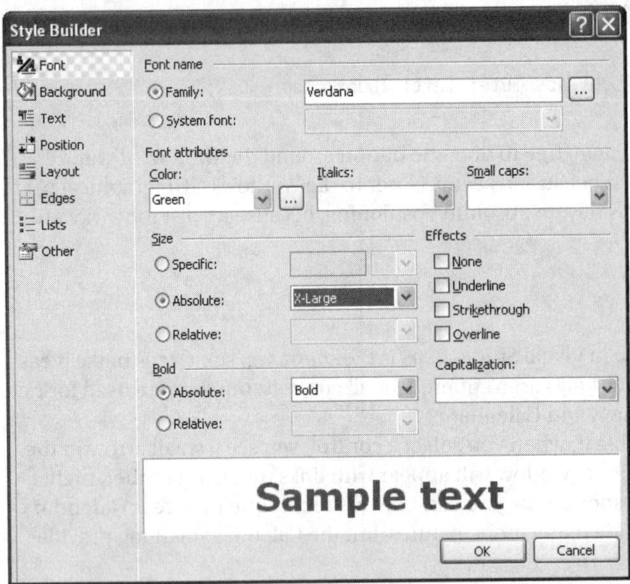

Figure 2-7. *Building HTML styles*

If you want to configure the HTML element as a server control so that you can handle events and interact with it in code, you need to right-click it in the web page and select Run As Server Control. This adds the required runat="server" attribute to the control tag. Alternatively, you could switch to source view and type this in on your own.

HTML Tables

One convenient way to organize content in a web page is to place it in the different cells of an HTML table using the <table> tag. In previous versions of Visual Studio, the design-time support for this strategy was poor. But in Visual Studio 2005, life gets easier. To try it, drag a table from the HTML tab of the Toolbox. You'll start with a standard 3×3 table, but you can quickly transform it using editing features that more closely resemble a word processor than a programming tool. Here are some of the tricks you'll want to use:

- To move from one cell to another in the table, press the Tab key or use the arrow keys. The current cell is highlighted with a blue border. Inside each cell you can type static HTML or drag and drop controls from the Toolbox.
- To add new rows and columns, right-click inside a cell, and choose from one of the many options in the Insert submenu to insert rows, columns, and individual cells.
- To resize a part of the table, just click and drag.
- To format a cell, right-click inside it, and choose Style. This shows the same Style Builder dialog box you saw in Figure 2-7.
- To work with several cells at once, hold down Ctrl while you click each cell. You can then right-click to perform a batch formatting operation.
- To merge cells (in other words, change two cells into one cell that spans two columns), just select the cells, right-click, and choose Merge.

With these conveniences, you might never need to resort to a design tool like Dreamweaver.

The Visual Studio IDE

Now that you've created a basic website, it's a good time to take a tour of the different parts of the Visual Studio interface. Figure 2-8 identifies each part of the Visual Studio window, and Table 2-1 describes each one.

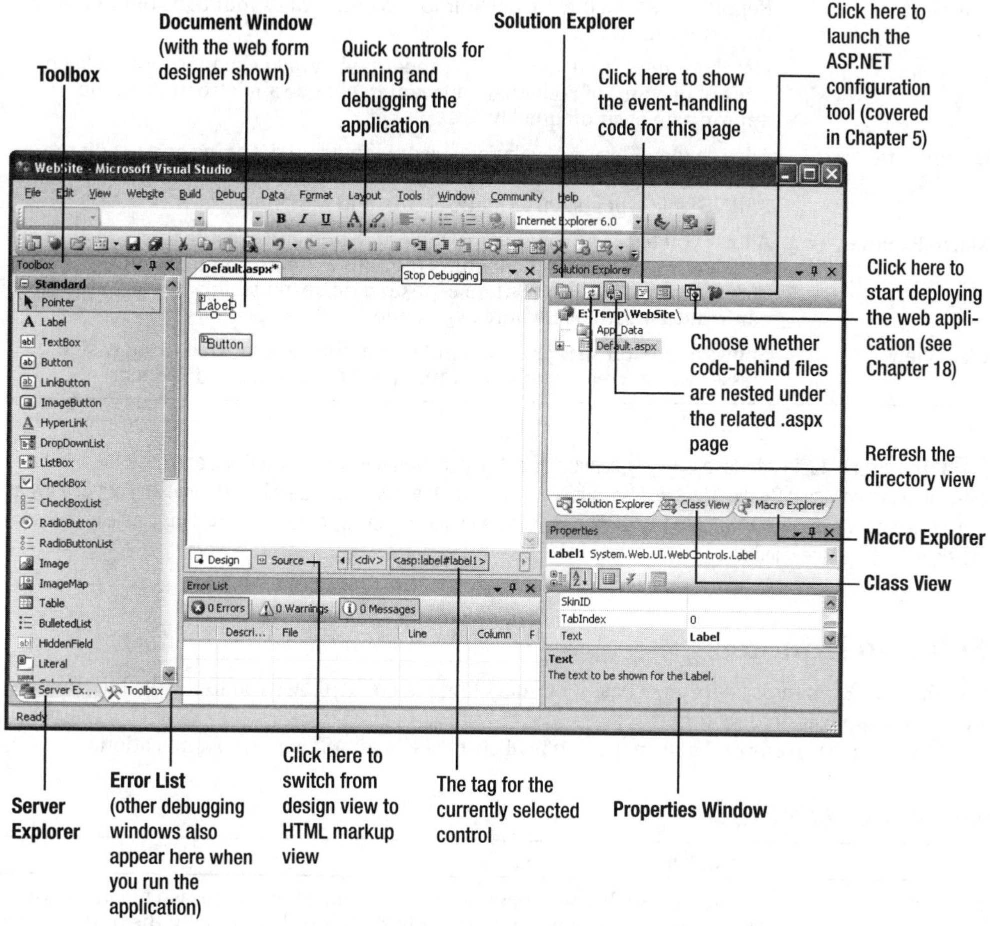

Figure 2-8. *The Visual Studio interface*

Table 2-1. *Visual Studio Windows*

Windows	Description
Solution Explorer	Lists the files and subfolders that are in the web application folder.
Toolbox	Shows ASP.NET's built-in server controls and any third-party controls or custom controls that you build yourself and add to the Toolbox. Controls can be written in any language and used in any language.

(Continued)

Table 2-1. *Continued*

Windows	Description
Server Explorer	Allows access to databases, system services, message queues, and other server-side resources.
Properties	Allows you to configure the currently selected element, whether it's a file in the Solution Explorer or a control on the design surface of a web form.
Error List	Reports on errors that Visual Studio has detected in your code but that you haven't resolved yet.
Task List	Lists comments that start with a predefined moniker so that you can keep track of portions of code that you want to change and also jump to the appropriate position quickly.
Document	Allows you to design a web page by dragging and dropping and to edit the code files you have within your Solution Explorer. Also supports non-ASP.NET file types, such as static HTML and XML files.
Macro Explorer	Allows you to see all the macros you've created and execute them. Macros are an advanced Visual Studio feature; they allow you to automate time-consuming tasks. Visual Studio exposes a rich extensibility model, and you can write a macro using pure .NET code.
Class View	Shows a different view of your application that is organized to show all the classes you've created (and their methods, properties, and events).

■ **Tip** The Visual Studio interface is highly configurable. You can drag the various windows and dock them to the sides of the main Visual Studio window. Also, some windows on the side automatically slide into and out of view as you move your mouse. If you want to freeze these windows in place, just click the thumbtack (or pin) icon in the top-right corner of the window.

Solution Explorer

The Solution Explorer is, at its most basic, a visual filing system. It allows you to see the files that are in the web application directory.

Table 2-2 lists some of the file types you're likely to see in an ASP.NET web application.

Table 2-2. *ASP.NET File Types*

File	Description
Ends with .aspx	These are ASP.NET web pages (the .NET equivalent of the .asp file in an ASP application). They contain the user interface and, optionally, the underlying application code. Users request or navigate directly to one of these pages to start your web application.
Ends with .ascx	These are ASP.NET user controls. User controls are similar to web pages, except that they can't be accessed directly. Instead, they must be hosted inside an ASP.NET web page. User controls allow you to develop an important piece of the user interface and reuse it in as many web forms as you want without repetitive code.
Ends with .asmx	These are ASP.NET web services. Web services work differently than web pages, but they still share the same application resources, configuration settings, and memory.

File	Description
web.config	This is the XML-based configuration file for your ASP.NET application. It includes settings for customizing security, state management, memory management, and much more. Visual Studio adds a web.config file when you need it. (For example, it adds a web.config file that supports debugging if you attempt to run your web application.) When you first create a website, you won't have a web.config file. You can add a web.config file manually if you need one.
global.asax	This is the global application file. You can use this file to define global variables and react to global events, such as when a web application first starts (see Chapter 5 for a detailed discussion). Visual Studio doesn't create a global.asax file by default—you need to add it if it's appropriate.
Ends with .vb	These are code-behind files that contain C# code. They allow you to separate the application from the user interface of a web page. The code-behind model is introduced in this chapter and used extensively in this book.

In addition, your web application can contain other resources that aren't ASP.NET file types. For example, your virtual directory can hold image files, HTML files, or CSS files. These resources might be used in one of your ASP.NET web pages, or they can be used independently.

Visual Studio distinguishes between different file types. When you right-click a file in the list, a context menu appears with the menu options that apply for that file type. For example, if you right-click a web page, you'll have the option of building it and launching it in a browser window.

Using the Solution Explorer, you can rename, rearrange, and add files. All these options are just a right-click away. To delete a file, just select it in the Solution Explorer, and press the Delete key.

You can also add new files by right-clicking the Solution Explorer and selecting Add ➤ Add New Item. You can add various different types of files, including web forms, web services, stand-alone classes, and so on. You can also copy files that already exist elsewhere on your computer (or an accessible network path) by selecting Add ➤ Add Existing Item. Use the Add ➤ New Folder to create a new subdirectory inside your web application. You can then drag web pages and other files into or out of this directory.

Visual Studio also checks for project management events such as when another process changes a file in a project you currently have open.. When this occurs, Visual Studio will notify you and give you the option to refresh the view of the file in the document window.

Document Window

The document window is the portion of Visual Studio that allows you to edit various types of files using different designers. Each file type has a default editor. To learn a file's default editor, simply right-click the file in the Solution Explorer, and then select Open With from the pop-up menu. The default editor will have the word *Default* alongside it.

Depending on the applications you've installed, you may see additional designers that plug into Visual Studio. For example, if you've installed FrontPage 2003, you'll have the option of editing web pages with a FrontPage designer (which actually opens your web page in a stand-alone FrontPage window).

Toolbox

The Toolbox works in conjunction with the document window. Its primary use is providing the controls that you can drag onto the design surface of a web form. However, it also allows you to store code and HTML snippets.

The content of the Toolbox depends on the current designer you're using as well as the project type. For example, when designing a web page, you'll see the set of tabs described in Table 2-3. Each tab contains a group of icons. You can see only one tab at a time. To view a tab, click the heading, and the icons will slide into view.

Table 2-3. *Toolbox Tabs for an ASP.NET Project*

Tab	Description
Standard	This tab includes the rich web server controls that are the heart of ASP.NET's web form model.
Data	These components allow you to connect to a database. This tab includes nonvisual data source controls that you can drop onto a form and configure at design time (without using any code) and data display controls such as grids.
Validation	These controls allow you to verify an associated input control against user-defined rules. For example, you can specify the input can't be empty, it must be a number, it must be greater than a certain value, and so on. Chapter 4 has more details.
Navigation	These controls are designed to display site maps and allow the user to navigate from one page to another. You'll learn about the navigation controls in Chapter 16.
Login	These controls provide prebuilt security solutions, such as login boxes and a wizard for creating users. You'll learn about the login controls in Chapter 20.
WebParts	This set of controls supports web parts, an ASP.NET model for building componentized, highly configurable web portals. You'll learn about WebParts in Chapter 29.
HTML	This tab allows you to drag and drop static HTML elements. If you want, you can also use this tab to create server-side HTML controls—just drop a static HTML element onto a page, right-click it, and choose Run As Server Control.
General	Provides a repository for code snippets and control objects. Just drag and drop them here, and pull them off when you need to use them later.

You can customize both the tabs and the items in each tab. To modify the tab groups, right-click a tab heading, and select Rename Tab, Add Tab, or Delete Tab. To add an item, right-click the blank space on the Toolbox, and Select Items. You can also drag items from one tab group to another.

Error List and Task List

The Error List and Task List are two versions of the same window. The Error List catalogs error information that's generated by Visual Studio when it detects problematic code. The Task List shows a similar view with to-do tasks and other code annotations you're tracking. Each entry in the Error List and Task List consists of a text description and, optionally, a link that leads you to a specific line of code somewhere in your project.

With the default Visual Studio settings, the Error List appears automatically whenever you build a project that has errors (see Figure 2-9).

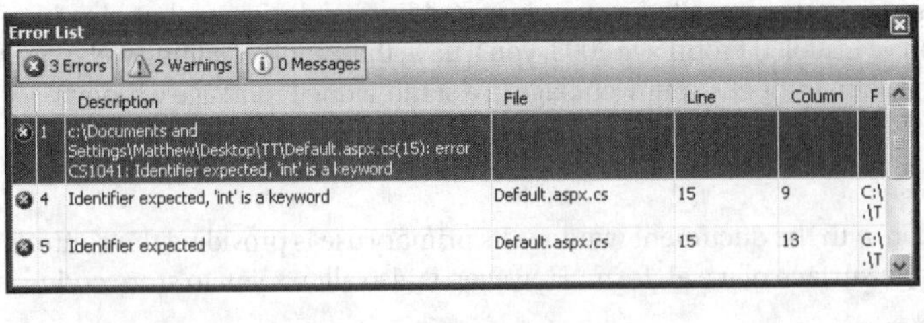

Figure 2-9. *Viewing build errors in a project*

To see the Task List, choose View ➤ Other Windows ➤ Task List. Two types of tasks exist—user tasks and comments. You can choose which you want to see from the drop-down list at the top of the Task List. User tasks are entries you've specifically added to the task list. You create these by clicking the Create User Task icon (which looks like a clipboard with a check mark) in the Task List. You can give your task a basic description, a priority, and a check mark to indicate when it's complete.

■**Note** As with breakpoints, any custom tasks you add by hand are stored in the hidden solution files. This makes them fairly fragile—if you rename or move your project, these tasks will disappear without warning (or without even a notification the next time you open the website).

The comment entries are more interesting, because they're added automatically and they link to a specific line in your code. To try the comment feature, move somewhere in your code, and enter the comment marker (') followed by the word *TODO* (which is commonly referred to as a *token tag*). Now type in some descriptive text:

```
' TODO: Replace this hard-coded value with a configuration file setting.
Dim  fileName As String = "c:\myfile.txt"
```

Because your comment uses the recognized token tag TODO, Visual Studio recognizes it and automatically adds it to the Task List (as shown in Figure 2-10).

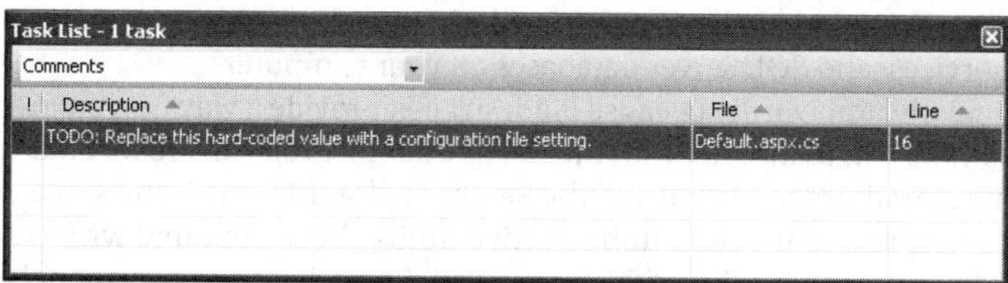

Figure 2-10. *Keeping track of tasks*

To move to the line of code, double-click the new task entry. Notice that if you remove the comment, the task entry is automatically removed as well.

Three token tags are built-in—HACK, TODO, and UNDONE. However, you can add more. Simply select Tools ➤ Options. In the Options dialog box, navigate to the Environment ➤ Task List tab. You'll see a list of comment tokens, which you can modify, remove, and add to. Figure 2-11 shows this window with a new ASP comment token that you could use to keep track of sections of code that have been migrated from classic ASP pages.

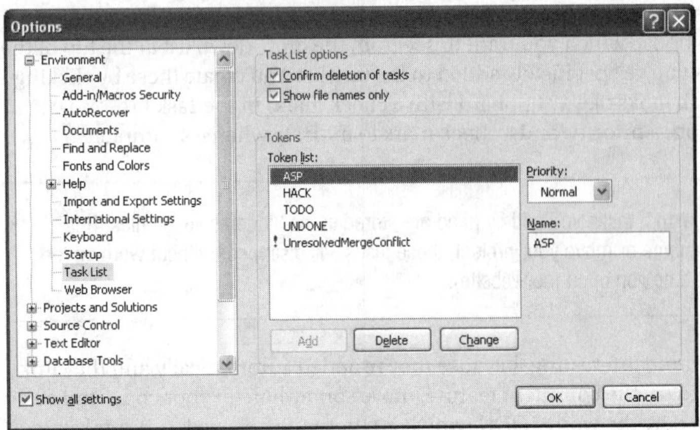

Figure 2-11. *Adding a new comment token*

Server Explorer

The Server Explorer provides a tree that allows you to explore various types of services on the current computer (and other servers on the network). It's similar to the Computer Management administrative tool. Typically, you'll use the Server Explorer to learn about available event logs, message queues, performance counters, system services, and SQL Server databases on your computer.

The Server Explorer is particularly noteworthy because it doesn't just provide a way for you to browse server resources; it also allows you to interact with them. For example, you can create databases, execute queries, and write stored procedures using the Server Explorer in much the same way that you would using the Enterprise Manager administrative utility that's included with SQL Server 2000 or SQL Server Management Studio in SQL Server 2005. To find out what you can do with a given item, right-click it. Figure 2-12 shows the Server Explorer window listing the databases in a local SQL Server and allowing you to retrieve all the records in the selected table.

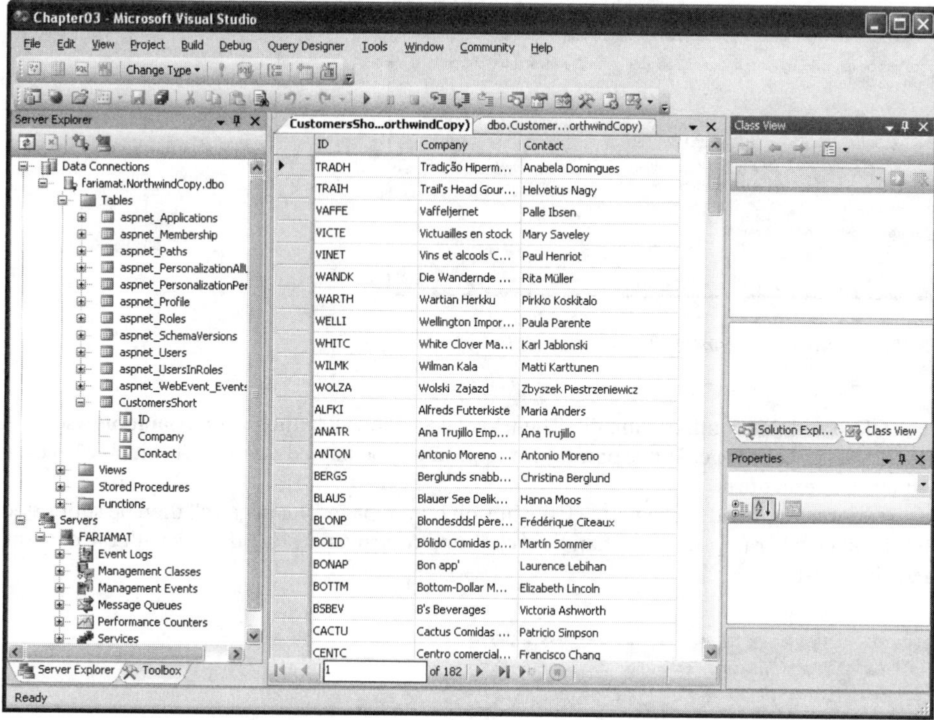

Figure 2-12. *Querying data in a database table*

The Code Editor

Many of Visual Studio's most welcome enhancements appear when you start to write the code that supports your user interface. To start coding, you need to switch to the code-behind view. To switch back and forth, you can use two buttons that are placed just above the Solution Explorer window. The tooltips identify these buttons as View Code and View Designer. When you switch to code view, you'll see the page class for your web page. You'll learn more about code-behind later in this chapter.

ASP.NET is event-driven, and everything in your web-page code takes place in response to an event. To create a simple event handler for the Button.Click event, double-click the button in design view. Here's a simple example that displays the current date and time in a label:

```
Protected Sub Button1_Click
      (ByVal sender As Object, ByVal e As System.EventArgs)
      Handles Button1.Click
   Label1.Text = "Current time: " &
   DateTime.Now.ToLongTimeString()
End Sub
```

To test this page, select Debug ➤ Start Debugging from the menu. Because this is the first time running any page in this application, Visual Studio will inform you that you need a configuration file that specifically enables debugging (see Figure 2-13).

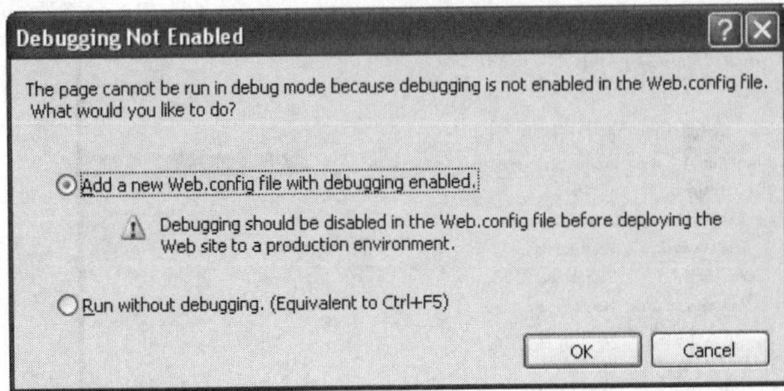

Figure 2-13. *Adding a web.config file automatically*

Click OK to add this configuration file. Then, Visual Studio will launch your default browser, with the URL set to your page. At this point, your request will be passed to ASP.NET, which will compile the page and execute it.

To test your event-handling logic, click the button on the page. The page will then be submitted to ASP.NET, which will run your event-handling code and return a new HTML page with the data (as shown in Figure 2-14).

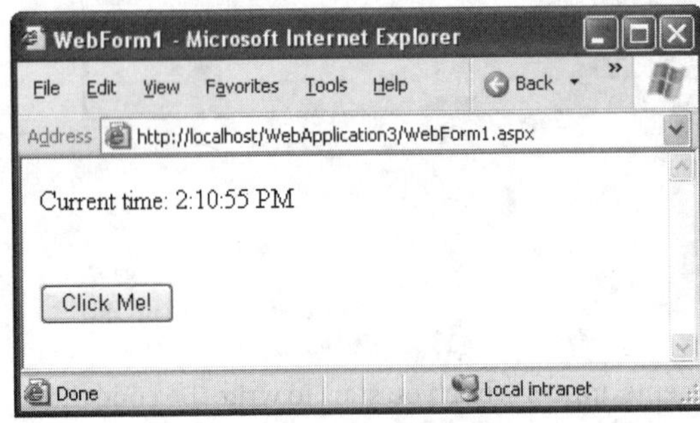

Figure 2-14. *Testing a simple web page*

Adding Assembly References

By default, ASP.NET makes a small set of commonly used .NET assemblies available to all web pages. These assemblies (listed in Table 2-4) are configured through a special machine-wide configuration file. You don't need to take any extra steps to use the classes in these assemblies.

Table 2-4. *Core Assemblies for ASP.NET Pages*

Assembly	Description
mscorlib.dll and System.dll	Includes the core set of .NET data types, common exception types, and numerous other fundamental building blocks.
System.Configuration.dll	Includes classes for reading and writing configuration information in the web.config file, including your custom settings.
System.Data.dll	Includes the data container classes for ADO.NET.
System.Drawing.dll	Includes classes representing colors, fonts, and shapes. Also includes the GDI+ drawing logic you need to build graphics on the fly.

Assembly	Description
System.Web.dll	Includes the core ASP.NET classes, including classes for building web forms, managing state, handling security, and much more.
System.Web.Services.dll	Includes classes for building web services—units of code that can be remotely invoked over HTTP.
System.Xml.dll	Includes .NET classes for reading, writing, searching, transforming, and validating XML.
System.EnterpriseServices.dll	Includes .NET classes for COM+ services such as transactions.
System.Web.Mobile.dll	Includes .NET classes for the mobile web controls, which are targeted for small devices such as web-enabled cell phones.

If you want to use additional features or a third-party component, you may need to import more assemblies. For example, if you want to use an Oracle database, you need to add a reference to the System.Data.OracleClient.dll assembly. To add a reference, right-click the project in the Solution Explorer, and select Add Reference from the context menu. The Add Reference dialog box will appear, with a list of registered .NET assemblies (see Figure 2-15).

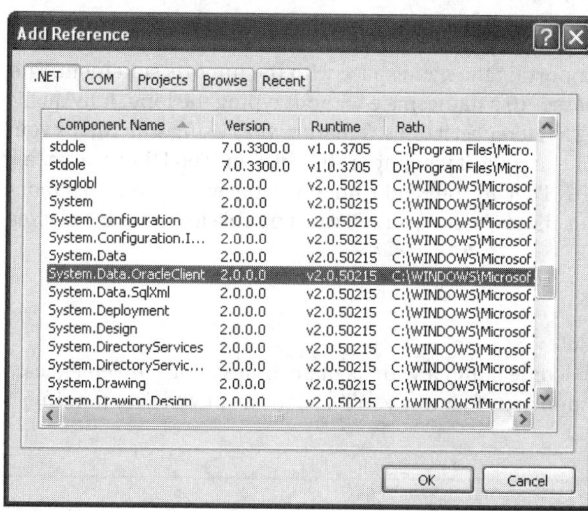

Figure 2-15. *Adding a reference*

In the Add Reference dialog box, select the component you want to use. If you want to use a component that isn't listed here, you'll need to click the Browse tab and select the DLL file from the appropriate directory.

When you add a reference, Visual Studio modifies the web.config file to indicate that you use this assembly. Here's an example of what you might see after you add a reference to the System.Data.OracleClient file:

```
<?xml version="1.0"?>
<configuration xmlns="http://schemas.microsoft.com/.NetConfiguration/v2.0">
  <system.web>
    <compilation debug="true">
      <assemblies>
        <add assembly="System.Data.OracleClient, Version=2.0.0.0, ..."/>
      </assemblies>
    </compilation>
    <!-- Other settings omitted. -->
  </system.web>
</configuration>
```

Chapter 5 explores the web.config file in greater detail.

If you add a reference to an assembly that isn't stored in the GAC (global assembly cache) on the development machine, Visual Studio will create a Bin subdirectory in your web application and copy the DLL into that directory. This step isn't required for assemblies in the GAC because they are shared with all the .NET applications on the computer.

■ **Note** Unlike previous versions of Visual Studio, in Visual Studio 2005 you won't see a list of assembly references in the Solution Explorer. Instead, you need to crack open the web.config file to get that information.

Adding a reference isn't the same as importing the namespace with the Imports statement. The Imports statement allows you to use the classes in a namespace without typing the long, fully qualified class names. However, if you're missing a reference, it doesn't matter what Using statements you include—the classes won't be available. For example, if you import the System.Web.UI namespace, you can write Page instead of System.Web.UI.Page in your code. But if you haven't added a reference to the System.Web.dll assembly that contains these classes, you still won't be able to access the classes in the System.Web.UI namespace.

IntelliSense and Outlining

As you program with Visual Studio, you'll become familiar with its many timesaving conveniences. The following sections outline the most important features you'll use (none of which is new in Visual Studio 2005).

■ **Tip** Visual Studio does include one new IntelliSense feature—XHTML (Extensible HTML) validation. You'll learn about this feature, and how to control the level of XHTML support you want, in Chapter 3.

Outlining

Outlining allows Visual Studio to "collapse" a subroutine, block structure, or region to a single line. It allows you to see the code that interests you, while hiding unimportant code. To collapse a portion of code, click the minus box next to the first line. Click the box again (which will now have a plus symbol) to expand it (see Figure 2-16).

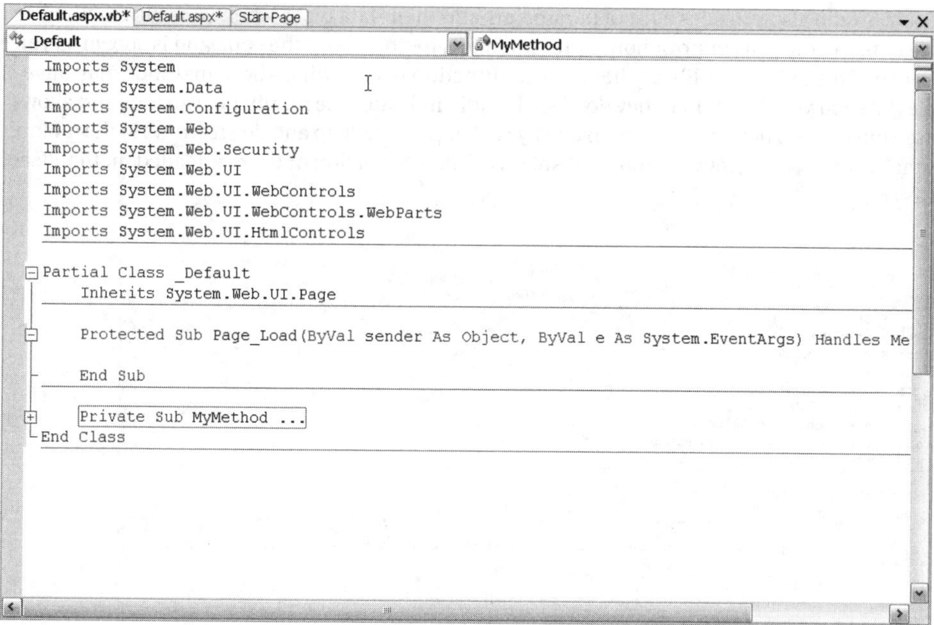

Figure 2-16. *Collapsing code*

Member List

Visual Studio makes it easy for you to interact with controls and classes. When you type a class or object name, Visual Studio pops up a list of available properties and methods (see Figure 2-17). It uses a similar trick to provide a list of data types when you define a variable and to provide a list of valid values when you assign a value to an enumeration.

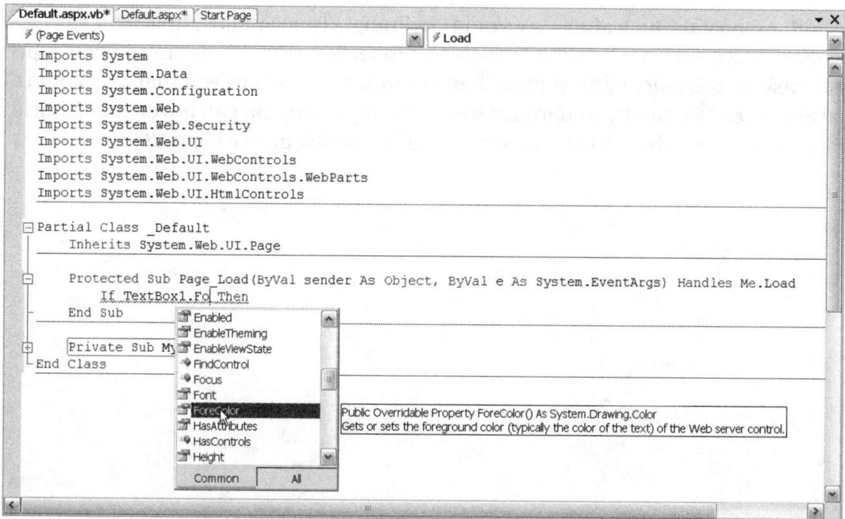

Figure 2-17. *IntelliSense at work*

Visual Studio also provides a list of parameters and their data types when you call a method or invoke a constructor. This information is presented in a tooltip above the code and is shown as you type. Because the .NET class library heavily uses function overloading, these methods may have multiple different versions. When they do, Visual Studio indicates the number of versions and allows you to see the method definitions for each one by clicking the small up and down arrows in the tooltip. Each time you click the arrow, the tooltip displays a different version of the overloaded method (see Figure 2-18).

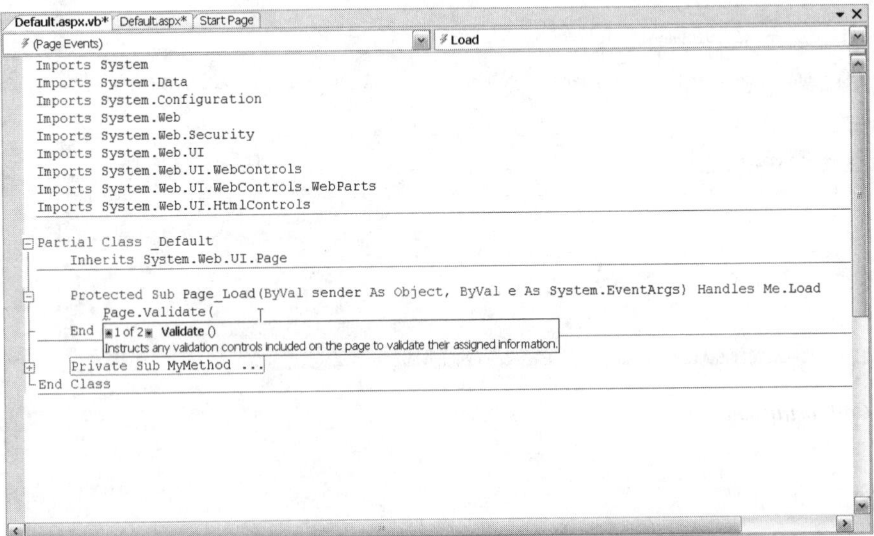

Figure 2-18. *IntelliSense with overloaded methods*

Error Underlining

One of the code editor's most useful features is error underlining. Visual Studio is able to detect a variety of error conditions, such as undefined variables, properties, or methods; invalid data type conversions; and missing code elements. Rather than stopping you to alert you that a problem exists, the Visual Studio editor quietly underlines the offending code. You can hover your mouse over an underlined error to see a brief tooltip description of the problem (see Figure 2-19).

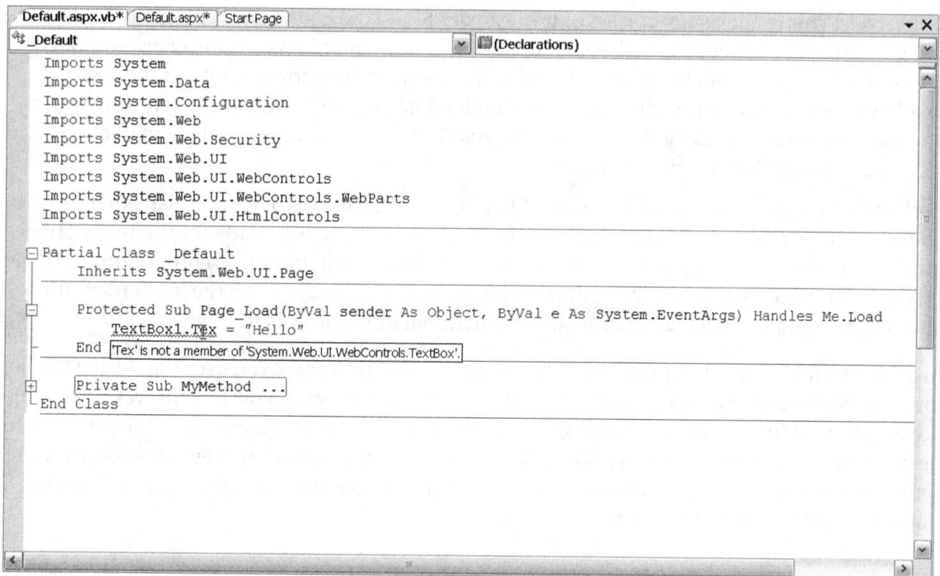

Figure 2-19. *Highlighting errors at design time*

Visual Studio won't flag your errors immediately. Instead, it will quickly scan through your code as soon as you try to compile it and mark all the errors it finds. If your code contains at least one error, Visual Studio will ask you whether it should continue. At this point, you'll almost always decide to cancel the operation and fix the problems Visual Studio has reported. (If you choose to continue, you'll actually wind up using the last compiled version of your application, because the .NET compilers can't build an application that has errors.)

■ Note You may find that as you fix errors and rebuild your project you discover more problems. That's because Visual Studio doesn't check for all types of errors at once. When you try to compile your application, Visual Studio scans for basic problems such as unrecognized class names. If these problems exist, they can easily mask other errors. On the other hand, if your code passes this basic level of inspection, Visual Studio checks for more subtle problems such as trying to use an unassigned variable.

The Coding Model

So far, you've learned how to design simple web pages, and you've taken a tour of the Visual Studio interface. But before you get to serious coding, it's important to understand a little more about the underpinnings of the ASP.NET code model. In this section, you'll learn about your options for using code to program a web page and how ASP.NET events wire up to your code.

Visual Studio supports two models for coding web pages and web services:

Inline code: This model is the closest to traditional ASP. All the code and HTML is stored in a single .aspx file. The code is embedded in one or more script blocks. However, even though the code is in a script block, it doesn't lose IntelliSense or debugging support, and it doesn't need to be executed linearly (like classic ASP code). Instead, you'll still react to control events and use subroutines. This model is handy because it keeps everything in one neat package, and it's popular for coding simple web pages.

Code-behind: This model separates each ASP.NET web page into two files: an .aspx markup file with the HTML and control tags, and a .vb code file with the source code for the page. This model provides better organization, and separating the user interface from programmatic logic is keenly important when building complex pages. In Visual Studio 2005, the implementation of the code-behind model has changed, but the overall philosophy is the same.

In .NET 1.0 and 1.1, the design tool you choose determines the model you use. With Visual Studio, you have the freedom to use either approach. When you add a new web page to your website (using Website ➤ Add New Item), the Place Code in a Separate File check box chooses whether you want to use the code-behind model (see Figure 2-20). Visual Studio remembers your previous setting for the next time you add a new page, but it's completely valid (albeit potentially confusing) to mix both styles of pages in the same application.

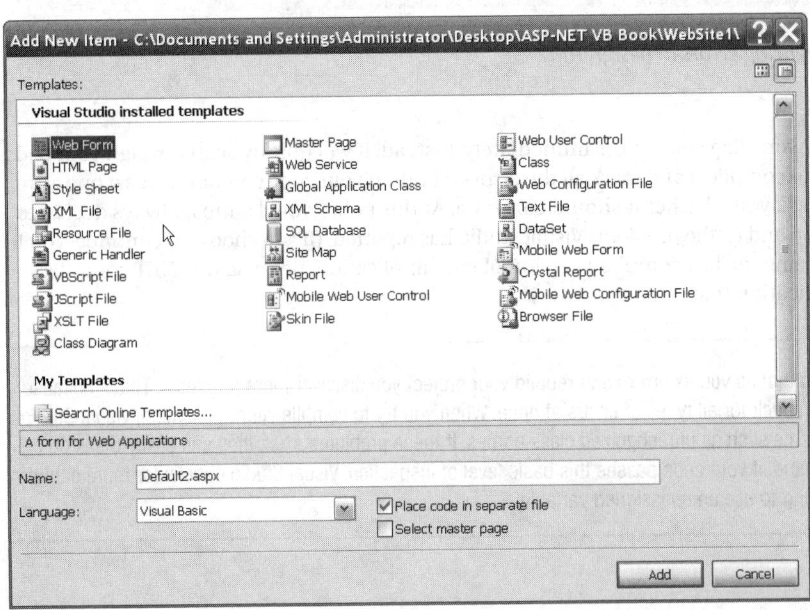

Figure 2-20. *Choosing the coding model*

To understand the difference, it helps to consider a simple page, like the following dynamic time example; this is TestFormInline.aspx, which shows how the page looks with inline code:

```
<%@ Page Language="vb" %>
<script runat="server">
  Protected Sub Button1_Click
    (ByVal sender As Object, ByVal e As System.EventArgs)
    Label1.Text = "Current time: " & DateTime.Now.ToLongTimeString()
  End Sub
```

```
</script>

<html xmlns="http://www.w3.org/1999/xhtml" >
<head runat="server">
  <title>Test Page</title>
</head>
<body>
  <form id="form1" runat="server">
  <div>
    <asp:Label ID="Label1" runat="server" Text="Click Me!">
    </asp:Label>
  <br />
  <br />
  <br />
  <asp:Button ID="Button1" runat="server"
      OnClick="Button1_Click" Text="Button" />
  </div>
  </form>
</body>
</html>
```

The following listings, TestFormCodeBehind.aspx and TestFormCodeBehind.aspx.vb, show how the page is broken up into two pieces using the code-behind model. This is TestFormCodeBehind.aspx:

```
<%@ Page Language="vb" AutoEventWireup="true" CodeFile="TestFormCodeBehind.aspx.vb"
        Inherits="TestFormCodeBehind"%>.aspx:

<html xmlns="http://www.w3.org/1999/xhtml" >
<head runat="server">
   <title>Test Page</title>
</head>
<body>
   <form id="form1" runat="server">
   <div>
      <asp:Label ID="Label1" runat="server" Text="Click Me!"></asp:Label><br />
      <br />
      <br />
      <asp:Button ID="Button1" runat="server" OnClick="Button1_Click"
      Text="Button" /></div>
   </form>
</body>
</html>
```

This is TestFormCodeBehind.aspx.vb:

```
Partial Class TestFormCodeBehind
          Inherits System.Web.UI.Page
    Protected Sub Button1_Click
      (ByVal sender As Object, ByVal e As System.EventArgs)
        Label1.Text = "Current time: " & DateTime.Now.ToLongTimeString()
    End Sub
End Class
```

The only real difference in this code is that the page class is no longer implicit—instead it is declared to contain all the page methods.

Overall, the code-behind model is preferred for complex pages. Although the inline code model is slightly more compact for small pages, as your code and HTML grows it becomes much easier to deal with both portions separately. The code-behind model is also conceptually cleaner, as it explicitly indicates the class you've created and the namespaces you've imported. Finally, the code-behind model introduces the possibility that a web designer may refine the markup in your pages without touching your code. This book uses the code-behind model for all examples.

How Code-Behind Files Are Connected to Pages

Every .aspx page starts with a Page directive. This Page directive specifies the language for the page, and it also tells ASP.NET where to find the associated code (unless you're using inline code, in which case the code is contained in the same file).

You can specify where to find the associated code in several ways. In previous versions of ASP.NET, it was common to use the Src attribute to point to the source code file or the Inherits attribute to indicate a compiled class name. However, both of these options have their idiosyncrasies. For example, with the Inherits attribute, you're forced to always precompile your code, which is tedious (and can cause problems in development teams, because the standard option is to compile every page into a single DLL assembly). But the real problem is that both approaches force you to declare every web control you want to use with a member variable. This adds a lot of boilerplate code.

In ASP.NET 2.0, you can solve the problem using a new language feature called *partial classes*, which let you split a single class into multiple source code files. Essentially, the model is the same as before, but the control declarations are shuffled into a separate file. You, the developer, never need to be distracted by this file—instead you can just access your web-page controls by name. Keen eyes will have spotted the word *partial* in the class declaration for your web-page code:

```
Partial Class TestFormCodeBehind
    Inherits System.Web.UI.Page
    ...
End Class
```

With this bit of infrastructure in place, the rest is easy. Your .aspx page links to the source code file using the CodeFile attribute, as shown here:

```
<%@ Page Language="vb" AutoEventWireup="true" CodeFile="TestFormCodeBehind.aspx.vb"
   Inherits="TestFormCodeBehind"%>
```

Notice that Visual Studio uses a slightly unusual naming syntax for the source code file. It has the full name of the corresponding web page, complete with the .aspx extension, followed by the .vb extension at the end. This is just a matter of convention, and it avoids a problem if you happen to create two different code-behind file types (for example, a web page and a web service) with the same name.

How Control Tags Are Connected to Page Variables

When you request your web page in a browser, ASP.NET starts by finding the associated code file. Then, it generates a variable declaration for each control that has a runat="server" attribute declaration. For example, imagine you have a text box named txtInput:

```
<asp:TextBox ID="txtInput" runat="server"/>
```

ASP.NET generates the following member variable declaration and merges it with your page class using the magic of partial classes:

```
Protected System.Web.UI.TextBox txtInput;
```

To make sure this system works, you must keep both the .aspx markup file (with the control tags) and the .vb file (with the source code) synchronized. If you edit control names in one piece using another tool (such as a text editor), you'll break the link, and your code won't compile.

Incidentally, you'll notice that control variables are always declared with the protected accessibility keyword. That's because of the way ASP.NET uses inheritance in the web-page model. The following three layers are at work:

- First, the Page class from the .NET class library defines the basic functionality that allows a web page to host other controls, render itself to HTML, and provide access to the traditional ASP objects such as Request, Response, and Session.
- Second, your code-behind class (for example, TestFormCodeBehind) inherits from the Page class to acquire the basic set of ASP.NET web-page functionality.
- Finally, the .aspx page (for example, HelloWorldPage.aspx) uses the code from the custom page class you created. This allows it to combine the user interface with the code that supports it.

Protected variables act like private variables with a key difference—they are accessible to derived classes. In other words, using protected variables in your code-behind class ensures that the variables are accessible in the derived page class. This allows ASP.NET to connect your control variables to your control tags at runtime.

How Events Are Connected to Event Handlers

Most of the code in an ASP.NET web page is placed inside event handlers that react to web control events. Using Visual Studio, you can add an event handler to your code in three ways:

Type it in by hand: In this case, you add the method directly to the page class. You must specify the appropriate parameters so that the signature of the event handler exactly matches the signature of the event you want to handle. You'll also need to edit the control tag so that it links the control to the appropriate event handler. (Alternatively, you can use delegates to wire this up programmatically.)

Double-click a control in design view: In this case, Visual Studio will create an event handler for that control's default event (and adjust the control tag accordingly). For example, if you double-click the page, it will create a Page.Load event handler. If you double-click a Button control, Visual Studio will create an event handler for the Click event.

Choose the event from the Properties window: Just select the control, and click the lightning bolt in the Properties window. You'll see a list of all the events provided by that control. Double-click in the box next to the event you want to handle, and Visual Studio will automatically generate the event handler in your page class and adjust the control tag.

The second and third options are the most convenient. The third option is the most flexible, because it allows you to select a method in the page class that you've already created. Just select the event in the Properties window, and click the drop-down arrow at the right. You'll see a list that includes all the methods in your class that match the signature this event requires. You can then choose a method from the list to connect it. Figure 2-21 shows an example where the Button.Click event is connected to the Button_Click() method in your page class. The only limitation of this technique is that it works exclusively with web controls, not server-side HTML controls.

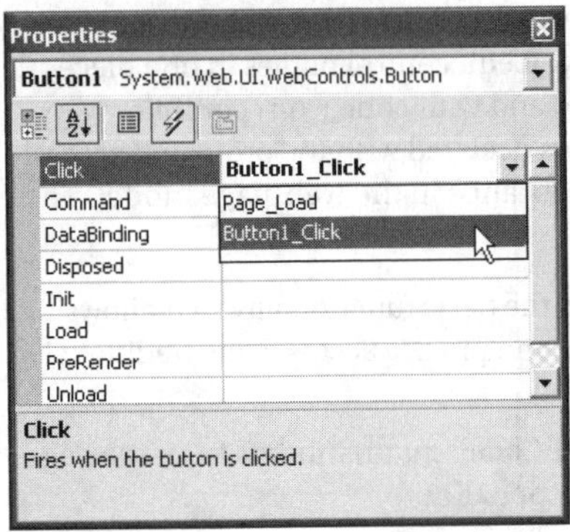

Figure 2-21. *Attaching an event handler*

Visual Studio 2005 uses *automatic event wire-up*, as indicated in the Page directive. Automatic event wire-up has two basic principles:

- All page event handlers are connected automatically based on the name of the event handler. In other words, the Page_Load() method is automatically called when the page loads. Visual Studio adds a comment to your page class to point out the commonly used event methods.
- All control event handlers are connected using attributes in the control tag. The attribute has the same name as the event, prefixed by the word *On*.

For example, if you want to handle the Click event of the Button control, you simply need to set the OnClick attribute in the control tag with the name of the event handler you want to use. Here's the change you need:

```
<asp:Button id="cmdOK" OnClick="cmdOK_Click" runat="server">
```

ASP.NET controls always use this syntax. Remember, because ASP.NET must connect the event handlers, the derived page class must be able to access the code-behind class. This means your event handlers must be declared with the protected or public keyword. (Protected is preferred, because it prevents other classes from seeing this method.)

Visual Studio Debugging

Visual Studio has always provided robust tools for debugging your web applications. In Visual Studio 2005, these tools remain essentially the same, with some minor enhancements that make it easier to drill into live objects and collections at runtime.

To debug a specific web page in Visual Studio, select that web page in the Solution Explorer, and click the Start Debugging button on the toolbar. (If you are currently editing the web page you want to test, you don't need to select it at all—just click Start Debugging to launch it directly.)

What happens next depends on the location of your project. If your project is stored on a remote web server or a local IIS virtual directory, Visual Studio simply launches your default browser and directs you to the appropriate URL. If you've used a file system application, Visual Studio starts its integrated web server on a dynamically selected port (which prevents it from conflicting with IIS, if it's installed). Then Visual Studio launches the default browser and passes it a URL that points to the local web server. Either way, the real work—compiling the page and creating the page objects—is passed along to the ASP.NET worker process.

■ Tip Visual Studio's built-in web server allows you to retrieve a file listing. This means if you create a web application named MyApp, you can make a request in the form of `http://localhost:port/MyApp` to see a list of pages. Then, just click the page you want to test. This process assumes your web application doesn't have a Default.aspx page—if it does, any requests for the website root automatically return this page.

The separation between Visual Studio, the web server, and ASP.NET allows for a few interesting tricks. For example, while your browser window is open, you can still make changes to the code and tags of your web pages. Once you've completed your changes, just save the page, and click the Refresh button in your browser to rerequest it. Although you'll always be forced to restart the entire page to see the results of any changes you make, it's still more convenient than rebuilding your whole project.

Fixing and restarting a web page is handy, but what about when you need to track down an elusive error? In these cases, you need Visual Studio's debugging smarts, which are described in the next few sections.

■ Note When you use the test web server, it runs all code using your user account. This is different from the much more limited behavior you'll see in IIS, which uses a less-privileged account to ensure security. It's important to understand the difference, because if your application accesses protected resources (such as the file system, a database, the registry, or an event log), you'll need to make sure you explicitly allow the IIS user. For more information about IIS and the hosting model, refer to Chapter 18.

Single-Step Debugging

Single-step debugging allows you to execute your code one line at a time. It's incredibly easy to use. Just follow these steps:

1. Find a location in your code where you want to pause execution, and start single-stepping (you can use any executable line of code but not a variable declaration, comment, or blank line). Click in the margin next to the line code, and a red breakpoint will appear (see Figure 2-22).

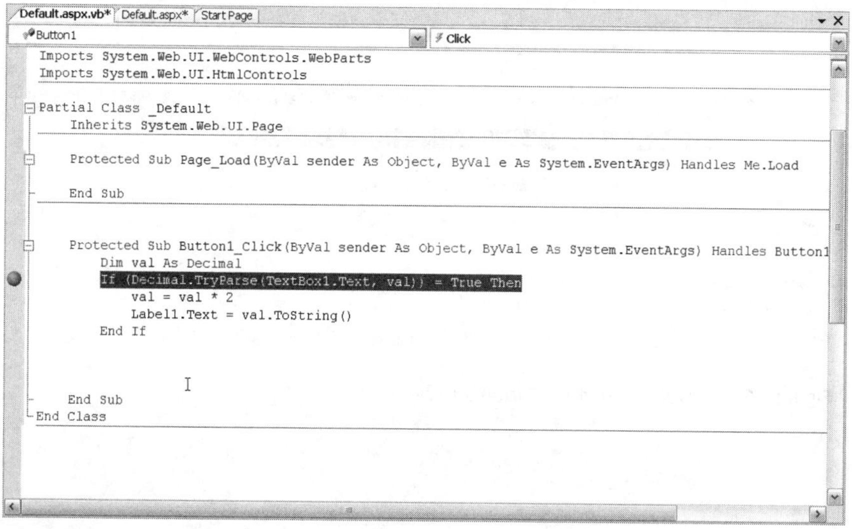

```
Imports System.Web.UI.WebControls.WebParts
Imports System.Web.UI.HtmlControls

Partial Class _Default
    Inherits System.Web.UI.Page

    Protected Sub Page_Load(ByVal sender As Object, ByVal e As System.EventArgs) Handles Me.Load

    End Sub


    Protected Sub Button1_Click(ByVal sender As Object, ByVal e As System.EventArgs) Handles Button1
        Dim val As Decimal
        If (Decimal.TryParse(TextBox1.Text, val)) = True Then
            val = val * 2
            Label1.Text = val.ToString()
        End If


    End Sub
End Class
```

Figure 2-22. *Setting a breakpoint*

2. Now start your program as you would ordinarily. When the program reaches your breakpoint, execution will pause, and you'll be switched back to the Visual Studio code window. The breakpoint statement won't be executed.
3. At this point, you have several options. You can execute the current line by pressing F8 or Shift+F8. The following line in your code will be highlighted with a yellow arrow, indicating that this is the next line that will be executed. You can continue like this through your program, running one line at a time by pressing F8 or Shift+F8 and following the code's path of execution. Or, you can exit break mode and resume running your code by pressing F5.

■ **Note** Instead of using shortcut keys such as F8, Shift+F8, and F5, you can use the buttons in the Visual Studio Debug toolbar. Alternatively, you can right-click the code window and choose an option from the context menu.

---

4. Whenever the code is in break mode, you can hover over variables to see their current contents. This allows you to verify that variables contain the values you expect (see Figure 2-23). If you hover over an object, you can drill down into all the individual properties by clicking a small plus symbol to expand it (see Figure 2-24).

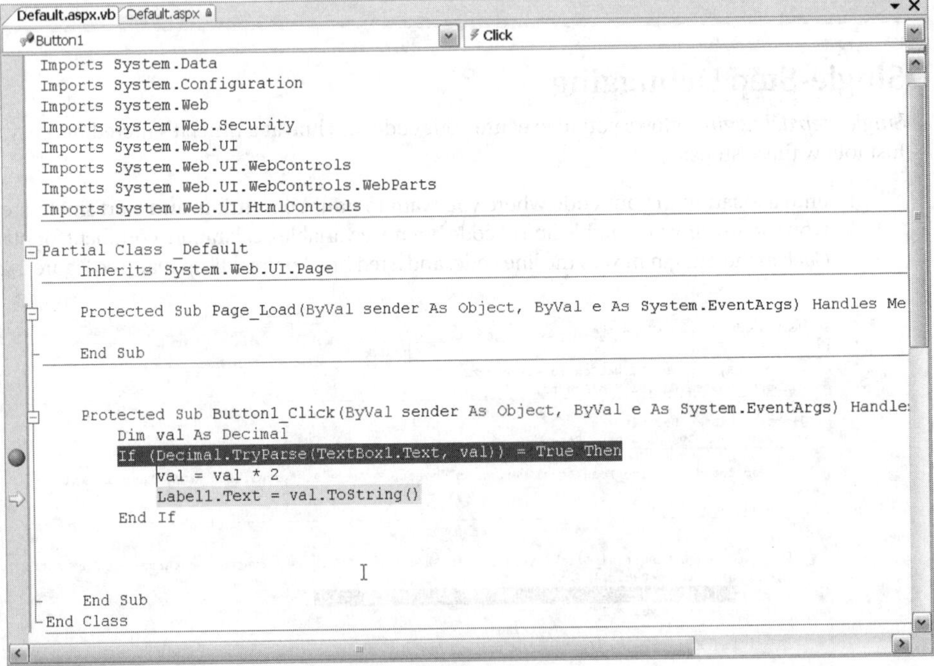

Figure 2-23. *Viewing variable contents in break mode*

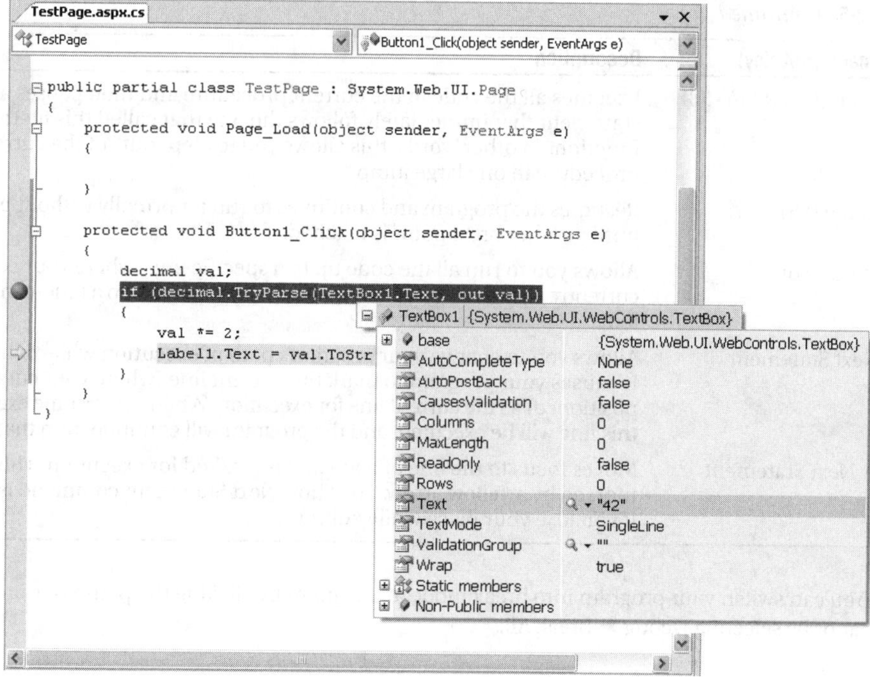

Figure 2-24. *Viewing object properties in break mode*

Tip You can even modify the values in a variable or property directly—just click inside the tooltip, and enter the new value. This allows you to simulate scenarios that are difficult or time-consuming to re-create manually or to test specific error conditions.

---

5. You can also use any of the commands listed in Table 2-5 while in break mode. These commands are available from the context menu by right-clicking the code window or by using the associated hot key.

Table 2-5. *Commands Available in Break Mode*

Command (Hot Key)	Description
Step Into (F8)	Executes the currently highlighted line and then pauses. If the currently highlighted line calls a procedure, execution will pause at the first executable line inside the method or function (which is why this feature is called stepping *into*).
Step Over (Shift+F8)	The same as Step Into, except that it runs procedures as though they are a single line. If you select the Step Over command while a procedure call is highlighted, the entire procedure will be executed. Execution will pause at the next executable statement in the current procedure.

(Continued)

Table 2-5. *Continued*

Command (Hot Key)	Description
Step Out (Ctrl+Shift+F8)	Executes all the code in the current procedure and then pauses at the statement that immediately follows the one that called this method or function. In other words, this allows you to step "out" of the current procedure in one large jump.
Continue (F5)	Resumes the program and continues to run it normally without pausing until another breakpoint is reached.
Run to Cursor	Allows you to run all the code up to a specific line (where your cursor is currently positioned). You can use this technique to skip a time-consuming loop.
Set Next Statement	Allows you to change your program's path of execution while debugging. It causes your program to mark the current line (where your cursor is positioned) as the current line for execution. When you resume execution, this line will be executed, and the program will continue from that point.
Show Next Statement	Moves focus to the line of code that is marked for execution. This line is marked by a yellow arrow. The Show Next Statement command is useful if you lose your place while editing.

You can switch your program into break mode at any point by clicking the pause button in the toolbar or by selecting Debug ➤ Break All.

Advanced Breakpoints

Choose Debug ➤ Windows ➤ Breakpoints to see a window that lists all the breakpoints in your current project. The Breakpoints window provides a hit count, showing you the number of times a breakpoint has been encountered (see Figure 2-25). You can jump to the corresponding location in code by double-clicking a breakpoint. You can also use the Breakpoints window to disable a breakpoint without removing it. That allows you to keep a breakpoint to use in testing later, without leaving it active. Breakpoints are automatically saved with the hidden solution file described earlier.

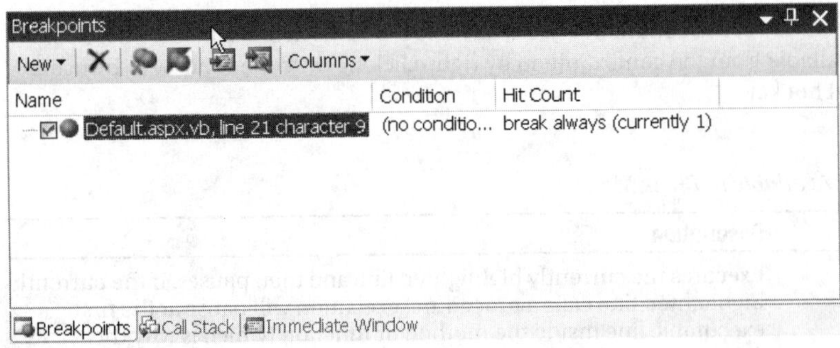

Figure 2-25. *The Breakpoints window*

Visual Studio allows you to customize breakpoints so they occur only if certain conditions are true. To customize a breakpoint, right-click it, and select Breakpoint Properties. In the window that appears, you can take one of the following actions:

- Click the Condition button to set an expression. You can choose to break when this expression is true or when it has changed since the last time the breakpoint was hit.
- Click the Hit Count button to create a breakpoint that pauses only after a breakpoint has been hit a certain number of times (for example, at least 20) or a specific multiple of times (for example, every fifth time).

Variable Watches

In some cases, you might want to track the status of a variable without switching into break mode repeatedly. In this case, it's more useful to use the Locals, Autos, and Watch windows, which allow you track variables across an entire application. Table 2-6 describes these windows.

Table 2-6. *Variable Tracking Windows*

Window	Description
Locals	Automatically displays all the variables that are in scope in the current procedure. This offers a quick summary of important variables.
Autos	Automatically displays variables that Visual Studio determines are important for the current code statement. For example, this might include variables that are accessed or changed in the previous line.
Watch	Displays variables you have added. Watches are saved with your project, so you can continue tracking a variable later. To add a watch, right-click a variable in your code, and select Add Watch; alternatively, double-click the last row in the Watch window, and type in the variable name.

Each row in the Locals, Autos, and Watch windows provides information about the type or class of the variable and its current value. If the variable holds an object instance, you can expand the variable and see its private members and properties. For example, in the Locals window you'll see the Me variable, which is a reference to the current page class. If you click the plus symbol next to this, a full list will appear that describes many page properties (and some system values), as shown in Figure 2-26.

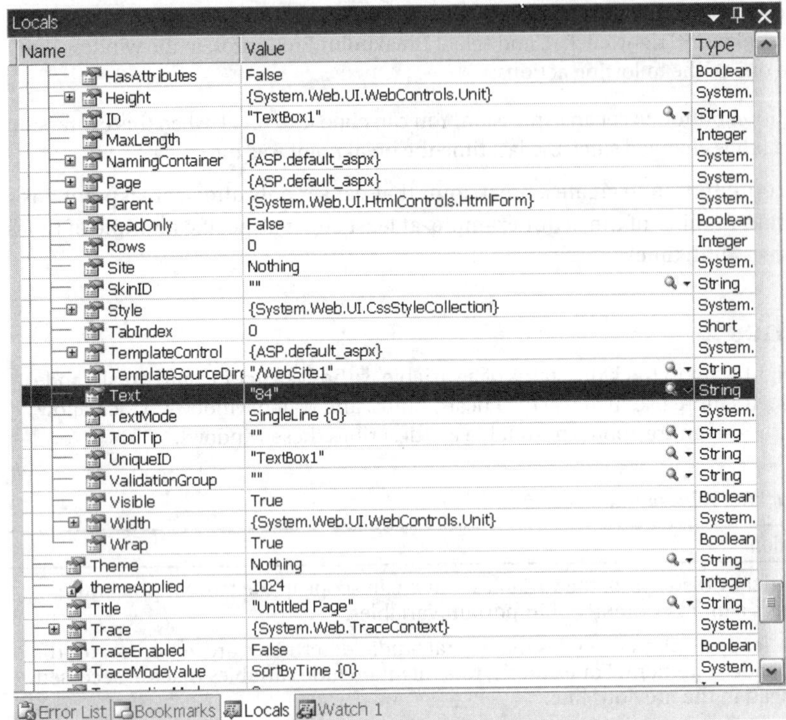

Locals
Name
Value
Type
HasAttributes
False
Boolean
Height
{System.Web.UI.WebControls.Unit}
System.
ID
"TextBox1"
String
MaxLength
0
Integer
NamingContainer
{ASP.default_aspx}
System.
Page
{ASP.default_aspx}
System.
Parent
{System.Web.UI.HtmlControls.HtmlForm}
System.
ReadOnly
False
Boolean
Rows
0
Integer
Site
Nothing
System.
SkinID
""
String
Style
{System.Web.UI.CssStyleCollection}
System.
TabIndex
0
Short
TemplateControl
{ASP.default_aspx}
System.
TemplateSourceDire
"/WebSite1"
String
Text
"84"
String
TextMode
SingleLine {0}
System.
ToolTip
""
String
UniqueID
"TextBox1"
String
ValidationGroup
""
String
Visible
True
Boolean
Width
{System.Web.UI.WebControls.Unit}
System.
Wrap
True
Boolean
Theme
Nothing
String
themeApplied
1024
Integer
Title
"Untitled Page"
String
Trace
{System.Web.TraceContext}
System.
TraceEnabled
False
Boolean
TraceModeValue
SortByTime {0}
System.
Error List
Bookmarks
Locals
Watch 1

Figure 2-26. *Viewing the current page class in the Locals window*

The Locals, Autos, and Watch windows allow you to change variables or properties while your program is in break mode. Just double-click the current value in the Value column, and type in a new value. If you are missing one of the watch windows, you can show it manually by selecting it from the Debug ➤ Windows submenu.

Visual Studio Macros

One of the most exciting frills of the Visual Studio development environment is its powerful macro and add-in framework (which is largely unchanged from previous versions of Visual Studio .NET). This framework, known as the Visual Studio Automation model, provides almost 200 objects that give you unprecedented control over the IDE, including the ability to access and manipulate the current project hierarchy, the collection of open windows, and the integrated debugger. One of the most convenient and flexible Automation tools is the macro facility.

The simplest macro is a keystroke recording. To create a simple keystroke macro, select Tools ➤ Macros ➤ Record Temporary Macro from the Visual Studio menu, and press the appropriate keystrokes. Once you're finished, click the stop button on the floating macro toolbar. You can now replay the recorded macro (with the Ctrl+Shift+P shortcut key).

■ **Note** Visual Studio allows only one recorded macro, which is overwritten every time you record a new one. To make a temporary macro permanent, you'll need to cut and paste the code into a different subroutine.

A good way to start learning about macros is to use the record facility and then look at the code it generates. Select Tool ➤ Macros ➤ Macro Explorer to see a window that shows a tree of macro modules and the macros they contain (see Figure 2-27). Each macro corresponds to a Visual Basic subroutine. (Unfortunately, C# is not supported.) To edit the macro you just created, right-click the TemporaryMacro subroutine in the RecordingModule, and select Edit.

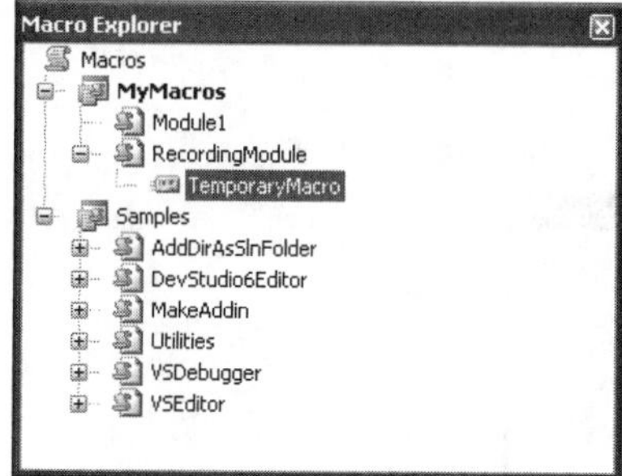

Figure 2-27. *The Macro Explorer*

Macro code uses a special DTE (design-time environment) object model. The DTE hierarchy provides the core features that allow you to interact with every aspect of the IDE. Some of the ingredients at your fingertips include the following:

- Window objects (used to close, rearrange, or otherwise manipulate open windows)
- Document objects (used to edit text)
- Solution and project objects (used to manage the underlying files and project collection)
- Tool-window objects (used to configure the IDE's interface)
- Debugging objects (used for tasks such as creating breakpoints and halting execution)
- Event objects (used to react to IDE events)
- Code-manipulation objects (used to analyze your project's code constructs)

For example, the following macro automatically lists all the files in the project that have been modified but not saved. The list is shown in the Output window.

```
Sub ListModifiedDocuments()
    Dim win As Window = DTE.Windows.Item(Constants.vsWindowKindCommandWindow)
    Dim target As Object

    ' If the current window is an Output window, use it. Otherwise, use a
    ' helper function to find and activate the window.
    If (DTE.ActiveWindow Is win) Then
        target = win.Object
    Else
         ' The GetOutputWindowPane is a helper function that can be downloaded
         ' from MSDN or Apress with the code download accompanying this book
        target = GetOutputWindowPane("Modified Documents")
        target.clear()
    End If

    ' Loop through all the open documents, and if unsaved changes are detected,
    ' write the document name to the Output window.
```

```
    Dim doc As Document
    For Each doc In DTE.Documents
        If Not doc.Saved Then
            target.OutputString(doc.Name & "    " & doc.FullName & _
              Microsoft.VisualBasic.Constants.vbCrLf)
        End If
    Next
End Sub
```

Figure 2-28 shows the result of running this macro.

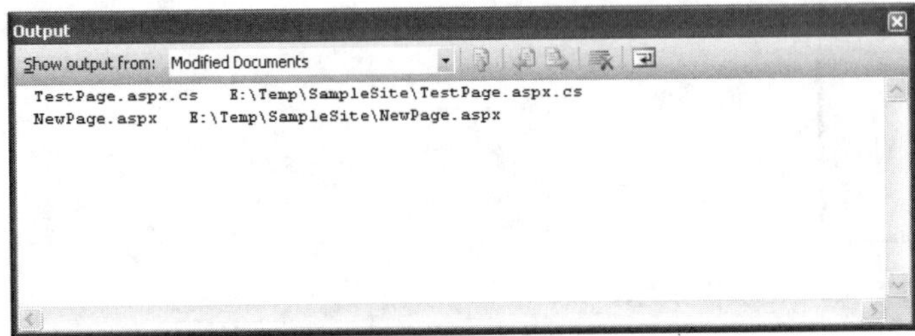

Figure 2-28. *Detecting changed documents*

You can run the Macro from the Tools ➤ Macro menu in Visual Studio 2005.

This is only one of several dozen useful macros that are included in the Samples macro project, which comes with Visual Studio 2005 (and the code download for this chapter). To learn more about Visual Studio macros and add-ins, you can consult a dedicated book on the subject. Several good titles exist for the previous version of Visual Studio .NET, including *Inside Microsoft Visual Studio .NET* (Microsoft Press, 2003).

■ **Tip** Many useful Visual Studio macros are installed by default with Visual Studio 2005. Look under the Samples group in the Macro Explorer, which has macros for adding comments, switching on and off line numbers, inserting dates and times, formatting code, and debugging. You can also download more advanced add-ins from `http://msdn.microsoft.com/vstudio/downloads/samples`. These samples can do everything from automating the build process and integrating with Outlook to spell-checking the text in your user interface.

ASP.NET Development Helper

Another interesting tool that's only begun its development is the ASP.NET Development Helper, a free tool created by Nikhil Kothari from the ASP.NET team. The central goal of the ASP.NET Development Helper is to improve the debugging experience for ASP.NET developers by enhancing the ability of the browser to participate in the debugging process. Currently, the ASP.NET Development Helper is limited to just a few useful features:

- It can report whether a page is in debug or tracing mode.
- It can display the view state information for a page.
- It can display the trace information for a page (and hide it from the page, making sure your layout isn't cluttered).
- It can clear the cache or trigger an application restart.

Many of these features haven't been covered yet, but you'll see a brief example of the ASP.NET Development Helper in the next chapter.

The design of the ASP.NET Development Helper is quite interesting. Essentially, it's built out of two pieces:

- An HTTP module that runs on the web server and makes additional information available to the client browser. (You'll learn about HTTP modules in Chapter 5.)
- An unmanaged browser plug-in that communicates with the HTTP module and displays the important information in a side panel in the browser (see Figure 2-29). The browser plug-in is designed exclusively for Internet Explorer, but at least one other developer has already created a Firefox version that works with the same HTTP module.

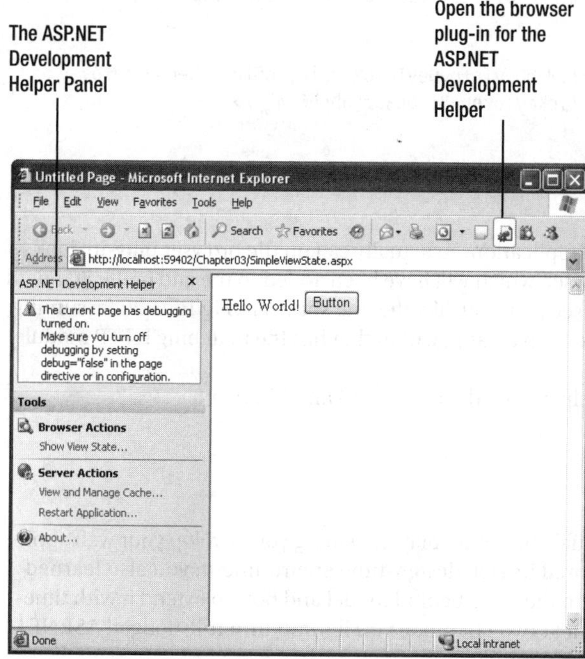

Figure 2-29. *The ASP.NET Development Helper*

To download the ASP.NET Development Helper, surf to `http://www.nikhilk.net/ASPNETDevHelperTool.aspx`. There you can download two DLLs, one for the HTTP module (WebDevInfo.dll) and one for the browser plug-in (WebDevInfo.BHO.dll). Copy these to any directory.

Next, you install the HTTP module with the following command:

```
Gacutil /I nStuff.WebDevInfo.dll
```

Then you need to add this module to the list of httpModules in your configuration. Open web.config (it should be in %windir%\Microsoft.NET\Framework\v2.0.50215\config or similar), and add the following entry to the <httpModules> section:

```
<add name="DevInfo" type="nStuff.WebDevInfo.DevInfoModule, nStuff.WebDevInfo,
   version=0.5.0.0, Culture=neutral, PublicKeyToken=8fc0e3af5abc6c4" />
```

Finally, install the browser extension with the following command line:

```
regsvr32 nStuff.WebDevInfo.BHO.dll
```

Next, you need install the assembly for the HTTP module into the GAC. You can do this by dragging and dropping in Windows Explorer, but it's generally easier to use the gacutil.exe utility. Start a Visual Studio command prompt (choose Programs ➤ Visual Studio 2005 ➤ Visual Studio Tools ➤ Visual Studio 2005 Command Prompt from the Start menu), and then run this command:

```
gacutil /i nStuff.WebDevInfo.dll
```

Now, when you want to use this tool with a web application, you need to modify the web.config file so it loads the HTTP module. The content you need depends on the exact version of the tool you're using, but it looks something like this:

```
<configuration xmlns="http://schemas.microsoft.com/.NetConfiguration/v2.0">
  <system.web>
    <httpModules>
      <add name="DevInfo" type="nStuff.WebDevInfo.DevInfoModule, nStuff.WebDevInfo,
Version=0.5.0.0, Culture=neutral, PublicKeyToken=8fc0e3af5abcb6c4" />
    </httpModules>
    ...
  </system.web>
</configuration>
```

Now, run one of the pages from this application. To actually call up the browser plug-in, look for a button (with a gear icon) in the browser, which will have been added to the end of the Standard toolbar. When you click this icon, you'll see a display like the one shown in Figure 2-29 (assuming you're currently viewing an ASP.NET page from an application that has the matching HTTP module loaded).

You'll see the ASP.NET Developer Helper at work in Chapter 3 and Chapter 6.

Summary

This chapter considered the role that Visual Studio can play in helping you develop your web applications. At the same time that you explored its rich design-time environment, you also learned about how it works behind the scenes with the code-behind model and how to extend it with time-saving features such as macros. In the next two chapters, you'll jump into full-fledged ASP.NET coding by examining web pages and server controls.

CHAPTER 3

Web Forms

ASP.NET pages (officially known as *web forms*) are a vital part of an ASP.NET application. They provide the actual output of a web application—the web pages that clients request and view in their browsers.

Although web pages aren't anything new, the concept of web *forms* is something entirely unique to ASP.NET. Essentially, web forms allow you to create a web application using the same control-based interface as a Windows application. To run an ASP.NET web form, the ASP.NET ISAPI extension reads the entire file, generates the corresponding objects, and fires a series of events. You react to these events using thoroughly object-oriented code.

This chapter provides in-depth coverage of web forms. You'll learn how they work and how you can use them to build simple pages. You'll also get an in-depth first look at the page-processing life cycle and the ASP.NET server-side control model.

WEB FORMS CHANGES IN .NET 2.0

The web forms model undergoes a minor tune-up in ASP.NET 2.0—there aren't many dramatic differences. Some of the changes take place behind the scenes—for example, pages now include even more events in their life cycle so they can plug into other ASP.NET features, such as themes and the new data binding model.

This chapter concentrates mostly on the core web forms model that was established in ASP.NET 1.0. However, you'll find a few refinements in this chapter. Here they are, in order of their appearance:

- *View state chunking*: Instead of placing all your view state information into a single field, you can tell ASP.NET to split it into several fields of a certain size. This feature is primarily intended to resolve issues with proxy servers that don't support really large hidden input fields.
- *XHTML support*: Web forms now render themselves using XHTML-compliant markup. This is a major shift from ASP.NET 1.*x*, and it's almost entirely painless.
- *Programmable page header*: The <head> portion of a web page is now exposed as an instance of the HtmlHead server control. Using this control, you can programmatically change the title, add metadata, or add linked stylesheets to the page.

If you're a seasoned ASP.NET 1.*x* developer, you can hone in on these additions as you work your way through this chapter.

Page Processing

One of the key goals of ASP.NET is to create a model that lets web developers rapidly develop web forms in the same way that Windows developers can build made-to-measure windows in a desktop application. Of course, web applications are very different from traditional rich client applications. There are two key stumbling blocks:

- *Web applications execute on the server*: For example, suppose you create a form that allows the user to select a product record and update its information. The user performs these tasks in the browser, but in order for you to perform the required operations (such as updating the database), your code needs to run on the web server. ASP.NET handles this divide with a technique called *postback*, which sends the page (and all user-supplied information) to the server when certain actions are performed. Once ASP.NET receives the page, it can then fire the corresponding server-side events to notify your code.
- *Web applications are stateless*: In other words, before the rendered HTML page is sent to the user, your web-page objects are destroyed and all client-specific information is discarded. This model lends itself well to highly scalable, heavily trafficked applications, but it makes it difficult to create a seamless user experience. ASP.NET includes several tools to help you bridge this gap; most notable is a persistence mechanism called *view state*, which automatically embeds information about the page in a hidden field in the rendered HTML.

In the following sections, you'll learn about both the postback and the view state features. Together, these mechanisms help abstract the underlying HTML and HTTP details, allowing developers to work in terms of objects and events.

HTML Forms

If you're familiar with HTML, you know that the simplest way to send client-side data to the server is using a <form> tag. Inside the <form> tag, you can place other <input> tags to represent basic (UI) user interface ingredients such as buttons, text boxes, list boxes, check boxes, and radio buttons.

For example, here's a form tag with a submit button, two check boxes, a text box, and a button, for a total of five <input> tags:

```
<html>
    <head>
        <title>Programmer Questionnaire</title>
    </head>
    <body>
        <form method="post" action="page.aspx">
            <p>Enter your first name: 
            <input type="text" name="FirstName"/><br>
            Enter your last name: 
            <input type="text" name="LastName"/><p>
            <p>You program with:<br>
               
            <input type="checkbox" name="VB"/>VB.NET<br>
               
            <input type="checkbox" name="CS"/>C#<br><br>
            <input type="submit" value="Submit" id="OK"/>
            </p>
        </form>
    </body>
</html>
```

Figure 3-1 shows what this basic page looks like in a web browser.

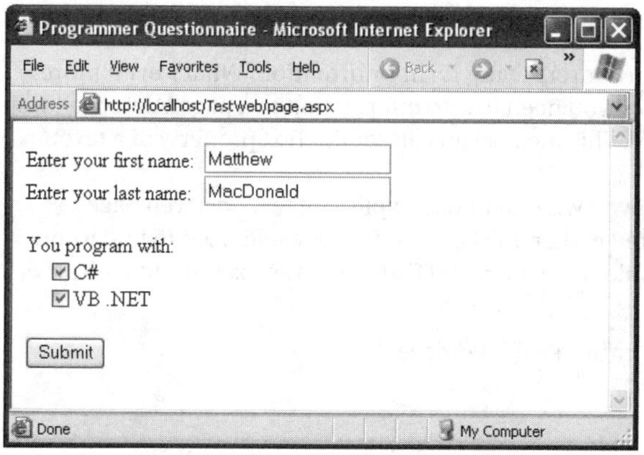

Figure 3-1. *A simple HTML form*

When the user clicks the submit button, the browser collects the current value of each control and pastes it together in a long string. This string is then sent back to the page indicated in the <form> tag (in this case, page.aspx) using an HTTP POST operation.

In this example, that means the web server might receive a request with this string of information:

```
FirstName=Matthew&LastName=MacDonald&CS=on&VB=on
```

The browser follows certain rules when constructing this string. Information is always sent as a series of name/value pairs separated by the ampersand (&) character. Each name/value pair is split with an equal (=) sign. Check boxes are left out unless they are checked, in which case the browser supplies the text *on* for the value. For the complete lowdown on the HTML forms standard, which is supported in every current browser, surf to `http://www.w3.org/TR/REC-html40/interact/forms.html`.

Virtually all server-side programming frameworks add a layer of abstraction over the raw form data. They parse this string and expose it in a more useful way. For example, JSP, ASP, and ASP.NET all allow you to retrieve the value of a form control using a thin object layer. In ASP and ASP.NET, you can look up values by name in the Request.Form collection. Here's an example in ASP.NET:

```
Dim firstName As String = Request.Form("FirstName")
```

This thin veneer over the actual POST message is helpful, but it's still a long way from a true object-oriented framework. That's why ASP.NET goes another step further. When a page is posted back to ASP.NET, it extracts the values, populates the Form collection (for backward compatibility with ASP code), and then configures the corresponding control objects. This means you can use the following much more intuitive syntax to retrieve information:

```
Dim firstName As String = txtFirstName.Text
```

This code also has the benefit of being type-safe. In other words, if you're retrieving the state of the check box, you'll receive a Boolean True or False value, instead of a string with the word *on*. In this way, developers are insulated from the quirks of HTML syntax.

■ **Note** In ASP.NET, all controls are placed inside a single <form> tag. This tag is marked with the runat="server" attribute, which allows it to work on the server side. ASP.NET does not allow you to create web forms that contain more than one server-side <form> tag, although it is possible to create a page that posts to another page using a technique called *cross-page posting*, which is discussed in Chapter 6.

Dynamic Interfaces

Clearly, the control model makes life easier for retrieving form information. What's even more remarkable is how it simplifies your life when you need to *add* information to a page. Almost all web control properties are readable and writable. This means you can set the Text property of a text box just as easily as you can read it.

For example, consider what happens if you want to update a piece of text on a web page to reflect some information the user has entered earlier. In classic ASP, you would need to find a convenient place to insert a script block that would write the raw HTML. Here's an example that displays a brightly colored welcome message:

```
Dim message As String = "<span style=""color:Red"">Welcome "
    & FirstName & " " & LastName & "</span>"
Response.Write(message)
```

On the other hand, life is much neater when you define a Label control in ASP.NET:

```
<asp:Label id="lblWelcome" runat="server" />
```

Now you can simply set its properties:

```
lblWelcome.Text = "Welcome " & FirstName & " " & LastName
lblWelcome.ForeColor = Color.Red
```

This code has several key advantages. First, it's much easier to write (and to write without errors). The savings seems fairly minor in this example, but it is much more dramatic when you consider a complete ASP.NET page that needs to dynamically render complex blocks of HTML that contain links, images, and styles.

Second, control-based code is also much easier to place inside a page. You can write your ASP.NET code wherever the corresponding action takes place. On the other hand, in classic ASP you need to worry about where the content appears on the page and arrange your script blocks code appropriately. If a page has several dynamic regions, it can quickly become a tangled mess of script blocks that don't show any clear relation or organization.

Another, subtler but equally dramatic, advantage of the control model is the way it hides the low-level HTML details. Not only does this allow you to write code without learning all the idiosyncrasies of HTML, but it also allows your pages to support a wider range of browsers. Because the control renders itself, it has the ability to tailor its output to support different browsers, enhanced client-side features, or even other HTML-related standards such as XHTML or WML (which is used in mobile browsers). Essentially, your code is no longer tightly coupled to the HTML standard.

The ASP.NET Event Model

Classic ASP uses a linear processing model. That means code on the page is processed from start to finish and is executed in order. Because of this model, classic ASP developers need to write a considerable amount of code even for simple pages. A classic example is a web page that has three different submit buttons for three different operations. In this case, your script code has to carefully distinguish which button was clicked when the page is submitted and then execute the right action using conditional logic.

ASP.NET provides a refreshing change with its new *event-driven* model. In this model, you add controls to a web form and then decide what events you want to respond to. Each event handler is wrapped up in a discrete method, which keeps the page code tidy and organized. This model is nothing new, but until the advent of ASP.NET it has been the exclusive domain of windowed UI programming in rich client applications.

So, how do ASP.NET events work? It's actually surprisingly straightforward. Here's a brief outline:

1. Your page runs for the first time. ASP.NET creates page and control objects, the initialization code executes, and then the page is rendered to HTML and returned to the client. The page objects are also released from server memory.
2. At some point, the user does something that triggers a postback, such as clicking a button. At this point, the page is submitted with all the form data by using ViewState information.
3. ASP.NET intercepts the returned page and re-creates the page objects, taking care to return them to the state they were in the last time the page was sent to the client.
4. Next ASP.NET checks what operation triggered the postback, and it raises the appropriate events (such as Button.Click), which your code can react to. Typically, at this point you'll perform some server-side operation (such as updating a database or reading data from a file) and then modify the control objects to display new information.
5. The modified page is rendered to HTML and returned to the client. The page objects are released from memory. If another postback occurs, ASP.NET repeats the process in steps 2 through 4.

In other words, ASP.NET doesn't just use the form data to configure the control objects for your page. It also uses it to decide what events to fire. For example, if it notices the text in a text box has changed since the last postback, it raises an event to notify your page. It's up to you whether you want to respond to this event.

■ Note Keep in mind that since HTML is completely stateless, and all state made available by ASP.NET is reconstituted, the event-driven model is really an emulation. ASP.NET performs quite a few tasks in the background in order to support this model, as you'll see in the following sections. The beauty of this concept is that the beginner programmer doesn't need to be familiar with the underpinnings of the system to take advantage of server-side events.

Automatic Postbacks

Of course, one gap exists in the event system described so far. Windows developers have long been accustomed to a rich event model that lets your code react to mouse movements, key presses, and the minutest control interactions. But in ASP.NET, client actions happen on the client side, and server processing takes place on the web server. This means a certain amount of overhead is always involved in responding to an event. For this reason, events that fire rapidly (such as a mouse move event) are completely impractical in the world of ASP.NET.

■ Note If you want to accomplish a certain UI effect, you might handle rapid events such as mouse movements with client-side JavaScript. (Or, better yet, you might use a custom ASP.NET control that already has these smarts built in, like some sort of pop-up menu.) However, all your business code must execute in the secure, feature-rich server environment.

If you're familiar with HTML forms, you know there is one basic way to submit a page—by clicking a submit button. If you're using the standard HTML server controls, this is still your only option. However, once the page is posted back, ASP.NET can fire other events at the same time (namely, events that indicate that the value in an input control has been changed).

Clearly, this isn't enough to build a rich web form. Fortunately, ASP.NET web controls extend this model with an *automatic postback* feature. With this feature, input controls can fire different events, and your server-side code can respond immediately. For example, you can trigger a postback when the user clicks a check box, changes the selection in a list, or changes the text in a text box and then moves to another field. These events still aren't as fine-grained as events in a Windows application, but they are a significant step up from the submit button.

Automatic Postbacks "Under the Hood"

To use automatic postback, you simply need to set the AutoPostBack property of a web control to True (the default is False, which ensures optimum performance if you don't need to react to a change event). When you do, ASP.NET uses the client-side abilities of JavaScript to bridge the gap between client-side and server-side code.

Here's how it works: if you create a web page that includes one or more web controls that are configured to use AutoPostBack, ASP.NET adds a JavaScript function to the rendered HTML page named __doPostBack(). When called, it triggers a postback, posting the page back to the web server with all the form information.

ASP.NET also adds two hidden input fields that the __doPostBack() function uses to pass information back to the server. This information consists of the ID of the control that raised the event and any additional information that might be relevant. These fields are initially empty, as shown here:

```
<input type="hidden" name="__EVENTTARGET" value="" />

<input type="hidden" name="__EVENTARGUMENT" value="" />
```

The `__doPostBack()` function has the responsibility for setting these values with the appropriate information about the event and then submitting the form. A sample `__doPostBack()` function is shown here:

```
<script type="text/javascript">

<!--
    function __doPostBack(eventTarget, eventArgument) {
        if(!theForm.onsubmit || (theForm.onsubmit() != false)) {
         theForm.__EVENTTARGET.value = eventTarget;
         theForm.__EVENTARGUMENT.value = eventArgument;
         theForm.submit();
        }
    }
// -->
</script>
```

Remember, ASP.NET generates the __doPostBack() function automatically. This code grows lengthier as you add more AutoPostBack controls to your page, because the event data must be set for each control.

Finally, any control that has its AutoPostBack property set to True is connected to the __doPostBack() function using the onClick or onChange attribute. These attributes indicate what action the browser should take in response to the client-side JavaScript events onClick and onChange.

The following example shows the tag for a list control named lstCountry, which posts back automatically. Whenever the user changes the selection in the list, the client-side onChange event fires. The browser then calls the __doPostBack() function, which sends the page back to the server.

```
<select id="lstCountry" onchange="__doPostBack('lstCountry','')"
        language="javascript">
```

In other words, ASP.NET automatically changes a client-side JavaScript event into a server-side ASP.NET event, using the __doPostBack() function as an intermediary. If you're a seasoned ASP developer, you may have manually created a solution like this for traditional ASP web pages. ASP.NET handles these details for you automatically, simplifying life a great deal.

■ **Tip** Remember, ASP.NET includes two control models: the bare-bones HTML server controls and the more fully functional web controls. Automatic postback is available only with web controls.

View State

The final ingredient in the ASP.NET model is the new *view state* mechanism. View state solves another problem that occurs because of the stateless nature of HTTP—lost changes.

Every time your page is posted back, you receive all the information that the user has entered in any <input> controls in the <form> tag. ASP.NET then loads the web page in its original state (based on the layout and defaults you've defined) and tweaks the page according to this new information. The problem is that in a dynamic web form, your code might change a lot more. For example, you might programmatically change the color of a heading, modify a piece of static text, hide or show a panel of controls, or even bind a full table of data to a grid. All these actions change the page from its initial state. However, none of them is reflected in the form data that's posted back. That means this information will be lost after every postback. Traditionally, statelessness has been overcome with the use of simple cookies, session-based cookies, and various other workarounds. All of these mechanisms require homemade (and sometimes painstaking) measures.

To deal with this limitation, ASP.NET has devised its own integrated state serialization mechanism. Essentially, once your page code has finished running (and just before the final HTML is rendered and sent to the client), ASP.NET examines all the properties of all the controls on your page. If any of these properties has been changed from its initial state, ASP.NET makes a note of this information in a name/value collection. Finally, ASP.NET takes all the information it has amassed and then serializes it as a Base64 string. (A Base64 string ensures that there aren't any special characters that wouldn't be valid HTML.) The final string is inserted in the <form> section of the page as a new hidden field.

When the page is posted back, ASP.NET follows these steps:

1. ASP.NET re-creates the page and control objects based on its defaults. Thus, the page has the same state that it had when it was first requested.
2. Next, ASP.NET deserializes the view state information and updates all the controls. This returns the page to the state it was in before it was sent to the client the last time.
3. Finally, ASP.NET adjusts the page according to the posted back form data. For example, if the client has entered new text in a text box or made a new selection in a list box, that information will be in the Form collection and ASP.NET will use it to tweak the corresponding controls. After this step, the page reflects the current state as it appears to the user.
4. Now your event-handling code can get involved. ASP.NET triggers the appropriate events, and your code can react to change the page, move to a new page, or perform a completely different operation.

Using view state is a great solution because server resources can be freed after each request, thereby allowing for scalability to support hundreds or thousands of requests without bogging the server down. However, it still comes with a price. Because view state is stored in the page, it results in a larger total page size. This affects the client doubly, because the client not only needs to receive a larger page, but the client also needs to send the hidden view state data back to the server with the next postback. Thus, it takes longer both to receive and post the page. For simple pages, this overhead is minimal, but if you configure complex, data-heavy controls such as the GridView, the view state information can grow to a size where it starts to exert a toll. In these cases, you can disable view state for a control by setting its EnableViewState property to False. However, in this case you need to reinitialize the control with each postback.

■ **Note** Even if you set EnableViewState to False, the control can still hold onto a smaller amount of view state information that it deems critical for proper functioning. This privileged view state information is known as *control state*, and it can never be disabled. However, in a well-designed control the size required for control state will be significantly smaller than the size of the entire view state. Control state is new in ASP.NET 2.0, and you'll see how it works when you design your own custom controls in Chapter 27.

ASP.NET uses view state only with page and control properties. ASP.NET doesn't take the same steps with member variables and other data you might use. However, as you'll learn later in this book, you can place other types of data into view state and retrieve this information manually at a later time.

Figure 3-2 provides an end-to-end look at page requests that puts all these concepts together.

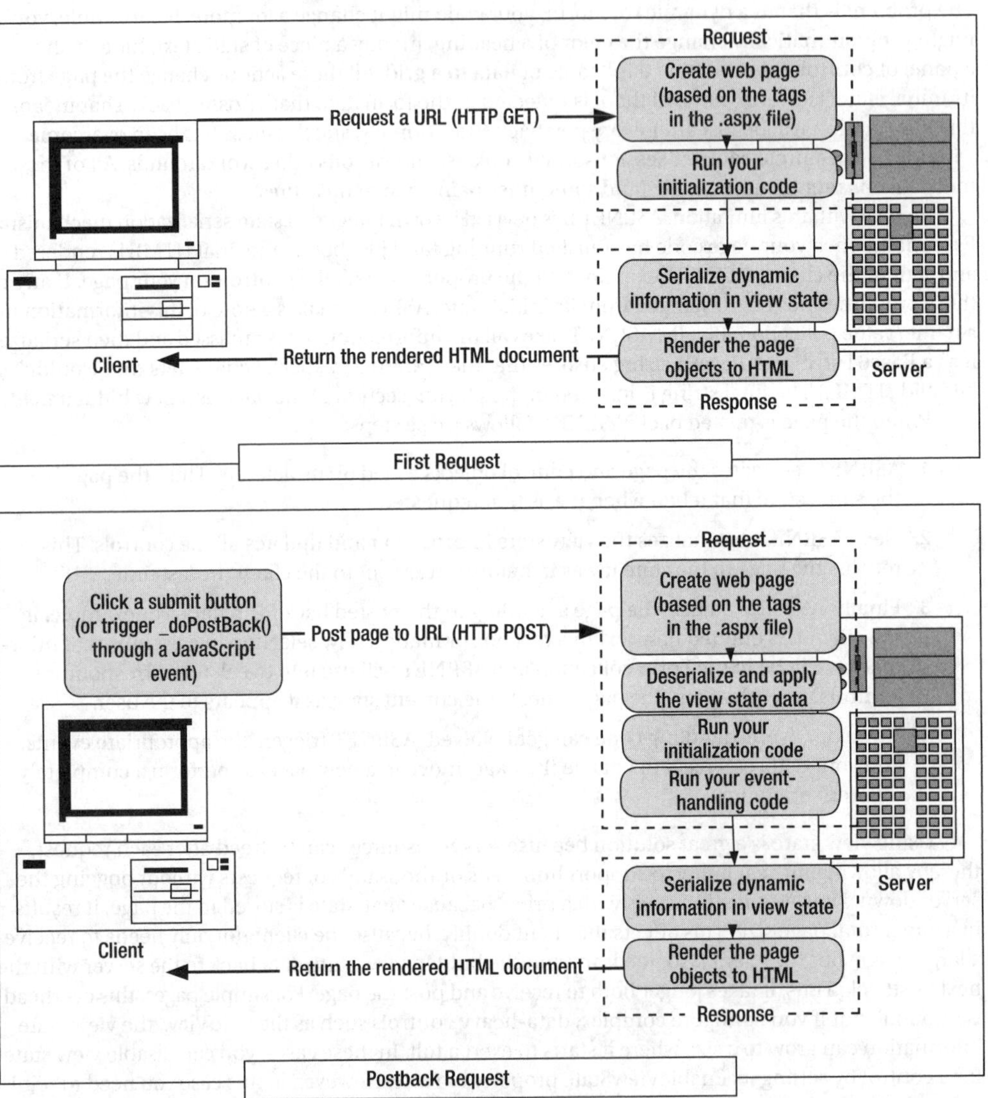

Figure 3-2. *ASP.NET page requests*

Note It is absolutely essential to your success as an ASP.NET programmer to remember that the web form is re-created with *every* round-trip. It does not persist or remain in memory longer than it takes to render a single request.

View State "Under the Hood"

If you look at the rendered HTML for an ASP.NET page, you can easily find the hidden input field with the view state information. The following example shows a page that uses a simple Label web control and sets it with a dynamic "Hello, world" message:

```
<html>
    <head runat="server">
        <title>Hello World Page</title>
    </head>
    <body>
    <form name="Form1" method="post" action="WebForm1.aspx" id="Form1">
      <div>
        <input type="hidden" name="__VIEWSTATE" value="/wEPDwUKLTE2MjY5MTY1
NQ9kFgICAw9kFgICAQ8PFgIeBFRleHQFDEhlbGxvIFdvcmxkIWRkZPsbiNOyNAufEt7OvNIbVYc
GWHqf" />

      </div>
      <div>
        <input type="submit" name="Button1" value="Button" id="Button1" />
        <span id="lbl">Hello, world</span>
      </div>
    </form>
    </body>
</html>
```

The view state string isn't human readable—it just looks like a series of random characters. However, it's important to note that a user who is willing to go to a little work can interpret this data quite easily. Here's a snippet of .NET code that does the job and writes the decoded information to a web page:

```
' viewStateString contains the view state information.
' Convert the Base64 string to an ordinary array of bytes
' representing ASCII characters.
Dim stringBytes As Byte() = Convert.FromBase64String(viewStateString)

' Deserialize and display the string.
Dim decodedViewState As String = System.Text.Encoding.ASCII.GetString(stringBytes)
lbl.Text = decodedViewState
```

In the web page, you'll see something like this:

```
?□□□□ -162691655□d□□□□□d□□□□□□□□□□-□Text□ Hello, worldddd?□???4 ?□????□U?□Xz
```

As you can see, the control text is clearly visible (along with some unprintable characters that render as blank boxes). This means that, in its default implementation, view state isn't a good place to store sensitive information that the client shouldn't be allowed to see—that sort of data should stay on the server. Additionally, you shouldn't make decisions based on view state that could compromise your application if the client tampers with the view state data.

Fortunately, it's possible to tighten up view state security quite a bit. You can enable automatic hash codes to prevent view state tampering, and you can even encrypt view state to prevent it from being decoded. These techniques raise hidden fields from a clumsy workaround to a much more robust and respectable piece of infrastructure. You'll learn about both of these techniques in Chapter 6.

■ **Note** If you've programmed with ASP.NET 1.*x*, you may have noticed that the view state serialization model in ASP.NET 2.0 isn't exactly the same. Instead of separating values with semicolons and angle brackets, ASP.NET 2.0 uses nonprintable characters, which makes parsing the string more efficient (because it's easier to distinguish the serialized data from the markers) and more compact. ASP.NET 2.0 also reduces the serialization size for many common data types, including Boolean values, integers, and strings that are repeated more than once (which is fairly common, because different controls often have the same property names). These seemingly minor changes can have a dramatic effect. Depending on the number of delimiters in the serialized view state, and the types of data types that are used, a data-heavy control can shrink its view state by half or more.

View State Chunking

The size of the hidden view state field has no limit. However, some proxy servers and firewalls refuse to let pages through if they have hidden fields greater than a certain size. To circumvent this problem, you can use *view state chunking*, which automatically divides view state into multiple fields to ensure that no hidden field exceeds a size threshold you set.

To use view state chunking, you simply need to set the maxPageStateFieldLength attribute of the <pages> element in the web.config file. This specifies the maximum view state size, in bytes. Here's an example that caps view state at 1 KB:

```
<configuration xmlns="http://schemas.microsoft.com/.NetConfiguration/v2.0">
    <system.web>
        <pages maxPageStateFieldLength = "1024" />
    </system.web>
</configuration>
```

When you request a page that generates a view state larger than this, several hidden input fields will be created:

```
<input type="hidden" name="__VIEWSTATEFIELDCOUNT" value="3" />
<input type="hidden" name="__VIEWSTATE" value="..." />
<input type="hidden" name="__VIEWSTATE1" value="..." />
<input type="hidden" name="__VIEWSTATE2" value="..." />
```

Remember, view state chunking is simply a mechanism for avoiding problems with certain proxies (which is a relatively rare occurrence). View state chunking does not improve performance (and adds a small amount of extra serialization overhead). As a matter of good design, you should strive to include as little information in view state as possible, which ensures the best performance.

XHTML Compliance

In a major shift from ASP.NET 1.*x*, the web controls in ASP.NET 2.0 are compliant with the XHTML 1.1 standard. However, it's still up to you to make sure the rest of your page behaves by the rules. ASP.NET doesn't take any steps to force XHTML compliance onto your page.

■ **Note** XHTML support doesn't add any functionality to your web pages that you wouldn't have with HTML 4.01. However, because XHTML is a stricter standard, it has a few benefits. For example, you can validate XHTML pages to catch minor errors that could trip up certain browsers. Most important, XHTML pages are also valid XML documents, which makes it easier for applications to read or analyze them programmatically and introduces the possibility of future extensibility. The current consensus is that XHTML will replace HTML in the future. You can learn more about XHTML by referring to the specification at `http://www.w3.org/TR/xhtml11`.

With a few exceptions, all the ASP.NET server controls render themselves using XHTML-compliant markup. That means this markup follows the rules of XHTML, which include the following:

- Tag and attribute names must be in lowercase.
- All elements must be closed, either with a dedicated closing tag (<p></p>) or using an empty tag that closes itself (<br />).
- All attribute values must be enclosed in quotes (for example, type="text").
- The id attribute must be used instead of the name attribute.

XHTML also removes support for certain features that were allowed in HTML, such as frames and inline formatting that doesn't use CSS. In most cases, a suitable XHTML alternative exists. However, one sticking point is the target attribute, which HTML developers can use to create links that open in new windows. The following ASP.NET controls may use the target attribute:

- AdRotator
- TreeNode
- HyperLink
- HyperLinkColumn
- BulletedList

Using the target attribute won't cause a problem in modern browsers. However, if you need to create a website that is completely XHTML-compliant, you should avoid these controls.

Note You won't gain much, if anything, by using XHTML today. However, some companies and organizations mandate the use of XHTML, namely, with a view to future standards. In the future, XHTML will make it easier to design web pages that are adaptable to a variety of different platforms, can be processed by other applications, and are extensible with new markup features. For example, you could use XSLT (XSL Transformations), another XML-based standard, to transform an XHTML document into another form. The same features won't be available to HTML pages.

Document Type Definitions

Every XHTML document begins with a *document type definition* that defines the type of XHTML your page uses. You place this immediately after the Page directive in the markup portion of your web page. That way, the document type definition will be rendered as the first line of your document, which is a requirement.

Here's an example that defines a web page that supports XHTML 1.1:

```
<%@ Page Language="vb" AutoEventWireup="true"
 CodeFile="TestPage.aspx.vb" Inherits="_TestPage" %>

<!DOCTYPE html PUBLIC "-//W3C//DTD XHTML 1.1//EN"
 "http://www.w3.org/TR/xhtml11/DTD/xhtml11.dtd">

<html xmlns="http://www.w3.org/1999/xhtml" >
<head runat="server">
    <title>Untitled Page</title>
</head>
<body>
```

```
    <form id="form1" runat="server">
    <div>
        ...
    </div>
    </form>
</body>
</html>
```

The page also defines the XML namespace for the <html> element. This is another detail that XHTML requires but ASP.NET doesn't supply automatically.

■ **Note** When you create a web page in Visual Studio, it sets the XML namespace for the <html> element, and it adds a doctype for XHTML 1.1. You can change this doctype (or even remove it entirely).

If you don't want to support the full XHTML 1.1 standard, you can make a few compromises. Some other common choices for doctype include *XHTML 1.0 transitional*, which enforces the structural rules of XHTML but allows HTML formatting features that have been replaced by stylesheets and are considered obsolete. Here's the doctype you need:

```
<!DOCTYPE html PUBLIC "-//W3C//DTD XHTML 1.0 Transitional//EN"
"http://www.w3.org/TR/xhtml1/DTD/xhtml1-transitional.dtd">
```

The XHTML transitional doctype considers HTML frames obsolete. If you need to create a frames page, consider the *XHTML 1.0 frameset doctype*:

```
<!DOCTYPE html PUBLIC "-//W3C//DTD XHTML 1.0 Frameset//EN"
"http://www.w3.org/TR/xhtml1/DTD/xhtml1-frameset.dtd">
```

Remember, the ASP.NET server controls will work equally well with any doctype (and they will work with browsers that support only HTML as well). It's up to you to choose the level of standards compliance (and backward compatibility) you want in your web pages.

■ **Note** If you're really intent on following the rules of the XHTML standard, you can choose to render your page using the MIME content type application/xhtml+xml instead of the standard text/html. This change is an XHTML recommendation, and it's designed to help browsers and other applications distinguish between ordinary HTML pages and XHTML. Unfortunately, at the time of this writing Internet Explorer still doesn't support the application/xhtml+xml content type (unlike almost all other modern browsers). If you still want to implement the change, just add the attribute ContentType="application/xhtml+xml" to the Page directive.

XHTML Validation

The core ASP.NET controls follow the rules of XHTML, but to make sure the finished page is XHTML-compliant, you need to make sure any static content you add *also* follows these rules. Visual Studio can help you with its own built-in validator. Just select the target standard from the drop-down list in the HTML Source Editing toolbar. For example, if you choose XHTML 1.1, Visual Studio flags structural errors and obsolete tags (see Figure 3-3).

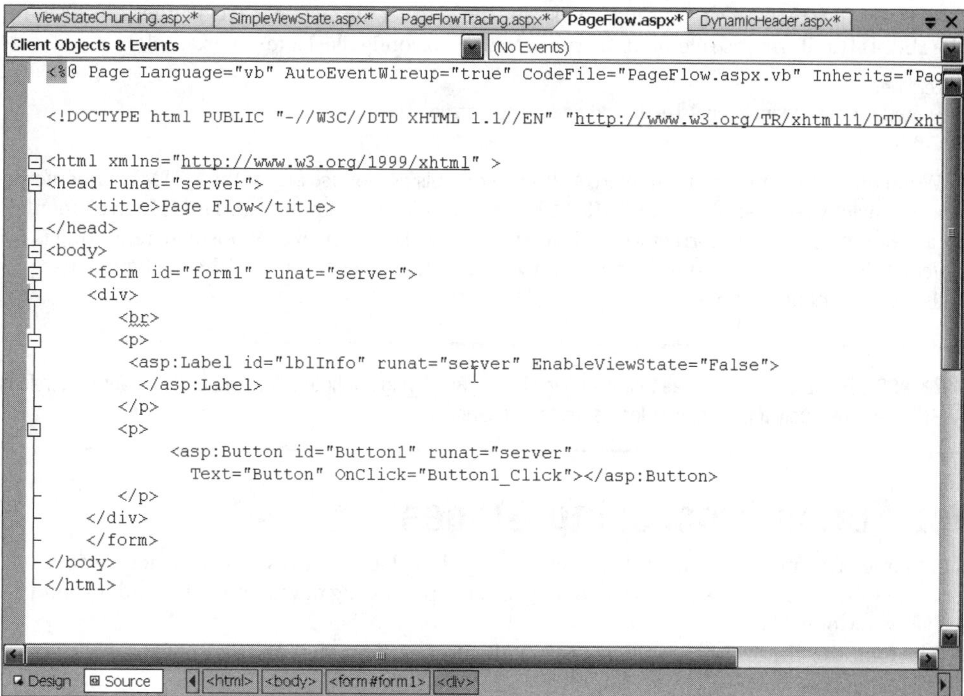

Figure 3-3. *Validating for XHTML 1.1 in Visual Studio*

Remember, if you violate the rules of XHTML, your browser probably won't flag the error. To create an XHTML-compliant page, you can use Visual Studio.NET IntelliSense, but that forces you to work with the page source, and it doesn't guarantee the final page won't contain an XHTML violation. (For example, you might use a third-party control that renders markup that isn't XHTML-compliant.) To give your pages the acid test, use a third-party validator that can request your page and scan it for errors.

One good resource is the free W3C validation service at `http://validator.w3.org`. Simply enter the URL to your web page, and click Check. You can also upload a file to check it, but in this case you must make sure you upload the final rendered page, not the .aspx source. You can see (and save) the rendered content for a page in Internet Explorer by choosing View ➤ Source.

Disabling XHTML Rendering

The ASP.NET server controls automatically use XHTML markup if the requesting browser supports HTML 4.0 or later. However, there may be rare cases when you want to disable XHTML-compliant rendering altogether. This might be the case if you have client-side JavaScript that relies on tags or attributes that aren't allowed in XHTML. To solve this problem, you can revert to the HTML rendering used in ASP.NET 1.*x*.

To revert to HTML-only rendering, you simple need to set the enableLegacyRendering attribute of the xhtml11Conformance element to True in your web.config file. Here's an example:

```
<system.web>
    <xhtml11Conformance enableLegacyRendering="true" />
</system.web>
```

When obsolete rendering is enabled, ASP.NET controls do not use any of the XHTML refinements that aren't strictly compatible with HTML 4.01. For example, they render standard HTML elements such as <br> instead of the correct XHTML version <br />. However, even if obsolete rendering is enabled, ASP.NET won't strip out the namespace in the <html> tag or remove the doctype if these details are present in your page.

■ **Note** ASP.NET makes no guarantee that the enableLegacyRendering attribute will be supported in future versions of ASP.NET, so use it only if it's required for a specific scenario.

Web Forms Processing Stages

On the server side, processing an ASP.NET web form takes place in stages. At each stage, various events are raised. This allows your page to plug into the processing flow at any stage and respond however you would like.

The following list shows the major stages in the process flow of an ASP.NET page:

- Page framework initialization
- User code initialization
- Validation
- Event handling
- Automatic data binding
- Cleanup

Remember, these stages occur independently for each web request. Figure 3-4 shows the order in which these stages unfold. More stages exist than are listed here, but those are typically used for programming your own ASP.NET controls and aren't handled directly by the page.

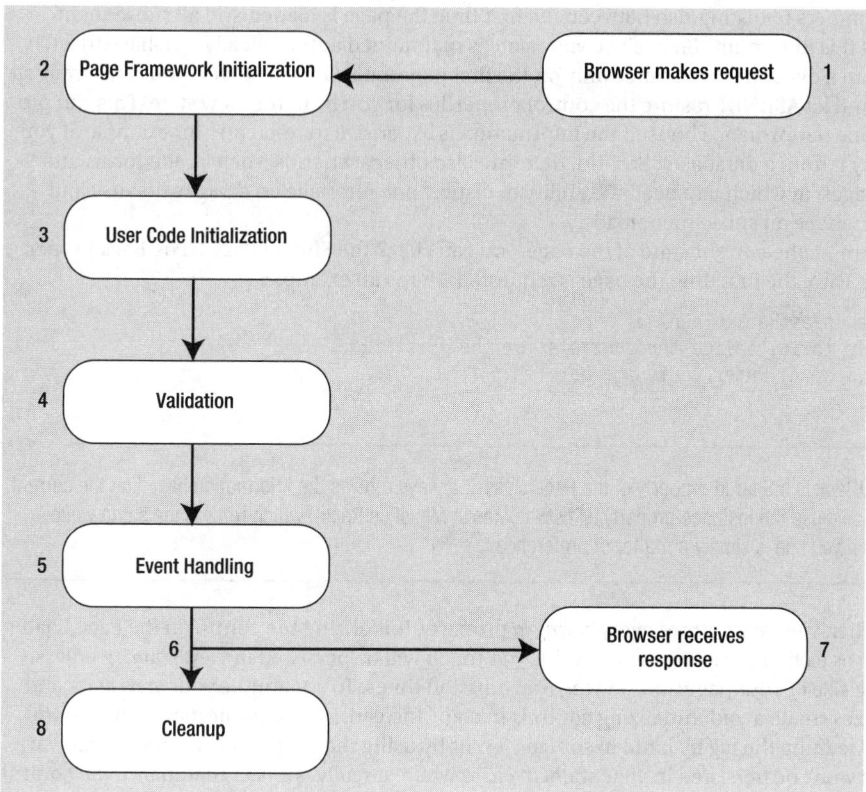

Figure 3-4. *ASP.NET page life cycle*

In the next few sections you'll learn about each stage and then examine a simple web page example.

Page Framework Initialization

This is the stage in which ASP.NET first creates the page. It generates all the controls you have defined with tags in the .aspx web page. In addition, if the page is not being requested for the first time (in other words, if it's a postback), ASP.NET deserializes the view state information and applies it to all the controls.

At this stage, the Page.Init event fires. However, this event is rarely handled by the web page, because it's still too early to perform page UI rendering.

User Code Initialization

At this stage of the processing, the Page.Load event is fired. Most web pages handle this event to perform any required initialization (such as filling in dynamic text or configuring controls).

The Page.Load event *always* fires, regardless of whether the page is being requested for the first time or whether it is being requested as part of a postback. Fortunately, ASP.NET provides a way to allow programmers to distinguish between the first time the page is loaded and all subsequent loads. Why is this important? First, since view state is maintained automatically, you have to fetch your data from a dynamic data source only on the first page load. On a postback, you can simply sit back, relax, and let ASP.NET restore the control properties for you from the view state. This can provide a dramatic performance boost if the information is expensive to re-create (for example, if you need to query it from a database). Second, there are also other scenarios, such as edit forms and drill-down pages, in which you need the ability to display one interface on a page's first use and a different interface on subsequent loads.

To determine the current state of the page, you can check the Shared Page.IsPostBack property, which will be False the first time the page is requested. Here's an example:

```
If (Not Page.IsPostBack) Then
  ' It's safe to initialize the controls for the first time.
  FirstName.Text = "Enter your name here"
End If
```

■ **Note** IsPostBack is a Shared property of the Page class. It always returns the information based on the current page. You can also use the instance property IsPostBack (as in Me.IsPostBack), which returns the same value. Which approach you use is simply a matter of preference.

Remember, view state stores every *changed* property. Initializing the control in the Page.Load event counts as a change, so any control value you touch will be persisted in view state, needlessly enlarging the size of your page and slowing transmission times. To streamline your view state and keep page sizes small, avoid initializing controls in code. Instead, set the properties in the control tag (either by editing the tag by hand in source view or by using the Properties window). That way, these details won't be persisted in view state. In cases where it really is easier to initialize the control in code, consider disabling view state for the control by setting EnableViewState to False and initializing the control every time the Page.Load event fires, regardless of whether the current request is a postback.

Validation

ASP.NET introduces new validation controls that can automatically validate other user input controls and display error messages. These controls fire after the page is loaded but before any other events take place. However, the validation controls are for the most part self-sufficient, which means you don't need to respond to the validation events. Instead, you can just examine whether the page is valid (using the Page.IsValid property) in another event handler. Chapter 4 discusses the validator controls in more detail.

Event Handling

At this point, the page is fully loaded and validated. ASP.NET will now fire all the events that have taken place since the last postback. For the most part, ASP.NET events are of two types:

Immediate response events: These include clicking a submit button or clicking some other button, image region, or link in a rich web control that triggers a postback by calling the __doPostBack() JavaScript function.

Change events: These include changing the selection in a control or the text in a text box. These events fire immediately for web controls if AutoPostBack is set to True. Otherwise, they fire the next time the page is posted back.

As you can see, ASP.NET's event model is still quite different from a traditional Windows environment. In a Windows application, the form state is resident in memory, and the application runs continuously. That means you can respond to an event immediately. In ASP.NET, everything occurs in stages, and as a result events are sometimes batched together.

For example, imagine you have a page with a submit button and a text box that doesn't post back automatically. You change the text in the text box and then click the submit button. At this point, ASP.NET raises all of the following events (in this order):

- Page.Init
- Page.Load
- TextBox.TextChanged
- Button.Click
- Page.PreRender
- Page.Unload

Remembering this bit of information can be essential in making your life as an ASP.NET programmer easier. There is an upside and a downside to the event-driven model. The upside is that the event model provides a higher level of abstraction, which keeps your code clear of boilerplate code for maintaining state. The downside is that it's easy to forget that the event model is really just an emulation. This can lead you to make an assumption that doesn't hold true (such as expecting information to remain in member variables) or a design decision that won't perform well (such as storing vast amounts of information in view state).

Automatic Data Binding

In Chapter 9, you'll learn about the data source controls (new in ASP.NET 2.0), which automate the data binding process. When you use the data source controls, ASP.NET automatically performs updates and queries against your data source as part of the page life cycle.

Essentially, two types of data source operations exist. Any changes (inserts, deletes, or updates) are performed after all the control events have been handled but just before the Page.PreRender event fires. Then, after the Page.PreRender event fires, the data source controls perform their queries and insert the retrieved data into any linked controls. This model makes instinctive sense, because if queries were executed before updates, you could end up with stale data in your web page. However, this model also introduces a necessary limitation—none of your other event handlers will have access to the most recent data, because it hasn't been retrieved yet.

This is the last stop in the page life cycle. Historically, the Page.PreRender event is supposed to signify the last action before the page is rendered into HTML (although, as you've just learned, some data binding work can still occur after the prerender stage). During the prerender stage, the page and control objects are still available, so you can perform last-minute steps such as storing additional information in view state.

To learn much more about the ASP.NET data binding story, refer to Chapter 9.

Cleanup

At the end of its life cycle, the page is rendered to HTML. After the page has been rendered, the real cleanup begins, and the Page.Unload event is fired. At this point, the page objects are still available, but the final HTML is already rendered and can't be changed.

Remember, the .NET Framework has a garbage collection service that runs periodically to release memory tied to objects that are no longer referenced. If you have any unmanaged resources to release, you should make sure you do this explicitly in the cleanup stage or, even better, before. When the garbage collector collects the page, the Page.Disposed event fires. This is the end of the road for the web page at the server. Control returns to the browser.

A Page Flow Example

No matter how many times people explain how something works, it's always more satisfying to see it for yourself (or break it trying to learn how it works). To satisfy your curiosity, you can build a sample web form test that illustrates the flow of processing. About the only thing this example won't illustrate is validation (which is discussed in the next chapter).

To try this, start by creating a new web form named PageFlow.aspx. In Visual Studio, you simply need to drag two controls (a label and button) onto the design surface from the Web Forms section of the toolbox. This generates a server-side <form> tag with the two control tags that you need in the .aspx file. Next, select the Label control. Using the Properties window, set the ID property to lblInfo and the EnableViewState property to False.

Here's the complete markup for the .aspx file:

```
<%@ Page language="vb" CodeFile="PageFlow.aspx.vb"
  AutoEventWireup="true" Inherits="PageFlow" %>
<html>
    <head runat="server">
        <title>Page Flow</title>
    </head>
    <body>
        <form id="form1" runat="server">
             <div>
                 <p>
                     <asp:Label id="lblInfo" runat="server" EnableViewState="False">
                     </asp:Label>
                 </p>
                 <p>
                     <asp:Button id="Button1" runat="server" Text="Button">
                     </asp:Button>
                 </p>
             </div>
        </form>
    </body>
</html>
```

The next step is to add your event handlers. When you're finished, the code-behind file will hold five event handlers that respond to different events, including Page.Init, Page.Load, Page.PreRender, Page.Unload, and Button.Click.

Page event handlers are a special case. Unlike other controls, you don't need to wire them up using attributes in your markup. Instead, page event handlers are automatically connected provided they use the correct method name. Here are the event handlers for various page events in the PageFlow example:

```
Protected Sub Page_Load(ByVal sender As Object, ByVal e As System.EventArgs)
  lblInfo.Text &= "Page.Load event handled.<br />"
  If Page.IsPostBack Then
    lblInfo.Text &= "<b>This is the second time you've seen this page.</b><br />"
  End If
End Sub

Protected Sub Page_Init(ByVal sender As Object, ByVal e As System.EventArgs)
  lblInfo.Text &= "Page.Init event handled.<br />"
End Sub
```

```
Protected Sub Page_PreRender(ByVal sender As Object, ByVal e As System.EventArgs)
  lblInfo.Text &= "Page.PreRender event handled.<br />"
End Sub

Protected Sub Page_Unload(ByVal sender As Object, ByVal e As System.EventArgs)
' This text never appears because the HTML is already
' rendered for the page at this point.
  lblInfo.Text &= "Page.Unload event handled.<br />"
End Sub
```

Each event handler simply adds to the text in the Text property of the label. When the code adds this text, it also uses embedded HTML tags such as <b> (to bold the text) and
 (to insert a line break). Another option would be to create separate Label controls and configure the style-related properties of each one.

■ **Note** In this example, the EnableViewState property of the label is set to False. This ensures that the text is cleared every time the page is posted back and the text that's shown corresponds only to the most recent batch of processing. If you left EnableViewState set to True, the list would grow longer with each postback, showing you all the activity that has happened since you first requested the page.

Additionally, you need to wire up an event handler for the Button.Click event, as shown here:

```
Protected Sub Button1_Click(ByVal sender As Object, ByVal e As System.EventArgs)
   lblInfo.Text &= "Button1.Click event handled.<br />"
End Sub
```

You may have noticed that the Button.Click event handler requires a different accessibility level than the page event handlers. The page event handlers are Private, and all control event handlers are Protected. To understand this difference, you need to reconsider the code model that was introduced in Chapter 2.

Page handlers are hooked up explicitly using the code editor. You simply select the (Page Events) item on the left menu, and the appropriate Event on the right menu. The declaration will be generated for you by the IDE.

Control event handlers are connected using a different mechanism—the control tag. They are bound at a later stage of processing, after the markup in the .aspx file and the code-behind class have been merged together. ASP.NET creates this merged class by deriving a new class from the code-behind class.

Here's where things get tricky. This derived class needs to be able to access the event handlers in the page so it can connect them to the appropriate controls. The derived class can access the event handlers only if they are Public (in which case any class can access them) or Protected (in which case any derived class can access them).

■ **Tip** Although it's acceptable for page event handlers to be Private, it's a common convention in ASP.NET 2.0 code to make all event handlers Protected, just for consistency and simplicity.

Figure 3-5 shows the ASP.NET page after clicking the button, which triggers a postback and the Button1.Click event. Note that even though this event caused the postback, Page.Init and Page.Load were both raised first.

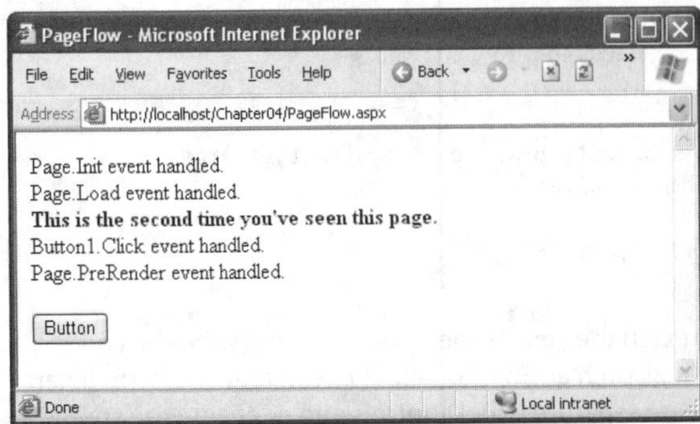

Figure 3-5. *ASP.NET order of operations*

The Page As a Control Container

Now that you've learned the stages of web forms processing, it's time to take a closer look at how the server control model plugs into this pipeline. To render a page, the web form needs to collaborate with all its constituent controls. Essentially, the web form renders itself and then asks all the controls on the page to render themselves. In turn, each of those controls can contain child controls; each is also responsible for their own rendering code. As these controls render themselves, the page assembles the generated HTML into a complete page. This process may seem a little complex at first, but it allows for an amazing amount of power and flexibility in creating rich web-page interfaces.

When ASP.NET first creates a page (in response to an HTTP request), it inspects the .aspx file. For each control tag it finds, it creates and configures a control object, and then it adds this control as a *child control* of the page. You can examine the Page.Controls collection to find all the child controls on the page.

Showing the Control Tree

Here's an example that looks for controls. Each time it finds a control, the code uses the `Reponse.Write()` command to write the control class type and control ID to the end of the rendered HTML page, as shown here:

```
For Each control As Control In Page.Controls
    Response.Write(control.GetType().ToString() _
        & " - <b>" & control.ID & "</b><br />")
Next control
' Separate this content from the rest of the page with a horizontal line.
Response.Write("<hr />")
```

This code can reside behind a button on your page or even in Page_Load().

Note The Response.Write() method is a holdover from classic ASP, and you should never use it in a real-world ASP.NET web application. It effectively bypasses the web control model, which leads to disjointed interfaces, compromises ASP.NET's ability to create markup that adapts to the target device, and almost always breaks XHTML compatibility. However, in this test page Response.Write() allows you to write raw HTML without generating any additional controls—which is a perfect technique for analyzing the controls on the page without disturbing them.

To test this code, you can add it to the Page.Load event handler. In this case, the rendered content will be written at the top of the page before the controls. However, when you run it, you'll notice some unexpected behavior. For example, consider the web form shown in Figure 3-6, which contains several controls, some of which are organized into a box using the Panel web control. It also contains two lines of static HTML text.

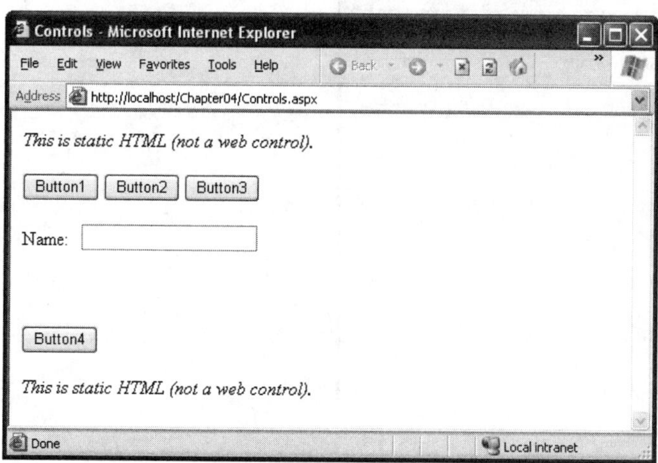

Figure 3-6. *A sample web page with multiple controls*

Here's the .aspx markup code for the page:

```
<%@ Page language="vb" CodeFile="MyControls.aspx.vb" AutoEventWireup="true"
        Inherits="MyControls" %>
<html>
  <head>
    <title>Controls</title>
  </head>
  <body>
    <p><i>This is static HTML (not a web control).</i></p>
    <form id="Controls" method="post" runat="server">
    <div>
      <asp:panel id="MainPanel" runat="server" Height="112px">
      <p><asp:Button id="Button1" runat="server" Text="Button1"/>
      <asp:Button id="Button2" runat="server" Text="Button2"/>
      <asp:Button id="Button3" runat="server" Text="Button3"/></p>
      <p><asp:Label id="Label1" runat="server" Width="48px">
       Name:</asp:Label>
      <asp:TextBox id="TextBox1" runat="server"></asp:TextBox></p>
      </asp:panel>
      <p><asp:Button id="Button4" runat="server" Text="Button4"/></p>
    </div>
    </form>
    <p><i>This is static HTML (not a web control).</i></p>
  </body>
</html>
```

When you run this page, you won't see a full list of controls. Instead, you'll see a list that names only three controls, as shown in Figure 3-7.

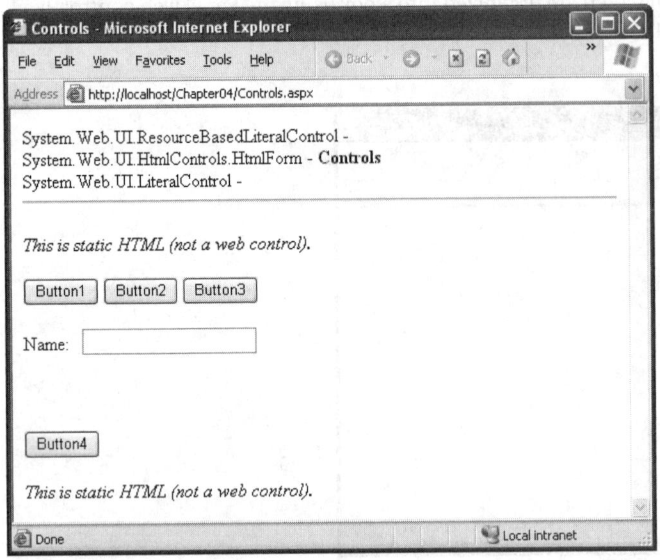

Figure 3-7. *Controls on the top layer of the page*

ASP.NET models the *entire* page using control objects, including elements that don't correspond to server-side content. For example, if you have one server control on a page, ASP.NET will create a LiteralControl that represents all the static content before the control and will create another LiteralControl that represents the content after it. Depending on how much static content you have and how you break it up between other controls, you may end up with multiple LiteralControl objects.

LiteralControl objects don't provide much in the way of functionality. For example, you can't set style-related information such as colors and font. They also don't have a unique server-side ID. However, you can manipulate the content of a LiteralControl using its Text property. The following code rewrites the earlier example so that it checks for literal controls, and, if present, it casts the base Control object to the LiteralControl type so it can extract the associated text:

```
For Each control As Control In Page.Controls
  Response.Write(control.GetType().ToString() _
      & " - <b>" & control.ID + "</b><br />")

    If TypeOf control Is LiteralControl Then
      ' Display the literal content (whitespace and all).
      Response.Write("*** Text: " & (CType(control, LiteralControl)).Text _
          & "<br />")
    End If
Next control
Response.Write("<hr>")
```

This example still suffers from a problem. You now understand the unexpected new content, but what about the missing content—namely, the other control objects on the page?

To answer this question, you need to understand that ASP.NET renders a page *hierarchically*. It directly renders only the top level of controls. If these controls contain other controls, they provide their own Controls properties, which provide access to their child controls. In the example page, as in all ASP.NET web forms, all the controls are nested inside the <form> tag. This means you need to inspect the Controls collection of the HtmlForm class to get information about the server controls on the page.

However, life isn't necessarily this straightforward. That's because there's no limit to how many layers of nested controls you can use. To really solve this problem and display all the controls on a page, you need to create a recursive routine that can tunnel through the entire control tree.

The following code shows the complete solution:

```
Partial Class Controls
   Inherits System.Web.UI.Page

  Protected Sub Page_Load(ByVal sender As Object, ByVal e As System.EventArgs)
      ' Start examining all the controls.
     DisplayControl(Page.Controls, 0)
     ' Add the closing horizontal line.
     Response.Write("<hr/>")
  End Sub

  Private Sub DisplayControl(ByVal controls As ControlCollection,
       ByVal depth As Integer)
    For Each control As Control In controls
      ' Use the depth parameter to indent the control tree.
     Response.Write(New String("-"c, depth * 4) & "> ")

      ' Display this control.
      Response.Write(control.GetType().ToString() & " - <b>" _
          & control.ID & "</b><br />")
      If control.Controls IsNot Nothing Then
        DisplayControl(control.Controls, depth + 1)
      End If
    Next control
  End Sub

End Class
```

Figure 3-8 shows the new result—a hierarchical tree that shows all the controls on the page and their nesting.

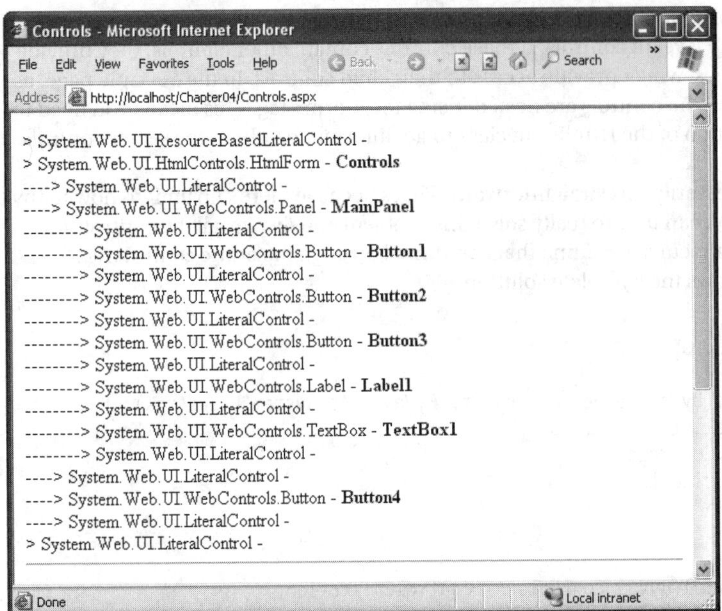

Figure 3-8. *A tree of controls on the page*

The Page Header

As you've seen, you can transform any HTML element into a server control with the runat="server" attribute, and a page can contain an unlimited number of HTML controls. In addition to the controls you add, a web form can also contain a single HtmlHead control, which provides server-side access to the <head> tag.

The control tree shown in the previous example doesn't include the HtmlHead control, because the runat="server" attribute hasn't been applied to the <head> tag. However, the Visual Studio default is to always make the <head> tag into a server-side control, in contrast to previous versions of ASP.NET.

As with other server controls, you can use the HtmlHead control to programmatically change the content that's rendered in the <head> tag. The difference is that the <head> tag doesn't correspond to actual content you can see in the web page. Instead, it includes other details such as the title, metadata tags (useful for providing keywords to search engines), and stylesheet references. To change any of these details, you use one of a small set of members that are defined in the IPageHeader interface. The HtmlHead control implements the IPageHeader interface. It includes the following properties:

Title: This is the title of the HTML page, which is usually displayed in the browser's title bar. You can modify this at runtime.

LinkedStyleSheets: This provides access to a collection of IStyleSheet objects (CSS stylesheets), one for each stylesheet that's linked to your web page through the header. You'll learn more about stylesheets in Chapter 15.

StyleSheet: This provides an IStyleSheet object that represents inline styles defined in the header.

Metadata: This provides a collection of metadata tags. You can add or remove entries at runtime.

Out of this list, the Metadata property is the most useful. Here's an example that sets some header information programmatically:

```
Page.Header.Title = "Dynamically Titled Page"
Page.Header.Metadata.Add("Keywords", ".NET, VB.NET, ASP.NET")
Page.Header.Metadata.Add("Description", "A great website to learn .NET")
```

■ **Tip** The HtmlHead control is handy in pages that are extremely dynamic. For example, if you build a data-driven website that serves promotional content from a database, you might want to change the keywords and title of the page depending on the content you use when the page is requested.

Dynamic Control Creation

Using the Controls collection, you can create a control and add it to a page programmatically. Here's an example that generates a new button and adds it to a Panel control on the page:

```
Protected Sub Page_Load(ByVal sender As Object, ByVal e As System.EventArgs)
  Dim newButton As Button = New Button()
  ' Assign some text and an ID so you can retrieve it later.
  newButton.Text = "* Dynamic Button *"
  newButton.ID = "newButton"
  ' Add the button to a Panel.
  MyPanel.Controls.Add(newButton)
End Sub
```

You can execute this code in any event handler. However, because the page is already created, this code always adds the new control at the end of the collection. In this example, that means the new button will end up at the bottom of the Panel control.

To get more control over where a dynamically added control is positioned, you can use a PlaceHolder. A PlaceHolder is a control that has no purpose except to house other controls. If you don't add any controls to the Controls collection of the PlaceHolder, it won't render anything in the final web page. However, Visual Studio gives a default representation that looks like an ordinary label at design time, so you can position it exactly where you want. That way, you can add a dynamic control between other controls.

```
' Add the button to a PlaceHolder.
PlaceHolder1.Controls.Add(newButton)
```

When using dynamic controls, you must remember that they will exist only until the next postback. ASP.NET will not re-create a dynamically added control. If you need to re-create a control multiple times, you should perform the control creation in the Page.Load event handler. This has the additional benefit of allowing you to use view state with your dynamic control. Even though view state is normally restored *before* the Page.Load event, if you create a control in the handler for the Page.Load event, ASP.NET will apply any view state information that it has after the Page.Load event handler ends. This process is automatic.

If you want to interact with the control later, you should give it a unique ID. You can use this ID to retrieve the control from the Controls collection of its container. You could find the control using recursive searching logic, as demonstrated in the control tree example, or you can use the Shared Page.FindControl() method, which searches the entire page for the control with the ID you specify. Here's an example that searches for the dynamically added control with the FindControl() method and then removes it:

```
Protected Sub cmdRemove_Click(ByVal sender As Object, ByVal e As System.EventArgs)
    ' Search for the button, no matter what level it's at.
    Dim foundButton As Button = CType(Page.FindControl("newButton"), Button)

    ' Remove the button.
    If foundButton IsNot Nothing Then
        foundButton.Parent.Controls.Remove(foundButton)
    End If
End Sub
```

Dynamically added controls can handle events. All you need to do is attach an event handler using delegate code. You *must* perform this task in your Page.Load event handler. As you learned earlier, all control-specific events are fired after the Page.Load event. If you wait any longer, the event handler will be connected after the event has already fired, and you won't be able to react to it any longer.

```
' Attach an event handler to the Button.Click event.
AddHandler newButton.Click, AddressOf Me.Button_Click
```

Figure 3-9 demonstrates all these concepts. It generates a dynamic button. When you click this button, the text in a label is modified. Two other buttons allow you to dynamically remove or re-create the button.

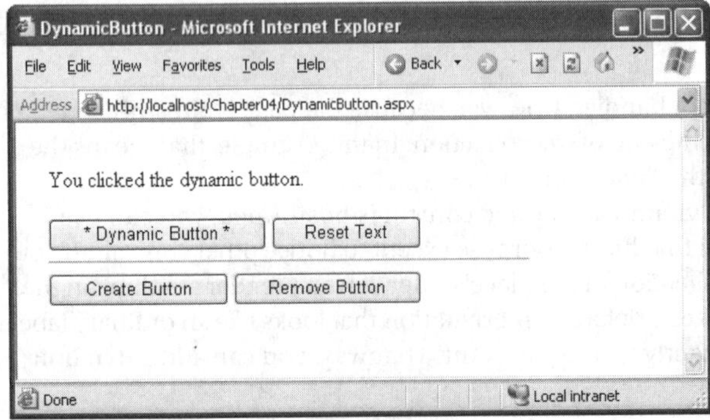

Figure 3-9. *Handling an event from a dynamically added control*

Dynamic control creation is particularly powerful when you combine it with user controls (reusable blocks of user interface that can combine a group of controls and HTML). You'll learn more about user controls in Chapter 14.

The Page Class

Now that you've explored the page life cycle and learned how a page contains controls, it's worth pointing out that the page itself is also instantiated as a type of control object. In fact, all web forms are actually instances of the ASP.NET Page class, which is found in the System.Web.UI namespace.

You may have already figured this out by noticing that every code-behind class explicitly derives from System.Web.UI.Page. This means that every web form you create is equipped with an enormous amount of out-of-the-box functionality. The Shared FindControl() method and the IsPostBack property are two examples you've seen so far. In addition, deriving from the Page class gives your code the following extremely useful properties:

- Session
- Application
- Cache
- Request
- Response
- Server
- User
- Trace

Many of these properties correspond to intrinsic objects that you could use in classic ASP web pages. However, in classic ASP you accessed this functionality through built-in objects that were available at all times. In ASP.NET, each of these built-in objects actually corresponds to a Page property that exposes an instance of a full-featured class.

The following sections introduce these objects.

Session, Application, and Cache

The Session object is an instance of the System.Web.SessionState.HttpSessionState class. It's designed to store any type of user-specific data that needs to persist between web-page requests. The Session object provides dictionary-style access to a set of name/value pairs that represents the user's data for that session. Session state is often used to maintain things such as the user's name, the user's ID, a shopping cart, or various other elements that are discarded when a given user is no longer accessing pages on the website.

The Application object is an instance of the System.Web.HttpApplicationState class. Like the Session object, it's also a name/value dictionary of data. However, this data is global to the entire application.

Finally, the Cache object is an instance of the System.Web.Caching.Cache class. It also stores global information, but it provides a much more scalable storage mechanism because ASP.NET can remove objects if server memory becomes scarce. Like the other state collections, it's essentially a name/value collection of objects, but you can also set specialized expiration policies and dependencies for each item.

Deciding how to implement state management is one of the key challenges of programming a web application. You'll learn much more about all these types of state management in Chapter 6.

Request

The Request object is an instance of the System.Web.HttpRequest class. This object represents the values and properties of the HTTP request that caused your page to be loaded. It contains all the URL parameters and all other information sent by a client. Much of the information provided by the Request object is wrapped by higher-level abstractions (such as the ASP.NET web control model), so it isn't nearly as important as it was in classic ASP. However, you might still use the Request object to find out what browser the client is using or to set and examine cookies.

Table 3-1 describes some of the more common properties of the Request object.

Table 3-1. *HttpRequest Properties*

Property	Description
PhysicalApplicationPath and PhysicalPath	PhysicalApplicationPath gets the ASP.NET application's virtual directory (URL), while PhysicalPath gets the "real" directory.
AnonymousID	This uniquely identifies the current user if you've enabled anonymous access. You'll learn how to use the new anonymous access features in Chapter 24.
Browser	This provides a link to an HttpBrowserCapabilities object, which contains properties describing various browser features, such as support for ActiveX controls, cookies, VBScript, and frames.
ClientCertificate	This is an HttpClientCertificate object that gets the security certificate for the current request, if there is one.
Cookies	This gets the collection cookies sent with this request. Chapter 6 discusses cookies.
FilePath and CurrentExecutionFilePath	These return the real file path (relative to the server) for the currently executing page. FilePath gets the page that started the execution process. This is the same as CurrentExecutionFilePath, unless you've transferred the user to a new page without a redirect (for example, using the Server.Transfer() method), in which case CurrentExecutionFilePath reflects the new page and FilePath indicates the original page.
Form	This represents the collection of form variables that were posted back to the page. In almost all cases, you'll retrieve this information from control properties instead of using this collection.
Headers and ServerVariables	These provide a name/value collection of HTTP headers and server variables. You can get the low-level information you need if you know the corresponding header or variable name.
IsAuthenticated and IsSecureConnection	These return True if the user has been successfully authenticated and if the user is connected over SSL (Secure Sockets Layer).
IsLocal	This returns True if the user is requesting the page from the current computer.
QueryString	This provides the parameters that were passed along with the query string. Chapter 6 shows how you can use the query string to transfer information between pages.
Url and UrlReferrer	These provide a Url object that represents the current address for the page and the page where the user is coming from (the previous page that linked to this page).
UserAgent	This is a string representing the browser type. Internet Explorer provides the value MSIE for this property.

Property	Description
UserHostAddress and UserHostName	These get the IP address and the DNS name of the remote client. You could also access this information through the ServerVariables collection. However, this information may not always be available.
UserLanguages	This provides a sorted string array that lists the client's language preferences. This can be useful if you need to create multilingual pages.

Response

The Response object is an instance of the System.Web.HttpResponse class, and it represents the web server's response to a client request. In classic ASP, the Response object was the only way to programmatically send HTML text to the client. Now server-side controls have nested, object-oriented methods for rendering themselves. All you have to do is set their properties. As a result, the Response object doesn't play nearly as central a role.

The HttpResponse does still provide some important functionality—namely, cookie features and the Redirect() method. The Redirect() method allows you to send the user to another page. Here's an example:

```
' You can redirect to a page in the current directory.
Response.Redirect("newpage.aspx")

' You can redirect to another website.
Response.Redirect("http://www.prosetech.com")
```

The Redirect() method requires a round-trip. Essentially, it sends a message to the browser that instructs it to request a new page. If you want to transfer the user to another page in the same web application, you can use a faster approach with the Server.Transfer()method.

■ **Tip** Another way also exists to get from one page to the next—*cross-page posting*. Using this technique, you can create a page that posts itself to another page, which allows you to effectively transfer all the view state information and the contents of any controls. You'll learn how to use this technique in Chapter 6.

Table 3-2 lists common HttpResponse members.

Table 3-2. *HttpResponse Members*

Member	Description
BufferOutput	When set to True (the default), the page isn't sent to the client until it's completely rendered and ready to be sent, as opposed to being sent piecemeal.
Cache	This references an HttpCachePolicy object that allows you to configure output caching. Chapter 11 discusses caching.
Cookies	This is the collection of cookies sent with the response. You can use this property to add additional cookies.
Expires and ExpiresAbsolute	You can use these properties to cache the rendered HTML for the page, improving performance for subsequent requests. You'll learn about this type of caching (known as *output caching*) in Chapter 11.

(Continued)

Table 3-2. *Continued*

Member	Description
IsClientConnected	This is a Boolean value indicating whether the client is still connected to the server. If it isn't, you might want to stop a time-consuming operation.
Write(), BinaryWrite(), and WriteFile()	These methods allow you to write text or binary content directly to the response stream. You can even write the contents of a file. These methods are de-emphasized in ASP.NET and shouldn't be used in conjunction with server controls.
Redirect()	This method transfers the user to another page in your application or a different website.

Server

The Server object is an instance of the System.Web.HttpServerUtility class. It provides a handful of miscellaneous helper methods and properties, as listed in Table 3-3.

Table 3-3. *HttpServerUtility Methods*

Method	Description
MachineName	A property representing the computer name of the server on which the page is running. This is the name the web server computer uses to identify itself to the rest of the network.
CreateObject()	Creates an instance of the COM object that is identified by its progID (programmatic ID). This is included for backward compatibility, because it will generally be easier to interact with COM objects using .NET's support for COM interop, which provides strongly typed interaction.
GetLastError()	Retrieves the exception object for the most recently encountered error (or a null reference, if there isn't one). This error must have occurred while processing the current request, and it must not have been handled. This is most commonly used in an application event handler that checks for error conditions (an example of which you'll see in Chapter 5).
HtmlEncode() and HtmlDecode()	Changes an ordinary string into a string with legal HTML characters (and back again).
UrlEncode() and UrlDecode()	Changes an ordinary string into a string with legal URL characters (and back again).
UrlTokenEncode () and UrlTokenDecode)	Performs the same work as UrlEncode() and UrlDecode(), except they work on a byte array that contains Base64-encoded data.
MapPath()	Returns the physical file path that corresponds to a specified virtual file path on the web server.
Transfer()	Transfers execution to another web page in the current application. This is similar to the Response.Redirect() method, but it's faster. It cannot be used to transfer the user to a site on another web server or to a non-ASP.NET page (such as an HTML page or an ASP page).

The Transfer() method is the quickest way to redirect the user to another page in your application. When you use this method, a round-trip is not involved. Instead, the ASP.NET engine simply loads the new page and begins processing it. As a result, the URL that's displayed in the client's browser won't change.

```
' You can transfer to a file in the current web application.
Server.Transfer("newpage.aspx")

' You can't redirect to another website.
' This attempt will cause an error.
Server.Transfer ("http://www.apress.com")
```

The MapPath() method is another useful method of the Server object. For example, imagine you want to load a file named info.txt from the current virtual directory. Instead of hard-coding the path, you can use Request.ApplicationPath() to get the current relative virtual directory and Server.MapPath() to convert this to an absolute physical path. Here's an example:

```
Dim physicalPath As String = Server.MapPath(Request.ApplicationPath & "/info.txt"))

' Now open the file.
Dim reader As New StreamReader(physicalPath)
' (Process the file here.)
reader.Close()
```

HTML and URL Encoding

The Server class also includes methods that change ordinary strings into a representation that can safely be used as part of a URL or displayed in a web page. For example, imagine you want to display this text on a web page:

```
To bold text use the <b> tag.
```

If you try to write this information to a page or place it inside a control, you would end up with this instead:

```
To bold text use the tag.
```

Not only will the text <b> not appear, but the browser will interpret it as an instruction to make the text that follows bold. To circumvent this automatic behavior, you need to convert potential problematic values to their special HTML equivalents. For example, < becomes < in your final HTML page, which the browser displays as the < character. Table 3-4 lists some special characters that need to be encoded.

Table 3-4. *Common HTML Entities*

Result	Description	Encoded Entity
	Nonbreaking space	
<	Less-than symbol	<
>	Greater-than symbol	>
&	Ampersand	&
"	Quotation mark	"

Here's an example that circumvents the problem using the Server.HtmlEncode() method:

```
Label1.Text = Server.HtmlEncode("To bold text use the <b> tag.")
```

You also have the freedom to use HtmlEncode for some input, but not for all of it if you want to insert a combination of text that could be invalid and HTML tags. Here's an example:

```
Label1.Text = "To <b>bold</b> text use the "
Label1.Text &= Server.HtmlEncode("<b>") + " tag."
```

Note Some controls circumvent this problem by automatically encoding tags. (The Label web control is not one of them. Instead, it gives you the freedom to insert HTML tags as you please.) For example, the basic set of HTML server controls include both an InnerText tag and an InnerHtml tag. When you set the contents of a control using InnerText, any illegal characters are automatically converted into their HTML equivalents. However, this won't help if you want to set a tag that contains a mix of embedded HTML tags and encoded characters.

The HtmlEncode() method is particularly useful if you're retrieving values from a database and you aren't sure if the text is valid HTML. You can use the HtmlDecode() method to revert the text to its normal form if you need to perform additional operations or comparisons with it in your code. Similarly, the UrlEncode() method changes text into a form that can be used in a URL, escaping spaces and other special characters. This step is usually performed with information you want to add to the query string.

It's worth noting that the HtmlEncode() method won't convert spaces to nonbreaking spaces. This means that if you have a series of space characters, the browser will display only a single space. Although this doesn't invalidate your HTML, it may not be the effect you want. To change this behavior, you can manually replace spaces with nonbreaking spaces using the String.Replace() method. Just make sure you perform this step after you encode the string, not before, or the nonbreaking space character sequence (&nbps;) will be replaced with character entities and treated as ordinary text.

```
' Encode illegal characters.
Dim line = Server.HtmlEncode(line)

' Replace spaces with nonbreaking spaces.
line = line.Replace(" ", " ")
```

Similarly, the HtmlEncode() method won't convert line breaks into the <br> tag. This means that hard returns will be ignored unless you specifically insert <br> tags.

Note The issue of properly encoding input is important for more than just ensuring properly displayed data. If you try to display data that has embedded <script> tags, you could inadvertently end up executing a block of JavaScript code on the client. Chapter 27 has more about this danger and the ASP.NET request validation feature that prevents it.

User

The User object represents information about the user making the request of the web server, and it allows you to test that user's role membership.

The User object always implements System.Security.Principal.IPrincipal. The specific class depends on the type of authentication you're using. For example, you can authenticate a user based on Windows account information using IIS or through cookie-based authentication with a dedicated login page. However, it's important to realize that the User object provides useful information only if your web application is performing some sort of authentication that restricts anonymous users.

Part 4 of this book deals with security in detail.

Trace

The Trace object is a general-purpose tracing tool (and an instance of the System.Web.TraceContext class). It allows you to write information to a log that is scoped at the page level. This log has detailed timing information so that not only can you use the Trace object for debugging but you can also use it for performance monitoring and timing. Additionally, the trace log also shows a compilation of miscellaneous information, grouped into several sections. Table 3-5 describes all the information you'll see.

Table 3-5. *Trace Log Information*

Section	Description
Request Details	This section includes some basic information about the request context, including the current session ID, the time the web request was made, and the type of web request and encoding.
Trace Information	This section shows the different stages of processing the page went through before being sent to the client. Each section has additional information about how long it took to complete, as a measure from the start of the first stage (From First) and as a measure from the start of the previous stage (From Last). If you add your own trace messages (a technique described shortly), they will also appear in this section.
Control Tree	The control tree shows you all the controls on the page, indented to show their hierarchy, similar to the control tree example earlier in this chapter. One useful feature of this section is the Viewstate column, which tells you how many bytes of space are required to persist the current information in the control. This can help you gauge whether enabling control state could affect page transmission times.
Session State and Application State	These sections display every item that is in the current session or application state. Each item is listed with its name, type, and value. If you're storing simple pieces of string information, the value is straightforward. If you're storing an object, .NET calls the object's ToString() method to get an appropriate string representation. For complex objects, the result may just be the class name.
Cookies Collection	This section displays all the cookies that are sent with the response, as well as the content and size of each cookie in bytes. Even if you haven't explicitly created a cookie, you'll see the ASP.NET_SessionId cookie, which contains the current session ID. If you're using forms-based authentication, you'll also see the security cookie.
Headers Collection	This section lists all the HTTP headers associated with the request.
Forms Collection	This section lists the posted-back form information.
QueryString Collection	This section lists the variables and values submitted in the query string.
Server Variables	This section lists all the server variables and their contents.

Tip Tracing complements Visual Studio debugging. In many cases, debugging is the best approach for solving problems while you are coding a web application, while tracing gives you an easier option if you need to troubleshoot problems that appear while the application is running on a web server. However, tracing provides a few services that debugging doesn't (at least not as easily), such as showing you the amount of information in view state and the time taken to process the page on the server. Tracing also works regardless of whether you build your application in debug mode (with the debug symbols) or release mode.

You can enable tracing in two ways. You can set the Trace.IsEnabled property to True at any point in your code, as follows:

```
Trace.IsEnabled = True
```

Usually, you'll do this in the Page.Load event handler. Another option is to use the Trace attribute in the Page directive:

```
<%@ Page language="vb" CodeFile="PageFlow.aspx.vb" AutoEventWireup="true"
        Inherits="PageFlow" Trace="true" %>
```

By default, trace messages are listed in the order they were generated. Alternatively, you can specify that messages should be sorted by category, using the TraceMode attribute in the Page directive, as follows:

```
<%@ Page language="vb" CodeFile="PageFlow.aspx.vb" AutoEventWireup="true"
    Inherits="PageFlow" Trace="true" TraceMode="SortByCategory" %>
```

or the TraceMode property of the Trace object in your code:

```
Trace.TraceMode = TraceMode.SortByCategory
```

Figure 3-10 shows a partial listing of trace information with the PageFlow example demonstrated earlier.

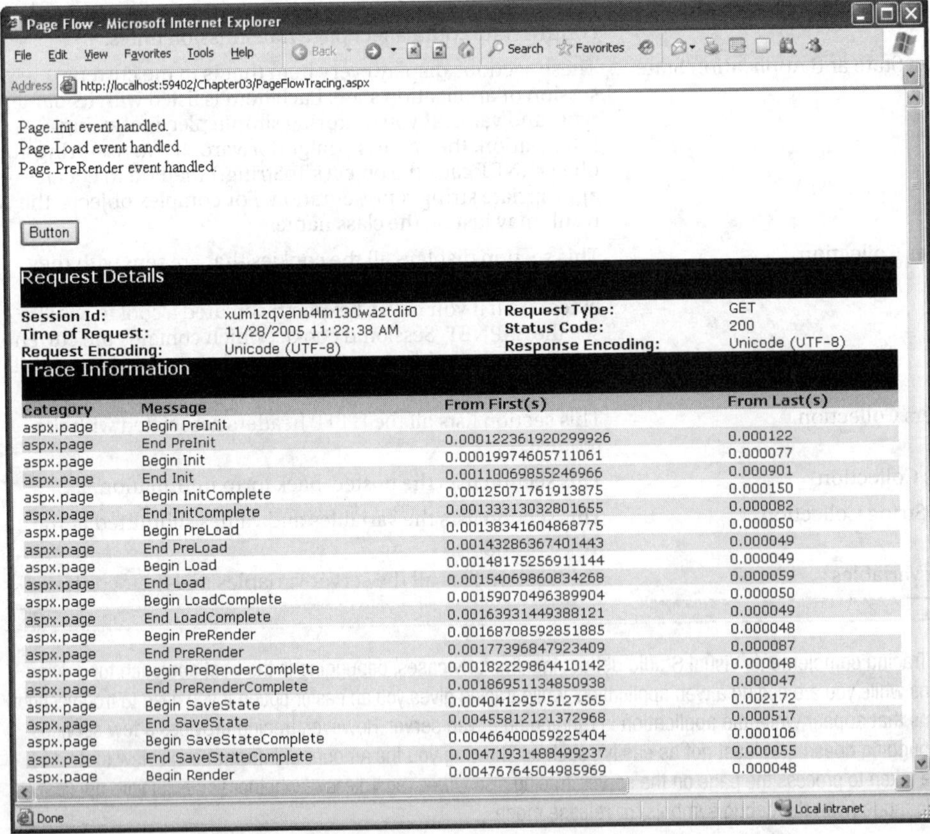

Request Details

Session Id:	xum1zqvenb4lm130wa2tdif0	Request Type:	GET
Time of Request:	11/28/2005 11:22:38 AM	Status Code:	200
Request Encoding:	Unicode (UTF-8)	Response Encoding:	Unicode (UTF-8)

Trace Information

Category	Message	From First(s)	From Last(s)
aspx.page	Begin PreInit		
aspx.page	End PreInit	0.000122361920299926	0.000122
aspx.page	Begin Init	0.00019974605711061	0.000077
aspx.page	End Init	0.00110069855246966	0.000901
aspx.page	Begin InitComplete	0.00125071761913875	0.000150
aspx.page	End InitComplete	0.00133313032801655	0.000082
aspx.page	Begin PreLoad	0.00138341604868775	0.000050
aspx.page	End PreLoad	0.00143286367401443	0.000049
aspx.page	Begin Load	0.00148175256911144	0.000049
aspx.page	End Load	0.00154069860834268	0.000059
aspx.page	Begin LoadComplete	0.00159070496389904	0.000050
aspx.page	End LoadComplete	0.00163931449388121	0.000049
aspx.page	Begin PreRender	0.00168708592851885	0.000048
aspx.page	End PreRender	0.00177396847923409	0.000087
aspx.page	Begin PreRenderComplete	0.00182229864410142	0.000048
aspx.page	End PreRenderComplete	0.00186951134850938	0.000047
aspx.page	Begin SaveState	0.00404129575127565	0.002172
aspx.page	End SaveState	0.00455812121372968	0.000517
aspx.page	Begin SaveStateComplete	0.00466400059225404	0.000106
aspx.page	End SaveStateComplete	0.00471931488499237	0.000055
aspx.page	Begin Render	0.00476764504985969	0.000048

Figure 3-10. *Basic trace information*

You can also write your own information to the trace log (the portion of the trace log that appears in the Trace Information section) using the Trace.Write() or Trace.Warn() method. These methods are equivalent. The only difference is that Warn() displays the message in red lettering, which makes it easier to distinguish from other messages in the list.

Here's a code snippet that writes a trace message when the user clicks a button:

```
Protected Sub Button1_Click(ByVal sender As Object, ByVal e As System.EventArgs)
    ' You can supply just a message, or include a category label,
    ' as shown here.
    Trace.Write("Button1_Click", "About to update the label.")
    lblInfo.Text &= "Button1.Click event handled.<br />"
    Trace.Write("Button1_Click", "Label updated.")
End Sub
```

When you write trace messages, they are automatically sent to all trace listeners. However, if you've disabled tracing for the page, the messages are simply ignored. Tracing messages are automatically HTML-encoded. This means tags such as <br /> and <b> are displayed as text, not interpreted as HTML.

Figure 3-11 shows the new entries that have been traced.

Trace Information

Category	Message	From First(s)	From Last(s)
aspx.page	Begin PreInit		
aspx.page	End PreInit	0.000139123827190327	0.000139
aspx.page	Begin Init	0.000217066694230691	0.000078
aspx.page	End Init	0.000311212737931776	0.000094
aspx.page	Begin InitComplete	0.000360380998143619	0.000049
aspx.page	End InitComplete	0.000416812751341302	0.000056
aspx.page	Begin LoadState	0.000465142916208624	0.000048
aspx.page	End LoadState	0.000799263593557282	0.000334
aspx.page	Begin ProcessPostData	0.000898438209325487	0.000099
aspx.page	End ProcessPostData	0.00102722552726673	0.000129
aspx.page	Begin PreLoad	0.00110349220361806	0.000076
aspx.page	End PreLoad	0.00115321919405958	0.000050
aspx.page	Begin Load	0.00119987316823786	0.000047
aspx.page	End Load	0.00125881920746911	0.000059
aspx.page	Begin ProcessPostData Second Try	0.00130575254676223	0.000047
aspx.page	End ProcessPostData Second Try	0.00135100969536631	0.000045
aspx.page	Begin Raise ChangedEvents	0.00139738430442975	0.000046
aspx.page	End Raise ChangedEvents	0.00144571446929708	0.000048
aspx.page	Begin Raise PostBackEvent	0.0014926478085902	0.000047
Button1_Click	About to update the label.	0.00488274347717377	0.003390
Button1_Click	Label updated.	0.00511154350622775	0.000229
aspx.page	End Raise PostBackEvent	0.00521826098009663	0.000107
aspx.page	Begin LoadComplete	0.00526882606588268	0.000051
aspx.page	End LoadComplete	0.00531715623075	0.000048
aspx.page	Begin PreRender	0.00536492766538764	0.000048
aspx.page	End PreRender	0.00543365148363828	0.000069
aspx.page	Begin PreRenderComplete	0.00548309910896497	0.000049
aspx.page	End PreRenderComplete	0.00552947371802841	0.000046
aspx.page	Begin SaveState	0.00672459767931399	0.001195
aspx.page	End SaveState	0.00711431201451581	0.000390
aspx.page	Begin SaveStateComplete	0.00719979773965686	0.000085
aspx.page	End SaveStateComplete	0.00725343584170614	0.000054
aspx.page	Begin Render	0.0073369660110433	0.000084
aspx.page	End Render	0.00856952489771745	0.001233

Figure 3-11. *Writing custom trace messages*

■ **Tip** Not only can you send your own trace messages, but you can also create an event handler that *receives* every trace message. Although this is a uncommon and specialized technique, you could use it to filter out messages that are of particular interest to you during development and log them accordingly. All you need to do is handle the Trace.TraceFinished event, which provides you with a collection of TraceContext objects representing each trace message.

Application Tracing

By default, tracing is enabled on a page-by-page basis. This isn't always convenient. In some cases, you want to collect trace statistics for a page and then view them later. ASP.NET supports this approach with application-level tracing.

To enable application-level tracing, you need to modify the web.config configuration file. Look for the <trace> element and enable it as shown here:

```
<configuration>
    <system.web>
        <trace enabled="true" requestLimit="10" pageOutput="false"
         traceMode="SortByTime" localOnly="true" />
    </system.web>
</configuration>
```

When you enable application-level tracing, you won't see the trace information unless you request the trace.axd application extension in your web application's root directory (`http://server/application/trace.axd`). This extension doesn't correspond to an actual file—instead, ASP.NET automatically intercepts the request and lists the most recently collected trace requests (as shown in Figure 3-12), provided you're making the request from the local machine or have enabled remote tracing. You can see the detailed information for any request by clicking the View Details link.

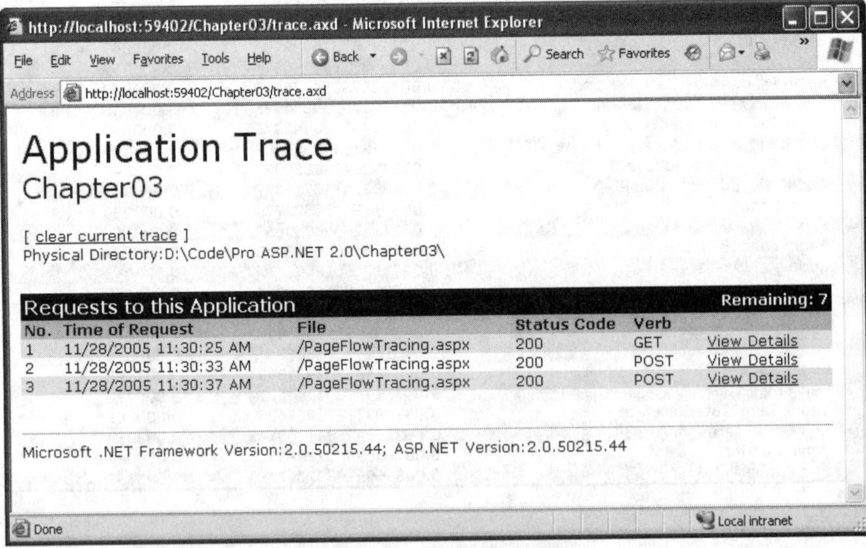

Figure 3-12. *Traced application request*

Table 3-6 describes the full list of tracing options in the web.config <trace> element.

Table 3-6. *Tracing Options*

Attribute	Values	Description
Enabled	True, False	Turns tracing on or off for all pages. This is the default setting for your web application—you can still override it on a page-by-page basis with the Page directive. Use the pageOutput setting to determine whether trace information is shown in the page or collected silently.
traceMode	SortByTime, SortByCategory	Determines the sort order of trace messages.
localOnly	True, False	Determines whether tracing information will be shown only to local clients (clients using the same computer) or can be shown to remote clients as well. By default, this is True and remote clients cannot see tracing information. In a production-level application, this should always be True to ensure security.
pageOutput	True, False	Determines whether tracing information will be displayed on the page (as it is with page-level tracing) or just stored on the server (application-level tracing). If you choose False to use application-level tracing, you'll still be able to view the collected information by requesting trace.axd from the virtual directory where your application is running.
requestLimit	Any integer (for example, 10)	When using application-level tracing, this is the number of HTTP requests for which tracing information will be stored. Unlike page-level tracing, this allows you to collect a batch of information from multiple requests. If you specify any value greater than 10,000, ASP.NET treats it as 10,000. When the maximum is reached, the behavior depends on the value of the mostRecent setting.
mostRecent	True, False	If True, ASP.NET keeps only the most recent trace messages. When the requestLimit maximum is reached, the information for the oldest request is abandoned every time a new request is received. If False (the default), ASP.NET stops collecting new trace messages when the limit is reached and ignores subsequent requests.

(Continued)

Table 3-6. *Continued*

Attribute	Values	Description
writeToDiagnosticsTrace	True, False	If True, all trace messages are also forwarded to the System.Diagnostics tracing infrastructure and received by any trace listeners you've configured using that model. The default is False. The System.Diagnostics trace features are not ASP.NET-specific and can be used in a wide variety of .NET applications. They may be used in ASP.NET as a way to automatically capture trace messages and enter them in an event log.

Tracing with the ASP.NET Development Helper

If you've installed the ASP.NET Development Helper introduced in Chapter 2 (and available at `http://www.nikhilk.net/ASPNETDevHelperTool.aspx`), you have another option for looking at tracing information—viewing it in a separate window. When the ASP.NET Developer Helper is running (both on the web server and web browser), it automatically removes trace information from the page. To access it, you can either uncheck the Hide Trace from Page check box (which shows it in the page) or click the Show Trace link.

Figure 3-13 shows this handy feature at work.

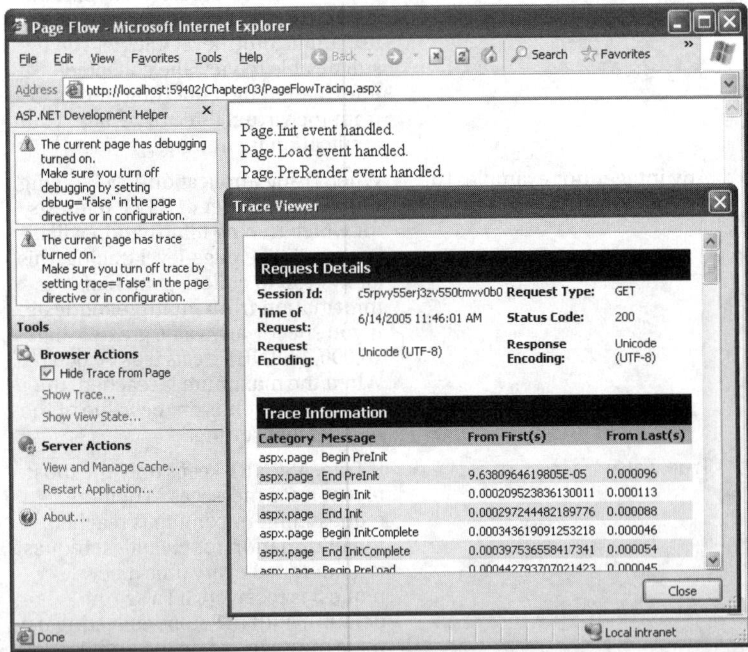

Figure 3-13. *Managing trace information with the ASP.NET Development Helper*

Accessing the HTTP Context in Another Class

Over the past several sections, you've seen how the Page class exposes a significant number of useful features that let you retrieve information about the current HTTP context. These details are available because they're provided as properties of the Page class. But what if you want to retrieve this information from inside another class, one that doesn't derive from Page?

Fortunately, another way exists to get access to all the HTTP context information. You can use the System.Web.HttpContext class. This class exposes a Shared property called Current, which returns an instance of the HttpContext class that represents all the information about the current request and response. It provides the same set of built-in ASP.NET objects as properties.

For example, here's how you would write a trace message from another component that doesn't derive from Page but is being used by a web page as part of a web request:

```
HttpContext.Current.Trace.Write("This message is from DB Component")
```

If you want to perform multiple operations, it may be slightly faster to retrieve a reference to the current context and then reuse it:

```
Dim current As HttpContext = HttpContext.Current
current.Trace.Write("This is message 1")
current.Trace.Write("This is message 2")
```

Summary

In this chapter you walked through a detailed examination of the ASP.NET page. You learned what it is and how it really works behind the scenes with postbacks and view state. You also learned the basics of the server control model, took a close look at the System.Web.UI.Page class, and learned how to use tracing. In the next chapter, you'll take a closer look at the web controls that ASP.NET gives you to build sophisticated pages.

CHAPTER 4

Server Controls

ASP.NET *server controls* are a fundamental part of the ASP.NET architecture. Essentially, server controls are classes in the .NET Framework that represent visual elements on a web form. Some of these classes are relatively straightforward and map closely to a specific HTML tag. Other controls are much more ambitious abstractions that render a more complex representation from multiple HTML elements.

In this chapter, you'll learn about the different types of ASP.NET server controls and how they're related. You'll also learn how to use validation controls to ensure that the user input matches specific rules before a web page is submitted to the server.

SERVER CONTROLS CHANGES IN .NET 2.0

ASP.NET 2.0 keeps the .NET 1.0 controls almost unchanged and adds a slew of new controls. However, you won't learn about these new controls in this chapter. Instead, you'll explore them as you examine various topics. For example, when you consider data binding, you'll learn about the GridView and DetailsView (Chapter 9 and Chapter 10); when you explore navigation, you'll use the TreeVew and Menu (Chapter 16); and when you create web portals, you'll use the new portal controls (Chapter 30).

In this chapter, you'll consider ASP.NET control basics. There are just a few new features, as listed here (in the order they appear in this chapter):

- *Control focus*: You can now programmatically set the ASP.NET control that will have focus when the page is rendered in the browser.
- *Default buttons*: You can now set the ASP.NET control that will be triggered when the user presses the Enter key while viewing a page.
- *BulletedList*: ASP.NET 2.0 provides a server-side abstraction for HTML ordered and unordered lists with the new BulletedList control.
- *Validation groups*: Rather than validate the entire page in an all-or-nothing operation, you can organize controls into logical groups that are validated independently.

Also, a few new features are built into the base control and web-page classes that you won't study in this chapter. One notable example is themes (Chapter 15).

Types of Server Controls

ASP.NET offers many different server controls, which fall into several categories. This chapter explores the controls in the following categories:

HTML server controls: These are classes that wrap the standard HTML tags and are declared with the runat="server" attribute. Apart from this attribute, the declaration for an HTML server control remains the same. Two examples include HtmlAnchor (for the <a> tag) and HtmlSelect (for the <select> tag). However, you can turn any HTML tag into a server control. If there isn't a direct corresponding class, ASP.NET will simply use the HtmlGenericControl class. To create one of these controls in Visual Studio, you need to drag an HTML element from the HTML tab of the Toolbox. Then, right-click the element, and choose Run As Server Control to add the runat="server" attribute.

Web controls: These classes duplicate the functionalities of the basic HTML tags but have a more consistent and meaningful set of properties and methods that make it easier for the developer to declare and access them. Some examples are the HyperLink, ListBox, and Button controls. In addition, several other types of ASP.NET controls (such as rich controls and validation controls) are commonly considered to be special types of web controls. In Visual Studio, you'll find the basic web forms controls in the Standard tab of the Toolbox.

Rich controls: These advanced controls have the ability to generate a large amount of HTML markup and even client-side JavaScript to create the interface. Examples include the Calendar, AdRotator, and TreeView controls. In Visual Studio, rich controls are also found in the Standard tab of the Toolbox.

Validation controls: This set of controls allows you to easily validate an associated input control against several standard or user-defined rules. For example, you can specify that the input can't be empty, that it must be a number, that it must be greater than a certain value, and so on. If validation fails, you can prevent page processing or allow these controls to show inline error messages in the page. In Visual Studio, these controls are found in the Validation tab of the Toolbox.

Additionally, you'll examine several more specialized control groupings in other chapters. These include the following:

Data controls: These controls include sophisticated grids and lists that are designed to display large amounts of data, with support for advanced features such as templating, editing, sorting, and pagination. This set also includes the data source controls that allow you to bind to different data sources declaratively, without writing extra code. You'll learn about the data controls in Chapter 9 and Chapter 10.

Navigation controls: These controls are designed to display site maps and allow the user to navigate from one page to another. You'll learn about the navigation controls in Chapter 16.

Login controls: These controls support forms authentication, an ASP.NET model for authenticating users against a database and tracking their status. Rather than writing your own interfaces to work with forms authentication, you can use these controls to get prebuilt, customizable login pages, password recovery, and user-creation wizards. You'll learn about the login controls in Chapter 21.

Web parts controls: This set of controls supports WebParts, an ASP.NET model for building componentized, highly configurable web portals. You'll learn about WebParts in Chapter 30.

ASP.NET mobile controls: This is a set of controls that resembles the web controls but is customized to support mobile clients such as PDAs, smart phones, and so on, by rendering pages to markup standards such as HTML 3.2 or WML 1.1. The mobile controls are highly adaptive, which means that when you create a page using these controls, the page can be rendered in several completely different ways depending on the device that's accessing the page. (This concept is also used in ordinary web controls on a lesser scale. They can generate XHTML or HTML 4.01 with JavaScript code or generate plain HTML 3.2 code according to the client browser's capabilities.)

ASP.NET mobile controls aren't covered in this book, although you can learn more from Derek Ferguson's *Mobile .NET* (Apress, 2001).

The Server Control Hierarchy

All server controls derive from the base Control class in the System.Web.UI namespace. This is true whether you're using HTML server controls, using web controls, or creating your own custom controls. It also applies to the Page class from which all web forms derive. Figure 4-1 illustrates the main branches of this inheritance chain.

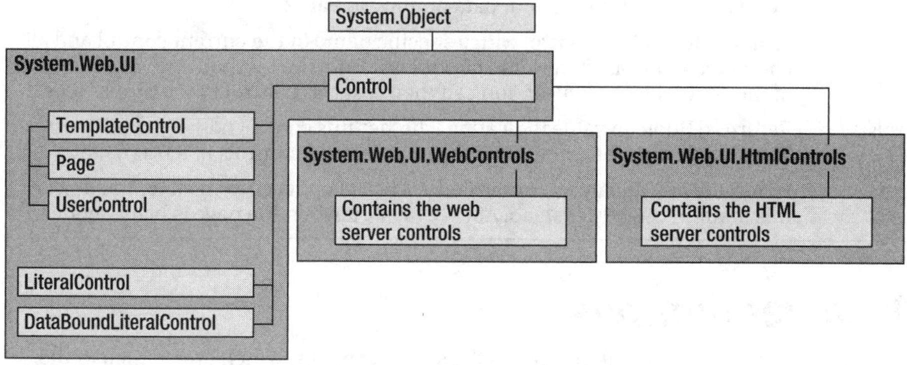

Figure 4-1. *Server control inheritance*

Because all controls derive from the base Control class, you have a basic common denominator that you can use to manipulate any control on the page, even if you don't know the specific control type. (For example, you could use this technique to loop through all the controls on the page and hide each one by setting the Visible property to false.) Table 4-1 and Table 4-2 describe the most commonly used members of the Control class.

Table 4-1. *Control Class Properties*

Property	Description
ClientID	Returns the identifier of the control, which is a unique name created by ASP.NET at the time the page is instantiated.
Controls	Returns the collection of child controls on the page. This is the "first level" of controls, some of which may be container controls that contain additional child controls of their own.
EnableViewState	Returns or sets a Boolean value indicating whether the control should maintain its state across postbacks of its parent page. This property is True by default.

(Continued)

Table 4-1. *Continued*

Property	Description
ID	Returns or sets the identifier of the control. In practice, this is the name through which you can access the control from the server-side scripts or the code-behind class.
Page	Returns a reference to the containing page object.
Parent	Returns a reference to the control's parent, which can be the page or another container control.
Visible	Returns or sets a Boolean value indicating whether the control should be rendered. If False, the control isn't just made invisible on the client—instead, the corresponding HTML tag is not generated.

Table 4-2. *Control Class Methods*

Method	Description
DataBind()	Binds the control and all of its child controls to the specified data source or expression. You'll learn about data binding in Part 2.
FindControl()	Searches for a child control with a specific name in the current control and all contained controls. If the child control is found, the method returns a reference of the general type Control. You can then cast this control to the proper type.
HasControls()	Returns a Boolean value indicating whether this control has any child controls. The control must be a container tag to have child controls (such as a <div> tag).
Render()	Writes the HTML output for the control based on its current state. You don't call this method directly. Instead, ASP.NET calls it when the page is being rendered.

HTML Server Controls

In the following sections you'll learn about the HTML server controls, which are defined in the namespace System.Web.UI.HtmlControls. Overall, there are about 20 distinct HTML server control classes. They're split into separate categories based on whether they are input controls (in which case they derive from HtmlInputControl) or can contain other controls (in which case they derive from HtmlContainerControl). Figure 4-2 shows the inheritance hierarchy.

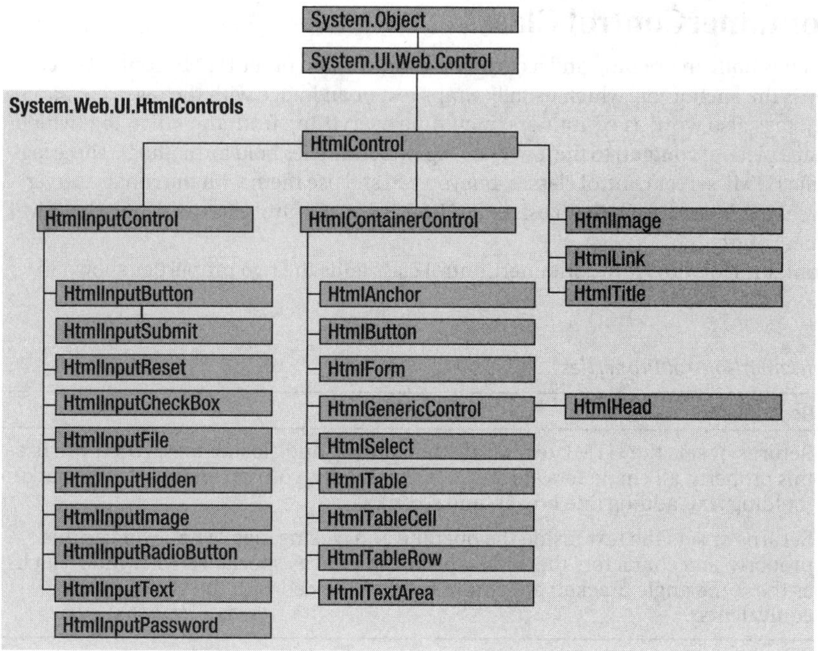

Figure 4-2. *HTML server controls*

The HtmlControl Class

All the HTML server controls derive from the base class HtmlControl. Table 4-3 shows the properties that the HtmlControl class adds to the base Control class.

Table 4-3. *HtmlControl Properties*

Property	Description
Attributes	Allows you to access or add attributes in the control tag. You can use this collection to add attributes that are not exposed by specific properties. (For example, you could add the onFocus attribute to a text box and specify some JavaScript code to configure what happens when the text box gets focus in the page.)
Disabled	Returns or sets the control's disabled state. If True, the control is usually rendered as a "grayed-out" control and is not usable.
Style	Returns a collection of CSS attributes that are applied to the control. In the web page you set this property as a semicolon-delimited list of style:value attributes. In Visual Studio, you can set this information using a designer by right-clicking the control and selecting Build Style.
TagName	Returns the control's tag name, such as a, img, and so on.

The HtmlContainerControl Class

Any HTML tag that has both an opening and a closing tag can contain other HTML content or controls. One example is the anchor tag, which usually wraps text or an image with the tags <a>...</a>. Many other HTML tags also work as containers, including everything from the <div> tag (which allows you to format a block of content) to the lowly <b> tag (which applies bold formatting). These tags don't map to specific HTML server control classes, but you can still use them with the runat="server" attribute. In this case, you interact with them using the HtmlGenericControl class, which itself derives from HtmlContainerControl.

To support containment, the HtmlContainerControl class adds the two properties shown in Table 4-4.

Table 4-4. *HtmlContainerControl Properties*

Property	Description
InnerHtml	Returns or sets the HTML text inside the opening and closing tags. When you use this property, all characters are left as is. This means you can embed HTML markup (bolding text, adding line breaks, and so on).
InnerText	Returns or sets the text inside the opening and closing tags. When you use this property, any characters that would be interpreted as special HTML syntax (such as the <, the angle bracket) are automatically replaced with the HTML entity equivalents.

The HtmlInputControl Class

The HTML input controls allow for user interaction. These include the familiar graphical widgets, including check boxes, text boxes, buttons, and list boxes. All of these controls are generated with the <input> tag. The type attribute indicates the type of input control, as in <input type="text"> (a text box), <input type="submit"> (a submit button), and <input type="file"> (controls for uploading a file).

Server-side input controls derive from HtmlInputControl, which adds the properties shown in Table 4-5.

Table 4-5. *HtmlInputControl Properties*

Property	Description
Name	Gets the unique identifier name for the HtmlInputControl.
Type	Gets the type of an HtmlInputControl. For example, if this property is set to text, the HtmlInputControl is a text box for data entry.
Value	Gets or sets the value associated with an input control. The value associated with a control depends on the type of control. For example, in a text box this property contains the text entered in the control. For buttons, this defines the text on the button.

The HTML Server Control Classes

Table 4-6 lists all the available HTML server controls and the specific properties and events that each one adds to the base class. As noted earlier, the declaration of HTML server controls on the page is the same as what you use for normal static HTML tags, with the addition of the runat="server" attribute. It is this attribute that allows ASP.NET to process them and translate them into instances of the corresponding .NET class. For this reason, the HTML server controls are a good option if you're converting your existing HTML or ASP page to an ASP.NET web form.

Table 4-6. *HTML Server Control Classes*

Tag Declaration	.NET Class	Specific Members
<a runat="server">	HtmlAnchor	HRef, Target, Title, Name, ServerClick event
<button runat="server">	HtmlButton	CausesValidation, ValidationGroup, ServerClick event
<form runat="server">	HtmlForm	Name, Enctype, Method, Target, DefaultButton, DefaultFocus
<img runat="server">	HtmlImage	Align, Alt, Border, Height, Src, Width
<input type="button" runat="server">	HtmlInputButton	Name, Type, Value, CausesValidation, ValidationGroup, ServerClick event
<input type="reset" runat="server">	HtmlInputReset	Name, Type, Value
<input type="submit" runat="server">	HtmlInputSubmit	Name, Type, Value, CausesValidation, ValidationGroup, ServerClick event
<input type="checkbox" runat="server">	HtmlInputCheckBox	Checked, Name, Type, Value, ServerClick event
<input type="file" runat="server">	HtmlInputFile	Accept, MaxLength, Name, PostedFile, Size, Type, Value
<input type="hidden" runat="server">	HtmlInputHidden	Name, Type, Value, ServerChange event
<input type="image" runat="server">	HtmlInputImage	Align, Alt, Border, Name, Src, Type, Value, CausesValidation, ValidationGroup, ServerClick event
<input type="radio" runat="server">	HtmlInputRadioButton	Checked, Name, Type, Value, ServerChange event
<input type="text" runat="server">	HtmlInputText	MaxLength, Name, Type, Value, ServerChange event
<input type="password" runat="server">	HtmlInputPassword	MaxLength, Name, Type, Value, ServerChange event
<select runat="server">	HtmlSelect	Multiple, SelectedIndex, Size, Value, DataSource, DataTextField, DataValueField, Items (collection), ServerChange event
<table runat="server">, <td runat="server">	HtmlTable	Align, BgColor, Border, BorderColor, CellPadding, CellSpacing, Height, Width, Rows (collection)

(Continued)

Table 4-6. *Continued*

Tag Declaration	.NET Class	Specific Members
<th runat="server">	HtmlTableCell	Align, BgColor, , BorderColor, ColSpan, Height, NoWrap, RowSpan, VAlign, Width
<tr runat="server">	HtmlTableRow	Align, BgColor, , BorderColor, Height, VAlign, Cells (collection)
<textarea runat="server">	HtmlTextArea	Cols, Name, Rows, Value, ServerChange event
Any other HTML tag with the runat="server" attribute	HtmlGenericControl	None

■ **Note** Two specialized HTML controls aren't shown in Table 4-6. These are the HtmlHead and HtmlTitle controls, which provide server-side access to the <head> portion of a web page. Using these controls, you can dynamically set the title, metadata, and linked stylesheets for the page. Chapter 3 shows an example.

The meaning of most of the HTML server control properties is quite obvious, because they match the underlying HTML tag attributes. This means there's no need to focus on each individual control. In the next few sections, you'll get an overview of some common techniques for using controls and dig a little deeper into their events and the common object model.

Setting Style Attributes and Other Properties

The following example shows how you can configure a standard HtmlInputText control (which represents the <input type="text"> tag). To read or set the current text in the text box, you use the Value property. If you want to configure the style information, you need to add new CSS style attributes using the Style collection. Finally, if you want to set other attributes that aren't exposed by any properties, you need to use the Attributes collection. This example uses the Attributes collection to associate some simple JavaScript code—showing an alert message box with the current value of the text box—to the client-side onFocus event of the control.

```
Protected Sub Page_Load(ByVal sender As Object, ByVal e As System.EventArgs)
  ' Perform the initialization only the first time the page is requested.
  ' After that, this information is tracked in view state.
  If (Not Page.IsPostBack) Then
    ' Set the style attributes to configure appearance.
    TextBox1.Style("font-size") = "20px"
    TextBox1.Style("color") = "red"
    ' Use a slightly different but equivalent syntax
    ' for setting a style attribute.
    TextBox1.Style.Add("background-color", "lightyellow")
    ' Set the default text.
    TextBox1.Value = "<Enter e-mail address here>"
    ' Set other nonstandard attributes.
    TextBox1.Attributes("onfocus") = "alert(TextBox1.value)"
  End If
End Sub
```

If you request the page, the following HTML code will be returned for the text box:

```
<input name="TextBox1" id="TextBox1" type="text"
style="WIDTH:410px;HEIGHT:46px;font-size:20px;color:red;
background-color:lightyellow;" size="63" value="&lt;Enter e-mail address here&gt;"
onfocus="alert(TextBox1.value)" />
```

Notice that the CSS style attribute also includes some information that wasn't explicitly set in the code. Instead, Visual Studio added this information (Width and Height) to the control tag when the control was resized in the development environment.

Figure 4-3 shows the resulting page when focus changes to the text box.

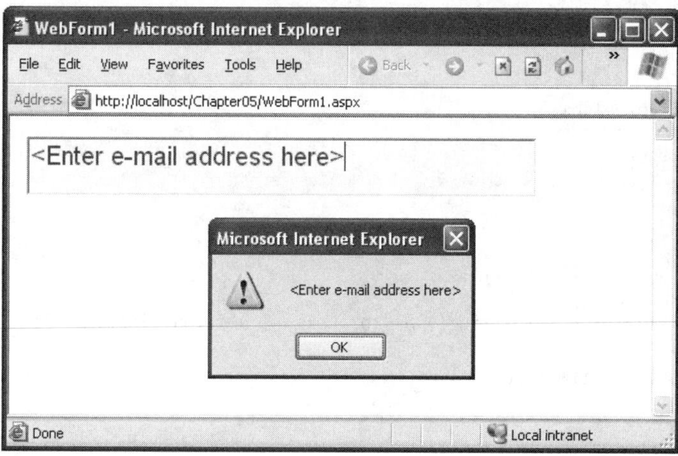

Figure 4-3. *Testing HTML server controls*

This process of control interaction is essentially the same for all HTML server controls. Style properties and attributes are always set in the same way. The only difference is that some controls expose additional properties that you can use. For example, the HtmlAnchor control exposes an HRef property that lets you set the target page for the link.

Programmatically Creating Server Controls

Sometimes you don't know in advance how many text boxes, radio buttons, table rows, or other controls you need because this might depend on other factors such as the number of records stored in a database or the user's input. With ASP.NET, the solution is easy—you can simply create instances of the HTML server controls you need, set their properties with the object-oriented approach used in the previous example, and then simply add them to the Controls collection of the containing page. This technique was introduced in the previous chapter, and it applies equally well to HTML server controls and web controls.

For example, the following code dynamically creates a table with five rows and four cells per row, sets their colors and text, and shows all this on the page. The interesting detail is that no control tags are declared in the .aspx file. Instead, everything is generated programmatically.

```
Protected Sub Page_Load(ByVal sender As Object, ByVal e As System.EventArgs)
    ' Create a new HtmlTable object.
    Dim table1 As New HtmlTable()
    ' Set the table's formatting-related properties.
    table1.Border = 1
    table1.CellPadding = 3
    table1.CellSpacing = 3
    table1.BorderColor = "red"

    ' Start adding content to the table.
    Dim row As HtmlTableRow
    Dim cell As HtmlTableCell
    For i As Integer = 1 To 5
        ' Create a new row, and set its background color.
        row = New HtmlTableRow()
        If i Mod 2=0 Then
            row.BgColor = ("lightyellow")
        Else
            row.BgColor = ("lightcyan")
        End If

        For j As Integer = 1 To 4
            ' Create a cell, and set its text.
            cell = New HtmlTableCell()
            cell.InnerHtml = "Row: " & i.ToString() & "<br>Cell: " & j.ToString()

            ' Add the cell to the current row.
            row.Cells.Add(cell)
        Next j

            ' Add the row to the table.
            table1.Rows.Add(row)
      Next i

    ' Add the table to the page.
    Me.Controls.Add(table1)
End Sub
```

This example contains nested loops. The outer loop creates a row. The inner loop then creates the cells and adds them to the Cells collection of the current row. When the inner loop ends, the code adds the entire row to the Rows collection of the table. The final step occurs when the outer loop is finished. At this point, the code adds the completed table to the Controls collection of the page.

Figure 4-4 shows the resulting page.

This example used a table because it gave a good opportunity to show how child controls (cells and rows) are added to the Controls collection of the parent, but of course this mechanism works with any other server control.

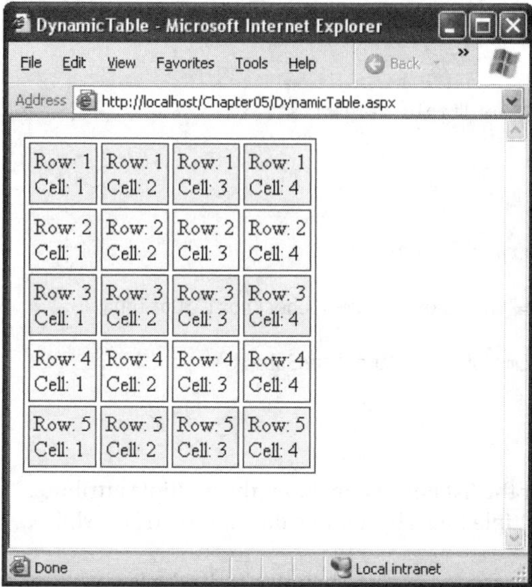

Figure 4-4. *A dynamically generated table*

Handling Server-Side Events

HTML server controls provide a sparse event model with two possible events: ServerClick and ServerChange. ServerClick gets processed on the server side. It's provided by most button controls, and it allows your code to take immediate action. This action might override the expected behavior. For example, if you intercept the click event of a hyperlink control (the <a> element), the user won't be redirected to a new page unless you provide extra code to forward the request.

The ServerChange event responds when a change has been made to a text or selection control. This event doesn't occur until the page is posted back (for example, after the user clicks a submit button). At this point, the ServerChange event occurs for all changed controls, followed by the appropriate ServerClick.

Table 4-7 shows which controls provide a ServerClick event and which ones provide a ServerChange event.

Table 4-7. *HTML Control Events*

Event	Controls That Provide It
ServerClick	HtmlAnchor, HtmlForm, HtmlButton, HtmlInputButton, HtmlInputImage
ServerChange	HtmlInputText, HtmlInputCheckBox, HtmlInputRadioButton, HtmlInputHidden, HtmlSelect, HtmlTextArea

The ServerClick and ServerChange Events

The following example demonstrates the ServerClick and ServerChange events and shows you the order in which they are raised. To create this example, you need a text box, list box, and check box.

Here are the controls on the page:

```
<form id="Form1" runat="server">
  <div>
    <select runat="server" id="List1" size="5" multiple Name="List1">
        <option>Option 1</option>
        <option>Option 2</option>
    </select>
    <br />
    <input type="text" runat="server" ID="Textbox1" Size="10"
     Name="Textbox1"><br />
    <input type="checkbox" runat="server" ID="Checkbox1" Name="Checkbox1">Option
     text<br />
    <input type="submit" runat="server" ID="cmdSubmit" Name="cmdSubmit"
     value="Submit Query">
  </div>
</form>
```

Note that this code declares two list items for the list box and includes the multiple attribute. This means that the user will be able to select multiple items by holding down the Ctrl key while clicking each entry.

The text box and the check box are attached to the same event handler, while the list box uses a separate event handler with different code—this is done because the event that handles the check box and text box isn't really doing anything specific for that control, just reporting that it was fired, and thus two event handlers aren't necessary. We want to produce different results for the list, so it has a separate event handler. The easiest way to set this up in Visual Studio is to create a text box event handler by double-clicking the text box. Then, rename the event handler to Ctrl_ServerChange(), and enter the code shown here:

```
Protected Sub Ctrl_ServerChange(ByVal sender As Object, ByVal e As System.EventArgs)
    Response.Write("<li>ServerChange detected for " _
        & (CType(sender, Control)).ID & "</li>")
End Sub
```

The actual event handler code is quite straightforward. It simply casts the sender object to a Control type, reads its ID property, and writes a message declaring that the event was detected.

Now, switch to the HTML source view, and edit the text box and check box tags to bind their ServerChange events to the new event handler, as shown here:

```
<input type="text" runat="server" ID="Textbox1" Size="10"
 Name="Textbox1" OnServerChange="Ctrl_ServerChange"><br />
<input type="checkbox" runat="server" ID="Checkbox1"
 Name="Checkbox1" OnServerChange="Ctrl_ServerChange">
```

■ **Note** Visual Studio provides a greater level of design-time support for events with web controls. When working with web controls, you can attach event handlers using a special event view in the Properties window—you just need to click the lightning bolt icon. With HTML server controls, this facility isn't available, although you can still coax Visual Studio into generating an event handler for the control's default event by double-clicking it

---

Next, double-click the HtmlSelect control to create an event handler for the list box. This event handler cycles through the control's Items collection and writes the value of all the selected items to the web page, as follows:

```
Protected Sub List1_ServerChange(ByVal sender As Object,
      ByVal e As System.EventArgs)
    Response.Write("<li>ServerChange detected for List1. " _
```

```
        & "The selected items are:</li><br />")
    For Each li As ListItem In List1.Items
        If li.Selected Then
            Response.Write("  - " & li.Value & "<br />")
        End If
    Next
End Sub
```

Finally, the submit button handles the ServerClick event, as shown here:

```
Protected Sub Submit1_ServerClick(ByVal sender As Object,
      ByVal e As System.EventArgs)
    Response.Write("<li>ServerClick detected for Submit1.</li>")
End Sub
```

As an added bonus, when the page is created, the event handler for the Page.Load event adds another three items to the list box, provided the page is being requested for the first time. This shows how easy it is to programmatically add list items.

```
Protected Sub Page_Load(ByVal sender As Object, ByVal e As System.EventArgs)
    If (Not Page.IsPostBack) Then
      List1.Items.Add("Option 3")
      List1.Items.Add("Option 4")
      List1.Items.Add("Option 5")
    End If
End Sub
```

To test this page, request it in the browser, select some items in the list box, type some characters in the text box, select the check box, and click the submit button to generate a postback. You should end up with something similar to what's shown in Figure 4-5.

Note that the order of change events is nondeterministic, and you shouldn't rely on these events occurring in any set order. However, you're likely to see events raised in the order in which the controls are declared. The only detail of which you're guaranteed is that all the change events fire before the ServerClick event that triggered the postback.

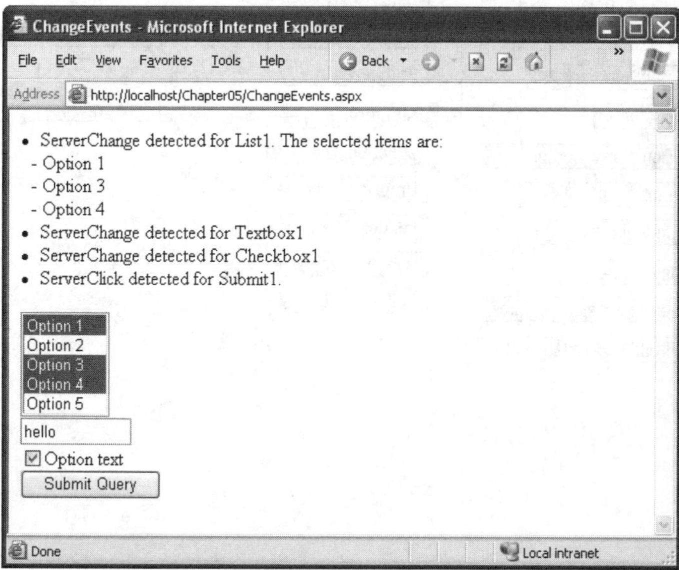

Figure 4-5. *Detecting change events*

Web Controls

HTML server controls provide a relatively fast way to migrate to ASP.NET, but not necessarily the best way. For one thing, the names of HTML controls and their attributes are not always intuitive, and they don't have the same design-time support for attaching event handlers. The HTML controls also have certain limitations, such as that style properties must be set through CSS syntax (which is more difficult than setting a direct property) and that change events can't be raised until the page is posted back in response to another action. Finally, HTML server controls can't provide user interface elements that aren't already defined in the HTML standard. If you want to create some sort of aggregate control that uses a combination of HTML elements to render a complex interface, you're on your own.

To address these issues, ASP.NET provides a higher-level web control model. All web controls are defined in the System.Web.UI.WebControl namespace and derive from the WebControl base class, which provides a more abstract, consistent model than the HTML server controls. Web controls also enable additional features, such as automatic postback. But the really exciting part is that many extended controls don't just map a single HTML tag but instead generate more complex output made up of several HTML tags and JavaScript code. Examples include lists of check boxes, radio buttons, calendars, editable grids, and so on.

Figure 4-6 shows a portion of the inheritance hierarchy for web controls.

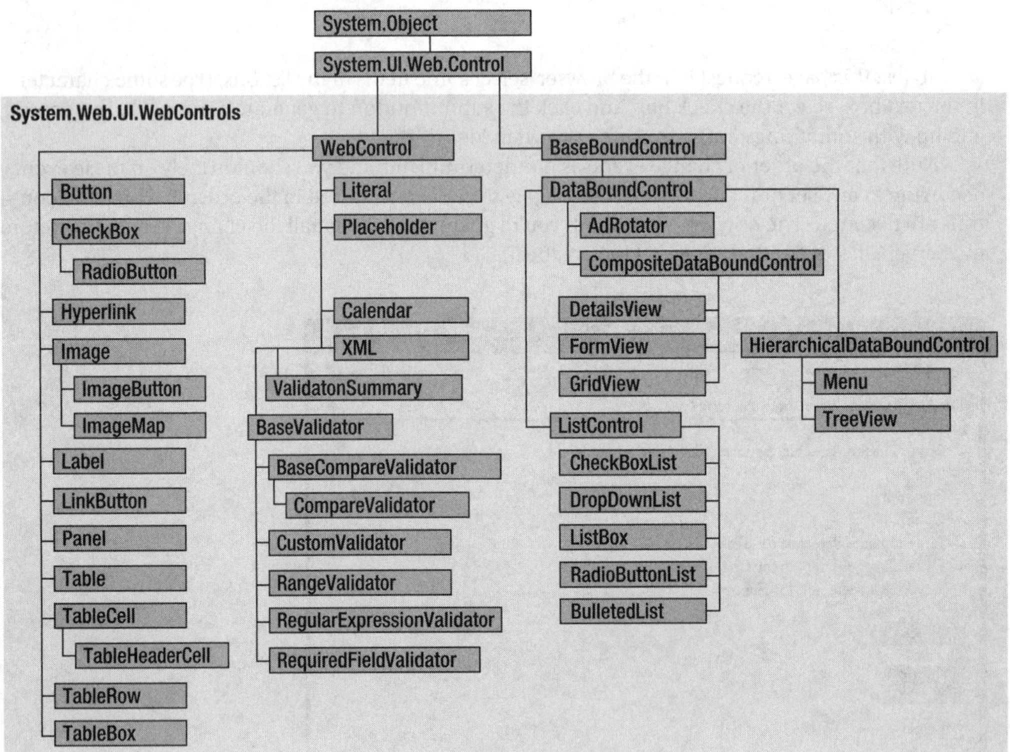

Figure 4-6. *Web controls*

The WebControl Base Class

All the web controls inherit from the WebControl class. The WebControl class also derives from Control. As a result, many of its properties and methods—such as Controls, Visible, and FindControl()—are similar to those of the HTML server controls. However, the WebControl class adds the properties shown in Table 4-8. Many of these properties wrap the CSS style attributes, such as the foreground or background color, the font, the height, the width, and so on. These properties allow you to configure the appearance of a web control much more easily (and with less chance of error).

Table 4-8. *WebControl Class Properties*

Property	Description
AccessKey	Returns or sets the keyboard shortcut that allows the user to quickly navigate to the control. For example, if set to A, the user can move the focus to this control by pressing Alt+A.
BackColor	Returns or sets the background color.
BorderColor	Returns or sets the border color.
BorderStyle	One of the values from the BorderStyle enumeration, including Dashed, Dotted, Double, Groove, Ridge, Inset, Outset, Solid, and None.
BorderWidth	Returns or sets the border width.
CssClass	Returns or sets the CSS style to associate with the control. The CSS style can be defined in a <style> section at the top of the page or in a separate CSS file referenced by the page.
Enabled	Returns or sets the control's enabled state. If false, the control is usually rendered grayed-out and is not usable.
Font	Returns an object with all the style information of the font used for the control's text. This property includes subproperties that can be set with the object-walker syntax shown later in this chapter.
ForeColor	Returns or sets the foreground color; for example, that of the text of the control.
Height	Returns or sets the control's height.
TabIndex	A number that allows you to control the tab order. The control with a TabIndex of 0 has the focus when the page first loads. Pressing Tab moves the user to the control with the next lowest TabIndex, provided it is enabled. This property is supported only in Internet Explorer 4.0 and higher.
ToolTip	Displays a text message when the user hovers the mouse above the control. Many older browsers don't support this property.
Width	Returns or sets the control's width.

Basic Web Control Classes

ASP.NET includes a web control that duplicates each HTML server control and provides the same functionality. These web controls inherit from WebControl and add their own properties and events. Table 4-9 summarizes these core controls and their specific members.

Table 4-9. *Basic Web Control Classes*

ASP.NET Tag Declaration	Generated HTML	Key Members
<asp:Button>	<input type="submit"/> or <input type="button"/>	Text, CausesValidation, PostBackUrl, ValidationGroup, Click event
<asp:CheckBox>	<input type="checkbox"/>	AutoPostBack, Checked, Text, TextAlign, CheckedChanged event
<asp:FileUpload>	<input type="file">	FileBytes, FileContent, FileName, HasFile, PostedFile, SaveAs()
<asp:HiddenField>	<input type="hidden">	Value
<asp:HyperLink>	<a>...</a>	ImageUrl, NavigateUrl, Target, Text
<asp:Image>	<img/>	AlternateText, ImageAlign, ImageUrl
<asp:ImageButton>	<input type="image"/>	CausesValidation, ValidationGroup, Click event
<asp:ImageMap>	<map>	HotSpotMode, HotSpots (collection), AlternateText, ImageAlign, ImageUrl
<asp:Label>	<span>...</span>	Text, AssociatedControlID
<asp:LinkButton>	<a><img/></a>	Text, CausesValidation, ValidationGroup, Click event
<asp:Panel>	<div>...</div>	BackImageUrl, DefaultButton, GroupingText, HorizontalAlign, Scrollbars, Wrap
<asp:RadioButton>	<input type="radio"/>	AutoPostBack, Checked, GroupName, Text, TextAlign, CheckedChanged event
<asp:Table>	<table>...</table>	BackImageUrl, CellPadding, CellSpacing, GridLines, HorizontalAlign, Rows (collection)
<asp:TableCell>	<td>...</td>	ColumnSpan, HorizontalAlign, RowSpan, Text, VerticalAlign, Wrap
<asp:TableRow>	<tr>...</tr>	Cells (collection), HorizontalAlign, VerticalAlign
<asp:TextBox>	<input type="test"/> or <input type="test"/> or <textarea>...</textarea>	AutoPostBack, Columns, MaxLength, ReadOnly, Rows, Text, TextMode, Wrap, TextChanged event

The properties of web controls are all fairly intuitive. One of the goals of web controls is to make it easier to set a control's attributes through properties with consistent names, without having to worry about the details of how they translate to HTML code (although having a good knowledge of HTML certainly helps). For this reason, this chapter won't describe and show examples for every type of control. Instead, we'll provide a general discussion that's useful for every control.

To start highlighting some of the key differences between HTML server controls and web controls, consider the following web control tag:

```
<asp:TextBox runat="server" ID="Textbox1" Text="This is a test"
  ForeColor="red" BackColor="lightyellow" Width="250px"
  Font-Name="Verdana" Font-Bold="True" Font-Size="20" />
```

Web controls are always declared on the page with the syntax <asp:controlname>, with the asp: prefix that makes them immediately recognizable as being different from the HTML controls. But this example also demonstrates a more dramatic difference—the way that style information is specified.

Essentially, this tag generates a text box control with a width of 250 pixels, a red foreground color, and a light yellow background. The text is displayed with the font Verdana, with a size of 20, and with bold formatting. The differences between the previous declaration and the respective declaration of a HTML tag are the following:

- The control is declared using its class name (TextBox) instead of the HTML tag name (input).
- The default content is set with the Text property, instead of a less-obvious Value attribute.
- The style attributes (colors, width, and font) are set by direct properties, instead of being grouped together in a single style attribute.

Web controls also have two special restrictions:

- Every control declaration must have a corresponding closing tag or the empty element /> syntax at the end of the opening tag. If you don't close the tag, you'll get a runtime error. Breaking this rule when working with HTML server controls has no adverse effect.
- All web controls must be declared within a server-side form tag (and there can be only one server-side form per page), even if they don't cause a postback. Otherwise, you'll get a runtime error. This rule is not necessary when working with HTML server controls, provided you don't need to handle postbacks.

If you request a page with this tag, you'll see that the control is translated into the following HTML tag when the page is rendered:

```
<input name="Textbox1" type="text" value="This is a test" id="Textbox1"
style="color:Red;background-color:LightYellow;font-family:Verdana;
font-size:20pt;font-weight:bold;width:250px;" />
```

Units

All the control properties that use measurements, including BorderWidth, Height, and Width, require the Unit structure, which combines a numeric value with a type of measurement (pixels, percentage, and so on). This means when you set these properties in a control tag, you must make sure to append px (for pixel) or % (for percentage) to the number to indicate the type of unit.

Here's an example with a Panel control that is 300 pixels high and has a width equal to 50 percent of the current browser window:

```
<asp:Panel Height="300px" Width="50%" id="pnl" runat="server" />
```

If you're assigning a unit-based property through code, you need to use one of the static methods of the Unit type. Use Pixel() to supply a value in pixels, and use Percentage() to supply a percentage value.

```
' Convert the number 300 to a Unit object
' representing pixels, and assign it.
pnl.Height = Unit.Pixel(300)

' Convert the number 50 to a Unit object
' representing percent, and assign it.
pnl.Width = Unit.Percentage(50)
```

You could also manually create a Unit object and initialize it using one of the supplied constructors and the UnitType enumeration. This requires a few more steps but allows you to easily assign the same unit to several controls.

```
' Create a Unit object.
Dim myUnit As New Unit(300, UnitType.Pixel)
```

```
' Assign the Unit object to several controls or properties.
pnl.Height = myUnit
pnl.Width = myUnit
```

Enumerated Values

Enumerations are used heavily in the .NET class library to group a set of related constants. For example, when you set a control's BorderStyle property, you can choose one of several predefined values from the BorderStyle enumeration. In code, you set an enumeration using the dot syntax:

```
ctrl.BorderStyle = BorderStyle.Dashed
```

In the .aspx file, you set an enumeration by specifying one of the allowed values as a string. You don't include the name of the enumeration type, which is assumed automatically.

```
<asp:TextBox BorderStyle="Dashed" Text="Border Test" id="txt"
 runat="server" />
```

Colors

The `ForeColor` and `BackColor` properties refer to a Color object from the System.Drawing namespace. You can create Color objects in several ways:

Using an ARGB (alpha transparency, red, green, blue) color value: You specify each value as integer.

Using a predefined .NET color name: You choose the correspondingly named read-only property from the Color class. These properties include all the HTML colors (for instance, Color.red).

Using an HTML color name: You specify this value as a string using the ColorTranslator class.

To use these any of techniques, you must import the System.Drawing namespace, as follows:

```
Imports System.Drawing
```

The following code shows several ways to specify a color in code:

```
' Create a color from an ARGB value.
Dim alpha As Integer = 255, red As Integer = 0
Dim green As Integer = 255, blue As Integer = 0
Dim ctrl.ForeColor = Color.FromARGB(alpha, red, green, blue)

' Create a color using a .NET name:
ctrl.ForeColor = Color.Crimson

' Create a color from an HTML code.
ctrl.ForeColor = ColorTranslator.FromHtml("Blue")
```

When defining a color in the .aspx file, you can use any one of the known color names, as follows:

```
<asp:TextBox ForeColor="Red" Text="Test" id="txt" runat="server" />
```

Refer to the MSDN documentation for a full list of color names. Alternatively, you can use a hexadecimal color number (in the format #<red><green><blue>), as shown here:

```
<asp:TextBox ForeColor="#ff50ff" Text="Test"
     id="txt" runat="server" />
```

Fonts

The Font property actually references a full FontInfo object, which is defined in the System.Web.UI.WebControls namespace. Every FontInfo object has several properties that define a font's name, size, and style. Even though the WebControl.Font property is read-only, you can modify all the FontInfo properties (shown in Table 4-10).

Table 4-10. *FontInfo Properties*

Property	Description
Name	A string indicating the font name (such as Verdana).
Names	An ordered array of strings containing font names.
Size	The size of the font as a FontUnit object.
Bold, Italic, Strikeout, Underline, and Overline	Boolean properties that either apply the given style attribute or ignore it.

In code, you can assign values to the various font properties as shown here:

```
ctrl.Font.Name = "Verdana"
ctrl.Font.Bold = True
```

You can also set the size using the FontUnit type:

```
' Specifies a relative size.
ctrl.Font.Size = FontUnit.Small

' Specifies an absolute size of 14 pixels.
ctrl.Font.Size = FontUnit.Point(14)
```

In the .aspx file, you need to use a special *object-walker* syntax to specify object properties such as font. The object-walker syntax uses a hyphen (-) to separate properties. For example, you could set a control with a specific font (Tahoma) and font size (40 point) like this:

```
<asp:TextBox Font-Name="Tahoma" Font-Size="40" Text="Size Test" id="txt"
 runat="server" />
```

or with a relative size, as follows:

```
<asp:TextBox Font-Name="Tahoma" Font-Size="Large" Text="Size Test"
 id="txt" runat="server" />
```

Of course, in the world of the Internet font names are just recommendations. If a given font isn't present on a client's computer, the browser attempts to substitute a similar font. (For more information on this font-substitution process, refer to the CSS specification at `http://www.w3.org/TR/REC-CSS2/fonts.html`.)

If you want to provide a list of possible fonts, you can use the FontInfo.Names property instead of the FontInfo.Name property. The Names property accepts an array of names that will be rendered as an ordered list (with greatest preference given to the names at the top of the list).

■ **Tip** The Names and Name property are kept synchronized, and setting either one affects the other. When you set the Names property, the Name property is automatically set to the first item in the array you used for the Names property. If you set the Name property, the Names property is automatically set with an array containing a single item. Therefore, you should use only the Name property or the Names property, but not both at once.

Focus

Unlike HTML server controls, every web control provides a Focus() method. The focus control has an effect only for input controls (controls that can accept keystrokes from the user). When the page is rendered in the client browser, the user starts in the focused control. The Focus() method is new in ASP.NET 2.0.

For example, if you have a form that allows the user to edit customer information, you might call the Focus() method on the first text box with customer address information. That way, the cursor appears in this text box immediately. Also, if the text box is partway down the form, the page scrolls to the correct position automatically. Once the page is rendered, the user can move from control to control using the time-honored Tab key.

Of course, if you're familiar with the HTML standard, you know there isn't any built-in way to give focus to an input control. Instead, you need to rely on JavaScript. This is the secret to ASP.NET's implementation. When your code is finished processing and the page is rendered, ASP.NET adds an extra block of JavaScript code to the end of your page. This JavaScript code simply sets the focus to the last control that had the Focus() method triggered. Here's an example:

```
<script type="text/javascript">
<!--
  WebForm_AutoFocus('TextBox2');// -->
</script>
```

If you haven't called Focus() at all, this code isn't emitted. If you've called it for more than one control, the JavaScript code uses the more recently focused control.

Rather than call the Focus() method programmatically, you can set a control so that it is always the first to get focused (unless you override it by calling the Focus() method). You do this by setting the DefaultFocus property, like so:

```
<form id="Form1" defaultfocus="TextBox2" runat="server">
```

As you can see, the focusing code relies on a JavaScript method named WebForm_AutoFocus(), which ASP.NET generates automatically. Technically, the JavaScript method is provided through an ASP.NET extension named WebResource.axd. The resource is named Focus.js. If you dig through the rendered HTML of your page, you'll find an element that links to this JavaScript file that looks something like this:

```
<script src="WebResource.axd?a=s&r=WebForms.js"></script>
```

You can type this request directly into your browser to download and examine the JavaScript document. It's quite lengthy, because it carefully deals with cases such as focusing on a nonfocusable control that contains a focusable child. However, the following code shows the heart of the focusing logic:

```
function WebForm_AutoFocus(focusId) {
    // Find the element based on the ID (code differs based on browser).
    var targetControl;
    if (__nonMSDOMBrowser) {
        targetControl = document.getElementById(focusId);
    }
    else {
        targetControl = document.all[focusId];
    }

    // Check if the control can accept focus or contains a child that can.
    var focused = targetControl;
    if (targetControl != null && (!WebForm_CanFocus(targetControl)) ) {
        focused = WebForm_FindFirstFocusableChild(targetControl);
    }
```

```
    // If there is a valid control, try to apply focus and scroll it into view.
    if (focused != null) {
        try {
            focused.focus();
            focused.scrollIntoView();
            if (window.__smartNav != null) {
                window.__smartNav.ae = focused.id;
            }
        }
        catch (e) {
        }
    }
}
```

As you can see, the first task this code performs is to test whether the current browser is an up-level version of Internet Explorer (and hence supports the Microsoft DOM). However, even if it isn't, the script code still performs the autofocusing, with only subtle differences.

Another way to manage focus is using access keys. For example, if you set the AccessKey property of a TextBox to A, then when the user presses Alt+A, focus will switch to the TextBox. Labels can also get into the game, even though they can't accept focus. The trick is to set the Label.AssociatedControlID property to specify a linked input control. That way, the label transfers focus to the control nearby.

For example, the following label gives focus to TextBox2 when the keystroke Alt+2 is pressed:

```
<asp:Label AccessKey="2" AssociatedControlID="TextBox2" runat="server">
 TextBox2:</asp:Label><asp:TextBox runat="server" ID="TextBox2" />
```

Access keys are also supported in non-Microsoft browsers, including Firefox.

The Default Button

Along with the idea of control focusing, ASP.NET 2.0 introduces a new mechanism that allows you to designate a default button on a web page. The default button is the button that is "clicked" when the user presses the Enter key. For example, on a form you might want to turn the submit button into a default button. That way, if the user hits Enter at any time, the page is posted back and the Button.Click event is fired for that button.

To designate a default button, you must set the HtmlForm.DefaultButton property with the ID of the respective control, as shown here:

```
<form id="Form1" defaultbutton="cmdSubmit" runat="server">
```

The default button must be a control that implements the IButtonControl interface. The interface is implemented by the Button, LinkButton, and ImageButton web controls but not by any of the HTML server controls.

In some cases, it makes sense to have more than one default button. For example, you might create a web page with two groups of input controls. Both groups may need a different default button. You can handle this by placing the groups into separate panels. The Panel control also exposes the DefaultButton property, which works when any input control it contains gets the focus.

Scrollable Panels

In ASP.NET 2.0, the Panel control gains the ability to scroll. This means you can fill your Panel controls with server controls or HTML, explicitly set the Height and Width properties of the panel so they won't be smaller than what's required, and then switch on scrolling by setting the ScrollBars property to Vertical, Horizontal, Both, or Auto (which shows scrollbars only when there's too much content to fit).

Here's an example:

```
<asp:Panel ID="Panel1" runat="server" Height="116px" Width="278px"
 BorderStyle="Solid" BorderWidth="1px" ScrollBars="Auto">
  This scrolls.
  <br /><br />
  <asp:Button ID="Button1" runat="server" Text="Button" />
  <asp:Button ID="Button2" runat="server" Text="Button" />
  <br />
  ...
</asp:Panel>
```

Figure 4-7 shows the result.

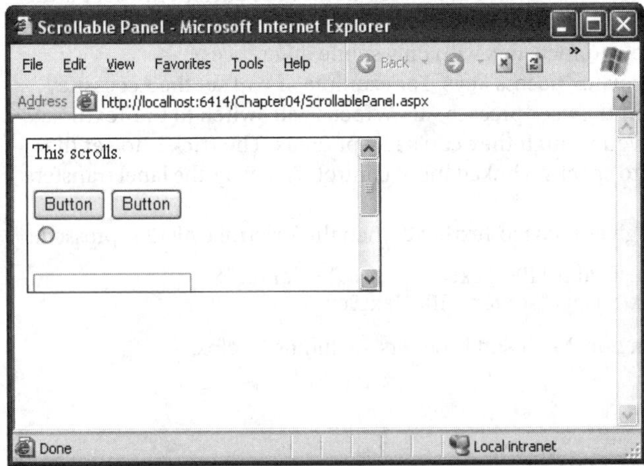

Figure 4-7. *A scrollable panel*

The panel is rendered as a <div> tag. The scrolling behavior is provided by setting the CSS overflow attribute, which is supported in most browsers (starting with Internet Explorer 4.0 and Netscape 6.0).

Handling Web Control Events

Server-side events for Web controls work in much the same way as the server events of the HTML server controls. Instead of the ServerClick events, there is a Click event, and instead of the generic ServerChange events there are specific events such as CheckedChanged (for the RadioButton and CheckButton) and TextChanged (for the TextBox), but the behavior remains the same.

The key difference is that web controls support the AutoPostBack feature described in the previous chapter, which uses JavaScript to capture a client-side event and trigger a postback. ASP.NET receives the posted-back page and raises the corresponding server-side event immediately.

To watch these events in action, it helps to create a simple event tracker application (see Figure 4-8). All this application does is add a new entry to a list control every time one of the events it is monitoring occurs. This allows you to see the order in which events are triggered and the effect of using automatic postback.

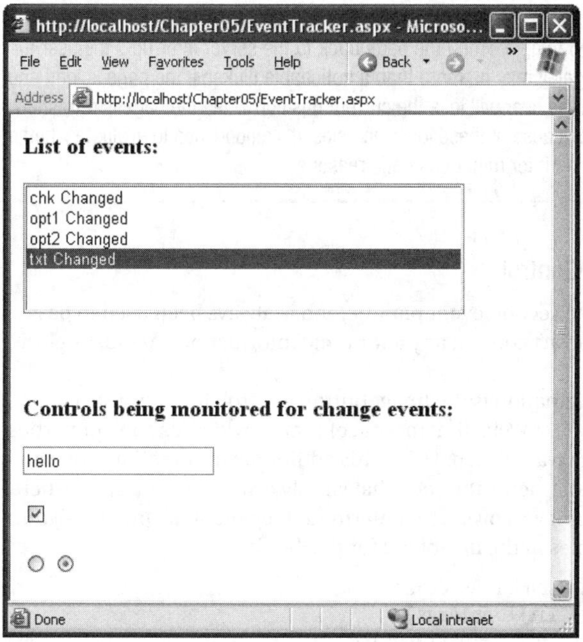

Figure 4-8. *The event tracker*

In this demonstration, all control change events are handled by the same event handler, `CtrlChanged`:

```
<form id="form1" runat="server">
  <div>
    <h3>List of events:</h3>
    <asp:ListBox id="lstEvents" runat="server" Height="107px" Width="355px"/>
    <br /><br />
    <h3>Controls being monitored for change events:</h3>
    <asp:TextBox id="txt" runat="server" AutoPostBack="true"
     OnTextChanged="CtrlChanged"/>
    <br /><br />
    <asp:CheckBox id="chk" runat="server" AutoPostBack="true"
     OnCheckedChanged="CtrlChanged"/>
    <br /><br />
    <asp:RadioButton id="opt1" runat="server" GroupName="Sample"
     AutoPostBack="true" OnCheckedChanged="CtrlChanged"/>
    <asp:RadioButton id="opt2" runat="server" GroupName="Sample"
     AutoPostBack="true" OnCheckedChanged="CtrlChanged"/>
  </div>
</form>
```

The event handler simply adds a new message to a list box and scrolls to the end:

```
Protected Sub CtrlChanged(ByVal sender As Object, ByVal e As EventArgs)
    Dim ctrlName As String = (CType(sender, Control)).ID
    lstEvents.Items.Add(ctrlName & " Changed")
    ' Select the last item to scroll the list so the most recent
    ' entries are visible.
    lstEvents.SelectedIndex = lstEvents.Items.Count - 1
End Sub
```

■ **Note** Automatic postback isn't always a good thing. Posting the page back to the server interrupts the user for a brief amount of time. If the page is large, the delay may be more than a noticeable flicker. If the page is long and the user has scrolled to the bottom of the page, the user will lose the current position when the page is refreshed and the view is returned to the top of the page. Because of these idiosyncrasies, it's a good idea to evaluate whether you really need postback and to refrain from using it for minor cosmetic reasons.

The Click Event and the ImageButton Control

In the examples you've looked at so far, the second event parameter has always been used to pass a System.EventArgs object. This object doesn't contain any additional information—it's just a glorified placeholder.

One control that does send extra information is the ImageButton control. It sends a special ImageClickEventArgs object (from the System.Web.UI namespace) that provides X and Y properties representing the location where the image was clicked. Using this additional information, you can create a server-side image map. For example, here's the code that simply displays the location where the image was clicked and checks whether it was over a predetermined region of the picture—you can find this code and many other examples in the download for this book:

```
Protected Sub ImageButton1_Click(ByVal sender As Object,
        ByVal e As System.Web.UI.ImageClickEventArgs)
    lblResult.Text = "You clicked at (" & e.X.ToString() & ", " _
        & e.Y.ToString() & "). "
    If (e.Y > 20) AndAlso (e.Y < 100) AndAlso (e.X > 20) AndAlso (e.X < 275) Then
        lblResult.Text &= "You clicked on the button surface."
    Else
        lblResult.Text &= "You clicked the button border."
    End If
End Sub
```

The sample web page shown in Figure 4-9 puts this feature to work with a simple graphical button. Depending on whether the user clicks the button border or the button surface, the web page displays a different message.

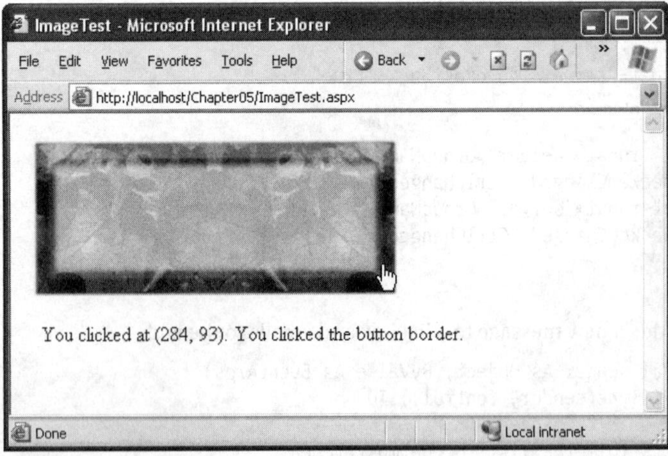

Figure 4-9. *Using an ImageButton control*

■ **Note** Another more powerful approach to handling image clicks is to create a server-side image map using the ImageMap control. The ImageMap control is demonstrated in Chapter 28, which deals with dynamic graphics.

The List Controls

The list controls are specialized web controls that generate list boxes, drop-down lists, and other repeating controls that can be either bound to a data source (such as a database or a hard-coded collection of values) or programmatically filled with items. Most list controls allow the user to select one or more items, but the BulletedList is an exception—it displays a static bulleted or numbered list. Table 4-11 shows all the list controls.

Table 4-11. *List Controls*

Control	Description
<asp:DropDownList>	A drop-down list populated by a collection of <asp:ListItem> objects. In HTML, it is rendered by a <select> tag with the size="1" attribute.
<asp:ListBox>	A list box list populated by a collection of <asp:ListItems> objects. In HTML, it is rendered by a <select> tag with the size="x" attribute, where x is the number of visible items.
<asp:CheckBoxList>	Its items are rendered as check boxes, aligned in a table with one or more columns.
<asp:RadioButtonList>	Like the <asp:CheckBoxList>, but the items are rendered as radio buttons.
<asp:BulletedList>	A static bulleted or numbered list. In HTML, it is rendered using the <ul> or <ol> tags. You can also use this control to create a list of hyperlinks.

All the list controls support the same base properties and methods as other web controls. In addition, they inherit from the System.Web.UI.WebControls.ListControl class, which exposes the properties in Table 4-12. You can fill the lists automatically from a data source (as you'll learn in Part 2), or you can fill them programmatically or declaratively, as you'll see in the next section.

Table 4-12. *ListControl Class Properties*

Member	Description
AutoPostBack	If True, the form is automatically posted back when the user changes the current selection.
Items	Returns a collection of ListItem objects (the items can also be added declaratively by adding the <asp:ListItem> tag in the ASPX page).
SelectedIndex	Returns or sets the index of the selected item. For lists with multiple selectable items, you should loop through the collection of Items and check the Selected property of each ListItem instead.
SelectedItem	Returns a reference to the first selected ListItem. For lists with multiple selectable items, you should loop through the collection of Items and check the Selected property of each ListItem instead.
DataSource	You can set this property to an object that contains the information you want to display (such as a DataSet, DataTable, or collection). When you call DataBind(), the list will be filled based on that object.

(Continued)

Table 4-12. *Continued*

Member	Description
DataMember	Used in conjunction with data binding when the data source contains more than one table (such as when the source is a DataSet). The DataMember identifies which table you want to use.
DataTextField	Used in conjunction with data binding to indicate which property or field in the data source should be used for the text of each list item.
DataValueField	Used in conjunction with data binding to indicate which property or field in the data source should be used for the value attribute of each list item (which isn't displayed but can be read programmatically for future reference).
DataTextFormatString	Sets the formatting string used to render the text of the list item (according to the DataTextField property).

In addition, the ListControl control class also defines a SelectedIndexChanged event, which fires when the user changes the current selection.

■ **Note** The SelectedIndexChanged event and the SelectedIndex and SelectedItem properties are not used for the BulletedList control.

The Selectable List Controls

The selectable list controls include the DropDownList, ListBox, CheckBoxList, and RadioButtonList controls—all the list controls except the BulletedList. They allow users to select one or more of the contained items. When the page is posted back, you can check which items were chosen.

By default, the RadioButtonList and CheckBoxList render their interfaces by creating multiple option buttons or check boxes. Both of these classes add a few more properties that allow you to manage the layout of these repeated items, as described in Table 4-13.

Table 4-13. *Added RadioButtonList and CheckBoxList Properties*

Property	Description
RepeatLayout	This specifies whether the check boxes or radio buttons will be rendered in a table (the default option) or inline. The values are Table and Flow, respectively.
RepeatDirection	This specifies whether the list of controls will be rendered horizontally or vertically.
RepeatColumns	This sets the number of columns, in case RepeatLayout is set to Table.
CellPadding, CellSpacing, TextAlign	If RepeatLayout is Table, these properties configure the spacing and alignment of the cells of the layout table.

Here's an example page that declares an instance of every selectable list control, adds items to each of them declaratively, and sets a few other properties:

```
<form id="form1" runat="server">
  <div>
    <asp:ListBox runat="server" ID="Listbox1" SelectionMode="Multiple" Rows="5">
        <asp:ListItem Selected="true">Option 1</asp:ListItem>
```

```
        <asp:ListItem>Option 2</asp:ListItem>
    </asp:ListBox>
    <br /><br />
    <asp:DropDownList runat="server" ID="DropdownList1">
        <asp:ListItem Selected="true">Option 1</asp:ListItem>
        <asp:ListItem>Option 2</asp:ListItem>
    </asp:DropDownList>
    <br /><br />
    <asp:CheckBoxList runat="server" ID="CheckboxList1" RepeatColumns="3" >
        <asp:ListItem Selected="true">Option 1</asp:ListItem>
       <asp:ListItem>Option 2</asp:ListItem>
    </asp:CheckBoxList>
    <br />
    <asp:RadioButtonList runat="server" ID="RadiobuttonList1"
     RepeatDirection="Horizontal" RepeatColumns="2">
        <asp:ListItem Selected="true">Option 1</asp:ListItem>
        <asp:ListItem>Option 2</asp:ListItem>
    </asp:RadioButtonList>
    <asp:Button runat="server" Text="Submit" OnClick="Button1_Click"/>
  </div>
</form>
```

When the page is loaded for the first time, the event handler for the Page.Load event adds three more items to each list control programmatically, as shown here:

```
Protected Sub Page_Load(ByVal sender As Object, ByVal e As System.EventArgs)
    If (Not Page.IsPostBack) Then
        For i As Integer = 3 To 5
            Listbox1.Items.Add("Option " & i.ToString())
            DropdownList1.Items.Add("Option " & i.ToString())
            CheckboxList1.Items.Add("Option " & i.ToString())
            RadiobuttonList1.Items.Add("Option " & i.ToString())
        Next i
    End If
End Sub
```

Finally, when the submit button is clicked, the selected items of each control are displayed on the page. For the controls with a single selection (DropDownList and RadioButtonList), this is just a matter of accessing the SelectedItem property. SelectedItem property. For the other controls that allow multiple selections, you must cycle through all the items in the Items collection and check whether the ListItem.Selected property is True. Here's the code that does both of these tasks:

```
Protected Sub Button1_Click(ByVal sender As Object, ByVal e As System.EventArgs)
    Response.Write("<b>Selected items for Listbox1:</b><br />")
    For Each li As ListItem In Listbox1.Items
        If li.Selected Then
        Response.Write("- " & li.Text & "<br />")
        End If
    Next
    Response.Write("<b>Selected item for DropdownList1:</b><br />")
    Response.Write("- " & DropdownList1.SelectedItem.Text & "<br />")

    Response.Write("<b>Selected items for CheckboxList1:</b><br />")
    For Each li As ListItem In CheckboxList1.Items
        If li.Selected Then
        Response.Write("- " & li.Text & "<br />")
        End If
    Next
```

```
    Response.Write("<b>Selected item for RadiobuttonList1:</b><br />")
    Response.Write("- " & RadiobuttonList1.SelectedItem.Text & "<br />")
End Sub
```

To test the page, load it, select one or more items in each control, and then click the button. You should get something like what's shown in Figure 4-10.

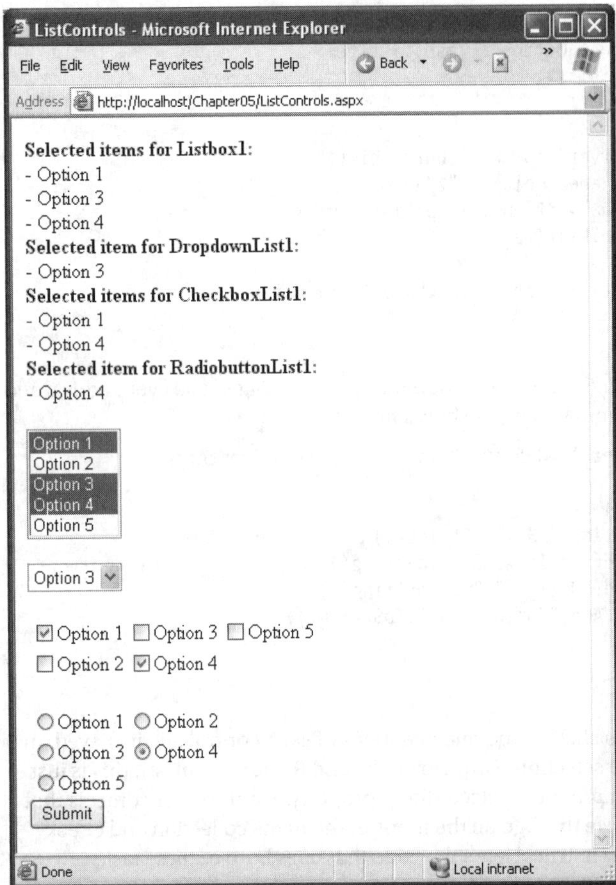

Figure 4-10. *Checking for selected items in the list controls*

■ **Tip** You can set the ListItem.Disabled property to True if you want an item in a RadioButtonList or CheckBoxList to be disabled. It will still appear in the page, but it will be grayed out and won't be selectable. The ListItem.Disabled is ignored for ListBox and DropDownList controls.

The BulletedList Control

The BulletedList control is the server-side equivalent of the <ul> (unordered list) or <ol> (ordered list) elements. As with all list controls, you set the collection of items that should be displayed through the Items property. Additionally, you can use the properties in Table 4-14 to configure how the items are displayed.

Table 4-14. *Added BulletedList Properties*

Property	Description
BulletStyle	Determines the type of list. Choose from Numbered (1, 2, 3...), LowerAlpha (a, b, c...) and UpperAlpha (A, B, C...), LowerRoman (i, ii, iii...) and UpperRoman (I, II, III...), and the bullet symbols Disc, Circle, Square, or CustomImage (in which case you must set the BulletStyleImageUrl property).
BulletImageUrl	If the BulletStyle is set to Custom, this points to the image that is placed to the left of each item as a bullet.
FirstBulletNumber	In an ordered list (using the Numbered, LowerAlpha, UpperAlpha, LowerRoman, or UpperRoman styles), this sets the first value. For example, if you set FirstBulletNumber to 3, the list might read 3, 4, 5 (for Numbered) or C, D, E (for UpperAlpha).
DisplayMode	Determines whether the text of each item is rendered as text (use Text, the default), a link button (use LinkButton) or a hyperlink (use HyperLink).

If you choose to set the DisplayMode to use hyperlinks, you can react to the Click event to determine which item was clicked. Here's an example:

```
Protected Sub BulletedList1_Click(ByVal sender As Object,
      ByVal e As BulletedListEventArgs)
    Dim itemText As String = BulletedList1.Items(e.Index).Text
    Label1.Text = "You choose item" & itemText
End Sub
```

Figure 4-11 shows multiple BulletedList controls with different DisplayMode values.

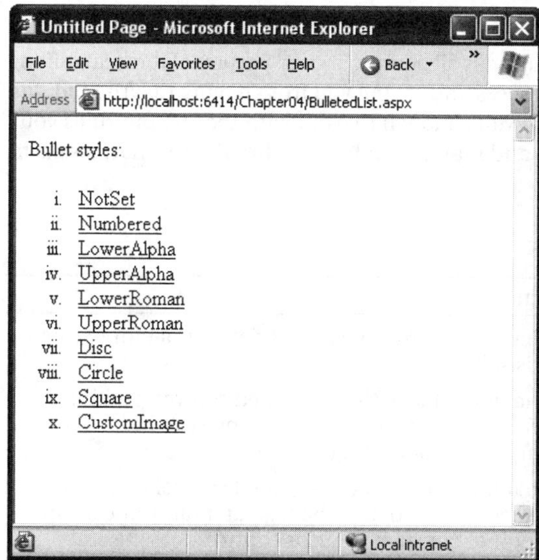

Figure 4-11. *Different BulletedList styles*

Input Validation Controls

One of the most common uses for web pages (and the reason that the HTML form tags were first created) is to collect data. Often, a web page will ask a user for some information and then store it in a back-end database. In almost every case, this data must be *validated* to ensure that you don't store useless, spurious, or contradictory information that might cause later problems.

Ideally, the validation of the user input should take place on the client side so that the user is immediately informed that there's something wrong with the input *before* the form is posted back to the server. If this pattern is implemented correctly, it saves server resources and gives the user faster feedback. However, regardless of whether client-side validation is performed, the form's data must also be validated on the server side. Otherwise, a shrewd attacker could hack the page by removing the client-side JavaScript that validates the input, saving the new page, and using it to submit bogus data.

Writing validation code by hand is a lengthy task, especially because the models for client-side programming (typically JavaScript) and server-side programming (in this case, ASP.NET) are quite different. The developers at Microsoft are well aware of this, so, in addition to the set of HTML and web controls, they also developed a set of *validation controls*. These controls can be declared on a web form and then bound to any other input control. Once bound to an input control, the validation control performs automatic client-side *and* server-side validation. If the corresponding control is empty, doesn't contain the correct data type, or doesn't adhere to the specified rules, the validator will prevent the page from being posted back altogether.

■ **Note** ASP.NET 2.0 adds exactly three new validation features. There's new support for placing input controls into validation groups, a new BaseValidator.SetFocusOnError property, and a new CustomValidator.ValidateEmptyText property.

The Validation Controls

ASP.NET includes six validation controls. These controls all perform a good portion of the heavy lifting for you, thereby streamlining the validation process and saving you from having to write tedious code. Even better, the validation controls are flexible enough to work with the custom rules you define, which makes your code more reusable and modular. Table 4-15 briefly summarizes each validator.

Table 4-15. *The Validation Controls*

Validation Control	Description
<asp:RequiredFieldValidator>	Checks that the control it has to validate is not empty when the form is submitted.
<asp:RangeValidator>	Checks that the value of the associated control is within a specified range. The value and the range can be numerical—a date or a string.
<asp:CompareValidator>	Checks that the value of the associated control matches a specified comparison (less than, greater than, and so on) against another constant value or control.
<asp:RegularExpressionValidator>	Checks whether the value of the control it has to validate matches the specified regular expression.
<asp:CustomValidator>	Allows you to specify any client-side JavaScript validation routine and its server-side counterpart to perform your own custom validation logic.
<asp:ValidationSummary>	Shows a summary with the error messages for each failed validator on the page (or in a pop-up message box).

It's important to note that you can use more than one validator for the same control. For example, you could use a validator to ensure that an input control is not empty and another to ensure that it contains data of a certain type. In fact, if you use the RangeValidator, CompareValidator, or RegularExpressionValidator, validation will automatically succeed if the input control is empty, because there is no value to validate. If this isn't the behavior you want, you should add a RequiredFieldValidator to the control. This ensures that two types of validation will be performed, effectively restricting blank values.

Although you can't validate RadioButton or CheckBox controls, you can validate the TextBox (the most common choice) and other controls such as ListBox, DropDownList, RadioButtonList, HtmlInputText, HtmlTextArea, and HtmlSelect. When validating a list control, the property that is being validated is the Value property of the selected ListItem object. Remember, the Value property is a hidden attribute that stores a piece of information in the HTML page for each list item, but it isn't displayed in the browser. If you don't use the Value attribute, you can't validate the control (validating the text of the selection isn't a supported option).

Technically, every control class has the option of designating one property that can be validated using the ValidationProperty attribute. For example, if you create your own control class named FancyTextBox, here's how you would designate the Text property as the property that supports validation:

```
<ValidationProperty("Text")> _
Public Class FancyTextBox
    Inherits WebControl
      ...
End Class
```

You'll learn more about how attributes, such as `ValidationProperty`, work with custom controls in Chapter 28.

The Validation Process

You can use the validation controls to verify a page automatically when the user submits it or to verify it manually in your code. The first approach is the most common.

When using automatic validation, the user receives a normal page and begins to fill in the input controls. When finished, the user clicks a button to submit the page. Every button has a CausesValidation property, which can be set to True or False. What happens when the user clicks the button depends on the value of the CausesValidation property.

If CausesValidation is False: ASP.NET will ignore the validation controls, the page will be posted back, and your event-handling code will run normally.

If CausesValidation is True (the default): ASP.NET will automatically validate the page when the user clicks the button. It does this by performing the validation for each control on the page. If any control fails to validate, ASP.NET will return the page with some error information, depending on your settings. Your click event-handling code may or may not be executed—meaning you'll have to specifically check in the event handler whether the page is valid.

Note Many other button-like controls that can be used to submit the page also provide the CausesValidation property. Examples include the LinkButton, ImageButton, and BulletedList.

Based on this description, you'll realize that validation happens automatically when certain buttons are clicked. It doesn't happen when the page is posted back because of a change event (such as choosing a new value in an AutoPostBack list) or if the user clicks a button that has CausesValidation set to False. However, you can still validate one or more controls manually and then make a decision in your code based on the results.

In browsers that support it, ASP.NET will automatically add code for client-side validation. In this case, when the user clicks a CausesValidation button, the same error messages will appear without the page needing to be submitted and returned from the server. This increases the responsiveness of the application. However, if the page validates successfully on the client side, ASP.NET will still revalidate it when it's received at the server. By performing the validation at both ends, your application can be as responsive as possible but still remain secure.

■ **Note** In ASP.NET 1.*x*, the validation controls emitted client-side JavaScript only for Internet Explorer browsers. Fortunately, ASP.NET 2.0 finally remedies the gap, with support for client-side scripts on Netscape and Firefox.

Figure 4-12 shows a page that uses validation with several text boxes and ends with a validation summary. In the following section, you'll learn about how you can use the different validators in this example.

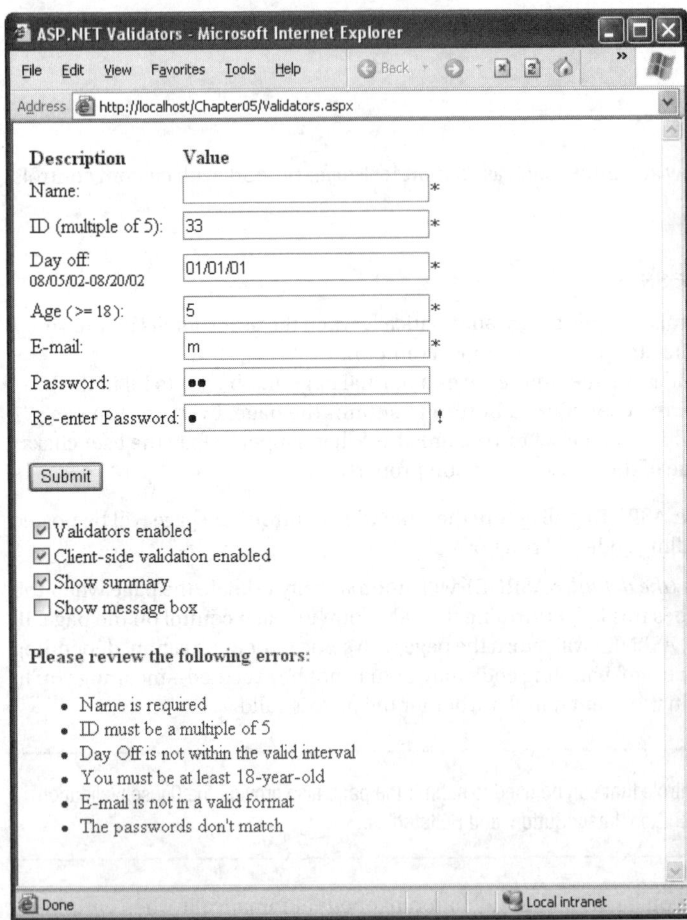

Figure 4-12. *Validating a sample page*

The BaseValidator Class

The validation control classes are found in the System.Web.UI.WebControls namespace and inherit from the BaseValidator class. This class defines the basic functionality for a validation control. Table 4-16 describes its properties.

Table 4-16. *BaseValidator Members*

Member	Description
ControlToValidate	Indicates the input control to validate.
Display	Indicates how the error message will be shown. If Static, the space required to show the message will be calculated and added to the space layout in advance. If Dynamic, the page layout will dynamically change to show the error string. Be aware that although the dynamic style could seem useful, if your layout is heavily based on table structures, it could change quite a bit if multiple strings are dynamically added, and this could confuse the user.
Enabled	A Boolean property that allows the user to enable or disable the validator. When the control is disabled, it does not validate anything. This property is usually used programmatically to change the enabled state according to the current page state or according to another application's settings.
ErrorMessage	Error string that will be shown in the errors summary by the ValidationSummary control, if present.
Text	The error text that will be displayed in the validator control if the attached input control fails its validation.
IsValid	This property is also usually read or set only from script code (or the code-behind class) to determine whether the associated input control's value is valid. This property can be checked on the server after a postback, but if the client-side validation is active and supported by the client browser, the execution won't get to the server if the value isn't valid. (In other words, you check this property just in case the client-side validation did not run.) Remember that you can also read the Page.IsValid property to know in a single step if all the input controls are in a valid state. Page.IsValid returns true only if all the contained controls are valid.
Validate()	This method revalidates the control and updates the IsValid property accordingly. The web page calls this method when a page is posted back by a CausesValidation control. You can also call it programmatically (for example, if you programmatically set the content of an input control and you want to check its validity).

In addition, the BaseValidator class has other properties such as BackColor, Font, ForeColor, and others that are inherited (and in some case overridden) from the base class TextControl (and the classes it inherits from, such as WebControl and Control). Every derived validator adds its own specific properties, which you'll see in the following sections.

The RequiredFieldValidator Control

The simplest available control is RequiredFieldValidator, whose only work is to ensure that the associated control is not empty. For example, the control will fail validation if a linked text box doesn't contain any content (or just contains spaces), instead of checking for blank values you can specify a default value using the InitialValue property. In this case, validation fails if the content in the control matches this InitialValue (indicating that the user hasn't changed it in any way).

Here is an example of a typical RequiredFieldValidator:

```
<asp:TextBox runat="server" ID="Name" />
<asp:RequiredFieldValidator runat="server"
  ControlToValidate="Name" ErrorMessage="Name is required"
  Display="dynamic">*
</asp:RequiredFieldValidator>
```

The validator declared here will show an asterisk (*) character if the Name text box is empty. This error text appears when the user tries to submit the form by clicking a button that has CausesValidation set to True. It also occurs on the client side in Internet Explorer 5.0 or above as soon as the user tabs to a new control, thanks to the client-side JavaScript.

If you want to place a specific message next to the validated control, you should replace * with an error message. (You don't need to use the ErrorMessage property. The ErrorMessage is required only if you want to show the summary of all the errors on the page using the ValidationSummary control, which you'll see later in this chapter.) Alternatively, for a nicer result, you could use an HTML <img> tag to use a picture (such as the common ! sign inside a yellow triangle) with a tooltip for the error message. You'll see this approach later in this chapter as well.

The RangeValidator Control

The RangeValidator control verifies that an input value falls within a predetermined range. It has three specific properties: Type, MinimumValue, and MaximumValue. The last two define the range of valid values, while Type defines the type of the data that will be typed into the input control and validated. The available values are Currency, Date, Double, Integer, and String.

The following example checks that the date entered falls within August 5 and August 20, 2005 (encoded in the form mm/dd/yyyy, so if your web server uses different regional settings, you'll have to change the date format):

```
<asp:TextBox runat="server" ID="DayOff" />
<asp:RangeValidator runat="server" Display="dynamic"
  ControlToValidate="DayOff" Type="Date"
  ErrorMessage="Day Off is not within the valid interval"
  MinimumValue="08/05/2005 MaximumValue="08/20/2005>*
</asp:RangeValidator>
```

The CompareValidator Control

The CompareValidator control compares a value in one control with a fixed value or, more commonly, a value in another control. For example, this allows you to check that two text boxes have the same data or that a value in one text box doesn't exceed a maximum value established in another.

Like the RangeValidator control, the CompareValidator provides a Type property that specifies the type of data you are comparing. It also exposes the ValueToCompare and ControlToCompare properties, which allow you to compare the value of the input control with a constant value or the value of another input control, respectively. You use only one of these two properties.

The Operator property allows you to specify the type of comparison you want to do. The available values are Equal, NotEqual, GreaterThan, GreaterThanEqual, LessThan, LessThanEqual, and DataTypeCheck. The DataTypeCheck value forces the validation control to check that the input has the required data type (specified through the Type property), without performing any additional comparison.

The following example compares an input with a constant value in order to ensure that the specified age is greater than or equal to 18:

```
<asp:TextBox runat="server" ID="Age" />
<asp:CompareValidator runat="server" Display="dynamic"
  ControlToValidate="Age" ValueToCompare="18"
  ErrorMessage="You must be at least 18 years old"
  Type="Integer" Operator="GreaterThanEqual">*
</asp:CompareValidator>
```

The next example compares the input values in two password text boxes to ensure that their value is the same:

```
<asp:TextBox runat="server" TextMode="Password" ID="Password" />
<asp:TextBox runat="server" TextMode="Password" ID="Password2" />
<asp:CompareValidator runat="server"
  ControlToValidate="Password2" ControlToCompare="Password"
  ErrorMessage="The passwords don't match"
  Type="String" Display="dynamic">
  <img src="imgError.gif" border="0" alt="The passwords don't match">
</asp:CompareValidator>
```

This example also demonstrates another useful technique. The previous examples have used an asterisk (*) to indicate errors. However, this control tag uses an <img> tag to show a small image file of an exclamation mark instead.

The RegularExpressionValidator Control

The RegularExpressionValidator control is a powerful tool in the ASP.NET developer's toolbox. It allows you to validate text by matching against a pattern defined in a *regular expression*. You simply need to set the regular expression in the ValidationExpression property.

Regular expressions are also powerful tools—they allow you to specify complex rules that specify the characters, and in what sequence (position and number of occurrences) they are allowed, in the string. For example, the following control checks that the text input in the text box is a valid e-mail address:

```
<asp:TextBox runat="server" ID="Email" />
<asp:RegularExpressionValidator runat="server"
  ControlToValidate="Email" ValidationExpression=".+@.{2,}\..{2,}"
  ErrorMessage="E-mail is not in a valid format" Display="dynamic">*
</asp:RegularExpressionValidator>
```

The expression .*@.{2,}\..{2,} specifies that the string that it's validating must begin with a number of characters (.+) and must contain an @ character, at least two more characters (the domain name), a period (escaped as \.), and, finally, at least two more characters for the domain extension. For example, marco@apress.com is a valid e-mail address, while marco@apress or marco.apress.com would fail validation. Using a more-complex regular expression, you could check that the domain name is valid, that the extension is not made up (see `http://www.icann.org` for a list of allowed domain name extensions), and so on. However, regular expressions obviously don't provide any way to check that a domain actually exists or is online.

Table 4-17 summarizes the commonly used syntax constructs (modifiers) for regular expressions.

Table 4-17. *Metacharacters for Matching Single Characters*

Character Escapes	Description
Ordinary characters	Characters other than .$^{[(|)*+?\ match themselves.
\b	Matches a backspace.
\t	Matches a tab.
\r	Matches a carriage return.
\v	Matches a vertical tab.
\f	Matches a form feed.
\n	Matches a newline.
\	If followed by a special character (one of .$^{[(|)*+?\), this character escape matches that character literal. For example, \+ matches the + character.

In addition to single characters, you can specify a class or a range of characters that can be matched in the expression. For example, you could allow any digit or any vowel in any position and exclude all the other characters. The metacharacters in Table 4-18 accomplish this.

Table 4-18. *Metacharacters for Matching Types of Characters*

Character Class	Description
.	Matches any character except \n.
[aeiou]	Matches any single character specified in the set.
[^aeiou]	Matches any character not specified in the set.
[3-7a-dA-D]	Matches any character specified in the specified ranges (in the example, the ranges are 3–7, a–d, A–D).
\w	Matches any word character; that is, any alphanumeric character or the underscore (_).
\W	Matches any nonword character.
\s	Matches any whitespace character (space, tab, form-feed, newline, carriage return, or vertical feed).
\S	Matches any nonwhitespace character.
\d	Matches any decimal character.
\D	Matches any nondecimal character.

Using more advanced syntax, you can specify that a certain character or class of characters must be present at least once, or between two and six times, and so on. The quantifiers are placed just after a character or a range of characters and allow you to specify how many times the preceding character must be matched (see Table 4-19).

Table 4-19. *Quantifiers*

Quantifier	Description
*	Zero or more matches
+	One or more matches
?	Zero or one matches

Quantifier	Description
{N}	N matches
{N,}	N or more matches
{N,M}	Between N and M matches

To demonstrate these rules with another easy example, consider the following regular expression:

```
[aeiou]{2,4}\+[1-5]*
```

A string that correctly matches this expression must start with two to four vowels, have a + sign, and terminate with zero or more digits between one and five. The .NET Framework documentation details many more expression modifiers.

Table 4-20 describes a few common (and useful) regular expressions.

Table 4-20. *Commonly Used Regular Expressions*

Content	Regular Expression	Description
E-mail address*	\S+@\S+\.\S+	Checks for an at (@) sign, dot (.), and only allowed nonwhitespace characters.
Password	\w+	Any sequence of word characters (letter, space, or underscore).
Specific-length password	\w{4,10}	A password that must be at least four characters long but no longer than ten characters.
Advanced password	[a-zA-Z]\w{3,9}	As with the specific-length password, this regular expression will allow four to ten total characters. The twist is that the first character must fall in the range of a–z or A–Z (that is to say, it must start with a nonaccented ordinary letter).
Another advanced password	[a-zA-Z]\w*\d+\w*	This password starts with a letter character, followed by zero or more word characters, one or more digits, and then zero or more word characters. In short, it forces a password to contain a number somewhere inside it. You could use a similar pattern to require two numbers or any other special character.
Limited-length field	\S{4,10}	Like the password example, this allows four to ten characters, but it allows special characters (asterisks, ampersands, and so on).
U.S. Social Security number	\d{3}-\d{2}-\d{4}	A sequence of three, two, then four digits, with each group separated by a dash. A similar pattern could be used when requiring a phone number.

* *Many different regular expressions of varying complexity can validate e-mail addresses. See* `http://www.4guysfromrolla.com/webtech/validateemail.shtml` *for a discussion of the subject and numerous examples.*

The CustomValidator Control

If the validation controls described so far are not flexible or powerful enough for you, and if you need more advanced or customized validation, then the CustomValidator control is what you need. The CustomValidator allows you to execute your custom client-side and server-side validation routines. You can associate these routines with the control so that validation is performed automatically. If the validation fails, the Page.IsValid property to False, as occurs with any other validation control.

The client-side and server-side validation routines for the CustomValidator are declared similarly. They both take two parameters: a reference to the validator and a custom argument object. This object provides a Value property that contains the current value of the associated input control (the value you have to validate) and an IsValid property through which you specify whether the input value is valid. If you want to check that a number is a multiple of five, for example, you could use a client-side JavaScript validation routine like this:

```
<script language="JavaScript">
  function EmpIDClientValidate(ctl, args)
  {
    // the value is a multiple of 5 if the modulo by 5 is 0
    args.IsValid=(args.Value%5 == 0);
  }
</script>
```

To associate this code with the control so that client-side validation is performed automatically, you simply need to set the ClientValidationFunction property to the name of the function (in this case, EmpIDClientValidate).ClientValidationFunction to the name of the function (in this case, EmpIDClientValidate).

Next, when the page is posted back, ASP.NET fires the CustomValidator.ServerValidate event. You handle this event to perform the same task using VB code. And although the JavaScript logic is optional, you must make sure you include a server-side validation routine to ensure the validation is performed in case the client is using a down-level browser (or tampers with the web-page HTML).

Here's the VB server-side equivalent of the validation routine shown earlier:

```
Protected Sub EmpIDServerValidate(ByVal sender As Object,
      ByVal args As ServerValidateEventArgs)
    Try
      args.IsValid = (Integer.Parse(args.Value) Mod 5 = 0)
    Catch
      ' An error is most likely caused by non-numeric data.
      args.IsValid = False
    End Try
End Sub
```

Finally, here's an example CustomValidator tag that uses these routines:

```
<asp:TextBox runat="server" ID="EmpID" />
<asp:CustomValidator runat="server" ControlToValidate="EmpID"
  ClientValidationFunction="EmpIDClientValidate"
  ErrorMessage="ID must be a multiple of 5" Display="dynamic">*
</asp:CustomValidator>
```

■ Tip In ASP.NET 2.0, the CustomValidator includes an additional property named ValidateEmtpyText, which is False by default. However, it's quite possible you might create a client-side function that attempts to assess empty values. If so, set ValidateEmtpyText to True to give the same behavior to your server-side event handler.

The ValidationSummary Control

The ValidationSummary control doesn't perform any validation. Instead, it allows you to show a summary of all the errors in the page. This summary displays the ErrorMessage value of each failed validator. The summary can be shown in a client-side JavaScript message box (if the ShowMessageBox property is true) or on the page (if the ShowSummary property is true).The summary can be shown in a client-side JavaScript message box (if the ShowMessageBox property is true) or on the page (if the ShowSummary property is true). You can set both ShowMessageBox and ShowSummary to true to show both types of summaries, since they are not exclusive. If you choose to display the summary on the page, you can choose a style with the DisplayMode property (possible values are SingleParagraph, List, and BulletList). Finally, you can set a title for the summary with the HeaderText property.HeaderText property.

The control declaration is straightforward:

```
<asp:ValidationSummary runat="server" ID="ValidationSum"
  ShowSummary="true" DisplayMode="BulletList"
  HeaderText="<b>Please review the following errors:</b>"
/>
```

Figure 4-13 shows an example with a validation summary that displays a bulleted summary on the page and in a message box.

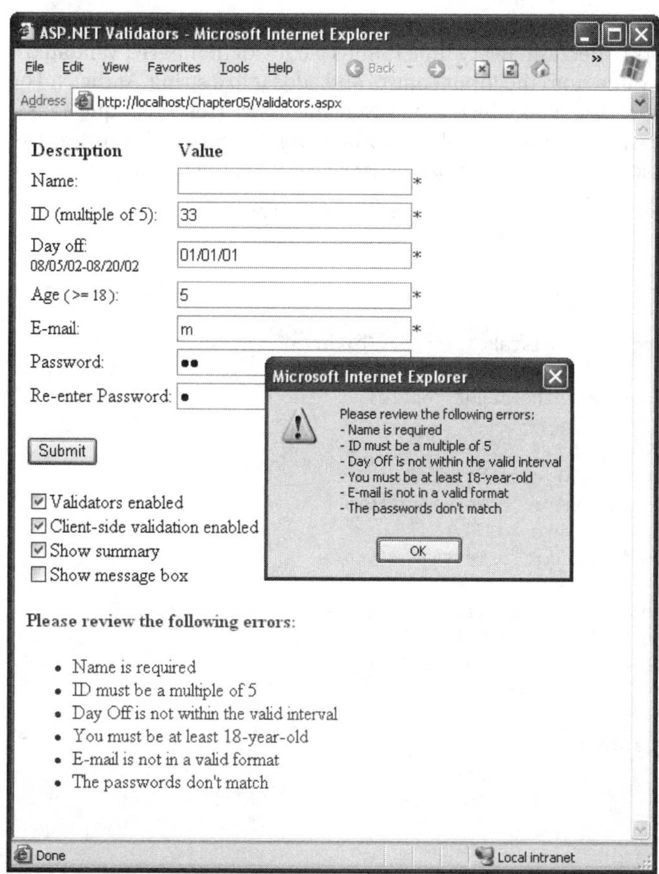

Figure 4-13. *The validation summary*

Using the Validators Programmatically

As with all other server controls, you can programmatically read and modify the properties of a validator. To access all the validators on the page, you can iterate over the Validators collection of the current page.

In fact, this technique is already demonstrated in the sample page shown in Figures 4-11 and 4-12. This page provides four check boxes that allow you to test the behavior of the validators with different options. When a check box is selected, it causes a postback. The event handler iterates over all the validators and updates them according to the new options, as shown here:

```
Protected Sub Options_Changed(ByVal sender As Object, ByVal e As System.EventArgs)
    For Each valCtl As BaseValidator In Page.Validators
        valCtl.Enabled=EnableValidators.Checked
        valCtl.EnableClientScript = EnableClientSide.Checked
    Next valCtl
    ValidationSum.ShowMessageBox = ShowMsgBox.Checked
    ValidationSum.ShowSummary = ShowSummary.Checked
End Sub
```

You can use a similar technique to perform custom validation. The basic idea is to add a button with CausesValidation set to False. When this button is clicked, manually validate the page or just specific validators using the Validate() method. Then examine the IsValid property and decide what to do.

The next example uses this technique. It examines all the validation controls on the page by looping through the Page.Validators collection. Every time it finds a control that hasn't validated successfully, it retrieves the invalid value from the input control and adds it to a string. At the end of this routine, it displays a message that describes which values were incorrect. This technique adds a feature that wouldn't be available with automatic validation, which uses the Shared ErrorMessage property. In that case, it isn't possible to include the actual incorrect values in the message.

```
Private Sub cmdOK_Click(ByVal sender As Object, ByVal e As EventArgs)
    ' Validate the page.
    Me.Validate()

    If (Not Me.IsValid) Then
       Dim errorMessage As String = "<b>Mistakes found:</b><br/>"

       ' Create a variable to represent the input control.
       Dim ctrlInput As TextBox

            ' Search through the validation controls.
            For Each ctrl As BaseValidator In Me.Validators
                If (Not ctrl.IsValid) Then
                    errorMessage &= ctrl.ErrorMessage & "<br>"
                    ctrlInput =
                        CType(Me.FindControl(ctrl.ControlToValidate), TextBox)
                    errorMessage &= " * Problem is with this input: "
                    errorMessage &= ctrlInput.Text & "<br/>"
                End If
            Next ctrl
            lblMessage.Text = errorMessage
    End If
End Sub
```

This example uses the Page.FindControl() method. It's required because the ControlToValidate property is just a string with the name of a control, not a reference to the actual control object. To find the control that matches this name (and retrieve its Text property), you need to use the FindControl() method. Once the code has retrieved the matching text box, it can perform other tasks such as clearing the current value, tweaking a property, or even changing the text box color.

Validation Groups

In more complex pages, you might have several distinct groups of pages, possibly in separate panels. In these situations, you may want to perform validation separately. For example, you might create a form that includes a box with login controls and a box underneath it with the controls for registering a new user. Each box includes its own submit button, and depending on which button is clicked, you want to perform the validation just for that section of the page.

ASP.NET 2.0 enables this scenario with a new feature called *validation groups*. To create a validation group, you need to put the input controls and the CausesValidation button controls into the same logical group. You do this by setting the ValidationGroup property of every control with the same descriptive string (such as "Form1" or "Login"). Every button control that provides a CausesValidation property also includes the ValidationGroup property. All validators acquire the ValidationGroup by inheriting from the BaseValidator class.

For example, the following page defines two validation groups, named Group1 and Group2:

```
<form id="form1" runat="server">
  <div>
    <asp:Panel ID="Panel1" runat="server">
        <asp:TextBox ID="TextBox1" ValidationGroup="Group1" runat="server" />
        <asp:RequiredFieldValidator ID="RequiredFieldValidator1"
         ErrorMessage="*Required" ValidationGroup="Group1"
         runat="server" ControlToValidate="TextBox1" />
        <asp:Button ID="Button1" Text="Validate Group1"
         ValidationGroup="Group1" runat="server" />
    </asp:Panel>
    <br />
    <asp:Panel Height="94px" ID="Panel2" runat="server" Width="125px">
        <asp:TextBox ID="TextBox2" ValidationGroup="Group2"
         runat="server" />
        <asp:RequiredFieldValidator ID="RequiredFieldValidator2"
         ErrorMessage="*Required" ValidationGroup="Group2"
         ControlToValidate="TextBox2" runat="server" />
        <asp:Button ID="Button2" Text="Validate Group2"
         ValidationGroup="Group2" runat="server" />
    </asp:Panel>
  </div>
</form>
```

Figure 4-14 shows the page. If you click the first button, only the first text box is validated. If you click the second button, only the second text box is validated.

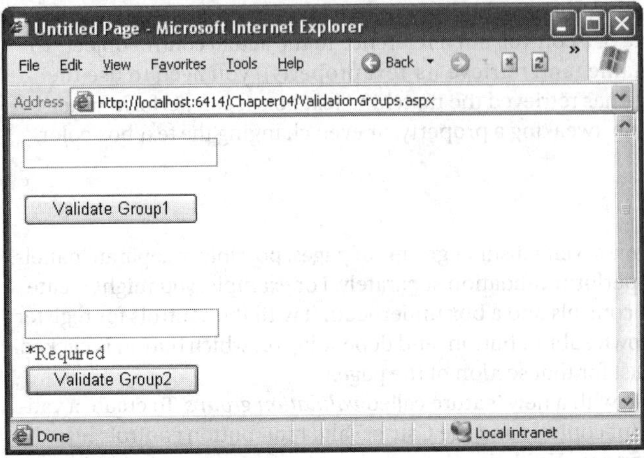

Figure 4-14. *Grouping controls for validation*

An interesting scenario is if you add a new button that doesn't specify any validation group. In this case, the button validates every control that isn't explicitly assigned to a named validation group. In this case, no controls fit the requirement, so the page is posted back successfully and deemed to be valid. If you want to make sure a control is always validated, regardless of the validation group of the button that's clicked, you'll need to create multiple validators for the control, one for each group (and one with no validation group). Alternatively, you might choose to manage complex scenarios such as these using server-side code.

In your code, you can work with the validation groups programmatically. You can retrieve the controls in a given validator group using the Page.GetValidators() method. Just pass the name of the group as the first parameter. You can then loop through the items in this collection and choose which ones you want to validate, as shown in the previous section.

Another option is to use the Page.Validate() method and specify the name of the validation group. For example, using the previous page, you could create a button with no validation group assigned and respond to the Click event with this code:

```
Protected Sub cmdValidateAll_Click(ByVal sender As Object, ByVal e As EventArgs)
    Label1.Text = "Valid: " & Page.IsValid.ToString()
    Page.Validate("Group1")
    Label1.Text &= "<br />Group1 Valid: " & Page.IsValid.ToString()
    Page.Validate("Group2")
    Label1.Text &= "<br />Group2 Valid: " & Page.IsValid.ToString()
End Sub
```

The first Page.IsValid check will return True, because the validators in the two groups weren't validated. After validating the first group, the Page.IsValid property will return True or False, depending on whether there is text in TextBox1. The same is true for the second group, only now you're checking for text in TextBox2.

The ASP.NET Rich Controls

Rich controls are web controls that model complex user interface elements. Although there isn't a strict definition for rich controls, the term commonly describes web controls that provide an object model that is distinctly separate from the underlying HTML representation. A typical rich control can often be programmed as a single object (and defined with a single control tag), but renders itself with a complex sequence of HTML elements and may even use client-side JavaScript.

To understand the difference, consider the Table control and the Calendar control. When you program with the Table control, you use objects that provide a thin wrapper over HTML table elements such as <table>, <tr>, and <td>. The Table control isn't considered a rich control. On the other hand, when you program with the Calendar, you work in terms of days, months, and selection ranges—concepts that have no direct correlation to the HTML markup that the Calendar renders. For that reason, the Calendar is considered a rich control.

ASP.NET includes numerous rich controls that are discussed elsewhere in this book, including data-based list controls, security controls, and controls tailored for web portals. The following list identifies the rich controls that don't fall into any specialized category:

AdRotator: A banner ad that displays one out of a set of images based on a predefined schedule that's saved in an XML file.

Calendar: A calendar that displays and allows you to move through months and days and to select a date or a range of days.

MultiView, View, and Wizard: You can think of these controls as more-advanced panels that let you switch between groups of controls on a page. The Wizard control even includes built-in navigation logic. You'll learn about these controls in Chapter 16.

Substitution: This control is really a placeholder that allows you to customize ASP.NET's output caching feature, which you'll tackle in Chapter 11.

TreeView: This is the most impressive of the rich controls. It allows you to show a hierarchical tree of items, perhaps as a data-bound list (see Chapter 12) or a navigational control (see Chapter 16).

Xml: Takes an XML file and an XSLT stylesheet file as input and displays the resulting HTML in a browser. You'll learn about the Xml control in Chapter 12.

The rich controls in this list all appear in the Standard tab of the Visual Studio Toolbox.

■ **Tip** The Internet contains many hubs for control sharing. One such location is Microsoft's own ASP.NET website (`http://www.asp.net`), which provides a control gallery where developers can submit their own ASP.NET web controls. Some of these controls are free (at least in a limited version), while others require a payment.

The AdRotator Control

The AdRotator randomly selects banner graphics from a list that's specified in an external XML schedule file.

Before creating the control, it makes sense to define the XML schedule file. Here's an example:

```
<Advertisements>
  <Ad>
    <ImageUrl>hdr_logo.gif</ImageUrl>
    <NavigateUrl>http://www.apress.com</NavigateUrl>
    <AlternateText>Apress - The Author's Press</AlternateText>
    <Impressions>20</Impressions>
    <Keyword>books</Keyword>
  </Ad>
  <Ad>
    <ImageUrl>javaOne.gif</ImageUrl>
    <NavigateUrl>http://www.sun.com</NavigateUrl>
    <AlternateText>Java from Sun</AlternateText>
    <Impressions>20</Impressions>
```

```
    <Keyword>Java</Keyword>
  </Ad>
  <!-- More ads can go here. -->
</Advertisements>
```

Each <Ad> element has a number of other important properties that configure the link, the image, and the frequency, as described in Table 4-21.

Table 4-21. *Advertisement File Elements*

Element	Description
ImageUrl	The image that will be displayed. This can be a relative link (a file in the current directory) or a fully qualified Internet URL.
NavigateUrl	The link that will be followed if the user clicks the banner.
AlternateText	The text that will be displayed instead of the picture if it cannot be displayed. This text will also be used as a tooltip in some newer browsers.
Impressions	A number that sets how often an advertisement will appear. This number is relative to the numbers specified for other ads. For example, a banner with the value 10 will be shown twice as often as the banner with the value 5.
Keyword	A keyword that identifies a group of advertisements. This can be used for filtering. For example, you could create ten advertisements and give half of them the keyword *Retail* and the other half the keyword *Computer*. The web page can then choose to filter the possible advertisements to include only one of these groups.

The actual `AdRotator` class only provides a limited set of properties. You specify both the appropriate advertisement file in the AdvertisementFile property and the type of window that the link should follow in the Target property. You can also set the KeywordFilter property so that the banner will be chosen from entries that have a specific keyword.

Here's an example that opens the link for an advertisement in a new window:

```
<asp:AdRotator runat="server" AdvertisementFile="Ads.xml" Target="_blank" />
```

Figure 4-15 shows the AdRotator control. Try refreshing the page. When you do, you'll see that a new advertisement is randomly selected each time.

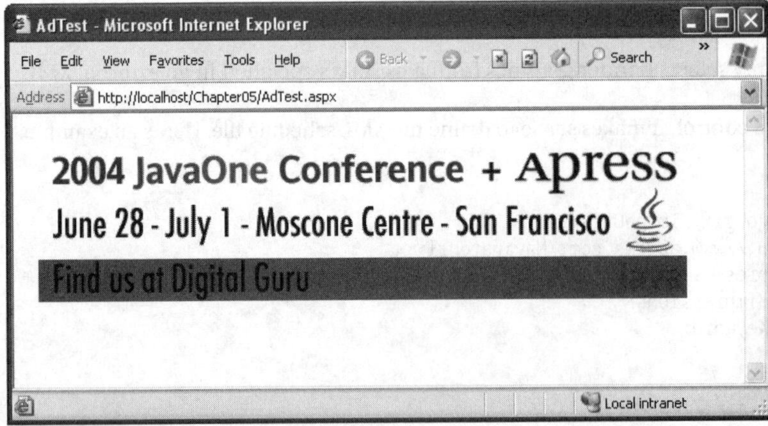

Figure 4-15. *The AdRotator control*

Additionally, you can react to the AdRotator.AdCreated event. This occurs when the page is being created and an image is randomly chosen from the file. This event provides you with information about the image that you can use to customize the rest of your page.

The event-handling code for this example simply configures a HyperLink control so that it corresponds with the randomly selected advertisement in the AdRotator:

```
Protected Sub Ads_AdCreated(ByVal sender As Object, ByVal e As AdCreatedEventArgs)
    ' Synchronize the Hyperlink control.
    lnkBanner.NavigateUrl = e.NavigateUrl

    ' Synchronize the text of the link.
    lnkBanner.Text = "Click here for information about our sponsor: "
    lnkBanner.Text &= e.AlternateText
End Sub
```

The Calendar Control

This control creates a functionally rich and good-looking calendar box that shows one month at a time. The user can move from month to month, select a date, and even select a range of days (if multiple selection is allowed). The Calendar control has many properties that, taken together, allow you to change almost every part of this control. For example, you can fine-tune the foreground and background colors, the font, the title, the format of the date, the currently selected date, and so on. The Calendar also provides events that enable you to react when the user changes the current month (VisibleMonthChanged), when the user selects a date (SelectionChanged), and when the Calendar is about to render a day (DayRender).

The following Calendar tag sets a few basic properties:

```
<asp:Calendar runat="server" ID="Calendar1"
  ForeColor="red" BackColor="lightyellow" />
```

The most important Calendar event is SelectionChanged, which fires every time a user clicks a date. Here's a basic event handler that responds to the SelectionChanged event and displays the selected date:

```
Protected Sub Calendar1_SelectionChanged
    (ByVal sender As Object, ByVal e As System.EventArgs)
    lblDates.Text = "You selected" & Calendar1.SelectedDate.ToLondDateString())
End Sub
```

■Note Every user interaction with the calendar triggers a postback. This allows you to react to the selection event immediately, and it allows the Calendar to rerender its interface, thereby showing a new month or newly selected dates. The Calendar does not use the AutoPostBack property.

You can also allow users to select entire weeks or months as well as single dates, or you can render the control as a static calendar that doesn't allow selection. The only fact you must remember is that if you allow month selection, the user can also select a single week or a day. Similarly, if you allow week selection, the user can also select a single day. The type of selection is set through the Calendar.SelectionMode property Calendar.SelectionMode property. You may also need to set the Calendar.FirstDayOfWeek property to configure how a week is selected. (For example, if you set FirstDayOfWeek to the enumerated value Monday, weeks will be selected from Monday to Sunday.)

When you allow multiple date selection (by setting Calendar.SelectionMode to something other than Day), you need to examine the SelectedDates property instead of the SelectedDate property. SelectedDates provides a collection of all the selected dates, which you can examine, as shown here:

```
Protected Sub Calendar1_SelectionChanged
    (ByVal sender As Object, ByVal e As System.EventArgs)
    lblDates.Text = "You selected these dates:<br>"
    For Each dt As DateTime In Calendar1.SelectedDates
      lblDates.Text += dt.ToLongDateString() & "<br>"
    Next dt
End Sub
```

The Calendar control exposes many more formatting-related properties, many of which map to the underlying HTML table representation (such as CellSpacing, CellPadding, Caption, and CaptionAlign). Additionally, you can individually tweak portions of the controls through grouped formatting settings called *styles* (which expose color, font, and alignment options). Example properties include DayHeaderStyle, DayStyle, NextPrevStyle, OtherMonthDayStyle, SelectedDayStyle, TitleStyle, TodayStyle, and WeekendDayStyle. You can change the subproperties for all of these styles using the Properties window.

Finally, by handling the DayRender event, you can completely change the appearance of the cell being rendered. The DayRender event is extremely powerful. Besides allowing you to tailor what dates are selectable, it also allows you to configure the cell where the date is located through the e.Cell property. (The Calendar control is really a sophisticated HTML table.) For example, you could highlight an important date or even add extra controls or HTML content in the cell. Here's an example that changes the background and foreground colors of the weekend days and also makes them nonclickable so that the user can't choose those days:

```
Protected Sub Calendar1_DayRender(ByVal sender As Object,
        ByVal e As DayRenderEventArgs)
    If e.Day.IsWeekend Then
    e.Cell.BackColor = System.Drawing.Color.Green
    e.Cell.ForeColor = System.Drawing.Color.Yellow
    e.Day.IsSelectable = False
    End If
End Sub
```

Figure 4-16 shows the result.

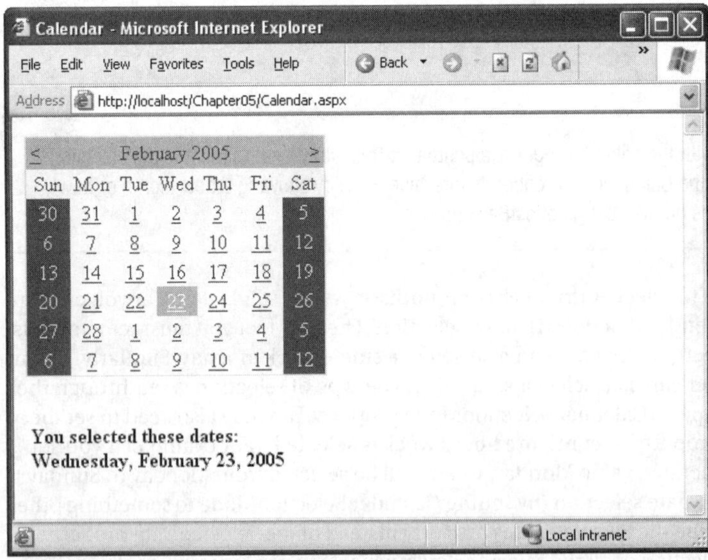

Figure 4-16. *The Calendar control*

■ **Tip** If you're using a design tool such as Visual Studio, you can even set an entire related color scheme using the built-in designer. Simply select the Auto Format link in the smart tag. You'll be presented with a list of predefined formats that set various style properties.

Summary

In this chapter you learned the basics of the core server controls included with ASP.NET, including HTML server controls, web controls, list controls, validation controls, and rich controls. You also learned how to use ASP.NET controls from your web-page code, access their properties, and handle their server-side events. Finally, you learned how to validate potentially problematic user input with the validation controls. In the next chapter, you'll learn how pages come together to form web applications.

CHAPTER 5

ASP.NET Applications

In traditional desktop programming, an *application* is an executable file with related support files. For example, a typical Windows application consists of a main executable file (EXE), supporting components (typically DLLs), and other resources such as databases and configuration files. An ASP.NET application follows a much different model.

On the most fundamental level, an ASP.NET application is a combination of files, pages, handlers, modules, and executable code that can be invoked from a virtual directory (and its subdirectories) on a web server. In this chapter, you'll learn why this distinction exists and take a closer look at how an ASP.NET application is configured and deployed. You'll also learn how to use components and HTTP handlers with an ASP.NET application.

WEB APPLICATION CHANGES IN .NET 2.0

The web application model remains essentially the same in ASP.NET 2.0. The most significant change is the improvement in the configuration model, which now boasts a programmable API and a graphical web-page interface.

Here are the changes you'll see, in the order they appear in this chapter:

- *Application directory structure*: ASP.NET 1.*x* had one special web application directory—the Bin directory, which houses compiled assemblies. ASP.NET 2.0 adds several more for source code, localizable resources, browser definitions, themes, and more.
- *Configuration API*: You can now use a handy set of classes to read *and* write almost any information in a configuration file.
- *The WAT*: The new WAT (website administration tool) uses the new configuration API to present an easy-to-use web-page interface for configuring common web.config settings.
- *Encryptable configuration sections*: Configuration files often contain sensitive data. Now you can protect them by encrypting any section.

If you're a seasoned ASP.NET 1.*x* developer, you can focus on these additions as you work your way through this chapter.

Anatomy of an ASP.NET Application

The difference between ASP.NET applications and rich client applications makes a lot of sense when you consider the ASP.NET execution model. Unlike a Windows application, the end user never runs an ASP.NET application directly. Instead, a user launches a browser such as Internet Explorer and requests a specific URL (such as `http://www.mysite.com/mypage.aspx`) over HTTP.

This request is received by a web server. When you're debugging the application in Visual Studio, you use a local-only test server. When you deploy the application, you use the IIS web server, as described in Chapter 18.

The web server has no concept of separate applications—it simply passes the request to the ASP.NET worker process. However, the ASP.NET worker process carefully segregates code execution into different application domains based on the virtual directory. Web pages and web services that are hosted in the same virtual directory (or one of its subdirectories) execute in the same *application domain*. Web pages and web services in different virtual directories execute in separate application domains.

■ **Note** A *virtual directory* is simply a directory that's exposed through a web server. In Chapter 18, you'll learn how to create virtual directories. When using the test server in Visual Studio, your web project directory is treated like a virtual directory. The only exception is that the test server supports only local connections (requests initiated from the current computer).

The Application Domain

An application domain is the .NET equivalent to a process—it's a boundary enforced by the CLR that ensures that one application can't influence (or see the in-memory data) of another. The following characteristics are a direct result of the application domain model:

- All the web pages and web services in a single web application share the same in-memory resources, such as global application data, per-user session data, and cached data. This information isn't directly accessible to other ASP.NET or ASP applications.
- All the web pages and web services in a single web application share the same core configuration settings. However, you can customize some configuration settings in individual subdirectories of the same virtual directory. For example, you can set only one authentication mechanism for a web application, no matter how many subdirectories it has. However, you can set different authorization rules in each directory to fine-tune who is allowed to access different groups of pages.
- All web applications raise global application events at various stages (when the application domain is first created, when it's destroyed, and so on). You can attach event handlers that react to these global application events using code in the global.asax file in your application's virtual directory.

In other words, the virtual directory is the basic grouping structure that delimits an ASP.NET application. You can create a legitimate ASP.NET application with a single web page (.aspx file) or web service (.asmx file). However, ASP.NET applications can include all of the following ingredients:

Web pages (.aspx files): These are the cornerstones of any ASP.NET application.

Web services (.asmx files): These allow you to share useful functions with applications on other computers and other platforms.

Code-behind files: Depending on the code model you're using, you may also have separate source code files. If these files are coded in VB .NET, they have the extension .vb.

A configuration file (web.config): This file contains a slew of application-level settings that configure everything from security to debugging and state management.

Global.asax: This file contains event handlers that react to global application events (such as when the application is first being started).

Other components: These are compiled assemblies that contain separate components you've developed or third-party components with useful functionality. Components allow you to separate business and data access logic and create custom controls.

Of course, a virtual directory can hold a great deal of additional resources that ASP.NET web applications will *use*, including stylesheets, images, XML files, and so on. In addition, you can extend the ASP.NET model by developing specialized components known as HTTP handlers and HTTP modules, which can plug into your application and take part in the processing of ASP.NET web requests.

■ **Note** It's possible to have file types that are owned by different ISAPI extensions in the same virtual directory. One example is if you mingle .aspx and .asp files. A more complex example is if you map .aspx web-page files to version 1.1 of ASP.NET and .asmx web service files to version 2.0. In these examples, the virtual directory corresponds to more than one application. These applications just happen to be accessible through the same virtual web directory. However, each application is mediated by a different ISAPI extension.

Application Lifetime

ASP.NET uses a *lazy initialization* technique for creating application domains. This means that the application domain for a web application is created the first time a request is received for a page or web service in that application.

An application domain can shut down for a variety of reasons, including if the web server itself shuts down. But, more commonly, applications restart themselves in new application domains in response to error conditions or configuration changes. For example, depending on the settings in the computer-wide machine.config file, an ASP.NET application may be periodically recycled when certain thresholds are reached. This model is designed to keep an application healthy and to detect characteristics that could indicate a problem has developed. Depending on your machine.config settings, application domains may be recycled based on the length of time the application domain has been running, the number of queued requests, or the amount of memory used (as described in Chapter 18).

ASP.NET automatically recycles application domains when you change the application. One example is if you modify the web.config file. Another example is if you replace an existing web-page file or DLL assembly file. In both of these cases, ASP.NET starts a new application domain to handle all future requests and keeps the existing application domain alive long enough to finish handling any outstanding requests (including queued requests).

■ **Tip** You can programmatically shut down a web application domain using the Shared HttpRuntime.UnloadAppDomain() method. (The application will restart itself automatically the next time it receives a request.) This technique is rarely used, but it can be useful if you're hosting a number of web applications on the same server and some are used only infrequently. In this case, the memory overhead of keeping the application domain alive may outweigh the increased speed of serving subsequent requests into the application.

Application Updates

One of the most remarkable features about the ASP.NET execution model is that you can update your web application without needing to restart the web server and without worrying about harming existing clients. This means you can add, replace, or delete files in the virtual directory at any time. ASP.NET then performs the same transition to a new application domain that it performs when you modify the web.config configuration file.

Being able to update any part of an application at any time, without interrupting existing requests, is a powerful feature. However, it's important to understand the architecture that makes it possible. Many developers make the mistake of assuming that it's a feature of the CLR that allows ASP.NET to seamlessly transition to a new application domain. But in reality, the CLR always locks assembly files when it executes them. To get around this limitation, ASP.NET doesn't actually use the ASP.NET files in the virtual directory. Instead, it uses another technique, called *shadow copy*, during the compilation process to create a copy of your files in c:\[WinDir]\Microsoft.NET\[Version]\Temporary ASP.NET Files. The ASP.NET worker process loads the assemblies from this directory, which means these assemblies are locked.

The second part of the story is ASP.NET's ability to detect when you change the original files. This detail is fairly straightforward—it simply relies on the ability of the Windows operating system to track directories and files and send immediate change notifications. ASP.NET maintains an active list of all assemblies loaded within a particular application's application domain and uses monitoring code to watch for changes and acts accordingly.

■ **Note** ASP.NET can use files that are stored in the GAC, a computer-wide repository of assemblies that includes staples such as the assemblies for the entire .NET Framework class library. You can also put your own assemblies into the GAC, but web applications are usually simpler to deploy and more straightforward to manage if you don't.

Application Directory Structure

Every web application should have a well-planned directory structure. Independently from the directory structure you design, ASP.NET defines a few directories with special meanings.

ASP.NET 1.*x* just introduced one special directory—the Bin directory. ASP.NET 2.0 introduces a few more, as described in Table 5-1.

Table 5-1. *Special ASP.NET Directories*

Directory	Description
Bin	Contains all the precompiled .NET assemblies (usually DLLs) that the ASP.NET web application uses. These assemblies can include precompiled web-page and web service classes, as well as other assemblies referenced by these classes.
App_Code	Contains source code files that are dynamically compiled for use in your application. These code files are usually separate components, such as a logging component or a data access library. The compiled code never appears in the Bin directory, because ASP.NET places it in the temporary directories used for dynamic compilation.
App_GlobalResources	This directory stores global resources that are accessible to every page in the web application. Chapter 17 has more about resources and localization.

Directory	Description
App_LocalResources	This directory serves the same purpose as App_GlobalResources, except these resources are accessible for their dedicated pages only. Chapter 17 has more about resources and localization.
App_WebReferences	Stores references to web services that the web application uses. This includes WSDL files and discovery documents. You'll learn about web services in Part 6.
App_Data	This directory is reserved for data storage, including SQL Server 2005 Express database files and XML files. Of course, you're free to store data files in other directories.
App_Browsers	This directory contains browser definitions stored in XML files. These XML files define the capabilities of client-side browsers for different rendering actions. Although ASP.NET does this globally (across the entire computer), the App_Browsers folder allows you to configure this behavior for separate web applications. See Chapter 27 for more information about how ASP.NET determines different browsers.
App_Themes	Stores the themes used by the web application. You'll learn more about themes in Chapter 15.

The Global.asax Application File

The global.asax file allows you to write event handlers that react to global events. Users never request the global.asax file directly. Instead, the global.asax file executes its code automatically in response to certain application events. The global.asax file provides a similar service to the global.asa file in classic ASP applications.

You write the code in a global.asax file in a similar way to a web form. The difference is that the global.asax doesn't contain any HTML or ASP.NET tags. Instead, it contains methods with specific, predefined names. For example, the following global.asax file reacts to the Application.EndRequest event, which happens just before the page is sent to the user.

```
<script language="vb" runat="server">
    Sub Application_OnEndRequest()
        Response.Write("<hr />This page was served at " & DateTime.Now.ToString())
    End Sub
</script>
```

Although it's not indicated in the global.asax file, every global.asax file defines the methods for a single class—the application class. The application class derives from HttpApplication, and as a result your code has access to all its Public and Protected members. This example uses the Response object, which is provided as a built-in property of the HttpApplication class, just like it's a built-in property of the Page class.

This event handler writes a footer at the bottom of the page with the date and time that the page was created. Because it reacts to the Application.EndRequest event, it executes every time a page is requested after all the event-handling code in that page has finished.

As with web forms, you can also separate the content of the global.asax file into two files, one that declares the file and another that contains the code. However, because there's no design surface for global.asax files, the division isn't required. Visual Studio doesn't give you the option to create a global.asax file with a separate code-behind class.

The global.asax file is optional, but a web application can have no more than one global.asax file, and it must reside in the root directory of the application, not in a subdirectory. To add a global.asax file to a project, select Website ➤ Add New Item, and choose the Global Application Class template.

When Visual Studio adds a global.asax file, it includes empty event handlers for the most commonly used application events. You simply need to insert your code in the appropriate method.

It's worth noting that application event handlers aren't attached in the same way as ordinary control events. The usual way to attach an application event handler is just to use the recognized method name. For example, if you create a protected method named Application_OnEndRequest(), ASP.NET automatically calls this method when the Application.EndRequest event occurs.

ASP.NET creates a pool of application objects when your application domain is first loaded and uses one to serve each request. This pool varies in size depending on the system and the number of available threads, but it typically ranges from 1 to 100 instances. Each request gets exclusive access to one of these application objects, and when the request ends, the object is reused. As different stages in application processing occur, ASP.NET calls the corresponding method, which triggers your code. Of course, if your methods have the wrong name, your implementation won't get called—instead, your code will simply be ignored.

Note The global application class that's used by the global.asax file should always be stateless. That's because application objects are reused for different requests as they become available. If you set a value in a member variable in one request, it might reappear in another request. However, there's no way to control how this happens or which request gets which instance of the application object. To circumvent this issue, don't use member variables unless they're declared as Shared variables (as discussed in Chapter 6).

Application Events

You can handle two types of events in the global.asax file:

- Events that always occur for every request. These include request-related and response-related events.
- Events that occur only under certain conditions.

The required events unfold in this order:

1. *Application_BeginRequest()*: This method is called at the start of every request, including requests for files that aren't web forms, such as web services.
2. *Application_AuthenticateRequest()*: This method is called just before authentication is performed. This is a jumping-off point for creating your own authentication logic.
3. *Application_AuthorizeRequest()*: After the user is authenticated (identified), it's time to determine the user's permissions. You can use this method to assign special privileges.
4. *Application_ResolveRequestCache()*: This method is commonly used in conjunction with output caching. With output caching (described in Chapter 11), the rendered HTML of a web form is reused, without executing any of your code. However, this event handler still runs.
5. At this point, the request is handed off to the appropriate handler. For example, for a web form request this is the point when the page is compiled (if necessary) and instantiated.
6. *Application_AcquireRequestState()*: This method is called just before session-specific information is retrieved for the client and used to populate the Session collection.
7. *Application_PreRequestHandlerExecute()*: This method is called before the appropriate HTTP handler executes the request.
8. At this point, the appropriate handler executes the request. For example, if it's a web form request, the event-handling code for the page is executed, and the page is rendered to HTML.

9. *Application_PostRequestHandlerExecute()*: This method is called just after the request is handled.

10. *Application_ReleaseRequestState()*: This method is called when the session-specific information is about to be serialized from the Session collection so that it's available for the next request.

11. *Application_UpdateRequestCache()*: This method is called just before information is added to the output cache. For example, if you've enabled output caching for a web page, ASP.NET will insert the rendered HTML for the page into the cache at this point.

12. *Application_EndRequest()*: This method is called at the end of the request, just before the objects are released and reclaimed. It's a suitable point for cleanup code.

Figure 5-1 shows the process of handling a single request.

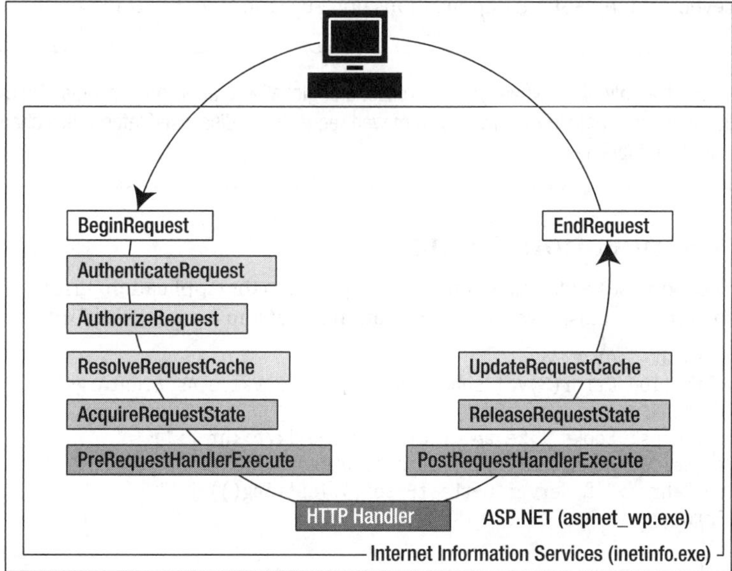

Figure 5-1. *The application events*

Some events don't fire with every request:

Application_Start(): This method is invoked when the application first starts up and the application domain is created. This event handler is a useful place to provide application-wide initialization code. For example, at this point you might load and cache data that will not change throughout the lifetime of an application, such as navigation trees, static product catalogs, and so on.

Session_Start(): This method is invoked each time a new session begins. This is often used to initialize user-specific information. Chapter 6 discusses sessions with state management.

Application_Error(): This method is invoked whenever an unhandled exception occurs in the application.

Session_End(): This method is invoked whenever the user's session ends. A session ends when your code explicitly releases it or when it times out after there have been no more requests received within a given timeout period (typically 20 minutes). This method is typically used to clean up any related data.

Application_End(): This method is invoked just before an application ends. The end of an application can occur because IIS is being restarted or because the application is transitioning to a new application domain in response to updated files or the process recycling settings.

Application_Disposed(): This method is invoked some time after the application has been shut down and the .NET garbage collector is about to reclaim the memory it occupies. This point is too late to perform critical cleanup, but you can use it as a last-ditch failsafe to verify that critical resources are released.

Application events are commonly used to perform application initialization, cleanup, usage logging, profiling, and troubleshooting. However, don't assume that your application will need to use global application events. Many ASP.NET applications don't use the global.asax file at all.

■ **Tip** The global.asax file isn't the only place where you can respond to global web application events. You can also create custom modules that participate in the processing of web requests, as discussed later in this chapter in the section "Extending the HTTP Pipeline."

Demonstrating Application Events

The following web application uses a global.asax file that responds to the Application_Error method. It intercepts the error and displays some information about it in a predefined format.

```
<script language="vb" runat="server">
    Protected Sub Application_Error(ByVal sender As Object, ByVal e As EventArgs)
        Response.Write("<b>")
        Response.Write("Oops! Looks like an error occurred!!</b><hr />")
        Response.Write(Server.GetLastError().Message.ToString())
        Response.Write("<hr />" & Server.GetLastError().ToString())
        Server.ClearError()
    End Sub
</script>
```

To test this application event handler, you need to create another web page that causes an error. Here's an example that generates an error by attempting to divide by zero when a page loads:

```
Protected Sub Page_Load(ByVal sender As Object, ByVal e As EventArgs)
    Dim i As Integer = 0
    Dim j As Integer = 1
    Dim k As Integer = j/i
End Sub
```

If you request this page, you'll see the display shown in Figure 5-2.

Typically, you wouldn't use the Application_Error() method to control the appearance of a web page, because it doesn't give you enough flexibility to deal with different types of errors (without coding painstaking conditional logic). Instead, you would probably configure custom error pages using the web.config file (as described in the next section). However, Application_Error() might be extremely useful if you want to log an error for future reference or even send an e-mail about it to a system administrator. In fact, in many events you'll need to use techniques such as these because the Response object won't be available. Two examples include the Application_Start() and Application_End() methods.

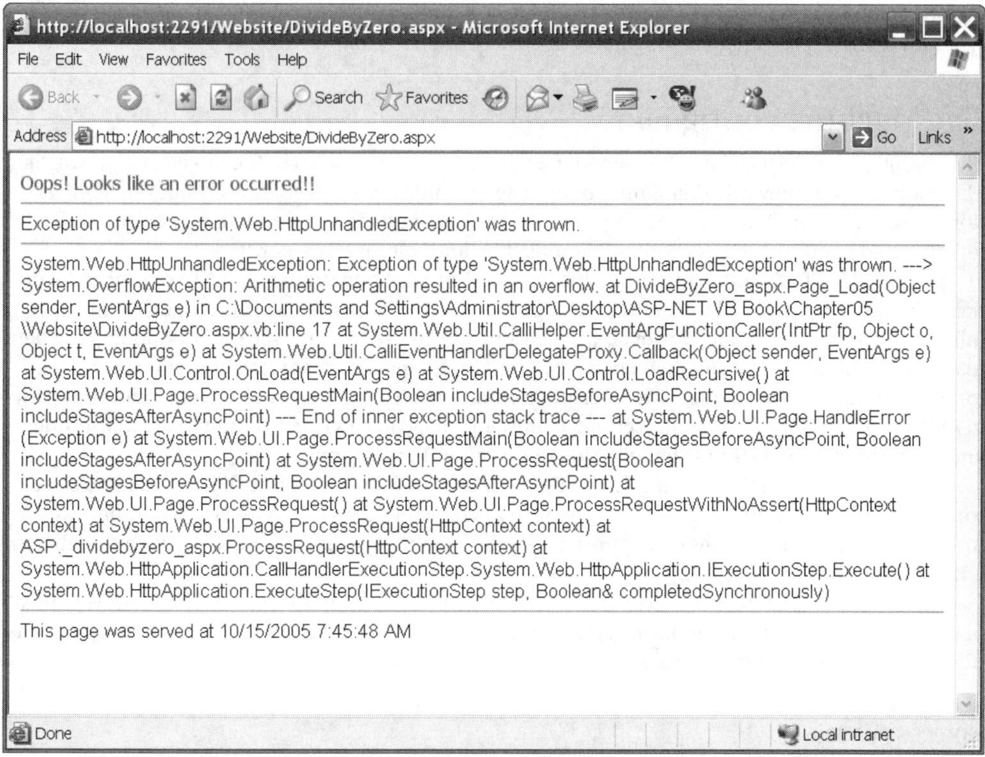

Figure 5-2. *Catching an unhandled error*

ASP.NET Configuration

Configuration in ASP.NET is managed with XML configuration files. All the information needed to configure an ASP.NET application's core settings, as well as the custom settings specific to your own application, is stored in these configuration files.

The ASP.NET configuration files have several advantages over traditional ASP configuration:

They are never locked: As described in the beginning of this chapter, you can update configuration settings at any point, and ASP.NET will smoothly transition to a new application domain.

They are easily accessed and replicated: Provided you have the appropriate network rights, you can modify a configuration file from a remote computer (or even replace it by uploading a new version via FTP). You can also copy a configuration file and use it to apply identical settings to another application or another web server that runs the same application in a web farm scenario.

They are easy to edit and understand: The settings in the configuration files are human-readable, which means they can be edited and understood without needing a special configuration tool.

With ASP.NET, you don't need to worry about configuring the IIS metabase or restarting the web server. However, you still can't perform a few tasks with a web.config file. For example, you can't create or remove a virtual directory. Similarly, you can't change file mappings. If you want the ASP.NET service to process requests for additional file types (such as HTML or a custom file type you define), you must use IIS Manager, as described in Chapter 18.

The Machine.config File

The configuration starts with a file named machine.config that resides in the directory c:\[WinDir]\Microsoft.NET\Framework\[Version]\Config. The machine.config file defines supported configuration file sections, configures the ASP.NET worker process, and registers providers that can be used for advanced features such as profiles, membership, and role-based security.

In ASP.NET 2.0, the machine.config file has been streamlined dramatically. To optimize the initialization process, many of the default settings that used to be in the machine.config file are now initialized programmatically. However, you can still look at the relevant settings by opening the new machine.config.comments file (which you can find in the same directory). It contains the full text for the standard settings along with descriptive comments (this is similar to the machine.config file in ASP.NET 1.*x*). Using the machine.config.comments file, you can learn about the default settings, and then you can add settings that override these values to machine.config.

Along with the machine.config file, ASP.NET 2.0 uses a root web.config file (in the same directory) that contains additional settings. The settings register ASP.NET's core HTTP handlers and modules, set up rules for browser support, and define security policy. In ASP.NET 1.*x*, these settings appeared in the machine.config file.

All the web applications on the computer inherit the settings in these two files. However, most of the settings are essentially plumbing features that you never need to touch. The following sections discuss the two most common exceptions.

<processModel>

This section allows you to configure how the ASP.NET worker process recycles application domains, and the Windows account it executes under, which determines its privileges. If you're using IIS 6 (the version included with Windows 2003 Server), many of these settings are ignored, and you can configure similar settings through the IIS Manager utility.

Chapter 18 has more information about the <processModel> element.

<machineKey>

This section allows you to set the server-specific key used for encrypting data and creating digital signatures. You can use encryption in conjunction with several ASP.NET features. ASP.NET uses it automatically to protect the forms authentication cookie, and you can also apply it to protected view state data (as described in Chapter 6). The key is also used for authentication with out-of-process session state providers.

Ordinarily, the <machineKey> element takes this form:

```
<machineKey validationKey="AutoGenerate,IsolateApps"
  decryptionKey="AutoGenerate,IsolateApps" validation="SHA1" />
```

The AutoGenerate,IsolateApps value indicates that ASP.NET will create and store machine-specific, application-specific keys. In other words, each application uses a distinct, automatically generated key. This prevents potential cross-site attacks.

If you don't need application-specific keys, you can choose to use a single key for all applications on the current computer, like so:

```
<machineKey validationKey="AutoGenerate"
  decryptionKey="AutoGenerate" validation="SHA1" />
```

If you're using a web farm and running the same application on multiple computers, both of these approaches raise a problem. If you request a page and it's handled by one server, and then you post back the page and it's handled by another server, the second server won't be able to decrypt the view state and the forms cookie from the first server. This problem occurs because the two web servers use different keys.

To resolve this problem, you need to define the key explicitly in the machine.config file. Here's an example of a <machineKey> element with the two key attributes defined:

```
<machineKey
  validationKey="61EA54E005915332011232149A2EEB317586824B265326CCDB3AD9ABDBE9D
6F24B0625547769E835539AD3882D3DA88896EA531CC7AFE664866BD5242FC2B05D"
  decryptionKey="61EA54E005915332011232149A2EEB317586824B265337AF"
  validation="SHA1" />
```

■ **Tip** You can also hard-code application-specific keys by adding a <machineKey> to the web.config file that you place in the application virtual directory. You'll need this approach if you're in a situation that combines the two scenarios described previously. (For example, you'll need this approach if you're running your application on multiple servers *and* these servers host multiple web applications that need individual keys.)

The validationKey value can be from 40 to 128 characters long. It is strongly recommended that you use the maximum length key available. The decryptionKey value can be either 16 or 48 characters long. If 16 characters are defined, standard DES (Data Encryption Standard) encryption is used. If 48 characters are defined, Triple DES (or 3DES) will be used. (This means DES is applied three times consecutively.) 3DES is much more difficult to break than DES, so it is recommended that you always use 48 characters for the decryptionKey. If the length of either of the keys is outside the allowed values, ASP.NET will return a page with an error message when requests are made to the application.

It doesn't make much sense to create the validation and decryption keys on your own. If you do, they're likely to be not sufficiently random, which makes them more subject to certain types of attacks. A better approach is to generate a strong random key using code and the .NET Framework cryptography classes (from the System.Security.Cryptography namespace).

The following is a generic code routine called CreateMachineKey() that creates a random series of bytes using a cryptographically strong random number generator. The CreateMachineKey() method accepts a single parameter that specifies the number of characters to use. The result is returned in hexadecimal format, which is required for the machine.config file.

```
Public Shared Function CreateMachineKey(ByVal length As Integer) As String
    ' Create a byte array.
    Dim random As Byte() = New Byte(length/2 - 1) {}

    ' Create a cryptographically strong random number generator.
    Dim rng As New RNGCryptoServiceProvider()

    ' Fill the byte array with random bytes.
    rng.GetBytes(random)

    ' Create a StringBuilder to hold the result once it is
    ' converted to hexadecimal format.
    Dim machineKey As New System.Text.StringBuilder(length)
```

```
    ' Loop through the random byte array and append each value
    ' to the StringBuilder.
    Dim i As Integer = 0
    Do While i < random.Length
        machineKey.Append(String.Format("{0:X2}", random(i)))
         i += 1
    Loop
    Return machineKey.ToString()
End Function
```

You can use this function in a web form to create the keys you need. For example, the following snippet of code creates a 48-character decryption key and a 128-character validation key, and it displays the values in two separate text boxes:

```
txtDecryptionKey.Text = CreateMachineKey(48)
txtValidationKey.Text = CreateMachineKey(128)
```

You can then copy the information and paste it into the machine.config file for each computer in the web farm. This is a much more convenient and secure approach than creating keys by hand. You'll learn much more about the cryptography classes in the System.Security.Cryptography namespace in Chapter 25.

The Web.config File

Every web application inherits the settings from the machine.config file. In addition, you can apply application-specific settings. For example, you might want to set a specific method for authentication, a type of debugging, a default language, or custom error pages. However, it's important to understand that you can't override every setting from the machine.config file. Certain settings, such as the process model settings, can't be changed on a per-application basis. Other settings are application-specific. If you use these settings, you must place the web.config file in the root virtual directory of your application (not in a subdirectory).

The entire content of an ASP.NET configuration file is nested in a root <configuration> element. This element contains a <system.web> element, which is used for ASP.NET settings. Inside the <system.web> element are separate elements for each aspect of configuration.

Here's the basic skeletal structure of the web.config file:

```
<?xml version="1.0" encoding="utf-8" ?>
<configuration xmlns="http://schemas.microsoft.com/.NetConfiguration/v2.0">
  <system.web>
    <!-- ASP.NET configuration sections go here. -->
  </system.web>
</configuration>
```

ASP.NET uses a multilayered configuration system that allows you to use different settings for different parts of your application. To use this technique, you need to create additional subdirectories inside your virtual directory. These subdirectories can contain their own web.config files with additional settings. ASP.NET uses *configuration inheritance* so that each subdirectory acquires the settings from the parent directory.

For example, consider the web request `http://localhost/A/B/C/MyPage.aspx`, where A is the root directory for the web application. In this case, multiple levels of settings come into play:

1. The default machine.config settings are applied first.
2. The web.config settings from the computer root are applied next. This web.config file is in the same Config directory as the machine.config file.
3. If there is a web.config file in the application root A, these settings are applied next.
4. If there is a web.config file in the subdirectory B, these settings are applied next.
5. If there is a web.config file in the subdirectory C, these settings are applied last.

In this sequence (shown in Figure 5-3), it's important to note that although you can have an unlimited number of subdirectories, the settings applied in step 1 and step 2 have special significance. That's because certain settings can be applied only at the machine.config level (such as the Windows account used to execute code), and other settings can be applied only at the application root level (such as the type of authentication your web application uses).

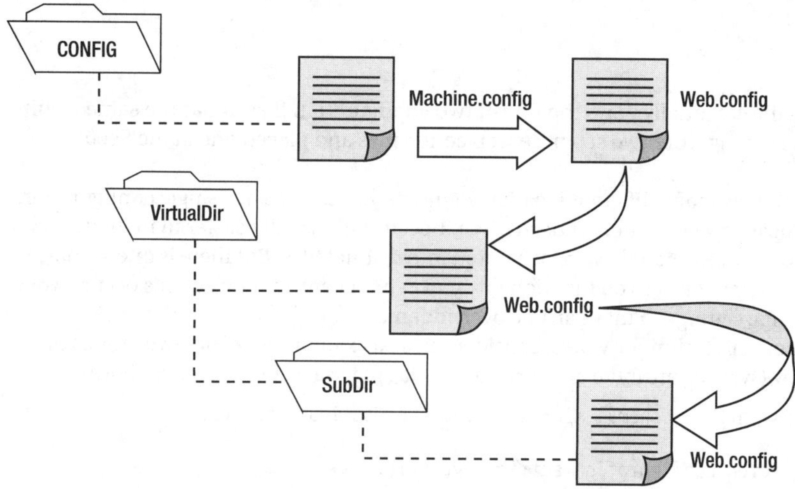

Figure 5-3. *Configuration inheritance*

In this way, subdirectories can specify just a small set of settings that differ from the rest of the web application. One reason you might want to use multiple directories in an application is to apply different security settings. Files that need to be secured would then be placed in a special directory with a web.config file that defines more stringent security settings than the root virtual directory.

If settings conflict, the settings from a web.config in a nested directory always override the settings inherited from the parent. However, one exception exists. You can designate specific *locked* sections that can't be changed. The next section describes this technique.

Using <location> Elements

The <location> element is an extension that allows you to specify more than one group of settings in the same configuration file.You use the path attribute of the <location> element to specific the subdirectory or file to which the settings should be applied.

For example, the following web.config file uses the <location> element to create two groups of settings—one for the current directory and one that applies only to files in the subdirectory named Secure:

```
<configuration xmlns="http://schemas.microsoft.com/.NetConfiguration/v2.0">
    <system.web>
        <!-- Basic configuration settings go here. -->
    </system.web>

    <location path="/Secure">
        <system.web>
            <!-- Configuration settings for the Secure subdirectory go here. -->
        </system.web>
    </location>
</configuration>
```

This web.config file essentially plays the role of two configuration files. It has the same result as if you had split the settings into two separate web.config files and placed one in the Secure subdirectory.

There's no limit to how many different location elements you can use in a single configuration file. However, the <location> element isn't used often, because it's usually easier to manage and update configuration settings when they are separated into distinct files. But there is one scenario where the <location> element gives you functionality you can't get any other way. This occurs when you want to lock specific settings so they can't be overridden.

To understand how this technique works, consider the next example. It defines two groups of settings and sets the allowOverride attribute of the <location> tag to false on one group, as shown here:

```
<configuration xmlns="http://schemas.microsoft.com/.NetConfiguration/v2.0">
    <system.web>
        <!-- Unprotected configuration settings go here. -->
    </system.web>
    <location allowOverride="false" >
        <system.web>
            <!-- Locked configuration settings go here. -->
        </system.web>
    </location>
</configuration>
```

In this case, you can't override any of the settings in the <location> section. If you try, ASP.NET will generate an unhandled exception when you request a page in the web application.

The allowOverride attribute of the <location> element is primarily useful for web hosting companies that want to make sure certain settings can't be changed. In this case, the administrator will modify the machine.config file on the web server and use the <location> element to lock specific sections.

Tip When you lock settings in the machine.config file, you have two choices. First, you can lock the settings for all applications by omitting the path attribute of the <location> tag. Second, you can lock settings for a specific application by setting the path attribute to the appropriate web application name.

Configuration Settings

The <system.web> element contains all the ASP.NET-specific configuration settings. These settings configure various aspects of your web application and enable services such as security, state management, and tracing.

Table 5-2 lists the basic child elements that the <system.web> element can contain and their purpose. This list is not complete and is intended only to give you a rough idea of the scope of ASP.NET configuration.

Table 5-2. *Some Basic Configuration Sections*

Element	Description
authentication	This element determines how you will verify a client's identity when the client requests a page. This is set at the application level.
authorization	This element controls which clients have access to the resources within the web application or current directory.
compilation	This element contains the <assemblies> element, which lists the assemblies your web application uses. These assemblies are then made available to your code (as long as they can be found in the Bin directory or the GAC). The <compilation> element can also contain mappings to language compilers, although this is typically done only at the machine.config level.
customErrors	This element allows you to set specific redirect URLs that should be used when specific (or default) errors occur. For example, this element could be used to redirect the user to a friendly replacement for the dreaded 404 (page not found) error.
identity	Controls the security identity of the ASP.NET application. You can use this setting to cause the web application to temporarily assume the identity of another Windows account and its permissions and restrictions. Typically, this is set at the application level.
sessionState	Configures the various options for maintaining session state for the application, such as whether to maintain it at all and where to maintain it (SQL, a separate Windows service, and so on). This is set at the application level.
trace	Configures tracing, an ASP.NET feature that lets you display diagnostic information in the page (or collect it for viewing separately).
webServices	Controls the many settings used for web services. This allows you to tweak the various protocol and configuration settings for communicating with any web service contained within the application.

You can include as few or as many configuration sections as you want. For example, if you need to specify special error settings, you could add just the <customErrors> section and leave out the others. Visual Studio adds comments to describe the purpose and syntax of various options. XML comments are bracketed with the <!-- and --> character sequences, as shown here:

```
<!-- This is the format for an XML comment. -->
```

Note Like all XML documents, the web.config file is case-sensitive. Every setting uses camel case and starts with a lowercase letter. That means you cannot write <CustomErrors> instead of <customErrors>.

The following sections give a brief overview of several of the more important sections.

<configuration>

<configuration> is the root element that contains all the configuration details. Every web.config file *must* have a configuration element. The <configuration> element can contain several other subelements, but in an ASP.NET application you're likely to see only two: <system.web> and <appSettings>.

<system.web>

<system.web> acts as a container for the predefined ASP.NET-specific settings, many of which are detailed in the following sections. The schema of the <system.web> section is fixed—in other words, you can't change the structure or add your own custom elements here.

Throughout this book, you'll consider different parts of the web.config file as you learn about features such as authentication, session state management, and tracing.

■ **Note** The configuration file architecture is a .NET standard, and other types of applications (such as Windows applications) can also use configuration files. For that reason, the root <configuration> element isn't tailored to web application settings. Instead, web application settings are contained inside the dedicated <system.web> section.

<customErrors>

This element allows you to configure the behavior of your application in response to various HTTP errors. For example, you can redirect the dreaded 404 error to a page that prints a user-friendly error message to the users of your web application by creating a section like this:

```
<customErrors defaultRedirect="standarderror.aspx" mode="remoteonly">
  <error statusCode="404" redirect="filenotfound.htm"/>
</customErrors>
```

In this example, if the error is code 404 (file not found), it will redirect the user to filenotfound.htm. If any other error occurs (including an HTTP error or an unhandled .NET exception in the web page), the user will be redirected to the page standarderror.aspx. Because the error mode is set to remoteonly, local administrators will see the actual error message rather than being redirected. Remote clients will see only the custom error page.

The following is a list of the modes supported for the mode attribute:

on: Indicates that custom errors are enabled. If no defaultRedirect attribute is supplied, users will see a generic error.

off: Custom errors are disabled. This allows full error details to be displayed.

remoteonly: Custom errors are shown only to remote clients while full detailed errors are displayed to local clients.

Keep in mind that the custom error settings you define in a configuration file come into effect only if ASP.NET is handling the request. For example, if you request the nonexistent page whateverpage.aspx in an application with the previous settings shown, you'll be redirected to filenotfound.aspx, because the .aspx file extension is registered to the ASP.NET service. However, if you request the nonexistent page whateverpage.html, ASP.NET will not process the request, and the default redirect setting specified in IIS will be used. Typically, this means that the user will see the page c:\[WinDir]\Help\IISHelp\common\404b.htm. You could change the set of registered ASP.NET file types to include .html and .htm files, but this will slow down performance for these file types (and give additional work to the ASP.NET worker process).

■**Note** What happens if an error occurs in the error page itself? If an error occurs in a custom error page (in this case, DefaultError.aspx), ASP.NET will not be able to handle it. It will not try to reforward the user to the same page. Instead, it will display the normal client error page with the generic message.

<connectionStrings>

This section, which is new in ASP.NET 2.0, allows you to define connection strings that will be used elsewhere in your application. Seeing as connection strings need to be reused exactly to support connection pooling and may need to be modified without recompiling the web application, it makes perfect sense to store them in the web.config file.

You can add as many connection strings as you want. For each one, you need to specify the ADO.NET provider name. (See Chapter 7 for more information.)

Here's an example that defines a single connection string:

```
<?xml version="1.0" encoding="utf-8" ?>
<configuration xmlns="http://schemas.microsoft.com/.NetConfiguration/v2.0">
  <connectionStrings>
    <add name="NorthwindConnection"
         connectionString=
  "Data Source=localhost;Integrated Security=SSPI;Initial Catalog=Northwind;"
         providerName="System.Data.SqlClient" />
  </connectionStrings>
  <system.web>...</system.web>
</configuration>
```

<appSettings>

You add custom settings to a web.config file in a special element called <appSettings>. Here's where the <appSettings> section fits into the web.config file:

```
<?xml version="1.0" encoding="utf-8" ?>
<configuration xmlns="http://schemas.microsoft.com/.NetConfiguration/v2.0">
  <appSettings>
    <!-- Custom application data goes here. -->
  </appSettings>
  <system.web>...</system.web>
</configuration>
```

The custom settings that you add are written as simple string variables. You might want to use a special web.config setting for several reasons. Often, you'll want the ability to record hard-coded but changeable information for connecting to external resources, such as database connection strings, file paths, and web service URLs. Because the configuration file can be modified at any time, this allows you to update the configuration of an application as its physical deployment characteristics change without needing to recompile it.

Custom settings are entered using an <add> element that identifies a unique variable name (the key) and the variable contents (the value). The following example adds two new custom configuration settings:

```
<?xml version="1.0" encoding="utf-8" ?>
<configuration xmlns="http://schemas.microsoft.com/.NetConfiguration/v2.0">
  <appSettings>
    <add key="websiteName" value="My New Website"/>
    <add key="welcomeMessage" value="Welcome to my new Website, friend!"/>
```

```
  </appSettings>
  <system.web>...</system.web>
</configuration>
```

Once you've added this information, .NET makes it extremely easy to retrieve it in your web-page code. You simply need to use the ConfigurationSettings class from the System.Configuration namespace. It exposes a Shared property called AppSettings, which contains a dynamically built collection of available application settings for the current directory. For example, if the ASP.NET page class referencing the AppSettings collection is at a location such as `http://localhost/MyApp/MyDirectory/MySubDirectory`, it is possible that the AppSettings collection contains settings from three different web.config files. The AppSettings collection makes that hierarchy seamless to the page that's using it.

To use the ConfigurationSettings class, it helps to first import the System.Configuration namespace so you can refer to the class without needing to use the long fully qualified name, as shown here:

```
Imports System.Configuration
```

Next, you simply need to retrieve the value by name. The following example fills two labels using the custom application information:

```
Protected Sub Page_Load(ByVal sender As Object, ByVal e As EventArgs)
    lblSiteName.Text = ConfigurationManager.AppSettings("websiteName")
    lblWelcome.Text = ConfigurationManager.AppSettings("welcomeMessage")
End Sub
```

Figure 5-4 shows the test web page in action.

Figure 5-4. *Retrieving custom application settings*

An error won't occur if you try to retrieve a value that doesn't exist. If you suspect this could be a problem, make sure to test for a null reference (Nothing in Visual Basic) before retrieving a value.

■ **Note** Values in the <appSettings> element of a configuration file are available to any class in your application or to any component that your application uses, whether it's a web form class, a business logic class, a data access class, or something else. In all these cases, you use the ConfigurationSettings class in the same way.

Reading and Writing Configuration Sections Programmatically

ASP.NET 2.0 introduces a new model for reading configuration files. It revolves around the new WebConfigurationManager and Configuration classes in the System.Web.Configuration namespace, which allow you to extract information from a configuration file at runtime. The WebConfigurationManager is the starting point. It provides the members shown in Table 5-3.

Table 5-3. *ConfigurationManager Members*

Member	Description
AppSettings	Provides access to any custom information you've added to the <appSettings> section of the application configuration file. Individual settings are provided through a collection that's indexed by name.
ConnectionStrings	Provides access to data in the <connectionStrings> section of the configuration file. Individual settings are provided through a collection that's indexed by name.
OpenWebConfiguration()	Returns a Configuration object that provides access to the configuration information for the specified web application.
OpenMachineConfiguration()	Returns a Configuration object that provides access to the configuration information that's defined for the web server (in the machine.config file).
RefreshSection()	Discards any information that has been retrieved for the indicated section. Next time you read any of the section's information, the WebConfigurationManager will reread it from disk.

You need to consider a number of factors when using these methods. When you retrieve information using the WebConfigurationManager.OpenWebConfiguration() method, it reflects the *cumulative* configuration for the current application. That means settings from the current web.config file are merged with those defined higher up the configuration hierarchy (for example, in a parent directory or in the machine.config file). To test this, you simply need to loop over the connection strings using code like this:

```
For Each connection As ConnectionStringSettings
    In WebConfigurationManager.ConnectionStrings
    Response.Write("Name: " & connection.Name & "<br />")
    Response.Write("Connection String: " _
        & connection.ConnectionString & "<br /><br />")
Next
```

Even if your application doesn't define any connection strings of its own, you'll see the default connection strings that are defined for the web server.

Tip Remember that in order to successfully use these methods, the ASP.NET worker process needs certain permissions (such as read access to the web directory). If you plan to change these settings programmatically, the worker process also requires write access. To protect against problems, you should always wrap your configuration calls in exception-handling code.

The WebConfigurationManager gives convenient access to two configuration sections: the <appSettings> section where you can define custom settings and the <connectionStrings> section used to define how your application connects to the database. You can get this information using the AppSettings and ConnectionStrings properties.

Using the configuration classes, you can also retrieve information about any other configuration section. However, you'll need to go to a little more work. The basic technique is to call WebConfigurationManager.OpenWebConfiguration() to retrieve a Configuration object that contains all the configuration information. Then, you can navigate to just the section that interests you using the Configuration.GetSection() method. The trick is that the GetSection() method returns a different type of object depending on the type of section. For example, if you're retrieving information from the <authentication> section, you'll receive an AuthenticationSection object, as shown here:

```
' Get the configuration for the current web application.
Dim config As Configuration =
        WebConfigurationManager.OpenWebConfiguration(Request.ApplicationPath)

' Search for the <authentication> element inside the <system.web> element.
Dim authSection As AuthenticationSection =
        CType(config.GetSection("system.web/authentication"), AuthenticationSection)
```

The search is performed using a pathlike syntax. You don't indicate the root <configuration> element, because all configuration sections are contained in that element.

Classes for every configuration section are defined in the class library in the System.Web.Configuration namespace (not the System.Configuration namespace, which includes only configuration classes that are generic to all .NET applications). All these classes inherit from the ConfigurationSection class.

Using a ConfigurationSection object allows you to retrieve a good deal of information about the current state of your application. Here's an example that displays information about the assemblies that are currently referenced:

```
Dim config As Configuration =
        WebConfigurationManager.OpenWebConfiguration(Request.ApplicationPath)

Dim compSection As CompilationSection =
        CType(config.GetSection("system.web/compilation"), CompilationSection)
For Each assm As AssemblyInfo In compSection.Assemblies
    Response.Write(assm.Assembly & "<br />")
Next
```

You can also modify most configuration sections programmatically through the Configuration class—in fact, ASP.NET relies on this functionality for its administrative web pages. You can modify the value directly, but you must call Configuration.Save() to commit the change. When modifying a setting, ASP.NET handles the update safely by using synchronization code to ensure that multiple clients can't commit a change simultaneously.

In your code, you're most likely to change settings in the <appSettings> section or the <connectionStrings> section. Here's an example that rewrites the application settings shown earlier so that it updates one of the settings after reading it:

```
Protected Sub Page_Load(ByVal sender As Object, ByVal e As EventArgs)
    Dim config As Configuration =
        WebConfigurationManager.OpenWebConfiguration(Request.ApplicationPath)

    lblSiteName.Text = config.AppSettings.Settings("websiteName").Value
    lblWelcome.Text = config.AppSettings.Settings("welcomeMessage").Value
```

```
    config.AppSettings.Settings("welcomeMessage").Value = "Welcome, again."
    config.Save()
End Sub
```

■ **Tip** This example reflects the cumulative configuration in the root web application directory, because it uses the Request.ApplicationPath when calling the OpenWebConfiguration() method. If you use the Request.CurrentExecutionFilePath instead, you'll get cumulative settings for the current directory. If the current directory is a subdirectory inside a web application, and if that subdirectory has its own web.config file, you'll see these additional settings.

Note that the web.config file is *never* a good solution for state management. Instead, it makes sense as a way to occasionally update a setting that, under normal circumstances, almost never changes. That's because changing a configuration setting has a significant cost. File access has never been known for blistering speed, and the required synchronization adds a certain amount of overhead. However, the real problem is that the cost of creating a new application domain (which happens every time a configuration setting changes) is significant. The next time you request the page, you'll see the effect—the request will complete much more slowly while the page is compiled to native machine code, cached, and loaded. Even worse, information in the Application and Caching collections will be lost, as well as any information in the Session collection if you're using the in-process session provider. (See Chapter 6 for more information.) Unfortunately, the new configuration model makes it all too easy to make the serious mistake of storing frequently changed values in a configuration file.

By default, the Configuration.Save() method persists only those changes you have made since creating the Configuration object. Settings are stored in the local web.config file, or one is created if needed. It's important to realize that if you change an inherited setting (for example, one that's stored in the machine.config file), then when you save the changes, you won't overwrite the existing value in the configuration file where it's defined. Instead, the new value will be saved in the local web.config file so that it overrides the inherited value for the current application only. You can also use the SaveAs() method to save configuration settings to another file.

When calling Configuration.Save(), you can use an overloaded version of the method that accepts a value from the ConfigurationSaveMode enumeration. Use Modified to save any value you changed, even if it doesn't differ from the inherited values. Use Full to save everything in the local web.config, which is useful if you're trying to duplicate configuration settings for testing or deploying. Finally, use Minimal to save only those changes that differ from the inherited levels—this is the default.

The Website Administration Tool (WAT)

You might wonder why the ASP.NET team went to all the trouble of creating a sophisticated tool like the WebConfigurationManager that performs too poorly to be used in a typical web application. The reason is because the WebConfigurationManager isn't really intended to be used in your web pages. Instead, it's designed to allow developers to build custom configuration tools that simplify the work of configuring web applications. ASP.NET even includes a graphical configuration tool that's entirely based on the WebConfigurationManager, although you'd never know it unless you dived into the code.

This tool is called the WAT, and it lets you configure various parts of the web.config file using a web-page interface. To run the WAT to configure the current web project in Visual Studio, select Website ➤ ASP.NET Configuration. A web browser window will appear inside Visual Studio (see Figure 5-5). Internet Explorer will automatically log you in under the current user account, allowing you to make changes.

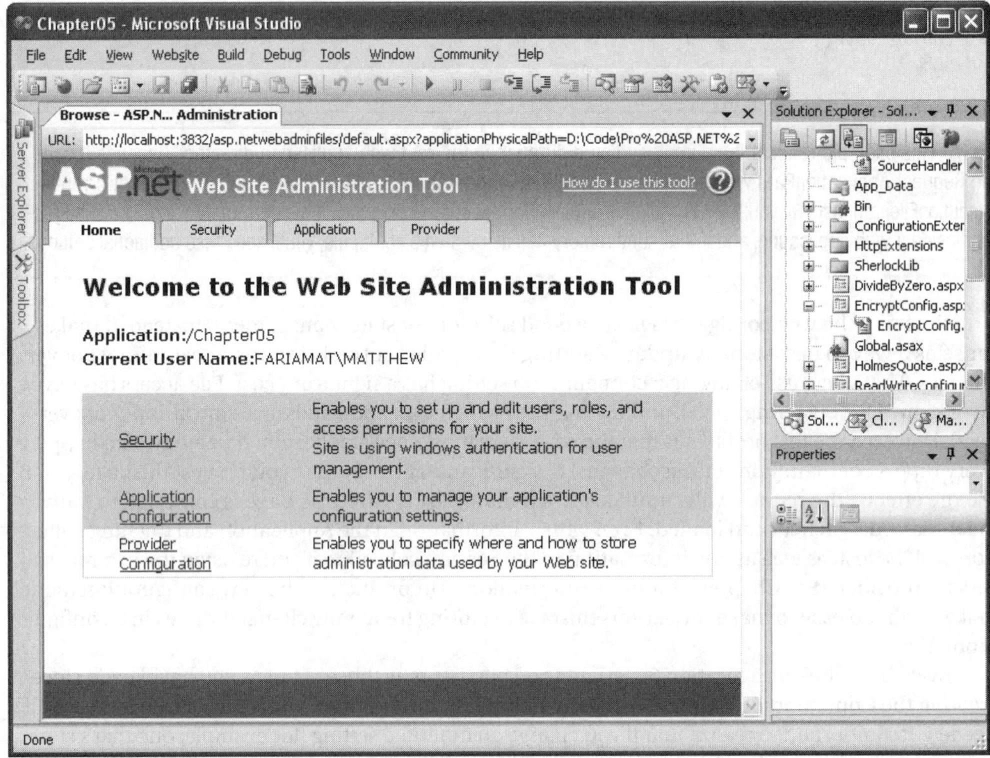

Figure 5-5. *Running the WAT*

You can use the WAT to automate the web.config changes you made in the previous example. To try this, click the Application tab. Using this tab, you can edit or remove application settings (select the Manage Application Settings link) or create a new setting (click the Create Application Settings link). Figure 5-6 shows how you can edit an application setting.

This is the essential idea behind the WAT. You make your changes using a graphical interface (a web page), and the WAT generates the settings you need and adds them to the web.config file for your application behind the scenes. Of course, the WAT has a number of settings for configuring more complex ASP.NET settings, and you'll see it at work throughout this book.

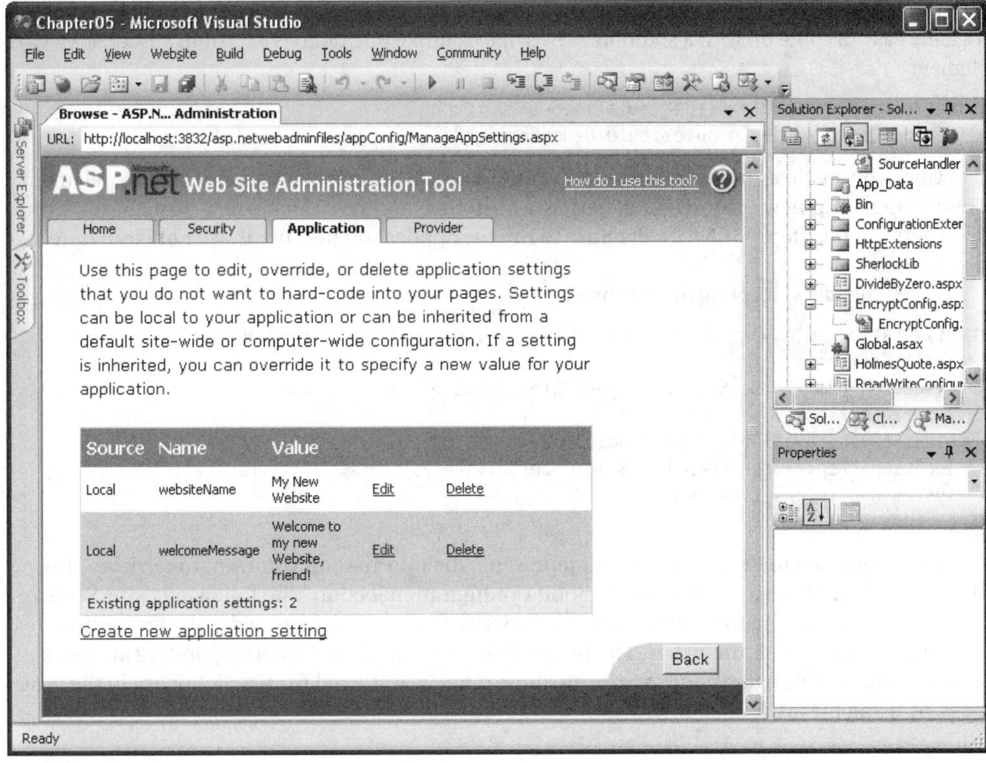

Figure 5-6. *Editing an application setting with the WAT*

Extending the Configuration File Structure

As you've seen, ASP.NET uses a modular, highly extensible configuration model. Not only can you extend the HTTP pipeline with HTTP handlers and HTTP modules, but you can also extend the structure of the web.config and machine.config configuration files with your own custom sections.

Earlier in this chapter, you learned how you can use the <appSettings> element to store custom information that your application uses. The <appSettings> element has two significant limitations. First, it doesn't provide a way to store structured information, such as lists or groups of related settings. Second, it doesn't give you the flexibility to deal with different types of data. Instead, the <appSettings> element is limited to single strings. Fortunately, you can extend the structure of the configuration file with arbitrary XML. You can then create a more specialized class that's able to read this information and convert it into the data type you want.

For example, imagine you want to store several related settings about how to contact a remote object in your web.config files. These settings indicate the location, user authentication information, and so on. Although you could enter this information using separate settings in the <appSettings> group, you'd face a few problems. For example, nothing would indicate which settings are logically related, which could lead to problems if one is updated and the other isn't.

If you don't need to fit your information into the limiting structure of the <appSettings> section, it's fairly easy to come up with a solution. Here's one example that defines a custom <orderService> element:

```
<orderService available="true" pollTimeout="00:01:00"
 location="tcp://OrderComputer:8010/OrderService"/>
```

Once you create a custom element, you need to define that section using a <section> element. This registers your new section and maps it to a custom data class (which you'll create next). If you don't perform this step, ASP.NET will refuse to run the application because it will notice an unrecognized section.

Here's the full web.config file you need:

```
<configuration xmlns="http://schemas.microsoft.com/.NetConfiguration/v2.0">
  <configSections>
    <section name="orderService" type="OrderService" />
  </configSections>
  <orderService available="true" pollTimeout="00:01:00"
   location="tcp://OrderComputer:8010/OrderService"/>
  <system.web>...</system.web>
</configuration>
```

Next, you need to define a class that represents the information you want to retrieve. This class must derive from System.Configuration.ConfigurationSection. The following OrderService class plays that role. It represents a single <orderService> element and provides the three attributes through strongly typed properties. The properties are mapped to the corresponding attribute names using the ConfigurationProperty attribute. They're retrieved from a dictionary in the base class, by using the attribute name.

```
Public Class OrderService
    Inherits ConfigurationSection

    <ConfigurationProperty("available", DefaultValue := False)> _
    Public Property Available() As Boolean
        Get
            Return CBool(MyBase.Item("available"))
        End Get
        Set
            MyBase.Item("available") = Value
        End Set
    End Property

    <ConfigurationProperty("pollTimeout", RequiredValue := True)> _
    Public Property PollTimeout() As TimeSpan
        Get
            Return CType(MyBase.Item("pollTimeout"), TimeSpan)
        End Get
        Set
            MyBase.Item("pollTimeout") = Value
        End Set
    End Property

    <ConfigurationProperty("location", RequiredValue := True)> _
    Public Property Location() As String
```

```
        Get
          Return CStr(MyBase.Item("location"))
        End Get
        Set
            MyBase.Item("location") = Value
        End Set
    End Property
End Class
```

Typically, you'll place this class and the section handler class in a separate DLL assembly. Then, you must copy the compiled assembly into the Bin directory of the web application where you want to use it by adding a reference in Visual Studio. However, a quicker approach is to add this class to a source code file in the App_Code subdirectory.

■ **Note** We'll discuss component reuse later in this chapter in the ".NET Components" section. For now, you can use the quicker App_Code approach rather than creating a full-fledged, separately compiled component.

ASP.NET uses dedicated classes called *section handlers* to process the information in a configuration file. In previous versions of ASP.NET, you were forced to create your own section handlers by hand. In ASP.NET 2.0, the WebConfigurationManager has the built-in smarts to parse a section of the configuration file's XML and deserialize it into the corresponding custom SectionHandler class.

Here's an example that retrieves your custom configuration settings and displays them in a page:

```
Dim config As Configuration =
      WebConfigurationManager.OpenWebConfiguration(Request.ApplicationPath)

Dim custSection As OrderService =
      CType(config.GetSection("orderService"), OrderService)

lblInfo.Text &= "Retrieved service information...<br />" &
             "<b>Location:</b> " & custSection.Location _
             & "<br /><b>Available:</b> " & _
             custSection.Available.ToString() & "<br /><b>Timeout:</b> " & _
            custSection.PollTimeout.ToString() & "<br /><br />"
```

Figure 5-7 shows the displayed data.

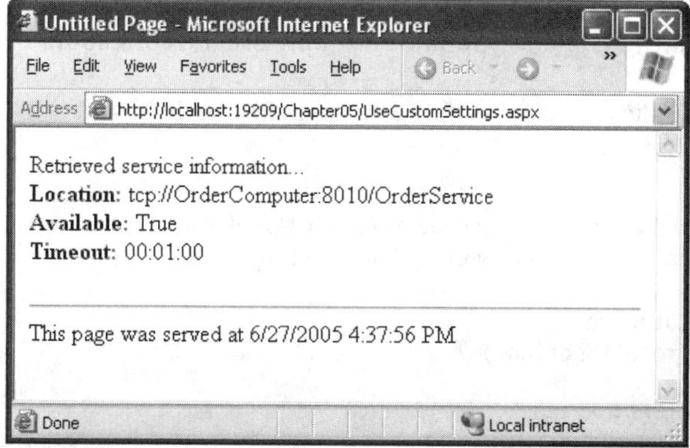

Figure 5-7. *Retrieving custom configuration data*

You can also change this custom section and update the web.config file in the same way as before.

Custom section handlers can get a fair bit more sophisticated. For example, you can use additional attributes to validate configuration string values (look for the attributes that derive from ConfigurationValidatorAttribute), and you can create sections with nested elements and more complex structures. For more information about extending ASP.NET configuration files, refer to the MSDN Help.

Encrypting Configuration Sections

ASP.NET never serves requests for configuration files, because they often contain sensitive information. However, even with this basic restriction in place, you may want to increase security by encrypting sections of a configuration file. This is a recommended practice for data such as connections and user-specific details. (Of course, any passwords should also be encrypted, although ideally they won't be placed in a configuration file at all.)

ASP.NET supports two encryption options:

RSA: The RSA provider allows you to create a key pair that is then used to encrypt the configuration data. The advantage is that you can copy this key between computers (for example, if you want to use the same configuration file with all the servers in a web farm). The RSA provider is used by default.

DPAPI: The DPAPI (data protection API) provider uses a protection mechanism that's built into Windows. Configuration files are encrypted using a machine-specific key. The advantage is that you don't need to manage or maintain the key. The disadvantage is that you can't use a configuration file encrypted in this way on any other computer.

With both of these options, encryption is completely transparent. When you retrieve a setting from an encrypted section, ASP.NET automatically performs the decryption and returns the plain text to your code (provided the required key is available). Similarly, if you modify a value programmatically and save it, encryption is performed automatically. However, you won't be able to edit that section of the web.config file by hand. But you *can* still use the WAT, the IIS snap-in, or your own custom code. When you use the configuration API, the decryption and encryption steps are performed automatically when you read from or write to a protected section.

Programmatic Encryption

To enable encryption programmatically, you need to retrieve the corresponding ConfigurationSection.SectionInformation object and then call the ProtectSection() method. Any existing data is encrypted at this point, and any changes you make from this point on are automatically encrypted. If you want to switch off encryption, you simply use the corresponding UnprotectSection() method.

Here's an example that encrypts the application section if it's unencrypted or switches off encryption if it is:

```
Dim config As Configuration =
        WebConfigurationManager.OpenWebConfiguration(Request.ApplicationPath)
Dim appSettings As ConfigurationSection = config.GetSection("appSettings")

If appSettings.SectionInformation.IsProtected Then
    appSettings.SectionInformation.UnprotectSection()
Else
    appSettings.SectionInformation.ProtectSection
        ("DataProtectionConfigurationProvider")
End If
config.Save()
```

Here's an excerpted version of what a protected <appSettings> section looks like:

```
<appSettings>
  <EncryptedData>
    <CipherData>
      <CipherValue>AQAAANCMnd8BFdERjHoAwE/Cl+sBAAAAIEokx++BEOmpDaPjVrJ/jQQAAAA
CAAAAAAADZgAAqAAAABAAAAClK6Kt++FOJoJrMZs12KWdAAAAAASAAACgAAAAEAAAAFYA23iGZF1pe
FwDPTKM2/1IAQAAYG/Y4cmSlEVs/a4yK7KXoYbWtjDsQBnMAcndmK3q+ODw/8...</CipherValue>
      </CipherData>
    </EncryptedData>
  </appSettings>
```

Note that you can't tell anything about the encrypted data, including the number of settings, the key names of settings, or their data types.

■ Note Some settings can't be encrypted because they are used outside ASP.NET (usually by the IIS web server). The <httpRuntime> section is one example.

Command-Line Encryption

Currently, no graphical tool exists for encrypting and decrypting configuration file settings. However, if you don't want to write code, you can use the aspnet_regiis.exe command-line utility, which is found in the directory c:\[WinDir]\Microsoft.NET\Framework\[Version]. To use this tool, you must have already created a virtual directory to set your application up in IIS. (See Chapter 18 for more about that process.)

When using aspnet_regiis to protect a portion of a configuration file, you need to specify these command-line arguments:

- The -pe switch specifies the configuration section to encrypt.
- The -app switch specifies your web application's virtual path.
- The -prov switch specifies the provider name.

Here's a the command-line that duplicates the earlier example for an application at `http://localhost/TestApp`:

```
aspnet_regiis -pe "appSettings" -app "/TestApp"
 -prov "DataProtectionConfigurationProvider"
```

.NET Components

A well-designed web application written for ASP.NET will include separate components that may be organized into distinct data and business tiers. Once you've created these components, you can use them from any ASP.NET web page or web service seamlessly.

You can create a component in two ways:

Create a new .vb file in the App_Code subdirectory: ASP.NET automatically compiles any code files in this directory and makes the classes they contain available to the rest of your web application. When you add a new class in Visual Studio, you'll be prompted to create the App_Code directory (if it doesn't exist yet) and place the file there.

Create a new class library project in Visual Studio: All the classes in this project will be compiled into a DLL assembly. Once you've compiled the assembly, you can use Visual Studio's Website ➤ Add Reference command to bring it into your web application. This step adds the assembly reference to your web.config file and copies the assembly to the Bin subdirectory of your application.

Both approaches have the same ultimate result. For example, if you code a database component, you'll access it in the same way regardless of whether it's a compiled assembly in the Bin directory or a source code file in the App_Code directory. Similarly, if you use ASP.NET's precompilation features (discussed in Chapter 18), both options will perform the same way. (If you don't, you'll find that the first request to your web application takes longer to execute when you use the App_Code approach, because an extra compilation step is involved.)

Although both approaches have essentially the same footprint, they aren't the same for code management. This is especially true in cases where you want to reuse the component in more than one web application (or even in different types of .NET applications). If you use the App_Code approach with multiple web applications, it's all too easy to make slight modifications and wind up with a mess of different versions of the same shared class. The second approach is also more practical for building large-scale applications with a team of developers, in which case you'll want the freedom to have different portions of the web application completed and compiled separately. For these reasons, the class library approach is always preferred for professional applications.

■ **Tip** The App_Code subdirectory should be used only for classes that are tightly coupled to your web application. Reusable units of functionality (such as business libraries, database components, validation routines, encryption utilities, and so on) should always be built as separate class libraries. The scaled-down Visual Web Developer 2005 Express Edition doesn't provide support for class library projects.

Creating a Component

The next example demonstrates a simple component that reads a random Sherlock Holmes quote from an XML file. (This XML file is available on the Internet and freely reusable via the GNU Public License.) The component consists of two classes—a Quotation class that represents a single quote and a SherlockQuotes class that allows you to read a random quote. Both of these classes are placed in the SherlockLib namespace.

The first listing shows the SherlockQuotes class, which loads an XML file containing quotes in QEL (Quotation Exchange Language, an XML dialect) when it's instantiated. The SherlockQuotes class provides a public GetRandom() quote method that the web-page code can use.

```
Imports System
Imports System.Xml

Namespace SherlockLib
    Public Class SherlockQuotes
        Private quoteDoc As XmlDocument
        Private quoteCount As Integer
        Public Sub New(ByVal fileName As String)
            quoteDoc = New XmlDocument()
            quoteDoc.Load(fileName)
            quoteCount = quoteDoc.DocumentElement.ChildNodes.Count
        End Sub

        Public Function GetRandomQuote() As Quotation
            Dim i As Integer
            Dim x As New Random()
            i = x.Next(quoteCount-1)
            Return New Quotation(quoteDoc.DocumentElement.ChildNodes(i))
        End Function
    End Class
End Namespace
```

Each time a random quotation is obtained, it is stored in a Quotation object. The listing for the Quotation class is as follows:

```
Imports System
Imports System.Xml

Namespace SherlockLib

    Public Class Quotation

        Private qsource As String
        Public Property Source() As String
            Get
                Return qsource
            End Get
            Set
                qsource = Value
            End Set
        End Property

        Private dteDate As String
        Public Property MyDate () As String
        Get
                Return dteDate
        End Get
            Set
                    dteDate = Value
            End Set
        End Property

        Private strQuotation As String
        Public Property QuotationText() As String
            Get
                    Return strQuotation
            End Get
            Set
                    strQuotation = Value
            End Set
        End Property

        Public Sub New(ByVal quoteNode As XmlNode)
          If quoteNode.SelectSingleNode("source") IsNot Nothing Then
            qsource = quoteNode.SelectSingleNode("source").InnerText
          End If
          If quoteNode.Attributes.GetNamedItem("date") IsNot Nothing Then
            dteDate = quoteNode.Attributes.GetNamedItem("date").Value
          End If
          strQuotation = quoteNode.FirstChild.InnerText
        End Sub
    End Class

End Namespace
```

Using a Component Through the App_Code Directory

The simplest way to quickly test this class is to copy the source code files to the App_Code subdirectory in a web application. You can take this step in Windows Explorer or use Visual Studio (Website ➤ Add Existing Item).

Now you might want to import the SherlockLib namespace in your web page to make its classes more readily available, as shown here:

```
Imports SherlockLib
```

Finally, you can use the class in your web-page code just as you would use a class from the .NET Framework. Here's an example that displays the quotation information on a web page:

```
Protected Sub Page_Load(ByVal sender As Object, ByVal e As System.EventArgs)
    ' Put user code to initialize the page here.
    Dim quotes As New SherlockQuotes(Server.MapPath("./sherlock-holmes.xml"))
    Dim quote As Quotation = quotes.GetRandomQuote()
    Response.Write("<b>" & quote.Source & "</b> (<i>" & quote.Date & "</i>)")
    Response.Write("<blockquote>" & quote.QuotationText & "</blockquote>")
End Sub
```

When you run this application, you'll see something like what's shown in Figure 5-8. Every time you refresh the page, you'll see a different quote.

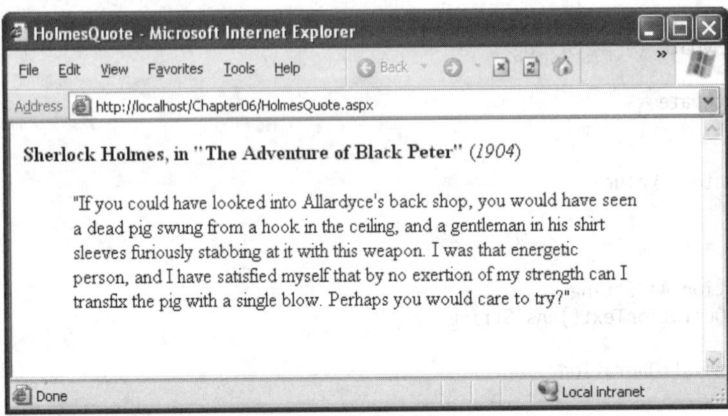

Figure 5-8. *Using the component in your web page*

■ **Note** When you use the App_Code directory, you face another limitation—you can use only one language. This limitation results from the way that ASP.NET performs its dynamic compilation. Essentially, all the classes in the App_Code directory are compiled into a single directory, so you can't mix C# and VB.

Using a Component Through the Bin Directory

Assuming your component provides a significant piece of functionality and that it may be reused in different applications, you'll probably want to create it using a separate project. This way, your component can be reused, tested, and versioned separately from the web application.

To create a separate component, you need to use Visual Studio to create a class library project. Although you can create this using a separate instance of Visual Studio, it's often easier to load both your class library project and your web application into Visual Studio at once to assist in debugging. This allows you to easily modify both the web application and the component code at the same time and single-step from a web-page event handler into a method in your component. To set this up, create your web application first. Then, select File ➤ Add ➤ New Project, and select the Class Library project type (see Figure 5-9). Notice that when you create a class library project, you don't specify a virtual directory. Instead, you choose a physical directory on your local hard drive where the source files will be stored.

■**Note** If you are using the scaled-down version of Visual Studio known as Visual Web Developer 2005 Express Edition, you won't be able to create class library projects. Your only alternative is to use the App_Code approach or build the class library with another version of Visual Studio.

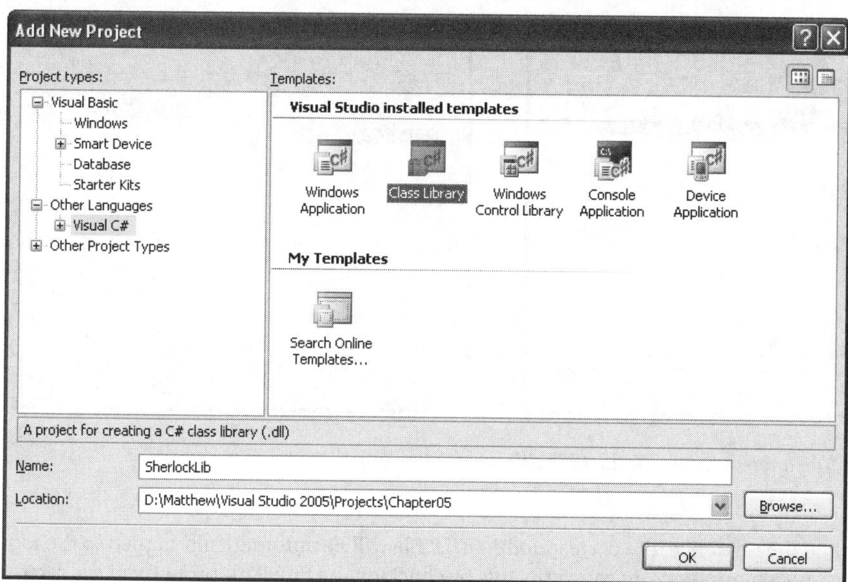

Figure 5-9. *Adding a class library project to a solution*

Once you've added the code to your class library project, you can compile your component by right-clicking the project in the Solution Explorer and choosing Build. This generates a DLL assembly that contains all the component classes.

To allow your web application to use this component, you need to add an assembly reference to the component. This allows Visual Studio to provide its usual syntax checking and IntelliSense. Otherwise, it will interpret your attempts to use the class as mistakes and refuse to compile your code.

To add a reference, choose Website ➤ Add Reference from your web application. The Add Reference dialog box includes several tabs:

.NET: This allows you to add a reference to a .NET assembly. You can choose from the list of well-known assemblies that are stored in the registry. Typically, you'll use this tab to add a reference to an assembly that's included as part of the .NET Framework.

COM: This allows you to add a reference to a legacy COM component. You can choose from a list of shared components that are installed in the Windows system directory. When you add a reference to a COM component, .NET automatically creates an intermediary wrapper class known as an *interop assembly*. You use the interop assembly in your .NET code, and the interop assembly interacts with the legacy component.

Projects: This allows you to add a reference to a .NET class library project that's currently loaded in Visual Studio. Visual Studio automatically shows a list of eligible projects. This is often the easiest way to add a reference to one of your own custom components.

Browse: This allows you to hunt for a compiled .NET assembly file (or a COM component) on your computer. This is a good approach for testing custom components if you don't have the source project or you don't want to load it into Visual Studio where you might inadvertently modify it.

Figure 5-10 compares two ways to add a reference to the SherlockLib component—by adding a reference to a currently loaded project and by adding a reference to the compiled DLL file.

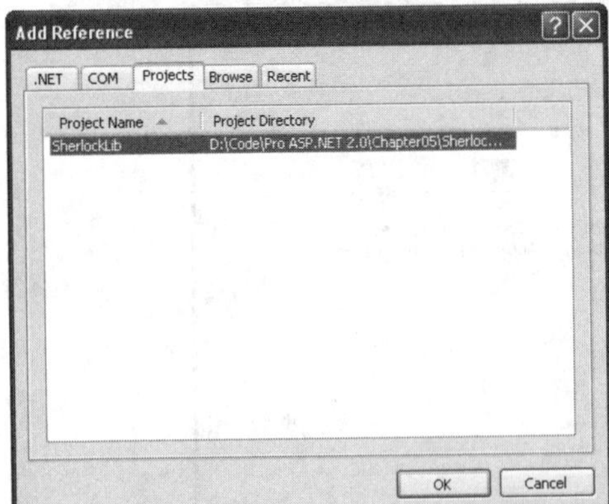

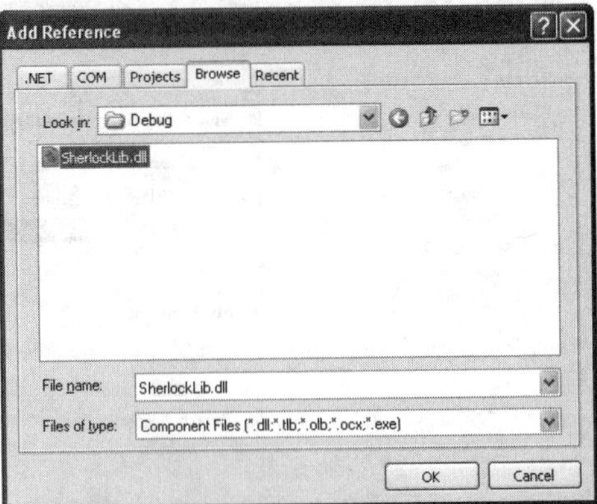

Figure 5-10. *Adding a reference to SherlockLib.dll*

Once you add the reference, the corresponding DLL file will be automatically copied to the Bin directory of your current project. You can verify this by checking the Full Path property of the reference in the Properties window or just by browsing to the directory in Windows Explorer. The nice thing is that this file will automatically be overwritten with the most recent compiled version of the assembly every time you run the web application.

It really is that easy. To use another component—either from your own business tier, from a third-party developer, or from somewhere else—all you need to do is add a reference to that assembly.

■ **Tip** ASP.NET also allows you to use assemblies with custom controls just as easily as you use assemblies with custom components. This allows you to bundle reusable user interface output and functionality into self-contained packages so that they can be used over and over again within the same or multiple applications. Part 4 has more information about this technique.

Extending the HTTP Pipeline

As explained earlier, the pipeline of application events isn't limited to requests for .aspx web forms. It also applies if you request web services or even create your own handlers to deal with custom file types.

Why would you want to create your own handler? For the most part, you won't. However, sometimes it's convenient to use a lower-level interface that still provides access to useful objects such as Response and Request but doesn't use the full control-based web form model. One example is if you want to create a web resource that dynamically renders a custom graphic (a technique demonstrated in Chapter 29). In this situation, you simply need to receive a request, check the URL parameters, and then return raw image data as a JPEG or GIF file. By avoiding the full web control model, you save some overhead, because ASP.NET does not need to go through as many steps (such as creating the web-page objects, persisting view state, and so on).

ASP.NET makes scenarios like these remarkably easy through its pluggable architecture. You can "snap in" new handlers for specialized file types just by adding configuration settings. But first, you need to take a closer look at the HTTP pipeline.

HTTP Handlers and HTTP Modules

Every request into an ASP.NET application is handled by a specialized component known as an *HTTP handler*. The HTTP handler is the backbone of the ASP.NET request-processing framework. ASP.NET uses different HTTP handlers to serve different file types. For example, the handler for web pages creates the page and control objects, runs your code, and renders the final HTML. The handler for web services has a slightly simpler task—it simply deserializes the SOAP message and invokes the corresponding code.

All HTTP handlers are defined in the <httpHandlers> section of a configuration file. The core set of HTTP handlers is defined in the root web.config file. Here's an excerpt of that file:

```
<httpHandlers>
    <add verb="*" path="trace.axd" type="System.Web.Handlers.TraceHandler"/>
    <add verb="*" path="*.config" type="System.Web.HttpForbiddenHandler"/>
    <add verb="*" path="*.vb" type="System.Web.HttpForbiddenHandler"/>
    <add verb="*" path="*.aspx" type="System.Web.UI.PageHandlerFactory"/>
    ...
</httpHandlers>
```

Inside the <httpHandlers> section you can place <add> elements that register new handlers and <remove> elements to unregister existing handlers. In this example, four classes are registered. All requests for trace.axd are handed to the TraceHandler, which renders an HTML page with a list of all the recently collected trace output (as described in Chapter 3). Requests for files that end in .config or .vb are handled by the HttpForbiddenHandler, which always generates an exception informing the user that these file types are never served. And files ending in .aspx are handled by the PageHandlerFactory. In this case, PageHandlerFactory isn't actually an HTTP handler. Instead, it's a factory class that will create the appropriate HTTP handler. This extra layer allows the factory to create a different handler or configure the handler differently depending on other information about the request.

ASP.NET also uses another ingredient in page processing, called *HTTP modules*. HTTP modules participate in the processing of a request by handling application events, much like the global.asax file. A given request can flow through multiple HTTP modules, but it always ends with a single HTTP handler. Figure 5-11 shows how the two interact.

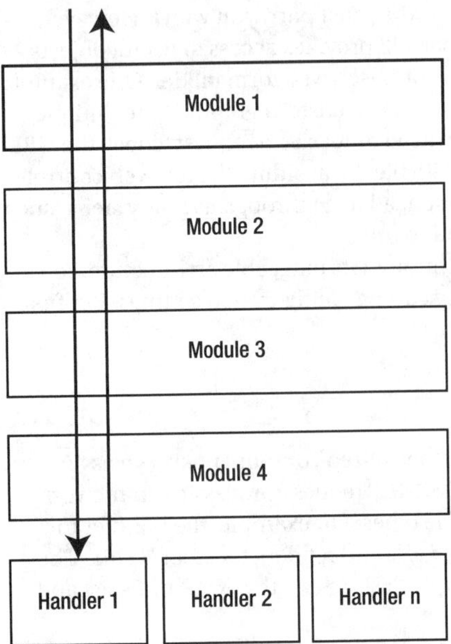

Figure 5-11. *The ASP.NET request-processing architecture*

ASP.NET uses a core set of HTTP modules to enable platform features such as caching, authentication, and error pages. You can add or remove HTTP modules with <add> and <remove> tags in the <httpModules> section of a configuration file. Here's an excerpt showing some of the HTTP modules that are defined in the machine.config file:

```
<httpModules>
    <add name="OutputCache" type="System.Web.Caching.OutputCacheModule"/>
    <add name="Session" type="System.Web.SessionState.SessionStateModule"/>
    <add name="WindowsAuthentication"
         type="System.Web.Security.WindowsAuthenticationModule"/>
    <add name="FormsAuthentication"
         type="System.Web.Security.FormsAuthenticationModule"/>
    ...
</httpModules>
```

One of the benefits of HTTP modules and HTTP handlers is that they provide an extensible architecture that allows you to easily plug in your own handlers and modules. In the past, developers who need these sort of features were forced to author their own ISAPI extensions (which play the same role as HTTP handlers) or ISAPI filters (which play the same role as HTTP modules). Both of these components are dramatically more complex to create.

■ **Note** ISAPI extensions and filters plug directly into IIS. HTTP handlers and modules play the same role, but they plug into ASP.NET. For example, imagine you create and register a custom HTTP handler. When the client issues a request for that file type, it will flow first from IIS to ASP.NET (through the ASP.NET ISAPI extension). Then ASP.NET will create and execute your handler. As a result, your handlers and modules never interact with IIS.

Creating a Custom HTTP Handler

If you want to work at a lower level than the web form model to support a specialized form of processing, you can implement your own HTTP handler.

To create a custom HTTP handler, you simply need to author a class that implements the IHttpHandler interface. You can place this class in the App_Code directory, or you can compile it as part of a stand-alone DLL assembly (in other words, a separate class library project). If you use the second approach, you need to add a reference to the project (as described earlier in this chapter). This step instructs Visual Studio to copy the compiled assembly into the Bin directory.

The IHttpHandler requires your class to implement two members, which are shown in Table 5-4.

Table 5-4. *IHttpHandler Members*

Member	Description
ProcessRequest()	ASP.NET calls this method when a request is received. It's where the HTTP handlers perform all the processing. You can access the intrinsic ASP.NET objects (such as Request, Response, and Server) through the HttpContext object that's passed to this method.
IsReusable	After ProcessRequest() finishes its work, ASP.NET checks this property to determine whether a given instance of an HTTP handler can be reused. If you return True, the HTTP handler object can be reused for another request of the same type current. If you return False, the HTTP handler object will simply be discarded.

The following code shows one of the simplest possible HTTP handlers you can create. It simply returns a fixed block of HTML with a message.

```
Imports System
Imports System.Web

Namespace HttpExtensions

    Public Class SimpleHandler
            Implements IHttpHandler

        Public Sub ProcessRequest(ByVal context As System.Web.HttpContext)
          Implements IHttpHandler.ProcessRequest
            Dim response As HttpResponse = context.Response
            response.Write("<html><body><h1>Rendered by the SimpleHandler")
            response.Write("</h1></body></html>")
        End Sub

        Public ReadOnly Property IsReusable() As Boolean
            Implements IHttpHandler.IsReusable
            Get
                    Return True
            End Get
        End Property

    End Class

End Namespace
```

■ **Note** If you create this extension as a class library project, you'll need to add a reference to the System.Web.dll assembly, which contains the bulk of the ASP.NET classes. Without this reference, you won't be able to use types such as IHttpHandler and HttpContext. (To add the reference, right-click the project name in the Solution Explorer, choose Add Reference, and find the assembly in the list in the .NET tab.)

Configuring a Custom HTTP Handler

Once you've created your HTTP handler class and made it available to your web application (either by placing it in the App_Code directory or by adding a reference), you're ready to use your extension. The next step is to alter the web.config file for the web application so that it registers your HTTP handler. Here's an example:

```
<httpHandlers>
    <add verb="*" path="test.simple"
         type="HttpExtensions.SimpleHandler,HttpExtensions" />
</httpHandlers>
```

When you register an HTTP handler, you specify three important details. The verb attribute indicates whether the request is an HTTP POST or HTTP GET request (use * for all requests). The path attribute indicates the file extension that will invoke the HTTP handler. In this example, the web.config section links the SimpleHandler class to the filename test.simple. Finally, the type attribute identifies the HTTP handler class. This identification consists of two portions. First is the fully qualified class name (in this example, HttpExtensions.SimpleHandler). That portion is followed by a comma and the name of the DLL assembly that contains the class (in this example, HttpExtensions.dll). Note that the .dll extension is always assumed, and you don't include it in the name.

If you're using the App_Code approach instead of a separately compiled assembly, you can omit the DLL name entirely, because ASP.NET generates it automatically.

```
<httpHandlers>
    <add verb="*" path="test.simple"
         type="HttpExtensions.SimpleHandler" />
</httpHandlers>
```

Visual Studio doesn't allow you to launch your HTTP handler directly. Instead, you need to run your web project and then type in a URL that includes test.simple. For example, if your web application URL is set to `http://localhost:19209/Chapter05` in the local server, you need to manually change it to `http://localhost:19209/Chapter05/test.simple`. You'll see the HTML shown in Figure 5-12.

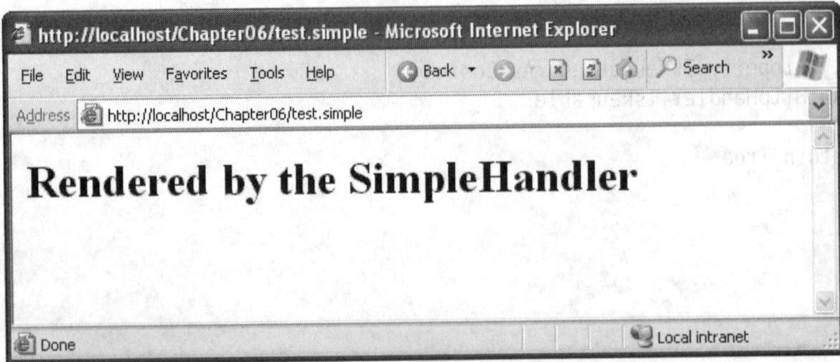

Figure 5-12. *Running a custom HTTP handler*

Using a custom HTTP handler isn't as convenient when you deploy your web application to an IIS web server. The problem is that the .simple extension won't be recognized by IIS. This means that by default it's handled by IIS on its own, not by ASP.NET. IIS simply checks for a file with that name, and if it exists, IIS returns the raw data from the file. If it doesn't, IIS returns an error message. To change this behavior, you need to add an IIS file mapping for your application that explicitly tells IIS to send all .simple requests to ASP.NET. Chapter 18 walks you through the process.

Registering HTTP Handlers Without Configuring IIS

Instead of using a web.config or machine.config file, ASP.NET provides an alternate approach for registering HTTP handlers—you can use the recognized extension .ashx. All requests that end in .ashx are automatically recognized as requests for a custom HTTP handler.

To create an .ashx file in Visual Studio, select Website ➤ Add New Item and choose Generic Handler (see Figure 5-13).

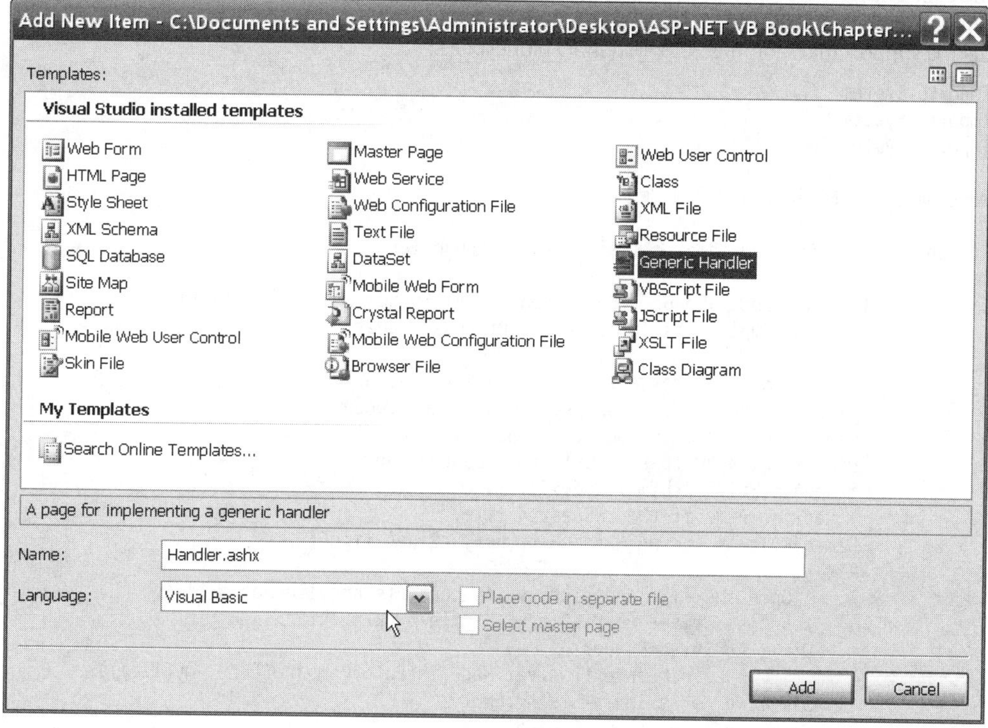

Figure 5-13. *Creating an .ashx file*

The .ashx file begins with a WebHandler directive. This WebHandler directive indicates the class that should be exposed through this file. Here's an example:

```
<%@ WebHandler Language="vb" Class="HttpExtensions.SimpleHandler" %>
```

The class name can correspond to a class in the App_Code directory or a class in a reference assembly. Alternatively, you can define the class directly in the .ashx file (underneath the WebHandler directive). Either way, when a client requests the .ashx file, the corresponding HTTP handler class is executed. If you save the previous example as the file simple.ashx, then whenever the client requests simple.ashx, your custom web handler will be executed. Best of all, the .ashx file type is registered in IIS, so you don't need to perform any IIS configuration when you deploy your application.

Whether you use a configuration file or an .ashx file is mostly a matter of preference. However, .ashx files are usually used for simpler extensions that are designed for a single web application. Configuration files also give you a little more flexibility. For example, you can register an HTTP handler to deal with all requests that end with a given extension, whereas an .ashx file only a request with a specific filename serves. Also, you can register an HTTP handler for multiple applications (by registering it in the web.config file and installing the assembly in the GAC). To achieve the same effect with an .ashx file, you need to copy the .ashx file to each virtual directory.

Creating an Advanced HTTP Handler

In the previous example, the HTTP handler simply returns a block of static HTML. However, you can create much more imaginative handlers. For example, you might read data that has been posted to the page or that has been supplied in the query string and use that to customize your rendered output. Here's a more sophisticated example that displays the source code for a requested file. It uses the file I/O support that's found in the System.IO namespace.

```
Imports System
Imports System.Web
Imports System.IO

Namespace HttpExtensions

    Public Class SourceHandler : Implements IHttpHandler

        Public Sub ProcessRequest(ByVal context As System.Web.HttpContext)
                Implements IHttpHandler.ProcessRequest

            ' Make the HTTP context objects easily available.
            Dim response As HttpResponse = context.Response
            Dim request As HttpRequest = context.Request
            Dim server As HttpServerUtility = context.Server
            response.Write("<html><body>")
            ' Get the name of the requested file.
            Dim myFile As String = request.QueryString("file")
            Try
                ' Open the file and display its contents one line at a time.
                response.Write("<b>Listing " & file & "</b><br />")
                Dim r As StreamReader =
                        File.OpenText(server.MapPath(Path.Combine("./", myFile)))
                Dim line As String = String.Empty
                Do While line IsNot Nothing
                    line = r.ReadLine()
                    If line IsNot Nothing Then
                        ' Make sure tags and other special characters are
                        ' replaced by their corresponding HTML entities so that
                        ' they can be displayed appropriately.
                        line = server.HtmlEncode(line)
                        ' Replace spaces and tabs with nonbreaking spaces
                        ' to preserve whitespace.
                        line = line.Replace(" ", " ")
```

```
                    line = line.Replace(Constants.vbTab,
                       "     ")
                    ' A more sophisticated source viewer might apply
                    ' color coding.
                    response.Write(line & "<br />")
                End If
            Loop
            r.Close()
        Catch err As Exception
            response.Write(err.Message)
        End Try
        response.Write("</html></body>")
    End Sub

    Public ReadOnly Property IsReusable() As Boolean
            Implements IHttpHandler.IsReusable
        Get
                Return True
        End Get
    End Property

  End Class

End Namespace
```

This code simply finds the requested file, reads its content, and uses a little string substitution (for example, replacing spaces with nonbreaking spaces and line breaks with the <br /> element) and HTML encoding to create a representation that can be safely displayed in a browser. You'll learn more about techniques for reading and manipulating files in Chapter 13.

Next, you can map the handler to a file extension, as follows:

```
<httpHandlers>
    <add verb="*" path="source.simple"
        type="HttpExtensions.SourceHandler,HttpExtensions"/>
</httpHandlers>
```

To test this handler, you can use a URL in this format:

```
http://localhost:[Port]/Chapter05/source.simple?file=HolmesQuote.aspx.vb
```

The HTTP handler will then show the source code for the .vb file, as shown in Figure 5-14.

Based on this example, you can probably imagine a variety of different ways you can use HTTP handlers. For example, you could render a custom image, perform an ad hoc database query, or return some binary data. These examples extend the ASP.NET architecture but bypass the web-page model. The result is a leaner, more efficient component.

You can also create HTTP handlers that work *asynchronously*. This means they create a new thread to do their work, instead of using one of the ASP.NET worker threads. This improves scalability in situations where you need to perform a task that takes a long amount of time but isn't CPU-intensive. A classic example is waiting to read an extremely slow network resource. ASP.NET allows a fixed set of worker threads to run only at one time (typically 25), so once this limit is reached additional requests will be queued, even if the computer has available CPU time. With asynchronous handlers, additional requests can be accepted, because the handler creates a new thread to process each request rather than using the worker process. Of course, there is a risk with this approach. Namely, if you create too many threads for the computer to manage efficiently, or if you try to do too much CPU-intensive work at once, the performance of the entire web server will be adversely affected. Asynchronous HTTP handlers are beyond the scope of this book, but you can read an excellent introduction from *MSDN Magazine* at `http://msdn.microsoft.com/msdnmag/issues/03/06/Threading`.

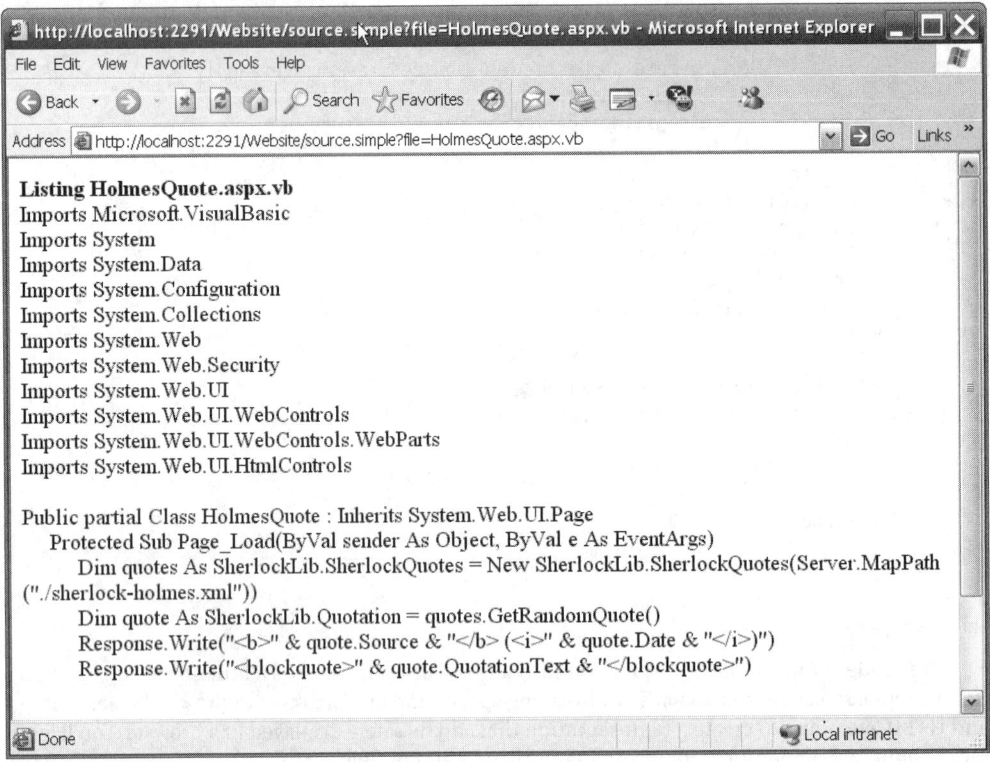

Figure 5-14. *Using a more sophisticated HTTP handler*

HTTP HANDLERS AND SESSION STATE

By default, HTTP handlers do not have access to client-specific session state. That's because HTTP handlers are generally used for lower-level tasks, and skipping the steps needed to serialize and retrieve session state information achieves a minor increase in performance. However, if you do need access to session state information, you simply need to implement one of the following two interfaces:

- IRequiresSessionState
- IReadOnlySessionState

If you require just read-only access to session state, you should implement the IRequiresSessionState interface. If you need to modify or add to session information, you should implement the IReadOnlySessionState interface. You should never implement both at the same time.

These two interfaces are just marker interfaces and do not contain any methods. That means you don't need to write any extra code to enable session support. For example, if you want to use read-only session state with the SimpleHandler class, you would declare it in this way:

```
Public Class SimpleHandler
    Implements IHttpHandler, IReadOnlySessionState
      ...
End Class
```

To actually access the Session object, you'll need to work through the HttpContext object that's submitted to the ProcessRequest() method. It provides a Session property.

Creating a Custom HTTP Module

It's just as easy to create custom HTTP modules as custom HTTP handlers. You simply need to author a class that implements the System.Web.IHttpModule interface. You can then register your module by adding it to the <httpModules> section of the web.config file. However, you don't need to configure IIS to use your HTTP modules. That's because modules are automatically used for every web request.

So, how does an HTTP module plug itself into the ASP.NET request-processing pipeline? It does so in the same way as the global.asax file. Essentially, when an HTTP module is created, it registers to receive specific global application events. For example, if the module is concerned with authentication, it will register itself to receive the authentication events. Whenever those events occur, ASP.NET invokes all the interested HTTP modules. The HTTP module wires up its events with delegate code in the Init() method.

The IHttpModule interface defines the two methods shown in Table 5-5.

Table 5-5. *IHttpModule Members*

Member	Description
Init()	This method allows an HTTP module to register its event handlers to receive the events of the HttpApplication object. This method provides the current HttpApplication object for the request as a parameter.
Dispose()	This method gives an HTTP module an opportunity to perform any cleanup before the object gets garbage collected.

The following class is a custom HTTP module that handles the event HttpApplication.AuthenticateRequest and then logs the user information to a new entry in the Windows event log using the EventLog class from the System.Diagnostics namespace. To use this example, the account used to run ASP.NET code must have permission to write to the event log.

```
Imports System
Imports System.Web
Imports System.Diagnostics

Namespace HttpExtensions
    Public Class LogUserModule
            Implements IHttpModule

        Public Sub Init(ByVal httpApp As HttpApplication)
                Implements IHttpModule.Init
            ' Attach application event handlers.
            AddHandler httpApp.AuthenticateRequest, AddressOf OnAuthentication
        End Sub

        Private Sub OnAuthentication(ByVal sender As Object, ByVal a As EventArgs)
            ' Get the current user identity.
            Dim name As String = HttpContext.Current.User.Identity.Name
            ' Log the user name.
            Dim log As New EventLog()
            log.Source = "Log User Module"
            log.WriteEntry(name & " was authenticated.")
        End Sub
```

```
        Public Sub Dispose() Implements IHttpModule.Dispose
        End Sub

    End Class

End Namespace
```

Now you can register the module with the following information in the web.config file. Here's an example that assumes it's compiled in a separated assembly named HttpExtensions.dll:

```
<httpModules>
    <add name="LogUserModule"
         type="HttpExtensions.LogUserModule,HttpExtensions" />
</httpModules>
```

To test this module, request any other page in the web application. Then check the entry in the Windows application event log. (To view the log, select Programs ➤ Administrative Tools ➤ Event Viewer from the Start menu.) Figure 5-15 shows the logged messages.

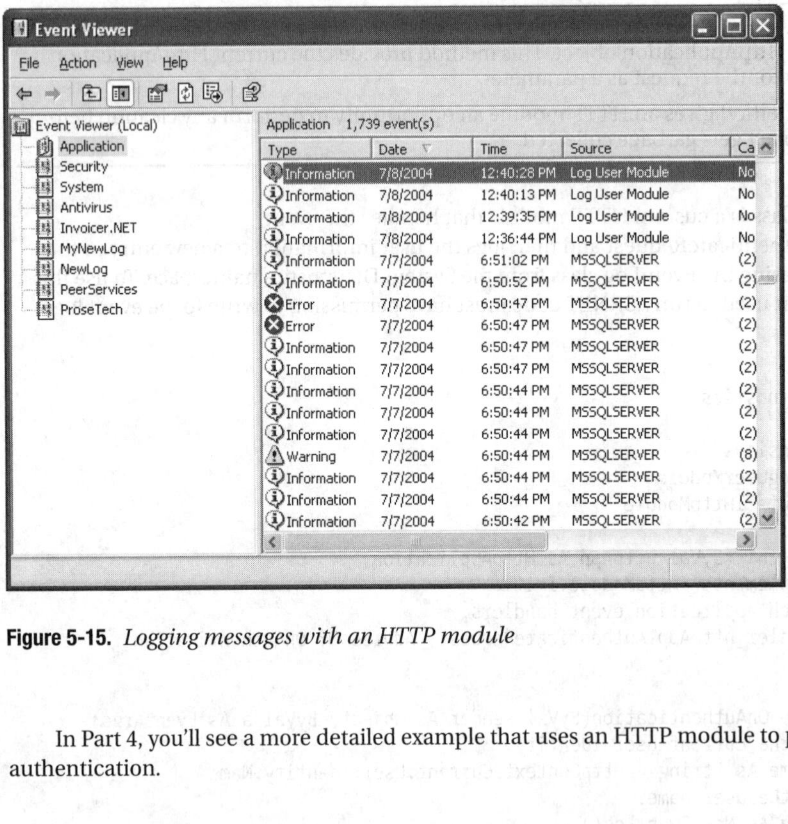

Figure 5-15. *Logging messages with an HTTP module*

In Part 4, you'll see a more detailed example that uses an HTTP module to perform custom authentication.

HANDLING EVENTS FROM OTHER MODULES

The previous example shows how you can handle application events in a custom HTTP module. However, some global events aren't provided by the HttpApplication class but are still quite important. These include events raised by other HTTP modules, such as the events fired to start and end a session.

Fortunately, you can wire up to these events in the Init() event; you just need a slightly different approach. The HttpApplication class provides a collection of all the modules that are a part of the current HTTP pipeline through the Modules collection. You can retrieve a module by name and then use delegate code to connect an event handler.

For example, if you want to connect an event handler named OnSessionStart() to the SessionStateModule.Start event, you could use code like this for the Init() method in your HTTP module:

```
Public Sub Init(ByVal httpApp As HttpApplication)
    Dim sessionMod As SessionStateModule = httpApp.Modules("Session")
    AddHandler sessionMod.Start, AddressOf OnSessionStart
End Sub
```

Summary

In this chapter, you took a closer look at what constitutes an ASP.NET application. After learning more about the life cycle of an application, you learned how to code global application event handlers with the global.asax file and how to set application configuration with the web.config file. Finally, you learned how to use separately compiled components in your web pages and how to extend the HTTP pipeline with your own handlers and modules.

CHAPTER 6

■ ■ ■

State Management

No web application framework, no matter how advanced, can change that HTTP is a stateless protocol. After every web request, the client disconnects from the server, and the ASP.NET engine discards the page objects. This architecture ensures that web applications can scale up to serve thousands of simultaneous requests without running out of server memory. The drawback is that your code needs to use other techniques to store information between web requests and retrieve it when needed.

In this chapter, you'll see how to tackle this challenge by maintaining information on the server and on the client using a variety of techniques. You'll also learn how to transfer information from one web page to another.

STATE MANAGEMENT CHANGES IN .NET 2.0

The standbys of state management remain the same in ASP.NET 2.0. That means the programming interface for session state, application state, view state, and the query string hasn't changed at all. However, session state now offers more configuration options, and you have a new way to transfer information between pages.

Here's a preview of the changes:

- *Cross-page postbacks*: In ASP.NET 1.*x*, a page could post only to itself. In ASP.NET 2.0, you can post from one page to another, transferring the page's state at the same time.
- *New session state settings*: Session state is now more configurable. You have options that allow you to use a custom SQL Server database (instead of one named ASPState), set timeouts, and configure how cookies are used and named.
- *Custom session state providers*: Microsoft has opened the session state model so that you can develop custom session state providers (and session ID providers) that store state in other data sources or generate session IDs using different algorithms.
- *Profiles*: Rather than coding your own database retrieval logic, you can use the new profile API to store user-specific information in a database. Best of all, this information is strongly typed, unlike session state. Profiles build on the ASP.NET authentication model.

Out of these four topics, you'll see only the first two in this chapter. Chapter 24 discusses profiles, because you need to use them in conjunction with Windows authentication or forms authentication. Custom session state providers are beyond the scope of this book. However, expect to see third-party session providers that allow you to use sessions with other relational databases.

ASP.NET State Management

ASP.NET includes a variety of options for state management. It features the same Session and Application state collections as traditional ASP (with a few enhancements) and an entirely new view state model. ASP.NET even includes a caching system that allows you to retain information without sacrificing server scalability. Each state management choice has a different lifetime, scope, performance overhead, and level of support.

Table 6-1, Table 6-2, and Table 6-3 show an at-a-glance comparison of your state management options.

Table 6-1. *State Management Options Compared (Part 1)*

	View State	Query String	Custom Cookies
Allowed Data Types	All serializable .NET data types.	A limited amount of string data.	String data.
Storage Location	A hidden field in the current web page.	The browser's URL string.	The client's computer (in memory or a small text file, depending on its lifetime settings).
Lifetime	Retained permanently for postbacks to a single page.	Lost when the user enters a new URL or closes the browser. However, can be stored in a bookmark.	Set by the programmer. It can be used in multiple pages and can persist between visits.
Scope	Limited to the current page.	Limited to the target page.	The whole ASP.NET application.
Security	By default it's insecure, although you can use Page directives to enforce encryption and hashing.	Clearly visible and easy for the user to modify.	Insecure and can be modified by the user.
Performance Implications	Storing a large amount of information will slow transmission but will not affect server performance.	None, because the amount of data is trivial.	None, because the amount of data is trivial.
Typical Use	Page-specific settings.	Sending a product ID from a catalog page to a details page.	Personalization preferences for a website.

Table 6-2. *State Management Options Compared (Part 2)*

	Session State	Application State
Allowed Data Types	All serializable .NET data types. Nonserializable types are supported if you are using the default in-process state service.	All .NET data types.
Storage Location	Server memory.	Server memory.
Lifetime	Times out after a predefined period (usually 20 minutes but can be altered globally or programmatically).	The lifetime of the application (typically, until the server is rebooted).
Scope	The whole ASP.NET application.	The whole ASP.NET application. Unlike most other types of methods, application data is global to all users.

	Session State	Application State
Security	Secure, because data is never transmitted to the client. However, subject to session hijacking if you don't use SSL.	Very secure, because data is never transmitted to the client.
Performance Implications	Storing a large amount of information can slow down the server severely, especially if there are a large number of users at once, because each user will have a separate copy of session data.	Storing a large amount of information can slow down the server, because this data will never time out and be removed.
Typical Use	Store items in a shopping basket.	Storing any type of global data.

Table 6-3. *State Management Options Compared (Part 3)*

	Profiles	Caching
Allowed Data Types	All serializable .NET data types. Nonserializable types are supported if you create a custom profile.	All .NET data types.
Storage Location	A back-end database.	Server memory.
Lifetime	Permanent.	Depends on the expiration policy you set but may possibly be released early if server memory becomes scarce.
Scope	The whole ASP.NET application. May also be accessed by other applications.	The same as application state (global to all users and all pages).
Security	Fairly secure, because although data is never transmitted, it is stored in a database that could be compromised.	Very secure, because data is never transmitted to the client.
Performance Implications	Large amounts of data can be stored easily, but there may be a nontrivial overhead in retrieving and writing the data for each request.	Storing a large amount of information may force out other, more useful cached information. However, ASP.NET has the ability to remove items early to ensure optimum performance.
Typical Use	Store customer account information.	Storing data retrieved from a database.

Clearly, there's no shortage of choices for managing state in ASP.NET! Fortunately, most of these state management systems expose a similar collection-based programming interface. The two exceptions are the query string (which is really a way of transferring information, not maintaining it) and profiles.

This chapter explores all the approaches to state management shown in Table 6-1 and Table 6-2 but not those in Table 6-3. Chapter 11 covers caching, an indispensable technique for optimizing access to limited resources such as databases. Chapter 24 covers profiles, a higher-level model for storing user-specific information that works in conjunction with ASP.NET authentication. However, before you can tackle either of these topics, you'll need to have a thorough understanding of state management basics.

In addition, you can always write your own custom state management code and use back-end server-side resources to store information. The most common example is one or more tables in a database. The drawback with using server-side resources is that they tend to slow down performance and can hurt scalability. For example, opening a connection to a database or reading information from a file takes time. In many cases, you can salvage these approaches by using caching to supplement your state management system. You'll explore your options for using and enhancing database access in Part 2.

View State

View state should be your first choice for storing information within the bounds of a single page. View state is used natively by the ASP.NET web controls. It allows them to retain their properties between postbacks. You can add your own data to the view state collection using a built-in page property called ViewState. The type of information you can store includes simple data types and your own custom objects.

Like most types of state management in ASP.NET, view state relies on a *dictionary collection*, where each item is indexed with a unique string name. For example, consider this code:

```
ViewState("Counter") = 1
```

This places the value 1 (or rather, an integer that contains the value 1) into the ViewState collection and gives it the descriptive name Counter. If there is currently no item with the name Counter, a new item will be added automatically. If there is already an item indexed under the name Counter, it will be replaced.

When retrieving a value, you use the key name. You also need to cast the retrieved value to the appropriate data type. This extra step is required because the ViewState collection stores all items as standard objects, which allows it to handle many different data types.

Here's the code that retrieves the counter from view state and converts it to an integer:

```
Dim counter As Integer
If ViewState("Counter") IsNot Nothing Then
    counter = CInt(ViewState("Counter"))
End If
```

If you attempt to look up a value that isn't present in the collection, you'll receive a NullReferenceException. To defend against this possibility, you should check for a null value before you attempt to retrieve and cast data that may not be present.

■**Note** ASP.NET provides many collections that use the same dictionary syntax. This includes the collections you'll use for session and application state as well as those used for caching and cookies. You'll see several of these collections in this chapter.

A View State Example

The following code demonstrates a page that uses view state. It allows the user to save a set of values (all the text that's displayed in all the text boxes of a table) and restore it later. This example uses recursive logic to dig through all child controls, and it uses the control ID for the view state key, because this is guaranteed to be unique in the page.

Here's the complete code:

```
Public partial Class ViewStateTest
        Inherits System.Web.UI.Page
    Protected Sub cmdSave_Click(ByVal sender As Object, ByVal e As System.EventArgs)
        ' Save the current text.
        SaveAllText(Page.Controls, True)
    End Sub

    Private Sub SaveAllText(ByVal controls As ControlCollection,
        ByVal saveNested As Boolean)
        For Each control As Control In controls
            If TypeOf control Is TextBox Then
                ' Store the text using the unique control ID.
                ViewState(control.ID) = (CType(control, TextBox)).Text
            End If

            If (control.Controls IsNot Nothing) AndAlso saveNested Then
                SaveAllText(control.Controls, True)
            End If
        Next control
    End Sub

    Protected Sub cmdRestore_Click(ByVal sender As Object,
        ByVal e As System.EventArgs)
        ' Retrieve the last saved text.
        RestoreAllText(Table1.Controls, True)
    End Sub

    Private Sub RestoreAllText(ByVal controls As ControlCollection,
        ByVal saveNested As Boolean)
        For Each control As Control In controls
            If TypeOf control Is TextBox Then
                If ViewState(control.ID) IsNot Nothing Then
                  CType(control, TextBox).Text = CStr(ViewState(control.ID))
                End If
            End If
            If (control.Controls IsNot Nothing) AndAlso saveNested Then
                RestoreAllText(control.Controls, True)
            End If
        Next control
    End Sub
End Class
```

Figure 6-1 shows the page in action.

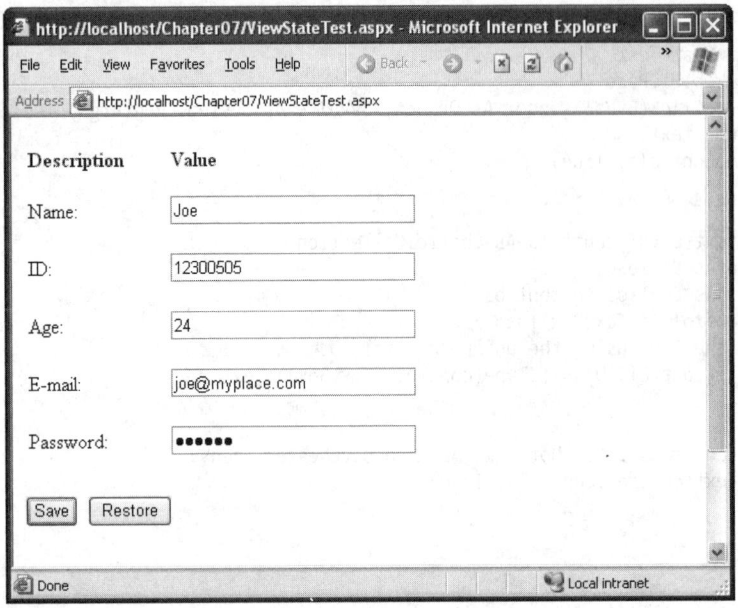

Figure 6-1. *Saving and restoring text using view state*

Storing Objects in View State

You can store your own objects in view state just as easily as you store numeric and string types. However, to store an item in view state, ASP.NET must be able to convert it into a stream of bytes so that it can be added to the hidden input field in the page. This process is called *serialization*. If your objects aren't serializable (and by default they aren't), you'll receive an error message when you attempt to place them in view state.

To make your objects serializable, you need to add the Serializable attribute before your class declaration. For example, here's an exceedingly simple Customer class:

```
<Serializable> _
Public Class Customer
    Public FirstName As String
    Public LastName As String

    Public Sub New(ByVal firstName As String, ByVal lastName As String)
        FirstName = firstName
        LastName = lastName
    End Sub
End Class
```

Because the Customer class is marked as serializable, it can be stored in view state:

```
' Store a customer in view state.
Dim cust New Customer("Marsala", "Simons")
ViewState("CurrentCustomer") = cust
```

Remember, when using custom objects, you'll need to cast your data when you retrieve it from view state.

```
' Retrieve a customer from view state.
Private cust As Customer
cust = CType(ViewState("CurrentCustomer"), Customer)
```

For your classes to be serializable, you must meet these requirements:

- Your class must have the Serializable attribute.
- Any classes it derives from must have the Serializable attribute.
- All the private variables of the class must be serializable data types. Any nonserializable data type must be decorated with the NonSerialized attribute (which means it is simply ignored during the serialization process).

Once you understand these principles, you'll also be able to determine what .NET objects can be placed in view state. You simply need to find the class information in the MSDN Help. Find the class you're interested in, and examine the documentation. If the class declaration is preceded with the Serializable attribute, the object can be placed in view state. If the Serializable attribute isn't present, the object isn't serializable, and you won't be able to store it in view state. However, you may still be able to use other types of state management, such as in-process session state, which is described later in the "Session State" section.

The following example rewrites the page shown earlier to use the Hashtable class. The Hashtable class is a serializable dictionary collection that's provided in the System.Collections namespace. Because it's serializable, it can be stored in view state without a hitch. To demonstrate this technique, the page stores all the control information for the page in the hashtable and then adds the hashtable to the view state for the page. When the user clicks the Display button, the hashtable is retrieved, and all the information it contains is displayed in a label.

```
Public partial Class ViewStateObjects
        Inherits System.Web.UI.Page
    ' This will be created at the beginning of each request.
    Private textToSave As New Hashtable()

    Protected Sub cmdSave_Click(ByVal sender As Object, ByVal e As System.EventArgs)
        ' Put the text in the Hashtable.
        SaveAllText(Table1.Controls, True)
        ' Store the entire collection in view state.
        ViewState("ControlText") = textToSave
    End Sub

    Private Sub SaveAllText(ByVal controls As ControlCollection,
        ByVal saveNested As Boolean)
        For Each control As Control In controls
            If TypeOf control Is TextBox Then
                ' Add the text to a collection.
                textToSave.Add(control.ID, (CType(control, TextBox)).Text)
            End If
            If (control.Controls IsNot Nothing) AndAlso saveNested Then
                SaveAllText(control.Controls, True)
            End If
        Next
    End Sub
```

```
    Protected Sub cmdDisplay_Click(ByVal sender As Object,
        ByVal e As System.EventArgs)
        If ViewState("ControlText") IsNot Nothing Then
            ' Retrieve the hashtable.
            Dim savedText As Hashtable = CType(ViewState("ControlText"), Hashtable)

            ' Display all the text by looping through the hashtable.
            lblResults.Text = String.Empty
            For Each item As DictionaryEntry In savedText
                lblResults.Text &= CStr(item.Key) & " = " _
                        & CStr(item.Value) & "<br />"
            Next
        End If
    End Sub
End Class
```

Figure 6-2 shows the result of a simple test, after entering some data, saving it, and retrieving it.

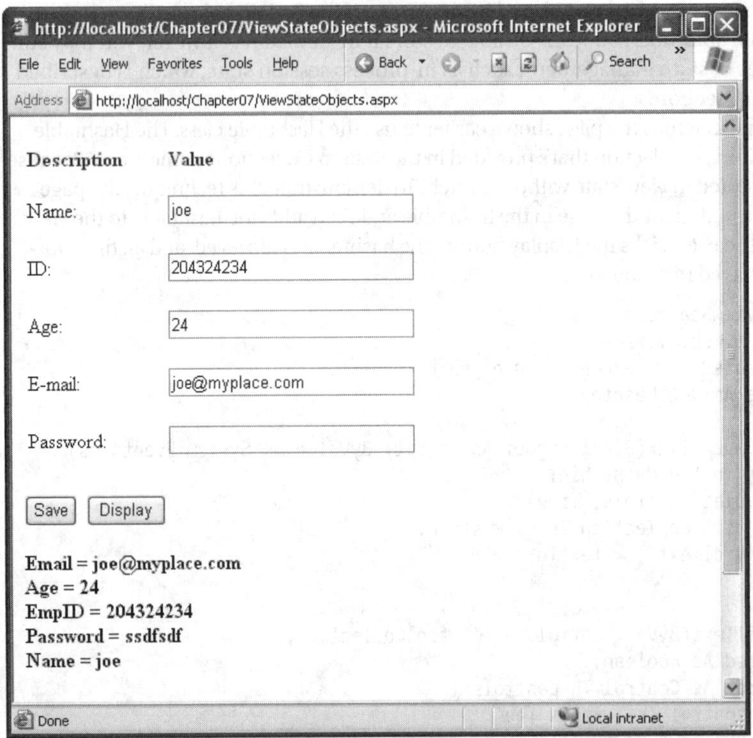

Figure 6-2. *Retrieving an object from view state*

Retaining Member Variables

Unlike control properties, member variables that you add to your web-page classes are never saved in view state. Interestingly, you can work around this limitation using view state.

You have two basic approaches. The first is to create a property procedure that wraps view state access. For example, in the previous web page you could provide the control text hashtable as a property like this:

```
Private Property ControlText() As Hashtable
    Get
        If ViewState("ControlText") IsNot Nothing Then
          Return CType(ViewState("ControlText"), Hashtable)
        Else
          Return New Hashtable()
        End If
    End Get
    Set
          ViewState("ControlText") = Value
    End Set
End Property
```

Now the rest of your page code can freely use the ControlText property, without worrying about how it's being retrieved.

The other approach is to save all your member variables to view state when the Page.PreRender event occurs and retrieve them when the Page.Load event occurs. That way, all your other event handlers can use the member variables normally.

Keep in mind when you use either of these techniques you must be careful not to store needless amounts of information. If you store unnecessary information in view state, it will enlarge the size of the final page output and can thus slow down page transmission times.

Assessing View State

View state is ideal because it doesn't take up any memory on the server and doesn't impose any arbitrary usage limits (such as a timeout). So, what might force you to abandon view state for another type of state management? Here are three possible reasons:

- You need to store mission-critical data that the user cannot be allowed to tamper with. (An ingenious user could modify the view state information in a postback request.) In this case, consider session state. Alternatively, consider using the countermeasures described in the next section. They aren't bulletproof, but they will *greatly* increase the effort an attacker would need in order to read or modify view state data.
- You need to store information that will be used by multiple pages. In this case, consider session state, cookies, or the query string.
- You need to store an extremely large amount of information, and you don't want to slow down page transmission times. In this case, consider using a database, or possibly session state.

The amount of space used by view state depends on the number of controls, their complexity, and the amount of dynamic information. If you want to profile the view state usage of a page, just turn on tracing by adding the Trace attribute to the Page directive, as shown here:

```
<%@ Page Language="vb" Trace="true" ... %>
```

Look for the Control Tree section. Although it doesn't provide the total view state used by the page, it does indicate the view state used by each individual control in the Viewstate Size Bytes column (see Figure 6-3). Don't worry about the Render Size Bytes column, which simply reflects the size of the rendered HTML for the control.

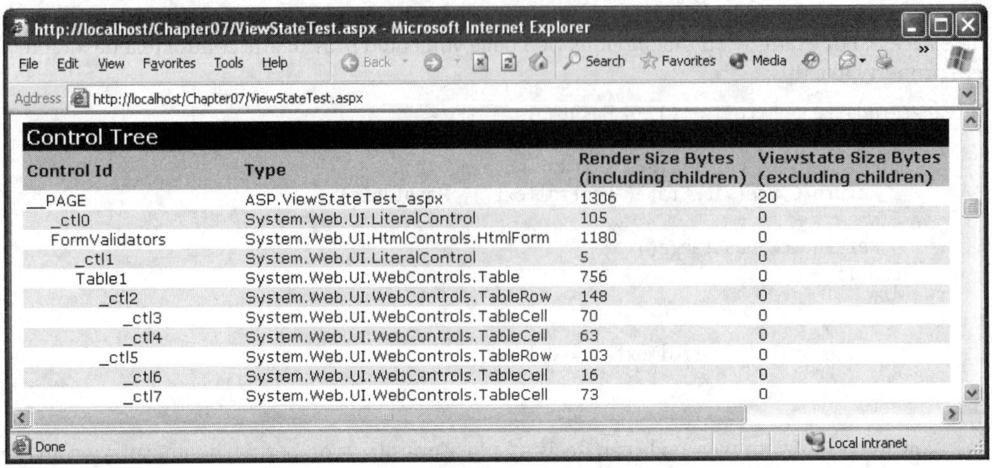
http://localhost/Chapter07/ViewStateTest.aspx - Microsoft Internet Explorer
File Edit View Favorites Tools Help
Back Search Favorites Media
Address http://localhost/Chapter07/ViewStateTest.aspx
Control Tree
Control Id | Type | Render Size Bytes (including children) | Viewstate Size Bytes (excluding children)
__PAGE | ASP.ViewStateTest_aspx | 1306 | 20
_ctl0 | System.Web.UI.LiteralControl | 105 | 0
FormValidators | System.Web.UI.HtmlControls.HtmlForm | 1180 | 0
_ctl1 | System.Web.UI.LiteralControl | 5 | 0
Table1 | System.Web.UI.WebControls.Table | 756 | 0
_ctl2 | System.Web.UI.WebControls.TableRow | 148 | 0
_ctl3 | System.Web.UI.WebControls.TableCell | 70 | 0
_ctl4 | System.Web.UI.WebControls.TableCell | 63 | 0
_ctl5 | System.Web.UI.WebControls.TableRow | 103 | 0
_ctl6 | System.Web.UI.WebControls.TableCell | 16 | 0
_ctl7 | System.Web.UI.WebControls.TableCell | 73 | 0
Done
Local intranet

Figure 6-3. *Determining the view state used in a page*

■Tip You can also examine the contents of the current view state of a page using the ASP.NET Development Helper described in Chapter 2.

To improve the transmission times of your page, it's a good idea to eliminate view state when it's not needed. Although you can disable view state at the application and page level, it makes most sense to disable it on a per-control basis. You won't need view state for a control in three instances:

- The control never changes. For example, a button with static text doesn't need view state.
- The control is repopulated in every postback. For example, if you have a label that shows the current time, and you set the current time in the Page.Load event handler, it doesn't need view state.
- The control is an input control, and it changes only because of user actions. After each postback, ASP.NET will populate your input controls using the submitted form values. This means the text in a text box or the selection in a list box won't be lost, even if you don't use view state.

■Tip Remember that view state applies to *all* the values that change, not just the text displayed in the control. For example, if you dynamically change the colors used in a label, you'll need to use view state even if you don't dynamically set the text. Technically, it's the control's responsibility to use view state, so it is possible to create a server control that doesn't retain certain values even if view state is enabled. This might be used to optimize performance in certain scenarios.

To turn off view state for a single control, set the EnableViewState property of the control to False. To turn off view state for an entire page and all its controls, set the EnableViewState property of the page to False, or use the EnableViewState attribute in the Page directive, as shown here:

```
<%@ Page Language="vb" EnableViewState="False" ... %>
```

Even when you disable view state for the entire page, you'll still see the hidden view state tag with a small amount of information. That's because ASP.NET always stores the control hierarchy for the page at a minimum, even if view state is disabled. There's no way to remove this last little fragment of data.

Trimming View State in a List Control

In some controls, disabling view state may break a feature on which you rely. Although the situation has improved with the creation of control state (a privileged section of view state used by the control, which you'll learn about in Chapter 27), some problems still remain. This is particularly the case with existing controls, which sometimes can't be updated to use control state without introducing behavior changes that could break existing ASP.NET 1.*x* pages.

One example is how list controls such as ListBox and DropDownList track selection. Imagine you create a page where you need to fill a drop-down list with hundreds of entries. If the list isn't expensive to create (for example, if you're retrieving it directly from memory or the cache), you might choose to disable view state for the list control and rebuild the list at the beginning of each postback. Here's an example that simply fills a list with numbers:

```
Protected Sub Page_Load(ByVal sender As Object, ByVal e As EventArgs)
    For i As Integer = 0 To 999
        lstBig.Items.Add(i.ToString())
    Next
End Sub
```

The problem this causes is that once you disable view state, you ensure that the user's list selection is lost every time the page is posted back. That means you won't be able to retrieve any information from the SelectedIndex or SelectedItem properties. Similarly, the SelectedIndexChanged won't fire.

You have one way to remedy this problem. Although the selection information is lost, the user's choice is actually still maintained in the Request.Forms collection (a collection of posted values that's present for backward compatibility with ASP pages). You can look up the selected value using the control name, and you can use code such as this to reset the proper selected index:

```
Protected Sub Page_Load(ByVal sender As Object, ByVal e As EventArgs)
    For i As Integer = 0 To 999
        lstBig.Items.Add(i.ToString())
    Next
    If Page.IsPostBack Then
        lstBig.SelectedItem.Text = Request.Form("lstBig")
    End If
End Sub
```

■ Note Clearly, this could represent a situation where you need to rethink your user interface to be more usable. For example, a better design might be to ask the user a preliminary question to narrow the number of list entries. You might even want to model the whole process with a Wizard control. But assuming you really do need a list with a huge number of entries, you'll need to understand how to optimize its view state usage.

View State Security

As described in earlier chapters, view state information is stored in a single Base64-encoded string that looks like this:

```
<input type="hidden" name="__VIEWSTATE" value="dDw3NDg2NTI5MDg7Oz4="/>
```

Because this value isn't formatted as clear text, many ASP.NET programmers assume that their view state data is encrypted. It isn't. A clever hacker could reverse-engineer this string and examine your view state data in a matter of seconds, as demonstrated in Chapter 3.

If you want to make view state secure, you have two choices. First, you can make sure that the view state information is tamper-proof by using a *hash code.*

You do this by adding the EnableViewStateMAC attribute to the Page directive in your .aspx file, as shown here:

```
<%@ Page EnableViewStateMAC="true" %>
```

A hash code is a cryptographically strong checksum. Essentially, ASP.NET calculates this checksum based on the current view state content and adds it to the hidden input field when it returns the page. When the page is posted back, ASP.NET recalculates the checksum and ensures that it matches. If a malicious user changes the view state data, ASP.NET will be able to detect the change, and it will reject the postback.

Hash codes are enabled by default, so if you want this functionality, you don't need to take any extra steps. Occasionally, developers choose to disable this feature to prevent problems in a web farm where different servers have different keys. (The problem occurs if the page is posted back and handled by a new server, which won't be able to verify the view state information.) To disable hash codes, you can use the EnableViewStateMac attribute of the <pages> element in the web.config or machine.config file, as shown here:

```
<configuration xmlns="http://schemas.microsoft.com/.NetConfiguration/v2.0">
  <system.web>
    <pages enableViewStateMac="False" />
    ...
  </system.web>
</configuration>
```

■ **Note** This step is strongly discouraged. It's much better to configure multiple servers to use the same key, thereby removing any problem. Chapter 5 describes how to do this.

Even when you use hash codes, the view state data will still be readable. To prevent users from getting any view state information, you can enable view state *encryption*. You can turn on encryption for an individual page using the ViewStateEncryptionMode property of the Page directive:

```
<%@Page ViewStateEncryptionMode="Always">
```

Or you can set the same attribute in the web.config configuration file:

```
<pages viewStateEncryptionMode="Always">
```

Either way, this enforces encryption. You have three choices for your view state encryption setting—always encrypt (Always), never encrypt (Never), or encrypt only if a control specifically requests it (Auto). The default is Auto, which means a control must call the Page.RegisterRequiresViewStateEncryption() method to request encryption. If no control calls this method to indicate it has sensitive information, the view state is not encrypted, thereby saving the encryption overhead. On the other hand, a control doesn't have absolute power—if it calls Page.RegisterRequiresViewStateEncryption() and the encryption mode is Never, the view state won't be encrypted.

When hashing or encrypting data, ASP.NET uses the computer-specific key defined in the <machineKey> section of the machine.config file, described in Chapter 5. By default, you won't actually see the definition for the <machineKey> because it's initialized programmatically. However, you can see the equivalent content in the machine.config.comments files, and you can explicitly add the <machineKey> element if you want to customize its settings.

■ **Tip** Don't encrypt view state data if you don't need to do so. The encryption will impose a performance penalty, because the web server needs to perform the encryption and decryption with each postback.

Transferring Information

One of the most significant limitations with view state is that it's tightly bound to a specific page. If the user navigates to another page, this information is lost. This problem has several solutions, and the best approach depends on your requirements.

The Query String

One common approach is to pass information using a query string in the URL. You will commonly find this approach in search engines. For example, if you perform a search on the Google website, you'll be redirected to a new URL that incorporates your search parameters. Here's an example:

```
http://www.google.ca/search?q=organic+gardening
```

The query string is the portion of the URL after the question mark. In this case, it defines a single variable named q, which contains the "organic+gardening" string.

The advantage of the query string is that it's lightweight and doesn't exert any kind of burden on the server. Unlike cross-page posting, the query string can easily transport the same information from page to page. It has some limitations, however:

- Information is limited to simple strings, which must contain URL-legal characters.
- Information is clearly visible to the user and to anyone else who cares to eavesdrop on the Internet.
- The enterprising user might decide to modify the query string and supply new values, which your program won't expect and can't protect against.
- Many browsers impose a limit on the length of a URL (usually from 1 to 2 KB). For that reason, you can't place a large amount of information in the query string and still be assured of compatibility with most browsers.

Adding information to the query string is still a useful technique. It's particularly well suited in database applications where you present the user with a list of items corresponding to records in a database, like products. The user can then select an item and be forwarded to another page with detailed information about the selected item. One easy way to implement this design is to have the first page send the item ID to the second page. The second page then looks that item up in the database and displays the detailed information. You'll notice this technique in e-commerce sites such as Amazon.com.

Using the Query String

To store information in the query string, you need to place it there yourself. Unfortunately, there is no collection-based way to do this. Typically, this means using a special HyperLink control, or you can use a Response.Redirect() statement like the one shown here:

```
' Go to newpage.aspx. Submit a single query string argument
' named recordID, and set to 10.
Dim recordID As Integer = 10
Response.Redirect("newpage.aspx?recordID=" & recordID.ToString())
```

You can send multiple parameters as long as you separate them with an ampersand (&), as shown here:

```
' Go to newpage.aspx. Submit two query string arguments:
' recordID (10) and mode (full).
Response.Redirect("newpage.aspx?recordID=10&mode=full")
```

The receiving page has an easier time working with the query string. It can receive the values from the QueryString dictionary collection exposed by the built-in Request object, as shown here:

```
Dim ID As String = Request.QueryString("recordID")
```

Note that information is always retrieved as a string, which can then be converted to another simple data type. Values in the QueryString collection are indexed by the variable name.

■Note Unfortunately, ASP.NET does not expose any mechanism to automatically verify or encrypt query string data. This facility could work in almost the same way as the view state protection. Without these features, query string data is easily subject to tampering. In Chapter 25, you'll take a closer look at the .NET cryptography classes and learn how you can use them to build a truly secure query string.

URL Encoding

One potential problem with the query string is using characters that aren't allowed in a URL. The list of characters that are allowed in a URL is much shorter than the list of allowed characters in an HTML document. All characters must be alphanumeric or one of a small set of special characters, including $-_.+!*'(),. Some browsers tolerate certain additional special characters (Internet Explorer is notoriously lax), but many do not.

If you're concerned that the data you want to store in the query string may not consist of URL-legal characters, you should use URL encoding. With URL encoding, special characters are replaced by escaped character sequences starting with the percent sign (%), followed by a two-digit hexadecimal representation. For example, the space becomes %20.

You can use the methods of the HttpServerUtility class to encode your data automatically. For example, the following shows how you would encode a string of arbitrary data for use in the query string. This replaces all the nonlegal characters with escaped character sequences.

```
Dim productName As String = "Flying Carpet"
Response.Redirect("newpage.aspx?productName=" & Server.UrlEncode(productName))
```

And here's how you could decode the same information:

```
Dim ID As String = Server.UrlDecode(Request.QueryString("recordID"))
```

Cross-Page Posting

One approach that's new in ASP.NET 2.0 is to trigger a postback to another page. This technique sounds conceptually straightforward, but it's a potential minefield, and if you're not careful, it can lead you to create pages that are tightly coupled to one another and difficult to enhance and debug.

The infrastructure that supports cross-page postbacks is a new property named PostBackUrl, which is defined by the IButtonControl interface and turns up in button controls such as ImageButton, LinkButton, and Button. To use cross-posting, you simply set PostBackUrl to the name of another web form. When the user clicks the button, the page will be posted to that new URL with the values from all the input controls on the current page.

Here's an example that defines a form with two text boxes and a button that posts to a page named CrossPage2.aspx:

```
<%@ Page Language="vb" AutoEventWireup="true" CodeFile="CrossPage1.aspx.vb"
    Inherits="CrossPage1" %>
<html>
<head runat="server">
    <title>CrossPage1</title>
</head>
<body>
    <form id="form1" runat="server" >
      <div>
            <asp:TextBox runat="server" ID="txtFirstName"></asp:TextBox>  
            <asp:TextBox runat="server" ID="txtLastName"></asp:TextBox>
            <asp:Button runat="server" ID="cmdSubmit"
            PostBackUrl="CrossPage2.aspx" Text="Submit" />
      </div>
    </form>
</body>
</html>
```

In CrossPage2.aspx, the page can interact with the CrossPage1.aspx objects using the Page.PreviousPage property. Here's an example:

```
Protected Sub Page_Load(ByVal sender As Object, ByVal e As EventArgs)
    If PreviousPage IsNot Nothing Then
        lblInfo.Text = "You came from a page titled " & PreviousPage.Header.Title
    End If
End Sub
```

Note that this page checks for a null reference (Nothing in Visual Basic) before attempting to access the PreviousPage object. If no PreviousPage object exists, then no cross-page postback exists.

ASP.NET uses some interesting sleight of hand to make this system work. The first time the second page accesses Page.PreviousPage, ASP.NET needs to create the previous page object. To do this, it actually starts the page processing but interrupts it just before the PreRender stage. Along the way, a stand-in Response object is created to silently catch and ignore any Response.Write() commands from the previous page. However, you still get some interesting side effects. For example, all the page events of the previous page are fired, including Page.Load, Page.Init, and even the Button.Click event, for the button that triggered the postback (if it's defined). Firing these events is mandatory, because they are required to properly initialize the page. Trace messages aren't ignored like Response messages are, which means you may see tracing information from both pages in a cross-posting situation.

Getting Page-Specific Information

In the previous example, the information you can retrieve from the previous page is limited to the members of the Page class. If you want to get more specific details, such as control values, you need to cast the PreviousPage reference to the appropriate type.

Here's an example that handles this situation properly, by checking first if the PreviousPage object is an instance of the expected source (CrossPage1):

```
Protected Sub Page_Load(ByVal sender As Object, ByVal e As EventArgs)
    If PreviousPage IsNot Nothing Then
        If TypeOf(PreviousPage) Is CrossPage1 Then
            ' (Read some information from the previous page.)
        End If
    End If
End Sub
```

You can solve this problem in another way. Rather than casting the reference manually, you can add the PreviousPageType control directive to your page, which indicates the expected type of the page initiating the cross-page postback. Here's an example:

```
<%@ PreviousPageType VirtualPath="CrossPage1.aspx" %>
```

However, this approach is more fragile because it limits you to a single type. You don't have the flexibility to deal with situations where more than one page might trigger a cross-page postback. For that reason, the casting approach is preferred.

■ **Tip** Seeing as the PostBackUrl property can point to only one page, it may seem that cross-page posting can accommodate a fixed relationship between just two pages. However, you can extend this relationship with various techniques. For example, you can modify the PostBackUrl property programmatically to choose a different target. Conversely, a cross-post target can test the PreviousPage property, checking if it is one of several different classes. You can then perform different tasks depending on what page initiated the cross-post.

Once you've cast the previous page to the appropriate page type, you still won't be able to directly access the control values. That's because the controls are declared as protected members. You can handle this by adding properties to the page class that wrap the control variables, like this:

```
Public ReadOnly Property FirstNameTextBox() As TextBox
    Get
            Return txtFirstName
    End Get
End Property
Public ReadOnly Property LastNameTextBox() As TextBox
    Get
            Return txtLastName
    End Get
End Property
```

However, this usually isn't the best approach. The problem is that it exposes too many details, giving the target page the freedom to read every control property. If you need to change the page later to use different input controls, it's difficult to maintain these properties. Instead, you'll probably be forced to rewrite code in both pages.

A better choice is to define specific, limited methods that extract just the information you need. Here's an example:

```
Public Function GetFullName() As String
            Return txtFirstName.Text & " " &  txtLastName.Text
End Function
```

This way, the relationship between the two pages is well documented and easily understood. If the controls in the source page change, you can probably still keep the same interface for the public methods. For example, if you changed the name entry to use different controls in the previous example, you would still be forced to revise the GetFullName() method. However, once your changes are confined to CrossPage1.aspx, you don't need to modify CrossPage2.aspx at all.

■ **Tip** In many cases, a better alternative to cross-page posting is to use some sort of control that simulates multiple pages or multiple steps, such as separate Panel controls or the MultiView or Wizard control. This offers much the same user experience and simplifies the coding model.

Performing Cross-Page Posting in Any Event Handler

As you learned in the previous section, cross-page posting is available only with controls that implement the IButtonControl interface. However, you can work around this limitation. You can use an overloaded method of Server.Transfer() to switch to a new ASP.NET page with the view state information left intact. You simply need to include the Boolean preserveForm parameter and set it to True, as shown here:

```
Server.Transfer("CrossPage2.aspx", True)
```

This gives you the opportunity to use cross-page posting anywhere in your web-page code.

Interestingly, you can distinguish between a cross-page post that's initiated directly through a button and the Server.Transfer() method. Although in both cases you can access Page.PreviousPage, if you use Server.Transfer(), the Page.PreviousPage.IsCrossPagePostBack property is False. Here's the pseudocode that explains it:

```
If PreviousPage Is Nothing Then
    ' The page was requested (or posted back) directly.
Else If PreviousPage.IsCrossPagePostBack Then
    ' A cross-page postback through a button.
Else
    ' A stateful transfer through Server.Transfer().
End If
```

Cross-Page Posting and Validation

Cross-page posting introduces a few wrinkles when you use it in conjunction with the validator controls described in Chapter 4. As you learned in Chapter 4, when you use the validator controls, you need to check the Page.IsValid property to ensure that the data the user entered is correct. Although users are usually prevented from posting invalid pages back to the server (thanks to some slick client-side JavaScript), this isn't always the case. For example, the client browser might not support JavaScript, or a malicious user could deliberately circumvent the client-side validation checks.

When you use validation in a cross-page posting scenario, the potential for some trouble exists. Namely, what happens if you use a cross-page postback and the source page has validation controls? Figure 6-4 shows an example with a RequiredFieldValidator that requires input in a text box.

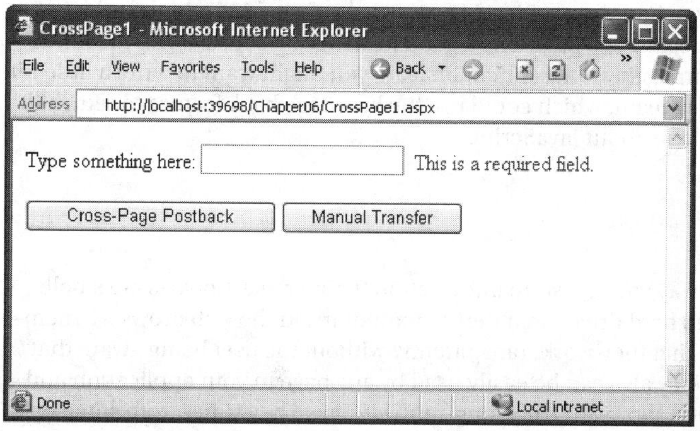

Figure 6-4. *Using a validator in a page that cross-posts*

If you click one of the buttons to perform the cross-page postback (both of which have CausesValidation set to True), you'll be prevented by the browser's client-side checks. Instead, the error message will appear. However, you should also check what happens when client-side scripting isn't supported by setting the RequiredFieldValidator.EnableClientScript property to False. (You can change it back to True once you perfect your code.) Now when you click one of the buttons, the page is posted back, and the new page appears.

To prevent this from happening, you obviously need to check the validity of the source page in the target page before you perform any other action by examining Page.IsValid. This is the standard line of defense used in any web form that employs validation. The difference is that if the page isn't valid, it's not sufficient to do nothing. Instead, you need to take the extra step of returning the user to the original page. Here's the code you need:

```
Protected Sub Page_Load(ByVal sender As Object, ByVal e As EventArgs)
    If PreviousPage IsNot Nothing Then
        If (Not PreviousPage.IsValid) Then
            ' Display an error message or just do nothing.
        Else
            ...
        End If
    End If
End Sub
```

It's still possible to improve on this code. Currently, when the user is returned to the original page, the error message won't appear, because the page is being re-requested (not posted back). To correct this issue, you can set a flag to let the source page know the target page has refused the page. Here's an example that adds this flag to the query string:

```
If (Not PreviousPage.IsValid) Then
    Response.Redirect(Request.UrlReferrer.AbsolutePath & "?err=true")
End If
```

Now the original page simply needs to check for the presence of this query string value and perform the validation accordingly. The validation causes error messages to appear for any invalid data:

```
Protected Sub Page_Load(ByVal sender As Object, ByVal e As EventArgs)
    If Request.QueryString("err") IsNot Nothing Then
      Page.Validate()
    End If
End Sub
```

You could do still more to try to improve the page. For example, if the user is in the midst of filling out a detailed form, re-requesting the page isn't a good idea, because it clears all the input controls and forces the user to start again from scratch. Instead, you might want to write a little bit of JavaScript code to the response stream, which could use the browser's back feature to return to the source page. Chapter 29 has more about JavaScript.

Custom Cookies

Custom cookies provide another way you can store information for later use. Cookies are small files that are created on the client's hard drive (or, if they're temporary, in the web browser's memory). One advantage of cookies is that they work transparently without the user being aware that information needs to be stored. They also can be easily used by any page in your application and even retained between visits, which allows for truly long-term storage. They suffer from some of the same drawbacks that affect query strings. Namely, they're limited to simple string information, and they're easily accessible and readable if the user finds and opens the corresponding file. These factors make them a poor choice for complex or private information or large amounts of data.

Some users disable cookies on their browsers, which will cause problems for web applications that require them. For the most part, cookies are widely adopted because so many sites use them. However, they can limit your potential audience, and they aren't suited for the embedded browsers used with mobile devices.

Before you can use cookies, you should import the System.Net namespace so you can easily work with the appropriate types, as shown here:

```
Imports System.Net
```

Cookies are fairly easy to use. Both the Request and Response objects (which are provided through Page properties) provide a Cookies collection. The important trick to remember is that you retrieve cookies from the Request object, and you set cookies using the Response object.

To set a cookie, just create a new System.Net. HttpCookie object. You can then fill it with string information (using the familiar dictionary pattern) and attach it to the current web response, as follows:

```
' Create the cookie object.
Dim cookie As New HttpCookie("Preferences")

' Set a value in it.
cookie("LanguagePref") = "English"

' Add it to the current web response.
Response.Cookies.Add(cookie)
```

A cookie added in this way will persist until the user closes the browser and will be sent with every request. To create a longer-lived cookie, you can set an expiration date, as shown here:

```
' This cookie lives for one year.
cookie.Expires = DateTime.Now.AddYears(1)
```

Cookies are retrieved by cookie name using the Request.Cookies collection, as shown here:

```
Dim  cookie As HttpCookie = Request.Cookies("Preferences")

' Check to see whether a cookie was found with this name.
' This is a good precaution to take,
' because the user could disable cookies,
' in which case the cookie will not exist.
Dim language As String
If cookie Is Not Nothing Then
    language = cookie("LanguagePref")
End If
```

The only way to remove a cookie is by replacing it with a cookie that has an expiration date that has already passed. The following code demonstrates this technique:

```
Dim cookie As New HttpCookie("LanguagePref")
cookie.Expires = DateTime.Now.AddDays(-1)
Response.Cookies.Add(cookie)
```

■ **Note** You'll find that some other ASP.NET features use cookies. Two examples are session state (which allows you to temporarily store user-specific information in server memory) and forms security (which allows you to restrict portions of a website and force users to access it through a login page).

Session State

Session state is the heavyweight of state management. It allows information to be stored in one page and accessed in another, and it supports any type of object, including your own custom data types. Best of all, session state uses the same collection syntax as view state. The only difference is the name of the built-in page property, which is Session.

Every client that accesses the application has a different session and a distinct collection of information. Session state is ideal for storing information such as the items in the current user's shopping basket when the user browses from one page to another. But session state doesn't come for free. Though it solves many of the problems associated with other forms of state management, it forces the web server to store additional information in memory. This extra memory requirement, even if it is small, can quickly grow to performance-destroying levels as hundreds or thousands of clients access the site.

Session Architecture

Session management is not part of the HTTP standard. As a result, ASP.NET needs to do some extra work to track session information and bind it to the appropriate response.

ASP.NET tracks each session using a unique 120-bit identifier. ASP.NET uses a proprietary algorithm to generate this value, thereby guaranteeing (statistically speaking) that the number is unique and that it's random enough so a malicious user can't reverse-engineer or guess what session ID a given client will be using. This ID is the only piece of information that is transmitted between the web server and the client. When the client presents the session ID, ASP.NET looks up the corresponding session, retrieves the serialized data from the state server, converts it to live objects, and places these objects into a special collection so they can be accessed in code. This process takes place automatically.

■ **Note** Every time you make a new request, ASP.NET generates a new session ID until you actually use session state to store some information. This behavior achieves a slight performance enhancement—in short, why bother to save the session ID if it's not being used?

At this point you're probably wondering where ASP.NET stores session information and how it serializes and deserializes it. In classic ASP, the session state is implemented as a free-threaded COM object that's contained in the asp.dll library. In ASP.NET, the programming interface is nearly identical, but the underlying implementation is quite a bit different.

As you saw in Chapter 5, when ASP.NET handles an HTTP request, it flows through a pipeline of different modules that can react to application events. One of the modules in this chain is the SessionStateModule (in the System.Web.SessionState namespace). The SessionStateModule generates the session ID, retrieves the session data from external state providers, and binds the data to the call context of the request. It also saves the session state information when the page is finished processing. However, it's important to realize that the SessionStateModule doesn't actually *store* the session data. Instead, the session state is persisted in external components, which are named *state providers*. Figure 6-5 shows this interaction.

Session state is another example of ASP.NET's pluggable architecture. A state provider is any class that implements the IStateClientManager interface, which means you can customize how session state works simply by building (or purchasing) a new .NET component. ASP.NET includes three prebuilt state providers, which allow you to store information in process, in a separate service, or in a SQL Server database.

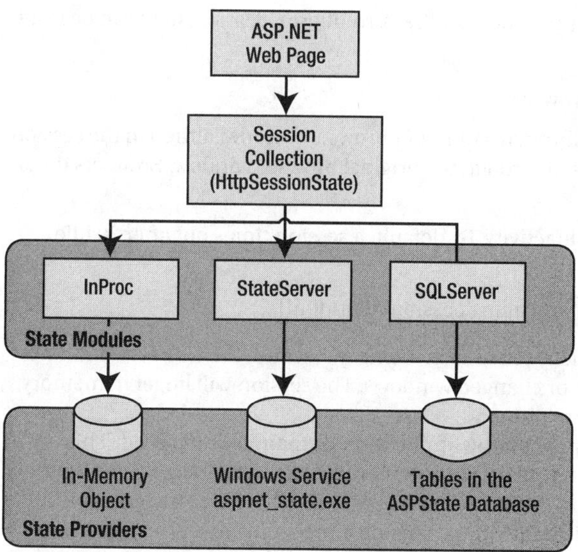

Figure 6-5. *ASP.NET session state architecture*

The final ingredient in the puzzle is how the cookie is tracked from one request to the next. For session state to work, the client needs to present the appropriate session ID with each request. You can accomplish this in two ways:

Using cookies: In this case, the session ID is transmitted in a special cookie (named ASP.NET_SessionId), which ASP.NET creates automatically when the session collection is used. This is the default, and it's also the same approach that was used in earlier versions of ASP.

Using modified URLs: In this case, the session ID is transmitted in a specially modified (or "munged") URL. This is a new feature in ASP.NET that allows you to create applications that use session state with clients that don't support cookies.

You'll learn more about how to configure cookieless sessions and different session state providers later in the "Configuring Session State" section.

Using Session State

You can interact with session state using the System.Web.SessionState.HttpSessionState class, which is provided in an ASP.NET web page as the built-in Session object. The syntax for adding items to the collection and retrieving them is basically the same as for adding items to the view state of a page.

For example, you might store a DataSet in session memory like this:

```
Session("ds") = ds
```

You can then retrieve it with an appropriate conversion operation:

```
ds = Ctype(Session("ds"),DataSet)
```

Session state is global to your entire application for the current user. Session state can be lost in several ways:

- If the user closes and restarts the browser.
- If the user accesses the same page through a different browser window, although the session will still exist if a web page is accessed through the original browser window. Browsers differ on how they handle this situation.
- If the session times out because of inactivity. By default, a session times out after 20 idle minutes.
- If the programmer ends the session by calling Session.Abandon().

In the first two cases, the session actually remains in memory, because the web server has no idea that the client has closed the browser or changed windows. The session will linger in memory, remaining inaccessible, until it eventually expires.

In addition, session state will be lost when the application domain is re-created. This process happens transparently when you update your web application or change a configuration setting. The application domain may also be recycled periodically to ensure application health, as described in Chapter 18. If this behavior is causing a problem, you can store session state information out of process, as described in the next section. With out-of-process state storage, the session information is retained even when the application domain is shut down.

Table 6-4 describes the methods and properties of the HttpSessionState class.

Table 6-4. *HttpSessionState Members*

Member	Description
Count	The number of items in the current session collection.
IsCookielessSession	Identifies whether this session is tracked with a cookie or with modified URLs.
IsNewSession	Identifies whether this session was just created for the current request. If there is currently no information in session state, ASP.NET won't bother to track the session or create a session cookie. Instead, the session will be re-created with every request.
Mode	Provides an enumerated value that explains how ASP.NET stores session state information. This storage mode is determined based on the web.config configuration settings discussed later in this chapter.
SessionID	Provides a string with the unique session identifier for the current client.
StaticObjects	Provides a collection of read-only session items that were declared by <object runat=server> tags in the global.asax. Generally, this technique isn't used and is a holdover from ASP programming that is included for backward compatibility.
Timeout	The current number of minutes that must elapse before the current session will be abandoned, provided that no more requests are received from the client. This value can be changed programmatically, giving you the chance to make the session collection longer term when required for more important operations.
Abandon()	Cancels the current session immediately and releases all the memory it occupied. This is a useful technique in a logoff page to ensure that server memory is reclaimed as quickly as possible.
Clear()	Removes all the session items but doesn't change the current session identifier.

Configuring Session State

You can configure session state through the <sessionState> element in the web.config file for your application. Here's a snapshot of all the available settings you can use:

```
<?xml version="1.0" encoding="utf-8" ?>
<configuration>
    <system.web>
        <!-- Other settings omitted. -->

        <sessionState
            mode="InProc"
            stateConnectionString="tcpip=127.0.0.1:42424" stateNetworkTimeout="10"
            sqlConnectionString="data source=127.0.0.1;Integrated Security=SSPI"
            sqlCommandTimeout="30" allowCustomSqlDatabase="False"
            useHostingIdentity="true"
            cookieless="UseCookies" cookieName="ASP.NET_SessionId"
            regenerateExpiredSessionId="False"
            timeout="20"
            customProvider=""
        />
    </system.web>
</configuration>
```

The session attributes are described in the following sections.

Mode

The mode session state settings allow you to configure what session state provider is used to store session state information between requests. The following sections explain your options.

Off

This setting disables session state management for every page in the application. This can provide a slight performance improvement for websites that are not using session state.

InProc

InProc is similar to how session state was stored in classic ASP. It instructs ASP.NET to store information in the current application domain. This provides the best performance but the least durability. If you restart your server, the state information will be lost.

InProc is the default option, and it makes sense for most small websites. In a web farm scenario, though, it won't work. To allow session state to be shared between servers, you must use the out-of-process or SQL Server state service. Another reason you might want to avoid InProc mode is because it makes for more fragile sessions. In ASP.NET, application domains are recycled in response to a variety of actions, including configuration changes, updated pages, and when certain thresholds are met (regardless of whether an error has occurred). If you find that your application domain is being restarted frequently and contributing to prematurely lost sessions, you can try to counter the effect by changing some of the process model settings (see Chapter 18), or you can change to one of the more robust session state providers.

Before you use either the out-of-process or the SQL Server state service, keep in mind that more considerations will apply:

- When using the StateServer or SqlServer mode, the objects you store in session state must be serializable. Otherwise, ASP.NET will not be able to transmit the object to the state service or store it in the database.
- If you're hosting ASP.NET on a web farm, you'll also need to take some extra configuration steps to make sure all the web servers are in sync. Otherwise, one might encode information in session state differently than another, which will cause a problem if the user is routed from one server to another during a session. The solution is to modify the <machineKey> section of the machine.config file so it's consistent across all servers. For more information, refer to Chapter 5.
- If you aren't using the in-process state provider, the SessionStateModule.End event won't be fired, and any event handlers for this event in the global.asax file or an HTTP module will be ignored.

StateServer

With this setting, ASP.NET will use a separate Windows service for state management. Even if you run this service on the same web server, it will be loaded outside the main ASP.NET process, which gives it a basic level of protection if the ASP.NET process needs to be restarted. The cost is the increased time delay imposed when state information is transferred between two processes. If you frequently access and change state information, this can make for a fairly unwelcome slowdown.

When using the StateServer setting, you need to specify a value for the stateConnectionString setting. This string identifies the TCP/IP address of the computer that is running the StateServer service and its port number (which is defined by ASP.NET and doesn't usually need to be changed). This allows you to host the StateServer on another computer. If you don't change this setting, the local server will be used (set as address 127.0.0.1).

Of course, before your application can use the service, you need to start it. The easiest way to do this is to use the Microsoft Management Console. Select Start ➤ Programs ➤ Administrative Tools ➤ Computer Management (you can also access the Administrative Tools group through the Control Panel). Then select the Services and Applications ➤ Services node. Find the service called ASP.NET State in the list, as shown in Figure 6-6.

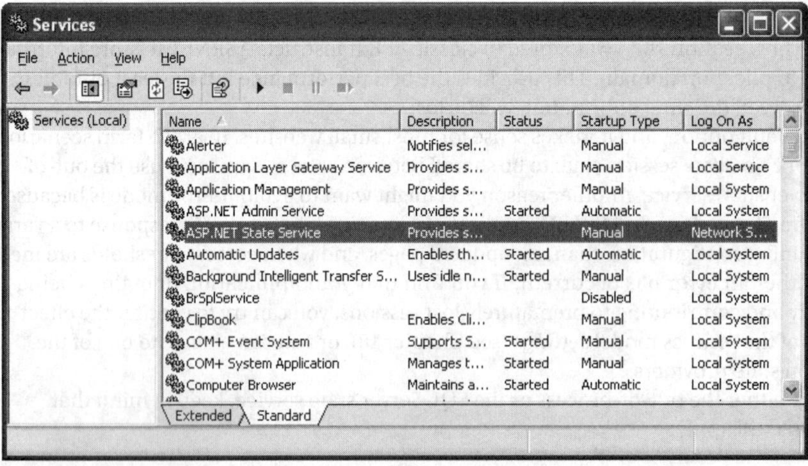

Figure 6-6. *The ASP.NET state service*

Once you find the service in the list, you can manually start and stop it by right-clicking it. Generally, you'll want to configure Windows to automatically start the service. Right-click it, select Properties, and modify the Startup Type setting to Automatic, as shown in Figure 6-7.

Figure 6-7. *Service properties*

■ **Note** When using StateServer mode, you can also set an optional stateNetworkTimeout attribute that specifies the maximum number of seconds to wait for the service to respond before canceling the request. The default is ten seconds.

SQL Server

This setting instructs ASP.NET to use an SQL Server database to store session information, as identified by the sqlConnectionString attribute. This is the most resilient state store but also the slowest by far. To use this method of state management, you'll need to have a server with SQL Server installed.

When setting the sqlConnectionString, you follow the same sort of pattern you use with ADO.NET data access (which is described in Part 2). Generally, you'll need to specify a data source (the server address) and a user ID and password, unless you're using SQL integrated security.

In addition, you need to install the special stored procedures and temporary session databases. These stored procedures take care of storing and retrieving the session information. ASP.NET includes a Transact-SQL script for this purpose called InstallSqlState.sql. It's found in the c:\[WinDir]\Microsoft.NET\Framework\[Version] directory. You can run this script using an SQL Server utility such as OSQL.exe or Query Analyzer. It needs to be performed only once. If you decide to change your state service, you can use UninstallSqlState.sql to remove the state tables.

The session state timeout still applies for SQL Server state management. That's because the InstallSqlState.sql script also creates a new SQL Server job named ASPState_Job_DeleteExpiredSessions. As long as the SQLServerAgent service is running, this job will be executed every minute.

Additionally, the state tables will be removed every time you restart SQL Server, no matter what the session timeout. That's because when you use InstallSqlState, the state tables are created in the tempdb database, which is a temporary storage area. If this isn't the behavior you want, you can use the InstallPersistSqlState.sql and UninstallPersistSqlState.sql scripts instead of InstallSqlState.sql and UninstallSqlState.sql. In this case, the state tables are created in the ASPState database and are permanent.

Ordinarily, the state database is always named ASPState. As a result, the connection string in the web.config file doesn't explicitly indicate the database name. Instead, it simply reflects the location of the server and the type of authentication that will be used:

```
<sessionState sqlConnectionString="data source=127.0.0.1;Integrated Security=SSPI"
... />
```

If you want to use a different database (with the same structure), simply set allowCustomSqlDatabase to True, and make sure the connection string includes the Initial Catalog setting, which indicates the name of the database you want to use:

```
<sessionState allowCustomSqlDatabase="False" sqlConnectionString=
"data source=127.0.0.1;Integrated Security=SSPI;Initial Catalog=CustDatabase"
... />
```

When using the SqlServer mode, you can also set an optional sqlCommandTimeout attribute that specifies the maximum number of seconds to wait for the database to respond before canceling the request. The default is 30 seconds.

Custom

When using custom mode, you need to indicate what session state store provider to use by supplying the customProvider attribute. The customProvider attribute points to the name of a class that's part of your web application in the App_Code directory or in a compiled assembly in the Bin directory or the GAC.

Creating a custom state provider is a low-level task that needs to be handled carefully to ensure security, stability, and scalability. Custom state providers are also beyond the scope of this book. However, if you'd like to try creating your own, you can find a sample at `http://weblogs.asp.net/ngur/articles/371952.aspx`.

Cookieless

You can set the cookieless setting to one of the values defined by the HttpCookieMode enumeration, as described in Table 6-5.

Table 6-5. *HttpCookieMode Values*

Value	Description
UseCookies	Cookies are always used, even if the browser or device doesn't support cookies or they are disabled. This is default. If the device does not support cookies, session information will be lost over subsequent requests, because each request will get a new ID.
UseUri	Cookies are never used, regardless of the capabilities of the browser or device. Instead, the session ID is stored in the URL.

Value	Description
UseDeviceProfile	ASP.NET chooses whether to use cookieless sessions by examining the BrowserCapabilities object. The drawback is that this object indicates what the device should support—it doesn't take into account that the user may have disabled cookies in a browser that supports them. Chapter 27 has more information about how ASP.NET identifies different browsers and decides whether they support features such as cookies.
AutoDetect	ASP.NET attempts to determine whether the browser supports cookies by attempting to set and retrieve a cookie (a technique commonly used on the Web). This technique can correctly determine whether a browser supports cookies but has them disabled, in which case cookieless mode is used instead.

Here's an example that forces cookieless mode (which is useful for testing):

```
<sessionState cookieless="UseUri" ... />
```

In cookieless mode, the session ID will automatically be inserted into the URL. When ASP.NET receives a request, it will remove the ID, retrieve the session collection, and forward the request to the appropriate directory. A munged URL is shown here:

```
http://localhost/WebApplication/(amfvyc55evojk455cffbq355)/Page1.aspx
```

Because the session ID is inserted in the current URL, relative links also automatically gain the session ID. In other words, if the user is currently stationed on Page1.aspx and clicks a relative link to Page2.aspx, the relative link includes the current session ID as part of the URL. The same is true if you call Response.Redirect() with a relative URL, as shown here:

```
Response.Redirect("Page2.aspx");
```

The only real limitation of cookieless state is that you cannot use absolute links, because they will not contain the session ID. For example, this statement causes the user to lose all session information:

```
Response.Redirect("http://localhost/WebApplication/Page2.aspx");
```

By default, ASP.NET allows you to reuse a session identifier. For example, if you make a request and your query string contains an expired session, ASP.NET creates a new session and uses that session ID. The problem is that a session ID might inadvertently appear in a public place—such as in a results page in a search engine. This could lead to multiple users accessing the server with the same session identifier and then all joining the same session with the same shared data.

To avoid this potential security risk, it's recommended that you include the optional regenerateExpiredSessionId attribute and set it to True whenever you use cookieless sessions. This way, a new session ID will be issued if a user connects with an expired session ID. The only drawback is that this process also forces the current page to lose all view state and form data, because ASP.NET performs a redirect to make sure the browser has a new session identifier.

Tip You can test whether a cookieless session is currently being used by checking the IsCookielessSession property of the Session object.

Timeout

Another important session state setting in the web.config file is the timeout. This specifies the number of minutes that ASP.NET will wait, without receiving a request, before it abandons the session.

```
<sessionState timeout="20" ... />
```

This setting represents one of the most important compromises of session state. A difference of minutes can have a dramatic effect on the load of your server and the performance of your application. Ideally, you will choose a time frame that is short enough to allow the server to reclaim valuable memory after a client stops using the application but long enough to allow a client to pause and continue a session without losing it.

You can also programmatically change the session timeout in code. For example, if you know a session contains an unusually large amount of information, you may need to limit the amount of time the session can be stored. You would then warn the user and change the timeout property. Here's a sample line of code that changes the timeout to ten minutes:

```
Session.Timeout = 10
```

Securing Session State

The information is session state is very secure, because it is stored exclusively on the server. However, the cookie with the session ID can easily become compromised. This means an eavesdropper could steal the cookie and assume the session on another computer.

Several workarounds address this problem. One common approach is to use a custom session module that checks for changes in the client's IP address (see `http://msdn.microsoft.com/msdnmag/issues/04/08/WickedCode` for a sample implementation). However, the only truly secure approach is to restrict session cookies to portions of your website that use SSL. That way, the session cookie is encrypted and useless on other computers.

If you choose to use this approach, it also makes sense to mark the session cookie as a secure cookie so that it will be sent *only* over SSL connections. That prevents the user from changing the URL from `https://` to `http://`, which would send the cookie without SSL. Here's the code you need:

```
Request.Cookies("ASP.NET_SessionId").Secure = True
```

Typically, you'll use this code immediately after the user is authenticated. Make sure at least one piece of information appears in session state so the session isn't abandoned (and then re-created later).

Another related security risk exists with cookieless sessions. Even if the session ID is encrypted, a clever user could use a social-engineering attack to trick a user into joining a specific session. All the malicious user needs to do is feed the user a URL with a valid session ID. When the user clicks the link, they join that session. Although the session ID is protected from this point onward, the attacker now knows what session ID is in use and can hijack the session at a later time.

Taking certain steps can reduce the likelihood of this attack. First, when using cookieless sessions, always regenerate ExpiredSessionId to True. This prevents the attacker from supplying a session ID that's expired. Next, explicitly abandon the current session before logging in a new user.

Application State

Application state allows you to store global objects that can be accessed by any client. Application state is based on the System.Web.HttpApplicationState class, which is provided in all web pages through the built-in Application object.

Application state is similar to session state. It supports the same type of objects, retains information on the server, and uses the same dictionary-based syntax. A common example with application state is a global counter that tracks how many times an operation has been performed by all of the web application's clients.

For example, you could create a global.asax event handler that tracks how many sessions have been created or how many requests have been received into the application. Or you can use similar logic in the Page.Load event handler to track how many times a given page has been requested by various clients. Here's an example of the latter:

```
Protected Sub Page_Load(ByVal sender As Object, ByVal e As EventArgs)
    Dim count As Integer = CInt(Application("HitCounterForOrderPage"))
    count += 1
    Application("HitCounterForOrderPage") = count
    lblCounter.Text = count.ToString()
End Sub
```

Once again, application state items are stored as objects, so you need to cast them when you retrieve them from the collection. Items in application state never time out. They last until the application or server is restarted or until the application domain refreshes itself (because of automatic process-recycling settings or an update to one of the pages or components in the application).

Application state isn't often used, because it's generally inefficient. In the previous example, the counter would probably not keep an accurate count, particularly in times of heavy traffic. For example, if two clients requested the page at the same time, you could have a sequence of events like this:

1. User A retrieves the current count (432).
2. User B retrieves the current count (432).
3. User A sets the current count to 433.
4. User B sets the current count to 433.

In other words, one request isn't counted because two clients access the counter at the same time. To prevent this problem, you need to use the Lock() and Unlock() methods, which explicitly allow only one client to access the Application state collection at a time, as follows:

```
Protected Sub Page_Load(ByVal sender As Object, ByVal e As EventArgs)
    ' Acquire exclusive access.
    Application.Lock()

    Dim count As Integer = CInt(Application("HitCounterForOrderPage"))
    count += 1
    Application("HitCounterForOrderPage") = count

    ' Release exclusive access.
    Application.Unlock()

    lblCounter.Text = count.ToString()
End Sub
```

Unfortunately, all other clients requesting the page will now be stalled until the Application collection is released. This can drastically reduce performance. Generally, frequently modified values are poor candidates for application state. In fact, application state is rarely used in the .NET world because its two most common uses have been replaced by easier, more efficient methods:

- In the past, application state was used to store application-wide constants, such as a database connection string. As you saw in Chapter 5, this type of constant can now be stored in the web.config file, which is generally more flexible because you can change it easily without needing to hunt through web-page code or recompile your application.
- Application state can also be used to store frequently used information that is time-consuming to create, such as a full product catalog that requires a database lookup. However, using application state to store this kind of information raises all sorts of problems about how to check if the data is valid and how to replace it when needed. It can also hamper performance if the product catalog is too large. A similar but much more sensible approach is to store frequently used information in the ASP.NET cache. Many uses of application state can be replaced more efficiently with caching.

Application state information is always stored in process. This means you can use any .NET data types. However, it also introduces the same two limitations that affect in-process session state. Namely, you can't share application state between the servers in a web farm, and you will always lose your application state information when the application domain is restarted—an event that can occur as part of ASP.NET's normal housekeeping.

■ **Note** Application state is included primarily for backward compatibility with classic ASP. In new applications, it's almost always better to rely on other mechanisms for global data, such as using databases in conjunction with the Cache object.

Shared Application Variables

You can store global application variables in one other way. You can add Shared member variables to the global.asax file (which was introduced in Chapter 5). These members are then compiled into the custom HttpApplication class for your web application and made available to all pages. Here's an example:

```
Public Shared fileList as String()
```

The key detail that allows this to work is that the variable is Shared. That's because ASP.NET creates a pool of HttpApplication classes to serve multiple requests. As a result, each request might be served with a different HttpApplication object, and each HttpApplication object has its own instance data. However, only one copy of the shared data exists, which is shared for all instances.

Another requirement is that you must supply the ClassName attribute in the Application directive. This assigns a name to the global application class, which you'll need to use to retrieve the Shared value you've just created.

Of course, for the best encapsulation (and the most flexibility), you should use property procedures:

```
Private Shared strFileListAs String()
Public Shared ReadOnly Property FileList() As String()
    Get
            Return strFileList
    End Get
End Property
```

When you add a member variable to the global.asax file, it has essentially the same characteristics as a value in the Application collection. In other words, you can use any .NET data type, the value is retained until the application domain is restarted, and state isn't shared across computers in a web farm. However, there's no automatic locking. Because multiple clients might try to access or modify a value at the same time, you should use the SyncLock statement to temporarily restrict the variable to a single thread. Depending on how your data is accessed, you might perform the locking in the web page (in which case you could perform several tasks at once with the locked data) or in the property procedures or methods in the global.asax file (in which case the lock would be held for the shortest possible time). Here's an example of property procedure that maintains a thread-safe global collection of metadata:

```
Private Shared metadata As New Dictionary(Of String, String)()
Public Sub AddMetadata(ByVal key As String, ByVal value As String)
    SyncLock metadata
        metadata(key) = value
    End SyncLock
End Sub
Public Function GetMetadata(ByVal key As String) As String
    SyncLock metadata
        Return metadata(key)
    End SyncLock
End Function
```

Using Shared member variables instead of the Application collection has two advantages. First, it allows you to write custom code in a property procedure. You could use this code to log how many times a value is being accessed to check whether the data is still valid or to re-create it. Here's an example that uses a *lazy initialization* pattern and creates the global object only when it's first requested:

```
Private Shared strFileListAs String()
Public Shared ReadOnly Property FileList() As String()
    Get
        If strFileListIs Nothing Then
            strFileList=
             Directory.GetFiles(HttpContext.Current.Request.PhysicalApplicationPath)
        End If
        Return strFileList
    End Get
End Property
```

This example uses the file access classes described in Chapter 13 to retrieve a list of files in the web application. This approach wouldn't be possible with the Application collection.

The other benefit of using Shared member variables is that the code that consumes them can be type-safe. Here's an example that uses the FileList property:

```
Protected Sub Page_Load(ByVal sender As Object, ByVal e As EventArgs)
    Dim builder As New StringBuilder()
    For Each file As String In Global.FileList
        builder.Append(file & "<br />")
    Next
    lblInfo.Text = builder.ToString()
End Sub
```

Notice that no casting step is required to gain access to the custom property you've added.

Summary

State management is the art of retaining information between requests. Usually, this information is user-specific (such as a list of items in a shopping cart, a user name, or an access level), but sometimes it's global to the whole application (such as usage statistics that track site activity). Because ASP.NET uses a disconnected architecture, you need to explicitly store and retrieve state information with each individual request. The approach you choose for storing this data can have a dramatic effect on the performance, scalability, and security of your application. To perfect your state management solution, you'll almost certainly want to consider adding caching into the mix, as described in Chapter 11.

PART 2

Data Access

CHAPTER 7

ADO.NET Fundamentals

A large number of computer applications—both desktop and web applications—are *data-driven*. These applications are largely concerned with retrieving, displaying, and modifying data.

Retrieving and processing data seems like a fairly straightforward task, but over the past decade the way applications use data has changed repeatedly. Developers have moved from simple client applications that use local databases to distributed systems that rely on centralized databases on dedicated servers. At the same time, data access technologies have evolved. If you've worked with Microsoft languages for some time, you've most likely heard of (and possibly used) an alphabet soup of data access technologies that includes ODBC, DAO, RDO, RDS, and ADO.

The .NET Framework includes its own data access technology, ADO.NET. ADO. NET consists of managed classes that allow .NET applications to connect to data sources (usually relational databases), execute commands, and manage disconnected data. The small miracle of ADO.NET is that it allows you to write more or less the same data access code in web applications that you write for client-server desktop applications, or even single-user applications that connect to a local database.

This chapter describes the architecture of ADO.NET and the ADO.NET data providers. You'll learn about ADO.NET basics such as opening a connection, executing a SQL statement or stored procedure, and retrieving the results of a query. You'll also learn how to prevent SQL injection attacks and use transactions.

Tip ASP.NET includes a new data binding framework that can hide the underlying ADO.NET plumbing in your web pages. You can skip to Chapter 9 to start learning about these features right away. However, to build truly scalable high-performance web applications, you'll need to write custom database code (and your own database components). That means you'll need a thorough understanding of the concepts presented in this chapter.

ADO.NET CHANGES IN .NET 2.0

If you're a seasoned .NET 1.*x* programmer, you're probably wondering what's new in the latest iteration of ADO.NET. Without a doubt, the greatest change for ASP.NET applications is the new data binding model (described in Chapters 9 and 10). The data binding model allows you to reduce the amount of code you write for data display, and it can even allow you to avoid writing any data access code at all (if you're willing to pay the price with pages that are less flexible and more difficult to optimize).

Even with the advent of the new data binding model, the underlying ADO.NET reality doesn't change that much. Many of the changes are internal (such as a more compact DataSet serialization format that requires less memory) or involve frills that aren't of much use in the average web application (such as the new SQL bulk copy feature for rapidly transferring an entire table between two database servers). Several more features were cut during the .NET 2.0 beta cycle (such as built-in paging support for getting part of a query, the ObjectSpaces system for relational mapping, and the XmlAdapter class for more powerful DataSet-to-XML conversions, to name just a few). These may turn up again in separate toolkits or later versions of .NET, but for now developers are out of luck.

So, what does that leave us with? Here are some genuinely interesting ADO.NET changes that are still around:

- *Provider factories*: The dream of generic data access code (code you can write once and use with multiple different databases) takes a giant leap forward in .NET 2.0 thanks to *provider factories*—new components that can create strongly typed Connection, Command, and DataAdapter objects on the fly. You'll learn about them in this chapter.
- *Change notification*: To build truly scalable web applications, you need to cache data that's retrieved from a database so it can be reused without connecting to the data source each time. However, caching introduces the possibility of out-of-date information. ADO.NET includes a new change notification feature that you can use to automatically remove cached data when the related records in the database change. You'll learn about this feature in Chapter 11.
- *Connection statistics*: It's a small frill, but the new connection-tracking features of the SqlConnection object might help you profile different data access strategies. They're introduced in this chapter.
- *SQL Server 2005*: SQL Server 2005 introduces a whole set of new features, and ADO.NET 2.0 supports them seamlessly. These features include user-defined data types that are based on .NET classes, as well as stored procedures written with .NET languages. For more information about these features, refer to a dedicated SQL Server 2005 book such as *A First Look at Microsoft SQL Server 2005 for Developers* (Addison-Wesley, 2004) or *Pro SQL Server 2005 Assemblies* (Apress, 2005).

The ADO.NET Architecture

ADO.NET uses a multilayered architecture that revolves around a few key concepts, such as Connection, Command, and DataSet objects. However, the ADO.NET architecture is quite a bit different from classic ADO.

One of the key differences between ADO and ADO.NET is how they deal with the challenge of different data sources. In ADO, programmers always use a generic set of objects, no matter what the underlying data source is. For example, if you want to retrieve a record from an Oracle database, you use the same Connection class you would use to tackle the same task with SQL Server. This isn't the case in ADO.NET, which introduces a new data provider model.

ADO.NET Data Providers

A *data provider* is a set of ADO.NET classes that allows you to access a specific database, execute SQL commands, and retrieve data. Essentially, a data provider is a bridge between your application and a data source.

The classes that make up a data provider include the following:

Connection: You use this object to establish a connection to a data source.

Command: You use this object to execute SQL commands and stored procedures.

DataReader: This object provides fast read-only, forward-only access to the data retrieved from a query.

DataAdapter: This object performs two tasks. First, you can use it to fill a DataSet (a disconnected collection of tables and relationships) with information extracted from a data source. Second, you can use it to apply changes to a data source, according to the modifications you've made in a DataSet.

ADO.NET doesn't include generic data provider objects. Instead, it includes different data providers specifically designed for different types of data sources. Each data provider has a specific implementation of the Connection, Command, DataReader, and DataAdapter classes that's optimized for a specific RBDMS (relational database management system). For example, if you need to create a connection to a SQL Server database, you'll use a connection class named SqlConnection.

■ **Note** This book uses generic names for provider-specific objects. In other words, instead of discussing the SqlConnection and OracleConnection object, you'll learn about all connection objects. Just keep in mind that there really isn't a generic Connection object—it's just convenient shorthand for referring to all the provider-specific connection objects, which work in a standardized fashion.

One of the key underlying ideas of the ADO.NET provider model is that it's *extensible*. In other words, developers can create their own providers for proprietary data sources. In fact, numerous proof-of-concepts examples are available that show how you can easily create custom ADO.NET providers to wrap nonrelational data stores, such as the file system or a directory service. Some third-party vendors also sell custom providers for .NET.

The .NET Framework is bundled with a small set of four providers:

SQL Server provider: Provides optimized access to a SQL Server database (version 7.0 or later).

OLE DB provider: Provides access to any data source that has an OLE DB driver. This includes SQL Server databases prior to version 7.0.

Oracle provider: Provides optimized access to an Oracle database (version 8*i* or later).

ODBC provider: Provides access to any data source that has an ODBC driver.

Figure 7-1 shows the layers of the ADO.NET provider model.

When choosing a provider, you should first try to find a native .NET provider that's customized for your data source. If you can't find a native provider, you can use the OLE DB provider, as long as you have an OLE DB driver for your data source. The OLE DB technology has been around for many years as part of ADO, so most data sources provide an OLE DB driver (including SQL Server, Oracle, Access, MySQL, and many more). In the rare situation when you can't find a dedicated .NET provider or an OLE DB driver, you can fall back on the ODBC provider, which works in conjunction with an ODBC driver.

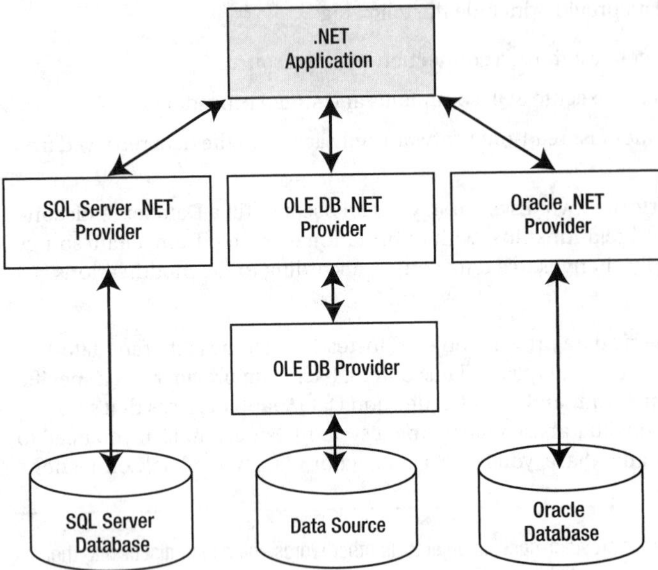

Figure 7-1. *The ADO.NET architecture*

■ **Tip** Microsoft includes the OLE DB provider with ADO.NET so that you can use your existing OLE DB drivers. However, if you can find a provider that's customized specifically for your data source, you should use it instead. For example, you can connect to a SQL Server database using either the SQL Server provider or the OLE DB provider, but the SQL Server provider will always perform best.

Standardization in ADO.NET

At first glance, it might seem that ADO.NET offers a fragmented model, because it doesn't include a generic set of objects that can work with multiple types of databases. As a result, if you change from one RDBMS to another, you'll need to modify your data access code to use a different set of classes.

But even though different .NET data providers use different classes, all providers are *standardized* in the same way. More specifically, each provider is based on the same set of interfaces and base classes. For example, every Connection object implements the IDbConnection interface, which defines core methods such as Open() and Close(). This standardization guarantees that every Connection class will work in the same way and expose the same set of core properties and methods.

Behind the scenes, different providers use completely different low-level calls and APIs. For example, the SQL Server provider uses the proprietary TDS (Tabular Data Stream) protocol to communicate with the server. The benefits of this model aren't immediately obvious, but they are significant:

- Because each provider uses the same interfaces and base classes, you can still write generic data access code (with a little more effort) by coding against the interfaces instead of the provider classes. You'll see this technique in action in the section "Provider-Agnostic Code."
- Because each provider is implemented separately, it can use proprietary optimizations. (This is different from the ADO model, where every database call needs to filter through a common layer before it reaches the underlying database driver.) In addition, custom providers can add nonstandard features that aren't included in other providers (such as SQL Server's ability to perform an XML query).

ADO.NET also has another layer of standardization: the DataSet. The DataSet is an all-purpose container for data that you've retrieved from one or more tables in a data source. The DataSet is completely generic—in other words, custom providers don't define their own custom versions of the DataSet class. No matter which data provider you use, you can extract your data and place it into a disconnected DataSet in the same way. That makes it easy to separate data *retrieval* code from data *processing* code. If you change the underlying database, you will need to change the data retrieval code, but if you use the DataSet and your information has the same structure, you won't need to modify the way you process that data.

Tip The next chapter covers the DataSet in much more detail. In this chapter, you'll learn the fundamentals—how to use ADO.NET to perform direct, connection-based access.

SQL Server 2005

ADO.NET 2.0 provides support for a few features that are limited to SQL Server 2005. These features include the following:

MARS (multiple active result sets): This allows you to have more than one query on the go at the same time. For example, you could query a list of customers and then query a list of orders without closing the first query. This technique is occasionally useful, but it's better if you can avoid the extra overhead.

User-defined data types: Using .NET code, you can define a custom class and then store instances of that class directly in a column of the database. This saves you the work of examining several fields in a row and then manually creating a corresponding data object to use in your application.

Managed stored procedures: SQL Server 2005 can host the CLR, which gives you the ability to write stored procedures in the database using pure .NET code.

SQL notifications: Notifications allow your code to respond when specific changes are made in a database. In ASP.NET, this feature is most commonly used to invalidate a cached data object when one or more records are updated. This is the only SQL Server 2005 feature that's also supported in SQL Server 7 and SQL Server 2000, albeit through a different mechanism.

Snapshot transaction isolation: This is a new transaction level that allows you to improve concurrency. It allows transactions to see a slightly older version of data while it's being updated by another transaction.

For the most part, this book concentrates on programming techniques that work with all relational databases. However, Chapter 11 covers SQL notifications because they are of great use in many ASP.NET applications, and they are also supported in earlier versions of SQL Server through a different technology. This chapter briefly covers snapshot isolation. For information about other features that are specific to SQL Server 2005, you may want to consult *A First Look at Microsoft SQL Server 2005 for Developers* (Addison-Wesley, 2004) and *Pro SQL Server 2005 Assemblies* (Apress, 2005).

Fundamental ADO.NET Classes

ADO.NET has two types of objects:

Connection-based objects: These are the data provider objects such as Connection, Command, DataAdapter, and DataReader. They execute SQL statements, connect to a database, or fill a DataSet. The connection-based objects are specific to the type of data source.

Content-based objects: These objects are really just "packages" for data. They include the DataSet, DataColumn, DataRow, DataRelation, and several others. They are completely independent of the type of data source and are found in the System.Data namespace.

In the rest of this chapter, you'll learn about the first level of ADO.NET—the connection-based objects, including Connection, Command, and DataReader. You won't learn about the higher-level DataAdapter yet, because the DataAdapter is designed for use with the DataSet and is discussed in Chapter 8. (Essentially, the DataAdapter is a group of related Command objects; these objects help you synchronize a DataSet with a data source.)

■ **Note** An ADO.NET provider is simply a set of ADO.NET classes (with an implementation of Connection, Command, DataAdapter, and DataReader) that's distributed in a class library assembly. Usually, all the classes in the data provider use the same prefix. For example, the prefix *Oracle* is used for the ADO.NET Oracle provider, and it provides an implementation of the Connection object named OracleConnection.

The ADO.NET classes are grouped into several namespaces. Each provider has its own namespace, and generic classes such as the DataSet are stored in the System.Data namespaces. Table 7-1 describes the namespaces.

Table 7-1. *The ADO.NET Namespaces*

Namespace	Description
System.Data	Contains the key data container classes that model columns, relations, tables, datasets, rows, views, and constraints. In addition, contains the key interfaces that are implemented by the connection-based data objects.
System.Data.Common	Contains base, mostly abstract classes that implement some of the interfaces from System.Data and define the core ADO.NET functionality. Data providers inherit from these classes to create their own specialized versions.
System.Data.OleDb	Contains the classes used to connect to an OLE DB provider, including OleDbCommand, OleDbConnection, and OleDbDataAdapter. These classes support most OLE DB providers but not those that require OLE DB version 2.5 interfaces.

Namespace	Description
System.Data.SqlClient	Contains the classes you use to connect to a Microsoft SQL Server database, including SqlDbCommand, SqlDbConnection, and SqlDBDataAdapter. These classes are optimized to use the TDS interface to SQL Server.
System.Data.OracleClient	Contains the classes required to connect to an Oracle database (version 8.1.7 or later), including OracleCommand, OracleConnection, and OracleDataAdapter. These classes are using the optimized Oracle Call Interface (OCI).
System.Data.Odbc	Contains the classes required to connect to most ODBC drivers. These classes include OdbcCommand, OdbcConnection, and OdbcDataAdapter. ODBC drivers are included for all kinds of data sources and are configured through the Data Sources icon in the Control Panel.
System.Data.SqlTypes	Contains structures that match the native data types in SQL Server. These classes aren't required but provide an alternative to using standard .NET data types, which require automatic conversion.

The Connection Class

The Connection class allows you to establish a connection to the data source that you want to interact with. Before you can do anything else (including retrieving, deleting, inserting, or updating data), you need to establish a connection.

The core Connection properties and methods are specified by the IDbConnection interface, which all Connection classes implement.

Connection Strings

When you create a Connection object, you need to supply a *connection string*. The connection string is a series of name/value settings separated by semicolons (;). The order of these settings is unimportant, as is the capitalization. Taken together, they specify the basic information needed to create a connection.

Although connection strings vary based on the RDBMS and provider you are using, a few pieces of information are almost always required:

The server where the database is located: In the examples in this book, the database server is always located on the same computer as the ASP.NET application, so the loopback alias localhost is used instead of a computer name.

The database you want to use: Most of the examples in this book use the Northwind database, which is installed by default with most editions of SQL Server.

How the database should authenticate you: The Oracle and SQL Server providers give you the choice of supplying authentication credentials or logging in as the current user. The latter choice is usually best, because you don't need to place password information in your code or configuration files.

For example, here's the connection string you would use to connect to the Northwind database on the current computer using integrated security (which uses the currently logged-in Windows user to access the database):

```
Dim connectionString As String =
    "Data Source=localhost;Initial Catalog=Northwind;Integrated Security=SSPI"
```

If integrated security isn't supported, the connection must indicate a valid user and password combination. For a newly installed SQL Server database, the sa (system administrator) account is usually present. Here's a connection string that uses this account:

```
Dim connectionString As String =
  "Data Source=localhost;Initial Catalog=Northwind; user id=sa;password=opensesame"
```

If you're using the OLE DB provider, your connection string will still be similar, with the addition of a provider setting that identifies the OLE DB driver. For example, you can use the following connection string to connect to an Oracle database through the MSDAORA OLE DB provider:

```
Dim connectionString As String =
    "Data Source=localhost;Initial Catalog=Sales; " _
     & "user id=sa;password=;Provider=MSDAORA"
```

And here's an example that connects to an Access database file:

```
Dim connectionString As String =
    "Provider=Microsoft.Jet.OLEDB.4.0; Data Source=C:\DataSources\Northwind.mdb"
```

■**Tip** If you're using a database other than SQL Server, you might need to consult the data provider documentation (or the .NET Framework class library reference) to determine the supported connection string values. For example, most databases support the Connect Timeout setting, which sets the number of seconds to wait for a connection before throwing an exception. (The SQL Server default is 15 seconds.)

When you create a Connection object, you can pass the connection string as a constructor parameter. Alternatively, you can set the ConnectionString property by hand, as long as you do it before you attempt to open the connection.

There's no reason to hard-code a connection string. As discussed in Chapter 5, the <connectionStrings> section of the web.config file is a handy place to store your connection strings. Here's an example:

```
<configuration xmlns="http://schemas.microsoft.com/.NetConfiguration/v2.0">
  <connectionStrings>
    <add name="Northwind" connectionString=
        "Data Source=localhost;Initial Catalog=Northwind;Integrated Security=SSPI"/>
  </connectionStrings>
  ...
</configuration>
```

You can then retrieve your connection string by name from the WebConfiguration➥ Manager.ConnectionStrings collection, like so:

```
Dim connectionString As String =
    WebConfigurationManager.ConnectionStrings("Northwind").ConnectionString
```

The following examples assume you've added this connection string to your web.config file.

Testing a Connection

Once you've chosen your connection string, managing the connection is easy—you simply use the Open() and Close() methods. You can use the following code in the Page.Load event handler to test a connection and write its status to a label:

```
' Create the Connection object.
Dim connectionString As String = _
    WebConfigurationManager.ConnectionStrings("Northwind").ConnectionString
Dim con As New SqlConnection(connectionString)

Try
    ' Try to open the connection.
    con.Open()
    lblInfo.Text = "<b>Server Version:</b> " & con.ServerVersion
    lblInfo.Text &= "<br /><b>Connection Is:</b> " & con.State.ToString()
Catch err As Exception
    ' Handle an error by displaying the information.
    lblInfo.Text = "Error reading the database. "
    lblInfo.Text &= err.Message
Finally
    ' Either way, make sure the connection is properly closed.
    ' Even if the connection wasn't opened successfully,
    ' calling Close() won't cause an error.
    con.Close()
    lblInfo.Text &= "<br /><b>Now Connection Is:</b> "
    lblInfo.Text &= con.State.ToString()
End Try
```

Figure 7-2 shows the results of running this code.

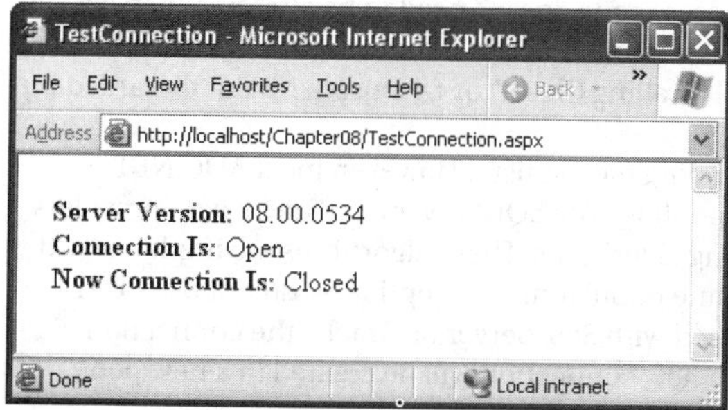

Figure 7-2. *Testing a connection*

Connections are a limited server resource. This means it's imperative to open the connection as late as possible and release it as quickly as possible. In the previous code sample, an exception handler makes sure that even if an unhandled error occurs, the connection will be closed in the finally block. If you don't use this design and an unhandled exception occurs, the connection will remain open until the garbage collector disposes the SqlConnection object.

An alternate approach is to wrap your data access code in a Using block. The Using statement declares that you are using a disposable object for a short period of time. As soon as the Using block ends, the CLR releases the corresponding object immediately by calling its Dispose() method. Interestingly, calling the Dispose() method of a Connection object is equivalent to calling Close(). That means you can rewrite the earlier example in the following, more compact, form:

```
Dim connectionString As String =
    WebConfigurationManager.ConnectionStrings("Northwind").ConnectionString
Dim con As SqlConnection = New SqlConnection(connectionString)

Using con
    con.Open()
    lblInfo.Text = "<b>Server Version:</b> " & con.ServerVersion
    lblInfo.Text &= "<br /><b>Connection Is:</b> " & con.State.ToString()
End Using

lblInfo.Text &= "<br /><b>Now Connection Is:</b> "
lblInfo.Text &= con.State.ToString()
```

The best part is that you don't need to write a finally block—the Using statement releases the object you're using even if you exit the block as the result of an unhandled exception.

Connection Pooling

Acquiring a connection takes a short, but definite, amount of time. In a web application in which requests are being handled efficiently, connections will be opened and closed endlessly as new requests are processed. In this environment, the small overhead required to establish a connection can become significant and limit the scalability of the system.

One solution is *connection pooling*. Connection pooling is the practice of keeping a permanent set of open database connections to be shared by sessions that use the same data source. This avoids the need to create and destroy connections all the time. Connection pools in ADO.NET are completely transparent to the programmer, and your data access code doesn't need to be altered. When a client requests a connection by calling Open(), it's served directly from the available pool, rather than re-created. When a client releases a connection by calling Close() or Dispose(), it's not discarded but returned to the pool to serve the next request.

ADO.NET does not include a connection pooling mechanism. However, most ADO.NET providers implement some form of connection pooling. The SQL Server and Oracle data providers implement their own efficient connection pooling algorithms. These algorithms are implemented entirely in managed code and—in contrast to some popular misconceptions—do not use COM+ enterprises services. For a connection to be reused with SQL Server or Oracle, the connection string matches exactly. If it differs even slightly, a new connection will be created in a new pool.

■ Tip SQL Server and Oracle connection pooling use a full-text match algorithm. That means any minor change in the connection string will thwart connection pooling, even if the change is simply to reverse the order of parameters or add an extra blank space at the end. For this reason, it's imperative that you don't hard-code the connection string in different web pages. Instead, you should store the connection string in one place—preferably the <connectionStrings> section of the web.config file.

With both the SQL Server and Oracle providers, connection pooling is enabled and used automatically. However, you can also use connection string parameters to configure pool size settings. Table 7-2 describes these parameters.

Table 7-2. *Connection Pooling Settings*

Setting	Description
Max Pool Size	The maximum number of connections allowed in the pool (defaults to 100). If the maximum pool size has been reached, any further attempts to open a connection are queued until a connection becomes available. (An error is raised if the Connection.Timeout value elapses before a connection becomes available.)
Min Pool Size	The minimum number of connections always retained in the pool (defaults to 0). This number of connections will be created when the first connection is opened, leading to a minor delay for the first request.
Pooling	When True (the default), the connection is drawn from the appropriate pool or, if necessary, is created and added to the appropriate pool.
Connection Lifetime	Specifies a time interval in seconds. If a connection is returned to the pool and its creation time is older than the specified lifetime, it will be destroyed. The default is 0, which disables this behavior. This feature is useful when you want to recycle a large number of connections at once.

Here's an example connection string that sets a minimum pool size:

```
Dim connectionString As String =
    "Data Source=localhost;Initial Catalog=Northwind;" _
        & "Integrated Security=SSPI;Min Pool Size=10"
Dim con As New SqlConnection(connectionString)

' Get the connection from the pool (if it exists)
' or create the pool with ten connections (if it doesn't).
con.Open()

' Return the connection to the pool.
con.Close()
```

Some providers include methods for emptying out the connection pool. For example, with the SqlConnection you can call the Shared ClearPool() and ClearAllPools() methods. When calling ClearPool(), you supply a SqlConnection, and all the matching connections are removed. ClearAllPools() empties out every connection pool in the current application domain. (Technically, these methods don't close the connections. They just mark them as invalid so that they will time out and be closed during the regular connection cleanup a few minutes later.) This functionality is rarely used—typically, the only case in which it's useful is if you know the pool is full of invalid connections (for example, as a result of restarting SQL Server) and you want to avoid an error.

■ **Tip** SQL Server and Oracle connection pools are always maintained as part of the global resources in an application domain. As a result, all the connections are lost if the application domain is restarted (for example, because of an update or in response to a certain threshold being reached). For the same reason, connection pools can't be reused between separate web applications on the same web server or between web applications and other .NET applications.

Connection Statistics

If you're using the SQL Server provider, you can retrieve some interesting statistics using the SqlConnection.RetrieveStatistics() method (new in .NET 2.0). RetrieveStatistics returns a hashtable with various low-level details that can help you analyze the performance of commands and the amount of work you've performed. Connection statistics aren't often used in a deployed application, but they are useful for diagnosing performance during the testing and profiling stage. For example, they provide one tool that you can use to determine how various data access strategies perform (other tools include the SQL Server administrative utilities, such as the SQL Profiler and Query Analyzer).

By default, connection statistics are disabled to improve performance. To use connection statistics, you need to set the SqlConnection.StatisticsEnabled property to True. This tells the SqlConnection class to collect information about every action it performs. At any point after, you can call the RetrieveStatistics() method to examine this information, or you can use ResetStatistics() to clear it out and start from scratch.

Here's an example that displays the number of bytes received by the connection since you enabled statistics:

```
Dim statistics As Hashtable = con.RetrieveStatistics()
lblBytes.Text = "Retrieved bytes: " & statistics("BytesRetrieved").ToString()
```

Statistics are provided in a loosely typed name/value collection. That means you need to know the specific name of a statistic in order to retrieve it. You can find the full list in the MSDN help, but here are a few of the most useful:

ServerRoundtrips: Indicates the number of times the connection has made a request to the database server. Typically, this value corresponds to the number of commands you've executed, but strategies such as command batching can affect it.

ConnectionTime: Indicates the cumulative amount of time the connection has been open.

BytesReceived: Indicates the total number of bytes retrieved from the database server (as a cumulative result of all the commands you've executed).

SumResultSets: Indicates the number of queries you've performed.

SelectRows: Records the total number of rows retrieved in every query you've executed.

The Command and DataReader Classes

The Command class allows you to execute any type of SQL statement. Although you can use a Command class to perform *data-definition* tasks (such as creating and altering databases, tables, and indexes), you're much more likely to perform *data-manipulation* tasks (such as retrieving and updating the records in a table).

The provider-specific Command classes implement standard functionality, just like the Connection classes. In this case, the IDbCommand interface defines the core set of Command methods that are used to execute a command over an open connection.

Command Basics

Before you can use a command, you need to choose the command type, set the command text, and bind the command to a connection. You can perform this work by setting the corresponding properties (CommandType, CommandText, and Connection), or you can pass the information you need as constructor arguments.

The command text can be a SQL statement, a stored procedure, or the name of a table. It all depends on the *type* of command you're using. Three types of commands exist, as listed in Table 7-3.

Table 7-3. *Values for the CommandType Enumeration*

Value	Description
CommandType.Text	The command will execute a direct SQL statement. The SQL statement is provided in the CommandText property. This is the default value.
CommandType.StoredProcedure	The command will execute a stored procedure in the data source. The CommandText property provides the name of the stored procedure.
CommandType.TableDirect	The command will query all the records in the table. The CommandText is the name of the table from which the command will retrieve the records. (This option is included for backward compatibility with certain OLE DB drivers only. It is not supported by the SQL Server data provider, and it won't perform as well as a carefully targeted query.)

For example, here's how you would create a Command object that represents a query:

```
Dim cmd As New SqlCommand()
cmd.Connection = con
cmd.CommandType = CommandType.Text
cmd.CommandText = "SELECT * FROM Employees"
```

And here's a more efficient way using one of the Command constructors. Note that you don't need to specify the CommandType, because CommandType.Text is the default.

```
Dim cmd As New SqlCommand("SELECT * FROM Employees", con)
```

Alternatively, to use a stored procedure, you would use code like this:

```
Dim cmd As New SqlCommand("GetEmployees", con)
cmd.CommandType = CommandType.StoredProcedure
```

These examples simply define a Command object; they don't actually execute it. The Command object provides three methods that you can use to perform the command, depending on whether you want to retrieve a full result set, retrieve a single value, or just execute a nonquery command. Table 7-4 lists these methods.

Table 7-4. *Command Methods*

Method	Description
ExecuteNonQuery()	Executes non-SELECT commands, such as SQL commands that insert, delete, or update records. The returned value indicates the number of rows affected by the command.
ExecuteScalar()	Executes a SELECT query and returns the value of the first field of the first row from the rowset generated by the command. This method is usually used when executing an aggregate SELECT command that uses functions such as COUNT() or SUM() to calculate a single value.
ExecuteReader()	Executes a SELECT query and returns a DataReader object that wraps a read-only, forward-only cursor.

The DataReader Class

A DataReader allows you to read the data returned by a SELECT command one record at a time, in a forward-only, read-only stream. This is sometimes called a *firehose cursor*. Using a DataReader is the simplest way to get to your data, but it lacks the sorting and relational abilities of the disconnected DataSet described in Chapter 8. However, the DataReader provides the quickest possible no-nonsense access to data.

Table 7-5 lists the core methods of the DataReader.

Table 7-5. *DataReader Methods*

Method	Description
Read()	Advances the row cursor to the next row in the stream. This method must also be called before reading the first row of data. (When the DataReader is first created, the row cursor is positioned just before the first row.) The Read() method returns True if there's another row to be read, or it returns False if it has gone beyond the last row.
GetValue()	Returns the value stored in the field with the specified column name or index, within the currently selected row. The type of the returned value is the closest .NET match to the native value stored in the data source. If you access the field by index and pass an invalid index that refers to a nonexistent field, you will get an IndexOutOfRangeException exception. You can also access the same value by name, which is slightly less efficient because the DataReader must perform a lookup to find the column with the specified name.
GetValues()	Saves the values of the current row into an array. The number of fields that are saved depends on the size of the array you pass to this method. You can use the DataReader.FieldCount property to determine the number of fields in a row, and you can use that information to create an array of the right size if you want to save all the fields.
GetInt32(),GetChar(), GetDateTime(), GetXxx()	These methods return the value of the field with the specified index in the current row, with the data type specified in the method name. Note that if you try to assign the returned value to a variable of the wrong type, you'll get an InvalidCastException exception.
NextResult()	If the command that generated the DataReader returned more than one rowset, this method moves the pointer to the next rowset (just before the first row).
Close()	Closes the reader. If the originator command ran a stored procedure that returned an output value, that value can be read only from the respective parameter after the reader has been closed.

The ExecuteReader() Method and the DataReader

The following example creates a simple query command to return all the records from the Employees table in the Northwind database. The command is created when the page is loaded.

```
Protected Sub Page_Load(ByVal sender As Object, ByVal e As System.EventArgs)
    ' Create the Command and the Connection objects.
    Dim connectionString As String =
        WebConfigurationManager.ConnectionStrings("Northwind").ConnectionString
    Dim con As New SqlConnection(connectionString)
    Dim sql As String = "SELECT * FROM Employees"
    Dim cmd As New SqlCommand(sql, con)
    ...
```

■ **Note** This SELECT query uses the * wildcard to retrieve all the fields, but in real-world code you should retrieve only the fields you really need in order to avoid consuming time to retrieve data you'll never use. It's also a good idea to limit the records returned with a WHERE clause if you don't need all the records.

The connection is then opened, and the command is executed through the ExecuteReader() method, which returns a SqlDataReader, as follows:

```
...
' Open the Connection and get the DataReader.
con.Open()
Dim reader As SqlDataReader = cmd.ExecuteReader()
...
```

Once you have the DataReader, you can cycle through its records by calling the Read() method in a while loop. This moves the row cursor to the next record (which, for the first call, means to the first record). The Read() method also returns a Boolean value indicating whether there are more rows to read. In the following example the loop continues until Read() returns False, at which point the loop ends gracefully.

The information for each record is then joined into a single large string. To ensure that these string manipulations performed quickly, a StringBuilder (from the System.Text namespace) is used instead of ordinary string objects.

```
...
' Cycle through the records, and build the HTML string.
Dim htmlStr As New StringBuilder("")
Do While reader.Read()
    htmlStr.Append("<li>")
    htmlStr.Append(reader("TitleOfCourtesy"))
    htmlStr.Append(" <b>")
    htmlStr.Append(reader.GetString(1))
    htmlStr.Append("</b>, ")
    htmlStr.Append(reader.GetString(2))
    htmlStr.Append(" - employee from ")
    htmlStr.Append(reader.GetDateTime(6).ToString("d"))
    htmlStr.Append("</li>")
Loop
...
```

This code reads the value of the TitleOfCourtesy field by accessing the field by name through the Item indexer. Because the Item property is the default indexer, you don't need to explicitly include the Item property name when you retrieve a field value. Next, the code reads the LastName and FirstName fields by calling GetString() with the field index (1 and 2 in this case). Finally, the code accesses the HireDate field by calling GetDateTime() with a field index of 6. All these approaches are equivalent and included to show the supported variation.

■ **Note** In this example, the StringBuilder ensures a dramatic increase in performance. If you use the & operator to concatenate strings instead, this operation would destroy and create a new string object every time. This operation is noticeably slower, especially for large strings. The StringBuilder object avoids this problem by allocating a buffer of memory for characters.

The final step is to close the reader and the connection and show the generated text in a server control:

```
    ...
    reader.Close()
    con.Close()
    HtmlContent.Text = htmlStr.ToString()
End Sub
```

If you run the page, you'll see the output shown in Figure 7-3.

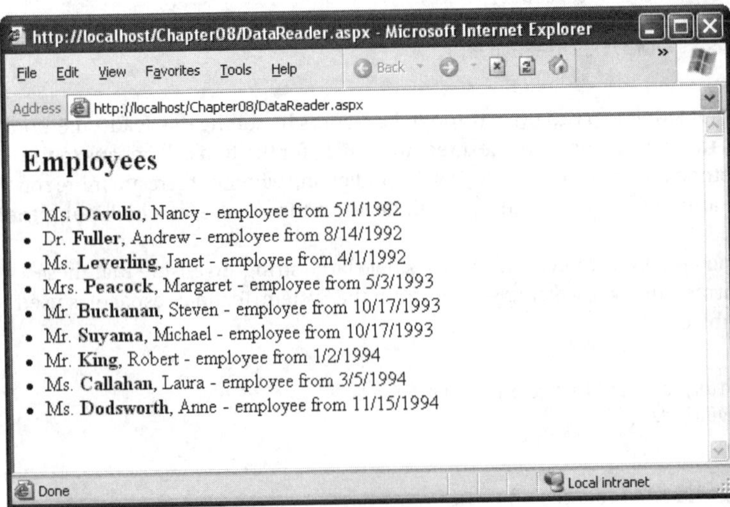

Figure 7-3. *Retrieving results with a DataReader*

In most ASP.NET pages, you won't take this labor-intensive approach to displaying data in a web page. Instead, you'll use the data controls described in later chapters. However, you're still likely to use the DataAdapter when writing data access code in a database component.

CommandBehavior

The ExecuteReader() method has an overloaded version that takes one of the values from the CommandBehavior enumeration as a parameter. One useful value is CommandBehavior.CloseConnection. When you pass this value to the ExecuteReader() method, the DataReader will close the associated connection as soon as you close the DataReader.

Using this technique, you could rewrite the code as follows:

```
Dim reader As SqlDataReader = cmd.ExecuteReader(CommandBehavior.CloseConnection)

' (Build the HTML string here.)

' No need to close the connection. You can simply close the reader.
reader.Close()
HtmlContent.Text = htmlStr.ToString()
```

This behavior is particularly useful if you retrieve a DataReader in one method and need to pass it to another method to process it. If you use the CommandBehavior.CloseConnection value, the connection will be automatically closed as soon as the second method closes the reader.

Another possible value is CommandBehavior.SingleRow, which can improve the performance of the query execution when you're retrieving only a single row. For example, if you are retrieving a single record using its unique primary key field (CustomerID, ProductID, and so on), you can use this optimization. You can also use Command.Behavior.SequentialAccess to read part of a binary field at a time, which reduces the memory overhead for large binary fields. You'll see this technique at work in Chapter 10.

The other values are less frequently used and aren't covered here. You can refer to the .NET documentation for a full list.

Processing Multiple Result Sets

The command you execute doesn't have to return a single result set. Instead, it can execute more than one query and return more than one result set as part of the same command. This is useful if you need to retrieve a large amount of related data, such as a list of products and product categories that, taken together, represent a product catalog.

A command can return more than one result set in two ways:

- If you're calling a stored procedure, it may use multiple SELECT statements.
- If you're using a straight text command, you may be able to batch multiple commands by separating commands with a semicolon (;). Not all providers support this technique, but the SQL Server database provider does.

Here's an example of a string that defines a batch of three SELECT statements:

```
Dim sql As String = "SELECT TOP 5 * FROM Employees;" _
  &  "SELECT TOP 5 * FROM Customers;SELECT TOP 5 * FROM Suppliers"
```

This string contains three queries. Together, they return the first five records from the Employees table, the first five from the Customers table, and the first five from the Suppliers table.

Processing these results is fairly straightforward. Initially, the DataReader will provide access to the results from the Employees table. Once you've finished using the Read() method to read all these records, you can call NextResult() to the next result set. When there are no more result sets, this method returns False.

You can even cycle through all the available result sets with a while loop, although in this case you must be careful not to call NextResult() until you finish reading the first result set.

Here's an example:

```
' Cycle through the records and all the rowsets,
' and build the HTML string.
Dim htmlStr As New StringBuilder("")
Dim i As Integer = 0
Do
    htmlStr.Append("<h2>Rowset: ")
    htmlStr.Append(i.ToString())
    htmlStr.Append("</h2>")

    Do While reader.Read()
        htmlStr.Append("<li>")
        ' Get all the fields in this row.
        Dim field As Integer = 0
        Do While field < reader.FieldCount
            htmlStr.Append(reader.GetName(field).ToString())
            htmlStr.Append(": ")
            htmlStr.Append(reader.GetValue(field).ToString())
            htmlStr.Append("   ")
            field += 1
```

```
            Loop
            htmlStr.Append("</li>")
        Loop
        htmlStr.Append("<br /><br />")
        i += 1
    Loop While reader.NextResult()

    ' Close the DataReader and the Connection.
    reader.Close()
    con.Close()

    ' Show the generated HTML code on the page.
    HtmlContent.Text = htmlStr.ToString()
```

Note that in this case all the fields are accessed using the GetValue() method, which takes the index of the field to read. That's because the code is designed generically to read all the fields of all the returned result sets, no matter what query you use. However, in a realistic database application, you would almost certainly know which tables to expect as well as the corresponding table and field names.

Figure 7-4 shows the page output.

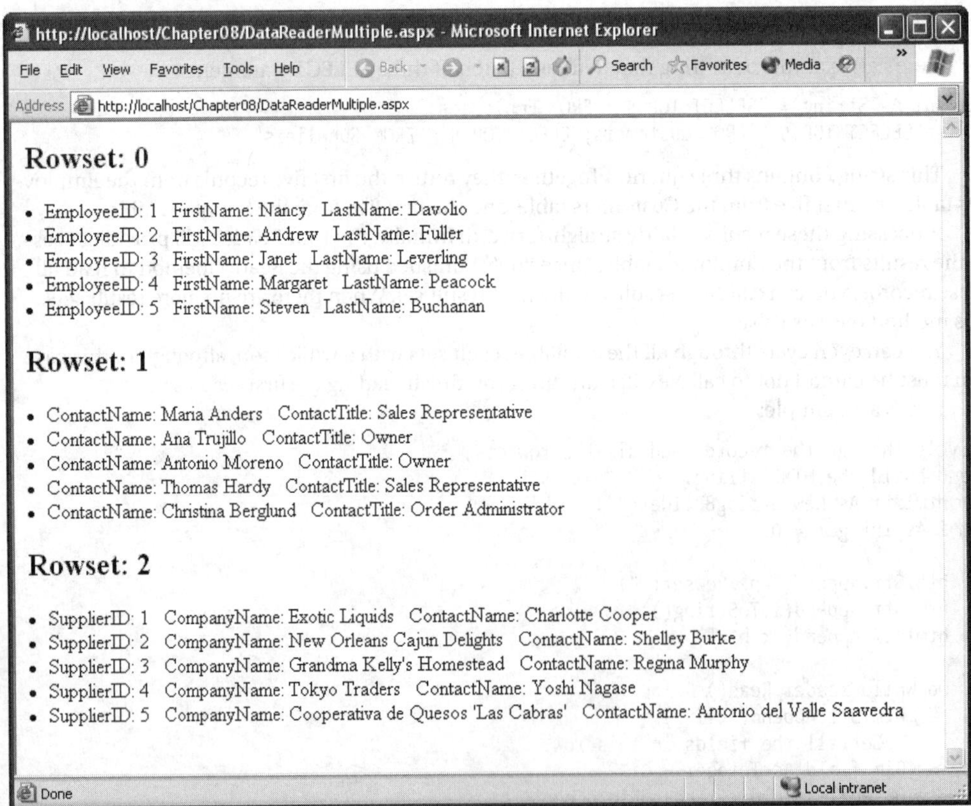

Figure 7-4. *Retrieving multiple result sets*

You don't always need to step through each record. If you're willing to show the data exactly as it is, with no extra processing or formatting, you can add a GridView control to your page and bind the DataReader to the GridView control in a single line. Here's the code you would use:

```
' Specify the data source.
GridView1.DataSource = reader

' Fill the GridView with all the records in the DataReader.
GridView1.DataBind()
```

You'll learn much more about data binding and how to customize it in Chapter 9 and Chapter 10.

The ExecuteScalar() Method

The ExecuteScalar() method returns the value stored in the first field of the first row of a result set generated by the command's SELECT query. This method is usually used to execute a query that retrieves only a single field, perhaps calculated by a SQL aggregate function such as COUNT() or SUM().

The following procedure shows how you can get (and write on the page) the number of records in the Employees table with this approach:

```
Dim con As New SqlConnection(connectionString)
Dim sql As String = " SELECT COUNT(*) FROM Employees "
Dim cmd As New SqlCommand(sql, con)

' Open the Connection, and get the COUNT(*) value.
con.Open()
Dim numEmployees As Integer = CInt(cmd.ExecuteScalar())
con.Close()

' Display the information.
HtmlContent.Text &= "<br />Total employees: <b>" _
        & numEmployees.ToString() & "</b><br />"
```

The code is fairly straightforward, but it's worth noting that you must cast the returned value to the proper type because ExecuteScalar() returns an object.

The ExecuteNonQuery() Method

The ExecuteNonQuery() method executes commands that don't return a result set, such as INSERT, DELETE, and UPDATE. The ExecuteNonQuery() method returns a single piece of information—the number of affected records.

Here's an example that uses a DELETE command by dynamically building a SQL string:

```
Dim con As New SqlConnection(connectionString)
Dim sql As String = "DELETE FROM Employees WHERE EmployeeID = " & empID.ToString()
Dim cmd As New SqlCommand(sql, con)

Try
    con.Open()
    Dim numAff As Integer = cmd.ExecuteNonQuery()
    HtmlContent.Text &=
        String.Format("<br />Deleted <b>{0}</b> record(s)<br />", numAff)
Catch exc As SqlException
    HtmlContent.Text &=
        String.Format("<b>Error:</b> {0}<br /><br />", exc.Message)
Finally
    con.Close()
End Try
```

SQL Injection Attacks

So far, all the examples you've seen have used hard-coded values. That makes the examples simple, straightforward, and relatively secure. It also means they aren't that realistic, and they don't demonstrate one of the most serious risks for web applications that interact with a database—*SQL injection attacks*.

In simple terms, SQL injection is the process of passing SQL code into an application, in a way that was not intended or anticipated by the application developer. This may be possible because of the poor design of the application, and it affects only applications that use SQL string building techniques to create a command with user-supplied values.

Consider the example shown in Figure 7-5. In this example, the user enters a customer ID, and the GridView shows all the rows for that customer. In a more realistic example the user would also need to supply some sort of authentication information such as a password. Or, the user ID might be based on a previous login screen, and the text box would allow the user to supply additional criteria such as a date range or the name of a product in the order.

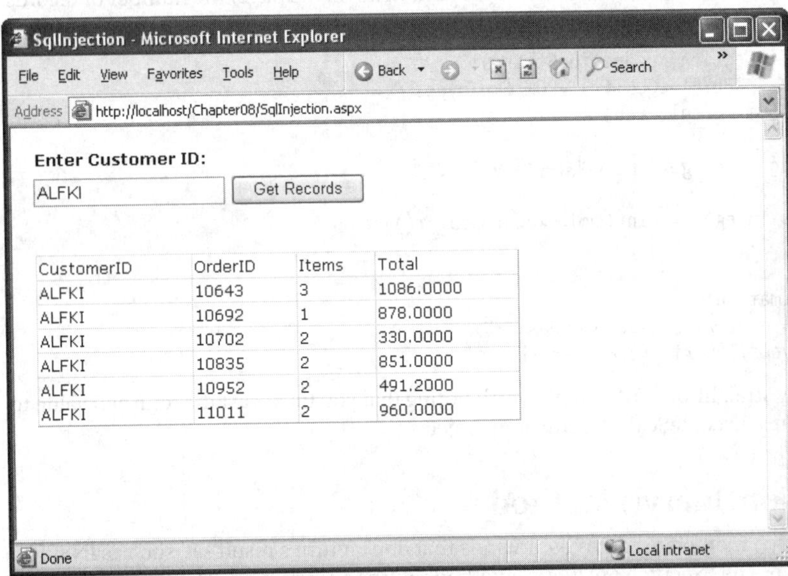

Figure 7-5. *Retrieving orders for a single customer*

The problem is how this command is executed. In this example, the SQL statement is built dynamically using a string building technique. The value from the txtID text box is simply pasted into the middle of the string. Here's the code:

```
Dim connectionString As String =
     WebConfigurationManager.ConnectionStrings("Northwind").ConnectionString
Dim con As New SqlConnection(connectionString)
Dim sql As String = "SELECT Orders.CustomerID, Orders.OrderID, " _
                    & "COUNT(UnitPrice) AS Items, SUM(UnitPrice * Quantity)" _
                    & " AS Total FROM Orders " & "INNER JOIN [Order Details] " _
                    & "ON Orders.OrderID = [Order Details].OrderID " _
                    & "WHERE Orders.CustomerID = '" _
                    & txtID.Text & "' " & "GROUP BY Orders.OrderID, Orders.CustomerID"
Dim cmd As New SqlCommand(sql, con)
```

```
con.Open()
Dim reader As SqlDataReader = cmd.ExecuteReader()
GridView1.DataSource = reader
GridView1.DataBind()
reader.Close()
con.Close()
```

In this example, a user might try to tamper with the SQL statement. Often, the first goal of such an attack is to receive an error message. If the error isn't handled properly and the low-level information is exposed to the attacker, that information can be used to launch a more sophisticated attack.

For example, imagine what happens if the user enters the following text into the text box:

```
ALFKI' OR '1'='1
```

Now consider the complete SQL statement that this creates:

```
SELECT Orders.CustomerID, Orders.OrderID, COUNT(UnitPrice) AS Items,
  SUM(UnitPrice * Quantity) AS Total FROM Orders
  INNER JOIN [Order Details]
  ON Orders.OrderID = [Order Details].OrderID
  WHERE Orders.CustomerID = 'ALFKI' OR '1'='1'
  GROUP BY Orders.OrderID, Orders.CustomerID
```

This statement returns all the order records. Even if the order wasn't created by ALFKI, it's still true that 1=1 for every row. The result is that instead of seeing the specific information for the current customer, all the information is exposed to the attacker, as shown in Figure 7-6. If the information shown on the screen is sensitive, such as Social Security numbers, dates of birth, or credit card information, this could be an enormous problem! In fact, simple SQL injection attacks exactly like this are often the source of problems that affect major e-commerce companies. Often, the vulnerability doesn't occur in a text box but appears in the query string (which can be used to pass a database value such as a unique ID from a list page to a details page).

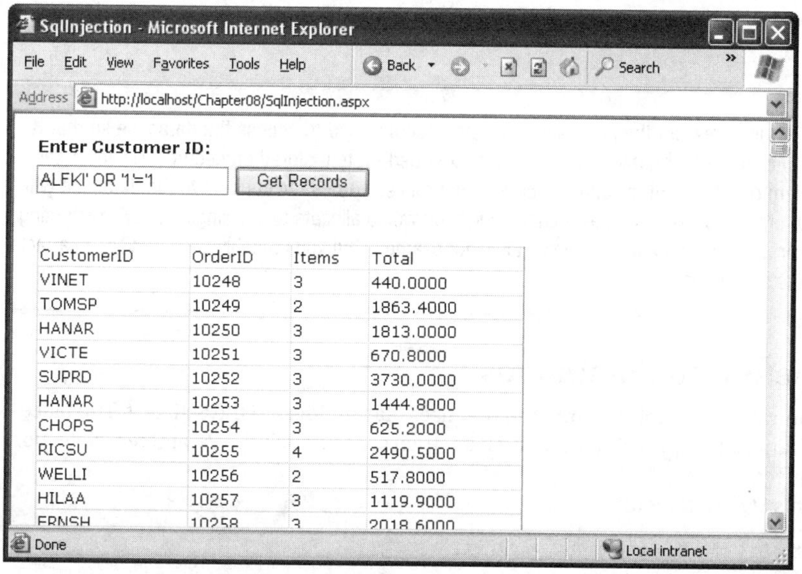

Figure 7-6. *A SQL injection attack that shows all rows*

More sophisticated attacks are possible. For example, the malicious user could simply comment out the rest of your SQL statement by adding two hyphens (--).This attack is specific to SQL Server, but equivalent exploits are possible in MySQL with the hash (#) symbol and in Oracle with the semicolon (;). Or the attacker could use a batch command to execute an arbitrary SQL command. With the SQL Server provider, the attacker simply needs to supply a semicolon followed by a new command. This exploit allows the user to delete the contents of another table, or even use the SQL Server xp_cmdshell system stored procedure to execute an arbitrary program at the command line.

Here's what the user would need to enter in the text box for a more sophisticated SQL injection attack to delete all the rows in the Customers table:

```
ALFKI'; DELETE * FROM Customers--
```

So, how can you defend against SQL injection attacks? You can keep a few good guidelines in mind. First, it's a good idea to use the TextBox.MaxLength property to prevent overly long entries if they aren't needed. That reduces the chance of a large block of script being pasted in where it doesn't belong. In addition, you should restrict the information given by error messages. If you catch a database exception, you should report only a generic message like "Data source error" rather than display the information in the Exception.Message property, which may indicate system vulnerabilities.

More important, you should take care to remove special characters. For example, you can convert all single quotation marks to two quotation marks, thereby ensuring that they won't be confused with the delimiters in your SQL statement:

```
Dim ID As String = txtID.Text.Replace("'", "''")
```

Of course, this introduces headaches if your text values really should contain apostrophes. It also suffers because some SQL injection attacks are still possible. Replacing apostrophes prevents a malicious user from closing a string value prematurely. However, if you're building a dynamic SQL statement that includes numeric values, a SQL injection attack just needs a single space. This vulnerability is often (and dangerously) ignored.

An even better approach is to use a parameterized command or a stored procedure that performs its own escaping and is impervious to SQL injection attacks. The following sections describe these techniques.

Tip Another good idea is to restrict the permissions of the account used to access the database so that it doesn't have the right to access other databases or execute extended system stored procedures. However, this can't remove the problem of SQL script injection, because the process you use to connect to the database will almost always require a broader set of privileges than the ones you would allocate to any single user. By restricting the account, you could prevent an attack that deletes a table, for example, but you probably can't prevent an attack that steals someone else's information.

Using Parameterized Commands

A parameterized command is simply a command that uses placeholders in the SQL text. The placeholders indicate dynamically supplied values, which are then sent through the Parameters collection of the Command object.

For example, this SQL statement:

```
SELECT * FROM Customers WHERE CustomerID = 'ALFKI'
```

would become something like this:

```
SELECT * FROM Customers WHERE CustomerID = @CustID
```

The placeholders are then added separately and automatically encoded.

The syntax for parameterized commands differs slightly for different providers. With the SQL Server provider, parameterized commands use named placeholders (with unique names). With the OLE DB provider, each hard-coded value is replaced with a question mark. In either case, you need to supply a Parameter object for each parameter, which you insert into the Command.Parameters collection. With the OLE DB provider, you must make sure you add the parameters in the same order that they appear in the SQL string. This isn't a requirement with the SQL Server provider, because the parameters are matched to the placeholders based on their names.

The following example rewrites the query to remove the possibility of a SQL injection attack:

```
Dim connectionString As String =
       WebConfigurationManager.ConnectionStrings("Northwind").ConnectionString
Dim con As New SqlConnection(connectionString)
Dim sql As String = "SELECT Orders.CustomerID, Orders.OrderID, " _
              & "COUNT(UnitPrice) AS Items, SUM(UnitPrice * Quantity) AS Total " _
              & "FROM Orders " & "INNER JOIN [Order Details] " & _
              & "ON Orders.OrderID = [Order Details].OrderID " & _
              & "WHERE Orders.CustomerID = @CustID " & _
              & "GROUP BY Orders.OrderID, Orders.CustomerID"
Private cmd As SqlCommand = New SqlCommand(sql, con)
cmd.Parameters.Add("@CustID", txtID.Text)
con.Open()
Dim reader As SqlDataReader = cmd.ExecuteReader()
GridView1.DataSource = reader
GridView1.DataBind()
reader.Close()
con.Close()
```

If you try to perform the SQL injection attack against this revised version of the page, you'll find it returns no records. That's because no order items contain a customer ID value that equals the text string ALFKI' OR '1'='1. This is exactly the behavior you want.

Calling Stored Procedures

Parameterized commands are just a short step from commands that call full-fledged stored procedures.

A stored procedure, of course, is a batch of one or more SQL statements that are stored in the database. Stored procedures are similar to functions in that they are well-encapsulated blocks of logic that can accept data (through input parameter) and return data (through result sets and output parameters). Stored procedures have many benefits:

They are easier to maintain: For example, you can optimize the commands in a stored procedure without recompiling the application that uses it.

They allow you to implement more secure database usage: For example, you can allow the Windows account that runs your ASP.NET code to use certain stored procedures but restrict access to the underlying tables.

They can improve performance: Because a stored procedure batches together multiple statements, you can get a lot of work done with just one trip to the database server. If your database is on another computer, this reduces the total time to perform a complex task dramatically.

Note SQL Server version 7 (and later) precompiles all SQL commands, including off-the-cuff SQL statements. That means you gain the benefit of compilation regardless of whether you are using stored procedures. However, stored procedures still tend to increase the performance benefits, because they limit the variation in SQL statements, thereby ensuring that a single compiled execution plan can be reused more often and more effectively. Also, because the database code is contained in the database, not the client, it's easier for a database administrator to fine-tune indexes and locks and to employ other optimization strategies.

Here's the SQL code needed to create a stored procedure for inserting a single record into the Employees table. This stored procedure isn't in the Northwind database initially, so you'll need to add it to the database (using a tool such as Enterprise Manager or Query Analyzer) before you use it.

```
CREATE PROCEDURE InsertEmployee(
@TitleOfCourtesy varchar(25),
@LastName        varchar(20),
@FirstName       varchar(10),
@EmployeeID      int OUTPUT)
AS

INSERT INTO Employees
  (TitleOfCourtesy, LastName, FirstName, HireDate)
  VALUES (@TitleOfCourtesy, @LastName, @FirstName, GETDATE());

SET @EmployeeID = @@IDENTITY
GO
```

This stored procedure takes three parameters for the employee's title of courtesy, last name, and first name. It returns the ID of the new record through the output parameter called @EmployeeID, which is retrieved after the INSERT statement using the @@IDENTITY function. This is one example of a simple task that a stored procedure can make much easier. Without using a stored procedure, it's quite awkward to try to determine the automatically generated identity value of a new record you've just inserted.

Next, you can create a SqlCommand to wrap the call to the stored procedure. This command takes the same three parameters as inputs and uses @@IDENTITY to get and then return the ID of the new record. Here is the first step, which creates the required objects and sets the InsertEmployee as the command text:

```
Dim connectionString As String =
      WebConfigurationManager.ConnectionStrings("Northwind").ConnectionString
Dim con As New SqlConnection(connectionString)

' Create the command for the InsertEmployee stored procedure.
Dim cmd As New SqlCommand("InsertEmployee", con)
cmd.CommandType = CommandType.StoredProcedure
```

Now you need to add the stored procedure's parameters to the Command.Parameters collection. When you do, you need to specify the exact data type and length of the parameter so that it matches the details in the database.

Here's how it works for a single parameter:

```
cmd.Parameters.Add(New SqlParameter("@TitleOfCourtesy", SqlDbType.NVarChar, 25))
cmd.Parameters("@TitleOfCourtesy").Value = title
```

The first line creates a new SqlParameter object; sets its name, type, and size in the constructor; and adds it to the Parameters collection. The second line assigns the value for the parameter, which will be sent to the stored procedure when you execute the command.

■ **Note** Some providers include an overload to the Parameter.Add() method that allows you to create a parameter object without specifying the data type. However, this approach usually requires some degree of *reflection*, which means the data provider must query the data source to find out the parameter details. The best-performing approach is to specify the data type details in full, even though they make for tedious code.

Now you can add the next two parameters in a similar way:

```
cmd.Parameters.Add(New SqlParameter("@LastName", SqlDbType.NVarChar, 20))
cmd.Parameters("@LastName").Value = lastName
cmd.Parameters.Add(New SqlParameter("@FirstName", SqlDbType.NVarChar, 10))
cmd.Parameters("@FirstName").Value = firstName
```

The last parameter is an output parameter, which allows the stored procedure to return information to your code. Although this Parameter object is created in the same way, you must make sure you specify it is an output parameter by setting its Direction property to Output. You don't need to supply a value.

```
cmd.Parameters.Add(New SqlParameter("@EmployeeID", SqlDbType.Int, 4))
cmd.Parameters("@EmployeeID").Direction = ParameterDirection.Output
```

Finally, you can open the connection and execute the command with the ExecuteNonQuery() method. When the command is completed, you can read the output value, as shown here:

```
con.Open()
Try
    Dim numAff As Integer = cmd.ExecuteNonQuery()
    HtmlContent.Text &= String.Format("Inserted <b>{0}</b> record(s)<br />", numAff)

    ' Get the newly generated ID.
    empID = CInt(cmd.Parameters("@EmployeeID").Value)
    HtmlContent.Text &= "New ID: " & empID.ToString()
Finally
    con.Close()
End Try
```

In the next chapter, you'll see a small but fully functional database component that does all its work through stored procedures.

Transactions

A *transaction* is a set of operations that must either succeed or fail as a unit. The goal of a transaction is to ensure that data is always in a valid, consistent state.

For example, consider a transaction that transfers $1,000 from account A to account B. Clearly there are two operations:

- It should deduct $1,000 from account A.
- It should add $1,000 to account B.

Suppose that an application successfully completes step 1, but, because of some error, step 2 fails. This leads to an inconsistent data, because the total amount of money in the system is no longer accurate. A full $1,000 has gone missing.

Transactions help avoid these types of problems by ensuring that changes are committed to a data source only if *all* the steps are successful. So, in this example, if step 2 fails, then the changes made by step 1 will not be committed to the database. This ensures that the system stays in one of its two valid states—the initial state (with no money transferred) and the final state (with money debited from one account and credited to another).

Transactions are characterized by four properties popularly called *ACID properties*. ACID is an acronym that represents the following concepts:

Atomic: All steps in the transaction should succeed or fail together. Unless *all* the steps from a transaction complete, a transaction is not considered complete.

Consistent: The transaction takes the underlying database from one stable state to another.

Isolated: Every transaction is an independent entity. One transaction should not affect any other transaction running at the same time.

Durable: Changes that occur during the transaction are permanently stored on some media, typically a hard disk, before the transaction is declared successful. Logs are maintained so that the database can be restored to a valid state even if a hardware or network failure occurs.

Note that even though these are ideal characteristics of a transaction, they aren't always absolutely attainable. One problem is that in order to ensure isolation, the RDBMS needs to lock data so that other users can't access it while the transaction is in progress. The more locks you use, and the coarser these locks are, the greater the chance that a user won't be able to perform another task while the transactions are underway. In other words, there's often a trade-off between user concurrency and isolation.

Transactions and ASP.NET Applications

You can use three basic transaction types in an ASP.NET web application. They are as follows (from least to most overhead):

Stored procedure transactions: These transactions take place entirely in the database. Stored procedure transactions offer the best performance, because they need only a single round-trip to the database. The drawback is that you also need to write the transaction logic using SQL statements (which may be not as easy as using pure C# or VB.NET).

Client-initiated (ADO.NET) transactions: These transactions are controlled programmatically by your ASP.NET web-page code. Under the covers, they use the same commands as a stored procedure transaction, but your code uses some ADO.NET objects that wrap these details. The drawback is that extra round-trips are required to the database to start and commit the transaction.

COM+ transactions: These transactions are handled by the COM+ runtime, based on declarative attributes you add to your code. COM+ transactions use a two-stage commit protocol and always incur extra overhead. They also require that you create a separate serviced component class. COM+ components are generally a good choice only if your transaction spans multiple transaction-aware resource managers, because COM+ includes built-in support for distributed transactions. For example, a single COM+ transaction can span interactions in a SQL Server database *and* an Oracle database. COM+ transactions are not covered in this chapter, although you will consider them briefly with web services in Chapter 31.

■ **Note** ADO.NET 2.0 introduces a new concept of *promotable transactions*. However, a promotable transaction isn't a new type of transaction—it's just a way to create a client-initiated transaction that can automatically escalate itself into a COM+ transaction if needed. You shouldn't use promotable transactions unless you need to, as they make it more difficult to predict the performance and scalability of your solution. You can learn more about promotable transactions in *Pro ADO.NET 2.0* (Apress, 2005).

Even though ADO.NET provides good support for transactions, you should not always use transactions. In fact, every time you use any kind of transaction, you automatically incur some overhead. Also, transactions involve some kind of locking of table rows. Thus, unnecessarily using transactions may harm the overall scalability of your application.

When implementing a transaction, you can follow these practices to achieve the best results:

- Keep transactions as short as possible.
- Avoid returning data with a SELECT query in the middle of a transaction. Ideally, you should return the data before the transaction starts.
- If you do retrieve records, fetch only the rows that are required so as to not lock too many resources and so as to keep performance as good as possible.
- Wherever possible, write transactions within stored procedures instead of using ADO.NET transactions.
- Avoid transactions that combine multiple independent batches of work. Put separate batches into separate transactions.
- Avoid updates that affect a large range of records if at all possible.

Tip As a rule of thumb, use a transaction only when your operation requires one. For example, if you are simply selecting records from a database, or firing a single query, you will not need a transaction. On the other hand, if you are inserting an Order record in conjunction with a series of related OrderItem records, you might want to use a transaction. In general, a transaction is never required for single-statement commands such as individual UPDATE, DELETE, or INSERT statements, because these are inherently transactional.

Stored Procedure Transactions

If possible, the best place to put a transaction is in stored procedure code. This ensures that the server-side code is always in control, which makes it impossible for a client to accidentally hold a transaction open too long and potentially cause problems for other client updates. It also ensures the best possible performance, because all actions can be executed at the data source without requiring any network communication. Generally, the shorter the span of a transaction, the better the concurrency of the database and the fewer the number of database requests that will be serialized (put on hold while a temporary record lock is in place).

Stored procedure code varies depending on the database you are using, but most RDBMSs support the SQL statement BEGIN TRANSACTION. Once you start a transaction, all subsequent statements are considered part of the transaction. You can end the transaction with the COMMIT or ROLLBACK statement. If you don't, the transaction will be automatically rolled back.

Here's a pseudocode example that performs a fund transfer between accounts. It's a simplified version that allows an account to be set to a negative balance.

```
CREATE Procedure TransferAmount
(
  @Amount Money,
  @ID_A int,
  @ID_B int
)
AS
  BEGIN TRANSACTION
    UPDATE Accounts SET Balance = Balance + @Amount WHERE AccountID = @ID_A
  IF (@@ERROR > 0)
    ROLLBACK
```

```
ELSE
  COMMIT
  UPDATE Accounts SET Balance = Balance - @Amount WHERE AccountID = @ID_B
IF (@@ERROR > 0)
  ROLLBACK
ELSE
  COMMIT
```

■Note In SQL Server, a stored procedure can also perform a distributed transaction (one that involves multiple data sources and is typically hosted on multiple servers). By default, every transaction begins as a local transaction, but if you access a database on another server, the transaction is automatically upgraded to a distributed transaction governed by the Windows DTC (Distributed Transaction Coordinator) service.

Client-Initiated ADO.NET Transactions

Most ADO.NET data providers include support for database transactions. Transactions are started through the Connection object by calling the BeginTransaction() method. This method returns a provider-specific Transaction object that's used to manage the transaction. All Transaction classes implement the IDbTransaction interface. Examples include SqlTransaction, OleDbTransaction, OracleTransaction, and so on.

The Transaction class provides two key methods:

Commit(): This method identifies that the transaction is complete and that the pending changes should be stored permanently in the data source.

Rollback(): This method indicates that a transaction was unsuccessful. Pending changes are discarded, and the database state remains unchanged.

Typically, you use Commit() at the end of your operation. However, if any exception is thrown along the way, you should call Rollback().

Here's an example that inserts two records into the Employees table:

```
Dim connectionString As String =
    WebConfigurationManager.ConnectionStrings("Northwind").ConnectionString
Dim con As New SqlConnection(connectionString)

Dim cmd1 As New SqlCommand(
    "INSERT INTO Employees (LastName, FirstName) VALUES ('Joe','Tester')")
Dim cmd2 As New SqlCommand(
    "INSERT INTO Employees (LastName, FirstName) VALUES ('Harry','Sullivan')")
Dim tran As SqlTransaction = Nothing

Try
    ' Open the connection, and create the transaction.
    con.Open()
    tran = con.BeginTransaction()

    ' Enlist two commands in the transaction.
    cmd1.Transaction = tran
    cmd2.Transaction = tran

    ' Execute both commands.
    cmd1.ExecuteNonQuery()
    cmd2.ExecuteNonQuery()
```

```
        ' Commit the transaction.
        tran.Commit()
    Catch
        ' In the case of error, roll back the transaction.
        tran.Rollback()
    Finally
        con.Close()
    End Try
```

Note that it's not enough to create and commit a transaction. You also need to explicitly enlist each Command object to be part of the transaction by setting the Command.Transaction property to the Transaction object. If you try to execute a command that isn't a part of the current transaction while the transaction is underway, you'll receive an error. However, in the future this object model might allow providers to support more than one simultaneous transaction on the same connection.

■ Tip Instead of using separate command objects, you could also execute the same object twice and just modify its CommandText property in between (if it's a dynamic SQL statement) or the value of its parameters (if it's a parameterized command). For example, if your command inserts a new record, you could use this approach to insert two records in the same transaction.

To test the rollback features of a transaction, you can insert the following line just before the Commit() method is called in the previous example:

```
Throw New ApplicationException()
```

This raises an exception, which will trigger a rollback and ensure that neither record is committed to the database.

Although an ADO.NET transaction revolves around the Connection and Transaction objects, the underlying commands aren't different from a stored procedure transaction. For example, when you call BeginTransaction() with the SQL Server provider, it sends a BEGIN TRANSACTION command to the database.

■ Tip A transaction should be completed as quickly as possible (started as late as possible and finished as soon as possible). Also, an active transaction puts locks on the various resources involved, so you should select only the rows you really require.

Isolation Levels

The *isolation level* determines how sensitive a transaction is to changes made by other in-progress transactions. For example, by default when two transactions are running independently of one another, records inserted by one transaction are not visible to the other transaction until the first transaction is committed.

The concept of isolation levels is closely related to the concept of locks, because by determining the isolation level for a given transaction you determine what types of locks are required. *Shared locks* are locks that are placed when a transaction wants to read data from the database. No other transactions can modify the data while shared locks exist on a table, row, or range. However, more than one user can use a shared lock to read the data simultaneously. *Exclusive locks* are the locks that prevent two or more transactions from modifying data simultaneously. An exclusive lock is issued when a transaction needs to update data and no other locks are already held. No other user can read or modify the data while an exclusive lock is in place.

Note SQL Server actually has several types of locks that work together to help prevent deadlocks and other situations. For more information, refer to the information about locking in the SQL Server Books Online help, which is installed with SQL Server.

In a SQL Server stored procedure, you can set the isolation level using the SET TRANSACTION ISOLATION LEVEL command. In ADO.NET, you can pass a value from the IsolationLevel enumeration to the Connection.BeginTransaction() method. Table 7-6 lists possible values.

Table 7-6. *Values of the IsolationLevel Enumeration*

Value	Description
ReadUncommitted	No shared locks are placed, and no exclusive locks are honored. This type of isolation level is appropriate when you want to work with all the data matching certain conditions, irrespective of whether it's committed. Dirty reads are possible, but performance is increased.
ReadCommitted	Shared locks are held while the data is being read by the transaction. This avoids dirty reads, but the data can be changed before a transaction completes. This may result in nonrepeatable reads or phantom rows. This is the default isolation level used by SQL Server.
RepeatableRead	In this case, shared locks are placed on all data that is used in a query. This prevents others from modifying the data, and it also prevents nonrepeatable reads. However, phantom rows are possible.
Serializable	A range lock is placed on the data you use, thereby preventing other users from updating or inserting rows that would fall in that range. This is the only isolation level that removes the possibility of phantom rows. However, it has an extremely negative effect on user concurrency and is rarely used in multiple user scenarios.
Snapshot	Stores a copy of the data your transaction accesses. As a result, the transaction won't see the changes made by other transactions. This approach reduces blocking, because even if other transactions are holding locks on the data a transaction with snapshot isolation will be able to read a copy of the data. This option is supported only in SQL Server 2005 and needs to be enabled through a database-level option.

The isolation levels in Table 7-6 are arranged from the least degree of locking to the highest degree of locking. The default, ReadCommitted, is a good compromise for most transactions. Table 7-7 summarizes the locking behavior for different isolation levels.

Table 7-7. *Isolation Levels Compared*

Isolation Level	Dirty Read?	Nonrepeatable Read?	Phantom Data?	Concurrency
Read uncommitted	Yes	Yes	Yes	Best
Read committed	No	Yes	Yes	Good
Repeatable read	No	No	Yes	Poor
Serializable	No	No	No	Very poor

Savepoints

Whenever you roll back a transaction, it nullifies the effect of every command you've executed since you started the transaction. But what happens if you want to roll back only part of an ongoing transaction? SQL Server handles this with a feature called *savepoints*.

Savepoints are markers that act like bookmarks. You mark a certain point in the flow of transaction, and then you can roll back to that point. You set the savepoint using the Transaction.Save() method. Note that the Save() method is available only for the SqlTransaction class, because it's not part of the standard IDbTransaction interface.

Here's a conceptual look at how you use a savepoint:

```
' Start the transaction.
Dim tran As SqlTransaction = con.BeginTransaction()

' (Enlist and execute some commands inside the transaction.)

' Mark a savepoint.
tran.Save("CompletedInsert")

' (Enlist and execute some more commands inside the transaction.)

' If needed, roll back to the savepoint.
tran.Rollback("CompletedInsert")

' Commit or roll back the transaction.
tran.Commit()
```

Note how the Rollback() method is used with the savepoint name as a parameter. If you want to roll back the whole transaction, simply omit this parameter.

■ Note Once you roll back to a savepoint, all the savepoints defined after that save point are lost. You must set them again if they are needed.

Nested Transactions

Savepoints allow a transaction to be arranged as a sequence of actions that can be rolled back individually. Nested transactions play essentially the same role as savepoints—they allow you to start smaller transactions inside a larger transaction that can be committed or rolled back individually. To initiate nested transactions, you must call the Begin() method of the Transaction object. This returns a new Transaction object, which you can use just like the original Transaction object.

The implementation of nested transactions is up to the data source. Some data sources, such as SQL Server, don't properly support nested transactions. In SQL Server, rolling back a nested transaction actually rolls back the entire transaction. For that reason, the Begin() method isn't provided for the SqlTransaction class. Instead, you can use savepoints for similar functionality.

Provider-Agnostic Code

For the most part, ADO.NET's provider model is an ideal solution for dealing with different data sources. It allows each database vendor to develop a native, optimized solution while enforcing a high level of consistency so that skilled developers don't need to relearn the basics.

However, the provider model isn't perfect. Although you can use standard interfaces to interact with Command and Connection objects, when you instantiate a Command or Connection object, you need to know the provider-specific, strongly typed class you want to use (such as SqlConnection). This limitation makes it difficult to build other tools or add-ins that use ADO.NET. For example, in Chapter 9 you'll consider the new ASP.NET data source controls, which allow you to create data-bound pages without writing a line of code. To provide this functionality, you need a way for the data control to create the ADO.NET objects that it needs behind the scenes. It wouldn't be possible to implement this feature without dramatic restrictions in .NET 1.*x*.

.NET 2.0 solves this problem and adds improved support for writing provider-agnostic code (code that can work with any database). The secret is a new factory model.

■ **Note** Provider-agnostic code is useful when building specialized components. It may also make sense if you anticipate the need to move to a different database in the future or if you aren't sure what type of database you'll use in the final version of an application. However, it also has drawbacks. Provider-agnostic code can't take advantage of some provider-specific features (such as XML queries in SQL Server) and is more difficult to optimize. For those reasons, it's uncommon in large-scale professional web applications.

Creating the Factory

The basic idea of the factory model is that you use a single factory object to create every other type of provider-specific object you need. You can then interact with these provider-specific objects in a completely generic way, through a set of common base classes.

The factory class is itself provider-specific—for example, the SQL Server provider includes a class named System.Data.SqlClient.SqlClientFactory. The Oracle provider uses System.Data.OracleClient.OracleClientFactory. At first glance, this might seem to stop you from writing provider-agnostic code. However, it turns out that there's a completely standardized class that's designed to dynamically find and create the factory you need. This class is System.Data.Common.DbProviderFactories. It provides a Shared GetFactory() method that returns the factory you need based on the provider name.

For example, here's the code that uses DbProviderFactories to get the SqlClientFactory:

```
Dim factory As String = "System.Data.SqlClient"
Dim provider As DbProviderFactory = DbProviderFactories.GetFactory(factory)
```

Even though the DbProviderFactories class returns a strongly typed SqlClientFactory object, you shouldn't treat it as such. Instead, your code should access it as a DbProviderFactory instance. That's because all factories inherit from DbProviderFactory. If you use only the DbProviderFactory members, you can write code that works with any factory.

The weak point in the code snippet shown previously is that you need to pass a string that identifies the provider to the DbProviderFactories.GetFactory() method. You would typically read this from an application setting in the web.config file. That way, you can write completely database-agnostic code and switch your application over to another provider simply by modifying a single setting.

■ **Tip** In practice, you'll need to store several provider-specific details in a configuration file. Not only do you need to retrieve the provider name, but you'll also need to get a connection string. You might also need to retrieve queries or stored procedure names if you want to avoid hard-coding them because they might change. It's up to you to determine the ideal trade-off between development complexity and flexibility.

For the DbProviderFactories class to work, your provider needs a registered factory in the machine.config or web.config configuration file. The machine.config file registers the four providers that are included with the .NET Framework:

```
<configuration>
  <system.data>
    <DbProviderFactories>
      <add name="Odbc Data Provider" invariant="System.Data.Odbc"
        type="System.Data.Odbc.OdbcFactory, ..." />
      <add name="OleDb Data Provider" invariant="System.Data.OleDb"
        type="System.Data.OleDb.OleDbFactory, ..." />
      <add name="OracleClient Data Provider" invariant="System.Data.OracleClient"
        type="System.Data.OracleClient.OracleClientFactory, ..." />
      <add name="SqlClient Data Provider" invariant="System.Data.SqlClient"
        type="System.Data.SqlClient.SqlClientFactory, ..." />
    </DbProviderFactories>
  </system.data>
  ...
</configuration>
```

This registration step identifies the factory class and assigns a unique name for the provider (which, by convention, is the same as the namespace for that provider). If you have a third-party provider that you want to use, you need to register it in the <DbProviders> section of the machine.config file (to access it across a specific computer) or a web.config file (to access it in a specific Web application). It's likely that the person or company that developed the provider will include a setup program to automate this task or the explicit configuration syntax.

Create Objects with Factory

Once you have a factory, you can create other objects, such as Connection and Command instances, using the DbProviderFactory.CreateXxx() methods. For example, the CreateConnection() method returns the Connection object for your data provider. Once again, you must assume you don't know what provider you'll be using, so you can interact with the objects the factory creates only through a standard base class.

Table 7-8 gives a quick reference that shows what method you need in order to create each type of data access object and what base class you can use to manipulate it safely.

Table 7-8. *Interfaces for Standard ADO.NET Objects*

Type of Object	Base Class	Example	DbProviderFactory Method
Connection	DbConnection	SqlConnection	CreateConnection()
Command	DbCommand	SqlCommand	CreateCommand()
Parameter	DbDataParameter	SqlParameter	CreateParameter()
DataReader	DbDataReader	SqlDataReader	CreateDataReader()
DataAdapter	DbDataAdapter	SqlDataAdapter	CreateDataAdapter()

■ **Note** As explained earlier in this chapter, the provider-specific objects also implement certain interfaces (such as IDbConnection). However, because some objects use more than one ADO.NET interface (for example, a DataReader implements both IDataRecord and IDataReader), the base class model simplifies the model.

A Query with Provider-Agnostic Code

To get a better understanding of how all these pieces fit together, it helps to consider a simple example. In this section, you'll see how to perform a query and display the results using provider-agnostic code. In fact, this example is an exact rewrite of the page shown earlier in Figure 7-3. The only difference is that it's no longer tightly bound to the SQL Server provider.

The first step is to set up the web.config file with the connection string, provider name, and query for this example:

```
<configuration xmlns="http://schemas.microsoft.com/.NetConfiguration/v2.0">
  <connectionStrings>
    <add name="Northwind" connectionString=
"Data Source=localhost;Initial Catalog=Northwind;Integrated Security=SSPI"/>
  </connectionStrings>
  <appSettings>
    <add key="factory" value="System.Data.SqlClient" />
    <add key="employeeQuery" value="SELECT * FROM Employees" />
  </appSettings>
  ...
</configuration>
```

Next, here's the factory-based code:

```
' Get the factory.
Dim factory As String = WebConfigurationManager.AppSettings("factory")
Dim provider As DbProviderFactory = DbProviderFactories.GetFactory(factory)

' Use this factory to create a connection.
Dim con As DbConnection = provider.CreateConnection()
con.ConnectionString =
        WebConfigurationManager.ConnectionStrings("Northwind").ConnectionString

' Create the command.
Dim cmd As DbCommand = provider.CreateCommand()
cmd.CommandText = WebConfigurationManager.AppSettings("employeeQuery")
cmd.Connection = con

' Open the Connection, and get the DataReader.
con.Open()
Dim reader As DbDataReader = cmd.ExecuteReader()

' The code for navigating through the reader and displaying the records
' is identical from this point on.
```

To give this example a real test, try modifying the web.config file to use a different provider. For example, you can access the same database through the OLE DB provider by making this change:

```
<configuration xmlns="http://schemas.microsoft.com/.NetConfiguration/v2.0">
  <connectionStrings>
    <add name="Northwind" connectionString="Provider=SQLOLEDB;Data Source=
localhost;Initial Catalog=Northwind;Integrated Security=SSPI"/>
  </connectionStrings>
  ...
</configuration>
```

Now when you run the page, you'll see the same list of records. The difference is that the DbDataFactories class creates OLE DB objects to work with your code.

■ **Note** The challenges of provider-agnostic aren't completely solved yet. Even with the provider factories, you still face a few problems. For example, there's no generic way to catch database exception objects (because different provider-specific exception objects don't inherit from a common base class). Also, different providers may have slightly different conventions with parameter names and may support specialized features that aren't available through the common base classes (in which case you need to write some thorny conditional logic).

Summary

In this chapter, you learned about the first level of database access with ADO.NET: connected access. In many cases, using simple commands and quick read-only cursors to retrieve results provides the easiest and most efficient way to write data access code for a web application. Along the way, you considered some advanced topics, including SQL injection attacks, transactions, and provider-agnostic code.

In the next chapter, you'll learn how to use these techniques to build your own data access classes and how to use ADO.NET's disconnected DataSet.

CHAPTER 8

Data Components and the DataSet

In the previous chapter, you had your first look at ADO.NET, and you examined connection-based data access. Now, it's time to bring your data access code into a well-designed application.

In a properly organized application, your data access code is never embedded directly in the code-behind for a page. Instead, it's separated into a dedicated data component. In this chapter, you'll see how to create a simple data access class of your own, adding a separate method for each data task you need to perform. Best of all, this data class isn't limited to code-intensive scenarios. In the next chapter, you'll see how to consume your class with ASP.NET's new data binding infrastructure.

This chapter also tackles disconnected data—the ADO.NET features that revolve around the DataSet and allow you to interact with data long after you've closed the connection to the data source. The DataSet isn't required in ASP.NET pages. However, it gives you more flexibility for navigating, filtering, and sorting your data—topics you'll consider in this chapter.

Tip The information you'll see in this chapter hasn't changed much from ASP.NET 1.*x*. You use the same techniques to build a good database component, and the DataSet works in the same way (along with a few refinements). For a more detailed look at ADO.NET and how you can use it with a variety of .NET application types, refer to *Pro ADO.NET 2.0* (Apress, 2005).

Building a Data Access Component

In professional applications, database code is not embedded directly in the client but encapsulated in a dedicated class. To perform a database operation, the client creates an instance of this class and calls the appropriate method. When data access components use static classes, all the methods are Shared, and then there is no need to create an instance of the class.

When defining a data class, you should follow the basic guidelines in this section. This will ensure that you create a well-encapsulated, optimized database component that can be executed in a separate process, if needed, and even used in a load-balancing configuration with multiple servers.

Open and close connections quickly: Open the database connection in every method call, and close it before the method ends. Connections should never be held open between client requests, and the client should have no control over how connections are acquired or when they are released. If the client does have this ability, it introduces the possibility that a connection might not be closed as quickly as possible or might be inadvertently left open, which hampers scalability. Examples of where include when you open a reader and return it to the client and when the client closes the reader the connection also gets closed.

Implement error handling: Use error handling to make sure the connection is closed even if the SQL command generates an exception. Remember, connections are a finite resource, and using them for even a few extra seconds can have a major overall effect on performance.

Follow stateless design practices: Accept all the information needed for a method in its parameters, and return all the retrieved data through the return value. If you create a class that maintains state, it cannot be easily implemented as a web service or used in a load-balancing scenario. Also, if the database component is hosted out of the process, each method call has a measurable overhead, and using multiple calls to set properties will take much longer than invoking a single method with all the information as parameters.

Don't let the client specify connection string information: This poses security risks, raises the possibility that an out-of-date client will fail, and compromises the ability of connection pooling, which requires matching connection strings.

Don't connect with the client's user ID: Introducing any variability into the connection string will thwart connection pooling, as you learned in the previous chapter. Instead, rely on role-based security or a ticket-based system whereby you authenticate users and prevent them from attempting to perform a restricted operation. This model is also faster than trying to perform a database query under an invalid security account and waiting for an error.

Don't let the client use wide-open queries: Every query should judiciously select only the columns it needs. Also, you should restrict the results with a WHERE clause whenever possible. For example, when retrieving order records, you might impose a minimum date range (or an SQL clause such as TOP 1000). Without these safeguards, your application may work well at first but will slow down as the database grows and clients perform large queries, which can tax both the database and the network.

A good, straightforward design for a database component uses a separate class for every database table (or logically related group of tables). The common database access methods such as inserting, deleting, and modifying a record are all wrapped in separate stateless methods. Finally, every database call uses a dedicated stored procedure. Figure 8-1 shows this carefully layered design.

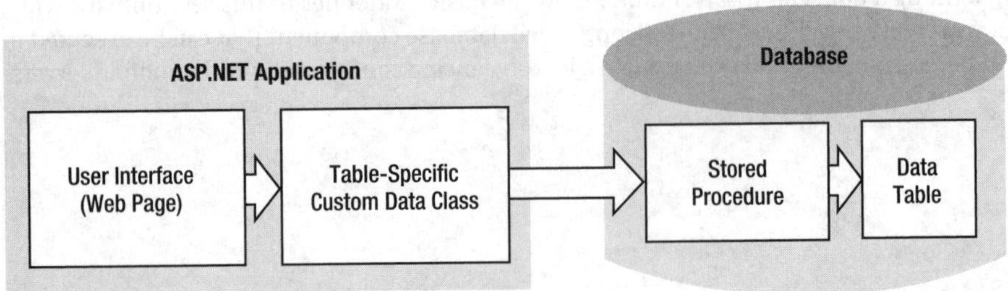

Figure 8-1. *Layered design with a database class*

The following example demonstrates a simple database component. Rather than placing the database code in the web page, it follows a much better design practice of separating the code into a distinct class that can be used in multiple pages. This class can then be compiled as part of a separate component if needed. Additionally, the connection string is retrieved from the <connectionStrings> section of the web.config file, rather than being hard-coded.

The data component actually consists of two classes—a data package class that wraps a single record of information and a database utility class that performs the actual database operations with ADO.NET code.

The Data Package

To make it easier to shuffle information to the Northwind database and back, it makes sense to create an EmployeeDetails class that provides all the fields as public properties. Here's the full code for this class:

```
Public Class EmployeeDetails
    Dim nEmployeeID As Integer
    Public Property EmployeeID() As Integer
        Get
                Return nEmployeeID
        End Get
        Set
                nEmployeeID = Value
        End Set
    End Property

    Dim strFirstName As String
    Public Property FirstName() As String
        Get
                Return strFirstName
        End Get
        Set
                strFirstName = Value
        End Set
    End Property

    Dim strLastName As String
    Public Property LastName() As String
        Get
                Return strLastName
        End Get
        Set
                strLastName = Value
        End Set
    End Property

    Dim strTitleOfCourtesy As String
    Public Property TitleOfCourtesy() As String
        Get
                Return strTitleOfCourtesy
        End Get
        Set
                strTitleOfCourtesy = Value
        End Set
    End Property


Public Sub New(ByVal nEmployeeID As Integer, ByVal strFirstName As String,
    ByVal strLastName As String, ByVal strTitleOfCourtesy As String)
```

```
        Me.employeeID = nEmployeeID
        Me.firstName = strFirstName
        Me.lastName = strLastName
        Me.titleOfCourtesy = strTitleOfCourtesy
    End Sub
End Class
```

Note that this class doesn't include all the information that's in the Employees table in order to make the example more concise.

The Stored Procedures

Before you can start coding the data access logic, you need to make sure you have the set of stored procedures you need in order to retrieve, insert, and update information. The following code shows the five stored procedures that are needed:

```
CREATE PROCEDURE InsertEmployee
(
    @EmployeeID      int OUTPUT,
    @FirstName       varchar(10),
    @LastName        varchar(20),
    @TitleOfCourtesy varchar(25)
)
AS
INSERT INTO Employees
  (TitleOfCourtesy, LastName, FirstName, HireDate)
  VALUES (@TitleOfCourtesy, @LastName, @FirstName, GETDATE());
SET @EmployeeID = @@IDENTITY
GO

CREATE PROCEDURE DeleteEmployee
(
    @EmployeeID      int
)
AS
DELETE FROM Employees WHERE EmployeeID = @EmployeeID
GO

CREATE PROCEDURE UpdateEmployee
(
    @EmployeeID      int,
    @TitleOfCourtesy varchar(25),
    @LastName        varchar(20),
    @FirstName       varchar(10)
)
AS
UPDATE Employees
    SET TitleOfCourtesy = @TitleOfCourtesy,
    LastName = @LastName,
    FirstName = @FirstName
    WHERE EmployeeID = @EmployeeID
GO
```

```
CREATE PROCEDURE GetAllEmployees
AS
SELECT EmployeeID, FirstName, LastName, TitleOfCourtesy FROM Employees
GO

CREATE PROCEDURE CountEmployees
AS
SELECT COUNT(EmployeeID) FROM Employees
GO

CREATE PROCEDURE GetEmployee
(
    @EmployeeID      int
)
AS
SELECT FirstName, LastName, TitleOfCourtesy FROM Employees
  WHERE EmployeeID = @EmployeeID
GO
```

The Data Utility Class

Finally, you need the utility class that performs the actual database operations. This class uses the stored procedures that were shown in the previous section.

In this example, the data utility class is named EmployeeDB. It encapsulates all the data access code and database-specific details. Here's the basic outline:

```
Public Class EmployeeDB
    Dim connectionString As String

    Public Sub New()
        ' Get default connection string.
        connectionString = WebConfigurationManager.ConnectionStrings(
                                                 "Northwind").ConnectionString
    End Sub
    Public Sub New(ByVal connectionStringName As String)
        ' Get the specified connection string.
        connectionString =
            WebConfigurationManager.ConnectionStrings(
                                              connectionStringName).ConnectionString
    End Sub

    Public Function InsertEmployee(ByVal emp As EmployeeDetails) As Integer
        ...
    End Function
    Public Sub DeleteEmployee(ByVal employeeID As Integer)
        ...
    End Sub
    Public Function GetEmployee() As EmployeeDetails
        ...
    End Function
    Public Function GetEmployees() As EmployeeDetails()
        ...
    End Function
    Public Function CountEmployees() As Integer
        ...
    End Function
End Class
```

■ **Note** You may have noticed that the EmployeeDB class uses instance methods, not static methods. That's because even though the EmployeeDB class doesn't store any state from the database, it does store the connection string as a private member variable. Because this is an instance class, the connection string can be retrieved every time the class is created, rather than every time a method is invoked. This approach makes the code a little clearer and allows it to be slightly faster (by avoiding the need to read the web.config file multiple times). However, the benefit is fairly small, so you can use static methods just as easily in your database components.

Each method uses the same careful approach, relying exclusively on a stored procedure to interact with the database. Here's the code for inserting a record:

```
Public Function InsertEmployee(ByVal emp As EmployeeDetails) As Integer
    Dim con As New SqlConnection(connectionString)
    Dim cmd As New SqlCommand("InsertEmployee", con)
    cmd.CommandType = CommandType.StoredProcedure
    cmd.Parameters.Add(New SqlParameter("@FirstName", SqlDbType.NVarChar, 10))
    cmd.Parameters("@FirstName").Value = emp.FirstName
    cmd.Parameters.Add(New SqlParameter("@LastName", SqlDbType.NVarChar, 20))
    cmd.Parameters("@LastName").Value = emp.LastName
    cmd.Parameters.Add(New SqlParameter("@TitleOfCourtesy", SqlDbType.NVarChar, 25))
    cmd.Parameters("@TitleOfCourtesy").Value = emp.TitleOfCourtesy
    cmd.Parameters.Add(New SqlParameter("@EmployeeID", SqlDbType.Int, 4))
    cmd.Parameters("@EmployeeID").Direction = ParameterDirection.Output

    Try
        con.Open()
        cmd.ExecuteNonQuery()
        Return CInt(cmd.Parameters("@EmployeeID").Value)
    Catch err As SqlException
        ' Replace the error with something less specific.
        ' You could also log the error now.
        Throw New ApplicationException("Data error.")
    Finally
        con.Close()
    End Try
End Function
```

As you can see, the method accepts data using the EmployeeDetails class. Any errors are caught, and the sensitive internal details are not returned to the web-page code. This prevents the web page from providing information that could lead to possible exploits. This would also be an ideal place to call another method in a logging component to report the full information in an event log or another database.

The GetEmployee() and GetEmployees() methods return the data using the EmployeeDetails package:

```
Public Function GetEmployee(ByVal employeeID As Integer) As EmployeeDetails
    Dim con As New SqlConnection(connectionString)
    Dim cmd As New SqlCommand("GetEmployee", con)
    cmd.CommandType = CommandType.StoredProcedure
    cmd.Parameters.Add(New SqlParameter("@EmployeeID", SqlDbType.Int, 4))
    cmd.Parameters("@EmployeeID").Value = employeeID
    Try
        con.Open()
        Dim reader As SqlDataReader = cmd.ExecuteReader(CommandBehavior.SingleRow)
```

```
        ' Get the first row.
        reader.Read()
        Dim emp As EmployeeDetails =
              New EmployeeDetails(CInt(reader("EmployeeID")),
              CStr(reader("FirstName")), CStr(reader("LastName")),
              CStr(reader("TitleOfCourtesy")))
        reader.Close()
        Return emp
    Catch err As SqlException
        Throw New ApplicationException("Data error.")
    Finally
        con.Close()
    End Try
End Function

Public Function GetEmployees() As EmployeeDetails
    Dim con As New SqlConnection(connectionString)
    Dim cmd As New SqlCommand("GetAllEmployees", con)
    cmd.CommandType = CommandType.StoredProcedure

    ' Create a collection for all the employee records.
    Dim employees As New ArrayList()
    Try
        con.Open()
        Dim reader As SqlDataReader = cmd.ExecuteReader()
        Do While reader.Read()
            Dim emp As New EmployeeDetails(CInt(reader("EmployeeID")),
                  CStr(reader("FirstName")), CStr(reader("LastName")),
                  CStr(reader("TitleOfCourtesy")))
            employees.Add(emp)
        Loop
        reader.Close()
        Return employees
    Catch err As SqlException
        Throw New ApplicationException("Data error.")
    Finally
        con.Close()
    End Try
End Function
```

The UpdateEmployee() method plays a special role. It determines the concurrency strategy of your database component (see the next section, "Concurrency Strategies").

Here's the code:

```
Public Sub UpdateEmployee(ByVal EmployeeID As Integer, ByVal firstName As String,
          ByVal lastName As String, ByVal titleOfCourtesy As String)
    Dim con As SqlConnection = New SqlConnection(connectionString)
    Dim cmd As SqlCommand = New SqlCommand("UpdateEmployee", con)
    cmd.CommandType = CommandType.StoredProcedure

    cmd.Parameters.Add(New SqlParameter("@FirstName", SqlDbType.NVarChar, 10))
    cmd.Parameters("@FirstName").Value = firstName
    cmd.Parameters.Add(New SqlParameter("@LastName", SqlDbType.NVarChar, 20))
    cmd.Parameters("@LastName").Value = lastName
    cmd.Parameters.Add(New SqlParameter("@TitleOfCourtesy", SqlDbType.NVarChar, 25))
    cmd.Parameters("@TitleOfCourtesy").Value = titleOfCourtesy
```

```
    cmd.Parameters.Add(New SqlParameter("@EmployeeID", SqlDbType.Int, 4))
    cmd.Parameters("@EmployeeID").Value = EmployeeID
    Try
        con.Open()
        cmd.ExecuteNonQuery()
    Catch err As SqlException
        Throw New ApplicationException("Data error.")
    Finally
        con.Close()
    End Try
End Sub
```

Finally, the DeleteEmployee() and CountEmployees() methods fill in the last two ingredients:

```
Public Sub DeleteEmployee(ByVal employeeID As Integer)
    Dim con As New SqlConnection(connectionString)
    Dim cmd As New SqlCommand("DeleteEmployee", con)
    cmd.CommandType = CommandType.StoredProcedure
    cmd.Parameters.Add(New SqlParameter("@EmployeeID", SqlDbType.Int, 4))
    cmd.Parameters("@EmployeeID").Value = employeeID
    Try
        con.Open()
        cmd.ExecuteNonQuery()
    Catch err As SqlException
        Throw New ApplicationException("Data error.")

    Finally
        con.Close()
    End Try
End Sub

Public Function CountEmployees() As Integer
    Dim con As SqlConnection = New SqlConnection(connectionString)
    Dim cmd As SqlCommand = New SqlCommand("CountEmployees", con)
    cmd.CommandType = CommandType.StoredProcedure
    Try
        con.Open()
        Return CInt(cmd.ExecuteScalar())
    Catch err As SqlException
        Throw New ApplicationException("Data error.")
    Finally
        con.Close()
    End Try
End Function
```

Concurrency Strategies

In any multiuser application, including web applications, there's the potential that more than one user will perform overlapping queries and updates. This can lead to a potentially confusing situation where two users, who are both in possession of the current state for a row, attempt to commit divergent updates. The first user's update will always succeed. The success or failure of the second update is determined by your *concurrency strategy*.

There are several broad approaches to concurrency management. The most important thing to understand is that you determine your concurrency strategy by the way you write your UPDATE commands (particularly the way you shape the WHERE clause).

Here are the most common examples:

Last-in-wins updating: This is a less restrictive form of concurrency control that always commits the update (unless the original row has been deleted). Every time an update is committed, all the values are applied. Last-in-wins makes sense if data collisions are rare. For example, you can safely use this approach if there is only one person responsible for updating a given group of records. Usually, you implement a last-in-wins by writing a WHERE clause that matches the record to update based on its primary key. The UpdateEmployee() method in the previous example uses the last-in-wins approach.

```
UPDATE Employees SET ... WHERE EmployeeID=@ID
```

Match-all updating: To implement this strategy, you add a WHERE clause that tries to match the current values of every field in the record to your UPDATE statement. That way, if even a single field has been modified, the record won't be matched and the change will not succeed. One problem with this approach is that compatible changes are not allowed. For example, if two users are attempting to modify different parts of the same record, the second user's change will be rejected, even though it doesn't conflict. Another, more significant, problem with the match-all updating strategy is that it leads to large, inefficient SQL statements. You can implement the same strategy more effectively with timestamps (see the next point).

```
UPDATE Employees SET ... WHERE EmployeeID=@ID AND FirstName=@FirstName
  AND LastName=@LastName ...
```

Timestamp-based updating: Most database systems support a timestamp column, which the data source updates automatically every time a change is performed. You do not need to modify the timestamp column manually. However, you can examine it for changes and thereby determine if another user has recently applied an update. If you write an UPDATE statement with a WHERE clause that incorporates the primary key and the current timestamp, you're guaranteed to update the record only if it hasn't been modified, just like with match-all updating.

```
UPDATE Employees SET ... WHERE EmployeeID=@ID AND TimeStamp=@TimeStamp
```

Changed-value updating: This approach attempts to apply just the changed values in an UPDATE command, thereby allowing two users to make changes at the same time if these changes are to different fields. The problem with this approach is it can be complex, because you need to keep track of what values have changed (in which case they should be incorporated in the WHERE clause) and what values haven't.

To get a better understanding of how this plays out, consider what happens if two users attempt to commit different updates to an employee record using a method such as UpdateEmployee(), which implements last-in-wins concurrency. The first user updates the mailing address. The second user changes the employee name and inadvertently reapplies the old mailing address at the same time. The problem is that the UpdateEmployee() method doesn't have any way to know what changes you are committing. This means that it pushes all the in-memory values back to the data source, even if these old values haven't been changed (and wind up overwriting someone else's update).

If you have large, complex records and you need to support different types of edits, the easiest way to solve a problem like this may be to create more-targeted methods. Instead of creating a generic UpdateEmployee() method, use more-targeted methods such as UpdateEmployeeAddress() or ChangeEmployeeStatus(). These methods can then execute more limited UPDATE statements that don't risk reapplying old values.

Testing the Component

Now it's a simple matter of creating a test page to use this database component. As with any other component, you must begin by adding a reference to the component assembly. Then you can import the namespace it uses to make it easier to access the EmployeeDetails and EmployeeDB classes. The only step that remains is to write the code that interacts with the classes. In this example, the code takes place in the Page.Load event handler.

First, the code retrieves and writes the number and the list of employees by using a private WriteEmployeesList() method that translates the details to HTML. Next, the code adds a record and lists the table content again. Finally, the code deletes the added record and shows the content of the Employees table one more time.

Here's the complete page code:

```
Public partial Class ComponentTest
    Inherits System.Web.UI.Page

    ' Create the database component so it's available anywhere on the page.
    Private db As EmployeeDB = New EmployeeDB()
    Protected Sub Page_Load(ByVal sender As Object, ByVal e As System.EventArgs)
        WriteEmployeesList()
        Dim empID As Integer =
            db.InsertEmployee(New EmployeeDetails(0, "Marco", "Bellinaso", "Mr"))
          HtmlContent.Text &= "<br />Inserted 1 employee.<br />"
        WriteEmployeesList()
         db.DeleteEmployee(empID)
        HtmlContent.Text &= "<br />Deleted 1 employee.<br />"
        WriteEmployeesList()
    End Sub

    Private Sub WriteEmployeesList()
        Dim htmlStr As StringBuilder = New StringBuilder("")
        Dim numEmployees As Integer = db.CountEmployees()
        htmlStr.Append("<br />Total employees: <b>")
        htmlStr.Append(numEmployees.ToString())
        htmlStr.Append("</b><br /><br />")
        Dim employees As List(Of EmployeeDetails) = db.GetEmployees()
        For Each emp As EmployeeDetails In employees
            htmlStr.Append("<li>")
            htmlStr.Append(emp.EmployeeID)
            htmlStr.Append(" ")
            htmlStr.Append(emp.TitleOfCourtesy)
            htmlStr.Append(" <b>")
            htmlStr.Append(emp.FirstName)
            htmlStr.Append("</b>, ")
            htmlStr.Append(emp.LastName)
            htmlStr.Append("</li>")
        Next emp
        htmlStr.Append("<br />")
        HtmlContent.Text &= htmlStr.ToString()
    End Sub
End Class
```

Figure 8-2 shows the page output.

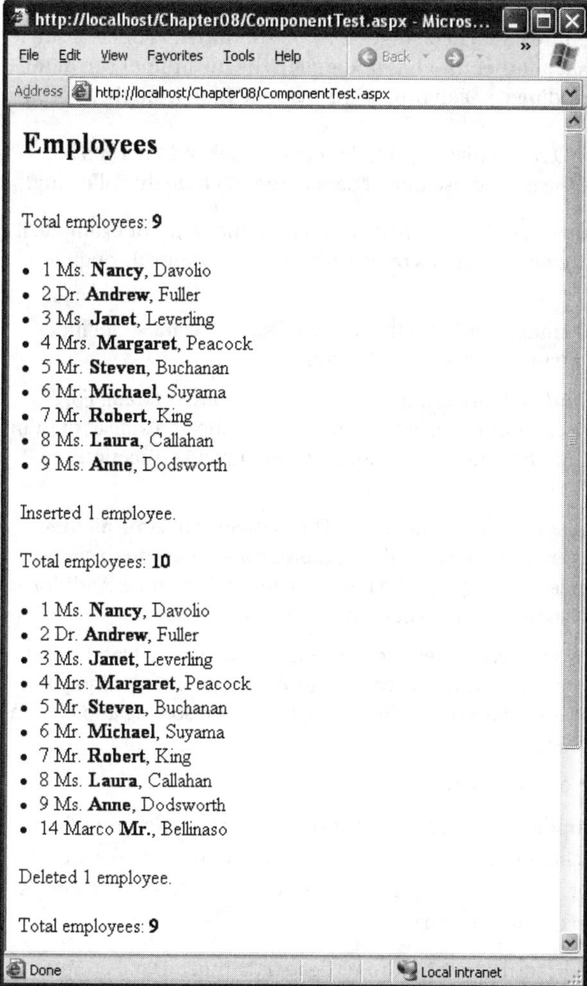

Figure 8-2. *Using a database component*

Disconnected Data

So far, all the examples you've seen have used ADO.NET's connection-based features. When using this approach, data ceases to have anything to do with the data source the moment it is retrieved. It's up to your code to track user actions, store information, and determine when a new command should be generated and executed.

ADO.NET emphasizes an entirely different philosophy with the DataSet object. When you connect to a database, you fill the DataSet with a copy of the information drawn from the database. You then close the connection to the database and continue working with the data while you are disconnected from the database. If you change the information in the DataSet, the information in the corresponding table in the database isn't changed. That means you can easily process and manipulate the data without worry, because you aren't using a valuable database connection. If necessary, you can reconnect to the original data source and apply all your DataSet changes in a single batch operation.

Of course, this convenience isn't without drawbacks, such as concurrency issues. Depending on how your application is designed, an entire batch of changes may be submitted at once. A single error (such as trying to update a record that another user has updated in the meantime) can derail the entire update process. With studious coding you can protect your application from these problems—but it requires additional effort.

Sometimes you might want to use ADO.NET's disconnected access model and the DataSet. Some of the scenarios in which a DataSet is easier to use than a data reader include the following:

- When you need a convenient object to send the data to another component (for example, if you're sharing information with other components or distributing it to clients through a .NET web service).
- When you need a convenient file format to serialize the data to disk (the DataSet includes built-in functionality that allows you to save it to an XML file).
- When you want to navigate backward and forward through a large amount of data. For example, you could use a DataSet to support a paged list control that shows a subset of information at a time. The DataReader, on the other hand, can move in only one direction: forward.
- When you want to navigate among several different tables. The DataSet can store all these tables, and information about the relations between them, thereby allowing you to create easy master-detail pages without needing to query the database more than once. Additionally, ADO.NET 2.0 has multiple active result sets to help manage this.
- When you want to use data binding with user interface controls. You can use a DataReader for data binding, but because the DataReader is a forward-only cursor, you can't bind your data to multiple controls. You also won't have the ability to apply custom sorting and filtering criteria, like you can with the DataSet.
- When you want to manipulate the data as XML.
- When you want to provide batch updates through a web service. For example, you might create a web service that allows a client to download a DataTable full of rows, make multiple changes, and then resubmit it later. At that point, the web service can apply all the changes in a single operation (assuming no conflicts occur).

In the remainder of this chapter, you'll learn about how to retrieve data into a DataSet. You'll also learn how to retrieve data from multiple tables, how to create relationships between these in-memory data tables, how to sort and filter data, and how to search for specific records. However, you won't consider the task of using the DataSet to perform updates. That's because the ASP.NET model lends itself more closely to direct commands, as discussed in the next section.

Web Applications and the DataSet

A common misconception is that the DataSet is required to ensure scalability in a web application. Now that you understand the ASP.NET request processing architecture, you can probably see that this isn't the case. A web application runs only for a matter of seconds (if that long—probably fractions of a second). This means that even if your web application uses direct cursor-based access, the lifetime of the connection is so short that it won't significantly reduce scalability, except in the mostly highly trafficked web applications.

In fact, the DataSet makes much more sense with distributed applications that use a rich Windows client. In this scenario, the clients can retrieve a DataSet from the server (perhaps using a web service), work with their DataSet objects for a long period of time, and reconnect to the system only when they need to update the data source with the batch of changes they've made. This allows the system to handle a much larger number of concurrent users than it would be able to if each client maintained a direct, long-lasting connection. It also allows you to efficiently share resources by caching data on the server and pooling connections between client requests.

The DataSet also acts as a neat package of information for rich client applications that are only intermittently connected to your system. For example, consider a traveling sales associate who needs to enter order information or review information about sales contacts on a laptop. Using the DataSet, an application on the user's laptop can store disconnected data locally and serialize it to an XML file. This allows the sales associate to build new orders using the cached data, even when no Internet connection is available. The new data can be submitted later when the user reconnects to the system.

So, where does all this leave ASP.NET web applications? Essentially, you have two choices. You can use the DataSet, or you can use direct commands to bypass the DataSet altogether. Generally speaking, you'll bypass the DataSet when adding, inserting, or updating records. However, you won't avoid the DataSet completely.

■ **Note** Web services represent the only real web application scenario in which you might decide to perform batch updating through a DataSet. In this case, a rich client application downloads the data as a DataSet, edits it, and resubmits the DataSet later to commit its changes.

XML Integration

The DataSet also provides native XML serialization. You don't need to even be aware of this to enjoy its benefits, such as being able to easily serialize a DataSet to a file or transmit the DataSet to another application through a web service. At its best, this feature allows you to share your data with clients written in different programming languages and running on other operating systems.

The XML integration in the DataSet also allows you to access the information in the DataSet as an XML document at any time. You can even modify values, remove rows, and add new records by modifying the XML without losing any information. This deep XML integration isn't required for a typical self-contained web application. In fact, if you modify relational data through an XML model, you can run into several types of problems that you won't face using the DataSet object directly, such as data type conversion problems and errors with duplicated data or violated relationships. Where the DataSet support for XML really shines is if you need to exchange the information in the DataSet with other applications and business processes.

You'll learn more about the DataSet support for XML in Chapter 12.

The DataSet Class

The DataSet is the heart of disconnected data access. The DataSet contains two important ingredients: a collection of zero or more tables (exposed through the Tables property) and a collection of zero or more relationships that you can use to link tables together (exposed through the Relations property). Figure 8-3 shows the basic structure of the DataSet.

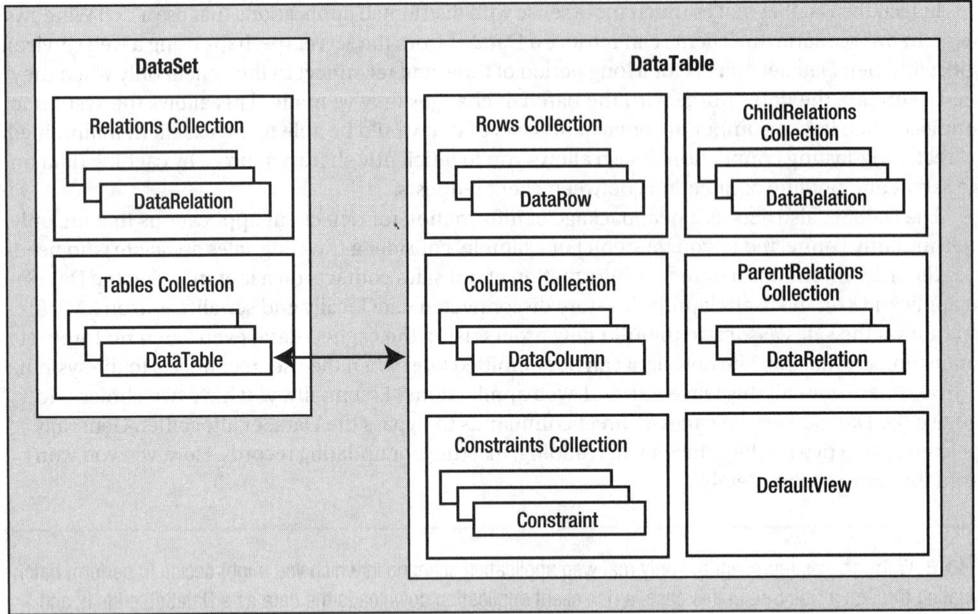

Figure 8-3. *Dissecting the DataSet*

■ **Note** Occasionally, novice ADO.NET developers make the mistake of assuming that the DataSet should contain all the information from a given table in the data source. This is not the case. For performance reasons, you will generally use the DataSet to work with a small subset of the total information in the data source. Also, the tables in the DataSet do not need to map directly to tables in the data source. A single table can hold the results of a query on one table, or it can hold the results of a JOIN query that combines data from more than one linked table.

As you can see in Figure 8-3, each record is represented as a DataRow object. To manage disconnected changes, the DataSet tracks versioning information for every DataRow. When you edit the value in a row, the original value is kept in memory, and the row is marked as changed. When you add or delete a row, the row is marked as added or deleted.

Always remember that the data in the data source is not touched at all when you work with the DataSet objects. Instead, all the changes are made locally to the DataSet in memory. The DataSet never retains any type of connection to a data source. If you want to extract records from a database and use them to fill a table in a DataSet, you need to use another ADO.NET object: a DataAdapter. The DataAdapter also allows you to update the data source according to the changes you make in the DataSet (although direct commands are a preferred approach to updating in ASP.NET).

The DataSet also has methods that can write and read XML data and schemas and has methods you can use to quickly clear and duplicate data. Table 8-1 outlines these methods. You'll learn more about XML in Chapter 12.

Table 8-1. *DataSet XML and Miscellaneous Methods*

Method	Description
GetXml() and GetXmlSchema()	Returns a string with the data (in XML markup) or schema information for the DataSet. The schema information is the structural information such as the number of tables, their names, their columns, their data types, and their relationships.
WriteXml() and WriteXmlSchema()	Persists the data and schema represented by the DataSet to a file or a stream in XML format.
ReadXml() and ReadXmlSchema()	Creates the tables in a DataSet based on an existing XML document or XML schema document. The XML source can be a file or any other stream.
Clear()	Empties all the data from the tables. However, this method leaves the schema and relationship information intact.
Copy()	Returns an exact duplicate of the DataSet, with the same set of tables, relationships, and data.
Clone()	Returns a DataSet with the same structure (tables and relationships) but no data.
Merge()	Takes another DataSet as input and merges it into the current DataSet, adding any new tables and merging any existing tables.

The DataTable Class

As you can see in Figure 8-3, each item in the DataSet.Tables collection is a DataTable. The DataTable contains its own collections—the Columns collection of DataColumn objects (which describe the name and data type of each field) and the Rows collection of DataRow objects (which contain the actual data in each record).

■Tip ADO.NET 2.0 adds a new CreateDataReader() method to the DataSet and DataTable classes. You can call this to return a DataReader-style object that lets you iterate over your disconnected data. This feature is particularly useful if you have existing code that expects a DataReader. The CreateDataReader() method returns a DataTableReader object, which derives from DbDataReader and implements the IDataReader interface, like all the DataReader objects.

The DataRow Class

Each DataRow object represents a single record in a table that has been retrieved from the data source. The DataRow is the container for the actual field values. You can access them by field name, as in myRow("FieldNameHere").

The DataAdapter Class

Each data provider has its own data adapter class, System.Data.SqlClient.SqlDataAdapter. The DataAdapter serves as a bridge between a single DataTable in the DataSet and the data source. It contains all the available commands for querying and updating the data source.

The DataAdapter provides three key methods, as listed in Table 8-2.

Table 8-2. *DataAdapter Methods*

Method	Description
Fill()	Adds a DataTable to a DataSet by executing the query in the SelectCommand. If your query returns multiple result sets, this method will add multiple DataTable objects at once. You can also use this method to add data to an existing DataTable.
FillSchema()	Adds a DataTable to a DataSet by executing the query in the SelectCommand and retrieving schema information only. This method doesn't add any data to the DataTable. Instead, it simply preconfigures the DataTable with detailed information about column names, data types, primary keys, and unique constraints.
Update()	Examines all the changes in a single DataTable and applies this batch of changes to the data source by executing the appropriate InsertCommand, UpdateCommand, and DeleteCommand operations.

To enable the DataAdapter to edit, delete, and add rows, you need to specify Command objects for the UpdateCommand, DeleteCommand, and InsertCommand properties of the DataAdapter. To use the DataAdapter to fill a DataSet, you must set the SelectCommand.

Figure 8-4 shows how a DataAdapter and its Command objects work together with the data source and the DataSet.

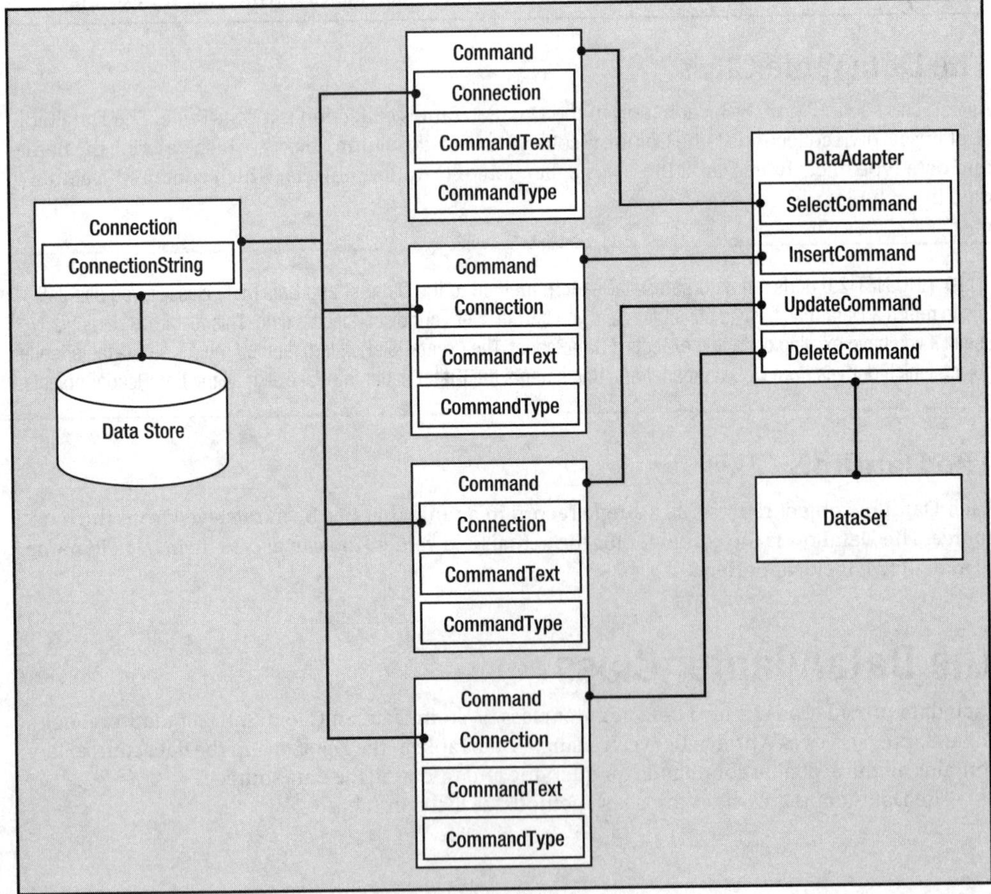

Figure 8-4. *How the DataAdapter interacts with the data source*

Filling a DataSet

In the following example, you'll see how to retrieve data from a SQL Server table and use it to fill a DataTable object in the DataSet. You'll also see how to display the data by using a Repeater control or by programmatically cycling through the records and displaying them one by one. All the logic takes place in the event handler for the Page.Load event.

First, the code creates the connection and defines the text of the SQL query:

```
Dim connectionString As String =
    WebConfigurationManager.ConnectionStrings("Northwind").ConnectionString
Dim con As New SqlConnection(connectionString)
Dim sql As String = "SELECT * FROM Employees"
```

The next step is to create a new instance of the SqlDataAdapter class that will retrieve the employee list. Although every DataAdapter supports four Command objects, only one of these (the SelectCommand) is required to fill a DataSet. To make life even easier, you can create the Command object you need and assign it to the DataAdapter.SelectCommand property in one step. You just need to supply a Connection object and query string in the DataAdapter constructor, as shown here:

```
Dim da As New SqlDataAdapter(sql, con)
```

Now you need to create a new, empty DataSet and use the DataAdapter. Fill() method to execute the query and place the results in a new DataTable in the DataSet. At this point, you can also specify the name for the table. If you don't, a default name (like `Table1`) will be used automatically. In the following example, the table name corresponds to the name of the source table in the database, although this is not a requirement:

```
Dim ds As New DataSet()
da.Fill(ds, "Employees")
```

Note that this code doesn't explicitly open the connection by calling Connection.Open(). Instead, the DataAdapter opens and closes the linked connection automatically when you call the Fill() method. As a result, the only line of code you should consider placing in an exception-handling block is the call to DataAdapter.Fill(). Alternatively, you can also open and close the connection manually. If the connection is open when you call Fill(), the DataAdapter will use that connection and won't close it automatically. This approach is useful if you want to perform multiple operations with the data source in quick succession and you don't want to incur the additional overhead of repeatedly opening and closing the connection each time.

The last step is to display the contents of the DataSet. A quick approach is to use the same technique that was shown in the previous chapter and build an HTML string by examining each record. The following code cycles through all the DataRow objects in the DataTable and displays the field values of each record in a bulleted list:

```
Dim htmlStr As New StringBuilder("")
For Each dr As DataRow In ds.Tables("Employees").Rows
    htmlStr.Append("<li>")
    htmlStr.Append(dr("TitleOfCourtesy").ToString())
    htmlStr.Append(" <b>")
    htmlStr.Append(dr("LastName").ToString())
    htmlStr.Append("</b>, ")
    htmlStr.Append(dr("FirstName").ToString())
    htmlStr.Append("</li>")
Next dr
```

Of course, the ASP.NET model is designed to save you from coding raw HTML. A much better approach is to bind the data in the DataSet to a data-bound control, which automatically generates the HTML you need based on a single template. Chapter 9 describes the data-bound controls in detail.

■ **Note** When you bind a DataSet to a control, such as a DataGridView, no data objects are stored in view state. The data control stores enough information to show only the data that's currently displayed. If you need to interact with a DataSet over multiple postbacks, you'll need to store it in the ViewState collection manually (which will greatly increase the size of the page) or the Session or Cache objects.

Working with Multiple Tables and Relationships

The next example shows a more advanced use of the DataSet that, in addition to providing disconnected data, uses table relationships. This example demonstrates how to retrieve some records from the Categories and Products tables of the Northwind database and how to create a relationship between them so that it's easy to navigate from a category record to all of its child products and create a simple report.

The first step is to initialize the ADO.NET objects and declare the two SQL queries (for retrieving categories and products), as shown here:

```
Dim connectionString As String =
    WebConfigurationManager.ConnectionStrings("Northwind").ConnectionString
Dim con As New SqlConnection(connectionString)

Dim sqlCat As String = "SELECT CategoryID, CategoryName FROM Categories"
Dim sqlProd As String = "SELECT ProductName, CategoryID FROM Products"

Dim da As New SqlDataAdapter(sqlCat, con)
Dim ds As New DataSet()
```

Next, the code executes both queries, adding two tables to the DataSet. Note that the connection is explicitly opened at the beginning and closed after the two operations, ensuring the best possible performance.

```
Try
    con.Open()

    ' Fill the DataSet with the Categories table.
    da.Fill(ds, "Categories")

    ' Change the command text, and retrieve the Products table.
    ' You could also use another DataAdapter object for this task.
    da.SelectCommand.CommandText = sqlProd
    da.Fill(ds, "Products")
Finally
    con.Close()
End Try
```

In this example, the same DataAdapter is used to fill both tables. This technique is perfectly legitimate, and it makes sense in this scenario because you don't need to reuse the DataAdapter to update the data source. However, if you were using the DataAdapter both to query data and to commit changes, you probably wouldn't use this approach. Instead, you would use a separate DataAdapter for each table so that you could make sure each DataAdapter has the appropriate insert, update, and delete commands for the corresponding table.

At this point you have a DataSet with two tables. These two tables are linked in the Northwind database by a relationship against the CategoryID field. This field is the primary key for the Categories table and the foreign key in the Products table. Unfortunately, ADO.NET does not provide any way to read a relationship from the data source and apply it to your DataSet automatically. Instead, you need to manually create a DataRelation that represents the relationship.

A relationship is created by defining a DataRelation object and adding it to the DataSet. Relations collection. When you create the DataRelation, you specify three constructor arguments: the name of the relationship, the DataColumn for the primary key in the parent table, and the DataColumn for the foreign key in the child table.

Here's the code you need for this example:

```
' Define the relationship between Categories and Products.
Dim relat As New DataRelation ( _
    "CatProds",
    ds.Tables("Categories").Columns("CategoryID"),
    ds.Tables("Products").Columns("CategoryID"))

' Add the relationship to the DataSet.
ds.Relations.Add(relat)
```

Once you've retrieved all the data, you can loop through the records of the Categories table and add the name of each category to the HTML string:

```
Dim htmlStr As New StringBuilder("")
' Loop through the category records, and build the HTML string.
For Each row As DataRow In ds.Tables("Categories").Rows
    htmlStr.Append("<b>")
    htmlStr.Append(row("CategoryName").ToString())
    htmlStr.Append("</b><ul>")
    ...
```

Here's the interesting part. Inside this block, you can access the related product records for the current category by calling the DataRow.GetChildRows() method. Once you have this array of product records, you can loop through it using a nested For Each loop. This is far simpler than the code you'd need in order to look up this information in a separate object or to execute multiple queries with traditional connection-based access.

The following piece of code demonstrates this approach, retrieving the child records and completing the outer For Each loop:

```
    ...
' Get the children (products) for this parent (category).
    Dim childRows As DataRow() = row.GetChildRows(relat)

    ' Loop through all the products in this category.
    For Each childRow As DataRow In childRows
      htmlStr.Append("<li>")
      htmlStr.Append(childRow("ProductName").ToString())
      htmlStr.Append("</li>")
    Next
    htmlStr.Append("</ul>")
Next
```

The last step is to display the HTML string on the page:

```
HtmlContent.Text = htmlStr.ToString()
```

The code for this example is now complete. If you run the page, you'll see the output shown in Figure 8-5.

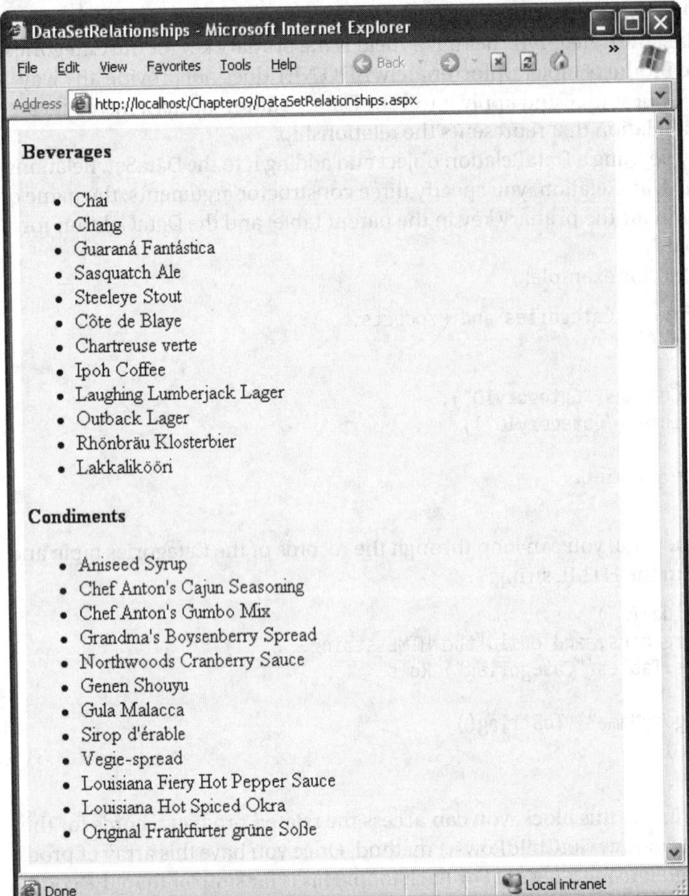

Figure 8-5. *A list of products in each category*

■ **Tip** A common question new ADO.NET programmers have is, when do you use JOIN queries and when do you use DataRelation objects? The most important consideration is whether you plan to update the retrieved data. If you do, using separate tables and a DataRelation object always offers the most flexibility. If not, you could use either approach, although the JOIN query may be more efficient because it involves only a single round-trip across the network, while the DataRelation approach often requires two to fill the separate tables.

REFERENTIAL INTEGRITY

When you add a relationship to a DataSet, you are bound by the rules of referential integrity. For example, you can't delete a parent record if there are linked child rows, and you can't create a child record that references a nonexistent parent, unless these are specified on the DataRelation where you can arrange for deletions on parent tables to cascade to the child tables. This can cause a problem if your DataSet contains only partial data. For example, if you have a full list of customer orders, but only a partial list of customers, it could appear that an order refers to a customer who doesn't exist just because that customer record isn't in your DataSet. One way to get around this problem is to create a DataRelation without creating the corresponding constraints. To do so, use the DataRelation constructor that accepts the Boolean createConstraints parameter and set it to False, as shown here:

```
Dim relat As New DataRelation("CatProds",
ds.Tables("Categories").Columns("CategoryID"),
        ds.Tables("Products").Columns("CategoryID"), False)
```

Searching for Specific Rows

The DataTable provides a useful Select() method that allows you to retrieve an array of DataRow objects based on an SQL expression. The expression you use with the Select() method plays the same role as the WHERE clause in a SELECT statement.

For example, the following code retrieves all the products that are marked as discontinued:

```
' Get the children (products) for this parent (category).
Dim matchRows As DataRow() = DataSet.Tables("Products").Select("Discontinued = 1")

' Loop through all the discontinued products, and generate a bulleted list.
htmlStr.Append("</b><ul>")
For Each row As DataRow In matchRows
          htmlStr.Append("<li>")
          htmlStr.Append(row("ProductName").ToString())
          htmlStr.Append("</li>")
Next
htmlStr.Append("</ul>")
```

In this example, the Select() method uses a fairly simple filter string. However, you're free to use more complex operators and a combination of different criteria. Additionally, you can use expressions. For more information, refer to the MSDN class library reference description for the DataColumn.Expression property, or refer to Table 8-3 and the discussion about filter strings in the "Filtering with a DataView" section.

■ **Note** The Select() method has one potential caveat—it doesn't support a parameterized condition. As a result, it's open to SQL injection attacks. Clearly, the SQL injection attacks that a malicious user could perform in this situation are fairly limited, because there's no way to get access to the actual data source or execute additional commands. However, a carefully written value could still trick your application into returning extra information from the table. If you create a filter expression with a user-supplied value, you might want to iterate over the DataTable manually to find the rows you want, instead of using the Select() method.

Using the DataSet in a Custom Data Class

There's no reason you can't use the DataSet or DataTable as the return value from a method in your custom data access class. For example, you could rewrite the GetAllEmployees() method shown earlier with the following DataSet code:

```
Public Function GetAllEmployees() As DataTable
    Dim con As New SqlConnection(connectionString)
    Dim cmd As New SqlCommand("GetEmployee", con)
    cmd.CommandType = CommandType.StoredProcedure
    cmd.Parameters.Add(New SqlParameter("@EmployeeID", SqlDbType.Int, 4))
    cmd.Parameters("@EmployeeID").Value = employeeID
    Dim sql as String = "Select * from Employees"
    Dim da As New SqlDataAdapter(sql, con)
    Dim ds As New DataSet()

    ' Fill the DataSet.
    Try
        da.Fill(ds, "Employees")
        Return ds.Tables("Employees")
    Catch
        Throw New ApplicationException("Data error.")
    End Try
End Function
```

Interestingly, when you use this approach, you have exactly the same functionality at your fingertips. For example, in the next chapter you'll learn to use the ObjectDataSource to bind to custom classes. The ObjectDataSource understands custom classes and the DataSet object equally well (and they have essentially the same performance).

The DataSet approach has a couple of limitations. Although the DataSet makes the ideal container for disconnected data, you may find it easier to create methods that return individual DataTable objects and even distinct DataRow objects (for example, as a return value from a GetEmployee() method). However, these objects don't have the same level of data binding support as the DataSet, so you'll need to decide between a clearer coding model (using the various disconnected data objects) and more flexibility (always using the full DataSet, even when returning only a single record). Another limitation is that the DataSet is weakly typed. That means there's no compile-time syntax checking or IntelliSense to make sure you use the right field names (unlike with a custom data access class such as EmployeeDetails). You can get around this limitation by building a typed DataSet, but it takes more work. For more information about creating a typed DataSet, refer to *Pro ADO.NET 2.0* (Apress, 2005).

Data Binding

Although there's nothing stopping you from generating HTML by hand as you loop through disconnected data, in most cases ASP.NET data binding can simplify your life quite a bit. Chapter 9 discusses data binding in detail, but before continuing to the DataView examples in this chapter you need to know the basics.

The key idea behind data binding is that you associate a link between a data object and a control, and then the ASP.NET data binding infrastructure takes care of building the appropriate output (be it web page, Windows form, etc.)

One of the data-bound controls that's easiest to use is the GridVew. The GridView has the built-in smarts to create an HTML table with one row per record and with one column per field.

To bind data to a data-bound control such as the GridView, you first need to set the DataSource property. This property points to the object that contains the information you want to display. In this case, it's the DataSet:

```
GridView1.DataSource = ds
```

Because data-bound controls can bind to only a single table (not the entire DataSet), you also need to explicitly specify what table you want to use. You can do that by setting the DataMember property to the appropriate table name, as shown here:

```
GridView1.DataMember = "Employees"
```

Finally, once you've defined where the data is, you need to call the control's DataBind() method to copy the information from the DataSet into the control. If you forget this step, the control will remain empty, and the information will not appear on the page.

```
GridView1.DataBind()
```

As a shortcut, you can call the DataBind() method of the current page, which walks over every control that supports data binding and calls the DataBind() method.

Note The following examples use data binding to demonstrate the filtering and sorting features of the GridView. You'll learn much more about data binding and the GridView control in Chapter 9 and Chapter 10.

The DataView Class

A DataView defines a view onto a DataTable object—in other words, a representation of the data in a DataTable that can include custom filtering and sorting settings. To allow you to configure these settings, the DataView has properties such as Sort and RowFilter. These properties allow you to choose what data you'll see through the view. However, they don't affect the actual data in the DataTable. For example, if you filter a table to hide certain rows, those rows will remain in the DataTable, but they won't be accessible through the DataView.

The DataView is particularly useful in data binding scenarios. It allows you to show just a subset of the total data in a table, without needing to process or alter that data if you need it for other tasks.

Every DataTable has a default DataView associated with it, although you can create multiple DataView objects to represent different views onto the same table. The default DataView is provided through the DataTable.DefaultView property.

In the following examples, you'll see how to create some grids that display records sorted by different fields and filtered against a given expression.

Sorting with a DataView

The next example uses a page with three GridView controls. When the page loads, it binds the same DataTable to each of the grids. However, it uses three different views, each of which sorts the results using a different field.

The code begins by retrieving the list of employees into a DataSet:

```
' Create the Connection, DataAdapter, and DataSet.
Dim connectionString As String =
      WebConfigurationManager.ConnectionStrings("Northwind").ConnectionString
Dim con As New SqlConnection(connectionString)
Dim sql As String = "SELECT TOP 5 EmployeeID, TitleOfCourtesy, LastName, " _
                          & "FirstName FROM Employees"

Dim da As New SqlDataAdapter(sql, con)
Dim ds As New DataSet()
```

```
' Fill the DataSet.
da.Fill(ds, "Employees")
```

The next step is to fill the GridView controls through data binding. To bind the first grid, you can simply use the DataTable directly, which uses the default DataView and displays all the data. For the other two grids, you must create a new DataView object. You can then set its Sort property explicitly.

```
' Bind the original data to #1.
grid1.DataSource = ds.Tables("Employees")

' Sort by last name, and bind it to #2.
Dim view2 As New DataView(ds.Tables("Employees"))
view2.Sort = "LastName"
grid2.DataSource = view2

' Sort by first name, and bind it to #3.
Dim view3 As New DataView(ds.Tables("Employees"))
view3.Sort = "FirstName"
grid3.DataSource = view3
```

Sorting a grid is simply a matter of setting the DataView.Sort property to a valid sorting expression. This example sorts by each view using a single field, but you could also sort by multiple fields, by specifying a comma-separated list. Here's an example:

```
view2.Sort = "LastName, FirstName"
```

■Note The sort is according to the data type of the column. Numeric and date columns are ordered from smallest to largest. String columns are sorted alphanumerically without regard to case, assuming the DataTable.CaseSensitive property is False (the default). Columns that contain binary data cannot be sorted. You can also use the ASC and DESC attributes to sort in ascending or descending order. You'll use sorting again and learn about DataView filtering in Chapter 10.

Once you've bound the grids, you still need to trigger the data binding process that copies the values from the DataTable into the control. You can do this for each control separately or for the entire page by calling Page.DataBind(), as in this example:

```
Me.DataBind()
```

Figure 8-6 shows the resulting page.

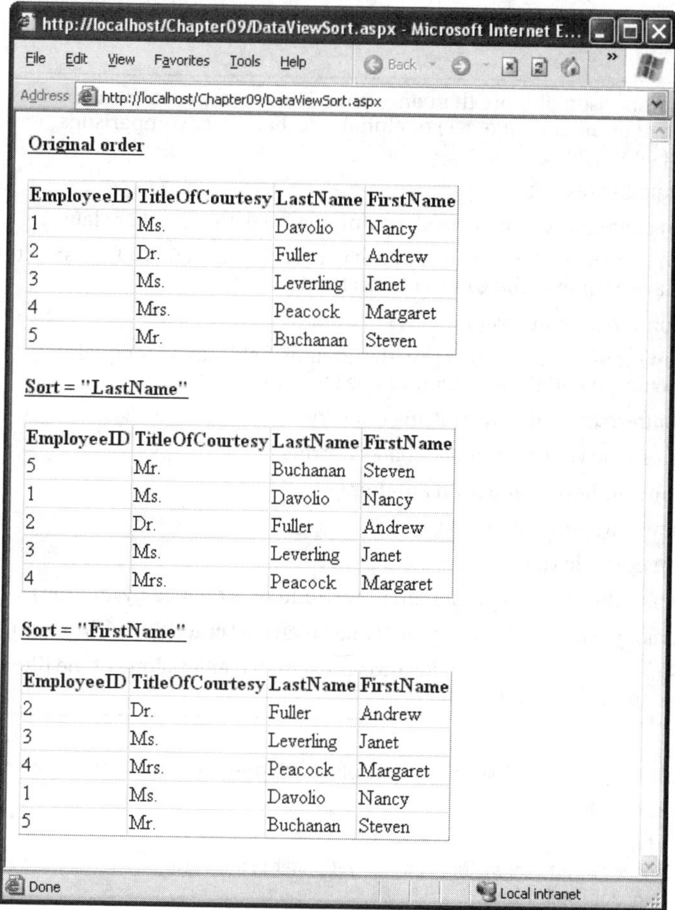

Figure 8-6. *Grids sorted in different ways*

Filtering with a DataView

You can also use a DataView to apply custom filtering so that only certain rows are included in the display. To accomplish this feat, you use the RowFilter property. The RowFilter property acts like a WHERE clause in a SQL query. Using it, you can limit results using logical operators (such as <, >, and =) and a wide range of criteria. Table 8-3 lists the most common filter operators.

Table 8-3. *Filter Operators*

Operator	Description
<, >, <=, and >=	Performs comparison of more than one value. These comparisons can be numeric (with number data types) or alphabetic dictionary comparisons (with string data types).
<> and =	Performs equality testing.
NOT	Reverses an expression. Can be used in conjunction with any other clause.
BETWEEN	Specifies an inclusive range. For example, "Units BETWEEN 5 AND 15" selects rows that have a value in the Units column from 5 to 15.
ISNULL	Tests the column for a null value.
IN(a,b,c)	A short form for using an OR clause with the same field. Tests for equality between a column and the specified values (a, b, and c).
LIKE	Performs pattern matching with string data types.
+	Adds two numeric values or concatenates a string.
-	Subtracts one numeric value from another.
*	Multiplies two numeric values.
/	Divides one numeric value by another.
%	Finds the modulus (the remainder after one number is divided by another).
AND	Combines more than one clause. Records must match all criteria to be displayed.
OR	Combines more than one clause. Records must match at least one of the filter expressions to be displayed.

The following example page includes three GridView controls. Each one is bound to the same DataTable but with different filter settings.

```
Dim connectionString As String =
    WebConfigurationManager.ConnectionStrings("Northwind").ConnectionString
Dim con As New SqlConnection(connectionString)
Dim sql As String = "SELECT ProductID, ProductName, UnitsInStock, " _
                                    & "UnitsOnOrder, Discontinued FROM Products"

Dim da As New SqlDataAdapter(sql, con)
Dim ds As DataSet = New DataSet()
da.Fill(ds, "Products")

' Filter for the Chocolade product.
Dim view1 As New DataView(ds.Tables("Products"))
view1.RowFilter = "ProductName = 'Chocolade'"
GridView1.DataSource = view1

' Filter for products that aren't on order or in stock.
Dim view2 As New DataView(ds.Tables("Products"))
view2.RowFilter = "UnitsInStock = 0 AND UnitsOnOrder = 0"
GridView2.DataSource = view2

' Filter for products starting with the letter P.
Dim view3 As New DataView(ds.Tables("Products"))
view3.RowFilter = "ProductName LIKE 'P%'"
GridView3.DataSource = view3

Me.DataBind()
```

Running the page will fill the three grids, as shown in Figure 8-7.

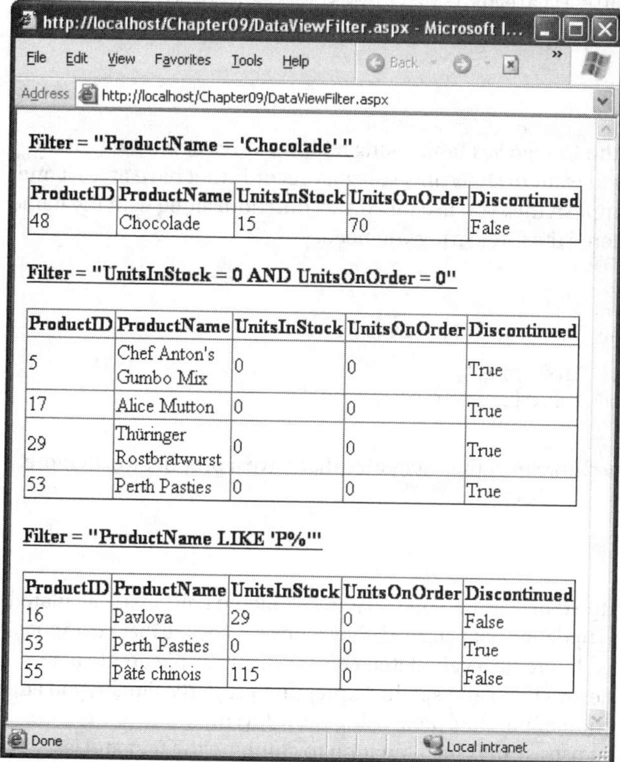

Figure 8-7. *Grids filtered in different ways*

■ **Tip** The DataView also includes a RowStateFilter property that you can use to filter a DataTable so it shows rows in a specific row state (inserted, deleted, modified, or unchanged). By default, this property is set to show all rows except those that have been marked as deleted.

Advanced Filtering with Relationships

The DataView allows for some surprisingly complex filter expressions. One of its little-known features is the ability to filter rows based on relationships. For example, you could display categories that contain more than 20 products, or you could display customers who have made a certain number of total purchases. In both of these examples, you need to filter one table based on the information in a related table.

To create this sort of filter string, you need to combine two ingredients:

- A table relationship that links two tables.
- An aggregate function such as AVG(), MAX(), MIN(), or COUNT(). This function acts on the data in the related records.

For example, suppose you've filled a DataSet with the Categories and Products tables and defined this relationship:

```
' Define the relationship between Categories and Products.
Dim relat As New DataRelation("CatProds",
                              ds.Tables("Categories").Columns("CategoryID"),
                              ds.Tables("Products").Columns("CategoryID"))

' Add the relationship to the DataSet.
ds.Relations.Add(relat)
```

You can now filter the display of the Categories table using a filter expression based on the Products table. For example, imagine you want to show only category records that have at least one product worth more than $50. To accomplish this, you use the MAX() function, along with the name of the table relationships (CatProds). Here's the filter string you need:

```
MAX(Child(CatProds).UnitPrice) > 50
```

And here's the code that applies this filter string to the DataView:

```
Dim view1 As New DataView(ds.Tables("Categories"))
view1.RowFilter = "MAX(Child(CatProds).UnitPrice) > 50"
GridView1.DataSource = view1
```

The end result is that the GridView shows only the categories that have a product worth more than $50.

Calculated Columns

In addition to the fields retrieved from the data source, you can add calculated columns. Calculated columns are ignored when retrieving and updating data. Instead, they represent a value that's computed using a combination of existing values. To create a calculated column, you simply create a new DataColumn object (specifying its name and type) and set the Expression property. Finally, you add the DataColumn to the Columns collection of the DataTable using the Add() method.

As an example, here's a column that uses string concatenation to combine the first and last name into one field:

```
Dim fullName As New DataColumn("FullName", GetType(String),
        "TitleOfCourtesy + ' ' + LastName + ', ' + FirstName")
ds.Tables("Employees").Columns.Add(fullName)
```

Tip Of course, you can also execute a query that creates calculated columns. However, that approach makes it more difficult to update the data source later, and it creates more work for the data source. For that reason, it's often a better solution to create calculated columns in the DataSet.

You can also create a calculated column that incorporates information from related rows. For example, you might add a column in a Categories table that indicates the number of related product rows. In this case, you need to make sure you first define the relationship with a DataRelation object. You also need to use a SQL aggregate function such as AVG(), MAX(), MIN(), or COUNT().

Here's an example that creates three calculated columns, all of which use aggregate functions and table relationships:

```
Dim connectionString As String =
    WebConfigurationManager.ConnectionStrings("Northwind").ConnectionString
Dim con As New SqlConnection(connectionString)
Dim sqlCat As String = "SELECT CategoryID, CategoryName FROM Categories"
Dim sqlProd As String = "SELECT ProductName, CategoryID, UnitPrice FROM Products"
Dim da As New SqlDataAdapter(sqlCat, con)
Dim ds As New DataSet()
```

```
Try
    con.Open()
    da.Fill(ds, "Categories")
    da.SelectCommand.CommandText = sqlProd
    da.Fill(ds, "Products")
Finally
    con.Close()
End Try

' Define the relationship between Categories and Products.
Dim relat As New DataRelation("CatProds",
                                ds.Tables("Categories").Columns("CategoryID"),
                                ds.Tables("Products").Columns("CategoryID"))
' Add the relationship to the DataSet.
ds.Relations.Add(relat)

' Create the calculated columns.
Dim count As New DataColumn("Products (#)", GetType(Integer),
        "COUNT(Child(CatProds).CategoryID)")
Dim max As New DataColumn("Most Expensive Product", GetType(Decimal),
        "MAX(Child(CatProds).UnitPrice)")
Dim min As New DataColumn("Least Expensive Product", GetType(Decimal),
        "MIN(Child(CatProds).UnitPrice)")

' Add the columns.
ds.Tables("Categories").Columns.Add(count)
ds.Tables("Categories").Columns.Add(max)
ds.Tables("Categories").Columns.Add(min)

' Show the data.
GridView1.DataSource = ds.Tables("Categories")
GridView1.DataBind()
```

Figure 8-8 shows the resulting page.

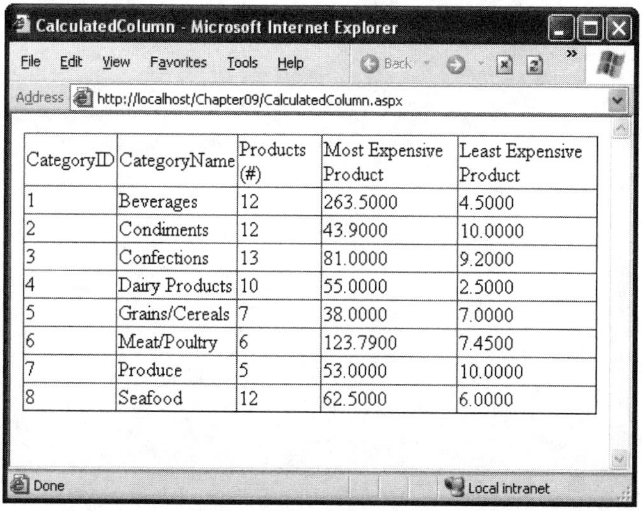

CalculatedColumn - Microsoft Internet Explorer

http://localhost/Chapter09/CalculatedColumn.aspx

CategoryID	CategoryName	Products (#)	Most Expensive Product	Least Expensive Product
1	Beverages	12	263.5000	4.5000
2	Condiments	12	43.9000	10.0000
3	Confections	13	81.0000	9.2000
4	Dairy Products	10	55.0000	2.5000
5	Grains/Cereals	7	38.0000	7.0000
6	Meat/Poultry	6	123.7900	7.4500
7	Produce	5	53.0000	10.0000
8	Seafood	12	62.5000	6.0000

Figure 8-8. *Showing calculated columns*

Note Keep in mind that these examples simply demonstrate convenient ways to filter and aggregate data. These operations are only part of *presenting* your data properly. The other half of the equation is proper formatting. In Chapter 9 and Chapter 10, you'll learn a lot more about the GridView so that you can show currency values in the appropriate format and customize other details such as color, sizing, column order, and fonts. For example, by setting the format, you can change 4.5000 to the more reasonable display value, $4.50.

Summary

In this chapter, you learned how to create basic database components and took an in-depth look at the DataSet and DataView. In the next chapter, you'll continue working with the same database component and the DataSet—albeit through a new layer. You'll learn how the data source controls wrap the ADO.NET world with a higher-level abstraction and let you build rich data-bound pages with minimal code.

If you do want to learn about all the features of the DataSet, including those that are tailored to distributed and rich client applications, you may want to consult *Programming Microsoft ADO.NET 2.0: Core Reference* (Microsoft Press, 2005) or *Pro ADO.NET 2.0* (Apress, 2005).

CHAPTER 9

■ ■ ■

Data Binding

Almost every web application has to deal with data, whether it's stored in a database, an XML file, a structured file, or something else. Retrieving this data is only part of the challenge—a modern application also needs a convenient, flexible, and attractive way to display the data in a web page.

Fortunately, ASP.NET includes a rich and full-featured model for *data binding*. Data binding allows you to bind the data objects you've retrieved to one or more web controls, which will then show the data automatically. That means you don't need to write time-consuming logic to loop through rows, read multiple fields, and manipulate individual controls.

ASP.NET 2.0 goes one step further with a new set of *data source controls*. A data source control allows you to define a declarative link in your ASPX markup between the page and a data source (such as a database or a custom data access component). Data source controls are notable for the way they plug into the data binding infrastructure. Once you've configured a data source control, you can hook it up to your web controls at design time, and ASP.NET will take care of all the data binding details. In fact, by using a data source control, you can create a sophisticated page that allows you to query and update a database—all without writing a single line of code.

Tip Of course, in a professional application you probably *will* write code to customize various aspects of the data binding process, such as error handling. That's why you'll be happy to discover that the data binding model and data source controls are remarkably extensible. In the past, countless data binding models have failed because of a lack of flexibility.

In this chapter, you'll learn how data binding and the data source controls work. You'll learn a straightforward approach to using the data source controls and the best practices you'll need to make them truly practical. This distinction is important, because it's easy to use the data source controls to build pages that are difficult to maintain and impossible to optimize properly. When used correctly, data source controls don't need to prevent good design practices—in fact, informed developers can plug their own custom data access classes into the data binding framework without sacrificing a thing.

But before you can tackle the data source controls, you need to start at the beginning—with a description of ASP.NET data binding.

DATA BINDING CHANGES IN ASP.NET 2.0

Although basic data binding hasn't changed, the data source controls are an ASP.NET 2.0 innovation. Even if you're an ASP.NET 1.*x* guru, you'll want to pay special attention to the changes described in this chapter.

Basic Data Binding

Data binding is a feature that allows you to associate a data source to a control and have that control automatically display your data. The key characteristic of data binding is that it's *declarative*, not programmatic. That means data binding is defined outside your code, alongside the controls in the .aspx page. The advantage is that it helps you achieve a cleaner separation between your controls and your code in a web page.

In ASP.NET, most web controls (including TextBox, LinkButton, Image, and many more) support *single-value* data binding. With single-value binding, you can bind a control property to a data source, but the control can display only a single value. The property you bind doesn't need to represent something directly visible on the page. For example, not only can you bind the text of the hyperlink by setting the Hyperlink.Text property, but you can also bind the NavigateUrl property to specify the target destination of the link. To use single-value binding, you create data binding expressions.

Many web controls support *repeated-value* binding, which means they can render a set of items. Repeated-value controls often create lists and grids (the ListBox and GridView are two examples). If a control supports repeated-value binding, it always exposes a DataSource property, which accepts a data object. When you set the DataSource property, you create the logical link from the server control to the data object that contains the data to render. However, this doesn't directly fill the control with that data. To accomplish that, you need the control's DataBind() method, which loops through the DataSource, extracts its data, and renders it to the page. Repeated-value binding is by far the more powerful type of data binding.

In the following sections, you'll consider both types of data binding.

Single-Value Binding

The controls that support single-value data binding allow you to bind some of their properties to a *data binding expression*. This expression is entered in the .aspx markup portion of the page (not the code-behind field) and enclosed between the <%# and %> delimiters. Here's an example:

```
<%# expression_goes_here %>
```

This may look like a script block, but it isn't. If you try to write any code inside this tag, you will receive an error. The only thing you can add is valid data binding expressions. For example, if you have a Public or Protected variable on your page named EmployeeName, you could write the following:

```
<%# EmployeeName %>
```

To evaluate a data binding expression such as this, you must call the Page.DataBind() method on the page object within your code. (For example, call Me.DataBind() within a web-page class.) When you call DataBind(), ASP.NET will examine all the expressions on your page and replace them with the corresponding value (in this case, the current value that's defined for the EmployeeName variable). If you forget to call the DataBind() method, the data binding expression won't be filled in—instead, it just gets tossed away when your page is rendered to HTML.

The source for single-value data binding can include the value of a property, member variable, or return value of a function (as long as the property, member variable, or function has an accessibility of Protected or Public). It can also be any other expression that can be evaluated at runtime, such as a reference to another control's property, a calculation using operators and literal values, and so on. The following data binding expressions are all valid:

```
<%# GetUserName(ID) %>
<%# 1 + (2 * 20) %>
<%# "John " + "Smith" %>
<%# Request.Browser.Browser %>
```

You can place your data binding expressions just about anywhere on the page, but usually you'll assign a data binding expression to a property in the control tag. Here's an example page that uses several data binding expressions:

```
<html>
  <body>
    <form method=post runat="server">
      <asp:Image ID="image1" runat="server" ImageUrl='<%# FilePath %>' /><br />
      <asp:Label ID="label1" runat="server" Text='<%# FilePath %>' /><br />
      <asp:TextBox ID="textBox1" runat="server" Text='<%# GetFilePath() %>' /><br />
      <asp:HyperLink ID="hyperLink1" runat="server"
        NavigateUrl='<%# LogoPath.Value %>' Font-Bold="True" Text="Show logo" />
      <br />
      <input type="hidden" ID="LogoPath" runat="server" value="apress.gif">
      <b><%# FilePath %></b><br />
      <img src="<%# GetFilePath() %>">
    </form>
    </body>
</html>
```

As you can see, not only can you bind the Text property of a Label and a TextBox, but you can also use other properties such as the ImageUrl of an Image, the NavigateUrl property of a HyperLink, and even the src attribute of a static HTML <img> tag. You can also put the binding expression elsewhere in the page without binding to any property or attribute. For example, the previous web page has a binding expression between the <b> and </b> tags. When it's processed, the resulting text will be rendered on the page and rendered in bold type. You can even place the expression outside the <form> section, as long as you don't try to insert a server-side control there.

The expressions in this sample page refer to a FilePath property, a GetFilePath() function, and the Value property of a server-side hidden field that's declared on the same page. To complete this page, you need to define these ingredients in script blocks or in the code-behind class: ()

```
Protected Function GetFilePath() As String
    Return "apress.gif"
End Function

Protected ReadOnly Property FilePath() As String
    Get
        Return "apress.gif"
    End Get
End Property
```

In this example, the property and function return only a hard-coded string. However, you can also add just about any code to generate the value for the data binding expression dynamically.

It's important to remember that the data binding expression does not directly set the property to which it's bound. It simply defines a connection between the control's property and some other piece of information. To cause the page to evaluate the expression, run the appropriate code, and assign the appropriate value, you must call the DataBind() method of the containing page, as shown here:

```
Protected Sub Page_Load(ByVal sender As Object, ByVal e As System.EventArgs)
  Me.DataBind()
End Sub
```

Figure 9-1 shows what you'll see when you run this page.

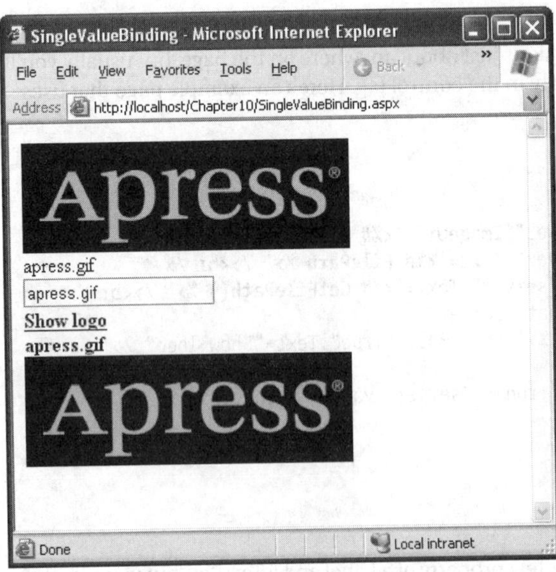

Figure 9-1. *Single-value data binding in various controls*

You'll see data binding expressions again when you create templates for more advanced controls in Chapter 10.

Other Types of Expressions

Data binding expressions are always wrapped in the <%# and %> characters. ASP.NET 2.0 also adds support for different types of expressions, commonly known as *$ expressions* because they incorporate the $ character. Technically, a $ expression is a code sequence that you can add to an .aspx page and that will be evaluated by an expression builder when the page is rendered. The expression builder processes the expression and replaces it with a string value in the final HTML.

Currently, ASP.NET includes a built-in expression builder that allows you to extract custom application settings and connection string information from the web.config file. For example, if you want to retrieve an application setting named appName from the <appSettings> portion of the web.config file, you can use the following expression:

```
<asp:Literal Runat="server" Text="<%$ AppSettings:appName %>" />
```

Several differences exist between $ expressions and data binding expressions:

- Data binding expressions start with the <%# character sequence, and $ expressions use <%$.
- Unlike data binding expressions, you don't need to call the DataBind() method to evaluate $ expressions. Instead, they're always evaluated when the page is rendered.

- Unlike data binding expressions, $ expressions can't be inserted anywhere in a page. Instead, you need to wrap them in a control tag and use the expression result to set a control property. That means if you just want to show the result of an expression as ordinary text, you need to wrap it in a Literal tag (as shown in the previous example). The Literal control outputs its text to plain, unformatted HTML.

The first part of a $ expression indicates the name of the expression builder. For example, the AppSettings:appName expression works because a dedicated AppSettingsExpression builder is registered to handle all expressions that begin with *AppSettings*. Similarly, ASP.NET includes a ResourceExpressionBuilder for inserting resources (see Chapter 17) and a ConnectionStringExpressionBuilder that retrieves connection information from the <connectionStrings> section of the web.config file. Here's an example that uses the ConnectionStringExpressionBuilder:

```
<asp:Literal Runat="server" Text="<%$ ConnectionStrings:Northwind %>" />
```

Displaying a connection string isn't that useful. But this technique becomes much more useful when you combine it with the SqlDataSource control you'll examine later in this chapter, in which case you can use it to quickly supply a connection string from the web.config file:

```
<asp:SqlDataSource ConnectionString="<%$ ConnectionStrings:Northwind %>" ... />
```

Technically, $ expressions don't involve data binding. But they work in a similar way and have a similar syntax.

Custom Expression Builders

One of the most innovative features of $ expressions is that you can create your own expression builders that plug into this framework. This is a specialized technique that, while neat, isn't always practical. As you'll see, custom $ expressions make the most sense if you're developing a distinct feature that you want to incorporate into more than one web application.

For example, imagine you want a way to create a custom expression builder that allows you to insert random numbers. You want to be able to write a tag such as this to show a random number between 1 and 6:

```
<asp:Literal Runat="server" Text="<%$ RandomNumber:1,6 %>" />
```

Unfortunately, creating a custom expression builder isn't quite as easy as you probably expect. The problem is how the code is compiled. When you compile a page that contains an expression, the expression evaluating the code also needs to be compiled with it. However, you don't want the expression to be evaluated at that point—instead, you want the expression to be reevaluated each time the page is requested. To make this possible, your expression builder needs to generate a generic segment of code that performs the appropriate task.

The technology that enables this is CodeDOM (Code Document Object Model)—a model for dynamically generating code constructs. Every expression builder includes a method named GetCodeExpression() that uses CodeDOM to generate the code needed for the expression. In other words, if you want to create a RandomNumberExpressionBuilder, you need to create a GetCodeExpression() method that uses CodeDOM to generate a segment of code for calculating random numbers. Clearly, it's not that straightforward—and for anything but trivial code, it's quite lengthy.

All expression builders must derive from the base ExpressionBuilder class (which is found in the System.Web.Compilation namespace). Here's how you might declare an expression builder for random number generation:

```
Imports System.Web.Compilation
Imports System.CodeDom
Imports System.ComponentModel

Public Class RandomNumberExpressionBuilder
 Inherits ExpressionBuilder
    ...
End Class
```

To simplify life, it helps to create a Shared method that performs the task you need (in this case, random number generation):

```
Public Shared Function GetRandomNumber(ByVal lowerLimit As Integer,
      ByVal upperLimit As Integer) As String
   Dim rand As New Random()
   Dim randValue As Integer = rand.Next(lowerLimit, upperLimit + 1)
   Return randValue.ToString()
End Function
```

The advantage of this approach is that when you use CodeDOM, you simply generate the single line of code needed to call the GetRandomNumber() method (rather than the code needed to generate the random number).

Now, you need to override the GetCodeExpression() method. This is the method that ASP.NET calls when it finds an expression that's mapped to your expression builder (while compiling the page). At this point, you need to examine the expression, verify no errors are present, and then generate the code for calculating the expression result (using a CodeExpression object from the System.CodeDom namespace). This dynamically generated piece of code will be executed every time the page is requested.

Here's the first part of the GetCodeExpression() method:

```
Public Overrides Function GetCodeExpression(ByVal entry As BoundPropertyEntry,
      ByVal parsedData As Object,
      ByVal context As ExpressionBuilderContext) As CodeExpression
   ' entry.Expression is the number string
   ' without the prefix (for example "1,6").
   If (Not entry.Expression.Contains(",")) Then
     Throw New ArgumentException("Must include two numbers separated by a comma.")
   Else
     ' Get the two numbers.
     Dim numbers As String() = entry.Expression.Split(","c)

     If numbers.Length <> 2 Then
       Throw New ArgumentException("Only include two numbers.")
     Else
       Dim lowerLimit, upperLimit As Integer
       If Int32.TryParse(numbers(0), lowerLimit) AndAlso
             Int32.TryParse(numbers(1), upperLimit) Then
             ...
```

So far, all the operations have been performed in normal code. That's because the two numbers are specified in the expression, so they won't change each time the page is requested. However, the random number should be allowed to change each time, so now you need to switch to CodeDOM to create a dynamic segment of code. The basic strategy is to construct a CodeExpression that calls the Shared GetRandomNumber() method.

Here's the rest of the code:

```
            ...
        ' Specify the class.
        Dim type As Type = entry.DeclaringType
        Dim descriptor As PropertyDescriptor =
                TypeDescriptor.GetProperties(type)(entry.PropertyInfo.Name)

        ' Define the parameters.
        Dim expressionArray As CodeExpression() = New CodeExpression(1) {}
        expressionArray(0) = New CodePrimitiveExpression(lowerLimit)
        expressionArray(1) = New CodePrimitiveExpression(upperLimit)

        ' Define the expression that invokes the method.
        Return New CodeCastExpression(descriptor.PropertyType,
                New CodeMethodInvokeExpression(New
            CodeTypeReferenceExpression(
               MyBase.GetType()), "GetRandomNumber", expressionArray))
        Else
            Throw New ArgumentException("Use valid integers.")
        End If
      End If
    End If
End Function
```

Now you can copy this expression builder to the App_Code folder (or compile it separately and place the DLL assembly in the Bin folder).

Finally, to use this expression builder in a web application, you need to register it in the web.config file and map it to the prefix you want to use:

```
<configuration xmlns="http://schemas.microsoft.com/.NetConfiguration/v2.0">
  <system.web>
    <compilation debug="true">
      <expressionBuilders>
        <add expressionPrefix="RandomNumber"
             type="RandomNumberExpressionBuilder"/>
      </expressionBuilders>
    </compilation>
    ...
  </system.web>
</configuration>
```

Now you can use expressions such as <%$ RandomNumber:1,6 %>. These expressions are automatically handled by your custom expression builder, which generates a new random number in the desired range each time the page runs.

The possibilities for expression builders are intriguing. They enable many extensibility scenarios, and third-party tools are sure to take advantage of this feature. However, if you intend to use an expression in a single web application or in a single web page, you'll find it easier to just use a data binding expression that calls a custom method in your page. For example, you could create a data binding expression like this:

```
<%# GetRandomNumber(1,6) %>
```

And add a matching Public or Protected method in your page, like this:

```
Protected Function GetRandomNumber(ByVal lowerLimit As Integer,
       ByVal upperLimit As Integer) As String
    ...
End Function
```

Just remember to call DataBind() on the page object to evaluate your expression.

Repeated-Value Binding

Repeated-value binding allows you to bind an entire list of information to a control. This list of information is represented by a data object that wraps a collection of items. This could be a collection of custom objects (for example, with an ordinary ArrayList or Hashtable) or a collection of rows (for example, with a data reader such as SqlDataReader or a DataSet).

ASP.NET includes several basic list controls that support repeated-value binding:

- All controls that render themselves using the <select> tag, including the HtmlSelect, ListBox, and DropDownList controls
- The CheckBoxList and RadioButtonList controls, which render each child item with a separate check box or radio button
- The BulletedList control, which creates a list of bulleted or numbered points

All these controls display a single-value field of a property from each data item. When dealing with one of these controls, you'll find the properties listed in Table 9-1.

Table 9-1. *Data Properties for List Controls*

Property	Description
DataSource	This is a data object that contains the data to display. This data object must implement a supported interface, typically ICollection.
DataSourceID	Instead of supplying the data object programmatically (using code), you can link your list control to a data source control by setting this property. The data source control will generate the required data object automatically. You can use either the DataSource property or the DataSourceID property, but not both.
DataTextField	Every data source represents a collection of data items. A list control can display only a single value from each list item. The DataTextField indicates the field (in the case of a row) or property (in the case of an object) of the data item that contains the value to display in the page.
DataTextFormatString	Specifies an optional format string that the control will use to format each DataTextValue before displaying it.
DataValueField	This property is similar to the DataTextField property, but the value from the data item isn't displayed in the page—instead, it's stored in the value attribute of the underlying HTML tag. This allows you to retrieve the value later in your code. The primary use of this field is to store a unique ID or primary key field so you can use it later to retrieve more data when the user selects a specific item.

All the list controls are essentially the same. The only differences are the way they render themselves in HTML and whether or not they support multiple selection.

Figure 9-2 shows a test page that displays all the list controls, along with some text that displays the current selection for the controls.

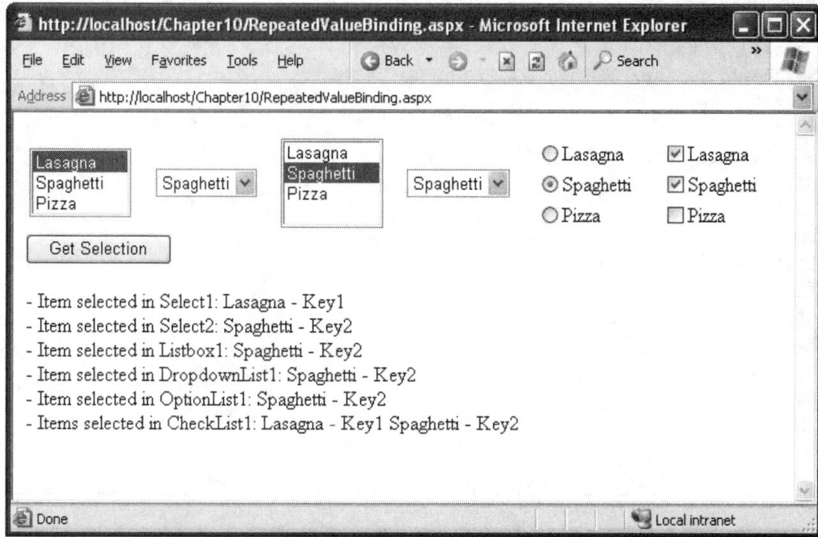

Figure 9-2. *Repeated-value data binding in list controls*

The controls are declared as follows:

```
<select runat="server" ID="Select1" size="3"
  DataTextField="Key" DataValueField="Value" />
<select runat="server" ID="Select2"
  DataTextField="Key" DataValueField="Value" />
<asp:ListBox runat="server" ID="Listbox1"
  DataTextField="Key" DataValueField="Value" />
<asp:DropDownList runat="server" ID="DropdownList1"
  DataTextField="Key" DataValueField="Value" />
<asp:RadioButtonList runat="server" ID="OptionList1"
  DataTextField="Key" DataValueField="Value"/>
<asp:CheckBoxList runat="server" ID="CheckList1"
  DataTextField="Key" DataValueField="Value" />
<asp:Button runat="server" Text="Get Selection" ID="cmdGetSelection"
      OnClick="cmdGetSelection_Click" />
<br /><br />
<asp:Literal runat="server" ID="Result" EnableViewState="False"/>
```

The last control, the Literal control, displays information about the selected items. Its EnableViewState attribute is set to False so that its content will be cleared after every postback.

When the page loads for the first time, the following code creates a data source and assigns it to all the list controls. In this example, the data object is a Hashtable collection, which contains a series of strings. The Value of the Hashtable collection item returns the actual item text (which is used for the DataTextField), while the Key of the Hashtable collection item returns the key under which the item is indexed.

Here's the code for creating and binding the collection:

```
Protected Sub Page_Load(ByVal sender As Object, ByVal e As System.EventArgs)
    If (Not Page.IsPostBack) Then
        ' Create the data source.
        Dim ht As Hashtable = New Hashtable(3)
        ht.Add("Lasagna", "Key1")
        ht.Add("Spaghetti", "Key2")
        ht.Add("Pizza", "Key3")

        ' Set the DataSource property for the controls.
        Select1.DataSource = ht
        Select2.DataSource = ht
        Listbox1.DataSource = ht
        DropdownList1.DataSource = ht
        CheckList1.DataSource = ht
        OptionList1.DataSource = ht

        ' Bind the controls.
        Page.DataBind()
    End If
End Sub
```

■ **Note** Every control that supports repeated-value data binding includes a DataBind() method. You could call this method to bind a specific control. However, when you call the DataBind() method on a Page object, the Page object calls DataBind() on every contained control, simplifying your life.

When the user clicks the button, the code adds the name and values of all the selected items to the label. Here's the code that accomplishes this task:

```
Protected Sub cmdGetSelection_Click(ByVal sender As Object,
      ByVal e As System.EventArgs)
    Result.Text &= "- Item selected in Select1: " _
          & Select1.Items(Select1.SelectedIndex).Text _
          & " - " & Select1.Value & "<br />"
    Result.Text &= "- Item selected in Select2: " _
          & Select2.Items(Select2.SelectedIndex).Text _
          & " - " & Select2.Value & "<br />"
    Result.Text &= "- Item selected in Listbox1: " _
          & Listbox1.SelectedItem.Text _
          & " - " & Listbox1.SelectedItem.Value & "<br />"
    Result.Text &= "- Item selected in DropdownList1: " _
          & DropdownList1.SelectedItem.Text & " - " _
          & DropdownList1.SelectedItem.Value & "<br />"
    Result.Text &= "- Item selected in OptionList1: " _
          & OptionList1.SelectedItem.Text & " - " _
          & OptionList1.SelectedItem.Value & "<br />"
    Result.Text &= "- Items selected in CheckList1: "
    For Each li As ListItem In CheckList1.Items
        If li.Selected Then
            Result.Text += li.Text & " - " & li.Value & " "
        End If
    Next
End Sub
```

Binding to a DataReader

The previous example used a Hashtable as the data source. Basic collections certainly aren't the only kind of data source you can use with list data binding. Instead, you can bind any data structure that implements the ICollection interface or one of its derivatives. The following list summarizes many of these data classes:

- All in-memory collection classes, such as Collection, ArrayList, Hashtable, and Dictionary
- An ADO.NET data reader object, which provides connection-based, forward-only, and read-only access to the database
- The ADO.NET DataView, which provides a view onto a single disconnected DataTable object
- Any other custom object that implements the ICollection interface

For example, imagine you want to fill a list box with the full name of all the employees contained in the Employees table of the Northwind database. Figure 9-3 shows the result you want to produce.

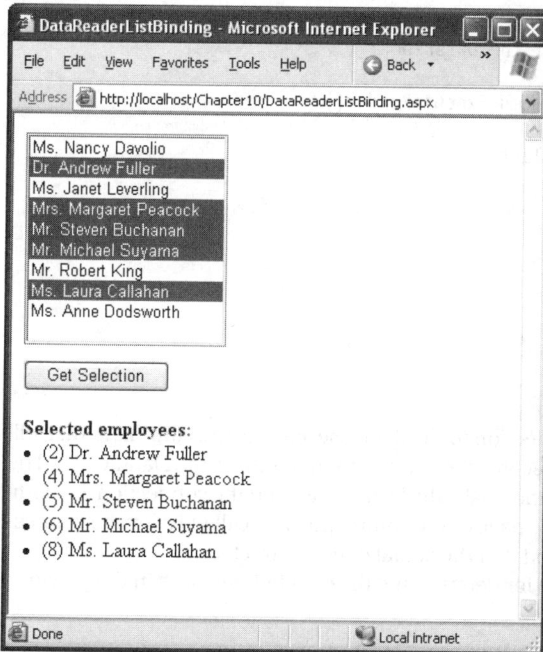

Figure 9-3. *Data binding with a DataReader*

The information in this example includes each person's title of courtesy, first name, and last name, which are stored in three separate fields. Unfortunately, the DataTextField property expects the name of only a single field. You cannot use data binding to concatenate these three pieces of data and create a value for the DataTextField. However, you can solve this issue with an easy but powerful trick—using a calculated column. You simply need to modify the SELECT query so that it creates a calculated column that consists of the information in the three fields. You can then use this column for the DataTextField. The SQL command that you need to accomplish this is as follows:

```
SELECT EmployeeID, TitleOfCourtesy + ' ' +
  FirstName + ' ' + LastName As FullName FROM Employees
```

The data-bound list box is declared on the page as follows:

```
<asp:ListBox runat="server" ID="lstNames" SelectionMode="Multiple"
  DataTextField="FullName" DataValueField="EmployeeID"/>
```

When the page loads, it retrieves the records from the database and binds them to the list control. This example uses a DataReader as the data source, as shown here:

```
Protected Sub Page_Load(ByVal sender As Object, ByVal e As System.EventArgs)
    If (Not Page.IsPostBack) Then
        ' Create the Command and the Connection.
        Dim connectionString As String =
            WebConfigurationManager.ConnectionStrings("Northwind").ConnectionString
        Dim sql As String = "SELECT EmployeeID, TitleOfCourtesy + ' ' + " _
            & "FirstName + ' ' + LastName As FullName FROM Employees"
        Dim con As New SqlConnection(connectionString)
        Dim cmd As New SqlCommand(sql, con)

        Try
            ' Open the connection, and get the DataReader.
            con.Open()
            Dim reader As SqlDataReader = cmd.ExecuteReader()

            ' Bind the DataReader to the list.
            lstNames.DataSource = reader
            lstNames.DataBind()
            reader.Close()
        Finally
            ' Close the connection.
            con.Close()
        End Try
    End If
End Sub
```

The previous code sample creates a connection to the database, creates the command that will select the data, opens the connection, and executes the command that returns the DataReader. The returned DataReader is bound to the list box, and finally the DataReader and the connection are both closed. Note that the DataBind() method of the page or the control must be called *before* the connection is closed. It's not until you call this method that the actual data is extracted.

The last piece of this example is the code for determining the selected items. As in the previous example, this code is quite straightforward:

```
Protected Sub cmdGetSelection_Click(ByVal sender As Object,
               ByVal e As System.EventArgs)
    Result.Text &= "<b>Selected employees:</b>"
    For Each li As ListItem In lstNames.Items
        If li.Selected Then
          Result.Text &= String.Format("<li>({0}) {1}</li>", li.Value, li.Text)
        End If
    Next li
End Sub
```

If you want to use a DropDownList, a CheckListBox, or a RadioButtonList instead of a ListBox, you need to change only the control declaration. The rest of the code that sets up the data binding remains the same.

The Rich Data Controls

In addition to the simple list controls, ASP.NET includes some rich data controls that support repeated-value binding. The rich data controls are quite a bit different from the simple list controls—for one thing, they are designed primarily for data binding. They also have the ability to display several properties or fields from each data item, often in a table-based layout or according to a template you've defined; they support higher-level features such as editing; and they provide several events that allow you to plug into the control's inner workings at various points.

The rich data controls include the following:

GridView: The GridView is an all-purpose grid control for showing large tables of information. It supports selecting, editing, sorting, and paging. The GridView is the heavyweight of ASP.NET data controls. It's also the successor to the ASP.NET 1.*x* DataGrid.

DetailsView: The DetailsView is ideal for showing a single record at a time, in a table that has one row per field. The DetailsView supports editing and optional paging controls that allow you to browse through a sequence of records.

FormView: Like the DetailsView, the FormView shows a single record at a time, supports editing, and provides paging controls for moving through a series of records. The difference is that the FormView is based on templates, which allow you to combine fields in a much more flexible layout that doesn't need to be based on a table.

■Note In addition to the controls in this list, some of ASP.NET's more specialized controls support data binding. These include the Menu and TreeView controls (see Chapter 16) and the AdRotator control (see Chapter 4).

You'll explore the rich data controls in detail in Chapter 10. However, it's worth taking a look at a quick example now with the GridView, because you'll use it to work through a variety of examples in this chapter.

Like the list controls, the GridView provides a DataSource property for the data object and a DataBind() that triggers it to read the data object and display each record. However, you don't need to use properties such as DataTextField and DataValueField, because the GridView automatically generates a column for every property (if you're binding to a custom object) or every field (if you're binding to a row). Here's all you need to get this basic representation:

```
<asp:GridView ID="GridView1" runat="server" AutoGenerateColumns="True" />
```

Now, define a query that selects several fields from the Employees table:

```
Dim sql As String = "SELECT EmployeeID, FirstName, LastName, Title, City " _
      & "FROM Employees"
```

You can bind the GridView to a DataReader in the same way you bound the list control in the previous example. Only the name of the control changes:

```
grid.DataSource = reader
grid.DataBind()
```

Figure 9-4 shows the GridView this code creates.

Of course, you can do a lot more to configure the appearance of the GridView and can use advanced features such as sorting, paging, and editing. You'll learn about these features throughout this chapter and in the next chapter. You can also give your GridView a quick face-lift by choosing Auto Format from the GridView's smart tag.

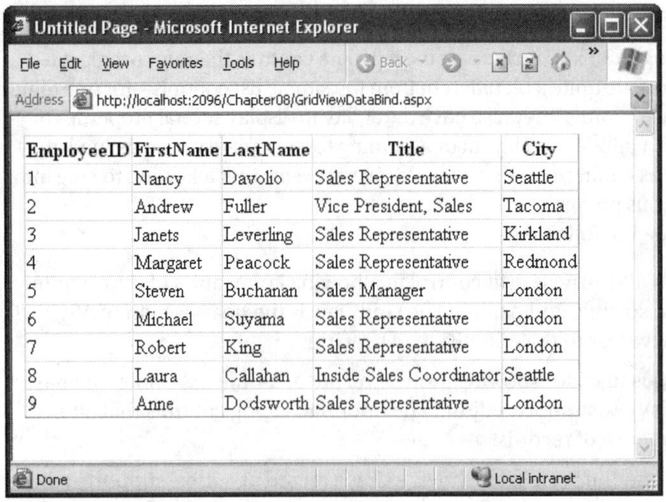

EmployeeID	FirstName	LastName	Title	City
1	Nancy	Davolio	Sales Representative	Seattle
2	Andrew	Fuller	Vice President, Sales	Tacoma
3	Janets	Leverling	Sales Representative	Kirkland
4	Margaret	Peacock	Sales Representative	Redmond
5	Steven	Buchanan	Sales Manager	London
6	Michael	Suyama	Sales Representative	London
7	Robert	King	Sales Representative	London
8	Laura	Callahan	Inside Sales Coordinator	Seattle
9	Anne	Dodsworth	Sales Representative	London

Figure 9-4. *The bare-bones GridView*

Binding to a DataView

You will encounter a few limitations when you bind directly to a DataReader. Because the DataReader is a forward-only cursor, you can't bind your data to multiple controls. You also won't have the ability to apply custom sorting and filtering criteria on the fly. Finally, unless you take care to code your page using generic interfaces such as IDataReader, you lock your code into the data provider you're currently using, making it more difficult to modify or adapt your code in the future. To solve these problems, you can use the disconnected ADO.NET data objects.

If you fill a disconnected DataSet, you can bind that to one or more controls, and you can tailor the sorting and filtering criteria. The DataSet is also completely generic—no matter which data provider you use to fill your DataSet, the DataSet itself (and the data binding code) looks the same.

Technically, you never bind directly to a DataSet or DataTable object. Instead, you bind to a DataView object. A DataView represents a view of the data in a specific DataTable. That means the following:

```
grid.DataSource = dataTable
grid.DataBind()
```

is equivalent to this:

```
grid.DataSource = dataTable.DefaultView
grid.DataBind()
```

It's important to note that every DataTable includes a default DataView object that's provided through the DataTable.DefaultView property. This sleight of hand allows you bind directly to the DataTable. If you do, ASP.NET actually uses the default DataView automatically. The default DataView doesn't apply any sort order and doesn't filter out any rows. If you want to tweak these settings, you can either configure the default DataView or create your own and explicitly bind it.

Data Source Controls

In Chapter 7 and Chapter 8, you saw how you can directly connect to a database, execute a query, loop through the records in the result set, and display them on a page. In this chapter, you've already seen that you have a simpler option; with data binding, you can write your data access logic and then show the results in the page with no looping or control manipulation required. Now, it's time to introduce *another* convenience—data source controls. With data source controls, you can avoid writing any data access code.

■ **Note** As you'll soon see, there's often a gap between what you *can* do and what you *should* do. In most professional, large-scale applications, you'll still need to write and fine-tune your data access code for optimum performance, data aggregation, error handling, logging, and so on. Even if you do, you can still use the data source controls—just don't expect to escape without writing any code!

The data source controls include any control that implements the IDataSource interface. The .NET Framework includes the following data source controls:

SqlDataSource: This data source allows you to connect to any data source that has an ADO.NET data provider. This includes SQL Server, Oracle, and the OLE DB or ODBC data sources, as discussed in Chapter 7. When using this data source, you don't need to write the data access code.

ObjectDataSource: This data source allows you to connect to a custom data access class, such as the one you saw in Chapter 8. This is the preferred approach for large-scale professional web applications.

XmlDataSource: This data source allows you to connect to an XML file. You'll learn more in Chapter 12.

SiteMapDataSource: This data source allows you to connect to a .sitemap file that describes the navigational structure of your website. You'll learn more in Chapter 16.

You can find all the data source controls in the Data tab of the Toolbox in Visual Studio. Data source controls are new in ASP.NET 2.0, and it's expected that more will become available, both from Microsoft and from third-party vendors.

When you drop a data source control onto your web page, it shows up as a gray box in Visual Studio. However, this box won't appear when you run your web application and request the page (see Figure 9-5).

If you perform more than one data access task in the same page (for example, you need to be able to query two tables), you'll need more than one data access control. If you find that the clutter of data source controls is disturbing your page layout at design time, just select View ➤ Non Visual Controls from the menu to hide them. You can still select each data source control from the Properties window when you want to configure it.

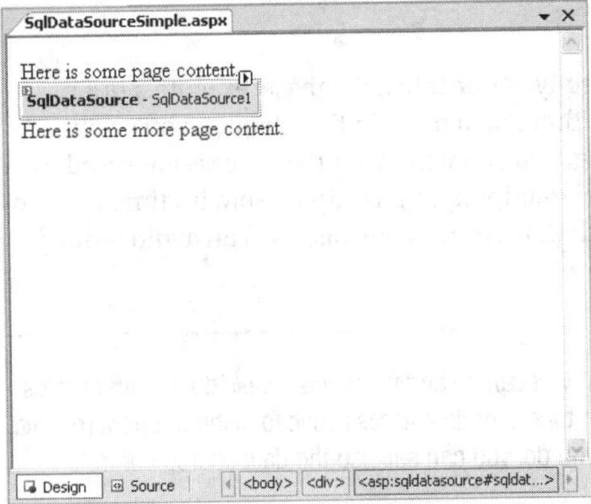

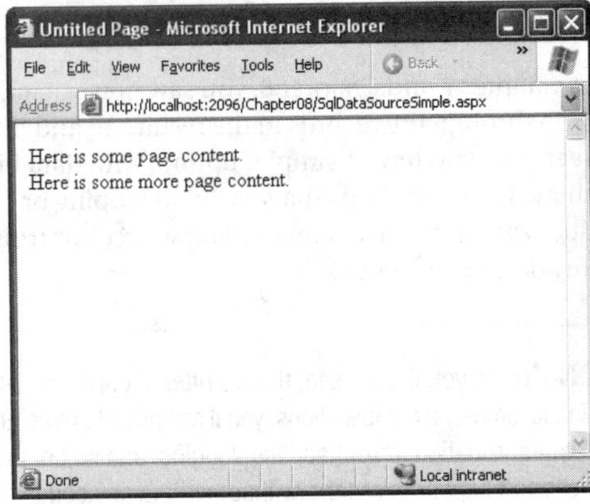

Figure 9-5. *A data source control at design time and runtime*

The Page Life Cycle with Data Binding

Data source controls can perform two key tasks:

- They can retrieve data from a data source and supply it to linked controls.
- They can update the data source when edits take place in linked controls.

In ASP.NET 1.*x*, creating data-bound pages was complicated because you needed to understand the page life cycle, or you risked binding the page at the wrong time. Of course, in ASP.NET 2.0 you *still* need to understand the basics of the page life cycle because you'll run into situations where you need to work with or extend the data binding model. For example, you might want to add data or set a selected item in a control after it has been bound to the data source. Depending on the scenario, you might be able to respond to data source control events, but they aren't always fired at the point you need to perform your logic.

Essentially, data binding tasks take place in this order:

1. The page object is created (based on the .aspx file).
2. The page life cycle begins, and the Page.Init and Page.Load events fire.
3. All other control events fire.
4. The data source controls perform any updates. If a row is being updated, the Updating and Updated events fire. If a row is being inserted, the Inserting and Inserted events fire. If a row is being deleted, the Deleting and Deleted events fire.
5. The Page.PreRender event fires.
6. The data source controls perform any queries and insert the retrieved data in the linked controls. The Selecting and Selected events fire at this point.
7. The page is rendered and disposed.

In the rest of this chapter, you'll look in detail at the SqlDataSource and the ObjectDataSource and see how you can use both to enable a variety of data binding scenarios with the rich GridView control.

■Tip Even if you plan to use the ObjectDataSource for binding your pages, you should begin by reading "The SqlDataSource" section, which will explain many of the basics about data source controls, including parameters, key fields, and two-way data binding.

The SqlDataSource

Data source controls turn up in the .aspx markup portion of your web page like ordinary controls. Here's an example:

```
<asp:SqlDataSource ID="SqlDataSource1" runat="server" ... />
```

The SqlDataSource represents a database connection that uses an ADO.NET provider. However, this has a catch. The SqlDataSource needs a generic way to create the Connection, Command, and DataReader objects it requires. The only way this is possible is if your data provider includes a data provider factory, as discussed in Chapter 7. The factory has the responsibility of creating the provider-specific objects that the SqlDataSource needs in order to access the data source.

As you know, .NET ships with these four provider factories:

- System.Data.SqlClient
- System.Data.OracleClient
- System.Data.OleDb
- System.Data.Odbc

These are registered in the machine.config file, and as a result you can use any of them with the SqlDataSource. You choose a data source by setting the provider name. Here's a SqlDataSource that connects to a SQL Server database:

```
<asp:SqlDataSource ProviderName="System.Data.SqlClient" ... />
```

The next step is to supply the required connection string—without it, you cannot make any connections. Although you can hard-code the connection string directly in the SqlDataSource tag, you should always place it in the <connectionStrings> section of the web.config file to guarantee greater flexibility and ensure you won't inadvertently change the connection string, which minimizes the effectiveness of connection pooling.

For example, if you create this connection string:

```
<configuration xmlns="http://schemas.microsoft.com/.NetConfiguration/v2.0">
  <connectionStrings>
    <add name="Northwind"
          connectionString="Data Source=localhost;Initial Catalog=Northwind;
          Integrated Security=SSPI"/>
  </connectionStrings>
  ...
</configuration>
```

you would specify it in the SqlDataSource using a $ expression like this:

```
<asp:SqlDataSource ConnectionString="<%$ ConnectionStrings:Northwind %>" ... />
```

Once you've specified the provider name and connection string, the next step is to add the query logic that the SqlDataSource will use when it connects to the database.

Selecting Records

You can use each SqlDataSource control you create to retrieve a single query. Optionally, you can also add corresponding commands for deleting, inserting, and updating rows. For example, one SqlDataSource is enough to query and update the Customers table in the Northwind database. However, if you need to independently retrieve or update Customers and Orders information, you'll need two SqlDataSource controls.

The SqlDataSource command logic is supplied through four properties: SelectCommand, InsertCommand, UpdateCommand, and DeleteCommand, each of which takes a string. The string you supply can be inline SQL (in which case the corresponding SelectCommandType, InsertCommandType, UpdateCommandType, or DeleteCommandType property should be Text, the default) or the name of a stored procedure (in which case the command type is StoredProcedure). You need to define commands only for the types of actions you want to perform. In other words, if you're using a data source for read-only access to a set of records, you need to define only the SelectCommand property.

■ **Note** If you configure a command in the Properties window, you'll see a property named SelectQuery instead of SelectCommand. The SelectQuery is actually a virtual property that's displayed as a design-time convenience. When you edit the SelectQuery (by clicking the ellipsis next to the property name), you can use a special designer to write the command text (the SelectCommand) and add command parameters (the SelectParameters).

Here's a complete SqlDataSource that defines a SELECT command for retrieving records from the Employees table:

```
<asp:SqlDataSource ID="sourceEmployees" runat="server"
  ProviderName="System.Data.SqlClient"
  ConnectionString="<%$ ConnectionStrings:Northwind %>"
  SelectCommand= "SELECT EmployeeID, FirstName,
  LastName, Title, City FROM Employees"/>
```

■ **Tip** You can write the data source logic by hand or by using a design-time wizard that lets you create a connection and then create the command logic in a graphical query builder. To launch this tool, select the data source control, and choose Configure Data Source from the smart tag.

Once you've created the data source, you can reap the benefits—namely, the ability to bind your controls at design time, rather than writing logic in the event handler for the Page.Load event. Here's how it works:

1. Select the data source control, and click Refresh Schema in the smart tag. This step triggers the data source control to connect to the database and retrieve the column information for your query. The advantage is this column information will now be available in handy drop-down boxes in the appropriate part of the Properties window. (If you don't take this step, or the database isn't available at design time, you'll need to type in field names by hand.)

2. Add a ListBox to your form. Set the ListBox.DataSourceID property to the data source control. You can choose it from a drop-down list that shows all the data sources on the form (see Figure 9-6).

3. Set the ListBox.DataTextField to the column you want to display (in this case, choose EmployeeID). The list of fields should also be provided in a drop-down list (see Figure 9-6).

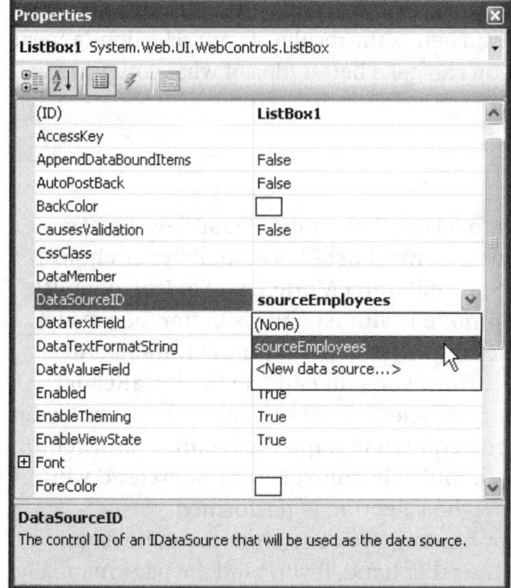

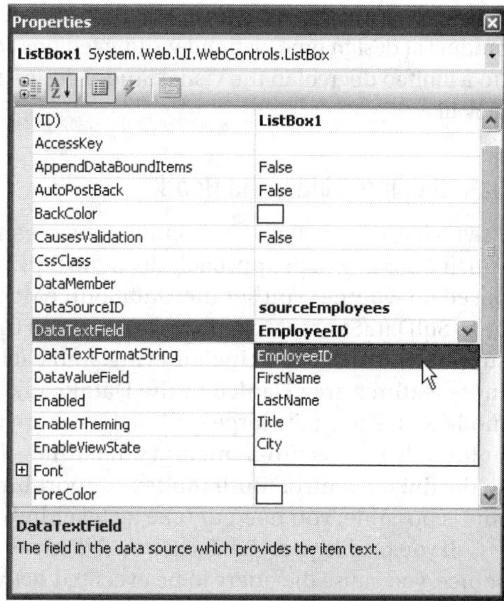

Figure 9-6. *Binding a list control to a data source field*

4. You can use the same steps to bind a rich data control. Add a GridView to your page, and set the GridView.DataSourceID property to the same data source. You don't need to set any field information, because the GridView can display multiple fields. You'll see the column headings from your query appear on the design surface of your page immediately.

5. Run your page. Don't worry about executing the command or calling DataBind() on the page—ASP.NET performs both of those tasks automatically. You'll see a data-bound page like the one in Figure 9-7.

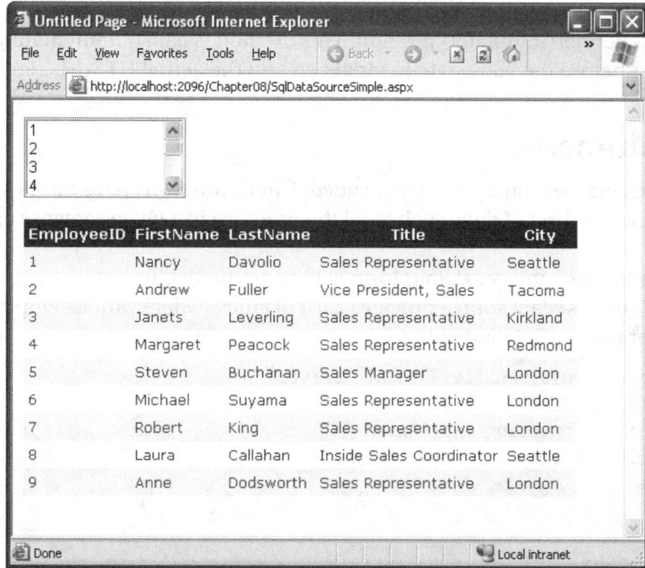

Figure 9-7. *A simple data-bound page with no code*

Clearly, the great advantage of the data source controls is that they allow you to configure data binding at design time, without writing tedious code. Even better, the results of your selections appear (to a limited degree) in the Visual Studio designer so you can get a better idea of what your form will look like.

Data Binding "Under the Hood"

As you learned earlier in this chapter, you can bind to a DataReader or a DataView. So, it's worth asking, which approach does the SqlDataSource control use? It's actually your choice, based on whether you set the DataSourceMode to SqlDataSourceMode.DataSet (the default) or to SqlDataSourceMode.DataReader. The DataSet mode is almost always better, because it supports advanced sorting, filtering, and caching settings that depend on the DataSet. All these features are disabled in the DataReader mode. However, you can use the DataReader mode with extremely large grids, as it's more memory-efficient. That's because the DataReader holds only one record in memory at a time—just long enough to copy the record's information to the linked control. Both modes support binding to multiple controls. To understand why this is possible, you need to take a closer look at how the selection is performed.

If you profile your database, you'll discover that by binding two controls to the same data source, you cause the query to be executed *twice*. On the other hand, if you bind the page manually, you have the ability to bind the same object to two different controls, which means you need to execute the query only once. Clearly, the SqlDataSource imposes a bit of unnecessary extra overhead here, but if you're aware of it you can design accordingly. First, you should consider caching, which the SqlDataSource supports natively (see Chapter 11 for a full discussion). Second, realize that most of the time you *won't* be binding more than one control to a data source. That's because the rich data controls—the GridVew, DetailsView, and FormsView—have the ability to present multiple pieces of data in a flexible layout. If you use these controls, you'll need to bind only one control, which allows you to steer clear of this limitation.

It's also important to note that data binding is performed at the end of your web-page processing, just before the page is rendered. That means the Page.Load event will fire, followed by any control events, followed by the Page.PreRender event, and only then will the data binding take place. The data binding is performed on every postback (unless you redirect to another page). If you need to write code that springs into action *after* the data binding is complete, you can override the Page.OnPreRenderComplete() method. This method is called immediately after the PreRender stage but just before the view state is serialized and the actual HTML is rendered.

Parameterized Commands

In the previous example, the complete query was hard-coded. Often, you won't have this flexibility. Instead, you'll want to retrieve a subset of data, such as all the products in a given category or all the employees in a specific city.

The following example creates a master-details form using parameters. To create this example, you need two data sources. The first data source provides a list of cities (where various employees live). Here's the definition for this SqlDataSource:

```
<asp:SqlDataSource ID="sourceEmployeeCities" runat="server"
 ProviderName="System.Data.SqlClient"
 ConnectionString="<%$ ConnectionStrings:Northwind %>"
 SelectCommand="SELECT DISTINCT City FROM Employees">
</asp:SqlDataSource>
```

This data source fills a drop-down list with city values:

```
<asp:DropDownList ID="lstCities" runat="server"
  DataSourceID="sourceEmployeeCities" DataTextField="City" AutoPostBack="True">
</asp:DropDownList>
```

The list control has automatic postback enabled, which ensures that the page is posted back every time the list selection is changed, giving your page the chance to update its data-bound controls accordingly. The other option is to create a dedicated button (such as Select) next to the list control for initiating the postback.

When you select a city, the second data source retrieves all the employees in that city. Here's the definition for the second data source:

```
<asp:SqlDataSource ID="sourceEmployees" runat="server"
 ProviderName="System.Data.SqlClient"
 ConnectionString="<%$ ConnectionStrings:Northwind %>"
 SelectCommand="SELECT EmployeeID, FirstName, LastName,
 Title, City FROM Employees WHERE City=@City">
  <SelectParameters>
    <asp:ControlParameter ControlID="lstCities" Name="City"
     PropertyName="SelectedValue" />
  </SelectParameters>
</asp:SqlDataSource>
```

The trick here is the query is written using a parameter. Parameters are always indicated with an @ symbol, as in @City. You can define as many symbols as you want, but you must map each parameter to another value. In this example, the value for the @City parameter is taken from the lstCities.SelectedValue property. However, you could just as easily modify the ControlParameter tag to bind to another property or control.

Now when you run the page, you can view the employees in a specific city (see Figure 9-8).

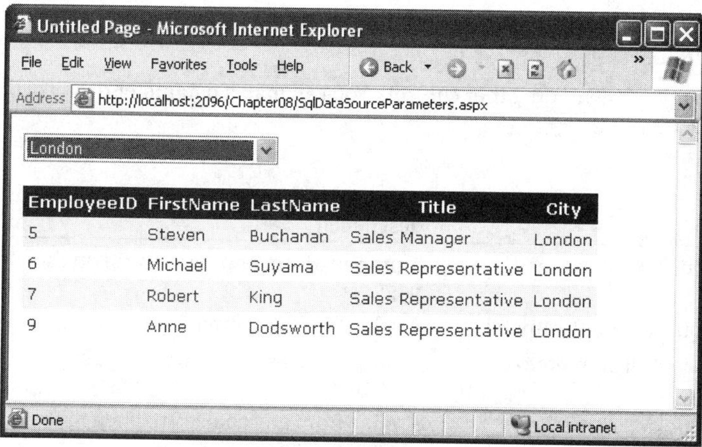

Figure 9-8. *Selecting records based on control selection*

It's important to understand the benefits and limitations of this example. First, when you create a parameterized command in a SqlDataSource tag, the parameters are properly encoded and

SQL injection attacks aren't a problem (as discussed in Chapter 7). Second, all the data-bound controls you create rebind themselves after every postback. This means that when you select a city, the page will be posted back and both queries will be executed. This is probably extra database work you don't require, assuming the list of cities does not change frequently. Once again, this is a good place to consider caching. (See Chapter 11 for details.)

Stored Procedures

You can adapt this example to work with a stored procedure just as easily. For example, if you have the following stored procedure in your database:

```
CREATE PROCEDURE GetEmployeesByCity
  @City varchar(15)
AS
  SELECT EmployeeID, FirstName, LastName, Title,
  City FROM Employees WHERE City=@City
GO
```

you can change the sourceEmployees data source, as shown here:

```
<asp:SqlDataSource ID="sourceEmployees" runat="server"
 ProviderName="System.Data.SqlClient"
 ConnectionString="<%$ ConnectionStrings:Northwind %>"
 SelectCommand="GetEmployeesByCity" SelectCommandType="StoredProcedure">
  <SelectParameters>
    <asp:ControlParameter ControlID="lstCities" Name="City"
      PropertyName="SelectedValue" />
  </SelectParameters>
</asp:SqlDataSource>
```

Not only does this give you all the benefit of stored procedures, but it also streamlines the .aspx portion of your page by removing the actual SQL query, which can be quite lengthy in a real-world page.

More Parameterized Commands

Parameter values aren't necessarily drawn from other controls. You can map a parameter to any of the parameter types defined in Table 9-2.

Table 9-2. *Parameter Types*

Source	Control Tag	Description
Control property	<asp:ControlParameter>	A property from another control on the page.
Query string value	<asp:QueryStringParameter>	A value from the current query string.
Session state value	<asp:SessionParameter>	A value stored in the current user's session.
Cookie value	<asp:CookieParameter>	A value from any cookie attached to the current request.
Profile value	<asp:ProfileParameter>	A value from the current user's profile (see Chapter 24).
A form variable	<asp:FormParameter>	A value posted to the page from an input control. Usually, you'll use a control property instead, but you might need to grab a value straight from the Forms collection if you've disabled view state for the corresponding control.

You don't need to remember the different tag names, as Visual Studio provides a handy editor that lets you create your command and define your parameters (see Figure 9-9). To see this dialog box, click the ellipsis (...) next to the SelectQuery property in the Properties window. When you type a command that uses one or more parameters, click the Refresh Parameters button, and the list of parameters will appear. You can then choose the mapping for each parameter by making a choice in the Parameter Source box.

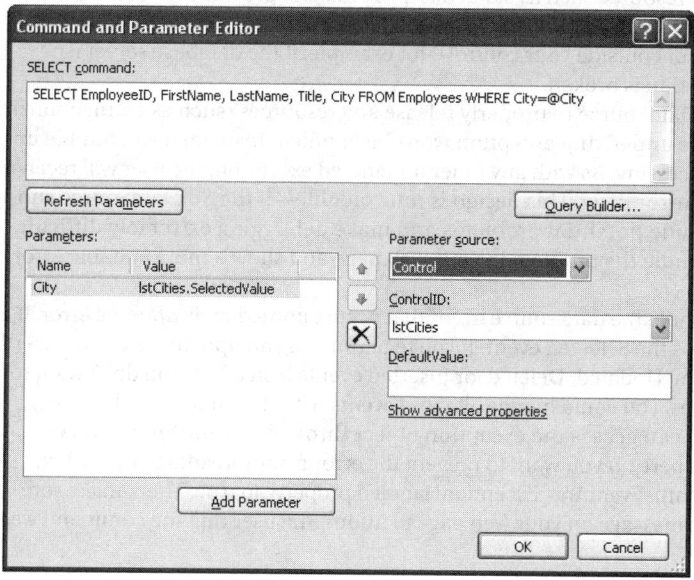

Figure 9-9. *Configuring parameter binding at design time*

For example, you could split the earlier example into two pages. In the first page, define a list control that shows all the available cities:

```
<asp:SqlDataSource ID="sourceEmployeeCities" runat="server"
 ProviderName="System.Data.SqlClient"
 ConnectionString="<%$ ConnectionStrings:Northwind %>"
 SelectCommand="SELECT DISTINCT City FROM Employees">
</asp:SqlDataSource>
<asp:ListBox ID="lstCities" runat="server" DataSourceID="sourceEmployeeCities"
 DataTextField="City"></asp:ListBox><br />
```

Now, you'll need a little extra code to copy the selected city to the query string and redirect the page. Here's a button that does just that:

```
Protected Sub cmdGo_Click(ByVal sender As Object, ByVal e As EventArgs)
    Response.Redirect("QueryParameter2.aspx?city=" & lstCities.SelectedValue)
End Sub
```

Finally, the second page can bind the GridView according to the city value that's supplied in the query string:

```
<asp:SqlDataSource ID="sourceEmployees" runat="server"
 ProviderName="System.Data.SqlClient"
 ConnectionString="<%$ ConnectionStrings:Northwind %>"
 SelectCommand="GetEmployeesByCity" SelectCommandType="StoredProcedure">
```

```
  <SelectParameters>
    <asp:QueryStringParameter Name="City" QueryStringField="city" />
  </SelectParameters>
</asp:SqlDataSource>
```

Handling Errors

When you deal with an outside resource such as a database, you need to protect your code with a basic amount of error-handling logic. Even if you've avoided every possible coding mistake, you still need to defend against factors outside your control—for example, if the database server isn't running or the network connection is broken.

You can count on the SqlDataSource to properly release any resources (such as connections) if an error occurs. However, the underlying exception won't be handled. Instead, it will bubble up to the page and derail your processing. As with any other unhandled exception, the user will receive a cryptic error message or an error page. This design is unavoidable—if the SqlDataSource suppressed exceptions, it could hide potential problems and make debugging extremely difficult. However, it's a good idea to handle the problem in your web page and show a more suitable error message.

To do this, you need to handle the data source event that occurs immediately *after* the error. If you're performing a query, that's the Selected event. If you're performing an update, delete, or insert operation, you would handle the Updated, Deleted, or Inserted events instead. (If you don't want to offer customized error messages, you could handle all these events with the same event handler.)

In the event handler, you can access the exception object through the SqlDataSource➥StatusEventArgs.Exception property. If you want to prevent the error from spreading any further, simply set the SqlDataSourceStatusEventArgs.ExceptionHandled property to true. Then, make sure you show an appropriate error message on your web page to inform the user that the command was not completed.

Here's an example:

```
Protected Sub sourceEmployees_Selected(ByVal sender As Object,
      ByVal e As SqlDataSourceStatusEventArgs)
    If e.Exception IsNot Nothing Then
        ' Mask the error with a generic message (for security purposes).
        lblError.Text = "An exception occurred performing the query."

        ' Consider the error handled.
        e.ExceptionHandled = True
    End If
End Sub
```

Updating Records

Selecting data is only half of the equation. The SqlDataSource can also apply changes. The only catch is that not all controls support updating. For example, the humble ListBox doesn't provide any way for the user to edit values, delete existing items, or insert new ones. Fortunately, ASP.NET's rich data controls—including the GridView, DetailsView, and FormView—all have editing features that you can switch on.

The first step is to define suitable commands for the operations you want to perform, such as inserting (InsertQuery), deleting (DeleteQuery), and updating (UpdateQuery). If you know that you will allow the user to perform only certain operations (such as updates) but not others (such as insertions and deletions), you can safely omit the commands you don't need.

You define the InsertCommand, DeleteCommand, and UpdateCommand in the same way you define the command for the SelectCommand property—by using a parameterized query. For example, here's a SqlDataSource that defines a basic update command that updates every field:

```
<asp:SqlDataSource ID="sourceEmployees" runat="server"
 ProviderName="System.Data.SqlClient"
 ConnectionString="<%$ ConnectionStrings:Northwind %>"
 SelectCommand="SELECT EmployeeID, FirstName, LastName, Title, City FROM Employees"
 UpdateCommand="UPDATE Employees SET FirstName=@FirstName, LastName=@LastName,
 Title=@Title, City=@City FROM Employees WHERE EmployeeID=@EmployeeID">
</asp:SqlDataSource>
```

In this example, the parameter names aren't chosen arbitrarily. As long as you give each parameter the same name as the field it affects and preface it with the @ symbol (so FirstName because @FirstName), you don't need to define the parameter. That's because the ASP.NET data controls automatically submit a collection of parameters with the new values before triggering the update. Each parameter in the collection uses this naming convention.

To try this, create a page with the SqlDataSource shown previously and a linked GridView control. Now, take the following steps to enable editing:

1. Select the GridView. In the smart tag, choose the Add New Column link.
2. In the Choose a Field Type box, select CommandField. Then, select the Edit/Update check box and the Show Cancel Button check box. Make sure all other check boxes are unchecked.
3. Click OK to add the column with editing controls.

When you complete these steps, the GridView editing controls appear in an additional column. When you run the page and the GridView is bound and displayed, the edit column shows an Edit link next to every record. When clicked, this link switches the corresponding row into edit mode. All fields are changed to text boxes (with the exception of read-only fields), and the Edit link is replaced with an Update link and a Cancel link (see Figure 9-10).

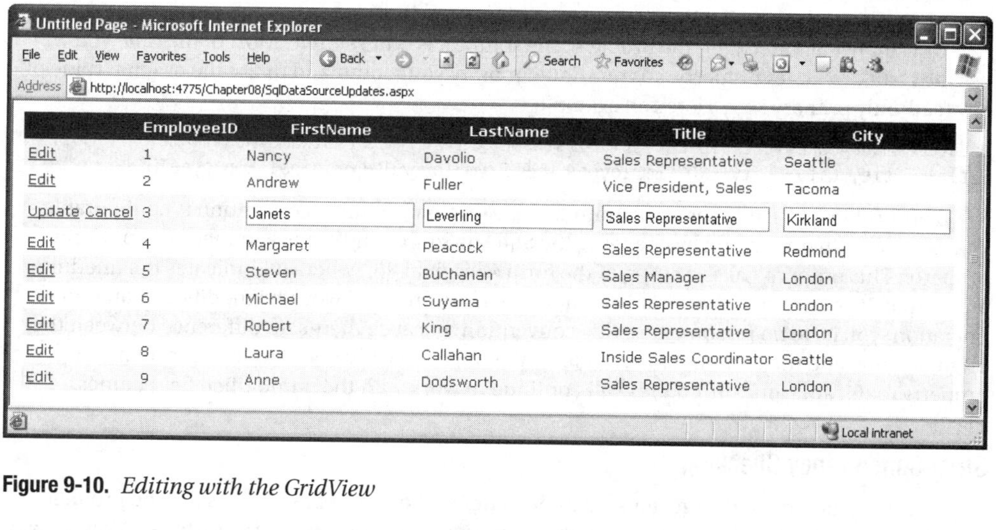

	EmployeeID	FirstName	LastName	Title	City
Edit	1	Nancy	Davolio	Sales Representative	Seattle
Edit	2	Andrew	Fuller	Vice President, Sales	Tacoma
Update Cancel	3	Janets	Leverling	Sales Representative	Kirkland
Edit	4	Margaret	Peacock	Sales Representative	Redmond
Edit	5	Steven	Buchanan	Sales Manager	London
Edit	6	Michael	Suyama	Sales Representative	London
Edit	7	Robert	King	Sales Representative	London
Edit	8	Laura	Callahan	Inside Sales Coordinator	Seattle
Edit	9	Anne	Dodsworth	Sales Representative	London

Figure 9-10. *Editing with the GridView*

The Cancel link returns the row to its initial state. The Update link passes the values to the SqlDataSource.UpdateParameters collection (using the field names) and then triggers the SqlDataSource.Update() method to apply the change to the database. Once again, you don't have to write any code.

You can create similar parameterized commands for the DeleteCommand and InsertCommand. To enable deleting and inserting, you need to add a column to the GridView that has the ShowInsertButton and ShowDeleteButton properties set to True.

■ **Note** The GridView is an extremely flexible control. Templates, one of its many features, allow you to define the controls and markup used when editing a record. This is handy if you want to enable editing through drop-down lists, add validation controls, or just fine-tune the appearance of a row in edit mode. You'll learn about templates in Chapter 10.

Updating and KeyFields

All the rich data controls include a DataKeyNames property. This property indicates which field (or fields) are considered primary keys.

To use this feature, you must set the DataKeyNames property with a comma-separated list of one or more key fields. Often, you'll have only one key field, as shown here:

```
<asp:GridView ID="gridEmployees" runat="server" DataSourceID="sourceEmployees"
 DataKeyNames="EmployeeID" ... >
```

Key fields are given special treatment. For example, the GridView makes it possible to easily retrieve the key information for a given row. Additionally, when you commit an update to a row, the data control passes the *original* value of the key fields, as well as the changed value (unless it's read-only). The original value is used in a WHERE clause to locate the row so you can perform the update. To avoid confusion, the parameter that contains the original value is automatically given the prefix *original_*. For example, the @EmployeeID parameter becomes @original_EmployeeID.

This difference can lead to a potential problem. You may begin using a parameter name such as @EmployeeID and then set the DataKeyName property to get access to another feature, such as selection. When you attempt to perform an update, you'll receive an error indicating the parameter @EmployeeID can't be found. What makes this problem even more confusing is that you can take certain actions in Visual Studio—such as refreshing the schema for your data control—that will automatically set the DataKeyName property without warning you.

Now that you understand the problem, the solution is quite simple. Most of the time you will use the DataKeyNames property, so you should modify your command to use the original value of any read-only primary keys. Here's an example:

```
UpdateCommand="UPDATE Employees SET FirstName=@FirstName, LastName=@LastName,
Title=@Title, City=@City FROM Employees WHERE EmployeeID=@original_EmployeeID">
```

This problem has another workaround. The @original_ naming convention is configurable. You can use a different prefix by changing the SqlDataSource.OldValuesParameterFormatString property. This property takes a string of the form @original_{0}, where {0} indicates the unadulterated name. If you are sure that your key values are read-only and won't be modified in an update operation, you have no reason to use this convention, because there's no difference between the original name and the current name. So, simply change the OldValuesParameterFormatString property to {0}, and your commands will continue to work with the unmodified field names.

Strict Concurrency Checking

The update command in the previous example matches the record based on its ID. The problem with this approach is that the update command updates every field indiscriminately—it has no way to distinguish between fields that are and aren't changed. As a result, you can end up obliterating the changes of another user, if they are made between the time the page is requested and the time the page is updated.

For example, imagine Chen and Lucy are viewing the same table of employee records. Lucy commits a change to the address of an employee. A few seconds later, Chen commits a name change to the same employee record. However, that update command not only applies the new name, but it also overwrites every field with the values in Chen's page—effectively replacing the address Lucy entered with the old address.

To defend against this sort of problem, you can enforce stricter concurrency checking. One way to do this is to create a command that performs the update only if every field matches. Here's what that command would look like:

```
UpdateCommand="UPDATE Employees SET FirstName=@FirstName, LastName=@LastName,
Title=@Title, City=@City FROM Employees WHERE EmployeeID=@original_EmployeeID AND
FirstName=@original_FirstName AND LastName=@original_LastName AND
Title=@original_Title AND City=@original_City">
```

The problem is that the command doesn't have access to the original values of every field—instead, it has only the original value of any key fields. You could define every field in the table as a key field, but this is certain to cause confusion. A better solution is to set the SqlDataSource.ConflictDetection property to ConflictOptions.CompareAllValues instead of ConflictOptions.OverwriteChanges (the default). The data control will then supply the original value of *every* field, and the command will work as written.

■ **Tip** Commands that compare values are often inefficient, because they require more data to be sent over the network and mean more comparison work for the database. A better solution is to use a timestamp field. If the row is unchanged, the timestamp will always match. In this case, you would hide the timestamp column from the data control but set the DataKeyFields property to include it, so you could use it when constructing your command.

Updating with Stored Procedures

The update example works just as readily with stored procedures. In this case, you simply supply the stored procedure name for the UpdateCommand:

```
UpdateCommand="UpdateEmployee" UpdateCommandType="StoredProcedure"
```

However, this has a catch. As you've learned, the parameter names are based on the field names. If the stored procedure uses the same parameter names, the update works without a hitch. However, if the stored procedure parameter names are slightly different, the update will fail.

■ **Tip** The order of parameters is irrelevant. Only the names are important. The SqlDataSource does a case-insensitive comparison, so your parameters can have different capitalization.

For example, consider an UpdateEmployee stored procedure that takes parameters like this:

```
CREATE PROCEDURE UpdateEmployee
(
  @EmployeeID         int,
  @TitleOfCourtesy    varchar(25),
  @Last               varchar(20),
  @First              varchar(10)
)
AS
...
```

In this example, the FirstName and LastName fields map to parameters named @First and @Last. Unfortunately, there's no declarative way to correct this problem and map these parameters to their correct names. Instead, you need to define the new parameters and write a little custom code.

The first step is to add two parameters to the SqlDataSource.UpdateParameters collection. Unfortunately, you can't create these while the update is in progress. Instead, you need to add them to the SqlDataSource tag:

```
<asp:SqlDataSource ID="sourceEmployees" runat="server"
 ProviderName="System.Data.SqlClient"
 ConnectionString="<%$ ConnectionStrings:Northwind %>" SelectCommand=
 "SELECT EmployeeID, FirstName, LastName, TitleOfCourtesy FROM Employees"
 UpdateCommand="UpdateEmployee" UpdateCommandType="StoredProcedure"
 OnUpdating="sourceEmployees_Updating" >
  <UpdateParameters>
    <asp:Parameter Name="First" Type="String" />
    <asp:Parameter Name="Last" Type="String" />
  </UpdateParameters>
</asp:SqlDataSource>
```

Note that the parameter names don't include the @ symbol when you define them in the SqlDataSource tag.

The next step is to react to the SqlDataSource.Updating event, which fires immediately before the update is committed. You can then set the value for the @First and @Last parameters and remove the @FirstName and @LastName parameters from site. Here's the code you need:

```
Protected Sub sourceEmployees_Updating(ByVal sender As Object, _
                ByVal e As SqlDataSourceCommandEventArgs)
    e.Command.Parameters("@First").Value = e.Command.Parameters("@FirstName").Value
    e.Command.Parameters("@Last").Value = e.Command.Parameters("@LastName").Value
    e.Command.Parameters.Remove(e.Command.Parameters("@FirstName"))
    e.Command.Parameters.Remove(e.Command.Parameters("@LastName"))
End Sub
```

This represents a fairly typical scenario in which the no-code data binding won't work. Overall, if you can design your stored procedures and classes to work with the data source controls, you'll avoid writing a great deal of code. On the other hand, if you introduce the data source controls to an existing application with a fixed database schema and database components, it may take a fair bit of extra code to fit these pieces together.

Disadvantages of the SqlDataSource

As you've seen, when you use the SqlDataSource, you can often avoid writing any data access code. However, you also sacrifice a fair bit of flexibility. Here are the most significant disadvantages:

Data access logic embedded in the page: To create a SqlDataSource control, you need to hard-code the SQL statements in your web page. This means you can't fine-tune your query without modifying your web page. In an enterprise application, this limitation isn't acceptable, as it's common to revise the queries after the application is deployed in response to profiling, indexes, and expected loads.

■ **Tip** You can improve this situation a fair bit by restricting your use of the SqlDataSource to stored procedures. However, in a large-scale web application, the data access code will be maintained, tested, and refined separately from the business logic (and it may even be coded by different developers). The SqlDataSource just doesn't give you that level of flexibility.

Maintenance in large applications: Every page that accesses the database needs its own set of SqlDataSource controls. This can turn into a maintenance nightmare, particularly if you have several pages using the same query (each of which requires a duplicate instance of the SqlDataSource). In a component-based application, you'll use a higher-level model. The web pages will communicate with a data access library, which will contain all the database details.

Lack of flexibility: Every data access task requires a separate SqlDataSource. If you want to provide a user with multiple ways to view or query data, this can swamp your page with data sources objects, one for each command variant. This can get complicated—fast.

Inapplicability to other data tasks: The SqlDataSource doesn't properly represent some types of tasks. The SqlDataSource is intended for data display and data editing scenarios. However, this model breaks down if you need to connect to the database and perform another task, such as placing a shipment request into an order pipeline or logging an event. In these situations, you'll need custom database code. It will simplify your application if you have a single database component that encapsulates these tasks along with data retrieval and updating operations.

■ **Note** In fact, in a well-abstracted multitier application, your web page may call a method such as Business.PlaceOrder() without worrying about whether this operation involves saving an order record in a database, sending a message to a message queue, communicating with a remote component, or using a combination of all these tasks.

To get around these limitations, you should consider the ObjectDataSource. The ObjectDataSource allows you to bind your page to a custom data access component. Best of all, you get almost all the same frills, such as design-time data binding and no need to write code in your web page.

The ObjectDataSource

The ObjectDataSource allows you to create a declarative link between your web-page controls and a data access component that queries and updates data. The ObjectDataSource is remarkably flexible and can work with a variety of different components. However, to use it, your data access class must conform to a few rules:

- It must be stateless. That's because the ObjectDataSource will create an instance only when needed and destroy it at the end of every request.
- It must have a default, no-argument constructor.
- All the logic must be contained in a single class. (If you want to use different classes for selecting and updating your data, you'll need to wrap them in another higher-level class.)
- None of the linked methods (for selecting or updating records) can be static.
- It must provide the query results when a single method is called.
- The query results are several records, which can be represented as a collection, an array, or a list object that implements IEnumerable. Each record should be a custom object that exposes all its data through public properties.

You can work around many of these rules by handling ObjectDataSource events and writing custom code. However, if you want your data access class to plug into the data-binding model seamlessly without extra work, you should observe these guidelines.

Selecting Records

For example, consider the data-bound page in Figure 9-8. You can create the same page using the custom data access component developed in Chapter 8. You can refer to Chapter 8 to see the full code, which has the following structure:

```
Public Class EmployeeDB
    Public Function InsertEmployee(ByVal emp As EmployeeDetails) As Integer
        ...
    End Function
    Public Sub DeleteEmployee(ByVal employeeID As Integer)
        ...
    End Sub
    Public Function GetEmployee() As EmployeeDetails
        ...
    End Function
    Public Function GetEmployees() As EmployeeDetails()
        ...
    End Function
    Public Function CountEmployees() As Integer
        ...
    End Function
End Class
```

The first step to use this class in your page is to define the ObjectDataSource and indicate the name of the class that contains the data access methods. You do this by specifying the fully qualified class name with the TypeName property:

```
<asp:ObjectDataSource ID="ObjectDataSource1" runat="server"
 TypeName="DatabaseComponent.EmployeeDB" ... />
```

Note For this to work, the DatabaseComponent.EmployeeDB class must exist in the App_Code folder or be compiled in an assembly in the Bin folder.

Once you've attached the ObjectDataSource to a class, the next step is to point it to the methods it can use to select and update records.

The ObjectDataSource defines SelectMethod, DeleteMethod, UpdateMethod, and InsertMethod properties that you use to link your data access class to various tasks. Each property takes the name of the method in the data access class. In this example, you simply need to enable querying, so you need to set the SelectMethod property:

```
<asp:ObjectDataSource ID="sourceEmployees" runat="server"
 TypeName="DatabaseComponent.EmployeeDB" SelectMethod="GetEmployees" />
```

Remember, the GetEmployees() method returns an array of EmployeeDetails objects. These objects fit the criteria of the ObjectDataSource—they provide all the appropriate record data through public properties.

Once you've set up the ObjectDataSource, you can bind your web-page controls in the same way you do with the SqlDataSource. You can even use the same drop-down lists in the Properties window, provided you click the Refresh Schema link in the ObjectDataSource smart tag first. When you click Refresh Schema, Visual Studio retrieves the property names and data types by reflecting on the EmployeeDetails class.

Here's the complete page code, without the formatting details for the GridView:

```
<asp:ObjectDataSource ID="sourceEmployees" runat="server"
 TypeName="DatabaseComponent.EmployeeDB" SelectMethod="GetEmployees"/>
<asp:ListBox ID="ListBox1" runat="server" DataSourceID="sourceEmployees"
 DataTextField="EmployeeID"></asp:ListBox>
<br />
<asp:GridView ID="GridView1" runat="server" DataSourceID="sourceEmployees">
</asp:GridView>
```

Figure 9-11 shows the result.

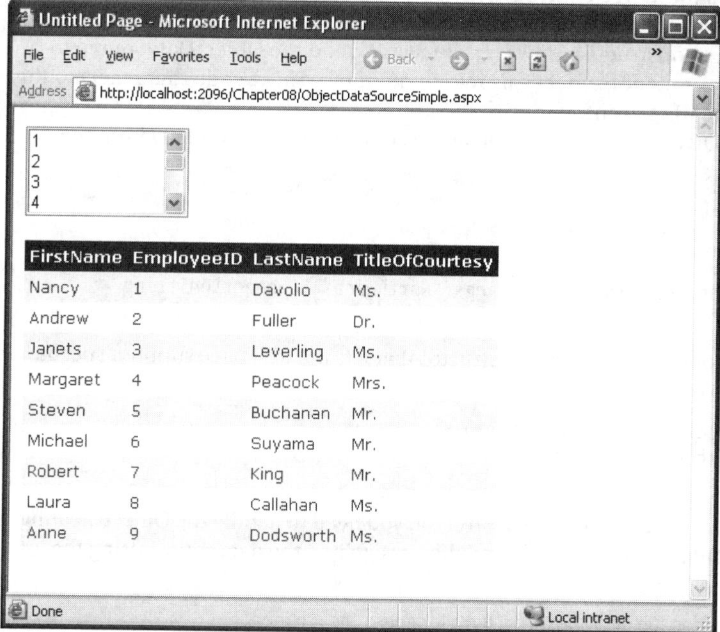

Figure 9-11. *Binding to a data access class*

From the user's perspective, this example is equivalent to the SqlDataSource page shown in Figure 9-8. The only difference is that by default, the columns are shown in the order that the properties are declared in the class, whereas the SqlDataSource shows them in the order they're listed in the query. You can easily change the ordering of columns by customizing the GridView.

The apparent similarities conceal some real behind-the-scenes differences. In this example, the web page doesn't require any hard-coded SQL details. Instead, all the work is handed off to the EmployeeDB class. When you run the page, the ListBox and GridView will request data from the ObjectDataSource, which will call the EmployeeDB.GetEmployees() method to retrieve the data (once for each control). This data is then bound and displayed in both controls, with no code required.

■**Note** Remember, the EmployeeDB class uses error-handling blocks to make sure connections are properly closed, but it doesn't catch exceptions. (Best design practices are to let the exception notify the web page, which can then decide how best to inform the user.) You can handle errors with the ObjectDataSource in the same way you handle them with the SqlDataSource—first, handle the Selected, Inserted, Updated, or Deleted event; second, check for an exception; and third, mark it as handled. For more information, see the "Handling Errors" section earlier in the chapter.

Using a Parameterized Constructor

A key part of extending the data source controls takes place through event handling. For example, by default the ObjectDataSource is able to create your custom data access class only if it provides a zero no-argument constructor. However, you can extend the ObjectDataSource to work with data access classes that don't meet this requirement by writing code that reacts to the ObjectDataSource.ObjectCreating event.

The current EmployeesDB class retrieves the database connection string directly from the web.config file, as shown here:

```
Private connectionString As String
Public Sub New()
    connectionString =
        WebConfigurationManager.ConnectionStrings("Northwind").ConnectionString
End Sub
```

However, you might want to add another constructor that lets the web page supply a specific connection string of its choosing:

```
Public Sub New(ByVal connectionString As String)
    Me.connectionString = connectionString
End Sub
```

To force the ObjectDataSource to use this constructor, you need to handle the ObjectCreating event, create the EmployeeDB instance yourself, and then assign it to the data source using the ObjectDataSourceEventArgs:

```
Protected Sub sourceEmployees_ObjectCreating(ByVal sender As Object,
        ByVal e As ObjectDataSourceEventArgs)
    e.ObjectInstance = New DatabaseComponent.EmployeeDB("...")
End Sub
```

Clearly, you could perform more complex initialization in the ObjectCreating event. For example, you could call an initialization method, choose to instantiate one of several derived classes, and so on.

■**Tip** The data source controls expose a rich event model. Events tend to fall into two categories. Events ending in *ing* such as ObjectCreating occur while a task is underway and give you the chance to cancel or customize what's happening. Events ending in *ed* such as ObjectCreated occur when the task is finished and are suitable for logging the action, synchronizing other controls, and handling errors.

You can also react to the ObjectDisposing event to perform cleanup. The ObjectDisposing event is fired just before the data access object is released (before the page is served). Usually, you won't need to use the ObjectDisposing event because a better alternative exists—place your cleanup code in a dedicated Dispose() method inside your data access class. As long as you implement IDisposable, the ObjectDataSource will automatically call your Dispose() method. (To get a painless implementation of IDisposable for free, just derive your data access class from the System.ComponentModel.Component class and override the Dispose() method.)

Using Method Parameters

Earlier, you saw how you could use the SqlDataSource to execute parameterized commands. The same feat is possible with the ObjectDataSource, if you provide a suitable select method that accepts one or more parameters. You can then map each parameter to a control value, query string argument, and so on.

To try this, you can use the EmployeeDB.GetEmployee() method, which retrieves a single employee by ID number. Here's the method declaration:

```
Public Function GetEmployee(ByVal employeeID As Integer) As EmployeeDetails
    ...
End Function
```

The test page provides a list with all the employee IDs. This list control uses the GetEmployees() method through an Object data source:

```
<asp:ObjectDataSource ID="sourceEmployeesList" runat="server"
 SelectMethod="GetEmployees" TypeName="DatabaseComponent.EmployeeDB"/>
<asp:ListBox ID="lstEmployees" runat="server" DataSourceID="sourceEmployeesList"
 DataTextField="EmployeeID" AutoPostBack="True"/>
```

When you choose an ID, the page posts back and uses a second data source to call GetEmployee(). The employeeID value is taken from the selected item in the list:

```
<asp:ObjectDataSource ID="sourceEmployee" runat="server"
 SelectMethod="GetEmployee" TypeName="DatabaseComponent.EmployeeDB"/>
  <SelectParameters>
    <asp:ControlParameter ControlID="lstEmployees" Name="employeeID"
     PropertyName="SelectedValue" />
  </SelectParameters>
</asp:ObjectDataSource>
```

The name you define for the parameter *must* match the parameter name you use in the method exactly. When the ObjectDataSource calls the method, it uses reflection to examine the method, and it examines the parameter names to determine the order of arguments. This system allows you to use overloaded methods, because the ObjectDataSource is able to correctly identify the overload you want based on the number of parameters you define and their names.

■ **Tip** The data types are not used in the matching process—instead, the ObjectDataSource will attempt to convert the parameter value into the data type of the matching parameter using the appropriate type converter for that data type. If this process fails, an exception is raised.

Now, the single employee record returned from GetEmployee() is displayed in another rich data control—the DetailsView. By default, the DetailsView creates a basic table with one row for each field or property in the data item. Here's a basic declaration for the DetailsView:

```
<asp:DetailsView ID="DetailsView1" runat="server" AutoGenerateRows="True"/>
```

You have one more detail to fill in. The first time the page is requested, there won't be any selected value in the lstEmployees control. However, the DetailsView will still try to bind itself, so the ObjectDataSource will call GetEmployee(). The employeeID parameter is Nothing but the actual value that's passed is 0, because integers aren't nullable. When the GetEmployee() method executes the query, it doesn't find a matching record with an employeeID of 0. This is an error condition, and an exception is thrown.

You could solve this problem by revising the GetEmployee() method to return Nothing in this situation. However, it makes more sense to catch the binding attempt and explicitly cancel it when there's no employeeID parameter. You can do this by handling the ObjectDataSource.Selecting event and looking for the employeeID parameter in the ObjectDataSourceSelectingEventArgs.InputParameters collection, which has every parameter you're using indexed by name.

```
Protected Sub sourceEmployee_Selecting(ByVal sender As Object,
      ByVal e As ObjectDataSourceSelectingEventArgs)
    If e.InputParameters("employeeID") Is Nothing Then
    e.Cancel = True
    End If
End Sub
```

This is the only code you need to write for the page. Figure 9-12 shows the page in action.

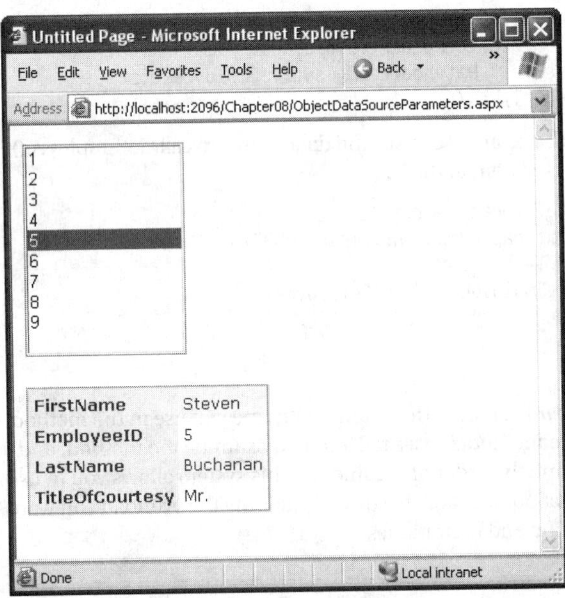

Figure 9-12. *Binding to a single employee record*

Updating Records

The ObjectDataSource provides the same type of support for updatable data binding as the SqlDataSource. The first step is to specify the UpdateMethod, which needs to be a Public instance method in the same class:

```
<asp:ObjectDataSource ID="sourceEmployees" runat="server"
 TypeName="DatabaseComponent.EmployeeDB"
 SelectMethod="GetEmployees" UpdateMethod="UpdateEmployee" />
```

The challenge is in making sure the UpdateMethod has the right signature. As with the SqlDataSource, updates, inserts, and deletes automatically receive a collection of parameters from the linked data control. These parameters have the same names as the corresponding properties in the class.

To understand how this works, it helps to consider a basic example. Assume you create a grid that shows a list of EmployeeDetails objects. You also add a column with edit links. When the user commits an edit, the GridView fills the ObjectDataSource.UpdateParameters collection with one parameter for each property of the EmployeeDetails class, including EmployeeID, FirstName, LastName, and TitleOfCourtesy. Then, the ObjectDataSource searches for a method named UpdateEmployee() in the EmployeeDB class. This method must have the same parameters, with the same names.

That means this method is a match:

```
Public Sub UpdateEmployee(ByVal employeeID As Integer, ByVal firstName As String,
        ByVal lastName As String, ByVal titleOfCourtesy As String)
    ...
End Sub
```

This method is not a match, because the names don't match exactly:

```
Public Sub UpdateEmployee(ByVal id As Integer, ByVal first As String,
        ByVal last As String, ByVal titleOfCourtesy As String)
    ...
End Sub
```

This is not a match, because there's an additional parameter:

```
Public Sub UpdateEmployee(ByVal employeeID As Integer, ByVal firstName As String,
        ByVal lastName As String, ByVal titleOfCourtesy As String,
        ByVal useOptimisticConcurrency As Boolean)
    ...
End Sub
```

The method matching algorithm is not case-sensitive, and it doesn't consider the order or data type of the parameters. It simply tries to find a method with the right number of parameters and the same names. As long as that method is present, the update can be committed automatically, without any custom code.

■ **Note** Remember, if you set the DataKeyNames property of the rich data control, the names of key fields will be changed (based on the ObjectDataSource.OldValuesParameterFormatString property). See the section "Updating and Key Fields" earlier in this chapter for more information.

Updating with a Data Object

One problem with the UpdateEmployee() method shown in the previous example is that the method signature is a little cumbersome—you need one parameter for each property in the data object. Seeing as you already have a definition for the EmployeeDetails class, it makes sense to create an UpdateEmployee() method that uses it and gets all its information from an EmployeeDetails object. Here's an example:

```
Public Sub UpdateEmployee(ByVal emp As EmployeeDetails)
    ...
End Sub
```

The ObjectDataSource supports this approach. However, to use it, you must set the DataObjectTypeName to the full name of the class you want to use. Here's how it works:

```
<asp:ObjectDataSource ID="sourceEmployees" runat="server"
 TypeName="DatabaseComponent.EmployeeDB"
 DataObjectTypeName="DatabaseComponent.EmployeeDetails"
 ... />
```

Once this is in place, the ObjectDataSource will match only the UpdateMethod, DeleteMethod, or InsertMethod if it has a single parameter that accepts the type specified in DataObjectTypeName. Additionally, your data object must follow some rules:

- It must provide a default (zero-argument) constructor.
- For every parameter, there must be a property with the same name. (Public variables are ignored.)
- All properties must be Public and writable.

You're free to add code to your data object class. For example, you can add methods, constructors, validation and event-handling logic in your property procedures, and so on.

Dealing with Nonstandard Method Signatures

Sometimes you may run into a problem in which the property names of your data class don't exactly match the parameter names of your update method. If all you need is a simple renaming job, you need to perform the task that was described in the "Updating with Stored Procedures" section earlier, although the syntax is slightly different.

First, you define the additional parameters you need, with the correct names. For example, maybe you need to rename the EmployeeDetails.EmployeeID property to a parameter named id in the update method. Here's the new parameter you need:

```
<asp:ObjectDataSource ID="sourceEmployees" runat="server"
 TypeName="DatabaseComponent.EmployeeDB" SelectMethod="GetEmployees"
 UpdateMethod="UpdateEmployee" OnUpdating="sourceEmployees_Updating" >
  <UpdateParameters>
    <asp:Parameter Name="id" Type="Int32" />
  </UpdateParameters>
</asp:ObjectDataSource>
```

Second, you react to the ObjectDataSource.Updating event, setting the value for these parameters and removing the ones you don't want:

```
Protected Sub sourceEmployees_Updating(ByVal sender As Object,
              ByVal e As ObjectDataSourceMethodEventArgs)
    e.InputParameters("id") = e.InputParameters("EmployeeID")
    e.InputParameters.Remove("EmployeeID")
End Sub
```

■ **Tip** The same approach used here for updating applies when you're performing inserts and deletes. The only difference is that you handle the Inserting and Deleting events instead.

You can use a similar approach to add extra parameters. For example, if your method requires a parameter with information that's not contained in the linked data control, just define it as one of the UpdateParameters and then set the value when the ObjectDataSource.Updating event fires.

If you're more ambitious, you can even decide to programmatically point the ObjectDataSource to a different update method in the same class:

```
sourceEmployees.UpdateMethod = "UpdateEmployeeStrict"
```

You'll use this approach to solve a common problem in the section "The Limits of the Data Source Controls" later in this chapter.

In fact, to get really adventurous you could set the ConflictDetection property to ConflictOptions.CompareAllValues so that the old and new values are submitted in the UpdateParameters collection. You can then examine these parameters, determine what fields have changed, and call a different method (with different parameters accordingly). Unfortunately, this isn't a zero-code scenario, and you might end up writing some awkward code for updating and removing parameters. Still, it gives you a valuable extra layer of flexibility.

Handling Identity Values in an Insert

So far, all the examples you've seen have used parameters to supply values to an update operation. However, you can also create a parameter to *return* a result. With the SqlDataSource, you can use this option to get access to an output parameter. With the ObjectDataSource, you can use this technique to capture the return value.

To see this in action, it's worth considering the InsertEmployee() method, which adds an employee record and returns the newly generated unique ID value as an integer:

```
Public Function InsertEmployee(ByVal emp As EmployeeDetails) As Integer
    ...
End Function
```

You don't need to use the identity value. As you've seen already, linked data controls are bound *after* any updates are committed, which ensures that the updated information always appears in the linked controls. However, you might want to use the identity for another purpose, such as displaying a confirmation message. To capture this identity value, you need to define a parameter:

```
<asp:ObjectDataSource ID="sourceEmployees" runat="server"
 TypeName="DatabaseComponent.EmployeeDB"
 DataObjectTypeName="DatabaseComponent.EmployeeDetails"
 SelectMethod="GetEmployees"
 InsertMethod="InsertEmployee" OnInserted="sourceEmployees_Inserted">
  <InsertParameters>
    <asp:Parameter Direction="ReturnValue" Name="EmployeeID" Type="Int32" />
  </InsertParameters>
</asp:ObjectDataSource>
```

Now you can retrieve the parameter by responding to the Inserted event, which fires after the insert operation is finished:

```
Protected Sub sourceEmployees_Inserted(ByVal sender As Object,
        ByVal e As ObjectDataSourceStatusEventArgs)
    If e.Exception Is Nothing Then
        lblConfirmation.Text = "Inserted record " & e.ReturnValue.ToString()
    End If
End Sub
```

The Limits of the Data Source Controls

As a whole, the data source controls are a remarkable innovation for ASP.NET developers. However, you'll still run into situations where you need to step beyond their bounds—or even abandon them completely. In the following sections, you'll see how to use the SqlDataSource and ObjectDataSource to deal with a common design requirement—additional options in a master-details list.

The Problem

Earlier, you saw an example that allowed users to browse a list of cities in different regions using two linked controls—a DropDownList and a GridView. Best of all, this example could be created using a SqlDataSource or an ObjectDataSource; either way, it doesn't require any custom code. Figure 9-9 shows this example.

As convenient as this example is, it presents a problem that's difficult to fix. Because it's impossible to create a drop-down list that doesn't have a selected item (unless it's empty), the first city in the list is automatically selected. Many web applications use a different behavior and add an extra item at the top of the list with text such as "(Choose a City)". Selecting this first item has no effect. Additionally, you might want to add an item that allows you to see *every* city in a single list. Figure 9-13 shows the result you want.

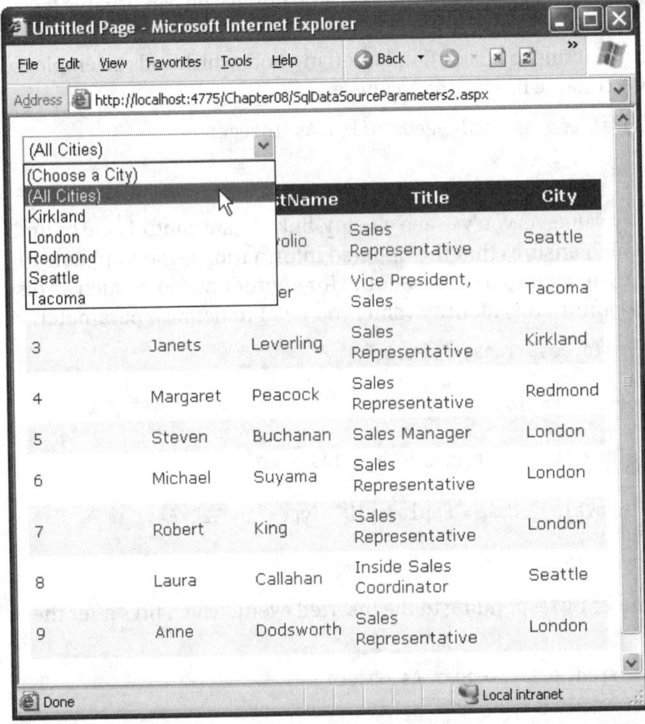

Figure 9-13. *Data binding with extra options*

So, how can you implement this model with data binding? One of the few weaknesses in the data binding model is that you never explicitly handle or create the data object that's bound to the control. As a result, you don't have the chance to add an extra item. In fact, this example has two challenges—determining how to add the extra options to the list and reacting when they are selected to override the automatic query logic.

Adding the Extra Items

This problem has a few possible workarounds, but none is perfect. You could rewrite the query so that it returns a result set with an extra hard-coded item. Here's an example:

```
SELECT '(Choose a City)' AS City UNION SELECT DISTINCT City FROM Employees
```

The problem with this approach is that it forces you to add presentation details to the data layer. If your query is in a dedicated stored procedure (which is always a good idea), it will be difficult to reuse this query for other purposes, and it will be awkward to maintain the page.

A better choice is to insert this fixed piece of string into the DropDownList programmatically. However, you can't take this step before the data binding takes place, because the data binding process will wipe it from the list. You could override the Page.OnPreRenderComplete() method to perform this task. However, that raises new complications. For one thing, the GridView will have already been filled with data based on the initial DropDownList selection. (Even if you solve this problem, there are other issues related to how changes are detected in the DropDownList selection.)

Ultimately, you'll need to resort to programmatic data binding. In normal operation, data source controls are invoked automatically when a linked control needs data or is ready to commit an update. However, a lesser known fact is that you can also take charge of data source controls programmatically, by calling methods such as Select(), Update(), Insert(), and Delete(). Of course, it's up to you to bind the data you retrieve from Select() and supply the changed data for when committing an update.

To put this into practice, start by removing the DropDownList.DataSourceID property . Instead of using this property, you'll bind the control when the page first loads. This gives you the chance to insert the items immediately, before any other data binding actions take place:

```
Protected Sub Page_Load(ByVal sender As Object, ByVal e As EventArgs)
    If (Not Page.IsPostBack) Then
        ' Trigger the sourceEmployeeCities query, and bind the results.
        lstCities.DataSource =
                sourceEmployeeCities.Select(DataSourceSelectArguments.Empty)
        lstCities.DataBind()

        ' Add the two new items, and select the first.
        lstCities.Items.Insert(0, "(Choose a City)")
        lstCities.Items.Insert(1, "(All Cities)")
        lstCities.SelectedIndex = 0
    End If
End Sub
```

In this example, the data binding for the list control is performed only once, when the page is requested for the first time. After that, the values in view state are used instead. This code is identical for the SqlDataSource and the ObjectDataSource. That's not true for the remainder of the example.

Handling the Extra Options with the SqlDataSource

The next challenge is to intercept clicks on either of the first two items. You can accomplish this by handling the data source Selecting event, which occurs just before the query is executed. You can then check the parameters that are about to be supplied and cancel the operation if needed.

Here's the complete code:

```
Protected Sub sourceEmployees_Selecting(ByVal sender As Object,
    ByVal e As SqlDataSourceSelectingEventArgs)
  If CStr(e.Command.Parameters("@City").Value) = "(Choose a City)" Then
      ' Do nothing.
      e.Cancel = True
  Else If CStr(e.Command.Parameters("@City").Value) = "(All Cities)" Then
      ' Manually change the command.
      e.Command.CommandText = "SELECT * FROM Employees"
  End If
End Sub
```

This brute-force approach—changing the command using a hard-coded query—is ugly. Another approach is to cancel the operation, call another method that returns the appropriate data, and bind that. However, that forces you to do a fair bit of work manually, and mixing manual and automatic data binding can quickly get confusing. Unfortunately, no perfect solution exists.

Handling the Extra Options with the ObjectDataSource

The object data source handles the problem better, because it gives you the option to reroute the command to another method. If you find that a full list of employees is required, you can remove the City parameter altogether and use a no-parameter method for retrieving all the employees.

Here's how it works:

```
Protected Sub sourceEmployees_Selecting(ByVal sender As Object,
          ByVal e As ObjectDataSourceSelectingEventArgs)
  If e.InputParameters("employeeID") Is Nothing Then
  e.Cancel = True
  End If
  If CStr(e.InputParameters("City").Value) = "(Choose a City)" Then
      ' Do nothing.
      e.Cancel = True
  ElseIf CStr(e.InputParameters("City").Value) = "(All Cities)" Then
      ' Manually change the method.
      sourceEmployees.SelectMethod = "GetAllEmployees"
      e.InputParameters.Remove("City")
  End If
End Sub
```

This solution isn't possible with the SqlDataSource, because the command logic is embedded into the data source control. Still, this approach can easily be abused and lead to code that is difficult to maintain. For example, you won't receive any warning if you rename, remove, or modify the parameters for the GetAllEmployees() method. In this case, you'll receive an error only when you run the page and click the (All Cities) option.

Summary

In this chapter, you looked at data binding expressions and the ASP.NET data source controls in detail. Along the way, you started using the GridView, ASP.NET's premier rich data control. In the next chapter, you'll explore the three most powerful data-bound controls in detail: the GridView, DetailsView, and FormView. You'll also learn how they work with a few data source features that this chapter didn't cover, such as sorting and filtering.

CHAPTER 10

■ ■ ■

Rich Data Controls

In the previous chapter, you saw how to use the data source controls to perform queries, both with and without the assistance of a custom data access class. Along the way, you used some of ASP.NET's rich data controls, such as the GridView. However, you haven't delved into all the features these controls provide.

In this chapter, you'll take a closer look at the GridView, DetailsView, and FormView and learn how to fine-tune formatting and take control of features such as selection, sorting, filtering, and templates. You'll also learn about advanced scenarios such as showing images, calculating summaries, and creating a master-details list in a single control.

ASP.NET 1.X TEMPLATED CONTROLS

ASP.NET 2.0 still provides the templated controls that were introduced with ASP.NET 1.0. These include the DataGrid, DataList, and Repeater. Most ASP.NET programmers won't use any of these controls any longer except for backward compatibility (in fact, they aren't discussed in this book).

- *DataGrid*: The DataGrid is completely replaced by the GridView, which provides the same set of features (and more) and simplifies the coding mode. By default, the DataGrid doesn't appear in the Visual Studio 2005 Toolbox.
- *DataList*: The DataList is mostly replaced by the GridView, which provides a similar set of templates and much simpler coding model. However, you could still use the DataList if you want to create a multicolumn table, where each cell is a separate record. The GridView doesn't support this unusual design, because it forces every record to occupy a separate row.
- *Repeater*: The Repeater still plays the same role as a bare-bones template-based control. Although it doesn't provide many features or frills, you might use it to create customized data displays. The Repeater doesn't add any built-in elements, so you aren't locked into a table-based format. However, getting the result you want takes a lot of work because the Repeater doesn't include higher-level features such as selection and editing.

The chapter focuses exclusively on the new ASP.NET 2.0 data controls: the GridView, DetailsView, and FormView. If you are interested in using the older 1.*x* controls, refer to the previous edition of this book.

The GridView

If you've programmed with ASP.NET 1.*x*, you've probably used the similar DataGrid control. Faced with the challenge of enhancing the DataGrid while preserving backward compatibility, the ASP.NET team decided to create an entirely new control to implement their improvements. This control is the GridView.

The GridView is an extremely flexible grid control for showing data. It includes a wide range of hard-wired features, including selection, paging, and editing, and it is extensible through templates. The great advantage of the GridView over the DataGrid is its support for code-free scenarios. Using the GridView, you can accomplish many common tasks, such as paging and selection, without writing any code. With the DataGrid, you were forced to handle events to implement the same features.

■ **Note** The DataGrid is still available in ASP.NET 2.0, and it now supports binding to a data source control. Although you can't find it in the Toolbox, you can add it by right-clicking the Toolbox and selecting Choose Items. As a rule of thumb, the DataGrid should be used only for backward compatibility and existing ASP.NET websites (where it still works quite well). When creating a new website, use the GridView instead.

Defining Columns

The GridView examples you've seen so far have set the GridView.AutoGenerateColumns property to True. When this property is set, the GridView uses reflection to examine that data object and finds all the fields (of a record) or properties (of a custom object). It then creates a column for each one, in the order that it finds it.

This automatic column generation is good for creating quick test pages, but it doesn't give you the flexibility you'll usually want. For example, what if you want to hide columns, change their order, or configure some aspect of their display, such as the formatting or heading text? In all of these cases, you'll need to set AutoGenerateColumns to False and define the columns yourself in the <Columns> section of the GridView control tag.

■ **Tip** It's possible to have AutoGenerateColumns set to True and define columns in the <Columns> section. In this case, the columns you explicitly defined are added before the autogenerated columns. This technique was used in the previous chapter to create a GridView with automatically generated bound columns and a manually defined column with edit controls. However, for the most flexibility you'll usually want to explicitly define every column.

Each column can be any of several different types, as described in Table 10-1. The order of your column tags determines the right-to-left order of columns in the GridView.

Table 10-1. *Column Types*

Column	Description
BoundField	This column displays text from a field in the data source.
ButtonField	This column displays a button for each item in the list.
CheckBoxField	This column displays a check box for each item in the list. It's used automatically for True/False fields (in SQL Server, these are fields that use the bit data type).
CommandField	This column provides selection or editing buttons.
HyperlinkField	This column displays its contents (a field from the data source or static text) as a hyperlink.

Column	Description
ImageField	This column displays image data from a binary field (providing it can be successfully interpreted as a supported image format).
TemplateField	This column allows you to specify multiple fields, custom controls, and arbitrary HTML using a custom template. It gives you the highest degree of control but requires the most work.

The most basic column type is the BoundField, which binds to one field in the data object. For example, here's the definition for a single data-bound column that displays the EmployeeID field:

```
<asp:BoundField DataField="EmployeeID" HeaderText="ID" />
```

This achieves one improvement over the autogenerated column—the header text has been changed from EmployeeID to just ID.

When you first create a GridView, the AutoGenerateColumns property is set to False. When you bind it to a data source control, nothing changes. However, if you click the Refresh Schema link of the data source control, the AutoGenerateColumns property is flipped to True, and Visual Studio adds a <BoundField> tag for each field it finds in the data source. This approach has several advantages:

- You can easily fine-tune your column order, column headings, and other details by tweaking the properties of your column object.
- You can hide columns you don't want to show by removing the column tag. (However, don't overuse this technique, because it's better to cut down on the amount of data you're retrieving if you don't intend to display it.)

Tip You can also hide columns programmatically. To hide a column, use the Columns collection for the GridView. For example, setting GridView1.Columns(2).Visible to False hides the third column. Hidden columns are left out of the rendered HTML altogether.

- Explicitly defined columns are faster than autogenerated columns. That's because autogenerated columns force the GridView to reflect on the data source at runtime.
- You can add extra columns to the mix for selecting, editing, and more.

Tip If you modify the data source so that it returns a different set of columns, you can regenerate the GridView columns. Just select the GridView, and click the Refresh Schema link in the smart tag. This step will wipe out any custom columns you've added (such as editing controls).

Here's a complete GridView declaration with explicit columns:

```
<asp:GridView ID="gridEmployees" runat="server" DataSourceID="sourceEmployees"
 AutoGenerateColumns="False">
  <Columns>
    <asp:BoundField DataField="EmployeeID" HeaderText="ID" />
    <asp:BoundField DataField="FirstName" HeaderText="First Name" />
    <asp:BoundField DataField="LastName" HeaderText="Last Name" />
    <asp:BoundField DataField="Title" HeaderText="Title" />
```

```
    <asp:BoundField DataField="City" HeaderText="City" />
  </Columns>
</asp:GridView>
```

When you explicitly declare a bound field, you have the opportunity to set other properties. Table 10-2 lists these properties.

Table 10-2. *BoundField Properties*

Property	Description
DataField	The name of the field (for a row) or property (for an object) of the data item that you want to display in this column.
DataFormatString	A format string that formats the field. This is useful for getting the right representation of numbers and dates.
ApplyFormatInEditMode	If True, the format string will be used to format the value even when it appears in a text box in edit mode. The default is False, which means only the underlying normal will be used (1143.02 instead of $1,143.02).
FooterText, HeaderText, and HeaderImageUrl	Sets the text in the header and footer region of the grid, if this grid has a header (ShowHeader is True) and Footer (ShowFooter is True). The header is most commonly used for a descriptive label such as the field name, while the footer can contain a dynamically calculated value such as a summary (a technique demonstrated in the section "Summaries in the GridView" toward the end of this chapter). To show an image in the header *instead* of text, set the HeaderImageUrl property.
ReadOnly	If True, the value for this column can't be changed in edit mode. No edit control will be provided. Primary key fields are often read-only.
InsertVisible	If False, the value for this column can't be set in insert mode. If you want a column value to be set programmatically or based on a default value defined in the database, you can use this feature.
Visible	If False, the column won't be visible in the page (and no HTML will be rendered for it). This property gives you a convenient way to programmatically hide or show specific columns, changing the overall view of the data.
SortExpression	An expression that can be appended to a query to perform a sort based on this column. Used in conjunction with sorting, as described in the "Sorting the GridView" section.
HtmlEncode	If True (the default), all text will be HTML encoded to prevent special characters from mangling the page. You could disable HTML encoding if you want to embed a working HTML tag (such as a hyperlink), but this approach isn't safe. It's always a better idea to use HTML encoding on all values and provide other functionality by reacting to GridView selection events.
NullDisplayText	The text that will be displayed for a null value. The default is an empty string, although you could change this to a hard-coded value, such as "(not specified)."
ConvertEmptyStringToNull	If this is True, before an edit is committed all empty strings will be converted to null values.
ControlStyle, HeaderStyle, FooterStyle, and ItemStyle	Configures the appearance for just this column, overriding the styles for the row. You'll learn more about styles throughout this chapter.

If you don't want to configure columns by hands, select the GridView, and click the ellipsis (...) next to the Columns property in the Properties window. You'll see a Fields dialog box that lets you add, remove, and refine your columns (see Figure 10-1).

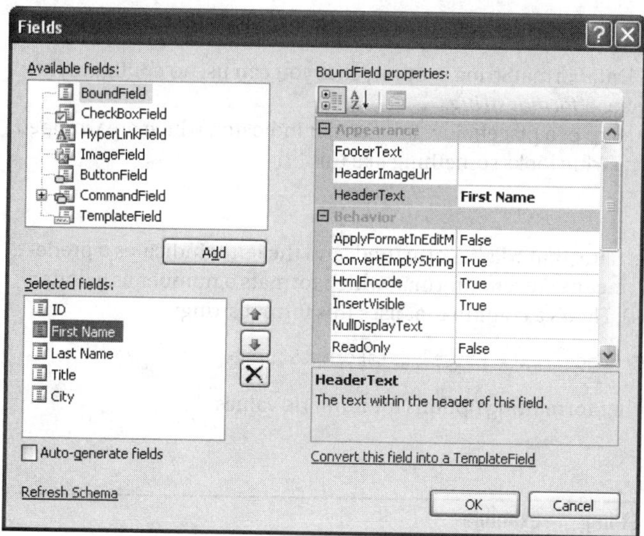

Figure 10-1. *Configuring columns in Visual Studio*

Now that you understand the underpinnings of the GridView, you've still only started to explore its higher-level features. In the following sections, you'll tackle these topics:

Formatting: How to format rows and data values

Selecting: How to let users select a row in the GridView and respond accordingly

Sorting: How to dynamically reorder the GridView in response to clicks on a column header

Paging: How to divide a large result set into multiple pages of data, using both automatic and custom paging code

Templates: How to take complete control of layout, formatting, and editing by defining templates

Formatting the GridView

Formatting consists of several related tasks. First, you want to ensure that dates, currencies, and other number values are presented in the appropriate way. You handle this job with the DataFormatString property. Next, you'll want to apply the perfect mix of colors, fonts, borders, and alignment options to each aspect of the grid, from headers to data items. The GridView supports these features through styles. Finally, you can intercept events, examine row data, and apply formatting to specific data points programmatically. In the following sections, you'll consider each of these techniques.

The GridView itself also exposes several formatting properties that are self-explanatory and aren't covered here. These include GridLines (for adding or hiding table borders), CellPadding and CellSpacing (for controlling the overall spacing between cells), and Caption and CaptionAlign (for adding a title to the top of the grid).

■ **Tip** Want to create a GridView that scrolls—inside a web page? It's easy. Just place the GridView inside a Panel control, set the appropriate size for the panel, and set the Panel.ScrollBars to Auto, Horizontal, Vertical, or Both.

Formatting Fields

Each BoundField column provides a DataFormatString property that you can use to configure the appearance of numbers and dates using a *format string*.

Format strings are generally made up of a placeholder and format indicator, which are wrapped inside curly brackets. A typical format string looks something like this:

```
{0:C}
```

In this case, the 0 represents the value that will be formatted, and the letter indicates a predetermined format style. In this case, C means currency format, which formats a number as a dollar figure (so 3400.34 becomes $3,400.34). Here's a column that uses this format string:

```
<asp:BoundField DataField="Price" HeaderText="Price" DataFormatString="{0:C}" />
```

Table 10-3 shows some of the other formatting options for numeric values.

Table 10-3. *Numeric Format Strings*

Type	Format String	Example
Currency	{0:C}	$1,234.50 Brackets indicate negative values: ($1,234.50). Currency sign is locale-specific: (?1,234.50).
Scientific (Exponential)	{0:E}	1.234.50E+004
Percentage	{0:P}	45.6%
Fixed Decimal	{0:F?}	Depends on the number of decimal places you set. {0:F3} would be 123.400. {0:F0} would be 123.

You can find other examples in the MSDN Help. For date or time values, there is also an extensive list. For example, if you want to write the BirthDate value in the format month/day/year (as in 12/30/05), you use the following column:

```
<asp:BoundField DataField="BirthDate" HeaderText="Birth Date"
 DataFormatString="{0:MM/dd/yy}" />
```

Table 10-4 shows some more examples.

Table 10-4. *Time and Date Format Strings*

Type	Format String	Syntax	Example
Short Date	{0:d}	M/d/yyyy	10/30/2005
Long Date	{0:D}	dddd, MMMM dd, yyyy	Monday, January 30, 2005
Long Date and Short Time	{0:f}	dddd, MMMM dd, yyyy HH:mm aa	Monday, January 30, 2005 10:00 AM
Long Date and Long Time	{0:F}	dddd, MMMM dd, yyyy HH:mm:ss aa	Monday, January 30, 2005 10:00:23 AM

Type	Format String	Syntax	Example
ISO Sortable Standard	{0:s}	yyyy-MM-dd HH:mm:ss	2005-01-30 10:00:23
Month and Day	{0:M}	MMMM dd	January 30
General	{0:G}	M/d/yyyy HH:mm:ss aa (depends on locale-specific settings)	10/30/2002 10:00:23 AM

The format characters are not specific to the GridView. You can use them with other controls, with data-bound expressions in templates (as you'll see later in this chapter), and as parameters for many methods. For example, the Decimal and DateTime types expose their own ToString() methods that accept a format string, allowing you to format values manually.

Styles

The GridView exposes a rich formatting model that's based on *styles*. Altogether, you can set eight GridView styles, as described in Table 10-5.

Table 10-5. *Numeric Format Strings*

Style	Description
HeaderStyle	Configures the appearance of the header row that contains column titles, if you've chosen to show it (if ShowHeader is True).
RowStyle	Configures the appearance of every data row.
AlternatingRowStyle	If set, applies additional formatting to every other row. This formatting acts in addition to the RowStyle formatting. For example, if you set a font using RowStyle, it is also applied to alternating rows, unless you explicitly set a different font through the AlternatingRowStyle.
SelectedRowStyle	Configures the appearance of the row that's currently selected. This formatting acts in addition to the RowStyle formatting.
EditRowStyle	Configures the appearance of the row that's in edit mode. This formatting acts in addition to the RowStyle formatting.
EmptyDataRowStyle	Configures the style that's used for the single empty row in the special case where the bound data object contains no rows.
FooterStyle	Configures the appearance of the footer row at the bottom of the GridView, if you've chosen to show it (if ShowFooter is True).
PagerStyle	Configures the appearance of the row with the page links, if you've enabled paging (set AllowPaging to True).

Styles are not simple single-value properties. Instead, each style exposes a Style object that includes properties for choosing colors (ForeColor and BackColor), adding borders (BorderColor, BorderStyle, and BorderWidth), sizing the row (Height and Width), aligning the row (HorizontalAlign and VerticalAlign), and configuring the appearance of text (Font and Wrap). These style properties allow you to refine almost every aspect of an item's appearance. And if you don't want to hard-code all the appearance settings in the web page, you can set the CssClass property of the style object reference to a stylesheet class that's defined in a linked stylesheet (see Chapter 15 for more about styles).

Defining Styles

When setting style properties, you can use two similar syntaxes (and you'll see both of them in this chapter). First, you can use the object-walker syntax to indicate the extended style properties as tag attributes. Here's an example:

```
<asp:GridView runat="server" ID="grid"
  <RowStyle-ForeColor="DarkBlue" ... >
  ...
</asp:GridView>
```

Alternatively, you can add nested tags, as shown here:

```
<asp:GridView runat="server" ID="grid" ...>
  <RowStyle ForeColor="DarkBlue" ... />
  ...
</asp:GridView>
```

Both of these approaches are equivalent. However, you make one other decision when setting style properties. You can specify global style properties that affect every column in the grid (as in the previous examples), or you can define column-specific styles. To create a column-specific style, you need to add style attributes or a nested tag inside the appropriate column tag, as shown here:

```
<asp:GridView runat="server" ID="grid" ...>
  <Columns>
    <asp:BoundField DataField="EmployeeID" HeaderText="ID" ItemStyle-Width="30px" />
    ...
  </Columns>
</asp:GridView>
```

Or equivalently, you can use a nested tag:

```
<asp:GridView runat="server" ID="grid" ...>
  <Columns>
    <asp:BoundField DataField="EmployeeID" HeaderText="ID">
      <ItemStyle Width="30px"/>
    </asp:BoundField>
    ...
  </Columns>
</asp:GridView>
```

This technique is often used to define specific column widths. If you don't define a specific column width, ASP.NET makes each column just wide enough to fit the data it contains (or, if wrapping is enabled, to fit the text without splitting a word over a line break). If values range in size, the width is determined by the largest value or the width of the column header, whichever is larger. However, if the grid is wide enough, you might want to expand a column so it doesn't appear to be crowded against the adjacent columns. In this case, you need to explicitly define a larger width.

Here's a fully formatted GridView tag:

```
<asp:GridView ID="GridView1" runat="server" DataSourceID="sourceEmployees"
 Font-Names="Verdana" Font-Size="X-Small" ForeColor="#333333"
 CellPadding="4" GridLines="None" AutoGenerateColumns="False">

  <HeaderStyle BackColor="#990000" Font-Bold="True" ForeColor="White" />
  <RowStyle BackColor="#FFFBD6" ForeColor="#333333" />
  <AlternatingRowStyle BackColor="White" />

  <Columns>
```

```
    <asp:BoundField DataField="EmployeeID" HeaderText="ID">
      <ItemStyle Font-Bold="True" BorderWidth="1"  />
    </asp:BoundField>
    <asp:BoundField DataField="FirstName" HeaderText="First Name" />
    <asp:BoundField DataField="LastName" HeaderText="Last Name" />
    <asp:BoundField DataField="City" HeaderText="City">
      <ItemStyle BackColor="LightSteelBlue" />
    </asp:BoundField>
    <asp:BoundField DataField="Country" HeaderText="Country">
      <ItemStyle BackColor="LightSteelBlue" />
    </asp:BoundField>
    <asp:BoundField DataField="BirthDate" HeaderText="Birth Date"
     DataFormatString="{0:MM/dd/yyyy}" />
    <asp:BoundField DataField="Notes" HeaderText="Notes">
      <ItemStyle Wrap="True" Width="400"/>
    </asp:BoundField>
  </Columns>
</asp:GridView>
```

This example uses GridView properties to set the font and adjust the cell spacing and cell gridlines. It uses styles to bold headings and configure the background of rows and alternating rows. Additionally, column-specific style settings highlight the location information with a different background, bold the ID values, and explicitly size the Notes column. A DataFormatString is used to format all date values in the BirthDate field. Figure 10-2 shows the final result.

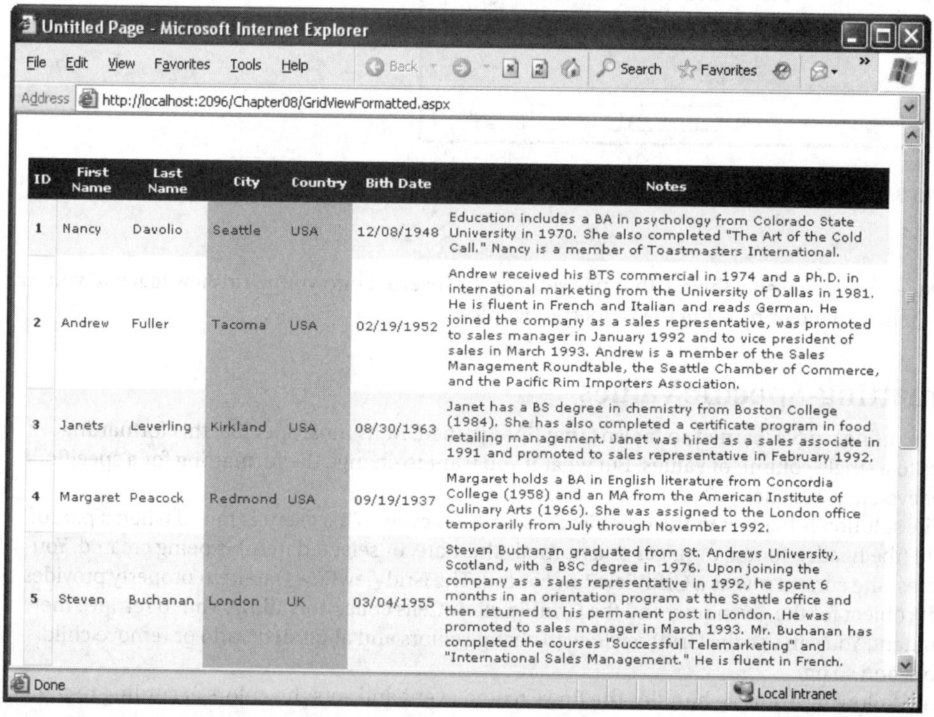

Figure 10-2. *A formatted GridView*

Configuring Styles with Visual Studio

There's no reason to code style properties by hand in the GridView control tag, because the GridView provides rich design-time support. To set style properties, you can use the Properties window to modify the style properties. For example, to configure the font of the header, expand the HeaderStyle property to show the nested Font property, and set that. The only limitation of this approach is that it doesn't allow you to set style for individual columns—if you need that trick, you must first call up the Fields dialog box (shown in Figure 10-1) by editing the Columns property. Then, select the appropriate column, and set the style properties accordingly.

You can even set a combination of styles using a preset theme by clicking the Auto Format link in the GridView smart tag. Figure 10-3 shows the Auto Format dialog box with some of the preset styles you can choose. Select Remove Formatting to clear all the style settings.

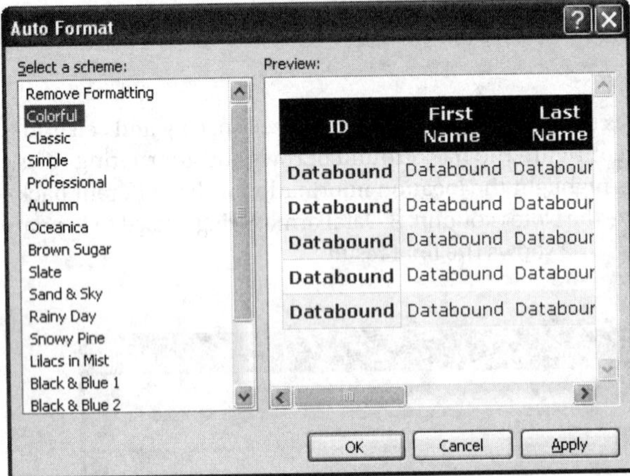

Figure 10-3. *Automatically formatting a GridView*

Once you've chosen a theme, the style settings are inserted into your GridView tag, and you can tweak them by hand or by using the Properties window.

Formatting-Specific Values

The formatting you've learned so far isn't that fine-grained. At its most specific, this formatting applies to a single column of values. But what if you want to change the formatting for a specific row, or even just a single cell?

The solution is to react to the GridView.RowCreated event. This event is raised when a part of the grid (the header, footer, or pager or a normal, alternate, or selected item) is being created. You can access the current row as a GridViewRow control. The GridViewRow.DataItem property provides the data object for the given row, and the GridViewRow.Cells collection allows you to retrieve the row content. You can use the GridViewRow to change colors and alignment, add or remove child controls, and so on.

The following example handles the RowCreated event and sets the colors according to the following rules:

- The item's background color is set to pink and the foreground color is set to maroon if the title of courtesy is a title for a female—in this case Ms. or Mrs.
- The item's background color is set to dark blue and the foreground color is set to light cyan if the title of courtesy is Mr.
- For other generic titles such as Dr., the item is rendered with the background color specified by the DataGrid.BackColor property.

Here is the complete code for the RowCreated event handler that implements these rules:

```
Protected Sub GridView1_RowCreated(
    ByVal sender As Object, ByVal e As GridViewRowEventArgs)
  If e.Row.RowType = DataControlRowType.DataRow Then
    ' Get the title of courtesy for the item that's being created.
    Dim title As String =
      CStr(DataBinder.Eval(e.Row.DataItem, "TitleOfCourtesy"))

    ' If the title of courtesy is "Ms.", "Mrs.", or "Mr.",
    ' change the item's colors.
    If title = "Ms." OrElse title = "Mrs." Then
      e.Row.BackColor = System.Drawing.Color.LightPink
      e.Row.ForeColor = System.Drawing.Color.Maroon
    ElseIf title = "Mr." Then
      e.Row.BackColor = System.Drawing.Color.LightCyan
      e.Row.ForeColor = System.Drawing.Color.DarkBlue
    End If
  End If
End Sub
```

First, the code checks if the item being created is an item or an alternate item. If neither of these, it means that the item is another interface element, such as the pager, footer, or header, and the procedure does nothing. If the item is of the right type, the code extracts the TitleOfCourtesy field from the data bound item and compares it to some hard-coded string values.

Figure 10-4 shows the resulting page.

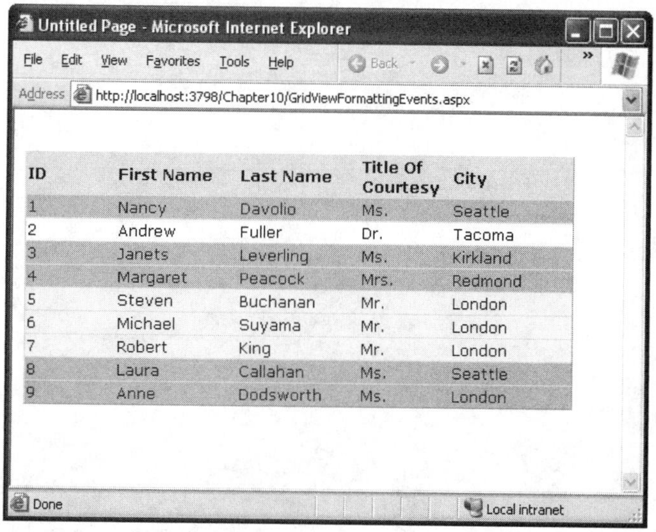
Untitled Page - Microsoft Internet Explorer
File Edit View Favorites Tools Help
Back
Address http://localhost:3798/Chapter10/GridViewFormattingEvents.aspx
ID First Name Last Name Title Of Courtesy City
1 Nancy Davolio Ms. Seattle
2 Andrew Fuller Dr. Tacoma
3 Janets Leverling Ms. Kirkland
4 Margaret Peacock Mrs. Redmond
5 Steven Buchanan Mr. London
6 Michael Suyama Mr. London
7 Robert King Mr. London
8 Laura Callahan Ms. Seattle
9 Anne Dodsworth Ms. London
Done
Local intranet

Figure 10-4. *Formatting individual rows based on values*

Tip This example uses the DataBinder.Eval() method to retrieve a piece of information from the data item using reflection. Alternatively, you could cast the e.Row.DataItem to the correct type (such as EmployeeDetails for the ObjectDataSource), DataRowView (for the SqlDataSource in DataSet mode), or DbDataRecord (for the SqlDataSource in DataReader mode). However, the DataBinder.Eval() approach works in all these scenarios (at the cost of being slightly slower).

This isn't the most useful example of using the RowCreated event, but it demonstrates how you can handle the event and read all the important information for the item. You could use much more imaginative formatting to change the way the pager's links are represented, add new buttons to the pager or header, render values that you want to highlight with special fonts and colors, create total and subtotal rows, and more.

GridView Row Selection

Selecting a row means that the user can highlight or change the appearance of a row by clicking some sort of button or link. When the user clicks the button, not only will the row change its appearance, but also your code will have the opportunity to handle the event.

The GridView provides built-in support for selection. You simply need to add a CommandField column with the ShowSelectButton property set to True. The CommandField can be rendered as a hyperlink, a button, or a fixed image. You choose the type using the ButtonType property. You can then specify the text through the SelectText property or specify the link to the image through the SelectImageUrl property.

Here's an example that displays a select button:

```
<asp:CommandField ShowSelectButton="True" ButtonType="Button"
 SelectText="Select" />
```

And here's an example that shows a small clickable icon:

```
<asp:CommandField ShowSelectButton="True" ButtonType="Image"
 SelectImageUrl="select.gif" />
```

Figure 10-5 shows both types of select buttons. Clicking either one selects the row.

Figure 10-5. *GridView selection*

When you click a select button, the page is posted back, and a series of steps unfolds. First, theGridView.SelectedIndexChanging event fires, which you can intercept to cancel the operation. Next, the GridView.SelectedIndex property is adjusted to point to the selected row. Finally, the GridView.SelectedIndexChanged event fires, which you can handle if you want to manually update other controls to reflect the new selection. When the page is rendered, the selected row is given the SelectedRowStyle.

■ **Note** For selection to work, you must configure the SelectedRowStyle so that selected rows look different from normal rows. Usually, selected rows will have a different BackColor property.

Using Selection to Create a Master-Details Form

As demonstrated in the previous chapter, you can bind other data sources to a property in a control using parameters. For example, you could add two GridView controls and use information from the first GridView to perform a query in the second.

In the case of the GridView, the property you need to bind is SelectedIndex. However, this has one problem. SelectedIndex returns a zero-based index number representing where the row occurs in the grid. This isn't the information you need to insert into the query that gets the related records. Instead, you need a key field from the corresponding row.

Fortunately, the GridView makes it easy to retrieve this information using the SelectedDataKeys property. To use this feature, you must set the GridView.DataKeyNames property, with a comma-separated list of one or more key fields. Each name you supply must match one of the properties of the bound object or one of the fields of the bound record.

Usually, you'll have only one key field, as shown here:

```
<asp:GridView ID="gridEmployees" runat="server" DataSourceID="sourceEmployees"
 DataKeyNames="EmployeeID" ... >
```

Now you can bind the second data source to this field. Here's an example that uses the EmployeeID in a join query to find all the matching records from the Territories table:

```
<asp:SqlDataSource ID="sourceRegions" runat="server"
 ConnectionString="<%$ ConnectionStrings:Northwind %>"
 ProviderName="System.Data.SqlClient" SelectCommand="SELECT Employees.EmployeeID,
Territories.TerritoryID, Territories.TerritoryDescription FROM Employees INNER JOIN
EmployeeTerritories ON Employees.EmployeeID = EmployeeTerritories.EmployeeID
INNER JOIN Territories ON EmployeeTerritories.TerritoryID = Territories.TerritoryID
WHERE (Employees.EmployeeID = @EmployeeID)" >
  <SelectParameters>
    <asp:ControlParameter ControlID="gridEmployees" Name="EmployeeID"
     PropertyName="SelectedDataKey.Values[&quot;EmployeeID&quot;]" />
    </SelectParameters>
</asp:SqlDataSource>
```

This example defines a SqlDataSource that executes a SELECT statement to get a result set. This method requires a single parameter—the EmployeeID of the selected employee record. The EmployeeID value is retrieved from the SelectedDataKey.Values collection. You can look up the EmployeeID field by its index position (which is 0 in this example, because there's only one field in the DataKeyNames list) or by name. The only trick when performing a name lookup is that you need to replace the quotation marks with the corresponding HTML character entity (").

Figure 10-6 shows this master-details form, which contains the regions assigned to an employee whenever an employee record is selected.

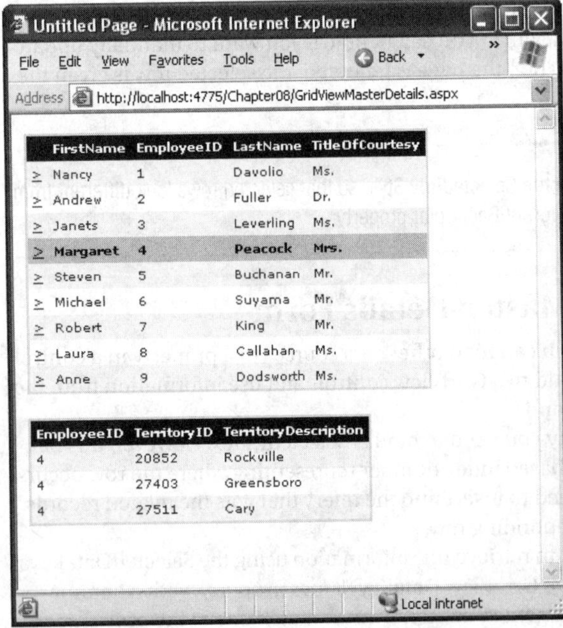

Figure 10-6. *A master-details page*

The SelectedIndexChanged Event

As the previous example demonstrates, you can set up master-details forms declaratively, without needing to write any code. However, there are many cases when you'll need to react to the SelectedIndexChanged event. For example, you might want to redirect the user to a new page (possibly with the selected value in the query string). Or, you might want to adjust other controls on the page.

For example, here's the code you need to add a label describing the child table shown in the previous example:

```
Protected Sub gridEmployees_SelectedIndexChanged(
      ByVal sender As Object, ByVal e As System.EventArgs)
    Dim index As Integer = gridEmployees.SelectedIndex

    ' You can retrieve the key field from the SelectedDataKey property.
    Dim ID As Integer = CInt(gridEmployees.SelectedDataKey.Values("EmployeeID"))

    ' You can retrieve other data directly from the Cells collection,
    ' as long as you know the column offset.
    Dim firstName As String = gridEmployees.SelectedRow.Cells(2).Text
    Dim lastName As String = gridEmployees.SelectedRow.Cells(3).Text

    lblRegionCaption.Text = "Regions that " & firstName & " " _
        & lastName & " (employee " & ID.ToString() & ") is responsible for:"
End Sub
```

Figure 10-7 shows the result.

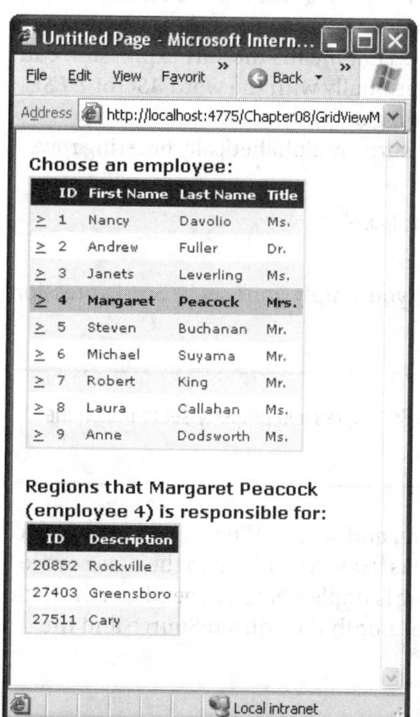

Figure 10-7. *Handling the SelectedIndexChanged event*

Using a Data Field As a Select Button

You don't need to create a new column to support row selection. Instead, you can turn an existing column into a link. This technique is commonly used to allow users to select rows in a table by the unique ID value.

To use this technique, remove the CommandField column and add a ButtonField column instead. Then, set the DataTextField to the name of the field you want to use.

```
<asp:ButtonField ButtonType="Link" DataTextField="EmployeeID" />
```

This field will be underlined and turned into a link that, when clicked, will post back the page and trigger the GridView.RowCommand event. You could handle this event, determine which row has been clicked, and programmatically set the SelectedIndex property. However, you can use an easier method. Instead, just configure the link to raise the SelectedIndexChanged event by specifying a CommandName with the text *Select*, as shown here:

```
<asp:ButtonField CommandName="Select" ButtonType="Link"
 DataTextField="EmployeeID" />
```

Now clicking the data field automatically selects the record.

Sorting the GridView

The GridView sorting features allow the user to reorder the results in the GridView by clicking a column header. It's convenient—and easy to implement.

To enable sorting, you must set the GridView. AllowSorting property to True. Next, you need to define a SortExpression for each column that can be sorted. In theory, a sort expression can use any syntax that's understood by the data source control. In practice, a sort expression almost always takes the form used in the ORDER BY clause of a SQL query. That means the sort expression can include a single field or a list of comma-separated fields, optionally with the word *ASC* or *DESC* added after the column name to sort in ascending or descending order.

Here's how you could define the FirstName column so it sorts by alphabetically ordering rows by first name:

```
<asp:BoundField DataField="FirstName" HeaderText="First Name"
 SortExpression="FirstName"/>
```

Note that if you don't want a column to be sort-enabled, you simply don't set its SortExpression property.

■ **Tip** If you use autogenerated columns, each bound column has its SortExpression property set to match the DataField property.

Once you've associated a sort expression with the column and set the AllowSorting property to True, the GridView will render the headers with clickable links. However, it's up to the data source control to implement the actual sorting logic. How the sorting is implemented depends on the data source you're using. Not all data sources support sorting, but both the SqlDataSource and the ObjectDataSource do.

Sorting with the SqlDataSource

In the case of the SqlDataSource, sorting is performed using the built-in sorting capabilities of the DataView class. Essentially, when the user clicks a column link, the DataView.Sort property is set to the sorting expression for that column.

■ Note As explained in Chapter 8, every DataTable is linked to a default DataView. The DataView is a window onto the DataTable, and it allows you to apply sorting and filtering without altering the structure of the underlying table. You can use a DataView programmatically, but when you use the SqlDataSource it's used implicitly, behind the scenes. However, it's available only when the DataSourceMode property is set to SqlDataSourceMode.DataSet.

With DataView sorting, the data is retrieved unordered from the database, and the results are sorted in memory. This is not the speediest approach (sorting in memory requires more overhead and is slower than having SQL Server do the same work), but it is more scalable when you add caching to the mix. That's because you can cache a single copy of the data and sort it dynamically in several different ways. (Chapter 11 has much more about this essential technique.) Without DataView sorting, a separate query is needed to retrieve the newly sorted data.

Figure 10-8 shows a sortable GridView with column links. Note that no custom code is required for this scenario.

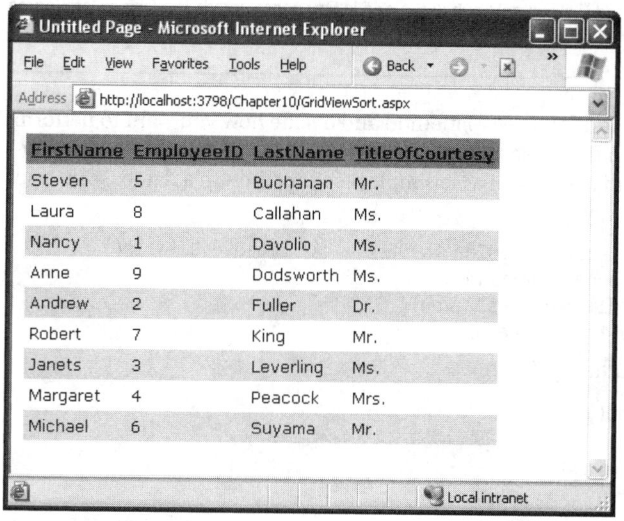

Untitled Page - Microsoft Internet Explorer

File Edit View Favorites Tools Help Back

Address http://localhost:3798/Chapter10/GridViewSort.aspx

FirstName	EmployeeID	LastName	TitleOfCourtesy
Steven	5	Buchanan	Mr.
Laura	8	Callahan	Ms.
Nancy	1	Davolio	Ms.
Anne	9	Dodsworth	Ms.
Andrew	2	Fuller	Dr.
Robert	7	King	Mr.
Janets	3	Leverling	Ms.
Margaret	4	Peacock	Mrs.
Michael	6	Suyama	Mr.

Local intranet

Figure 10-8. *Automatic sorting by LastName*

The sort is according to the data type of the column. Numeric and date columns are ordered from smallest to largest. String columns are sorted alphanumerically without regard to case, assuming the underlying DataTable.CaseSensitive property is False (the default setting). Columns that contain binary data cannot be sorted.

Sorting with the ObjectDataSource

The ObjectDataSource provides two options:

- If your select method returns a DataSet or DataTable, the ObjectDataSource can use the same automatic sorting used with the SqlDataSource.
- If your select method returns a custom collection, you need to provide a selection method that accepts a sort expression and performs the sorting. Once again, this behavior gives you enough flexibility to build a solution, but it's not necessarily the ideal arrangement. For example, instead of building a GetEmployees() method that can perform sorting, it might make more sense to create a custom EmployeeDetails collection class with a Sort() method. Unfortunately, the ObjectDataSource won't support this pattern.

To use the sort parameter, you need to create a select method that accepts a single string parameter. You must then set the ObjectDataSource.SortParameterName property to identify the name of that parameter, as shown here:

```
<asp:ObjectDataSource ID="sourceEmployees" runat="server"
 TypeName="DatabaseComponent.EmployeeDB"
 SelectMethod="GetEmployees" SortParameterName="sortExpression" />
```

■Note When you set SortParameterName, the ObjectDataSource will always call the version of your method that accepts a sort expression. If the data isn't sorted (for example, when the grid is first constructed), the ObjectDataSource will simply pass an empty string as the sort expression.

Now you have to implement the GetEmployees() method and decide how you want to perform the sorting. The easiest approach is to fill a disconnected DataSet so you can rely on the sorting functionality of the DataView. Here's an example of a GetEmployees() method in a database component that performs the sorting in this way:

```
Public Function GetEmployees(ByVal sortExpression As String) As EmployeeDetails()
    Dim con As New SqlConnection(connectionString)
    Dim cmd As New SqlCommand("GetAllEmployees", con)
    cmd.CommandType = CommandType.StoredProcedure
    Dim adapter As New SqlDataAdapter(cmd)

    Dim ds As DataSet = New DataSet()
    Try
        con.Open()
        adapter.Fill(ds, "Employees")
    Catch err As SqlException
        ' Replace the error with something less specific.
        ' You could also log the error now.
        Throw New ApplicationException("Data error.")
    Finally
        con.Close()
    End Try
    ' Apply sort.
    Dim view As DataView = ds.Tables(0).DefaultView
    view.Sort = sortExpression

    ' Create a collection for all the employee records.
    Dim employees As New ArrayList()
```

```
    For Each row As DataRowView In view
        Dim emp As New EmployeeDetails(CInt(row("EmployeeID")),
                CStr(row("FirstName")), CStr(row("LastName")),
                CStr(row("TitleOfCourtesy")))
        employees.Add(emp)
    Next
    Return CType(employees.ToArray(GetType(EmployeeDetails)), EmployeeDetails())
End Function
```

Another approach is to change the actual query you're executing in response to the sort expression. This way, your database can perform the sorting. This approach is a little more complicated, and no perfect option exists. Here are the two most common possibilities:

- You could dynamically construct a SQL statement with an ORDER BY clause. However, this risks SQL injection attacks, unless you validate your input carefully.
- You could write conditional logic to examine the sort expression and execute different queries accordingly (either in your select method or in the stored procedure). This code is likely to be fragile and involves a fair bit of string parsing.

Sorting and Selection

If you use sorting and selection at the same time, you'll discover another issue. To see this problem in action, select a row, and then sort the data by any column. You'll see that the selection will remain, but it will shift to a new item that has the same index as the previous item. In other words, if you select the second row and perform a sort, the second row will still be selected in the new page, even though this isn't the record you selected. The only way to solve this problem is to programmatically change the selection every time a header link is clicked.

The simplest option is to react to the GridView.Sorted event to clear the selection, as shown here:

```
Protected Sub GridView1_Sorted(
        ByVal sender As Object, ByVal e As GridViewSortEventArgs)
    ' Clear selected index.
    GridView1.SelectedIndex = -1
End Sub
```

In some cases you'll want to go even further and make sure a selected row remains selected when sorting changes. The trick here is to store the selected value of the key field in view state each time the selected index changes:

```
Protected Sub GridView1_SelectedIndexChanged(
        ByVal sender As Object, ByVal e As EventArgs)
    ' Save the selected value.
    If GridView1.SelectedIndex <> -1 Then
        ViewState("SelectedValue") = GridView1.SelectedValue.ToString()
    End If
End Sub
```

Now, when the grid is bound to the data source (for example after a sort operation), you can reapply to the last selected index:

```
Protected Sub GridView1_DataBound(ByVal sender As Object, ByVal e As EventArgs)
    If ViewState("SelectedValue") IsNot Nothing Then
        Dim selectedValue As String = CStr(ViewState("SelectedValue"))

        ' Reselect the last selected row.
        For Each row As GridViewRow In GridView1.Rows
            Dim keyValue As String =
```

```
                GridView1.DataKeys(row.RowIndex).Value.ToString()
            If keyValue = selectedValue Then
                GridView1.SelectedIndex = row.RowIndex
                Return
            End If
        Next
    End If
End Sub
```

Keep in mind that this approach can be confusing if you also have enabled paging (which is described later in the section "Paging the GridView"). That's because a sorting operation might move the current row to another page, rendering it not visible but keeping it selected. This is a perfectly valid situation from a code standpoint but confusing in practice.

Advanced Sorting

The GridView's sorting is straightforward—it supports sorting by any sortable column in ascending order. In some applications, the user has more sorting options or can order lengthy result sets with more complex sorting expressions.

Your first avenue for improving sorting with the GridView is to handle the GridView.Sorting event, which occurs just before the sort is applied. At this point, you can change the sorting expression. For example, you could use this to implement an ascending/descending sort pattern. With this pattern, you click a column once to apply an ascending sort and a second time to apply a descending sort. This is similar to the sorting that's built into Windows Explorer.

Here's the code you need to implement this approach:

```
Protected Sub GridView1_Sorting(
        ByVal sender As Object, ByVal e As GridViewSortEventArgs)
    ' Check to see the if the current sort (GridView1.SortExpression)
    ' matches the requested sort (e.SortExpression).
    ' This code tries to match the beginning of the GridView
    ' sort expression. The final ASC or DESC part is ignored.
    If GridView1.SortExpression.StartsWith(e.SortExpression) Then
        ' This sort is being applied to the same field for the second time.
        ' Reverse it.
        If GridView1.SortDirection = SortDirection.Ascending Then
            ' This takes care of automatically adding the "DESC"
            ' to the end of the sort expression.
            e.SortDirection = SortDirection.Descending
        End If
    End If
End Sub
```

You could use similar logic to turn clicks on different columns into a compound sort. For example, you might want to check if the user clicks LastName and then FirstName. In this case, you could apply a LastName+FirstName sort.

```
Protected Sub GridView1_Sorting(
        ByVal sender As Object, ByVal e As GridViewSortEventArgs)
    If e.SortExpression = "FirstName"
        AndAlso GridView1.SortExpression = "LastName" Then
        ' Based on the current sort and the requested sort, a compound
        ' sort makes sense.
        e.SortExpression = "LastName, FirstName"
    End If
End Sub
```

You could take this sorting approach one step further and cascade searches over any arbitrary collection of columns by storing the user's past sort selections in view state and using them to build a larger sort expression.

One more technique is available to you. You can sort the GridView programmatically by calling the GridView.Sort() method and supplying a sort expression. This could come in handy if you want to presort a lengthy data report before presenting it to the user. It also makes sense if you want to allow the user to choose from a list of predefined sorting options (listed in another control) rather than use column-header clicks.

Figure 10-9 shows an example. When an item is selected from the list, the sort is applied with this code:

```
Protected Sub lstSorts_SelectedIndexChanged(
        ByVal sender As Object, ByVal e As EventArgs)
    GridView1.Sort(lstSorts.SelectedValue, SortDirection.Ascending)
End Sub
```

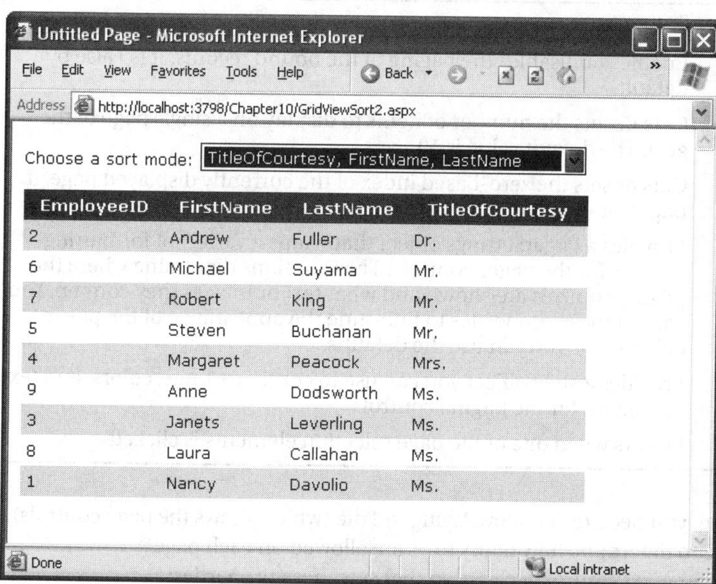

Figure 10-9. *Giving sorting options through another control*

Paging the GridView

All the examples of repeated-value binding that you've seen so far show all the records of the data source on a single web page. However, this isn't always ideal in real-world situations. Connecting to a data source that contains hundreds or even thousands of records would produce an extremely large page that would take a prohibitively long amount of time to render and transmit to the client browser.

Most websites that display data in tables or lists support record *pagination*, which means showing a fixed number of records per page and providing links to navigate to the previous or next pages to display other records. For example, you have no doubt seen this functionality in search engines that can return thousands of matches.

The GridView control has built-in support for pagination. You can use simple pagination with both the SqlDataSource and ObjectDataSource. If you're using the ObjectDataSource, you also have the ability to customize the way the paging works for a more efficient and scalable solution.

Automatic Paging

By setting a few properties and handling an event, you can make the GridView control manage the paging for you. The GridView will create the links to jump to the previous or next pages and will display the records for the current page without requiring you to manually extract the records by yourself. Before discussing the advantages and disadvantages of this approach, let's see what you need to get this working.

The GridView provides several properties designed specifically to support paging, as shown in Table 10-6.

Table 10-6. *Paging Members of the DataGrid*

Property	Description
AllowPaging	Enables or disables the paging of the bound records. It is False by default.
PageSize	Gets or sets the number of items to display on a single page of the grid. The default value is 10.
PageIndex	Gets or sets the zero-based index of the currently displayed page, if paging is enabled.
PagerSettings	Provides a PagerSettings object that wraps a variety of formatting options for the pager controls. These options determine where the paging controls are shown and what text or images they contain. You can set these properties to fine-tune the appearance of the pager controls, or you can use the defaults.
PagerStyle	Provides a style object you can use to configure fonts, colors, and text alignment for the paging controls.
PageIndexChanged event	Occurs when one of the page selection elements is clicked.

To use automatic paging, you need to set AllowPaging to True (which shows the page controls), and you need to set PageSize to determine how many rows are allowed on each page.

Here's an example of a DataGrid control declaration that sets these properties:

```
<asp:GridView ID="GridView1" runat="server" DataSourceID="sourceProducts"
 PageSize="5" AllowPaging="True" ...>
  ...
</asp:GridView>
```

This is enough to start using paging. Figure 10-10 shows an example with five records per page (for a total of 16 pages).

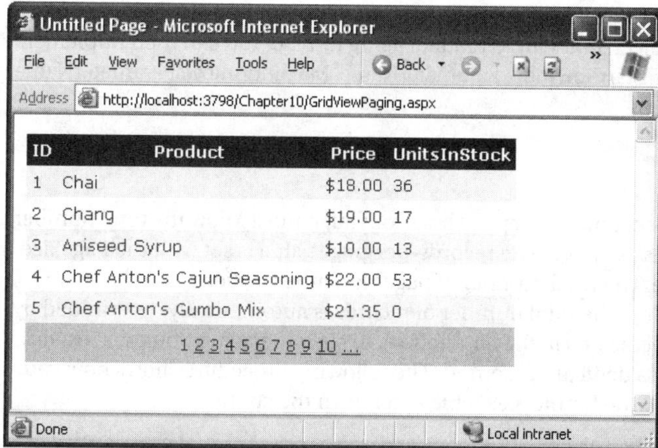

Figure 10-10. *Paging five records at a time*

Automatic paging works with any data source that implements ICollection. This means that the SqlDataSource supports automatic paging, as long as you use DataSet mode. (The DataReader mode won't work.) Additionally, the ObjectDataSource also supports paging, assuming your custom data access class returns an object that implements ICollection—arrays, strongly typed collections, and the disconnected DataSet are all valid options.

Automatic paging is a simulation—it doesn't reduce the amount of data you need to query from the database. One problem with paging is that all of the data must be bound every time the user changes the current page. In other words, if you split a table into ten pages and the user steps through each one, you will end up performing the same work ten times (and multiplying the overall database workload for the page by a factor of ten).

Fortunately, you can make automatic paging much more efficient by implementing caching (see Chapter 11). This allows you to reuse the same data object for multiple requests. Of course, storing the DataSet in the cache may not be the ideal solution if you're using paging to deal with an extremely large query. In this case, the amount of memory required to keep the full DataSet in the cache is prohibitively large. That's when custom pagination enters the scene.

Custom Pagination with the ObjectDataSource

Custom pagination requires you to take care of extracting and binding only the current page of records for the GridView. The GridView no longer selects the rows that should be displayed automatically. However, the GridView still provides the pager bar with the autogenerated links that allow the user to navigate through the pages.

Although custom pagination is more complex than automatic pagination, it also allows you to minimize the bandwidth usage and avoid storing a large data object in server-side memory. On the other hand, most custom pagination strategies requery the database with each postback, which means you may be creating more work for the database.

Tip To determine whether custom pagination is better than automatic paging with caching, you need to evaluate the way you use data. The larger the amount of data the GridView is using, the more likely you'll need to use custom pagination. On the other hand, the slower the database server and the heavier its load, the more likely you'll want to reduce repeated calls by caching the full data object. Ultimately, you may need to profile your application to determine the optimum paging strategy.

The ObjectDataSource is the only data source to support custom pagination. The first step to take control of custom paging is to set ObjectDataSource.EnablePaging to True. You can then implement paging through three more properties: StartRowIndexParameterName, MaximumRowsParameterName, and SelectCountMethod.

Counting the Records

To have the GridView create the correct number of page links for you, it must know the total number of records and the number of records per page. The records-per-page value is set with the PageSize property, as in the previous example. The total number of pages is a little trickier.

When using automatic pagination, the total number of records is automatically determined by the GridView based on the number of records in the data source. In custom paging, you must explicitly calculate the total number using a dedicated method. The following procedure shows how you can retrieve the number of records of the Employees table and return the count:

```
Public Function CountEmployees() As Integer
    ' Create the Command and the Connection.
    Dim sql As String = "SELECT COUNT(*) FROM Employees"
    Dim con As New SqlConnection(connectionString)
    Dim cmd As New SqlCommand(sql, con)
    con.Open()

    ' Execute the command and Return its outcome
    Return CInt(cmd.ExecuteScalar())
    con.Close()
End Function
```

This example uses the COUNT() aggregate function to calculate the number of records in the table and returns that information using the ExecuteScalar() method of the Command object. This method is bound to the ObjectDataSource using the SelectCountMethod property:

```
<asp:ObjectDataSource ID="sourceEmployees" runat="server" EnablePaging="True"
 SelectCountMethod="CountEmployees" ... />
```

When you use custom paging, the SelectCountMethod is executed for every postback. If you want to reduce database work at the risk of providing an incorrect count, you could cache this information and reuse it.

A Stored Procedure to Get Paged Records

The next part of the solution is a little trickier. Instead of retrieving a collection with all the employee records, the GetEmployees() method must retrieve records for the current page only. To accomplish this feat, this example uses a stored procedure named GetEmployeePage. This stored procedure copies all the employee records into a temporary table that has one additional column—a unique autoincrementing ID that will number each row. Next, the stored procedure retrieves a selection from that table that corresponds to the requested page of data, using the supplied @Start and @Count parameters.

Here's the complete stored procedure code:

```
CREATE PROCEDURE GetEmployeePage
(
    @Start int, @Count int
)
AS
-- create a temporary table with the columns we are interested in
CREATE TABLE #TempEmployees
(
```

```
  ID                int IDENTITY PRIMARY KEY,
  EmployeeID        int,
  LastName          nvarchar(20),
  FirstName         nvarchar(10),
  TitleOfCourtesy   nvarchar(25),
)

-- fill the temp table with all the employees
INSERT INTO #TempEmployees
(
  EmployeeID, LastName, FirstName, TitleOfCourtesy
)
SELECT
  EmployeeID, LastName, FirstName, TitleOfCourtesy
FROM
  Employees ORDER BY EmployeeID ASC

-- declare two variables to calculate the range of records
-- to extract for the specified page
DECLARE @FromID int
DECLARE @ToID int
-- calculate the first and last ID of the range of records we need
SET @FromID = @Start
SET @ToID =  @Start + @Count - 1

-- select the page of records
SELECT * FROM #TempEmployees WHERE ID >= @FromID AND ID <= @ToID
GO
```

■ **Note** This stored procedure uses a SQL Server–specific approach. Other databases might have other possible optimizations. For example, Oracle databases allow you to use the ROWNUM operator in the WHERE clause of a query to return a range of rows. For example, the query SELECT * FROM Employees WHERE ROWNUM > 100 AND ROWNUM < 200 retrieves the page of rows from 101 to 199.

The Paged Selection Method

The final step is to create an overload of the GetEmployees() method that performs paging. This method receives two arguments—the index of the row that starts the page (starting at 0) and the page size (maximum number of rows). You specify the parameter names you want to use for these two details through the StartRowIndexParameterName and MaximumRowsParameterName properties. If not set, the defaults are startRowIndex and maximumRows.

Here's the GetEmployees() method you need to use the stored procedure shown in the previous example:

```
Public Function GetEmployees(ByVal startRowIndex As Integer,
            ByVal maximumRows As Integer) As EmployeeDetails()
    Dim con As New SqlConnection(connectionString)
    Dim cmd As New SqlCommand("GetEmployeePage", con)
    cmd.CommandType = CommandType.StoredProcedure
    cmd.Parameters.Add(New SqlParameter("@Start", SqlDbType.Int, 4))
    cmd.Parameters("@Start").Value = startRowIndex + 1
    cmd.Parameters.Add(New SqlParameter("@Count", SqlDbType.Int, 4))
    cmd.Parameters("@Count").Value = maximumRows
```

```
    ' Create a collection for all the employee records.
    Dim employees As ArrayList = New ArrayList()
    Try
        con.Open()
        Dim reader As SqlDataReader = cmd.ExecuteReader()
        Do While reader.Read()
            Dim emp As New EmployeeDetails(CInt(reader("EmployeeID")),
                CStr(reader("FirstName")), CStr(reader("LastName")),
                CStr(reader("TitleOfCourtesy")))
            employees.Add(emp)
        Loop
        reader.Close()

        Return CType(employees.ToArray(GetType(EmployeeDetails)), EmployeeDetails())
    Catch err As SqlException
        Throw New ApplicationException("Data error.")
    Finally
        con.Close()
    End Try
End Function
```

When you run this page, you'll see that the output is the same as the output generated by the previous page using automatic pagination, and the pager controls work the same way.

Customizing the Pager Bar

The GridView paging controls are remarkably flexible. In their default representation, you'll see a series of numbered links (see Figure 10-10). However, you customize them thoroughly using the PagerStyle property (for foreground and background colors, the font, color, size, and so on) and the PagerSettings property. The most important detail in the PagerSettings.Mode property, which specifies how to render the paging links according to one of several styles, as described in Table 10-7.

Table 10-7. *Pager Modes*

Mode	Description
Numeric	The grid will render as many links to other pages as specified by the PageButtonCount property. If that number of links is not enough to link to every page of the grid, the pager will display ellipsis links (...) that, when clicked, display the previous or next set of page links.
NextPrevious	The grid will render only two links for jumping to the previous and next pages. If you choose this option, you can also define the text for the two links through the NextPageText and PreviousPageText properties (or use image links through NextPageImageUrl and PreviousPageImageUrl).
NumericFirstLast	The same as Numeric, except there are additional links for the first page and the last page.
NextPreviousFirstLast	The same as NextPrevious, except there are additional links for the first page and the last page. You can set the text for these links through FirstPageText and LastPageText properties (or images through FirstPageImageUrl and LastPageImageUrl).

If you don't like the default pager bar, you can implement your own using the template feature described in the next section by creating a PagerTemplate. You can then use any control you want, such as a text box where the user can type the index of the page and a button to submit the request and load the new page. The code for extracting and binding the records for the current page would remain the same.

GridView Templates

So far, the examples have used the DataGrid control to show data in using separate bound columns for each field. If you want to place multiple values in the same cell, or have the unlimited ability to customize the content in a cell by adding HTML tags and server controls, you need to use a TemplateField.

The TemplateField allows you to define a completely customized *template* for a column. Inside the template you can add control tags, arbitrary HTML elements, and data binding expressions. You have complete freedom to arrange everything the way you want.

For example, imagine you want to create a column that combines the first name, last name, and courtesy fields. To accomplish this trick, you can construct an ItemTemplate like this:

```
<asp:TemplateField HeaderText="Name">
  <ItemTemplate>
    <%# Eval("TitleOfCourtesy") %> <%# Eval("FirstName") %>
    <%# Eval("LastName") %>
  </ItemTemplate>
</asp:TemplateField>
```

Now when you bind the GridView, the GridView fetches the data from the data source and walks through the collection of items. It processes the ItemTemplate for each item, evaluates the data binding expressions, and adds the rendered HTML to the table. This template is quite simple—it simply defines three data-binding expressions. When evaluated, these expressions are converted to ordinary text.

■ **Note** If you attempt to bind a field that isn't present in your result set, you'll receive a runtime error. If you retrieve additional fields that are never bound to any template, no problem will occur.

You'll notice that these expressions use Eval(), which is a Shared method of the System.Web.UI.DataBinder class. Eval() is an indispensable convenience—it automatically retrieves the data item that's bound to the current row, uses reflection to find the matching field (for a row) or property (for a custom object), and retrieves the value. This process of reflection adds a little bit of extra work. However, this overhead is unlikely to add much time to the processing of a request. Without the Eval() method, you'd need to access the data object through the Container.DataItem property and use typecasting code like this:

```
<%# CType(Container.DataItem, EmployeeDetails)("FirstName") %>
```

The problem with this approach is that you need to know the exact type of data object. For example, the data-binding expression shown previously assumes you're binding to an array of EmployeeDetails objects through the ObjectDataSource. If you switch to the SqlDataSource, or if you rename the EmployeeDetails class, your page will break. On the other hand, if you use the Eval() method, your data binding expressions will keep working as long as the data object has a property with the given name. In other words, using the Eval() method allows you to create pages that are loosely bound to your data access layer.

■ **Tip** When binding to a SqlDataSource in DataSet mode, the data item is a DataRowView. When binding to a SqlDataSource in DataReader mode, the data item is a DbDataRecord.

The Eval() method also adds the extremely useful ability to format data fields on the fly. To use this feature, you must use the overloaded version of the Eval() method that accepts an additional format string parameter. Here's an example:

```
<%# Eval("BirthDate", "{0:MM/dd/yy}") %>
```

You can use any of the format strings defined in Table 10-3 and Table 10-4 with the Eval() method.

You're free to mix templated columns with other column types. Or, you could get rid of every other column and put all the information from the Employees table into one formatted template:

```
<asp:GridView ID="gridEmployees" runat="server" DataSourceID="sourceEmployees"
 AutoGenerateColumns="False" ...>
  <!-- Styles omitted. -->

  <Columns>
    <asp:TemplateField HeaderText="Employees">
      <ItemTemplate>
        <b>
          <%# Eval("EmployeeID") %> -
          <%# Eval("TitleOfCourtesy") %> <%# Eval("FirstName") %>
          <%# Eval("LastName") %>
        </b>
        <hr />
        <small><i>
          <%# Eval("Address") %><br />
          <%# Eval("City") %>, <%# Eval("Country") %>,
          <%# Eval("PostalCode") %><br />
          <%# Eval("HomePhone") %></i>
          <br /><br />
          <%# Eval("Notes") %>
        </small>
      </ItemTemplate>
    </asp:TemplateField>
  </Columns>
</asp:GridView>
```

Figure 10-11 shows the result.

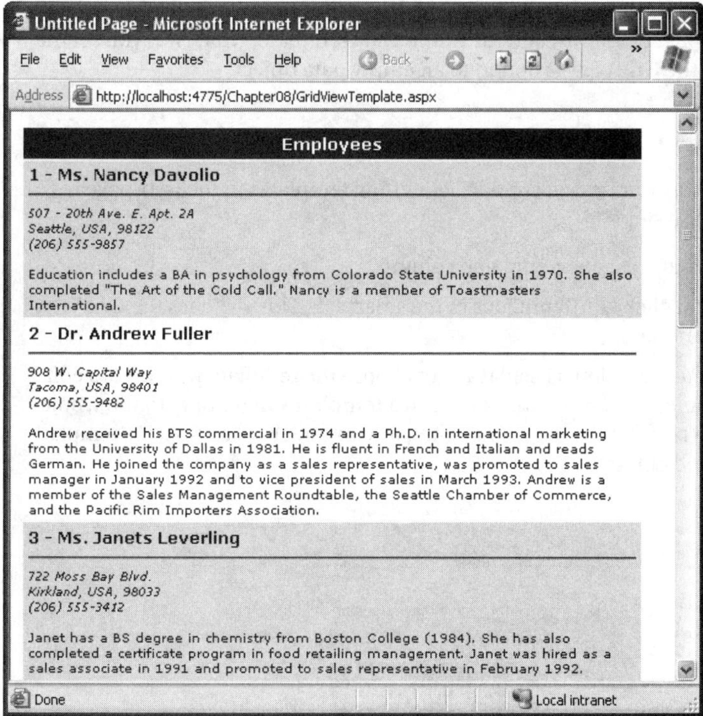

Figure 10-11. *Creating a templated column*

Using Multiple Templates

The previous example used a single template to configure the appearance of data items. However, the ItemTemplate isn't the only template that the GridView provides. In fact, the GridView allows you to configure various aspects of its appearance with a number of templates. Inside every template column, you can use the templates listed in Table 10-8.

Table 10-8. *GridView Templates*

Mode	Description
HeaderTemplate	Determines the appearance and content of the header cell
FooterTemplate	Determines the appearance and content of the footer cell
ItemTemplate	Determines the appearance and content of each data cell (if you aren't using the AlternatingItemTempalte) or every odd-numbered data cell (if you are)
AlternatingItemTemplate	Used in conjunction with the ItemTemplate to format even-numbered and odd-numbered rows differently
EditItemTemplate	Determines the appearance and controls used in edit mode

Out of the templates listed in Table 10-8, the EditItemTemplate is one of the most useful, as it gives you the ability to control the editing experience for the field. If you don't use templated fields, you're limited to ordinary text boxes, and you won't have any validation. The GridView also defines two templates that you can use outside of any column. These are the PagerTemplate, which lets you customize the appearance of pager controls, and the EmptyDataTemplate, which lets you set the content that should appear if the GridView is bound to an empty data object.

Editing Templates in Visual Studio

Visual Studio 2005 includes greatly improved support for editing templates in the web-page designer. To try this, follow these steps:

1. Create a GridView with at least one templated column.
2. Select the GridView and click Edit Templates in the smart tag. This switches the GridView into template editing mode.
3. In the smart tag, use the drop-down Display list to choose the template you want to edit (see Figure 10-12). You can choose either of the two templates that apply to the whole GridView (EmptyDataTemplate or PagerTemplate), or you can choose a specific template for one of the templated columns.

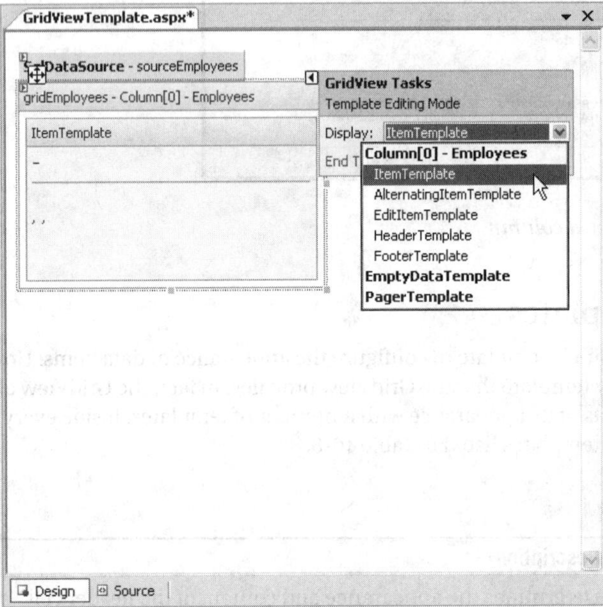

Figure 10-12. *Editing a template in Visual Studio*

4. Enter your content in the control. You can type in static content, drag-and-drop controls, and so on.
5. When you're finished choose End Template Editing from the smart tag.

Binding to a Method

One of the benefits of templates is that they allow you to use data binding expressions that extend the ways you can format and present bound data. One key technique that recurs in many scenarios is using a method in your page class to process a field value. This removes the limitations of simple data binding and lets you incorporate dynamic information and conditional logic.

For example, you might create a column where you want to display an icon next to each row. However, you don't want to use a static icon—instead, you want to choose the best image based on the data in the row. Figure 10-13 shows an example where check marks indicate when there is a large quantity of a given item in stock (more than 50 units) and an *X* indicates when stock is fully depleted.

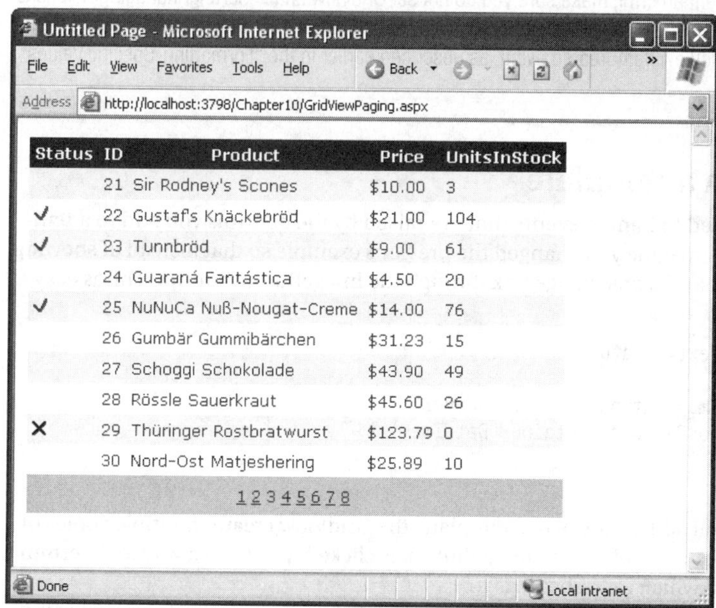

Figure 10-13. *Flagging rows conditionally*

Here's how you would define the status column:

```
<asp:TemplateField HeaderText="Status">
  <ItemTemplate>
    <img src='<%# GetStatusPicture(Container.DataItem) %>' />
  </ItemTemplate>
</asp:TemplateField>
```

And here's the GetStatusPicture() method that examines the data item and chooses the right picture URL:

```
Protected Function GetStatusPicture(ByVal dataItem As Object) As String
    Dim units As Integer =
        Integer.Parse(DataBinder.Eval(dataItem, "UnitsInStock").ToString())
    If units = 0 Then
        Return "Cancel.gif"
    ElseIf units > 50 Then
        Return "OK.gif"
    Else
        Return "blank.gif"
    End If
End Function
```

This technique turns up in many scenarios. For example, you could use it to adjust prices to take into consideration the current exchange rates. Or, you could use it to translate a numeric code into a more meaningful piece of text. You might even want to create completely calculated columns—for example, use the EmployeeDateOfBirth field to calculate a value for an EmployeeAge column.

■ **Note** If you use data binding expressions to bind to methods, you can no longer use callbacks to optimize the GridView refresh process. To prevent an error, make sure you do not set GridView.EnableSortingAndPagingCallbacks to True. If you don't want to sacrifice the callback features, you can get similar functionality by modifying the item when it first appears using the GridView.ItemCreated event, as described earlier in the "Formatting-Specific Values" section of this chapter.

Handling Events in a Template

In some cases, you might need to handle events that are raised by the controls you add to a templated column. For example, imagine you changed the previous example so that instead of showing a static status icon, it created a clickable image link through the ImageButton control. This is easy enough to accomplish:

```
<asp:TemplateField HeaderText="Status">
  <ItemTemplate>
    <asp:ImageButton ID="ImageButton1" runat="server"
     ImageUrl='<%# GetStatusPicture(Container.DataItem) %>' />
  </ItemTemplate>
</asp:TemplateField>
```

The problem is that if you add a control to a template, the GridView creates multiple copies of that control, one for each data item. When the ImageButton is clicked, you need a way to determine which image was clicked and which row it belongs to.

The way to resolve this problem is to use an event from the GridView, *not* the contained button. The RowCommand event serves this purpose, because it fires whenever any button is clicked in any template. This process, where a control event in a template is turned into an event in the containing control, is called *event bubbling.*

Of course, you still need a way to pass information to the RowCommand event to identify the row where the action took place. The secret lies in two string properties of all button controls: CommandName and CommandArgument. CommandName sets a descriptive name you can use to distinguish clicks on your ImageButton from clicks on other button controls in the GridView. The CommandArgument supplies a piece of row-specific data you can use to identify the row that was clicked. You can supply this information using a data binding expression.

Here's the revised ImageButton tag:

```
<asp:TemplateField HeaderText="Status">
  <ItemTemplate>
    <asp:ImageButton ID="ImageButton1" runat="server"
     ImageUrl='<%# GetStatusPicture(Container.DataItem) %>'
     CommandName="StatusClick" CommandArgument='<%# Eval("ProductID") %>' />
  </ItemTemplate>
</asp:TemplateField>
```

And here's the code you need to respond when an ImageButton is clicked:

```
Protected Sub GridView1_RowCommand(
      ByVal sender As Object, ByVal e As GridViewCommandEventArgs)
```

```
    If e.CommandName = "StatusClick" Then
      lblInfo.Text = "You clicked product #" & e.CommandArgument.ToString()
    End If
End Sub
```

This example simply displays the ProductID in a label.

Tip Remember, you can simplify your life using the GridView's built-in selection support. Just set the CommandName to Select and handle the SelectedIndexChanged event, as described in the section "Using a Data Field As a Select Button" earlier in this chapter. Although this approach gives you easy access to the clicked row, it won't help you if you want to provide multiple buttons that perform different tasks.

Editing with a Template

One of the best reasons to use a template is to provide a better editing experience. In the previous chapter, you saw how the GridView provides automatic editing capabilities—all you need to do is switch a row into edit mode by setting the GridView.EditIndex property. The easiest way to make this possible is to add a CommandField column with the ShowEditButton set to True. Then, the user simply needs to click a link in the appropriate row to begin editing it. At this point, every label in every column is replaced by a text box (unless the field is read-only).

The standard editing support has several limitations:

It's not always appropriate to edit values using a text box: Certain types of data are best handled with other controls (such as drop-down lists), large fields need multiline text boxes, and so on.

You get no validation: It would be nice to restrict the editing possibilities so that currency figures can't be entered as negative numbers, and so on. You can do that by adding validator controls to an EditItemTemplate.

It's often ugly: A row of text boxes across a grid takes up too much space and rarely seems professional.

In a templated column, you don't have these issues. Instead, you explicitly define the edit controls and their layout using the EditItemTemplate. This can be a somewhat laborious process.

Here's an edit template that allows editing of a single field—the Notes field:

```
<EditItemTemplate>
  <b>
    <%# Eval("EmployeeID") %> -
    <%# Eval("TitleOfCourtesy") %> <%# Eval("FirstName") %>
    <%# Eval("LastName") %>
  </b>
  <hr />
  <small><i>
    <%# Eval("Address") %><br />
    <%# Eval("City") %>, <%# Eval("Country") %>,
    <%# Eval("PostalCode") %><br />
    <%# Eval("HomePhone") %></i>
    <br /><br />
    <asp:TextBox Text='<%# Bind("Notes") %>' runat="server" id="textBox"
     TextMode="MultiLine" Width="413px" />
  </small>
</EditItemTemplate>
```

When binding an editable value to a control, you must use the Bind() method in your data binding expression instead of the ordinary Eval() method. Only the Bind() method creates the two-way link, ensuring that updated values will be sent back to the server.

Another important fact to keep in mind is that when the GridView commits an update, it will submit only the bound, editable parameters. In the previous example, this means the GridView will pass back a single @Notes parameter for the Notes field. This is important, because when you write your parameterized update command (if you're using the SqlDataSource), you must use only one parameter, as shown here:

```
UpdateCommand="UPDATE Employees SET Notes=@Notes WHERE EmployeeID=@EmployeeID"
```

Similarly, if you're using the ObjectDataSource, you must make sure your update method takes only one parameter, named Notes.

Figure 10-14 shows the row in edit mode.

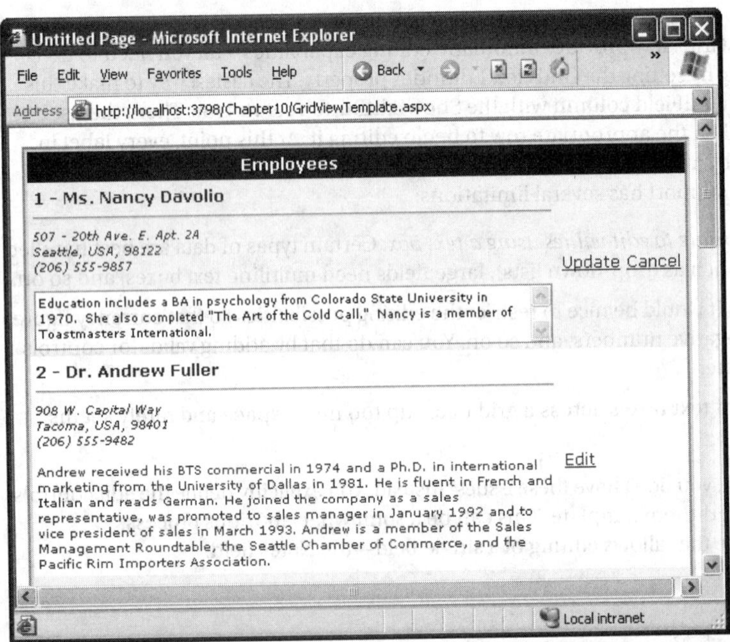

Figure 10-14. *Editing with a template*

Editing with Advanced Controls

Template based-editing really shines if you need to bind to more interesting controls, such as lists. For example, you could change the previous example to make the TitleOfCourtesy field editable through a drop-down list. Here's the template you need, with the new details in bold:

```
<EditItemTemplate>
  <b>
    <%# Eval("EmployeeID") %> -
    <asp:DropDownList runat="server" ID="EditTitle"
     SelectedIndex='<%# GetSelectedTitle(Eval("TitleOfCourtesy")) %>'
     DataSource='<%# TitlesOfCourtesy %>' />
```

```
    <%# Eval("TitleOfCourtesy") %> <%# Eval("FirstName") %>
    <%# Eval("LastName") %>
  </b>
  <hr />
  <small><i>
    <%# Eval("Address") %><br />
    <%# Eval("City") %>, <%# Eval("Country") %>,
    <%# Eval("PostalCode") %><br />
    <%# Eval("HomePhone") %></i>
    <br /><br />
    <asp:TextBox Text='<%# Bind("Notes") %>' runat="server" id="textBox"
     TextMode="MultiLine" Width="413px" />
  </small>
</EditItemTemplate>
```

This template allows the user to pick a title of courtesy from a limited selection of possible titles. To create this list, you need to resort to a little trick—setting the DropDownList.DataSource with a data binding expression that points to a custom property. This custom property can then return a suitable data source with the available titles of courtesy.

Here's the definition for the TitlesOfCourtesy property in the web-page class:

```
Protected ReadOnly Property TitlesOfCourtesy() As String()
    Get
            Return New String(){"Mr.", "Dr.", "Ms.", "Mrs."}
    End Get
End Property
```

■ **Note** This list of titles of courtesy is by no means complete. There are also Miss, Lord, Lady, Sir, None, and so on. For a real-world application the titles could come from a database table or configuration file.

This step ensures that the drop-down list is populated, but it doesn't solve the related problem of making sure the right title is selected in the list for the current value. The best approach here is to bind the SelectedIndex to a custom method that takes the current title and returns the index of that value. In this example, the GetSelectedTitle() method performs this task. It takes a title as input and returns the index of the respective value in the array returned by TitlesOfCourtesy.

```
Protected Function GetSelectedTitle(ByVal title As Object) As Integer
    Return Array.IndexOf(TitlesOfCourtesy, title.ToString())
End Function
```

This code searches the array using the static Array.IndexOf() method. Note that you must explicitly cast the title to a string. That's because the DataBinder.Eval() method returns an object, not a string, and that value is passed to the GetSelectedTitle() method.

Figure 10-15 shows the drop-down list in action.

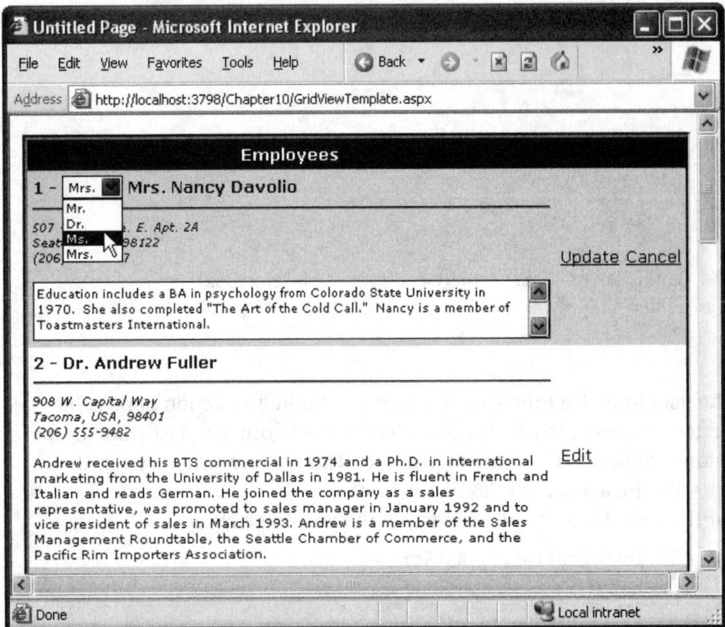

Figure 10-15. *Editing with a drop-down list of values*

Unfortunately, this still doesn't complete the example. Now you have a list box that is populated in edit mode, with the correct item automatically selected. However, if you change the selection, the value isn't sent back to the data source. In this example, you could tackle the problem by using the Bind() method with the SelectedValue property, because the text in the control exactly corresponds to the text you want to commit to the record. However, sometimes life isn't as easy, because you need to translate the value into a different database representation. In this situation, the only option is to handle the RowUpdating event, find the list control in the current row, and extract the text. You can then dynamically add the extra parameter, as shown here:

```
Protected Sub gridEmployees_RowUpdating(
      ByVal sender As Object, ByVal e As GridViewUpdateEventArgs)
    ' Get the reference to the list control.
    Dim title As DropDownList =
      CType(gridEmployees.Rows(e.RowIndex).FindControl("EditTitle"), DropDownList)

    ' Add it to the parameters.
    e.NewValues.Add("TitleOfCourtesy", title.Text)
End Sub
```

This will now successfully update both the Notes field and the TitleOfCourtesy. As you can see, editable templates give you a great deal of power, but they often aren't quick to code.

■ **Tip** To make an even more interesting EditItemTemplate, you could add validator controls to verify input values, as discussed in Chapter 4.

Editing Without a Command Column

So far, all the examples you've seen have used a CommandField that automatically generates edit controls. However, now that you've made the transition over to a template-based approach, it's worth considering how you can add your own edit controls.

It's actually quite easy. All you need to do is add a button control to the item template and set the CommandName to Edit. This automatically triggers the editing process, which fires the appropriate events and switches the row into edit mode:

```
<ItemTemplate>
  <b>
    <%# Eval("EmployeeID") %> - <%# Eval("TitleOfCourtesy") %>
    <%# Eval("TitleOfCourtesy") %> <%# Eval("FirstName") %>
    <%# Eval("LastName") %>
  </b>
  <hr />
  <small><i>
    <%# Eval("Address") %><br />
    <%# Eval("City") %>, <%# Eval("Country") %>,
    <%# Eval("PostalCode") %><br />
    <%# Eval("HomePhone") %></i>
    <br /><br />
    <%# Eval("Notes") %>
    <br /><br />
    <asp:LinkButton runat="server" Text="Edit"
     CommandName="Edit" ID="Linkbutton1" />
  </small>
</ItemTemplate>
```

In the edit item template, you need two more link buttons with a CommandName of Update and Cancel, respectively:

```
<EditItemTemplate>
  <b>
    <%# Eval("EmployeeID") %> -
    <asp:DropDownList runat="server" ID="EditTitle"
     SelectedIndex='<%# GetSelectedTitle(Eval("TitleOfCourtesy")) %>'
     DataSource='<%# TitlesOfCourtesy %>' />
    <%# Eval("TitleOfCourtesy") %> <%# Eval("FirstName") %>
    <%# Eval("LastName") %>
  </b>
  <hr />
  <small><i>
    <%# Eval("Address") %><br />
    <%# Eval("City") %>, <%# Eval("Country") %>,
    <%# Eval("PostalCode") %><br />
    <%# Eval("HomePhone") %></i>
    <br /><br />
    <asp:TextBox Text='<%# Bind("Notes") %>' runat="server" id="textBox"
     TextMode="MultiLine" Width="413px" />
    <br /><br />
    <asp:LinkButton runat="server" Text="Update"
     CommandName="Update" ID="Linkbutton1" />
    <asp:LinkButton runat="server" Text="Cancel"
     CommandName="Cancel" ID="Linkbutton2" />
  </small>
</EditItemTemplate>
```

As long as you use these names, the GridView editing events will fire and the data source controls will react in the same way as if you were using the automatically generated editing controls. Figure 10-16 shows the custom edit buttons.

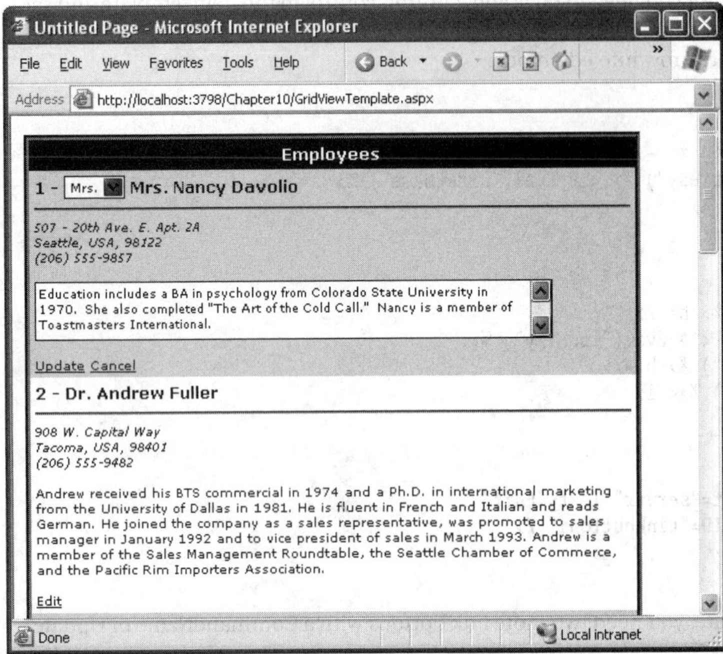

Figure 10-16. *Custom edit controls*

The DetailsView and FormView

The GridView excels at showing a dense table with multiple rows of information. However, sometimes you want to provide a detailed look at a single record. Although you could work out a solution using a template column in a GridView, ASP.NET also includes two controls that are tailored for this purpose: the DetailsView and FormView. Both show a single record at a time but can include optional pager buttons that let you step through a series of records (showing one per page). The difference between the DetailsView and the FormView is their support for templates. The DetailsView is built out of field objects, in the same way that the GridView is built out of column objects. On the other hand, the FormView is based on templates that work in the same way as a GridView templated column, which requires a little more work but gives you much more flexibility.

Now that you understand the features of the GridView, you can get up to speed with the DetailsView and FormView quite quickly. That's because both the DetailsView and the FormView borrow a portion of the GridView model.

The DetailsView

The DetailsView is designed to display a single record at a time. It places each piece of information (be it a field or a property) in a separate row of a table.

You saw how to create a basic DetailsView to show the currently selected record in Chapter 9. The DetailsView can also bind to a collection of items. In this case, it shows the first item in the group. It also allows you to move from one record to the next using paging controls, if you've set the AllowPaging property to True. You can configure the paging controls using the PagerStyle and PagerSettings properties in the same way as you tweak the pager for the GridView. The only difference is that there's no support for custom paging, which means the full data source object is always retrieved.

Figure 10-17 shows the DetailsView when it's bound to a set of employee records, with full employee information.

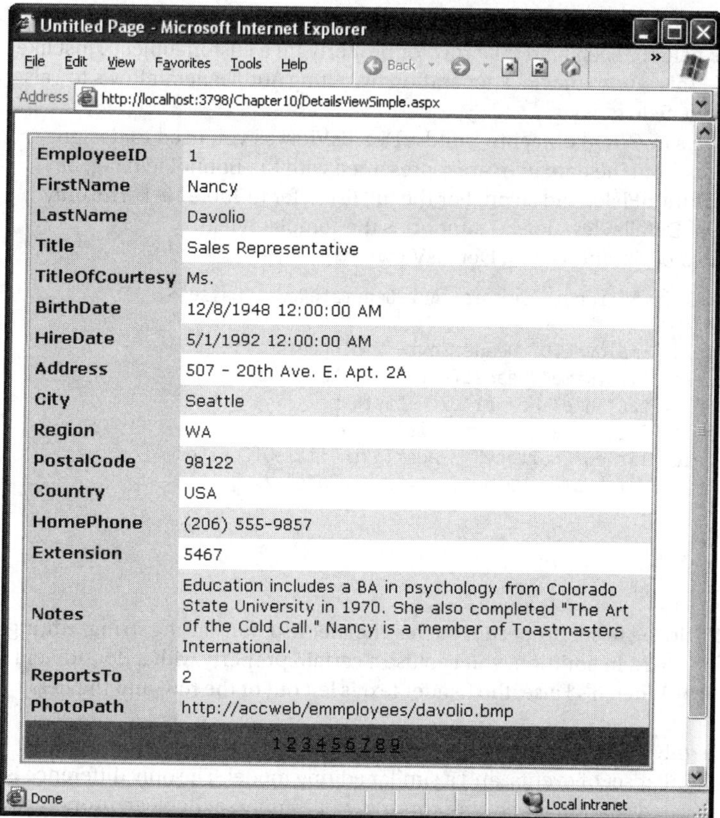

Figure 10-17. *The DetailsView with paging*

It's tempting to use the DetailsView pager controls to make a handy record browser. Unfortunately, this approach can be quite inefficient. First, a separate postback is required each time the user moves from one record to another (whereas a grid control can show multiple records at once). But the real drawback is that each time the page is posted back, the full set of records is retrieved, even though only a single record is shown. If you choose to implement a record browser page with the DetailsView, at a bare minimum you must enable caching to reduce the database work (see Chapter 11).

Often, a better choice is to create your own pager controls using a subset of the full data. For example, you could create a drop-down list and bind this to a data source that queries just the employee names. Then, when a name is selected from the list, you could retrieve the full details for just that record using another data source. Of course, several metrics can determine which approach is best, including the size of the full record (how much bigger it is than just the first and last name), the usage patterns (whether the average user browses to just one or two records or needs to see them all), and how many records there are in total. (You can afford to retrieve them all at once if there are dozens of records, but you need to think twice if there are thousands.)

Defining Fields

The DetailsView uses reflection to generate the fields it shows. That means it examines the data object and creates a separate field for each field (in a row) or property (in a custom object), just like the GridView. You can disable this automatic field generation by setting AutoGenerateRows to False. It's then up to you to declare the field objects.

Interestingly, you use the same field object to build a DetailsView as you used to design a GridView. For example, fields from the data item are represented with the BoundField tag, buttons can be created with the ButtonField, and so on. For the full list, refer to Table 10-1. The only GridView column type that the DetailsView doesn't support is the TemplateField.

Here's a portion of the field declarations for a DetailsView

```
<asp:DetailsView ID="DetailsView1" runat="server" AutoGenerateRows="False">
  <Fields>
    <asp:BoundField DataField="EmployeeID" HeaderText="EmployeeID" />
    <asp:BoundField DataField="FirstName" HeaderText="FirstName" />
    <asp:BoundField DataField="LastName" HeaderText="LastName" />
    <asp:BoundField DataField="Title" HeaderText="Title" />
    <asp:BoundField DataField="TitleOfCourtesy" HeaderText="TitleOfCourtesy" />
    <asp:BoundField DataField="BirthDate" HeaderText="BirthDate" />
    ...
  </Fields>
  ...
</asp:DetailsView>
```

You can use the BoundField tag to set properties such as header text, formatting string, editing behavior, and so on (see Table 10-2). In addition, you can use a certain property with a BoundField that has no effect in a GridView. When it's False, the header text is left out of the row, and the field data takes up both cells.

The field model isn't the only part of the GridView that the DetailsView control adopts. It also uses a similar set of styles, a similar set of events, and a similar editing model. The only difference is that instead of creating a dedicated column for editing controls, you simply set Boolean properties such as AutoGenerateDeleteButton, AutoGenerateEditButton, and AutoGenerateInsertButton. The links for these tasks are added to the bottom of the DetailsView. When you add or edit a record, the DetailsView always uses standard text box controls such as the GridView (see Figure 10-18). For more editing flexibility, you'll want to use the FormView control.

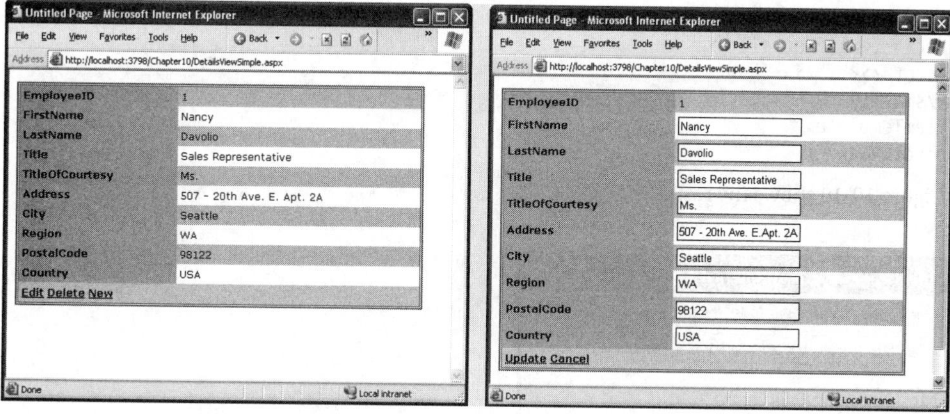

Figure 10-18. *Editing in the DetailsView*

The FormView

The DetailsView supports every type of GridView column except for templated columns. If you need the ultimate flexibility of templates, the FormView provides a template-only control for displaying and editing a single record.

The beauty of the FormView template model is that it matches the model of the TemplateField in the GridView quite closely. This means you have the following templates to work with:

- ItemTemplate
- EditItemTemplate
- InsertItemTemplate
- FooterTemplate
- HeaderTemplate
- EmptyDataTemplate
- PagerTemplate

This means you can take the exact template content you put in a TemplateField in a GridView and place it inside the FormView. Here's an example based on the earlier templated GridView:

```
<asp:FormView ID="FormView1" runat="server" DataSourceID="sourceEmployees">
  <ItemTemplate>
    <b>
      <%# Eval("EmployeeID") %> -
      <%# Eval("TitleOfCourtesy") %> <%# Eval("FirstName") %>
      <%# Eval("LastName") %>
    </b>
    <hr />
    <small><i>
      <%# Eval("Address") %><br />
      <%# Eval("City") %>, <%# Eval("Country") %>,
      <%# Eval("PostalCode") %><br />
      <%# Eval("HomePhone") %></i>
```

```
        <br /><br />
        <%# Eval("Notes") %>
        <br /><br />
      </small>
    </ItemTemplate>
</asp:FormView>
```

Figure 10-19 shows the result.

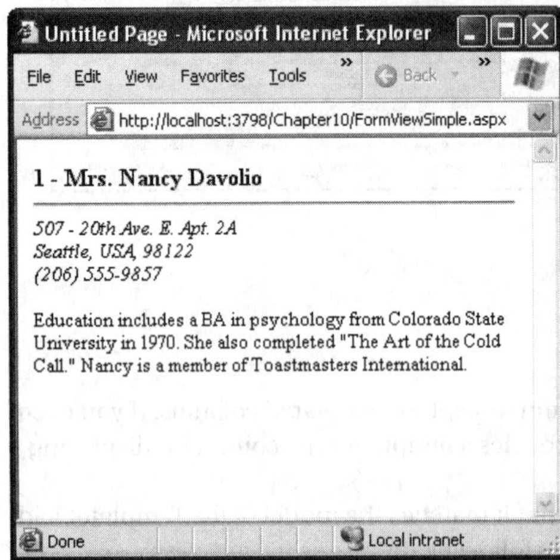

Figure 10-19. *A GridView with a footer summary*

If you want to support editing, you need to add button controls that trigger the Edit and Update process, as described in the section "Editing with a Template" in the GridView section.

Advanced Grids

In the following sections, you'll consider a few ways to extend the GridView. You'll learn how to show summaries, create a complete master-details report on a single page, and display image data that's drawn from a database. You'll also see an example that uses advanced concurrency handling to warn the user about potential conflicts when updating a record.

Summaries in the GridView

Although the prime purpose of a GridView is to show a set of records, you can also add some more interesting information, such as summary data. The first step is to add the footer row by setting the GridView.ShowFooter property to True. This displays a shaded footer row (which you can customize freely), but it doesn't show any data. To take care of that task, you need insert the content into the GridView.FooterRow.

For example, imagine you're dealing with a list of products. A simple summary row could display the total or average product price. In the next example, the summary row displays the total value of all the in-stock products.

The first step is to decide when to calculate this information. If you're using manual binding, you could retrieve the data object and use it to perform your calculations before binding it to the GridView. However, if you're using declarative binding, you need another technique. You have two basic options—you can retrieve the data from the data object before the grid is bound, or you can retrieve it from the grid itself after the grid has been bound. The following example uses the latter approach because it gives you the freedom to use the same calculation code no matter what data source was used to populate the control. It also gives you the ability to total just the records that are displayed on the current page, if you've enabled paging. The disadvantage is that your code is tightly bound to the GridView, because you need to pull out the information you want by position, using hard-coded column index numbers.

The basic strategy is to react to the GridView.DataBound event. This occurs immediately after the GridView is populated with data. At this point, you can't access the data source any longer, but you can navigate through the GridView as a collection of rows and cells. Once this total is calculated, it's inserted into the footer row.

Here's the complete code:

```
Protected Sub GridView1_DataBound(ByVal sender As Object, ByVal e As EventArgs)
    Dim valueInStock As Decimal = 0

    ' The Rows collection includes rows only on the current page
    ' (not "virtual" rows).
    For Each row As GridViewRow In GridView1.Rows
        Dim price As Decimal = Decimal.Parse(row.Cells(2).Text)
        Dim unitsInStock As Integer = Integer.Parse(row.Cells(3).Text)
        valueInStock += price * unitsInStock
    Next
    ' Update the footer.
    Dim footer As GridViewRow = GridView1.FooterRow

    ' Set the first cell to span over the entire row.
    footer.Cells(0).ColumnSpan = 3
    footer.Cells(0).HorizontalAlign = HorizontalAlign.Center

    ' Remove the unneeded cells.
    footer.Cells.RemoveAt(2)
    footer.Cells.RemoveAt(1)

    ' Add the text.
    footer.Cells(0).Text = "Total value in stock (on this page): " _
            & valueInStock.ToString("C")
End Sub
```

The summary row has the same number of columns as the rest of the grid. As a result, if you want your text to be displayed over multiple cells (as it is in this example), you need to configure cell spanning by setting the ColumnSpan property of the appropriate cell. In this example, the first cell spans over three columns (itself, and the next two on the right). Figure 10-20 shows the final result.

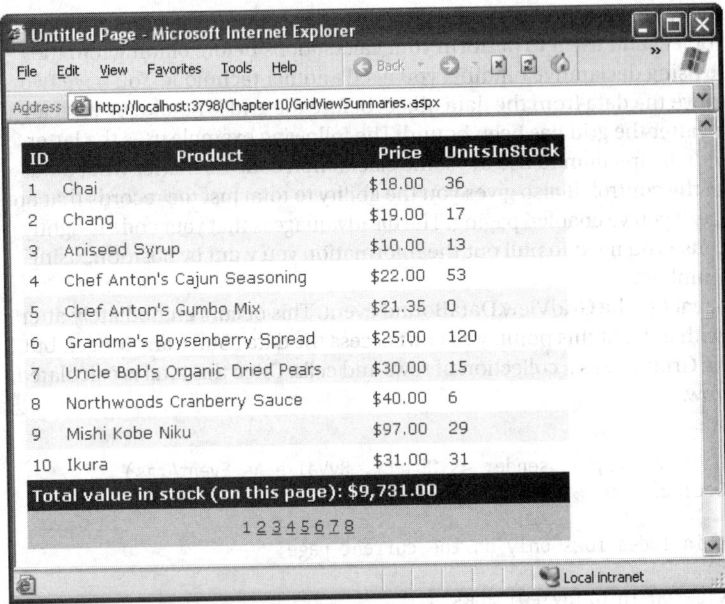

Figure 10-20. *A GridView with a footer summary*

A Parent/Child View in a Single Table

Earlier in this chapter, you saw a master/detail page that used a GridView and DetailsView. This gives you the flexibility to show the child records for just the currently selected parent record. However, sometimes you want to create a parent/child report that shows all the records from the child table, organized by parent. For example, you could use this to create a complete list of products organized by category. The next example demonstrates how you show a complete, subgrouped product list in a single grid.

The basic technique is to create a GridView for the parent table that contains an embedded GridView for each row. These child GridView controls are inserted into the parent GridView using a TemplateField. The only trick is that you can't bind the child GridView controls at the same time that you bind the parent GridView, because the parent rows haven't been created yet. Instead, you need to wait for the GridView.DataBound event to fire in the parent.

In this example, the parent GridView defines two columns, both of which are the TemplateField type. The first column combines the category name and category description:

```
<asp:TemplateField HeaderText="Category">
  <ItemStyle VerticalAlign="Top" Width="20%"></ItemStyle>
  <ItemTemplate>
    <br />
    <b><%# Eval("CategoryName") %></b>
    <br /><br />
    <%# Eval("Description" ) %>
    <br />
  </ItemTemplate>
</asp:TemplateField>
```

The second column contains an embedded GridView of products, with two bound columns. Here's an excerpted listing that omits the style-related attributes:

```
<asp:TemplateField HeaderText="Products">
  <ItemStyle VerticalAlign="Top"></ItemStyle>
  <ItemTemplate>
    <asp:GridView runat="server">
      <Columns>
        <asp:BoundField DataField="ProductName"
         HeaderText="Product Name"></asp:BoundField>
        <asp:BoundField DataField="UnitPrice"
         HeaderText="Unit Price" DataFormatString="{0:C}"></asp:BoundField>
      </Columns>
    </asp:GridView>
  </ItemTemplate>
</asp:TemplateField>
```

Now all you need to do is create two data sources, one for retrieving the list of categories and the other for retrieving all products in a specified category. The first query fills the parent GridView, and the second query is called multiple times to fill the child GridView.

You can bind the first grid directly to the data source, as shown here:

```
<asp:GridView id="gridMaster" runat="server" DataKeyNames="CategoryID"
 DataSourceID="sourceCategories" OnRowDataBound="gridMaster_RowDataBound" ... >
```

This part of the code is typical. The trick is to bind the child GridView controls. If you leave out this step, the child GridView controls won't appear.

To bind the child GridView controls, you need to react to the GridView.RowDataBound event, which fires every time a row is generated and bound to the parent GridView. At this point, you can retrieve the child DataGrid control from the second column and bind it to the product information by programmatically calling the Select() method of the data source. To ensure that you show only the products in the current category, you must also retrieve the CategoryID field for the current item and pass it as a parameter. Here's the code you need:

```
Protected Sub gridMaster_RowDataBound(
      ByVal sender As Object, ByVal e As GridViewRowEventArgs)
    ' Look for data items.
    If e.Row.RowType = DataControlRowType.DataRow Then
        ' Retrieve the GridView control in the second column.
        Dim gridChild As GridView = CType(e.Row.Cells(1).Controls(1), GridView)

        ' Set the CategoryID parameter so you get the products
        ' in the current category only.
        Dim catID As String =
           gridMaster.DataKeys(e.Row.DataItemIndex).Value.ToString()
        sourceProducts.SelectParameters(0).DefaultValue = catID

        ' Get the data object from the data source.
        Dim data As Object = sourceProducts.Select(DataSourceSelectArguments.Empty)

        ' Bind the grid.
        gridChild.DataSource = data
        gridChild.DataBind()
    End If
End Sub
```

Figure 10-21 shows the resulting grid.

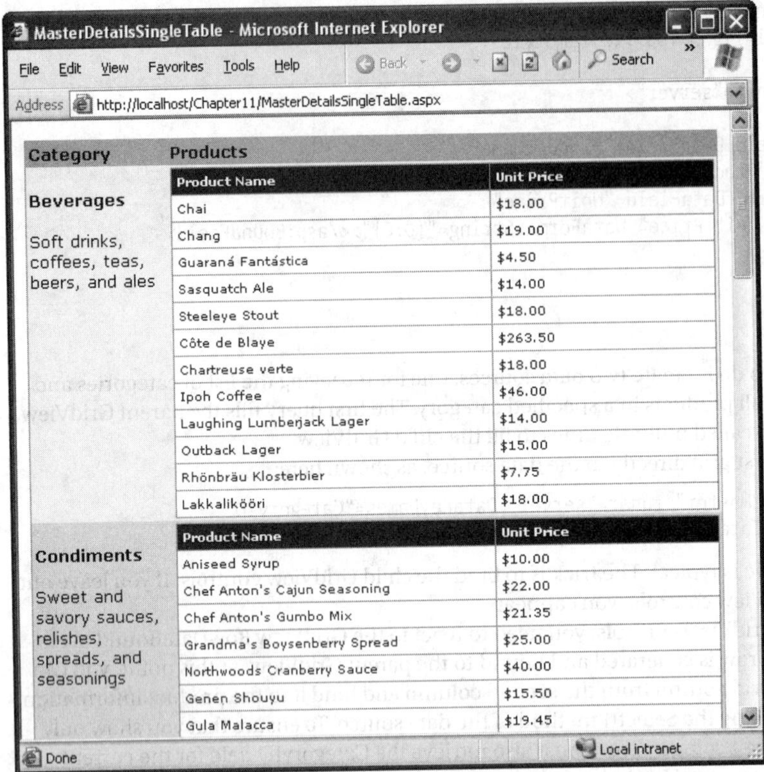

Figure 10-21. *A parent grid with embedded child grids*

Serving Images from a Database

The data examples in this chapter retrieve text, numeric, and date information. However, databases often have the additional challenge of storing binary data such as pictures. For example, you might have a Products table that contains pictures of each item in a binary field. Retrieving this data in an ASP.NET web page is fairly easy, but displaying it is not as simple.

The basic problem is that in order to show an image in an HTML page, you need to add an image tag that links to a separate image file through the src attribute. Here's an example:

```
<img src="myfile.gif" />
```

Unfortunately, this isn't much help if you need to show image data dynamically. Although you can set the src attribute in code, you have no way to set the image *content* programmatically. You could first save the data to an image file on the web server's hard drive, but that approach would be dramatically slower, waste space, and raise the possibility of concurrency errors if multiple requests are being served at the same time and they are all trying to write the same file.

You can solve this problem in two ways. One approach is to store all your images in separate files. Then your database record simply needs to store the filename, and you can bind the filename to a server-side image. This is a perfectly reasonable solution, but it doesn't help in situations where you want to store images in the database so you can take advantage of the abilities of the RDBMS to cache data, log usage, and back up everything.

In these situations, the solution is to use a separate ASP.NET resource that returns the binary data directly. You can then use this binary data in other web pages in controls. To tackle this task, you also need to step outside the data binding and write custom ADO.NET code. The following sections will develop the solution you need piece by piece.

■ **Tip** As a general rule of thumb, storing images in a database works well as long as the images are not enormous (for example, more than 50 MB) and do not need to be frequently edited by other applications.

Displaying Binary Data

ASP.NET isn't restricted to returning HTML content. In fact, you can use the Response.BinaryWrite() method to return raw bytes and completely bypass the web-page model.

The following page uses this technique with the pub_info table in the pubs database (another standard database that's included with SQL Server). It retrieves the logo field, which contains binary image data. The page then writes this data directly to the page, as shown here:

```
Protected Sub Page_Load(ByVal sender As Object, ByVal e As System.EventArgs)
    Dim connectionString As String =
      WebConfigurationManager.ConnectionStrings("Pubs").ConnectionString
    Dim con As New SqlConnection(connectionString)
    Dim SQL As String = "SELECT logo FROM pub_info WHERE pub_id='1389'"
    Dim cmd As New SqlCommand(SQL, con)

    Try
        con.Open()
        Dim r As SqlDataReader = cmd.ExecuteReader()
        If r.Read() Then
            Dim bytes As Byte() = CType(r("logo"), Byte())
            Response.BinaryWrite(bytes)
        End If
        r.Close()
    Finally
        con.Close()
    End Try
End Sub
```

Figure 10-22 shows the result. It doesn't appear terribly impressive (the logo data isn't that remarkable), but you could easily use the same technique with your own database, which can include much richer and larger images.

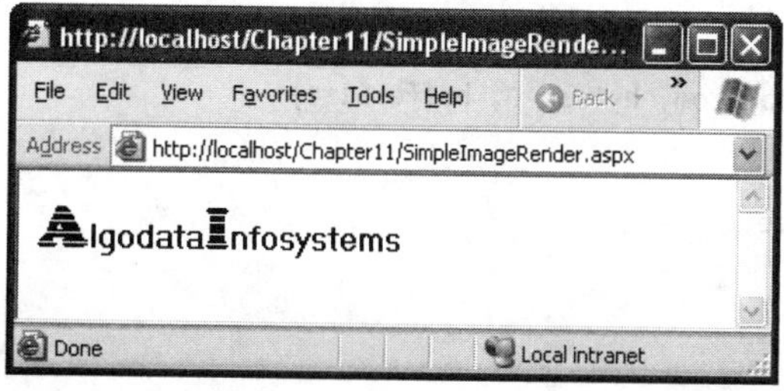

Figure 10-22. *Displaying an image from a database*

When you use BinaryWrite(), you are stepping away from the web-page model. If you add other controls to your web page, they won't appear. Similarly, Response.Write() won't have any effect, because you are no longer creating an HTML page. Instead, you're retuning image data. You'll see how to solve this problem and optimize this approach in the following sections.

Reading Binary Data Efficiently

Binary data can easily grow to large sizes. However, if you're dealing with a large image file, the example shown previously will demonstrate woefully poor performance. The problem is that it uses the DataReader, which loads a single record into memory at a time. This is better than the DataSet (which loads the entire result set into memory at once), but it still isn't ideal if the field size is large.

There's no good reason to load an entire 2 MB picture into memory at once. A much better idea would be to read it piece by piece and then write each chunk to the output stream using Response.BinaryWrite(). Fortunately, the DataReader has a sequential access feature that supports this design. To use sequential access, you simply need to supply the CommandBehavior.SequentialAccess value to the Command.ExecuteReader() method. Then you can move through the row one block at a time, using the DataReader.GetBytes() method.

When using sequential access, you need to keep a couple of limitations in mind. First, you must read the data as a forward-only stream. Once you've read a block of data, you automatically move ahead in the stream, and there's no going back. Second, you must read the fields in the same order they are returned by your query. For example, if your query returns three columns, the third of which is a binary field, you must return the values of the first and second fields before accessing the binary data in the third field. If you access the third field first, you will not be able to access the first two fields.

Here's how you would revise the earlier page to use sequential access:

```
Protected Sub Page_Load(ByVal sender As Object, ByVal e As System.EventArgs)
    Dim connectionString As String =
        WebConfigurationManager.ConnectionStrings("Pubs").ConnectionString
    Dim con As New SqlConnection(connectionString)
    Dim SQL As String = "SELECT logo FROM pub_info WHERE pub_id='1389'"
    Dim cmd As New SqlCommand(SQL, con)

    Try
        con.Open()
        Dim r As SqlDataReader = cmd.ExecuteReader(CommandBehavior.SequentialAccess)

        If r.Read() Then
            Dim bufferSize As Integer = 100 ' Size of the buffer.
            Dim bytes As Byte() = New Byte(bufferSize - 1) {} ' The buffer of data.
            Dim bytesRead As Long ' The number of bytes read.
            Dim readFrom As Long = 0 ' The starting index.

            ' Read the field 100 bytes at a time.
            Do
                bytesRead = r.GetBytes(0, readFrom, bytes, 0, bufferSize)
                Response.BinaryWrite(bytes)
                readFrom += bufferSize
            Loop While bytesRead = bufferSize
        End If
        r.Close()
    Finally
        con.Close()
    End Try
End Sub
```

The GetBytes() method returns a value that indicates the number of bytes retrieved. If you need to determine the total number of bytes in the field, you simply need to pass a null reference (Nothing) instead of a buffer when you call the GetBytes() method.

Integrating Images with Other Content

The Reponse.BinaryWrite() method creates a bit of a challenge if you want to integrate image data with other controls and HTML. That's because when you use BinaryWrite() to return raw image data, you lose the ability to add any extra HTML content.

To attack this problem, you need to create another page that calls your image-generating code. The best way to do this is to replace your image-generating page with a dedicated HTTP handler that generates image output. This way, you save the overhead of the full ASP.NET web form model, which you aren't using anyway. (Chapter 5 introduces HTTP handlers.)

Creating the HTTP handler you need is quite easy. You simply need to implement the IHttpHandler interface and implement the ProcessRequest() method. The HTTP handler will retrieve the ID of the record you want to display from the query string.

Here's the complete HTTP handler code:

```
Public Class ImageFromDB : Implements IHttpHandler
    Public Sub ProcessRequest(ByVal context As HttpContext)
        Implements IHttpHandler.ProcessRequest

        Dim connectionString As String =
            WebConfigurationManager.ConnectionStrings("Pubs").ConnectionString

        ' Get the ID for this request.
        Dim id As String = context.Request.QueryString("id")
        If id Is Nothing Then
                Throw New ApplicationException("Must specify ID.")
        End If

        ' Create a parameterized command for this record.
        Dim con As New SqlConnection(connectionString)
        Dim SQL As String = "SELECT logo FROM pub_info WHERE pub_id=@ID"
        Dim cmd As New SqlCommand(SQL, con)
        cmd.Parameters.AddWithValue("@ID", id)

        Try
            con.Open()
            Dim r As SqlDataReader =
                 cmd.ExecuteReader(CommandBehavior.SequentialAccess)

            If r.Read() Then
                Dim bufferSize As Integer = 100 ' Size of the buffer.
                Dim bytes As Byte() = New Byte(bufferSize - 1) {} ' The buffer.
                Dim bytesRead As Long ' The # of bytes read.
                Dim readFrom As Long = 0 ' The starting index.

                ' Read the field 100 bytes at a time.
                Do
                    bytesRead = r.GetBytes(0, readFrom, bytes, 0, bufferSize)
                    context.Response.BinaryWrite(bytes)
                    readFrom += bufferSize
                Loop While bytesRead = bufferSize
            End If
            r.Close()
```

```
        Finally
            con.Close()
        End Try
    End Sub

    Public ReadOnly Property IsReusable() As Boolean
      Implements IHttpHandler.IsReusable
        Get
            Return True
        End Get
    End Property
End Class
```

Once you've created the HTTP handler, you need to register it in the web.config file, as shown here:

```
<httpHandlers>
  <add verb="GET" path="ImageFromDB.ashx"
    type="ImageFromDB" />
</httpHandlers>
```

Now you can retrieve the image data by requesting the HTTP handler URL, with the ID of the row that you want to retrieve. Here's an example:

```
ImageFromDB.ashx?ID=1389
```

To show this image content in another page, you simply need to set the src attribute of an image to this URL, as shown here:

```
<img src="ImageFromDB.ashx?ID=1389"/>
```

Figure 10-23 shows a page with multiple controls and logo images. It uses the following ItemTemplate in a GridView:

```
<ItemTemplate>
  <table border='1'><tr><td>
    <img src='ImageFromDB.ashx?ID=<%# Eval("pub_id")%>'/>
    </td></tr></table>
  <b><%# Eval("pub_name") %></b>
  <br />
  <%# Eval("city") %>,
  <%# Eval("state") %>,
  <%# Eval("country") %>
  <br /><br />
</ItemTemplate>
```

And it binds to this data source:

```
<asp:SqlDataSource ID="sourcePublishers"
 ConnectionString="<%$ ConnectionStrings:Pubs %>"
 SelectCommand="SELECT * FROM publishers" runat="server"/>
```

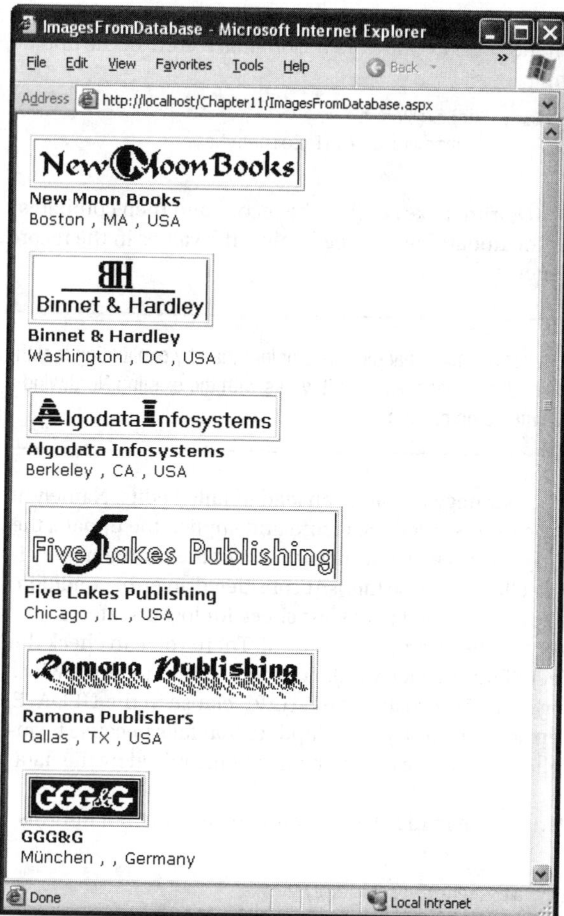

Figure 10-23. *Displaying database images in ASP.NET web page*

This current HTTP handler approach works well if you want to build a detail page with information about a single record. For example, you could show a list of publishers and then display the image for the appropriate publisher when the user makes a selection. However, this solution isn't as efficient if you want to show image data for every publisher at once, such as in a list control. The approach still works, but it will be inefficient because it uses a separate request to the HTTP handler (and hence a separate database connection) to retrieve each image. You can solve this problem by creating an HTTP handler that checks for image data in the cache before retrieving it from the database. Before you bind the GridView, you would then perform a query that returns all the records with their image data and load each image into the cache.

Detecting Concurrency Conflicts

As discussed in Chapter 8, if a web application allows multiple users to make changes, it's quite possible for two or more edits to overlap. Depending on the way these edits overlap and the concurrency strategy you're using (see the section "Concurrency Strategies" in Chapter 8 for more information), this could inadvertently result in committing stale values back to the database.

To prevent this problem, developers often use match-all or timestamp-based concurrency. The idea here is that the UPDATE statement must match every value from the original record, or the update won't be allowed to continue. Here's an example:

```
UPDATE Shippers SET CompanyName=@CompanyName, Phone=@Phone
 WHERE ShipperID=@original_ShipperID AND CompanyName=@original_CompanyName
 AND Phone=@original_Phone
```

SQL Server uses the index on the ShipperID primary key to find the record and then compares the other fields to make sure it matches. Now the update can succeed only if the values in the record match what the user saw when making the changes.

■ **Note** As indicated in Chapter 8, timestamps are a better way to handle this problem than by explicating matching every field. However, this example uses the match-all approach because it works with the existing Northwind database. Otherwise, you would need to add a new timestamp column.

The problem with a match-all concurrency strategy is that it can lead to failed edits. Namely, if the record has changed in between the time the user queried the record and applied the update, the update won't succeed. In fact, the data-bound controls won't even warn you of the problem; they'll just execute the UPDATE statement without any effect, because this isn't considered an error condition.

If you decide to use match-all concurrency, you'll need to at least check for lost updates. You can do this by handling the ItemUpdated event of the appropriate control. There you can check the RowsAffected property of the EventArgs object. If this property is 0, no records were updated, which is almost always because another edit changed the record and the WHERE clause in the UPDATE statement couldn't match anything. (Other errors, such as trying an update that fails because it violates a key constraint or tries to commit invalid data *does* result in an error being raised by the data source.)

Here's an example that checks for a failed update in the DetailsView control and then informs the user of the problem:

```
Protected Sub DetailsView1_ItemUpdated(ByVal sender As Object,
                                       ByVal e As DetailsViewUpdatedEventArgs)
    If e.AffectedRows = 0 Then
        lblStatus.Text = "A conflicting change has already been made to this " _
          & " record by another user. No records were updated."
    End If
End Sub
```

Unfortunately, this doesn't make for the most user-friendly web application. It's particularly a problem if the record has several fields, or if the fields take detailed information, because these edits are simply discarded, forcing the user to start from scratch.

A better solution is to give the user a choice. Ideally, the page would show the current value of the record (taking any recent changes into account) and allow the user to apply the original edited values, cancel the update, or make additional refinements and then apply the update. It's actually quite easy to build a page that provides these niceties.

First, start with a DetailsView that allows the user to edit individual records from the Shippers table in the Northwind database. (The Shippers table is fairly easy to use with match-all concurrency because it has only three fields. Larger tables work better with the equivalent timestamp-based approach.)

Here's an abbreviated definition of the DetailsView you need:

```
<asp:DetailsView ID="detailsEditing" runat="server"
 DataKeyNames="ShipperID" AllowPaging="True" AutoGenerateRows="False"
 DataSourceID="sourceShippers" OnItemUpdated="DetailsView1_ItemUpdated" ...>
```

```
    <Fields>
      <asp:BoundField DataField="ShipperID" ReadOnly="True" />
      <asp:BoundField DataField="CompanyName" />
      <asp:BoundField DataField="Phone" />
      <asp:CommandField ShowEditButton="True" />
    </Fields>
    ...
</asp:DetailsView>
```

The data source control that's bound to the DetailsView uses a match-all UPDATE expression to implement strict concurrency:

```
<asp:SqlDataSource ID="sourceShippers" runat="server"
 ConnectionString="<%$ ConnectionStrings:Northwind %>"
  SelectCommand="SELECT * FROM Shippers" UpdateCommand="UPDATE Shippers SET
CompanyName=@CompanyName, Phone=@Phone WHERE ShipperID=@original_ShipperID AND
CompanyName=@original_CompanyName AND Phone=@original_Phone"
 ConflictDetection="CompareAllValues">
  <UpdateParameters>
    <asp:Parameter Name="CompanyName" />
    <asp:Parameter Name="Phone" />
    <asp:Parameter Name="original_ShipperID" />
    <asp:Parameter Name="original_CompanyName" />
    <asp:Parameter Name="original_Phone" />
  </UpdateParameters>
</asp:SqlDataSource>
```

You'll notice the SqlDataSource.ConflictDetection property is set to CompareAllValues, which ensures that the values from the original record are submitted as parameters (using the prefix defined by the OldValuesParameterFormatString property).

Most of the work takes place in response to the DetailsView.ItemUpdated event. Here, the code catches all failed updates and explicitly keeps the DetailsView in edit mode.

```
Protected Sub DetailsView1_ItemUpdated(
        ByVal sender As Object, ByVal e As DetailsViewUpdatedEventArgs)
    If e.AffectedRows = 0 Then
        e.KeepInEditMode = True
    ...
```

But the real trick is to rebind the data control. This way, all the original values in the DetailsView are reset to match the values in the database. That means the update can succeed (if the user tries to apply it again).

```
...
        detailsEditing.DataBind()
...
```

Rebinding the grid is the secret, but there's still more to do. To maintain the values that the user is trying to apply, you need to manually copy them back into the newly bound data control. This is easy but a little tedious.

```
...
' Repopulate the DetailsView with the edit values.
Dim txt As TextBox
txt = CType(detailsEditing.Rows(1).Cells(1).Controls(0), TextBox)
txt.Text = CStr(e.NewValues("CompanyName"))
txt = CType(detailsEditing.Rows(2).Cells(1).Controls(0), TextBox)
txt.Text = CStr(e.NewValues("Phone"))
...
```

At this point, you have a data control that can detect a failed update, rebind itself, and reinsert the values the user's trying to apply. That means if the user clicks Update a second time, the update will now succeed (assuming the record isn't changed yet again by another user).

However, this still has one shortcoming. The user might not have enough information at this point to decide whether to apply the update. Most likely, they'll want to know what changes were made before they overwrite them. One way to handle this problem is to list the current values in a label or another control. In this example, the code simply unhides a Panel control that contains another DetailsView:

```
    ...
    ErrorPanel.Visible = True
    End If
End Sub
```

The error panel describes the problem with an informative error message and contains a second DetailsView that binds to the matching row to show the current value of the record in question.

```
<asp:Panel ID="ErrorPanel" runat="server" Visible="False" EnableViewState="False">
  There is a newer version of this record in the database.<br />
  The current record has the values shown below.<br />
  <br />
  <asp:DetailsView ID="detailsConflicting" runat="server"
    AutoGenerateRows="False" DataSourceID="sourceUpdateValues" ...>
    <Fields>
      <asp:BoundField DataField="ShipperID" />
      <asp:BoundField DataField="CompanyName" />
      <asp:BoundField DataField="Phone" />
    </Fields>
    ...
  </asp:DetailsView>
  <br />
  * Click <b>Update</b>to override these values with your changes.<br />
  * Click <b>Cancel</b>to abandon your edit. 
  <asp:SqlDataSource ConnectionString="<%$ ConnectionStrings:Northwind %>"
   ID="sourceUpdateValues" runat="server"
   SelectCommand="SELECT * FROM Shippers WHERE (ShipperID = @ShipperID)"
   OnSelecting="sourceUpdateValues_Selecting">
    <SelectParameters>
      <asp:ControlParameter ControlID="detailsEditing" Name="ShipperID"
       PropertyName="SelectedValue" Type="Int32" />
    </SelectParameters>
  </asp:SqlDataSource>
</asp:Panel>
```

There's one last detail. To save overhead, there's no point in performing the query for the second DetailsView unless it's absolutely necessary because a concurrency error occurred. To implement this logic, the code reacts to the SqlDataSource.Selecting event and cancels the query if the error panel isn't currently visible.

```
Private SqlDataSource_Selecting(ByVal sender As Object,
        ByVal e As SqlDataSourceSelectingEventArgs) As sourceUpdateValues
    If (Not ErrorPanel.Visible) Then
            e.Cancel = True
    End If
End Function
```

To try this example, open two copies of the page in separate browser windows and put both into edit mode for the same row. Apply the first change, and then apply the second one. When you attempt to apply the second one, the error panel will appear, with the explanation (see Figure 10-24). You can then choose to continue with the edit by clicking Update or to abandon it by clicking Cancel.

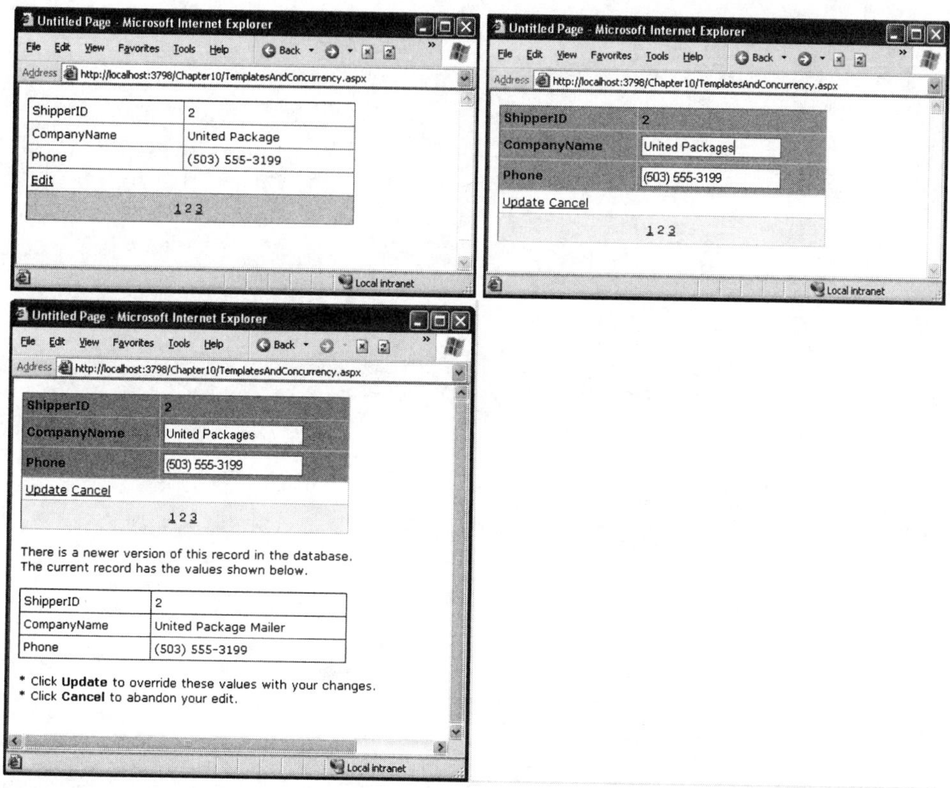

Figure 10-24. *Detecting a concurrency error during an edit*

Summary

In this chapter, you considered everything you need to build rich data-bound pages. You took an exhaustive tour of the GridView and considered its support for formatting, selection, sorting, paging, templates, and editing. You also considered the more modest DetailsView and FormView. Finally, the chapter wrapped up by looking at several common advanced scenarios with data-bound pages.

CHAPTER 11

Caching

One of the most valuable features in ASP.NET 1.*x* is caching, and in ASP.NET 2.0 a good story gets even better.

Caching is the technique of storing an in-memory copy of some information that's expensive to create. For example, you could cache the results of a complex query so that subsequent requests don't need to access the database at all. Instead, they can grab the appropriate object directly from server memory—a much faster proposition. The real beauty of caching is that unlike many other performance-enhancing techniques, caching bolsters both performance *and* scalability. Performance is better because the time taken to retrieve the information is cut down dramatically. Scalability is improved because you work around bottlenecks such as database connections. As a result, the application can serve more simultaneous page requests with fewer database operations.

Of course, storing information in memory isn't always a good idea. Server memory is a limited resource; if you try to store too much, some of that information will be paged to disk, potentially slowing down the entire system. That's why the best caching strategies (such as those hard-wired into ASP.NET) are self-limiting. When you store information in a cache, you expect to find it there on a future request, most of the time. However, the lifetime of that information is at the discretion of the server. If the cache becomes full or other applications consume a large amount of memory, information will be selectively evicted from the cache, ensuring that performance is maintained. It's this self-sufficiency that makes caching so powerful (and so complicated to implement on your own).

With ASP.NET, you get first-rate caching for free, and you have a variety of options. You can cache the completely rendered HTML for a page, a portion of that HTML, or arbitrary objects. You can also customize expiration policies and set up dependencies so that items are automatically removed when other resources—such as files or database tables—are modified.

CACHING CHANGES IN .NET 2.0

ASP.NET 2.0 improves its already impressive caching model. Here is a list of changes, in their order of appearance in this chapter:

- *The Substitution control*: Use this control to define some dynamic content on a cached page. The end result is that this content is always rendered at runtime, even when the rest of the page is pulled from the output cache.
- *Cache profiles*: Managing a site with dozens of cached pages can be tedious, because if you need to tweak caching settings, then you need to modify each page. With cache profiles, you can define your settings in the web.config file and apply them to a batch of pages.
- *The disk output cache*: You can now explicitly tell ASP.NET to save cached information to a disk, as well as in memory. This allows a cached item to linger much longer—even if it's removed from memory or the application restarts. Disk caching is enabled by default, but you can configure it or disable it.
- *SQL cache dependencies*: You can remove cached data objects when the related data in the database changes, using one of ASP.NET's hottest new features.
- *Custom dependencies*: Need to automatically invalidate cached items when other resources change? Now the CacheDependency class is unsealed so you can derive your own custom dependencies.

You'll learn about these innovations in this chapter.

Understanding ASP.NET Caching

Many developers who learn about caching see it as a bit of a frill, but nothing could be further from the truth. Used intelligently, caching can provide a twofold, threefold, or even tenfold performance improvement by retaining important data for just a short period of time.

ASP.NET really has two types of caching. Your applications can and should use both types, because they complement each other:

Output caching: This is the simplest type of caching. It stores a copy of the final rendered HTML page that is sent to the client. The next client that submits a request for this page doesn't actually run the page. Instead, the final HTML output is sent automatically. The time that would have been required to run the page and its code is completely reclaimed.

Data caching: This is carried out manually in your code. To use data caching, you store important pieces of information that are time-consuming to reconstruct (such as a DataSet retrieved from a database) in the cache. Other pages can check for the existence of this information and use it, thereby bypassing the steps ordinarily required to retrieve it. Data caching is conceptually the same as using application state, but it's much more server-friendly because items will be removed from the cache automatically when it grows too large and performance could be affected. Items can also be set to expire automatically.

Also, two specialized types of caching build on these models:

Fragment caching: This is a specialized type of output caching—instead of caching the HTML for the whole page, it allows you to cache the HTML for a portion of it. Fragment caching works by storing the rendered HTML output of a user control on a page. The next time the page is executed, the same page events fire (and so your page code will still run), but the code for the appropriate user control isn't executed.

Data source caching: This is the caching that's built into the data source controls, including the SqlDataSource, ObjectDataSource, and XmlDataSource. Technically, data source caching uses data caching. The difference is that you don't need to handle the process explicitly. Instead, you simply configure the appropriate properties, and the data source control manages the caching storage and retrieval.

In this chapter, you'll consider every caching option. You'll begin by considering the basics of output caching and data caching. Next, you'll consider the caching in the data source controls. Finally, you'll explore one of ASP.NET's hottest new features—linking cached items to tables in a database with SQL cache dependencies.

Output Caching

With output caching, the final rendered HTML of the page is cached. When the same page is requested again, the control objects are not created, the page lifecycle doesn't start, and none of your code executes. Instead, the cached HTML is served. Clearly, output caching gets the theoretical maximum performance increase, because all the overhead of your code is sidestepped.

■ Note An ASP.NET page may use other static resources (such as images) that aren't handled by ASP.NET. Don't worry about caching these items. IIS automatically handles the caching of files in a more efficient way than the ASP.NET cache.

Declarative Output Caching

To see output caching in action, you can create a simple page that displays the current time of day. Figure 11-1 shows an example.

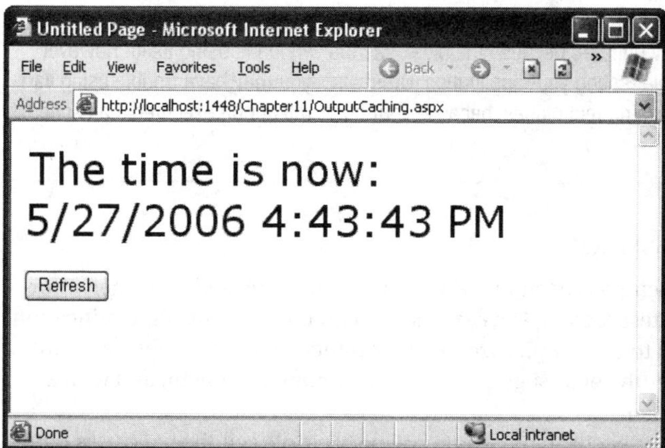

Figure 11-1. *Caching an entire page*

The code for this page is straightforward. It simply sets the date to appear in a label when the Page.Load event fires:

```
Protected Sub Page_Load(ByVal sender As Object, ByVal e As EventArgs)
    lblDate.Text = "The time is now:<br />"
    lblDate.Text &= DateTime.Now.ToString()
End Sub
```

You have two ways to add this page to the output cache. The most common approach is to insert the OutputCache directive at the top of your .aspx file, as shown here:

```
<%@ OutputCache Duration="20" VaryByParam="None" %>
```

In this example, the Duration attribute instructs ASP.NET to cache the page for 20 seconds. The VaryByParam attribute is also required, but you'll learn about its effect in the next section.

When you run the test page, you'll discover some interesting behavior. The first time you access the page, the current date will be displayed. If you refresh the page a short time later, however, the page will not be updated. Instead, ASP.NET will automatically send the cached HTML output to you (assuming 20 seconds haven't elapsed, and therefore the cached copy of the page hasn't expired). When the cached page expires, ASP.NET will run the page code again, generate a new cached copy, and use that for the next 20 seconds.

Twenty seconds may seem like a trivial amount of time, but in a high-volume site, it can make a dramatic difference. For example, you might cache a page that provides a list of products from a catalog. By caching the page for 20 seconds, you limit database access for this page to three operations per minute. Without caching, the page will try to connect to the database once for each client and could easily make dozens of requests in a minute.

Of course, just because you request that a page should be stored for 20 seconds doesn't mean it actually will be. The page could be evicted from the cache early if the system finds that memory is becoming scarce. This allows you to use caching freely, without worrying too much about hampering your application by using up vital memory.

■ **Tip** When you recompile a cached page, ASP.NET will automatically remove the page from the cache. This prevents problems where a page isn't properly updated because the older, cached version is being used. However, you might still want to disable caching while testing your application. Otherwise, you may have trouble using variable watches, breakpoints, and other debugging techniques, because your code will not be executed if a cached copy of the page is available.

Caching and the Query String

One of the main considerations in caching is deciding when a page can be reused and when information must be accurate up to the latest second. Developers, with their love of instant gratification (and lack of patience), generally tend to overemphasize the importance of real-time information. You can usually use caching to efficiently reuse slightly stale data without a problem, and with a considerable performance improvement.

Of course, sometimes information needs to be dynamic. One example is if the page uses information from the current user's session to tailor the user interface. In this case, full page caching just isn't appropriate (although fragment caching may help). Another example is if the page is receiving information from another page through the query string. In this case, the page is too dynamic to cache—or is it?

The current example sets the VaryByParam attribute to None, which effectively tells ASP.NET that you need to store only one copy of the cached page, which is suitable for all scenarios. If the request for this page adds query string arguments to the URL, it makes no difference—ASP.NET will always reuse the same output until it expires. You can test this by adding a query string parameter manually in the browser window (such as ?a=b).

Based on this experiment, you might assume that output caching isn't suitable for pages that use query string arguments. But ASP.NET actually provides another option. You can set the VaryByParam attribute to * to indicate that the page uses the query string and to instruct ASP.NET to cache separate copies of the page for different query string arguments, as shown here:

```
<%@ OutputCache Duration="20" VaryByParam="*" %>
```

Now when you request the page with additional query string information, ASP.NET will examine the query string. If the string matches a previous request, and a cached copy of that page exists, it will be reused. Otherwise, a new copy of the page will be created and cached separately.

To get a better idea how this process works, consider the following series of requests:

1. You request a page without any query string parameter and receive page copy A.
2. You request the page with the parameter ProductID=1. You receive page copy B.
3. Another user requests the page with the parameter ProductID=2. That user receives copy C.
4. Another user requests the page with ProductID=1. If the cached output B has not expired, it's sent to the user.
5. The user then requests the page with no query string parameters. If copy A has not expired, it's sent from the cache.

You can try this on your own, although you might want to lengthen the amount of time that the cached page is retained to make it easier to test.

Caching with Specific Query String Parameters

Setting VaryByParam="*" allows you to use caching with dynamic pages that vary their output based on the query string. This approach could be extremely useful for a product detail page, which receives a product ID in its query string. With vary-by-parameter caching, you could store a separate page for each product, thereby saving a trip to the database. However, to gain performance benefits you might have to increase the cached output lifetime to several minutes or longer.

Of course, this technique has some potential problems. Pages that accept a wide range of different query string parameters (such as a page that receives numbers for a calculation, client information, or search keywords) just aren't suited to output caching. The possible number of variations is enormous, and the potential reuse is low. Though these pages will be evicted from the cache when the memory is needed, they could inadvertently force other more important information from the cache first or slow down other operations.

In many cases, setting VaryByParam to the wildcard asterisk (*) is unnecessarily vague. It's usually better to specifically identify an important query string variable by name. Here's an example:

```
<%@ OutputCache Duration="20" VaryByParam="ProductID" %>
```

In this case, ASP.NET will examine the query string looking for the ProductID parameter. Requests with different ProductID parameters will be cached separately, but all other parameters will be ignored. This is particularly useful if the page may be passed additional query string information that it doesn't use. ASP.NET has no way to distinguish the "important" query string parameters without your help.

You can specify several parameters, as long as you separate them with semicolons, as follows:

```
<%@ OutputCache Duration="20" VaryByParam="ProductID;CurrencyType" %>
```

In this case, the query string will cache separate versions, provided the query string differs by ProductID or CurrencyType.

■ **Note** Output caching works well with pages that vary only based on server-side data (for example, the data in a database) and the data in query string. However, output caching doesn't work if the page output depends on user-specific information such as session data or cookies. Output caching also won't work with event-driven pages that use forms. In these cases, events will be ignored, and a static page will be re-sent with each postback, effectively disabling the page. To avoid these problems, use fragment caching instead to cache a portion of the page or use data caching to cache specific information.

Custom Caching Control

Varying by query string parameters isn't the only option when storing multiple cached versions of a page. ASP.NET also allows you to create your own procedure that decides whether to cache a new page version or reuse an existing one. This code examines whatever information is appropriate and then returns a string. ASP.NET uses this string to implement caching. If your code generates the same string for different requests, ASP.NET will reuse the cached page. If your code generates a new string value, ASP.NET will generate a new cached version and store it separately.

One way you could use custom caching is to cache different versions of a page based on the browser type. That way, Netscape browsers will always receive Netscape-optimized pages, and Internet Explorer users will receive Internet Explorer–optimized HTML. To set up this sort of logic, you start by adding the OutputCache directive to the pages that will be cached. Use the VaryByCustom attribute to specify a name that represents the type of custom caching you're creating. The following example uses the name browser because pages will be cached based on the client browser:

```
<%@ OutputCache Duration="10" VaryByParam="None" VaryByCustom="browser" %>
```

Next, you need to create the procedure that will generate the custom caching string. This procedure must be coded in the global.asax application file (or its code-behind file) and must use the following syntax:

```
Public Overrides Function GetVaryByCustomString(ByVal context As HttpContext,
      ByVal arg As String) As String
    ' Check for the requested type of caching.
    If arg = "browser" Then
      ' Determine the current browser.
      Dim browserName As String
      browserName = Context.Request.Browser.Browser
      browserName &= Context.Request.Browser.MajorVersion.ToString()

      ' Indicate that this string should be used to vary caching.
      Return browserName
    Else
      Return MyBase.GetVaryByCustomString(context, arg)
    End If
End Function
```

The GetVaryByCustomString() function passes the VaryByCustom name in the arg parameter. This allows you to create an application that implements several types of custom caching in the same function. Each different type would use a different VaryByCustom name (such as Browser, BrowserVersion, or DayOfWeek). Your GetVaryByCustomString() function would examine the VaryByCustom name and then return the appropriate caching string. If the caching strings for different requests match, ASP.NET will reuse the cached copy of the page. Or, to look at it another way, ASP.NET will create and store a separate cached version of the page for each caching string it encounters.

Interestingly, the base implementation of the GetVaryByCustomString() already includes the logic for browser-based caching. That means you don't need to code the method shown previously. The base implementation of GetVaryByCustomString() creates the cached string based on the browser name and major version number. If you want to change how this logic works (for example, to vary based on name, major version, and minor version), you could override the GetVaryByCustomString() method, as in the previous example.

■ **Note** Varying by browser is an important technique for cached pages that use browser-specific features. For example, if your page generates client-side JavaScript that's not supported by all browsers, you should make the caching dependent on the browser version. Of course, it's still up to your code to identify the browser and choose what JavaScript to render. You'll learn more about adaptive pages and JavaScript in Part 5.

The OutputCache directive also has a third attribute that you can use to define caching. This attribute, VaryByHeader, allows you to store separate versions of a page based on the value of an HTTP header received with the request. You can specify a single header or a list of headers separated by semicolons. You could use this technique with multilingual sites to cache different versions of a page based on the client browser language, as follows:

```
<%@ OutputCache Duration="20" VaryByParam="None"
    VaryByHeader="Accept-Language" %>
```

Caching with the HttpCachePolicy Class

Using the OutputCache directive is generally the preferred way to cache a page, because it separates the caching instruction from the rest of your code. The OutputCache directive also makes it easy to configure several advanced properties in one line.

However, you have another choice: You can write code that uses the built-in special Response.Cache property, which provides an instance of the System.Web.HttpCachePolicy class. This object provides properties that allow you to turn on caching for the current page.

In the following example, the date page has been rewritten so that it automatically enables caching when the page is first loaded. This code enables caching with the SetCacheability() method, which specifies that the page will be cached on the server and that any other client can use the cached copy of the page. The SetExpires() method defines the expiration date for the page, which is set to be the current time plus 60 seconds.

```
Protected Sub Page_Load(ByVal sender As Object, ByVal e As EventArgs)
    ' Cache this page on the server.
    Response.Cache.SetCacheability(HttpCacheability.Public)

    ' Use the cached copy of this page for the next 60 seconds.
    Response.Cache.SetExpires(DateTime.Now.AddSeconds(60))

    ' This additional line ensures that the browser can't
    ' invalidate the page when the user clicks the Refresh button
    ' (which some rogue browsers attempt to do).
    Response.Cache.SetValidUntilExpires(True)

    lblDate.Text = "The time is now:<br />" & DateTime.Now.ToString()
End Sub
```

Programmatic caching isn't as clean from a design point of view. Embedding the caching code directly in your page is often awkward, and it's always messy if you need to include other initialization code in your page. Remember, the code in the Page.Load event handler runs only if your page isn't in the cache (either because this is the first request for the page, because the last cached version has expired, or because the request parameters don't match).

■ **Tip** Make sure you use the Response.Cache property of the page, *not* the Cache property. The Cache property isn't used for output caching—instead, it gives you access to the data cache (discussed in the "Data Caching" section).

Post-Cache Substitution and Fragment Caching

In some cases, you may find that you can't cache an entire page, but you would still like to cache a portion that is expensive to create and doesn't vary. You have two ways to handle this challenge:

Fragment caching: In this case, you identify just the content you want to cache, wrap that in a dedicated user control, and cache just the output from that control.

Post-cache substitution: In this case, you identify just the dynamic content you don't want to cache. You then replace this content with something else using the Substitution control. Post-cache substitution is new in ASP.NET 2.0.

Out of the two, fragment caching is the easiest to implement. However, the decision of which you want to use will usually be based on the amount of content you want to cache. If you have a small, distinct portion of content to cache, fragment caching makes the most sense. Conversely, if you have only a small bit of dynamic content, post-cache substitution may be the more straightforward approach. Both approaches offer similar performance.

■ **Tip** The most flexible way to implement a partial caching scenario is to step away from output caching altogether and use data caching to handle the process programmatically in your code. You'll see this technique in the "Data Caching" section.

Fragment Caching

To implement fragment caching, you need to create a user control for the portion of the page you want to cache. You can then add the OutputCache directive to the user control. The result is that the page will not be cached, but the user control will. Chapter 14 discusses user controls.

Fragment caching is conceptually the same as page caching. It has only one catch—if your page retrieves a cached version of a user control, it cannot interact with it in code. For example, if your user control provides properties, your web-page code cannot modify or access these properties. When the cached version of the user control is used, a block of HTML is simply inserted into the page. The corresponding user control object is not available.

Post-Cache Substitution

The post-cache substitution feature (which is new in ASP.NET 2.0) revolves around a single method that has been added to the HttpResponse class. The method is WriteSubstitution(), and it accepts a single parameter—a delegate that points to a callback method that you implement in your page class. This callback method returns the content for that portion of the page.

Here's the trick: When the ASP.NET page framework retrieves the cached page, it automatically triggers your callback method to get the dynamic content. It then inserts your content into the cached HTML of the page. The nice thing is that even if your page hasn't been cached yet (for example, it's being rendered for the first time), ASP.NET still calls your callback in the same way to get the dynamic content. In essence, the whole idea is that you create a method that generates some dynamic content, and by doing so you guarantee that your method is always called, and its content is never cached.

The method that generates the dynamic content needs to be Shared. That's because ASP.NET needs to be able to call this method even when an instance of your page class isn't available. (Obviously, when your page is served from the cache, the page object isn't created.) The signature for the method is fairly straightforward—it accepts an HttpContext object that represents the current request, and it returns a string with the new HTML. Here's an example that returns a date with bold formatting:

```
Private Shared Function GetDate(ByVal context As HttpContext) As String
    Return "<b>" & DateTime.Now.ToString() & "</b>"
End Function
```

To get this in the page, you need to use the Response.WriteSubstitution() method at some point:

```
Protected Sub Page_Load(ByVal sender As Object, ByVal e As EventArgs)
    Response.Write("This date is cached with the page: ")
    Response.Write(DateTime.Now.ToString() & "<br />")
    Response.Write("This date is not: ")
    Response.WriteSubstitution(
        New HttpResponseSubstitutionCallback(AddressOf GetDate))
End Sub
```

Now, even if you apply caching to this page with the OutputCache directive, the date will still be updated for each request. That's because the callback bypasses the caching process. Figure 11-2 shows the result of running the page and refreshing it several times.

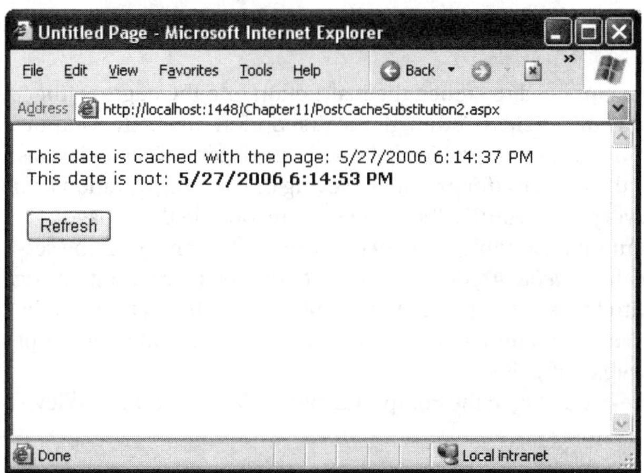

Figure 11-2. *Injecting dynamic content into a cached page*

The problem with this technique is that post-cache substitution works at a lower-level than the rest of your user interface. Usually, when you design an ASP.NET page, you don't use the Response object at all—instead, you use web controls, and those web controls use the Response object to generate their content. One problem is that if you use the Response object as shown in the previous example, you'll lose the ability to position your content with respect to the rest of the page. The only realistic solution is to wrap your dynamic content in some sort of control. That way, the control can use Response.WriteSubstitution() when it renders itself. You'll learn more about control rendering in Chapter 27.

However, if you don't want to go to the work of developing a custom control just to get the post-cache substitution feature, ASP.NET has one shortcut—a generic Substitution control that uses this technique to make all its content dynamic. You bind the Substitution control to a Shared method that returns your dynamic content, exactly as in the previous example. However, you can place the Substitution control alongside other ASP.NET controls, allowing you to control exactly where the dynamic content appears.

Here's an example that duplicates the earlier example using markup in the .aspx portion of the page:

```
This date is cached with the page:
<asp:Label ID="lblDate" runat="server" /><br />
This date is not:
<asp:Substitution ID="Substitution1" runat="server" MethodName="GetDate" />
```

Unfortunately, at design time you won't see the content for the Substitution control.

Remember, post-cache substitution allows you to execute only a Shared method. ASP.NET still skips the page life cycle, which means it won't create any control objects or raise any control events. If your dynamic content depends on the values of other controls, you'll need to use a different technique (such as data caching), because these control objects won't be available to your callback.

■ Note Custom controls are free to use Response.WriteSubstitution() to set their caching behavior. For example, the AdRotator uses this feature to ensure that the advertisement on a page is always rotated, even when the rest of the page is served from the output cache.

Cache Profiles

One problem with output caching is that you need to embed the instruction into the page—either in the .aspx markup portion or in the code of the class. Although the first option (using the Output-Cache) is relatively clean, it still produces management problems if you create dozens of cached pages. If you want to change the caching for all these pages (for example, moving the caching duration from 30 to 60 seconds), you need to modify every page. ASP.NET also needs to recompile these pages.

ASP.NET 2.0 introduces a new option that's suitable if you need to apply the same caching settings to a group of pages. This feature, called *cache profiles*, allows you to define the caching settings in a web.config file, associate a name with these settings, and then apply these settings to multiple pages using the name. That way, you have the freedom to modify all the linked pages at once simply by changing the caching profile in the web.config file.

To define a cache profile, you use the <add> tag in the <outputCacheProfiles> section, as follows. You assign a name and a duration.

```
<configuration>
  <system.web>
    <caching>
      <outputCacheSettings>
        <outputCacheProfiles>
          <add name="ProductItemCacheProfile" duration="60" />
        </outputCacheProfiles>
      </outputCacheSettings>
    </caching>
  ...
  </system.web>
</configuration>
```

You can now use this profile in a page through the CacheProfile attribute:

```
<%@ OutputCache CacheProfile="ProductItemCacheProfile" VaryByParam="None" %>
```

Interestingly, if you want apply other caching details, such as the VaryByParam behavior, you can set it either as an attribute in the OutputCache directive or as an attribute of the <add> tag for the profile. Just make sure you start with a lowercase letter if you use the <add> tag, because the property names are camel-cased, as are all configuration settings, and case is important in XML.

Caching to Disk

ASP.NET 2.0 has the ability to save cached responses in memory *and* to disk. The benefit of storing a cached item on disk is that even if it's removed from memory to ensure performance or because the web application was restarted or the application domain was recycled, the cached item remains available (although it's slightly more expensive to retrieve). Of course, cached items are removed both from memory and disk when they expire.

Essentially, disk caching allows ASP.NET to cache a much larger amount of data. Disk caching is enabled by default, and every web application is allocated 2 MB of space. However, you can configure the maximum size to use for disk caching and the location where cache information is stored using the web.config file. Here's an example that sets a maximum 20 MB disk cache:

```
<configuration>
  <system.web>
    <caching>
      <outputCache>
        <diskCache maxSizePerApp="20" />
      </outputCache>
    </caching>
  </system.web>
  ...
</configuration>
```

You can also disable disk caching altogether by supplying the enabled attribute and setting it to False or by changing the path where cached information is stored using the path attribute.

Finally, you can choose to create pages that opt out of disk caching altogether using the DiskCacheable attribute in the OutputCache directive (or the diskCacheable attribute in the cache profile that's defined in the web.config file).

```
<%@ OutputCache Duration="20" VaryByParam="None"
    DiskCacheable="False" %>
```

■ **Note** Obviously, caching to disk is much slower than caching in memory. However, in most cases it's still more expensive to connect to a database and perform a query. Disk caching is best suited to scenarios where you want to cache a large amount of data that's expensive to re-create.

Data Caching

Data caching is the most flexible type of caching, but it also forces you to take specific additional steps in your code to implement it. The basic principle of data caching is that you add items that are expensive to create to a special built-in collection object (called Cache). This object works much like the Application object. It's globally available to all requests from all clients in the application. However, a few key differences exist:

The Cache object is thread-safe: This means you don't need to explicitly lock or unlock the Cache collection before adding or removing an item. However, the objects in the Cache collection will still need to be thread-safe themselves. For example, if you create a custom business object, more than one client could try to use that object at once, which could lead to invalid data. You can code around this limitation in various ways. One easy approach that you'll see in this chapter is just to make a duplicate copy of the object if you need to work with it in a web page.

Items in the cache are removed automatically: ASP.NET will remove an item if it expires, if one of the objects or files it depends on is changed, or if the server becomes low on memory. This means you can freely use the cache without worrying about wasting valuable server memory, because ASP.NET will remove items as needed. But because items in the cache can be removed, you always need to check if a cached object exists before you attempt to use it. Otherwise, you'll run into a NullReferenceException.

Items in the cache support dependencies: You can link a cached object to a file, a database table, or another type of resource. If this resource changes, your cached object is automatically deemed invalid and released.

As with application state, the cached object is stored in process, which means it doesn't persist if the application domain is restarted and it can't be shared between computers in a web farm. This behavior is by design, because the cost of allowing multiple computers to communicate with an out-of-process cache mitigates some of its performance benefit. It makes more sense for each web server to have its own cache.

Adding Items to the Cache

As with the Application and Session collections, you can add an item to the Cache collection just by assigning to a new key name:

```
Cache("key") = item
```

However, this approach is generally discouraged because it does not allow you to have any control over the amount of time the object will be retained in the cache. A better approach is to use the Insert() method.

Table 11-1 lists the four versions of the Insert() method.

Table 11-1. *The Insert() Method Overloads*

Overload	Description
Cache.Insert(key, value);	Inserts an item into the cache under the specified key name, using the default priority and expiration. This is the same as using the indexer-based collection syntax and assigning to a new key name.
Cache.Insert(key, value, dependencies);	Inserts an item into the cache under the specified key name, using the default priority and expiration. The last parameter contains a CacheDependency object that links to other files or cached items and allows the cached item to be invalidated when these change.
Cache.Insert(key, value, dependencies, absoluteExpiration, slidingExpiration);	Inserts an item into the cache under the specified key name, using the default priority and the indicated sliding or absolute expiration policy (you cannot set both at once). This is the most commonly used version of the Insert() method.
Cache.Insert(key, value, dependencies, absoluteExpiration, slidingExpiration, priority, onRemoveCallback);	Allows you to configure every aspect of the cache policy for the item, including expiration, dependencies, and priority. In addition, you can submit a delegate that points to a method you want invoked when the item is removed.

The most important choice you make when inserting an item into the cache is the expiration policy. ASP.NET allows you to set a sliding expiration or an absolute expiration policy, but you cannot use both at the same time. If you want to use an absolute expiration, set the slidingExpiration parameter to TimeSpan.Zero. To set a sliding expiration policy, set the absoluteExpiration parameter to DateTime.Max.

With sliding expiration, ASP.NET waits for a set period of inactivity to dispose of a neglected cache item. For example, if you use a sliding expiration period of ten minutes, the item will be removed only if it is not used within a ten-minute period. Sliding expiration works well when you have information that is always valid but may not be in high demand, such as historical data or a product catalog. This information doesn't expire because it's no longer valid but shouldn't be kept in the cache if it isn't doing any good.

Here's an example that stores an item with a sliding expiration policy of ten minutes, with no dependencies:

```
Cache.Insert("MyItem", obj, Nothing,
    DateTime.MaxValue, TimeSpan.FromMinutes(10))
```

Note The similarity between caching with absolute expiration and session state is no coincidence. When you use the in-process state server for session state, it actually uses the cache behind the scenes! The session state information is stored in a private slot and given an expiration policy to match the timeout value. The session state item is not accessible through the Cache object.

Absolute expirations are best when you know the information in a given item can be considered valid only for a specific amount of time, such as a stock chart or weather report. With absolute expiration, you set a specific date and time when the cached item will be removed.

Here's an example that stores an item for exactly 60 minutes:

```
Cache.Insert("MyItem", obj, Nothing,
DateTime.Now.AddMinutes(60), TimeSpan.Zero)
```

When you retrieve an item from the cache, you must always check for a Nothing reference. That's because ASP.NET can remove your cached items at any time. One way to handle this is to add special methods that re-create the items as needed. Here's an example:

```
Private Function GetCustomerData() As DataSet
    If Cache("CustomerData") IsNot Nothing Then
        ' Return the object from the cache.
        Return CType(Cache("CustomerData"), DataSet)
    Else
        ' Re-create the item, and insert it into the cache.
        Dim customers As DataSet = QueryCustomerDataFromDatabase()
        Cache.Insert("CustomerData", customers)
        Return customers
    End If
End Function

Private Function QueryCustomerDataFromDatabase() As DataSet
    ' (Code to query the database goes here.)
End Function
```

Now you can retrieve the DataSet elsewhere in your code using the following syntax, without worrying about the caching details.

```
GridView1.DataSource = GetCustomerData()
```

For an even better design, move the QueryDataFromDatabase() method to a separate data component.

You have no way to clear the entire data cache, but you can enumerate through the collection using the DictionaryEntry class. This gives you a chance to retrieve the key for each item and allows you to empty the cache using code like this:

```
For Each item As DictionaryEntry In Cache
    Cache.Remove(item.Key.ToString())
Next item
```

Or you can retrieve a list of cached items, as follows:

```
Dim itemList As String = String.Empty
For Each item As DictionaryEntry In Cache
    itemList &= item.Key.ToString() & " "
Next item
```

This code is rarely used in a deployed application but is extremely useful while testing your caching strategies.

A Simple Cache Test

The following example presents a simple caching test. An item is cached for 30 seconds and reused for requests in that time. The page code always runs (because the page itself isn't cached), checks the cache, and retrieves or constructs the item as needed. It also reports whether the item was found in the cache.

All the caching logic takes place when the Page.Load event fires.

```
Protected Sub Page_Load(ByVal sender As Object, ByVal e As EventArgs)
    If Me.IsPostBack Then
        lblInfo.Text &= "Page posted back.<br />"
    Else
        lblInfo.Text &= "Page created.<br />"
    End If

    If Cache("TestItem") Is Nothing Then
        lblInfo.Text &= "Creating TestItem...<br />"
        Dim testItem As DateTime = DateTime.Now

        lblInfo.Text &= "Storing TestItem in cache "
        lblInfo.Text &= "for 30 seconds.<br />"
        Cache.Insert("TestItem", testItem, Nothing,
                DateTime.Now.AddSeconds(30), TimeSpan.Zero)
    Else
        lblInfo.Text &= "Retrieving TestItem...<br />"
        Dim testItem As DateTime = CDate(Cache("TestItem"))
        lblInfo.Text &= "TestItem is '" & testItem.ToString()
        lblInfo.Text &= "'<br />"
    End If
    lblInfo.Text &= "<br />"
End Sub
```

Figure 11-3 shows the result after the page has been loaded and posted back several times in the 30-second period.

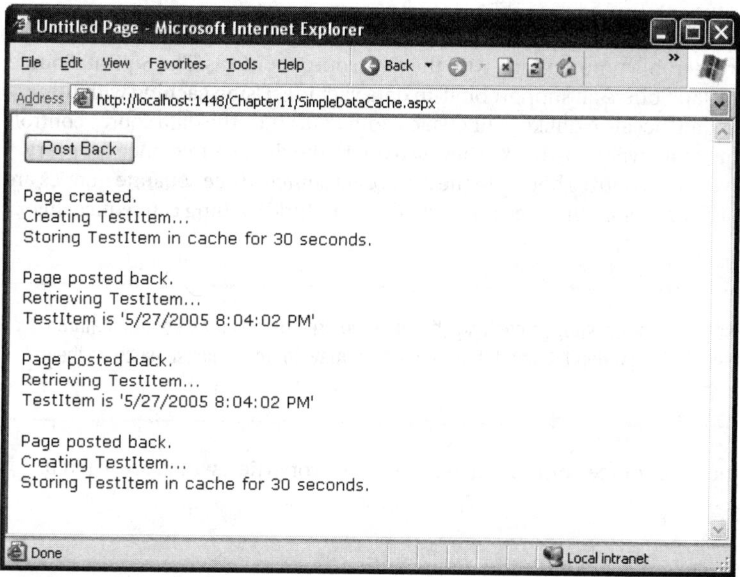

Figure 11-3. *Retrieving data from the cache*

Cache Priorities

You can also set a priority when you add an item to the cache. The priority only an effect has if ASP.NET needs to perform *cache scavenging*, which is the process of removing cached items early because memory is becoming scarce. In this situation, ASP.NET will look for underused items that haven't yet expired. If it finds more than one similarly underused item, it will compare the priorities to determine which one to remove first. Generally, you would set a higher cache priority for items that take more time to reconstruct in order to indicate its heightened importance.

To assign a cache priority, you choose a value from the CachePriority enumeration. Table 11-2 lists all the values.

Table 11-2. *Values of the CachePriority Enumeration*

Value	Description
High	These items are the least likely to be deleted from the cache as the server frees system memory.
AboveNormal	These items are less likely to be deleted than Normal priority items.
Normal	These items have the default priority level. They are deleted only after Low or BelowNormal priority items have been removed.
BelowNormal	These items are more likely to be deleted than Normal priority items.
Low	These items are the most likely to be deleted from the cache as the server frees system memory.
NotRemovable	These items will ordinarily not be deleted from the cache as the server frees system memory.

Caching with the Data Source Controls

In Chapter 9, you spent considerable time working with the data source controls. The SqlDataSource, ObjectDataSource, and XmlDataSource all support built-in data caching. Using caching with these controls is highly recommended, because unlike your own custom data code, the data source controls always requery the data source in every postback. They also query the data source once for every bound control, so if you have three controls bound to the same data source, three separate queries are executed against the database just before the page is rendered. Even a little caching can reduce this overhead dramatically.

■ **Note** Although many data source controls support caching, it's not a required data source control feature, and you'll run into data source controls that don't support it or for which it may not make sense (such as the SiteMapDataSource).

To support caching, the data source controls all use the same properties, which are listed in Table 11-3.

Table 11-3. *Values for the CacheItemRemovedReason Enumeration*

Property	Description
EnableCaching	If True, caching is switched on. It's False by default.
CacheExpirationPolicy	Uses a value from the DataSourceCacheExpiry enumeration—Absolute for absolute expiration (which times out after a fixed interval of time) or Sliding for sliding expiration (which resets the time window every time the data object is retrieved from the cache).
CacheDuration	The number of seconds to cache the data object. If you are using sliding expiration, the time limit is reset every time the object is retrieved from the cache. The default, DataSourceCacheExpiry.Infinite keeps cached items perpetually.
CacheKeyDependency and SqlCacheDependency	Allows you to make a cached item dependent on another item in the data cache (CacheKeyDependency) or on a table in your database (SqlCacheDependency).Dependencies are discussed in the "Cache Dependencies" section.

Caching with SqlDataSource

When you enable caching for the SqlDataSource control, you cache the results of the SelectQuery. However, if you create a select query that takes parameters, the SqlDataSource will cache a separate result for every set of parameter values.

For example, imagine you create a page that allows you to view employees by city. The user selects the desired city from a list box, and you use a SqlDataSource control to fill in the matching employee records in a grid (see Figure 11-4). This example was first presented in Chapter 9.

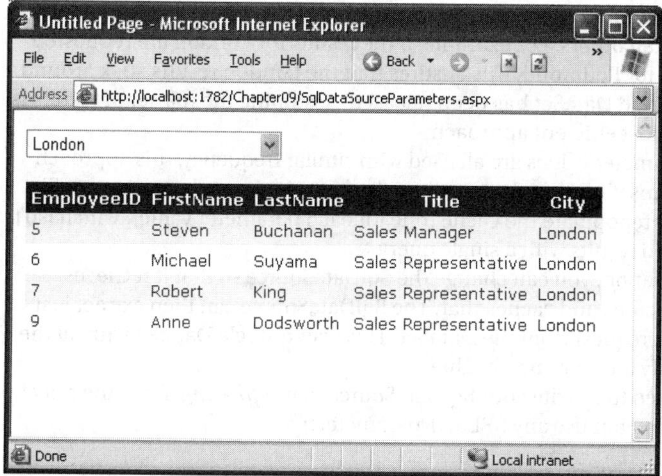

Figure 11-4. *Retrieving data from the cache*

To fill the grid, you use the following SqlDataSource:

```
<asp:SqlDataSource ID="sourceEmployees" runat="server"
 ProviderName="System.Data.SqlClient"
 ConnectionString="<%$ ConnectionStrings:Northwind %>"
 SelectCommand="SELECT EmployeeID, FirstName, LastName, Title, City FROM Employees
WHERE City=@City">
  <SelectParameters>
    <asp:ControlParameter ControlID="lstCities" Name="City"
     PropertyName="SelectedValue" />
  </SelectParameters>
</asp:SqlDataSource>
```

In this example, each time you select a city, a separate query is performed to get just the matching employees in that city. The query is used to fill a DataSet, which is then cached. If you select a different city, the process repeats, and the new DataSet is cached separately. However, if you pick a city that you or another user has already requested, the appropriate DataSet is fetched from the cache (provided it hasn't yet expired).

■ **Note** SqlDataSource caching works only when the DataSourceMode property is set to DataSet (the default). That's because the DataReader object can't be efficiently cached, because it represents a live connection to the database.

Caching separate results for different parameter values works well if some parameter values are used much more frequently than others. For example, if the results for London are requested much more often than the results for Redmond, this ensures that the London results stick around in the cache even when the Redmond DataSet has been released. Assuming the full set of results is extremely large, this may be the most efficient approach.

On the other hand, if the parameter values are all used with similar frequency, this approach isn't as suitable. One of the problems it imposes is that when the items in the cache expire, you'll need multiple database queries to repopulate the cache (one for each parameter value), which isn't as efficient as getting the combined results with a single query.

If you fall into the second situation, you can change the SqlDataSource so that it retrieves a DataSet with all the employee records and caches that. The SqlDataSource can then extract just the records it needs to satisfy each request from the DataSet. This way, a single DataSet with all the records is cached, which can satisfy any parameter value.

To use this technique, you need to rewrite your SqlDataSource to use *filtering*. First, the select query should return all the rows and not use any SELECT parameters:

```
<asp:SqlDataSource ID="sourceEmployees" runat="server"
 SelectCommand="SELECT EmployeeID, FirstName, LastName, Title, City FROM Employees"
 ...>
</asp:SqlDataSource>
```

Second, you need to define the filter expression. This is the portion that goes in the WHERE clause of a typical SQL query, and you write it in the same was as you used the DataView.RowFilter property in Chapter 9. (In fact, the SqlDataSource uses the DataView's row filtering abilities behind the scenes.) However, this has a catch—if you're supplying the filter value from another source (such as a control), you need to define one or more placeholders, using the syntax {0} for the first placeholder, {1} for the second, and so on. You then supply the filter values using the <FilterParameters> section, in much the same way you supplied the select parameters in the first version.

Here's the completed SqlDataSource tag:

```
<asp:SqlDataSource ID="sourceEmployees" runat="server"
 ProviderName="System.Data.SqlClient"
 ConnectionString="<%$ ConnectionStrings:Northwind %>"
 SelectCommand="SELECT EmployeeID, FirstName, LastName, Title, City FROM Employees"
 FilterExpression="City='{0}'" EnableCaching="True">
  <FilterParameters>
    <asp:ControlParameter ControlID="lstCities" Name="City"
     PropertyName="SelectedValue" />
  </FilterParameters>
</asp:SqlDataSource>
```

■ **Tip** Don't use filtering unless you are using caching. If you use filtering without caching, you are essentially retrieving the full result set each time and then extracting a portion of its records. This combines the worst of both worlds—you have to repeat the query with each postback, and you fetch far more data than you need each time.

Caching with ObjectDataSource

The ObjectDataSource caching works on the data object returned from the SelectMethod. If you are using a parameterized query, the ObjectDataSource distinguishes between requests with different parameter values and caches them separately. Unfortunately, the ObjectDataSource caching has a significant limitation—it works only when the select method returns a DataSet or DataTable. If you return any other type of object, you'll receive a NotSupportedException.

This limitation is unfortunate, because there's no technical reason you can't cache custom objects in the data cache. If you want this feature, you'll need to implement data caching inside your method, by manually insert your objects into the data cache and retrieving them later. In fact, caching inside your method can be more effective, because you have the ability to share the same cached object in multiple methods. For example, you could cache a DataTable with a list of product categories and use that cached item in both the GetProductCategories() and GetProductsByCategory() methods.

■ **Tip** The only consideration you should keep in mind is to make sure you use unique cache key names that aren't likely to collide with the names of cached items that the page might use. This isn't a problem when using the built-in data source caching, because it always stores its information in a hidden slot in the cache.

If your custom class returns a DataSet or DataTable, and you do decide to use the built-in ObjectDataSource caching, you can also use filtering as discussed with the SqlDataSource control. Just instruct your ObjectDataSource to call a method that gets the full set of data, and set the FilterExpression to retrieve just those items that match the current view.

Cache Dependencies

As time passes, the data source may change in response to other actions. However, if your code uses caching, you may remain unaware of the changes and continue using out-of-date information from the cache. To help mitigate this problem, ASP.NET supports *cache dependencies*. Cache dependencies allow you to make a cached item dependent on another resource so that when that resource changes the cached item is removed automatically.

ASP.NET includes three types of dependencies:

- Dependencies on other cache items
- Dependencies on files or folders
- Dependencies on a database query

In the following section, you'll consider the first two options. Toward the end of this chapter, you'll learn about SQL dependencies, and you'll learn how to create your own custom dependencies—two tasks that are new in ASP.NET 2.0.

File and Cache Item Dependencies

To create a cache dependency, you need to create a CacheDependency object and then use it when adding the dependent cached item. For example, the following code creates a cached item that will automatically be evicted from the cache when an XML file is changed, deleted, or overwritten:

```
' Create a dependency for the ProductList.xml file.
Dim prodDependency As New CacheDependency(Server.MapPath("ProductList.xml"))

' Add a cache item that will be dependent on this file.
Cache.Insert("ProductInfo", prodInfo, prodDependency)
```

If you point the CacheDependency to a folder, it watches for the addition, removal, or modification of any files in that folder. Modifying a subfolder (for example, renaming, creating, or removing a subfolder) also violates the cache dependency. However, changes further down the directory tree (such as adding a file into a subfolder or creating a subfolder in a subfolder) don't have any effect.

The CacheDependency provides several constructors. You've already seen how it can make a dependency based on a file by using the filename constructor. You can also specify a directory that needs to be monitored for changes, or you can use a constructor that accepts an array of strings that represent multiple files or directories.

Yet another constructor accepts an array of filenames and an array of cache keys. The following example uses this constructor to create an item that is dependent on another item in the cache:

```
Cache("Key1") = "Cache Item 1"

' Make Cache["Key2"] dependent on Cache["Key1"].
Dim dependencyKey As String() = New String(0) {}
dependencyKey(0) = "Key1"
Dim dependency As New CacheDependency(Nothing, dependencyKey)

Cache.Insert("Key2", "Cache Item 2", dependency)
```

Next, when Cache("Key 1") changes or is removed from the cache, Cache("Key 2") will automatically be dropped.

■ **Tip** CacheDependency monitoring begins as soon as the object is created. If the XML file changes before you have added the dependent item to the cache, the item will expire immediately once it's added. If that's not the behavior you want, use the overloaded constructor that accepts a DateTime object. This DateTime indicates when the dependency monitoring will begin.

Figure 11-5 shows a simple test page that is included with the online samples for this chapter. It sets up a dependency, modifies the file, and allows you to verify that the cache item has been dropped from the cache.

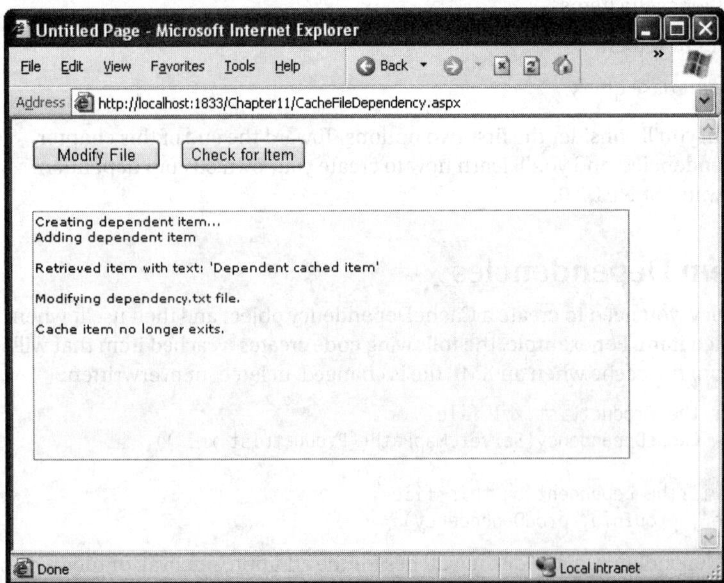

Figure 11-5. *Testing cache dependencies*

Aggregate Dependencies

Sometimes, you might want to combine dependencies to create an item that's dependent on more than one other resource. For example, you might want to create an item that's invalidated if any one of three files changes. Or, you might want to create an item that's invalidated if a file changes or another cached item is removed. Creating these rules is easy with the new AggregateCacheDependency class introduced in ASP.NET 2.0.

The AggregateCacheDependency can wrap any number of CacheDependency objects. All you need to do is supply your CacheDependency objects in an array using the AggregateCacheDependency.Add() method.

Here's an example that makes a cached item dependent on two files:

```
Dim dep1 As New CacheDependency(Server.MapPath("ProductList1.xml"))
Dim dep2 As New CacheDependency(Server.MapPath("ProductList2.xml"))

' Create the aggregate.
Dim dependencies As CacheDependency() = New CacheDependency(){dep1, dep2}
Dim aggregateDep As New AggregateCacheDependency()
aggregateDep.Add(dependencies)

' Add the dependent cache item.
Cache.Insert("ProductInfo", prodInfo, aggregateDep)
```

This example isn't particularly practical, because you can already supply an array of files when you create a CacheDependency object to get the same effect. The real value of AggregateCacheDependency appears when you need to wrap different types of objects that derive from CacheDependency. Because the AggregateCacheDependency.Add() supports any CacheDependency-derived object, you could create a single dependency that incorporates a file dependency, a SQL cache dependency, and even a custom cache dependency.

The Item Removed Callback

ASP.NET also allows you to write a callback method that will be triggered when an item is removed from the cache. This might be useful if you need to clean up other related resources (such as a temporary file on the hard drive). However, you shouldn't use this callback to re-create the item and reinsert the removed item into the cache. Not only will this waste time generating data that might not be immediately required, but it will also thwart ASP.NET's attempt to reduce memory usage when server resources are scarce.

You can place the method that handles the callback in your web-page class, or you can use a Shared method in another accessible class. However, you should keep in mind that this code won't be executed as part of a web request. That means you can't interact with web-page objects or notify the user.

The following example uses a cache callback to make two interdependent items—a feat that wouldn't be possible with dependencies alone. Two items are inserted in the cache, and when either one of those items is removed, the item-removed callback removes the other.

```
Public partial Class ItemRemovedCallbackTest
        Inherits System.Web.UI.Page

    Protected Sub Page_Load(ByVal sender As Object, ByVal e As System.EventArgs)
        If (Not Me.IsPostBack) Then
            lblInfo.Text &= "Creating items...<br />"
            Dim itemA As String = "item A"
            Dim itemB As String = "item B"
```

```
            Cache.Insert("itemA", itemA, Nothing, DateTime.Now.AddMinutes(60),
               TimeSpan.Zero, CacheItemPriority.Default,
                AddressOf ItemRemovedCallback)
            Cache.Insert("itemB", itemB, Nothing, DateTime.Now.AddMinutes(60),
                TimeSpan.Zero, CacheItemPriority.Default,
                AddressOf ItemRemovedCallback)
        End If
    End Sub

    Protected Sub cmdCheck_Click(ByVal sender As Object,
                ByVal e As System.EventArgs)
        Dim itemList As String = String.Empty
        For Each item As DictionaryEntry In Cache
            itemList &= item.Key.ToString() & " "
        Next item
        lblInfo.Text &= "<br />Found: " & itemList & "<br />"
    End Sub

    Protected Sub cmdRemove_Click(ByVal sender As Object,
                ByVal e As System.EventArgs)
        lblInfo.Text &= "<br />Removing itemA.<br />"
        Cache.Remove("itemA")
    End Sub

    Private Sub ItemRemovedCallback(ByVal key As String, ByVal value As Object,
              ByVal reason As CacheItemRemovedReason)
        ' This fires after the request has ended, when the
        ' item is removed.

        ' If either item has been removed, make sure
        ' the other item is also removed.
        If key = "itemA" OrElse key = "itemB" Then
            Cache.Remove("itemA")
            Cache.Remove("itemB")
        End If
    End Sub
End Class
```

Figure 11-6 shows a test of this page.

The callback also provides your code with additional information, including the removed item and the reason it was removed. Table 11-4 shows possible reasons.

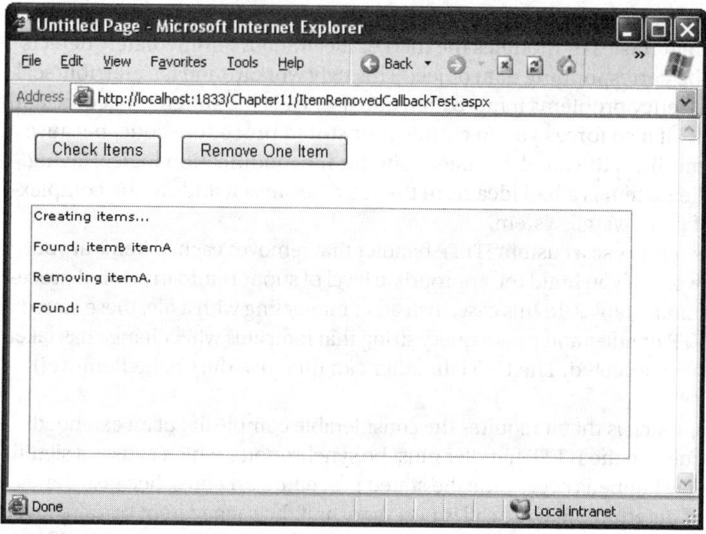

Figure 11-6. *Testing a cache callback*

Table 11-4. *Values for the CacheItemRemovedReason Enumeration*

Value	Description
DependencyChanged	Removed because a file or key dependency changed
Expired	Removed because it expired (according to its sliding or absolute expiration policy)
Removed	Removed programmatically by a Remove method call or by an Insert method call that specified the same key
Underused	Removed because ASP.NET decided it wasn't important enough and wanted to free memory

Understanding SQL Cache Notifications

SQL cache dependencies are one of the most widely touted new ASP.NET 2.0 features—the ability to automatically invalidate a cached data object (such as a DataSet) when the related data is modified in the database. This feature is supported in both SQL Server 2005 and in SQL Server 2000, although the underlying plumbing is quite a bit different.

To understand how SQL cache dependencies work, it's important to understand a few flawed solutions that developers have been forced to resort to in the past.

One common technique is to use a marker file. With this technique, you add the data object to the cache and set up a file dependency. However, the file you use is empty—it's just a marker file that's intended to indicate when the database state changes.

Here's how it works. When the user calls a stored procedure that modifies the table you're interested in, your stored procedure removes or modifies the marker file. ASP.NET immediately detects the file change and removes the corresponding data object. This ugly workaround isn't terribly scalable and can introduce concurrency problems if more than one user calls the stored procedure and tries to remove the file at once. It also forces you to clutter your stored procedure code, because every stored procedure that modifies the database needs similar file modification logic. Having a database interact with the file system is a bad idea from the start, because it adds to the complexity and reduces the security of your overall system.

Another common approach is to use a custom HTTP handler that removes cached items at your request. Once again, this only works if you build the appropriate level of support into the stored procedures that modify the corresponding tables. In this case, instead of interacting with a file, these stored procedures call the custom HTTP handler and pass a query string that indicates what change has taken place or what cache key has been affected. The HTTP handler can then use the Cache.Remove() method to get rid of the data.

The problem with this approach is that it requires the considerable complexity of an extended stored procedure. Also, the request to the HTTP handler must be synchronous, which causes a significant delay. Even worse, this delay happens every time the stored procedure executes, because the stored procedure has no way of determining if the call is necessary or if the cached item has already been removed. As a result, the overall time taken to execute the stored procedure increases significantly, and the overall scalability of the database suffers. Like the marker file approach, it works well in small scenarios but can't handle large-scale, complex applications. Both of these approaches introduce a whole other set of complications in web farm scenarios with multiple servers.

What's needed is an approach that can deliver notifications asynchronously, and in a scalable and reliable fashion. In other words, the database server should notify ASP.NET without stalling the current connection. Just as importantly, it should be possible to set up the cache dependency in a loosely coupled way so that stored procedures don't need to be aware of the caching that's in place. The database server should watch for changes that are committed by any means, including from a script, an inline SQL command, or a batch process. Even if the change doesn't go through the expected stored procedures, the change should still be noticed, and the notification should still be delivered to ASP.NET. Finally, the notification method needs to support web farms.

Microsoft put together a team of architects from the ASP.NET, SQL Server, ADO.NET, and IIS groups to concoct a solution. They came up with two different architectures, depending on the database server you're using. Both of them use the same SqlCacheDependency class, which derives from the CacheDependency class you saw earlier.

■ **Tip** Using SQL cache dependencies still entails more complexity than just using a time-based expiration policy. If it's acceptable for certain information to be used without reflecting all the most recent changes (and developers often overestimate the importance of up-to-the-millisecond live information), you may not need it at all.

Cache Notifications in SQL Server 2000 or SQL Server 7

ASP.NET uses a polling model for SQL Server 2000 and SQL Server 7. Older versions of SQL Server and other databases aren't supported (although third parties can implement their own solutions by creating a custom dependency class).

With the polling model, ASP.NET keeps a connection open to the database and uses a dedicated thread to check periodically if a table has been updated. The effect of tying up one connection in this way isn't terribly significant, but the extra database work involved with polling does add some database overhead. For the polling model to be effective, the polling process needs to be quicker and lighter than the original query that extracts the data.

Enabling Notifications

Before you can use SQL Server cache invalidation, you need to enable notifications for the database. This task is performed with the aspnet_regsql.exe command-line utility, which is located in the c:\[WinDir]\Microsoft.NET\Framework\[Version] directory. To enable notifications, you need to use the -ed command-line switch. You also need to identify the server (use -E for a trusted connection and -S to choose a server other than the current computer) and the database (use -d). Here's an example that enables notifications for the Northwind database on the current server:

```
aspnet_regsql -ed -E -d AspNet
```

■ Tip You'll see aspnet_regsql used throughout this book. It's required to create the tables for other new ASP.NET 2.0 features such as membership, profiles, and role management.

When you take this step, a new table named SqlCacheTablesForChangeNotification is added to the database named AspNet (which must already exist). The SqlCacheTablesForChangeNotification table has three columns: tableName, notificationCreated, and changeId. This table is used to track changes. Essentially, when a change takes place, a record is written into this table. The SQL Server polling queries this table.

This design achieves a number of benefits:

- Because the change notification table is much smaller than the table with the cached data, it's much faster to query.
- Because the change notification table isn't used for other tasks, reading these records won't risk locking and concurrency issues.
- Because multiple tables in the same database will use the same notification table, you can monitor several tables at once without materially increasing the polling overhead.

Figure 11-7 shows an overview of how SQL Server 2000 cache invalidation works.

The aspnet_regsql utility adds several stored procedures to the database, as listed in Table 11-5.

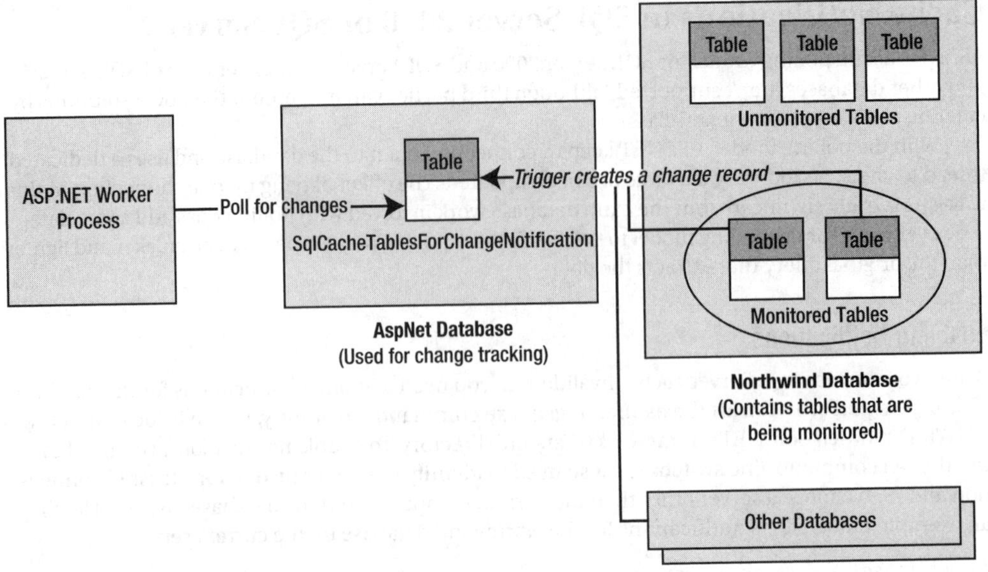

Figure 11-7. *Monitoring a database for changes in SQL Server 2000*

Table 11-5. *Stored Procedures for Managing Notifications*

Name	Description
AspNet_SqlCachePollingStoredProcedure	Gets the list of changes from the AspNet_SqlCacheTablesForChange➥Notification table. You can use this to perform the polling.
AspNet_SqlCacheQueryRegisteredTablesStoredProcedure	Extracts just the table names from the AspNet_SqlCacheTablesForChange➥Notification table. You can use this to get a quick look at all the registered tables.
AspNet_SqlCacheRegisterTableStoredProcedure	Sets a table up to support notifications. This process works by adding a notification trigger to the table, which will fire when any row is inserted, deleted, or updated.
AspNet_SqlCacheUnRegisterTableStoredProcedure	Takes a registered table and removes notification trigger so that notifications won't be generated.
AspNet_SqlCacheUpdateChangeIdStoredProcedure	The notification trigger calls this stored procedure to update the AspNet_SqlCacheTablesForChange➥Notification, thereby indicating that the table has changed.

Even once you've created the SqlCacheTablesForChangeNotification table, you still need to enable notification support for each individual table. You can do this manually using the SqlCacheRegisterTableStoredProcedure, or you can rely on aspnet_regsql, using the -et parameter to turn on the notifications and the -t parameter to name the table. Here's an example that enables notifications for the Employees table:

```
aspnet_regsql -et -E -d Northwind -t Employees
```

This step generates the notification trigger for the Employees table.

How Notifications Work

Now you have all the ingredients in place to use the notification system. For example, imagine you cache the results of a query like this:

```
SELECT * FROM Employees
```

This query retrieves records from the Employees table. To check for changes that might invalidate your cached object, you need to know if any record in the Employees table is inserted, deleted, or updated. You can watch for these operations using triggers. For example, here's the trigger on the Employees table that aspnet_regsql creates:

```
CREATE TRIGGER dbo.[Employees_AspNet_SqlCacheNotification_Trigger]
  ON [Employees]
  FOR INSERT, UPDATE, DELETE AS BEGIN

  SET NOCOUNT ON
  EXEC dbo.AspNet_SqlCacheUpdateChangeIdStoredProcedure N'Employees'
END
```

The AspNet_SqlCacheUpdateChangeIdStoredProcedure stored procedure simply increments the changeId for the table:

```
CREATE PROCEDURE dbo.AspNet_SqlCacheUpdateChangeIdStoredProcedure
  @tableName NVARCHAR(450)
AS

  BEGIN
  UPDATE dbo.AspNet_SqlCacheTablesForChangeNotification WITH (ROWLOCK)
    SET changeId = changeId + 1
    WHERE tableName = @tableName
  END
GO
```

The AspNet_SqlCacheTablesForChangeNotification contains a single record for every table you're monitoring. As you can see, when you make a change in the table (such as inserting a record), the changeId column is incremented by 1. ASP.NET queries this table repeatedly and keeps track of the most recent changeId values for every table. When this value changes in a subsequent read, ASP.NET knows that the table has changed.

This hints at one of the major limitations of cache invalidation as implemented in SQL Server 2000 and SQL Server 7. *Any* change to the table is deemed to invalidate *any* query for that table. In other words, if you use this query:

```
SELECT * FROM Employees WHERE City='London'
```

The caching still works in the same way. That means if any employee record is touched, even if the employee resides in another city (and therefore isn't one of the cached records), the notification is still sent and the cached item is considered invalid. Keeping track of what changes do and do not invalidate a cached data object is simply too much work for SQL Server 2000 (although it is possible in SQL Server 2005).

■Tip The implementation of cache invalidation with SQL Server 2000 has more overhead than the implementation with SQL Server 2005 and isn't as fine-grained. As a result, it doesn't make sense for tables that change frequently or for narrowly defined queries that retrieve only a small subset of records from a table.

Enabling ASP.NET Polling

The next step is to instruct ASP.NET to poll the database. You do this on a per-application basis. In other words, every application that uses cache invalidation will hold a separate connection and poll the notification table on its own.

To enable the polling service, you use the <sqlCacheDepency> element in the web.config file. You set the enabled attribute to True to turn it on, and you set the pollTime attribute to the number of milliseconds between each poll. (The higher the poll time, the longer the potential delay before a change is detected.) You also need to supply the connection string information.

For example, this web.config file checks for updated notification information every 15 seconds:

```
<configuration xmlns="http://schemas.microsoft.com/.NetConfiguration/v2.0">
  <connectionStrings>
    <add name="Northwind" connectionString=
"Data Source=localhost;Initial Catalog=Northwind;Integrated Security=SSPI"/>
  </connectionStrings>

  <system.web>
    <caching>
      <sqlCacheDependency enabled="True" pollTime="15000" >
        <databases>
          <add name="Northwind" connectionStringName="Northwind" />
        </databases>
      </sqlCacheDependency>
    </caching>
    ...
  </system.web>
</configuration>
```

Creating the Cache Dependency

Now that you've seen how to set up your database to support SQL Server notifications, the only remaining detail is the code, which is quite straightforward. You can use your cache dependency with programmatic data caching, a data source control, and output caching.

For programmatic data caching, you need to create a new SqlCacheDependency and supply that to the Cache.Insert() method, much as you did with file dependencies. In the SqlCacheDependency constructor, you supply two strings. The first is the name of the database you defined in the <add> element in the <sqlCacheDependency> section of the web.config file. The second is the name of the linked table.

Here's an example:

```
' Create a dependency for the Employees table.
Dim empDependency As New SqlCacheDependency("Northwind", "Employees")

' Add a cache item that will be invalidated if this table changes.
Cache.Insert("Employees", dsEmployees, empDependency)
```

To perform the same trick with output caching, you simply need to set the SqlCacheDependency property with the database dependency name and the table name, separated by a colon:

```
<%@ OutputCache Duration="600" SqlDependency="Northwind:Employees"
    VaryByParam="none" %>
```

You can also set the dependency using programmatic output caching with the Response.AddCacheDependency() method:

```
Response.AddCacheDependency(empDependency)

' Use output caching for this page (for 60 seconds or until the table changes).
Response.Cache.SetCacheability(HttpCacheability.Public)
Response.Cache.SetExpires(DateTime.Now.AddSeconds(60))
Response.Cache.SetValidUntilExpires(True)
```

Finally, the same technique works with the SqlDataSource and ObjectDataSource controls:

```
<asp:SqlDataSource EnableCaching="True"
 SqlCacheDependency="Northwind:Employees" ... />
```

To try a complete example, you can use the downloadable code for this chapter.

Cache Notifications in SQL Server 2005

SQL Server 2005 gets closest to the ideal notification solution, because the notification infrastructure is built into the database with a messaging system called *Service Broker*. The Service Broker manages *queues*, which are database objects that have the same standing as tables, stored procedures, or views.

Essentially, you can instruct SQL Server 2005 to send notifications for specific events using the CREATE EVENT NOTIFICATION command. ASP.NET offers a higher-level model—you register a query, and ASP.NET automatically instructs SQL Server 2005 to send notifications for any operations that would affect the results of that query. This mechanism works in a similar way to indexed views. Every time you perform an operation, SQL Server determines whether your operation affects a registered command. If it does, SQL Server sends a notification message and stops the notification process.

When using notification with SQL Server, you get the following benefits over SQL Server 2000:

Notification is much more fine-grained: Instead of invalidating your cached object when the table changes, SQL Server 2005 invalidates your object only when a row that affects your query is inserted, updated, or deleted.

Notification is more intelligent: A notification message is sent when the first time the data is changed, but not if the data is changed again (unless you re-register for notification messages by adding an item back to the cache).

No special steps are required to set up notification: You do not run aspnet_regsql or add polling settings to the web.config file.

Notifications work with SELECT queries and stored procedures. However, some restrictions exist for the SELECT syntax you can use. To properly support notifications, your command must adhere to the following rules:

- You must fully qualify table names in the form [Owner].table, as in dbo.Northind.Employees (not just Employees).
- Your query cannot use an aggregate function, such as COUNT(), MAX(), MIN(), or AVERAGE().
- You cannot select all columns with the wildcard * (as in SELECT * FROM Employees). Instead, you must specifically name each column so that SQL Server can properly track changes that do and do not affect the results of your query.

Here's an acceptable command:

```
SELECT EmployeeID, FirstName, LastName, City FROM Northwind.dbo.Employees
```

These are the most important rules, but the SQL Server Books Online has a lengthy list of caveats and exceptions. If you break one of these rules, you won't receive an error. However, the notification message will be sent as soon as you register the command, and the cached item will be invalidated immediately.

Creating the Cache Dependency

You use a different syntax to use SQL cache dependencies with SQL Server 2005. That's because it's not enough to simply identify the database name and table—instead, SQL Server needs to know the exact command.

If you use programmatic caching, you must create the SqlCacheDependency using the constructor that accepts a SqlCommand object. Here's an example:

```
' Create the ADO.NET objects.
Dim con As SqlConnection =
      WebConfigurationManager.ConnectionStrings("Northwind").ConnectionString
Dim query As String =
      "SELECT EmployeeID, FirstName, LastName, City FROM Northwind.dbo.Employees"
Dim cmd As New SqlCommand(query, con)
Dim adapter As New SqlDataAdapter(cmd)

' Fill the DataSet.
Dim ds As New DataSet()
adapter.Fill(ds, "Employees")

' Create the dependency.
Dim empDependency As New SqlCacheDependency(cmd)

' Add a cache item that will be invalidated if one of its records changes
' (or a new record is added in the same range).
Cache.Insert("Employees", ds, empDependency)
```

If you're using the OutputCache directive or a data source control, ASP.NET takes care of the registration for you. You simply need to supply the string value CommandNotification, as shown here:

```
<%@ OutputCache Duration="600" SqlDependency="CommandNotification"
   VaryByParam="none" %>
```

Custom Cache Dependencies

ASP.NET gives you the ability to create your own custom cache dependencies by deriving from CacheDependency, in much the same way that SqlCacheDependency does. This feature allows you (or third-party developers) to create dependencies that wrap other databases or to create resources such as message queues, Active Directory queries, or even web service calls.

Designing a custom CacheDependency is remarkably easy. All you need to do is start some asynchronous task that checks when the dependent item has changed. When it has, you call the base CacheDependency.NotifyDependencyChanged() method. In response, the base class updates the values of the HasChanged and UtcLastModified properties, and ASP.NET will remove any linked item from the cache.

You can use one of several techniques to create a custom cache dependency. Here are some typical examples:

Start a timer: When this timer fires, poll your resource to see if it has changed.

Start a separate thread: On this thread, check your resource and, if necessary, pause between checks by sleeping the thread.

Attach an event handler to another component: When the event fires, check your resource. For example, you could use this technique with the FileSystemWatcher to watch for a specific type of file change (such as file deletion).

In every case, you perform the basic initialization (attaching event handlers, creating a separate thread, and so on) in the constructor for your dependency.

A Basic Custom Cache Dependency

The following example shows an exceedingly simple custom cache dependency class. This class uses a timer to periodically check if a cached item is still valid.

The first step is to create the class by deriving from CacheDependency:

```
Public Class TimerTestCacheDependency
    Inherits CacheDependency
    ...
End Class
```

When the dependency is first created, you can set up the timer. In this example, the polling time isn't configurable—it's hard-coded at 5 seconds. That means every 5 seconds the timer fires and the dependency check runs.

```
Private timer As Timer
Private pollTime As Integer = 5000

Public Sub New()
    ' Check immediately, and then wait the poll time
    ' for each subsequent check (same as CacheDependency behavior).
    timer = New Timer( AddressOf CheckDependencyCallback, Me, 0, pollTime)
End Sub
```

As a test, the dependency check simply counts the number of times it's called. Once it's called for the fifth time (after a total of about 25 seconds), it invalidates the cached item. The important part of this example is how it tells ASP.NET to remove the dependent item. All you need to do is call the base CacheDependency.NotifyDependencyChanged() method, passing in a reference to the event sender (the current class) and any event arguments.

```
Private count As Integer = 0

Private Sub CheckDependencyCallback(ByVal sender As Object)
    ' Check your resource here. If it has changed, notify ASP.NET:
    count += 1
    If count > 4 Then
        ' Signal that the item is expired.
        MyBase.NotifyDependencyChanged(Me, EventArgs.Empty)

        ' Don't fire this callback again.
        timer.Dispose()
    End If
End Sub
```

The last step is to override DependencyDispose() to perform any cleanup that you need. DependencyDispose() is called soon after you use the NotifyDependencyChanged() method to invalidate the cached item. At this point, the dependency is no longer needed.

```
Protected Overrides Sub DependencyDispose()
    ' Cleanup code goes here.
    If timer IsNot Nothing Then
        timer.Dispose()
    End If
End Sub
```

Once you've created a custom dependency class, you can use it in the same was as the CacheDependency class, by supplying it as a parameter when you call Cache.Insert():

```
Dim dependency As New TimerTestCacheDependency()
Cache.Insert("MyItem", item, dependency)
```

A Custom Cache Dependency Using Message Queues

Now that you've seen how to create a basic custom cache dependency, it's worth considering a more practical example. The following MessageQueueCacheDependency monitors a Windows Messaging Queuing (formerly known as MSMQ) queue. As soon as that queue receives a message, the item is considered expired (although you could easily extend the class so that it waits to receive a specific message). The MessageQueueCacheDependency class could come in handy if you're building the backbone of a distributed system and you need to pass messages between components on different computers to notify them when certain actions are performed or changes are made.

Before you can create the MessageQueueCacheDependency, you need to add a reference to the System.Messaging.dll and import the System.Messaging namespace where the MessageQueue and Message classes reside. Then you're ready to build the solution.

In this example, the MessageQueueCacheDependency is able to monitor any queue. When you instantiate the dependency, you supply the queue name (which includes the location information). To perform the monitoring, the MessageQueueCacheDependency fires its private WaitForMessage() method asynchronously. This method waits until a new message is received in the queue, at which point it calls NotifyDependencyChanged() to invalidate the cached item.

Here's the complete code for the MessageQueueCacheDependency:

```
Public Class MessageQueueCacheDependency
    Inherits CacheDependency

    ' The queue to monitor.
    Private queue As MessageQueue

    Public Sub New(ByVal queueName As String)
        queue = New MessageQueue(queueName)

        ' Wait for the queue message on another thread.
        ThreadPool.QueueUserWorkItem(AddressOf WaitForMessage)
    End Sub

    Private Sub WaitForMessage(ByVal state As Object)
        ' Check your resource here (the polling).
        ' This blocks until a message is sent to the queue.
        Dim msg As Message = queue.Receive()
        ' (If you're looking for something specific, you could
        '  perform a loop and check the Message object here
        '  before invalidating the cached item.)
        MyBase.NotifyDependencyChanged(Me, EventArgs.Empty)
    End Sub
End Class
```

To test this, you can use a revised version of the file-dependency testing page shown earlier (see Figure 11-8).

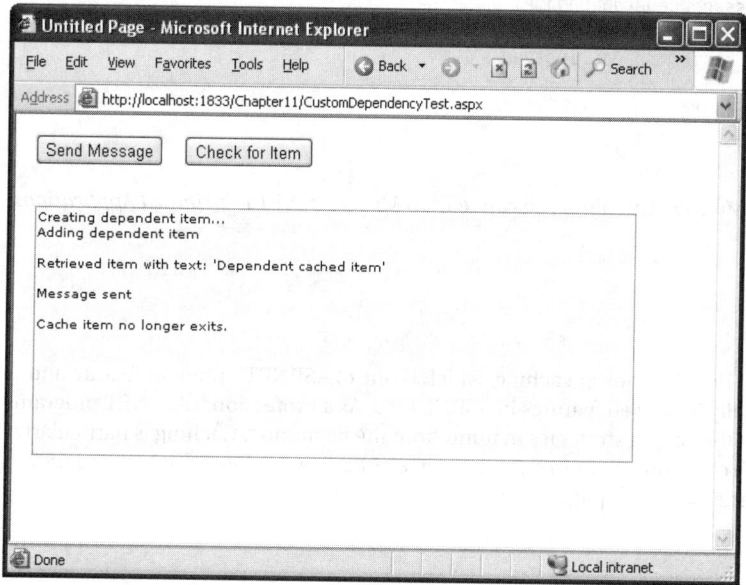

Figure 11-8. *Testing a message queue dependency*

This page creates a new private cache on the current computer and then adds a new item to the cache with a dependency on that queue:

```
Dim queueName As String = ".\Private$\TestQueue"
' The leading . represents the current computer.
' The following Private$ indicates it's a private queue for this computer.
' The TestQueue is the queue name (you can modify this part).

Protected Sub Page_Load(ByVal sender As Object, ByVal e As EventArgs)
    If (Not Me.IsPostBack) Then
        ' Set up the queue.
        Dim queue As MessageQueue
        If MessageQueue.Exists(queueName) Then
            queue = New MessageQueue(queueName)
        Else
            queue = MessageQueue.Create(".\Private$\TestQueue")
        End If

        lblInfo.Text &= "Creating dependent item...<br />"
        Cache.Remove("Item")
        Dim dependency As New MessageQueueCacheDependency(queueName)
        Dim item As String = "Dependent cached item"
        lblInfo.Text &= "Adding dependent item<br />"
        Cache.Insert("Item", item, dependency)
    End If
End Sub
```

When you click Send Message, a simple text message is sent to the queue, which will be received almost instantaneously by the custom dependency class:

```
Protected Sub cmdModify_Click(ByVal sender As Object, ByVal e As EventArgs)
    Dim queue As New MessageQueue(queueName)

    ' (You could send a custom object instead
    '  of a string.)
    queue.Send("Invalidate!")
    lblInfo.Text &= "Message sent<br />"
End Sub
```

To learn more about Message Queuing, you can refer to *Microsoft .NET Distributed Applications* (Microsoft Press, 2003).

Summary

In this chapter, you took a detailed look at caching, which is one of ASP.NET's premier feature and one of the most dramatically improved features in ASP.NET 2.0. As a professional ASP.NET programmer, you should design with caching strategies in mind from the beginning. Caching is particularly important when using the data source controls, which can exert a sizeable footprint because they repeat their database queries for every page request.

CHAPTER 12

■ ■ ■

XML

Ever since XML (Extensible Markup Language) first arrived on the scene in the late 1990s, it has been the focus of intense activity and overenthusiastic speculation. Based on nothing but ordinary text, XML offers a means of sharing data between just about any two applications, whether they're new or old, written in different languages, built by distinct companies, or even hosted on different operating systems. Now that XML has come of age, it's being steadily integrated into different applications, problem domains, and industries.

Microsoft's .NET Framework uses XML heavily and gives ASP.NET applications a rich set of features for using and manipulating XML data. In this chapter, you'll learn how to work with XML in streams and strings. Additionally, you'll look at the new XML data binding features in .NET 2.0. XML data binding works analogously to data binding with the SqlDataSource and ObjectDataSource controls. It lets you extract XML content from a file and show that data in a bound control, all without requiring you to write a single line of code.

XML CHANGES IN .NET 2.0

.NET 2.0 refines its XML classes but keeps the overall model almost the same. At one point, early in the beta cycle, there were more ambitious plans to make XPathNavigator the new standard for editing XML and to outfit it with a high-powered set of editing features. However, the cost of forcing developers to rework their code was considered too great.

ASP.NET 2.0 does have one innovation when it comes to XML—the new XmlDataSource control. With this control, you can bind to XML data sources just as easily as you bind to databases and data objects. However, this has a few limitations. For example, the XmlDataSource is best suited to XML content in a file, and it doesn't support two-way binding. For those reasons, you'll still need to use the XML classes in .NET in many scenarios.

The XmlDataSource control is described in the "XML Data Binding" section later in this chapter.

When Does Using XML Make Sense?

The question that every new ASP.NET developer asks (and many XML proponents don't answer) is, when does it make sense to use XML in an ASP.NET web application? It makes sense in a few core scenarios:

- You need to manipulate data that's already stored in XML. This situation might occur if you want to exchange data with an existing application that uses a specific flavor of XML.
- You want to use XML to store your data and open the possibilities of future integration. Because you use XML, you know other third-party applications can be designed to read this data in the future.
- You want to use a technology that depends on XML. For example, web services (discussed in Part 6) use various standards that are all based on XML.

Many ASP.NET features use XML behind the scenes. For example, web services use a higher-level model that's built on top of the XML infrastructure. You don't need to directly manipulate XML to use web services—instead, you can work through an abstraction of objects. Similarly, you don't need to manipulate XML to read information from ASP.NET configuration files, use the DataSet, or rely on other .NET Framework features that have XML underpinnings. In all these situations, XML is quietly at work, and you gain the benefits of XML without needing to deal with it by hand.

XML makes the most sense in *application integration* scenarios. However, there's no reason you can't use an XML format to store your own proprietary data. If you do, you'll gain a few minor conveniences, such as the ability to use .NET classes to read XML data from a file. When storing complex, highly structured data, the convenience of using these classes rather than designing your own custom format and writing your own file-parsing logic is significant. It will also make it easier for other developers to understand the system you've created and to reuse or enhance your work.

■ **Note** One of the most important concepts developers must understand is that there are two decisions when storing data—choosing the way data will be structured (the logical format) and choosing the way data will be stored (the physical data store). XML is a choice of format, not a choice of storage. This means if you decide to store data in an XML format, you still need to decide whether that XML will be inserted into a database field, inserted into a file, or just kept in memory in a string or some other type of object. It should also be noted that SQL Server 2005, Oracle 10g and some other databases have extensive native support for storing XML data and querying it within the database.

An Introduction to XML

In its simplest form, the XML specification is a set of guidelines, defined by the W3C (World Wide Web Consortium), for describing structured data in plain text. Like HTML, XML is a markup language based on tags within angled brackets. As with HTML, the textual nature of XML makes the data highly portable and broadly deployable. In addition, you can create and edit XML documents in any standard text editor.

Unlike HTML, XML does not have a fixed set of tags. Instead, XML is a *metalanguage* that allows for the creation of *other* markup languages. In other words, XML sets out a few simple rules for naming and ordering elements, and you create your own data format with your own custom elements.

For example, the following document shows a custom XML format that stores a product catalog. It starts with some generic product catalog information, followed by a product list with itemized information about two products.

```
<?xml version="1.0" ?>
<productCatalog>
    <catalogName>Acme Fall 2003 Catalog</catalogName>
```

```
    <expiryDate>2005-01-01</expiryDate>
    <products>
        <product id="1001">
            <productName>Magic Ring</productName>
            <productPrice>342.10</productPrice>
        </product>
        <product id="1002">
            <productName>Flying Carpet</productName>
            <productPrice>982.99</productPrice>
        </product>
    </products>
</productCatalog>
```

This example uses elements such as <productCatalog>, <product>, and <catalogName> to indicate the document structure. However, you're free to use whatever element names describe your data best.

It's because of this flexibility that XML has become extremely successful. Of course, flexibility also has drawbacks. Because XML doesn't define any standard data formats, it's up to you to create data formats that represent product catalogs, invoices, customer lists, and so on. Different companies can easily store similar data using completely different tag names and structures. And even though any application can parse XML data, the writer and the reader of that data still need to agree on a common set of tags and structure in order for the reader to be able to *interpret* that data and extract meaningful information.

Usually, third-party organizations define standards for particular problem domains and industries. For example, if you need to store a mathematical equation in XML, you'll probably choose the MathML format, which is an XML-based format that defines a specific set of tags and a specific structure. Similarly, hundreds more standard XML formats exist for real estate listings, music notation, legal documents, patient records, vector graphics, and much more. Creating a robust, usable XML format takes some experience, so it's always best to use a standardized, agreed-upon, XML-based markup language when possible.

The Advantages of XML

When XML was first introduced, its success was partly due to its simplicity. The rules of XML are much shorter and simpler than the rules of its predecessor, SGML (Standard Generalized Markup Language), and simple XML documents are human-readable. However, in the intervening years many other supporting standards have been added to the XML mix, and as a result, using XML in a professional application isn't simple at all.

■ **Note** Although XML is human-readable in theory, it's often difficult to understand complex documents, and only computer applications, not developers, can read many types of XML.

But if anything, XML is much more useful today than it ever was before. The benefits of using XML in a modern application include the following:

Adoption: XML is ubiquitous. Many companies are using XML to store and exchange data or are actively considering it. Whenever data needs to be shared, XML is automatically the first (and often the only) choice that's examined.

Extensibility and flexibility: XML imposes no rules about data semantics and does not tie companies into proprietary networks, unlike EDI (Electronic Data Interchange). As a result, XML can fit any type of data and is cheaper to implement.

Related standards and tools: Another reason for XML's success is the tools (such as parsers) and the surrounding standards (such as XML Schema, XPath, DOM and XSLT) that help in creating and processing XML documents. As a result, programmers in nearly any language have ready-made components for reading XML, verifying that XML is valid, verifying XML against a set of rules (known as a *schema*), searching XML, and transforming one format of XML into another.

XML acts like the glue that allows different systems to work together. It helps standardize business processes and transactions between organizations. But XML is not just suited for data exchange between companies. Many programming tasks today are all about *application* integration—web applications integrate multiple web services, e-commerce sites integrate legacy inventory and pricing systems, and intranet applications integrate existing business applications. All these applications are held together by the exchange of XML documents.

Well-Formed XML

XML is a fairly strict standard. This strictness is designed to preserve broad compatibility. HTML, on the other hand, is much more lenient. As a result, it's quite possible to create an HTML web page with errors (such as mismatched end tags) that will be successfully rendered in one browser but interpreted differently in another. When it comes to storing business data, this type of error could cause catastrophic problems.

To prevent this sort of problem, all XML parsers perform a few basic quality checks. If an XML document does not meet these standards, it's rejected outright. If the XML document does follow these rules, it's deemed to be *well formed.* Well-formed XML isn't necessarily correct XML—for example, it could still contain incorrect data—but an XML processor can parse it.

To be considered well formed, an XML document must meet these criteria:

- Every start tag must have an end tag.
- An empty element must end with />, or </elementname> (i.e. <X></X>).
- Elements can never overlap. In other words, <person><firstName></firstName></person> is valid, but <person><firstName></person></firstName> is not.
- A document can have only one root element.
- All attributes must have quotes around the value. These can be a single (') or a double (") quote.
- The document must not contain illegal characters.
- An element cannot contain two attributes with the same name.
- Comments and processing instructions can't be placed inside tags.

■ **Tip** To quickly test if an XML document is well formed, try opening it in Internet Explorer. If there is an error, Internet Explorer will report a message and flag the offending line.

XML Namespaces

As the XML standard gained ground, dozens of XML markup languages (often called *XML grammars*) were created, and many of them are specific to certain industries, processes, and types of information. In many cases, it becomes important to extend one type of markup with additional company-specific elements, or even create XML documents that combine several different XML grammars. This poses a problem. What happens if you need to combine two XML grammars that use elements with the same names? How do you tell them apart? A related, but more typical, problem occurs when an application needs to distinguish between XML grammars in a document. For example, consider an XML document that has order-specific information using a standard called OrderML and client-specific information using a standard called ClientML. This document is sent to an order-fulfillment application that's interested only in the OrderML details. How can it quickly filter out the information that it needs and ignore the unrelated details?

The solution is the XML Namespaces standard. The core idea behind this standard is that every XML markup language has its own namespace that uniquely identifies all related elements. Technically, namespaces *disambiguate* elements by making it clear to which markup language they belong.

All XML namespaces use URIs (universal resource identifiers). Typically, these URIs look like a web-page URL. For example, `http://www.mycompany.com/mystandard` is a typical name for a namespace. Though the namespace looks like it points to a valid location on the Web, this isn't required (and shouldn't be assumed). URIs are used for XML namespaces because they are more likely to be unique. Usually, if you create a new XML language, you'll use a URI that points to a domain or website you control. That way, you can be sure that no one else is likely to use that URI. However, the namespace doesn't need to be a URI—any sequence of text is acceptable. Two common alternatives are URNs and GUIDs.

Tip Namespace names must match exactly. If you change the capitalization in part of a namespace, add a trailing / character, or modify any other detail, the XML parser will interpret it as a different namespace.

To specify that an element belongs to a specific namespace, you simply need to add the xmlns attribute to the start tag and indicate the namespace. For example, the element shown here is part of the `http://mycompany/OrderML` namespace. If you don't take this step, the element will not be part of any namespace.

```
<order xmlns="http://mycompany/OrderML"></order>
```

It would be cumbersome if you needed to type in the full namespace URI every time you wrote an element in an XML document. Fortunately, when you assign a namespace in this fashion, it becomes the default namespace for all child elements. For example, in the XML document shown here, the <order> and <orderItem> elements are both placed in the `http://mycompany/OrderML` namespace:

```
<?xml version="1.0"?>
<order xmlns="http://mycompany/OrderML">
    <orderItem>...</orderItem>
    <orderItem>...</orderItem>
</order>
```

You can declare a new namespace for separate portions of the document. The easiest way to deal with this is to use *namespace prefixes*. Namespace prefixes are short character sequences that you can insert in front of a tag name to indicate its namespace. You define the prefix in the xmlns attribute by inserting a colon (:) followed by the characters you want to use for the prefix.

Here's an order document that uses namespace prefixes to map different elements into two different namespaces:

```
<?xml version="1.0"?>
<ord:order xmlns:ord="http://mycompany/OrderML"
 xmlns:cli="http://mycompany/ClientML">
   <cli:client>
       <cli:firstName>...</cli:firstName>
       <cli:lastName>...</cli:lastName>
   </cli:client>
```

```
    <ord:orderItem>...</ord:orderItem>
    <ord:orderItem>...</ord:orderItem>
</ord:order>
```

Namespace prefixes are simply used to map an element to a namespace. The actual prefix you use isn't important as long as it remains consistent.

XML Schemas

A good part of the success of the XML standard is due to its remarkable flexibility. Using XML, you can create exactly the markup language you need. This flexibility also raises a few problems. With developers around the world using your XML format, how do you ensure that everyone is following the rules?

The solution is to create a formal document that states the rules of your custom markup language, which is called a *schema*. These rules won't include syntactical details (such as the requirement to use angle brackets or properly nest tags) because these requirements are already part of the basic XML standard. Instead, the schema document will list the logical rules that pertain to your type of data. They include the following:

Document vocabulary: This determines what element and attribute names are used in your XML documents.

Document structure: This determines where tags can be placed and can include rules specifying that certain tags must be placed before, after, or inside others. You can also specify how many times an element can occur.

Supported data types: This allows you to specify whether data is ordinary text or must be able to be interpreted as numeric data, date information, and so on.

Allowed data ranges: This allows you to set constraints that restrict numbers to certain ranges or that allow only specific values.

The XML Schema standard defines the rules you need to follow when creating a schema document. The following is an XML schema that defines the rules for the product catalog document shown earlier:

```
<?xml version="1.0"?>
<xsd:schema xmlns:xsd="http://www.w3.org/2001/XMLSchema">
  <xsd:element name="productCatalog">
    <xsd:complexType>
      <xsd:sequence>
        <xsd:element name="catalogName" type="xsd:string"/>
        <xsd:element name="expiryDate" type="xsd:date"/>

        <xsd:element name="products">
          <xsd:complexType>
            <xsd:sequence>
              <xsd:element name="product"
               type="product" maxOccurs="unbounded" />
            </xsd:sequence>
          </xsd:complexType>
        </xsd:element>
      </xsd:sequence>
    </xsd:complexType>
  </xsd:element>

  <xsd:complexType name="product">
    <xsd:sequence>
```

```
            <xsd:element name="productName" type="xsd:string"/>
            <xsd:element name="productPrice" type="xsd:decimal"/>
            <xsd:element name="inStock" type="xsd:boolean"/>
        </xsd:sequence>
        <xsd:attribute name="id" type="xsd:integer"/>
    </xsd:complexType>
</xsd:schema>
```

Every schema document is an XML document that begins with a root <schema> element. Inside the <schema> element are two types of definitions—the <element> element, which defines the structure the target document must follow, and one or more <complexType> elements, which define smaller data structures that are used to define the document structure.

The <element> tag is really the heart of the schema, and it's the starting point for all validation. In this example, the <element> tag identifies that the product catalog must begin with a root element named <productCatalog>. Inside the <productCatalog> element is a sequence of three elements. The first, <catalogName>, contains ordinary text. The second, <expiryDate>, includes text that fits the rules for date representation, as set out in the schema standard. The final element, <products>, contains a list of <product> elements.

Each <product> element is a complex type, and the type is defined with the <complexType> element at the end of the schema document. This <product> complex type consists of a sequence of three elements with product information. The elements must store this information as text (<productName>), a decimal value (<productPrice>), and a Boolean value (<inStock>), respectively.

■ **Note** A full discussion of XML Schema is beyond the scope of this book. However, if you want to learn more, you can consider the excellent online tutorials at `http://www.w3schools.com/schema` or the standard itself at `http://www.w3.org/XML/Schema`.

Writing and Reading XML Programmatically

The .NET Framework allows you to manipulate XML data with a set of classes in the System.Xml namespace (and other namespaces that begin with System.Xml). These types fully support the XML DOM (Document Object Model) Level 2 Core, as defined by the W3C. It also adds classes and methods that make it easier to read and write XML documents; navigate through nodes, attributes, and elements; and query, transform, and manipulate XML data in various ways.

Writing XML Files

The .NET Framework provides two approaches for writing XML data to a file:

- You can use DOM techniques to build the document in memory using the XmlDocument class and write it to a file when you're finished by calling the Save() method. The XmlDocument represents XML using a tree of node objects.
- You can write the document directly to a stream using the XmlTextWriter. This outputs data as you write it, node by node.

The XmlDocument is a good choice if you need to perform other operations on XML content after you create it, such as searching it, transforming it, or validating it. It's also the only way to write an XML document in a nonlinear way, because it allows you to insert new nodes anywhere. However, the XmlTextWriter provides a much simpler and better performing model for writing directly to a file, because it doesn't store the whole document in memory at once.

Tip You can use both the XmlDocument and the XmlTextWriter to create XML data that isn't stored in a file. Both of these classes allow you to write information to any stream, and the XmlDocument allows you to retrieve the raw XML as string data. Using techniques such as these, you could build an XML document and then insert it into another storage location such as a text-based field in a database table.

The next web-page example shows how to use the XmlTextWriter to create a well-formed XML file. The first step is to create a private WriteXML() method that will handle the job. It begins by creating an XmlTextWriter object and passing the physical path of the file you want to create as a constructor argument.

```
Private Sub WriteXML()
    Dim xmlFile As String = Server.MapPath("DvdList.xml")
    Using writer As XmlTextWriter = XmlWriter.Create(xmlFile, Nothing)
    ...
```

The XmlTextWriter has properties such as Formatting and Indentation, which allow you to specify whether the XML data will be automatically indented with the typical hierarchical structure and to indicate the number of spaces to use as indentation. You can set these two properties as follows:

```
...
writer.Formatting = Formatting.Indented
writer.Indentation = 3
...
```

Tip Remember, in a datacentric XML document, whitespace is almost always ignored. But by adding indentation, you create a file that is easier for a human to read and interpret, so it can't hurt.

Now you're ready to start writing the file. The WriteStartDocument() method writes the XML declaration with version 1.0 (<?xml version="1.0"?>), as follows:

```
writer.WriteStartDocument()
```

The WriteComment() method writes a comment. You can use it to add a message with the date and time of creation:

```
writer.WriteComment("Created @ " & DateTime.Now.ToString())
```

Next, you need to write the real content—the elements, attributes, and so on. This example builds an XML document that represents a DVD list, with information such as the title, the director, the price, and a list of actors for each DVD. These records will be child elements of a parent <DvdList> element, which must be created first:

```
writer.WriteStartElement("DvdList")
```

Now you can create the child nodes. The following code opens a new <DVD> element:

```
writer.WriteStartElement("DVD")
```

Now the code writes two attributes, representing the ID and the related category. This information is added to the start tag of the <DVD> element.

```
...
writer.WriteAttributeString("ID", "1")
writer.WriteAttributeString("Category", "Science Fiction")
...
```

The next step is to add the elements with the information about the DVD inside the <DVD> element. These elements won't have child elements of their own, so you can write them and set their values more efficiently with a single call to the WriteElementString() method. WriteElementString() accepts two arguments: the element name and its value (always as string), as shown here:

```
...
 ' Write some simple elements.
writer.WriteElementString("Title", "The Matrix")
writer.WriteElementString("Director", "Larry Wachowski")
writer.WriteElementString("Price", "18.74")
...
```

Next is a child <Starring> element that lists one or more actors. Because this element contains other elements, you need to open it and keep it open with the WriteStartElement() method. Then you can add the contained child elements, as shown here:

```
...
writer.WriteStartElement("Starring")
writer.WriteElementString("Star", "Keanu Reeves")
writer.WriteElementString("Star", "Laurence Fishburne")
...
```

At this point the code has written all the data for the current DVD. The next step is to close all the opened tags, in reverse order. To do so, you just call the WriteEndElement() method once for each element you've opened. You don't need to specify the element name when you call WriteEndElement(). Instead, each time you call WriteEndElement() it will automatically write the closing tag for the last opened element.

```
...
' Close the <Starring> element.
writer.WriteEndElement()

' Close the <DVD> element.
writer.WriteEndElement()
...
```

Now let's create another <DVD> element using the same approach:

```
...
writer.WriteStartElement("DVD")

' Write a couple of attributes to the <DVD> element.
writer.WriteAttributeString("ID", "2")
writer.WriteAttributeString("Category", "Drama")

' Write some simple elements.
writer.WriteElementString("Title", "Forrest Gump")
writer.WriteElementString("Director", "Robert Zemeckis")
writer.WriteElementString("Price", "23.99")

' Open the <Starring> element.
writer.WriteStartElement("Starring")

' Write two elements.
writer.WriteElementString("Star", "Tom Hanks")
writer.WriteElementString("Star", "Robin Wright")

' Close the <Starring> element.
writer.WriteEndElement()
```

```
' Close the <DVD> element.
writer.WriteEndElement()
...
```

This is quite straightforward, isn't it? To complete the document, you simply need to close the <DvdList> item, with yet another call to WriteEndElement(). You can then close the XmlTextWriter, as shown here:

```
    ...
    writer.WriteEndElement()
    writer.Close()
End Sub
```

To try this code, call the WriteXML() procedure from the Page.Load event handler. It will generate an XML file named DvdList.xml in the current folder, as shown in Figure 12-1.

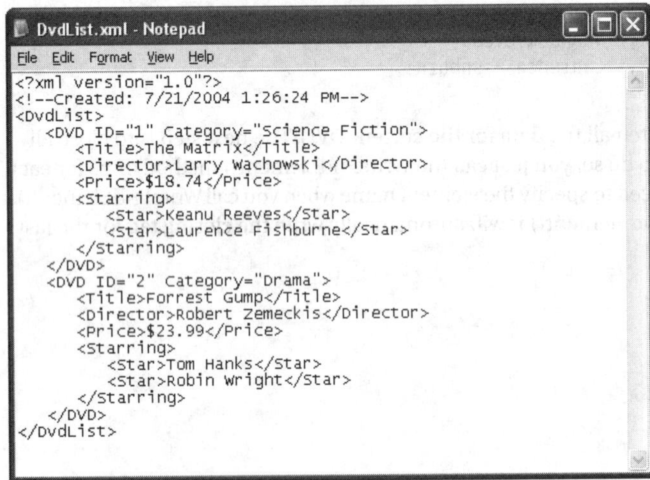

Figure 12-1. *A dynamically created XML document*

■Note Keep in mind that when you use the XmlTextWriter to create an XML file, you face all the limitations that you face when writing any other type of file in a web application. In other words, you need to take safeguards (such as generating unique filenames) to ensure that two different clients don't run the same code and try to write the same file at once. Chapter 13 has more information about file access and dealing with these types of problems.

Reading XML Files

The following are ways to read and navigate the content of an XML file:

> *Using XmlDocument*: You can load the document using the XmlDocument class mentioned earlier. This holds all the XML data in memory once you call Load() to retrieve it from a file or stream. It also allows you to modify that data and save it back to the file later. The XmlDocument class implements the full XML DOM.

Using XPathNavigator: You can load the document into an XPathNavigator (which is located in the System.Xml.XPath namespace). Like the XmlDocument, the XPathNavigator holds the entire XML document in memory. However, it offers a slightly faster, more streamlined model than the XML DOM, along with enhanced searching features. Unlike the XmlDocument, it doesn't provide the ability to make changes and save them.

Using XmlTextReader: You can read the document one node at a time using the XmlTextReader class. This is the least expensive approach in terms of server resources, but it forces you to examine the data sequentially from start to finish.

The following sections demonstrate each of these approaches to loading the DVD list XML document.

Using the XML DOM

Figure 12-2 shows the final web page that reads the DVDList.xml document and displays a list of elements, using different levels of indenting to show the overall structure.

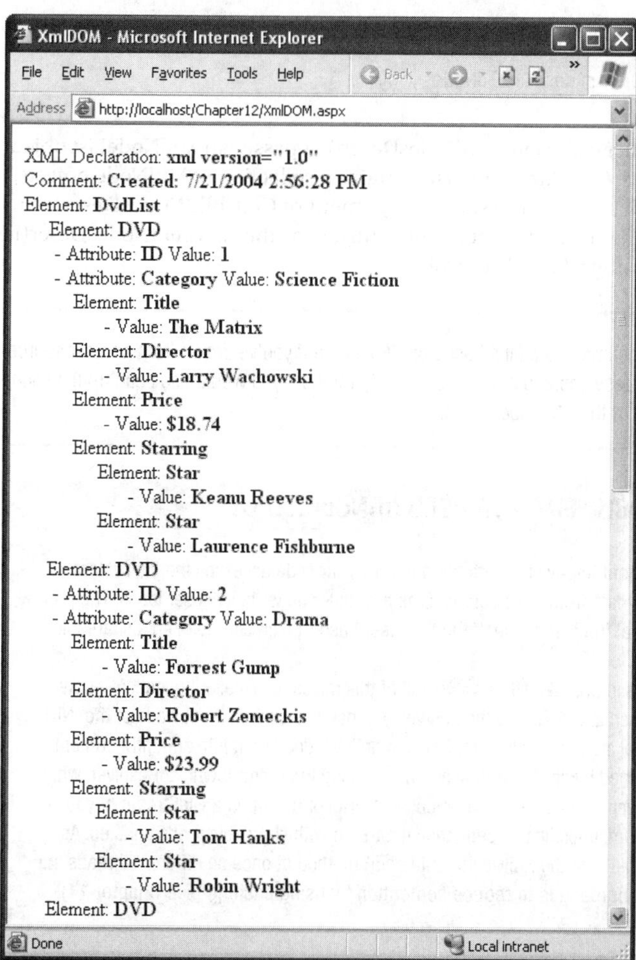

Figure 12-2. *Retrieving information from an XML document*

The XmlDocument stores information as a tree of nodes. A *node* is the basic ingredient of an XML file and can be an element, an attribute, a comment, or a value in an element. A separate XmlNode object represents each node, and nodes are grouped together in *collections*.

You can retrieve the first level of nodes through the XmlDocument.ChildNodes property. In this example, that property provides access to the <DvdList> element. The <DvdList> element contains other child nodes, and these nodes contain still more nodes and the actual values. To drill down through all the layers of the tree, you need to use recursive logic, as shown in this example.

When the example page loads, it creates an XmlDocument object and calls the Load() method, which retrieves the XML data from the file. It then calls a recursive function in the page class named GetChildNodesDescr().GetChildNodesDescr() takes an XmlNodeList object as an input and the index of the nesting level. It then returns the string with the content for that node and all its child nodes and attributes.

```
Private Sub Page_Load(ByVal sender As Object, ByVal e As System.EventArgs)
    Dim xmlFile As String = Server.MapPath("DvdList.xml")

    ' Load the XML file in an XmlDocument.
    Dim doc As XmlDocument = New XmlDocument()
    doc.Load(xmlFile)

    ' Write the description text.
    XmlText.Text = GetChildNodesDescr(doc.ChildNodes, 0)
End Sub
```

When the Page.Load event handler calls GetChildNodesDescr(), it passes an XmlNodeList object that represents the first level of nodes. (The XmlNodeList contains a collection of XmlNode objects, one for each node.) The code also passes 0 as the second argument of GetChildNodesDescr() to indicate that this is the first level of the structure. The string returned by the GetChildNodesDescr() method is then shown on the page using a Literal control.

■ **Tip** What if you want to create an XmlDocument and fill it based on XML content you've drawn from another source, such as a field in a database table? In this case, instead of using the Load() method, you would use LoadXml(), which accepts a string that contains the content of the XML document.

THE XMLDOCUMENT AND USER CONCURRENCY

In a web application, it's extremely important to pay close attention to how your code accesses the file system. If you aren't careful, a web page that reads data from a file can become a disaster under heavy user loads. The problem occurs when two users access a file at the same time. If the first user hasn't taken care to open a shareable stream, the second user will receive an error.

You'll learn more about these issues in Chapter 13. However, all of this raises an excellent question—how does the XmlDocument.Load() method open a file? To find the answer, you need to dig into the IL code of the .NET Framework. What you'll find is that several steps actually unfold to load an XML document into an XmlDocument object. First, the path you supply is examined by an XmlUrlResolver and passed to an XmlDownloadResolver, which determines whether it needs to make a web request (if you've supplied a URL) or can open a FileStream (if you've supplied a path). If it can use the FileStream, it explicitly opens the FileStream with shareable reads enabled. As a result, if more than one user loads the file with the XmlDocument.Load() method at once on different threads, no conflict will occur. Of course, the best approach is to reduce contention by using caching (see Chapter 11).

The interesting part is the GetChildNodesDescr() method. It first creates a string with three spaces for each indentation level that it will later use as a prefix for each line added to the final HTML text.

```
Private Function GetChildNodesDescr(ByVal nodeList As XmlNodeList,
      ByVal level As Integer) As String
    Dim indent As String = ""
    Dim i As Integer=0
    Do While i<level
        indent &= "     "
        i += 1
    Loop
    ...
```

Next, the GetChildNodesDescr() method cycles through all the child nodes of the XmlNodeList. For the first call, these nodes include the XML declaration, the comment, and the <DvdList> element. An XmlNode object exposes properties such as NodeType, which identifies the type of item (for example, Comment, Element, Attribute, CDATA, Text, EndElement, Name, and Value). The code checks for node types that are relevant in this example and adds that information to the string, as shown here:

```
...
    Dim str As New StringBuilder("")
    For Each node As XmlNode In nodeList
        Select Case node.NodeType
            Case XmlNodeType.XmlDeclaration
                str.Append("XML Declaration: <b>")
                str.Append(node.Name)
                str.Append(" ")
                str.Append(node.Value)
                str.Append("</b><br />")
            Case XmlNodeType.Element
                str.Append(indent)
                str.Append("Element: <b>")
                str.Append(node.Name)
                str.Append("</b><br />")
            Case XmlNodeType.Text
                str.Append(indent)
                str.Append(" - Value: <b>")
                str.Append(node.Value)
                str.Append("</b><br />")
            Case XmlNodeType.Comment
                str.Append(indent)
                str.Append("Comment: <b>")
                str.Append(node.Value)
                str.Append("</b><br />")
        End Select
...
```

Note that not all types of nodes have a name or a value. For example, for an element such as Title, the name is Title, but the value is empty, because it's stored in the following Text node.

Next, the code checks whether the current node has any attributes (by testing if its Attributes collection is null). If it does, the attributes are processed with a nested foreach loop:

```
...
        If node.Attributes IsNot Nothing Then
            For Each attrib As XmlAttribute In node.Attributes
                str.Append(indent)
```

```
                str.Append(" - Attribute: <b>")
                str.Append(attrib.Name)
                str.Append("</b> Value: <b>")
                str.Append(attrib.Value)
                str.Append("</b><br />")
            Next
        End If...
```

Lastly, if the node has child nodes (according to its HasChildNodes property), the code recursively calls the GetChildNodesDescr function, passing to it the current node's ChildNodes collection and the current indent level plus 1, as shown here:

```
    ...
    If node.HasChildNodes Then
        str.Append(GetChildNodesDescr(node.ChildNodes, level+1))
    End If
    Next
    Return str.ToString()
End Function
```

When the whole process is finished, the outer foreach block is closed, and the function returns the content of the StringBuilder object.

Using the XPathNavigator

The XPathNavigator works similarly to the XmlDocument class. It loads all the information into memory and then allows you to move through the nodes. The key difference is that it uses a cursor-based approach that allows you to use methods such as MoveToNext() to move through the XML data. An XPathNavigator can be positioned on only one node a time.

You can create an XPathNavigator from an XmlDocument using the XmlDocument. CreateNavigator() method. Here's an example (note that you will need to import System.Xml.XPath or use the version in the code download):

```
Private Sub Page_Load(ByVal sender As Object, ByVal e As System.EventArgs)
    Dim xmlFile As String = Server.MapPath("DvdList.xml")

    ' Load the XML file in an XmlDocument.
    Dim doc As New XmlDocument()
    doc.Load(xmlFile)

    ' Create the navigator.
    Dim xnav As XPathNavigator = doc.CreateNavigator()
    XmlText.Text = GetXNavDescr(xnav, 0)
End Sub
```

In this case, the returned object is passed to the GetXNavDescr() recursive method, which returns the HTML code that represents the XML structure, as in the previous example.

The code of the GetXNavDescr() method is a bit different from the GetChildNodesDescr() method in the previous example, because it takes an XPathNavigator object that is positioned on a single node, not a collection of nodes. That means you don't need to loop through any collections. Instead, you can simply examine the information for the current node, as follows:

```
Private Function GetXNavDescr(ByVal xnav As XPathNavigator,
        ByVal level As Integer) As String
    Dim indent As String = ""
    Dim i As Integer=0
    Do While i<level
      indent &= "     "
```

```
        i += 1
    Loop
    Dim str As New StringBuilder("")
    Select Case xnav.NodeType
        Case XPathNodeType.Root
            str.Append("<b>ROOT</b>")
            str.Append("<br />")
        Case XPathNodeType.Element
            str.Append(indent)
            str.Append("Element: <b>")
            str.Append(xnav.Name)
            str.Append("</b><br />")
        Case XPathNodeType.Text
            str.Append(indent)
            str.Append(" - Value: <b>")
            str.Append(xnav.Value)
            str.Append("</b><br />")
        Case XPathNodeType.Comment
            str.Append(indent)
            str.Append("Comment: <b>")
            str.Append(xnav.Value)
            str.Append("</b><br />")
    End Select
    ...
```

Note that the values for the NodeType property are almost the same, except for the enumeration name, which is XPathNodeType instead of XmlNodeType. That's because the XPathNavigator uses a smaller, more streamlined set of nodes. One of the nodes it doesn't support is the XmlDeclaration node type.

The function checks if the current node has any attributes. If so, it moves to the first one with a call to MoveToFirstAttribute() and loops through all the attributes until the MoveToNextAttribute() method returns False. At that point it returns to the parent node, which is the node originally referenced by the object. Here's the code that carries this out:

```
...
If xnav.HasAttributes Then
        xnav.MoveToFirstAttribute()
        Do
            str.Append(indent)
            str.Append(" - Attribute: <b>")
            str.Append(xnav.Name)
            str.Append("</b> Value: <b>")
            str.Append(xnav.Value)
            str.Append("</b><br />")
        Loop While xnav.MoveToNextAttribute()

        ' Return to the parent.
        xnav.MoveToParent()
    End If
...
```

The function does a similar thing with the child nodes by moving to the first one with MoveToFirstChild() and recursively calling itself until MoveToNext() returns False, at which point it moves back to the original node, as follows:

```
    ...
    If xnav.HasChildren Then
        xnav.MoveToFirstChild()
```

```
        Do
            str.Append(GetXNavDescr(xnav, level+1))
        Loop While xnav.MoveToNext()

        ' Return to the parent.
        xnav.MoveToParent()
    End If
    Return str.ToString()
End Function
```

This code produces almost the same output as shown in Figure 12-2.

Searching an XML Document

In some situations, you don't need to process the entire XML document. Instead, you need to extract a single piece of information. The next section will review some techniques that allow you to do just that.

GetElementsbyTagName

If you know the element name, you can use the XmlDocument.GetElementsByTagName() method, which searches an entire document and returns an XmlNodeList that contains all the matching XmlNode objects.

For example, the following code retrieves the title of each DVD in the document:

```
' Load the XML file.
Dim xmlFile As String = Server.MapPath("DvdList.xml")
Dim doc As New XmlDocument()
doc.Load(xmlFile)

' Find all the <Title> elements anywhere in the document.
Dim str As New StringBuilder()
Dim nodes As XmlNodeList = doc.GetElementsByTagName("Title")
For Each node As XmlNode In nodes
    str.Append("Found: <b>")

    ' Show the text contained in this <Title> element.
    str.Append(node.ChildNodes(0).Value)
    str.Append("</b><br />")
Next
XmlText.Text = str.ToString()
```

Figure 12-3 shows the result of running this code in a web page.

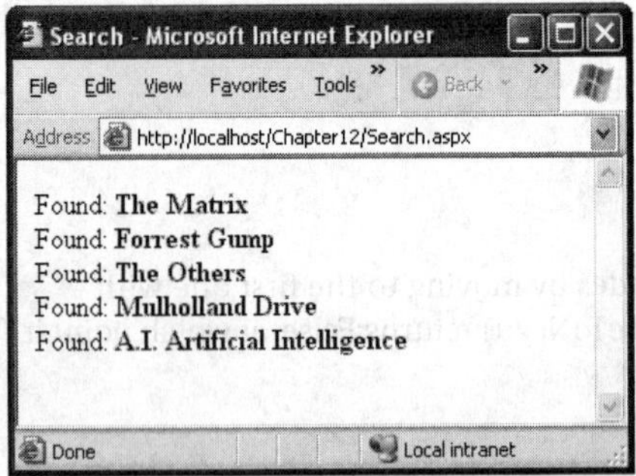

Figure 12-3. *Searching for information in an XML document*

You can also search portions of an XML document by using the method XmlElement.GetElementsByTagName() on a specific element. In this case, the XmlDocument searches all the descendant nodes looking for a match. To use this method, first retrieve an XmlNode that corresponds to an element and then cast this object to an XmlElement. The following example demonstrates how to use this technique to find the stars of a specific movie:

```
' Load the XML file.
Dim xmlFile As String = Server.MapPath("DvdList.xml")
Dim doc As New XmlDocument()
doc.Load(xmlFile)

' Find all the <Title> elements anywhere in the document.
Dim str As New StringBuilder()
Dim nodes As XmlNodeList = doc.GetElementsByTagName("Title")

For Each node As XmlNode In nodes
    str.Append("Found: <b>")

    ' Show the text contained in this <Title> element.
    Dim name As String = node.ChildNodes(0).Value
    str.Append(name)
    str.Append("</b><br />")

    If name = "Forrest Gump" Then
        ' Find the stars for just this movie.
        ' First you need to get the parent node
        ' (which is the <DVD> element for the movie).
        Dim parent As XmlNode = node.ParentNode

        ' Then you need to search down the tree.
        Dim childNodes As XmlNodeList = _
                (CType(parent, XmlElement)).GetElementsByTagName("Star")
        For Each childNode As XmlNode In childNodes
            str.Append("    Found Star: ")
            str.Append(childNode.ChildNodes(0).Value)
            str.Append("<br />")
        Next childNode
    End If
Next
XmlText.Text = str.ToString()
```

Figure 12-4 shows the result of this test.

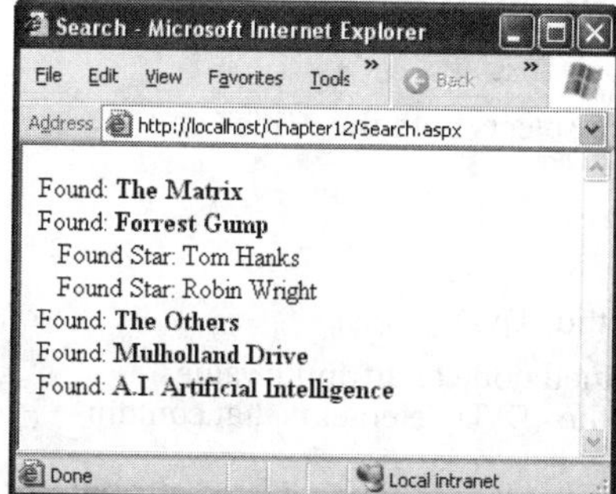

Figure 12-4. *Searching portions of an XML document*

The code you've seen so far assumes that none of the elements has a namespace. More sophisticated XML documents will always include a namespace and may even have several of them. In this situation, you can use the overload of the method GetElementsByTagName(), which requires a namespace name as a string argument, as shown here:

```
' Retrieve all <order> elements in the OrderML namespace.
Dim nodes As XmlNodeList =
      doc.GetElementsByTagName("order", "http://mycompany/OrderML")
```

Additionally, you can supply an asterisk (*) for the element name if you want to match all tags in the specified namespace:

```
' Retrieve all elements in the OrderML namespace.
Dim nodes As XmlNodeList =
      doc.GetElementsByTagName("*", "http://mycompany/OrderML")
```

Searching an XML Document with XPath

The GetElementsByTagName() method is fairly limited. It allows you to search based on the name of an element only. You can't filter based on other criteria, such as the value of the element or attribute content. XPath is a much more powerful standard that allows you to retrieve the portions of a document that interest you.

XPath uses a pathlike notation. For example, the path / identifies the root of an XML document, and /DvdList identifies the root <DvdList> element. The path /DvdList/DVD selects every <DVD> element that is a direct child element of the <DvdList>.

These ingredients are enough to build many basic templates, although the XPath standard also defines special selection criteria that can filter out only the nodes in which you are interested. Table 12-1 provides an overview of XPath syntax.

Table 12-1. *Basic XPath Syntax*

Expression	Meaning
/	Starts an absolute path from the root node. /DvdList/DVD selects all <DVD> elements that are children of the root <DvdList> element.
//	This is the recursive descent operator that searches for descendants rather than children. //DVD/Title selects all the <Title> elements that are descendants of a <DVD> element.
@	Selects an attribute of a node. /DvdList/DVD/@ID selects the attribute named ID from the <DVD> element.
*	Selects a child element in the path. /DvdList/DVD/* selects all the elements that are direct children of the <DVD> element (which include <Title>, <Director>, <Price>, and <Starring> in this example).
|	Combines multiple paths. /DvdList/DVD/ | Title//DvdList/DVD/Director selects both the <Title> and <Director> elements in the <DVD> element.
.	Indicates the current node.
..	Indicates the parent node. If the current node is <Title>, then .. refers to the <DVD> node.
[]	Define selection criteria that can test a contained node or attribute value. /DvdList/DVD[Title='Forrest Gump'] selects the <DVD> elements that contain a <Title> element with the indicated value. /DvdList/DVD[@ID='1'] selects the <DVD> elements with the indicated attribute value. You can use the *and* keyword to combine criteria.

Expression	Meaning
starts-with	This function retrieves elements based on what text a contained element starts with. /DvdList/DVD[starts-with(Title, 'P')] finds all <DVD> elements that have a <Title> element that contains text that starts with the letter *P*.
position	This function retrieves elements based on position. /DvdList/DVD[position()=2] selects the second <DVD> element. A handy shorthand for this is to use [2]. Note also that numbering begins at '1' not '0'.
count	This function counts the number of nodes with the matching name. count(DVD) returns the number of <DVD> elements.

To execute an XPath expression in .NET, you can use the Select() method of the XPathNavigator or the SelectNodes() or SelectSingleNode() method of the XmlDocument class. The following code uses this technique to retrieve specific information:

```
' Load the XML file.
Dim xmlFile As String = Server.MapPath("DvdList.xml")
Dim doc As New XmlDocument()
doc.Load(xmlFile)

' Retrieve the title of every science-fiction movie.
Dim nodes As XmlNodeList =
        doc.SelectNodes("/DvdList/DVD[@Category='Science Fiction']/Title")

' Display the titles.
Dim str As New StringBuilder()
For Each node As XmlNode In nodes
    str.Append("Found: <b>")

    ' Show the text contained in this <Title> element.
    str.Append(node.ChildNodes(0).Value)
    str.Append("</b><br />")
Next
XmlText.Text = str.ToString()
```

Figure 12-5 shows the results.

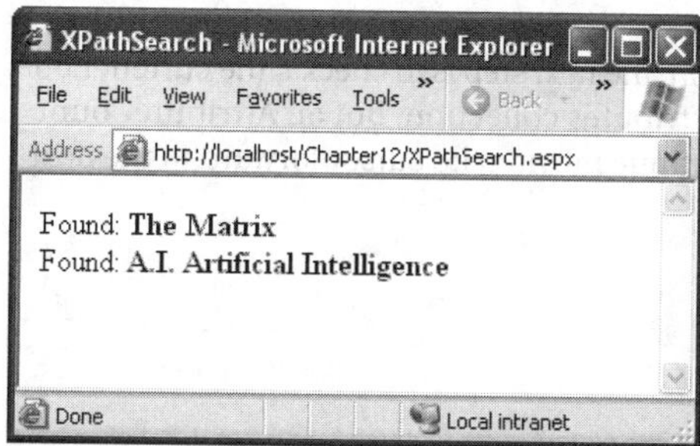

Figure 12-5. *Extracting information with XPath*

Using the XmlTextReader

Reading an XML file with an XmlTextReader object is the simplest approach, but it also provides the least flexibility. The file is read in sequential order, and you can't freely move to the parent, child, and sibling nodes as you can with XmlDocument and XPathNavigator. Instead, you read a node at a time from a stream.

The following code starts by loading the source file in an XmlTextReader object. It then begins a loop that moves through the document one node at time. To move from one node to the next, you call the XmlTextReader.Read() method. This method returns True until it moves past the last node, at which point it returns False. This is similar to the approach used by the data reader classes in ADO.NET such as the SqlDataReader class, which retrieves query results from a database.

Here's an example:

```
Private Sub ReadXML()
    Dim xmlFile As String = Server.MapPath("DvdList.xml")

    ' Create the reader.
    Dim reader As New XmlTextReader(xmlFile)
    Dim str As StringBuilder = New StringBuilder()

    ' Loop through all the nodes.
    Do While reader.Read()
        Select Case reader.NodeType
            Case XmlNodeType.XmlDeclaration
                str.Append("XML Declaration: <b>")
                str.Append(reader.Name)
                str.Append(" ")
                str.Append(reader.Value)
                str.Append("</b><br />")
            Case XmlNodeType.Element
                str.Append("Element: <b>")
                str.Append(reader.Name)
                str.Append("</b><br />")
            Case XmlNodeType.Text
                str.Append(" - Value: <b>")
                str.Append(reader.Value)
                str.Append("</b><br />")
        End Select
        ...
```

After handling the types of nodes you're interested in, the next step is to check if the current node has attributes. The XmlTextReader doesn't have an Attributes collection, but an AttributeCount property returns the number of attributes. You can continue moving the cursor forward to the next attribute until MoveToNextAttribute() returns False.

```
        ...
        If reader.AttributeCount > 0 Then
            Do While reader.MoveToNextAttribute()
                str.Append(" - Attribute: <b>")
                str.Append(reader.Name)
                str.Append("</b> Value: <b>")
                str.Append(reader.Value)
                str.Append("</b><br />")
            Loop
        End If
    Loop
```

```
    ' Close the reader and show the text.
    reader.Close()
    XmlText.Text = str.ToString()
End Sub
```

In the last two lines the procedure concludes by flushing the content in the buffer and closing the reader. When using the XmlTextReader, it's imperative you finish your task and close the reader as soon as possible, because it retains a lock on the file, unlike the XmlDocument, which loads all the information into memory when you call the Load() method.

If you run this code now, you'll see a web page that's quite similar to the earlier examples with the XmlDocument and XPathNavigator.

The XmlTextReader provides additional methods that help make reading XML even faster and more convenient if you know what structure to expect. For example, you can use MoveToContent(), which skips over irrelevant nodes (such as comments, whitespace, and the XML declaration) and stops on the declaration of the next element.

You can also use the ReadStartElement() method, which reads an element start tag and performs basic validation at the same time. When you call ReadStartElement(), you specify the name of the element you expect to appear next in the document. The XmlTextReader calls MoveToContent() and then verifies that the current element has the name you've specified. If it doesn't, an exception is thrown. You can also use ReadEndElement() method to skip over whitespace and read the closing tag for the element.

Finally, if you want to read an element that contains only text data, you move over the start tag, content, and end tag by using the ReadElementString() method and by specifying the element name. The data you want is returned as a string.

Here's the code that extracts data from the XML list using this more streamlined approach:

```
' Create the reader.
Dim xmlFile As String = Server.MapPath("DvdList.xml")
Dim reader As New XmlTextReader(xmlFile)

Dim str As New StringBuilder()
reader.ReadStartElement("DvdList")

' Read all the <DVD> elements.
Do While reader.Read()
    If (reader.Name = "DVD") AndAlso
            (reader.NodeType = XmlNodeType.Element) Then
        reader.ReadStartElement("DVD")
        str.Append("<ul><b>")
        str.Append(reader.ReadElementString("Title"))
        str.Append("</b><li>")
        str.Append(reader.ReadElementString("Director"))
        str.Append("</li><li>")
        str.Append(String.Format("{0:C}",
              Decimal.Parse(reader.ReadElementString("Price"))))
        str.Append("</li></ul>")
    End If
Loop
' Close the reader and show the text.
reader.Close()
XmlText.Text = str.ToString()
```

Figure 12-6 shows the result.

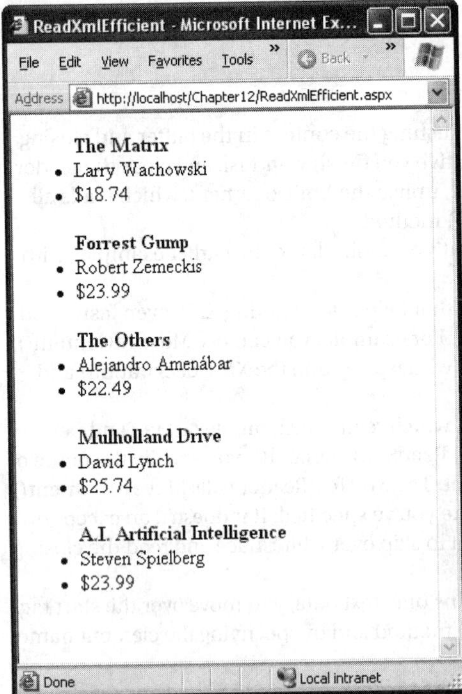

Figure 12-6. *Efficient XML reading*

Validating XML Files

So far you've seen a number of strategies for reading and parsing XML data. If you try to read badly formed XML content using any of these approaches, you'll receive an error. In other words, all these classes require well-formed XML. However, none of the examples you've seen so far has validated the XML to check that it follows any application-specific rules.

As described at the beginning of this chapter, XML formats are commonly codified with an XML schema that lays out the required structure and data types. For the DVD list document, you can create an XML schema that looks like this:

```
<?xml version="1.0" ?>
<xs:schema id="DvdList" xmlns="" xmlns:xs="http://www.w3.org/2001/XMLSchema"
  xmlns:msdata="urn:schemas-microsoft-com:xml-msdata">
    <xs:element name="DvdList">
        <xs:complexType>
            <xs:sequence maxOccurs="unbounded">
                <xs:element name="DVD" type="DVDType" />
            </xs:sequence>
        </xs:complexType>
    </xs:element>

    <xs:complexType name="DVDType">
        <xs:sequence>
            <xs:element name="Title" type="xs:string" />
            <xs:element name="Director" type="xs:string"  />
            <xs:element name="Price" type="xs:decimal"  />
```

```
            <xs:element name="Starring" type="StarringType" />
        </xs:sequence>
        <xs:attribute name="ID" type="xs:integer" />
        <xs:attribute name="Category" type="xs:string" />
    </xs:complexType>

    <xs:complexType name="StarringType">
        <xs:sequence maxOccurs="unbounded">
            <xs:element name="Star" type="xs:string"/>
        </xs:sequence>
    </xs:complexType>
</xs:schema>
```

This schema defines two complex types, representing the list of stars (named StarringType) and the list of DVDs (named DVDType). The structure of the document is defined using an <element> tag.

To validate an XML document against a schema, you use the XmlReader.Create method, passing it an object of type XmlReaderSettings. This object can be instantiated with the schema to validate against, and initialized as a validator of a schema.

You'll need to import the following namespaces:

```
Imports System.Xml
Imports System.IO
Imports System.Xml.Schema
```

The following example shows how you can create XmlReader.Create and pass it an XmlReaderSettings object to set your reader up for schema-based validation.

```
Dim xmlFile As String = Server.MapPath("DvdList.xml")
Dim xsdFile As String = Server.MapPath("DvdList.xsd")

Dim sc as XmlSchemaSet = new XmlSchemaSet()
sc.Add("urn:dvd-schema",xsdFile)

Dim settings as New XmlReaderSettings()
settings.ValidationType = ValidationType.Schema
settings.Schemas = sc

' Open the XML file.
Dim vr As XmlReader = XmlReader.Create(xmlFile,settings)

' Read through the document.
Do While vr.Read()
    ' Process document here.
    ' If an error is found, an exception will be thrown.
Loop
vr.Close()
```

Using the current file, this code will succeed, and you'll be able to access the current node through the XmlReader object. However, consider what happens if you make the minor modification shown here:

```
<DVD ID="A" Category="Science Fiction">
```

Now when you try to validate the document, an XmlSchemaException (from the System.Xml.Schema namespace) will be thrown, alerting you to the invalid data type—the letter *A* in an attribute that is designated for integer values.

Instead of catching errors, you can react to the ValidationEventHandler event of the XmlReaderSettings object. If you react to this event, you'll be provided with information about the error, but no exception will be thrown. To connect an event handler to this event, create a new ValidationEventHandler delegate and assign it to the XmlReaderSettings.ValidationEventHandler event just before you start to read the XML file:

```
' Connect to the method named MyValidateHandler.
AddHandler settings.ValidationEventHandler, AddressOf ValidateHandler
```

The event handler receives a ValidationEventArgs class, which contains the exception, a message, and a number representing the severity:

```
Private Sub ValidateHandler(ByVal sender As Object, ByVal e As ValidationEventArgs)
    lblInfo.Text &= "Error: " & e.Message & "<br />"
End Sub
```

To try the validation, you can use the XmlValidation.aspx page in the online samples. This page allows you to validate a valid DVD list as well as another version with incorrect data and an incorrect tag. Figure 12-7 shows the result of a failed validation attempt.

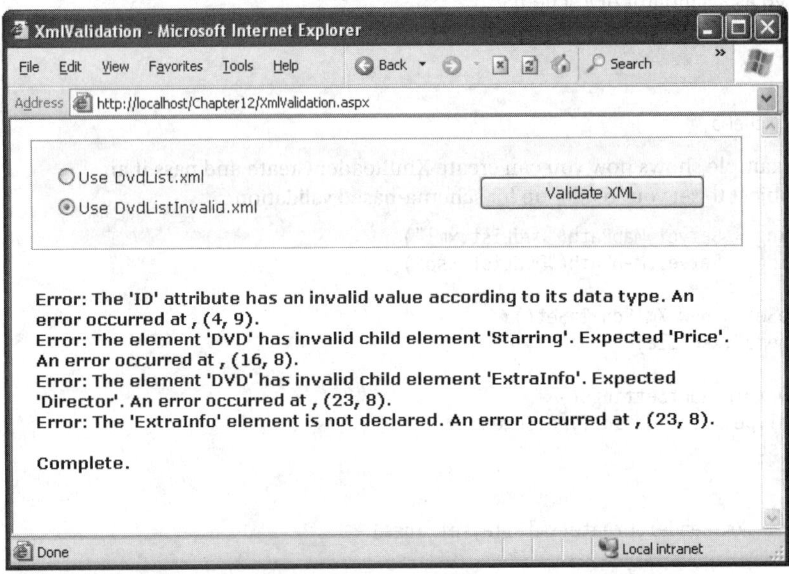

Figure 12-7. *The validation test page*

Displaying XML Content with XSL

Another related standard is XSL (Extensible Stylesheet Language), which is an XML-based language for creating stylesheets. *Stylesheets* (also known as *transforms*) are special documents that can be used (with the help of an XSLT processor) to convert your XML documents into other documents. For example, you can use an XSLT stylesheet to transform one type of XML to a different XML structure. Or you could use a stylesheet to convert your XML into another text-based document such as an HTML page, as you'll see with the next example.

■ **Note** Of course, XSL stylesheets shouldn't be confused with CSS (Cascading Style Sheets), a standard used to format HTML. Chapter 15 discusses CSS.

Before you can perform a transformation, you need to create an XSL stylesheet that defines how the conversion should be applied. XSL is a complex standard—in fact, it can be considered a genuine language of its own with conditional logic, looping structures, and more.

■ Note A full discussion of XSLT is beyond the scope of this book. However, if you want to learn more, you can consider a book such as Jeni Tennison's *Beginning XSLT* (Apress, 2004), the excellent online tutorials at `http://www.w3schools.com/xsl`, or the standard itself at `http://www.w3.org/Style/XSL`.

A Basic Stylesheet

To transform the DVD list into HTML, you'll use the simple stylesheet shown here:

```
<xsl:stylesheet xmlns:xsl="http://www.w3.org/1999/XSL/Transform" version="1.0">
  <xsl:template match="/">
    <html>
    <body>
      <xsl:apply-templates select="/DvdList/DVD" />
    </body>
    </html>
  </xsl:template>

  <xsl:template match="DVD">
    <hr/>
    <h3><u><xsl:value-of select="Title" /></u></h3>
    <b>Price: </b> <xsl:value-of select="Price" /><br/>
    <b>Director: </b> <xsl:value-of select="Director" /><br/>
    <xsl:apply-templates select="Starring" />
  </xsl:template>

  <xsl:template match="Starring">
    <b>Starring:</b><br />
    <xsl:apply-templates select="Star" />
  </xsl:template>

  <xsl:template match="*">
    <li><xsl:value-of select="." /></li>
  </xsl:template>
</xsl:stylesheet>
```

Every XSL file has a root <stylesheet> element. The <stylesheet> element can contain one or more templates (the sample file has four). In this example, the first <template> element matches the root node. When it finds it, it outputs the tags necessary to start an HTML page and then uses the <apply-templates> command to branch off and perform processing for any contained <DVD> elements, as follows:

```
<xsl:template match="/">
  <html>
  <body>
    <xsl:apply-templates select="/DvdList/DVD" />
  </body>
  </html>
</xsl:template>
```

Each time the <DVD> tag is matched, a horizontal line is added, and a heading is created. Information about the <Title>, <Price>, and <Director> tag is extracted and written to the page using the <value-of> command. Here's the full template:

```
<xsl:template match="DVD">
  <hr/>
  <h3><u><xsl:value-of select="Title" /></u></h3>
  <b>Price: </b> <xsl:value-of select="Price" /><br/>
  <b>Director: </b> <xsl:value-of select="Director" /><br/>
  <xsl:apply-templates select="Starring" />
</xsl:template>
```

Using XslCompiledTransform

Using this template and the XsCompiledlTransform class (contained in the System.Xml.Xsl namespace), you can transform the DVD list into formatted HTML. Here's the code that performs this transformation and saves the result to a new file:

```
Dim xslFile As String = Server.MapPath("DvdList.xsl")
Dim xmlFile As String = Server.MapPath("DvdList.xml")
Dim htmlFile As String = Server.MapPath("DvdList.htm")
Dim transf As New XslCompiledTransform()
transf.Load(xslFile)
transf.Transform(xmlFile, htmlFile)
```

Alternatively, you could use an overload of the Transform method to directly write to the Response buffer like this:

```
transf.Transform(xmlFile,Nothing,Response.OutputStream)
```

Figure 12-8 shows the resulting page.

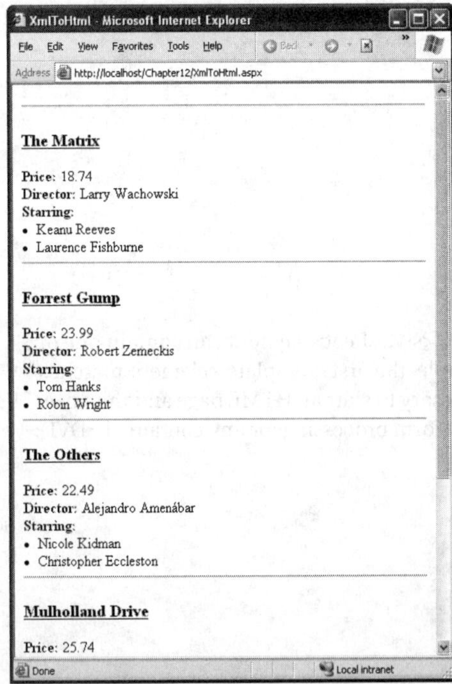

Figure 12-8. *Transforming XML to HTML*

Using the Xml Control

In some cases you might want to combine transformed HTML output with other content and web controls. In this case, you can use the Xml control. The Xml control displays the result of an XSL transformation in a discrete portion of a page.

For example, consider the previous XSLT example, which transformed DvdList.xml using DvdList.xsl. Using the Xml control, all you need is a single tag that sets the DocumentSource and TransformSource properties, as shown here:

```
<asp:Xml runat="server"
  DocumentSource="DvdList.xml" TransformSource="DvdList.xsl" />
```

The best part of this example is that all you need to do is set the XML input and the XSL transform file. You don't need to manually initiate the conversion.

XML Data Binding

Now that you've learned how to read, write, and display XML by hand, it's worth considering a shortcut that can save a good deal of code—the XmlDataSource control.

The XmlDataSource control works in a declarative way that's analogous to the SqlDataSource and ObjectDataSource controls you learned about in Chapter 9. However, it has two key differences:

- The XmlDataSource extracts information from an XML file, rather than a database or data access class. It provides other controls with an XmlDocument object for data binding.
- XML content is hierarchical and can have an unlimited number of levels. By contrast, the SqlDataSource and ObjectDataSource return flat tables of data.

The XmlDataSource also provides a few features in common with the other data source controls, including caching and rich design support that shows the schema of your data in bound controls.

In the following sections, you'll see how to use the XmlDataSource in simple and complex scenarios.

Nonhierarchical Binding

The simplest way to deal with the hierarchical nature of XML data is to ignore it. In other words, you can bind the XML data source directly to an ordinary grid control such as the GridView.

The first step is to define the XML data source and point it to the file that has the content you want to use:

```
<asp:XmlDataSource ID="sourceDVD" runat="server"
 DataFile="DvdList.xml" />
```

Now you can bind the GridView with automatically generated columns, in the same way you bind it to any other data source:

```
<asp:GridView ID="GridView1" runat="server" AutoGenerateColumns="True"
 DataSourceID="sourceDVD">
...
</asp:GridView>
```

■ **Note** Remember, you don't need to use automatically generated columns. If you refresh the schema at design time, Visual Studio will read the DvdList.xml file, determine its structure, and define the corresponding GridView columns explicitly.

Now, when you run the page, the XmlDataSource will extract the data from the DvdList.xml file, provide it to the GridView as an XmlDocument object, and call DataBind(). Because the XmlDocument implements the IEnumerable interface, the GridView can walk through its structure in much the same way as it walks through a DataView. It traverses the XmlDocument.Nodes collection and gets all the attributes for each XmlNode.

■ **Tip** You can use the XmlDataSource programmatically. Call the GetXmlDocument method on an XmlDataSource object to cause it to return the file's content as an XmlDocument object.

However, this has a catch. As explained earlier, the XmlDocument.Nodes collection contains only the first level of nodes. Each of these nodes can contain nested nodes through its own XmlNode.Nodes collection. However, the IEnumerable implementation that the XmlDocument uses doesn't take this into account. It walks over only the upper level of XmlNode objects, and as a result you'll see only the top level of nodes, as shown in Figure 12-9.

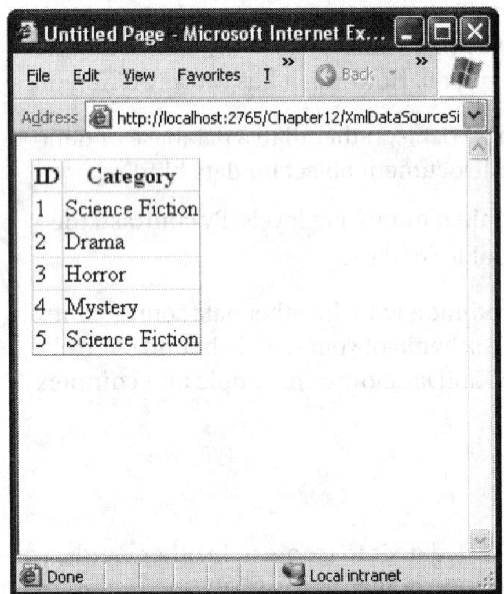

Figure 12-9. *Flattening XML with data binding*

You can make this binding explicit by defining columns for each attribute:

```
<asp:GridView ID="GridView1" runat="server" AutoGenerateColumns="False"
 DataSourceID="sourceDVD">
  <Columns>
    <asp:BoundField DataField="ID" HeaderText="ID" SortExpression="ID" />
    <asp:BoundField DataField="Category" HeaderText="Category"
     SortExpression="Category" />
  </Columns>
</asp:GridView>
```

In other words, if you don't customize the XML data binding process, you can bind only to the top-level of nodes, and you can display text only from the attributes of that node. Furthermore, if there is more than one type of top-level node, the bound control uses the schema of the first node. In other words, if you have a document like this:

```
<DvdList>
  <Retailer ID="..." Name="...">...</Retailer>
  <Retailer ID="..." Name="...">...</Retailer>

  <DVD ID="..." Category="...">...</DVD>
  <DVD ID="..." Category="...">...</DVD>
  <DVD ID="..." Category="...">...</DVD>
</DvdList>
```

the GridView will inspect the first node and create an ID and Name column. It will then attempt to display ID and name information for each node. If no matching attribute is found (for example, the <DVD> specifies a name), then that value will be left blank. Similarly, the Category attribute won't be used, unless you explicitly define it as a column.

All of this raises an obvious question—how do you display other information from deeper down in the XML document? You have a few options:

- You can use XPath to filter out the important elements.
- You can use an XSL transformation to flatten the XML into the structure you want.
- You can nest one data control inside another (similar to the way that the master-child details grid was created in Chapter 10).
- You can use a control that supports hierarchical data. The only ready-made .NET control that fits is the TreeView.

You'll see all of these techniques in the following sections.

Using XPath Binding Expressions

Ordinarily, when you bind an XmlNode, you display only attribute values. However, you can get the text from nested elements using XPath data binding expressions.

The most flexible way to do this is to use a template that defines XPath data binding expressions. XPath data binding expressions are similar to Eval() expressions, except instead of supplying the name of the field you want to display, you supply an XPath expression based on the current node.

For example, here's an XPath expression that starts at the current node, looks for a child element called Title, and gets associated element text:

```
<%# XPath("Title")%>
```

Here's an XPath expression that filters out the text of an ID attribute for the current node:

```
<%# XPath("@ID")%>
```

Tip You can use the XPath data binding syntax with your own custom data objects, but it isn't easy. The only requirement is that the data item must implement the IXPathNavigable interface.

Finally, here's a GridView with a simple set of XPath expressions:

```
<asp:GridView ID="GridView1" runat="server" AutoGenerateColumns="False"
 DataSourceID="sourceDVD">
  <Columns>
    <asp:TemplateField HeaderText="DVD">
      <ItemTemplate>
        <b><%# XPath("Title") %></b><br />
        <%# XPath("Director") %><br />
```

```
      </ItemTemplate>
    </asp:TemplateField>
  </Columns>
</asp:GridView>
```

As with the Eval() method, you can use an optional second parameter with a format string:

```
<%# XPath("Price", "{0:c}") %>
```

Figure 12-10 shows the result.

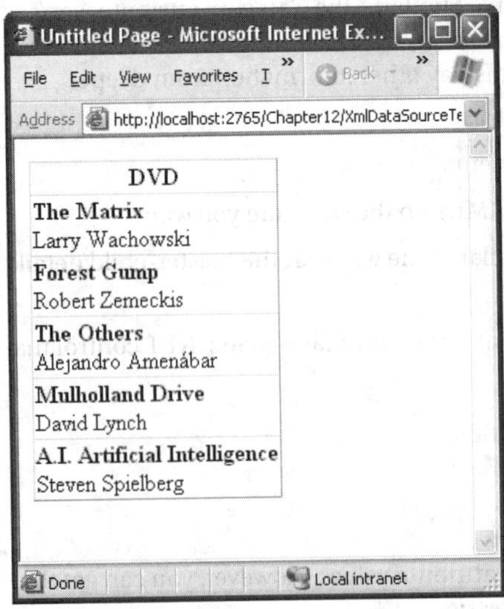

Figure 12-10. *XML data binding with templates*

■Note Unfortunately, you need to use a template to gain the ability to write XPath data binding expressions. That limits the usefulness of other controls (such as drop-down lists) in XML data binding scenarios. Although you can bind them to attributes without any problem, you can't bind them to show element content.

You can also use XPath to prefilter out XmlDataSource objects. For example, imagine you want to create a grid that shows a list of stars rather than a list of movies. To accomplish this, you need to use the XPath support that's built into the XmlDataSource to prefilter the results.

To use XPath, you need to supply the XPath expression that selects the data you're interested in by using the XmlDataSource.XPath property. This XPath expression extracts an XmlNodeList, which is then made available to the bound controls.

```
<asp:XmlDataSource ID="sourceDVD" runat="server" DataFile="DvdList.xml"
 XPath="/DvdList/DVD/Starring/Star" />
```

If that expression returns a list of nodes, and all the information you need to display is found in attributes, you don't need to perform any extra steps. However, if the information is in element text, you need to create a template.

In this example, the template simply displays the text for each <Star> node:

```
<asp:GridView ID="GridView1" runat="server" DataSourceID="sourceDVD"
 AutoGenerateColumns="False">
  <Columns>
    <asp:TemplateField HeaderText="DVD">
      <ItemTemplate>
        <%# XPath(".") %><br />
      </ItemTemplate>
    </asp:TemplateField>
  </Columns>
```

Figure 12-11 shows the result.

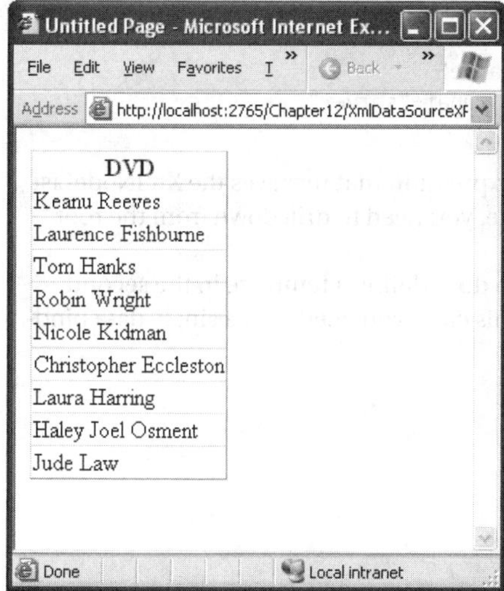

Figure 12-11. *Using XPath to filter out results*

You can create a simple record browser using the XmlDataSource.XPath property. Just let the user choose an ID from another control (such as a drop-down list), and then set the XPath property accordingly:

```
sourceDVD.XPath = "/DVDList/DVD[@ID=" & dropDownList1.SelectedValue & "]"
```

This works because data binding isn't performed until the end of the page life cycle.

Nested Grids

Another option is to show nested elements by nesting one grid control inside another. This allows you to deal with much more complex XML structures.

The remarkable part is that ASP.NET provides support for this approach without requiring you to write any code. This is notable, especially because it *does* require code to create the nested master-details grid display demonstrated in Chapter 10.

The next example uses nested grids to create a list of movies, with a separate list of starring actors in each movie. To accomplish this, you begin by defining the outer grid. Using a template, you can display the title and director information as follows. Note that the XmlDataSource isn't pre-filtered with an XPath in this case:

```
<asp:GridView ID="GridView1" runat="server" AutoGenerateColumns="False"
 DataSourceID="sourceDVD">
  <Columns>
    <asp:TemplateField HeaderText="DVD">
      <ItemTemplate>
        <b><%#XPath("./Title") %></b><br />
        <%#XPath("./Director") %><br />
        <br /><i>Starring...</i><br />
        ...
```

Now, you need to define another GridView control inside the template of the first GridView. The trick is in the DataSource property, which you can set using a new XPathSelect() data binding statement, as shown here:

```
...
<asp:GridView id="GridView2" AutoGenerateColumns="False"
 DataSource='<%# XPathSelect("./Starring/Star") %>' runat="server">
...
```

When you call XPathSelect(), you supply the XPath expression that retrieves the XmlNodeList based on a search starting at the current node. In this case, you need to drill down from the root <DvdList> element to the group of <Star> elements.

Once you've set the right data source, all you need to do is define a template in the second GridView that displays the appropriate information. In this case, you need only a single data binding expression to get the element text:

```
          ...
          <Columns>
            <asp:TemplateField>
              <ItemTemplate>
                <%# XPath(".") %><br />
              </ItemTemplate>
            </asp:TemplateField>
          </Columns>
        </asp:GridView>

      </ItemTemplate>
    </asp:TemplateField>
  </Columns>
</asp:GridView>
```

Figure 12-12 shows the grid, with a little extra formatting added for good measure.

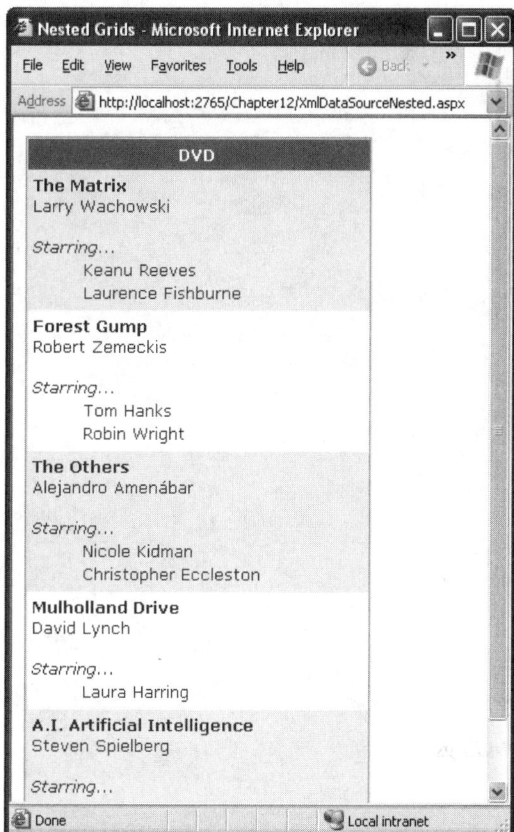

Figure 12-12. *Showing XML with nested grids*

■ **Tip** In this example, you might want to consider using the Repeater to show the actor names. That way, you have the flexibility to show the list in a more compact format, without using a table.

Hierarchical Binding with the TreeView

Some controls have the built-in smarts to show hierarchical data. In .NET, a good example is the TreeView. When you bind the TreeView to an XmlDataSource, it uses the XmlDataSource.GetHierarchcialView() method and displays the full structure of the XML document (see Figure 12-13).

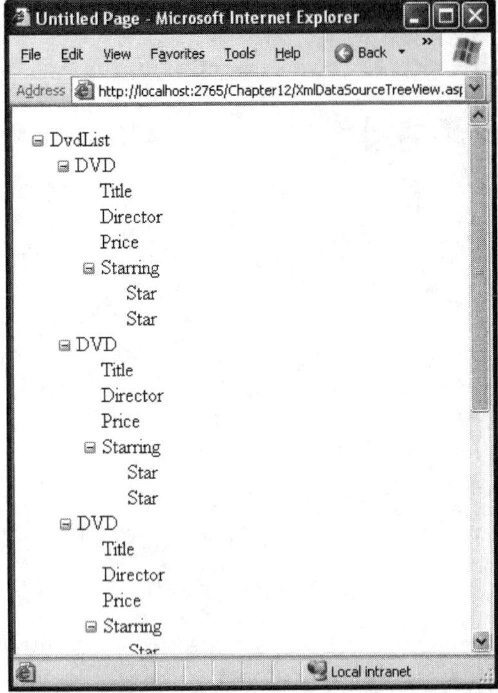

Figure 12-13. *Automatically generated TreeView bindings*

The TreeView's default XML representation still leaves a lot to be desired. It shows only the document structure (the element names), not the document content (the element text). It also ignores attributes. To improve this situation, you need to set the TreeView.AutomaticallyGenerateDataBindings property to False, and you then need to explicitly map different parts of the XML document to TreeView nodes.

```
<asp:TreeView ID="TreeView1" runat="server" DataSourceID="sourceDVD"
 AutoGenerateDataBindings="False">
  ...
</asp:TreeView>
```

TreeView controls contain a <DataBinding> configuration section that specifies how they are bound to the underlying data. To create a TreeView mapping, you need to add <TreeNodeDataBinding> elements to this section. You must start with the root element and then add a binding for each level you want to show. You cannot skip any levels.

Here's an example:

```
<DataBindings>
  <asp:TreeNodeBinding DataMember="DVDList" Text="Root" Value="Root" />
  <asp:TreeNodeBinding DataMember="DVD" TextField="ID" />
  <asp:TreeNodeBinding DataMember="Title" TextField="#InnerText" />
</DataBindings>
```

■ **Note** The approach you use to customize bindings with a TreeView is not completely finalized and may change in the final release of ASP.NET 2.0.

Each <TreeNodeDataBinding> must name the node it binds to (through the DataMember property), the text it should display (TextField), and the hidden value for the node (Value). Unfortunately, both TextField and Value are designed to bind to attributes. If you want to bind to element content, you can use an ugly hack and specify the #InnerText code. However, this shows *all* the inner text, including text inside other more deeply nested nodes.

The next example expands on the previous; it defines a basic set of nodes to show the movie title information:

```
<asp:TreeView ID="TreeView1" runat="server" DataSourceID="sourceDVD"
 AutoGenerateDataBindings="False">
  <DataBindings>
    <asp:TreeNodeBinding DataMember="DvdList" Text="Root" Value="Root" />
    <asp:TreeNodeBinding DataMember="DVD" TextField="ID" />
    <asp:TreeNodeBinding DataMember="Title" TextField="#InnerText" />
  </DataBindings>
</asp:TreeView>
```

Figure 12-14 shows the result.

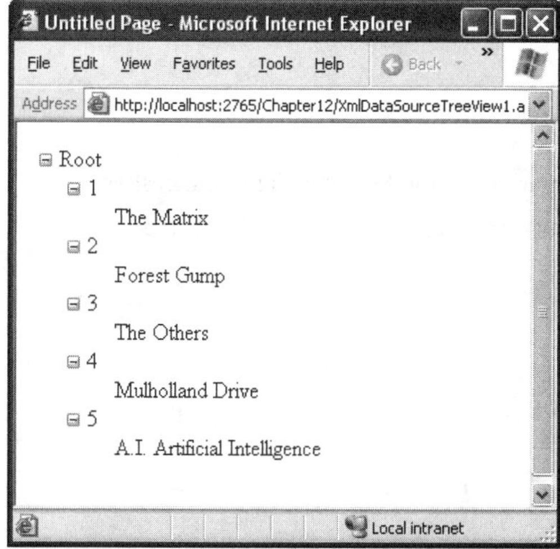

Figure 12-14. *Binding to specific content*

To get a more practical result with TreeView data binding, you need to use an XSL transform to create a more suitable structure, as described in the next section.

■ **Tip** To learn how to format the TreeView, including how to tweak gridlines and node pictures, refer to Chapter 16.

Using XSLT to Prepare Data for Binding in a TreeView

The XmlDataSource has similar built-in support for XSL transformations. The difference is that you don't use the stylesheet to convert the XML to HTML. Instead, you use it to convert the source XML document into an XML structure that's easier to data bind. For example, you might generate an XML document with just the results you want and generate a flattened structure (with elements converted into attributes) for easier data binding.

To specify a stylesheet, you can set the XmlDataSource.TransformFile property to point to a file with the XSL transform, or you can supply the stylesheet as a single long string using the XmlDataSource. Transform property. You can use both stylesheets and XPath expressions, but the stylesheet is always applied first.

```
<asp:XmlDataSource ID="sourceDVD" runat="server" DataFile="DvdList.xml"
  TransformFile="DVDTreeList.xsl" />
```

One good reason to use the XSLT features of the XmlDataSource is to get your XML data ready for display in a hierarchical control such as the TreeView. For example, imagine you want to create a list of stars grouped by movie. You also want to put all the content into attributes so it's easy to bind.

Here's the final XML you'd like:

```
<Movies>
  <DVD ID="1" Title="The Matrix">
    <Star Name="Keanu Reeves" />
    <Star Name="Laurence Fishburne" />
  </DVD>
  <DVD ID="2" Title="Forest Gump">
    <Star Name="Tom Hanks" />
    <Star Name="Robin Wright" />
  </DVD>
  ...
</Movies>
```

You can transform the original XML into this markup using the following XSL stylesheet:

```
<xsl:stylesheet xmlns:xsl="http://www.w3.org/1999/XSL/Transform" version="1.0">

  <xsl:output method="xml"/>
  <xsl:template match="/">
    <!-- Rename the root element. -->
    <xsl:element name="Movies">
      <xsl:apply-templates select="/DvdList/DVD" />
    </xsl:element>
  </xsl:template>

  <xsl:template match="DVD">
    <!-- Keep the DVD element with the same name. -->
    <xsl:element name="{name()}">
      <!-- Keep the ID attribute. -->
      <xsl:attribute name="ID">
        <xsl:value-of select="@ID"/>
      </xsl:attribute>
      <!-- Put the nested <Title> text into an attribute. -->
      <xsl:attribute name="Title">
        <xsl:value-of select="Title/text()"/>
      </xsl:attribute>
      <xsl:apply-templates select="Starring" />
    </xsl:element>
  </xsl:template>
```

```
  <xsl:template match="Starring">
    <xsl:element name="Stars">
      <!-- Put the nested <Star> text into an attribute. -->
      <xsl:attribute name="Name">
        <xsl:value-of select="Star/text()"/>
      </xsl:attribute>
    </xsl:element>
  </xsl:template>

</xsl:stylesheet>
```

Now you can bind this to the TreeView and display it with this set of bindings:

```
<asp:TreeView ID="TreeView1" runat="server" DataSourceID="sourceDVD"
 AutoGenerateDataBindings="False">
  <DataBindings>
    <asp:TreeNodeBinding DataMember="Movies" Text="Movies" />
    <asp:TreeNodeBinding DataMember="DVD" TextField="Title" />
    <asp:TreeNodeBinding DataMember="Stars" TextField="Name" />
  </DataBindings>
</asp:TreeView>
```

Binding to XML Content from Other Sources

So far, all the examples you've seen have bound to XML content in a file. This is the standard scenario for the XmlDataSource control, but it's not your only possibility. The other option is to supply the XML as text through the XmlDataSource.Data property.

You can set the Data property at any point before the binding takes place. One convenient time is during the Page.Load event:

```
Protected Sub Page_Load(ByVal sender As Object, ByVal e As EventArgs)
    Dim xmlContent As String
    ' (Retrieve XML content from another location.)
    sourceDVD.Data = xmlContent
End Sub
```

■Tip If you use this approach, you may find it's still a good idea to set the XmlDataSource.DataFile property at design time in order for Visual Studio to load the schema information about your XML document and make it available to other controls. Just remember to remove this setting when you're finished developing, as the DataFile property overrides the Data property if they are both set.

This allows you to read XML content from another source (such as a database) and still work with the bound data controls. However, it requires adding some custom code.

Even if you do use the XmlDataSource.Data property, XML data binding still isn't nearly as flexible as the .NET XML classes you learned about earlier in this chapter. One of the key limitations is that the XML content needs to be loaded into memory all at once as a string object. If you're dealing with large XML documents, or you just need to ensure the best possible scalability for your web application, you might be able to reduce the overhead considerably by using the XmlReader instead, even though it will require much more code. Handling the XML parsing process yourself also gives you unlimited flexibility to rearrange and aggregate your data into a meaningful summary, which isn't always easy using XSLT alone.

■ **Note** If you *do* use the XmlDataSource to display XML data from a file, make sure you use caching to reduce the number of times that the file needs to be opened with the CacheDuration, CacheDependency, and CachePolicy properties. If your file changes infrequently, you'll be able to keep it in the cache indefinitely, which guarantees good performance. On the other hand, if you need to update the underlying XML document frequently, you're likely to run into multiuser concurrency headaches, as discussed in Chapter 13.

Updating XML Through the XmlDataSource

Unlike the SqlDataSource and the ObjectDataSource, the XmlDataSource doesn't support editable binding. You can confirm this fact with a simple test—just bind the XmlDataSource to GridView, and add a CommandField with edit buttons. When you try to commit the update, you'll get an error informing you that the data source doesn't support this feature.

However, the XmlDataSource does provide a Save() method. This method replaces the file specified in the DataFile property with the current XML content. Although you need to add code to call the Save() method, some developers have used this technique to provide editable XML data binding.

The basic technique is as follows: when the user commits a change in a control, your code retrieves the current XML content as an XmlDocument object by calling the XmlDataSource.GetXmlDocument() method. Then, your code finds the corresponding node and makes the change using the features of XmlDocument (as described earlier in this chapter). You can find and edit specific nodes, remove nodes, or add nodes. Finally, your code must call the XmlDataSource.Save() method to commit the change.

Although this approach works perfectly well, it's not necessarily a great way to design a website. The XML manipulation code can become quite long, and you're likely to run into concurrency headaches if two users make different changes to the same XmlDocument at once. If you need to change XML content, it's almost always a better idea to implement the logic you need in a separate component, using the XML classes described earlier.

XML and ADO.NET

Now that you've taken an exhaustive look at general-purpose XML and .NET, it's worth taking a look at a related topic—the XML support that's built into ADO.NET.

ADO.NET supports XML through the disconnected DataSet and DataTable objects. Both have the built-in intelligence to convert their collection rows into an XML document. You might use this functionality for several reasons. For example, you might want to share data with another application on another platform. Or you might simply use the XML format to serialize to disk so you can retrieve it later. In this case, you still use the same methods, although the actual data format isn't important.

Table 12-2 lists all the XML methods of the DataSet.

Table 12-2. *DataSet Methods for Using XML*

Method	Description
GetXml()	Retrieves the XML representation of the data in the DataSet as a single string.
WriteXml()	Writes the contents of the DataSet to a file or a TextWriter, XmlWriter, or Stream object. You can choose a write mode that determines if change tracking information and schema information is also written to the file.

Method	Description
ReadXml()	Reads XML data from a file or a TextReader, XmlReader, or Stream object and uses it to populate the DataSet.
GetXmlSchema()	Retrieves the XML schema for the DataSet XML as a single string. No data is returned.
WriteXmlSchema()	Writes just the XML schema describing the structure of the DataSet to a file or a TextWriter, XmlWriter, or Stream object. You can choose to include the schema at the beginning of the document.
ReadXmlSchema()	Reads an XML schema from a file or a TextReader, XmlReader, or Stream object and uses it to configure the structure of the DataSet.
InferXmlSchema()	Reads an XML document with DataSet contents from a file or a TextReader, XmlReader, or Stream object and uses it to infer what structure the DataSet should have. This is an alternate approach to using the ReadXmlSchema() method, but it doesn't guarantee that all the data type information is preserved.

■ **Note** .NET 2.0 adds support for XML directly to the DataTable class. This means you can use the ReadXml(), WriteXml(), ReadXmlSchema(), and WriteXmlSchema() methods of the DataTable to read or write XML for a single table in a DataSet.

Converting the DataSet to XML

Using the XML methods of the DataSet is quite straightforward, as you'll see in the next example. This example uses two GridView controls on a page. The first DataSet is filled directly from the Employees table of the Northwind database. (The code isn't shown here because it's similar to what you've seen in the previous chapters.) The second DataSet is filled using XML.

Here's how it works: once the DataSet has been created, you can generate an XML schema file describing the structure of the DataSet and an XML file containing the contents of every row. The easiest approach is to use the WriteXmlSchema() and WriteXml() methods of the DataSet. These methods provide several overloads, including a version that lets you write data directly to a physical file. When you write the XML data, you can choose between several slightly different formats by specifying an XmlWriteMode. You can indicate that you want to save both the data and the schema in a single file (XmlWriteMode.WriteSchema), only the data (XmlWriteMode.IgnoreSchema), or the data with both the current and the original values (XmlWriteMode.DiffGram).

Here's the code that you need in order to save a DataSet to an XML file:

```
Dim xmlFile As String = Server.MapPath("Employees.xml")
ds.WriteXml(xmlFile, XmlWriteMode.WriteSchema)
```

This code creates an Employees.xml file in the current folder.

Now you can perform the reverse step by creating a new DataSet object and filling it with the data contained in the XML file using the DataSetReadXml() method as follows:

```
Dim dsXml As New DataSet("Northwind")
dsXml.ReadXml(xmlFile)
```

If you want to see the structure of the generated Employees.xml file, you can open it in Internet Explorer, as shown in Figure 12-15. Notice how the first part contains the schema that describes the structure of the table (name, type, and size of the fields), followed by the data itself.

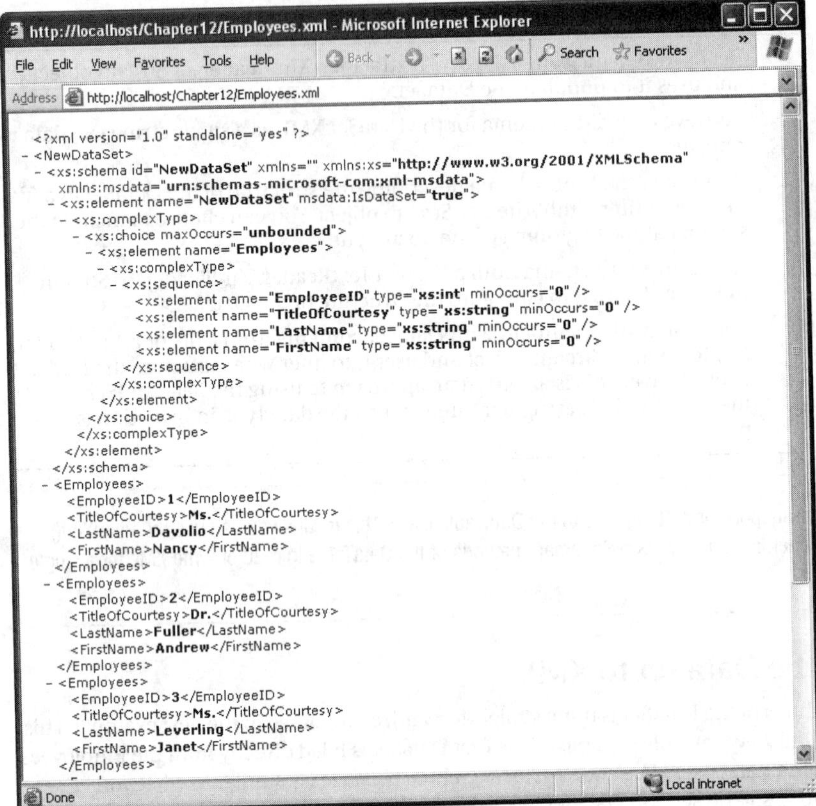

Figure 12-15. *Examining the DataSet XML*

The DataSet XML follows a predefined format with a few simple rules:

- The root document element is the DataSet.DataSetName (for example, Northwind).
- Each row in every table is contained in a separate element, using the name of the table. The example with one table means that there are multiple <Employees> elements.
- Every field in the row is contained as a separate tag in the table row tag. The value of the field is stored as text inside the tag.

Unfortunately, the DataSet doesn't make it possible for you to alter the overall structure. If you need to convert the DataSet to another form of XML, you need to manipulate it by using XSLT or by loading it into an XmlDocument object.

Accessing a DataSet As XML

Another option provided by the DataSet is the ability to access it through an XML interface. This allows you to perform XML-specific tasks (such as hunting for a tag or applying an XSL transformation) with the data you've extracted from a database. To do so, you create an XmlDataDocument that wraps the DataSet. When you create the XmlDataDocument, you supply the DataSet you want as a parameter, as follows:

```
Dim dataDocument As XmlDataDocument = New XmlDataDocument(myDataSet)
```

Now you can look at the DataSet in two ways. Because the XmlDataDocument inherits from the XmlDocument class, it provides all the same properties and methods for examining nodes and modifying content. You can use this XML-based approach to deal with your data, or you can manipulate the DataSet through the XmlDataDocument.DataSet property. In either case, the two views are kept automatically synchronized—when you change the DataSet, the XML is updated immediately, and vice versa. This can lead to a large performance hit, so exercise caution in using it.

For example, consider the pubs database, which includes a table of authors. Using the XmlDataDocument, you could examine a list of authors as an XML document and then apply an XSL transformation with the help of the Xml web control. Here's the complete code you'd need:

```
' Create the ADO.NET objects.
Dim con As New SqlConnection(connectionString)
Dim SQL As String = "SELECT * FROM authors WHERE city='Oakland'"
Dim cmd As New SqlCommand(SQL, con)
Dim adapter As New SqlDataAdapter(cmd)
Dim ds As New DataSet("AuthorsDataSet")

' Retrieve the data.
con.Open()
adapter.Fill(ds, "AuthorsTable")
con.Close()

' Create the XmlDataDocument that wraps this DataSet.
Dim dataDoc As New XmlDataDocument(ds)

' Display the XML data (with the help of an XSLT) in the XML web control.
XmlControl.Document = dataDoc
XmlControl.TransformSource = "authors.xslt"
```

Here's the XSL stylesheet that does the work of converting the XML data into ready-to-display HTML:

```
<?xml version="1.0" encoding="UTF-8" ?>
<xsl:stylesheet xmlns:xsl="http://www.w3.org/1999/XSL/Transform" version="1.0">
  <xsl:template match="AuthorsDataSet">
    <h1>The Author List</h1>
      <xsl:apply-templates select="AuthorsTable"/>
    <i>Created through XML and XSLT</i>
  </xsl:template>

  <xsl:template match="AuthorsTable">
    <p><b>Name: </b><xsl:value-of select="au_lname"/>,
    <xsl:value-of select="au_fname"/><br/>
    <b>Phone: </b> <xsl:value-of select="phone"/></p>
  </xsl:template>
</xsl:stylesheet>
```

Figure 12-16 shows the processed data in HTML form.

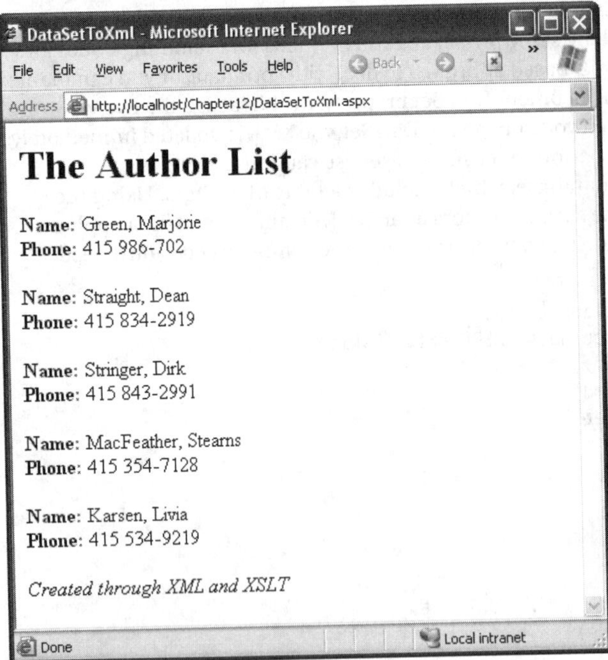

Figure 12-16. *Displaying the results of a query through XML and XSLT*

Remember that when you interact with your data as XML, all the customary database-oriented concepts such as relationships and unique constraints go out the window. The only reason you should interact with your DataSet as XML is if you need to perform an XML-specific task. You shouldn't use XML manipulation to replace the approaches used in earlier chapters to update data. In most cases, you'll find it easier to use advanced controls such as the GridView, rather than creating a dedicated XSL stylesheet to transform data into the HTML you want to display.

Executing an XML Query

SQL Server 2000 and later provide built-in support for XML. You can execute any query and return the results as an XML fragment by adding the FOR XML clause to your query. This feature is completely separate from the XML features of the DataSet. However, it gives you another way to retrieve data from one or more tables in a database and work with it as XML.

■ **Note** An XML fragment contains valid XML syntax, but isn't necessarily a valid document of its own. Usually, this is because there is no root element. An XML document requires all elements to be nested in a single root element.

The FOR XML clause supports a specialized syntax that allows you to specify the exact structure and naming of the resulting document. However, this syntax doesn't conform to any XML standard, and it's notoriously messy. As a result, XML queries often use one of the two default XML representations that SQL Server provides. The first is FOR XML AUTO.

For example, if you execute this query:

```
SELECT FirstName, LastName FROM Employees FOR XML AUTO
```

you'll receive results like this:

```
<Employees FirstName="Nancy" LastName="Davolio"/>
<Employees FirstName="Andrew" LastName="Fuller"/>
<Employees FirstName="Janet" LastName="Leverling"/>
...
```

As you can see, each record is a separate element, with all the fields as attributes. The other easy option is FOR XML AUTO, ELEMENTS. Here's an example:

```
SELECT FirstName, LastName FROM Employees FOR XML AUTO, ELEMENTS
```

In this case, the data you'll receive uses separate elements for each row and each field, as shown here:

```
<Employees>
  <FirstName>Nancy</FirstName>
  <LastName>Davolio</LastName>
</Employees>
<Employees>
  <FirstName>Andrew</FirstName>
  <LastName>Fuller</LastName>
</Employees>
<Employees>
  <FirstName>Janet</FirstName>
  <LastName>Leverling</LastName>
</Employees>
...
```

Tip You can also fine-tune the format in much more painstaking detail using the FOR XML EXPLICIT syntax. For example, this allows you to convert some fields to attributes and others to elements. Refer to the SQL Server Books Online for more information. Unfortunately, the FOR XML query syntax is specific to SQL Server and isn't supported by other database products. Note also that SQL Server 2005 has much better support for XML, including a native XML data type and the facility to do XQuery operations.

To perform an XML query, you must use the SqlCommand.ExecuteXmlReader() method. This method returns an XmlReader with the results of your query as an XML fragment. You can move through the XmlReader one node at a time in a forward-only direction in the same way you use the XmlTextReader. In fact, XmlTextReader derives from XmlReader.

Here's the code needed to retrieve and display a customer list on a web page:

```
' Define the command.
Dim customerQuery As String =
      "SELECT FirstName, LastName FROM Employees FOR XML AUTO, ELEMENTS"
Dim con As New SqlConnection(connectionString)
Dim com As New SqlCommand(customerQuery, con)

' Execute the command.
Dim str As New StringBuilder()
Try
    con.Open()
    Dim reader As XmlReader = com.ExecuteXmlReader()

    Do While reader.Read()
        ' Process each employee.
```

```
        If (reader.Name = "Employees") AndAlso
              (reader.NodeType = XmlNodeType.Element) Then
            reader.ReadStartElement("Employees")
            str.Append(reader.ReadElementString("FirstName"))
            str.Append(" ")
            str.Append(reader.ReadElementString("LastName"))
            str.Append("<br />")
            reader.ReadEndElement()
        End If
    Loop
    reader.Close()
Finally
    con.Close()
End Try
XmlText.Text = str.ToString()
```

Of course, life gets much more interesting when you combine an XML query with some of the other standards you've seen in this chapter, such as XPath searching or XSL transformation. These techniques aren't for everyone, but they do give you the ability to transform your data into virtually any XML representation.

Summary

In this chapter, you got a taste of ASP.NET's XML features. The class libraries for interacting with XML are available to any .NET application, whether it's a Windows application, a web application, or a simple command-line tool. They provide one of the most fully featured toolkits for working with XML and other standards such as XPath, XML Schema, and XSLT.

XML is a vast topic, and there is much more to cover, such as advanced navigation, search and selection techniques, validation, and serialization. If you want to learn more about XML in .NET, you may want to refer to *Pro .NET XML* (Apress, 2005). But remember that you should use XML only where it's warranted. XML is a great tool for persisting file-based data in a readable format and for sharing information with other application components and services. However, it doesn't replace the core data management techniques you've seen in previous chapters.

CHAPTER 13

Files and Streams

Most web applications rely heavily on databases to store information. Databases are unmatched in multiuser scenarios. They handle simultaneous access without a hitch, and they support caching and low-level disk optimizations that guarantee blistering performance. Quite simply, an RDBMS offers the most robust and best-performing storage for data.

Of course, most web developers inevitably face a scenario where they need to access data in other locations, such as the file system. Common examples include reading information produced by another application, writing a quick-and-dirty log for testing purposes, and creating a management page that allows administrators to upload files and view what's currently on the server. In this chapter, you'll learn how to use the classes in the System.IO namespace to get file system information, work with file paths as strings, write and read files, and serialize objects.

FILE ACCESS CHANGES IN .NET 2.0

The classes for retrieving file information and for reading and writing streams remain essentially the same in .NET 2.0, with a few useful additions. Here are the changes you'll see in this chapter, in their order of appearance:

- *The DriveInfo class*: Along with the existing DirectoryInfo and FileInfo classes, the DriveInfo class allows you to get information about a logical drive on the current computer. It's primarily useful for determining free and used space.
- *The FileUpload control*: FileUpload works almost the same as the HtmlInput control, allowing a user to upload files from a browser. It has one minor convenience—it sets the encoding type of the <form> tag automatically, dodging a common mistake.
- *Compression*: The new System.IO.Compression namespace provides classes that let you compress data using the industry-standard GZIP algorithm.

Working with the File System

The simplest level of file access just involves retrieving information about existing files and directories and performing typical file system operations such as copying files and creating directories. These tasks don't involve actually opening or writing a file (both of which are tasks you'll learn about later in this chapter).

The .NET Framework provides a few basic classes for retrieving file system information. They are all located in the System.IO namespace (and, incidentally, can be used in desktop applications in the same way they are used in web applications). They include the following:

Directory and File: These classes provide Shared methods that allow you to retrieve information about any files and directories that are visible from your server.

DriveInfo, DirectoryInfo, and FileInfo: These classes use similar instance methods and properties to retrieve the same information.

These two sets of classes provide similar methods and properties. The key difference is that you need to create a DirectoryInfo or FileInfo object before you can use any methods, whereas the Shared methods of the Directory and File classes are always available. Typically, the Directory and File classes are more convenient for one-off tasks. On the other hand, if you need to retrieve several pieces of information, it's better to create DirectoryInfo and FileInfo objects. That way you don't need to keep specifying the name of the directory or file each time you call a method. It's also faster. That's because the FileInfo and DirectoryInfo classes perform their security checks once—when you create the object instance. The Directory and File classes perform a security check every time you invoke a method.

The Directory and File Classes

The Directory and File classes provide a number of useful methods. Table 13-1 and Table 13-2 tell the whole story. Note that every method takes the same parameter: a fully qualified path name identifying the directory or file you want the operation to act on.

Table 13-1. *Directory Methods*

Method	Description
CreateDirectory()	Creates a new directory. If you specify a directory inside another nonexistent directory, ASP.NET will thoughtfully create *all* the required directories.
Delete()	Deletes the corresponding empty directory. To delete a directory along with its contents (subdirectories and files), add the optional second parameter of True.
Exists()	Returns True or False to indicate whether the specified directory exists.
GetCreationTime(), GetLastAccessTime(), and GetLastWriteTime()	Returns a Date object that represents the time the directory was created, accessed, or written to. Each "Get" method has a corresponding "Set" method, which isn't shown in this table.
GetDirectories(), GetFiles(), and GetLogicalDrives()	Returns an array of strings, one for each subdirectory, file, or drive in the specified directory (depending on which method you're using). The GetDirectories and GetFiles methods can also accept a second parameter that specifies a search expression (such as ASP*.*). Drive letters are in the format of c:\.
GetParent()	Parses the supplied directory string and tells you what the parent directory is. You could do this on your own by searching for the \ character (or, more generically, the Path.DirectorySeparatorChar), but this function makes life a little easier.
GetCurrentDirectory() and SetCurrentDirectory()	Allows you to set and retrieve the current directory, which is useful if you need to use relative paths instead of full paths. Generally, you shouldn't rely on these functions—use full paths instead.
Move()	Accepts two parameters: the source path and the destination path. The directory and all its contents can be moved to any path, as long as it's located on the same drive.
GetAccessControl()	Returns a System.Security.AccessControl.DirectorySecurity object. You can use this object to examine the Windows ACLs (access control lists) that are applied on this directory and even change them programmatically.

Table 13-2. *File Methods*

Method	Description
Copy()	Accepts two parameters: the fully qualified source filename and the fully qualified destination filename. To allow overwriting, use the version that takes a Boolean third parameter and set it to True.
Delete()	Deletes the specified file but doesn't throw an exception if the file can't be found.
Exists()	Indicates True or False whether a specified file exists.
GetAttributes() and SetAttributes()	Retrieves or sets an enumerated value that can include any combination of the values from the FileAttributes enumeration.
GetCreationTime(), GetLastAccessTime(), and GetLastWriteTime()	Returns a DateTime object that represents the time the file was created, accessed, or last written to. Each "Get" method has a corresponding "Set" method, which isn't shown in this table.
Move()	Accepts two parameters: the fully qualified source filename and the fully qualified destination filename. You can move a file across drives and even rename it while you move it (or rename it without moving it).
Create() and CreateText()	Creates the specified file and returns a FileStream object that you can use to write to it. CreateText() performs the same task but returns a StreamWriter object that wraps the stream.
Open(), OpenRead(), OpenRead(), and OpenText()	Opens a file (provided it exists). OpenText() and OpenRead() open a file in read-only mode, returning a FileStream or StreamReader. OpenWrite() opens a file in write-only mode, returning a FileStream.
ReadAllText(), ReadAllLines(), and ReadAllBytes()	Reads the entire file and returns its contents as a single string, an array of strings (one for each line), or an array of bytes. Use this method only for very small files. For larger files, use streams to read one chunk at a time and reduce the memory overhead.
WriteAllText(), WriteAllLines(), and WriteAllBytes()	Writes an entire file in one shot using a supplied string, array of strings (one for each line), or array of bytes. If the file already exists, it is overwritten.
GetAccessControl()	Returns a System.Security.AccessControl.FileSecurity object. You can use this object to examine the Windows ACLs that are applied on this directory and even change them programmatically.

■ **Tip** The only feature that the File class lacks (and the FileInfo class provides) is the ability to retrieve the size of a specified file.

The File and Directory methods are completely intuitive. For example, you could use this code to write a dynamic list displaying the name of each file in the current directory:

```
Dim strDirectoryName As String = "c:\Temp"

' Retrieve the list of files, and display it in the page.
Dim fileList As String() = Directory.GetFiles(ftpDirectory)
For Each file As String In fileList
    lstFiles.Items.Add(file)
Next
```

Because the list of files is simply an ordinary list of strings, it can easily be bound to a list control, resulting in the following more efficient syntax for displaying the files on a page:

```
Dim strDirectoryName As String = "c:\Temp"
lstFiles.DataSource = Directory.GetFiles(ftpDirectory)
lstFiles.DataBind()
```

Note For this code to work, the account that is used to run the ASP.NET worker process must have rights to the directory you're using. Otherwise, a SecurityException will be thrown when your web page attempts to access the file system. You can modify the permissions for a directory by right-clicking the directory, selecting Properties, and choosing the Security tab. If you are using the default ASP.NET settings with IIS 5, you need to grant read and write permissions to the ASPNET account. (With IIS 6, the local network account is used instead.) Alternatively, you might find it easier to modify the account that ASP.NET uses so you don't need to change these permissions at all. For more information, refer to Chapter 18, which explains how to configure the account used for ASP.NET applications.

The DirectoryInfo and FileInfo Classes

The DirectoryInfo and FileInfo classes mirror the functionality in the Directory and File classes. In addition, they make it easy to walk through directory and file relationships. For example, you can easily retrieve the FileInfo objects of files in a directory represented by a DirectoryInfo object.

Note that while the Directory and File classes expose only methods, DirectoryInfo and FileInfo provide a combination of properties and methods. For example, while the File class had separate GetAttributes() and SetAttributes() methods, the FileInfo class exposes a read-write Attributes property.

Another nice thing about the DirectoryInfo and FileInfo classes is that they share a common set of properties and methods because they derive from the common FileSystemInfo base class. Table 13-3 describes the members they have in common.

Table 13-3. *DirectoryInfo and FileInfo Members*

Member	Description
Attributes	Allows you to retrieve or set attributes using a combination of values from the FileAttributes enumeration.
CreationTime, LastAccessTime, and LastWriteTime	Allows you to set or retrieve the creation time, last access time, and last write time using a Date object.
Exists	Returns True or False depending on whether the file or directory exists. In other words, you can create FileInfo and DirectoryInfo objects that don't actually correspond to current physical directories, although you obviously won't be able to use properties such as CreationTime and methods such as MoveTo().
FullName, Name, and Extension	Returns a string that represents the fully qualified name, the directory or filename (with extension), or the extension on its own, depending on which property you use.
Delete()	Removes the file or directory, if it exists. When deleting a directory, it must be empty, or you must specify an optional parameter set to True.
Refresh()	Updates the object so it's synchronized with any file system changes that have happened in the meantime (for example, if an attribute was changed manually using Windows Explorer).
Create()	Creates the specified directory or file.
MoveTo()	Copies the directory and its contents or the file. For a DirectoryInfo object, you need to specify the new path; for a FileInfo object, you specify a path and filename.

In addition, the FileInfo and DirectoryInfo classes have a couple of unique members, as indicated in Table 13-4 and Table 13-5.

Table 13-4. *Unique DirectoryInfo Members*

Member	Description
Parent and Root	Returns a DirectoryInfo object that represents the parent or root directory.
CreateSubdirectory()	Creates a directory with the specified name in the directory represented by the DirectoryInfo object. It also returns a new DirectoryInfo object that represents the subdirectory.
GetDirectories()	Returns an array of DirectoryInfo objects that represent all the subdirectories contained in this directory.
GetFiles()	Returns an array of FileInfo objects that represent all the files contained in this directory.

Table 13-5. *Unique FileInfo Members*

Member	Description
Directory	Returns a DirectoryInfo object that represents the parent directory.
StrDirectoryName	Returns a string that identifies the name of the parent directory.
Length	Returns a long (64-bit integer) with the file size in bytes.
CopyTo()	Copies a file to the new path and filename specified as a parameter. It also returns a new FileInfo object that represents the new (copied) file. You can supply an optional additional parameter of True to allow overwriting.
Create() and CreateText()	Creates the specified file and returns a FileStream object that you can use to write to it. CreateText() performs the same task but returns a StreamWriter object that wraps the stream.
Open(), OpenRead(), OpenText(), and OpenWrite()	Opens a file (provided it exists). OpenRead() and OpenText() open a file in read-only mode, returning a FileStream or StreamReader. OpenWrite() opens a file in write-only mode, returning a FileStream.

When you create a DirectoryInfo or FileInfo object, you specify the full path in the constructor, as shown here:

```
Dim myDirectory As New DirectoryInfo("c:\Temp")
Dim myFile As New FileInfo("c:\Temp\readme.txt")
```

When you create a new DirectoryInfo or FileInfo object, you'll receive an exception if the path you used isn't properly formed (for example, if it contains illegal characters). However, the path doesn't need to correspond to a real physical file or directory. If you're not sure, you can use Exists to check whether your directory or file really exists.

If the file or directory doesn't exist, you can always use a method such as Create() to create it. Here's an example:

```
' Define the new directory and file.
Dim myDirectory As New DirectoryInfo("c:\Temp\Test")
Dim myFile As New FileInfo("c:\Temp\Test\readme.txt")

' Now create them. Order here is important.
' You can't create a file in a directory that doesn't exist yet.
myDirectory.Create()
Dim stream As FileStream = myFile.Create()
stream.Close()
```

The FileInfo and DirectoryInfo objects retrieve information from the file system the first time you query a property. They don't check for new information on subsequent use. This could lead to inconsistency if the file changes in the meantime. If you know or suspect that file system information has changed for the given object, you should call the Refresh() method to retrieve the latest information.

The DirectoryInfo class doesn't provide any property for determining the total size information. However, you can calculate the size of all the files in a particular directory quite easily by totaling the FileInfo.Length contribution of each one.

Before you take this step, you need to decide whether to include subdirectories in the total. The following method lets you use either approach:

```
Private Shared Function GetDirectorySize(ByVal directory As DirectoryInfo,
      ByVal includeSubdirectories As Boolean) As Long
    Dim totalSize As Long = 0

    ' Add up each file.
    Dim files As FileInfo() = directory.GetFiles()
    For Each file As FileInfo In files
        totalSize += file.Length
    Next

    ' Add up each subdirectory, if required.
    If includeSubdirectories Then
        Dim dirs As DirectoryInfo() = directory.GetDirectories()
        For Each dir As DirectoryInfo In dirs
            totalSize += CalculateDirectorySize(dir, True)
        Next
    End If
    Return totalSize
End Function
```

For information about free space, you need to use the DriveInfo class.

The DriveInfo Class

The DriveInfo class (new in .NET 2.0) allows you to retrieve information about a drive on your computer. Few pieces of information will interest you—typically, the DriveInfo class is just used to retrieve the total amount of used and free space.

Table 13-6 shows the DriveInfo members. Unlike the FileInfo and DriveInfo classes, there is no Drive class to provide instance versions of these methods.

Table 13-6. *DriveInfo Members*

Member	Description
TotalSize	Gets the total size of the drive, in bytes. This includes allocated and free space.
TotalFreeSpace	Gets the total amount of free space, in bytes.
AvailableFreeSpace	Gets the total amount of available free space, in bytes. Available space may be less than the total free space if you've applied disk quotas limiting the space that the ASP.NET process can use.
DriveFormat	Returns the name of the file system used on the drive (such as NTFS or FAT32).
DriveType	Returns a value from the DriveType enumeration, which indicates whether the drive is a fixed, network, CD-ROM, RAM, or removable drive. (It returns Unknown if the drive's type cannot be determined.)

Member	Description
IsReady	Returns whether the drive is ready for reading or writing operations. Removable drives are considered "not ready" if they don't have any media. For example, if there's no CD in a CD drive, IsReady will return False. In this situation, it's not safe to query the other DriveInfo properties. Fixed drives are always read.
Name	Returns the drive letter name of the drive (such as C: or E:).
VolumeLabel	Returns the descriptive volume label for the drive. In an NTFS-formatted drive, the volume label can be up to 32 characters. If not set, this property returns Nothing.
RootDirectory	Returns a DirectoryInfo object for the root directory in this drive.
GetDrives()	Retrieves an array of DriveInfo objects, representing all the logical drives on the current computer.

■ **Tip** Attempting to read from a drive that's not ready (for example, a CD drive that doesn't currently have a CD in it) will throw an exception. To avoid this problem, check the DriveInfo.IsReady property and attempt to read other properties only if the DriveInfo.IsReady property returns True.

Working with Attributes

The Attributes property of the FileInfo and DirectoryInfo classes represent the file system attributes for the file or directory. Because every file and directory can have a combination of attributes, the Attributes property contains a combination of values from the FileAttributes enumeration. Table 13-7 describes these values.

Table 13-7. *Values for the FileAttributes Enumeration*

Value	Description
Archive	The item is archived. Applications can use this attribute to mark files for backup or removal, although it's really just a holdover from older DOS-based operating systems.
Compressed	The item is compressed.
Device	Not currently used. Reserved for future use.
Directory	The item is a directory.
Encrypted	This item is encrypted. For a file, this means that all data in the file is encrypted. For a directory, this means that encryption is the default for newly created files and directories.
Hidden	This item is hidden and thus is not included in an ordinary directory listing. However, you can still see it in Windows Explorer.
Normal	This item is normal and has no other attributes set. This attribute is valid only if used alone.
NotContentIndexed	This item will not be indexed by the operating system's content indexing service.
Offline	This file is offline and not currently available.
ReadOnly	This item is read-only.
ReparsePoint	This file contains a reparse point, which is a block of user-defined data associated with a file or a directory in an NTFS file system.

(Continued)

Table 13-7. *Continued*

Value	Description
SparseFile	The file is a sparse file. Sparse files are typically large files with data consisting of mostly zeros. This item is supported only on NTFS file systems.
System	The item is part of the operating system or is used exclusively by the operating system.
Temporary	This item is temporary and can be deleted when the application is no longer using it.

To examine the attributes on a file, you can use the GetAttributes() method and the FileAttributes enumeration as shown here:

```
If (File.GetAttributes(path) And FileAttributes.Hidden) = FileAttributes.Hidden Then
    ...
Next
```

You can also call the ToString() method of the Attributes property. This returns a string with a comma-separated list of attributes:

```
' This displays a string in the format "ReadOnly, Archive, Encrypted"
lblInfo.Text = myFile.Attributes.ToString()
```

When testing for a single specific attribute, you need to use bitwise arithmetic. For example, consider the following faulty code:

```
If myFile.Attributes = FileAttributes.ReadOnly Then
    ...
End If
```

This test succeeds only if the read-only attribute is the *only* attribute for the current file. This is rarely the case. If you want to successfully check whether the file is read-only, you need this code instead:

```
If (myFile.Attributes And FileAttributes.ReadOnly) = FileAttributes.ReadOnly Then
    ...
End If
```

This test succeeds because it filters out just the read-only attribute. Essentially, the Attributes setting consists (in binary) of a series of ones and zeros, such as 00010011. Each 1 represents an attribute that is present, and each 0 represents an attribute that is not. When you use the And operator with an enumerated value, it automatically performs a *bitwise and* operation, which compares each digit against each digit in the enumerated value. For example, if you combine a value of 00100001 (representing an individual file's archive and read-only attributes) with the enumerated value 00000001 (which represents the read-only flag), the resulting value will be 00000001. It will have a 1 only where it can be matched in both values. You can then test this resulting value against the FileAttributes.ReadOnly enumerated value using the equal sign.

Similar logic allows you to verify that a file does *not* have a specific attribute:

```
If Not(myFile.Attributes And FileAttributes.ReadOnly)
  = FileAttributes.ReadOnly Then
    ...
End If
```

When setting an attribute, you must also use bitwise arithmetic. In this case, it's needed to ensure that you don't inadvertently wipe out the other attributes that are already set.

```
' This adds just the read-only attribute.
myFile.Attributes = myFile.Attributes Or FileAttributes.ReadOnly

' This removes just the read-only attribute.
myFile.Attributes = myFile.Attributes And Not FileAttributes.ReadOnly
```

Note Some attributes can't be set programmatically. For example, the Encrypted attributed is set by the operating system only if you are using EFS (Encrypting File System) to encrypt files.

Filter Files with Wildcards

The DirectoryInfo and Directory objects both provide a way to search the current directories for files or directories that match a specific filter expression. These search expressions can use the standard ? and * wildcards. The ? wildcard represents any single character, and the * wildcard represents any sequence of zero or more characters.

For example, the following code snippet retrieves the names of all the files in the c:\temp directory that have the extension .txt. The code then iterates through the retrieved FileInfo collection of matching files and displays the name and size of each one.

```
Dim dir As New DirectoryInfo("c:\temp")

' Get all the files with the .txt extension.
Dim files As FileInfo() = dir.GetFiles("*.txt")

' Process each file.
For Each file as FileInfo in files
    ...
Next
```

You can use a similar technique to retrieve directories that match a specified search pattern by using the overloaded DirectoryInfo.GetDirectories() method.

The GetFiles() and GetDirectories() methods search only the current directory. If you want to perform a search through all the contained subdirectories, you'd need to use recursive logic.

Retrieving File Version Information

File version information is the information you see when you look at the properties of an EXE or DLL file in Windows Explorer. Version information commonly includes a version number, the company that produced the component, trademark information, and so on.

The FileInfo and File classes don't provide a way to retrieve file version information. However, you can retrieve it quite easily using the Shared GetVersionInfo() method of the System.Diagnostics.FileVersionInfo class. The following example uses this technique to get a string with the complete version information and then displays it in a label:

```
Dim fileName As String = "c:\Windows\explorer.exe"
Dim info As FileVersionInfo = FileVersionInfo.GetVersionInfo(fileName)
lblInfo.Text = info.FileVersion
```

Table 13-8 lists the properties you can read.

Table 13-8. *FileVersionInfo Properties*

Property	Description
FileVersion, FileMajorPart, FileMinorPart, FileBuildPart, and FilePrivatePart	Typically, a version number is displayed as [MajorNumber].[MinorNumber].[BuildNumber].[Private PartNumber]. These properties allow you to retrieve the complete version as a string (FileVersion) or each individual component as a number.
FileName	Gets the name of the file that this instance of FileVersionInfo describes.
OriginalFilename	Gets the name the file was created with.
InternalName	Gets the internal name of the file, if one exists.
FileDescription	Gets the description of the file.
CompanyName	Gets the name of the company that produced the file.
ProductName	Gets the name of the product this file is distributed with.
ProductVersion, ProductMajorPart, ProductMinorPart, ProductBuildPart, and ProductPrivatePart	These properties allow you to retrieve the complete product version as a string (ProductVersion) or each individual component as a number.
IsDebug	Gets a Boolean value that specifies whether the file contains debugging information or is compiled with debugging features enabled.
IsPatched	Gets a Boolean value that specifies whether the file has been modified and is not identical to the original shipping file of the same version number.
IsPreRelease	Gets a Boolean value that specifies whether the file is a development version, rather than a commercially released product.
IsPrivateBuild	Gets a Boolean value that specifies whether the file was built using standard release procedures.
IsSpecialBuild	Gets a Boolean value that specifies whether the file is a special build.
SpecialBuild	If IsSpecialBuild is True, this property contains a string that specifies how the build differs from an ordinary build.
Comments	Gets the comments associated with the file.
Language	Gets the default language string for the version info block.
LegalCopyright	Gets all copyright notices that apply to the specified file.
LegalTrademarks	Gets the trademarks and registered trademarks that apply to the file.

The Path Class

If you're working with files, you're probably also working with file and directory paths. Path information is stored as an ordinary string, which can lead to a number of problems ranging from minor headaches to serious security breaches.

For example, imagine you write the following block of code to add a filename to a path:

```
Dim dirInfo As New DirectoryInfo("c:\temp\")
Dim file As String = "test.txt"
Dim strPath As String = dirInfo.FullName & "\" & file
```

At first, this code appears to work correctly. However, a problem occurs with the last line if you try to process the root directory. Here's an example of the error:

```
Dim dirInfo As New DirectoryInfo("c:\")
Dim file As String = "test.txt"
Dim strPath As String = dirInfo.FullName & "\" & file
```

The problem here is that the FullName property never returns a trailing backslash. For example, c:\temp\ becomes just c:\temp. However, there's one exception—the root directory c:\, which always includes a trailing backslash. As a result, this seemingly logical code generates the nonsensical path c:\\test.txt and fails.

The proper solution is to use the System.IO.Path class, which provides Shared helper methods that perform common path manipulation tasks. In this case, the Combine() method neatly solves the problem and works with any directory and file, as follows:

```
Dim dirInfo As New DirectoryInfo("c:\")
Dim file As String = "test.txt"
Dim strPath As String = Path.Combine(dirInfo.FullName, file)
```

Minor hiccups like this are bothersome, but they aren't serious. A more significant problem is the security risk of a *canonicalization error*. Canonicalization errors are a specific type of application error that can occur when your code assumes that user-supplied values will always be in a standardized form. Canonicalization errors are low-tech but quite serious, and they usually have the result of allowing a user to perform an action that should be restricted.

One infamous type of canonicalization error is SQL injection, whereby a user submits incorrectly formatted values to trick your application into executing a modified SQL command. (Chapter 7 covered SQL injection in detail.) Other forms of canonicalization problems can occur with file paths and URLs.

For example, consider the following method that returns file data from a fixed document directory:

```
Dim file As New FileInfo(Server.MapPath("Documents\" & txtBox.Text))
' (Read the file and display it in another control.)
```

This code looks simple enough. It concatenates the user-supplied filename with the Documents path, thereby allowing the user to retrieve data from any file in this directory. The problem is that filenames can be represented in multiple formats. Instead of submitting a valid filename, an attacker can submit a qualified filename such as ..\filename. The concatenated path of WebApp\Documents\..\filename will actually retrieve a file from the parent of the Documents directory (WebApp). A similar approach will allow the user to specify any filename on the web application drive. Because the web service is limited only according to the restrictions of the ASP.NET worker process, the user may be allowed to download a sensitive server-side file.

The fix for this code is fairly easy. Once again, you can use the Path class. This time, you use the GetFileName() method to extract just the final filename portion of the string, as shown here:

```
Dim fileName = Path.GetFileName(txtBox.Text)
Dim file As New FileInfo(Server.MapPath(
        Path.Combine("Documents", fileName))
```

This ensures that the user is constrained to the correct directory. If you are dealing with URLs, you can work similar magic with the System.Uri type. For example, here's how you might remove query string arguments from a URI and make sure it refers to a given server and virtual directory:

```
Dim uriString As String = "http://www.wrongsite.com/page.aspx?cmd=run"

Dim theuri As New Uri(uriString)
Dim page As String = System.IO.Path.GetFileName(theuri.AbsolutePath)
' page is now just "page.aspx"

Dim baseUri As New Uri("http://www.rightsite.com")
theuri = New Uri(baseUri, page)
' uri now stores the path http://www.rightsite.com/page.aspx
```

Table 13-9 lists the methods of the Path class.

Table 13-9. *Path Methods*

Methods	Description
Combine()	Combines a path with a filename or a subdirectory.
ChangeExtension()	Modifies the current extension of the file in a string. If no extension is specified, the current extension will be removed.
GetStrDirectoryName()	Returns all the directory information, which is the text between the first and last directory separators (\).
GetFileName()	Returns just the filename portion of a path.
GetFileNameWithoutExtension()	This method is similar to GetFileName(), but it omits the extension from the returned string.
GetFullPath()	This method has no effect on an absolute path, and it changes a relative path into an absolute path using the current directory. For example, if c:\Temp\ is the current directory, calling GetFullPath() on a filename such as test.txt returns c:\Temp\test.txt.
GetPathRoot()	Retrieves a string with the root (for example, C:\), provided that information is in the string. For a relative path, it returns a null reference.
HasExtension()	Returns True if the path ends with an extension.
IsPathRooted()	Returns True if the path is an absolute path and False if it's a relative path.

Although the Path class contains methods for drilling down the directory structure (adding subdirectories to directory paths), it doesn't provide any methods for going back up (removing subdirectories from directory paths). However, you can work around this limitation by using the Combine() method with the relative path .., which means "move one directory up." For good measure, you can also use the GetFullPath() method on the result to return it to a normal form.

Here's an example:

```
Dim strPath As String = "c:\temp\subdir"

strPath = Path.Combine(path, "..")
' path now contains the string "c:\temp\subdir\.."

strPath = Path.GetFullPath(path)
' path now contains the string "c:\temp"
```

■ **Note** In most cases, an exception will be thrown if you supply a path that contains illegal characters to one of these methods. However, path names that contain a wildcard character (* or ?) will not cause the methods to throw an exception.

A File Browser

Using the concepts you've learned so far, it's quite straightforward to put together a simple file-browsing application. Rather than iterating through collections of files and directories manually, this example handles everything using the GridView and some data binding code.

Figure 13-1 shows this program in action as it displays the contents of the c:\Documents and Settings directory.

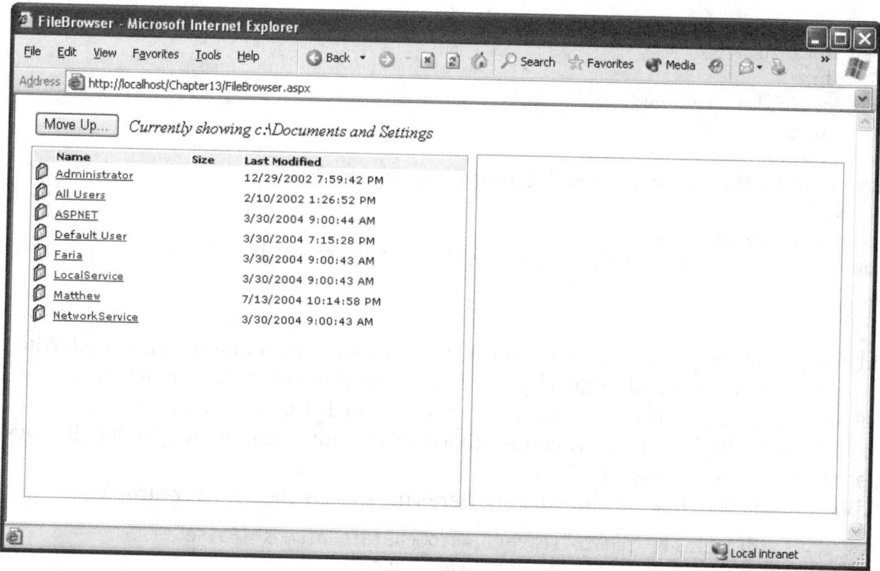

Figure 13-1. *Browsing the file system*

The directory listing is built using two separate GridView controls, one on top of the other. The topmost GridView shows the directories, and the GridView underneath shows files. The only visible differences to the user are that the directories don't display length information and have a folder icon next to their names. The ShowHeader property of the second GridView is set to False so that the two grids blend into each other fairly seamlessly. And because the GridView controls are stacked together, as the list of directories grows the list of files moves down the page to accommodate it.

Technically, you could handle the directory and file listing using one GridView object. That's because all FileInfo and DirectoryInfo objects have a common parent—the FileSystemInfo object. However, in this grid you want to show the size in bytes of each file, and you want to differentiate the appearance (in this case, through different icons). Because the DirectoryInfo object doesn't provide a Length property, trying to bind to it in a more generic list of FileSystemInfo objects would cause an error.

■ Note This problem has another, equally effective solution. You could create a single GridView but not bind directly to the FileInfo.Length property. Instead, you would bind to a method in the page class that examines the current data object and return either the length (for FileInfo objects) or a blank string (for DirectoryInfo objects). You could construct a similar method to hand out the correct icon URL.

Here's the declaration for the GridView control that provides the file list, without the formatting-specific style properties:

```
<asp:GridView ID="gridDirList" runat="server" AutoGenerateColumns="False"
 OnSelectedIndexChanged="gridDirList_SelectedIndexChanged"
 GridLines="None" CellPadding="0" CellSpacing="1"
 DataKeyNames="FullName">
```

```
  <Columns>
    <asp:TemplateField>
      <ItemTemplate>
        <img src="folder.jpg" />
      </ItemTemplate>
    </asp:TemplateField>
    <asp:ButtonField DataTextField="Name" CommandName="Select"
     HeaderText="Name" />
    <asp:BoundField HeaderText="Size" />
    <asp:BoundField DataField="LastWriteTime" HeaderText="Last Modified" />
  </Columns>
</asp:GridView>
```

This grid binds to an array of DirectoryInfo objects and displays the Name, Size, and LastWriteTime properties. In addition, the FullName property is designated as a key field so that you can return the full path after the user clicks one of the directories. You'll also notice that one of the columns doesn't actually display any information—that's the BoundColumn for length that displays header text, but it doesn't link to any data field.

The GridView for the files follows immediately. Here's the slightly shortened control tag:

```
<asp:GridView ID="gridFileList" runat="server" AutoGenerateColumns="False"
 OnSelectedIndexChanged="gridFileList_SelectedIndexChanged"
 GridLines="None" CellPadding="0" CellSpacing="1" DataKeyNames="FullName">

  <SelectedRowStyle BackColor="#C0FFFF" />
  <Columns>
    <asp:TemplateField>
      <ItemTemplate>
        <img src="file.jpg" />
      </ItemTemplate>
    </asp:TemplateField>
    <asp:ButtonField DataTextField="Name" CommandName="Select" />
    <asp:BoundField DataField="Length" />
    <asp:BoundField DataField="LastWriteTime" />
  </Columns>
</asp:GridView>
```

Note that the GridView for displaying files must define a SelectedRowStyle because it supports file selection.

The next step is to write the code that fills these controls. The star of the show is a Private method named ShowDirectoryContents(), which retrieves the contents of the current folder and binds the two GridView controls. Here's the complete code:

```
Private Sub ShowDirectoryContents(ByVal strPath As String)
    ' Define the current directory.
    Dim dir As New DirectoryInfo(path)

    ' Get the DirectoryInfo and FileInfo objects.
    Dim files As FileInfo() = dir.GetFiles()
    Dim dirs As DirectoryInfo() = dir.GetDirectories()
```

```
        ' Show the directory listing.
        lblCurrentDir.Text = "Currently showing " & path
        gridFileList.DataSource = files
        gridDirList.DataSource = dirs
        Page.DataBind()

        ' Clear any selection.
        gridFileList.SelectedIndex = -1

        ' Keep track of the current path.
        ViewState("CurrentPath") = path
    End Sub
```

When the page first loads, it calls this method to show the current application directory:

```
Protected Sub Page_Load(ByVal sender As Object, ByVal e As System.EventArgs)
    If (Not Page.IsPostBack) Then
        ShowDirectoryContents(Server.MapPath("."))
    End If
End Sub
```

You'll notice that the ShowDirectoryContents() method stores the currently displayed directory in view state. That allows the Move Up button to direct the user to a directory that's one level above the current directory:

```
Protected Sub cmdUp_Click(ByVal sender As Object, ByVal e As System.EventArgs)
    Dim strPath As String = CStr(ViewState("CurrentPath"))
    strPath = Path.Combine(strPath, "..")
    strPath = Path.GetFullPath(strPath)
    ShowDirectoryContents(strPath)
End Sub
```

To move down through the directory hierarchy, the user simply needs to click a directory link. This is raised as a SelectedIndexChanged event. The event handler then displays the new directory:

```
Protected Sub gridDirList_SelectedIndexChanged(
        ByVal source As Object, ByVal e As EventArgs)
    ' Get the selected directory.
    Dim dir As String = CStr(gridDirList.DataKeys(gridDirList.SelectedIndex).Value)

    ' Now refresh the directory list to
    ' show the selected directory.
    ShowDirectoryContents(dir)
End Sub
```

But what happens if a user selects a file from the second GridView? In this case, the code retrieves the full file path, creates a new FileInfo object, and binds it to a FormView control, which uses a template to display several pieces of information about the file. Figure 13-2 shows the result.

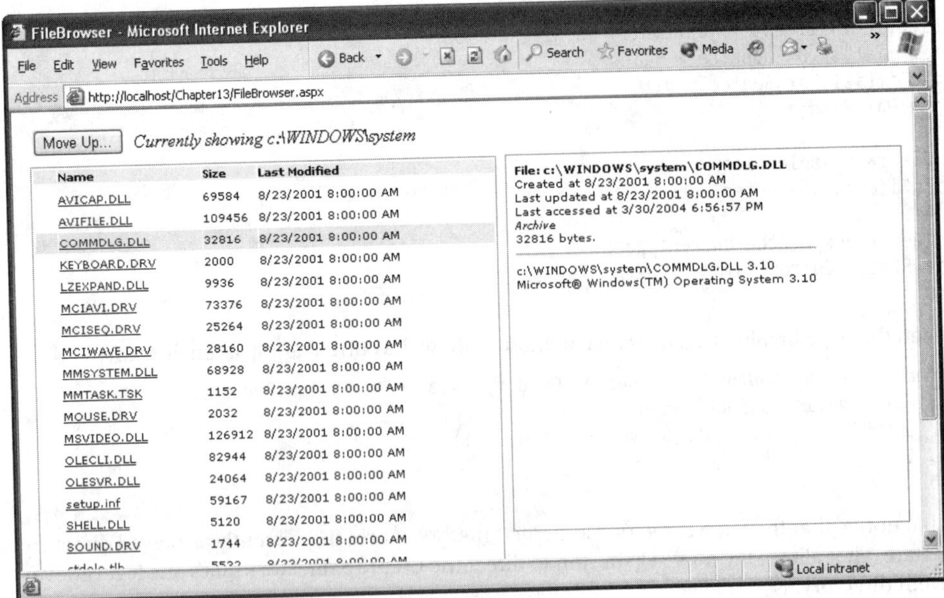

Figure 13-2. *Examining a file*

Here's the code that binds the file information when a file is selected:

```
Protected Sub gridFileList_SelectedIndexChanged(
      ByVal sender As Object, ByVal e As System.EventArgs)
    ' Get the selected file.
    Dim file As String =
      CStr(gridFileList.DataKeys(gridFileList.SelectedIndex).Value)

    ' The FormView shows a collection (or list) of items.
    ' To accommodate this model, you must add the file object
    ' to a collection of some sort.
    Dim files As ArrayList = New ArrayList()
    files.Add(New FileInfo(file))

    ' Now show the selected file.
    formFileDetails.DataSource = files
    formFileDetails.DataBind()
End Sub
```

The FormView uses the following template:

```
<asp:FormView id="formFileDetails" runat="server">
  <ItemTemplate>
    <b>File:
    <%# DataBinder.Eval(Container.DataItem, "FullName") %></b><br>
    Created at
    <%# DataBinder.Eval(Container.DataItem, "CreationTime") %><br>
    Last updated at
    <%# DataBinder.Eval(Container.DataItem, "LastWriteTime") %><br>
    Last accessed at
    <%# DataBinder.Eval(Container.DataItem, "LastAccessTime") %><br>
    <i><%# DataBinder.Eval(Container.DataItem, "Attributes") %></i><br>
```

```
    <%# DataBinder.Eval(Container.DataItem, "Length") %> bytes.
    <hr>
    <%# GetVersionInfoString(DataBinder.Eval(Container.DataItem, "FullName")) %>
  </ItemTemplate>
</asp:DataList>
```

The data binding expressions are fairly straightforward. The only one that needs any expression is the GetVersionInfoString() method. This method is coded inside the page class. It creates a new FileVersionInfo object for the file and uses that to extract the version information and product name.

```
Protected Function GetVersionInfoString(ByVal strPath As Object) As String
    Dim info As FileVersionInfo = FileVersionInfo.GetVersionInfo(CStr(path))
    Return info.FileName & " " & info.FileVersion & "<br>" _
         & info.ProductName & " " & info.ProductVersion
End Function
```

Of course, most developers have FTP tools and other utilities that make it easier to manage files on a web server. However, this page provides an excellent example of how to use the .NET file and directory management classes. With a little more work, you could transform it into a full-featured administrative tool for a web application.

Reading and Writing Files with Streams

The .NET Framework uses a *stream* model in several areas of the framework. Streams are abstractions that allow you to treat different data sources in a similar way—as a stream of ordered bytes. All .NET stream classes derive from the base System.IO.Stream class. Streams represent data in a memory buffer, data that's being retrieved over a network connection, and data that's being retrieved from or written to a file.

Here's how you create a new file and write an array of bytes to it through a FileStream:

```
Dim fStream As FileStream = Nothing
Try
    fStream = New FileStream(fileName, FileMode.Create)
    fStream.Write(bytes)
Finally
    If fStream IsNot Nothing Then
        fStream.Close()
    End If
End Try
```

In this example, the FileMode.Create value is specified in the FileStream constructor to indicate that you want to create a new file. You can use any of the FileMode values described in Table 13-10.

Table 13-10. *Values of the FileMode Enumeration*

Value	Description
Append	Opens the file if it exists and seeks to the end of the file, or creates a new file.
Create	Specifies that the operating system should create a new file. If the file already exists, it will be overwritten.
CreateNew	Specifies that the operating system should create a new file. If the file already exists, an IOException is thrown.
Open	Specifies that the operating system should open an existing file.
OpenOrCreate	Specifies that the operating system should open a file if it exists; otherwise, a new file should be created.
Truncate	Specifies that the operating system should open an existing file. Once opened, the file will be truncated so that its size is 0 bytes.

And here's how you can open a FileStream and read its contents into a byte array:

```
Dim fStream As FileStream = Nothing
Try
    fStream = New FileStream(fileName, FileMode.Open)
    Dim dataArray As Byte() = New Byte(fStream.Length - 1) {}

    Dim i As Integer = 0
    Do While i < fStream.Length
        dataArray(i) = fStream.ReadByte()
        i += 1
    Loop
Finally
    If fStream IsNot Nothing Then
        fStream.Close()
    End If
End Try
```

On their own, streams aren't that useful. That's because they work entirely in terms of single bytes and byte arrays. .NET includes a more useful higher-level model of writer and reader objects that fill the gaps. These objects wrap stream objects and allow you to write more complex data, including common data types such as integers, strings, and dates. You'll see readers and writers at work in the following sections.

■ Tip Whenever you open a file through a FileStream, remember to call the FileStream.Close() method when you're finished. This releases the handle on the file and makes it possible for someone else to access the file. In addition, because the FileStream class is disposable, you can use it with the Using statement, which ensures that the FileStream is closed as soon as the block ends.

Text Files

You can write to a file and read from a file using the StreamWriter and StreamReader classes in the System.IO namespace. When creating these classes, you simply pass the underlying stream as a constructor argument. For example, here's the code you need to create a StreamWriter using an existing FileStream:

```
Dim fStream As New FileStream("c:\myfile.txt", FileMode.Create)
Dim w As New StreamWriter(fStream)
```

You can also use one of the Shared methods included in the File and FileInfo classes, such as CreateText() or OpenText(). Here's an example that uses this technique to get a StreamWriter:

```
Dim w As StreamWriter = File.CreateText("c:\myfile.txt")
```

This code is equivalent to the earlier example.

TEXT ENCODING

You can represent a string in binary form using more than one way, depending on the encoding you use. The most common encodings include the following:

- *ASCII*: Encodes each character in a string using 7 bits. ASCII-encoded data can't contain extended Unicode characters. When using ASCII encoding in .NET, the bits will be padded, and the resulting byte array will have 1 byte for each character.
- *Full Unicode (or UTF-16)*: Represents each character in a string using 16 bits. The resulting byte array will have 2 bytes for each character.
- *UTF-7 Unicode*: Uses 7 bits for ordinary ASCII characters and multiple 7-bit pairs for extended characters. This encoding is primarily for use with 7-bit protocols such as mail, and it isn't regularly used.
- *UTF-8 Unicode*: Uses 8 bits for ordinary ASCII characters and multiple 8-bit pairs for extended characters. The resulting byte array will have 1 byte for each character (provided there are no extended characters).

.NET provides a class for each type of encoding in the System.Text namespace. When using the StreamReader and StreamWriter, you can specify the encoding you want to use with a constructor argument, or you can simply use the default UTF-8 encoding.

Here's an example that creates a StreamWriter that uses ASCII encoding:

```
Dim fStream As New FileStream("c:\myfile.txt", FileMode.Create)
Dim w As New StreamWriter(fStream, System.Text.Encoding.ASCII)
```

Once you have the StreamWriter, you can use the Write() or WriteLine() method to add information to the file. Both of these methods are overloaded so that they can write many simple data types, including strings, integers, and other numbers. These values are essentially all converted into strings when they're written to a file, and they must be converted back into the appropriate types manually when you read the file. To make this process easier, you should put each piece of information on a separate line by using WriteLine() instead of Write(), as shown here:

```
w.WriteLine("ASP.NET Text File Test") ' Write a string.
w.WriteLine(1000) ' Write a number.
```

When you finish with the file, you must make sure you close it. Otherwise, the changes may not be properly written to disk, and the file could be locked open. At any time, you can also call the Flush() method to make sure all data is written to disk, as the StreamWriter will perform some in-memory caching of your data to optimize performance (which is usually exactly the behavior you want).

```
' Tidy up.
w.Flush()
w.Close()
```

When reading information, you use the Read() or ReadLine() method of the StreamReader. The Read() method reads a single character, or the number of characters you specify, into the buffer that you specify. It returns an Integer containing the number of characters read. The ReadLine() method returns a string with the content of an entire line. ReadLine() starts at the first line and advances the position to the end of the file, one line at a time.

Here's a code snippet that opens and reads the file created in the previous example:

```
Dim r As StreamReader = File.OpenText("c:\myfile.txt")
Dim inputString As String
inputString = r.ReadLine()    ' = "ASP.NET Text File Test"
inputString = r.ReadLine()    ' = "1000"
```

ReadLine() returns a null reference when there is no more data in the file. This means you can read all the data in a file using code like this:

```
' Read and display the lines from the file until the end
' of the file is reached.
Dim line As String
Do
    line = r.ReadLine()
    If line IsNot Nothing Then
        ' (Process the line here.)
    End If
Loop While line IsNot Nothing
```

■ **Tip** You can also use the ReadToEnd() method to read the entire contents of the file and return it as a single string. The File class also includes some shortcuts with Shared methods such as ReadAllText() and ReadAllBytes(), which are suitable for small files only.

Binary Files

You can also write to a binary file. Binary data uses space more efficiently but also creates files that aren't readable. If you open a binary file in Notepad, you'll see a lot of extended characters (politely known as *gibberish*).

To open a file for binary writing, you need to create a new BinaryWriter object. The constructor accepts a stream, which you can create by hand or retrieve using the File.OpenWrite() method. Here's the code to open the file c:\binaryfile.bin for binary writing:

```
Dim w As New BinaryWriter(File.OpenWrite("c:\binaryfile.bin"))
```

.NET concentrates on stream objects, rather than the source or destination for the data. This means you can write binary data to any type of stream, whether it represents a file or some other type of storage location, using the same code. In addition, writing to a binary file is almost the same as writing to a text file, as you can see here:

```
Dim str As String = "ASP.NET Binary File Test"
Dim myInt As Integer = 1000
w.Write(str)
w.Write(myInt)

w.Flush()
w.Close()
```

Unfortunately, when you read data, you need to know the data type you want to retrieve. To retrieve a string, you use the ReadString() method. To retrieve an integer, you must use ReadInt32(), as follows:

```
Dim r As New BinaryReader(File.OpenRead("c:\binaryfile.bin"))
Dim str As String
Dim myInt As Integer
str = r.ReadString()
myInt = r.ReadInt32()
```

■ **Note** There's no easy way to jump to a location in a text or binary file without reading through all the information in order. While you can use methods such as Seek() on the underlying stream, you need to specify an offset in bytes. This involves some fairly involved calculations to determine variable sizes. If you need to store a large amount of information and move through it quickly, you need a dedicated database, not a binary file.

Uploading Files

ASP.NET includes two controls that allow website users to upload files to the web server. Once the web server receives the posted file data, it's up to your application to examine it, ignore it, or save it to a back-end database or a file on the web server.

The controls that allow file uploading are HtmlInputFile (an HTML server control) and FileUpload (an ASP.NET web control). Both represent the <input type="file"> HTML tag. The only real difference is that the FileUpload control takes care of automatically setting the encoding of the form to multipart/form data. If you use the HtmlInputFile control, it's up to you to make this change using the enctype attribute of the <form> tag—if you don't, the HtmlInputFile control won't work.

Declaring the FileUpload control is easy. It doesn't expose any new properties or events that you can use through the control tag.

```
<asp:FileUpload ID="Uploader" runat="server" />
```

The <input type="file"> tag doesn't give you much choice as far as the user interface is concerned (it's limited to a text box that contains a filename and a Browse button). When the user clicks Browse, the browser presents an Open dialog box and allows the user to choose a file. This behavior is hard-wired into the browser, and you can't change it. Once the user selects a file, the filename is filled into the corresponding text box. However, the file isn't uploaded yet—that happens later, when the page is posted back. At this point, all the data from all the input controls (including the file data) is sent to the server. For that reason, it's common to add a Button control to post back the page.

To get information about the posted file content, you can access the FileUpload.PostedFile object. You can save the content by calling the PostedFile.SaveAs() method, as demonstrated in the following example.

Here's the event-handling code for the Button.Click event:

```
Protected Sub cmdUpload_Click(ByVal sender As Object, ByVal e As System.EventArgs)
    ' Check whether a file was submitted.
    If Uploader.PostedFile.ContentLength <> 0 Then
        Try
            If Uploader.PostedFile.ContentLength > 1064 Then
                ' This exceeds the size limit you want to allow.
                ' You should check the size to prevent a denial of
                ' service attack that attempts to fill up your
                ' web server's hard drive.
                ' You might also want to check the amount of
                ' remaining free space.
                lblStatus.Text = "Too large. This file is not allowed"
    Else
                ' Retrieve the physical directory path for the Upload
                ' subdirectory.
                Dim destDir As String = Server.MapPath("./Upload")
                ' Extract the filename part from the full path of the
                ' original file.
                Dim fName As String = Path.GetFileName(Uploader.PostedFile.FileName)
                ' Combine the destination directory with the filename.
                Dim destPath As String = Path.Combine(destDir, fName)
                ' Save the file on the server.
```

```
                Uploader.PostedFile.SaveAs(destPath)
                lblStatus.Text = "Thanks for submitting your file"
            End If
        Catch err As Exception
            lblStatus.Text = err.Message
        End Try
    End If
End Sub
```

In the example, if a file has been posted to the server and isn't too large, the file is saved using the HttpPostedFile.SaveAs() method. To determine the physical path you want to use, the code combines the destination directory (Upload) with the name of the posted file using the Shared utility methods of the Path class.

Figure 13-3 shows the page after the file has been uploaded.

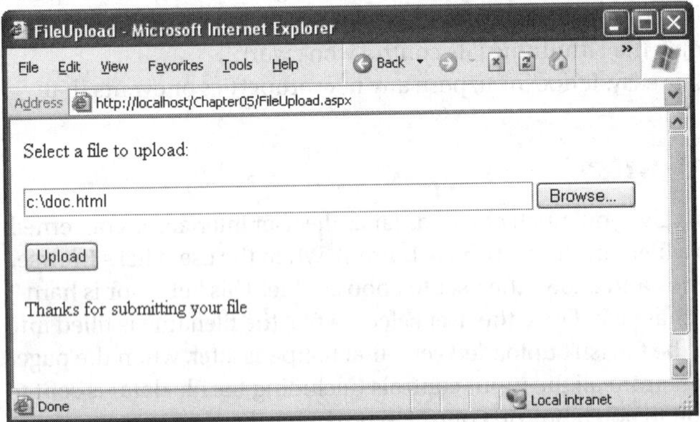

Figure 13-3. *Uploading a file*

You can also interact with the posted data through the stream model, rather than just saving it to disk. To get access to the data, you use the FileUpload.PostedFile.InputStream property. For example, you could use the following code to display the content of a posted file (assuming it's text-based):

```
' Display the whole file content.
Dim r As New StreamReader(Uploader.PostedFile.InputStream)
lblStatus.Text = r.ReadToEnd()
r.Close()
```

Note By default, the maximum size of the uploaded file is 4 MB. If you try to upload a bigger file, you'll get a runtime error. To change this restriction, modify the maxRequestLength attribute of the <httpRuntime> setting in the application's web.config file. The size is specified in kilobytes, so <httpRuntime maxRequestLength="8192"/> sets the maximum file size to 8 MB.

Making Files Safe for Multiple Users

Although it's fairly easy to create a unique filename, what happens in the situation where you really do need to access the same file to serve multiple different requests? Although this situation isn't ideal (and often indicates that a database-based solution would work better), you can use certain techniques to defend yourself.

One approach is to open your files with sharing, which allows multiple processes to access the same file at the same time. To use this technique, you need to use the four-parameter FileStream constructor that allows you to select a FileMode. Here's an example:

```
Dim fs As New FileStream(fileName, FileMode.Open, FileAccess.Read, FileShare.Read)
```

This statement allows multiple users to open the file for reading at the same time. However, no one will be able to update the file.

■Tip Another technique that works well if multiple users need to access the same data, especially if this data is frequently used and not excessively large, is to load the data into the cache (as described in Chapter 11). That way, multiple users can simultaneously access the data without a hitch. Of course, this approach may not suit your needs if another process is responsible for creating or periodically updating the file, in which case you can't be sure the data you've cached is up-to-date.

It is possible to have multiple users open the file in read-write mode by specifying a different FileAccess value (such as FileAccess.Write or FileAccess.ReadWrite). In this case, Windows will dynamically lock small portions of the file when you write to them (or you can use the FileStream.Lock() method to lock down a range of bytes in the file). If two users try to write to the same locked portion at once, an exception can occur. Because web applications have high concurrency demands, this technique is not recommended and is extremely difficult to implement properly. It also forces you to use low-level byte-offset calculations, where it is notoriously easy to make small, aggravating errors.

So, what is the solution when multiple users need to update a file at once? One option is to create separate user-specific files for each request. Another option is to tie the file to some other object and use locking. The following sections explain these techniques.

Creating Unique Filenames

One solution for dealing with user-concurrency headaches with files is to avoid the conflict altogether by using different files for different users. For example, imagine you want to store a user-specific log. To prevent the chance for an inadvertent conflict if two web pages try to use the same log, you can use the following two techniques:

- Create a user-specific directory for each user.
- Add some information to the filename, such as a timestamp, GUID (global unique identifier), or random number. This reduces the chance of duplicate filenames to a small possibility.

The following sample page demonstrates this technique. It defines a method for creating filenames that are statistically guaranteed to be unique. In this case, the filename incorporates a GUID.

Here's the private method that generates a new unique filename:

```
Private Function GetFileName() As String
    ' Create a unique filename.
    Dim fileName As String = "user." & Guid.NewGuid().ToString()

    ' Put the file in the current web application path.
    Return Path.Combine(Request.PhysicalApplicationPath, fileName)
End Function
```

■ **Note** A GUID is a 128-bit integer. GUID values are tremendously useful in programming because they're statistically unique. In other words, you can create GUID values continuously with little chance of ever creating a duplicate. For that reason, GUIDs are commonly used to uniquely identify queued tasks, user sessions, and other dynamic information. They also have the advantage over sequential numbers in that they can't easily be guessed. The only disadvantage is that GUIDs are long and almost impossible to remember (for an ordinary human being). GUIDs are commonly represented in strings as a series of lowercase hexadecimal digits, like 382c74c3-721d-4f34-80e5-57657b6cbc27.

Using the GetFileName() method, you can create a safer logging application that writes information about the user's actions to a text file. In this example, all the logging is performed by calling a Log() method, which then checks for the filename and assigns a new one if the file hasn't been created yet. The text message is then added to the file, along with the date and time information.

```
Private Sub Log(ByVal message As String)
    ' Check for the file.
    Dim mode As FileMode
    If ViewState("LogFile") Is Nothing Then
        ' First, create a unique user-specific filename.
        ViewState("LogFile") = GetFileName()

        ' The log file must be created.
        mode = FileMode.Create
    Else
        ' Add to the existing file.
        mode = FileMode.Append
    End If

    ' Write the message.
    ' A Using block ensures the file is automatically closed,
    ' even in the case of error.
    Dim fileName As String = CStr(ViewState("LogFile"))
    Using fs As New FileStream(fileName, mode)
        Dim w As New StreamWriter(fs)
        w.WriteLine(DateTime.Now)
        w.WriteLine(message)
        w.Close()
    End Using
End Sub
```

For example, a log message is added every time the page is loaded, as shown here:

```
Protected Sub Page_Load(ByVal sender As Object, ByVal e As System.EventArgs)
    If (Not Page.IsPostBack) Then
        Log("Page loaded for the first time.")
    Else
        Log("Page posted back.")
    End If
End Sub
```

The last ingredients are two button event handlers that allow you to delete the log file or show its contents, as follows:

```
Protected Sub cmdRead_Click(ByVal sender As Object, ByVal e As System.EventArgs)
    If ViewState("LogFile") IsNot Nothing Then
```

```
            Dim fileName As String = CStr(ViewState("LogFile"))
            Using fs As New FileStream(fileName, FileMode.Open)
                Dim r As New StreamReader(fs)
                ' Read line by line (allows you to add
                ' line breaks to the web page).
                Dim line As String
                Do
                    line = r.ReadLine()
                    If line IsNot Nothing Then
                        lblInfo.Text &= line & "<br>"
                    End If
                Loop While line IsNot Nothing
                r.Close()
            End Using
        End If
End Sub

Protected Sub cmdDelete_Click(ByVal sender As Object, ByVal e As System.EventArgs)
    If ViewState("LogFile") IsNot Nothing Then
        File.Delete(CStr(ViewState("LogFile")))
    End If
End Sub
```

Figure 13-4 shows the web page displaying the log contents.

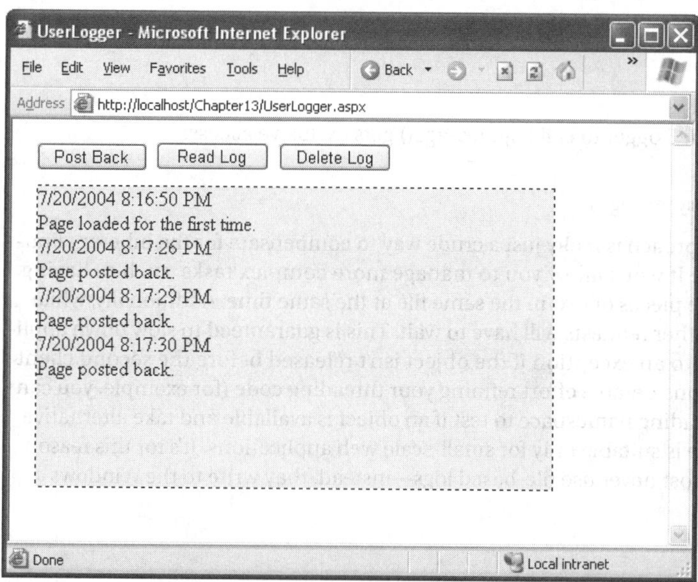

Figure 13-4. *A safer way to write a user-specific log*

Locking File Access Objects

Of course, in some cases you *do* need to update the same file in response to actions taken by multiple users. One approach is to use *locking*. The basic technique is to create a separate class that performs all the work of retrieving the data. Once you've defined this class, you can create a single global instance of it and add it to the Application collection. Now you can use the VB SyncLock statement to ensure that only one thread can access this object at a time (and hence only one thread can attempt to open the file at once).

For example, imagine you create the following Logger class, which updates a file with log information when you call the LogMessage() method, as shown here:

```
Public Class Logger
    Public Sub LogMessage(strIn as String)
        SyncLock Me
            ' (Open the file and update it.)
        End SyncLock
    End Sub
End Class
```

The Logger class locks the current Logger instance before accessing the log file, creating a *critical section*. This ensures that only one thread can execute the LogMessage() code on a particular Logger object, removing the danger of file conflicts.

However, for this to work you must make sure every class is using the same instance of the Logger object. You have a number of options here—for example, you could respond to the HttpApplication.Start event in the global.asax file to create a global instance of the Logger class and store it in the Application collection. This may cause scalability problems as all other threads could get blocked. Another option is to expose a single Logger instance through a Shared variable in the global.asax file, as shown here:

```
Private log = New Logger()
Public ReadOnly Property Log() As Logger
    Get
        Return log
    End Get
End Property
```

Now any page that uses the Logger to call LogMessage() gets exclusive access:

```
' Update the file safely.
Application.Log.LogMessage(myMessage)
```

Keep in mind that this approach is really just a crude way to compensate for the inherent limitations of a file-based system. It won't allow you to manage more complex tasks, such as having individual users read and write pieces of text in the same file at the same time. Additionally, while a file is locked for one client, other requests will have to wait. This is guaranteed to slow down application performance and lead to an exception if the object isn't released before the second client times out. Unless you invest considerable effort refining your threading code (for example, you can use classes in the System.Threading namespace to test if an object is available and take alternative action if it isn't), this technique is suitable only for small-scale web applications. It's for this reason that ASP.NET applications almost never use file-based logs—instead, they write to the Windows event log or a database.

Compression

.NET 2.0 adds built-in support for compressing data in any stream. This trick allows you to compress data that you write to any file. The support comes from two classes in the new System.IO.Compression namespace: GZipStream and DeflateStream. Both of these classes represent similarly efficient lossless compression algorithms.

To use compression, you need to wrap the real stream with one of the compression streams. For example, you could wrap a FileStream (for compressing data as it's written to disk) or a MemoryStream (for compressing data in memory). Using a MemoryStream, you could compress data before storing it in a binary field in a database or sending it to a web service.

For example, imagine you want to compress data saved to a file. First, you create the FileStream:

```
Dim fStream As New FileStream("c:\myfile.txt", FileMode.Create)
```

Next, you create a GZipStream or DeflateStream, passing in the FileStream and a CompressionMode value that indicates whether you are compressing or decompressing data:

```
Dim compressStream As New GZipStream(fileStream, CompressionMode.Compress)
```

To write your actual data, you use the Write() method of the compression stream, not the FileStream. The compression stream compresses the data and then passes the compressed data to the underlying FileStream. If you want to use a higher-level writer, such as the StreamWriter or BinaryWriter, you supply the compression stream instead of the FileStream:

```
Dim w As New StreamWriter(compressStream)
```

Now you can perform your writing through the writer object. When you're finished, flush the GZipStream so that all the data ends up in the file:

```
w.Flush()
fileStream.Close()
```

Reading a file is just as straightforward. The difference is that you create a compression stream with the CompressionMode.Decompress option, as shown here:

```
Dim fStream As New FileStream("c:\myfile.bin", FileMode.Open)
Dim decompressStream As New GZipStream(fileStream, CompressionMode.Decompress)
Dim r As New StreamReader(decompressStream)
```

■ **Note** Although GZIP is an industry-standard compression algorithm (see `http://www.gzip.org` for information), that doesn't mean you can use third-party tools to decompress the compressed files you create. The problem is that although the compression algorithm may be the same, the file format is not. Namely, the files you create won't have header information that identifies the original compressed file.

Serialization

You can use one more technique to store data in a file—*serialization*. Serialization is a higher-level model that's built on .NET streams. Essentially, serialization allows you to convert an entire live object into a series of bytes and write those bytes into a stream object such as the FileStream. You can then read those bytes back later to re-create the original object.

For serialization to work, your object must all meet the following criteria:

- The object must have a Serializable attribute preceding the class declaration.
- All the Public, Protected, Internal and Private variables of the class must be serializable.
- If the class derives from another class, all parent classes must also be serializable.

Here's a serializable class that you could use to store log information:

```
<Serializable()> _
Public Class LogEntry
    Private strMessage As String
    Private dteDate As DateTime
```

```
    Public Property Message() As String
        Get
                Return strMessage
        End Get
        Set
                strMessage = Value
        End Set
    End Property
    Public Property DateTime() As String
        Get
                Return dteDate
        End Get
        Set
                dteDate = Value
        End Set
    End Property

    Public Sub New(ByVal strMessage As String)
        Me.strMessage = strMessage
        Me.dteDate = DateTime.Now
    End Sub
End Class
```

■ **Tip** In some cases, a class might contain data that shouldn't be serialized. For example, you might have a large field you can recalculate or re-create easily, or you might have some sensitive data that could pose a security request. In these cases, you can add a NonSerialized attribute before the appropriate variable to indicate it shouldn't be persisted. When you re-create the class, nonserialized variables will return to their default values.

You may remember serializable classes from earlier in this book. Classes need to be serializable in order to be stored in the view state for a page or put into an out-of-process session state store. In those cases, you let .NET serialize the object for you automatically. However, you can also manually serialize a serializable object and store it in a file or another data source of your choosing (such as a binary field in a database).

To convert a serializable object into a stream of bytes, you need to use a class that implements the IFormatter interface. The .NET Framework includes two such classes: BinaryFormatter, which serializes an object to a compact binary representation, and SoapFormatter, which uses the SOAP XML format and results in a longer text-based message. The BinaryFormatter class is found in the System.Runtime.Serialization.Formatters.Binary namespace, and SoapFormatter is found in the System.Runtime.Serialization.Formatters.Soap namespace. (To use SoapFormatter, you also need to add a reference to the assembly System.Runtime.Serialization.Formatters.Soap.dll.) Both methods serialize all the Private, Protected, Internal and Public data in a class, along with the assembly and type information needed to ensure that the object can be deserialized exactly.

To create a simple example, let's consider what you need to do to rewrite the logging page shown earlier to use object serialization instead of writing data directly to the file. The first step is to change the Log() method so that it creates a LogEntry object and uses the BinaryFormatter to serialize it into the existing file, as follows:

```
Private Sub Log(ByVal message As String)
    ' Check for the file.
    Dim mode As FileMode
    If ViewState("LogFile") Is Nothing Then
        ViewState("LogFile") = GetFileName()
        mode = FileMode.Create
```

```
    Else
        mode = FileMode.Append
    End If

    ' Write the message.
    Dim fileName As String = CStr(ViewState("LogFile"))
    Using fs As New FileStream(fileName, mode)
        ' Create a LogEntry object.
        Dim entry As New LogEntry(message)

        ' Create a formatter.
        Dim formatter As New BinaryFormatter()

        ' Serialize the object to a file.
        formatter.Serialize(fs, entry)
    End Using
End Sub
```

The last step is to change the code that fills the label with the complete log text. Instead of reading the raw data, it now deserializes each saved instance using the BinaryFormatter, as shown here:

```
Protected Sub cmdRead_Click(ByVal sender As Object, ByVal e As System.EventArgs)
    If ViewState("LogFile") IsNot Nothing Then
        Dim fileName As String = CStr(ViewState("LogFile"))
        Using fs As New FileStream(fileName, FileMode.Open)
            ' Create a formatter.
            Dim formatter As New BinaryFormatter()

            ' Get all the serialized objects.
            Do While fs.Position < fs.Length
                ' Deserialize the object from the file.
                Dim entry As LogEntry = CType(formatter.Deserialize(fs), LogEntry)

                ' Display its information.
                lblInfo.Text &= entry.Date.ToString() & "<br>"
                lblInfo.Text &= entry.Message & "<br>"
            Loop
        End Using
    End If
End Sub
```

So, exactly what information is stored when an object is serialized? Both the BinaryFormatter and the SoapFormatter use a proprietary .NET serialization format that includes information about the class, the assembly that contains the class, and all the data stored in the class member variables. Although the binary format isn't completely interpretable, if you display it as ordinary ASCII text, it looks something like this:

```
?ÿÿÿÿ? ?GApp_Web_a7ve1ebl, Version=0.0.0.0, Culture=neutral, PublicKeyToken=null??
?LogEntry??message?date????Page loaded for the first time. ????
```

The SoapFormatter produces more readily interpretable output, although it stores the same information (in a less compact form). The assembly information is compressed into a namespace string, and the data is enclosed in separate elements:

```
<SOAP-ENV:Envelope xmlns:xsi="http://www.w3.org/2001/XMLSchema-instance"
 xmlns:xsd="http://www.w3.org/2001/XMLSchema"
 xmlns:SOAP-ENC="http://schemas.xmlsoap.org/soap/encoding/"
 xmlns:SOAP-ENV="http://schemas.xmlsoap.org/soap/envelope/"
 xmlns:clr="http://schemas.microsoft.com/soap/encoding/clr/1.0"
```

```
 SOAP-ENV:encodingStyle="http://schemas.xmlsoap.org/soap/encoding/">
  <SOAP-ENV:Body>
    <a1:LogEntry id="ref-1"
     xmlns:a1=
"http://schemas.microsoft.com/clr/assem/App_Web_m9gesigu%2C%20Version%3D0.0.0.0%2C
%20Culture%3Dneutral%2C%20PublicKeyToken%3Dnull ">
      <message id="ref-3">Page loaded for the first time.</message>
      <date>2005-09-21T22:50:04.8677568-04:00</date>
    </a1:LogEntry>
  </SOAP-ENV:Body>
</SOAP-ENV:Envelope>
```

Clearly, this information is suitable just for .NET-only applications. However, it provides the most convenient, compact way to store the contents of an entire object.

Summary

In this chapter, you learned how to use the .NET classes for retrieving file system information. You also examined how to work with files and how to serialize objects. Along the way you learned how data binding can work with the file classes, how to plug security holes with the Path class, and how to deal with file contention in multiuser scenarios. You also considered data compression using GZIP.

PART 3

■■■

Building ASP.NET Websites

CHAPTER 14

User Controls

The core set of ASP.NET controls is broad and impressive. It includes controls that encapsulate basic HTML tags and controls that provide a rich higher-level model, such as the Calendar, TreeView, and data controls. Of course, even the best set of controls can't meet the needs of every developer. Sooner or later, you'll want to get under the hood, start tinkering, and build your own user interface components.

In .NET, you can plug into the web forms framework with your own controls in two ways. You can develop either of the following:

User controls: A *user control* is a small section of a page that can include static HTML code and web server controls. The advantage of user controls is that once you create one, you can reuse it in multiple pages in the same web application. You can even add your own properties, events, and methods.

Custom server controls: *Custom server controls* are compiled classes that programmatically generate their own HTML. Unlike user controls (which are declared like web-form pages in a plain-text file), server controls are always precompiled into DLL assemblies. Depending on how you code the server control, you can render the content from scratch, inherit the appearance and behavior from an existing web control and extend its features, or build the interface by instantiating and configuring a group of constituent controls.

In this chapter, you'll explore the first option—user controls. User controls are a great way to standardize repeated content across all the pages in a website. For example, imagine you want to provide a consistent way for users to enter address information on several different pages. To solve this problem, you could create an address user control that combines a group of text boxes and a few related validators. You could then add this address control to any web form and program against it as a single object.

User controls are also a good choice when you need to build and reuse site headers, footers, and navigational aids. (Master pages, which are discussed in Chapter 15, complement user controls by giving you a way to standardize web-page layout.) In all of these examples, you could avoid user controls entirely and just copy and paste the code wherever you need to do so. However, if you do, you'll run into serious problems once you need to modify, debug, or enhance the controls in the future. Because multiple copies of the user interface code will be scattered throughout your website, you'll have the unenviable task of tracking down each copy and repeating your changes. Clearly, user controls provide a more elegant, object-oriented approach.

USER CONTROL CHANGES IN ASP.NET 2.0

User controls are essentially unchanged from ASP.NET 1.*x*. The only differences are the new code-behind model (which matches the new code-behind model for web pages) and better design-time support that lets you see a user control on the design surface of a page inside Visual Studio.

User Control Basics

User control (.ascx) files are similar to ASP.NET web-form (.aspx) files. Like web forms, user controls are composed of a user interface portion with control tags (the .ascx file) and can use inline script or a .vb code-behind file. User controls can contain just about anything a web page can, including static HTML content and ASP.NET controls, and they also receive the same events as the Page object (like Load and PreRender) and expose the same set of intrinsic ASP.NET objects through properties (such as Application, Session, Request, and Response).

The key differences between user controls and web pages are as follows:

- User controls begin with a Control directive instead of a Page directive.
- User controls use the file extension .ascx instead of .aspx, and their code-behind files inherit from the System.Web.UI.UserControl class. In fact, the UserControl class and the Page class both inherit from the same TemplateControl class, which is why they share so many of the same methods and events.
- User controls can't be requested directly by a client. (ASP.NET will give a generic "that file type is not served" error message to anyone who tries.) Instead, user controls are embedded inside other web pages.

Creating a Simple User Control

To create a user control in Visual Studio, select Website ➤ Add New Item, and choose the Web User Control template.

The following is the simplest possible user control—one that merely contains static HTML. This user control represents a header bar.

```
<%@ Control Language="vb" AutoEventWireup="true"
    CodeFile="Header.ascx.vb" Inherits="Header" %>
<table width="100%" border="0" bgcolor="blue">
    <tr>
        <td><font face="Verdana,Arial" size="6" color="yellow"><b>
            User Control Test Page</b></font>
        </td>
    </tr>
    <tr>
        <td align="right"><font size="3" color="white"><b>
            An Apress Creation (c) 2005</b></font>   
        </td>
    </tr>
</table>
```

You'll notice that the Control directive identifies the code-behind class. However, the simple header control doesn't require any custom code to work, so you can leave the class empty:

```
Public Partial Class Header
        Inherits System.Web.UI.UserControl
End Class
```

As with ASP.NET web forms, the user control is a partial class, because it's merged with a separate portion generated by ASP.NET. That automatically generated portion has the member variables for all the controls you add at design time.

Now to test the control, you need to place it on a web form. First, you need to tell the ASP.NET page that you plan to use that user control with the Register directive, as shown here:

```
<%@ Register TagPrefix="apress" TagName="Header" Src="Header.ascx" %>
```

This line identifies the source file that contains the user control using the Src attribute. It also defines a tag prefix and tag name that will be used to declare a new control on the page. In the same way that ASP.NET server controls have the <asp: ... > prefix to declare the controls (for example, <asp:TextBox>), you can use your own tag prefixes to help distinguish the controls you've created. This example uses a tag prefix of apress and a tag named Header.

The full tag is shown in this page:

```
<%@ Page Language="vb" AutoEventWireup="true" CodeFile="HeaderTest.aspx.vb"
    Inherits="HeaderTest" %>
<%@ Register TagPrefix="apress" TagName="Header" Src="Header.ascx" %>
<html>
    <head>
        <title>HeaderHost</title>
    </head>
    <body>
        <form id="Form1" method="post" runat="server">
            <apress:Header id="Header1" runat="server"></apress:Header>
        </form>
    </body>
</html>
```

At a bare minimum, when you add a user control to your page, you should give it a unique ID and indicate that it runs on the server, like all ASP.NET controls. Figure 14-1 shows the sample page with the custom header.

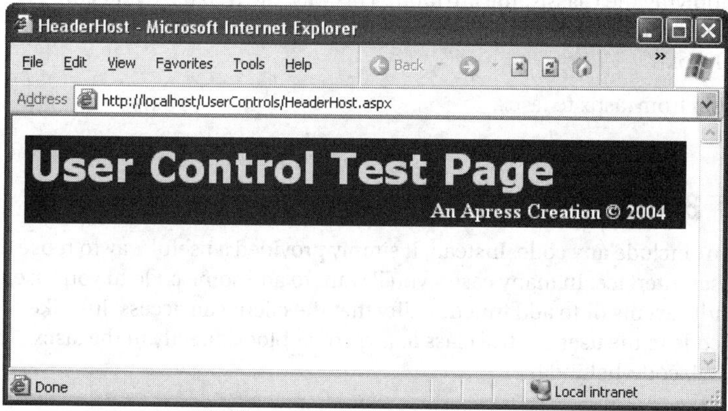

Figure 14-1. *Testing the header user control*

In Visual Studio, you don't need to code the Register directive by hand. Instead, once you've created your user control, simply select the .ascx in the Solution Explorer and drag it onto the drawing area of a web form. Visual Studio will automatically add the Register directive for you as well as an instance of the user control tag.

The header control is the simplest possible user control example, but it can already provide some realistic benefits. Think about what might happen if you had to manually copy the header's HTML code into all your ASP.NET pages, and then you had to change the title, add a contact link, or something else. You would need to change and upload all the pages again. With a separate user control, you just update that one file. Best of all, you can use any combination of HTML, user controls, and server controls on an ASP.NET web form.

Note The design-time support for user controls is greatly improved in ASP.NET 2.0. Now you can see a real representation of the user control at design time (rather than a blank gray box), and you can use the smart tag to quickly jump to the corresponding .ascx file. Best of all, when you add the user control to a web page, Visual Studio makes the corresponding user control object available to your code automatically, as you'll see in later examples.

Converting a Page to a User Control

Sometimes the easiest way to develop a user control is to put it in a web page first, test it on its own, and then translate the page to a user control. Even if you don't follow this approach, you might still end up with a portion of a user interface that you want to extract from a page and reuse in multiple places.

Overall, this process is a straightforward cut-and-paste operation. However, you need to watch for a few points:

- Remove all <html>, <body>, and <form> tags. These tags appear once in a page, so they can't be added to user controls (which might appear multiple times in a single page).
- If there is a Page directive, change it to a Control directive and remove the attributes that the Control directive does not support, such as AspCompat, Buffer, ClientTarget, CodePage, Culture, EnableSessionState, EnableViewStateMac, ErrorPage, LCID, ResponseEncoding, Trace, TraceMode, and Transaction.
- If you aren't using the code-behind model, make sure you still include a class name in the Control directive by supplying the ClassName attribute. This way, the web page that consumes the control can be strongly typed, which allows it to access properties and methods you've added to the control.
- Change the file extension from .aspx to .ascx.

Adding Code to a User Control

The previous user control didn't include any code. Instead, it simply provided a useful way to reuse a static block of a web-page user interface. In many cases, you'll want to add some code to your user control creation, either to handle events or to add functionality that the client can access. Just like a web form, you can add this code to the user control class in a <script> block directly in the .ascx file, or you can use a separate .vb code-behind file.

Handling Events

To get a better idea of how this works, the next example creates a simple TimeDisplay user control with some event-handling logic. This user control encapsulates a single LinkButton control. Whenever the link is clicked, the time displayed in the link is updated. The time is also refreshed when the control first loads.

Here's the user control, using inline code with a <script> block:

```
<%@ Control Language="vb" ClassName="TimeDisplay" %>
<asp:LinkButton runat="server" ID="lnkTime" OnClick="lnkTime_Click"/>

<script language="vb" runat="server">
Protected Sub Page_Load(ByVal sender As Object, ByVal e As EventArgs)
    If (Not Page.IsPostBack) Then
        RefreshTime()
    End If
End Sub

Protected Sub lnkTime_Click(ByVal sender As Object, ByVal e As EventArgs)
    RefreshTime()
End Sub

Public Sub RefreshTime()
    lnkTime.Text = DateTime.Now.ToLongTimeString()
End Sub
</script>
```

Note that the lnkTime_Click event handler calls a method named RefreshTime(). Because this method is public, the code on the hosting web form can trigger a label refresh programmatically by calling the method at any time. Another important detail is the ClassName attribute in the Control directive. This indicates that the code will be compiled into a user control named TimeDisplay, with the methods in the script block.

Figure 14-2 shows the resulting control.

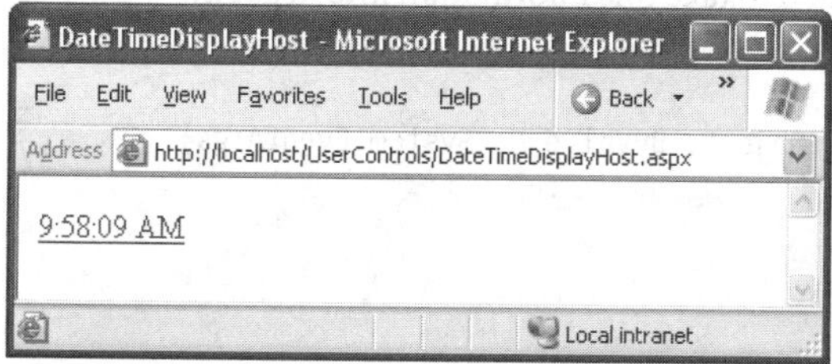

Figure 14-2. *A user control that handles its own events*

The code takes a turn for the better if you split it into a separate .ascx portion and a .vb code-behind file. In this case, the Control directive must specify the Src attribute with the name of the user control source code file *or* the Inherits attribute with the name of the compiled class. User controls created always use the Inherits attribute, as shown here:

```
<%@ Control Language="vb" AutoEventWireup="true"
    CodeFile="TimeDisplay.ascx.vb" Inherits="TimeDisplay" %>
<asp:LinkButton id="lnkTime" runat="server" OnClick="lnkTime_Click" />
```

And here's the corresponding code-behind class:

```
Partial Class TimeDisplay
    Inherits System.Web.UI.UserControl

    Private Sub Page_Load1(ByVal sender As Object,
              ByVal e As System.EventArgs) Handles Me.Load
```

```
        If Not Page.IsPostBack Then
            RefreshTime()
        End If
    End Sub

    Protected Sub lnkTime_Click(ByVal sender As Object, ByVal e As System.EventArgs)
        RefreshTime()
    End Sub

    Public Sub RefreshTime()
        lnkTime.Text = DateTime.Now.ToLongTimeString()
    End Sub

End Class
```

Note that in this example, the user control receives and handles a Page.Load event. This event and event handler are completely separate from the Page.Load event that the web form can respond to (although they both are raised as a consequence of the same thing—a page being created). This makes it easy for you to add initialization code to a user control.

Adding Properties

Currently, the TimeDisplay user control allows only limited interaction with the page that hosts it. All you can really do in your web-form code is call RefreshTime() to update the display. To make a user control more flexible and much more reusable, developers often add properties.

The next example shows a revised TimeDisplay control that adds a public Format property. This property accepts a standard .NET format string, which configures the format of the displayed date. The RefreshTime() method has been updated to take this information into account.

```
Public Class TimeDisplay
        Inherits System.Web.UI.UserControl
    Protected Sub Page_Load(ByVal sender As Object, ByVal e As System.EventArgs)
        If (Not Page.IsPostBack) Then
            RefreshTime()
        End If
    End Sub

    Private strFormat As String
    Public Property Format() As String
        Get
                Return strFormat
        End Get
        Set
                strFormat = Value
        End Set
    End Property

    Protected Sub lnkTime_Click(ByVal sender As Object, ByVal e As System.EventArgs)
        RefreshTime()
    End Sub

    Public Sub RefreshTime()
        If strFormat = String.Empty Then
            lnkTime.Text = DateTime.Now.ToLongTimeString()
        Else
            ' This will throw an exception for invalid format strings,
            ' which is acceptable.
```

```
            lnkTime.Text = DateTime.Now.ToString(format)
        End If
    End Sub
End Class
```

In the hosting page, you have two choices. You can set the Format property at some point in your code by manipulating the control object, as shown here:

```
TimeDisplay1.Format = "dddd, dd MMMM yyyy HH:mm:ss tt (GMT z)"
```

Your second option is to configure the user control when it's first initialized by setting the value in the control tag, as shown here:

```
<apress:TimeDisplay id="TimeDisplay1"
  Format="dddd, dd MMMM yyyy HH:mm:ss tt (GMT z)" runat="server" />
<hr />
<apress:TimeDisplay id="TimeDisplay2" runat="server" />
```

In this example, two versions of the TimeDisplay control are created, one with a control that displays the date in the default format and another one with a custom format applied. Figure 14-3 shows the resulting page on the browser.

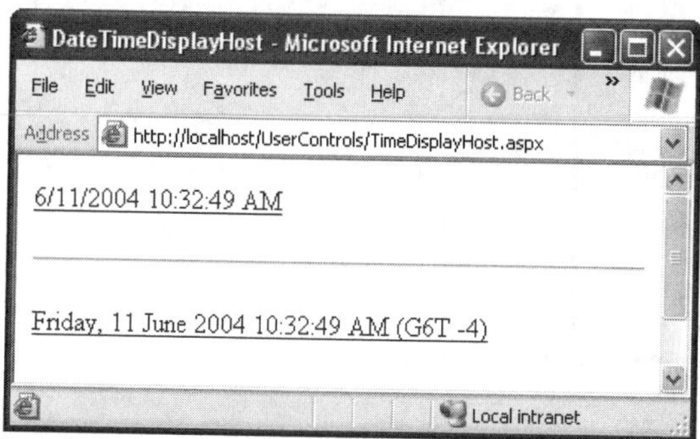

Figure 14-3. *Two instances of a dynamic user control*

■ **Tip** If you use simple property types such as int, DateTime, float, and so on, you can still set them with string values when declaring the control on the host page. ASP.NET will automatically convert the string to the property type defined in the class. Technically, ASP.NET employs a type converter—a special type of object often used to convert data types to and from string representations, which is described in Chapter 28.

When you begin adding properties to a user control, it becomes more important to understand the sequence of events. Essentially, page initialization follows this order:

1. The page is requested.
2. The user control is created. If you have any default values for your variables, or if you perform any initialization in a class constructor, it's applied now.
3. If any properties are set in the user control tag, these are applied now.
4. The Page.Load event in the page executes, potentially initializing the user control.
5. The Page.Load event in the user control executes, potentially initializing the user control.

Once you understand this sequence, you'll realize that you shouldn't perform user control initialization in the Page.Load event of the user control that might overwrite the settings specified by the client.

Using Custom Objects

Many user controls are designed to *abstract* away the details of common scenarios with a higher-level control model. For example, if you need to enter address information, you might group several text box controls into one higher-level AddressInput control. When you're modeling this sort of control, you'll need to use more-complex data than individual strings and numbers. Often, you'll want to create custom classes designed expressly for communication between your web page and your user control.

To demonstrate this idea, the next example develops a LinkTable control that renders a set of hyperlinks in a formatted table. Figure 14-4 shows the LinkTable control.

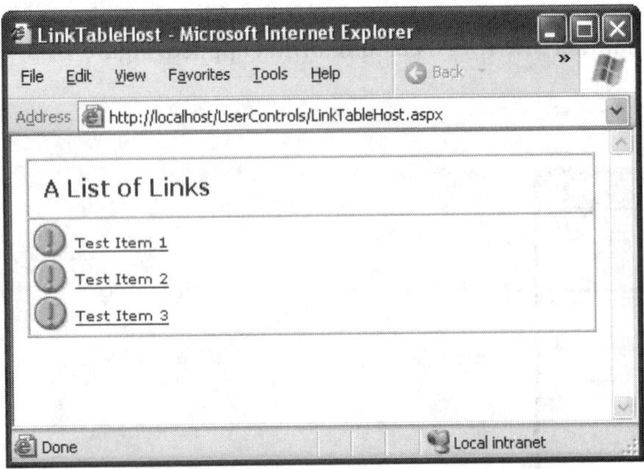

Figure 14-4. *A user control that displays a table of links*

To support this control, you need a custom class that defines the information needed for each link:

```
Public Class LinkTableItem
    Private strText As String
    Public Property Text() As String
        Get
                Return strText
        End Get
        Set
                strText = Value
        End Set
    End Property

    Private strUrl As String
    Public Property Url() As String
        Get
                Return strUrl
        End Get
        Set
```

```
                strUrl = Value
            End Set
        End Property

        ' Default constructor.
        Public Sub New()
        End Sub

        Public Sub New(ByVal text_in As String, ByVal url_in As String)
            Me.strText = text
            Me.strUrl = url_in
        End Sub
    End Class
```

This class could be expanded to include other details, such as an icon that should appear next to the control. The LinkTable simply uses the same icon for every item.

Next, consider the code-behind class for the LinkTable. It defines a Title property that allows you to set a caption and an Items collection that accepts an array of LinkTableItem objects, one for each link that you want to display in the table.

```
Public Partial Class LinkTable
        Inherits System.Web.UI.UserControl
    Public Property Title() As String
        Get
                Return lblTitle.Text
        End Get
        Set
                lblTitle.Text = Value
        End Set
    End Property

    Private lstItems As LinkTableItem()
    Public Property Items() As LinkTableItem()
        Get
            Return lstItems
        End Get
        Set
            lstItems = Value

            ' Refresh the grid.
            listContent.DataSource = lstItems
            listContent.DataBind()
        End Set
    End Property
End Class
```

The control itself uses data binding to render most of its user interface. Whenever the Items property is set or changed, a DataList in the LinkTable control is rebound to the item collection. The DataList contains a single template that, for each link, displays each HyperLink control, which appears with an exclamation mark icon next to it.

```
<%@ Control Language="vb" AutoEventWireup="false"
      Codebehind="LinkTable.ascx.vb" Inherits="LinkTable" %>
<table border="1" width="100%" cellspacing="0" cellpadding="2" height="43">
    <tr>
        <td width="100%" height="1">
          <asp:Label id="lblTitle" runat="server" ForeColor="#C00000"
            Font-Bold="True" Font-Names="Verdana" Font-Size="Small">
```

```
            [Title Goes Here]</asp:Label>
        </td>
    </tr>
    <tr>
        <td width="100%" height="1">
          <asp:DataList id="listContent" runat="server">
            <ItemTemplate>
              <img height="23" src="exclaim.gif"
                       width="25" align="absMiddle" border="0">
                <asp:HyperLink id="HyperLink1"
                       NavigateUrl='<%#DataBinder.Eval(Container.DataItem, "Url")%>'
                       Font-Names="Verdana" Font-Size="XX-Small" ForeColor="#0000cd"
                       Text='<%#DataBinder.Eval(Container.DataItem, "Text")%>'
                       runat="server">
                </asp:HyperLink>
             </ItemTemplate>
          </asp:DataList>
        </td>
    </tr>
</table>
```

Finally, here's the typical web-page code you would use to define a list of links and display it by binding it to the LinkTable user control:

```
Protected Sub Page_Load(ByVal sender As Object, ByVal e As System.EventArgs)
    ' Set the title.
    LinkTable1.Title = "A List of Links"

    ' Set the hyperlinked item list.
    Dim items As LinkTableItem() = New LinkTableItem(2) {}
    items(0) = New LinkTableItem("Test Item 1", "http://www.apress.com")
    items(1) = New LinkTableItem("Test Item 2", "http://www.apress.com")
    items(2) = New LinkTableItem("Test Item 3", "http://www.apress.com")
    LinkTable1.Items = items
End Sub
```

Once it's configured, the web-page code never needs to interact with this control again. When the user clicks one of the links, the user is just forwarded to the new destination without needing any additional code. Another approach would be to design the LinkTable so that it raises a server-side click event. You'll see that approach in the next section.

Adding Events

Another way that communication can occur between a user control and a web page is through events. With methods and properties, the user control reacts to a change made by the web-page code. With events, the story is reversed—the user control notifies the web page about an action, and the web-page code responds.

Usually, you'll delve into events when you create a user control that the user can interact with. After the user takes a certain action—such as clicking a button or choosing an option from a list—your user control intercepts a web control event and then raises a new, higher-level event to notify your web page.

The first version of LinkTable control is fairly functional, but it doesn't use events. Instead, it simply creates the requested links. To demonstrate how events can be used, the next example revises the LinkTable so that it notifies the user when an item is clicked. Your web page can then determine what action to take based on which item was clicked.

The first step to implement this design is to define the events. Remember that to define an event you must use the event keyword with a delegate that represents the signature of the event. The .NET standard for events specifies that every event should use two parameters. The first one provides a reference to the control that sent the event, and the second one incorporates any additional information. This additional information is wrapped into a custom EventArgs object, which inherits from the System.EventArgs class. (If your event doesn't require any additional information, you can just use the generic System.EventArgs object, which doesn't contain any additional data. Many events in ASP.NET, such as Page.Load or Button.Click, follow this pattern.)

In the LinkTable example, it makes sense to transmit basic information about what link was clicked. To support this design, you can create the following EventArgs object, which adds a read-only property that has the corresponding LinkTableItem object:

```
Public Class LinkTableEventArgs
        Inherits EventArgs
    Private selItem As LinkTableItem
    Public ReadOnly Property SelectedItem() As LinkTableItem
        Get
                Return selItem
        End Get
    End Property

    Private bCancel As Boolean = False
    Public Property Cancel() As Boolean
        Get
                Return bCancel
        End Get
        Set
                bCancel = Value
        End Set
    End Property

    Public Sub New(ByVal theItem As LinkTableItem)
        selectedItem = theItem
    End Sub
End Class
```

Notice that the LinkTableEventArgs defines two new details—a SelectedItem property that allows the user to get information about the item that was clicked and a Cancel property that the user can set to prevent the LinkTable from navigating to the new page. One reason you might set Cancel is if you want to respond to the event in your web-page code and handle the redirect yourself. For example, you might want to show the target link in a server-side <iframe> or use it to set the content for an <img> tag rather than navigating to a new page.

Next, you need to create a new delegate that represents the LinkClicked event signature. Here's what it should look like:

```
Public Delegate Sub LinkClickedEventHandler(ByVal sender As Object,
      ByVal e As LinkTableEventArgs)
```

Using the LinkClickedEventHandler, the LinkTable class defines a single event:

```
Public Event LinkClicked As LinkClickedEventHandler
public event LinkClicked as LinkClickedEventHandler
```

To intercept the server click, you need to replace the HyperLink control with a LinkButton, because only the LinkButton raises a server-side event. (The HyperLink simply renders as an anchor that directs the user straight to the target when clicked.) Here's the new template you need:

```
<ItemTemplate>
  <img height="23" src="exclaim.gif"
   width="25" align="absMiddle" border="0">
  <asp:LinkButton id="HyperLink1" Font-Names="Verdana" Font-Size="XX-Small"
   ForeColor="#0000cd" runat="server"
   Text='<%# DataBinder.Eval(Container.DataItem, "Text") %>'
   CommandArgument='<%# DataBinder.Eval(Container.DataItem, "Url") %>'>
  </asp:LinkButton>
</ItemTemplate>
```

You can then intercept the server-side click event and forward it along to the web page as a LinkClicked event. Here's the code you need:

```
Protected Sub listContent_ItemCommand(ByVal source As Object,
      ByVal e As DataListCommandEventArgs)
    If LinkClicked IsNot Nothing Then
        ' Get the HyperLink object that was clicked.
        Dim link As LinkButton = CType(e.Item.Controls(1), LinkButton)

        ' Construct the event arguments.
        Dim item As New LinkTableItem(link.Text, link.CommandArgument)
        Dim args As New LinkTableEventArgs(item)

        ' Fire the event.
        LinkClicked(Me, args)

        ' Navigate to the link if the event recipient didn't
        ' cancel the operation.
        If (Not args.Cancel) Then
            Response.Redirect(item.Url)
        End If
    End If
End Sub
```

Note that when you raise an event, you must first check to see if the event variable contains a null reference. If it does, it signifies that no event handlers are registered yet (perhaps the control hasn't been created). Trying to fire the event at this point will generate a null reference exception. If the event variable isn't Nothing, you can fire the event by using the name and passing along the appropriate event parameters.

Consuming this event isn't quite as easy as it is for the standard set of ASP.NET controls. The problem is that user controls don't provide much in the way of design-time support. (Custom controls, which you'll look at in Chapter 27, do provide design-time support.) As a result, you can't use the Properties window to wire up the event handler at design time. Instead, you need to write the event handler and the code that attaches it yourself.

Here's an example of an event handler that has the required signature (as defined by the LinkClickedEventHandler):

```
Protected Sub LinkClicked(ByVal sender As Object, ByVal e As LinkTableEventArgs)
    lblInfo.Text = "You clicked '" & e.SelectedItem.Text _
        & "' but this page chose not to direct you to '" & e.SelectedItem.Url & "'."
    e.Cancel = True
End Sub
```

You have two options to wire up the event handler. You can do it manually in the Page.Load event handler using delegate code:

```
AddHandler LinkTable1.LinkClicked, AddressOf LinkClicked
```

Alternatively, you can do it in the control tag. Just add the prefix On in front of the event name, as shown here:

```
<apress:LinkTable ID="LinkTable1" runat="server" OnLinkClicked="LinkClicked" />
```

Figure 14-5 shows the result when a link is clicked.

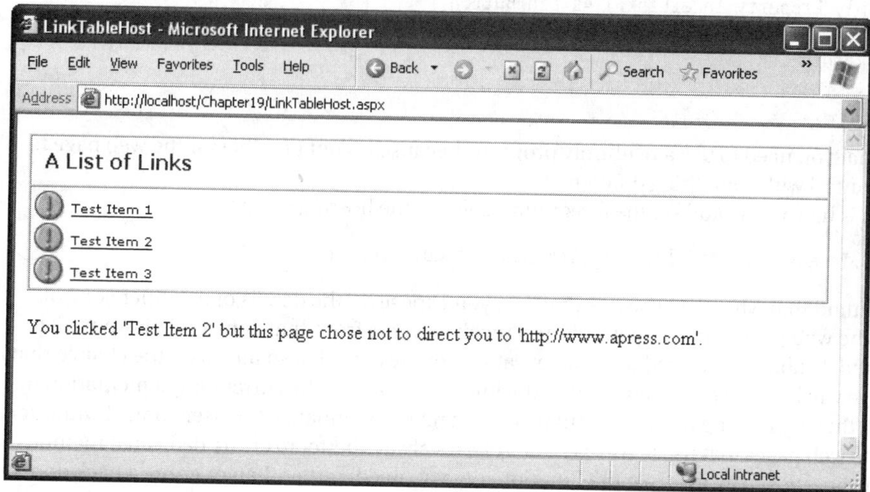

Figure 14-5. *A user control that fires an event*

Exposing the Inner Web Control

One important detail to remember is that the user control's constituent controls can be accessed only by the user control. This means the web page that hosts the user control can receive the events, set the properties, or call the methods of these contained controls. For example, in the TimeDisplay user control the web page has no ability to access the LinkButton control that it uses.

Usually, this behavior is exactly what you want. It means your user control can add public properties to expose specific details without giving the web page free rein to tamper with everything and potentially introduce invalid or inconsistent changes. For example, if you want to give the web page the ability to tweak the foreground color of the LinkButton control, you might add a ForeColor property to your user control. Here's an example:

```
Public Property ForeColor() As Color
    Get
            Return lnkTime.ForeColor
    End Get
    Set
            lnkTime.ForeColor = Value
    End Set
End Property
```

To change the foreground color in your web-page code, you would now use code like this:

```
TimeDisplay1.ForeColor = System.Drawing.Color.Green
```

This example maps the lnkTime.ForeColor property to the ForeColor property of the user control. This trick is usually the best approach, but it can become tedious if you need to expose a large number of properties. For example, your user control might render a table, and you might want to let the user configure the formatting of each table cell.

In this case, it might make sense to expose the complete control object. Here's an example that exposes the lnkTime control for the TimeDisplay user control:

```
Public ReadOnly Property InnerLink() As LinkButton
    Get
            Return lnkTime
    End Get
End Property
```

Notice that you need to use a read-only property, because it's not possible for the web page to replace the control with something different.

Now this is how you would set the foreground color in the hosting page:

```
TimeDisplay1.InnerLink.ForeColor = System.Drawing.Color.Green
```

Keep in mind that when you use this practice, you expose *all* the details of the inner control. This means the web page can call methods and receive events from that control. This approach gives unlimited flexibility, but it reduces the reusability of the code. It also increases the chance that your web page will become tightly coupled to the internal details of the current implementation of your control, thereby making it less likely that you can revise or enhance the user control without disrupting the web pages that use it. As a general rule, it's always better to create dedicated methods, events, and properties to expose just the functionality you need, rather than opening a back door that could be used to create messy workarounds.

Dynamically Loading User Controls

So far you've seen how you can add server controls to a page by registering the type of user control and adding the corresponding tag. You can also create user controls dynamically—in other words, create them on the fly using nothing but a little web-page code.

This technique is similar to the technique you used to add ordinary web controls dynamically (as described in Chapter 3). As with ordinary controls, you should do the following:

- Add user controls when the Page.Load event fires (so that your user control can properly restore its state and receive postback event).
- Use container controls and the PlaceHolder control to make sure the user controls end up exactly where you want.
- Give the user control a unique name by setting its ID property. You can use this information to retrieve a reference to the control when you need it with the Page.FindControl() method.

This has one additional wrinkle. You can't create a user control object directly, like you can with an ordinary control. That's because user controls aren't entirely based on code—they also require the control tags that are defined in the .ascx file. To use a user control, ASP.NET needs to process this file and initialize the corresponding child control objects.

To perform this step, you need to call the Page.LoadControl() method. When you call LoadControl(), you pass the filename of the .ascx user control markup file. LoadControl() returns a UserControl object, which you can then add to the page and cast to the specific class type to access control-specific functionality.

Here's an example that loads the TimeDisplay user control dynamically and adds it to the page using a PlaceHolder control:

```
Dim ctrl as TimeDisplay = _ CTYpe(Page.LoadControl("TimeDisplay.ascx"), TimeDisplay)
PlaceHolder1.Controls.Add(ctrl)
```

Despite this slightly awkward detail, dynamically loading is a powerful technique when used in conjunction with user controls. It's commonly used to create highly configurable portal frameworks.

Portal Frameworks

Although it takes a fair bit of boilerplate code to create a complete portal framework, you can see the most important principles with a simple example. Consider the page shown in Figure 14-6. It includes a panel that contains three controls—a DropDownList, a Label, and a PlaceHolder control.

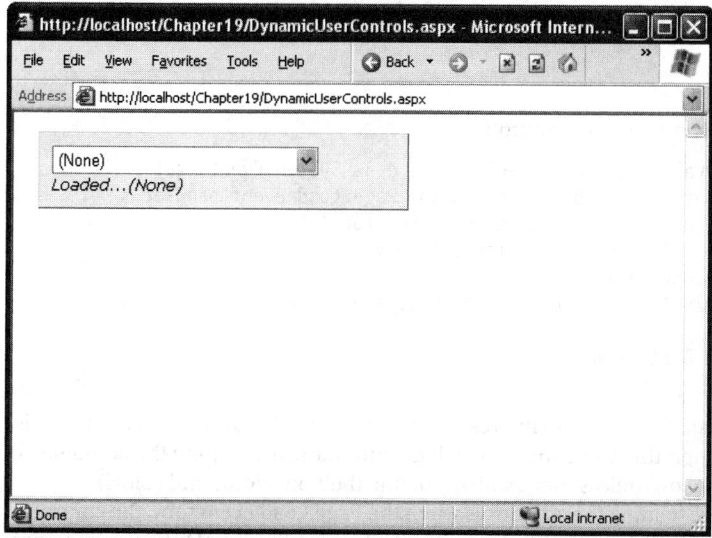

Figure 14-6. *A panel for holding user controls*

When the user selects an item from the drop-down list, the page posts back, and the appropriate user control is loaded dynamically and inserted into the placeholder. Figure 14-7 shows the result.

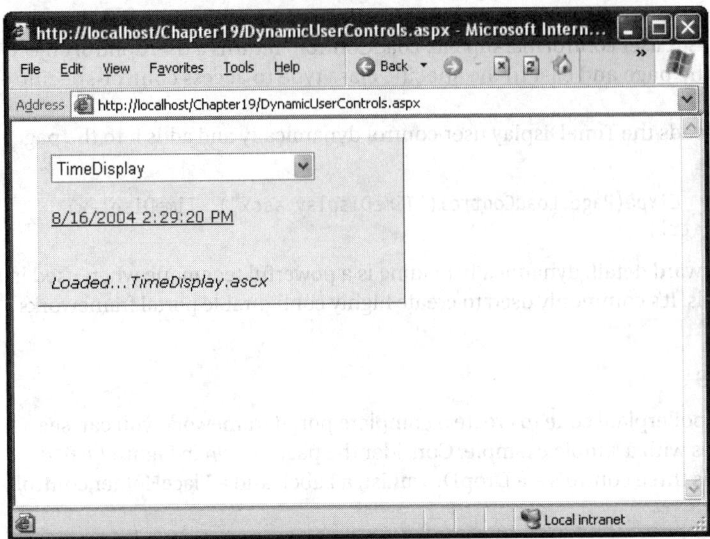

Figure 14-7. *A dynamically loaded user control*

Here's the code that loads the selected control:

```
Protected Sub Page_Load(ByVal sender As Object, ByVal e As System.EventArgs)
    ' Remember that the control must be loaded in the Page.Load event handler.
    ' The DropDownList.SelectedIndexChanged event fires too late.
    Dim ctrlName As String = listControls.SelectedItem.Value
    If ctrlName.EndsWith(".ascx") Then
        placeHolder.Controls.Add(Page.LoadControl(ctrlName))
    End If
    lbl.Text = "Loaded..." & ctrlName
End Sub
```

This example demonstrates a number of interesting features. First, because the PlaceHolder is stored in a formatted container, the user controls you load automatically acquire the container's font, background color, and so on (unless they explicitly define their own fonts and colors).

Best of all, because you're loading these controls when the Page.Load event fires, the control objects are able to handle their own events. You can try this by loading the TimeDisplay user control and then clicking the link to refresh the time.

■Note Because the TimeDisplay control isn't loaded until the page is posted back at least once, it won't show the time until you click the link at least once. Instead, it will start with the generic control name text. You can solve this problem in a number of ways, including calling the RefreshTime() method from your web page when the control is loaded. An even better approach is to create an interface for all your user controls that defines certain basic methods, such as InitializeControl(). That way, you can initialize any control generically. Most portal frameworks use interfaces to provide this type of standardization.

It's not too difficult to extend this example to provide an entire configurable web page. All you need to do is create more panels and organize them on your web page (possibly using tables and other panels to group them). This might seem like a tedious task, but you can actually use it quite effectively by writing some generic code that deals with all the panels on your page. One option is to create a user control that loads other user controls. Another approach is a custom method, as shown here, which handles user control loading for three panels:

```
Protected Sub Page_Load(ByVal sender As Object, ByVal e As System.EventArgs)
    LoadControls(div1)
    LoadControls(div2)
    LoadControls(div3)
End Sub

Private Sub LoadControls(ByVal container As Control)
    Dim list As DropDownList = Nothing
    Dim ph As PlaceHolder = Nothing
    Dim lbl As Label = Nothing

    ' Find the controls for this panel.
    For Each ctrl As Control In container.Controls
        If TypeOf ctrl Is DropDownList Then
            list = CType(ctrl, DropDownList)
        Else If TypeOf ctrl Is PlaceHolder Then
            ph = CType(ctrl, PlaceHolder)
        Else If TypeOf ctrl Is Label Then
            lbl = CType(ctrl, Label)
        End If
    Next

    ' Load the dynamic content into this panel.
    Dim ctrlName As String = list.SelectedItem.Value
    If ctrlName.EndsWith(".ascx") Then
        ph.Controls.Add(Page.LoadControl(ctrlName))
    End If
    lbl.Text = "Loaded..." & ctrlName
End Sub
```

Figure 14-8 shows this example in action.

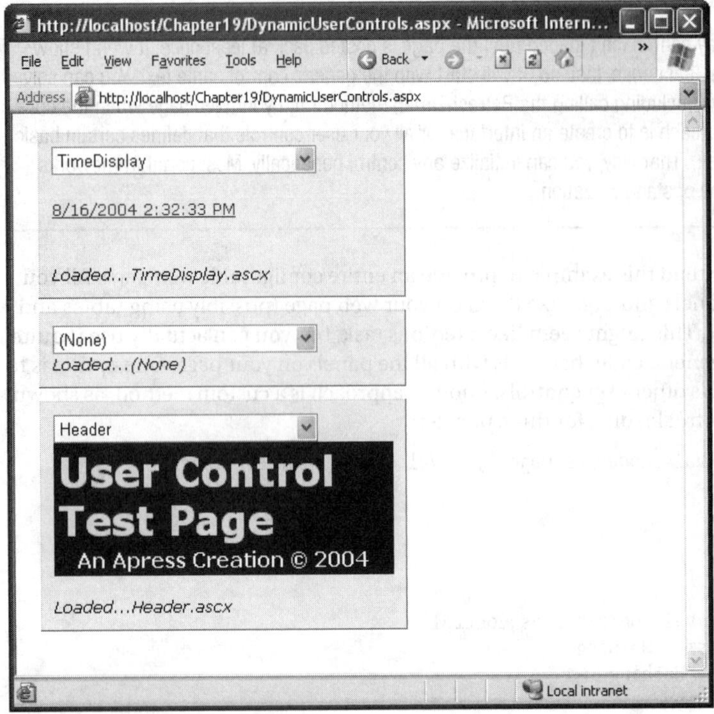

Figure 14-8. *A dynamic web page with multiple user controls*

Using this technique to build an entire web portal framework is possible, but it requires significant work before it would be practical. Creating this framework is a tedious, time-consuming task. In Chapter 30 you'll learn about a *web parts*, a native ASP.NET solution for building web portals that doesn't force you to reinvent the wheel. Web parts are based, at least in part, on user controls.

Partial Page Caching

In Chapter 11, you learned how you can cache a web page by adding the OutputCache directive to the .aspx page. This type of caching, called *output caching*, caches a rendered HTML version of the page, which ASP.NET can reuse automatically for future requests without executing any of your page code.

One of the drawbacks with response caching is that it works on an all-or-nothing basis. It doesn't work if you need to render a portion of your page dynamically. For example, you might want to cache a table that's filled with records read from a data source so that you can limit the round-trips to the database server, but you might still need to get a fresh output for the rest of the page. If that's your situation, user controls can provide exactly what you're looking for because they can cache their own output. This feature is called *partial caching*, or *fragment caching*, and it works in almost the same way as output caching. The only difference is that you add the OutputCache directive to the user control, instead of the page.

To test this feature, add the following line to the .ascx portion of a user control such as the TimeDisplay:

```
<%@ OutputCache Duration="10" VaryByParam="None" %>
```

Now in the hosting page you'll see that the displayed time won't change for ten seconds. Refreshing the page has no effect. The VaryByParam parameter has the same meaning as it did with web pages—it allows to you to generate and cache fresh HTML output when the parameters in the query string portion of the URL change.

Alternatively, you can enable caching by adding the following attribute to the declaration of your user control class:

```
<PartialCaching(10)> _
Public Class MyUserControl
        Inherits UserControl
          ...
End Class
```

There's one caveat when using fragment caching. When a user control is cached, the user control essentially becomes a block of static HTML. As a result, the user control object won't be available to your web-page code. Instead, ASP.NET instantiates one of two more generic object types, depending on how the user control was created. If the user control was created declaratively (by adding a user tag to the web page), a StaticPartialCachingControl object is added. If the user control was created programmatically (using the LoadControl() method), a PartialCachingControl object is added. ASP.NET places the object into the logical position that a user control would occupy in the page's control hierarchy if it were not cached. However, these objects are just placeholders—they won't allow you to interact with the user control through its properties or methods. If you aren't sure if caching is in effect, you should test for a null reference before you attempt to use the user control object.

VaryByControl

If your user control contains input controls, it's difficult to use caching. The problem occurs if the content in the input controls affects the cached content that the user control displays. With ordinary caching, you're stuck reusing the same copy of the user control, regardless of what the user types into an input control. (A similar problem exists with web pages, which is why it seldom makes sense to cache a web page that includes input controls.)

The VaryByControl property solves this problem. VaryByControl takes a semicolon-delimited string of control names that are used to vary the cached content in the same way that VaryByParameter varies the cached content for query string values.

For example, consider the following user control:

```
<%@ Control Language="vb" AutoEventWireup="true"
    CodeFile="VaryByControl.ascx.vb" Inherits="VaryByControl" %>

<asp:DropDownList id="lstMode" runat="server" Width="187px">
  <asp:ListItem>Large</asp:ListItem>
  <asp:ListItem>Small</asp:ListItem>
  <asp:ListItem>Medium</asp:ListItem>
</asp:DropDownList> <br />
<asp:button ID="Button1" text="Submit" OnClick="SubmitBtn_Click" runat=server/>
<br /><br />
Control generated at:<br /> <asp:label id="TimeMsg" runat="server" />
```

When the button is clicked, it displays the current date in one of three formats:

```
Protected Sub Page_Load(ByVal sender As Object, ByVal e As EventArgs)
    Select Case lstMode.SelectedIndex
        Case 0
            TimeMsg.Font.Size = FontUnit.Large
        Case 1
            TimeMsg.Font.Size = FontUnit.Small
```

```
        Case 2
            TimeMsg.Font.Size = FontUnit.Medium
    End Select
        TimeMsg.Text = DateTime.Now.ToString("F")
End Sub
```

It's not sufficient to keep one cached copy of this page, because the display format changes depending on the selection in the lstMode control (see Figure 14-9).

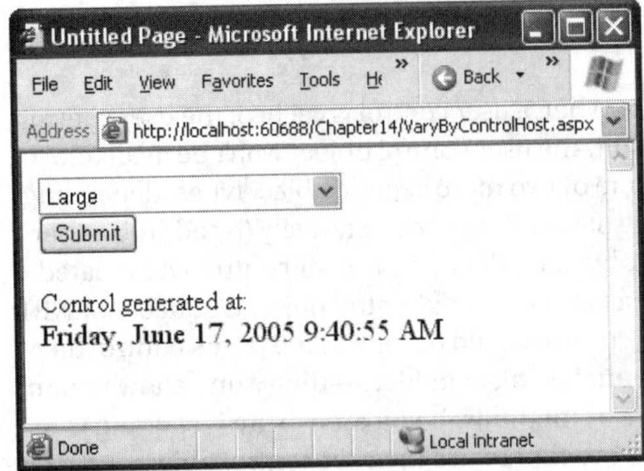

Figure 14-9. *Content that varies by control selection*

You can handle this using the VaryByControl attribute and referring specifically to this control:

```
<%@ OutputCache Duration="30" VaryByControl="lstMode" %>
```

When you try this example, you'll see a different date for each option, which emphasizes that ASP.NET maintains a separate cached copy for each list selection.

Sharing Cached Controls

If you use the same user control in ten different pages, ASP.NET will cache ten separate versions of that control. This gives each page the chance to customize the user control the first time is executed, before the user control is cached. However, in many cases you might find that you reuse the same user control on multiple pages and you don't need to introduce page-specific customizations. In this case, you can save memory by telling ASP.NET to share the cached copy of the control.

ASP.NET enables this scenario through the Shared property of the OutputCache directive. The Shared property works only when you are applying the directive to a user control, not a web form. Here's an example:

```
<%@ OutputCache Duration="10" VaryByParam="None" Shared="True" %>
```

You can also make the same request by adding the PartialCaching attribute to the class declaration for the user control:

```
<PartialCaching(10, Nothing, Nothing, Nothing, True)> _
Public Class MyUserControl
        Inherits UserControl
    ...
End Class
```

The Nothing parameters here represent VaryByParameter, VaryByControl, and VaryByCustom.

Summary

In this chapter, you learned how to create some simple and some sophisticated user controls. You also saw how to load user controls dynamically and how to cache them. Though user controls are easy to create, they don't solve every custom control challenge. In fact, user controls are quite limited in scope (they can't be easily shared across applications), and they have limited design-time support (for example, you can't attach event handlers in the Properties window). User controls also lack advanced features and aren't well suited to rendering HTML and JavaScript on the fly. To improve on this situation, you can step up to custom controls, which are much more sophisticated and quite a bit more complicated to create. Chapter 27 describes custom controls.

■ **Note** Although server controls are more powerful than user controls, most of the concepts you've learned in this chapter apply to server controls in the same way that they apply to user controls. For example, you can create server controls that include properties and methods, use custom objects, fire events, and expose child controls.

CHAPTER 15

■ ■ ■

Themes and Master Pages

Building a professional web application involves much more than designing individual web pages. You also need the tools to integrate your web pages into a complete, unified website. In this chapter, you'll consider two new ASP.NET features that let you do that.

First up is a feature called *themes*, which let you define the formatting details for various controls and seamlessly reuse these formats in multiple pages. Themes make it much easier to standardize your website's look and feel and tweak it later. Once a theme is in place, you can give your entire website a face-lift just by changing the theme definition.

A more impressive innovation is *master pages*, which let you create reusable page templates. Using a master page, you can define the layout for your website pages, complete with all the usual details such as headers, menu bars, and ad banners. Once you've formalized this structure, you can use the master page throughout your website, ensuring that all pages have the same design. Visitors can then surf from one section to another without noticing any change.

In this chapter, you'll learn how to use themes and master pages, two features that are new in ASP.NET 2.0, to standardize your websites.

Standardizing Website Formatting

The first step you can follow to integrate your website is to adopt a consistent visual style. In other words, standardize ruthlessly. If you want to tweak the font or border of a button, make sure you change it for *every* button you include.

Being consistent isn't always easy. To help manage the details, you can use CSS or themes.

Cascading Style Sheets

One of the most common ways to apply standardized formatting is to use CSS (Cascading Style Sheets). CSS provides a cross-platform solution for formatting web pages that works in conjunction with HTML 4 and is supported by virtually all modern browsers. In fact, early versions of Visual Studio automatically generated a Styles.vbs file for you to use in your website. (Later versions of Visual Studio abandoned this practice in favor of less clutter.)

Tip You can get the technical lowdown on CSS at `http://www.w3.org/Style/CSS`, or you can visit `http://www.w3schools.com/css` for a thorough tutorial.

With CSS, you use a stylesheet to define a set of formatting presets. You then link this stylesheet to the appropriate control using the CssClass property. To try it and add an (almost) empty stylesheet to your web project, choose Website ➤ Add New Item in Visual Studio. Then select Style Sheet, and click OK.

Stylesheets consist of *rules*. Each rule defines how a single ingredient in your web page should be formatted. For example, if you want to define a rule for formatting headings, you start by defining a rule with a descriptive name, like this:

```
.heading1
{
}
```

Each rule name has two parts. The portion before the period indicates the tag to which the rule applies. In this example, nothing appears before the period, which means the rule can apply to any tag. The portion after the period is a unique name (called the CSS *class name*) that you choose to identify your rule.

Once you've defined a rule, you can add the appropriate formatting information. Here's an example that sets the heading1 style to a large sans-serif font with a green foreground color:

```
.heading1
{
    font-weight: bold;
    font-size: large;
    color: limegreen;
    font-family: Verdana, Arial, Sans-Serif;
}
```

■ **Tip** If hand-writing CSS rules seems like too much work, don't worry—Visual Studio allows you to build a style rule using the same designer you use to format HTML tags. To use this feature, start by adding your rule declaration. Then, right-click between the two curly braces, and select Build Style. You'll see the familiar Style Builder dialog box where you can point and click your way to custom fonts, borders, backgrounds, and alignment.

A typical stylesheet defines a slew of rules. In fact, stylesheets are often used to formally define the formatting for every significant piece of a website's user interface. The following stylesheet serves this purpose. It defines three rules (heading1, heading2, and blockText) and a body rule that is applied to all tags automatically as a baseline for formatting.

```
body
{
    font-family: Verdana, Arial, Sans-Serif;
    font-size: small;
}

.heading1
{
    font-weight: bold;
    font-size: large;
    color: limegreen;
}
.heading2
{
    font-weight: bold;
    font-size: medium;
    font-style: italic;
    color: darkkhaki;
}
```

```
.blockText
{
    padding: 10px;
    background-color: lightyellow;
    border-style: solid;
    border-width: thin;
}
```

To use a rule in a web page, you first need to link the page to the appropriate stylesheet. You do this by adding a <link> tag in the <head> section of your page. The link tag references the file with the styles you want to use. Here's an example that allows the page to use styles defined in the file StyleSheet.vbs, assuming it's in the same folder as the web page:

```
<link href="StyleSheet.vbs" rel="stylesheet" type="text/css" />
```

■ **Tip** For a Visual Studio shortcut, select the underlying page (so that the DOCUMENT object appears in the Properties window), and then set the StyleSheet property to the stylesheet filename. This adds the <link> tag automatically. You can also drag the stylesheet onto the design surface of a page to trigger the same outcome.

Now you can bind any static HTML element or control to your style rules. For example, if you want an ordinary label to use the heading1 format, set the Label.vbsStyle property to heading1, as shown here:

```
<asp:Label ID="Label1" runat="server" Text="This Label Uses heading1"
 CssClass="heading1"></asp:Label>
```

You'll immediately see the result of the new formatting in the design window. Figure 15-1 shows a page that uses several CSS styles.

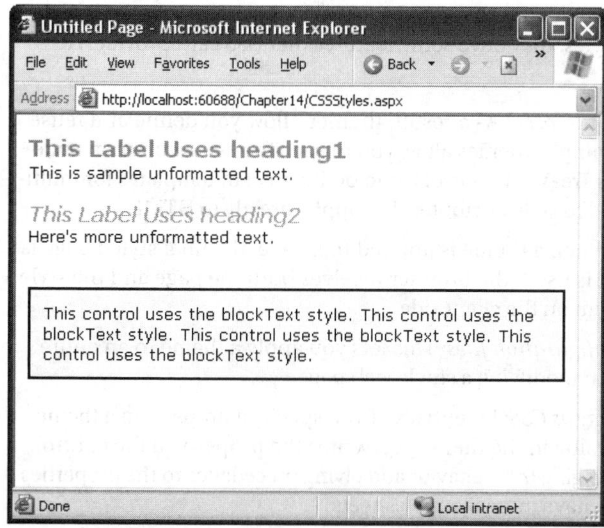

Figure 15-1. *Using CSS styles to format a page*

You can also create rules that are applied to HTML tags automatically. To do this, specify the tag name for the rule name. Here's a rule that affects all <h2> tags on the page that uses the stylesheet:

```
h2
{ ... }
```

Although this automatic stylesheet application sounds useful, it's less convenient in ASP.NET because you're usually dealing with controls, not individual HTML tags. You can't always be certain what tags will be used to render a given control, so it's best to explicitly specify the rule you want to use through the class name.

Using stylesheets accomplishes two things. First, it standardizes your layout so that you can quickly format new pages without introducing minor mistakes or idiosyncrasies. Second, it separates the formatting information so that it doesn't appear in your web pages at all, allowing you to modify the format without tracking down each page or recompiling your code. And although CSS isn't a .NET-centric standard, Visual Studio still provides rich support for it.

Themes

With the convenience of CSS styles, you might wonder why developers need anything more. The problem is that CSS rules are limited to a fixed set of style attributes. They allow you to reuse specific formatting details (fonts, borders, foreground and background colors, and so on), but they obviously can't control other aspects of ASP.NET controls. For example, the CheckBoxList control includes properties that control how it organizes items into rows and columns. Although these properties affect the visual appearance of the control, they're outside the scope of CSS, so you need to set them by hand. Additionally, you might want to define part of the behavior of the control along with the formatting. For example, you might want to standardize the selection mode of a Calendar control or the wrapping in a TextBox. This obviously isn't possible through CSS.

Themes, a new feature in ASP.NET 2.0, fill this gap. Like CSS, themes allow you to define a set of style attributes that you can apply to controls in multiple pages. However, unlike CSS, themes aren't implemented by the browser. Instead, they're a native ASP.NET solution that's implemented on the server. Although themes don't replace styles, they have some features that CSS can't provide. Here are the key differences:

Themes are control-based, not HTML-based: As a result, themes allow you define and reuse almost any control property. For example, themes allow you to specify a set of common node pictures and use them in numerous TreeView controls or to define a set of templates for multiple GridView controls. CSS is limited to style attributes that apply directly to HTML.

Themes are applied on the server: When a theme is applied to a page, the final styled page is sent to the user. When a stylesheet is used, the browser receives both the page and the style information and then combines them on the client side.

Themes can be applied through configuration files: This lets you apply a theme to an entire folder or your whole website without modifying a single web page.

Themes don't cascade in the same way as CSS: Essentially, if you specify a property in a theme *and* in the individual control, the value in the theme overwrites the property in the control. However, you have the choice of changing this behavior and giving precedence to the properties in the page, which makes themes behave more like stylesheets.

It would be overstating it to say that themes replace CSS. Instead, themes represent a higher-level model. To implement your formatting properties, ASP.NET will frequently render inline style rules. In addition, if you've crafted the perfect stylesheet, you can still use it. It's up to you whether you want to use one or both solutions. As you'll see later in this chapter (in the section "Using CSS in a Theme"), it's possible to use a stylesheet as part of a theme.

Theme Folders and Skins

All themes are application-specific. To use a theme in a web application, you need to create a folder that defines it. You need to place this folder in a folder named App_Theme, which must be inside the top-level directory for your web application. In other words, a web application named SuperCommerce might have a FunkyTheme theme in the SuperCommerce\App_Theme\FunkyTheme folder.

An application can contain definitions for multiple themes, as long as each theme is in a separate folder. Only one theme can be active on a given page at a time. In the "Applying Themes Dynamically" section, you'll discover how you can dynamically change the active theme when your page is processing.

To actually make your theme accomplish something, you need to create at least one *skin* file in the theme folder. A skin file is a text file with the .skin extension. ASP.NET never serves skin files directly—instead, they're used behind the scenes to define a theme.

A skin file is essentially a list of control tags—with a twist. The control tags in a skin file don't need to completely define the control. Instead, they need to set only the properties you want to standardize. For example, if you're trying to apply a consistent color scheme, you might be interested in setting properties such as ForeColor and BackColor only. When you add a control tag for the ListBox control, it might look like this:

```
<asp:ListBox runat="server" ForeColor="White" BackColor="Orange"/>
```

The runat="server" portion is always required. Everything else is optional. The id attribute is not allowed in a theme, because it's required to uniquely identify each control.

It's up to you whether you create multiple skin files or place all your control tags in a single skin file. Both approaches are equivalent, because ASP.NET treats all the skin files in a theme directory as part of the same theme definition. Often, it makes sense to separate the control tags for complex controls (such as the data controls) into separate skin files. Figure 15-2 shows the relationship between themes and skins in more detail.

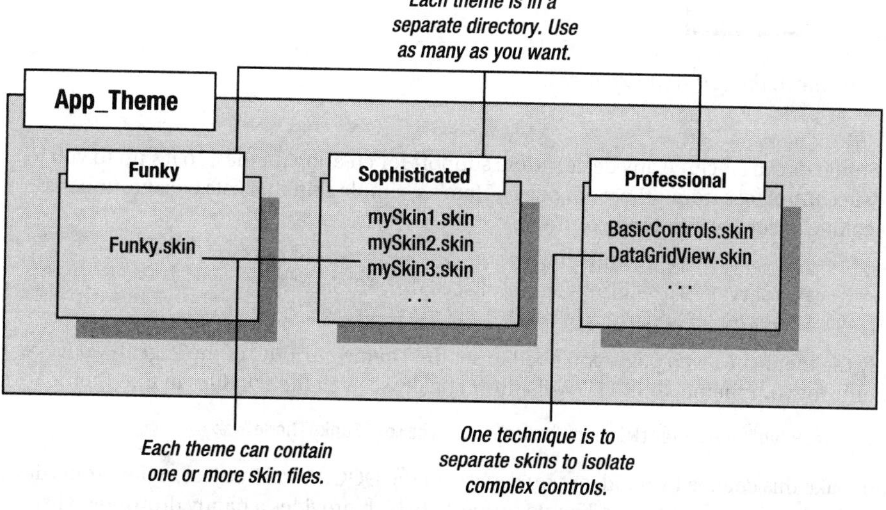

Figure 15-2. *Themes and skins*

ASP.NET also supports global themes. These are themes you place in the [WinDir]\Microsoft.Net\Framework\[Version]\Themes folder. However, it's recommended that you use local themes, even if you want to create more than one website that has the same theme. Using local themes makes it easier to deploy your web application, and it gives you the flexibility of introducing site-specific differences in the future.

If you have a local theme with the same name as a global theme, the local theme takes precedence, and the global theme is ignored. The themes are *not* merged together.

Tip ASP.NET doesn't ship with any predefined themes. That means you'll need to create your own from scratch or download sample themes from other websites such as `http://www.asp.net`.

Applying a Simple Theme

To add a theme to your project, select Website ➤ Add New Item and choose Skin File. Visual Studio will warn you that skin files need to be placed in a subfolder of the App_Themes folder and will ask you if that's what you intended. If you choose Yes, Visual Studio will create a folder with the same name as your theme file. You can then rename the folder and the file to whatever you'd like to use. Figure 15-3 shows an example with a theme that contains a single skin file.

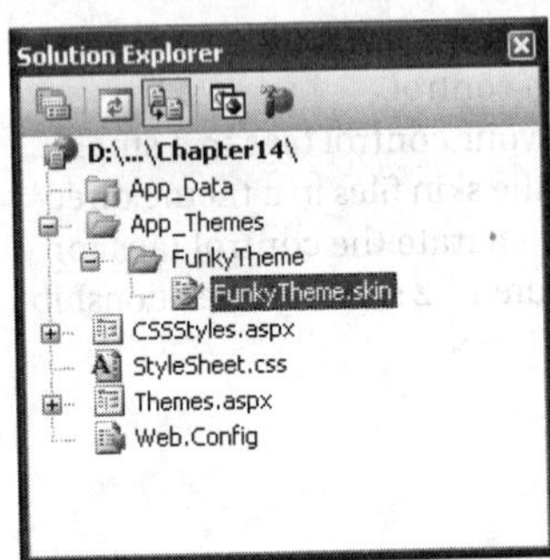

Figure 15-3. *A theme in the Solution Explorer*

Visual Studio doesn't include any design-time support for creating themes, so it's up to you to copy and paste control tags from other web pages. Here's a sample skin that sets background and foreground colors for several common controls:

```
<asp:ListBox runat="server" ForeColor="White" BackColor="Orange"/>
<asp:TextBox runat="server" ForeColor="White" BackColor="Orange"/>
<asp:Button runat="server" ForeColor="White" BackColor="Orange"/>
```

To apply the theme in a web page, you need to set the Theme attribute of the Page directive to the folder name for your theme. (ASP.NET will automatically scan all the skin files in that theme.)

```
<%@ Page Language="vb" AutoEventWireup="true" ... Theme="FunkyTheme" %>
```

You can make this change by hand, or you can select the DOCUMENT object in the Properties window at design time and then set the Theme property (which provides a handy drop-down list of all your web application's themes). Visual Studio will modify the Page directive accordingly.

When you apply a theme to a page, ASP.NET considers each control on your web page and checks your skin files to see if they define any properties for that control. If ASP.NET finds a matching tag in the skin file, the information from the skin file overrides the current properties of the control.

Figure 15-4 shows the result of applying the FunkyTheme to a simple page. The first picture shows the Themes.aspx page in its natural state, with no theme. The second picture shows the same page with the FunkyTheme applied. All the settings in FunkyTheme are applied to the controls in Themes.aspx, even if they overwrite values you've explicitly set in the page (such as the background for the list box). However, details that were in the original page but that don't conflict with the theme (such as the custom font for the buttons) are left in place.

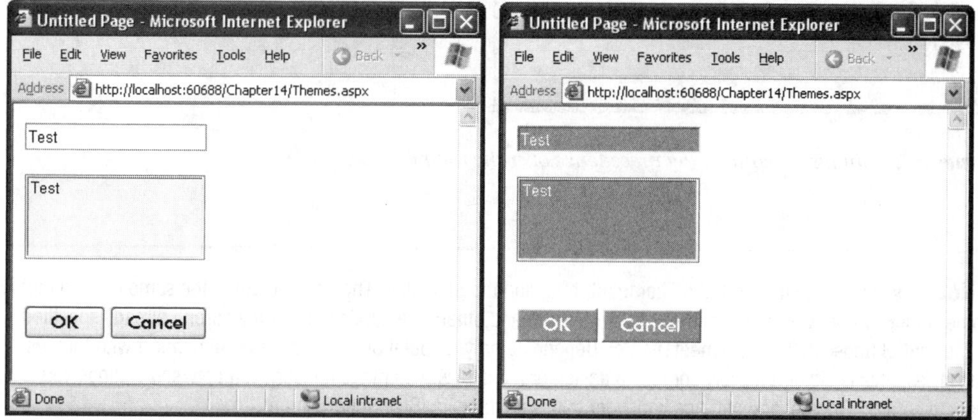

Figure 15-4. *A simple page before and after applying a theme*

Handling Theme Conflicts

As you've seen, when properties conflict between your controls and your theme, the theme wins. However, in some cases you might want to change this behavior so that your controls can fine-tune a theme by specifically overriding certain details. ASP.NET gives you this option, but it's an all-or-nothing setting that applies to all the controls on the entire page.

To make this change, just use the StyleSheetTheme attribute instead of the Theme attribute in the Page directive. (The StyleSheetTheme setting works more like CSS.) Here's an example:

```
<%@ Page Language="vb" AutoEventWireup="true" ... StyleSheetTheme="FunkyTheme" %>
```

Now the custom yellow background of the ListBox takes precedence over the background color specified by the theme. Figure 15-5 shows the result—and a potential problem. Because the foreground color has been changed to white, the lettering is now difficult to read. Overlapping formatting specifications can cause glitches such as this, which is why it's often better to let your themes take complete control by using the Theme attribute.

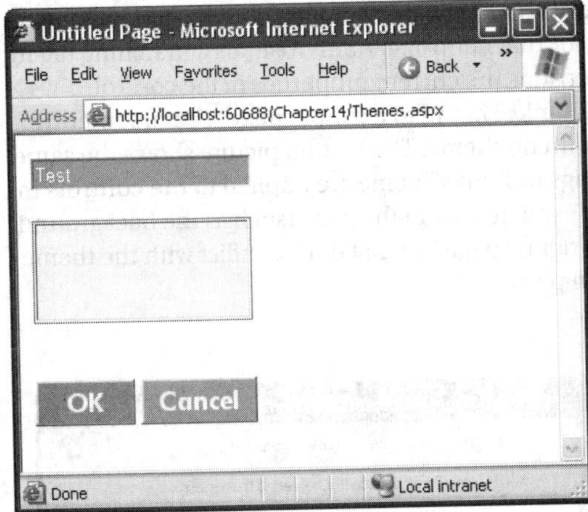

Figure 15-5. *Giving the control tag precedence over the theme*

■ **Note** It's possible to use both the Theme attribute and the StyleSheetTheme attribute at the same time so that some settings are always applied (those in the Theme) and others are applied only if they aren't already specified in the control (those in the StyleSheetTheme). Depending on your point of view (and level of comfort with themes and styles), this is either a terribly confusing design or a useful way to make a distinction between settings you want to enforce (Theme) and settings you want to use as defaults (StyleSheetTheme).

Another option is to configure specific controls so they opt out of the theming process entirely. To do this, simply set the EnableTheming property of the control to false. ASP.NET will still apply the theme to other controls on the page, but it will skip over the control you've configured.

```
<asp:Button ID="Button1" runat="server" ... EnableTheming="false" />
```

Creating Multiple Skins for the Same Control

Having each control locked into a single format is great for standardization, but it's probably not flexible enough for a real-world application. For example, you might have several types of text boxes that are distinguished based on where they're used or what type of data they contain. Labels are even more likely to differ, depending on whether they're being used for headings or for body text. Fortunately, ASP.NET allows you to create multiple declarations for the same control.

Ordinarily, if you create more than one theme for the same control, ASP.NET will give you a build error stating that you can have only a single default skin for each control. To get around this problem, you need to create a named skin by supplying a SkinID attribute. Here's an example:

```
<asp:ListBox runat="server" ForeColor="White" BackColor="Orange" />
<asp:TextBox runat="server" ForeColor="White" BackColor="Orange" />
<asp:Button runat="server" ForeColor="White" BackColor="Orange" />
<asp:TextBox runat="server" ForeColor="White" BackColor="DarkOrange"
 Font-Bold="True" SkinID="Dramatic"/>
<asp:Button runat="server" ForeColor="White" BackColor="DarkOrange"
 Font-Bold="True" SkinID="Dramatic"/>
```

The catch is that named skins aren't applied automatically like default skins. To use a named skin, you need to set the SkinID of the control on your web page to match. You can choose this value from a drop-down list that Visual Studio creates based on all your defined skin names, or you can type it in by hand:

```
<asp:Button ID="Button1" runat="server" ... SkinID="Dramatic" />
```

If you don't like the opt-in model for themes, you can make all your skins named. That way, they'll never be applied unless you set the control's SkinID.

■ **Note** Using named themes is similar to using CSS rules that are based on class name (as shown at the beginning of this chapter). CSS class rules are applied only if you set the class attribute of the corresponding HTML tag.

ASP.NET is intelligent enough to catch if you try to use a skin name that doesn't exist, in which case you'll get a build warning. The control will then behave as though you set EnableTheming to false, which means it will ignore the corresponding default skin.

■ **Tip** The SkinID doesn't need to be unique. It just has to be unique for each control. For example, imagine you want to create an alternate set of skinned controls that use a slightly smaller font. These controls match your overall theme, but they're useful on pages that display a large amount of information. In this case, you can create new Button, TextBox, and Label controls and give each one the same skin name (such as Smaller).

Skins with Templates and Images

So far, the theme examples have applied relatively simple properties. However, you can create much more detailed control tags in your skin file. Most control properties support themes. If a property can't be declared in a theme, you'll receive a build error when you attempt to launch your application.

■ **Note** Control developers can choose which properties you can set in a skin file by applying the Themeable attribute to the property declaration. If this attribute isn't present, the property can't be set in a theme. You'll learn more about custom control attributes in Chapter 28.

For example, many controls support styles that specify a range of formatting information. The data controls are one example, and the Calendar control provides another. Here's how you might define Calendar styles in a skin file to match your theme:

```
<asp:Calendar ID="Calendar1" runat="server" BackColor="White" ForeColor="Black"
 BorderColor="Black" BorderStyle="Solid" CellSpacing="1"
 Font-Names="Verdana" Font-Size="9pt" Height="250px" Width="500px"
 NextPrevFormat="ShortMonth" SelectionMode="Day">
  <SelectedDayStyle BackColor="DarkOrange" ForeColor="White" />
  <DayStyle BackColor="Orange" Font-Bold="True" ForeColor="White" />
  <NextPrevStyle Font-Bold="True" Font-Size="8pt" ForeColor="White" />
  <DayHeaderStyle Font-Bold="True" Font-Size="8pt" ForeColor="#333333"
   Height="8pt" />
  <TitleStyle BackColor="Firebrick" BorderStyle="None" Font-Bold="True"
   Font-Size="12pt" ForeColor="White" Height="12pt" />
  <OtherMonthDayStyle BackColor="NavajoWhite" Font-Bold="False"
   ForeColor="DarkGray" />
</asp:Calendar>
```

This skin defines the font, colors, and styles of the Calendar. It also sets the selection mode, the formatting of the month navigation links, and the overall size of the calendar. As a result, all you need to use this formatted calendar is the following streamlined tag:

```
<asp:Calendar ID="Calendar1" runat="server" />
```

Figure 15-6 shows how this Calendar control would ordinarily look and how it looks when the page uses the corresponding theme.

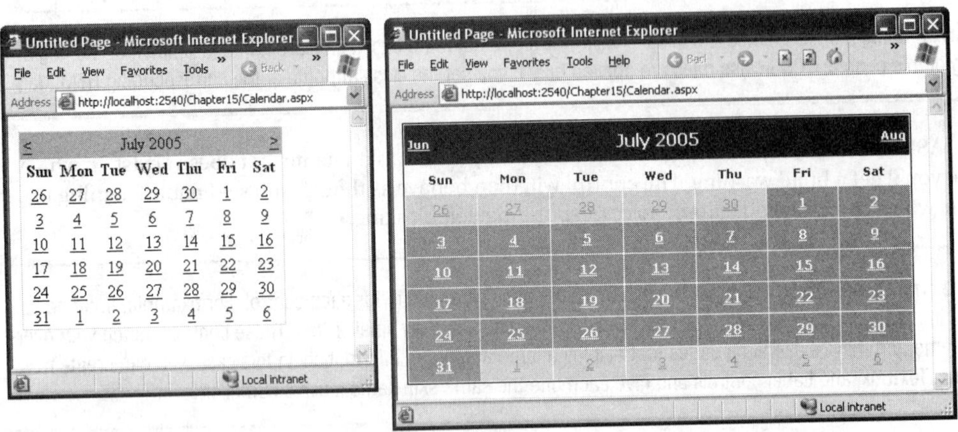

Figure 15-6. *An unformatted Calendar on an unthemed and themed page*

■ **Caution** When you create skins that specify details such as sizing, be careful. When these settings are applied to a page, they could cause the layout to change with unintended consequences. If you're in doubt, set a SkinID so that the skin is applied only if the control specifically opts in.

Another powerful technique is to reuse images by making them part of your theme. For example, imagine you perfect an image that you want to use for OK buttons throughout your website and you have another image for all the cancel buttons. The first step in implementing this design is to add the images to your theme folder. For the best organization, it makes sense to create one or more subfolders just for holding images. In Figure 15-7, the images are stored in a folder named ButtonImages.

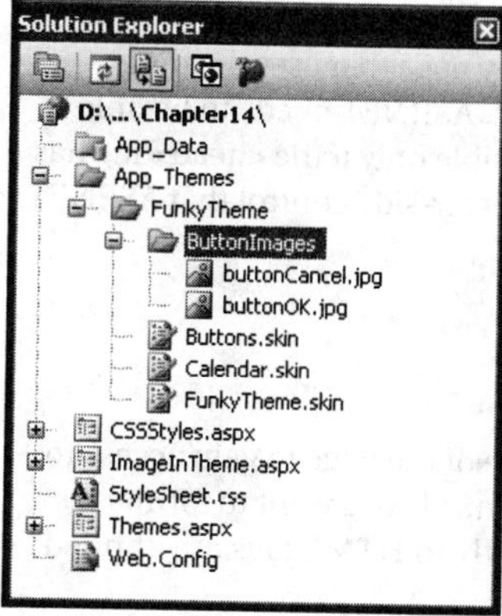

Figure 15-7. *Adding images to a theme*

Now you need to create the skins that use these images. In this case, both of these tags should be named skins. That's because you're defining a specific type of standardized button that should be available to the page when needed. You *aren't* defining a default style that should apply to all buttons.

```
<asp:ImageButton runat="server" SkinID="OKButton"
 ImageUrl="ButtonImages/buttonOK.jpg" />
<asp:ImageButton runat="server" SkinID="CancelButton"
 ImageUrl="ButtonImages/buttonCancel.jpg" />
```

When you add a reference to an image in a skin file, always make sure the image URL is relative to the theme folder, not the folder where the page is stored. When this theme is applied to a control, ASP.NET automatically inserts the Themes\ThemeName portion at the beginning of the URL.

Now to apply these images, simply create an ImageButton in your web page that references the corresponding skin name:

```
<asp:ImageButton ID="ImageButton1" runat="server" SkinID="OKButton" />
<asp:ImageButton ID="ImageButton2" runat="server" SkinID="CancelButton" />
```

You can use the same technique to create skins for other controls that use images. For example, you can standardize the node pictures used in a TreeView, the bullet image used for the BulletList control, or the icons used in a DataGridView.

Using CSS in a Theme

ASP.NET also gives you the ability to use a stylesheet as part of a theme. You might use this feature for a few reasons:

- You want to style HTML elements that might not correspond to server controls.
- You prefer to use a stylesheet because it is more standardized or because it can also be used to format static HTML pages.
- You have already invested effort in creating a stylesheet, and you don't want to create themes to implement the same formatting.

To use a stylesheet in a theme, you first need to add the stylesheet to your theme folder. ASP.NET searches this folder for all .vbs files and dynamically binds them to any page that uses the theme.

This has one catch, however. To bind the page to the stylesheet, ASP.NET needs to be able to insert a <link> tag in the <head> section of the web page. This is possible only if the <head> tag has the runat="server" attribute. This turns the <head> element into a server-side control that ASP.NET can modify to insert the stylesheet links.

```
<head runat="server">
    <title>...</title>
</head>
```

Once this is in place, you simply need to set the Theme attribute of the page to gain access to the stylesheet rules. You can then set the CssClass property of the controls you want to format, as you saw earlier in the chapter. Any style rules that are linked directly to HTML tags are applied automatically.

You can use as many stylesheets as you want in a theme. ASP.NET will add multiple <link> tags, one for each stylesheet in the theme.

You can include more than one cascading stylesheet in a theme. If you add multiple cascading stylesheets, then the server-side <head runat="Server" /> tag will automatically generate links for each stylesheet.

Applying Themes Through a Configuration File

Using the Page directive, you can bind a theme to a single page. However, you might decide that your theme is ready to be rolled out for the entire web application. The cleanest way to apply this theme is to configure the <pages> element in the web.config file for your application, as shown here:

```
<configuration>
  <system.web>
    <pages theme="FunkyTheme" />
  </system.web>
</configuration>
```

If you want to use the stylesheet behavior so that the theme doesn't overwrite conflicting control properties, use the StyleSheetTheme attribute instead of theme:

```
<configuration>
  <system.web>
    <pages StyleSheetTheme="FunkyTheme" />
  </system.web>
</configuration>
```

Either way, when you specify a theme in the web.config file, the theme you specify will be applied throughout all the pages in your website, provided these pages don't have their own theme settings. If a page specifies the Theme attribute, the page setting will take precedence over the web.config setting.

Using this technique, it's just as easy to apply a theme to part of a web application. For example, you can create a separate web.config file for each subfolder and use the <pages> setting to configure different themes.

■ **Tip** If you apply themes through a configuration file, you can still disable them for specific pages. Just include the EnableTheming attribute in the Page directive, and set it to false. No themes will be applied to the page.

Applying Themes Dynamically

In some cases, themes aren't used to standardize website appearance but to make that appearance configurable for each user. In this scenario, your web application gives the user the chance to specify the theme that your pages will use.

This technique is remarkably easy. All you need to do is set the Page.Theme or Page.StyleSheet property dynamically in your code. The trick is that this step needs to be completed in the Page.Init event stage. After this point, attempting to set the property causes a compilation error.

Here's an example that applies a dynamic theme by reading the theme name from the current Session collection:

```
Protected Sub Page_PreInit(ByVal sender As Object, ByVal e As EventArgs)
    If Session("Theme") Is Nothing Then
        ' No theme has been chosen. Choose a default
        ' (or set a blank string to make sure no theme
        ' is used).
        Page.Theme = String.Empty
    Else
        Page.Theme = CStr(Session("Theme"))
    End If
End Sub
```

Of course, you could also store the selected theme in a cookie, a session state, a profile (see Chapter 24), or any other user-specific location.

If you want to create a page that allows the user to choose a theme, you need a little more sleight of hand. The problem is that the user's selection can't be read until after the page has been loaded and has passed the PreInit stage. However, at this point, it is too late to set the theme. One way around this problem is to trigger a refresh by redirecting the page back to itself. The most efficient way to accomplish this is to use Server.Transfer() so that all the processing takes place on the server. (Response.Redirect() sends a redirect header to the client and so requires an extra round-trip.)

Here's the code that presents the list of selections when the page loads and then records the selection and transfers the page when a button is clicked:

```
Protected Sub Page_Load(ByVal sender As Object, ByVal e As EventArgs)
    If (Not Page.IsPostBack) Then
        ' Fill the list box with available themes
        ' by reading the folders in the App_Themes folder.
        Dim themeDir As New DirectoryInfo(Server.MapPath("App_Themes"))
        lstThemes.DataTextField = "Name"
        lstThemes.DataSource = themeDir.GetDirectories()
        lstThemes.DataBind()
    End If
End Sub

Protected Sub cmdApply_Click(ByVal sender As Object, ByVal e As EventArgs)
    ' Set the chosen theme.
    Session("Theme") = lstThemes.SelectedValue

    ' Refresh the page.
    Server.Transfer(Request.FilePath)
End Sub
```

Figure 15-8 shows the resulting page.

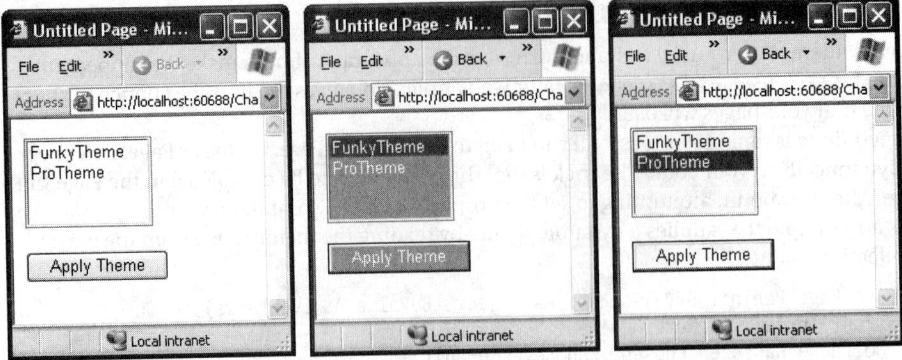

Figure 15-8. *Allowing the user to choose a theme*

If you use named skins, you can set the SkinID of a control declaratively when you design the page, or you can specify it dynamically in your code.

■ **Caution** If you use named skins, you'll need to be careful that every theme uses the same names and provides tags for the same controls. If a control specifies the SkinID attribute and ASP.NET can't find a matching skin for that control in the theme, the control won't be themed, and it will keep its current formatting.

Standardizing Website Layout

Standardizing the formatting of your website is only half the battle. You also need to make sure that common elements, such as your website header and site navigation controls, appear in the same position on every page.

The challenge is to create a simple, flexible layout that can be replicated throughout your entire website. You can use three basic approaches:

User controls: User controls allow you to define a "pagelet"—a portion of a web page, complete with markup and server-side code, that can be reused on as many web forms as you want. User controls are a great way to standardize a common page element. However, they can't solve the layout problem on their own, because there's no way to ensure that user controls are placed in the same position on every page. Chapter 14 describes user controls.

HTML frames: Frames, a basic tool of HTML, allow you to show more than one page in a browser window at once. The key disadvantage of frames is that each page is retrieved through a separate request to the server, and as a result the code on each page must be completely independent. That means a page in one frame can't communicate with or influence a page in another frame (at least not through server-side code). The one advantage that frames give that can't be duplicated by any other feature is isolated scrolling, which means each frame can be scrolled separately.

Master pages: Master pages are a new innovation in ASP.NET that are designed specifically for standardizing web-page layout. Master pages are web-page templates that can define fixed content and declare the portion of the web page where you can insert custom content. If you use the same master page throughout your website, you're guaranteed to keep the same layout. Best of all, if you change the master page definition after applying it, all the web pages that use it inherit the change automatically.

In ASP.NET, master pages are the preferred option, and you'll see them at work throughout the rest of this chapter. Frames offer a clumsier programming model but are required if you want to fix a portion of your page in place while allowing scrolling in another section. If you want to learn more about frames, refer to Chapter 29 for the basics and for several ASP.NET workarounds.

Master Page Basics

Many loyal ASP developers were surprised to find that ASP.NET 1.0 and 1.1 didn't include any facility for creating page templates—a must for building a coherent site. Although some workarounds were proposed, these custom solutions still had drawbacks and often didn't integrate well with the Visual Studio design environment. Adding to the disappointment was that Windows Forms (the .NET toolkit for Windows user interfaces) included a model for reusable form templates, although even that was far from perfect. Finally, ASP.NET 2.0 fills the gap with a comprehensive new feature called *master pages*.

To provide a practical, flexible solution for page templating, a number of requirements must be met:

- The ability to define a portion of a page separately and reuse it on multiple pages.
- The ability to create a locked-in layout that defines editable regions. Pages that reuse this template are then constrained to adding or modifying content in the allowed regions.
- The ability to allow some customization of the elements you reuse on each page.
- The ability to bind a page to a page template declaratively (with no code) or to bind to a page dynamically at runtime.
- The ability to design a page that uses a page template with a tool such as Visual Studio.

Master pages meet all of these requirements. They provide a system for reusing templates, a way to limit how templates can be modified, and rich design-time support.

For this to work, ASP.NET defines two new types of pages: master pages and content pages. A *master page* is a page template. Like an ordinary ASP.NET web page, it can contain any combination of HTML, web controls, and even code. In addition, master pages can include *content placeholders*—defined regions that can be modified. Each *content page* references a single master page and acquires its layout and content. In addition, the content page can add page-specific content in any of the placeholders. In other words, the content page fills in the missing pieces that the master page doesn't define.

For example, in a typical website, a master page might include a fixed element such as a header and a content placeholder for the rest of the page. The content page then acquires the header for free and supplies additional content.

To take a closer look at how this works, it helps to consider the example presented in the following sections.

A Simple Master Page

To create a master page in Visual Studio, select Website ➤ Add New Item from the menu. Select Master Page, give it a filename, and click OK.

A master page is similar to an ordinary ASP.NET web form. Like a web form, the master page can include HTML, web controls, and code (either in an inline script block or in a separate file). One difference is that while web forms start with the Page directive, a master page starts with a Master directive that specifies the same information, as shown here:

```
<%@ Master Language="vb" AutoEventWireup="true" CodeFile="SiteTemplate.master.vb"
    Inherits="SiteTemplate" %>
```

Another difference between master pages and ordinary web forms is that master pages can use the ContentPlaceHolder control, which isn't allowed in ordinary pages. The ContentPlaceHolder is a portion of the page where the content page can insert content. When you create a new master page in Visual Studio, you start with a blank page that includes a single ContentPlaceHolder control (see Figure 15-9), although you can add as many as you need.

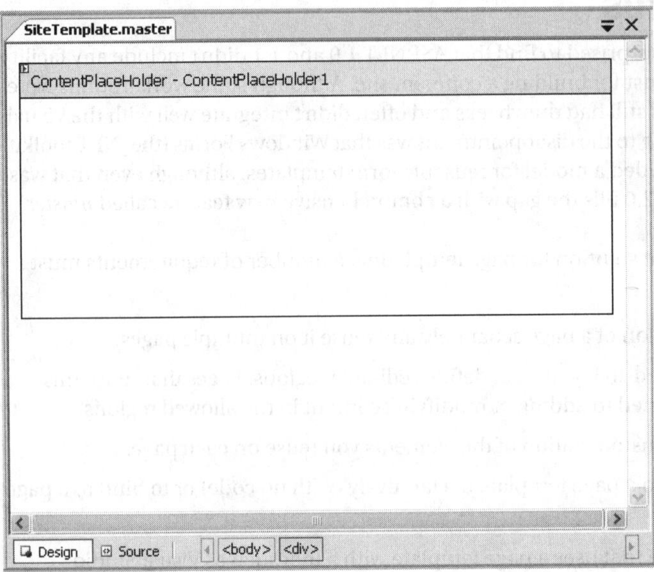

Figure 15-9. *A new master page*

The ContentPlaceHolder doesn't have any remarkable properties. Here's an example that creates a master page with a static banner followed by a ContentPlaceHolder and then a footer (shown in Figure 15-10):

```
<%@ Master Language="vb" AutoEventWireup="true" CodeFile="SiteTemplate.master.vb"
   Inherits="SiteTemplate" %>

<html xmlns="http://www.w3.org/1999/xhtml" >
<head runat="server">
    <title>Untitled Page</title>
</head>
<body>
    <form id="form1" runat="server">
    <table width="100%">
      <tr>
        <td bgcolor="black" style="...">
          <img align="left" src="headerleft.jpg" />
          <img align="right" src="headerright.jpg" />
          <br />My Site<br />
        </td>
      </tr>
    </table>
    <br />
    <asp:ContentPlaceHolder id="ContentPlaceHolder1" runat="server">
    </asp:ContentPlaceHolder>
```

```
    <br />
    <em>Copyright (c) 2005.</em>
    </form>
</body>
</html>
```

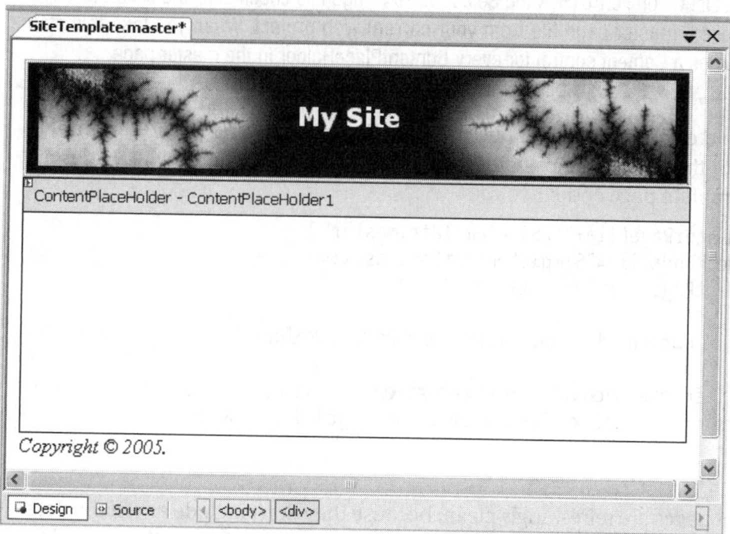

Figure 15-10. *A master page at design time*

Master pages can't be requested directly. To use a master page, you need to build a linked content page.

A Simple Content Page

To use your master page in another web page, you need to add the MasterPageFile attribute to the Page directive. This attribute indicates the filename of the master you want to use:

```
<%@ Page Language="vb" MasterPageFile="~/SiteTemplate.master" ... %>
```

Notice that the MasterPageFile attribute begins with the path ~/ to specify the root website folder. If you just specify the filename, ASP.NET checks a predetermined subfolder (named MasterPages) for your master page. If you haven't created this folder or your master page isn't there, it checks the root of your web folder next.

Setting the MasterPageFile attribute isn't enough to transform an ordinary page into a content page. The problem is that content pages have a single responsibility—to define the content that will be inserted in one or more ContentPlaceHolder controls (and to write any code you need for these controls). A content page doesn't define the page, because the outer shell is already provided by the master page. As a result, attempting to include elements such as <html>, <head>, and <body> will fail, because they're already defined in the master page.

To provide content for a ContentPlaceHolder, you use another specialized control, called Content. The ContentPlaceHolder control and the Content control have a one-to-one relationship. For each ContentPlaceHolder in the master page, the content page supplies a matching Content control (unless you don't want to supply any content at all for that region). ASP.NET links the Content control to the appropriate ContentPlaceHolder by matching the ID of the ContentPlaceHolder with the Content.ContentPlaceHolderID property of the corresponding Content control. If you create a Content control that references a nonexistent ContentPlaceHolder, you'll receive an error.

■ **Tip** To make it even easier to create a new content page, let Visual Studio guide you. Just select Website ➤ Add New Item from the menu. Select Web Form, click the Select Master Page File check box, and click OK. Visual Studio will prompt you to choose a master page file from your current web project. When you take this step, Visual Studio automatically creates a Content control for every ContentPlaceHolder in the master page.

Thus, to create a complete content page that uses the SiteTemplate master page, you simply need to fill in the content for the ContentPlaceHolder with the ID ContentPlaceHolder1. Here's an example that shows the complete page code:

```
<%@ Page Language="vb" MasterPageFile="~/SiteTemplate.master"
    AutoEventWireup="true" CodeFile="SimpleContentPage.aspx.vb"
    Inherits="SimpleContentPage" Title="Untitled Page" %>

<asp:Content ID="Content1" ContentPlaceHolderID="ContentPlaceHolder1"
  runat="Server">
<span style="...">Far out in the uncharted backwaters of the unfashionable end
of the western spiral arm of the Galaxy lies a small unregarded yellow sun.
</span>
</asp:Content>
```

As you can see, content pages are refreshingly clean, because they don't include any of the details defined in the master page. Even better, this makes it easy to update your website. All you need to is modify a single master page. As long as you keep the same ContentPlaceHolder controls, the existing content pages will keep working and will fit themselves into the new layout wherever you specify.

Figure 15-11 shows this sample content page.

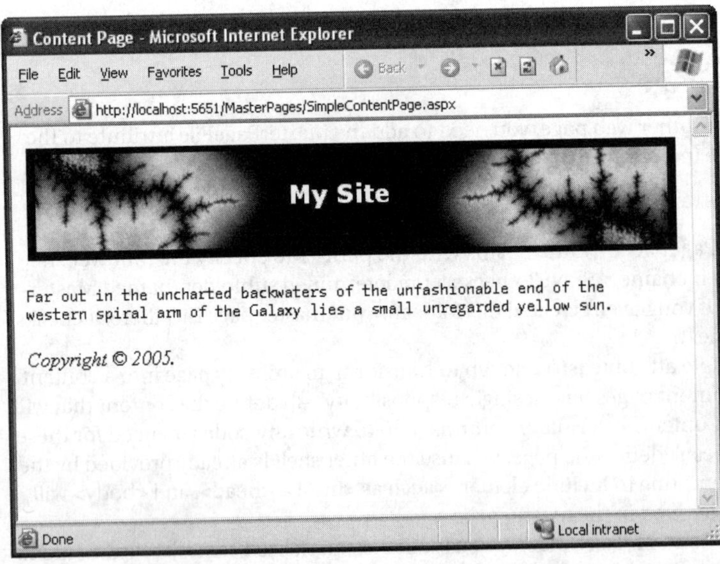

Figure 15-11. *A content page at runtime*

To get a better understanding of how master pages work under the hood, it's worth taking a look at a content page with tracing (add the Trace="True" attribute in the Page directive). That way you can study the control hierarchy. What you'll discover is that ASP.NET creates the control objects for the master page first, including the ContentPlaceHolder, which acts as a container. It then adds the controls from the content page into the ContentPlaceHolder.

Design-Time Quirks with Master Pages

The design-time representation of your content pages can range from excellent to poor. For the simple header and footer example, you'll see a fairly good representation of your content page that includes all the elements of the master page and the additional content you've added. The parts you've acquired from the master page will be shaded in gray, indicating you can't select or change them in any way. Instead, you'll be limited to inserting comments into the ContentPlaceHolder region, as shown in Figure 15-12.

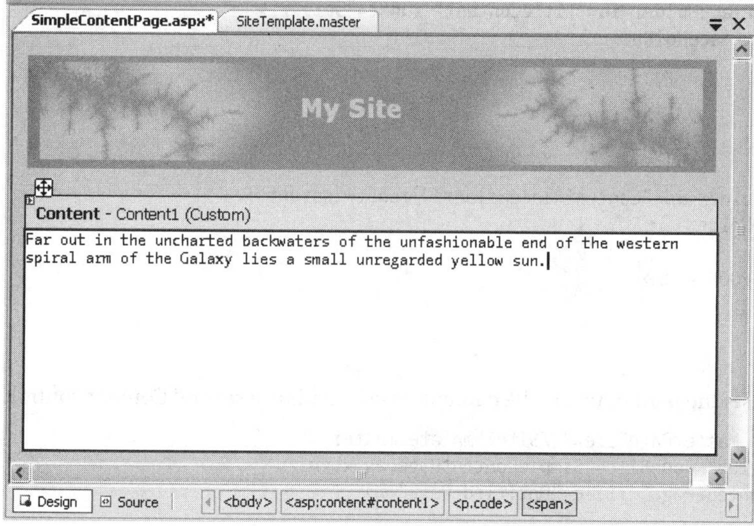

Figure 15-12. *A content page at design time*

■ **Tip** If a master page defines a ContentPlaceHolder but your content page doesn't define a corresponding Content control, you'll see a black box in its place. To add the required Content control, right-click that section of the page and choose Create Custom Content.

However, this design-time representation is a little misleading. That's because when you run the page, the ContentPlaceHolder section will expand or collapse to fit the content you place in it. If you've added volumes of text, the footer won't appear until the end. And if you've included only a single line of text, you'll see something more compact (as in Figure 15-11).

The main problem is how Visual Studio renders the ContentPlaceHolder and Content controls. Initially, these are shown as empty boxes that expand as you add content. However, no matter how little content you add, the design-time representation of this box won't shrink beyond a certain set size. As a result, your alignment won't be faithfully depicted for very small content regions.

To see a more dramatic example of this problem, try adding a second ContentPlaceHolder to the master and allowing the user to define a title in the header, with the preset graphics and font:

```
<%@ Master Language="vb" AutoEventWireup="true" CodeFile="SiteTemplate.master.vb"
    Inherits="SiteTemplate" %>

<html xmlns="http://www.w3.org/1999/xhtml" >
<head runat="server">
    <title>Untitled Page</title>
</head>
<body>
    <form id="form1" runat="server">
    <table width="100%">
      <tr>
        <td bgcolor="black" style="...">
          <img align="left" src="headerleft.jpg" />
          <img align="right" src="headerright.jpg" />
          <br />
          <asp:ContentPlaceHolder id="TitleContent" runat="server">
          </asp:ContentPlaceHolder>
          <br />
        </td>
      </tr>
    </table>
    <br />
    <asp:ContentPlaceHolder id="ContentPlaceHolder1" runat="server">
    </asp:ContentPlaceHolder>
    <br />
    <em>Copyright (c) 2005.</em>
    </form>
</body>
</html>
```

Now you can easily set the banner text in the content page by adding a second Content control:

```
<%@ Page Language="vb" MasterPageFile="~/SiteTemplate.master"
    AutoEventWireup="true" CodeFile="SimpleContentPage.aspx.vb"
    Inherits="SimpleContentPage" Title="Untitled Page" %>

<asp:Content ID="Content1" ContentPlaceHolderID="ContentPlaceHolder1"
  runat="Server">
<span style="...">Far out in the uncharted backwaters of the unfashionable end
of the western spiral arm of the Galaxy lies a small unregarded yellow sun.
</span>
</asp:Content>

<asp:Content ContentPlaceHolderID="TitleContent" ID="Content2" runat="server">
  Custom Title</asp:Content>
```

Figure 15-13 compares what you'll see at design time with what you'll see at runtime. Not only is the text unreadable (because the white font color from the master page isn't applied at design time), but also the layout is scrambled because of the minimum display size that the Content control uses at design time.

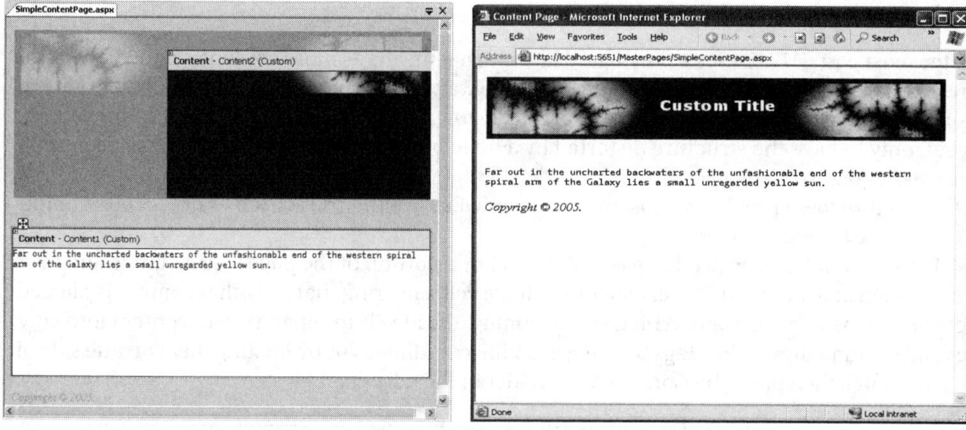

Figure 15-13. *The design-time and runtime view of a more complex content page*

■ **Tip** When creating master pages that don't use tables, make sure you include a <br /> line break after your ContentPlaceHolder, if needed. In the design environment, the ContentPlaceHolder is shown as a box that takes the full width of the design surface. As a result, content that appears after it always starts on the line underneath. However, if you haven't added a line break, in your content page you'll see a different behavior—namely, the content in the ContentPlaceHolder placeholder will run directly into the following content.

Default Content

When the master page defines a ContentPlaceHolder, it can also include default content—content that will be used only if the content page doesn't supply a corresponding Content control.

To get this effect, all you need to do is place the appropriate HTML or web controls in the ContentPlaceHolder tag. (You can do this by hand using the .aspx markup or just by dragging and dropping controls into the ContentPlaceHolder.)

Here's an example that adds default content to the banner text from the previous example:

```
<asp:ContentPlaceHolder id="TitleContent" runat="server">
Master Pages Website
</asp:ContentPlaceHolder>
```

If you create a content page in Visual Studio, you won't notice any immediate change. That's because Visual Studio automatically creates a <Content> tag for each ContentPlaceHolder. When a content page includes a <Content> tag, it automatically overrides the default content. However, if you delete the <Content> tag, you'll see the default content in its place—the new "Master Pages Website" banner text.

■ **Note** Content pages can't use just a portion of the default content or just edit it slightly. This isn't possible because the default content is stored only in the master page, not in the content page. As a result, you need to decide between using the default content as is or replacing it completely.

A More Practical Master Page

For the most part, HTML uses a flow-based layout. That means as more content is added, the page is reorganized and other content is bumped out the way. This layout can make it difficult to get the result you want with master pages. For example, if you aren't careful, you could craft the perfect layout, only to have the structure distorted by a huge block of information that's inserted into a <Content> tag.

To control these problems, most master pages will use either HTML tables or CSS positioning to control the layout.

With tables, the basic principle is to divide all or a portion of the page into columns and rows. You can then add a ContentPlaceHolder in a single cell, ensuring that the other content is aligned more or less the way you want. With CSS positioning, the idea is to separate your content into <div> tags and position these <div> tags by using absolute coordinates or by floating them on one side of the page. You'll then place the ContentPlaceHolder in the <div> tag.

Tip For some great examples of CSS-based layout, see the sites `http://www.csszengarden.com` and `http://www.bluerobot.com/web/layouts`.

The following example shows how you can use master pages to create a traditional web application with a header, footer, and navigation bar, all of which are defined with tables. Figure 15-14 shows how this structure is broken up into a table.

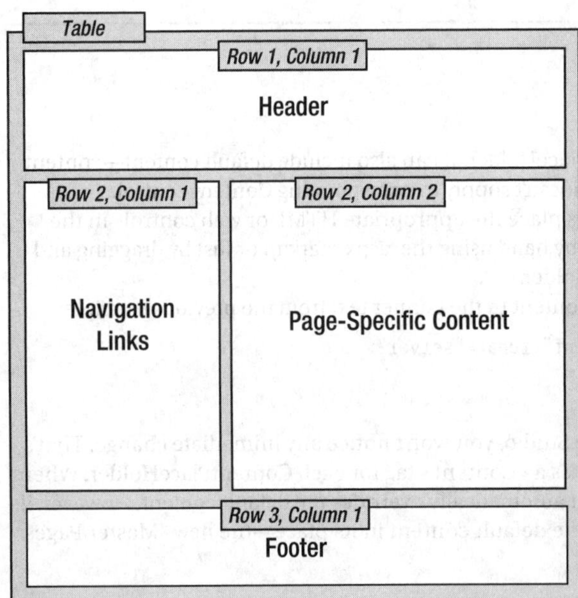

Figure 15-14. *A table-based layout*

Here's the markup for the table:

```
<table width="100%">
    <tr><td colspan="2">My Header</td></tr>
    <tr>
        <td width="150px">Navigation Controls</td>
        <td>
            <asp:ContentPlaceHolder id="ContentPlaceHolder1" runat="server">
            </asp:ContentPlaceHolder>
        </td>
     </tr>
     <tr><td colspan="2">My Footer</td></tr>
</table>
```

■**Tip** For a quick refresher on HTML tables, complete with information about how to specify borders, cell sizes, alignment, and more, refer to the examples at `http://www.w3schools.com/html/html_tables.asp`.

Figure 15-15 shows the resulting master page and a content page that uses the master page.

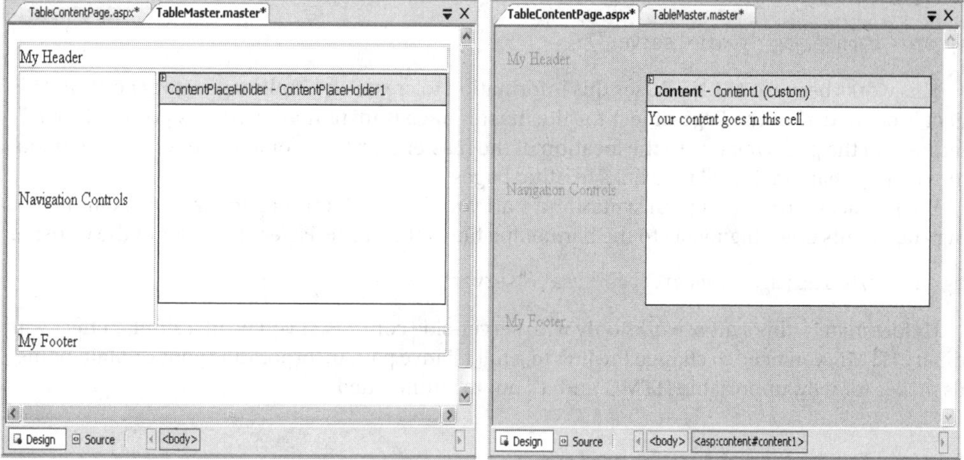

Figure 15-15. *A master page and content page that use a table*

To convert this example into something more practical, just replace the static text in the master page with the actual header, navigation controls, and footer you really want. All the child pages will acquire these features automatically. This is the first step for defining a practical structure for your entire website.

Master Pages and Relative Paths

One quirk that can catch unsuspecting developers is the way that master pages handle relative paths. If all you're using is static text, this issue won't affect you. However, if you've added <img> tags or any other HTML tag that points to another resource, problems can occur.

The problem shows up if you place the master page in a different directory from the content page that uses it. This is a recommended best practice for large websites. In fact, Microsoft encourages you to use a dedicated folder for storing all your master pages. However, if you're not suitably careful, this can cause problems when you use relative paths.

For example, imagine you put a master page in a subfolder named MasterPages and add the following <img> tag to the master page:

```
<img src="banner.jpg" />
```

Assuming the file \MasterPages\banner.jpg exists, this appears to work fine. The image will even appear in the Visual Studio design environment. However, if you create a content page in another subfolder, the path is interpreted relative to that folder. If the file doesn't exist there, you'll get a broken link instead of your graphic. Even worse, you could conceivably get the wrong graphic if another image has the same filename.

This problem occurs because the <img> tag is ordinary HTML. As a result, ASP.NET won't touch it. Unfortunately, when ASP.NET builds your content page, this tag is no longer appropriate.

To solve your problem, you could try to think ahead and write your URL relative to the content page where you want to use it. But this creates confusion, limits where your master page can be used, and has the unwelcome side effect of displaying your master page incorrectly in the design environment.

Another quick fix is to make your image tag into a server-side control, in which case ASP.NET will fix the mistake:

```
<img src="banner.jpg" runat="server"/>
```

This works because ASP.NET uses this information to create an HtmlImage server control. This object is created after the Page object for the master page is instantiated. At this point, ASP.NET interprets all the paths relative to the location of the master page. You could use the same technique to fix <a> tags that provide relative links to other pages.

You can also use the root path syntax and start your URL with the ~ character. For example, this <img> tag points unambiguously to the banner.jpg file in the MasterPages subfolder of the website:

```
<img src="~/MasterPages/banner.jpg" runat="server" />
```

Unfortunately, this syntax works only with server-side controls. If you want a similar effect with ordinary HTML, you need to change the link to a full relative path incorporating your domain name. This makes for ugly, unportable HTML, and it's not recommended.

Master Pages and Formatting

Master pages give you another technique you can use to apply consistent formatting across your entire website. For example, if you want a particular theme to always be used with a master page, simply set the Theme or StyleSheetTheme attribute of the Master directive. That way every content page gets the linked theme without any extra work required. Linking themes to master pages is a useful technique—it's easier than setting the theme for each page and not as clumsy as trying to apply it across an entire website through the web.config file.

Master pages provide a few other options for standardizing formatting. For example, you can link to a stylesheet without using themes by adding a <link> element in the <head> section of the master page.

You can also use a more fine-grained model and have your master page help you apply different formatting to different sections of a content page. All you need to do is set the appropriate foreground and background colors, fonts, and alignment options using container tags in the master page. For example, you might set these on a table, a table cell, or a <div> tag. The information from the content page can then flow seamlessly into these containers, acquiring the appropriate style attributes automatically.

Applying Master Pages Through a Configuration File

It's worth nothing that you can also apply a master page to all the pages in your website at once using the web.config file. All you need to do is add the <pages> attribute and set its masterPageFile attribute, as shown here:

```
<configuration>
  <system.web>
    <pages masterPageFile ="SiteTemplate.master"/>
  </system.web>
</configuration>
```

The problem is that this approach tends to be quite inflexible. Any web page you have that doesn't play by the rules (for example, includes a root <html> tag or defines a content region that doesn't correspond to a ContentPlaceHolder) will be automatically broken. If you must use this feature, don't apply it site-wide. Instead, create a subfolder for your content pages, and create a web.config file in just that subfolder to apply the master page.

■ **Note** Even if a master page is applied through the web.config, you have no guarantee that an individual page won't override your setting by supplying a MasterPageFile attribute in the Page directive. And if the MasterPageFile attribute is specified with a blank string, the page won't have any master page at all, regardless of what the web.config file specifies.

Advanced Master Pages

Using what you've learned, you can create and reuse master pages across your website. However, you can use other tricks and techniques to refine the way master pages work. In the following sections, you'll see how to interact with a master page from your content, how to set master pages dynamically, and how to nest one master page inside another.

Specifying a Title and Metatags for a Content Page

As you've seen, the master page always specifies the basic HTML skeleton of the page, including the outermost <html> tag and the <head> portion. This raises a potential problem. Namely, what if the content page needs to supply information for the <head> section of the page, such as a page title?

One option is to define a ContentPlaceHolder in the <head> section of the page to wrap the appropriate tags. However, this approach isn't valid, because the ContentPlaceHolder, like all ASP.NET controls, needs to be nested inside a server-side <form> tag. Fortunately, ASP.NET provides a solution. You can set the page title through the Title attribute of the Page directive.

The Title attribute overrides the title that's specified in the master page with something more appropriate for the particular content page. Here's an example:

```
<%@ Page Language="vb" MasterPageFile="~/SiteTemplate.master"
    AutoEventWireup="true" CodeFile="SimpleContentPage.aspx.vb"
    Inherits="SimpleContentPage" Title="Content Page" %>
```

This works only as long as the master page has the runat="server" attribute in the <head> tag, which is the default.

This approach isn't any help if you need to override other ingredients from the <head> section, such as the metatags or style tags. However, this problem has a solution. You can modify the <head> element programmatically. To do this, you need to retrieve a reference to the Page object for the master page, which you can access from the current page like this:

```
Private masterPage as Page = MyBase.Master.Page
```

Of course, the MyBase keyword is optional, but this makes it clear that Master is a property that's built into the base Page class. If the current page doesn't use a master page, the Master property returns Nothing.

Using the Page object, you can drill down to the server-side HtmlHead control, as described in Chapter 3. Here's an example that changes the title and adds metadata tags using this technique:

```
MyBase.Master.Page.Header.Title = "Content Page"
MyBase.Master.Page.Header.Metadata.Add("Keywords", "great,cool,revolutionary")
MyBase.Master.Page.Header.Metadata.Add("Description", "A truly great website.")
Typically, you'd execute this code when the content page's Page.Load event fires.
```

■ **Tip** Sometimes you might use initialization code in both the master page and the content page. In this situation, it's important to understand the order that the respective events fire. ASP.NET begins by creating the master page controls and then the child controls for the content page. It then fires the Page.Init event for the master page and follows it up by firing the Page.Init event for the content page. The same step occurs with the Page.Load event. Thus, customizations that you perform in the content page (such as changing the page title) will take precedence over changes you make at the same stage in the master page, if they conflict.

Interacting with the Master Page Class

One issue with master pages is how their model assumes you either want to copy something exactly across every page (in which case you include it in the master page) or vary it on each and every page (in which you add a ContentPlaceHolder for it and include the information in each content page). This distinction works well for many pages, but it runs into trouble if you want to allow a more nuanced interaction between the master page and content pages.

For example, you might want the master page to give a choice of three display modes. The content page would then choose the correct display mode, which would change the appearance of the master page. However, the content page shouldn't have complete freedom to change the master page indiscriminately. Instead, anything other than these three presets should be disallowed.

To enable scenarios such as these, you need some level of programmatic interaction between the content page and the master page. This isn't too difficult, because you can access the current instance of your master page using the Page.Master property, as described in the previous section.

The first step in allowing interaction between your content page and master page is to add public properties or methods to your master page class. The content page can then set these properties or call these methods accordingly. For example, maybe you want to make the banner text customizable (as shown in a previous example) but you don't want to let the content page insert any type of content there. Instead, you want to restrict it to a single descriptive string. To accomplish this, you can add a server-side label control to the header and provide access to that control through a BannerText property in the master page class:

```
Public Property BannerText() As String
    Get
        Return lblTitleContent.Text
    End Get
    Set
        lblTitleContent.Text = Value
    End Set
End Property
```

The content page can now change the text. The only caveat is that the Master property returns an object that's typed as the generic MasterPage class. You need to cast it to your specific master page class to get access to any custom members you've added.

```
Protected Sub Page_Load(ByVal sender As Object, ByVal e As EventArgs)
    Dim theMaster As CustomizableMasterPage
  _theMaster = CType(Master, CustomizableMasterPage)
    theMaster.BannerText = "Content Page #1"
End Sub
```

Another way to get strongly typed access to the master page is to add the MasterType directive to the content page. All you need to do is indicate the virtual path of the corresponding .master file:

```
<%@ MasterType VirtualPath="~/SiteTemplate.master" %>
```

Now you can use simpler strongly typed code when you access the master page:

```
Protected Sub Page_Load(ByVal sender As Object, ByVal e As EventArgs)
    Master.BannerText = "Content Page #1"
End Sub
```

You should note one point about these examples. When you navigate from page to another, all the web-page objects are re-created. This means that even if you move to another content page that uses the same master page, ASP.NET creates a different instance of the master page object. As a result, the Text property of the Label control in the header is reset to its default value (a blank string) every time the user navigates to a new page. To change this behavior, you need to store the information in another location (such as a cookie) and write initialization code in the master page to check for it.

You can also get access to an individual control on a master page through brute force. The trick is to use the MasterPage.FindControl() method to search for the object you want based on its unique name. When you have the control, you can then modify it directly. Here's an example that uses this technique to look for a label:

```
Dim lbl As Label
lbl = Master.FindControl("lblTitleContent")

If lbl IsNot Nothing Then
    lbl.Text = "Content Page #1"
End If
```

Of course, this type of interaction breaks all the rules of proper class-based design and encapsulation. If you really need to access a control in a master page, you are far better off wrapping it (or, ideally, just the properties you're interested in) by adding properties to your master page class. That way, the interaction between the content page and the master page is clear, documented, and loosely coupled. If your content page tinkers directly with the internals of another page, it's likely to lead to fragile code models with dependencies that break when you edit the master page.

Dynamically Setting a Master Page

Sometimes you might want to change your master page on the fly. This might occur in a few cases:

- Several types of users exist, and you want to adjust the complexity of the layout or the visible features according to the user. You may perform this customization based on user information managers have specified, or you might give the users the ability to set their own preferences.
- You are in partnership with another company, and you need your website to adjust itself to have a different look and layout accordingly. For example, you might cobrand your website, providing the same features with two or more different layouts.

Changing the master page programmatically is easy. All you need to do is set the Page.MasterPageFile property. The trick is that this step needs to be completed in the Page.Init event stage. After this point, attempting to set this property causes an exception.

You can implement this technique in much the same way that you implemented dynamic themes earlier in this chapter. However, this technique has a potential danger—a content page isn't necessarily compatible with an arbitrary master page. If your content page includes a Content tag that doesn't correspond to a ContentPlaceHolder in the master, an error will occur. To prevent this problem, you need to ensure that all the master pages you set dynamically include the same placeholders.

Nesting Master Pages

You can nest master pages so that one master page uses another master page. This is not used too often, but it could allow you to standardize your website to different degrees. For example, you might have two sections of your website. Each section might warrant its separate navigation controls. However, both sections may need the same header. In this case, you could create a top-level master page that adds the header. Here's an example:

```
<%@ Master Language="vb" AutoEventWireup="true"
    CodeFile="NestedMasterRoot.master.vb" Inherits="NestedMasterRoot" %>

<html xmlns="http://www.w3.org/1999/xhtml" >
<head runat="server">
    <title>Untitled Page</title>
</head>
<body bgcolor="#ccffff">
    <form id="form1" runat="server">
    <div>
        <h1>The Root</h1>
        <asp:ContentPlaceHolder  id="RootContent" runat="server">
        </asp:ContentPlaceHolder >
    </div>
    </form>
</body>
</html>
```

Next, you would create a second master page that uses the first master page (through the MasterPageFile attribute). This second master page would get the header from the first master page and could add the navigation controls in a panel on the left. Here's an example:

```
<%@ Master Language="vb" AutoEventWireup="true"
    CodeFile="NestedMasterSecondLevel.master.vb"
    Inherits="NestedMasterSecondLevel"
    MasterPageFile="~/NestedMasterRoot.master"%>
```

```
<asp:Content ID="Content1" ContentPlaceHolderID="RootContent" Runat="Server">
    <table width="100%" bgcolor="#ccff00">
      <tr>
        <td colspan="2">
          <h2>The Second Level</h2>
        </td>
      <tr>
        <td width="200px"></td>
        <td bgcolor="white">
          <asp:ContentPlaceHolder  id="NestedContent" runat="server">
          </asp:ContentPlaceHolder >
        </td>
      </tr>
    </table>
</asp:Content>
```

Presumably, your goal would be to create more than one version of the second master page, one for each section of your website. These would acquire the same standard header.

Finally, each content page could use one of the second-level master pages to standardize its layout:

```
<%@ Page Language="vb" MasterPageFile="~/NestedMasterSecondLevel.master"
    AutoEventWireup="true" CodeFile="NestedContentPage.aspx.vb"
    Inherits="NestedContentPage" Title="Untitled Page" %>

<asp:Content ID="Content1" ContentPlaceHolderID="NestedContent" Runat="Server">
<br />This is the nested content!<br />
</asp:Content>
```

Figure 15-16 shows the result.

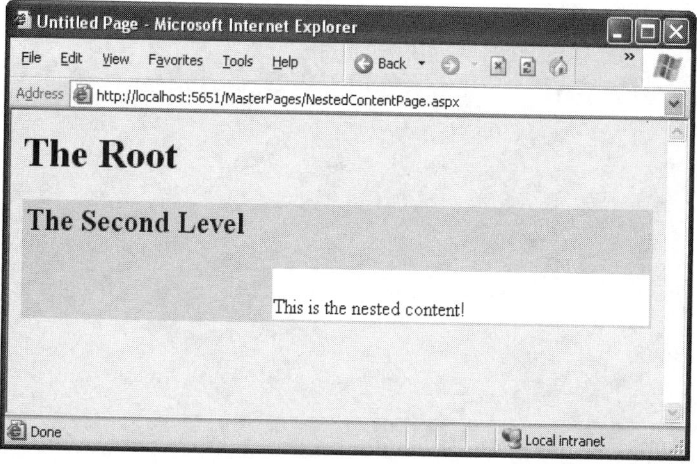

Figure 15-16. *A content page that uses a nested master page*

You can use as many layers of nested master pages as you want. However, be careful when implementing this approach—although it sounds like a nifty way to make a modular design, it can tie you down more than you realize. For example, you'll need to rework your master page hierarchy if you decide later that the two website sections need similar but slightly different headers. For that reason, it might be better to use only one level of master pages and copy the few common elements. In most cases, you won't be creating many master pages, so this won't add a significant amount of duplication.

■Caution Another significant issue with nested master pages is the lack of design-time support. In the previous example, you'll be able to access the design surface only for the root master page. You'll need to code the second-level master page and the content page by hand.

Summary

In this chapter you tackled two key enhancements that were introduced in ASP.NET 2.0: themes and master pages. Armed with these tools, you can create a complete, integrated web application that has a unified look and feel and a consistent layout. In the next chapter, you'll learn how to add navigation controls to the mix.

CHAPTER 16

■ ■ ■

Website Navigation

Navigation is a fundamental component of any website. ASP.NET 1.*x* had plenty of raw tools, but you were forced to cobble together your own navigation solutions. ASP.NET 2.0 addresses this gap by introducing a wide range of navigation features.

In this chapter, you'll tackle three core topics:

The MultiView and Wizard controls: These let you boil down a series of steps into a single page.

The new site map model: This lets you define the navigation structure of your website and bind it directly to rich controls. You'll also learn how to extend this framework to support different types of controls and different site map storage locations.

The rich navigational controls: These include the TreeView and Menu. Although these controls aren't limited to navigation, they're an ideal match. In this chapter, you'll learn about their wide range of features.

Using these controls, the site map model, and master pages, you can build a complete navigation system with minimal effort. Best of all, ASP.NET cleanly separates the data (the information about the structure of your website) from its implementation (the navigational controls). That means you can reorganize, replace, and rename web pages without disturbing your website or editing any code. All you need to do is make the corresponding changes to your application's site map file.

WEBSITE NAVIGATION CHANGES IN ASP.NET 2.0

The features discussed in this chapter are all new in ASP.NET 2.0. This means if you're a skilled ASP.NET 1.*x* developer, this is a chapter worth reading in detail.

Pages with Multiple Views

Most websites split tasks across several pages. For example, if you want to add an item to your shopping cart and take it to the checkout in an e-commerce site, you'll need to jump from one page to another. This is the cleanest approach, and it's easy to program—provided you use some sort of state management technique (from query strings to session state) to transfer information from one page to another.

In other situations, you might want to embed the code for several different pages inside a single page. For example, you might want to provide several views of the same data (such as a grid-based view and a chart-based view) and allow the user to switch from one view to the other without leaving the page. Or, you might want to handle a small multistep task (such as supplying user information for an account sign-up process), without worrying about how to transfer the relevant information.

■Tip From the user's point of view, it probably doesn't make much difference whether you use multiple pages or a page with multiple views. In a well-designed site, the only difference the user will see is that the multiple view approach keeps the same URL. The prime difference is the coding model. With multiple pages, you get improved separation but extra work in determining how the pages should interact (the way they share or transmit information). With multiple views, you lose your separation but get easier coding for small, nondivisible tasks.

In ASP.NET 1.*x*, the only way to model a page with multiple views was to add several Panel controls to a page so that each panel represents a single view or a single step. You can then set the Visible property of each Panel so that you see only one at a time. The problem with this approach is that it clutters your page with extra code for managing the panels. Additionally, it's not very robust—with a minor mistake, you can end up with two panels showing at the same time.

In ASP.NET 2.0, there's no need to design your own multiple view system from scratch. Instead, you can use one of two higher-level controls that make these designs much easier—the MultiView and the Wizard.

The MultiView Control

The MultiView is the simpler of the two multiple view controls. Essentially, the MultiView gives you a way to declare multiple views and show only one at a time. It has no default user interface—you get only whatever HTML and controls you add. The MultiView is equivalent to the custom panel approach explained earlier.

Creating a MultiView is suitably straightforward. You add the <asp:MultiView> tag to your .aspx page file and then add one <asp:View> tag inside it for each separate view:

```
<asp:MultiView ID="MultiView1" runat="server">
  <asp:View ID="View1" runat="server">...</asp:View>
  <asp:View ID="View2" runat="server">...</asp:View>
  <asp:View ID="View3" runat="server">...</asp:View>
</asp:MultiView>
```

Inside the <asp:View> tag, you add the HTML and web controls for that view:

```
<asp:MultiView ID="MultiView1" runat="server" ActiveViewIndex="0">
  <asp:View ID="View1" runat="server">
    <b>Showing View #1<br />
    <br />
    <asp:Image ID="Image1" runat="server"
     ImageUrl="~/cookies.jpg" /></b>
  </asp:View>
  <asp:View ID="View2" runat="server">
    <b>Showing View #2</b><br />
    <br />
    Text content.
  </asp:View>
  <asp:View ID="View3" runat="server">
    <b>Showing View #3</b><br />
    <br />
    <asp:Calendar ID="Calendar1" runat="server"></asp:Calendar>
  </asp:View>
</asp:MultiView>
```

■Tip You can also add views programmatically (like any other control) by instantiating a new view object and adding it to the MultiView with the Add() or AddAt() methods of the Views collection.

Visual Studio shows all your views at design time, one after the other (see Figure 16-1). You can edit these regions in the same way you design any other part of the page.

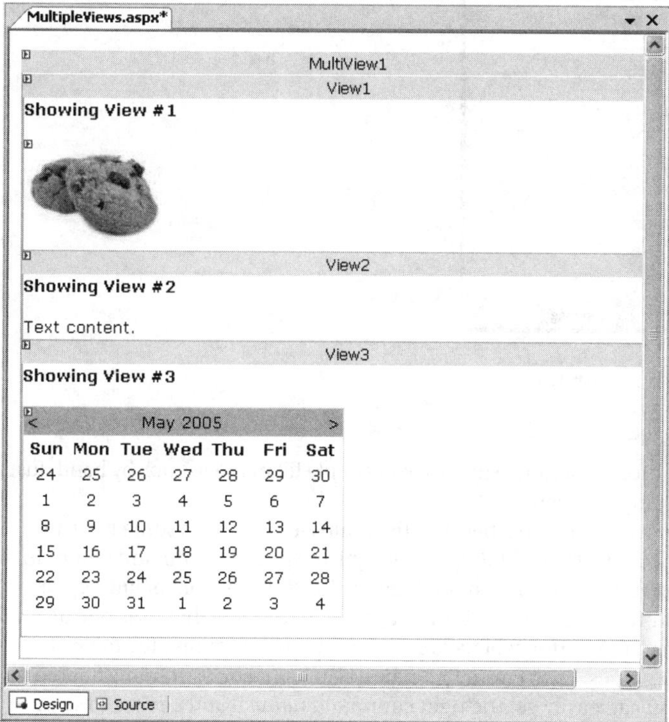

Figure 16-1. *Designing multiple views*

The MultiView.ActiveViewIndex determines what view will be shown. This is the only view that's rendered in the page. The default ActiveIndex value is –1, which means no view is shown. You need to set the ActiveIndex programmatically.

One option is to use a list control that lets users choose from the full list of views. Here's some sample code that binds the list of views to a list box:

```
Protected Sub Page_Load(ByVal sender As Object, ByVal e As EventArgs)
    If (Not Page.IsPostBack) Then
        DropDownList1.DataSource = MultiView1.Views
        DropDownList1.DataTextField = "ID"
        DropDownList1.DataBind()
    End If
End Sub
```

And here's the code that sets the current view based on the list index:

```
Protected Sub DropDownList1_SelectedIndexChanged(ByVal sender As Object,
            ByVal e As EventArgs)
    MultiView1.ActiveViewIndex = DropDownList1.SelectedIndex
End Sub
```

Figure 16-2 shows the result.

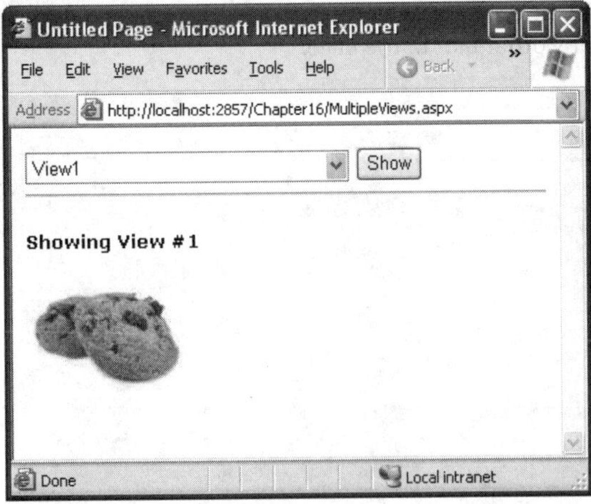

Figure 16-2. *Switching views with a list control*

If you want to give the views more descriptive names, you simply fill in the list box by hand. Just make sure the order matches the order of views.

You actually have no need to write this code, because the MultiView includes some built-in smarts. Like some of the rich data controls, the MultiView recognizes specific command names in button controls. (A button control is any control that implements IButtonControl, including the Button, ImageButton, and LinkButton.) If you add a button control to the view that uses one of these recognized command names, the button will have some automatic functionality. Table 16-1 lists all the recognized command names. Each command name also has a corresponding Shared field in the MultiView class, so you can easily get the right command name if you choose to set it programmatically.

Table 16-1. *Recognized Command Names for the MultiView*

Command Name	MultiView Field	Description
PrevView	PrevViewCommandName	Moves to the previous view.
NextView	NextViewCommandName	Moves to the next view.
SwitchViewByID	SwitchViewByIDCommandName	Moves to the view with a specific ID (string name). The ID is taken from the CommandArgument property of the button control.
SwitchViewByIndex	SwitchViewByIndexCommandName	Moves to the view with a specific numeric index. The index is taken from the CommandArgument property of the button control.

To try this, add this button to your first two views (remembering to change the ID for each one):

```
<asp:Button ID="cmdNext" runat="server" Text="Next >" CommandName="NextView" />
```

And add this button to your second and third views:

```
<asp:Button ID="cmdPrev" runat="server" Text="< Prev" CommandName="PrevView" />
```

Finally, make sure the drop-down list shows the correct view when you use the buttons by adding this code to handle the MutliView.ActiveViewIndexChanged event:

```
Protected Sub MultiView1_ActiveViewChanged(ByVal sender As Object,
      ByVal e As EventArgs)
   DropDownList1.SelectedIndex = MultiView1.ActiveViewIndex
End Sub
```

Now you can move from view to view using the buttons (see Figure 16-3).

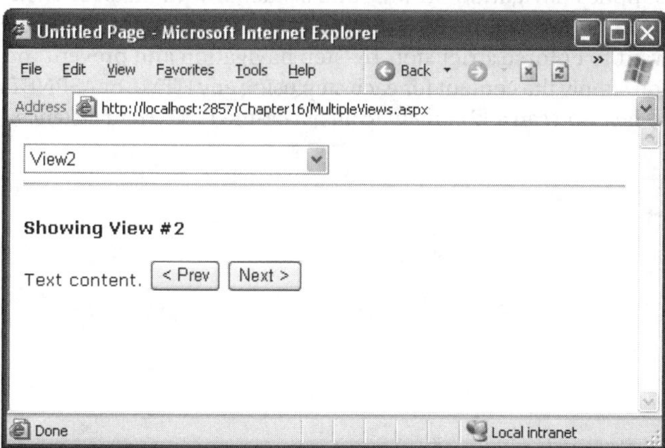

Figure 16-3. *Switching views with recognized command names*

THE PERFORMANCE OF MULTIVIEW PAGES

The most important detail you need to know about the MultiView is that unlike the rich data controls (the GridView, FormsView, and so on), the MultiView is *not* a naming container. This means that if you add a control named textBox1 to a view, you can't add another control named textBox1 to another view. In fact, in terms of the page model, there's no real difference between controls you add to a view and controls in the rest of the page. Either way, the controls you create will be accessible through member variables in your page class. This means it's easy to configure a control in the second view when an event is raised by a control in the first view.

As a result, the pages you create using the MultiView tend to be heavier than normal pages. That's because the entire control model—including the controls from every view—is created on every postback and persisted to view state. For the most part, this won't be a significant factor, unless you are manipulating a large number of controls programmatically (in which case you might want to turn EnableViewstate off for these controls) or you are using several data sources. For example, if you have three views and each view has a different data source control, each time the page is posted back all three data source controls will perform their queries, and every view will be bound, including those that aren't currently visible. To avoid this overhead, you can use the techniques described in Chapter 9, such as leaving your controls unbound and binding them programmatically, or canceling the binding process for views that aren't currently visible.

Of course, not all uses of the MultiView need to involve data binding. The perfect scenario for the MultiView is an extended set of input controls—for example, an online survey form that's split into separate views just to spare the user a lot of scrolling. This example works well with the MultiView because at the end when the survey is complete, you can read all the data from the controls of every view.

The Wizard Control

The Wizard control is a more glamorous version of the MultiView control. It also supports showing one of several views at a time, but it includes a fair bit of built-in yet customizable behavior, including navigation buttons, a sidebar with step links, styles, and templates.

Usually, wizards represent a single task, and the user moves linearly through them, moving from the current step to the one immediately following it (or the one immediately preceding it in the case of a correction). The ASP.NET Wizard control also supports nonlinear navigation, which means it allows you to decide to ignore a step based on the information the user supplies.

By default, the Wizard control supplies navigation buttons and a sidebar with links for each step on the left. You can hide the sidebar by setting the Wizard.DisplaySideBar property to false. Usually, you'll take this step if you want to enforce strict step-by-step navigation and prevent the user from jumping out of sequence. You supply the content for each step using any HTML or ASP.NET controls. Figure 16-4 shows the region where you can add content to an out-of-the-box Wizard instance.

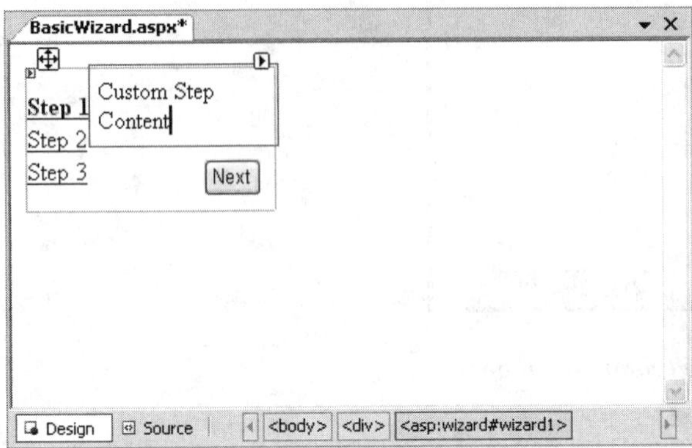

Figure 16-4. *The region for step content*

Wizard Steps

To create a wizard in ASP.NET, you simply define the steps and their content using <asp:WizardStep> tags. Each step takes a few basic pieces of information, as listed in Table 16-2.

Table 16-2. *WizardStep Properties*

Property	Description
Title	The descriptive name of the step. This name is used for the text of the links in the sidebar.
StepType	The type of step, as a value from the WizardStepType enumeration. This value determines the type of navigation buttons that will be shown for this step. Choices include Start (shows a Next button), Step (shows Next and Previous buttons), Finish (shows a Finish and Previous button), Complete (show no buttons and hides the sidebar, if it's enabled), and Auto (the step type is inferred from the position in the collection). The default is Auto, which means that the first step is Start, the last step is Finish, and all other steps are Step.
AllowReturn	Indicates whether the user can return to this step. If false, once the user has passed this step, the user will not be able to return. The sidebar link for this step will have no effect, and the Previous button of the following step will either skip this step or be hidden completely (depending on the AllowReturn value of the preceding steps).

The following wizard contains four steps that, taken together, represent a simple survey. The StepType adds a Complete step at the end, with a summary. The navigation buttons and sidebar links are added automatically.

```
<asp:Wizard ID="Wizard1" runat="server" Width="467px"
 BackColor="#EFF3FB" BorderColor="#B5C7DE" BorderWidth="1px">
  <WizardSteps>
    <asp:WizardStep ID="WizardStep1" runat="server" Title="Personal">
      <h3>Personal Profile</h3>
      Preferred Programming Language:
      <asp:DropDownList ID="lstLanguage" runat="server">
        <asp:ListItem>VB .NET</asp:ListItem>
        <asp:ListItem>C#</asp:ListItem>
        <asp:ListItem>J#</asp:ListItem>
        <asp:ListItem>Java</asp:ListItem>
        <asp:ListItem>C++</asp:ListItem>
        <asp:ListItem>C</asp:ListItem>
      </asp:DropDownList>
      <br />
    </asp:WizardStep>
    <asp:WizardStep ID="WizardStep2" runat="server" Title="Company">
      <h3>Comany Profile</h3>
      Number of Employees: <asp:TextBox ID="txtEmpCount" runat="server"/>
      Number of Locations: <asp:TextBox ID="txtLocCount" runat="server"/>
    </asp:WizardStep>
    <asp:WizardStep ID="WizardStep3" runat="server" Title="Software">
      <h3>Software Profile</h3>
      Licenses Required:
      <asp:CheckBoxList ID="lstTools" runat="server">
        <asp:ListItem>Visual Studio</asp:ListItem>
        <asp:ListItem>Office</asp:ListItem>
        <asp:ListItem>Windows 2003 Server</asp:ListItem>
        <asp:ListItem>SQL Server 2005</asp:ListItem>
        <asp:ListItem>BizTalk 2004</asp:ListItem>
      </asp:CheckBoxList>
    </asp:WizardStep>
    <asp:WizardStep ID="Complete" runat="server" Title="Complete"
     StepType="Complete">
      <br />
      Thank you for completing this survey.<br />
      Your products will be delivered shortly.<br />
    </asp:WizardStep>
  </WizardSteps>
</asp:Wizard>
```

Figure 16-5 shows the wizard steps.

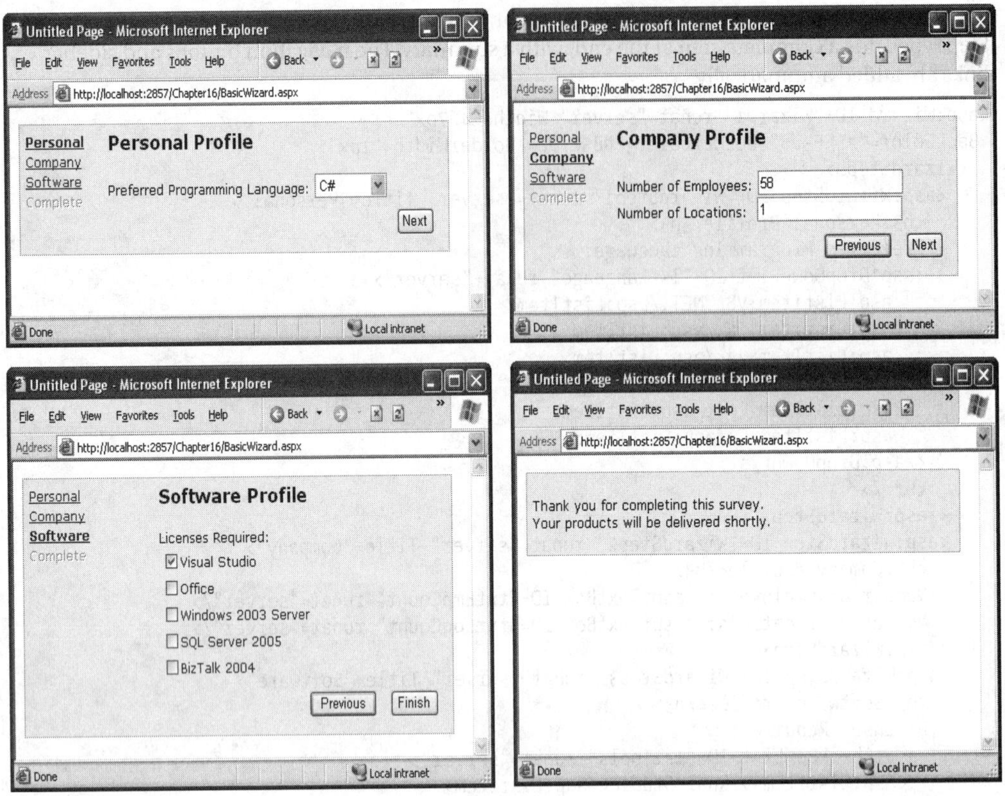

Figure 16-5. *A wizard with four steps*

Unlike the MultiView control, you can see only one step at a time in Visual Studio. To choose which step you're currently designing, select it from the smart tag, as shown in Figure 16-6. But be warned—every time you do, Visual Studio changes the Wizard.ActiveStepIndex property to the step you choose. Make sure you set this back to 0 before you run your application so it starts at the first step.

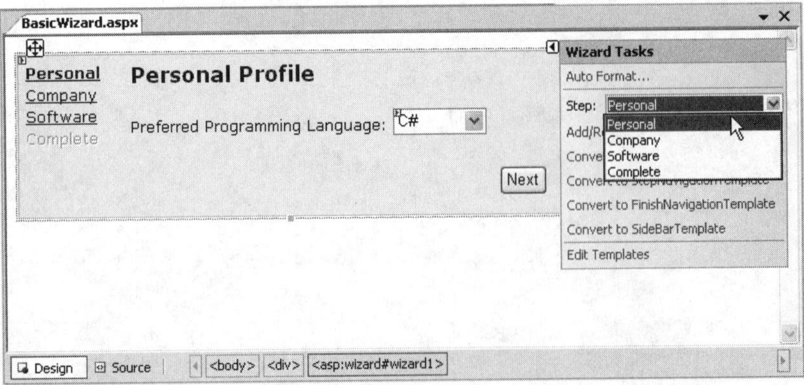

Figure 16-6. *Designing a step*

■ **Note** Remember, when you add controls to separate steps on a wizard, they are all instantiated and persisted in view state, regardless of the current step. If you need to slim down a complex wizard, you'll need to split it into separate pages, use the Server.Transfer() method to move from one page to the next, and tolerate a less elegant programming model.

Wizard Events

You can write the code that underpins your wizard by responding to several events (as listed in Table 16-3).

Table 16-3. *Wizard Events*

Event	Description
ActiveStepChanged	Occurs when the control switches to a new step (either because the user has clicked a navigation button or your code has changed the ActiveStepIndex property).
CancelButtonClick	Occurs when the Cancel button is clicked. The cancel button is not shown by default, but you can add it to every step by setting the Wizard.DisplayCancelButton property. Usually, a cancel button exits the wizard. If you don't have any cleanup code to perform, just set the CancelDestinationPageUrl property, and the wizard will take care of the redirection automatically.
FinishButtonClick	Occurs when the Finish button is clicked.
NextButtonClick and PreviousButtonClick	Occurs when the Next or Previous button is clicked on any step. However, because there is more than one way to move from one step to the next, it's better to handle the ActiveStepChanged event.
SideBarButtonClick	Occurs when a button in the sidebar area is clicked.

On the whole, two wizard programming models exist:

Commit-as-you-go: This makes sense if each wizard step wraps an atomic operation that can't be reversed. For example, if you're processing an order that involves a credit card authorization followed by a final purchase, you can't allow the user to step back and edit the credit card number. To support this model, you set the AllowReturn property to false on some or all steps, and you respond to the ActiveStepChanged event to commit changes for each step.

Commit-at-the-end: This makes sense if each wizard step is collecting information for an operation that's performed only at the end. For example, if you're collecting user information and plan to generate a new account once you have all the information, you'll probably allow a user to make changes midway through the process. You execute your code for generating the new account when the wizard is finished by reacting to the FinishButtonClick event.

To implement commit-at-the-end with the current example, just respond to the FinishButtonClick event. Here's an example that simply displays every selection in the summary:

```
Protected Sub Wizard1_FinishButtonClick(ByVal sender As Object,
      ByVal e As WizardNavigationEventArgs)
    Dim sb As New StringBuilder()
    sb.Append("<b>You chose: <br />")
    sb.Append("Programming Language: ")
    sb.Append(lstLanguage.Text)
    sb.Append("<br />Total Employees: ")
    sb.Append(txtEmpCount.Text)
```

```
        sb.Append("<br />Total Locations: ")
        sb.Append(txtLocCount.Text)
        sb.Append("<br />Licenses Required: ")
        For Each item As ListItem In lstTools.Items
            If item.Selected Then
                sb.Append(item.Text)
                sb.Append(" ")
            End If
        Next
        sb.Append("</b>")
        lblSummary.Text = sb.ToString()
    End Sub
```

For this to work, you must add a Label control named lblSummary to the summary step.

■ **Tip** If you want to find out the path the user has taken through your wizard, you can use the Wizard.GetHistory() method. It returns a collection of WizardStepBase objects that have been accessed so far, arranged in reverse chronological order. That means the first item in the collection represents the previous step, the second item represents the step before that, and so on.

Wizard Styles and Templates

Without a doubt, the Wizard control's greatest strength is the way it lets you customize its appearance. This means that if you want the basic model (a multistep process with navigation buttons and various events), you aren't locked into the default user interface.

Depending on how radically you want to change the wizard, you have different options. For less-dramatic modifications, you can set various top-level properties. For example, you can control the colors, fonts, spacing, and border style, as you can with any ASP.NET control. You can also tweak the appearance of every button. For example, to change the Next button, you can use the following properties: StepNextButtonType (use a button, link, or clickable image), StepNextButtonText (customize the text for a button or link), StepNextButtonImageUrl (set the image for an image button), and StepNextButtonStyle (use a style from a stylesheet). You can also add a header using the HeaderText property.

More control is available through styles. You can use styles to apply formatting options to various portions of the Wizard control just as you can use styles to format different parts of rich data controls such as the GridView. Table 16-4 lists all the styles you can use. As with other style-based controls, more specific style settings (such as SideBarStyle) override more general style settings (such as ControlStyle) when they conflict. Similarly, StartNextButtonStyle overrides NavigationButtonStyle on the first step.

Table 16-4. *Wizard Styles*

Style	Description
ControlStyle	Applies to all sections of the Wizard control
HeaderStyle	Applies to the header section of the Wizard control, which is visible only if you set some text in the HeaderText property
SideBarStyle	Applies to the sidebar area of the Wizard control
SideBarButtonStyle	Applies to just the buttons in the sidebar
StepStyle	Applies to the section of the control where you define the step content

Style	Description
NavigationStyle	Applies to the bottom area of the control where the navigation buttons are displayed
NavigationButtonStyle	Applies to just the navigation buttons in the navigation area
StartNextButtonStyle	Applies to the Next navigation button on the first step (when StepType is Start)
StepNextButtonStyle	Applies to the Next navigation button on intermediate steps (when StepType is Step)
StepPreviousButtonStyle	Applies to the Previous navigation button on intermediate steps (when StepType is Step)
FinishPreviousButtonStyle	Applies to the Previous navigation button on the last step (when StepType is Finish)
CancelButtonStyle	Applies to the Cancel button, if you have Wizard.DisplayCancelButton set to true

Finally, if you can't get the level of customization you want through properties and styles, you can use templates to completely define the appearance of the Wizard control. Ordinarily, you can supply the HTML only for the step content (as shown in Figure 16-1). With templates, you supply the HTML for one of the other regions, such as the header, sidebar, or buttons. All templates are declared separately from the step content. Figure 16-7 shows where templates fit in.

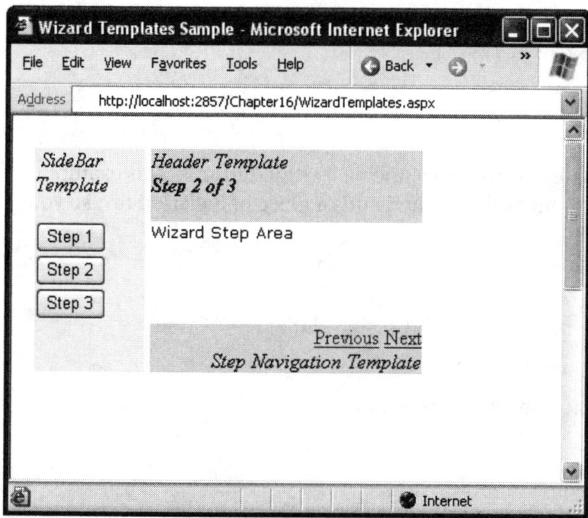

Figure 16-7. *Template regions in the Wizard control*

Table 16-5 shows the full list of templates.

Table 16-5. *Wizard Templates*

Style	Description
HeaderTemplate	Defines the content of the header region
SideBarTemplate	Defines the sidebar, which typically includes navigation links for each step
StartNavigationTemplate	Defines the navigation buttons for the first step (when StepType is Start)
StepNavigationTemplate	Defines the navigation buttons for intermediate steps (when StepType is Step)
FinishNavigationTemplate	Defines the navigation buttons for the final step (when StepType is Finish)

For example, here's a header template that uses a data binding expression to show the title of the current step:

```
<asp:Wizard ID="Wizard1" runat="server" ...>
  <WizardSteps>
    ...
  </WizardSteps>

  <HeaderTemplate>
    <i>Header Template</i> -
    <b><%= Wizard1.ActiveStep.Title %></b>
    <br /><br />
  </HeaderTemplate>
</asp:Wizard>
```

You can also add the following templates to customize the navigation buttons. This example keeps the standard buttons (by declaring them explicitly) and adds a piece of italicized text so you can see when each template is being used.

```
<StepNavigationTemplate>
  <i>StepNavigationTemplate</i><br />
  <asp:Button ID="StepPreviousButton" runat="server" CausesValidation="False"
   CommandName="MovePrevious"
  Text="Previous" />
  <asp:Button ID="StepNextButton" runat="server" Text="Next"
   CommandName="MoveNext" />
</StepNavigationTemplate>
<StartNavigationTemplate>
  <i>StartNavigationTemplate</i><br />
  <asp:Button ID="StartNextButton" runat="server" Text="Next"
   CommandName="MoveNext" />
  </StartNavigationTemplate>
  <FinishNavigationTemplate>
  <i>FinishNavigationTemplate</i><br />
  <asp:Button ID="FinishPreviousButton" runat="server" CausesValidation="False"
    Text="Previous" CommandName="MovePrevious" />
  <asp:Button ID="FinishButton" runat="server" Text="Finish"
   CommandName="MoveComplete" />
</FinishNavigationTemplate>
```

The secret to using templates is making sure you use the right command names so that the Wizard control will hook up the standard logic. Otherwise, you'll need to implement the navigation and sequencing code, which is tedious and error-prone. For example, clicking on a button with a command name of MoveNext automatically moves to the next step. If you are unsure about the correct command name to use, you can use a convenient shortcut. Select the Wizard control in Visual Studio, and choose one of the template-generation links in the smart tag, such as Convert to StartNavigationTemplate. When you do, Visual Studio inserts a template that duplicates the default button appearance and behavior.

Site Maps

If your website has more than a handful of pages, you'll probably need some sort of navigation system to let the user move one page to the next. As you saw in Chapter 15, you can use master pages to define a template for your site that includes a navigation bar. However, it's still up to you to fill this navigation bar with content.

Obviously, you can use the ASP.NET toolkit of controls to implement almost any navigation system, but it still requires you to perform all the hard work. Fortunately, ASP.NET adds a new set of navigation features that you can use to dramatically simplify the task.

As with all the best ASP.NET features, ASP.NET navigation is flexible, configurable, and pluggable. It consists of three components:

- A way to define the navigational structure of your website. This part is the XML site map, which is (by default) stored in a file.
- A convenient way to parse the site map file and convert its information into a suitable object model. This part is performed by the SiteMapDataSource control and the XmlSiteMapProvider.
- A way to use the site map information to display the user's current position and give the user the ability to easily move from one place to another. This part is provided through the controls you bind to the SiteMapDataSource control, which can include breadcrumb links, lists, menus, and trees.

You can customize or extend each of these ingredients separately. For example, if you want to change the appearance of your navigation controls, you simply need to bind different controls to the SiteMapDataSource. On the other hand, if you want to read a different format of site map information or read it from a different location, you need to change your site map provider.

Figure 16-8 shows how these pieces fit together.

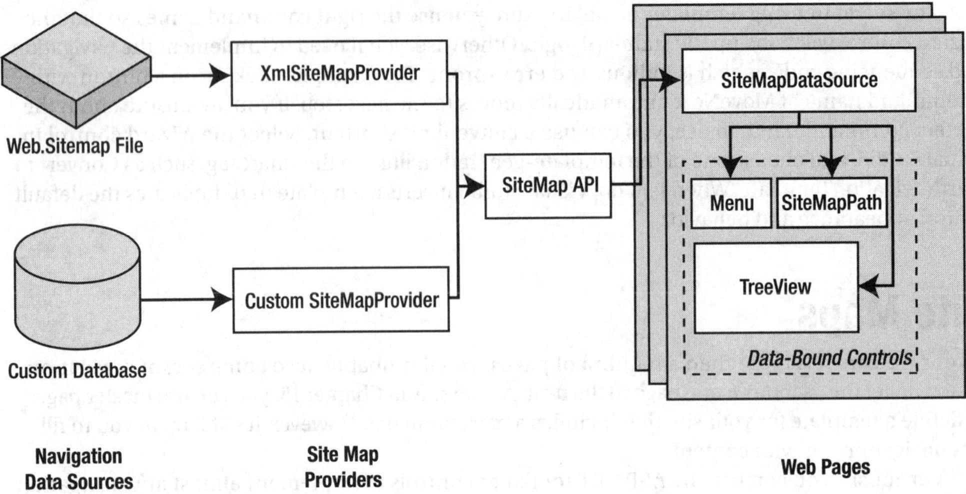

Figure 16-8. *ASP.NET navigation with site maps*

Defining a Site Map

The starting point in site map–based navigation is the site map provider. ASP.NET ships with a single site map provider, named XmlSiteMapProvider, which is able to retrieve site map information from an XML file. If you want to retrieve a site map from another location or in a custom format, you'll need to create your own site map provider—a topic covered in the section "Creating a Custom SiteMapProvider."

The XmlSiteMapProvider looks for a file named Web.sitemap in the root of the virtual directory. Like all site map providers, its task is to extract the site map data and create the corresponding SiteMap object. This SiteMap object is then made available to other controls through the SiteMapDataSource.

To try this, you need to begin by creating a Web.sitemap file and defining the website structure using the <siteMap> and <siteMapNode> elements:

```
<siteMap xmlns="http://schemas.microsoft.com/AspNet/SiteMap-File-1.0">
  <siteMapNode>
    <siteMapNode>...</siteMapNode>
    <siteMapNode>...</siteMapNode>
    ...
  </siteMapNode>
</siteMap>
```

To be valid, your site map must begin with the root <siteMap> node, followed by a single <siteMapNode> element, representing the default home page. You can nest other <siteMapNode> elements in the root <siteMapNode> as many layers deep as you want. Each site map node should have a title, description, and URL, as shown here:

```
<siteMapNode title="Home" description="Home" url="~/default.aspx">
```

In this example, the URL uses the new ~/ syntax, which indicates the root of the web application. This style isn't necessary, but it is strongly recommended, as it ensures that your site map links are interpreted correctly regardless of the current folder.

You can now use the <siteMapNode> to create a site map. The only other restriction is that you can't create two site map nodes with the same URL.

■**Note** The restriction to avoid duplicate URLs is not baked into the navigation system. It's simply required by the XmlSiteMapProvider, because the XmlSiteMapProvider uses the URL as a unique key. If you create your own site map provider or use a third-party provider, you may allow different URLs and require separate key information. However, you can't get around the rule that every site must begin with one root node, because that's implemented in the base SiteMapProvider class. (As you'll see shortly, you still have options for tailoring the display of the site map tree, but you must start with a single home node.)

Here's a sample site map:

```
<siteMap xmlns="http://schemas.microsoft.com/AspNet/SiteMap-File-1.0">
  <siteMapNode title="Home" description="Home" url="~/default.aspx">
    <siteMapNode title="Products" description="Our products"
      url="~/Products.aspx">
      <siteMapNode title="Hardware" description="Hardware choices"
        url="~/Hardware.aspx" />
      <siteMapNode title="Software" description="Software choices"
        url="~/Software.aspx" />
    </siteMapNode>
    <siteMapNode title="Services" description="Services we offer"
        url="~/Services.aspx">
        <siteMapNode title="Training" description="Training classes"
          url="~/Training.aspx" />
        <siteMapNode title="Consulting" description="Consulting services"
          url="~/Consulting.aspx" />
        <siteMapNode title="Support" description="Support plans"
          url="~/Support.aspx" />
    </siteMapNode>
  </siteMapNode>
</siteMap>
```

■**Tip** In this example, the Products and Services nodes have URLs, which means they are clickable (and take the user to specific pages). However, if you simply want to use these nodes as categories to arrange other links, just omit the url attribute. You'll still see the node in your bound controls; it just won't be rendered as a link.

Binding to a Site Map

Once you've defined the Web.sitemap file, you're ready to use it in a page. This is a great place to use master pages so that you can define the navigation controls as part of a template and reuse them with every page. Here's how you might define a basic structure in your master page that puts navigation controls on the left:

```
<form id="form1" runat="server">
  <table>
    <tr>
      <td style="width: 226px;vertical-align: top;">
        <!-- Navigation controls go here. -->
      </td>
      <td style="vertical-align: top;">
        <asp:ContentPlaceHolder id="ContentPlaceHolder1" runat="server" />
      </td>
    </tr>
  </table>
```

```
  <asp:SiteMapDataSource ID="SiteMapDataSource1" runat="server" />
</form>
```

Then, create a child with some simple static content:

```
<asp:Content ID="Content1" ContentPlaceHolderID="ContentPlaceHolder1"
  runat="Server">
    <br />
    <br />
    Default.aspx page (home).
</asp:Content>
```

The only remaining task is to choose the controls you want to use to display the site map data. One all-purpose solution is the TreeView control. You can add the TreeView and bind it to the SiteMapDataSource in the master page using the DataSourceID, as shown here:

```
<asp:TreeView ID="treeNav" runat="server" DataSourceID="SiteMapDataSource1" />
```

Alternatively, you could use the fly-out Menu control just as easily:

```
<asp:Menu ID="Menu1" runat="server" DataSourceID="SiteMapDataSource1" />
```

Figure 16-9 shows both options.

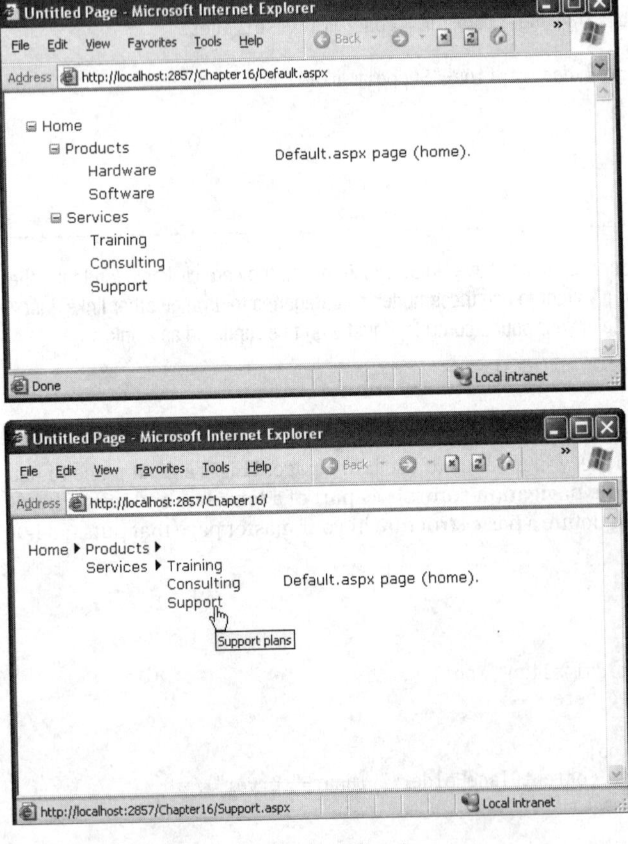

Figure 16-9. *TreeView and Menu navigation*

You can do a lot more to customize the appearance of your navigation controls and the processing of your site map. You'll consider these more advanced topics in the following sections.

Breadcrumbs

ASP.NET actually defines three navigation controls: the TreeView, Menu, and SiteMapPath. The SiteMapPath provides *breadcrumb navigation*, which means it shows the user's current location and allows the user to navigate back up the hierarchy to a higher level using links. Figure 16-10 shows an example with a SiteMapPath control when the user is on the Software.aspx page. Using the SiteMapPath control, the user can return to the Products.aspx page or the Home.aspx page.

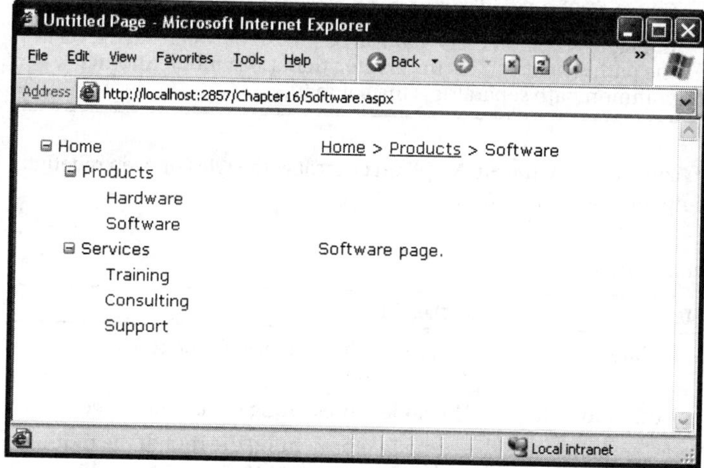

Figure 16-10. *Breadcrumb navigation with SiteMapPath*

Here's how you define the SiteMapPath control:

```
<asp:SiteMapPath ID="SiteMapPath1" runat="server" />
```

The SiteMapPath control is useful both for an at-a-glance view that provides the current position and for a way to move up the hierarchy. However, you always need to combine it with other navigation controls that let the user move down the site map hierarchy.

The SiteMapPath control is also thoroughly customizable. Table 16-6 lists some of its most commonly configured properties.

Table 16-6. *SiteMapPath Appearance-Related Properties*

Property	Description
ShowToolTips	Set this to false if you don't want the description text to appear when the user hovers over a part of the site map path.
ParentLevelsDisplayed	Sets the maximum number of parent levels that will be shown at once. By default, this setting is –1, which means all levels will be shown.
RenderCurrentNodeAsLink	If true, the portion of the page that indicates the current page is turned into a clickable link. By default, this is false because the user is already at the current page.
PathDirection	You have two choices: RootToCurrent (the default) and CurrentToRoot (which reverses the order of levels in the path).
PathSeparator	Indicates the characters that will be placed between each level in the path. The default is the greater-than (>) symbol. Another common path separator is the colon (:).

For even more control, you can configure the SiteMapPath control with styles or even redefine the controls and HTML with templates (see Table 16-7).

Table 16-7. *SiteMapPath Styles and Templates*

Style	Template	Applies To
NodeStyle	NodeTemplate	All parts of the path except the root and current node.
CurrentNodeStyle	CurrentNodeTemplate	The node representing the current page.
RootNodeStyle	RootNodeTemplate	The node representing the root. If the root node is the same as the current node, the current node template or styles are used.
PathSeparatorStyle	PathSeparatorTemplate	The separator between each node.

For example, the following SiteMapPath uses an arrow image as a separator and a fixed string of bold text for the root node. The final part of the path, which represents the current page, is italicized.

```
<asp:SiteMapPath ID="SiteMapPath1" runat="server">
  <PathSeparatorTemplate>
    <asp:Image ID="Image1" ImageUrl="~/images/arrow.jpg"
     runat="server" GenerateEmptyAlternateText="True" />
  </PathSeparatorTemplate>
  <RootNodeTemplate>
    <b>Root</b>
  </RootNodeTemplate>
  <CurrentNodeTemplate>
    <i><asp:Label ID="Label1" runat="server" Text='<%# Eval("title") %>'>
     </asp:Label></i>
  </CurrentNodeTemplate>
</asp:SiteMapPath>
```

Notice how the CurrentNodeTemplate uses a data binding expression to bind to the title property of the current node. You can also get the url and description attributes that you declared in the site map file in the same way.

Binding Portions of a SiteMap

In the examples so far, the page controls replicate the structure of the site map file exactly. However, this isn't always what you want. For example, you might not like the way the Home node sticks out because of the XmlSiteMapProvider rule that every site map must begin with a single root. To clean this up, you can set the SiteMapDataSource.ShowStartingNode property to false. Then, modify the site map file so it defines the Home entry in the first group of pages. (The root node won't be shown, so you can use a dummy node with any URL for it.)

Here's the revised site map:

```
<siteMap xmlns="http://schemas.microsoft.com/AspNet/SiteMap-File-1.0">
  <siteMapNode title="Root" description="Root" url="~/">
    <siteMapNode title="Home" description="Home" url="~/default.aspx"/>
    <siteMapNode title="Products" description="Our products"
      url="~/Products.aspx">
    ...
  </siteMapNode>
</siteMap>
```

Figure 16-11 shows the nicer result.

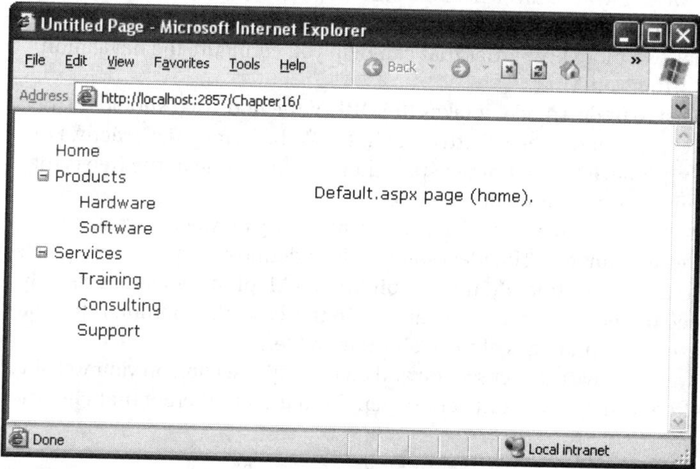

Figure 16-11. *A site map without the root node*

This example shows how you can ship the root node. Another option you have is to show just a portion of the complete site map, starting from the current node. For example, you might use a control such as the TreeView to show everything in the hierarchy starting from the current node. If the user wants to move up a level, they could use another control (such as a SiteMapPath).

To implement this design, simply set the SiteMapDataSource.StartFromCurrentNode property to true. The SiteMapPath will still show the complete hierarchy, allowing the user to move up to a higher-level page. However, other bound controls will show only pages beneath the current page, allowing the user to move down the hierarchy. You still have the choice of whether to use ShowStartingNode, but now it determines whether you show the current node (because that's the starting point for the navigation tree).

Figure 16-12 shows an example where both StartFromCurrentNode and ShowStartingNode are true. The current page is Software.aspx. The SiteMapPath shows higher-level pages, and the TreeView shows the nodes underneath the Software.aspx node.

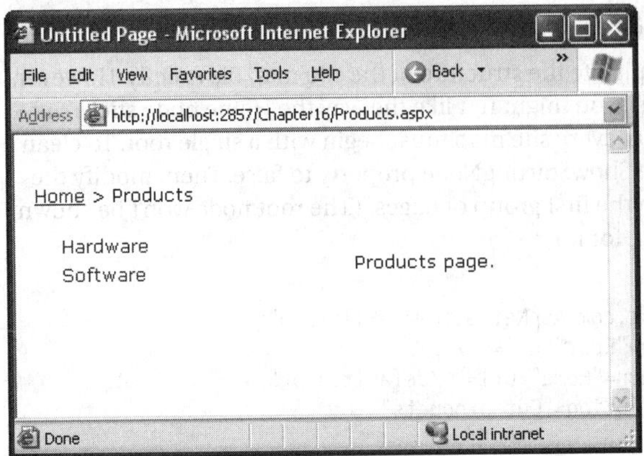

Figure 16-12. *Binding to child nodes only*

For this technique to work, ASP.NET must be able to find a page in the Web.sitemap file that matches the current URL. Otherwise, it won't know where the current position is, and it won't provide any navigation information to the bound controls.

The SiteMapDataSource has two more properties that can help you configure the navigation tree: StartingNodeOffset and StartingNodeUrl.

StartingNodeUrl is the easiest to understand—it takes the URL of the node that should be the first node in the tree. This value must match the url attribute in the Web.sitemap file exactly. For example, if you specify a StartingNodeUrl of "~/home.aspx", then the first node in the tree is the Home node, and you will see only nodes underneath that node.

The StartingNodeUrl property is particularly useful if you want to vary between a small number of different site maps (say, fewer than ten). The ideal solution is to define multiple site map files and bind to the one you want to use. Unfortunately, the default XmlSiteMapProvider supports only a single site map file, so you need to find a different mechanism. In this case, the solution is to separate the different site maps into distinct branches of the Web.sitemap file.

For example, imagine you want to have a dealer section and an employee section on your website. You might split this into two different structures and define them both under different branches in the same file, like this:

```
<siteMap xmlns="http://schemas.microsoft.com/AspNet/SiteMap-File-1.0" >
  <siteMapNode title="Root" description="Root" url="~/">
    <siteMapNode title="Dealer Home" description="Home" url="~/default.aspx">
      ...
    </siteMapNode>
    <siteMapNode title="Employee Home" description="Home" url="~/default_emp.aspx">
      ...
    </siteMapNode>
  </siteMapNode>
</siteMap>
```

Now, to bind the menu to the dealer view, you set the StartingNodeUrl property to "~/default.aspx". You can do this programmatically or, more likely, by creating an entirely different master page and implementing it in all your dealer pages. In your employee pages, you set StartingNodeUrl property to "~/default_emp.aspx". This way, you'll show only the pages under the Dealer Home branch of the site map.

You can even make your life easier by breaking a single site map into separate files using the siteMapFile attribute, like this:

```
<siteMap xmlns="http://schemas.microsoft.com/AspNet/SiteMap-File-1.0" >
  <siteMapNode title="Root" description="Root" url="~/">
    <siteMapNode siteMapFile="Dealers.sitemap" />
    <siteMapNode siteMapFile="Employees.sitemap" />
  </siteMapNode>
</siteMap>
```

Even with this technique, you're still limited to a single site map tree, and it always starts with the Web.sitemap file. However, you can manage your site map more easily because you can factor some of its content into separate files.

■Note This technique is greatly limited because the XmlSiteMapProvider doesn't allow duplicate URLs. That means there's no way to reuse the same page in more than one branch of a site map. Although you can try to work around this problem by creating different URLs that are equivalent (for example, by adding extra query string parameters on the end), this raises more headaches. If these limitations won't work in your scenario, the best approach is to design your own site map provider.

The SiteMapDataSource.StartingNodeOffset property takes the most getting used to. It takes an integer that instructs the SiteMapDataSource to move that many levels down the tree (if the number is positive) or up the tree (if the number is negative). The important detail that's often misunderstood is that when the SiteMapDataSource moves down the tree, it moves *toward* the current node. If it's already at the current node, or your offset takes it beyond the current node, the SiteMapDataSource won't know where to go, and you'll end up with a blank navigation control.

To understand how this works, it helps to consider an example. Imagine you're at this location in a website:

```
Home > Products > Software > Custom > Contact Us
```

If the SiteMapDataSource is starting at the Home node (the default), and you apply a StartingNodeOffset of 2, it will move down the tree two levels and bind this portion:

```
Software > Custom > Contact Us
```

That means you'll be able to jump to any links in the Software or Custom groups, but you won't be able to go anywhere else (at least not without stepping up a level first or clicking another control).

If you click the Custom link, the bound control will now show a tree with this information:

```
Products > Software > Custom
```

Now, what happens if you repeat the same test but set the site map provider to begin on another node? Consider what happens if you set StartFromCurrentNode to true. ASP.NET tries to move two levels down the hierarchy, starting from Contact Us. But because it's already at the current page, it has nowhere to go and can't get any navigational information.

On the other hand, if you set StartFromCurrentNode to true and use a StartingNodeOffset of –2, the SiteMapDataSource will move up two levels from Contact Us and bind this tree:

```
Software > Custom > Contact Us
```

It may take a bit of experimenting to decide the right combination of SiteMapDataSource settings that you want to use.

Programmatic Navigation

You aren't limited to no-code data binding in order to display navigation hierarchies. You can interact with the navigation information programmatically. Two reasons exist for using programmatic navigation:

To change the display of the page: For example, you can retrieve the current node information and use that to configure details such as the page heading and title.

To implement different navigation logic: For example, you might want to display just a portion of the full list of child nodes for the current page in a newsreader, or you might want to create Previous/Next navigation buttons.

The site map API is remarkably straightforward. To use it, you need to work with two classes from the System.Web namespace. The starting point is the SiteMap class, which provides the Shared properties CurrentNode (the site map node representing the current page) and RootNode (the root site map node). Both of these properties return a SiteMapNode object. Using the SiteMapNode, you can retrieve information from the site map, including the title, description, and URL values. You can branch out to consider related nodes using the navigational properties in Table 16-8.

■ Note You can also search for nodes using the methods of the current SiteMapProvider object, which is available through the SiteMap.Provider Shared property. For example, the SiteMap.Provider.FindSiteMapNode() method allows you to search for a node by its URL.

Table 16-8. *SiteMapNode Navigational Properties*

Property	Description
ParentNode	Returns the node one level up in the navigation hierarchy, which contains the current node. On the root node, this returns a null reference.
ChildNodes	Provides a collection of all the child nodes. Check the HasChildNodes property to determine if there are child nodes.
PreviousSibling	Returns the previous node that's at the same level (or a null reference if no such node exists).
NextSibling	Returns the next node that's at the same level (or a null reference if no such node exists).

To see this in action, consider the following code, which configures two labels on a page to show the heading and description information retrieved from the current node:

```
Protected Sub Page_Load(ByVal sender As Object, ByVal e As EventArgs)
    lblHead.Text = SiteMap.CurrentNode.Title
    lblDescription.Text = SiteMap.CurrentNode.Description
End Sub
```

The next example is a little more ambitious. It implements the Previous/Next links, which allow the user to traverse an entire set of subnodes. The code checks for the existence of sibling nodes, and if there aren't any in the required position, it simply hides the links.

```
Protected Sub Page_Load(ByVal sender As Object, ByVal e As EventArgs)
    If SiteMap.CurrentNode.NextSibling IsNot Nothing Then
        lnkNext.NavigateUrl = SiteMap.CurrentNode.NextSibling.Url
        lnkNext.Visible = True
```

```
    Else
        lnkNext.Visible = False
    End If
End Sub
```

Binding Other Controls

The TreeView and MenuView are two navigation controls that show hierarchical navigation information. (Both the TreeView and MenuView are described in more detail later in this chapter.) However, you aren't limited to these two controls—you can also use any ASP.NET control that supports data binding, from the ListBox to the GridView.

For example, you can bind the navigation information to a template in a rich data control and use data binding expression to extract the title, description, and URL information. Here's an example with a GridView:

```
<asp:GridView ID="listNavLinks" runat="server" DataSourceID="SiteMapDataSource1"
 AutoGenerateColumns="false" ShowHeader="False" BackColor="Linen" CellPadding="5">
  <Columns>
    <asp:TemplateField>
      <ItemTemplate>
        <a href='<%# Eval("Url") %>'><%# Eval("Title") %></a>
        <br />
        <%# Eval("Description") %>
      </ItemTemplate>
    </asp:TemplateField>
  </Columns>
</asp:GridView>
```

Figure 16-13 shows the result.

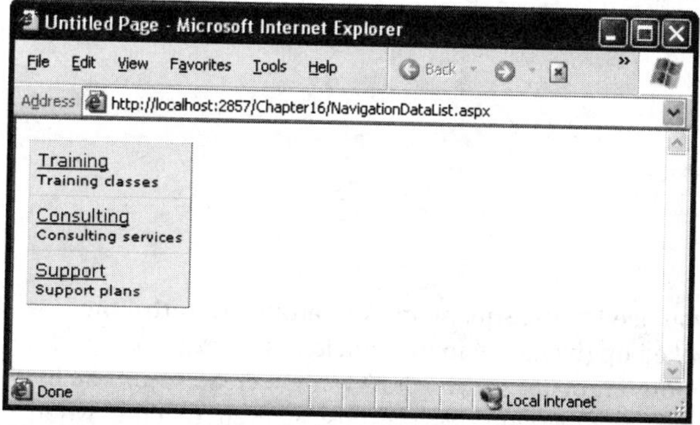

Figure 16-13. *Showing navigation links in a GridView template*

The only limitation in this example is that it shows links nested underneath the current page. It doesn't provide links to travel back up. You would need to add other controls to provide this functionality. You can use the SiteMapPath control along with the GridView, or you can use the SiteMap API. For example, you can use a LinkButton that, when clicked, runs this code to go up one level in the hierarchy:

```
Protected Sub cmdUp_Click(ByVal sender As Object, ByVal e As EventArgs)
    Response.Redirect(SiteMap.CurrentNode.ParentNode.Url)
End Sub
```

Unfortunately, you have no way to bind to nodes further down the hierarchy, as the SiteMapDataSource control doesn't support the XPath syntax demonstrated in Chapter 12. However, you can embed a nested control and bind it programmatically, using the same technique that's described in Chapter 10 in the "A Parent/Child View in a Single Table" section.

Adding Custom Site Map Information

In the site maps you've seen so far, the only information that's provided for a node is the title, description, and URL. This is the bare minimum of information that you'll want to use. However, the schema for the XML site map is open, which means you're free to insert custom attributes with your own data.

You might want to insert additional node data for a number of reasons. This additional information might be descriptive information that you intend to display or contextual information that describes how the link should work. For example, you could add attributes that specify a target frame or indicate that a link should be opened in a pop-up window. The only catch is that it's up to you to act on the information later. In other words, you need to configure your user interface so it uses this extra information.

For example, the following code shows a site map that uses a target attribute to indicate the frame where the link should be opened. This technique is useful if you're using frames-based navigation (rather than a master page), as described in Chapter 29. In this example, one link is set with a target of _blank so it will open in a new (pop-up) browser window.

```
<siteMap xmlns="http://schemas.microsoft.com/AspNet/SiteMap-File-1.0" >
  <siteMapNode title="Home" description="Root" url="~/Default.aspx">
    <siteMapNode title="Products" description="Our products"
     url="~/Products.aspx" target="_blank" />
    ...
  </siteMapNode>
</siteMap>
```

Now in your code, you have several options. If you're using a template in your navigation control, you can bind directly to the new attribute. Here's an example with the GridView from the previous section:

```
<ItemTemplate>
  <a href='<%# Eval("Url") %>'
   target='<%# Eval("[target]") %>'><%# Eval("Title") %></a>
  <br />
  <%# Eval("Description") %>
</ItemTemplate>
```

The one trick in this example is that you need to use square brackets around the attribute name to indicate that the value is being looked up (by name) in the data item's indexer.

If your navigation control doesn't support templates (or you don't want to create one), you'll need to find another approach. Both the TreeView and Menu classes expose an event that fires when an individual item is bound (TreeNodeDataBound and MenuItemDataBound). You can then customize the current item. To apply the new target, you use this code:

```
Protected Sub TreeView1_TreeNodeDataBound(ByVal sender As Object,
      ByVal e As TreeNodeEventArgs)
    SiteMapNode sn = CType(e.Node.DataItem, SiteMapNode)
    e.Node.Target = sn("target")
End Sub
```

Notice that you can't retrieve the custom attribute from a strongly typed property. Instead, you retrieve it by name using the SiteMapNode indexer.

■Note You can also create a custom SiteMapProvider that returns instances of a custom SiteMapNode-derived class. However, a significant amount of extra code is required, and as a result it's often not worth the trouble.

Creating a Custom SiteMapProvider

To really change how the ASP.NET navigation model works, you need to create your own site map provider. You might choose to create a custom site map provider for several reasons:

- You need to store site map information in a different data source (such as a relational database).
- You need to store site map information with a different schema from the XML format expected by ASP.NET. This is most likely if you have an existing system in place for storing site maps.
- You need a highly dynamic site map that's generated on the fly. For example, you might want to generate a different site map based on the current user, the query string parameters, and so on.
- You need to change one of the limitations in the XmlSiteMapProvider implementation. For example, maybe you want the ability to have nodes with duplicate URLs.

You have two choices when implementing a custom site map provider. All site map providers derive from the abstract base class SiteMapProvider in the System.Web namespace. You can derive from this class to implement a new provider from scratch. However, if you want to keep the same logic but use a different data store, just derive from the StaticSiteMapProvider class instead. It gives you a basic implementation of many methods, including the logic for node storing and searching.

In the following sections, you'll see a custom provider that lets you store site map information in a database.

Storing Site Map Information in a Database

In this example, all navigation links are stored in a single database table. Because databases don't lend themselves easily to hierarchical data, you need to be a little crafty. In this example, each navigation link is linked to a parent link in the same table, except for the root node. This means that although the navigational links are flattened into one table, you can re-create the right structure by starting with the home page and then searching for the subset of rows at each level.

Figure 16-14 shows the SiteMap table with some sample data that roughly duplicates the site map you saw earlier in this chapter.

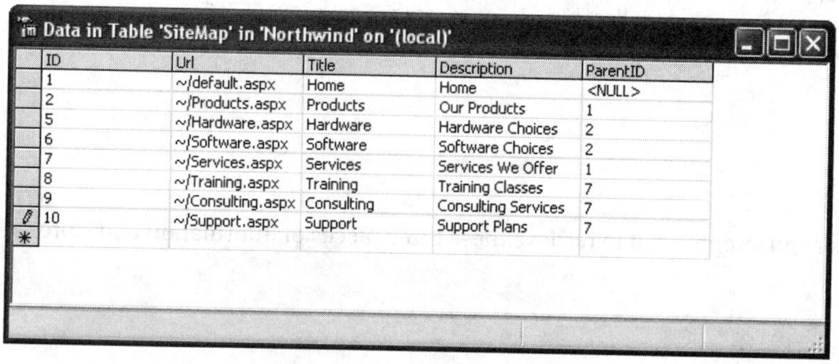

Data in Table 'SiteMap' in 'Northwind' on '(local)'

ID	Url	Title	Description	ParentID
1	~/default.aspx	Home	Home	<NULL>
2	~/Products.aspx	Products	Our Products	1
5	~/Hardware.aspx	Hardware	Hardware Choices	2
6	~/Software.aspx	Software	Software Choices	2
7	~/Services.aspx	Services	Services We Offer	1
8	~/Training.aspx	Training	Training Classes	7
9	~/Consulting.aspx	Consulting	Consulting Services	7
10	~/Support.aspx	Support	Support Plans	7

Figure 16-14. *The SiteMap table*

In this solution, the site map provider won't access the table directly. Instead, it will use a stored procedure. This gives some added flexibility and potentially allows you to store your navigation information with a different schema, as long as you return a table with the expected column names from your stored procedure.

Here's the stored procedure used in this example:

```
CREATE PROCEDURE GetSiteMap AS
SELECT * FROM SiteMap
GO
```

Creating the Site Map Provider

Because this site map provider doesn't change the underlying logic of site map navigation, you can derive from StaticSiteMapProvider instead of deriving from SiteMapProvider and reimplementing all the tracking and navigation behavior (which is a much more tedious task).

Here's the class declaration for the provider:

```
Public Class SqlSiteMapProvider
    Inherits StaticSiteMapProvider
    ...
End Class
```

The first step is to override the Initialize() method to get all the information you need from the web.config file. The Initialize() method gives you access to the configuration element that defines the site map provider.

In this example, your provider needs three pieces of information:

- The connection string for the database.
- The name of the stored procedure that returns the site map.
- The provider name for the database. This allows you to use provider-agnostic coding (as described in Chapter 7). In other words, you can support SQL Server, Oracle, or another database equally easily, as long as there's a .NET provider factory installed.

You can configure your web application to use the custom provider (SqlSiteMapProvider) and supply the required three pieces of information using the <siteMap> section of the web.config file:

```
<configuration xmlns="http://schemas.microsoft.com/.NetConfiguration/v2.0">
  <system.web>
    <siteMap defaultProvider="SqlSiteMapProvider">
      <providers>
        <add name="SqlSiteMapProvider" type="SqlSiteMapProvider"
          providerName="System.Data.SqlClient"
          connectionString=
"Data Source=localhost;Initial Catalog=Northwind;Integrated Security=SSPI"
          storedProcedure="GetSiteMap" />
      </providers>
    </siteMap>
    ...
  </system.web>
</configuration>
```

Now in your provider you simply need to retrieve these three pieces of information and store them for later:

```
Private connectionString As String
Private providerName As String
Private storedProcedure As String
```

```
    Public Overrides Sub Initialize(ByVal name As String,
      ByVal attributes As System.Collections.Specialized.NameValueCollection)
        If (Not IsInitialized) Then
            MyBase.Initialize(name, attributes)

            ' Retrieve the web.config settings.
            providerName = attributes("providerName")
            connectionString = attributes("connectionString")
            storedProcedure = attributes("storedProcedure")

            If String.IsNullOrEmpty(providerName) Then
              Throw New Exception("The provider name was not found.")
            Else If String.IsNullOrEmpty(connectionString) Then
              Throw New Exception("The connection string was not found.")
            Else If String.IsNullOrEmpty(storedProcedure) Then
              Throw New Exception("The stored procedure name was not found.")
            End If

            initialized = True
        End If
    End Sub

    Private initialized As Boolean = False
    Public Overridable ReadOnly Property IsInitialized() As Boolean
        Get
                Return initialized
        End Get
    End Property
```

The real work that the provider does is in the BuildSiteMap() method, which constructs the SiteMapNode objects that make up the navigation tree. In the lifetime of an application, you'll typically construct the SiteMapNode once and reuse it multiple times. To make that possible, the provider needs to store the site map in memory:

```
Private rootNode As SiteMapNode
```

The root SiteMapNode contains the first level of nodes, which then contain the next level of nodes, and so on. Thus, the root node is the starting point for the whole navigation tree.

You override the BuildSiteMap() method to actually create the site map. The first step is to check if the site map has already been generated and then create it. Because multiple pages could share the same instance of the site map provider, it's a good idea to lock the object before you update any shared information (such as the in-memory navigation tree).

```
Public Overrides Function BuildSiteMap() As SiteMapNode
    SyncLock Me
        ' Don't rebuild the map unless needed.
        ' If your site map changes often, consider using caching.
        If rootNode Is Nothing Then
            ' Start with a clean slate.
            Clear()
            ...
```

Next, you need to use create the database provider and use it to call the stored procedure that gets the navigation history. The navigation history is stored in a DataSet (a DataReader won't work because you need back-and-forth navigation to traverse the structure of the site map).

```
...
' Get all the data (using provider-agnostic code).
Dim provider As DbProviderFactory = DbProviderFactories.GetFactory(providerName)
```

```
' Use this factory to create a connection.
Dim con As DbConnection = provider.CreateConnection()
con.ConnectionString = connectionString

' Create the command.
Dim cmd As DbCommand = provider.CreateCommand()
cmd.CommandText = storedProcedure
cmd.CommandType = CommandType.StoredProcedure
cmd.Connection = con

' Create the DataAdapter.
Dim adapter As DbDataAdapter = provider.CreateDataAdapter()
adapter.SelectCommand = cmd

' Get the results in a DataSet.
Dim ds As New DataSet()
adapter.Fill(ds, "SiteMap")
Dim dtSiteMap As DataTable = ds.Tables("SiteMap")
...
```

The next step is to navigate the DataTable to create the SiteMapNode objects, beginning with the root node. You can find the root node by searching for the node with no parent (where ParentID is null). In this example, no attempt is made to check for all the possible error conditions (such as duplicate root nodes).

```
...
' Get the root node.
Dim drwRoot As DataRow = dtSiteMap.Select("ParentID IS NULL")(0)
...
```

Now to create a SiteMapNode, you need to supply the key, URL, title, and description. In the default implementation of a site map provider, the key and URL are the same, which makes searching by URL easier. The custom SqlSiteMapProvider also uses this convention.

```
...
rootNode = New SiteMapNode(Me, drwRoot("Url").ToString(), _
                      drwRoot("Url").ToString(), drwRoot("Title").ToString(), _
                      drwRoot("Description").ToString())
...
```

Now it's time to fill in the rest of the hierarchy. This is a step that needs to be performed recursively so that you can drill down through a hierarchy that's an unlimited number of levels deep. To make this work, the SqlSiteMapProvider uses a private AddChildren method, which fills in one level at a time. Once this process is complete, the root node that provides access to the full site map is returned.

```
            ...
            Dim rootID As String = drwRoot("ID").ToString()

            ' Fill down the hierarchy.
            AddChildren(rootNode, rootID, dtSiteMap)
        End If
    End SyncLock
    Return rootNode
End Function
```

The AddChildren() method simply searches the DataTable for records where the ParentID is the same as the current ID—in other words, it finds all the parents for the current node. Each time it finds a child, it adds the child to the SiteMapNode.ChildNodes collection using the AddNode method that's inherited from StaticSiteMapProvider.

Here's the complete code:

```
Private Sub AddChildren(ByVal rootNode As SiteMapNode, ByVal rootID As String,
    ByVal dtSiteMap As DataTable)
    Dim childRows As DataRow() = dtSiteMap.Select("ParentID = " & rootID)
    For Each row As DataRow In childRows
        Dim childNode As New SiteMapNode(Me, row("Url").ToString(), _
          row("Url").ToString(), row("Title").ToString(), _
          row("Description").ToString())
        Dim rowID As String = row("ID").ToString()

        ' Use the SiteMapNode AddNode method to add
        ' the SiteMapNode to the ChildNodes collection.
        AddNode(childNode, rootNode)

        ' Check for children in this node.
        AddChildren(childNode, rowID, dtSiteMap)
    Next row
End Sub
```

The only limitation in the AddChildren() method is that it doesn't attempt to apply any sort of positioning. Instead, entries are added in the order they appear in the database. Changing this behavior isn't difficult. To do so, you need to add a SortOrder column to the database table. Then, you could sort the records before adding them using an overload of the DataTable.Select() method.

The only remaining details are to fill a few other required overloads that retrieve the site map information:

```
Protected Overrides Function GetRootNodeCore() As SiteMapNode
    Return BuildSiteMap()
End Function

Public Overrides ReadOnly Property RootNode() As SiteMapNode
    Get
        Return BuildSiteMap()
    End Get
End Property

Protected Overrides Sub Clear()
    SyncLock Me
        rootNode = Nothing
        MyBase.Clear()
    End SyncLock
End Sub
```

This completes the example. You can now request the same pages you created earlier, using the new site map provider (as configured in the web.config file). The custom provider plugs in easily and neatly. The new information will flow through the custom provider and arrive in your pages without any indication that the underlying plumbing has changed.

URL Mapping

In some situations, you might want to have several URLs lead to the same page. This might be the case for a number of reasons—maybe you want to implement your logic in one page and use query string arguments but still provide shorter and easier-to-remember URLs to your website users (often called *friendly* URLs). Or maybe you have renamed a page, but you want to keep the old URL functional so it doesn't break user bookmarks. Although web servers sometimes provide this type of functionality, ASP.NET 2.0 now includes its own URL mapping feature.

The basic idea behind ASP.NET URL mapping is that you map a request URL to a different URL. The mapping rules are stored in the web.config file, and they're applied before any other processing takes place. Of course, for ASP.NET to apply the remapping, it must be processing the request, which means the request URL must use a file type extension that's mapped to ASP.NET. (See Chapter 18 for more information about how to configure ASP.NET to handle file extensions that it wouldn't ordinarily handle.)

You define URL mapping in the <urlMappings> section of the web.config file. You supply two pieces of information—the request URL (as the attribute url) and the new destination URL (mappedUrl). Here's an example:

```
<configuration xmlns="http://schemas.microsoft.com/.NetConfiguration/v2.0">
  <system.web>
    <urlMappings enabled="true">
      <add url="~/Category.aspx"
       mappedUrl="~/Default.aspx?category=default" />
      <add url="~/Software.aspx"
       mappedUrl="~/Default.aspx?category=software" />
    </urlMappings>
    ...
  </system.web>
</configuration>
```

To make a match, the incoming URL must be requesting the same page. However, the case of the request URL is ignored, as are query string arguments. Unfortunately, there's no support for advanced matching rules, such as wildcards or regular expressions.

When you use URL mapping, the redirection is performed in the same way as the Server.Transfer() method, which means there is no round-trip and the URL in the browser will still show the original request URL, not the new page. In your code, the Request.Path and Request.QueryString properties reflect the new (mapped) URL. The Request.RawUrl property returns the original friendly request URL.

This can introduce some complexities if you use it in conjunction with site maps—namely, does the site map provider try to use the original request URL or the destination URL when looking for the current node in the site map? The answer is both. It begins by trying to match the request URL (provided by Request.RawUrl property), and if no value is found, it then uses the Request.Path property instead. This is the behavior of the XmlSiteMapProvider, so you could change it in a custom provider if desired.

The TreeView Control

The TreeView is the most impressive new control in ASP.NET 2.0. Not only does it allow you to render rich tree views, it also supports filling portions of the tree on demand (and without refreshing the entire page). But most important, it supports a wide range of styles that can transform its appearance. By setting just a few basic properties, you can change the TreeView from a help topic index to a file and folder directory listing. In fact, the TreeView doesn't have to be rendered as a tree at all—it can also tackle nonindented hierarchical data such as a table of contents with the application of just a few style settings.

You've already seen two basic TreeView scenarios. In Chapter 12, you used a TreeView to display bound XML data. In this chapter, you used a TreeView to display site map data. Both of these examples used the ability of the TreeView to bind to hierarchical data sources. But you can also fill a TreeView by binding to an ordinary data source (in which case you'll get only a single level of nodes) or by creating the nodes yourself, either programmatically or through the .aspx declaration.

The latter option is the simplest. For example, by adding <asp:TreeNode> tags to the <Nodes> section of a TreeView control, you can create several nodes:

```
<asp:TreeView runat="server">
  <Nodes>
    <asp:TreeNode Text="Products">
      <asp:TreeNode Text="Hardware"/>
    </asp:TreeNode>
    <asp:TreeNode Text="Services"/>
  </Nodes>
</asp:TreeView>
```

And here's how you can add a TreeNode programmatically when the page loads:

```
Dim newNode As New TreeNode("Software")

' Add as a child of the first root node
' (the Products node in the previous example).
TreeView1.Nodes(0).ChildNodes.Add(newNode)
```

When the TreeView is first displayed, all the nodes are shown. You can control this behavior by setting the TreeView.ExpandDepth property. For example, if ExpandDepth is 2, only the first three levels are shown (level 0, level 1, and level 2). You can also programmatically collapse and expand nodes by setting the TreeNode.Expanded property to true or false.

This just scratches the surface of how a TreeView works. To get the most out of the TreeView, you need to understand how to customize several other details for a TreeNode.

The TreeNode

Each node in the tree is represented by a TreeNode object. As you already know, every TreeNode has an associated piece of text, which is displayed in the tree. The TreeNode object also provides navigation properties such as ChildNodes (the collection of nodes it contains) and Parent (the containing node, one level up the tree). Along with this bare minimum, the TreeNode provides all the useful properties detailed in Table 16-9.

Table 16-9. *TreeNode Properties*

Property	Description
Text	The text displayed in the tree for this node.
ToolTip	The tooltip text that appears when you hover over the node text.
Value	Stores a nondisplayed value with additional data about the node (such as a unique ID you'll use when handling click events to identify the node or look up more information).
NavigateUrl	If set, it automatically forwards the user to this URL when this node is clicked. Otherwise, you'll need to react to the TreeView.SelectedNodeChanged event to decide what action you want to perform.
Target	If the NavigateUrl property is set, this sets the target window or frame for the link. If Target isn't set, the new page is opened in the current browser window. The TreeView also exposes a Target property, which you can set to apply a default target for all TreeNode instances.
ImageUrl	The image that's displayed next to this node.
ImageToolTip	The tooltip text for the image displayed next to the node.

One unusual detail about the TreeNode is that it can be in one of two modes. In *selection mode*, clicking the node posts back the page and raises the TreeView.SelectedNodeChanged event. This is the default mode for all nodes. In *navigation mode*, clicking a node navigates to a new page, and the SelectedNodeChanged event is not raised. The TreeNode is placed in navigation mode as soon as you set the NavigateUrl property to anything other than an empty string. A TreeNode that's bound to site map data is in navigational mode, because each site map node supplies URL information.

The next example fills a TreeView with the results of a database query. You want to use the TreeView's ability to show hierarchical data to create a master-details list. Because ASP.NET doesn't include any data source control that can query a database and expose the results as a hierarchical data source, you can't use data binding. Instead, you need to programmatically query the table and create the TreeNode structure by hand.

Here's the code that implements this approach:

```
Protected Sub Page_Load(ByVal sender As Object, ByVal e As EventArgs)
    If (Not Page.IsPostBack) Then
        Dim ds As DataSet = GetProductsAndCategories()

        ' Loop through the category records.
        For Each row As DataRow In ds.Tables("Categories").Rows
            ' Use the constructor that requires just text
            ' and a nondisplayed value.
            Dim nodeCategory As New TreeNode(row("CategoryName").ToString(),
                row("CategoryID").ToString())

            TreeView1.Nodes.Add(nodeCategory)

            ' Get the children (products) for this parent (category).
            Dim childRows As DataRow() = row.GetChildRows(ds.Relations(0))

            ' Loop through all the products in this category.
            For Each childRow As DataRow In childRows
                    Dim nodeProduct As New TreeNode(
                                childRow("ProductName").ToString(),
                                childRow("ProductID").ToString())
                    nodeCategory.ChildNodes.Add(nodeProduct)
                Next childRow

                    ' Keep all categories collapsed (initially).
                    nodeCategory.Collapse()
        Next row
    End If
End Sub
```

Now when a node is clicked, you can handle the SelectedNodeChanged event to show the node information:

```
Protected Sub TreeView1_SelectedNodeChanged(ByVal sender As Object,
    ByVal e As EventArgs)
    If TreeView1.SelectedNode Is Nothing Then
            Return
    End If
    If TreeView1.SelectedNode.Depth = 0 Then
        lblInfo.Text = "You selected Category ID: "
    ElseIf TreeView1.SelectedNode.Depth = 1 Then
        lblInfo.Text = "You selected Product ID: "
    End If
    lblInfo.Text &= TreeView1.SelectedNode.Value
End Sub
```

Figure 16-15 shows the result.

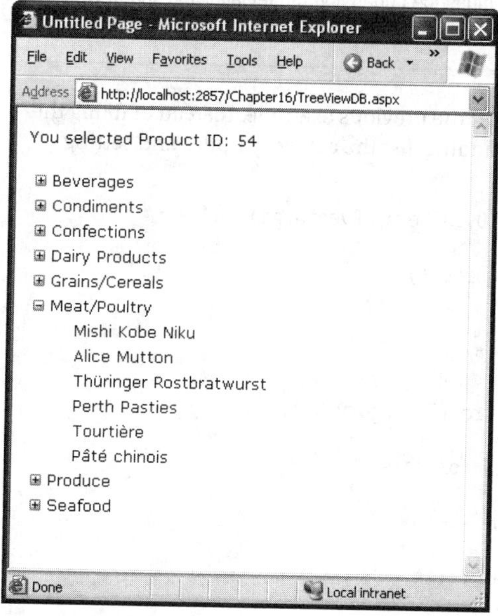

Figure 16-15. *Filling a TreeView with database data*

A few options exist to simplify the page code in this example. One option is to bind to XML data instead of relational data. Seeing as SQL Server 2000 and later have the ability to perform XML queries with FOR XML, you could retrieve the data shaped in a specific XML markup and then bind it through the XmlDataSource control. The only trick is that because the XmlDataSource assumes you'll be binding to a file, you need to set the Data property by hand with the XML extracted from the database.

Populating Nodes on Demand

If you have an extremely large amount of data to display in a TreeView, you probably don't want to fill it in all at once. Not only will that increase the time taken to process the initial request for the page, it will also dramatically increase the size of the page and the view state. Fortunately, the TreeView includes a populate-on-demand feature that makes it easy to fill in branches of the tree as they are expanded. Even better, you can use populate-on-demand on selected portions of the tree, as you see fit.

To use populate-on-demand, you set the PopulateOnDemand property to true for any TreeNode that has content you want to fill in at the last minute. When the user expands this branch, the TreeView will fire a TreeNodePopulate event, which you can use to add the next level of nodes. If you want, this level of nodes can contain another level of nodes that are populated on demand.

Although the programming model remains fixed, the TreeView actually supports two techniques for filling in the on-demand nodes. When the TreeView.PopulateNodesFromClient property is true (the default), the TreeView performs a client-side callback to retrieve the nodes it needs from your event, without posting back the entire page. If PopulateNodesFromClient is false, or if it's true but the TreeView detects that the current browser doesn't appear to support client callbacks, the TreeView triggers a normal postback to get the same result. The only difference is that the entire page will be refreshed in the browser, generating a less seamless interface. (It also allows other page events to fire, such as control change events.)

Note Chapter 29 has more information about how client callbacks work and how you can use them directly. However, the TreeView support is particularly nice because it hides the underlying model, allowing you to write an ordinary .NET event handler.

You can use the populate-on-demand feature with the previous example. Instead of filling the whole tree when the page loads, you would begin by adding just the category nodes and setting them to populate on demand:

```
Protected Sub Page_Load(ByVal sender As Object, ByVal e As EventArgs)
    If (Not Page.IsPostBack) Then
        Dim dtCategories As DataTable = GetCategories()

        ' Loop through the category records.
        For Each row As DataRow In dtCategories.Rows
            Dim nodeCategory As New TreeNode(
                row("CategoryName").ToString(), row("CategoryID").ToString())

            ' Use the populate-on-demand feature for this
            ' node's children.
            nodeCategory.PopulateOnDemand = True

            ' Make sure the node is collapsed at first,
            ' so it's not populated immediately.
            nodeCategory.Collapse()
            TreeView1.Nodes.Add(nodeCategory)
        Next row
    End If
End Sub
```

Now you need to react to the TreeNodePopulate event to fill a category when it's expanded. In this example, only the on-populate nodes are categories. However, if there were several types, you would check the TreeNode.Depth to determine what type of node is being expanded.

```
Protected Sub TreeView1_TreeNodePopulate(ByVal sender As Object,
      ByVal e As TreeNodeEventArgs)
    Dim categoryID As Integer = Integer.Parse(e.Node.Value)
    Dim dtProducts As DataTable = GetProducts(categoryID)

    ' Loop through the product records.
    For Each row As DataRow In dtProducts.Rows
        ' Use the constructor that requires just text
        ' and a nondisplayed value.
        Dim nodeProduct As New TreeNode(
              row("ProductName").ToString(), row("ProductID").ToString())

        e.Node.ChildNodes.Add(nodeProduct)
    Next row
End Sub
```

A given node is populated on-demand only once. After that, the values remain available on the client, and no callback is performed if the same node is collapsed and expanded.

■ **Note** The client-side callback feature can be tampered with, just like any posted data. For example, a malicious user could create a page that requests you to fill in an arbitrary CategoryID, even if you haven't added the category to the tree. If you are displaying a subset of data from a table that contains sensitive information, you should validate that the node is allowed before populating it.

TreeView Styles

The TreeView has a fine-grained style model that lets you completely control its appearance. Each style applies to a type of node. Styles are represented by the TreeNodeStyle class, which derives from the more conventional Style class.

As with other rich controls, the styles give you options to set background and foreground colors, fonts, and borders. Additionally, the TreeNodeStyle class adds the node-specific style properties shown in Table 16-10. These properties deal with the node image and the spacing around a node.

Table 16-10. *TreeNodeStyle Added Properties*

Property	Description
ImageUrl	The URL for the image shown next to the node
NodeSpacing	The space (in pixels) between the current node and the node above and below
VerticalPadding	The space (in pixels) between the top and bottom of the node text and border around the text
HorizontalPadding	The space (in pixels) between the left and right of the node text and border around the text
ChildNodesPadding	The space (in pixels) between the last child node of an expanded parent node and the following sibling node

---

■ **Tip** The TreeView does not support associating two pictures with a node, one for the collapsed state and one for the expanded state. However, you can change the appearance of the collapse/expand buttons rendered next to every node.

Because a TreeView is rendered using an HTML table, you can set the padding of various elements to control the spacing around text, between nodes, and so on. One other property that comes into play is TreeView.NodeIndent, which sets the number of pixels of indentation (from the left) in each subsequent level of the tree hierarchy. Figure 16-16 shows how these settings apply to a single node.

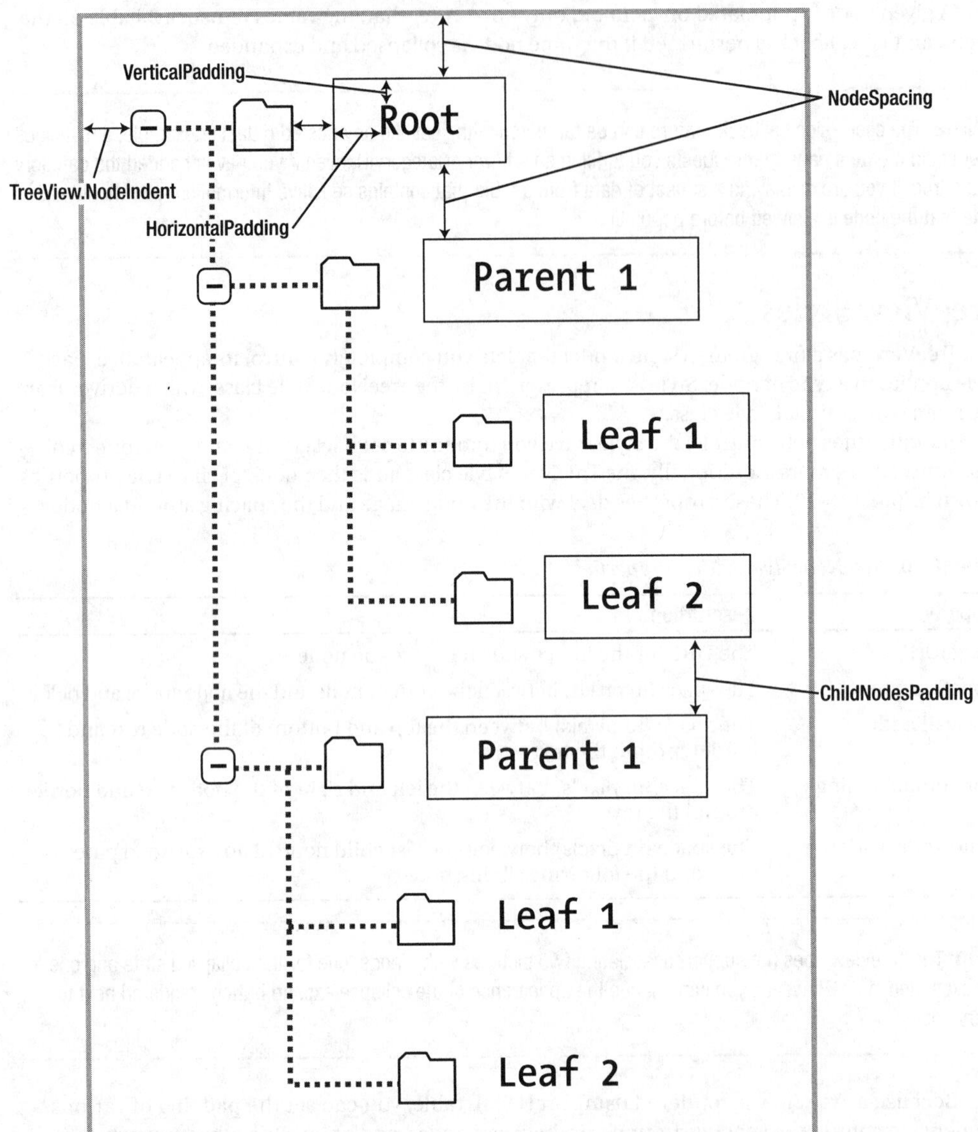

Figure 16-16. *Node spacing*

The TreeView also allows you to configure some of its internal rendering through higher-level properties. You can turn off the node lines in a tree using the TreeView.ShowExpandCollapse property. You can also use the CollapseImageUrl and ExpandImageUrl properties to set the expanded and collapsed indicators of the TreeView (usually represented by plus and minus icons) and the BlankImageUrl property to set what's displayed next to nodes that have no children. Finally, you can show check boxes next to every node (set TreeView.ShowCheckBoxes to true) or individual nodes (see TreeNode.ShowCheckBox). You can determine whether a given node is checked by examining the TreeNode.Checked property.

Applying Styles to Node Types

The TreeView allows you to individually control the styles for different types of nodes—for example, root nodes, nodes that contain other nodes, selected nodes, and so on.

To apply node style settings to all the nodes of a tree, you can use the TreeView.NodeStyle property. You can isolate individual regions of the TreeView using a more specific style, as listed in Table 16-11.

Table 16-11. *TreeView Style Properties*

Property	Description
NodeStyle	Applies to all nodes.
RootNodeStyle	Applies only to the first-level (root) nodes.
ParentNodeStyle	Applies to any node that contains other nodes, except root nodes.
LeafNodeStyle	Applies to any node that doesn't contain child nodes and isn't a root node.
SelectedNodeStyle	Applies to the currently selected node.
HoverNodeStyle	Applies to the node the user is hovering over with the mouse. These settings are applied only in up-level clients that support the necessary dynamic script.

Styles are listed in this table in order of most general to most specific. That means the SelectedNodeStyle style settings override any conflicting settings in a RootNodeStyle, for example. (If you don't want a node to be selectable, set the TreeNode.SelectAction to None.) However, the RootNodeStyle, ParentNodeStyle, and LeafNodeStyle settings never conflict, because the definitions for root, parent, and leaf nodes are mutually exclusive. You can't have a node that is simultaneously a parent and a root node, for example—the TreeView simply designates this as a root node.

Applying Styles to Node Levels

Being able to apply styles to different types of nodes is interesting, but a more useful feature is being able to apply styles based on the node *level*. That's because most trees use a rigid hierarchy (for example, the first level of nodes represents categories, the second level represents products, the third represents orders, and so on). In this case, it's not so important to determine whether a node has children. Instead, it's important to determine the node's depth.

The only problem is that a TreeView can have a theoretically unlimited number of node levels. Thus, it doesn't make sense to expose properties such as FirstLevelStyle, SecondLevelStyle, and so on. Instead, the TreeView has a LevelStyles collection that can have as many entries as you want. The level is inferred from the position of the style in the collection, so the first entry is considered the root level, the second entry is the second node level, and so on. For this system to work, you must follow the same order, and you must include an empty style placeholder if you want to skip a level without changing the formatting.

For example, here's a TreeView that doesn't use any indenting but instead differentiates levels by applying different amounts of spacing and different fonts:

```
<asp:TreeView runat="server" HoverNodeStyle-Font-Underline="true"
 ShowExpandCollapse="false" NodeIndent="0">
  <LevelStyles>
    <asp:TreeNodeStyle ChildNodesPadding="10" Font-Bold="true" Font-Size="12pt"
     ForeColor="DarkGreen"/>
    <asp:TreeNodeStyle ChildNodesPadding="5" Font-Bold="true" Font-Size="10pt" />
    <asp:TreeNodeStyle ChildNodesPadding="5"
               Font-UnderLine="true" Font-Size="10pt" />
  </LevelStyles>
  ...
</asp:TreeView>
```

If you apply this to the category and product list shown in earlier examples, you'll see a page like the one shown in Figure 16-17.

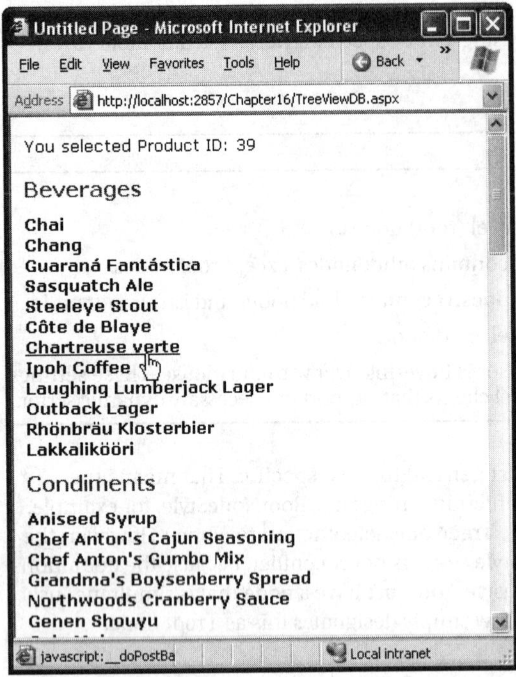

Figure 16-17. *A nonindented TreeView*

TreeView Themes

Using the right combination of style settings can dramatically transform your TreeView. However, for those less artistically inclined (or those who don't have the right set of images handy), it's comforting to know that Microsoft has made many classic designs available in a skin file. This skin file includes formatting settings and links to graphics that allow you to implement many common TreeView designs. Using these themes, you can easily adapt the TreeView to display anything from logged errors to an MSN Messenger contact list.

As with any skin file, you can apply these settings to a TreeView simply by attaching the skin file to the page and setting the TreeView.SkinID property to the skin you want to use. (See Chapter 15 for the full details.) Visual Studio makes this even easier—just click the Auto Format link in the smart tag, and you'll be able to choose from one of several built-in skins. Figure 16-18 shows some of your options.

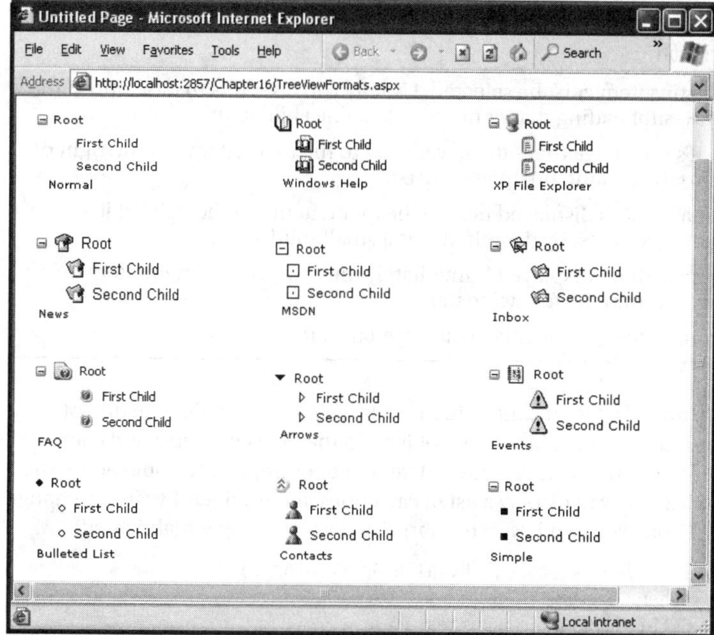

Figure 16-18. *Different looks for a TreeView*

Menu Control

The new ASP.NET 2.0 Menu control is another rich control that supports hierarchical data. Like the TreeView, you can bind the Menu to a data source, or you can fill it by hand (declaratively or programmatically) using MenuItem objects.

The MenuItem class isn't quite as rich as the TreeNode class—for example, MenuItem objects don't support check boxes or the ability to programmatically set their expanded/collapsed state. However, they still have many similar properties, including those for setting images, determining whether the item is selectable, and specifying a target link. Table 16-12 has the defaults.

Table 16-12. *MenuItem Properties*

Property	Description
Text	The text displayed in the menu for this item (when displayed).
ToolTip	The tooltip text that appears when you hover over the menu item.
Value	Stores a nondisplayed value with additional data about the menu item (such as a unique ID you'll use when handling click events to identify the node or look up more information).
NavigateUrl	If set, when this node is clicked, it automatically forwards the user to this URL. Otherwise, you'll need to react to the Menu.MenuItemClick event to decide what action you want to perform.
Target	If the NavigateUrl property is set, this sets the target window or frame for the link. If Target isn't set, the new page is opened in the current browser window. The Menu also exposes a Target property, which you can set to apply a default target for all MenuItem instances.

(Continued)

Table 16-12. *Continued*

Property	Description
Selectable	If false, this item can't be selected. Usually you'll set this to false only if the item is a subheading that contains selectable child items.
ImageUrl	If set, it's the image that's displayed next to the menu item (on the right of the text). By default, no image is used.
PopOutImageUrl	The image that's displayed next to the menu item (on the right) if it contains subitems. By default, this is a small solid arrow.
SeparatorImageUrl	The image that's displayed immediately underneath this menu item, to separate it from the following item.
ImageToolTip	The tooltip text for the image displayed next to the node.

You can walk over the structure of a Menu control in much the same way as the structure of a TreeView. The Menu contains a collection of MenuItem objects in the Items property, and each MenuItem has a ChildItems collection that contains nested items. For example, you could adapt the previous example that used the TreeView to display a list of categories and products by simply changing a few class names. Here's the code you need, with the surprisingly few changes highlighted:

```
Protected Sub Page_Load(ByVal sender As Object, ByVal e As EventArgs)
    If (Not Page.IsPostBack) Then
        Dim ds As DataSet = GetProductsAndCategories()

        ' Loop through the category records.
        For Each row As DataRow In ds.Tables("Categories").Rows
            ' Use the constructor that requires just text
            ' and a nondisplayed value.
            Dim itemCategory As MenuItem =
              New MenuItem(row("CategoryName").ToString(), _
              row("CategoryID").ToString())

            Menu1.Items.Add(itemCategory)

            ' Get the children (products) for this parent (category).
            Dim childRows As DataRow() = row.GetChildRows(ds.Relations(0))

            ' Loop through all the products in this category.
            For Each childRow As DataRow In childRows
                Dim itemProduct As MenuItem =
                        New MenuItem(childRow("ProductName").ToString(), _
                        childRow("ProductID").ToString())
                itemCategory.ChildItems.Add(itemProduct)
            Next
        Next
    End If
End Sub
```

```
Protected Sub Menu1_MenuItemClick(ByVal sender As Object,
      ByVal e As System.Web.UI.WebControls.MenuEventArgs)
    If Menu1.SelectedItem.Depth = 0 Then
        lblInfo.Text = "You selected Category ID: "
    ElseIf Menu1.SelectedItem.Depth = 1 Then
        lblInfo.Text = "You selected Product ID: "
    End If
    lblInfo.Text &= Menu1.SelectedItem.Value
End Sub
```

Figure 16-19 shows the result.

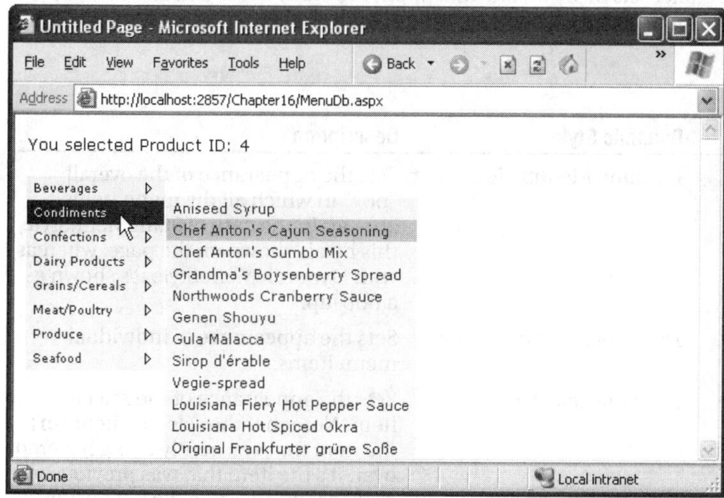

Figure 16-19. *Displaying a menu with information from a database*

Overall, the Menu and TreeView controls expose strikingly similar programming models, even though they render themselves quite differently. They also have a similar style-based formatting model. But a few noteworthy differences exist:

- The Menu displays a single submenu. The TreeView can expand an arbitrary number of node branches at a time.
- The Menu displays a root level of links in the page. All other items are displayed using fly-out menus that appear over any other content on the page. The TreeView shows all its items inline in the page.
- TreeView supports on-demand filling and client callbacks. The Menu does not.
- The Menu supports templates. The TreeView does not.
- The TreeView supports check boxes for any node. The Menu does not.
- The Menu supports horizontal and vertical layouts, depending on the Orientation property. The TreeView supports only vertical layout.

Menu Styles

The Menu control provides an overwhelming number of styles. Like the TreeView, the Menu derives a custom class from the Style base class—in fact, it derives two (MenuStyle and MenuItemStyle). These styles add spacing properties (ItemSpacing, HorizontalPadding, and VerticalPadding). However, you can't set menu item images through the style, because there is no ImageUrl property.

Much like the TreeView, the Menu supports defining different menu styles for different menu levels. However, the key distinction that the Menu control encourages you to adopt is between *static* items (the root level items that are displayed in the page when it's first generated) and *dynamic* items (the items in fly-out menus that are added when the user moves the mouse over a portion of the menu). In most websites, there is a definite difference in the styling of these two elements. To support this, the Menu class defines two parallel sets of styles, one that applies to static items and one that applies to dynamic items, as shown in Table 16-13.

Table 16-13. *Menu Styles*

Static Style	Dynamic Style	Description
StaticMenuStyle	DynamicMenuStyle	Sets the appearance of the overall "box" in which all the menu items appear. In the case of StaticMenuStyle, this box is shown on the page, whereas with DynamicMenuStyle it's shown as a pop-up.
StaticMenuItemStyle	DynamicMenuItemStyle	Sets the appearance of individual menu items.
StaticDynamicSelectedStyle	DynamicSelectedStyle	Sets the appearance of the selected item. Note that the selected item isn't the item that's currently being hovered over. It's the item that was previously clicked (and triggered the last postback).
StaticHoverStyle	DynamicHoverStyle	Sets the appearance of the item that the user is hovering over with the mouse.

Along with these styles, you can set level-specific styles so that each level of menu and submenu is different. You do this using three collections: LevelMenuItemStyles, LevelSubMenuStyles, LevelSelectedStyles. These collections apply to ordinary menus, menus that contain other items, and selected menu items, respectively.

It might seem like there's a fair bit of unnecessary work here in separating dynamic and static styles. The reason for this model becomes obvious when you consider another remarkable feature of the Menu control—it allows you to choose the number of static levels. By default, there is only one static level, and everything else is displayed as a fly-out menu when the user hovers over the corresponding parent. But you can set the Menu.StaticDisplayLevels property to change all that. If you set it to 2, for example, the first two levels of the menu will be rendered in the page, using the static styles. (You can control the indentation of each level using the StaticSubMenuIndent property.)

Figure 16-20 shows the previous example with this change. Note that the items still change as you hover over them, and selection works in the same way. If you want, you can make your entire menu static.

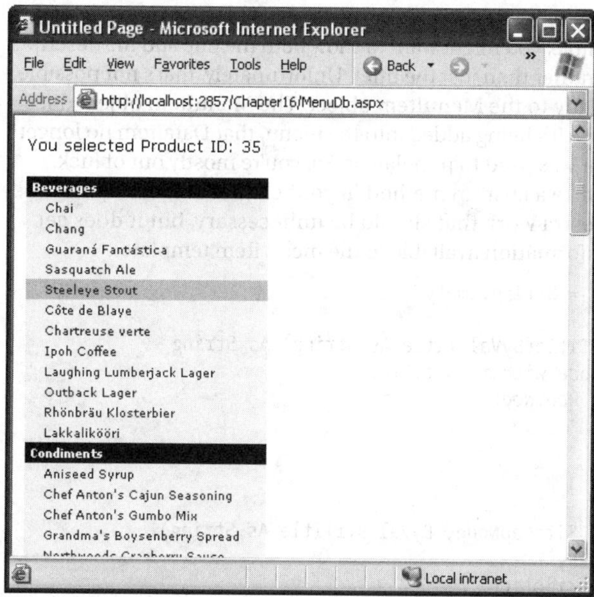

Figure 16-20. *A menu with two static levels*

■ **Tip** The Menu control exposes many more top-level properties for tweaking specific rendering aspects. For example, you can set the delay before a pop-up menu disappears (DisappearAfter), the default images used for expansion icons and separators, the scrolling behavior (which kicks into gear when the browser window is too small to fit a pop-up menu), and much more. Consult MSDN for a full list of properties.

Menu Templates

The Menu control also supports templates through the StaticMenuItemTemplate and DynamicMenuItemTemplate properties. These templates determine the HTML that's rendered for each menu item, giving you complete control.

Interestingly, whether you fill the Menu class declaratively or programmatically, you can still use a template. From the template's point of view, you're always binding to a MenuItem object. That means your template always needs to extract the value for the item from the MenuItem.Text property, as shown here:

```
<asp:Menu ID="Menu1" runat="server">
  <StaticItemTemplate>
    <%# Eval("Text") %>
  </StaticItemTemplate>
</asp:Menu>
```

One reason you might want to use the template features of the Menu is to show multiple pieces of information from a data object. For example, you might want to show both the title and the description from the SiteMapNode for this item (rather than just the title). Unfortunately, that's not possible. The problem is that the Menu binds directly to the MenuItem object. The MenuItem object does expose a DataItem property, but by the time it's being added into the menu, that DataItem no longer has the reference to the SiteMapNode that was used to populate it. So, you're mostly out of luck.

If you're really desperate, you can write a custom method in your class that looks up the SiteMapNode based on its URL. This is extra work that should be unnecessary, but it does get the job done of making the description information available to the menu item template.

```
Private matchingDescription As String = String.Empty

Protected Function GetDescriptionFromTitle(ByVal title As String) As String
    ' This assumes there's only one node with this title.
    Dim node As SiteMapNode = SiteMap.RootNode
    SearchNodes(node, title)
    Return matchingDescription
End Function

Private Sub SearchNodes(ByVal node As SiteMapNode, ByVal strTitle As String)
    If node.Title = strTitle Then
        matchingDescription = node.Description
        Return
    Else
        For Each child As SiteMapNode In node.ChildNodes
            ' Perform recursive search.
            SearchNodes(child, strTitle)
        Next
    End If
End Sub
```

Now you can use the GetDescriptionFromTitle() method in a template:

```
<asp:Menu ID="Menu1" runat="server" DataSourceID="SiteMapDataSource1">
  <StaticItemTemplate>
    <%# Eval("Text") %><br />
    <small>
    <%# GetDescriptionFromTitle(CType(Container.DataItem,MenuItem).Text) %>
    </small>
  </StaticItemTemplate>
  <DynamicItemTemplate>
    <%# Eval("Text") %><br />
    <small>
    <%# GetDescriptionFromTitle(CType(Container.DataItem,MenuItem).Text) %>

    </small>
  </DynamicItemTemplate>
</asp:Menu>
```

Finally, you can declare data bindings for the Menu control that specifically map out what property in the bound object should be used for the MenuItem text. This isn't much help if you want to display both the title and description, because it accepts only one field. However, it's fairly easy to show the title as the text and the description as the tooltip text:

```
<asp:Menu ID="Menu1" runat="server" DataSourceID="SiteMapDataSource1">
  <DataBindings>
    <asp:MenuItemBinding DataMember="SiteMapNode" TextField="Title"
     ToolTipField="Description" />
  </DataBindings>
</asp:Menu>
```

Summary

In this chapter you explored a variety of navigation features. You started with the multipane MultiView and Wizard controls. You then delved into the new navigation model and learned how to define site maps, bind the navigation data, and extend the site map provider infrastructure. Finally, you considered two rich controls that are especially suited for navigation data, the TreeView and Menu.

CHAPTER 17

■ ■ ■

Resources and Localization

Because more and more companies are reaching international markets through the Internet, supporting different cultures through your applications is essential for being successful. The .NET Framework comes with an integrated infrastructure for creating international applications.

Basically, the common language runtime (CLR) supports a mechanism for packaging and deploying resources with any type of application. The CLR and the base class library of the .NET Framework come with several classes for managing and accessing resources in applications. These classes are located in the System.Resources and System.Globalization namespaces.

In this chapter, you will learn all the necessary details for working with resources in ASP.NET applications and for creating international ASP.NET applications based on embedded resources and the integrated localization support.

Resources in .NET Applications

Usually applications use a number of images and strings for purposes such as toolbar or menu icons, menu captions, and label captions. Changing those strings and images can get really ugly if you put them directly in the source code. To make changing those strings and images in the program as easy as possible without having to go through the entire source code and search for them, you can put them in separate files and change them in only one place.

The .NET Framework and the CLR offer great support for this approach through embedded *resources*. You can put every string, image, and other type of data that should not exist directly in source code in separate resource files. Usually these resources are compiled into the binaries of the application itself. Therefore, they are automatically deployed with the application, and no extra deployment steps are necessary.

The primary use case for resources is localization. Using resources, you can define values for control properties (such as the text of a Label control) in different resource files—one for each culture the application supports. Each of these resource files contains strings (key/value pairs) for the localized properties of the control translated into the corresponding culture. At runtime the CLR loads these resources from the appropriate embedded resource files and applies them to the control's properties.

But localization is not the only useful application for resources. In Windows applications, resources are also used for toolbar, menu, and status icons so that they don't need to be deployed separately with the application (which is not common for web applications). You can also use resources in custom installer classes for embedding additional deployment scripts (such as database creation scripts or COM+ catalog modifications) so that you don't need to deploy them separately within the deployment process.

The definitions for resources are usually stored in .resx files. These .resx resource files are just XML files containing either string values or references to external files. These strings and referenced files are then compiled as embedded resources into the binaries of the application. You can add resources to your project by selecting Add ➤ Assembly Resource File.

The following example shows an excerpt of a sample .resx file. The file contains simple strings as well as a reference to an external image file.

```
<root>
    <resheader name="resmimetype">
        <value>text/microsoft-resx</value>
    </resheader>
    <resheader name="version">
        <value>2.0</value>
    </resheader>
    ...
    <data name="Binary Code Sm"
                type="System.Resources.ResXFileRef, System.Windows.Forms">
        <value>
            Binary Code Sm.png;System.Drawing.Bitmap, System.Drawing,
            Version=2.0.0.0, Culture=neutral, PublicKeyToken=b03f5f7f11d50a3a
        </value>
    </data>
    <data name="LegendAge">
        <value xml:space="preserve">Age</value>
    </data>
    <data name="LegendFirstname">
        <value xml:space="preserve">Firstname</value>
    </data>
    <data name="LegendLastname">
        <value xml:space="preserve">Lastname</value>
    </data>
</root>
```

■ **Note** This is just an excerpt of the .resx file. Visual Studio usually generates a bunch of comments and the XML schema for the resource file in the same XML file automatically.

Another way of compiling files as embedded resources in the application is to add them to the project and select the value Embedded Resource for the BuildAction property in the Properties window for the file. But this works only for Windows projects such as class libraries, Windows services, or Windows Forms applications. For ASP.NET applications, you have to take the approach introduced in this chapter. In any case, you can then access resources programmatically through the ResourceManager class.

■ **Note** You can also add resources as text files to the application. These text files consist of key/value pairs, one per line, in the format key = value. They can be compiled with the resgen.exe tool into a binary format with the file extension .resources. You can then add such .resources files as embedded resources (BuildAction=EmbeddedResource) to your application. But because this is the old way of managing resources, we suggest not using it.

While going through the following web application sample, you will learn how you can use resources both for populating control properties and for getting some other information such as document templates for report generation. The web application requires users to enter their first name, last name, and age. Based on this information, the application generates a simple Microsoft Word document. For this purpose, a template of the Microsoft Word document to be generated is bound to an XML schema, saved in XML format, and added as an embedded resource.

■ **Note** The XML features of Microsoft Office 2003 introduced in this chapter require Microsoft Word 2003 Professional Edition on the client (not on the server). If you don't have Microsoft Word 2003, you can test the same concepts with your own custom file templates. If you want to learn more details about Microsoft Office 2003 and XML, browse to `http://msdn.microsoft.com/office`.

All strings as well as the Microsoft Word document used in the application are embedded as resources. After adding an assembly resource file to the project, Visual Studio offers a resource editor for modifying the contents of the .resx file. It enables you to add strings as well as any other type of file to the project, as shown in Figure 17-1.

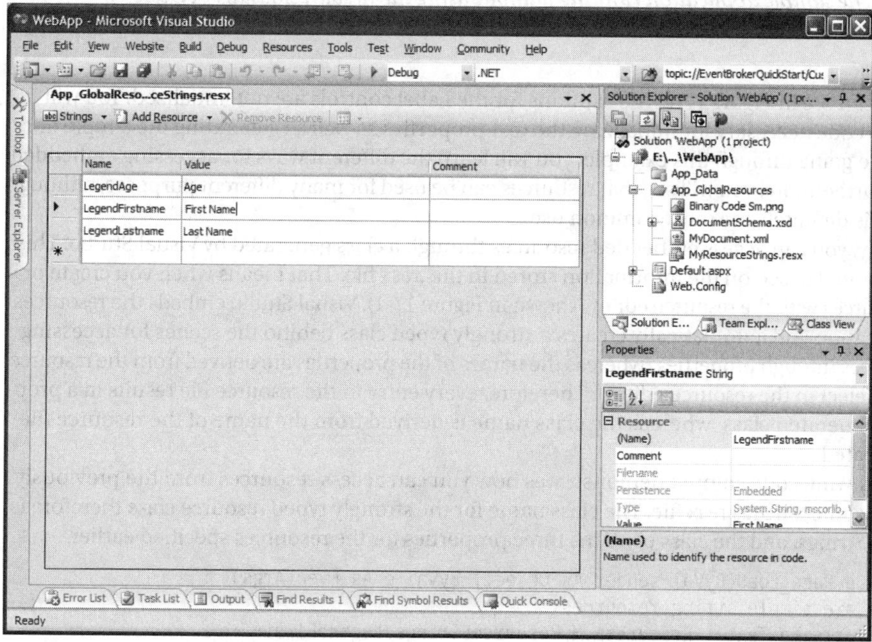

Figure 17-1. *The Visual Studio 2005 resource editor*

Through Add ➤ Add Existing File, you can add any external file stored in any format on the hard disk to the project. These files are automatically added to one of the resource directories of the ASP.NET website and compiled as embedded resources into the resulting binaries. Visual Studio and ASP.NET distinguish between global resources and local resources. *Global resources* are accessible from within any page of the application, and *local resources* exist on a per-page basis and are accessible from within their page only. Further, .resx files added to the App_GlobalResources folder are accessible from within all pages of the application. Figure 17-2 shows the current layout of the application running without using these embedded resources.

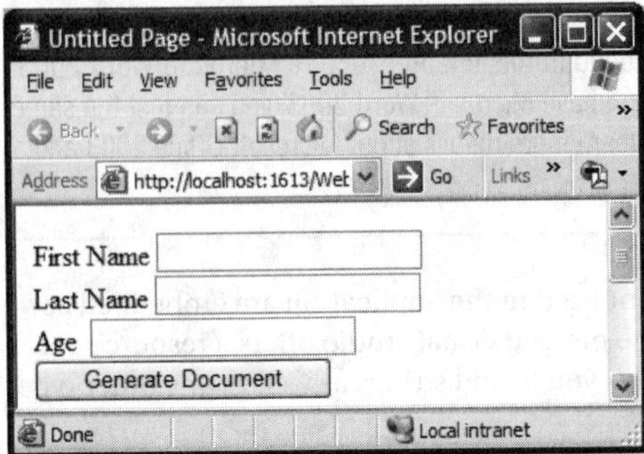

Figure 17-2. *The sample application running without using the ResourceManager class*

As you can see in Figure 17-2, the captions for the Label controls are not initialized. You will now add the code necessary for initializing the text properties as well as generating the simple document. While going through this example, you will learn the different ways for accessing embedded resources. Furthermore, you will see that resources can be used for many different purposes, although localization is definitely the most common use.

Basically, you can access embedded resources through a class generated by Visual Studio. This class is generated based on the information stored in the .resx file. That means when you create or modify resources with the resource editor (shown in Figure 17-1), Visual Studio embeds the resources in the application and automatically creates a strongly typed class behind the scenes for accessing these resources through properties (whereas the names of the properties are derived from the resource names you select in the resource editor). Therefore, every entry in the resource file results in a property of this generated class, whereas the class name is derived from the name of the resource file you have created.

The following code snippet demonstrates how you can access resources from the previously added MyResourceStrings.resx file. The class name for the strongly typed resource class therefore is MyResourceStrings, and the class contains three properties for the resources specified earlier.

```
Protected Sub Page_Load(ByVal sender As Object, ByVal e As EventArgs)
    ' These are simple string resources.
    LegendFirstname.Text = Resources.MyResourceStrings.LegendFirstname
    LegendLastname.Text = Resources.MyResourceStrings.LegendLastname
    LegendAge.Text = Resources.MyResourceStrings.LegendAge

    ' This is the XML document added to the resources as a file.
    DocumentXml.DocumentContent = Resources.MyResourceStrings.MyDocument
End Sub
```

Note Later, in the "Localization of Web Applications" section, you will see how Visual Studio 2005 and ASP.NET 2.0 provide much better support for localizing captions and other properties of controls. In this part of the chapter, we just want to show you the low-level API for managing any type of resources, not just localization resources.

Internally, the generated class uses an instance of the ResourceManager class, which is defined in the System.Resources namespace. The instance of this class is accessible through the generated class's ResourceManager property. Internally, the property procedures for accessing the embedded resources themselves are just wrappers around calls of one of the GetXxx methods (that is, GetString or GetStream) of this ResourceManager instance. For example, the resource that is accessible through the generated property procedure Resources.MyResourceStrings.LegendAge is also accessible through ResourceManager.GetString("LegendAge"), as shown in Figure 17-3.

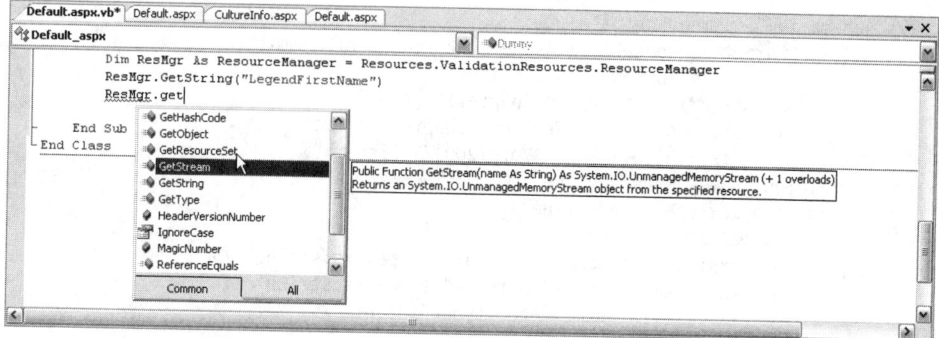

Figure 17-3. *The ResourceManager class's methods*

The ResourceManager property of the generated class creates an instance of the resource manager automatically, as shown in the following code snippet. Of course, anybody can do this.

```
Dim ResMgr As New ResourceManager("Resources.MyResourceStrings",
                System.Reflection.Assembly.GetAssembly
                (GetType(Resources.MyResourceStrings)))
```

The first parameter specifies the base name for the resources that should be loaded by the ResourceManager class. The second parameter specifies the assembly into which the resources have been compiled. If the resources are compiled into the assembly that executes this code, using the GetExecutingAssembly() method of the System.Reflection.Assembly class is sufficient. Mostly this is true for class libraries or classic Windows applications. ASP.NET is a little bit different, as it generates and compiles the assemblies automatically. Internally, the ASP.NET infrastructure actually creates different assemblies for the page code and global resources. And the name of the dynamically generated assembly is basically unknown, as it is determined by the infrastructure as well. Therefore, using the GetExecutingAssembly() method won't work. Alternatively, using the GetAssembly method with the type description of the generated resource class is a possible way of creating a custom instance of the ResourceManager class, because this type resides in the assembly created by ASP.NET for the embedded resources contained in this class.

As you know how to use resources now, you will see some code for generating the Microsoft Word document when the user clicks the button on the page. For this purpose, you can leverage the XML functionality of Microsoft Word 2003 by completing the following steps:

1. First, create a Microsoft Word document as usual and then save it as an XML document instead of the binary DOC format. You can select the format in the File Types list of the Save dialog box in Microsoft Word.

2. Next, create an XML schema. You must connect this XML schema to the Microsoft Word document through the XML Structure task pane. You get the task pane by selecting View ➤ Task Pane and then clicking the title of the task pane. From the menu, select XML Structure. This task pane allows you to add an XML schema to the document and attach the XML schema's elements to sections of the Microsoft Word document. Your application will use the elements defined in this XML schema for finding the appropriate sections in the document for generating contents through System.Xml. (You can find details about System.Xml in Chapter 12.)

3. Finally, add the XML Word document as a resource to your solution with the previously introduced resource editor (refer to Figure 17-1). The XML schema to create your solution is as follows. After you have created the schema, you can create the Word document and bind the schema to the document through the XML Structure task pane. Figure 17-4 shows the Word document with XML elements associated (and shows the XML Structure task pane).

```
<xs:schema id="DocumentSchema"
        targetNamespace="uri:AspNetPro20/Chapter17/Demo1"
        elementFormDefault="qualified"
        xmlns="uri:AspNetPro20/Chapter17/Demo1"
        xmlns:mstns="uri:AspNetPro20/Chapter17/Demo1"
        xmlns:xs="http://www.w3.org/2001/XMLSchema">
    <xs:element name="MyPersonType">
        <xs:complexType mixed="true">
            <xs:all>
                <xs:element name="Firstname" type="xs:string" />
                <xs:element name="Lastname" type="xs:string" />
                <xs:element name="Age" type="xs:int" />
            </xs:all>
        </xs:complexType>
    </xs:element>
</xs:schema>
```

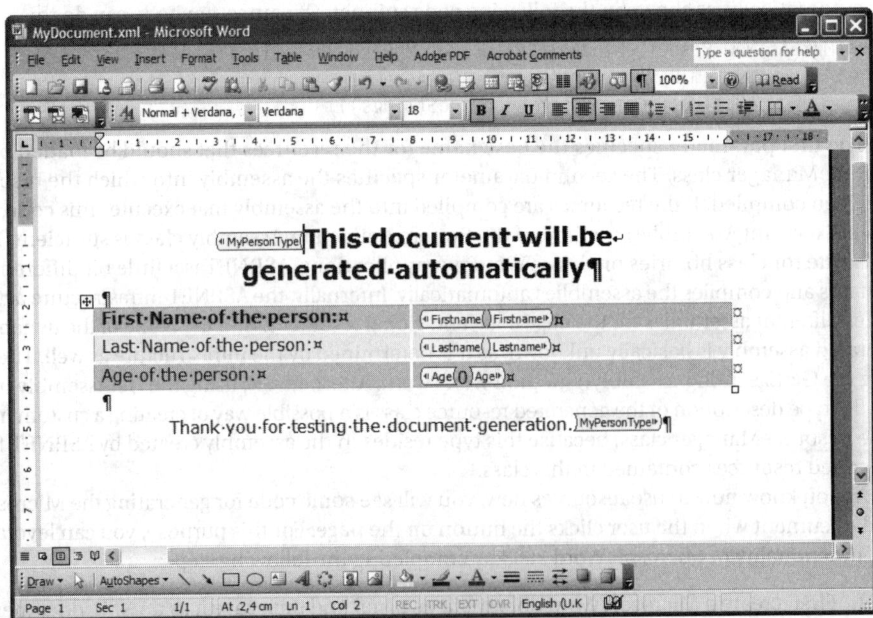

Figure 17-4. *The Microsoft Word document connected with the XML schema*

Generating the Microsoft Word document based on the XML template created previously requires nothing more than loading it from the embedded resources into an instance of XmlDocument. (You can find more information about XML in Chapter 12.) When taking a closer look at the Microsoft Word document that has been saved as XML, you will see that the XML elements defined by the schema are directly incorporated into the XML elements that define the Microsoft Word formatting and contents.

The following listing shows an excerpt of the Microsoft Word document saved as an XML file (which has been embedded as a resource in your application):

```
<?xml version="1.0" encoding="UTF-8" standalone="yes" ?>
<?mso-application progid="Word.Document"?>
<w:wordDocument xmlns:w="http://schemas.microsoft.com/office/word/2003/wordml"
...
  xmlns:ns1="uri:AspNetPro20/Chapter17/Demo1">
  <o:DocumentProperties>
    <o:Title>This document will automatically be generated:</o:Title>
    <o:Author>VB.NET Trainings</o:Author>
    <o:LastAuthor>VB.NET Trainings</o:LastAuthor>
    <o:Revision>8</o:Revision>
    <o:TotalTime>0</o:TotalTime>
...
...
  <w:body>
    <wx:sect>
      <ns1:MyPersonType>
        <w:p>
          <w:r>
            <w:rPr>
              <w:rFonts w:ascii="Verdana" w:h-ansi="Verdana" />
              <wx:font wx:val="Verdana" />
              <w:b />
              <w:sz w:val="36" />
              <w:sz-cs w:val="36" />
              <w:lang w:val="EN-GB" />
            </w:rPr>
            <w:t>This document will be</w:t>
          </w:r>
...
...
            <ns1:Firstname>
              <w:tc>
                <w:tcPr>
                  <w:tcW w:w="4606" w:type="dxa" />
                </w:tcPr>
                <w:p>
                    ...
                </w:p>
              </w:tc>
            </ns1:Firstname>
...
      </ns1:MyPersonType>
    </wx:sect>
  </w:body>
</w:wordDocument>
```

As you can see, the elements defined in the previously created XML schema are included directly in the Microsoft Word XML file. All the other tags you can see define the formatting and the other options that make up a complete Microsoft Word document. That means all the things that were encapsulated in the binary format of Microsoft Word documents (the DOC format) are now available as XML as well. This is what makes processing Microsoft Word documents on the server side from within web applications as easy as processing XML files. The XML schema that defines the Microsoft Word XML elements is well documented and can be downloaded (including the documentation) from `http://msdn.microsoft.com/office`. You need to know two things about this example; first, you can load this Microsoft Word document into an instance of XmlDocument and then change its contents through simple XML operations such as cloning nodes or adding new nodes. Second, you need to know the meaning of one special XML tag: the <w:r /> tag tag>, which is called *word run*. A word run is an XML fragment of a Microsoft Word document that encapsulates simple text within a paragraph. Therefore, if you want to programmatically enter text into a specific position within the XML Microsoft Word document, you have to complete the following steps:

1. Open the Microsoft Word document with System.Xml.XmlDocument.
2. Execute an XPath query for finding an element of your custom XML schema, such as the ns1:Firstname element in the document presented earlier.
3. Then execute another XPath query on the node returned from the last XPath query for finding the next word run (<w:r />>) below the custom XML node (ns1:Firstname).
4. Finally, within the <w:r> tag, you can add a <w:t> tag (Microsoft Word text) that then contains the text you want to add to the Microsoft Word document.

The following code shows how you can open the Microsoft Word document with the XmlDocument class. It then executes an XPath query for finding the ns1:Firstname element within the document. After it has found this element, it changes the InnerXml to a word run that contains just the text entered by the user into the ASP.NET TextBox control. Afterward, it does the same steps for the ns1:Lastname and ns1:Age sections.

```
Protected Sub GenerateAction_Click(ByVal sender As Object, ByVal e As EventArgs)
    Dim doc As New XmlDocument()
    doc.LoadXml(Resources.MyResourceStrings.MyDocument)

    Dim TextNode As XmlNode
    Dim NsMgr As New XmlNamespaceManager(doc.NameTable)
    NsMgr.AddNamespace("ns1", "uri:AspNetPro20/Chapter17/Demo1")
    NsMgr.AddNamespace("w", "http://schemas.microsoft.com/office/word/2003/wordml")

    TextNode = doc.SelectSingleNode("//ns1:Firstname//w:p", NsMgr)
    TextNode.InnerXml = String.Format("<w:r><w:t>{0}</w:t></w:r>",
        TextFirstname.Text)

    TextNode = doc.SelectSingleNode("//ns1:Lastname//w:p", NsMgr)
    TextNode.InnerXml = String.Format("<w:r><w:t>{0}</w:t></w:r>",
        TextLastname.Text)

    TextNode = doc.SelectSingleNode("//ns1:Age//w:p", NsMgr)
    TextNode.InnerXml = String.Format("<w:r><w:t>{0}</w:t></w:r>", TextAge.Text)

    ' Clear the response.
    Response.Clear()
    Response.ContentType = "application/msword"
    Response.Write(doc.OuterXml)
    Response.End()
End Sub
```

Because the XML Microsoft Word document itself has been added as an embedded resource to your application, you can retrieve it through the generated resources class as was done in the previous code sample. Actually, the string template <w:r><w:t>{0}</w:r></w:t> used for adding the text to the Word document is a perfect candidate to be embedded as a resource.

Localization of Web Applications

The infrastructure presented in the first part of this chapter provides the fundamentals for localizing any type of .NET-based application, including Windows applications, class libraries, services, and (of course) web applications.

Before you learn about the technical details for localizing applications, we will discuss the major challenges in doing do. Figure 17-5 shows some challenges of localizing a web application.

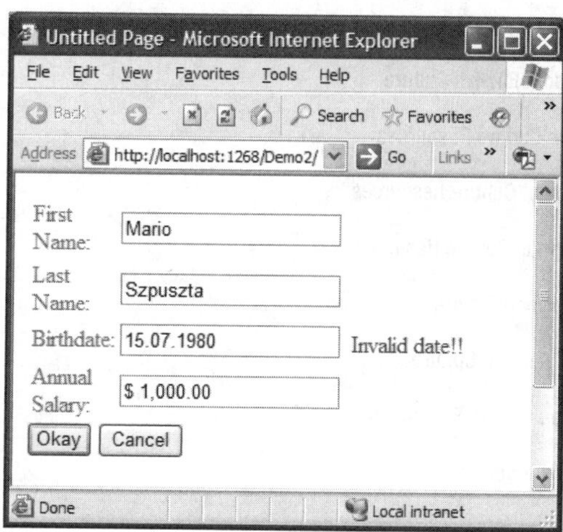

Figure 17-5. *Sample application showing localization challenges*

Although this is a simple example, it demonstrates some of the core challenges for localizing web applications. The simplest challenge, of course, is localizing the strings for the captions of the labels as well as the buttons. Also, you must localize the format for the currency values and for the dates and times. For that purpose, you need to localize the validation expression of the validation control.

Finally, when parsing the information in the code for storing it in a database or for other processing steps, you need to consider the format for dates, times, and currency values. All these values might be different and therefore customized from culture to culture.

Localization and the Common Language Runtime

Usually resources are created for every culture the application should support. In the earlier example, you learned how to create resources for the default culture, because we didn't specify any culture-specific information. These resources are used by the CLR as a last resort in the localization process.

The CLR defines a behavior for finding culture-specific resources. With that said, every set of resources has to define a base name that is specified through the first part of the name of the resource file. The second part of the name, which has been omitted in the first example of this chapter, defines the culture. If the culture portion in the name is not specified, the resources defined in the resource file are used as default resources. For example, if the base name of an embedded resource file is MyResourceStrings.resx, then the culture-specific name will be MyResourceStrings.en-US.resx.

The CLR defines a hierarchy of cultures and languages, as you can see in Figure 17-6. (For a complete list of cultures and their hierarchies, refer to the CultureInfo class in the MSDN documentation.)

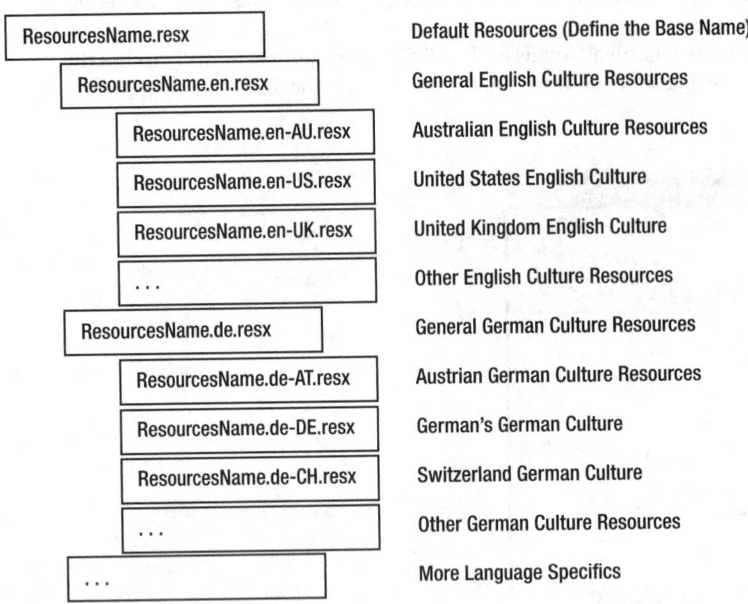

Figure 17-6. *The culture hierarchy defined by the CLR*

The CLR automatically finds culture-specific resources based on these hierarchies. Basically, it tries to find the closest matching set of resources for the current culture settings. More general culture resources are always used as a fallback if specific culture resources are not available. Further, if no culture resources are embedded for the current culture in the application, the CLR automatically uses the default resources embedded in the application. If the default resources don't include a value for the requested resource, the CLR throws an exception.

When loading resources through the ResourceManager class, you always specify the base name only. Therefore, when resource files with the names MyResourceStrings.resx and MyResourceStrings.en-US.resx have been added to the project, you use only the base name when instantiating the ResourceManager class, no matter which culture is going to be used. For example:

```
Dim ResMgr As New ResourceManager("Resources.MyResourceStrings",
          System.Reflection.Assembly.GetAssembly
                   (GetType(Resources.MyResourceStrings)))
```

■ **Note** ASP.NET automatically prefixes names for resources with the Resources prefix. So, the base name for (global) resources added to a web application project always has the format Resources.MyResourceFileName. When adding resources to a class library, for example, you can omit the Resources prefix.

Specifying culture-specific resource files is not mandatory. The CLR can load culture-specific resources from the resource files based on a "current" culture. But what is the current culture? HTTP specifies an HTTP header entry enabling the browser to send culture-specific information from the client to the server. Based on this information, you can create an instance of the CultureInfo class, as shown in the following section.

CultureInfo Class

Any culture-specific information is stored in an instance of the CultureInfo class. This class is defined in the System.Globalization namespace. It enables querying information such as the name of the culture, its date formats, its number formats, and the currency formats. The following code creates an instance of CultureInfo based on the language sent by the browser:

```
Protected Sub Page_Load(ByVal sender As Object, ByVal e As EventArgs)
    Dim ci As CultureInfo
    If (Not Request.UserLanguages Is Nothing) AndAlso
                 (Request.UserLanguages.Length > 0) Then
        ci = New CultureInfo(Request.UserLanguages(0))
        Thread.CurrentThread.CurrentUICulture = ci
    Else
        ci = Thread.CurrentThread.CurrentUICulture
    End If

    Dim MessageBuilder As New StringBuilder()
    MessageBuilder.Append("Current culture info: ")
    MessageBuilder.Append("<br/>")
    MessageBuilder.AppendFormat("-) Name: {0}", ci.Name)
    MessageBuilder.Append("<br/>")
    MessageBuilder.AppendFormat("-) ISO Name: {0}", ci.ThreeLetterISOLanguageName)
    MessageBuilder.Append("<br/>")
    MessageBuilder.Append("-) Currency Symbol: " & ci.NumberFormat.CurrencySymbol)
    MessageBuilder.Append("<br/>")
    MessageBuilder.Append("-) Long Date Pattern: " _
        & ci.DateTimeFormat.LongDatePattern)

    LegendCI.Text = MessageBuilder.ToString()
End Sub
```

The Request object includes a property called UserLanguages. This property includes language information the browser sent through the HTTP header to the server. But sending culture information through the HTTP header is optional and therefore might not be available to the web application. In that case, you can specify a default culture in the web.config file as follows:

```
<globalization enableClientBasedCulture="true"
               culture="de-DE"
               uiCulture="de-DE"/>
```

The settings specified in this element of the configuration are automatically set onto the Thread.CurrentThread.CurrentUICulture and Thread.CurrentThread.CurrentCulture properties. The CLR uses these properties for finding the appropriate data in the embedded resources as well as for controlling formatting functions such as ToString() or Parse of different, culture-aware types such as DateTime or Decimal.

Therefore, if the browser sends culture-specific information from the client, you need to override the settings, as demonstrated in the previous code example at the beginning of the Page_Load event. The CurrentCulture property affects the behavior of formatting functions. For example, if you call DateTime.Now.ToString or DateTime.Now.Parse, it uses the date format based on the CurrentCulture property of the thread. The same is true for number formats.

On the other hand, the ResourceManager uses CurrentUICulture to look up culture-specific resources. That means when a request is received from the browser, ASP.NET automatically initializes the property CurrentUICulture of the System.Threading.Thread.CurrentThread instance. Based on this CurrentUICulture property, as well as the culture hierarchy defined by the CLR (shown in Figure 17-6), the ResourceManager class automatically retrieves localized resources from the appropriate embedded resources when calling one of the GetXxx methods. Table 17-1 demonstrates some examples of this behavior if the following resource files are present for an application:

MyResources.resx: Default resources with values for Firstname, Lastname, Age, and DocumentName

MyResources.en.resx: Default resources for English cultures with values for Firstname, Lastname, and Age

MyResources.de.resx: Default resources for German cultures with values for Firstname, Lastname, and Age

MyResources.de-DE.resx: Resources for the German's German culture with values for Firstname and Lastname

MyResources.de-AT.resx: Resources for the Austrian's German culture with values for Firstname and Lastname

Table 17-1. *Examples for the ResourceManager's Behavior in Certain Situations*

CurrentUICulture	Method Call	Result
en-US	GetString("Firstname")	The value Firstname of MyResources.en.resx is used, as no resources exist for the US English culture in the application.
en-UK	GetString("Firstname")	The value Firstname of MyResources.en.resx, as no resources exist for the UK English culture in the application.
en-US	GetString("DocName")	The value DocumentName of MyResources.resx is used, as no value is specified in the resource file for the English culture for the key DocName.
de-DE	GetString("Firstname")	The value Firstname of MyResources.de-DE.resx is used.
de-DE	GetString("Age")	The value Age of MyResources.de.resx is used, as the value is not specified in the file MyResources.de-DE.resx.
de-AT	GetString("Lastname")	The value Lastname of MyResources.de-AT.resx is used.
de-AT	GetString("DocumentName")	The value DocumentName of MyResources.resx is used, as this value doesn't exist in MyResources.de-AT.resx as well as in MyResources.de.resx.

Local Resources for a Single Page

The classes you have seen up until now provide the basic infrastructure for localizing .NET-based applications of any type. With ASP.NET 1.*x*, you had to use this infrastructure for manually localizing the contents of your controls.

Fortunately, this has changed with the release of ASP.NET 2.0 and Visual Studio 2005, which now support the web developer in the same fashion Windows Forms did for localization from the start. For localizing a page, just select Tools ➤ Generate Local Resources. Visual Studio then generates a resource file in the App_LocalResources folder, which includes the values for every control of the page currently open in design view. Figure 17-7 shows the resources generated for the earlier example.

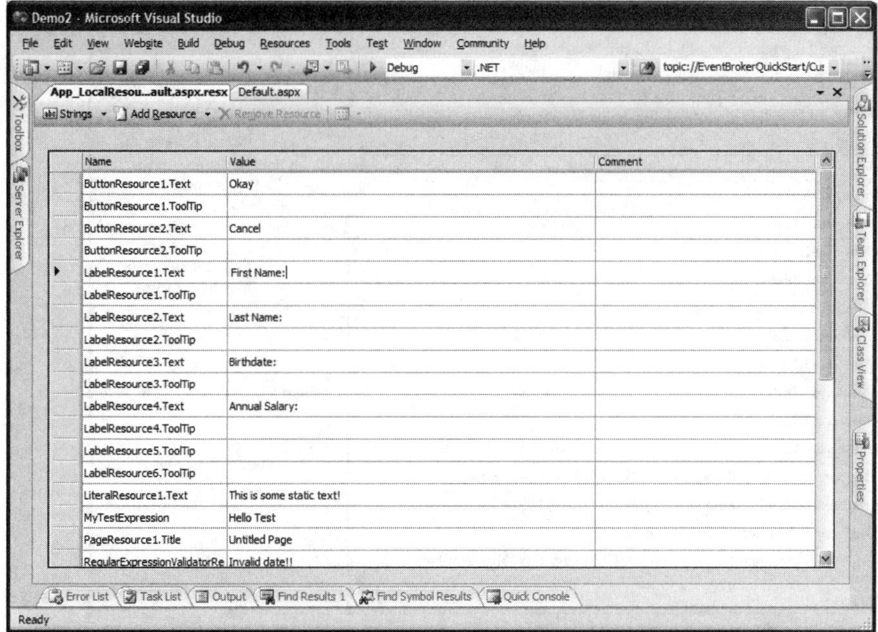

Figure 17-7. *Generated resources for the application introduced in Figure 17-5*

Visual Studio generates resources for several properties of each control. The resources are always prefixed with the name of the control and postfixed with the name of the property. Visual Studio automatically generates the default resources for the controls of the page only. You must add any further culture-specific resources manually by copying the generated resources and giving them the appropriate name (for example, Default.aspx.en-US.resx).

The resource generation tool creates an entry for every property that is marked with the <Localizable()> attribute (from the System.ComponentModel namespace) in the control. Therefore, if you want to create a custom, localizable control, you have to mark all <Localizable()> properties with this attribute, like so:

```
<Localizable(True)> _
Public Property MyProperty() As String
    Get
           ...
    End Get
    Set
           ...
    End Set
End Property
```

Copying the resources created previously and renaming this copy to Default.aspx.de.resx adds the culture-specific resources for the German culture to the application; the runtime is then able to initialize the control properties based on the CurrentUICulture of the thread with the strings contained in the embedded resource file for this culture. Figure 17-8 shows the adapted resource file, Figure 17-9 shows the result of browsing with German locale settings, and Figure 17-10 show the results of browsing with English locale settings.

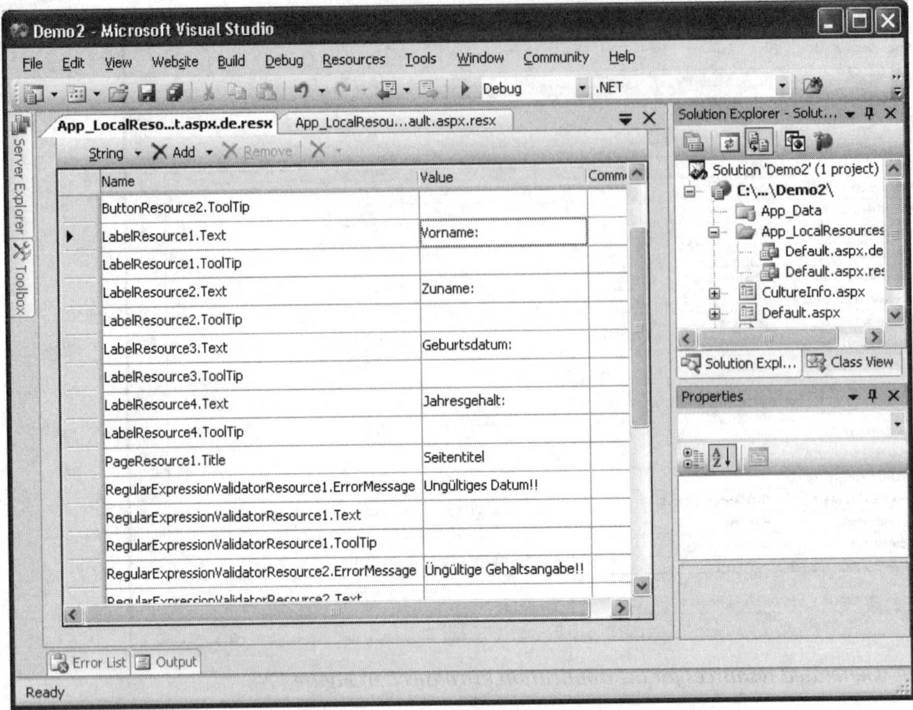

Figure 17-8. *Added resource file for a different culture*

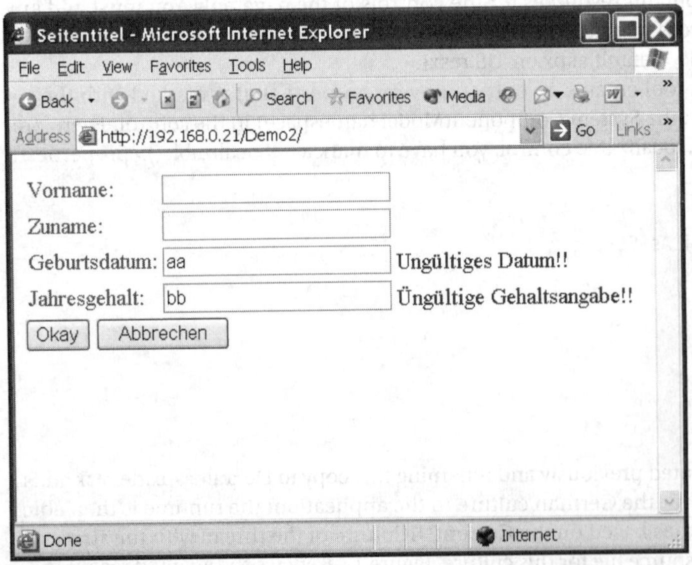

Figure 17-9. *Browsing with German locale settings*

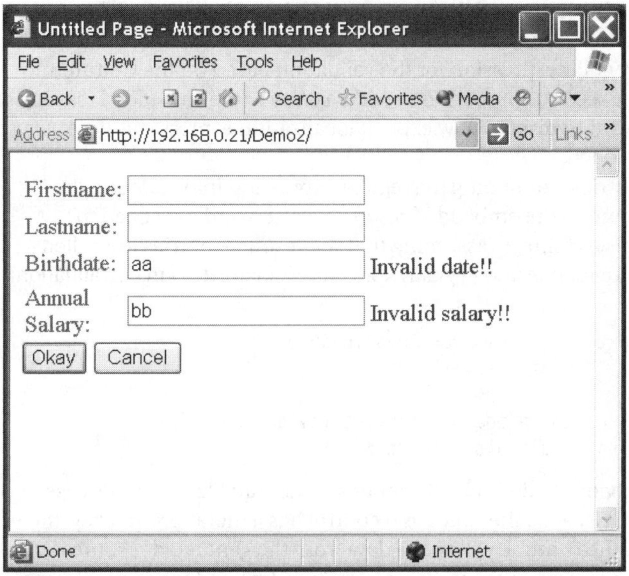

Figure 17-10. *Browsing with English locale settings*

In addition to generating the resource file, Visual Studio has changed the page's source code. For every <Localizable()> property of each control placed on the page, it has added a localization expression, as shown in the following code snippet:

```
<asp:Label ID="LegendFirstname" runat="server" Text="Firstname:"
        meta:resourcekey="LabelResource1"></asp:Label>
```

Localization expressions are identified by the meta:resourceKey attribute of the tag. During the page-parsing process, the runtime goes through the controls and generates the necessary code for getting the resource through the ResourceManager class. The declarative property assignments remain untouched and will be displayed in the design mode.

The localization expression in the previous code snippet is a so-called implicit localization expression. *Implicit localization expressions* are something like shortcuts to resource keys included in the embedded resources for a page. They have to adhere to the naming conventions used by Visual Studio for generating the resources (for example, Resourcekey.Propertyname). Implicit localization expressions just specify the base resource key for the embedded resource without a property name. Property names are derived from the second part of the name.

Therefore, you can use implicit localization expressions for <Localizable()> properties only. Further, they don't work for global applications resources. Another way to bind control properties to resources is using *explicit localization expressions*. These offer enhanced flexibility by enabling binding of any control property to embedded resources, and they work with global application resources as well. You will learn about explicit localization expressions in the next section, which gives details about global resources.

If you take a closer look at the generated resource files in Figures 17-7 and 17-8, you will see that you are not done yet. Although the RegularExpressionValidator control is included in the generated resources, the validation expression property is not included, because it is not marked with the <Localizable()> attribute. But the validation of both the birth date and the annual salary has to happen based on the culture settings of the user browsing to the page, because US visitors want to add their birth date in the format they are used to (and the same goes for Germans, Austrians, and other visitors).

Therefore, you need to do some additional work before you are finished localizing the application. Basically, two ways for localizing the validation of those two text fields are available. The first one is to automatically generate the regular expression for the validation based on the CultureInfo object created for the user's culture. The second approach is to add an entry to the embedded resources for the validation expression. As we want to discuss how explicit localization expressions work, we will show how to take the second approach.

First, you have to add two new entries, containing the regular expression for validating the user's birth date and annual salary input, to the embedded resources. Afterward, you need to change the definition of those controls as follows (assuming that the resource entries are called RegularExpressionValidatorResource1.Validation and RegularExpressionValidatorResource2.Validation):

```
<asp:RegularExpressionValidator
   ControlToValidate="BirthdateText" ErrorMessage="Invalid date!!"
   ID="RegularExpressionValidator1" runat="server"
   ValidationExpression=
      '<%$ Resources: RegularExpressionValidatorResource1.Validation %>'
   meta:resourcekey="RegularExpressionValidatorResource1" />
```

You can probably see that the previous validator still contains some static text—in this case ErrorMessage. Don't worry about that. Because the validation control has a meta:resourcekey, the control will ignore the static text, and the runtime will get its data from the generated resources. As soon as a control has such a meta:resourcekey attribute, it ignores static text and reads all information from embedded, localized resources. In the case of the ValidationExpression, you have to use explicit localization expressions, because automatic localization is not provided for this property. The general format for explicit localization expressions follows this syntax:

```
<%$ Resources: [ApplicationKey, ] ResourceKey %>
```

The application key identifies shared application resources and therefore can be omitted when accessing local resources. Figure 17-11 shows that localized properties are marked with special icons in the Properties window. The localization expressions themselves leverage the new expression engine included with ASP.NET 2.0.

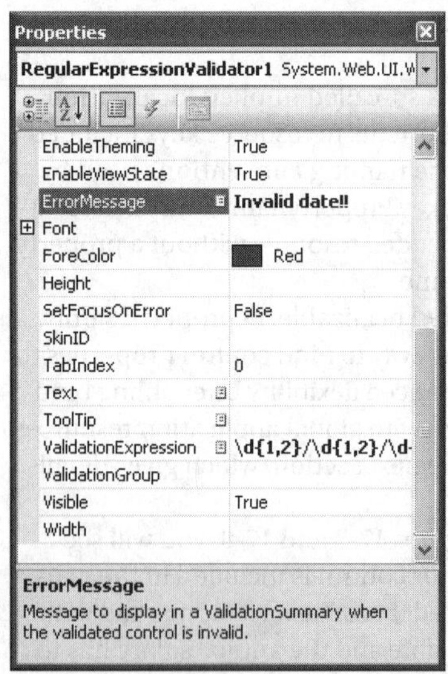

Figure 17-11. *Localized attributes marked in the Properties window*

You can edit expressions for all properties through the new expression editor. The Properties window includes a new Expressions property on the top. When you click the ellipsis button, the expression editor opens, as shown in Figure 17-12. The ClassKey property specifies the ApplicationKey parameter for the explicit localization expression, and the other one specifies the resource key. Actually, it specifies the name of the class generated for the global resources.

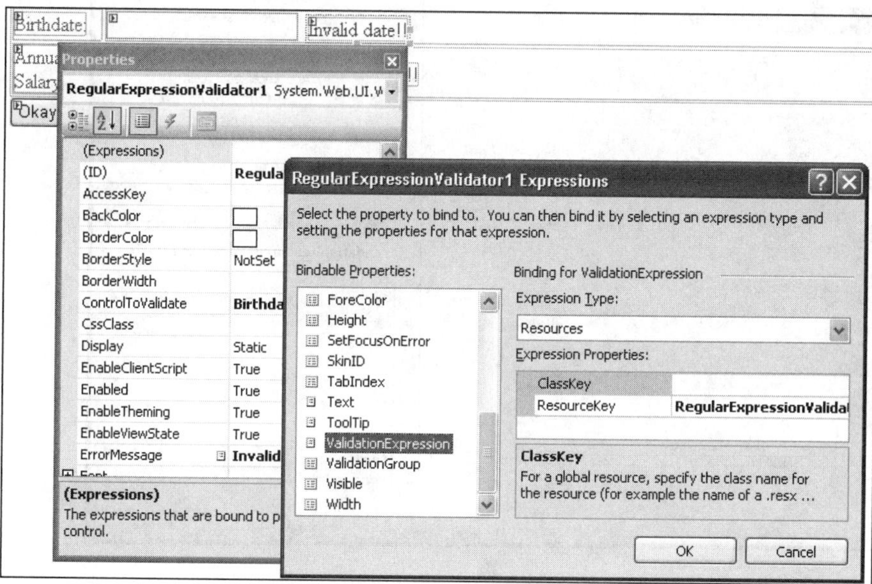

Figure 17-12. *The new expression editor*

Sharing Resources Between Pages

Generating local resources for a single page might lead to a duplication of resource strings or other resource information. Therefore, it is definitely useful to share resources between pages through global resources.

The tool support for shared resources in terms of generating and binding resources to controls is not as good as with local page resources. In the first example of this chapter, you saw how to use application global resources that can be shared across multiple pages. When adding assembly resources to a project, Visual Studio asks if it should place those resources into the global resource directory. If the resources are placed into this directory, they are accessible from within all pages.

As the validation expressions for date formats and number formants used earlier are definitely good candidates to be reused in several pages of the application, it is useful to put them into a global resource file. For this purpose you just need to add a new, global resource file and then add the values to those resources, as shown in Figure 17-13.

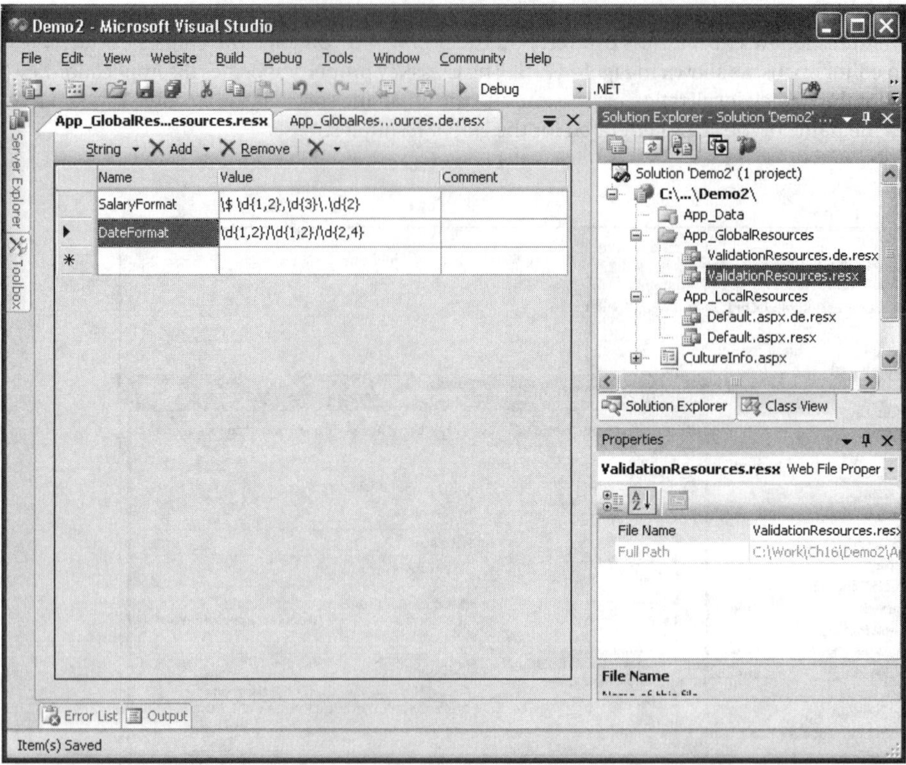

Figure 17-13. *Global resources added to the application*

Now you have to adopt the explicit localization expression for the two validation controls. For this purpose you have to change the name and add the ApplicationKey parameter. Because you named the global resource file ValidationResources.resx previously, this will be the value for the ApplicationKey property (without the .resx extension).

```
<asp:RegularExpressionValidator  ControlToValidate="BirthdateText"
    ErrorMessage="Invalid date!!" ID="RegularExpressionValidator1"
    runat="server"
    ValidationExpression='<%$ Resources:ValidationResources, DateFormat %>'
    meta:resourcekey="RegularExpressionValidatorResource1" />
```

Another big difference between local and global resources is how you access these resources programmatically. Although global resources can be accessed strongly typed through the generated resource class page, local resources have to be accessed through the GetLocalResourceObject method.

```
Me.GetLocalResourceObject("LabelResource1.Text")
```

■ **Note** Localization expressions and other type of expressions work for controls with the attribute runat="server" only. They are processed on the server side by the localization infrastructure of ASP.NET. Therefore, if you want to localize HTML controls with implicit or explicit localization expressions, you have to add the runat="server" attribute.

Basically, Visual Studio generates resources for every <Localizable()> property of every control of a page or user control opened in design view in the already described naming format of Resourcekey.Propertyname. If a property of a control is already bound to a resource through an explicit localization expression, resource generation for this property is omitted completely. Therefore, for localizing the other properties, it still includes the meta:resourceKey attribute for the control.

By the way, Visual Studio automatically generates a resource entry for the page's title and adds a meta:resourceKey attribute to the Page directive. And you can apply explicit localization expressions to the Page directive, like so:

```
<%@ Page Language="vb" ... Culture="auto"
                           UICulture="auto"
                           meta:resourcekey="PageResource1" %>
<%@ Page Language="vb" ... Culture="auto"
                           UICulture="auto"
        Title='<%$ Resources:ValidationResources, DateFormat %>' %>
```

The first example implicitly binds the page's properties such as the title to local resources, and the second example binds the page's title property to a global resource with the name DateFormat stored in the global ValidationResources class.

Furthermore, you can specify the default culture and UI culture settings at the page level in addition to the configuration in the web.config file demonstrated earlier.

Localizing Static Text

We have discussed how to use HTML controls with the attribute runat="server" for localization only. As they are processed on the server side, localizing properties of those controls is fairly easy. But what about static text and text directions?

Well, the answer is straightforward. ASP.NET 2.0 includes a new control based on the well-known Literal control that was introduced with the first version of ASP.NET. This new Localize control just needs to be wrapped around the static text, as shown in the following code snippet:

```
<asp:Localize runat=server
     meta:resourcekey="LiteralResource1"> is some static text!</asp:Localize>
```

If this control is wrapped around some text, this text portion of the page is automatically included in the resource generation process like any other control. The big difference between the Literal control and the Localize control is the behavior of the designer. Although the content of the Literal control cannot be edited in the designer, text wrapped into a Localize control can be edited like any other text content of the page.

Text Directions

Finally, you need a way to specify the text direction in international applications, because some cultures read from left to right and others read from right to left.

You can use a couple of controls in ASP.NET, such as the Panel control and the WebPart control, to deal with this. Therefore, it makes sense to define a property in either the global resources or the local resources for the text direction and to use explicit localization expressions for setting the direction property of these controls. For setting this property directly in the root element of your HTML file, you must use the runat="server" attribute to the <html> tag itself, and then you can apply explicit localization expressions to it, as shown in the following code excerpt:

```
<html runat="server"
      dir='<%$ Resources:ValidationResources, TextDirection %>'
      xmlns="http://www.w3.org/1999/xhtml" >
...
</html>
```

Summary

In this chapter you learned the fundamentals of creating international web applications with ASP.NET. First, you learned how .NET manages resources for applications and how you can access those resources programmatically. Furthermore, you saw that resources are not only useful for localization but also for other things, such as embedded default templates for reports (these can act as a fallback solution if no templates exist in other directories), additional setup scripts, or XML fragments used by your application.

Second, you learned about how the CLR manages culture-specific resources. The CLR selects embedded resources based on the CultureInfo set on the Thread.CurrentUICulture property. It includes a fallback mechanism (often referenced as *hub and spoke*) for locating resources by searching from the closest matching culture resources to the more general culture resources in a defined hierarchy of cultures. If it cannot find a matching culture, it uses the application's default culture for localization.

Finally, you learned how ASP.NET and Visual Studio support you with localizing web applications through local page resources as well as shared application resources. You learned how to access these resources programmatically as well as declaratively through implicit and explicit localization expressions.

CHAPTER 18

Website Deployment

Deploying an ASP.NET web application is just the process of copying the directory structure of your application and its files to the target server. Of course, once you've copied your application, you need to configure databases, configure security settings, and fine-tune the web server appropriately. The web server used in most scenarios is the one shipping with Windows—IIS. Using IIS, you can configure what directories are exposed as *virtual directories* and are thereby accessible to other clients that make calls over the network or the Internet.

In this chapter, you'll learn about the architecture of IIS 5 and 6, and you'll learn how to configure IIS. Afterward, you'll learn the specifics for deploying ASP.NET-based web applications, including the compilation model, side-by-side deployment with different versions of ASP.NET, and Visual Studio's deployment features. You'll also tackle a couple of advanced deployment topics, including the VirtualPathProvider (which lets you deploy web application pages to a database instead of the file system) and ASP.NET health monitoring (which helps you keep an eye on the state of your application in a production environment).

Internet Information Services (IIS)

IIS is, at its core, a Windows service that is responsible for processing requests received on specific ports. For this purpose, a service called the World Wide Web Publishing Service runs on the system. This service listens on a couple of TCP/IP network ports, usually port 80 for normal HTTP and port 443 for HTTPS. The service is managed by the IIS management console (also referred to as IIS Manager), where you can create multiple websites. For every website, you can register multiple ports, and at least one is necessary. A default installation consists of one default website running on port 80, as you can see in Figure 18-1.

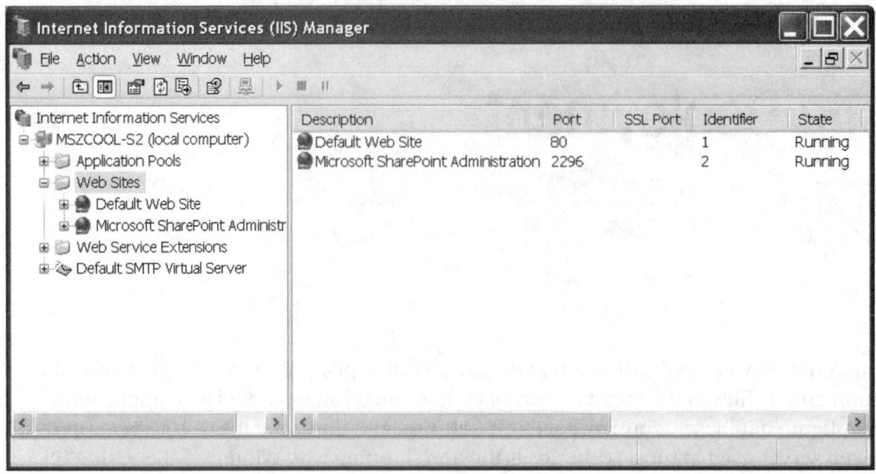

Figure 18-1. *IIS management console*

Any incoming request on one of the registered ports for the configured websites is passed through the Windows network stack to IIS (actually the World Wide Web Publishing Service), which processes the request and returns a response to the client again through the Windows network stack.

So-called virtual directories are created for a web application running in a website of the web server. Basically, every virtual directory maps to a physical directory. This makes the contents of the physical directory accessible through web technologies such as HTTP. Actually, the virtual directory is nothing more than a configuration entry in IIS for sharing a local physical path for access through the web server.

The complete configuration (which means any configured website or virtual directory with all its settings) is stored in a file, called a *metabase*, on the local system. The IIS metabase is a binary database in IIS 5.*x* and an XML-based data store in IIS 6.*x*, and it can be configured through the IIS management console (shown in Figure 18-1).

IIS and URL Processing

Web applications are accessed over HTTP by clients typing a URL into a browser. The browser passes this request to the server (in this case IIS), which actually processes the request.

When IIS receives a request, its first step is to examine the requested URL. A typical URL for a web application might take the following format:

```
http://WebServer/OnlineStore/catalog.aspx
```

If the website configured on the server does not run on the default port, 80, you have to specify the site's port in the URL. The following example accesses the same page on the same server but uses the port number 1234 because the website is running on this port and not on port 80.

```
http://WebServer:1234/OnlineStore/catalog.aspx
```

In this case, the first portion (WebServer:1234) identifies the name of the web server computer on a local network and the port. The second portion (OnlineStore) identifies the virtual directory where the ASP.NET application is stored. The third portion (catalog.aspx) indicates the requested file. The file extension gives IIS the necessary information for deciding how the request will be processed. Every file extension is registered in IIS and connected with the so-called ISAPI extension, as shown in Figure 18-2.

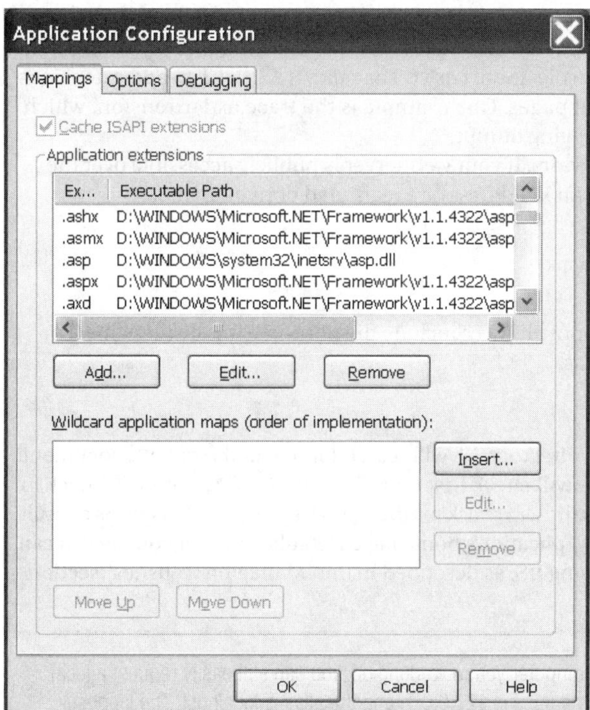

Figure 18-2. *ISAPI filter configurations*

As you can see, every file extension is connected to a DLL file. Actually, these DLLs are the ISAPI extensions responsible for processing requests for URLs, with a requested file having a specific file extension connected with this ISAPI DLL. For example, the file extension .asp is connected with the asp.dll ISAPI extension. That means the classic ASP runtime is defined within this ISAPI extension.

Any file extensions, such as .aspx and .asmx, that should be processed by the ASP.NET runtime are connected with the appropriate aspnet_isapi.dll ISAPI extension. These entries are automatically added to the IIS configuration when installing the .NET Framework on the target machine. As every version of the .NET Framework resides in a separate directory, every web application can be configured with the necessary version of the ASP.NET ISAPI extension. Therefore, using multiple versions of ASP.NET side by side (for example, ASP.NET 1.0, 1.1, and 2.0) for different web applications is possible without any types of side effects. You will learn more about side-by-side execution later in the section "ASP.NET Side-By-Side Execution."

■ **Tip** With ASP.NET 1.0 and 1.1, you had to ensure that every virtual directory was mapped to the correct version of the ASP.NET ISAPI extension by configuring the virtual directory with the command-line tool aspnet_regiis.exe, because the installation of the .NET Framework 1.1 automatically configured every virtual directory for ASP.NET 1.1. That means after you installed .NET 1.1, every ASP.NET application automatically executed with the 1.1 runtime version. If you still wanted to use the 1.0 version of the runtime, you had to call the aspnet_regiis.exe tool included with .NET 1.0 to register the ISAPI extensions for the virtual directory appropriately. ASP.NET 2.0 installs an additional property page to the virtual directory properties that allows you to configure a virtual directory for a specific version of ASP.NET by just selecting the version from a combo box. This property page then automatically configures all the mappings correctly for you.

Because the file requested in the previous URL has the extension .aspx, IIS recognizes that it's a request for an ASP.NET resource, and it passes the request to ASP.NET. Interestingly enough, IIS will pass the request to ASP.NET even if the file doesn't exist. That allows ASP.NET to add extensions that don't actually correspond to physical pages. One example is the trace.axd extension, which allows local developers to see recent debugging output.

Of course, URLs can come in many flavors. If your web server is publicly accessible over the Internet, clients might connect to it using an IP address or a registered domain name.

Here are two examples:

```
http://145.0.5.5/OnlineStore/catalog.aspx
http://www.MyBusiness.com/catalog.aspx
```

Finally, you've no doubt noticed that not all URLs include the portion with the filename. For example, you might make a request like this:

```
http://WebServer/OnlineStore
```

In this case, if OnlineStore is a virtual directory, IIS will search for one of the default documents and automatically run that. By default IIS will check first for a Default.htm file, then will check for Default.asp, index.htm, iisstart.asp, and finally will check for the ASP.NET file Default.aspx. As a result, it's always a good idea to name your web application's home page Default.aspx. (Of course, you can configure this list of default documents using IIS, as described in the "Managing Websites" section of this chapter.)

■ **Tip** Even if you don't know the name of the computer you're working on, you can still easily request a local page using the loopback address. The loopback address is 127.0.0.1, and the alias is localhost. The loopback address and alias always point to the current computer and are extremely useful while testing. For example, you can enter `http://localhost/OnlineStore/catalog.aspx` to request an ASP.NET page from the OnlineStore virtual directory on the local computer.

■ **Tip** As mentioned previously, you can configure multiple websites on one IIS server. Every website has to run on a separate port. This port has to be specified in the URL, as shown previously when accessing a web application running in one site, except the port has the default value of 80. Basically that means you can have only one website running on port 80. But IIS supports the notion of host headers. In the website's properties in the Advanced Web Site Identification dialog box, you can configure a host header for the website. Using this setting you can have multiple websites running on the same port. (Of course, every website then needs a different value for the host header setting.) Your web server needs to be made accessible through multiple machine names, whereas every machine name maps to a configured host header value. In that case, IIS determines the website that contains the web application that serves the request based on the requested web server's machine name. It compares the machine name with the host header values of the websites and selects the website with the host header name that matches this machine name.

Request Processing with IIS and ASP.NET

When IIS receives a request for static content, such as an HTML page or a graphic, it serves the file immediately (assuming there aren't any settings that prevent this file from being accessed in the current security context). Any file registered with a specific ISAPI DLL is not processed by IIS directly but through the registered ISAPI DLL.

That said, for an ASP.NET request, IIS just performs some preprocessing steps, such as checking security, and then forwards the request to the aspnet_isapi.dll extension. But the extension itself doesn't process the request. Although the processing models are different between IIS 5.*x* and IIS 6.0, the ISAPI extension forwards the request in any case to the managed ASP.NET runtime, as you can see in the high-level architecture shown in Figure 18-3.

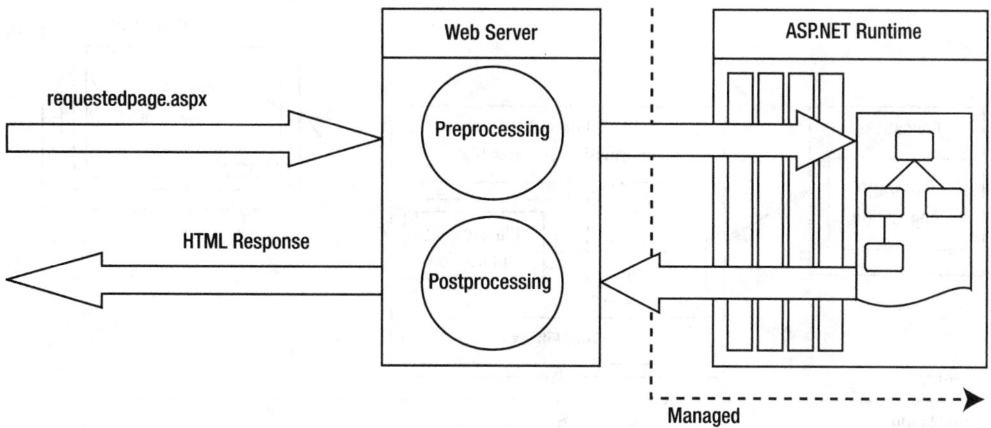

Figure 18-3. *High-level ASP.NET architecture*

As you can see in Figure 18-3, the ASP.NET runtime works completely independently from the actual web server. That said, you now know why Visual Studio is able to use the integrated Visual Web Developer Web Server. The Visual Web Developer Web Server is just another host for the ASP.NET runtime, and you can even create your own ASP.NET runtime host.

For the rest of this chapter, we will focus on processing requests with IIS and ASP.NET. As with IIS 6.0, a completely new developed version of IIS has been released; you will see that there are some significant differences between IIS 6.0 and previous versions of IIS in terms of the underlying process model.

IIS 5.*x* Process Model

IIS 5.*x* is designed to run on Windows 2000 and Windows XP systems. As mentioned previously, requests are not processed directly by the aspnet_isapi.dll ISAPI extension. In fact, the ASP.NET ISAPI extension is just a dispatcher. It receives requests and forwards these requests to the ASP.NET runtime, which runs completely in the context of the CLR.

When hosting ASP.NET web applications on IIS 5.*x*–based systems, the ASP.NET runtime actually runs in a separate worker process called aspnet_wp.exe. This worker process hosts the ASP.NET runtime and performs the actual request processing. Within the worker process, ASP.NET applications are isolated through AppDomains so that one web application cannot accidentally damage the memory of another web application. The ASP.NET ISAPI extension automatically starts the process if it is not running.

Any other ISAPI extension (either written in C++ or written in classic Visual Basic) runs either directly in the web server process or in an external dllhost.exe process for advanced isolation, as demonstrated in Figure 18-4.

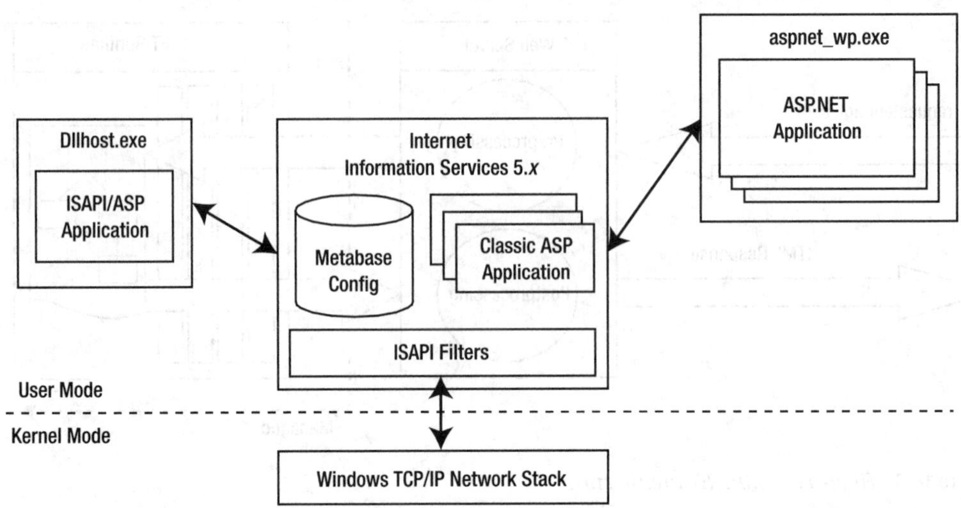

Figure 18-4. *The IIS 5.x process model*

As soon as the isolation level for a classic ISAPI extension–based application is set to High, IIS executes the ISAPI application in a separate dllhost.exe process. As mentioned, ASP.NET applications run in their own, isolated worker process. The applications are isolated through application domains. *Application domains* are mechanisms of the CLR for isolating .NET components running in the same host process for security and reliability reasons. In addition, this worker process provides a completely configurable process model that defines several settings for increasing the reliability of web applications; settings include process recycling, worker process memory limits, request queuing, and much more. Table 18-1 outlines the most important settings of the <processModel> element in the machine.config configuration file. (You can find a complete list in the documentation for the <processModel> element on MSDN Online.)

Table 18-1. *The <processModel> Element in the machine.config File*

Configuration	Description
enable	Enables or disables the ASP.NET process model. If the process model is enabled, the ASP.NET runtime is executed in its own worker process. If not, ASP.NET applications are executed directly in the web server process.
timeout	Specifies how long ASP.NET waits for a worker process before it creates a new instance of the worker process. Therefore, if a worker process hangs for some reason, other ASP.NET applications are still available, because the runtime creates a new worker process.
idleTimeout	Every worker process requires some resources in memory. Therefore, if requests come in infrequently, the runtime can shut down the process for saving resources. This value specifies how long the runtime waits for shutting down the worker process if it is idle and not processing any requests.
shutdownTimeout	In a normal situation the ASP.NET runtime sends a signal to the worker process for shutting down normally. If the worker process takes longer for shutting down than configured with this setting, it just kills the worker process abnormally.

Configuration	Description
requestLimit	If the number of requests processed by a worker process exceeds this number, the runtime launches another worker process. The old worker process completes processing the requests of the previously attached requests and shuts down afterward.
requestQueueLimit	If the number of requests in the worker process's queue to be processed exceeds this number, ASP.NET returns a 503 (server too busy) error. This is useful in particular for mitigating denial-of-service attacks in terms of required resources. (If too many requests come in and every request requires a large amount of memory, the resources on the server might not be enough.) You should carefully configure this setting. The other problem is that if you configure this setting with a too-low number, probably too many users would get a 503 error. This could result in a denial-of-service attack again in terms of blocking real users' requests while an attacker is flooding the server with senseless requests. Therefore, the setting alone is not enough for mitigating denial-of-service attacks (although it's hard mitigating them in general). Finding the appropriate application architecture and avoiding things such as storing lots of data for anonymous users are essential tasks.
restartQueueLimit	Specifies the maximum number of requests queued while waiting for the worker process to restart after an abnormal termination.
memoryLimit	Specifies the maximum amount of memory in percent of the total memory available on a system that can be used by the worker process. If this amount is exceeded, the runtime automatically launches a new process, reassigns requests to this new process, and shuts down the old process. But remember, even if you have a system with more than 2GB of RAM and have configured this setting appropriately, you might get an out-of-memory exception if the process requires more than 2GB of RAM. The reason for that is that the operating system itself by default doesn't allow a process to have more than 2GB. By enabling the so-called 4GB RAM TUNING feature on the operating system, a process can have up to 3GB of RAM.
webGarden	This setting is especially important for multiprocessor environments. Basically, it allows the runtime to start more than one worker process on one machine for request processing if the machine has more than one CPU. Actually, you can start exactly one process per CPU if web gardening is enabled for improving the performance of your web application. This setting is used together with the cpuMask setting.
cpuMask	This setting is used in conjunction with the webGarden setting. If web gardening is enabled, this setting specifies a bitmask that enables web application processing for different CPUs in the system. Every CPU is represented by a bit, and if this bit is set to 1, the ASP.NET runtime starts a worker process for the CPU. The bitmask is stored as a hexadecimal value in this setting.
username	Every process on a Windows system has to run under a specific identity. The user name of the process model element specifies the identity under which the worker process will run. Each access to the file system or to any other unmanaged operating system resources is verified against the process's identity. The default for this setting is Machine, which actually is a special setting that identifies the local machine's ASPNET user account.

(Continued)

Table 18-1. *Continued*

Configuration	Description
password	Specifies the password for the user account used for the worker process. By default this is set to the value AutoGenerate, which uses the password automatically generated during the installation of the .NET Framework.
responseDeadlockInterval	The ASP.NET runtime "pings" the worker process in regular intervals to verify if it is still alive. The process has to respond to this ping in the time specified in this setting. If the process hangs for any reason and doesn't respond in the time specified here, the runtime starts a new instance of the process and reassigns all requests in the request queue.
maxWorkerThreads	Allows you to configure the number of threads used for processing requests within one worker process.
maxIoThreads	Specifies the maximum number of IO threads per worker process instance.

As successful as it is, this process model has two significant flaws. First, if an application running directly in the web server process crashes, it can crash the whole web server. For that reason, the IIS product team added the possibility of configuring isolation levels and executing web applications in separate processes, which solves this problem. However, by default this behavior is not applied to ASP.NET applications, because they run in the external ASP.NET worker process (aspnet_wp.exe). It just affects classic ASP applications or any other type of ISAPI extension (such as PHP, Perl, or custom C++ ISAPI extensions). To apply this behavior to ASP.NET, you have to disable the process model through the <processModel> element in machine.config, as described previously. Disabling the ASP.NET process model means you cannot use the process model features described. Furthermore, it means that for every process an instance of the CLR has to be loaded. Of course, you should keep in mind that loading more instances of the CLR means that more memory is required.

Second, when taking a closer look at Figure 18-4, you can probably see that the process model has another, much bigger problem. Take a close look at the request flow in Figure 18-4! You'll see two context switches within the flow: The first one happens between the kernel mode network stack and the web server running in user mode, and the second context switch happens between the web server process and the external dllhost.exe or aspnet_wp.exe worker process. Context switches are expensive operations, especially if processes are running under different users. Data marshaling has to happen, and data must be exchanged between processes. To increase performance and reliability, the IIS product team has significantly changed the architecture of IIS with the release of Windows Server 2003, as you will see in the section "IIS 6.0 Process Model" of this chapter.

Custom Identities for the Worker Process

As you have seen already in Table 18-1, the <processModel> element includes a user name and password combination. By default the user name is set to Machine, and the password is set to Autogenerate. This setting automatically selects the ASPNET account, which is a low-privileged account generated with the installation of ASP.NET. Of course, the password is generated during installation as well and therefore unknown (which is not really a problem, because the ASPNET user is not intended to be used for interactive logon sessions).

Of course, if your code needs additional permissions (and it often will to access a file, database, registry key, and so on), you can either grant ASPNET these permissions or instruct ASP.NET to use a different account. In some cases, such as accessing network resources, it is necessary to create a separate user account. In this case you can enter the user name and password of another user in the <processModel> element, as follows:

```
<processModel enable="True" ...
              userName="MyUser" password="{the@password1}" ... />
```

Of course, the fact that the user name and password are not encrypted in this file is not really beautiful. Even worse, the new configuration encryption cannot be used with the <processModel> element. Fortunately, another tool (which needs to be downloaded separately) exists for encrypting this data (as well as user name and password settings stored in the <identity> configuration entry). This tool is aspnet_setreg.exe, and you can download it from the Microsoft website. The .NET runtime automatically decrypts the information. (This functionality has been added with a patch for ASP.NET 1.0 and is included in ASP.NET 1.1.)

IIS 6.0 Process Model

Windows Server 2003 was the first operating system released after the launch of the Trustworthy Computing Initiative. IIS 6.0, therefore, is the first web server from Microsoft developed completely within the parameters of the new security directives created during this initiative. These directives have changed the whole development process in relation to security.

Actually, IIS 6.0 is not just a product upgrade; it's a complete rewrite of the product with security and reliability taken into consideration from the first moment of the development life cycle for the product. The basic concepts such as websites, virtual directories, and the metabase (which is stored as XML in IIS 6.0) are still the same and configured in the same way, but the way the server processes requests is significantly different, as you can see in Figure 18-5.

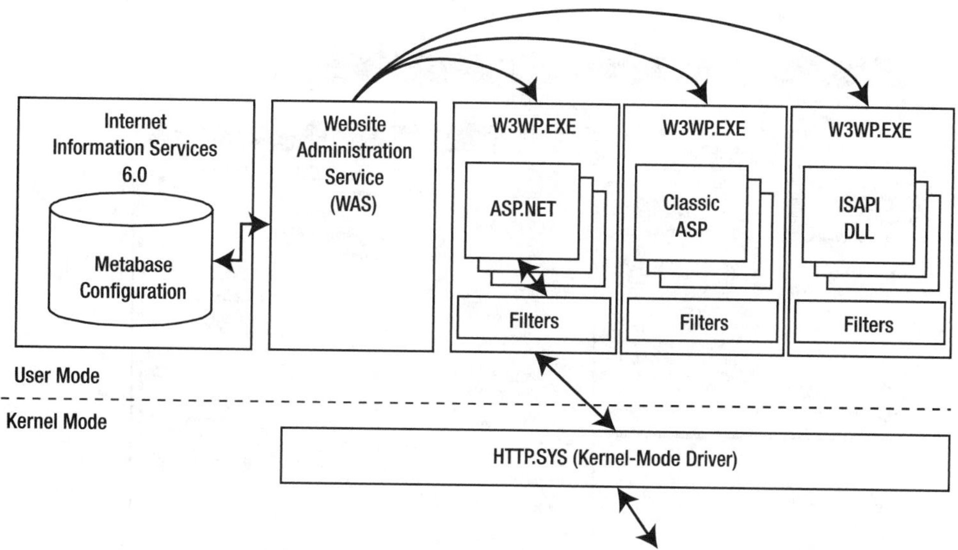

Figure 18-5. *The IIS 6.0 process model*

The web server is now split into several components. Instead of receiving requests from the TCP/IP network stack, Windows Server 2003 includes a kernel mode driver called HTTP.SYS, which is responsible for receiving HTTP requests from clients. The kernel mode forwards requests to any process that registers itself for specific URLs. Therefore, any application that registers with the kernel mode driver can receive HTTP requests without running a whole web server.

Note The method described previously will be used in the next generation of the operating system not only for HTTP but also for several other protocols. The next generation of the messaging system, code-named Indigo, will leverage this infrastructure as a hosting model as well. The hosting model is currently referenced as WebHost and provides the basic runtime environment for several protocols (TCP, SOAP, and so on).

IIS leverages this infrastructure for launching so-called W3C worker processes (W3WP.EXE). Every worker process runs one or more applications, either ASP.NET-based applications or other types of web applications. These worker processes provide a mechanism for isolation. As applications are running in separate processes, a crash of one application doesn't affect other applications at all. In addition, IIS 6.0 introduces WAS, which monitors the activities of worker processes. If a worker process fails, WAS automatically restarts the process so that the application is still available after the crash. Furthermore, you can configure a separate identity for every worker process. This allows you to configure additional isolation through permissions of the account that's configured for the worker process.

The worker processes are configured through *application pools* in the IIS management console, which includes new configuration options for this process model. For every application pool, the web server creates an instance of a worker process. Web applications (virtual directories) are assigned to these application pools. Each application pool can run as many applications as you want. The configuration for the application pools on one application replaces the isolation level known from IIS 5.*x* configurations. Figure 18-6 shows the IIS management console with the application pools as well as the property page of one virtual directory with the application pool configured.

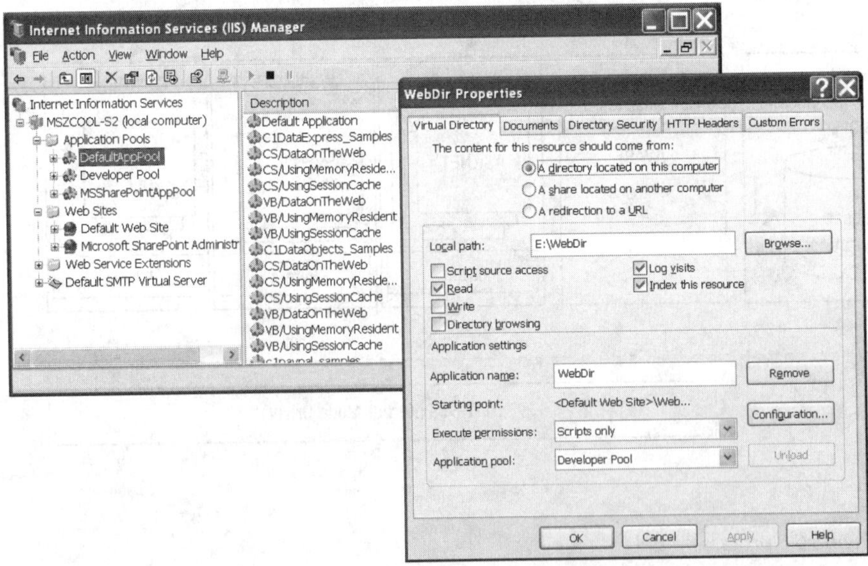

Figure 18-6. *Application pools and an application configured for one pool*

Application pools allow you to easily configure different web applications to run under different accounts with different resource usage limits, use multiple CPUs, and provide even more robust web application isolation. Of course, the drawback is that these separate instances of the IIS worker process load separate instances of the CLR, which consumes additional memory.

Note Remember, the worker process isn't limited to a single task. Both the ASP.NET worker process and the IIS worker process run multiple threads at the same time so that they can serve simultaneous requests from different users.

As mentioned, all the reliability and security options are configured at the application pool level in IIS 6.0. Therefore, when running ASP.NET on IIS 6.0, the classic ASP.NET process model with the configuration of the <processModel> element in machine.config is disabled, because all the options introduced for the <processModel> are configured for IIS 6.0 worker processes now.

Note You can use IIS 6.0 in IIS 5.*x* compatibility mode, which runs the web server with the process model introduced by IIS 5.*x*. In that case, the ASP.NET process model of course is enabled again. Keep in mind that using this process model leads to all the disadvantages of the old process model discussed previously. Although the process model in IIS 6.0 is different, your application basically is not affected by this change except that you activate recycling features and web gardening features of the application pool. As soon as you do that, you have to keep in mind that your application process will be shut down when recycling, which means that features such as session state or any other information is lost if you just keep it directly in the process. For ASP.NET applications you can configure session state to be stored either in an external process or in SQL Server to handle this problem. For classic ASP applications or other types of applications such as PHP, Perl, or custom ISAPI extensions, you have to handle this in your application on your own.

Every setting introduced with the ASP.NET process model maps to a corresponding setting for application pools in IIS 6.0. Table 18-2 gives an overview of which setting in the <processModel> element maps to which setting of an application pool.

Table 18-2. *IIS 6.0 Equivalents for the <processModel> Settings*

IIS 6.0 Setting	Configuration Tab	<processModel> Setting	Description
	Health	enable	Enables/disables the ASP.NET <processModel>.
Enable Pinging	Health	timeout	Pinging is performed by WAS for detecting the worker process's health state. It is nothing more than a local RPC to the process, and if the worker process doesn't respond in an appropriate time, it kills the process and starts a new one.

(Continued)

Table 18-2. *Continued*

IIS 6.0 Setting	Configuration Tab	<processModel> Setting	Description
Rapid-Fail protection	Health		Rapid fail protection is used together with pinging. If a process crashes several times within a specified amount of time, the web server can be configured to not restart it again. This enables you to avoid the situation of bothering the server with continuously restarting a worker process and therefore having less time available for processing requests of other worker processes.
Startup time limit	Health		Specifies the maximum amount of time a worker process may take for starting up. If the worker process needs more time, startup is canceled by WAS.
Shutdown time limit	Health	shutdownTimeout	Specifies the maximum amount of time the worker process may take for a normal shutdown. If the worker process needs more time for shutting down, WAS just kills the process.
Idle timeout	Performance	idleTimeout	If the worker process has no request to handle for the amount of time specified in this setting, WAS shuts it down.
Request queue limit	Performance	requestQueueLimit	Limits the number of requests in the kernel request queue to avoid flooding the server with requests.
Enable CPU monitoring	Performance		Specifies the maximum CPU charge for a worker process. If the worker process charges the CPU more than configured here, you can configure IIS to shut it down or keep it alive and in quarantine for debugging (called *orphaning*).

IIS 6.0 Setting	Configuration Tab	<processModel> Setting	Description
Web Garden	Performance	webGarden	This setting allows you configure IIS so that it creates multiple processes for one application pool. Each of these processes is then able to process requests for a web application. Actually, IIS 6.0 can launch multiple processes for a pool even if the machine has just one CPU.
SMPProcessorAffinityMask		cpuMask	Currently this setting can be edited only in the IIS metabase.xml file stored in the <DRIVE>:\WINDOWS\SYSTEM32\INTESRV directory. Together with the SMPAffinitized attribute set to True, it allows you to specify the CPU mask for web gardening on multiprocessor machines.
Recycle in minutes	Recycling		Allows you to specify that the worker process will be restarted based on the specified time interval.
Recycle in number of requests	Recycling	requestLimit	Recycles a worker process after it has processed the specified number of requests.
Recycle at following times	Recycling		IIS 6.0 allows you to specify dedicated times for worker process recycling.
		restartQueueLimit	See the documentation for the <processModel> element.
Memory Recycling	Recycling	memoryLimit	IIS 6.0 allows you to specify two separate memory limits. The first one is the memory used by the application, and the second option specifies the virtual memory (used plus reserved memory) of the application.

(Continued)

Table 18-2. *Continued*

IIS 6.0 Setting	Configuration Tab	<processModel> Setting	Description
Application pool identity	Identity	username	Specifies the user identity for an application pool. The default is the restricted Network Service account with least privileges. You can change this setting either to the local system that has a couple of additional privileges on the local machine or to the local system (what is not recommended, as you should run your applications always with the least privileges; you can find more information on that in Part 4).
Application pool identity	Identity	password	Specifies the password for the application pool's identity.
		responseDeadlockInterval	See the <processModel> configuration options.
		maxWorkerThreads	See the <processModel> configuration options.
		maxIoThreads	See the <processModel> configuration options.

This overview should give you a fairly good understanding of how IIS and ASP.NET work together. However, there's a lot more to learn before you can consider yourself an experienced web administrator. In particular, IIS 6 is a sophisticated program with a slew of powerful options. To learn more about these features, consult the online documentation (one good resource is the Microsoft site `http://www.microsoft.com/windowsserver2003/techinfo/_overview/iis.mspx`) or a dedicated book on IIS administration. However, you'll learn enough in this book to create, configure, and test web applications in virtual directories with IIS.

Installing IIS

Even though IIS is included with Windows, it's not installed by default. That's because Microsoft recognizes that allowing Internet access to any part of your computer is a security risk, and it's not an operation that should be performed automatically if it's not needed.

■ **Note** IIS is available only if your computer is running Windows 2000, Windows 2000 Server, Windows XP Professional, or Windows Server 2003. Each version of Windows has a slightly different version or configuration of IIS. As a general rule of thumb, when you want to publish your website, you should use a server version of Windows to host it. Desktop versions, such as Windows 2000 and Windows XP Professional, are fine for development testing, but they implement a connection limit of ten simultaneous users, which makes them much less suitable for real-world use. Windows Server 2003 is different from the other operating systems, as by default IIS 6.0 is installed in a locked-down mode processing static content and ASP.NET applications only. Other types of applications, even classic ASP, must be explicitly enabled by administrators.

The process of configuring IIS depends on the version of Windows you have installed. The next two sections lead you through the steps you need to perform.

Installing IIS 5

On a Windows 2000, Windows 2000 Server, or Windows XP Professional computer, you can follow these steps to install IIS:

1. Click Start, and select Settings ➤ Control Panel.
2. Choose Add or Remove Programs.
3. Click Add/Remove Windows Components.
4. If Internet Information Services is checked (see Figure 18-7), you already have this component installed. Otherwise, click it and click Next to install the required IIS files. You'll need to have your Windows setup CD handy.

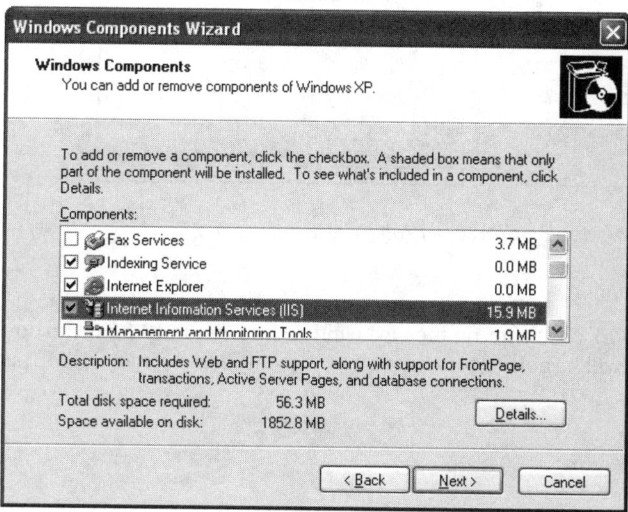

Figure 18-7. *IIS is currently installed.*

Installing IIS 6

If you're using Windows Server 2003, you can install IIS through the Add/Remove Windows Components dialog box, but it's more likely that you'll use the Manage Your Server Wizard. Here's how it works:

1. Select Add or Remove a Role from the main Manage Your Server window. This launches the Configure Your Server Wizard.
2. Click Next to continue past the introductory window. The setup wizard will test your available and enabled network connections and then continue to the next step.
3. Now you choose the roles to enable. Select Application Server (IIS, ASP.NET) from the list, as shown in Figure 18-8, and click Next.

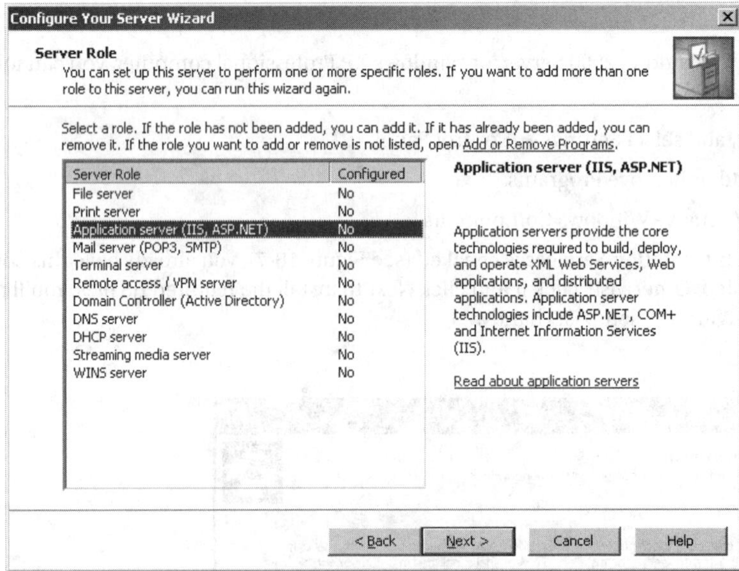

Figure 18-8. *Choosing an application server role*

4. Click the Enable ASP.NET check box on the next window (see Figure 18-9). If you don't, IIS will be enabled, but it will be able to serve static content only like ordinary HTML pages. Click Next to continue.

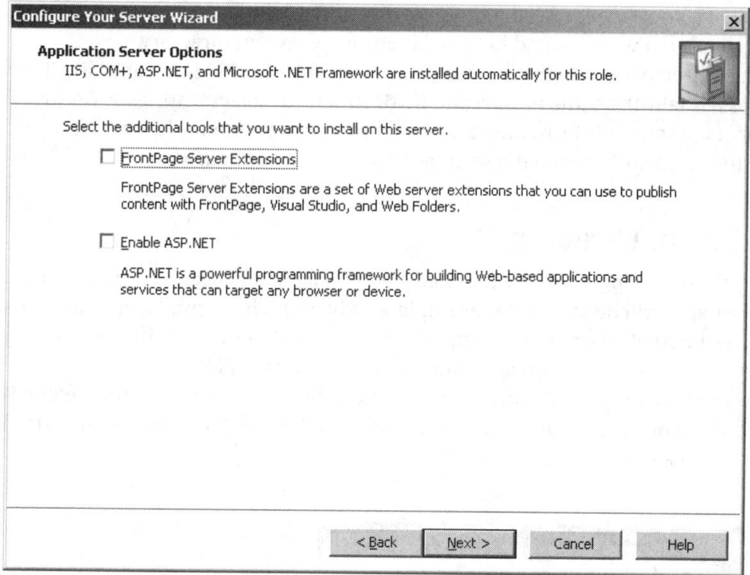

Figure 18-9. *Enabling other services*

5. The next window shows a summary of the options you've chosen. Click Next to continue installing IIS 6.0 and ASP.NET. Once the process is complete, you'll see a final confirmation message.

■ **Note** The rest of this chapter describes website administration with IIS 5, which is usually used when developing a website. However, if you're starting out with IIS 6, you'll still be able to use most of the instructions in this chapter, but you may want to supplement your knowledge with the online help for IIS 6 or a dedicated book about IIS 6 administration.

Managing Websites

When IIS is installed, it automatically creates a directory named c:\Inetpub\wwwroot, which represents your website. Any files in this directory will appear as though they're in the root of your web server.

To add more pages to your web server, you can copy HTML, ASP, or ASP.NET files directly to the c:\Inetpub\wwwroot directory. For example, if you add the file TestFile.html to this directory, you can request it in a browser through the URL `http://localhost/TestFile.html`. You can even create subdirectories to group-related resources. For example, you can access the c:\Inetpub\wwwroot\MySite\MyFile.html file through a browser using the URL `http://localhost/MySite/MyFile.html`. If you're using Visual Studio .NET to create new web projects, you'll find that it automatically generates new subdirectories in the wwwroot directory. So, if you create a web application named WebApplication1, the files will be stored in c:\Inetpub\wwwroot\WebApplication1 and will be made available through `http://localhost/_WebApplication1`.

Using the wwwroot directory is straightforward, but it makes for poor organization. To properly use ASP or ASP.NET, you should create a new *virtual directory* for each web application you create.

With a virtual directory, you can expose any physical directory (on any drive on your computer) on your web server as though it were located in the c:\Inetpup\wwwroot directory.

To create virtual directories, you need to use the administrative IIS Manager utility. The steps for doing this are essentially the same in IIS 5 and IIS 6. To start it, select Settings ➤ Control Panel ➤ Administrative Tools ➤ Internet Information Services from the Start menu. The next few sections walk you through the steps and explain the settings that you can configure.

Creating a Virtual Directory

When you're ready to create a new website, the first step you'll usually take is to create the physical directory where the pages will be stored (for example, c:\MySite). The second step is to expose this physical directory as a virtual directory through IIS. This means that the website becomes publicly accessible to other computers that connect to your computer over HTTP.

To create a new virtual directory for an existing physical directory, right-click the Default Website item in the IIS tree, and choose New ➤ Virtual Directory from the context menu. A wizard will start to manage the process, as shown in Figure 18-10.

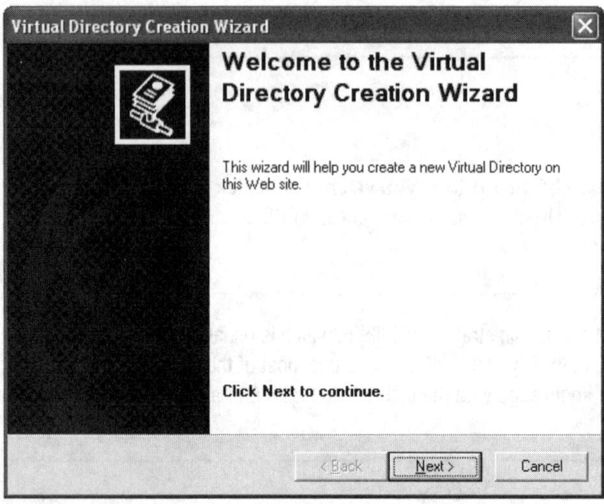

Figure 18-10. *The Virtual Directory Creation Wizard*

As you step through the wizard, you'll need to provide three pieces of information: an alias, a directory, and a set of permissions. The following sections describe these settings.

Alias

The alias is the name a remote client will use to access the files in this virtual directory. For example, if your alias is MyApp and your computer is MyServer, you can request pages using URLs such as `http://MyServer/MyApp/MyPage.aspx`.

Directory

The directory is the physical directory on your hard drive that will be exposed as a virtual directory. For example, c:\Intetpub\wwwroot is the physical directory that is used for the root virtual directory of your web server. IIS will provide access to all the allowed file types in this directory.

Permissions

Finally, the wizard asks you to set permissions for your virtual directory, as shown in Figure 18-11. You can set several permissions:

Read: This is the most basic permission—it's required in order for IIS to provide any requested files to the user. If this is disabled, the client will not be able to access ASP or ASP.NET pages or access static files such as HTML and images. Note that even when you enable read permission, several other layers of security are possible in IIS. For example, some file types (such as those that correspond to ASP.NET configuration files) are automatically restricted, even if they're in a directory that has read permission.

Run scripts: This permission allows the user to request an ASP or ASP.NET page. If you enable read but don't allow script permission, the user will be restricted to static file types such as HTML documents. ASP and ASP.NET pages require a higher permission because they could conceivably perform operations that would damage the web server or compromise security.

Execute: This permission allows the user to run an ordinary executable file or CGI application. This is a possible security risk as well and shouldn't be enabled unless you require it (which you won't for ordinary ASP or ASP.NET applications).

Write: This permission allows the user to add, modify, or delete files on the web server. This permission should never be granted, because it could easily allow the client computer to upload and then execute a dangerous script file (or, at the least, use all your available disk space). Instead, use an FTP site, or create an ASP.NET application that allows the user to upload specific types of information or files.

Browse: This permission allows you to retrieve a full list of files in the virtual directory, even if the contents of those files are restricted. Browse is generally disabled, because it allows users to discover additional information about your website and its structure as well as exploit possible security holes. On the other hand, it's quite useful for testing, so you might want to enable it on a development computer.

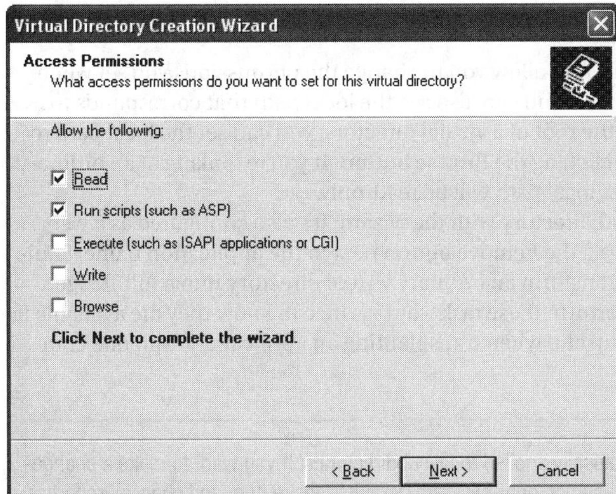

Figure 18-11. *Virtual directory permissions*

To host an ASP.NET application, you need to enable only the read and execute permissions (the first two check boxes). If you're using a development computer that will never act as a live web server, you can allow additional permissions. Keep in mind, however, that this could allow other users on a local network to access and modify files in the virtual directory. You can also change the virtual directory permissions after you have created the virtual directory.

Virtual Directories and Web Applications

You can manage all the virtual directories on your computer in the IIS utility by expanding the tree under the Default Website item. You'll notice that items in the tree have three types of icons:

Ordinary folder: This represents a subdirectory inside another virtual directory. For example, if you create a virtual directory and then add a subdirectory to the physical directory, it will be displayed here.

Folders with a globe: This represents a virtual directory.

Package folders: This represents a virtual directory that is also a web application. By default, when you use the wizard to create a virtual directory, it's also configured as a web application. This means it will share a common set of resources and run in its own application domain.

When you create a virtual directory with the Virtual Directory Creation Wizard, it's also configured as a web application. This is almost always what you want. If your virtual directory *isn't* a web application, you won't be able to control its ASP.NET configuration settings, and you won't be able to create a web application in it using Visual Studio .NET.

Folder Settings

IIS makes it easy to configure virtual directories after you've created them. Simply right-click the virtual directory in the list, and choose Properties. The Properties window will appear, with its information divided into several tabs. The following sections describe some of the most important settings.

Virtual Directory

The Virtual Directory tab includes options that allow you to change the permissions you set when creating the virtual directory with the wizard. You can also see the local path that corresponds to this virtual directory. If you're looking at the root of a virtual directory, you can set the local path to point to a different physical directory by clicking the Browse button. If you're looking at an ordinary subdirectory *inside* a virtual directory, the local path will be read-only.

Remember, when you create a virtual directory with the wizard, it's also configured as a web application. You can change this by clicking the Remove button next to the application name. Similarly, you can click the Create button to transform an ordinary virtual directory into a full-fledged application. Usually you won't need to perform these tasks, but it's nice to know they are available if you need to make a change. They can be useful when transplanting an application from one computer to another.

■ **Note** Any changes you make will be automatically applied to all subdirectories. If you want to make a change that will affect all the virtual directories on your server, right-click the Default Website item and choose Properties. The change will be cascaded down to all the subdirectories that are contained in the current virtual directory. If your change conflicts with the custom settings that you've set for a virtual directory, IIS will warn you. It will present a list of the directories that will be affected and give you the chance to specify exactly which ones you want to change and which ones you want to leave as is.

File Mappings

As explained earlier in this chapter, IIS hands off requests for ASP pages to the ASP ISAPI extension and sends requests for ASP.NET pages to the ASP.NET ISAPI extension. Furthermore, you have seen that IIS decides the designated ISAPI extension based on the filename extension of the requested URL. Actually, you can configure these file mappings on a per–virtual directory basis. When ASP.NET is installed, it modifies the IIS metabase to add the mappings for file types that it needs to process. To view these file mappings, click the Configuration button on the Virtual Directory tab. You'll see the dialog box shown in Figure 18-12.

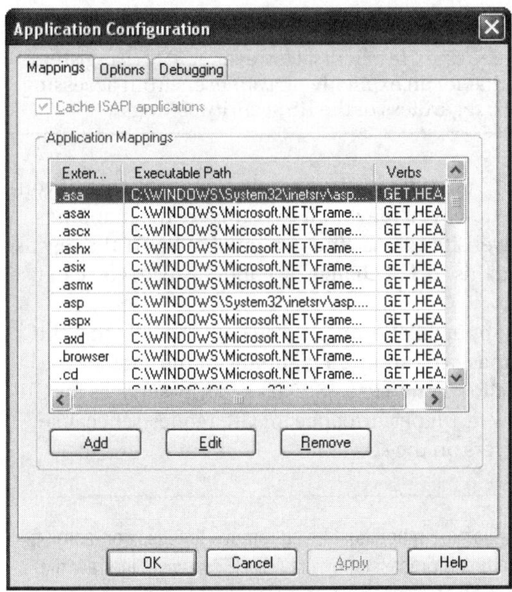

Figure 18-12. *File mappings*

Table 18-3 lists the ASP.NET file mappings.

Table 18-3. *The ASP.NET File Mappings*

File Extension	Description
.aspx	These are ASP.NET web pages.
.ascx	These are ASP.NET user controls. User controls are similar to web pages, except that they can't be accessed directly. Instead, they must be hosted inside an ASP.NET web page.
.asmx	These are ASP.NET web services, which allow you to expose useful functionality to other applications over HTTP.
.asax	This extension is used for the global application file, which you can use to react to global events, such as when a web application first starts.
.ashx	This extension is used for HTTP handlers, which allow you to process requests without using the full-fledged ASP.NET web-page model.

(Continued)

Table 18-3. *Continued*

File Extension	Description
.axd	This extension is used for the trace.axd application extension, which allows you to view trace messages while debugging.
.rem and .soap	These extensions identify that IIS is hosting an object that can be called by .NET remoting. The remoting technology is similar to web services, but it's a proprietary .NET solution that doesn't have the same features for cross-platform capability.
.cs, .csproj, .vb, .vbproj, .licx, .config, .resx, .webinfo, and .vsdisco	These file types are used by ASP.NET, but they can't be directly requested by clients. However, ASP.NET registers them so that it can explicitly *prevent* users from accessing these files, regardless of the IIS security settings.

Is there any reason you should explicitly change an ASP.NET file mapping? Probably not. If you have multiple versions of ASP.NET installed at one time, you may want to configure the mappings differently in different directories. That way, each website can use the version of ASP.NET that it was compiled with. However, there's no reason to make this sort of change by hand. Instead, you can use the aspnet_regiis.exe command-line utility.

In other cases, you might want to add a file mapping. For example, you could specify that the ASP.NET service will handle any requests for GIF images by adding a mapping for the .gif file type that points to the aspnet_isapi.dll file. This would allow you to use ASP.NET security services for GIF file requests. (Note that this sort of change can slow down performance for GIF requests, because these requests will need to trickle through more layers on the server.)

■ **Caution** You should never remove any of the ASP.NET file type mappings! If you remove the .aspx or .asmx file types, web pages and web services won't work. Instead of being processed by the ASP.NET service, the raw file will be sent directly to the browser. If you remove other files types such as .vb or .config, you'll compromise security. ASP.NET will no longer process requests for these types of files, which means that malicious users will be able to request them through IIS and inspect the code and configuration information for your web application.

More About Filename Extensions

In many cases it's useful to map your own file extensions to the ASP.NET runtime so that these file extensions are processed by ASP.NET (or, more exactly, your web application). For this purpose, you have to perform the following steps:

1. Use the IIS management console to map your filename extension to the appropriate version of the ASP.NET ISAPI DLL, as described earlier in this chapter.
2. Create a custom HTTP handler in your solution. A HTTP handler is a class that implements the IHttpHandler interface. The handler implements just one simple method called ProcessRequest. Within this method you add code for processing the request with the previously specified filename extension. In this way, for example, you can include code that reads a JPG image from a database instead of the file system. You can furthermore include functionality for caching the images or any type of information using the ASP.NET cache.
3. Configure the HTTP handler in the application's web.config file so that the ASP.NET runtime knows that a file extension has to be processed with the previously created HTTP handler.

In Chapter 22 you will learn about the details for mapping filename extensions to the ASP.NET runtime and creating an HTTP handler when it comes to securing custom filename extensions through the ASP.NET runtime.

Documents

This tab allows you to specify the default documents for a virtual directory. For example, consider the virtual directory `http://localhost/MySite`. A user can request a specific page in this directory using a URL such as `http://localhost/MySite/MyPage1.aspx`. But what happens if the user simply types `http://localhost/MySite` into a web browser?

In this case, IIS will examine the list of default documents defined for that virtual directory. It will scan the list from top to bottom and return the first matching page. Using the list in Figure 18-13, IIS will check first for a Default.htm file and then for Default.asp, index.htm, iisstart.asp, and Default.aspx. If none of these pages is found, IIS will return the HTTP 404 (page not found) error.

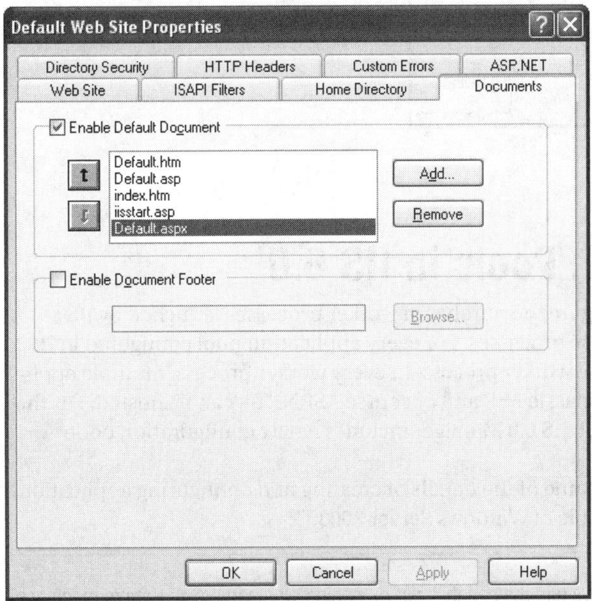

Figure 18-13. *The default document list*

You can configure the default document list by removing entries or adding new ones. Most ASP.NET applications simply use Default.aspx as their home page.

Custom Errors

The Custom Errors tab allows you to specify an error page that will be displayed for specific types of HTTP errors (see Figure 18-14). You can use ASP.NET configuration to replace HTTP errors or application errors with custom messages. However, these techniques won't work if the web request never makes it to the ASP.NET service (for example, if the user requests an HTML file that doesn't exist). In this case, you may want to supplement custom ASP.NET error handling with the appropriate IIS error pages for other generic error conditions.

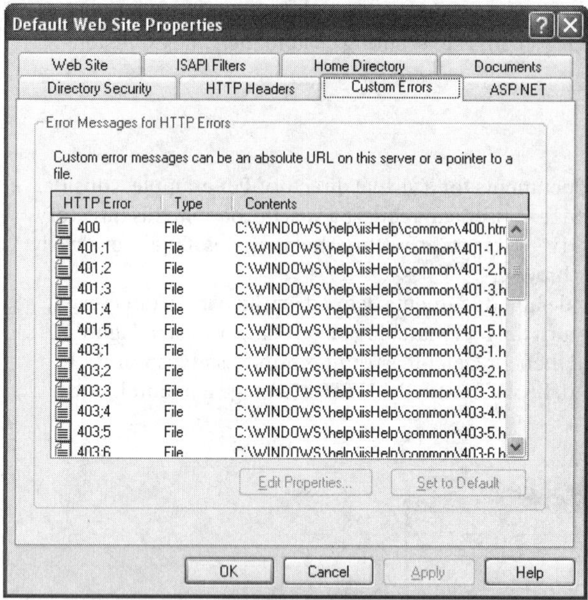

Figure 18-14. *IIS custom errors*

Managing Application Pools in IIS 6.0

Through application pools you can configure the number of worker processes launched by IIS as well as more configuration details for these processes. For every application pool configured in IIS Manager, the web server starts at least one worker process. In every worker process, multiple applications of any type—from ISAPI DLLs to classic ASP and of course ASP.NET—can be hosted. For the purpose of managing the application pool, IIS 6.0 Manager includes a new configuration node (refer to Figure 18-6).

In this section, you will learn about some of the details of creating and configuring application pools with the new IIS management console of Windows Server 2003.

Note The IIS management console has always had the capability of managing web servers on remote machines. You just had to add the server in IIS Manager to the root node, and then you were able to configure this remote machine. Of course, if you are using Windows XP running IIS 5.*x*, the IIS management console doesn't know about application pools; therefore, you can't manage them from Windows XP machines. For that purpose, Microsoft offers a tool called IIS 6.0 Manager for Windows XP on the Microsoft downloads page, which can be installed on Windows XP machines for administering IIS 6.0 instances (`http://www.microsoft.com/downloads/details.aspx?FamilyID=f9c1fb79-c903-4842-9f6c-9db93643fdb7&DisplayLang=en`).

Creating Application Pools

As you have seen already, the IIS 6.0 Manager displays application pools in a separate configuration node. A default installation consists of one application pool called the DefaultAppPool. This application pool runs as a network service, and every web application in the default website is configured to run in this application pool.

You may want to create additional application pools for other applications on a web server for several reasons:

Stability problems: Maybe you want to run older applications with some stability problems in a separate application pool so that these problems don't affect other applications.

Memory leaks: A resource-intensive application or an old application with a memory leak is a good candidate for regular recycling. In this case, you can create a separate pool and configure process recycling. Applications running in other pools are not affected by these settings.

Security: Security configuration might be another reason for encapsulating applications in separate pools. For example, if you have web applications that require specific permissions (such as accessing only specific SQL Server databases or the Windows certificate store), you can create your own Windows user having the necessary permissions, configure a new application pool with this user, and then run web applications that require only these specific permissions in this pool. All the other applications in other application pools still run under the low-privileged Network Service account.

Administration: In web hosting scenarios you can isolate administrative applications as well as applications for different customers (or groups of customers) through application pools; this way, web applications from one customer don't have access to resources such as databases or the file system of other customers' applications because of the permissions for a configured application pool identity.

As you can see, several useful scenarios exist for creating separate application pools for different applications or groups of applications. Application pools (worker processes) provide you with a mechanism for isolating these applications based on different criteria such as security or reliability.

■ **Caution** Recycling an application pool (worker process) basically means stopping the old process and starting a new instance of a worker process for the application pool. Therefore, any data stored in the process space of the worker process is lost when the pool is recycled. That said, an application needs to be "designed" for recycling, or recycling should take place at a time where traffic on the website is not heavy. Designing applications for recycling involves the same steps as designing an application for a web farm; using external session state, for example, is one of the key needs for preparing an application for recycling because usually session state is stored in the process space of the worker process. Fortunately, ASP.NET comes with a mechanism for externalizing session state and storing session data either in an external state server process or in SQL Server. In that case, session state is not lost if a process is recycled (or in the case of the web farm the request is processed by another server in the farm).

You can create applications pools just by double-clicking the Application Pools node (or an existing application pool) and selecting New ➤ Application Pool from the context menu, as demonstrated in Figure 18-15.

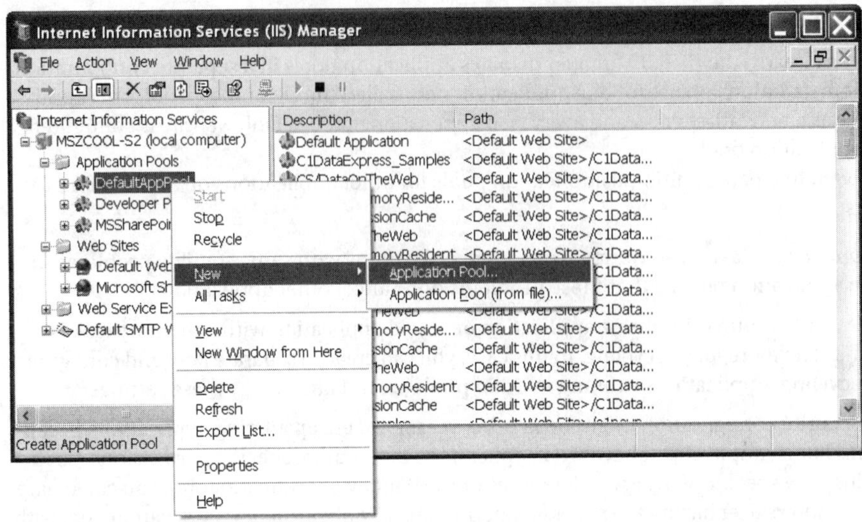

Figure 18-15. *First step for creating an application pool*

You can create an application pool either with the Add New Application Pool dialog box or through a previously exported XML configuration file (created by selecting All Tasks ➤ Save Configuration to a File from the context menu shown in Figure 18-15). When selecting the first option (just a new application pool), then you have two possibilities, as shown in Figure 18-16.

Add New Application Pool
Application pool ID: AppPool #1
Application pool settings
Use default settings for new application pool
Use existing application pool as template
Application pool name: DefaultAppPool
OK Cancel Help

Figure 18-16. *Creating a new application pool*

You can create the application pool with a set of default settings defined by IIS, or you can create the pool based on the settings already present in another application pool. As soon as you have created the application pool, you will see it in the list of application pools, and you can configure it by right-clicking it and selecting Properties from the context menu, as shown in Figure 18-17.

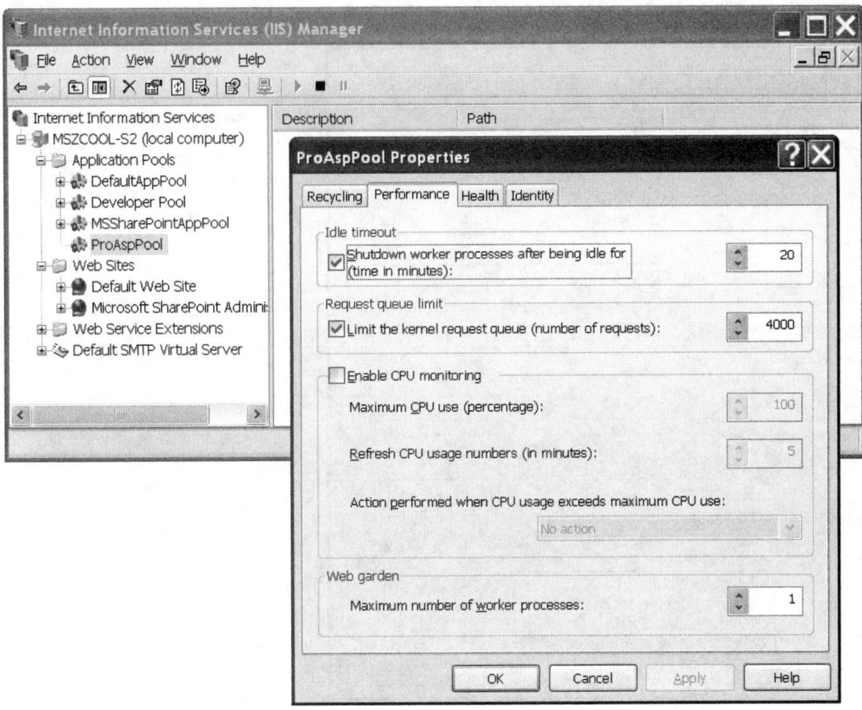

Figure 18-17. *The properties of an application pool*

Basically, you can create as many application pools as you want; IIS doesn't know any limits—theoretically. Of course, every process needs a basic set of resources; therefore, the number of processes is limited by the resources of the web server machine.

Application Pools and Web Applications

Once you have created an application pool, you can run web applications within this pool. As mentioned previously, isolating web applications takes place through application pools now; therefore, when configuring virtual directories and websites, the application pool setting replaces the old Isolation Mode setting introduced with IIS 5.*x*, as you can see in Figure 18-18.

Figure 18-18. *Configuring the application pool*

For configuring an application pool, just right-click the virtual directory for which you want to configure the application pool and then change the setting to the pool you want the application to run in.

You don't need to restart anything—neither the web server nor the application pool itself. The application runs in the new pool from the moment you click the OK or Apply button.

Custom Application Pool Identities

As previously mentioned, one of the useful isolation strategies you can implement with application pools is security. For every application with special security permissions, you can create a separate Windows user having those permissions and configure an application pool with this Windows user as an identity. Then only applications that require these permissions will be put into this application pool.

■ Tip By the way, application pools are a perfect way to use Windows authentication when connecting to SQL Server. This is more secure than SQL authentication, as you don't have to store user names and passwords in your web.config file. Also, it uses Kerberos if a KDC (in terms of Windows, an Active Directory with a primary domain controller) is in place. You just create a new Windows user, configure the application pool with the user, add the user to the SQL Server database the application needs to access, and then configure the application to run in this application pool. Applications running in other pools then don't have access to the database (except you configure them with the same identity or add the identity of another pool to the SQL Server database's users).

You can configure the identity for every application pool by just right-clicking the pool in the IIS management console, selecting Properties, and then going to the Identity tab of the property page, as demonstrated in Figure 18-19.

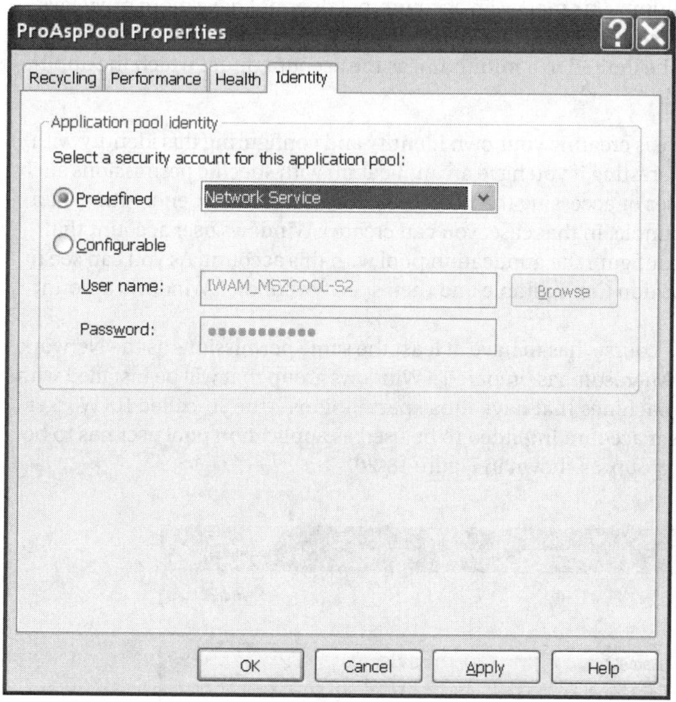

Figure 18-19. *Configuring the application pool identity*

In this dialog box, you basically have two options: The first one is selecting from a couple of predefined accounts, and the second one is selecting your own user account by specifying the Windows user name and password for this account.

■ **Note** IIS uses the same mechanism for storing these credentials as the Windows Service Control Manager does. It encrypts the credentials using the data protection API (DPAPI) of the system with a private key from the operating system and stores the encryption version in the metabase. Of course, this system's private key is accessible only when you have access to the local machine and the appropriate permissions on the machine.

The predefined accounts you can select are as follows:

Network Service: This is a restricted account with much fewer privileges than the Local System account. This account is intended to be used for applications that require access to the network and need to be accessed from other machines.

Local Service: This account is more restricted than the Network Service account and intended to be used for services that don't require additional network access. Services running on this account don't have the permission for accessing other network resources; they can access local resources only.

Local System: The well-known Local System account, of course, still exists. But we recommend never, ever using this account for web applications of any type, as this is the most powerful account of a system. It can perform any action on the local system, so any application running under this account can also do this. Basically, your strategy should always be running applications with a "least-privileged" account—this means an account that does not have more privileges than the application actually should need. Therefore, if someone is able to break (hack) the application, the damage will be limited to a minimum, as the account under which the application is running is restricted.

The other possibility you have is creating your own identity and configuring this identity with the application pool. This gets interesting if you have an application with specific permissions such as accessing only specific databases or accessing the Windows certificate store for encrypting data based on X509 certificates, for example. In that case, you can create a Windows user account that has these permissions and then configure the application pool with this account. As you can see in Figure 18-19, you can select the option Configurable and then specify your own Windows account for the application pool.

But this Windows account, of course, has to have at least the same permissions as the Network Service account has. Fortunately, Microsoft has prepared a Windows group that will be installed with IIS 6.0 on Windows Server 2003 machines that have those permissions—the so-called IIS Worker Process Group (IIS_WPG). Any user account intended to be used as application pool user has to be a member of this worker process group, as shown in Figure 18-20.

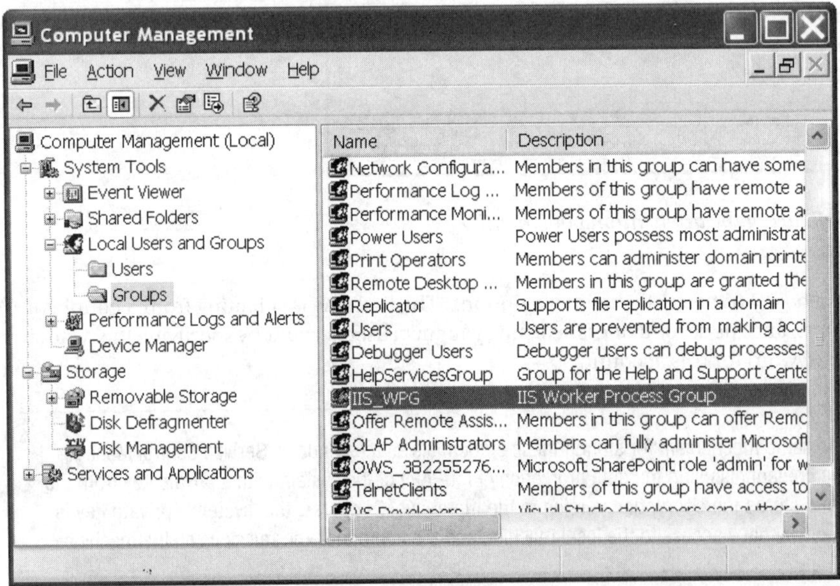

Figure 18-20. *The IIS Worker Process Group*

When you open the properties for this group, you will see that Network Service itself is a member of this group and therefore gets all the necessary permissions to be used as the identity for application pools. The group grants the user special permissions such as the permission for running as a service process in background. It also grants access to the necessary directories such as the temporary ASP.NET files stored in c:\WINDOWS\Microsoft.NET\Framework\[Version]\Temporary ASP.NET Files, where ASP.NET stores the dynamically compiled version of the different pages.

■Caution When configuring the identity for an application pool, you need to restart the pool. That's because every process runs under a valid identity; therefore, the identity must be known at the point of time when the process is started. Changing application pool configuration doesn't restart the application pool; therefore, it still runs under the old identity until it gets restarted. So, you have to restart the process so it starts under the newly configured account.

If your application needs access to any other directory granted by IIS_WPG, you must grant access to the identity configured for the application pool explicitly. You even have to grant access to the file system directories where the files of your web application itself are located. Otherwise, the application pool will not be able to access these files, and therefore the application won't work. But basically that's it: adding the user to IIS_WPG, granting access to resources necessary for your application (your file system directories or anything else your application tries to access), and configuring the application pool with the identity are the only steps necessary.

■Tip If your application calls complex web services or uses the XmlSerializer class, it might need access to the c:\WINDOWS\TEMP directory as well because the serializer stores dynamically created assemblies for serialization and deserialization in this directory. Therefore, if your web application crashes with an "access denied" exception when calling web services or serializing/deserializing XML documents, just verify whether the application pool's identity has access to this directory.

Deploying Your ASP.NET Applications

Deploying ASP.NET web applications is usually nothing more than copying the directory structure of your application to the target machine and configuring the environment. For simple applications, that's almost always true. But if your application uses databases or accesses other resources, you have to perform some additional steps. Here are some common factors that will require additional configuration steps:

Copy all required application files to the target machine: You don't need to do anything else. But if you are using global assemblies accessed through the GAC, you have to verify whether these assemblies are in place. If not, you have to install them using the gacutil.exe command-line utility of the .NET Framework.

Create and configure the database for the application: It's important to not only create the database and its tables but also to configure the database server logins and database users. Don't forget that if you are using integrated authentication for connecting to a SQL Server database, you must configure the account under which ASP.NET is executed (the application pool account or aspnet_wp.exe account) as a user for the application's database.

Configure IIS as required for the application: Therefore, create necessary application pools, share the application directory as a virtual directory, and configure the virtual directory appropriately.

Set up Windows account permissions for the worker process user: The user under which the worker process (either aspnet_wp.exe or w3wp.exe in IIS 6.0) needs access to the application directories (at least read if the application doesn't write anything to these directories). If your application accesses other resources such as the registry or event log, you have to configure the permission for the worker process account to access these resources.

Add IIS file mappings: Add IIS file mappings if you want to process any URLs with filename extensions that are different from the extensions registered on a default ASP.NET installation.

Configure ASP.NET through the web.config file for production environments: In other words, add (or modify) any connection strings and application settings as well as security and authorization settings, session state settings, and globalization settings appropriately.

In some cases it is also required to modify machine.config: For example, if you are in a web hosting environment and your application runs on multiple web servers for load balancing, you have to synchronize any encryption keys used for encrypting forms authentication tickets or view state on all those machines. These keys are stored in machine.config and need to be equal on every machine in the web farm so that one machine is able to decrypt information encrypted by another machine that previously processed the request.

Definitely when it comes to deployment, you should know about a couple of useful things. First, before running ASP.NET applications the first time on a server, it might be useful to verify whether ASP.NET has been installed appropriately. Then you have to decide which version of ASP.NET your application requires. Actually, as with every other .NET Framework application, you can run as many ASP.NET runtimes side by side as you want. And of course don't forget to turn off the debug configuration option in the <compilation> section of web.config.

```
<configuration>
  <system.web>
   <!-- Other settings omitted. -->
   <compilation defaultLanguage="vb" debug="false" />
  </system.web>
<configuration>
```

When debugging is enabled, the compiled ASP.NET web-page code will be larger and execute more slowly. Additionally, temporary compilation files won't be deleted automatically. For that reason, debugging should be used only while testing your web application.

Of course, you don't need to deploy any project and solution files (*.sln, *.vbproj, *.csproj, and so on) used by Visual Studio. In the case of using precompilation (either the classic one as used in ASP.NET 1.*x* or the site precompilation based on aspnet_compiler as introduced in the section "Compilation Models" of this chapter), source code files (*.cs, *.vb) and resource files (*.resx) don't need to be deployed. And of course, as you probably won't debug on production machines, you don't need any *.pdb files there as well.

Verifying the ASP.NET Installation

After installing ASP.NET, it's a good idea to test that it's working. All you need to do is create a simple ASP.NET page, request it in a browser, and make sure it's processed successfully.

To perform this test, create a new physical directory on your computer. Now, use the Create Virtual Directory Wizard to expose this directory as a virtual directory named Test. Finally, create a new file in this directory using Notepad. Name this file test.aspx. The filename isn't that important, but the extension is. It's the .aspx extension that tells IIS that this file needs to be processed by the ASP.NET engine.

Inside the test.aspx file, paste the following code:

```
<html>
<body>
<h1>The date is <% Response.Write(DateTime.Now.ToShortDateString()) %>
</h1>
</body>
</html>
```

When you request this file in a browser, ASP.NET will load the file, execute the embedded code statement (which retrieves the current date and inserts it into the page), and then return the final HTML page. This example isn't a full-fledged ASP.NET web page, because it doesn't use the web control model you learned about in the first part of this book. However, it's still enough to test that ASP.NET is working properly. When you enter `http://localhost/Test/_test.aspx` in the browser, you should see a page that looks like the one shown in Figure 18-21.

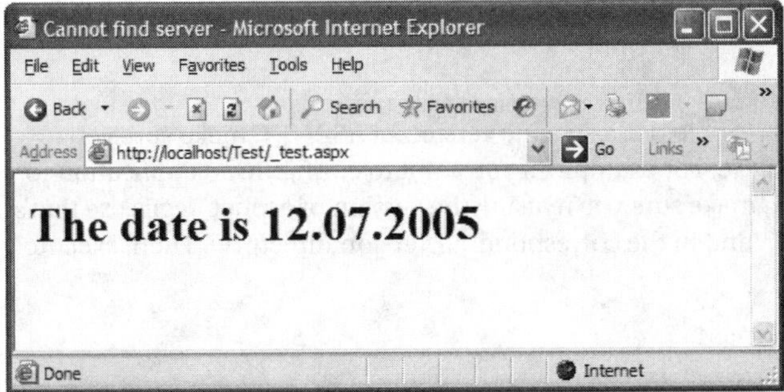

Figure 18-21. *ASP.NET is correctly installed.*

If you see only the plain text, as in Figure 18-22, ASP.NET isn't installed correctly. This problem commonly occurs if ASP.NET is installed but the ASP.NET file types aren't registered in IIS. In this case, ASP.NET won't actually process the request. Instead, the raw page will be sent directly to the user, and the browser will display only the content that isn't inside a tag or script block.

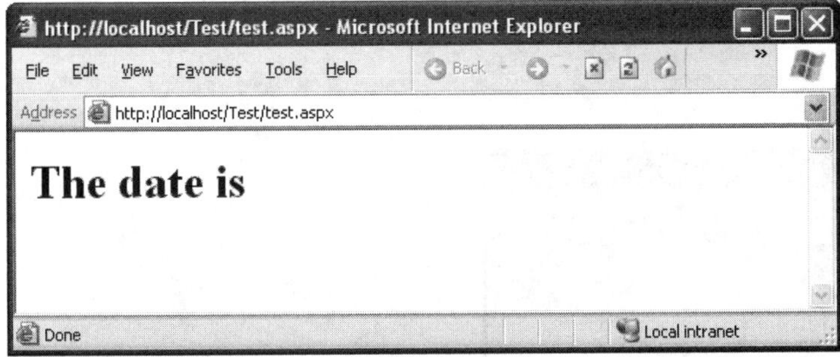

Figure 18-22. *ASP.NET isn't installed or configured correctly.*

You can usually solve this problem by repairing your IIS file mappings using the aspnet_regiis.exe utility described earlier. Here's the syntax you'll need:

```
c:\[WinDir]\Microsoft.NET\Framework\[Version]\aspnet_regiis.exe -i
```

Microsoft provides more detailed information about troubleshooting and aspnet_regiis.exe in a knowledge-base article at `http://support.microsoft.com/_default.aspx?scid=kb;en-us;325093`.

ASP.NET Side-By-Side Execution

As you already have seen a couple of times in this chapter, IIS forwards the request to an ISAPI extension DLL based on the filename extension of the URL request. Because every version of ASP.NET ships with its own ISAPI extension, it's easy to configure ASP.NET for side-by-side usage.

Just assign the ASP.NET file extension with the appropriate ISAPI extension of the version required, and the application runs with the required version of ASP.NET. This ISAPI extension is stored in the c:\WINDOWS\Microsoft.NET\Framework\[Version] directory, and its name is aspnet_isapi.dll. The following are a few examples of the tasks you can perform with aspnet_regiis.exe.

If you want to list all the versions of ASP.NET that are installed on the computer, and the matching ISAPI extensions, execute this command:

```
aspnet_regiis -lv
```

To configure a specific virtual directory to use a specific version of ASP.NET, make sure you're using the right version of aspnet_regiis.exe. For example, if you want to configure an application to use ASP.NET 2.0 instead of ASP.NET 1.1, make sure you're using the version of aspnet_regiis.exe that's included with the .NET 2.0 Framework (and in the corresponding version directory). Then, execute a command line like this:

```
aspnet_regiis -s W3SVC/1/ROOT/SampleApp1
```

This command maps the SampleApp1 virtual directory to use the version of ASP.NET that corresponds with the version of aspnet_regiis.exe. The first part of the path, W3SVC/1/ROOT/, identifies the web root of the current computer. Finally, if you need to migrate all the applications in one fell swoop, you can use the following command:

```
aspnet_regiis -i
```

This command also comes in handy if your IIS file mappings are set incorrectly (for example, if you installed IIS after you installed ASP.NET, the ASP.NET file mappings were not applied). But since ASP.NET 2.0 you can also use the graphical configuration tool that integrates into the IIS management console. Just right-click, select Properties for the virtual directory you want to configure, and open the newly integrated ASP.NET tab in the configuration. It allows you to select the version of ASP.NET, as shown in Figure 18-23.

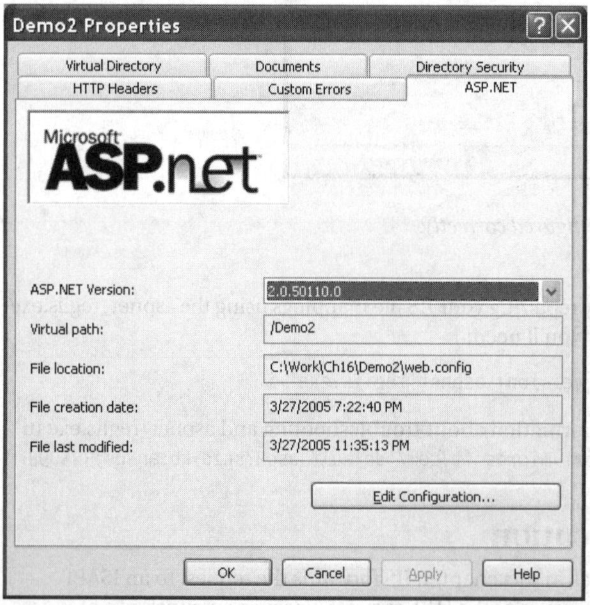

Figure 18-23. *Selecting the appropriate version of ASP.NET*

Configure HTTP Runtime Settings

The ASP.NET configuration builds upon the basic configuration of the web server itself, as you saw in the previous chapters. Furthermore, you have seen that you can configure lots of settings in terms of reliability and performance at the application pool level in IIS. But a couple of settings are not available there (but they were available in the old ASP.NET <processModel> configuration).

These settings are typical for the CLR and the ASP.NET runtime in particular. You can configure such settings through a special section in the web.config file for an ASP.NET web application—the <httpRuntime> section that resides directly below the <system.web> element in the configuration file. Table 18-4 shows the most important settings of the <httpRuntime> element; for a complete list, take a look at MSDN Online.

Table 18-4. *Most Important Settings of the <httpRuntime> Configuration Element*

Setting	Description
AppRequestQueueLimit	Specifies the maximum number of requests that ASP.NET will queue for the application. Request queuing takes place if ASP.NET does not have enough threads for processing the requests (threads are configured either in the <processModel> or through the minFreeThreads setting).
enable	If this setting is False, the application will not work any more, because the ASP.NET runtime doesn't create an AppDomain for the application and therefore doesn't process any requests targeted to this application.
enableKernelOutputCache	IIS 6.0 (and later) comes with a mechanism for caching data directly in the HTTP.SYS kernel mode driver's memory. This option specifies whether ASP.NET leverages this feature.
EnableVersionHeader	If this setting is set to True, ASP.NET outputs a version header.
ExecutionTimeout	Indicates the maximum number of seconds that a request is allowed to execute before being automatically shut down by ASP.NET.
idleTimeOut	As you know, ASP.NET ensues application isolation within a single process through application domains. For every configured web application (in IIS an application having a separate virtual directory), it creates an instance for an application domain. This setting specifies how long an application domain runs idle before ASP.NET releases the resources and shuts down the application domain.
maxRequestLength	This setting specifies the maximum size for uploaded files in kilobytes. Files that are uploaded through the FileUpload control are limited by this setting. The default is 4096 KB (4 MB).
MinFreeLocalRequestFreeThreads	The minimum number of free threads that ASP.NET keeps available to allow execution of new local requests (requests submitted on the local machine).
minFreeThreads	The minimum number of free threads to allow execution of new requests. If the number of requests requires more threads, the requests will be queued by the ASP.NET runtime.
CompilationTempDirectory	Specifies the directory used as temporary file storage for dynamic compilation.

(Continued)

Table 18-4. *Continued*

Setting	Description
requestPriority	Enables you to set priorities for web pages as they are processed by the ASP.NET runtime. This is interesting if you want to have a website or a part of a website running in the same worker process be more responsive than others. A typical example for that is an administrative page that has to be responsive in all cases. Sites or parts of a website configured with the value High will be processed faster and before lower prioritized parts of the website by the ASP.NET runtime.

Compilation Models

As you already know, ASP.NET comes with a compilation model for dynamically compiling assemblies out of tag-based code and actual source code. The application itself is always executed as a compiled version for increasing performance. Of course, special directories play an important role for dynamic compilation, as explained previously. ASP.NET offers three ways for compiling web applications:

Classic precompilation: ASP.NET introduced this model with its first release. With this compilation model, parts of the website are precompiled (of course, any referenced assemblies as well as the code-behind portions with the page processing logic), and others such as the tag-based code files (ASPX or ASMX files) are dynamically compiled at runtime with the first request. This model can be used only with the classic code-behind model where the actual page inherits from the compiled base class with the page logic.

Dynamic compilation: The application is deployed with all tag and source code files, and ASP.NET completely compiles the application on the fly. The advantage of this approach is that making changes just in tag files or even source code files is possible on the fly, and the application is automatically compiled after a change occurs. Of course, the big disadvantage is that dynamic compilation takes place on the first request, and therefore the first request after a change in code will need more time than subsequent requests (and to be honest, in large production systems we don't suggest making changes directly in source code without testing them first in test environments). This mechanism has been available since ASP.NET 2.0.

Site precompilation: ASP.NET 2.0 introduces a new model for precompilation that allows compiling the whole website into binaries so that no code files, even tag files such as ASPX or ASMX files, are completely compiled into binaries and deployed as binaries onto the target machine.

When creating a new website project, ASP.NET by default selects the dynamic compilation model. That means all the code and pages are stored as tag and source code files on the file system, and ASP.NET dynamically compiles them. Therefore, the first request will require a little bit more time as ASP.NET compiles the whole page. In that case, it might be better to deploy the site already in a compiled format, which you can do with site precompilation. For site precompilation, you have to use a separate tool for compiling the web application called aspent_compiler.exe. The compiler is stored in the Microsoft .NET Framework directory. The compiler has to be launched on your test/development machine before you deploy the entire website. Basically, the tool takes the following parameters:

```
aspnet_compiler -m metabase path
                -v virtual directory path
                -p physical path
                target directory
```

Therefore, you can specify either a metabase path, the virtual path, or the file system path for the application to be compiled as well as a target directory for the application. In Figure 18-24 you can see the aspnet_compiler.exe tool in action.

```
Visual Studio 2005 Command Prompt

E:\Ch18>aspnet_compiler -v none -p e:\Ch18\SampleCompile e:\SampleCompileBin
Utility to precompile an ASP.NET application
Copyright (C) Microsoft Corporation. All rights reserved.


E:\Ch18>dir ..\SampleCompileBin
 Volume in drive E is My Data
 Volume Serial Number is A8BB-9631

 Directory of E:\SampleCompileBin

12.07.2005  23:57    <DIR>          .
12.07.2005  23:57    <DIR>          ..
12.07.2005  23:57    <DIR>          bin
12.07.2005  23:57                86 Default.aspx
12.07.2005  23:57                50 PrecompiledApp.config
05.04.2005  00:06             1.671 Web.Config
               3 File(s)          1.807 bytes
               3 Dir(s)   6.058.528.768 bytes free

E:\Ch18>_
```

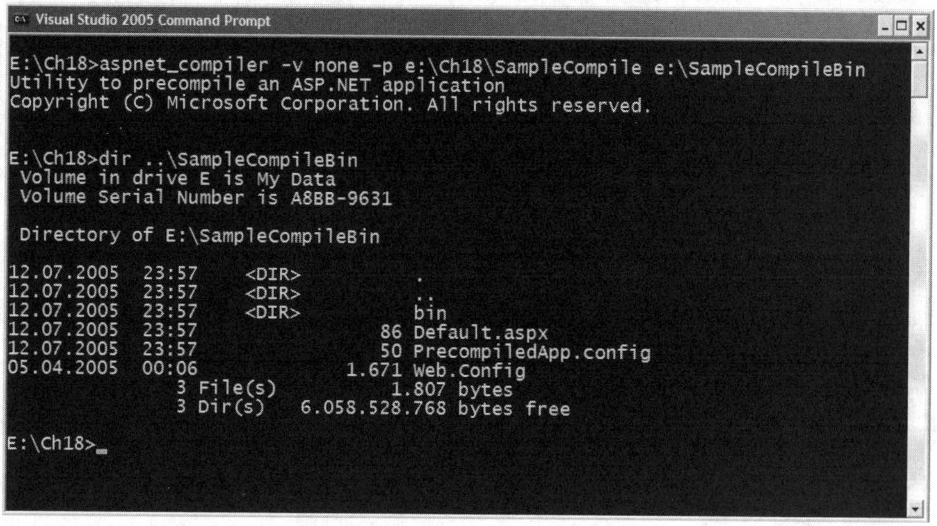

Figure 18-24. *The aspnet_compiler.exe tool in action*

As you can see, the compiler creates several files in the target directory. But when taking a closer look at the Default.aspx file, you'll recognize that it doesn't contain any useful tags; it just contains the information "This is a marker file generated by the precompilation tool, and should not be deleted!" All the actual code and tags are compiled into the binaries located in the Bin directory. Now you can just copy the resulting directory structure to the target machine and share the directory as virtual directory, and the application is ready to run.

Deploying with Visual Studio

Visual Studio offers an option for directly deploying websites from within the development environment onto a web server. This option supports multiple protocols such as FTP and FrontPage Server Extensions. Selecting Copy Web Site from the Web Site menu from within Visual Studio opens the dialog box shown in Figure 18-25.

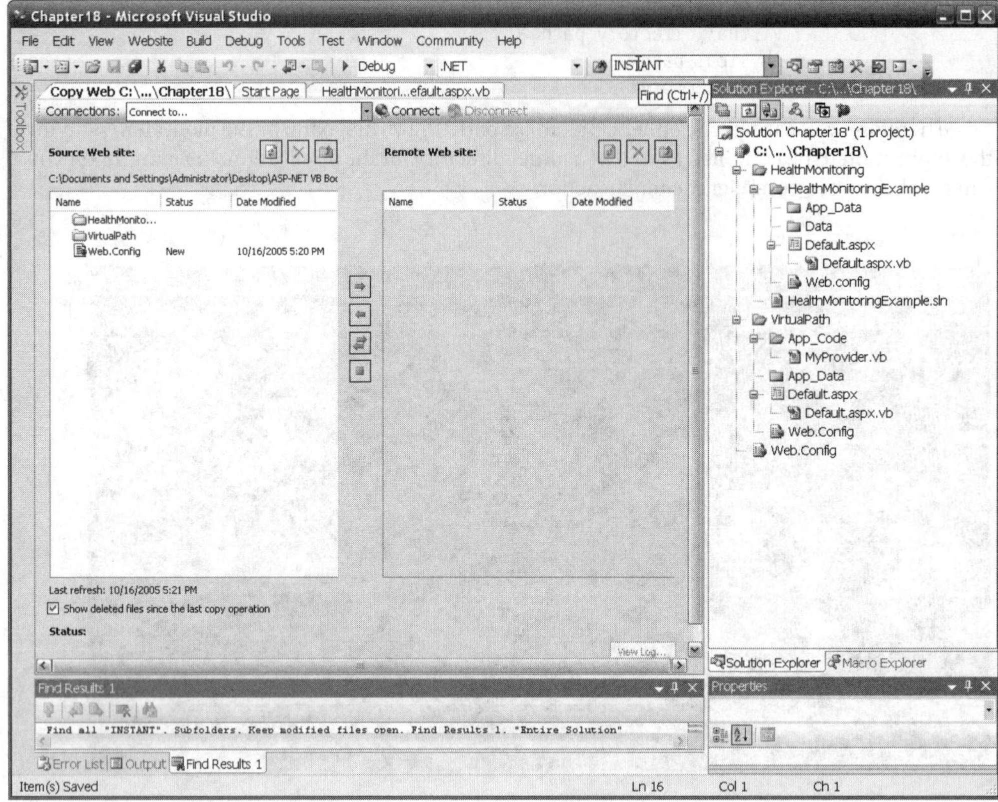

Figure 18-25. *The Visual Studio deployment option*

The dialog box shows you the website on the left side and the remote machine on the right side. For connecting to a remote machine, just click the button next to the Connect To drop-down list. This fires up another dialog box, as shown in Figure 18-26, for selecting the target website. As you can see, besides to a local directory or local IIS instance, remote sites can be accessed either through FTP or FrontPage Server Extensions.

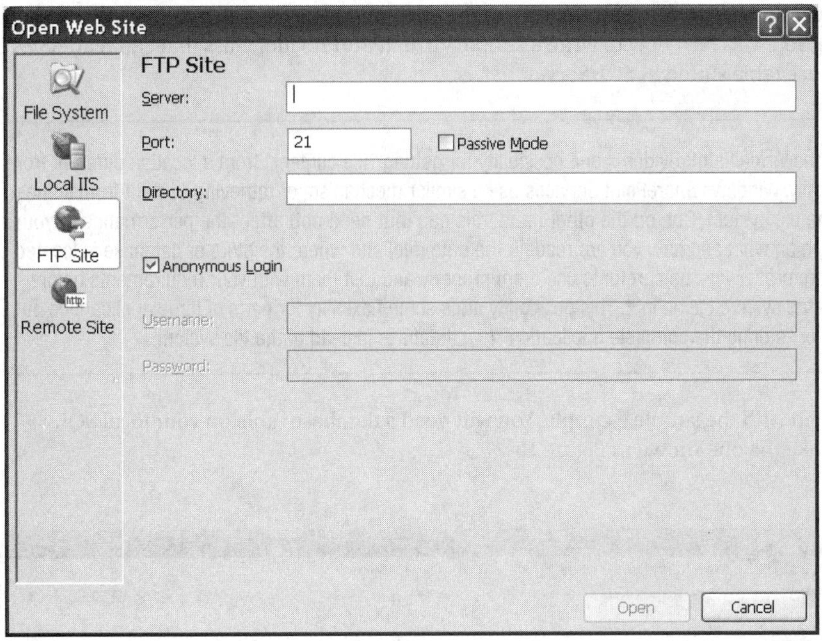

Figure 18-26. *Selecting the target website*

After connecting to the server, you can select files and directories from the left panel (which displays the content of your project) and move them over to the previously selected server. Of course, in the case of FTP or FrontPage Server Extensions, the website must already be configured on the remote machine.

The VirtualPathProvider in ASP.NET 2.0

The VirtualPathProvider class is a special part of the basic ASP.NET framework. It allows you to implement some sort of "virtual URL" accessible on the server. This gives you the possibility of generating a response for a URL dynamically without having an ASPX or HTML file stored on the hard disk.

Why is that interesting, and why will you learn about that in this chapter? Well, the VirtualPathProvider class gives you the additional possibility of deploying your web application (or, rather, parts of your web application). Actually, you have the possibility of storing "pages" of the web application somewhere else than on the file system without writing your own basic page framework that uses information in the database for dynamically creating controls and adding them to the page. You just can retrieve the whole file from the database and pass it to the ASP.NET runtime for further processing. The runtime treats the information retrieved from the database (or any other data store) like a physical page located on the file system. And that's not all. You can use the VirtualPathProvider class for accessing other features such as themes and skins from a different location than the file system. With such a possibility you can write fully customizable applications by providing some management system that allows you to upload new themes and skins into a database (perhaps on a per-user or per–user group basis) that are accessed by the runtime through the VirtualPathProvider class you have written.

The best way to understand the possibilities of the VirtualPathProvider class is to walk through a simple example. You will learn how to write a simple VirtualPathProvider class that can read ASPX files from a database table stored in SQL Server.

Note Of course, the VirtualPathProvider is one possibility for getting "file content" from a location different from the file system. Actually, Windows SharePoint Services use a similar mechanism of retrieving content from somewhere other than the file system. But, on the other hand, this can (but need not) affect the performance of your application depending on what and how you are reading the data (file) and where the store or database is located in your network. Therefore, always be careful to use them properly and test them with your requirements before actually building a large system based in it. This possibility adds some flexibility for parts of large applications but should not be used for "storing the complete application" in a database instead of the file system.

Let's get started with the simple example. You will need a database table on your local SQL Server that looks like the one shown in Figure 18-27.

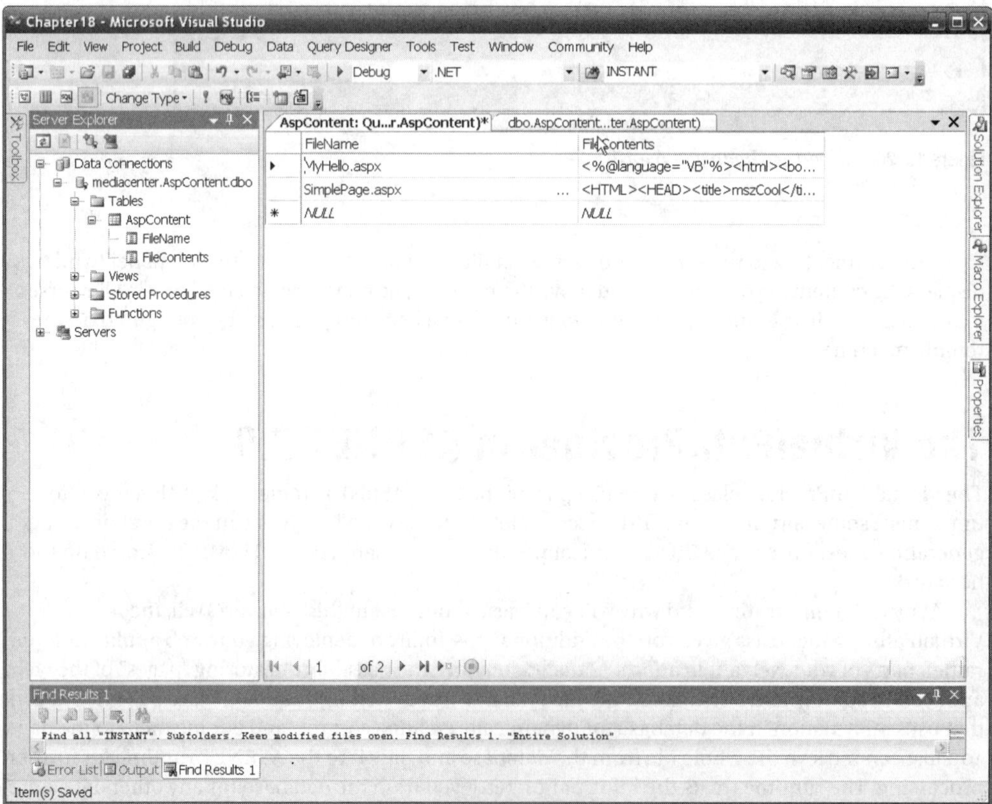

Figure 18-27. *The SQL Server database used for the VirtualPathProvider*

As you can see, the table includes a filename (which is the primary key as well) and the actual content. The content can be any type of code ASP.NET understands. Because you are serving just simple pages in the sample, the content can be anything the page parser is able to compile. After that, you can create a new website. Of course, both—files stored physically on the file system and files stored virtually in the database—should be accessible. You have to take that into consideration when writing your own implementation for the VirtualPathProvider class.

Therefore, when creating a new website, you just leave the Default.aspx page in place and modify its code as follows:

```
<%@ Page Language="vb" AutoEventWireup="true"
        CodeFile="Default.aspx.vb" Inherits="Default" %>

<!DOCTYPE html PUBLIC "-//W3C//DTD XHTML 1.1//EN"
   "http://www.w3.org/TR/xhtml11/DTD/xhtml11.dtd">

<html xmlns="http://www.w3.org/1999/xhtml" >
<head runat="server">
    <title>Untitled Page</title>
</head>
<body>
    <form id="form1" runat="server">
    <div>
      <b>This is the physical page</b><br />
      Served last time at <%= DateTime.Now.ToString() %>
    </div>
    </form>
</body>
</html>
```

Next, you have to create your implementation of the VirtualPathProvider class. The VirtualPathProvider class is defined in the System.Web.Hosting namespace. Just add a new class to the app_code directory and inherit from VirtualPathProvider. The class needs to implement at least the following methods:

```
Public Class MyProvider
        Inherits System.Web.Hosting.VirtualPathProvider
   Public Shared Sub Appinitialize()
     Dim fileProvider As New MyProvider()
     System.Web.Hosting.HostingEnvironment.RegisterVirtualPathProvider(fileProvider)
   End Sub

    Public Overrides Function FileExists(ByVal virtualPath As String) As Boolean
        Throw New Exception("The method or operation is not implemented.")
    End Function

    Public Overrides Function GetFile(ByVal virtualPath As String)
        As System.Web.Hosting.VirtualFile
        Throw New Exception("The method or operation is not implemented.")
    End Function
End Class
```

In addition, the VirtualPathProvider class has functions for verifying a directory (DirectoryExists) and getting file hashes (GetFileHash) as well as cache verification (GetCacheDependency) that should be overridden for more complex solutions. Furthermore, currently it requires you to implement a Shared method called AppInitialize. If the method is present in a VirtualPathProvider class, it is automatically called by the framework. Within this method, you create an instance of your own provider and register it for the hosting environment. If you don't do that, the framework simply won't know about your virtual provider and therefore will not use it at all.

As you can see in the previous code snippet, the GetFile method needs to return a virtual file. This virtual file is then used by the ASP.NET hosting framework for opening the file. Therefore, it provides an Open method. The Open method needs to return the contents for the entry in your database, but how will the content for your database get there? The VirtualFile class itself doesn't accept any parameters except the virtual path of the file. And—not really surprisingly—it is abstract.

So, the solution is simple—you have to create your own implementation of VirtualFile and override the Open method. This method then returns a stream to the ASP.NET infrastructure, which actually returns the contents of your database file. The following is the implementation of the simple VirtualFile class:

```
Public Class MyVirtualFile
      Inherits System.Web.Hosting.VirtualFile
   Private _FileContent As String

   Public Sub New(ByVal virtualPath As String, ByVal fileContent As String)
      MyBase.New(virtualPath)
      _FileContent = fileContent
   End Sub

   Public Overrides Function Open() As Stream
      Dim strm As New MemoryStream()
      Dim writer As New StreamWriter(strm, Encoding.Unicode)

      writer.Write(_FileContent)
      writer.Flush()
      strm.Seek(0, SeekOrigin.Begin)
      Return strm
   End Function
End Class
```

The class's constructor gets the virtual path as well as the content of the file. In the Open method, the string with the actual content gets saved to a MemoryStream, and this stream is then returned. ASP.NET uses the stream for reading the contents as if they were read from the file system—thanks to the abstraction of bytes through Stream classes.

The next step is to complete the VirtualPathProvider class. It needs to read the actual data for the files from the database. If a file doesn't exist in the database, the provider just forwards the request to its previous provider (which has been selected by the infrastructure while registering in the Shared AppInitialize method). Add a method for retrieving the contents from the database to the MyProvider class introduced previously:

```
Private Function GetFileFromDB(ByVal virtualPath As String) As String
   Dim contents As String
   Dim fileName As String = virtualPath.Substring(virtualPath.IndexOf("/"c, 1) + 1)

   ' Read the file from the database.
   Dim conn As New SqlConnection()
   conn.ConnectionString = "data source=(local);Integrated " _
            & "Security=SSPI;initial catalog=AspContent"
   conn.Open()
```

```
    Try
        Dim cmd As New SqlCommand("SELECT FileContents FROM AspContent " & _
                "WHERE FileName=@fn", conn)
        cmd.Parameters.Add("@fn", fileName)
        contents =cmd.ExecuteScalar().toString()
        If contents Is Nothing Then
            contents = String.Empty
        End If
    Catch
        contents = String.Empty
    Finally
        conn.Close()
    End Try
    Return contents
End Function
```

The GetFileFromDB function does nothing other than get the filename from the virtual path and then read the contents for the filename from the database. (Remember, the filename is the primary key in the database defined, as shown in Figure 18-27.) This method is then used by both, the FileExists method as well as the GetFile method, as shown in the following code snippet:

```
    Public Overrides Function FileExists(ByVal virtualPath As String) As Boolean
        Dim contents As String = Me.GetFileFromDB(virtualPath)
        Return contents <> String.Empty
End Function

    Public Overrides Function GetFile(ByVal virtualPath As String)
      As System.Web.Hosting.VirtualFile
        Dim contents As String = Me.GetFileFromDB(virtualPath)
        If contents = String.Empty Then
            Return Previous.GetFile(virtualPath)
        Else
            Return New MyVirtualFile(virtualPath, contents)
        End If
    End Function
```

With those functions in place, the application is ready to run. Of course, the VirtualPathProvider class works for resources connected with the ASP.NET ISAPI extension only. Therefore, if you want to use your own filename extensions in your application, you first have to connect this extension with the aspnet_isapi.dll ISAPI filter extension. Figure 18-28 shows the application in action. You can see three browsers in the figure, one trying to access the physical file, a second trying to access a file from the database, and a third trying to access a resource that is not available, neither in the database nor on the file system.

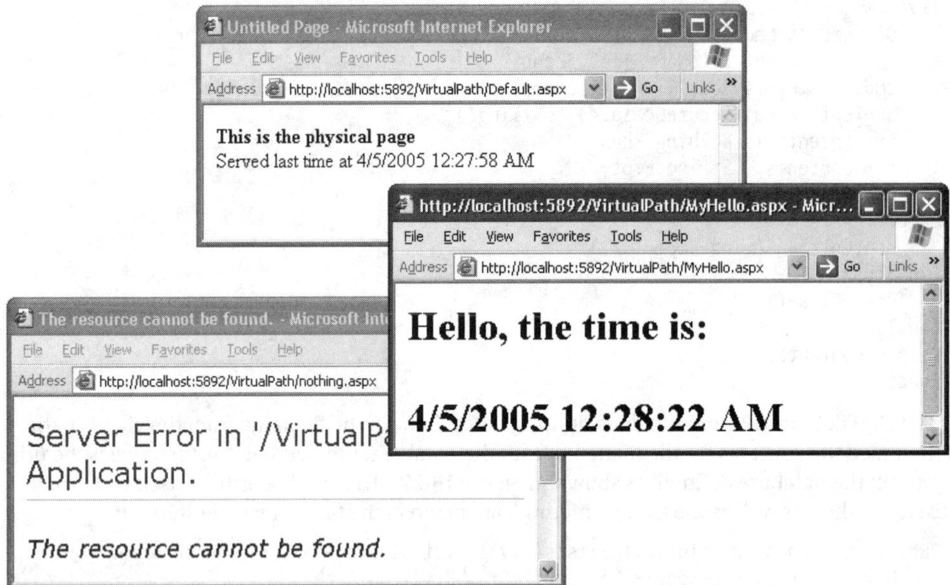

Figure 18-28. *The VirtualPathProvider in action*

Health Monitoring in ASP.NET 2.0

Health monitoring is a process for verifying the application's state while being operated in production environments. It is used for several reasons, such as catching errors, getting notified in case of errors, analyzing the performance of the application, getting information about the payload for the application, and much more. Monitoring usually is implemented through a mechanism called *instrumentation*, which is a technique used for adding events, performance counters, and tracing capabilities to an application.

Through these tracing capabilities, administrators, operational staff, and developers have the possibility of monitoring the application based on several aspects. However, instrumentation is something that has to be integrated into the application's architecture in a way that makes monitoring useful and convenient.

ASP.NET 2.0 ships with an integrated health-monitoring system that is completely consumable through a health-monitoring API. Therefore, the instrumentation capabilities are integrated into the platform itself. You will now learn about the fundamentals of this instrumentation system.

Understanding the Basic Structure

The system is split up into two major parts: types of events that are implemented in a set of event classes and providers that are responsible for processing different types of events. You can see this when looking at the basic structure of the health-monitoring configuration that is part of the web.config configuration file:

```
<healthMonitoring Enabled="true|false" heartBeatInterval="time interval">
    <providers>... </providers>
    <eventMappings>... </eventMappings>
    <profiles>... </profiles>
    <rules>... </rules>
</healthMonitoring>
```

Through the <providers> element you can configure a number of providers responsible for event processing. The events that can be processed are registered through the <eventMappings> element. The connection between providers and events is drawn through the <rules> element, which defines the provider responsible for processing an event and some additional parameters.

The <rules> section on its own may reference profiles that are defined in the <profiles> section. These profiles are some additional parameters that can be used for configuring the behavior of the event processing mechanism. Examples for such parameters are the number of times the event has to happen until it is raised by the monitoring system and the time that has to take place between two events.

Events and Providers

The reasons for splitting events and providers into two components are of course extensibility and flexibility. The event itself defines a situation that has become reality in the application, and the provider specifies how the event will be processed. ASP.NET ships with several event providers for catching the following types of events that are all defined in the System.Web.Management namespace:

- Heartbeats are events that are raised in a regular interval defined in the web.config configuration file. They provide you with information about the running process in regular intervals for monitoring memory consumption, CPU processor load, and much more. The class that implements this event is the WebHeartBeatEvent class.
- Application lifetime events enable you to catch several events raised during the application's life cycle such as startup, shutdown, session starts, session ends, and much more. These types of events are encapsulated in the WebApplicationLifetimeEvent class.
- The WebAuditEvent class encapsulates security audit events such as failed logons or attempts for accessing resources without the necessary permissions.
- Request-based and response-based events are encapsulated in the WebRequestEvent class. You can catch several types of events such as the start of a request, its end, information about response generated, and much more.
- Finally, you can catch and monitor several types of errors, either general application errors happening on startup/shutdown or request-based errors. These errors are encapsulated in the WebErrorEvent class for general errors and the WebRequestErrorEvent class for request-specific errors.

All these events are already registered with corresponding friendly names in the machine-wide configuration of the default installation of ASP.NET. Of course, if you create your own type of event generated by the application, you can register it in the <eventMappings> section of the <healthMonitoring> section in the web.config file. The syntax is basically the same as shown for the default events in machine.config in the following code snippet:

```
<healthMonitoring>
    <eventMappings>
        <add name="All Events"
             type="System.Web.Management.WebBaseEvent,
                  System.Web,Version=2.0.0.0,Culture=neutral,
                  PublicKeyToken=b03f5f7f11d50a3a"
           startEventCode="0" endEventCode="2147483647" />
        <add name="HeartBeats" type="System.Web.Management.WebHeartBeatEvent,
                                    System.Web,Version=2.0.0.0,Culture=neutral,
                                    PublicKeyToken=b03f5f7f11d50a3a"
           startEventCode="0" endEventCode="2147483647" />
        ...
    </eventMappings>
</healthMonitoring>
```

Of course, just a couple of events are registered in the machine-wide configuration. You can find a full list of the events with their friendly names in Table 18-5.

Table 18-5. *List of Events Available on a Default Installation*

Event Name	Event Type	Description
All Events	WebBaseEvent	Mapping for all events available, as all events inherit from this class.
HeartBeats	WebHeartBeatEvent	Heartbeat event for delivering information about the process in regular intervals.
Application Lifetime Events	WebApplicationLifetimeEvent	Delivers application-specific events such as startup or shutdown.
Request Processing Events	WebRequestEvent	Basic configuration for delivering all request processing events available.
All Errors	WebBaseErrorEvent	Catches all types of error events, as this is the base class for errors in general.
Infrastructure Errors	WebErrorEvent	While All Errors focuses on all errors happening within the web application, this type of error includes infrastructure errors of the ASP.NET runtime itself as well.
Request Processing Errors	WebRequestErrorEvent	Errors that occur within the processing of one request.
All Audits	WebAuditEvent	Catches all types of audits, as this is the general base class for audit events.
Failure Audits	WebFailureAuditEvent	Catches all audits designated to failures such as invalid logins or "access denied" errors.
Success Audits	WebSuccessAuditEvent	Catches all audits designated to succeeding operations.

Basically, any type of provider can process these events. Again, the system ships with a couple of providers, but only some of them are really configured in the machine-wide configuration, as shown in the following code snippet:

```
<healthMonitoring...>
    <providers>
        <add name="EventLogProvider"
             type="System.Web.Management.EventLogWebEventProvider,
                   System.Web,Version=2.0.0.0,Culture=neutral,
                   PublicKeyToken=b03f5f7f11d50a3a" />
        <add name="SqlWebEventProvider" ConnectionStringName="LocalSqlServer"
             maxEventDetailsLength="1073741823"
             buffer="false" bufferMode="Notification"
             type="System.Web.Management.SqlWebEventProvider,
                   System.Web,Version=2.0.0.0,Culture=neutral,
                   PublicKeyToken=b03f5f7f11d50a3a" />
        <add name="WmiWebEventProvider"
             type="System.Web.Management.WmiWebEventProvider,
```

```
                    System.Web,Version=2.0.0.0,Culture=neutral,
                    PublicKeyToken=b03f5f7f11d50a3a" />
    </providers>
</healthMonitoring>
```

Although only the three providers shown in the previous code snippet are configured by default, the framework ships with five providers. If you need another provider, just write a class inherited from the ProviderBase class of the namespace System.Configuration.Provider, and register the provider in the <providers> section of the <healthMonitoring> section in your own web.config in the same way as in the previous code snippet. The framework ships with the following providers:

EventLogWebEventProvider: EventLogWebEventProvider is responsible for adding different types of events to the Windows event log of the local system.

MailWebEventProvider: MailWebEventProvider is a provider for sending events via SMTP to a configured e-mail address. The e-mail address is added as a parameter to the provider entry in the same way as the ConnectionStringName parameter of the SqlWebEventProvider shown in the previous code snippet.

SqlWebEventProvider: SqlWebEventProvider offers the possibility for storing events into a SQL Server–based database. Of course, the database requires some standard tables for the provider in place. The SQL scripts for creating and dropping those tables are available in the InstallWebEventSqlProvider.sql as well as UninstallWebEventSqlProvider.sql files in the .NET Framework directory.

TraceWebEventProvider: TraceWebEventProvider enables you to catch and add events to the ASP.NET trace, which can be viewed through the trace.axd handler of the runtime.

WmiWebEventProvider: WmiWebEventProvider allows you to publish events through WMI. You can catch these events like you do any other type of WMI event through the System.Management API or the unmanaged WMI provider APIs available for Windows.

Now that you know events define situations that might happen in the application and providers define the delivery mechanism for those events (which means how these events are processed), you can configure a simple application for using the health-monitoring infrastructure. You just need to take any of the samples created previously, or create a new website with an empty Default.aspx page, and add the following configuration to the web.config file:

```
<healthMonitoring enabled="true">
  <providers>
    <add name="EmailProvider"
         type="System.Web.Management.SimpleMailWebEventProvider"
         from="testhealth@vpcbase.local"
         to="testdest@vpc.local"
         subjectPrefix="Testing Health"
         buffer="true" bufferMode="Notification"/>
  </providers>
  <rules>
    <add provider="EmailProvider"
         name="All App Events"
         eventName="Application Lifetime Events"/>
  </rules>
</healthMonitoring>
```

In the previous example, you have added the e-mail provider for sending an e-mail in case of every application lifetime event. The defined element in the <rules> section connects the previously configured e-mail provider to the actual events. For the rule definition, you should use the friendly name defined for the registered event in the <eventMappings> section.

■ **Tip** If you want to test this scenario quickly, you can use the POP3 server that ships with Windows Server 2003. When you set up the POP3 server, you can either configure it to create mailboxes based on Windows accounts or use password-based authentication and therefore create a user name/password combination for every mailbox you configure. After you have installed the POP3 server, just create a mailbox, launch Microsoft Outlook, and configure the previously configured mailbox. (The SMTP and POP3 server are both localhost in that case.) Afterward, you just need to configure the SMTP server for the ASP.NET application through the web administration site that results in adding the necessary configuration entries to the web.config file of the application. When starting and shutting down the application together with the web server, you will receive the appropriate events for the application.

Summary

In this chapter you learned how to configure your web application on the target environment. For this step, IIS—the web hosting software included with Windows—plays a key role; you saw the different aspects of installing and configuring IIS on Windows 2000/XP and Windows Server 2003 systems.

You also learned about the process architecture of IIS 5.*x* and IIS 6.0, and you learned about the differences between those two architectures. While IIS 5.*x* uses a single process model and ASP.NET executes in a separate worker process called aspnet_wp.exe for executing managed applications, IIS 6.0 favors the more secure and reliable worker process model where you can configure as many processes as you want for running your web applications. Every worker process is configured through so-called application pools. Based on these pools you can configure recycling settings, performance and health settings, and a custom identity for every process. By default each process runs under the restricted Network Service account, but if additional permissions are required, you can configure your own identity.

Then you learned about how Windows and IIS share web applications through virtual directories. You learned how to configure those virtual directories and how to put them into their designated application pool when using IIS 6.0. You also learned how to create and configure application pools.

In addition, you learned all the details about deploying ASP.NET applications to the target environment. Although deploying ASP.NET applications merely requires copying them onto the target web server and sharing the directory as a virtual directory through IIS, you need to keep a couple of things in mind, such as validating the ASP.NET configuration, selecting the appropriate ASP.NET runtime because more than one version of ASP.NET can be installed on the target machine, and viewing the details of the different compilation possibilities when it comes to ASP.NET deployment.

Finally, we discussed the fundamentals of the health-monitoring subsystem included with ASP.NET. This system gives you a basic infrastructure to instrument and monitor ASP.NET web applications based on events and providers. Events are just states that can become true in a web application, and providers are components for processing those events.

Basically the topics you learned in this chapter are the most important topics for website deployment. In addition, you might want to refer to the command-line administration available since IIS 6.0. Together with some other scripts (such as database scripts imported through osql.exe), they provide a mechanism for deploying ASP.NET web applications with simple scripts automatically.

PART 4

Security

CHAPTER 19

■ ■ ■

The ASP.NET Security Model

Security is an essential part of web applications and should be taken into consideration from the first stage of the development process. Essentially, security is all about protecting your assets from unauthorized actors. You use several mechanisms to this end, including identifying users, granting or denying access to sensitive resources, and protecting the data that's stored on the server and transmitted over the wire. In all of these cases, you need an underlying framework that provides basic security functionality. ASP.NET fills this need with built-in functionality that you can use for implementing security in your web applications.

The ASP.NET security framework includes classes for authenticating and authorizing users as well as for dealing with authenticated users in your applications. Furthermore, the .NET Framework on its own provides you with a set of base classes for implementing confidentiality and integrity through encryption and digital signatures.

With ASP.NET 2.0, the security infrastructure is extended significantly with a higher-level model for managing users and roles, both programmatically and with built-in administrative tools. This functionality (which is accessible through the membership and roles APIs) builds on the existing security infrastructure that has been present since ASP.NET 1.*x*. Best of all, this security infrastructure is completely extensible through the provider design pattern, as you'll see in Chapter 26.

This chapter provides a road map to the security features in ASP.NET. In subsequent chapters, you'll dig deeper into each of the topics covered in this chapter. Here, you'll get a quick introduction to the key features of .NET security. You'll see how the .NET authentication providers and authorization modules are structured, and you'll learn how the user's security context is represented with identity and principal objects. Most important, you'll get a basic understanding of how you can incorporate security into your application architecture and design, and you'll see what the most important factors are for creating secure software.

What It Means to Create Secure Software

Although the security framework provided by .NET and ASP.NET is powerful, it's essential to keep some basic principles in mind and use the features correctly and at the right time. In all too many projects, security is treated as an afterthought, and architects and developers fail to consider it in the early stages. But when you don't keep security in mind from the beginning—which means in your application architecture and design—how can you use all the security features offered by the .NET Framework correctly and at the right time?

Therefore, it's essential to include security from the first moment of your development process. That's the only way to make the right security-related decisions when creating your architecture and designs.

Understanding Potential Threats

Creating a secure architecture and design requires that you have an in-depth understanding of your application's environment. You can't create secure software if you don't know who has access to your application and where possible points of attack might be. Therefore, the most important factor for creating a secure application architecture and design lies in a good understanding of environmental factors such as users, entry points, and potential possible threats with points of attack.

That's why *threat modeling* has become more important in today's software development processes. Threat modeling is a structured way of analyzing your application's environment for possible threats, ranking those threats, and then deciding about mitigation techniques based on those threats. With this approach, a decision for using a security technology [such as authentication or Secure Sockets Layer (SSL) encryption] is always based on an actual reason, the threat itself.

But threat modeling is important for another reason. As you probably know, not all potential threats can be mitigated with security technologies such as authentication or authorization. In other words, some of them can't be solved technically. For example, a bank's online solution can use SSL for securing traffic on its website. But how do users know they are actually using the bank's page and not a hacker's fake website? Well, the only way of course to know this is to look at the certificate used for establishing the SSL channel. But users have to be aware of that, and therefore you have to inform them of this somehow. So, the "mitigation technique" is not a security technology. It just involves making sure all your registered users know how to look at the certificate. (Of course, you can't force them to do so, but if your information is designed appropriately, you might get most of them to do it.) Threat modeling as an analysis method helps you determine issues such as these, not merely the technical issues.

Threat modeling is a big topic that is beyond the scope of this book; refer to Michael Howard and David LeBlanc's *Writing Secure Code, Second Edition* (Microsoft Press, 2002) or Frank Swiderski and Window Snyder's *Threat Modeling* (Microsoft Press, 2004).

Secure Coding Guidelines

Of course, a secure architecture and design alone doesn't make your application completely secure. It's only one of the most important factors. After you have created a secure architecture and design, you have to write secure code as well. Again, *Writing Secure Code, Second Edition* (Microsoft Press, 2002) is an excellent source for detailed information for every developer. In terms of web applications, you should always keep the following guidelines in mind when writing code:

Never trust user input: Assume that every user is evil until you have proven the opposite. Therefore, always strongly validate user input. Write your validation code in a way that it verifies input against only allowed values and not invalid values. (There are always more invalid values than you might be aware of at the time of writing the application.)

Never use string concatenation for creating SQL statements: Always use parameterized statements so that your application is not SQL injectable, as discussed in Chapter 7.

Never output data entered by a user directly on your web page before validating and encoding it: The user might enter some HTML code fragments (for example, scripts) that lead to cross-site scripting vulnerabilities. Therefore, always use HttpUtility.HtmlEncode() for escaping special characters such as < or > before outputting them on the page, or use a web control that performs this encoding automatically.

Never store sensitive data, business-critical data, or data that affects internal business rule decisions made by your application in hidden fields on your web page: Hidden fields can be changed easily by just viewing the source of the web page, modifying it, and saving it to a file. Then an attacker simply needs to submit the locally saved, modified web page to the server. Browser plug-ins are available to make this approach as easy as writing e-mails with Microsoft Outlook.

Never store sensitive data or business-critical data in view state: View state is just another hidden field on the page, and it can be decoded and viewed easily. If you use the EnableViewStateMAC=True setting for your page, view state will be signed with a message authentication code that is created based on a machine key of the web server's machine.config. We recommend using EnableViewStateMAC=True as soon as you include data in your view state that should not be changed by users browsing your web page. See Chapter 6 for more about protecting view state.

Enable SSL when using Basic authentication or ASP.NET forms authentication: Chapter 20 discusses forms authentication. SSL is discussed later in this chapter in the section "Understanding SSL."

Protect your cookies: Always protect your authentication cookies when using forms authentication, and set timeouts as short as possible and only as long as necessary.

Use SSL: In general, if your web application processes sensitive data, secure your whole website using SSL. Don't forget to protect even image directories or directories with other files not managed by the application directly through SSL.

Of course, these are just a few general, important issues. To get a complete picture of the situation in terms of your concrete application, you have to create threat models in order to compile a complete list of potential dangers. In addition, invest in ongoing education, because hackers' techniques and technologies evolve just as other techniques and technologies do.

If you forget about just one of these guidelines, all the other security features are more or less useless. Never forget the following principle: security is only as good as your weakest link.

Understanding Gatekeepers

A good way for increasing the security of your application is to have many components in place that are enforcing security. *Gatekeepers* are a conceptual pattern that applies a pipelining model to a security infrastructure. This model helps you tighten your security.

The gatekeeper model assumes that a secure application has always more security mechanisms in place than necessary. Each of these mechanisms is implemented as a gatekeeper that is responsible for enforcing some security-related conditions. If one of these gatekeepers fails, the attacker will have to face the next gatekeeper in the pipeline. The more gatekeepers you have in your application, the harder the attacker's life will be. Actually, this model supports a core principle for creating secure applications: be as secure as possible, and make attackers' lives as hard as possible.

In Figure 19-1, you can see a pipeline of gatekeepers. At the end of the pipeline, you can see the protected resource (which can be anything, even your custom page code). The protected resource will be accessed or executed only if every gatekeeper grants access. If just one gatekeeper denies access, the request processing is returned to the caller with a security exception.

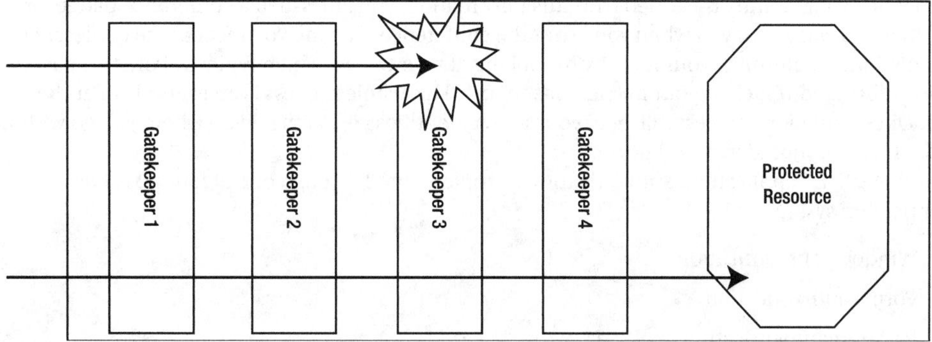

Figure 19-1. *A pipeline of gatekeepers*

Implementing a central security component in such a way is generally a good idea. You can also secure your business layer in this way. The ASP.NET application infrastructure leverages this mechanism as well. ASP.NET includes several gatekeepers, each one enforcing a couple of security conditions and therefore protecting your application. In the next sections of this chapter, you will learn which gatekeepers the ASP.NET framework includes and what the responsibilities of those gatekeepers are.

Understanding the Levels of Security

Basically, for mainstream web applications, the fundamental tasks for implementing security (besides the issues you identify during your threat modeling session) are always the same:

Authentication: First, you have to authenticate users. Authentication asks the question, who goes here? It determines who is working with your application on the other end.

Authorization: Second, as soon as you know who is working with your application, your application has to decide which operations the user may execute and which resources the user may access. In other words, authorization asks the question, what is your clearance level?

Confidentiality: While the user is working with the application, you have to ensure that nobody else is able to view sensitive data processed by the user. Therefore, you have to encrypt the channel between the client's browser and the web server. Furthermore, you possibly have to encrypt data stored on the backend (or in the form of cookies on the client) if even database administrators or other staff of the company where the web application is hosted may not view the data.

Integrity: Finally, you have to make sure data transmitted between the client and the server is not changed by unauthorized actors. Digital signatures provide you with a way to mitigate this type of threat.

ASP.NET includes a basic infrastructure for performing authentication and authorization. The .NET Framework base class library includes some classes in the System.Security namespace for encrypting and signing data. Furthermore, SSL is a standardized way for ensuring confidentiality and integrity for data transmitted between the client browser and the web server. Now you will take a closer look at each of these concepts.

Authentication

Authentication is the process of discovering a user's identity and ensuring the authenticity of this identity. The process of authentication is analogous to checking in at a conference registration table. First, you provide some credentials to prove your identity (such as a driver's license or a passport). Second, once your identity is verified with this information, you are issued a conference badge, or *token*, that you carry with you when you are at the conference. Anyone you meet at the conference can immediately determine your identity by looking at your badge, which typically contains basic identity information, such as your first and last name. This whole process is an example of authentication. Once your identity is established, your token identifies you so that everywhere you go within a particular area, your identity is known.

In an ASP.NET application, authentication is implemented through one of four possible authentication systems:

- Windows authentication
- Forms authentication
- Passport authentication
- A custom authentication process

In each of these, the user provides credentials when logging in. The user's identity is tracked in different ways depending on the type of authentication. For example, the Windows operating system uses a 96-bit number called a SID (security identifier) to identify each logged-on user. In ASP.NET forms authentication (which is covered in detail in Chapter 20), the user is given a forms authentication ticket, which is a combination of values that are encrypted and placed in a cookie.

All authentication does is allow the application to identify who a user is on each request. This works well for personalization and customization, because you can use the identity information to render user-specific messages on the web pages, alter the appearance of the website, add custom content based on user preferences, and so on. However, on its own, authentication isn't enough to restrict the tasks that a user is allowed to perform based on that user's identity. For that, you need authorization, described in a moment. However, before you learn about authorization, you will take a look at impersonation, which is related to authentication.

Impersonation

Impersonation is the process of executing code in the context (or on behalf) of another user identity. By default, all ASP.NET code is executed using a fixed machine-specific account (typically ASPNET on IIS 5.*x* or Network Service on IIS 6.0). To execute code using another identity, you can use the built-in impersonation capabilities of ASP.NET. You can use a predefined user account, or you can assume the user's identity, if the user has already been authenticated using a Windows account.

You might want to use impersonation for two reasons:

To give each web application different permissions: In IIS 5, the default account that's specified in the machine.config file is used for all web applications on the computer. If you want to give different web applications different permissions, you can use impersonation to designate different Windows accounts for each application. That's especially important for hosting scenarios where you want to isolate web applications of different customers appropriately (so that, for example, a web application of customer A is not able to access directories or databases from a web application of customer B).

To use existing Windows user permissions: For example, consider an application that retrieves information from various files that already have user-specific or group-specific permissions set. Rather than code the authorization logic in your ASP.NET application, you can use impersonation to assume the identity of the current user. That way, Windows will perform the authorization for you, checking permissions as soon as you attempt to access a file.

These two scenarios are fundamentally different. In the first scenario, impersonation defines a single, specific account. In this case, no matter what user accesses the application, and no matter what type of user-level security you use, the code will run under the account you've set. In the second scenario, the users must be authenticated by IIS. The web-page code will then execute under the identity of the appropriate user. You'll learn more about these options in Chapter 20.

Authorization

Authorization is the process of determining the rights and restrictions assigned to an authenticated user. In the conference analogy, authorization is the process of being granted permission to a particular type of session, such as the keynote speech. At most conferences it is possible to purchase different types of access, such as full access, preconference only, or exhibition hall only. This means if you want to attend the keynote address at Microsoft's Professional Developer Conference to hear what Bill Gates has to say, you must have the proper permissions (the correct conference pass). As you enter the keynote presentation hall, a member of staff will look at your conference badge. Based on the information on the badge, the staff member will let you pass or will tell you that you cannot enter. This is an example of authorization. Depending on information related to your identity, you are either granted or denied access to the resources you request.

The conference example is a case of *role-based authorization*—authorization being based on the role or group the user belongs to, not on who the user is. In other words, you are authorized to enter the room for the keynote address based on the role (type of pass), not your specific identity information (first and last name). In many cases, role-based authorization is preferable because it's much easier to implement. If the staff member needed to consult a list with the name of each allowed guest, the process of authorization would be much more awkward. The same is true in a web application, although the roles are more likely to be managers, administrators, guests, salespeople, clients, and so on.

In a web application, different types of authorization happen at different levels. For example, at the topmost level, your code can examine the user identity and decide whether to continue with a given operation. On a lower level, you can configure ASP.NET to deny access to specific web pages or directories for certain users or roles. At an even lower level, when your code performs various tasks such as connecting to a database, opening a file, writing to an event log, and so on, the Windows operating system checks the permissions of the Windows account that's executing the code. In most situations, you won't rely on this bottommost level, because your code will always run under a fixed account. In IIS 5.*x*, this is the account named ASPNET. In IIS 6.0, this is the fixed Network Service account. (In both cases, you can override the default account, as described in Chapter 18.)

Sound reasons exist for using a fixed account to run ASP.NET code. In almost all applications, the rights allocated to the user don't match the rights needed by your application, which works on behalf of the user. Generally, your code needs a broader set of permissions to perform incidental tasks, and you won't want to give these permissions to every user who might access your web application. For example, your code may need to create a log record when a failure occurs, even though the current user isn't allowed to directly write to the Windows event log, file, or database. Similarly, ASP.NET applications always require rights to the c:\[WinDir]\Microsoft.NET\[Version]\Temporary ASP.NET Files directory to create and cache a compiled machine-language version of your web pages. Finally, you might want to use an authentication system that has nothing to do with Windows. For example, an e-commerce application might verify user e-mail addresses against a server-side database. In this case, the user's identity doesn't correspond to a Windows account.

In a few rare cases, you'll want to give your code the ability to temporarily assume the identity of the user. This type of approach is much more common when creating ASP.NET applications for local networks where users already have a carefully defined set of Windows privileges. In this case, you need to supplement your security arsenal with impersonation, as described in Chapter 22.

Confidentiality and Integrity

Confidentiality means ensuring that data cannot be viewed by unauthorized users while being transmitted over a network or stored in a data store such as a database. *Integrity* is all about ensuring that nobody can change the data while it is transmitted over a network or stored in a data store. Both are based on encryption.

Encryption is the process of scrambling data so that it's unreadable by other users. Encryption in ASP.NET is a completely separate feature from authentication, authorization, and impersonation. You can use it in combination with these features or on its own.

As mentioned previously, you might want to use encryption in a web application for two reasons:

To protect communication (data over the wire): For example, you might want to make sure an eavesdropper on the public Internet can't read a credit card number that's used to purchase an item on your e-commerce site. The industry-standard approach to this problem is to use SSL. SSL also implements digital signatures for ensuring integrity. SSL isn't implemented by ASP.NET. Instead, it's a feature provided by IIS. Your web-page (or web service) code is identical whether or not SSL is used.

To protect permanent information (data in a database or in a file): For example, you might want to store a user credit card in a database record for future use. Although you could store this data in plain text and assume the web server won't be compromised, this is never a good idea. Instead, you should use the encryption classes that are provided with .NET to manually encrypt data before you store it.

It's worth noting that the .NET encryption classes aren't directly tied to ASP.NET. In fact, you can use them in any type of .NET application. You'll learn about encryption and digital signatures as well as how to take control of custom encryption in Chapter 25.

Pulling It All Together

So, how do authentication, authorization, and impersonation all work together in a web application?

When users first come to your website, they are anonymous. In other words, your application doesn't know (and doesn't care) who they are. Unless you authenticate them, this is the way it stays.

By default, anonymous users can access any ASP.NET web page. But when a user requests a web page that doesn't permit anonymous access, several steps take place (as shown in Figure 19-2):

1. The request is sent to the web server. Since the user identity is not known at this time, the user is asked to log in (using a custom web page or a browser-based login dialog box). The specific details of the login process depend on the type of authentication you're using.
2. The user provides their credentials, which are then verified, either by your application (in the case of forms authentication) or automatically by IIS (in the case of Windows authentication).
3. If the user credentials are legitimate, the user is granted access to the web page. If their credentials are not legitimate, then the user is prompted to log in again, or they are redirected to a web page with an "access denied" message.

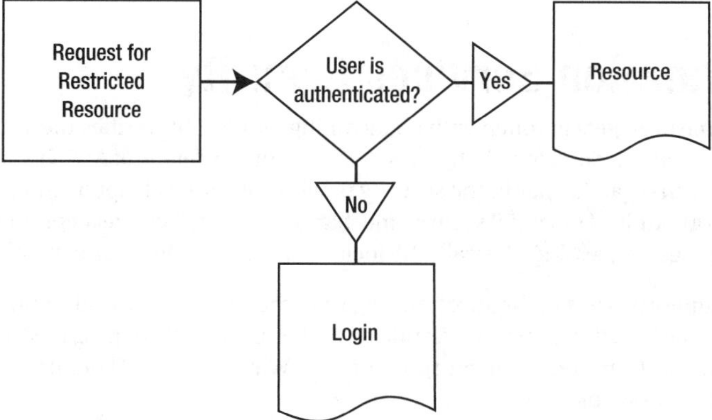

Figure 19-2. *Requesting a web page that requires authentication*

When a user requests a secure web page that allows only specific users or users in specific roles, the process is similar, but an extra step takes place (see Figure 19-3):

1. The request is sent to the web server. Since the user identity is not known at this time, the user is asked to log in (using a custom web page or a browser-based login dialog box). The specific details of the login process depend on the type of authentication you're using.
2. The user provides their credentials, which are verified with the application. This is the authentication stage.
3. The authenticated user's credentials or roles are compared to the list of allowed users or roles. If the user is in the list, then they are granted access to the resource; otherwise, access is denied.
4. Users who have access denied are either prompted to log in again, or they are redirected to a web page with an "access denied" message.

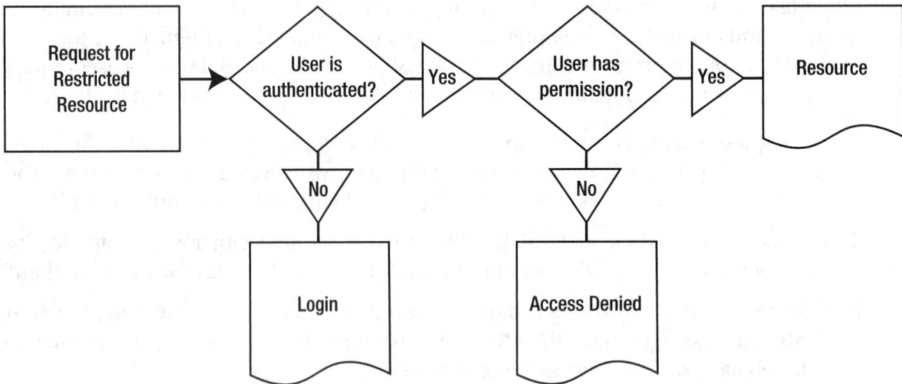

Figure 19-3. *Requesting a web page that requires authentication and authorization*

Internet Information Services Security

Before the ASP.NET runtime even gets in touch with an incoming request, IIS verifies the security according to its own configuration. Therefore, before you learn about the details of ASP.NET security, you have to learn about the first gatekeeper in the security pipeline of your web application—IIS.

IIS provides you with a couple of essential security mechanisms that act as gatekeepers before ASP.NET starts with the request processing. Basically, IIS includes the following security mechanisms:

Authentication: IIS supports Basic authentication, Digest authentication, Passport authentication, and Windows authentication as well as certificate authentication through an SSL channel. Any authentication IIS performs results in an authenticated Windows user. Therefore, IIS supports authenticating Windows users only.

Authorization: IIS provides built-in support of IP address restrictions and evaluation of Windows ACLs.

Confidentiality: Encryption can be enforced through SSL.

In the following sections, you will learn about the details of IIS security configuration. The other subsequent security chapters will go into the details of the ASP.NET security infrastructure. You have to keep IIS security always in mind, because it affects how ASP.NET behaves with different security settings applied in web.config.

For example, if your ASP.NET application wants to use Windows authentication, you should configure IIS to use either Windows or Basic (or Digest) authentication. If your ASP.NET web application doesn't want to use Windows accounts (and therefore use custom or forms authentication), you must configure IIS to allow anonymous access.

IIS Authentication

As previously mentioned, IIS supports several authentication mechanisms. Any other configuration setting security (and therefore authentication) is configured on a per-website basis. You can find the security settings on the Directory Security tab of a virtual directory's properties. Figure 19-4 shows the authentication options of IIS.

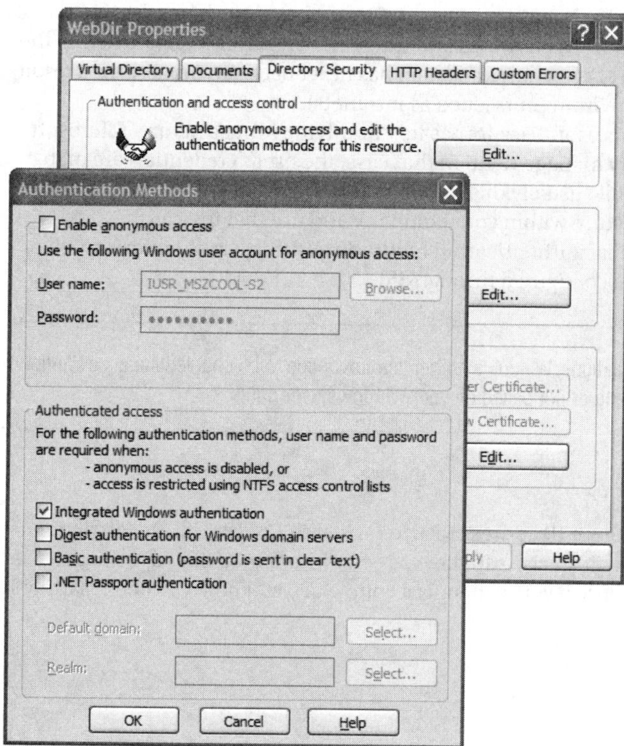

Figure 19-4. *IIS authentication options*

Of course, anonymous access gives everyone access to the web page. It overrides any other authentication setting of IIS because IIS authenticates only if it is necessary (and of course if anonymous authentication is enabled, no additional authentication steps are necessary for saving round-trips). Further, if you have configured anonymous authentication in IIS, you still can use ASP.NET-based security to authenticate users either with ASP.NET-integrated mechanisms such as forms authentication or a custom type of authentication, as you will learn later in this chapter and in subsequent chapters.

Windows authentication configures IIS to validate the credentials of the user against a Windows account configured either on the local machine or within the domain. When working within a domain, domain users don't need to enter their user name and password if already logged onto a client machine within the network, because the client's authentication ticket is passed to the server for authentication automatically.

IIS also supports Basic authentication. This is an authentication method developed by the W3C that defines an additional HTTP header for transmitting user names and passwords across the wire. But pay attention: Nothing is encrypted. The information will be transmitted Base64 encoded. Therefore, you should only use Basic authentication with SSL. As is the case with Windows authentication, the credentials entered by the user are evaluated against a Windows account. But the way the credentials are transferred over the wire is different. While Basic authentication transmits the information through the HTTP header, Windows authentication uses either NTLM or Kerberos for transmitting the information.

Digest authentication is similar to Basic authentication. Instead of sending the credentials Base64 encoded across the wire, it hashes the user's password and transmits the hashed version across the wire. Although this sounds more secure, Digest authentication has never become common. As a result, it's rarely used outside of controlled environments (such as intranets).

Passport authentication uses Microsoft Passport as its underlying infrastructure. Microsoft Passport implements a central identity management. In that case, the user's credentials are managed by a separate Passport server. While usually this infrastructure is hosted by Microsoft, you can also host your own Passport infrastructure within your company and use that instead.

Finally, IIS supports one additional authentication method, certificate authentication, that cannot be found in Figure 19-3, as it is configured through SSL.

■ **Note** For debugging ASP.NET web applications, Windows authentication needs to be enabled because Windows determines whether you are allowed to debug or not based on your Windows user rights.

IIS Authorization

Figure 19-5 shows how you can configure IP address restrictions with IIS. IP address restrictions provide you with a possibility of restricting access to the web server from machines specified in the list of granted machines. This makes sense if you want only a couple of well-known business partners to be able to access your web server.

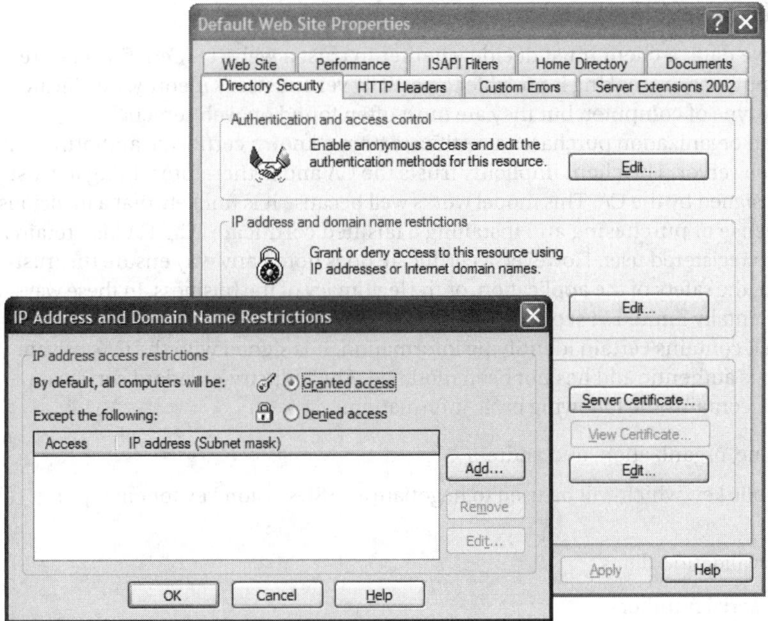

Figure 19-5. *IP address restrictions in IIS*

IIS and Secure Sockets Layer

The SSL technology encrypts communication over HTTP. SSL is supported by a wide range of browsers and ensures that information exchanged between a client and a web server can't be easily deciphered by an eavesdropper. SSL is important for hiding sensitive information such as credit card numbers and confidential company details, but it's also keenly important for user authentication. For example, if you create a login page where the user submits a user name and password, you must use SSL to encrypt this information. Otherwise, a malicious user could intercept the user credentials and use them to log onto the system.

IIIS provides SSL out of the box. Because SSL operates underneath HTTP, using SSL does not change the way you deal with HTTP requests. All the encryption and decryption work is taken care of by the SSL capabilities of the web server software (in this case, IIS). The only difference is that the URL for addresses protected by SSL begins with `https://` rather than `http://`. SSL traffic also flows over a different port (typically web servers use port 443 for SSL requests and port 80 for normal requests).

For a server to support SSL connections, it must have an installed X.509 certificate (the name X.509 was chosen to correspond with the X.500 directory standard). To implement SSL, you need to purchase a certificate, install it, and configure IIS appropriately. We'll cover these steps in the following sections.

Understanding Certificates

Before sending sensitive data, a client must decide whether to trust a website. *Certificates* were designed to serve this purpose, by making it possible to partially verify a user's identity. Certificates can be installed on any type of computer, but they are most often found on web servers.

With certificates, an organization purchases a certificate from a known certificate authority (CA) and installs it on its web server. The client implicitly trusts the CA and is therefore willing to trust certificate information signed by the CA. This model works well because it is unlikely that a malicious user will go to the expense of purchasing and installing a falsified certificate. The CA also retains information about each registered user. However, a certificate does not in any way ensure the trustworthiness of the server, the safety of the application, or the legitimacy of the business. In these ways, certificates are fundamentally limited in scope.

The certificate itself contains certain identifying information. It is signed with the CA's private key to guarantee that it is authentic and has not been modified. The industry-standard certificate type, known as x.509v3, contains the following basic information:

- The holder's name, organization, and address
- The holder's public key, which will be used to negotiate an SSL session key for encrypting communication
- The certificate's validation dates
- The certificate's serial number

In addition, a certificate might also include business-specific information, such as the certificate holder's industry, the length of time they have been in business, and so on.

The two biggest certificate authorities are as follows:

Thawte: `http://www.thawte.com`

VeriSign: `http://www.verisign.com`

If you don't need the identity validation function of CAs (for example, if your certificates will be used only on a local intranet), you can create and use your own certificates and configure all clients to trust them. This requires Active Directory and Certificate Server (which is a built-in part of Windows 2003 Server and Windows 2000 Server). For more information, consult a dedicated book about Windows network administration.

Understanding SSL

As described in the previous section, every certificate includes a public key. A public key is part of an *asymmetric key pair*. The basic idea is that the public key is freely provided to anyone who is interested. The corresponding private key is kept carefully locked away and is available only to the server. The interesting twist is that anything that's encrypted with one of the keys is decipherable with the other. That means a client can retrieve the public key and use it to encode a secret message that can be decrypted only with the corresponding private key. In other words, the client can create a message that only the server can read.

This process is called *asymmetric encryption*, and it's a basic building block of SSL. An important principle of asymmetric encryption is that you can't determine a private key by analyzing the corresponding public key. To do so would be computationally expensive (even more difficult than cracking one of the encrypted messages). However, asymmetric encryption also has its limitations—namely, it's much slower and generates much larger messages than symmetric encryption.

Symmetric encryption is the type of encryption that most people are intuitively familiar with. It uses the same secret key to encrypt a message as to decrypt it. The drawback with symmetric encryption is that both parties need to know the secret value in order to have a conversation.

However, you can't transmit this information over the Internet, because a malicious user might intercept it and then be able to decipher the following encrypted conversation. The great trick of SSL is to combine asymmetric and symmetric encryption. Asymmetric encryption manages the initial key exchange—in other words, agrees on a secret value. Then, this secret value symmetrically encrypts all subsequent messages, which ensures the best possible performance.

The whole process works like this:

1. The client sends a request to connect to the server.
2. The server signs its certificate and sends it to the client. This concludes the handshake portion of the exchange.
3. The client checks whether the certificate was issued by a CA it trusts. If so, it proceeds to the next step. In a web browser scenario, the client may warn the user with an ominous-sounding message if it does recognize the CA and allow the user to decide whether to proceed.
4. The client compares the information in the certificate with the information received from the site (including its domain name and its public key). The client also verifies that the server-side certificate is valid, has not been revoked, and is issued by a trusted CA. Then the client accepts the connection.
5. The client tells the server what encryption keys it supports for communication.
6. The server chooses the strongest shared key length and informs the client.
7. Using the indicated key length, the client randomly generates a symmetric encryption key. This will be used for the duration of the transaction between the server and the client. It ensures optimum performance, because symmetric encryption is much faster than asymmetric encryption.
8. The client encrypts the session key using the server's public key (from the certificate), and then it sends the encrypted session key to the server.
9. The server receives the encrypted session key and decrypts it using its private key. Both the client and server now have the shared secret key, and they can use it to encrypt all communication for the duration of the session.

You'll notice that the symmetric key is generated randomly and used only for the duration of a session. This limits the security risk. First, it's harder to break encrypted messages using cryptanalysis, because messages from other sessions can't be used. Second, even if the key is determined by a malicious user, it will remain valid only for the course of the session.

Another interesting point is that the client must generate the symmetric key. This is because the client has the server's public key, which can be used to encrypt a message that only the server can read. The server does not have corresponding information about the client and thus cannot yet encrypt a message. This also means that if the client supplies a weak key, the entire interaction could be compromised. For example, older versions of the Netscape browser used a weak random number generator to create the symmetric key. This would make it much easier for a malicious user to guess the key.

Installing Certificates in IIS

When deploying an application, you will probably want to purchase certificates from a genuine CA such as VeriSign. This is particularly the case with websites and Internet browsers, which recognize a limited number of certificate authorities automatically. If you use a test certificate to encrypt communication with a secured portion of a website, for example, the client browser will display a warning that the certificate is not from a known CA.

IIS Manager allows you to create a certificate request automatically. First, start IIS Manager. Expand the Web Sites group, right-click your website item (often titled Default Web Site), and choose Properties. Under the Directory Security tab, you'll find a Server Certificate button (see Figure 19-6).

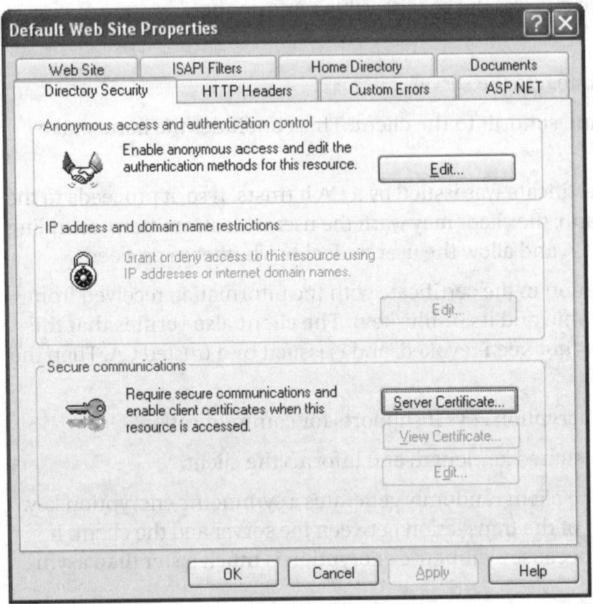

Figure 19-6. *Configuring directory security*

Click the Server Certificate button to start the IIS Certificate Wizard (see Figure 19-7). This wizard requests some basic organization information and generates a request file. You'll also need to supply a bit length for the key—the higher the bit length, the stronger the key.

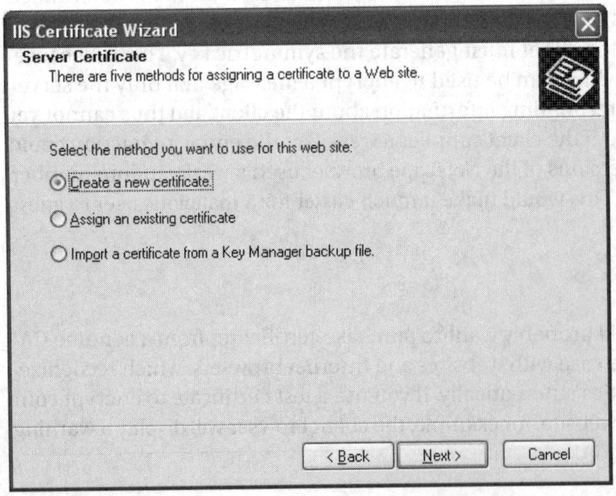

IIS Certificate Wizard
Server Certificate
There are five methods for assigning a certificate to a Web site.
Select the method you want to use for this web site:
Create a new certificate.
Assign an existing certificate
Import a certificate from a Key Manager backup file.
< Back
Next >
Cancel

Figure 19-7. *Creating a server certificate request*

The generated file can be saved as a text file, but it must ultimately be e-mailed to a CA. A sample (slightly abbreviated) request file is as follows:

```
Webmaster: administrator@certificatecompany.com
Phone: (555) 555-5555
Server: Microsoft Key Manager for IIS Version 4.0

Common-name: www.yourcompany.com
Organization: YourOrganization

-----BEGIN NEW CERTIFICATE REQUEST-----
MIIB1DCCAToCAQAwgZMxCzAJBgNVBAYTAlVTMREwDwYDVQQIEwhOZXcgWW9yazEQ
MA4GA1UEBxMHQnVmZmFsbzEeMBwGA1UEChMVVW5pdmVyc2l0eSBhdCBCdWZmYWxv
MRwwGgYDVQQLExNSZXNlYXJjaCBGb3VuZGF0aW9uMSEwHwYDVQQDExh3d3cucmVz
ZWFyY2guYnVmZmFsby5lZHUwgZ8wDQYJKoZIhvcNAQEBBQADgYOAMIGJAoGBALJO
hbsCagHN4KMbl7uzOGwvcjJeWH8JqIUFVFi352tnoA15PZfCxW18KNtFeBtrbOpf
-----END NEW CERTIFICATE REQUEST-----
```

The CA will return a certificate that you can install according to its instructions. By convention, you should run all SSL communication over port 443 and serve normal web traffic over port 80.

Encoding Information with SSL

Once you've installed the certificate, it's fairly easy to use SSL communication. The only other step is to modify your request to use a URL that starts with `https://` instead of the `http://` prefix. Typically, this means tweaking a Response.Redirect() statement in your code. Because all the encryption and decryption occurs just before the message is sent (or immediately after it is retrieved), your application does not need to worry about deciphering the data manually, manipulating byte arrays, using the proper character encoding, and so on.

At the server side, you can also enforce SSL connections so that it is impossible to interact with a web service without encrypting communication. Simply right-click the website in IIS Manager, and select the Directory Security tab. In the Secure Communications section, click the Edit button (which is available only after a certificate is installed). Then, choose Require Secure Channel (see Figure 19-8).

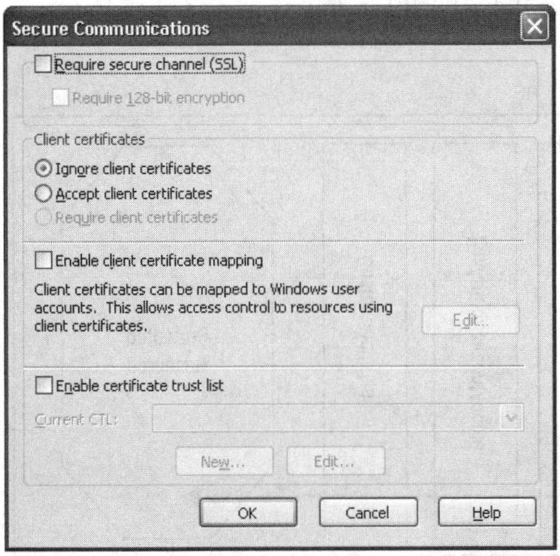

Figure 19-8. *Enforcing SSL access*

Keep in mind that there are good reasons not to enforce an SSL connection for an entire virtual directory. For example, you might want to secure some method calls in a web service but not secure others that don't return sensitive information. This allows you to increase performance and reduce the work performed by the server. If needed, you can check for a secure connection in your code and then throw an exception or redirect the user if SSL is required but not present.

Here's an example that checks whether the current request is transmitted over a secure connection using the HttpRequest.IsSecureConnection property:

```
If Request.IsSecureConnection Then
    ' (Application code goes here.)
Else
    ' Redirect with https to ensure the page is accessed over SSL.
    Response.Redirect("https://www.mySite.com/account.asmx")
End If
```

■ **Note** A common mistake is to use localhost or any other aliases for the server host name in an SSL connection. This will not work, because the client attempts to verify that the CN (common name) part of the subject name of the server certificate matches the host name found in the HTTP request during the handshake portion of the SSL exchange.

With SSL, all traffic will be encrypted, not just the sensitive data. For this reason, many web servers use a hardware accelerator to improve the performance of encryption with SSL.

■ **Note** Remember, SSL is not tied to ASP.NET in any way. If you want to learn more about SSL, consult a book dedicated to security and IIS such as *IIS Security* (Osbourne/McGraw-Hill, 2002).

ASP.NET Security Architecture

ASP.NET implements the concept of gatekeepers (introduced previously) through HTTP modules. Each module is a class implementing the interface IHttpModule, and each module acts as a gatekeeper of the ASP.NET infrastructure. Of course, HTTP modules are used for other tasks, but lots of them are security related. As you can see in Figure 19-9, ASP.NET includes several authentication and authorization modules.

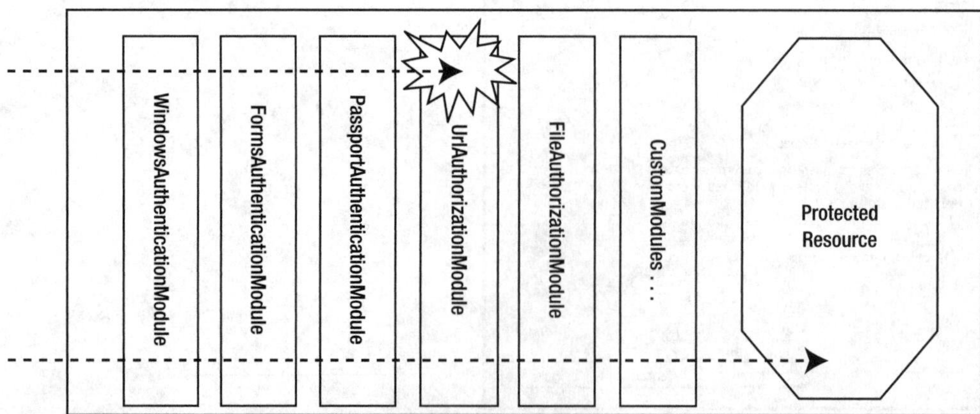

Figure 19-9. *The ASP.NET security gatekeepers as IHttpModule classes*

Because web applications use the stateless HTTP, no information is retained for the user between requests. As a result, the user must be authenticated and authorized at the beginning of each request. ASP.NET handles this by firing global application events. Authentication modules can handle these events to perform user authentication. Not all requests require authentication or authorization. However, the related events always fire. These events are handled by the configured HTTP modules demonstrated in Figure 19-9. Of course, you can handle the events through the global application class as well (these events are defined in the code-behind class of the global.asax file), but for higher reusability we recommend creating separate Http modules, because it is really easy to create them.

The two primary events you need to deal with are the AuthenticateRequest and AuthorizeRequest events. These aren't the only events that fire, but these are the most useful. Figure 19-10 shows the order of security-related application events.

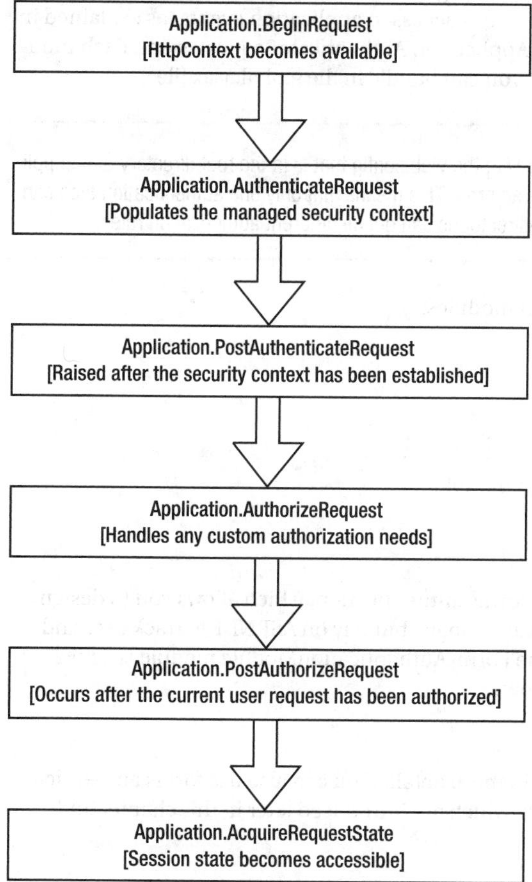

Figure 19-10. *Security-related application events*

■ **Note** Session state is not accessible until *after* the authorization and authentication events have fired. This prevents you from storing user identity information in session state. Instead, you must use other mechanisms.

The AuthenticateRequest event is raised by the HttpApplication object when a request requires authentication. Once the user is authenticated (typically supplying some sort of user credential such as a cookie with user information), the next step is to make sure the user identity information is readily available for the rest of the page-processing cycle. To accomplish this, you must create a new object with user information and attach it to the User property of the current HttpContext.

The AuthorizeRequest event is raised after the user has been authenticated in the AuthenticateRequest event. Authorization modules use AuthorizeRequest to check whether the user is authorized for the resource they are requesting.

Authentication

Authentication is implemented in ASP.NET through specialized HTTP modules, as demonstrated in Figures 19-9 and 19-10. You choose which authentication module you want to use with the <authentication> element in the web.config configuration file. All authentication modules implement the IHttpModule interface, which provides access to application events (as explained in Chapter 5). This allows them to handle the HttpApplication.AuthenticateRequest event. Each module also exposes its own Authenticate event that you can handle in the global.asax file.

Note The <authentication> element can be used only in the web.config that is in the root directory of an application. Attempting to use it in a subdirectory will cause an error. This means that only one authentication type can be defined for each application. However, different subdirectories can define different authorization rules.

ASP.NET provides three core authentication modules:

- FormsAuthenticationModule
- WindowsAuthenticationModule
- PassportAuthenticationModule

The following sections briefly describe each module.

The FormsAuthenticationModule

The FormsAuthenticationModule module uses forms authentication, which allows you to design your own login pages, write your own authentication logic, but rely on ASP.NET to track user and role information using an encrypted cookie. The FormsAuthenticationModule module is active when the <authorization> element is set as follows:

```
<authentication mode="Forms" />
```

Chapter 20 explores forms authentication in more detail. (You can also use forms authentication with the membership API and the roles API, which are introduced later in this chapter and covered in detail in Chapter 20.)

The WindowsAuthenticationModule

The WindowsAuthenticationModule module works in conjunction with IIS to perform Windows authentication. This module is active when the <authentication> element in the web.config file is set as follows:

```
<authentication mode="Windows" />
```

Chapter 22 explores Windows authentication in more detail.

The PassportAuthenticationModule

PassportAuthenticationModule is active when the <authentication> element in the web.config file is set as follows:

```
<authentication mode="Passport" />
```

The PassportAuthenticationModule module provides a wrapper for Microsoft's Passport authentication service. When using Passport, users are authenticated using the information in Microsoft's Passport database (the same technology that powers the free Hotmail e-mail system). The advantage of Passport is that you can use existing user credentials (such as an e-mail address and password), without forcing users to go through a separate registration process. The disadvantage is that you need to enter into a licensing agreement with Microsoft and pay a yearly fee based on use.

ASP.NET doesn't include full support for Passport authentication. To use it successfully, you'll need to download and install the Passport .NET SDK on your web server. This book doesn't cover Passport, but you can learn more (and download the SDK) at `http://www.microsoft.com/net/services/passport`.

Authorization

Once a user is authenticated, information such as the user's name and security context is automatically made available by the ASP.NET infrastructure. You can access this information through the HttpContext.Current.User object and use this information to implement authorization in your code. Furthermore, ASP.NET includes the following prebuilt modules for implementing authorization:

UrlAuthorization: The UrlAuthorization module works based on the content of the <authorization> configuration in the web.config files of different directories of your web application. It can restrict access to both directories and files, based on the user's name or the roles assigned to the user.

FileAuthorization: When using Windows authentication in intranets, ASP.NET automatically uses the FileAuthorization module for authorizing Windows users against files accessed by ASP.NET based on Windows Access Control Lists (ACLs). Therefore, each Windows user must have at least read access rights on the files of the web applications in that case. This module works with Windows authentication only—but without impersonation.

When impersonating users in Windows environments, you can even configure ACLs on registry entries or any other resource on the machine, and Windows does authorization based on the Windows user for you.

■ Caution Using impersonation is tricky (if not dangerous). It requires you to properly configure ACL entries on every object for every group, or sometimes even every user. A simple configuration mistake can lead to a security hole in your application. When the number of users (and Windows groups) grows, the situation gets more and more complex, and therefore configuration errors may happen. You shouldn't use impersonation if it's not really necessary. You should always prefer to create custom application roles and perform authorization based on these roles.

Furthermore, you can implement authorization by writing custom code in your pages or components used by the web application. In that case, you refer to the HttpContext.Current.User object and make decisions based on role membership or the user's name directly. You will learn more about how to design and implement authorization in Chapter 23. But before learning about the details of authentication and authorization, you must understand the meaning of the security context.

The Security Context

Regardless of the authentication system, ASP.NET uses the same underlying model to represent user and role information. Users who log into a web application are granted a *principal* and an *identity* based on the credentials they have provided. The principal object represents the current security context of the user. It combines the user itself (the identity) with information stored in the account records for the current user such as the roles, privileges, and much more. It therefore allows you to perform role-based authorization, and it provides a reference to the corresponding identity object. The identity object represents the successfully authenticated user and therefore provides user information such as the user name.

The IPrincipal Interface

All principal objects implement the IPrincipal interface, which defines a core set of functionality. When you access the User property of the current web page (System.Web.UI.Page) or from the current HTTP context (HttpContext.Current), you're accessing an IPrincipal object that represents the security context of the current user.

The IPrincipal interface defines a single property named Identity, which retrieves an IIdentity object that provides information about the current user. The IPrincipal interface also defines a single method named IsInRole(), which allows you to test whether the current user is a member of a specific role.

Here's an example that uses the IsInRole() method to test whether the current user is a member of a role named Admin:

```
If HttpContext.Current.User.IsInRole("Admin") Then
    ' (Do something.)
End If
```

When using Windows authentication or forms authentication, the principal object is created automatically. However, it's also possible to create a principal object on the fly, with user and role information that you extract from another location, such as a custom database. You'll see examples of both techniques in later chapters.

The IIdentity Interface

Like the IPrincipal interface, the IIdentity interface provides consistency no matter what authentication scheme you use. All identity objects must implement IIdentity.

The IIdentity interface defines the basic information needed to represent the current user. At a minimum, this includes the following three read-only properties:

AuthenticationType: Returns the type of authentication used as a string (forms, Passport, NTLM, or a custom authentication type)

IsAuthenticated: Returns a Boolean value that indicates whether the user has been authenticated (True) or is anonymous (False)

Name: Returns the name of the current user as a string

You can access the IIdentity object that represents the current user through the IPrincipal object. Here's an example that uses this technique to check whether the user has been authenticated:

```
If HttpContext.Current.User.Identity.IsAuthenticated Then
    lblUserName.Text = HttpContext.Current.User.Identity.Name & " is logged in"
End If
```

The type of identity object depends on the type of authentication used. All in all, four identity classes are included in the .NET Framework:

System.Web.Security.FormsIdentity: Represents a user who is logged on using forms authentication.

System.Security.Principal.WindowsIdentity: Represents a Windows user account.

System.Web.Security.PassportIdentity: Provides a class to be used by the PassportAuthenticationModule.

System.Security.Principal.GenericIdentity: Represents a generic user identity. (You can use this to create identities if you're creating a custom authentication system.)

Membership and Roles APIs

As you will see in Chapter 20, when using forms authentication, you need to authenticate your users against a custom store. This means you must do much more than create a basic login page for validating user names and passwords. Of course, you need a way to manage users as well as assign users to roles. With ASP.NET 1.*x* you had to create such management tools and components for programmatic management on your own. ASP.NET 2.0 provides this infrastructure through the membership API, the roles API, and the profiles API.

Membership API

The membership API is a complete user management system. It helps you create, edit, and delete users, and it includes functionality for password recovery. You can use the API for programmatically performing all these management tasks, or you can use the ASP.NET web configuration tool for the graphical administration of your users. With this infrastructure you can save lots of time, as you don't have to create your own user administration application anymore because it already exists within the ASP.NET 2.0 framework. Furthermore, it includes functionality for validating a user name and password combination entered by the user.

You will learn more details about the membership API in Chapter 21.

Roles API

In many cases authorization is performed on groups of users called *roles*. One role can contain many users, and a user can be assigned to many roles. ASP.NET 2.0 includes a ready-to-use API that allows you to assign users to roles as needed. Again, you can do this programmatically through the roles API or with the ASP.NET web configuration utility.

In Chapter 23, you will learn about the details of using the roles API in your applications.

Profiles API

Of course, if your web application authenticates users, these users may want to persist settings on your website for subsequent visits. Typically, for this use case you implement so-called user profiles that persist settings on a per-user basis between different visits of your website. The big difference between user profiles and session state is that profiles are persistent across multiple sessions. Again, ASP.NET 2.0 includes a ready-to-use infrastructure for managing profiles in your application.

In Chapter 24, you will learn how you can use the profiles API in your application.

Extending Membership, Roles, and Profiles

ASP.NET needs to store all the information of users, roles, and profiles somewhere. By default it stores the data in a SQL Server database. But the whole infrastructure is completely extensible through so-called custom providers. Membership, roles, and profile providers are components that are responsible for storing user, role, and profile information in a data store. While ASP.NET 2.0 ships with a profile for SQL Server, you can create and configure custom providers to store this information anywhere you want. Best of all, the whole API accesses these providers through well-defined interfaces, which means your application can be written completely provider independent. That means changing a provider will not affect your application in any way!

You will learn more about custom providers in Chapter 26.

Summary

With ASP.NET, programmers finally have a comprehensive, full-featured set of security tools. As with many other features in the world of ASP.NET, the presence of a security framework simply means that there is less work for you to do to implement a variety of authentication and authorization scenarios.

CHAPTER 20

Forms Authentication

In the previous chapter, you learned about the basic structure of ASP.NET security. In this chapter, you will learn how you can authenticate your users using forms authentication. You should use this type of authentication whenever you do not want to use Windows-based accounts in your applications.

In such cases, you need your own authentication infrastructure with a custom login page that validates a user name and password against a custom store such as your own database. This infrastructure then establishes the security context on each request again (in many cases, such systems work based on cookies). If you've ever authenticated users with ASP 3.0, you've probably created such authentication mechanisms on your own.

Fortunately, ASP.NET includes a complete infrastructure for implementing such systems. ASP.NET handles the cookies and establishes the security context on each request for you. This infrastructure is called *forms authentication*, and you'll learn how it works in this chapter.

Note The basic forms authentication infrastructure works the same way as in previous versions of ASP.NET. It includes only a handful of new settings in its configuration schema, covered in the section "Configuring Forms Authentication." If you have experience with ASP.NET 1.*x* and forms authentication, you can skip this chapter and proceed with Chapter 21.

Introducing Forms Authentication

Forms authentication is a *ticket-based* (also called *token-based*) system. This means when users log in, they receive a ticket with basic user information. This information is stored in an encrypted cookie that's attached to the response so it's automatically submitted on each subsequent request.

When a user requests an ASP.NET page that is not available for anonymous users, the ASP.NET runtime verifies whether the forms authentication ticket is available. If it's not available, ASP.NET automatically redirects the user to a login page. At that moment, it's your turn. You have to create this login page and validate the credentials within this login page. If the user is successfully validated, you just tell the ASP.NET infrastructure about the success (by calling a method of the FormsAuthentication class), and the runtime automatically sets the authentication cookie (which actually contains the ticket) and redirects the user to the originally requested page. With this request, the runtime detects that the authentication cookie with the ticket is available and grants access to the page. You can see this process in Figure 20-1.

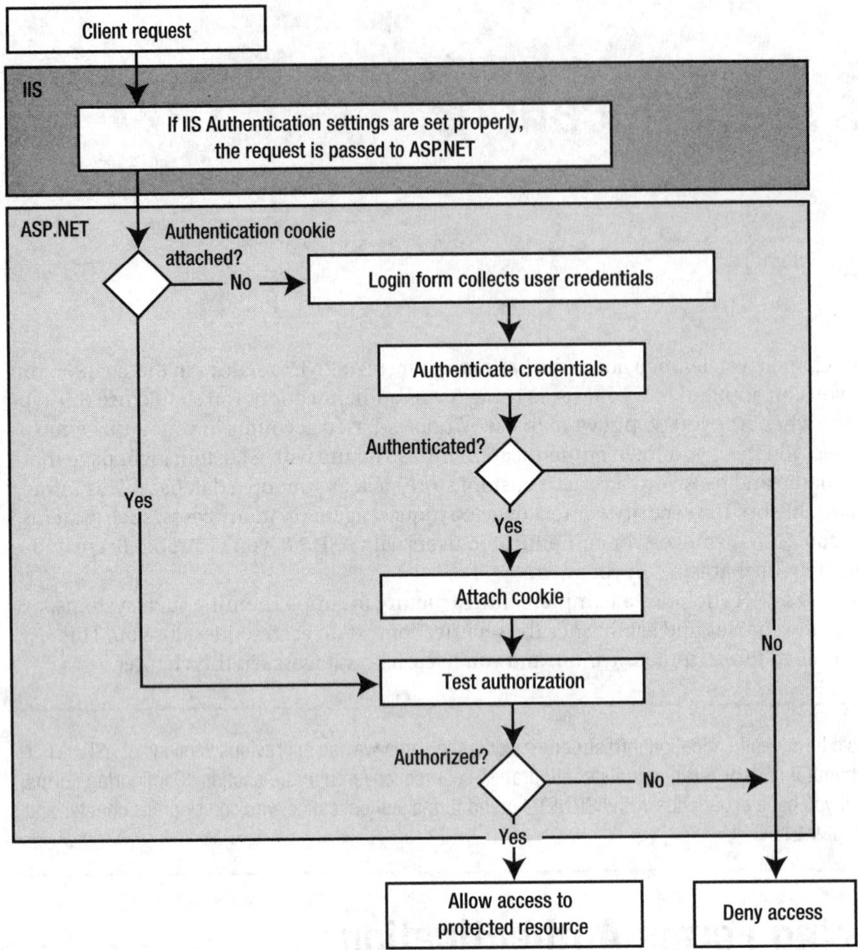

Figure 20-1. *The forms authentication process*

All you need to do is configure forms authentication in the web.config file, create the login page, and validate the credentials in the login page.

Why Use Forms Authentication?

Cookie authentication is an attractive option for developers for a number of reasons:

- You have full control over the authentication code.
- You have full control over the appearance of the login form.
- It works with any browser.
- It allows you to decide how to store user information.

Let's look at each of these in turn.

Controlling the Authentication Code

Because forms authentication is implemented entirely within ASP.NET, you have complete control over how authentication is performed. You don't need to rely on any external systems, as you do with Windows or Passport authentication. You can customize the behavior of forms authentication to suit your needs, as you will see in the section "Persistent Cookies in Forms Authentication."

Controlling the Appearance of the Login Form

You have the same degree of control over the appearance of forms authentication as you do over its functionality. In other words, you can format the login form in any way you like.

This flexibility in appearance is not available in the other authentication methods. Windows authentication needs the browser to collect credentials, and Passport authentication requires that users leave your website and visit the Passport site to enter their credentials.

Working with a Range of Browsers

Forms authentication uses standard HTML as its user interface, so all browsers can handle it. Because you can format the login form in any way you like, you can even use forms authentication with browsers that do not use HTML, such as those on mobile devices. To do this, you need to detect the browser being used and provide a form in the correct format for the device (such as WML for mobile phones).

■Caution Forms authentication uses standard HTML forms for collecting and submitting the user's credentials. Therefore, you have to use Secure Sockets Layer (SSL) to encrypt and transmit the user's credentials securely. If you don't use SSL, the information is transmitted as clear text in the postback data in the request to the server.

Storing User Information

Forms authentication stores users in the web.config file by default, but, as you will see in the section "Custom Credentials Store," you can store the information anywhere you like. You just need to create the code that accesses the data store and retrieves the required information. (And if you use the membership API introduced in Chapter 21, you even don't need to do that.) A common example is to store the user information in a custom database.

This flexibility in the storage of user information also means you can control how user accounts are created and administered, and you can attach additional information to user accounts.

By comparison, Windows authentication (discussed in Chapter 22) is much less flexible. It requires that you set up a Windows user account for each user you want to authenticate. This is obviously a problem if you want to serve a large number of users or if you want to register users programmatically. It also doesn't allow you to store additional information about users. (In the case of Active Directory, you have the possibility of extending the schema, but this is something that needs to be planned well.) Instead, you have to store this information separately. Passport authentication has similar limitations. Although Passport stores more user information, it doesn't allow you to add custom information, and it doesn't allow you to take part in user registration or account management.

Why Would You *Not* Use Forms Authentication?

So far, you've considered the reasons that make forms authentication an attractive choice for user authentication. However, forms authentication also has downsides:

- You have to create the user interface for users to log in.
- You have to maintain a catalog with user credentials.
- You have to take additional precautions against the interception of network traffic.

The following sections explore these issues. You can solve the first two of these downsides by using the membership API framework, which offers prebuilt controls and a prebuilt schema for credential storage and runs on SQL Server databases out of the box. You will learn about the membership API framework in Chapter 21.

Creating Your Own Login Interface

As mentioned earlier, forms authentication gives you control over the interface that users use to log into your web application. Along with its benefits, this approach also creates extra work, because you have to build the login page. Other forms of authentication supply some prebuilt portions. For instance, if you're using Windows authentication, the browser provides a standard dialog box. In Passport authentication, the user interface of the Passport site is always used for logging in.

Creating the login page for forms authentication doesn't require a lot of work, though. It's just worth noting that forms authentication is merely a framework for building an authentication system, rather than an all-in-one system that's complete and ready to use.

The new membership API, on the other hand, includes a prebuilt login control that can be used either on a separate login page or within any page of your application that provides a prebuilt login user interface. This user interface is customizable and communicates with the membership API to log the user in automatically. The control does most of the work of creating custom login pages. In most cases, creating a custom login page requires nothing more than adding an .aspx page to your solution with a login control on it. You don't need to catch any events or write any code if you are fine with the default behavior of the control (which will usually be the case). You will learn more details about this control in Chapter 21.

Maintaining User Details

When you use forms authentication, you are responsible for maintaining the details of the users who access your system. The most important details are the credentials that the user needs in order to log into the system. Not only do you need to devise a way to store them, but you also need to ensure that they are stored securely. Also, you need to provide some sort of administration tools for managing the users stored in your custom store.

The membership API framework ships with a prebuilt schema for storing credentials in a SQL Server database. So, you can save lots of time using this existing schema; furthermore, the schema is extensible. Still, you are responsible for backing up the credentials store securely so that you can restore it in case of a system failure.

All these considerations don't apply to most other types of authentication. In Windows authentication, user credentials are stored by the underlying operating system. Windows uses a variety of techniques to keep them secure automatically so that you don't need to perform any work of your own. In Passport authentication, the credentials are stored securely on Passport servers.

Intercepting Network Traffic

When a user enters credentials for forms authentication, the credentials are sent from the browser to the server in plain-text format. This means anyone intercepting them will be able to read them. This is obviously an insecure situation.

The usual solution to this problem is to use SSL (as described in the previous chapter). Now, a valid argument might be that you just need to use SSL for securing the login page, not the entire application. You can configure forms authentication to encrypt and sign the cookie, and therefore it's extremely difficult for an attacker to get any information from it. In addition, the cookie should not contain any sensitive information and therefore won't include the password that was used for authentication.

But what if the attacker intercepts the unencrypted traffic and just picks the (already encrypted) cookie and uses it for replay? The attacker doesn't need to decrypt it; she just needs to send the cookie with her own request across the wire. You can mitigate such a *replay attack* only if you run the entire website with SSL.

Other authentication mechanisms don't require this extra work. With Windows authentication, you can use a protocol that automatically enforces a secure login process (with the caveat that this is not supported by all browsers and all network environments). With Passport authentication, the login process is handled transparently by the Passport servers, which always use SSL.

Why Not Implement Cookie Authentication Yourself?

Cookie authentication is, on the surface, a fairly straightforward system. You might wonder why you shouldn't just implement it yourself using cookies or session variables.

The answer is the same reason developers don't implement features in ASP.NET ranging from session state to the web control framework. Not only does ASP.NET save you the trouble, but it also provides an implementation that's secure, well tested, and extensible. Some of the advantages provided by ASP.NET's implementation of forms authentication include the following:

- The authentication cookie is secure.
- Forms authentication is a well-tested system.
- Forms authentication integrates with the .NET security classes.

Keeping the Authentication Cookie Secure

Cookie authentication seems simple, but if it's not implemented correctly, you can be left with an insecure system. On their own, cookies are not a safe place to store sensitive information, because a malicious user can easily view and edit cookie data. If your authentication is based on unprotected cookies, attackers can easily compromise your system.

By default, the forms authentication module encrypts its authentication information before placing it in a cookie. It also attaches a hash code and validates the cookies when they return to the server to verify that no changes have been made. The combination of these two processes makes these cookies very secure and saves you from needing to write your own security code. Most examples of homemade cookie authentication are far less secure.

Forms Authentication Is Well Tested

Forms authentication is an integral part of ASP.NET, so it has already been used in a number of web applications and websites. Because so many people use the same system, flaws are quickly discovered, publicized, and solved. As long as you keep up-to-date with patches, you have a high level of protection. On the other hand, if you create your own cookie authentication system, you do not have the advantage of this widespread testing. The first time you'll notice a vulnerability will probably be when your system is compromised.

Integrating with the ASP.NET Security Framework

All types of ASP.NET authentication use a consistent framework. Forms authentication is fully integrated with this security framework. For example, it populates the security context (IPrincipal) object and user identity (IIdentity) object, as it should. This makes it easy to customize the behavior of forms authentication.

The Forms Authentication Classes

The most important part of the forms authentication framework is the FormsAuthenticationModule, which is an HttpModule class that detects existing forms authentication tickets in the request. If the ticket is not available and the user requests a protected resource, it automatically redirects the request to the login page configured in your web.config file before this protected resource is even touched by the runtime.

If the ticket is present, the module automatically creates the security context by initializing the HttpContext.Current.User property with a default instance of GenericPrincipal, which contains a FormsIdentity instance with the name of the currently logged-in user. Basically, you don't work with the module directly. Your interface to the module consists of the classes in Table 20-1, which are part of the System.Web.Security namespace.

Table 20-1. *The Forms Authentication Framework Classes*

Class Name	Description
FormsAuthentication	This is the primary class for interacting with the forms authentication infrastructure. It provides basic information about the configuration and allows you to create the ticket, set the cookie, and redirect from the login page to the originally requested page if the validation of credentials was successful.
FormsAuthenticationEventArgs	This module raises an Authenticate event that you can catch. The event arguments passed are encapsulated in an instance of this class. It contains basic information about the authenticated user.
FormsAuthenticationTicket	This class represents the user information that will be encrypted and stored in the authentication cookie.
FormsIdentity	This class is an implementation of IIdentity that is specific to forms authentication. The key addition to the FormsIdentity class is the Ticket property, which exposes the authentication ticket. This allows you to store and retrieve additional information in the ticket.
FormsAuthenticationModule	This is the core of the forms authentication infrastructure that establishes the security context and performs the automatic page redirects to the login page if necessary.

Mostly you will use the FormsAuthentication class and the FormsIdentity class, which represents a successfully authenticated user in your application. Next you will learn how to use forms authentication in your application.

Implementing Forms Authentication

Basically, you need to complete the following steps to use forms authentication in your application:

1. Configure forms authentication in the web.config file.
2. Configure IIS to *allow* anonymous access to the virtual directory, and configure ASP.NET to *restrict* anonymous access to the web application.
3. Create a custom login page that collects and validates a user name and password and then interacts with the forms authentication infrastructure for creating the ticket.

The following sections describe these steps.

■ Note The cookie is encrypted with a machine-specific key that's defined in the machine.config file. Usually, this detail isn't important. However, in a web farm you need to make sure all servers use the same key so that one server can decrypt the cookie created by another.

Configuring Forms Authentication

You have to configure forms authentication appropriately in your web.config file. Remember from the previous chapter that every web.config file includes the <authentication /> configuration section. Forms authentication works if you configure this section with the value Forms for the mode attribute:

```
<authentication mode="Forms">
    <!-- Detailed configuration options -->
</authentication>
```

The <authentication /> configuration is limited to the top-level web.config file of your application. If the mode attribute is set to Forms, ASP.NET loads and activates the FormsAuthenticationModule, which does most of the work for you. The previous configuration basically uses default settings for forms authentication that are hard-coded into the ASP.NET runtime. You can override any default settings by adding settings to the <system.web> section of the machine.config file. You can override these default settings in your application by specifying additional settings in the <forms /> child tag of this section. The following code snippet shows the complete set of options for the forms tag:

```
<authentication mode="Forms">
    <!-- Detailed configuration options -->
    <forms name="MyCookieName"
           loginUrl="MyLogin.aspx"
           timeout="20"
           slidingExpiration="true"
           cookieless="AutoDetect"
           protection="All"
           requireSSL="false"
           enableCrossAppRedirects="false"
           defaultUrl="MyDefault.aspx"
           domain="www.mydomain.com"
           path="/" />
</authentication>
```

The properties are listed in the order you will use them in most cases. Table 20-2 describes the details of these properties and their default configuration.

Table 20-2. *The Forms Authentication Options*

Option	Default	Description
name	.ASPXAUTH	The name of the HTTP cookie to use for authentication (defaults to .ASPXAUTH). If multiple applications are running on the same web server, you should give each application's security cookie a unique name.
loginUrl	login.aspx	Defines which page the user should be redirected to in order to log into the application. This could be a page in the root folder of the application, or it could be in a subdirectory.

(Continued)

Table 20-2. *Continued*

Option	Default	Description
timeout	30	The number of minutes before the cookie expires. ASP.NET will refresh the cookie when it receives a request, as long as half of the cookie's lifetime has expired. The expiry of cookies is a significant concern. If cookies expire too often, users will have to log in often, and the usability of your application may suffer. If they expire too seldom, you run a greater risk of cookies being stolen and misused.
slidingExpiration	False	This attribute enables or disables sliding expiration of the authentication cookie. If enabled, the expiration of an authentication cookie will be reset by the runtime with every request a user submits to the page. This means with every request the expiration of the cookie will be extended.
cookieless	UseDeviceProfile	Allows you to specify whether the runtime uses cookies for sending the forms authentication ticket to the client. Possible options are AutoDetect, UseCookies, UseUri, and UseDeviceProfile.
protection	All	Allows you to specify the level of protection for the authentication cookie. The option All encrypts and signs the authentication cookie. Other possible options are None, Encryption (encrypts only), and Validation (signs only).
requireSSL	False	If set to True, this property has the effect that the browser simply doesn't transmit the cookie if SSL is not enabled on the web server. Therefore, forms authentication will not work in this case if SSL is not activated on the web server.
enableCrossAppRedirects	False	Enables cross-application redirects when using forms authentication for different applications on your server. Of course, this makes sense only if both applications rely on the same credential store and use the same set of users and roles.
defaultUrl	Default.aspx	If the FormsAuthenticationModule redirects a request from the user to the login page, it includes the originally requested page when calling the login page. Therefore, when returning from the login page, the module can use this URL for a redirect after the credentials have been validated successfully. But what if the user browses to the login page directly? This option specifies the page to redirect to if the user accesses the login page directly by typing its URL into the address bar of the browser.
domain	Your host	Specifies the domain for which this cookie is valid. Overriding this property is useful if you want to enable the cookie to be used for more applications on your web server.
path	/	The path for cookies issued by the application. The default value (/) is recommended, because case mismatches can prevent the cookie from being sent with a request.

As explained in Table 20-2, you can disable cookie validation and encryption. However, it's reasonable to wonder why you would want to remove this protection. The only case in which you might make this choice is if you are not authenticating users for security reasons but simply identifying users for personalization purposes. In these cases, it does not really matter if a user impersonates another user, so you might decide that the overhead of encrypting, decrypting, and validating the authentication cookies will adversely affect performance without offering any benefits. Think carefully before taking this approach, however—you should use this approach only in situations where it really does not matter if the authentication system is subverted.

Credentials Store in web.config

When using forms authentication, you have the choice of where to store credentials for the users. You can store them in a custom file or in a database; basically, you can store them anywhere you want if you provide the code for validating the user name and password entered by the user with the values stored in your credential store.

The easiest place to store credentials is directly in the web.config file through the <credentials /> subelement of the <forms /> configuration tag introduced previously.

```
<authentication mode="Forms">
    <!-- Detailed configuration options -->
    <forms name="MyCookieName"
           loginUrl="MyLogin.aspx"
           timeout="20">
        <credentials passwordFormat="Clear">
            <user name="Admin" password="(Admin1)"/>
            <user name="Mario" password="Szpuszta"/>
            <user name="Matthew" password="MacDonald"/>
        </credentials>
    </forms>
</authentication>
```

■ **Note** First, using web.config as a credential store is possible for simple solutions with just a few users only. In larger scenarios, you should use the membership API, which is described in Chapter 21. Second, you can hash password values for credentials stored in the web.config file. Hashing is nothing more than applying one-way encryption to the password. This means the password will be encrypted in a way that it can't be decrypted any more. You will learn how you can hash passwords correctly when creating a custom membership provider in Chapter 26.

Denying Access to Anonymous Users

As mentioned earlier, you do not need to restrict access to pages in order to use authentication. It is possible to use authentication purely for personalization so that anonymous users view the same pages as authenticated users (but see slightly different, personalized content). However, to demonstrate the redirection functionality of forms authentication, it's useful to create an example that denies access to anonymous users. This will force ASP.NET to redirect anonymous users to the login page.

Chapter 23 describes authorization in detail. For now, you'll use the simple technique of denying access to all unauthenticated users. To do this, you must use the <authorization> element of the web.config file to add a new authorization rule, as shown here:

```
<configuration>
    <system.web>
        <!-- Other settings omitted. -->
        <authorization>
```

```
            <deny users="?" />
        </authorization>
    </system.web>
</configuration>
```

The question mark (?) is a wildcard character that matches all anonymous users. By including this rule in your web.config file, you specify that anonymous users are not allowed. Every user must be authenticated, and every user request will require the forms authentication ticket (which is a cookie). If you request a page in the application directory now, ASP.NET will detect that the request isn't authenticated and attempt to redirect the request to the login page (which will probably cause an error, unless you've already created this page).

■Tip Unlike the <authentication> element, the <authorization> element is not limited to the web.config file in the root of the web application. Instead, you can use it in any subdirectory, thereby allowing you to set different authorization settings for different groups of pages. You'll learn much more about authorization in Chapter 23.

Creating a Custom Login Page

Next, you have to create a custom login page. This page collects a user name and password from the user and validates it against the credentials stored in the credential store. If credentials are stored in web.config, this is extremely easy; it's not much harder having credentials stored in any other store such as an external database.

The login page you have to create must contain the parts shown in Figure 20-2. Furthermore, you must include the code for validating the credentials.

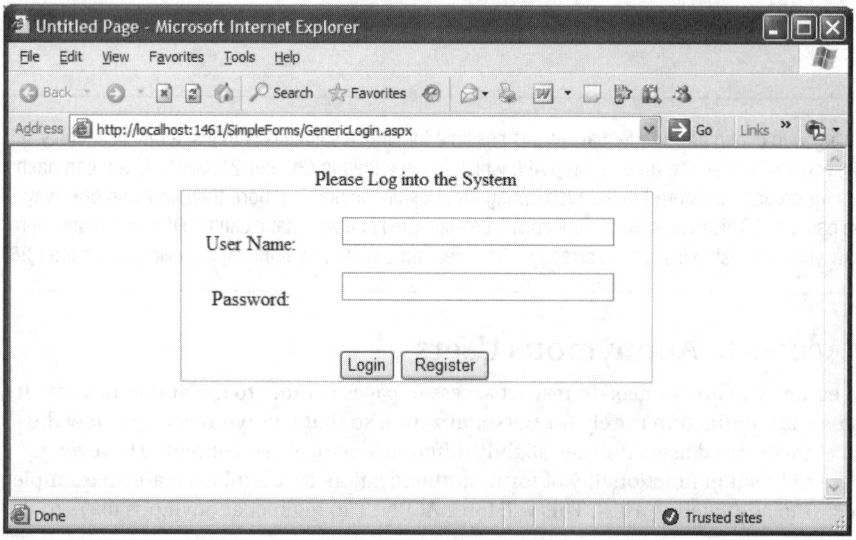

Figure 20-2. *A typical login page for a web application*

The ASP.NET page shown in Figure 20-2 contains the text boxes for entering the values. Note that the URL includes the originally requested page as a query parameter. This parameter is used by the FormsAuthentication class later for redirecting to the originally requested page. If not present, it uses the page configured in the defaultUrl attribute of the <forms /> configuration tag.

What you cannot see in Figure 20-2 are validation controls. Validation controls are especially important to let the user enter only valid values for a user name and a password. Remember what we mentioned in the previous chapter: Never trust user input. Validation adheres to this principle by ensuring that only valid values are entered. Here you can see all the controls contained on the login page:

```
<form id="form1" runat="server">
  <div style="text-align: center">
  Please Log into the System<br />
  <asp:Panel ID="MainPanel" runat="server" Height="90px" Width="380px"
      BorderColor="Silver" BorderStyle="Solid" BorderWidth="1px">
      <br />
      <table width="100%" border="0" cellpadding="0" cellspacing="0">
          <tr>
              <td width="30%" style="height: 43px">
                  User Name:</td>
              <td width="70%" style="height: 43px">
                  <asp:TextBox ID="UsernameText"
                               runat="server" Width="80%" />
                  <asp:RequiredFieldValidator
                      ID="UsernameRequiredValidator" runat="server"
                      ErrorMessage="*" ControlToValidate="UsernameText" />
                  <br />
                  <asp:RegularExpressionValidator
                      ID="UsernameValidator" runat="server"
                      ControlToValidate="UsernameText"
                      ErrorMessage="Invalid username"
                      ValidationExpression="[\w| ]*" />
              </td>
          </tr>
          <tr>
              <td width="30%" style="height: 26px">
                  Password:</td>
              <td width="70%" style="height: 26px">
                  <asp:TextBox ID="PasswordText" runat="server"
                               Width="80%" TextMode="Password" />
                  <asp:RequiredFieldValidator ID="PwdRequiredValidator"
                      runat="server" ErrorMessage="*"
                      ControlToValidate="PasswordText" />
                  <br />
                  <asp:RegularExpressionValidator ID="PwdValidator"
                      runat="server" ControlToValidate="PasswordText"
                      ErrorMessage="Invalid password"
                      ValidationExpression='[\w| !"§$%&amp;/()=\-?\*]*' />
              </td>
          </tr>
      </table>
      <br />
      <asp:Button ID="LoginAction" runat="server"
                  OnClick="LoginAction_Click" Text="Login" /><br />
      <asp:Label ID="LegendStatus" runat="server"
                 EnableViewState="False" Text="" />
  </asp:Panel>
  </div>
</form>
```

As mentioned previously, the validation controls serve two purposes. First, the RequiredFieldValidator controls ensure that both a user name and password are entered in a valid format containing only the characters allowed for user names and passwords. Second, the RegularExpressionValdiator controls ensure that only valid values are entered in the User Name text field and in the Password text field. For example, the user name may contain letters, digits, and spaces only. Therefore, the validation expression looks like this:

```
ValidationExpression="[\w| ]*"
```

The \w character class is equivalent to [a-zA-Z_0-9], and the space afterward allows spaces in the user name. The password, for example, may also contain special characters. Therefore, the validation expression looks different from the previous one, as shown here:

```
ValidationExpression='[\w| !"§$%&amp;/()=\-?\*]*'
```

Note that the single quote is used for enclosing the attribute value, because this uses the double quote as the allowed special character. Furthermore, because the attribute is contained in the tag code (and therefore the HTML entity), & indicates that the ampersand (&) character is allowed in the password. You can see the validation controls in action in Figure 20-3.

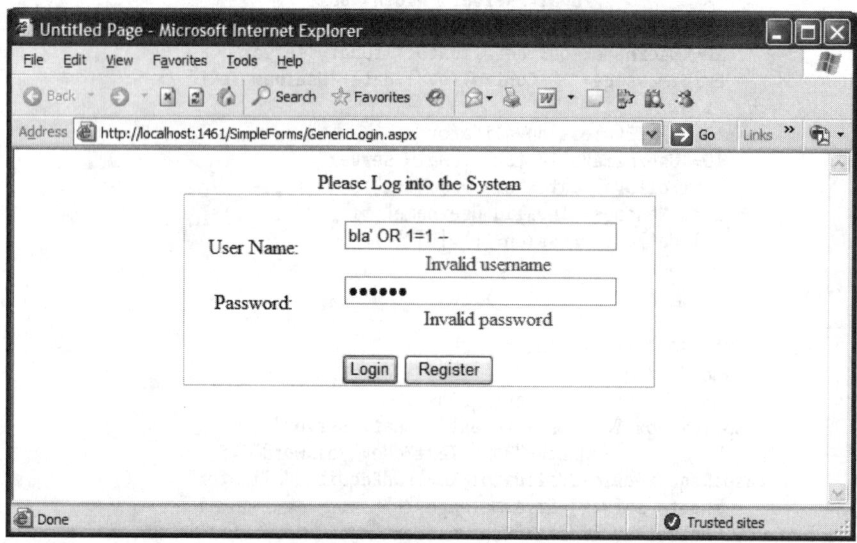

Figure 20-3. *Validation controls in action*

As you can see in Figure 20-3, with validation controls in place you can stop users from entering values for the user name or password that would lead to a SQL injection attack. In addition to using parameterized SQL queries (introduced in Chapter 7), you should always use validation controls to mitigate this type of attack in your applications.

The last step for creating the login page is to write the code for validating the credentials against the values entered by the user. You have to add the necessary code to the Click event of the login button. Because the following Click event is using the credentials store of the web.config file, validation is fairly easy:

```
Protected Sub LoginAction_Click(ByVal sender As Object, ByVal e As EventArgs)
    Page.Validate()
    If (Not Page.IsValid) Then
        Return
    End If
```

```
    If FormsAuthentication.Authenticate(UsernameText.Text, PasswordText.Text) Then
        ' Create the ticket, add the cookie to the response,
        ' and redirect to the originally requested page.
        FormsAuthentication.RedirectFromLoginPage(UsernameText.Text, False)
    Else
        ' User name and password are not correct
        LegendStatus.Text = "Invalid username or password!"
    End If
End Sub
```

■ **Note** Because forms authentication uses standard HTML forms for entering credentials, the user name and password are sent over the network as plain text. This is an obvious security risk—anyone who intercepts the network traffic will be able to read the user names and passwords that are entered into the login form. For this reason, it is strongly recommended that you encrypt the traffic between the browser and the server using SSL (as described in Chapter 19), at least while the user is accessing the login page.

Furthermore, it's important to include the Page.IsValid condition at the beginning of this procedure. The reason for this is that validation controls by default use JavaScript for client-side validation. When calling Page.Validate(), the validation takes place on the server. This is important for browsers that either have JavaScript turned off or don't support it. Therefore, if you don't include this part, validation will not happen if the browser doesn't support JavaScript or doesn't have JavaScript enabled. So, you should always include server-side validation in your code.

The FormsAuthentication class provides two methods that are used in this example. The Authenticate() method checks the specified user name and password against those stored in the web.config file and returns a Boolean value indicating whether a match was found. Remember that the methods of FormsAuthentication are Shared, so you do not need to create an instance of FormsAuthentication to use them—you simply access them through the name of the class.

```
If FormsAuthentication.Authenticate(UsernameText.Text, PasswordText.Text) Then
...
End If
```

If a match is found for the supplied credentials, you can use the RedirectFromLoginPage() method, as shown here:

```
FormsAuthentication.RedirectFromLoginPage(UsernameText.Text, False)
```

This method performs several tasks at once:

1. It creates an authentication ticket for the user.
2. It encrypts the information from the authentication ticket.
3. It creates a cookie to persist the encrypted ticket information.
4. It adds the cookie to the HTTP response, sending it to the client.
5. It redirects the user to the originally requested page (which is contained in the query string parameter of the login page request's URL).

The second parameter of RedirectFromLoginPage() indicates whether a persistent cookie should be created. Persistent cookies are stored on the user's hard drive and can be reused for later visits. Persistent cookies are described in the section "Persistent Cookies in Forms Authentication" later in this chapter.

Finally, if Authenticate() returns False, an error message is displayed on the page. Feedback such as this is always useful. However, make sure it doesn't compromise your security. For example, it's all too common for developers to create login pages that provide separate error messages depending on whether the user has entered a user name that isn't recognized or a correct user name with the wrong password. This is usually not a good idea. If a malicious user is trying to guess a user name and password, the user's chances increase considerably if your application gives this sort of specific feedback.

Logging Out

Logging a user out of forms authentication is as simple as calling the FormsAuthentication.SignOut() method. You can create a logout button and add this code, as shown here:

```
Protected Sub SignOutAction_Click(ByVal sender As Object, ByVal e As EventArgs)
    FormsAuthentication.SignOut()
    FormsAuthentication.RedirectToLoginPage()
End Sub
```

When you call the SignOut() method, you remove the authentication cookie. Depending on the application, you may want to redirect the user to another page when the user logs out. If the user requests another restricted page, the request will be redirected to the login page. You can also redirect to the login page immediately after calling the sign-out method. Or you can use the Response.Redirect method.

■ Tip In a sophisticated application, your login page might not actually be a page at all. Instead, it might be a separate portion of the page—either a distinct HTML frame or a separately coded user control. Using these techniques, you can keep a login and logout control visible on every page. The membership API framework includes ready-to-use controls for providing this type of functionality.

Hashing Passwords in web.config

Forms authentication includes the possibility of storing the password in different formats. In the <credentials /> configuration section, the format of the password is specified through the passwordFormat attribute, which has three valid values:

Clear: The passwords are stored as clear text in the <user /> elements of the <credentials /> section.

MD5: The hashed version of the password is stored in the <user /> elements, and the algorithm used for hashing the password is the MD5 hashing algorithm.

SHA1: The <user /> elements in the <credentials /> section of the web.config file contain the hashed password, and the algorithm used for hashing the password is the SHA1 algorithm.

When using the hashed version of the passwords, you have to write a tool or some code that hashes the passwords for you and stores them in the web.config file. For storing the password, you should then use the FormsAuthentication.HashPasswordForStoringInConfigFile method instead of passing in the clear-text password as follows:

```
Dim hashedPwd As String =
   FormsAuthentication.HashPasswordForStoringInConfigFile(clearTextPassword, "SHA1")
```

The first parameter specifies the clear-text password, and the second one specifies the hash algorithm you should use. The result of the method call is the hashed version of the password.

If you want to modify users stored in web.config as shown previously, you have to use the configuration API of the .NET Framework. You cannot edit this section with the web-based configuration tool. The following code snippet shows how you can modify the section through the configuration API:

```
Dim MyConfig As Configuration = WebConfigurationManager.OpenWebConfiguration("~/")

Dim SystemWeb As ConfigurationSectionGroup = MyConfig.SectionGroups("system.web")
Dim AuthSec As AuthenticationSection =
        CType(SystemWeb.Sections("authentication"), AuthenticationSection)
AuthSec.Forms.Credentials.Users.Add
        (New FormsAuthenticationUser(UserText.Text, PasswordText.Text))

MyConfig.Save()
```

Of course, only privileged users such as website administrators should be allowed to execute the previous code, and the process executing the code must have write access to your web.config file. Also, this sort of code should not be included in the actual web application. You should include it in an administration application only. You will learn more about hashing passwords in Chapter 25.

Cookieless Forms Authentication

New to ASP.NET 2.0 is that the runtime supports cookieless forms authentication out of the box. In ASP.NET 1.*x* you had to write this functionality on your own. If you don't want the runtime to use cookies, you configure this through the cookieless attribute of the <forms /> tag in the <authentication /> section.

```
<authentication mode="Forms">
    <!-- Detailed configuration options -->
    <forms name="MyCookieName"
           loginUrl="MyLogin.aspx"
           cookieless="AutoDetect" />
</authentication>
```

The cookieless option includes the possible settings in Table 20-3.

Table 20-3. *Cookieless Options in the <forms /> Configuration*

Option	Description
UseCookies	Forces the runtime to use cookies when working with forms authentication. This requires the client browser to support cookies.
UseUri	If this configuration option is selected, cookies will not be used for authentication. Instead, the runtime encodes the forms authentication ticket into the request URL, and the infrastructure processes this specific portion of the URL for establishing the security context.
AutoDetect	Results in the use of cookies if the client browser supports cookies. Otherwise, URL encoding of the ticket will be used. This is established through a probing mechanism.
UseDeviceProfile	Results in the use of cookies or URL encoding based on a device profile configuration stored on the web server. These profiles are stored in .browser files in the <drive>:\<windows directory>\Microsoft.NET\Framework\v2.0.50215\CONFIG\Browsers directory.

Custom Credentials Store

As mentioned previously, the credential store in web.config is useful for simple scenarios only. You won't want to use web.config as the credential store for a number of reasons:

Potential lack of security: Even though users aren't able to directly request the web.config file, you may still prefer to use a storage medium where you can secure access more effectively. As long as this information is stored on the web server, passwords are accessible to any administrator, developer, or tester who has access.

No support for adding user-specific information: For example, you might want to store information such as addresses, credit cards, personal preferences, and so on.

Poor performance with a large number of users: The web.config file is just a file, and it can't provide the efficient caching and multiuser access of a database.

Therefore, in most applications you will use your own custom credential store for user name and password combinations, and mostly it will be a database such as SQL Server. In ASP.NET 1.*x*, you had to implement this scenario on your own. In your login form you then had to connect to the database, verify whether the user exists, compare the password stored in the database to the one entered by the user, and then call FormsAuthentication.RedirectFromLoginPage if the user name and password entered by the user were valid. The following example demonstrates this, and it assumes that you have written a function MyAuthenticate that connects to a SQL Server database and reads the corresponding user entry. It returns True if the entered user name and password match the ones stored in the database.

```
Protected Sub LoginAction_Click(ByVal sender As Object, ByVal e As EventArgs)
    Page.Validate()
    If (Not Page.IsValid) Then
        Exit Sub
    End If

    If Me.MyAuthenticate(UsernameText.Text, PasswordText.Text) Then
        FormsAuthentication.RedirectFromLoginPage(UsernameText.Text, False)
    Else
        LegendStatus.Text = "Invalid username or password!"
    End If
End Sub
```

Fortunately, ASP.NET 2.0 provides a ready-to-use infrastructure as well as a complete set of security-related controls that do this for you. The membership API includes a SQL Server–based data store for storing users and roles and functions for validating user names and passwords against users of this store without knowing any details about the underlying database, as you will learn in Chapter 21. Furthermore, this infrastructure is completely extensible through custom providers, as you will learn in Chapter 26.

Persistent Cookies in Forms Authentication

The examples you've seen so far have used a nonpersistent authentication cookie to maintain the authentication ticket between requests. This means that if the user closes the browser, the cookie is immediately removed. This is a sensible step that ensures security. It's particularly important with shared computers to prevent another user from using a previous user's ticket. Nonpersistent cookies also make *session hijacking* attacks (where a malicious user gains access to the network and steals another user's cookie) more difficult and more limited.

Despite the increased security risks of using persistent authentication cookies, it is appropriate to use them in certain situations. If you are performing authentication for personalization rather than for controlling access to restricted resources, you may decide that the usability advantages of not requiring users to log in on every visit outweigh the increased danger of unauthorized use.

Once you have decided to use persistent cookies, implementing them is easy. You simply need to supply a value of True rather than False for the second parameter of the RedirectFromLoginPage() or SetAuthCookie() method of the FormsAuthentication class. Here's an example:

```
FormsAuthentication.RedirectFromLoginPage(UsernameTextBox.Text,True)
```

By default, persistent cookies do not expire unless the FormsAuthentication.SignOut() method is used. Persistent cookies are not affected by the timeout attribute that is set in the <forms> element of the web.config file. If you want the persistent cookie to eventually expire sometime in the future, you have to use the GetAuthCookie() method of FormsAuthentication, set the expiry date and time, and then write the cookie to the HTTP response yourself.

The following example rewrites the code that authenticates the user when the login button is clicked. It creates a persistent cookie but performs additional steps to limit the cookie's life span to ten days:

```
Protected Sub LoginAction_Click(ByVal sender As Object, ByVal e As EventArgs)
    Page.Validate()
    If (Not Page.IsValid) Then
        Exit Sub
    End If

    If FormsAuthentication.Authenticate(UsernameText.Text, PasswordText.Text) Then
        ' Create the authentication cookie
        Dim AuthCookie As HttpCookie
        AuthCookie = FormsAuthentication.GetAuthCookie(UsernameText.Text, True)
        AuthCookie.Expires = DateTime.Now.AddDays(10)

        ' Add the cookie to the response
        Response.Cookies.Add(AuthCookie)

        ' Redirect to the originally requested page
        Response.Redirect(
            FormsAuthentication.GetRedirectUrl(UsernameText.Text, True))
    Else
        ' User name and password are not correct
        LegendStatus.Text = "Invalid username or password!"
    End If
End Sub
```

The code for checking the credentials is the same in this scenario. The only difference is that the authentication cookie isn't added automatically. Instead, it's created with a call to GetAuthCookie(), which returns a new instance of HttpCookie, as shown here:

```
Dim AuthCookie As HttpCookie
AuthCookie = FormsAuthentication.GetAuthCookie(UsernameText.Text, True)
```

Once you've created the authentication cookie, you can retrieve the current date and time (using the DateTime.Now static property), add ten days to it (using the DateTime.AddDays() method), and use this value as the expiry date and time of the cookie:

```
AuthCookie.Expires = DateTime.Now.AddDays(10)
```

Next, you have to add the cookie to the HTTP response:

```
Response.Cookies.Add(AuthCookie)
```

Finally, you can redirect the user to the originally requested URL, which you can obtain by using the GetRedirectUrl() method:

```
Response.Redirect(FormsAuthentication.GetRedirectUrl(
    UsernameText.Text, True))
```

The end result is a cookie that will persist beyond the closing of the browser but that will expire after ten days, at which point the user will need to reenter credentials to log into the website.

Summary

In this chapter, you learned how to use forms authentication to implement authentication systems that simplify life and provide a great deal of flexibility. You also learned how to protect passwords and how you can use any data source for credential storage. In the next chapter, you'll learn about the new features that are built on top of forms authentication and that make it even easier to create login pages and deal with user authentication without writing all the code yourself.

CHAPTER 21

Membership

On one hand, forms authentication solves the critical fundamentals for implementing secure, custom login forms for your ASP.NET applications. On the other hand, the tasks you have to accomplish for implementing the login forms and communicating with the underlying credential store are almost always the same for every web application, and they're tedious. You should keep in mind one more point: Forms authentication provides the infrastructure for authenticating users only. If you are using a custom credentials store, you have to write administration applications for managing users.

That's what the ASP.NET team received as feedback from the developer community. Therefore, the team has added the new membership API to ASP.NET 2.0; the membership API is a framework based on top of the existing forms authentication infrastructure. When using the membership API, you even don't need to implement login pages or credential storage. In this chapter, you will learn about the details of the membership API.

Introducing the ASP.NET Membership API

The membership API framework provides you with a complete set of user management functions out of the box:

- The ability to create and delete users either programmatically or through the ASP.NET web configuration utility.
- The ability to reset passwords with the possibility of automatically sending password reset e-mails to the users if an e-mail address is stored for the affected user.
- The ability to automatically generate passwords for users if these users are created programmatically in the background. Of course, these passwords can be sent to these users automatically if e-mail addresses are available for them.
- The ability to find users in the underlying data store as well as retrieve lists of users and details for every user.
- A set of prebuilt controls for creating login pages and registration pages and for displaying login states and different views for authenticated and unauthenticated users.
- A layer of abstraction for your application so that the application has no dependency on the underlying data store through the so-called membership provider classes. Any functionality listed until now therefore works completely independently from the underlying data store, and the data store can be replaced with other types of data stores without needing to modify the application at all.

Figure 21-1 shows the fundamental architecture of the membership API, which consists of providers, an API, and controls for creating appropriate user interfaces.

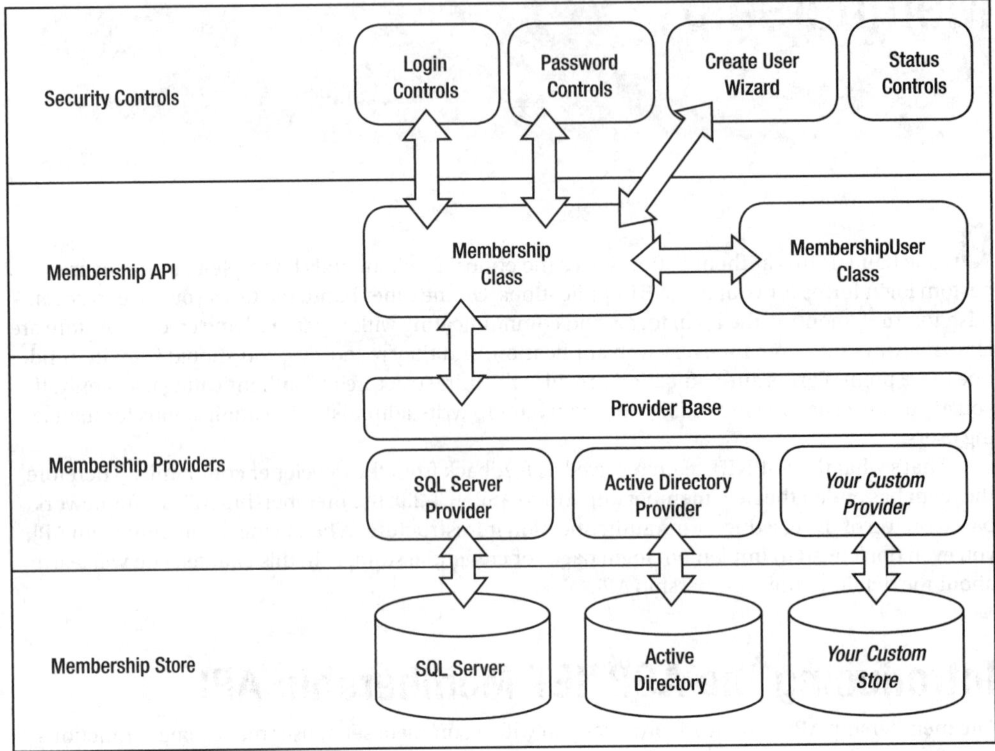

Figure 21-1. *Architecture of the membership API*

The membership API is designed to work completely independently from its underlying data store. You, as the application developer, primarily work with the controls provided by ASP.NET as well as the Membership class. The Membership class provides you with a set of methods for programmatically accessing users and roles of the store. These methods work with a membership provider. This provider implements the access to the underlying data store. Table 21-1 describes the membership components.

Table 21-1. *The Membership API Components*

Component	Description
Membership	The Membership class is the primary point of interaction with the membership API. It provides a couple of methods for managing users, validating users, and resetting user passwords.
MembershipCreateUserException	An exception is thrown if an error occurs when you try to create a user through the Membership class.
MembershipUser	Represents a single user stored in a membership API credential store. This object contains all information about this user and is returned through several methods of the Membership class such as GetUsers.

Component	Description
MembershipUserCollection	A collection of membership users. For example, the GetUsers method of the Membership class returns an instance of this collection.
MembershipProvider	This is the base class that you derive from if you want to create a custom membership provider that authenticates users against your custom credential store.
MembershipProviderCollection	A collection of available membership providers on the machine and for this web application.
SqlMembershipProvider	An implementation of the MembershipProvider class that works with SQL Server databases.
ActiveDirectoryMembershipProvider	An implementation of the MembershipProvider class that works with Active Directory.
ActiveDirectoryMembershipUser	This class inherits all the functionality from MembershipUser and adds some Active Directory–specific properties.

ASP.NET ships with a provider for SQL Server and Active Directory (which enables you to create custom login pages for users stored in Active Directory). But the idea of providers is that they give you the ability to completely extend the infrastructure. Therefore, you can write your own membership provider, which is basically a class that inherits from System.Web.Security.MembershipProvider. Membership providers are primarily configured through your web.config configuration file, which includes a new <membership /> section. You will learn more about custom membership providers in Chapter 26.

■**Note** Although the membership API supports Active Directory as a provider, there is still a big difference between using Windows authentication and using the membership API for authenticating users in your web application. When you configure your application to use membership APIs, which are actually based on forms authentication, credentials are sent as clear text across the line (except you should use SSL), and a forms authentication ticket is used for authentication, as you learned in the previous chapter. On the other hand, when configuring Windows authentication, the user is authenticated either through NTLM or through Kerberos (in the case of Windows 2000 or Windows Server 2003 domains). Both methods are much more secure, because credentials are never sent across the line.

The membership API is just used for managing and authenticating users. It does not implement any authorization functionality and doesn't provide you with functionality for managing user roles. For this purpose, you have to use the roles API. You will learn more about authorization and the role management functionality in Chapter 23.

Using the Membership API

Before you can use the ASP.NET membership API and the security controls of ASP.NET, you have to complete a few steps:

1. Configure forms authentication in your web.config file as usual, and deny access to anonymous users.
2. Set up the membership data store. For example, if you are using SQL Server, you have to create a couple of tables and stored procedures in a SQL Server database of your choice.

3. Configure the database connection string and the membership provider you want to use in the application's web.config file.
4. Create users in your membership store using the ASP.NET web configuration utility or using a custom administration page.
5. Create a login page that uses the prebuilt Login control, or create a login page that uses the Membership class for validating the entered credentials and authenticating the user.

You can perform every configuration step except the provider configuration through the ASP.NET WAT (Website Administration Tool), which includes a security wizard. Just select the Web Site ➤ ASP.NET Configuration menu from within Visual Studio. Figure 21-2 shows the WAT.

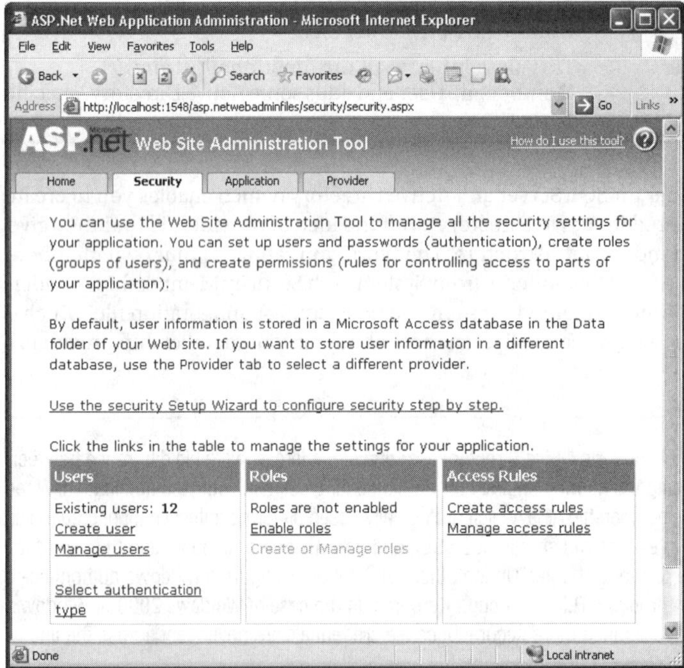

Figure 21-2. *Setting up security in the WAT*

If you are using ASP.NET on a machine with SQL Server 2005, you don't even need to set up a data store and configure a membership provider. Just launch the security wizard in the WAT, as shown in Figure 12-2, and start by adding users to your membership storage. The required underlying data store will be created automatically for you when you create the first user. It will be created automatically even if you programmatically access the membership store, because this functionality is provided through the SqlMembershipProvider.

But if you want to use your own database for data storage, you have to configure the membership provider and connection information for the provider before you launch the security wizard. You will learn more about the configuration steps and how the membership API works behind the scenes in the next sections of this chapter.

Configuring Forms Authentication

The membership API is based on top of forms authentication and provides you with an out-of-the-box infrastructure for managing and authenticating users. Therefore, as the first step, you have to configure your application for forms authentication as usual. But you will structure the solution a little bit differently this time. Often, the root directory of the web application grants access to anonymous users, while restricted resources are stored in subdirectories with restricted access. These subdirectories have their own web.config file that denies access to anonymous users. As soon as someone tries to access resources stored in this secured directory, the ASP.NET runtime automatically redirects the user to the login page. Typically, the root directory, which is accessible to anonymous users, includes features such as a login page and a registration page. You can see the structure of the web application in Figure 21-3, which displays the Solution Explorer of an already structured Visual Studio project.

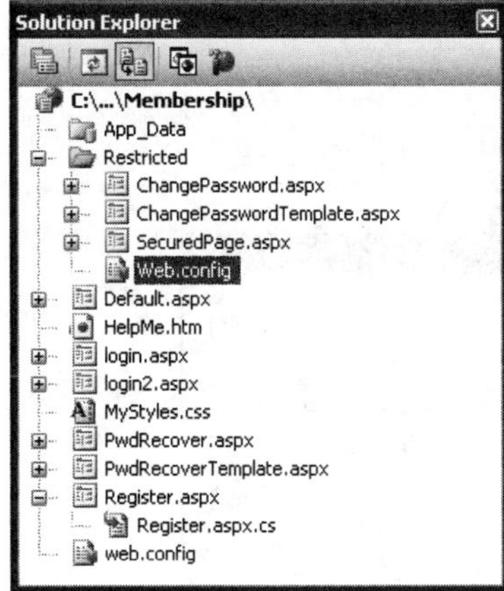

Figure 21-3. *The folder and file structure of a web application with a secured area*

Therefore, in the root directory of the web application, you just configure forms authentication by including the following:

```
<system.web>
    <authentication mode="Forms" />
</system.web>
```

As you can see, this configuration specifies forms authentication and allows anonymous access to the pages. In the secured subdirectory, you add an extra web.config file with the following contents:

```
<configuration xmlns="http://schemas.microsoft.com/.NetConfiguration/v2.0">
    <system.web>
        <authorization>
            <deny users="?" />
        </authorization>
    </system.web>
</configuration>
```

This configuration denies any anonymous user access to the website's secured subfolder. If someone who is not authenticated tries to access resources placed in this directory, the ASP.NET runtime automatically redirects the user to the (publicly available) login page. Of course, you have to create the login page on your own, but it's much easier and much less work with the membership API, as you will see when you learn about the Login control in the section "Using the Security Controls."

Creating the Data Store

When using the membership API, you have to set up a data store that will be used by your membership provider. In the case of SQL Server, this means just creating a couple of database tables in either an existing or a new SQL Server database. Fortunately, the .NET Framework ships with a tool called aspnet_regsql.exe that can create the tables for you automatically. In the case of a custom provider, you have to prepare and configure the data store used by the custom provider according to the custom provider's documentation.

You can use the aspnet_regsql.exe tool in two ways: either through a wizard interface or through the command line. If you just launch the tool without any parameters, it fires up the wizard interface that guides you through the process of creating a database, as shown in Figure 21-4.

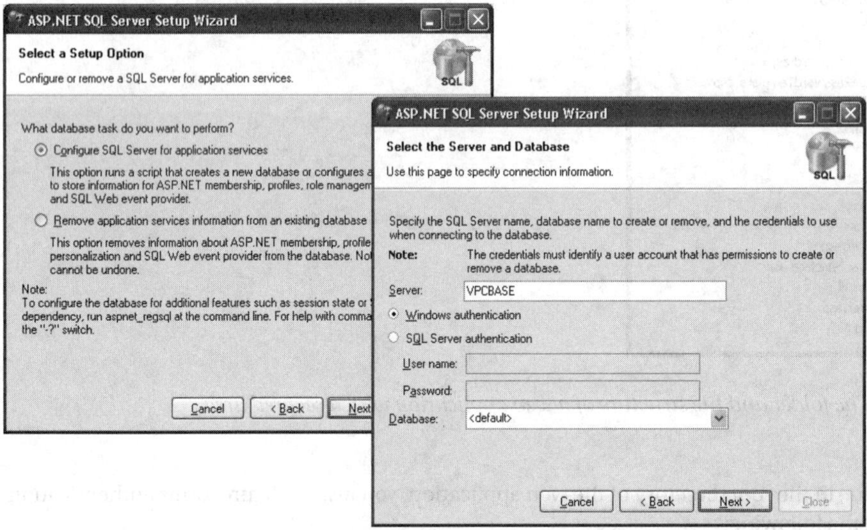

Figure 21-4. *The apsnet_regsql.exe wizard user interface*

The wizard provides you with the option of either creating the necessary database or removing the tables from an existing database. If you select the <default> option for the database, it looks for a database called aspnetdb on the server you have specified. If it doesn't exist already, it creates this database and creates the tables in this database. If the tables already exist in the target database, the wizard leaves them as they are.

As already mentioned, you can use the aspnet_regsql.exe tool from the command line as well. Actually, that's a good way to automate your application's setup—just call this tool from the command line and automatically set up the ASP.NET database tables required by your application. For example, to set up the membership API database tables, you can execute the following command:

```
aspnet_regsql -S (local) -E -A all -d MyDatabase
```

Figure 21-5 shows the result of executing this command.

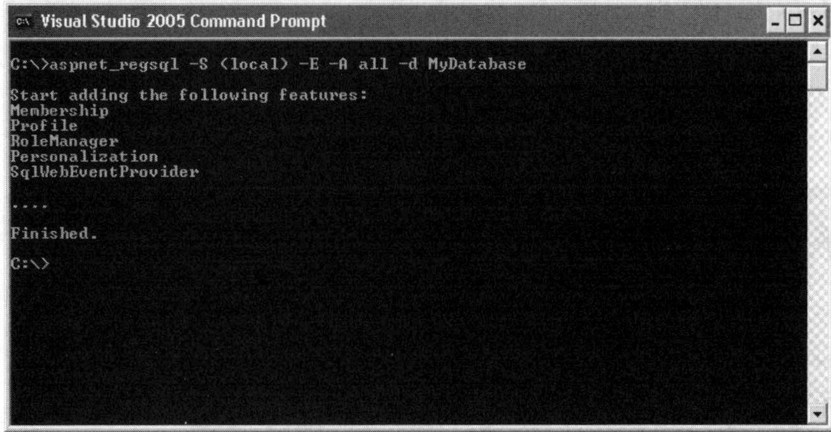

Figure 21-5. *Executing aspnet_regsql.exe for installing the database*

Table 21-2 describes the command-line switches of the aspnet_regsql.exe tool needed for the membership API and related ASP.NET application services.

Table 21-2. *Command-Line Switches of aspnet_regsql.exe*

Switch	Description
-S servername	Specifies the SQL Server and instance for which you want to install the ASP.NET database tables.
-U username	The SQL Server database user with which you want to connect to SQL Server.
-P password	If the -U switch is specified, you need to specify the password switch as well.
-E	If you don't specify -U and -P, you automatically connect through Windows authentication to the SQL Server instance specified in -S. With -E, you can explicitly specify to connect through Windows authentication to the SQL Server.
-C	Allows you to specify a full-fledged ODBC or OLEDB connection string for connecting to the database.
-sqlexportonly	Creates the SQL scripts for the specified option without installing them on a dedicated SQL Server instance.
-A	Installs application services. The valid options for this switch are all, m, r, p, c, and w. The command in the previous example used the option all for installing all application services; m is dedicated to membership. r means role services, p means ASP.NET profiles for supporting user profiles, and c stands for personalization of web part pages.
-R	Uninstalls application services. This switch supports the same option as -A and uninstalls the corresponding database tables for the application services.
-d	Lets you optionally specify the name of the database into which you want to install the application services. If you don't specify this parameter, a database named aspnetdb is created automatically (as is the case with the <default> option for the database in the wizard interface).

The aspnet_regsql.exe tool contains a couple of additional switches for installing SQL Server–based session state as well as for configuring the SQL cache dependency. For session state, please refer to Chapter 6. You will learn more about caching and cache dependencies in Chapter 11.

Database Scripts for ASP.NET Services

The aspnet_regsql.exe tool executes a couple of scripts for creating (or dropping) the membership-related database and database tables. These scripts ship with the .NET Framework; you can find them in the .NET Framework directory, as shown in Figure 21-6.

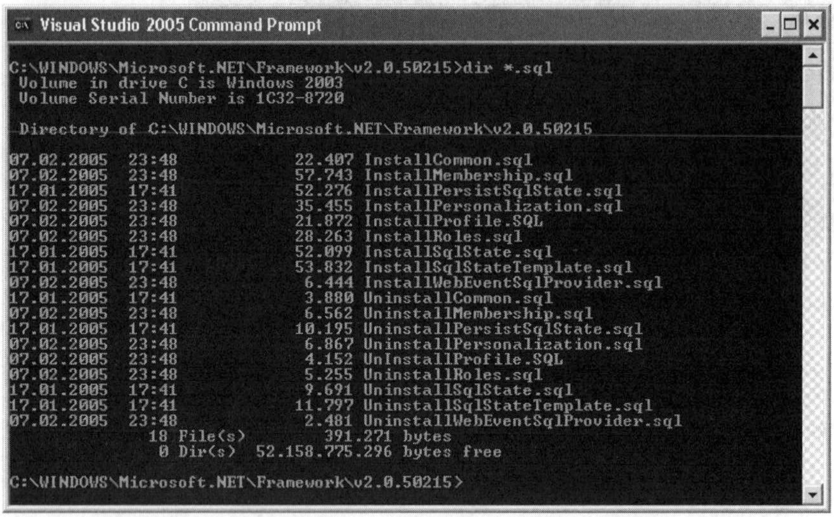

```
Visual Studio 2005 Command Prompt

C:\WINDOWS\Microsoft.NET\Framework\v2.0.50215>dir *.sql
 Volume in drive C is Windows 2003
 Volume Serial Number is 1C32-8720

 Directory of C:\WINDOWS\Microsoft.NET\Framework\v2.0.50215

07.02.2005  23:48            22.407 InstallCommon.sql
07.02.2005  23:48            57.743 InstallMembership.sql
17.01.2005  17:41            52.276 InstallPersistSqlState.sql
07.02.2005  23:48            35.455 InstallPersonalization.sql
07.02.2005  23:48            21.872 InstallProfile.SQL
07.02.2005  23:48            28.263 InstallRoles.sql
17.01.2005  17:41            52.099 InstallSqlState.sql
17.01.2005  17:41            53.832 InstallSqlStateTemplate.sql
07.02.2005  23:48             6.444 InstallWebEventSqlProvider.sql
17.01.2005  17:41             3.880 UninstallCommon.sql
07.02.2005  23:48             6.562 UninstallMembership.sql
17.01.2005  17:41            10.195 UninstallPersistSqlState.sql
07.02.2005  23:48             6.867 UninstallPersonalization.sql
07.02.2005  23:48             4.152 UnInstallProfile.SQL
07.02.2005  23:48             5.255 UninstallRoles.sql
17.01.2005  17:41             9.691 UninstallSqlState.sql
17.01.2005  17:41            11.797 UninstallSqlStateTemplate.sql
07.02.2005  23:48             2.481 UninstallWebEventSqlProvider.sql
              18 File(s)        391.271 bytes
               0 Dir(s)  52.158.775.296 bytes free

C:\WINDOWS\Microsoft.NET\Framework\v2.0.50215>
```

Figure 21-6. *The SQL scripts for installing and uninstalling SQL databases*

Basically, two types of scripts exist: InstallXXX and the corresponding UninstallXXX scripts. When an InstallXXX script installs a set of database tables such as the set needed for the membership API, the corresponding UninstallXXX script drops the same tables and databases. Table 21-3 describes the install scripts included with the .NET Framework.

Table 21-3. *Membership API Installation Scripts*

Script	Description
InstallCommon.sql	Installs some common tables and stored procedures necessary for both the membership and roles APIs. This includes tables for identifying ASP.NET applications that use other ASP.NET features such as the membership API, role service, or personalization.
InstallMembership.sql	Installs the database tables, stored procedures, and triggers used by the membership API. This includes tables for users, additional user properties, and stored procedures for accessing this information.
InstallRoles.sql	Installs all database tables and stored procedures required for associating users with application roles. These roles will be used for authorization, as you will learn in Chapter 23.
InstallPersonalization.sql	Contains DDL for creating any table and stored procedure required for creating personalized portal applications with web parts.
InstallProfile.sql	Creates all the necessary tables and stored procedures for supporting ASP.NET 2.0 user profiles.

Script	Description
InstallSqlState.sql	Installs tables for persistent session state in the TEMP database of SQL Server. That means every time the SQL Server service is shut down, the session state gets lost.
InstallPersistSqlState.sql	Installs tables for persistent session state in a separate ASPState database. That means the state stays alive even if the SQL Server service gets restarted.

You can execute these scripts by either using osql.exe or using sqlcmd.exe. osql.exe is included with SQL Server 2000 editions, and sqlcmd.exe is included with SQL Server 2005 editions for executing scripts from the command line. For example, to install the common database tables on a SQL Server Express Edition, you can execute the following command:

```
sqlcmd -S (local)\SQLExpress -E -i InstallCommon.sql
```

The -S switch specifies the server and instance name for the target SQL Server. Usually you will not use an instance name (which is specified after the \), but SQL Server Express Edition will be installed as a named instance so that you can install more versions and instances of SQL Server on the same machine. Therefore, for SQL Server Express Edition, you have to specify the instance name, which is SQLExpress by default. With the -E switch you specify to access SQL Server through Windows authentication, and finally through the -i switch you can specify the input SQL script that should be executed. Figure 21-7 shows the result of executing the previous command.

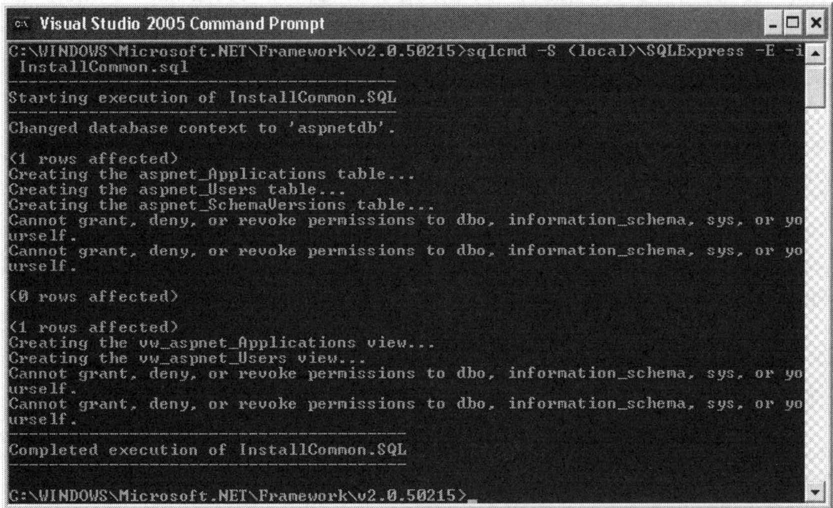

Figure 21-7. *Installing ASP.NET database tables on SQL Server Express*

File-Based SQL Server Store

SQL Server 2005 supports a file-only database mode that allows you to access SQL Server databases directly through their MDF files without creating or attaching them in a SQL Server instance. With this feature it is possible to just copy the application's database file with the application files onto the target server and run the application. The SQL Server provider then uses a connection string that accesses the database file directly. SQL Server automatically attaches the database (temporarily) and allows you to access it directly through the file without any additional configuration steps. The only prerequisite of course is that SQL Server 2005 is installed on the target machine.

These database files are located in the special App_Data subdirectory of the application. When running ASP.NET with the default configuration, this file will be created automatically for you. But what causes the file to be created for you? Well, the answer is quite simple: When a feature that requires a specific type of functionality is used for the first time, the provider automatically creates the database file with the necessary contents. Therefore, when you first run the security wizard you saw previously, the database will be created automatically when you create the first user. This functionality is provided by the SqlMembershipProvider class. (The actual implementation is also included in a utility class used by all SQL provider classes, such as like the SqlRoleProvider.)

Configuring Connection String and Membership Provider

With the default configuration and SQL Server 2005 (Express Edition or the full version) installed, you don't have to prepare the data store and configure a membership provider, because the ASP.NET runtime uses the file-based SQL Server 2005 provider and automatically creates the database file for you.

But if you want to use your own SQL Server database, or even your custom membership provider and store, you have to configure the provider as well as the connection string to the membership store database appropriately. For this purpose, you have to touch the web.config file directly or edit the configuration through the IIS MMC snap-in if you are running your application on IIS.

In the case of using SQL Server storage (or other database-based storage), you have to configure the connection string as your first step. You can do this through the <connectionStrings /> section of the web.config file. For example, if you want to use a local database called MyDatabase where you have installed the database tables through the aspnet_regsql.exe tool as shown previously, you have to configure the connection string as follows (remember, the <connectionStrings /> section is located directly below the <configuration /> element):

```
<connectionStrings>
    <add name="MyMembershipConnString"
         connectionString="data source=(local);Integrated Security=SSPI;
         initial catalog=MyDatabase" />
</connectionStrings>
```

After you have configured the connection string for your custom membership storage, you must configure the membership provider for the application. For this purpose, you have to add the <membership /> section to your web.config file (if it's not already there) below the <system.web /> section, as follows:

```
<system.web>

    <authentication mode="Forms" />
    <authorization>
        <deny users="?"/>
    </authorization>

    <membership defaultProvider="MyMembershipProvider">
        <providers>
            <add name="MyMembershipProvider"
                    connectionStringName="MyMembershipConnString"
                    applicationName="MyMembership"
```

```
                enablePasswordRetrieval="false"
                enablePasswordReset="true"
                requiresQuestionAndAnswer="true"
                requiresUniqueEmail="true"
                passwordFormat="Hashed"
                type="System.Web.Security.SqlMembershipProvider" />
      </providers>
    </membership>

</system.web>
```

Within the <membership /> section, you can add multiple providers as child elements of the <providers /> section. In the previous code, you can see a valid configuration for the included SqlMembershipProvider. It's important to not forget about the defaultProvider attribute. This attribute indicates the membership provider that will be used if you don't override the used provider in your code. Configured providers are shown in the ASP.NET web configuration when selecting the option Select a Different Provider for Each Feature, as shown in Figure 21-8.

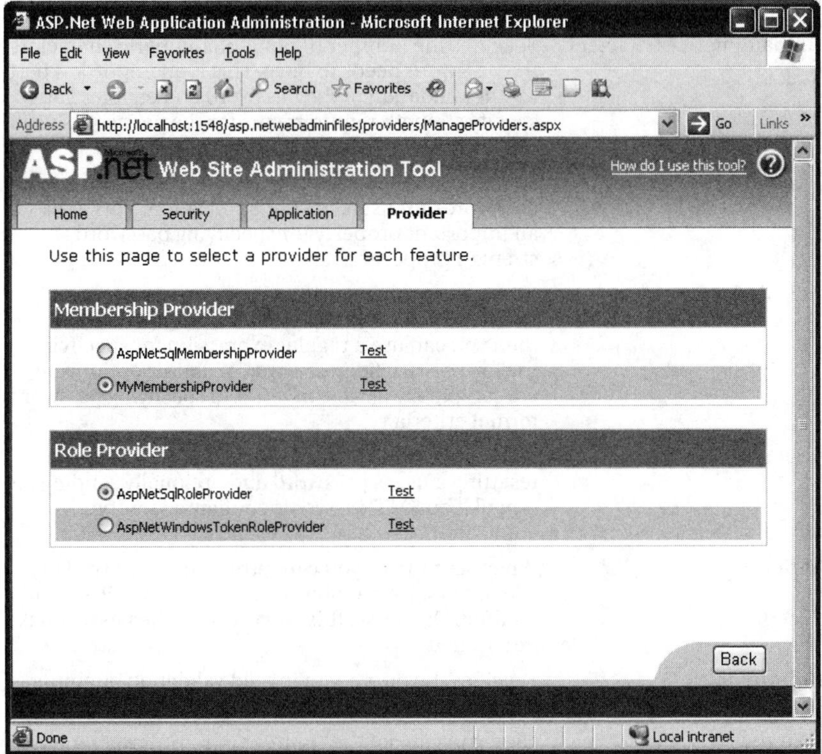

Figure 21-8. *The configured provider selected in the WAT*

Table 21-4 describes the properties you can configure for the SqlMembershipProvider.

Table 21-4. *The SqlMembershipProvider's Properties*

Property	Description
Name	Specifies a name for the membership provider. You can choose any name you want. This name can be used later for referencing the provider when programmatically accessing the list of configured membership providers. Furthermore, this name will be used by the WAT to display the provider.
ApplicationName	Specifies the name of the application for which the membership provider manages users and their settings.
Description	An optional description for the membership provider.
PasswordFormat	Gets or sets the format in which passwords will be stored in the underlying credential store. Valid options are Clear for clear-text password storage, Encrypted for encrypting passwords in the data store (uses the locally configured machine key for encryption), and Hash for hashing passwords stored in the underlying membership store.
MinRequiredNonAlphanumericCharacters	Specifies the number of nonalphanumeric characters the password needs to have. This is an important part for the validation of the password and enables you to specify strength requirements for the passwords used by your users.
MinRequiredPasswordLength	Allows you to specify the minimum length of passwords for users of your application. This is also an important property for specifying password strength properties.
PasswordStrengthRegularExpression	If the previously mentioned properties are not sufficient for specifying password strength conditions, then you can use a regular expression for specifying the format of valid passwords. With this option you are completely flexible in terms of specifying password format criteria.
EnablePasswordReset	The membership API contains functionality for resetting a user's password and optionally sending an e-mail if an SMTP server is configured for the application.
EnablePasswordRetrieval	When set to True, you can retrieve the password of a MembershipUser object by calling its GetPassword method. Of course, this works only if the password is not hashed.
MaxInvalidPasswordAttempts	Specifies the number of invalid validation attempts before the user gets locked.
PasswordAttemptWindow	Here you can set the number of minutes in which a maximum number of invalid password or password question-answer attempts are allowed before the user is completely locked out from the application. In that case, the user gets locked out, so the administrator must activate the account again.

Property	Description
RequiresQuestionAndAnswer	Specifies whether the password question with an answer is required for this application. This question can be used if the user has forgotten his password. With the answer he gets the possibility of retrieving an automatically generated, new password via e-mail.
RequiresUniqueEmail	Specifies whether e-mail addresses must be unique for every user in the underlying membership store.

Now, after you have set up the data store and configured the membership provider, you can test your configuration by creating users through the WAT. The utility includes a link for testing the configuration by connecting to the database with the configured membership provider, as shown in Figure 21-9.

Figure 21-9. *Testing the membership provider configuration*

Creating and Authenticating Users

To create new users in your previously created membership provider store, launch the WAT by selecting the Website ➤ ASP.NET Web Configuration menu from within Visual Studio. Now switch to the Security tab, and select Create User, as shown in Figure 21-10.

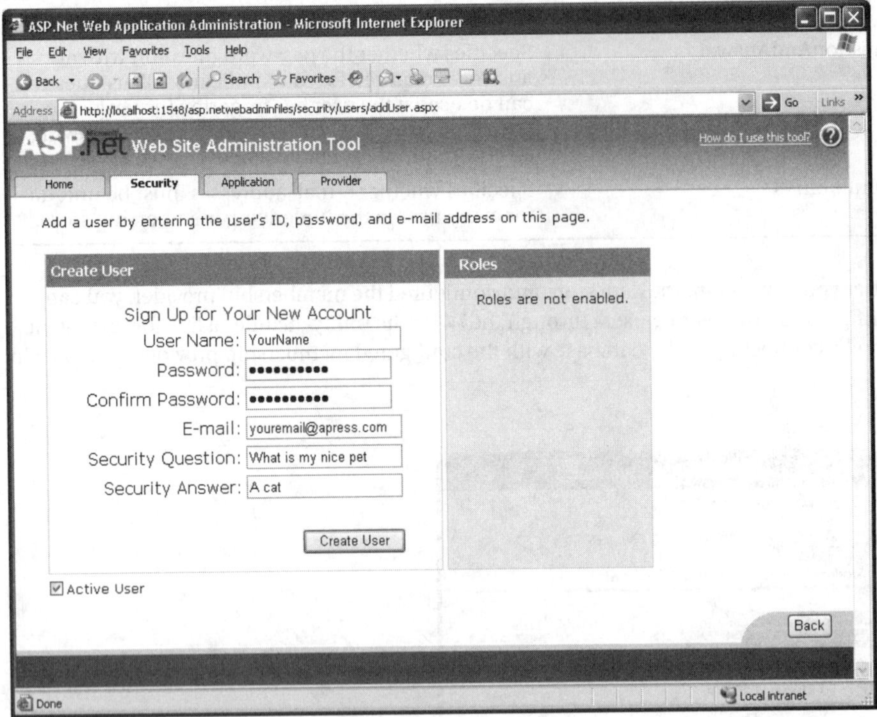

Figure 21-10. *Creating users with the WAT*

After you have created a couple of users, you can connect to the database through Visual Studio's Server Explorer and look at the aspnet_Users and aspnet_membership tables in the database, as shown in Figure 21-11.

SQL Server Enterprise Manager - [Data in Table 'aspnet_Users' in 'MyDatabase' on '(LOCAL)']

ApplicationId	UserId	UserName	LoweredUserName	MobileAlias	IsAnonymous	LastActivityDate
{47695139-0F22-4	{D65A0B56-CFB1-	12345	12345	<NULL>	0	30.04.2005 23:
{47695139-0F22-4	{A5858CE7-4DF1-	bli	bli	<NULL>	0	01.05.2005 00:
{47695139-0F22-4	{907AEA3D-2B7B-	heyyou	heyyou	<NULL>	0	30.04.2005 22:
{47695139-0F22-4	{CE05AF3B-D935-	marioszp	marioszp	<NULL>	0	30.04.2005 11:
{47695139-0F22-4	{FE40804F-668F-4	mcool	mcool	<NULL>	0	01.05.2005 00:
{47695139-0F22-4	{683981E9-50A8-4	msz	msz	<NULL>	0	30.04.2005 22:
{47695139-0F22-4	{7B89D2B8-3A3A-	new1	new1	<NULL>	0	30.04.2005 22:
{47695139-0F22-4	{07F5CA1A-80DE-	po	po	<NULL>	0	30.04.2005 23:
{47695139-0F22-4	{96768A82-0CD8-	thebest	thebest	<NULL>	0	01.05.2005 00:
{47695139-0F22-4	{ECB77888-30E2-4	thefirst	thefirst	<NULL>	0	30.04.2005 22:
{47695139-0F22-4	{888A19D4-4DD2-	tttt1	tttt1	<NULL>	0	01.05.2005 00:
{47695139-0F22-4	{AF30A5B6-1C77-	user1	user1	<NULL>	0	28.04.2005 20:

Figure 21-11. *The aspnet_Users table in the membership database*

Both the password and the answer for the password question are stored as a salted hash in the database because you have selected the passwordFormat="Hashed" option for the provider in the <membership> configuration section. After you have added users to the membership store, you can authenticate those users with the membership API. For that purpose, you have to create a login page that queries the user name and password from the user and then validates those credentials against the credential store, as follows:

```
Protected Sub LoginAction_Click(ByVal sender As Object, ByVal e As EventArgs)
    If Membership.ValidateUser(UsernameText.Text, PasswordText.Text) Then
        FormsAuthentication.RedirectFromLoginPage(UsernameText.Text, False)
    Else
        LegendStatus.Text = "Invalid user name or password!"
    End If
End Sub
```

You don't need to know about which provider is actually used by the application. If you want to use a different membership provider, you just need to change the configuration so that the membership API uses this different provider. Your application doesn't know about any details of the underlying provider. Furthermore, in the next section you will learn about the new security controls. You will see that you don't need to create the controls for the login page manually any more.

Using the Security Controls

Of course, you still have to create the login page again and again. But ASP.NET 2.0 ships with several new controls that simplify the process of creating the login page as well as other related functionality. In this section, you will learn more about the new security controls included with ASP.NET. These security controls rely on the underlying forms authentication and the membership API infrastructure. Table 21-5 describes the security controls that ship with ASP.NET.

Table 21-5. *The New ASP.NET Security Controls*

Control	Primary Purpose
Login	The Login control is a composite control that solves the most common task for forms authentication–based applications—displaying a user name and password textbox with a login button. Furthermore, if events are caught through custom event procedures, it automatically validates the user against the default membership provider.
LoginStatus	The login status is a simple control that validates the authentication state of the current session. If the user is not authenticated, it offers a login button that redirects to the configured login page. Otherwise, it displays a sign-out button for the possibility of logging off.
LoginView	This is really a powerful control that allows you to display different sets of controls for authenticated and unauthenticated users. Furthermore, it allows you to display different controls for users who are in different roles, as you will see in Chapter 23.
PasswordRecovery	This allows the user to retrieve the password if the user has provided an e-mail address during registration. It requests the user name from the user and then automatically displays a user interface that displays the password question and requests the appropriate answer from the user. If the answer is correct, it uses the membership API to send the password to the user.
ChangePassword	This control is a composite control that requests the old password from the user and lets the user enter a new password including the password confirmation.
CreateUserWizard	Includes a complete wizard that guides the user (or an administrator) through the creation process of a user.

You can use these controls with any other control. For example, you can use the Login control either on your main page or on a separate login page. Every control works in the same way: if you don't catch any custom events, all these controls work with the membership API by default. As soon as you catch events provided by the controls, you are responsible for completing the task. For example, the Login control supports an Authenticate event. If you don't catch this event, it uses the membership API automatically. But if you catch this event, you are responsible for validating user credentials on your own.

The Login Control

The Login control provides you with a ready-to-use user interface that queries the user name and password from the user and offers a login button for actually logging the user in. Figure 21-12 shows an example of the Login control in action.

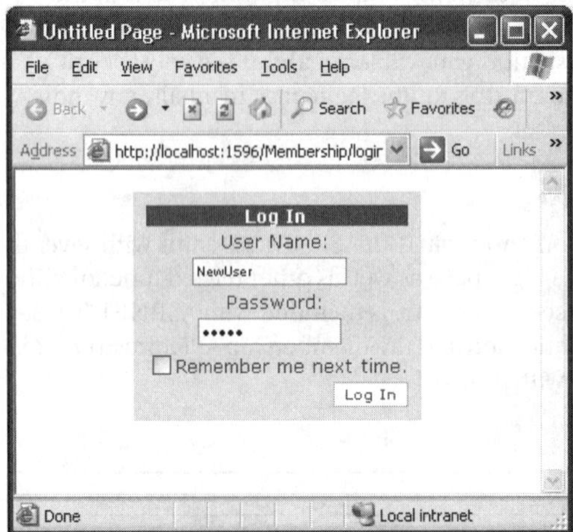

Figure 21-12. *The Login control in action*

Behind the scenes the Login control is nothing more than an ASP.NET composite control. It's completely extensible in that it allows you to override any layout styles and properties as well as catch events thrown by the control for overriding its default behavior. If you leave the Login control as it is and you don't catch any of its events, it automatically uses the membership provider configured for your application. The simplest form of a Login control on your page is as follows:

```
<form id="form1" runat="server">
    <div style="text-align: center">
        <asp:Login ID="Login1" runat="server">
        </asp:Login>
    </div>
</form>
```

You can use several properties for changing the appearance of the control. You can use the different style settings supported by the Login control as follows:

```
<form id="form1" runat="server">
<div style="text-align: center">
    <asp:Login ID="Login1" runat="server"
```

```
                BackColor="aliceblue" BorderColor="Black" BorderStyle="double">
        <LoginButtonStyle BackColor="darkblue" ForeColor="White" />
        <TextBoxStyle BackColor="LightCyan" ForeColor="Black" Font-Bold="True" />
        <TitleTextStyle Font-Italic="True" Font-Bold="True" Font-Names="Verdana" />
    </asp:Login>
</div>
</form>
```

You can also use CSS classes for customizing the Login control's appearance. Every style property supported by the Login control includes a CssClass property. As is the case for every other ASP.NET control, this property allows you to set a CSS class name for your Login control that was added to the website previously. Imagine you added the following CSS style sheet with the filename MyStyles.css to your project:

```
.MyLoginTextBoxStyle
{
    cursor: crosshair;
    background-color: yellow;
    text-align: center;
    border-left-color: black;
    border-bottom-color: black;
    border-top-style: dotted;
    border-top-color: black;
    border-right-style: dotted;
    border-left-style: dotted;
    border-right-color: black;
    border-bottom-style: dotted;
    font-family: Verdana;
    vertical-align: middle;
}
```

The content of the CSS file defines the style .MyLoginTextBoxStyle that you will use for the text boxes displayed on your Login control. You can include this style file in your login page so that you can use the style for the Login control as follows:

```
<html xmlns="http://www.w3.org/1999/xhtml" >
<head runat="server">
    <title>Untitled Page</title>
    <link href="MyStyles.css" rel="stylesheet" type="text/css" />
</head>
<body>
    <form id="form1" runat="server">
    <div style="text-align: center">
        <asp:Login ID="Login1" runat="server"
                   BackColor="aliceblue"
                   BorderColor="Black" BorderStyle="double">
            <LoginButtonStyle BackColor="darkblue" ForeColor="White" />
            <TextBoxStyle CssClass="MyLoginTextBoxStyle" />
            <TitleTextStyle Font-Italic="True" Font-Bold="True"
                            Font-Names="Verdana" />
        </asp:Login>
    </div>
    </form>
</body>
</html>
```

■**Note** If you try running the page and if the CSS file is placed in a directory where anonymous access is denied, the styles will not be applied to the Login control because the CSS file is protected by the ASP.NET runtime (because its file extension is mapped to ASP.NET). This is also the case if you deny access to anonymous users in the root directory and put your CSS file there. Therefore, if you want to use CSS files with the Login control (where the user is definitely the anonymous user), either you have to put the CSS file into a directory that allows anonymous users access or you have to add the following configuration for the CSS file to your web.config file:

```
<location path="MyStyles.css">
    <system.web>
        <authorization>
            <allow users="*" />
        </authorization>
    </system.web>
</location>
```

We prefer having publicly available resources in a separate folder and restricting access to any other location of the web application, or the other way round. You will learn more about authorization and the configuration steps for it in Chapter 23.

Table 21-6 lists the styles supported by the Login control. Every style works in the same way. You can set color and font properties directly, or you use the CssClass property for assigning a CSS class.

Table 21-6. *The Styles Supported by the Login Control*

Style	Description
CheckBoxStyle	Defines the style properties for the Remember Me check box.
FailureStyle	Defines the style for the text displayed if the login was not successful.
HyperLinkStyle	The Login control allows you to define several types of hyperlinks, for example, to a registration page. This style defines the appearance of these hyperlinks.
InstructionTextStyle	The Login control allows you to specify help text that is displayed directly in the Login control. This style defines the appearance of this text.
LabelStyle	Defines the style for the User Name and Password labels.
LoginButtonStyle	Defines the style for the login button.
TextBoxStyle	Defines the style for the User Name and Password text boxes.
TitleTextStyle	Defines a style for the title text of the Login control.
ValidatorTextStyle	Defines styles for validation controls that are used for validating the user name and password.

The styles are customizable not only for the Login control. Any content displayed in the control is customizable through several properties. For example, you can select the text displayed for the login button, and you have the choice of displaying a login link instead of a login button (which is the default). Furthermore, you can add several hyperlinks to your Login control, such as a hyperlink to a help text page or a hyperlink to a registration page. Of course, both pages must be available for anonymous users, because the help should be provided to anonymous users (remember, if someone sees the Login control, she potentially is an anonymous user). If you want to include some additional links in your Login control, modify the previously displayed control as follows:

```
<asp:Login ID="Login1" runat="server"
           BackColor="aliceblue"
```

```
            BorderColor="Black" BorderStyle="double"
            CreateUserText="Register"
            CreateUserUrl="Register.aspx" HelpPageText="Additional Help"
            HelpPageUrl="HelpMe.htm"
            InstructionText="Please enter your user name and password for <br>
                             logging into the system.">
    <LoginButtonStyle BackColor="DarkBlue" ForeColor="White" />
    <TextBoxStyle CssClass="MyLoginTextBoxStyle" />
    <TitleTextStyle Font-Italic="True" Font-Bold="True" Font-Names="Verdana" />
</asp:Login>
```

This code displays two additional links—one for a help page and one for a registration page—and adds some short, instructional text below the heading of the Login control. The styles discussed previously are applied to these properties. Table 21-7 describes the relevant properties for customizing the Login control.

Table 21-7. *The Relevant Customization Properties for the Login Control*

Property	Description
TitleText	The text displayed as the heading of the control.
InstructionText	You have already used this property in the previous code snippet, which contains text that is displayed below the heading of the control.
FailureText	This is the text displayed by the Login control if the login attempt was not successful.
UserNameLabelText	The text displayed as a label in front of the user name text box.
PasswordLabelText	The text displayed as a label in front of the password text box.
UserName	Initial value filled into the user name text box.
UsernameRequiredErrorMessage	Error message displayed if the user has not entered a user name.
PasswordRequiredErrorMessage	Error message displayed if the user has not entered a password.
LoginButtonText	The text displayed for the login button.
LoginButtonType	The login button can be displayed as a link, button, or image. For this purpose, you have to set this property appropriately. Supported values are Link, Button, and Image.
LoginButtonImageUrl	If you display the login button as an image, you have to provide a URL to an image that is displayed for the button.
DestinationPageUrl	If the login attempt was successful, the Login control redirects the user to this page. This property is empty by default. If empty, it uses the forms authentication infrastructure for redirecting either to the originally requested page or to the defautlUrl configured in web.config for forms authentication.
DisplayRememberMe	Enables you to show and hide the Remember Me check box. By default this property is set to True.
FailureAction	Defines the action the control performs after a login attempt failed. The two valid options are Refresh and RedirectToLoginPage. The first one refreshes just the current page, and the second one redirects to the configured login page. Of course, the second one is useful if you use the control anywhere else instead of the login page.

(Continued)

Table 21-7. *Continued*

Property	Description
RememberMeSet	Defines the default value for the Remember Me check box. By default this option is set to False, which means the check box is not checked by default.
VisibleWhenLoggedIn	If set to False, the control automatically hides itself if the user is already logged in. If set to True (default), the Login control is displayed even if the user is already logged in.
CreateUserUrl	Defines a hyperlink to a page in the website that allows you to create (register!) a user. Therefore, this is typically used for enabling the user to access a registration page. Typically this page displays the CreateUserWizard control.
CreateUserText	Defines the text displayed for the CreateUserUrl hyperlink.
CreateUserIconUrl	Defines a URL to an image displayed together with the text for the CreateUserUrl hyperlink.
HelpPageUrl	URL for redirecting the user to a help page.
HelpPageText	Text displayed for the hyperlink configured in the HelpPageUrl property.
HelpPageIconUrl	URL to an icon displayed together with the text for the HelpPageUrl hyperlink.
PasswordRecoveryUrl	URL for redirecting the user to a password recovery page. This page is used if the user has forgotten the password. Typically this page displays the PasswordRecovery control.
PasswordRecoveryText	The text displayed for the hyperlink configured in PasswordRecoveryUrl.
PasswordRecoveryIconUrl	Icon displayed together with the text for the PasswordRecoveryUrl.

Templates and the Login Control

As you can see, the control is nearly completely customizable through these properties. But as you probably have seen, you cannot define any validation expressions for validating the input. Of course, you can do validation on the server side within the event procedures offered by the Login control. However, generally, if you want to add any controls to the Login control, you can't do that through the properties introduced previously. For example, what if you have an additional text box for strong authentication with a second password or user access key as on some governmental pages?

Fortunately, the Login control supports templates just as other controls such as the GridView control do. With templates, you can customize the contents of the Login control without any limitations. You can add any controls you want to your Login control. You can use a custom template for the Login control through the LayoutTemplate tag as follows:

```
<asp:Login ID="LoginCtrl" runat="server"
        BackColor="aliceblue"
        BorderColor="Black"
        BorderStyle="double">
    <LayoutTemplate>
        <h4>Log-In to the System</h4>
        <table>
            <tr>
            <td>
            User Name:
            </td>
            <td>
```

```
            <asp:TextBox ID="UserName" runat="server" />
            <asp:RequiredFieldValidator ID="UserNameRequired"
                        runat="server"
                        ControlToValidate="UserName"
                        ErrorMessage="*" />
            <asp:RegularExpressionValidator ID="UsernameValidator"
                        runat="server"
                        ControlToValidate="UserName"
                        ValidationExpression="[\w| ]*"
                        ErrorMessage="Invalid User Name" />
            </td>
            </tr>
            <tr>
            <td>
            Password:
            </td>
            <td>
            <asp:TextBox ID="Password" runat="server" TextMode="Password" />
            <asp:RequiredFieldValidator ID="PasswordRequired"
                        runat="server"
                        ControlToValidate="Password"
                        ErrorMessage="*" />
            <asp:RegularExpressionValidator ID="RegularExpressionValidator1"
                        runat="server"
                        ControlToValidate="Password"
                        ValidationExpression='[\w| !"§$%&amp;/()=\-?\*]*'
                        ErrorMessage="Invalid Password" />
            </td>
            </tr>
        </table>
        <asp:CheckBox ID="RememberMe" runat="server" Text="Remember Me" />
        <asp:Literal ID="FailureText" runat="server" /><br />
        <asp:Button ID="Login" CommandName="Login"
                runat="server" Text="Login"  />
    </LayoutTemplate>
</asp:Login>
```

With the right controls and the correct ID values for these controls in place, you don't need to write any code for handling events. The code just works as usual except that you define the set of controls and the layout of these controls. Actually, the Login control requires at least two text boxes with the IDs UserName and Password. If those two text boxes are missing (or don't have these ID values), the control throws an exception. All the other controls are optional, but if you specify corresponding ID values (such as Login for the login button), the Login control automatically handles their events and behaves as when you used the predefined layouts for the control. Table 21-8 lists the special ID values, their required control types, and whether they are required or optional.

Table 21-8. *Special Controls for the Login Template*

Control ID	Control Type	Required?
UserName	System.Web.UI.WebControls.Textbox	Yes
Password	System.Web.UI.WebControls.Textbox	Yes
RememberMe	System.Web.UI.WebControls.CheckBox	No
FailureText	System.Web.UI.WebControls.Literal	No
Login	Any control that supports event bubbling and a CommandName	No

The control with the ID Login can be any control that supports event bubbling and a CommandName property. It is important that you set the CommandName property to Login, because otherwise it will not be recognized in the event-handling process by the Login control. You can also add controls with other IDs that are not related to the Login control at all. The previous code includes RequiredFieldValidator and RegularExpressionValidator controls for validating the user name and password fields appropriately. If you don't add a control with the CommandName set to Login, you have to handle the event of the control yourself and write the appropriate code for validating the user name and password and for redirecting to the originally requested page.

When using the LayoutTemplate, many of the properties originally offered by the control are not available anymore. Only the following properties are available when using the template:

- DestinationPageUrl
- VisibleWhenLoggedIn
- FailureAction
- MembershipProvider
- Password
- Username
- RememberMeSet

All the style properties and several properties for configuring text contents of default controls are not available any more, because you can add them manually as separate controls or static text to the template for the Login control.

Programming the Login Control

The Login control supports a couple of events and properties that you can use to customize the behavior of the control. This gives you complete control over customizing the Login control (used along with the other customization possibilities such as templates or custom style properties). The Login control supports the events listed in Table 21-9.

Table 21-9. *The Events of the Login Control*

Event	Description
LoggingIn	Raised before the user gets authenticated by the control.
LoggedIn	Raised after the user has been authenticated by the control.
LoginError	Raised when the login of the user failed for some reason (such as a wrong password or user name).
Authenticate	Raised to authenticate the user. If you catch this event, you have to authenticate the user on your own, and the Login control completely relies on your authentication code.

You can catch the first three events (in the previous table) to perform some actions before the user gets authenticated, after the user has been authenticated, and if an error has happened during the authentication process. For example, you can use the LoginError event to automatically redirect the user to the password recovery page after a specific number of attempts, as follows:

```
Protected Sub Page_Load(ByVal sender As Object, ByVal e As EventArgs)
    If (Not Me.IsPostBack) Then
        ViewState("LoginErrors") = 0
    End If
End Sub
```

```
Protected Sub LoginCtrl_LoginError(ByVal sender As Object, ByVal e As EventArgs)
    ' Increase the number of invalid logins
    Dim ErrorCount As Integer = CInt(ViewState("LoginErrors")) + 1
    ViewState("LoginErrors") = ErrorCount

    ' Now validate the number of errors
    If (ErrorCount > 3) AndAlso (LoginCtrl.PasswordRecoveryUrl <> String.Empty) Then
        Response.Redirect(LoginCtrl.PasswordRecoveryUrl)
    End If
End Sub
```

The Login control fires the events in the order shown in Figure 21-13.

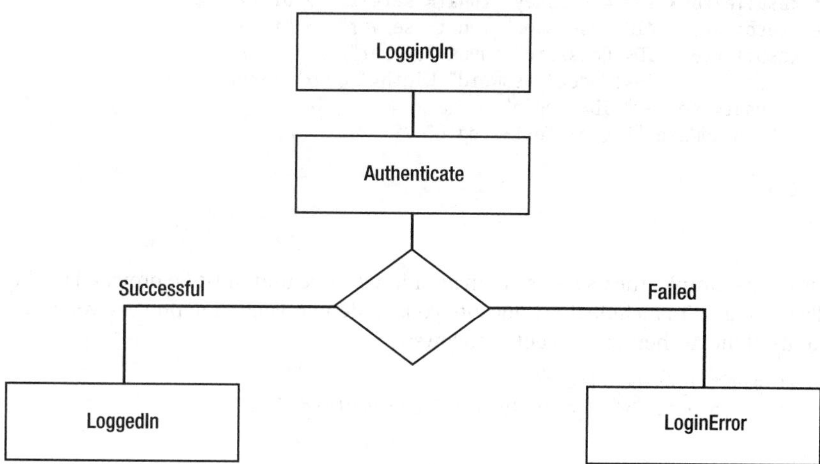

Figure 21-13. *The order of the Login control events*

As mentioned previously, if you catch the event, you have to add your own code for validating the user name and password. The Authenticate property supports an instance of AuthenticateEventArgs to the parameter list. This event argument class supports one property called Authenticated. If you set this property to True, the Login control assumes that authentication was successful and raises the LoggedIn event. If set to False, it displays the FailureText and raises the LoginError event.

```
Protected Sub LoginCtrl_Authenticate(
        ByVal sender As Object, ByVal e As AuthenticateEventArgs)
    If YourValidationFunction(LoginCtrl.UserName, LoginCtrl.Password) Then
        e.Authenticated = True
    Else
        e.Authenticated = False
    End If
End Sub
```

As you can see, you have direct access to the entered values through the UserName and Password properties that contain the text entered in the corresponding text boxes. If you are using template controls and require the value of another control in addition to the controls with the IDs UserName and Password, you can use the control's FindControl method to get the control. This method requires the ID of the control and returns an instance of System.Web.UI.Control. You then just cast the control to the appropriate type and read the values you require for your custom credential validation method. The following Login control uses a template with an additional control that you will use later in the Authenticate event in your code:

```
<asp:Login ID="OtherLoginCtrl" runat="server"
           BackColor="aliceblue"
           BorderColor="Black"
           BorderStyle="double"
           PasswordRecoveryUrl="~/pwdrecover.aspx"
           OnAuthenticate="OtherLoginCtrl_Authenticate">

    <LayoutTemplate>
        <font face="Courier New">
        Userskey: <asp:Textbox ID="AccessKey" runat="server" /><br />
        User Name: <asp:TextBox ID="UserName" runat="server" /><br />
        Password: <asp:TextBox ID="Password" runat="server"
                               TextMode="password" Width="149px" /><br />
        <asp:Button runat="server" ID="Login"
                    CommandName="Login" Text="Login" />
        </font>
    </LayoutTemplate>

</asp:Login>
```

In the previous code example, the user's key is an additional value that must be provided by the user for successfully logging in. To include this value into your credential-validation process, you have to modify the contents of the Authenticate event as follows:

```
Protected Sub OtherLoginCtrl_Authenticate(
        ByVal sender As Object, ByVal e As AuthenticateEventArgs)

    Dim AccessKeyText As TextBox =
        CType(OtherLoginCtrl.FindControl("AccessKey"), TextBox)

    If YourValidation(AccessKeyText.Text,
          OtherLoginCtrl.UserName, OtherLoginCtrl.Password) Then
        e.Authenticated = True
    Else
        e.Authenticated = False
    End If
End Sub
```

Of course, in this case you cannot use any default membership provider. You have to implement your own validation function that accepts these additional parameters. But the Login control forces you not to use membership at all. The validation function can be any type of function you want. You just need to set the e.Authenticated property appropriately. Then you can use the Login control for whatever login mechanism you want.

The LoginStatus Control

The LoginStatus control is a simple control that displays either a login link if the user is not authenticated or a logout link if the user is authenticated. The login link automatically redirects to the configured login page, and the logout link automatically calls the method FormsAuthentication.SignOut for logging off the user. The control is fairly simple, and therefore customization is simple as well.

```
<asp:LoginStatus ID="LoginStatus1" runat="server"
        LoginText="Sign In"
        LogoutText="Sign Out"
```

```
        LogoutPageUrl="~/Default.aspx"
        LogoutAction="Redirect" />
```

The LoginStatus control offers a couple of properties for customizing the text shown for the links and the URLs to redirect to when the user clicks the link. You can find the most important properties in Table 21-10.

Table 21-10. *Properties for Customizing the LoginStatus Control*

Property	Description
LoginText	The text displayed if the user is not signed in.
LoginImageUrl	A URL for an image displayed as an icon for the login link.
LogoutText	The text displayed if the user is authenticated.
LogoutImageUrl	A URL for an image displayed as icon for the logout link.
LogoutAction	Configures the action the control performs if the user clicks the logout link that is displayed when the user is authenticated. Valid options are Refresh, Redirect, and RedirectToLoginPage. The first option just refreshes the current page, the second option redirects to the page configured in the LogoutPageUrl, and the last option redirects to the login page.
LogoutPageUrl	A page to redirect to if the user clicks the logout link and the LogoutAction is set to Redirect.

The LoginView Control

This control is fairly simple but extremely powerful. It allows you to display a different set of controls for anonymous and authenticated users. Further, it even allows you to display different content based on which roles the currently logged-in user is assign to. But you will learn more about roles and their connection to the LoginView control in Chapter 23. For now you will learn how to display different content for anonymous users and for authenticated users.

The LoginView control is a template control with different types of templates—one for anonymous users, one for authenticated users, and one for supporting role-based templates. Within those templates, you just add the controls to display for the corresponding situation as follows (role-based templates are encapsulated into RoleGroup controls, but you will learn more about them in Chapter 23):

```
<asp:LoginView ID="LoginViewCtrl" runat="server">
    <AnonymousTemplate>
        <h2>You are anonymous</h2>
    </AnonymousTemplate>
    <LoggedInTemplate>
        <h2>You are logged in</h2>
        Submit your comment: <asp:TextBox runat="server" ID="CommentText" />
        <br />
        <asp:Button runat="server" ID="SubmitCommentAction" Text="Submit" />
    </LoggedInTemplate>
</asp:LoginView>
```

The previous control displays some simple text for anonymous users and some text in a text box together with a button for logged-in users, as shown in Figure 21-14. Furthermore, the control supports two events you can catch for initializing content controls of different templates appropriately before they are displayed:

- ViewChanging, which is raised before the control displays content defined in another template
- ViewChanged, which is raised after the control has changed the content display from one template to another

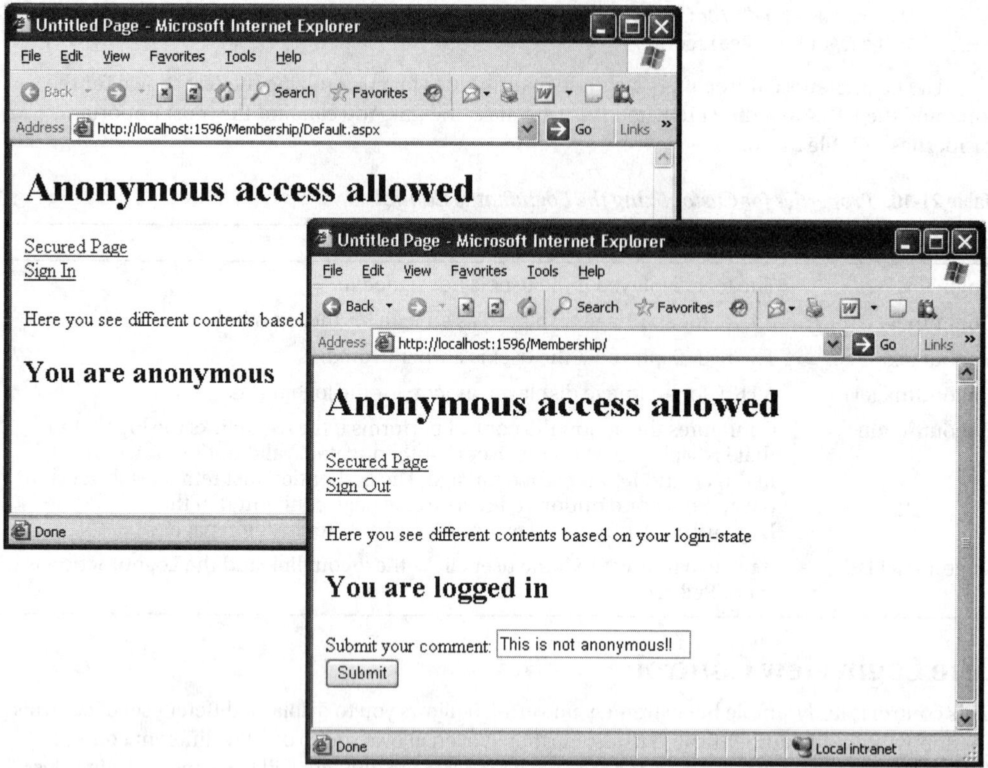

Figure 21-14. *The LoginView control for anonymous and authenticated users*

The PasswordRecovery Control

The PasswordRecovery control is useful if a user has forgotten his password. This queries the user name from the user and afterward automatically displays the password question stored for the user in the credential store. If the user enters the correct answer for the password question, the password is mailed automatically to the e-mail address configured for the user. Figure 21-15 shows the PasswordRecovery control in action.

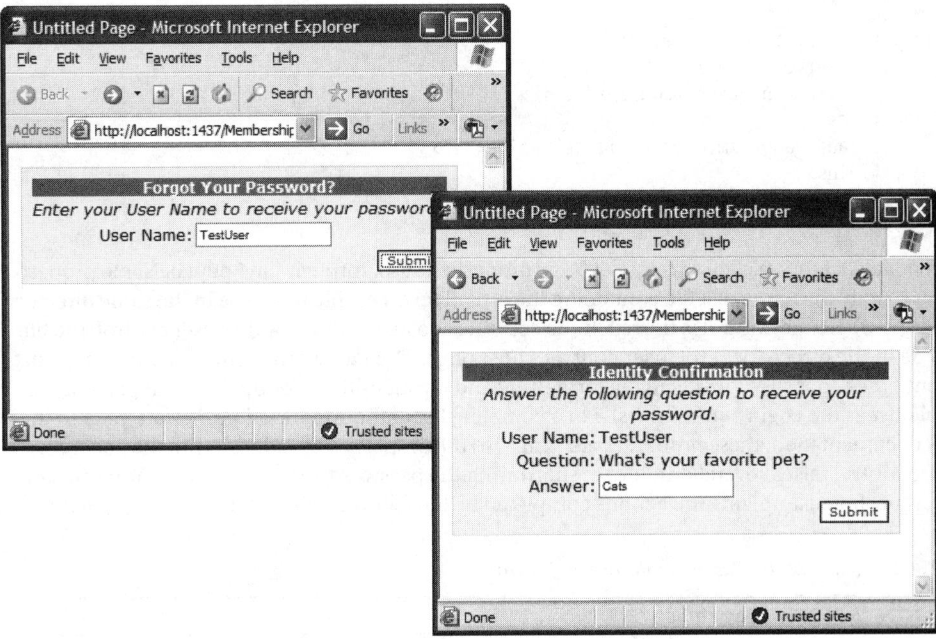

Figure 21-15. *The PasswordRecovery control in action*

The control includes three customizable view modes. First, the user has to enter his user name. When the user clicks the submit button, the control queries the password question through the membership API from the underlying credential store. Second, this question is then displayed, and the user is requested to enter the correct answer. When the user enters the correct answer, an automatically generated password or the stored password is sent to the user's e-mail address. This e-mail address was specified during the registration process (or when the user was created through the WAT). If sent successfully, the control displays a confirmation view. Any mail configuration takes place through the control's properties, as follows. Of course, the password itself can be sent to the user only if it is not hashed. Therefore, the membership provider must be configured in a way that it stores the passwords either encrypted or in clear-text format. If the membership provider stores the password in a hashed form, it automatically generates a new, random password and sends the new password in the e-mail.

```
<asp:PasswordRecovery ID=" PasswordRecoveryCtrl" runat="server"
                      BackColor="Azure"
                      BorderColor="Black" BorderStyle="solid">
    <MailDefinition From="proaspnet2@apress.com"
                    Subject="Forgotten Password"
                    Priority="High" />
    <TitleTextStyle Font-Bold="True" Font-Italic="True" BorderStyle="Dotted" />
    <TextBoxStyle BackColor="Yellow" BorderStyle="Double" />
    <FailureTextStyle Font-Bold="True" ForeColor="Red" />
</asp:PasswordRecovery>
```

The control requires an e-mail SMTP server for sending the e-mail message. Therefore, you have to configure the SMTP mail server in your web.config file, as follows:

```
<system.web>
    <smtpMail serverName="MyServer"
              serverPort="15"
              from="proaspnet2@apress.com">
        <fields>
            <add name="smtpauthenticate" value="2">
        </fields>
    </smtpMail>
</system.web>
```

The MailDefinition allows you to set basic properties. Also, through the BodyFileName property, you can specify the name of a file containing the e-mail text. This file has to be in the same directory as the page where the control is hosted. If the control is hosted within another user control, the file has to be in the directory of the user control's host page. The PasswordRecovery control supports different style properties for specifying formatting and layout options for the different parts of the control (just as the Login control does). For a complete list of the supported properties, refer to the MSDN documentation; these properties are similar to the properties introduced with the Login control. The control raises several different events during the password-recovery process. You can catch these events for customizing the actions completed by the control. Table 21-11 lists these events.

Table 21-11. *Events of the PasswordRecovery Control*

Event	Description
VerifyingUser	Raised before the control starts validating the user name entered. Validating the user name means looking for the user in the membership store and retrieving the password question information.
UserLookupError	If the user name entered in the user name text box doesn't exist in the membership store, this event is raised before the failure text is displayed.
VerifyingAnswer	When the user clicks the submit button in the second step, the answer for the question is compared to the one stored in the membership store. This event is raised before this action takes place.
AnswerLookupError	If the answer provided by the user is not correct, this event is raised by the control.
SendingEmail	This event is raised by the control after the answer submitted by the user has been identified as the correct answer and before the e-mail is sent through the mail server.
SendMailError	If the e-mail cannot be sent for some reason (for example, the mail server is not available), this event is raised by the control.

You can use these events for preparing information before that information gets processed by the control. For example, if you want to convert all letters in the user name to lowercase letters before the control compares contents with the data stored in the membership store, you can do this in the VerifyingUser event. Similarly, you can use the VerifyingAnswer for preprocessing information before it gets processed by the control. Both events get event arguments of type LoginCancelEventArgs, which contains a Cancel property. If you set this property to False, you can cancel the whole processing step.

When catching the SendingEmail event, you have the chance to modify the contents of the e-mail message before the control actually sends the e-mail to the user. The passed MailMessageEventArgs contains a Message property that represents the actual e-mail message. By modifying the Message's properties, such as the Attachments collection, you can add attachments, configure a CC address, or do anything else related to the e-mail message.

PasswordRecovery Templates

Like the Login control, the PasswordRecovery control can be customized completely if customization through the previously mentioned properties and styles is not sufficient for some reason. The control supports templates for every view:

- The UsernameTemplate contains all the controls displayed for the first step of the password-recovery process when the user is required to enter the user name.
- Controls for the second step, the password question step, are placed in the QuestionTemplate.
- Finally, the control supports a SuccessTemplate that consists of the controls displayed for the confirmation displayed after the password has been sent successfully to the user.

Every template has certain required controls. For example, the UsernameTemplate requires a text box for entering the user name. The QuestionTemplate requires a text box for entering the question, and of course the SuccessTemplate requires a Literal control for displaying the final confirmation message. A template PasswordRecovery control might look like this:

```
<asp:PasswordRecovery ID="PasswordTemplateCtrl" runat="server">
    <MailDefinition From="pwd@apress.com"
                    Priority="High"
                    Subject="Important information" />
    <UserNameTemplate>
        <span style="text-align: center">
        <font face="Courier New">
            <h2>Forgotten your Password?</h2>
            Please enter your user name:<br />
            <asp:TextBox ID="UserName" runat="server" />
            <br />
            <asp:Button ID="SubmitButton" CommandName="Submit"
                        runat="server" Text="Next" />
            <br />
            <span style="color: Red">
            <asp:Literal ID="FailureText" runat="server" />
            </span>
        </font>
        </span>
    </UserNameTemplate>
    <QuestionTemplate>
        <span style="text-align: center">
        <font face="Courier New">
            <h2>Forgotten your Password?</h2>
            Hello <asp:Literal ID="UserName" runat="server" />! <br />
            Please answer your password-question:<br />
            <asp:Literal ID="Question" runat="server" /><br />
            <asp:TextBox ID="Answer" runat="server" /><br />
            <asp:Button ID="SubmitButton" CommandName="Submit"
                        runat="Server" Text="Send Answer" /><br />
            <asp:Literal ID="FailureText" runat="server" />
            </span>
        </font>
        </span>
    </QuestionTemplate>
    <SuccessTemplate>
        Your password has been sent to your email address
        <asp:Label ID="EmailLabel" runat="server" />!
    </SuccessTemplate>
</asp:PasswordRecovery>
```

Again, if you use controls with the appropriate ID values and use the appropriate CommandName values for buttons, you don't have to write any code for the control to work, as in the previous examples where you didn't use templates. In the previous code, these special controls are in bold. Some of these controls are required for the templates, and others are optional. Table 21-12 lists the controls for PasswordRecovery templates.

Table 21-12. *Special Controls for PasswordRecovery Templates*

Template	ID	Control Type	Required?	Additional Comments
UsernameTemplate	UserName	System.Web.UI.WebControls.TextBox	Yes	
UsernameTemplate	SubmitButton	All controls that support event bubbling	No	CommandName must be set to Submit.
UsernameTemplate	FailureText	System.Web.UI.WebControls.Literal	No	
QuestionTemplate	UserName	System.Web.UI.WebControls.Literal	No	
QuestionTemplate	Question	System.Web.UI.WebControls.Literal	No	
QuestionTemplate	Answer	System.Web.UI.WebControls.TextBox	Yes	
QuestionTemplate	SubmitButton	All controls that support event bubbling	No	CommandName must be set to Submit.
QuestionTemplate	FailureText	System.Web.UI.WebControls.Literal	No	

Again, the submit button can be any control that supports event bubbling and a CommandName property. Typically you can use the controls Button, ImageButton, or LinkButton for this purpose. The CommandName must be set to Submit; otherwise, the command is not recognized by the control (the ID is not evaluated and can therefore be set to any value). The SuccessTemplate doesn't require any type of control with any special IDs. Therefore, you can add any control you want there; it's just for displaying the confirmation. In the previous example, it includes a Literal control that should display the e-mail address to which the password has been sent. You can set this Literal control through the SendingEmail event procedure. Again, you can use the FindControl method for finding the control (which is actually a child control of the password control) in the appropriate template, as follows:

```
Protected Sub PasswordTemplateCtrl_SendingMail(ByVal sender As Object,
        ByVal e As MailMessageEventArgs)
    Dim lbl As Label =
        CType(PasswordTemplateCtrl.SuccessTemplateContainer.FindControl
                    ("EmailLabel"), Label)
    lbl.Text = e.Message.To(0).Address
End Sub
```

Because the control includes more than one template, you cannot call the FindControl method directly on the PasswordRecovery control instance. You have to select the appropriate template container (UserNameTemplateContainer, QuestionTemplateContainer, or SuccessTemplateContainer). Afterward, you can work with the control as usual. In the previous example, you just set the text of the label to the first e-mail recipient. Of course, usually for a password recovery, the list has only one mail recipient.

The ChangePassword Control

You can use this control as a standard control for allowing the user to change her password. The control simply queries the user name as well as the old password from the user. Then it requires the user to enter the new password and confirm the new password. If the user is already logged on, the control automatically hides the text field for the user name and uses the name of the authenticated user. You can use the control on a secured page as follows:

```
<asp:ChangePassword ID="ChangePwdCtrl" runat="server"
                    BorderStyle="Groove" BackColor="aliceblue">
   <MailDefinition From="pwd@apress.com"
                   Subject="Changes in your profile"
                   Priority="High" />
   <TitleTextStyle Font-Bold="True" Font-Underline="True"
                   Font-Names="Verdana" ForeColor="blue" />
</asp:ChangePassword>
```

Again, the control includes a MailDefinition property with the same settings as the PasswordRecovery control. This is because after the password has been changed successfully, the control automatically can send an e-mail to the user's e-mail address if a mail server is configured for the web application. As all the other controls, this control is customizable through both properties and styles and a template-based approach. But this time two templates are required when customizing the control:

- The ChangePasswordTemplate displays the fields for entering the old user name and password as well as the new password including the password confirmation field.
- In the SuccessTemplate the success message is displayed.

The ChangePasswordTemplate requires you to add some special controls with special IDs and CommandName property values. You can find these control ID values and CommandName values in bold in the following code snippet:

```
<asp:ChangePassword ID="ChangePwdCtrl" runat="server">
    <ChangePasswordTemplate>
        Old Password: 
        <asp:TextBox ID="CurrentPassword" runat="server"
                     TextMode="Password" /><br />
        New Password: 
        <asp:TextBox ID="NewPassword" runat="server"
                     TextMode="Password" /><br />
        Confirmation: 
        <asp:TextBox ID="ConfirmNewPassword" runat="server"
                     TextMode="Password" /><br />
        <asp:Button ID="ChangePasswordPushButton" CommandName="ChangePassword"
                    runat="server" Text="Change Password" />
        <asp:Button ID="CancelPushButton" CommandName="Cancel"
                    runat="server" Text="Cancel" /><br />
        <asp:Literal ID="FailureText" runat="server"
                     EnableViewState="False" />
    </ChangePasswordTemplate>
    <SuccessTemplate>
        Your password has been changed!</td>
        <asp:Button ID="ContinuePushButton" CommandName="Continue"
                    runat="server" Text="Continue" />
    </SuccessTemplate>
</asp:ChangePassword>
```

Basically, the text box controls of the ChangePasswordTemplate are all required. The other controls are optional. If you select the ID properties and the CommandName properties for the buttons appropriately, you don't have to write any additional code.

The CreateUserWizard Control

The CreateUserWizard control is the most powerful control of the login controls. It enables you to create registration pages within a couple of minutes. This control is a wizard control with two default steps: one for querying general user information and one for displaying a confirmation message. Of course, as the CreateUserWizard inherits from the base Wizard control, you can add as many wizard steps as you want. But when you just add a CreateUserWizard control to your page as follows, the result is really amazing, as shown in Figure 21-16.

```
<asp:CreateUserWizard ID="RegisterUser" runat="server"
                       BorderStyle="Ridge" BackColor="aquamarine">
    <TitleTextStyle Font-Bold="True" Font-Names="Verdana" />
    <WizardSteps>
        <asp:CreateUserWizardStep runat="server">
        </asp:CreateUserWizardStep>
        <asp:CompleteWizardStep runat="server">
        </asp:CompleteWizardStep>
    </WizardSteps>
</asp:CreateUserWizard>
```

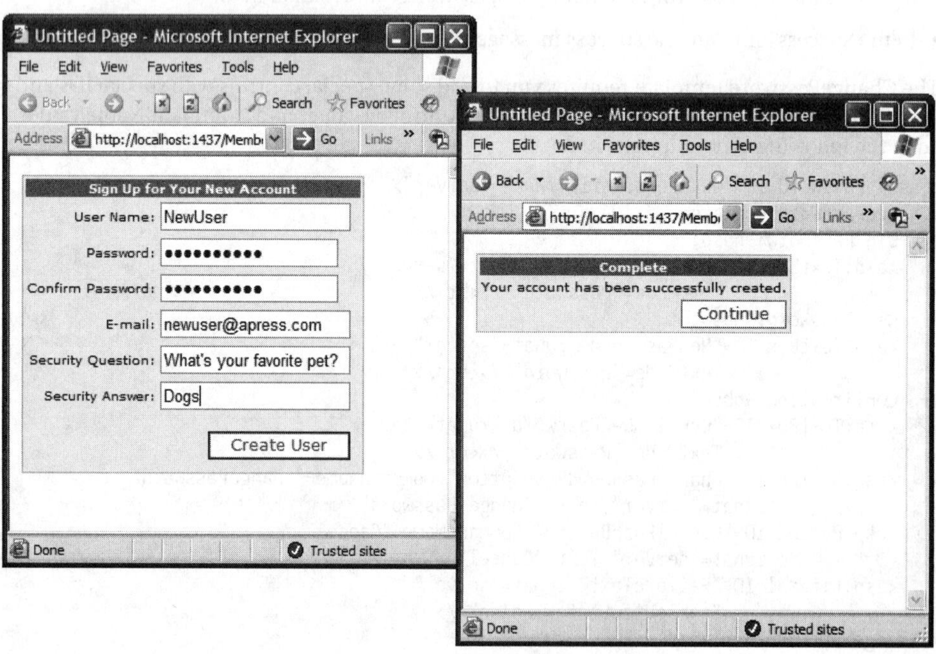

Figure 21-16. *A simple CreateUserWizard control*

The default appearance of the control is, again, customizable through properties and styles. The control offers lots of styles, but basically the meaning of the styles is similar to the styles covered for the previous controls. In fact, this control includes the most complete list of styles, as it includes most of the fields presented in the previous controls as well. When you use the CreateUserWizard control as shown previously, you don't need to perform any special configuration. It automatically uses the configured membership provider for creating the user, and it includes two steps: the default CreateUserWizardStep that creates controls for gathering the necessary information and the CompleteWizardStep for displaying a confirmation message. Both steps are customizable through styles and properties or through templates. Although you can customize these two steps, you cannot remove them. If you use templates, you are responsible for creating the necessary controls, as follows:

```
<asp:CreateUserWizard ID="RegisterUser" runat="server"
                      BorderStyle="Ridge" BackColor="aquamarine">
    <TitleTextStyle Font-Bold="True" Font-Names="Verdana" />
    <WizardSteps>
        <asp:CreateUserWizardStep runat="server">
            <ContentTemplate>
                <div align="right">
                <font face="Courier New">
                User Name:
                <asp:TextBox ID="UserName" runat="server" /><br />
                Password:
                <asp:TextBox ID="Password" runat="server"
                             TextMode="Password" /><br />
                Conform Password:
                <asp:TextBox ID="ConfirmPassword" runat="server"
                             TextMode="Password" /><br />
                Email:
                <asp:TextBox ID="Email" runat="server" /><br />
                Security Question:
                <asp:TextBox ID="Question" runat="server" /><br />
                Security Answer:
                <asp:TextBox ID="Answer" runat="server" /><br />
                <asp:Literal ID="ErrorMessage" runat="server"
                             EnableViewState="False" />
                </font>
                </div>
            </ContentTemplate>
        </asp:CreateUserWizardStep>
        <asp:CompleteWizardStep runat="server">
            <ContentTemplate>
                Your account has been successfully created.</td>
                <asp:Button ID="ContinueButton" CommandName="Continue"
                            runat="server" Text="Continue" />
            </ContentTemplate>
        </asp:CompleteWizardStep>
    </WizardSteps>
</asp:CreateUserWizard>
```

Because the control is a wizard control, the first step doesn't require any buttons because a Next button is automatically displayed by the hosting wizard control. Depending on the configuration of the membership provider, some of the controls are required, and others are not, as listed in Table 21-13.

Table 21-13. *Required Controls and Optional Controls*

ID	Type	Required?	Comments
UserName	System.Web.UI.WebControls.TextBox	Yes	Always required
Password	System.Web.UI.WebControls.TextBox	Yes	Always required
ConfirmPassword	System.Web.UI.WebControls.TextBox	Yes	Always required
Email	System.Web.UI.WebControls.TextBox	No	Required only if the RequireEmail property of the control is set to True
Question	System.Web.UI.WebControls.TextBox	No	Required only if the underlying membership provider requires a password question
Answer	System.Web.UI.WebControls.TextBox	No	Required only if the underlying membership provider requires a password question
ContinueButton	Any control that supports bubbling	No	Not required at all, but if present you need to set the CommandName to Continue

As soon as you start creating additional wizard steps, you will need to catch events and perform some actions within the event procedures. For example, if you collect additional information from the user with the wizard, you will have to store this information somewhere and therefore will need to execute some SQL statements against your database. Table 21-14 lists the events specific to the CreateUserWizard control. The control also inherits all the events you already know from the Wizard control.

Table 21-14. *The CreateUserWizard Events*

Event	Description
ContinueButtonClick	Raised when the user clicks the Continue button in the last wizard step.
CreatingUser	Raised by the wizard before it creates the new user through the membership API.
CreatedUser	After the control has been created successfully, the control raises this event.
CreateUserError	If the creation of the user was not successful, this event is raised.
SendingEmail	The control can send an e-mail to the created user if a mail server is configured. This event is raised by the control before the e-mail is sent so that you can modify the contents of the mail message.
SendMailError	If the control was unable to send the message—for example, because the mail server was unavailable—it raises this event.

Now you can just add a wizard step for querying additional user information, such as the first name and the last name, and automatically save this information to a custom database table. A valid point might be storing the information in the profile. But when running through the wizard, the user is not authenticated yet; therefore, you cannot store the information into the profile, as this is available for authenticated users only. Therefore, you either have to store it in a custom database table or include a possibility for the user to edit the profile after the registration process.

Furthermore, the CreatedUser event is raised immediately after the CreateUserWizardStep has been completed successfully. Therefore, if you want to save additional data within this event, you have to collect this information in previous steps. For this purpose, it's sufficient to place other wizard steps prior to the <asp:CreateUserWizardStep> tag. In any other case you have to save the information in one of the other events (for example, the FinishButtonClick event). But because you cannot make sure that the user really runs through the whole wizard and clicks the Finish button, it makes sense to collect all the required information prior to the CreateUserWizardStep and then save any additional information through the CreatedUser event.

```
<asp:CreateUserWizard ID="RegisterUser" runat="server"
                      BorderStyle="ridge" BackColor="aquamarine"
                      OnCreatedUser="RegisterUser_CreatedUser">
  <TitleTextStyle Font-Bold="True" Font-Names="Verdana" />
  <WizardSteps>
      <asp:WizardStep ID="NameStep" AllowReturn="True">
          Firstname:
          <asp:TextBox ID="FirstnameText" runat="server" /><br />
          Lastname:
          <asp:TextBox ID="LastnameText" runat="server" /><br />
          Age:
          <asp:TextBox ID="AgeText" runat="server" />
      </asp:WizardStep>
      <asp:CreateUserWizardStep runat="server">
          ...
      </asp:CreateUserWizardStep>
      <asp:CompleteWizardStep runat="server">
          ...
      </asp:CompleteWizardStep>
  </WizardSteps>
</asp:CreateUserWizard>
```

With the previous wizard step alignment, you now can store additional information in your data store when the CreatedUser event is raised by the control, as follows:

```
Private _Age As Short
Private _Firstname, _Lastname As String

Protected Sub Page_Load(ByVal sender As Object, ByVal e As EventArgs)
    If (Not Me.IsPostBack) Then
        _Age = -1
        If _Lastname = String.Empty Then
            _Firstname = _Lastname
        End If
    End If
End Sub

Protected Sub RegisterUser_CreatedUser(ByVal sender As Object, ByVal e As EventArgs)
    ' Find the correct wizard step
    Dim thestep As WizardStepBase = Nothing
    Dim i As Integer = 0
    Do While i < RegisterUser.WizardSteps.Count
        If RegisterUser.WizardSteps(i).ID = "NameStep" Then
            thestep = RegisterUser.WizardSteps(i)
            Exit Do
```

```
            End If
            i += 1
        Loop

        If thestep IsNot Nothing Then
            _Firstname = (CType(theStep.FindControl("FirstnameText"), TextBox)).Text
            _Lastname = (CType(theStep.FindControl("LastnameText"), TextBox)).Text
            _Age = Short.Parse((CType(theStep.FindControl("AgeTExt"), TextBox)).Text)

            ' Store the information
            Debug.WriteLine(String.Format("{0} {1} {2}", _Firstname, _Lastname, _Age))
        End If
    End Sub
```

In the CreatedUser event, the code just looks for the wizard step with the ID set to NameStep. Then it uses the FindControl method several times for getting the controls with the actual content. As soon as you have retrieved the controls, you can access their properties and perform any action you want with them.

In summary, the CreateUserWizard control is a powerful control based on top of the membership API and is customizable, just as the other login controls that ship with ASP.NET 2.0. With template controls, you have complete flexibility and control over the appearance of the login controls, and the controls still perform lots of work—especially interaction with membership—for you. And if you still want to perform actions yourself, you can catch several events of the controls.

Using the Membership Class

In the following sections of this chapter, you will learn how you can use the underlying membership programming interface that is used by all the controls and the whole membership API infrastructure you just used. You will see that the programming interface is simple. It consists of a class called Membership with a couple of properties and methods and a class called MembershipUser that encapsulates the properties for a single user. The methods of the Membership class perform fundamental operations:

- Creating new users
- Deleting existing users
- Updating existing users
- Retrieving lists of users
- Retrieving details for one user

Many methods of the Membership class accept an instance of MembershipUser as a parameter or return one or even a collection of MembershipUser instances. For example, by retrieving a user through the Membership.GetUser method, setting properties on this instance, and then passing it to the UpdateUser method of the Membership class, you can simply update user properties. The Membership class and the MembershipUser class both provide the necessary abstraction layer between the actual provider and your application. Everything you do with the Membership class depends on your provider. This means if you exchange the underlying membership provider, this will not affect your application if the implementation of the membership provider is complete and supports all features propagated by the MembershipProvider base class.

All classes used for the membership API are defined in the System.Web.Security namespace. The Membership class is just a class with lots of static methods and properties. You will now walk through the different types of tasks you can perform with the Membership class and related classes such as the MembershipUser.

Retrieving Users from the Store

The first task you will do is retrieve a single user and a list of users through the Membership class from the membership store. For this purpose, you just create a simple page with a GridView control for binding the users to the grid, as follows:

```
<html xmlns="http://www.w3.org/1999/xhtml" >
<head runat="server">
    <title>Untitled Page</title>
</head>
<body>
    <form id="form1" runat="server">
    <div>
        <asp:GridView ID="UsersGridView" runat="server"
                      DataKeyNames="UserName"
                      AutoGenerateColumns="False">
            <Columns>
                <asp:BoundField DataField="UserName" HeaderText="Username" />
                <asp:BoundField DataField="Email" HeaderText="Email" />
                <asp:BoundField DataField="CreationDate"
                                HeaderText="Creation Date" />
            </Columns>
        </asp:GridView>
        </div>
    </form>
</body>
</html>
```

As you can see, the GridView defines the UserName field as DataKeyName. This enables you to access the UserName value of the currently selected user directly through the grid's SelectedValue property. As most of the methods require the user name for retrieving more details, this is definitely useful. With this page in place, you can now add the following code to the Page_Load event procedure for loading the users from the membership store and binding them to the grid:

```
Public Partial Class _Default
        Inherits System.Web.UI.Page
    Private _MyUsers As MembershipUserCollection

    Protected Sub Page_Load(ByVal sender As Object, ByVal e As EventArgs)
        _MyUsers = Membership.GetAllUsers()
        UsersGridView.DataSource = _MyUsers

        If (Not Me.IsPostBack) Then
            UsersGridView.DataBind()
        End If
    End Sub
End Class
```

Figure 21-17 shows the application in action.

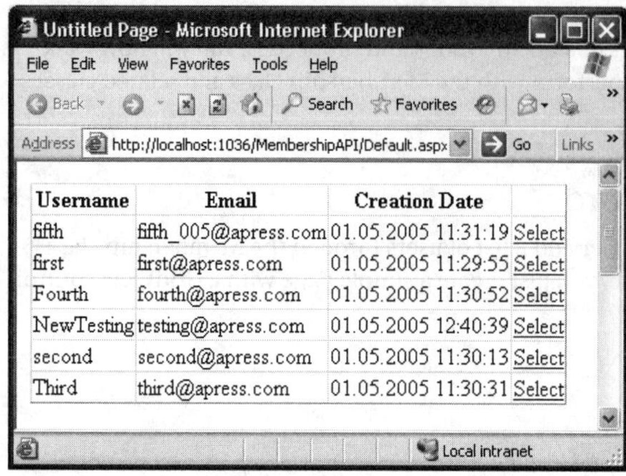

Figure 21-17. *The custom user management application in action*

As you can see, the Membership class includes a GetAllUsers method, which returns an instance of type MembershipUserCollection. You can use this collection just like any other collection. Every entry contains all the properties of a single user. Therefore, if you want to display the details of a selected user, you just need to add a couple of controls for displaying the contents of the selected user in the previously created page, as follows:

```
Selected User:<br />
<table border="1" bordercolor="blue">
    <tr>
        <td>User Name:</td>
        <td><asp:Label ID="UsernameLabel" runat="server" /></td>
    </tr>
    <tr>
        <td>Email:</td>
        <td><asp:TextBox ID="EmailText" runat="server" /></td>
    </tr>
    <tr>
        <td>Password Question:</td>
        <td><asp:Label ID="PwdQuestionLabel" runat="server" /></td>
    </tr>
    <tr>
        <td>Last Login Date:</td>
        <td><asp:Label ID="LastLoginLabel" runat="server" /></td>
    </tr>
    <tr>
        <td>Comment:</td>
        <td><asp:TextBox ID="CommentTextBox" runat="server"
                        TextMode="MultiLine" /></td>
    </tr>
    <tr>
        <td>
        <asp:CheckBox ID="IsApprovedCheck" runat="server" Text="Approved" />
        </td>
        <td>
        <asp:CheckBox ID="IsLockedOutCheck" runat="Server" Text="Locked Out" />
        </td>
    </tr>
</table>
```

You can then catch the SelectedIndexChanged event of the previously added GridView control for filling these fields with the appropriate values, as follows:

```
Protected Sub UsersGridView_SelectedIndexChanged
        (ByVal sender As Object, ByVal e As EventArgs)
    If UsersGridView.SelectedIndex >= 0 Then
        Dim Current As MembershipUser = _MyUsers(CStr(UsersGridView.SelectedValue))

        UsernameLabel.Text = Current.UserName
        PwdQuestionLabel.Text = Current.PasswordQuestion
        LastLoginLabel.Text = Current.LastLoginDate.ToShortDateString()
        EmailText.Text = Current.Email
        CommentTextBox.Text = Current.Comment
        IsApprovedCheck.Checked = Current.IsApproved
        IsLockedOutCheck.Checked = Current.IsLockedOut
    End If
End Sub
```

As you can see, the MembershipCollection object requires the user name for accessing users directly. Methods from the Membership class such as GetUser require the user name as well. Therefore, you used the UserName field as content for the DataKeyNames property in the GridView previously. With an instance of the MembershipUser in your hands, you can access the properties of the user as usual.

Updating Users in the Store

Updating a user in the membership store is nearly as easy as retrieving the user from the store. As soon as you have an instance of MembershipUser in your hands, you can update properties such as the e-mail and comments as usual. Then you just call the UpdateUser method of the Membership class. You can do that by extending the previous code by adding a button to your page and inserting the following code in the button's Click event-handling routine:

```
Protected Sub ActionUpdateUser_Click(ByVal sender As Object, ByVal e As EventArgs)
    If UsersGridView.SelectedIndex >= 0 Then
        Dim Current As MembershipUser = _MyUsers(CStr(UsersGridView.SelectedValue))

        Current.Email = EmailText.Text
        Current.Comment = CommentTextBox.Text
        Current.IsApproved = IsApprovedCheck.Checked

        Membership.UpdateUser(Current)

        ' Refresh the grids view
        UsersGridView.DataBind()
    End If
End Sub
```

The UpdateUser method just accepts the modified MembershipUser you want to update. Before the method is called, you have to update the properties on your instance. This has just one exception: the IsLockedOut property cannot be set. This property gets automatically set if the user has too many failed login attempts. If you want to unlock a user, you have to call the MembershipUser's UnlockUser method separately. Similar rules apply to the password. You cannot change the password directly by setting some properties on the MembershipUser. Furthermore, the MembershipUser class has no property for directly accessing the password at all. For this purpose, it supports a GetPassword method and a ChangePassword method that requires you to pass in the old and the new password. Retrieving the password through the GetPassword method is possible, but only if the password is not hashed in the underlying store. Therefore, GetPassword works only if the membership provider is configured to store the password either in clear text or encrypted in the underlying membership store.

Creating and Deleting Users

Creating users is as simple as using the rest of the membership API. You can create users by just calling the CreateUser method of the Membership class. Therefore, if you want to add the feature of creating users to your website, you can add a new page containing the necessary text boxes for entering the required information, then add a button, and finally catch the Click event of this button with the following code:

```
Protected Sub ActionAddUser_Click(ByVal sender As Object, ByVal e As EventArgs)
    Try
        Dim Status As MembershipCreateStatus

        Membership.CreateUser(UserNameText.Text, PasswordText.Text,
                UserEmailText.Text, PwdQuestionText.Text,
                PwdAnswerText.Text, True, Status)

        StatusLabel.Text = "User created successfully!"

    Catch ex As Exception
        Debug.WriteLine("Exception: " & ex.Message)
        StatusLabel.Text = "Unable to create user!"
    End Try
End Sub
```

The CreateUser exists with several overloads. The easiest overload just accepts a user name and a password, while the more complex versions require a password question and answer as well. The MembershipCreateStatus object returns additional information about the creation status of the user and is added as an output parameter because the method already returns a new instance of MembershipUser. Depending on the provider's configuration, your call to simpler versions of CreateUser will succeed or fail. For example, the default membership provider requires you to include a password question and answer; therefore, if you don't provide them, a call to CreateUser will result in an exception.

Deleting users is as simple as creating users. The Membership class offers a Delete method that requires you to pass the user name as a parameter. It deletes the user as well as all related information, if you want, from the underlying membership store.

Validating Users

Last but not least, the Membership class provides a method for validating a membership user. If a user has entered his user name and password in a login mask, you can use this method for programmatically validating the information entered by the user, as follows:

```
If Membership.ValidateUser(UserNameText.Text, PasswordText.Text) Then
    FormsAuthentication.RedirectFromLoginPage(UserNameText.Text, False)
Else
    ' Invalid username or password
End If
```

Summary

In this chapter, you learned about the membership API, which is new in ASP.NET 2.0. The membership API provides you with a full-fledged infrastructure for managing users of your application. You can use either the WAT, the new security controls, or the membership API for accessing these base services. Membership itself is provider-based. In other words, you can exchange the underlying store by changing the underlying provider without touching your application. In this chapter you used only SQL Server as a provider. In Chapter 26 you will learn the necessary details for creating and configuring a custom membership provider. In the next chapter, you'll look at a different approach of validating user identity—Windows authentication.

CHAPTER 22

■ ■ ■

Windows Authentication

Forms authentication is a great approach if you want to roll your own authentication system using a back-end database and a custom login page. But what if you are creating a web application for a smaller set of known users who already have Windows user accounts? In these situations, it makes sense to use an authentication system that can leverage the existing user and group membership information.

The solution is *Windows authentication*, which matches web users to Windows user accounts that are defined on the local computer or another domain on the network. In this chapter, you'll learn how to use Windows authentication in your web applications. You'll also learn how to apply impersonation to temporarily assume another identity.

Introducing Windows Authentication

Unlike forms authentication, Windows authentication isn't built into ASP.NET. Instead, Windows authentication hands over responsibility of authentication to IIS. IIS asks the browser to authenticate itself by providing credentials that map to a Windows user account. If the user is successfully authenticated, IIS allows the web-page request and passes the user and role information onto ASP.NET so that your code can act on it in much the same way that it works with identity information in a forms authentication scenario.

Figure 22-1 shows the end-to-end flow.

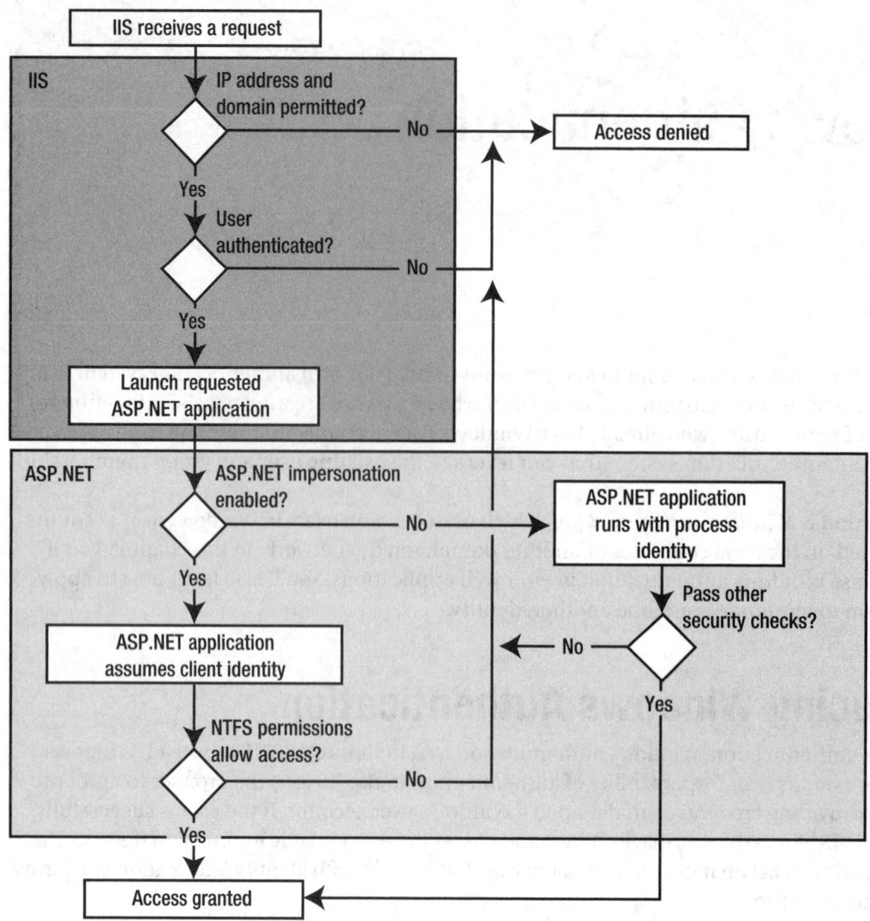

Figure 22-1. *The Windows authentication process*

Why Use Windows Authentication?

You would want to use Windows authentication for three main reasons:

- It involves little programming work on the developer's part.
- It allows you to use existing user logins.
- It allows you to use impersonation and Windows security.

The first reason is quite simple—using Windows authentication allows IIS and the client browser to take care of the authentication process so you don't need to create a login page, check a database, or write any custom code. Similarly, Windows already supports basic user account features such as password expiry, account lockout, and group membership.

The second, and most important, reason for using Windows authentication is that it allows you to leverage existing Windows accounts. Typically, you use Windows authentication for applications where the users are part of the same local network or intranet as your web server. That means you can authenticate users with the same credentials they use to log into their computers. Best of all, depending on the settings you use and the network architecture, you may be able to provide "invisible" authentication that works without forcing a separate login step. Instead, the browser simply uses the logged-in identity of the current user.

The third reason you might want to use Windows authentication is that it allows you to take advantage of existing Windows security settings. For example, you can control access to files by setting Windows file-access permissions. However, it's important to remember that these permissions don't take effect automatically. That's because by default your web application runs using a fixed account (typically ASPNET, as defined in the machine.config file). You can change this behavior by carefully using Windows authentication and impersonation, as described in the "Impersonation and Delegation on Windows Server 2003" section of this chapter.

Why Would You *Not* Use Windows Authentication?

So, why would you not want to use Windows authentication?

- It's tied to Windows users.
- It's tied to Windows client machines.
- It doesn't provide much flexibility or control and can't be customized easily.

The first problem is that Windows authentication won't work unless the users you are authenticating already have valid Windows accounts. In a public website, this probably isn't the case. Even if you could create a Windows account for each visitor, it wouldn't be as efficient as a database approach for large numbers of users. It also has a potential security risk, because Windows user accounts can have permissions to the web server computer or other network computers. You might not want to risk granting these abilities to your website users.

The second problem is that some of the authentication methods that IIS uses require users to have compatible software on their computers. This limits your ability to use Windows authentication for users who are using non-Microsoft operating systems or for users who aren't using Internet Explorer.

The final main problem is that Windows authentication doesn't give you any control over the authentication process. Also, you have no easy way to add, remove, and manage Windows account information programmatically or to store other user-specific information with the user credentials. As you learned in the previous chapter, all these features are easy to add to forms authentication, but they don't play any part in Windows authentication.

Mechanisms for Windows Authentication

When you implement Windows authentication, IIS uses one of three possible authentication strategies to authenticate each request it receives:

Basic authentication: The user name and password are passed as clear text. This is the only form of authentication supported by all browsers as part of the HTML standard.

Digest authentication: The user name and password are not transmitted. Instead, a cryptographically secure hash with this information is sent.

Integrated Windows authentication: The user name and password are not transmitted. Instead, the identity of a user already logged into Windows is passed automatically as a token. This is the only form of authentication that takes place transparently (without user intervention).

The following sections discuss these options.

■ **Note** There are other less commonly used protocols for Windows authentication. One example is certificate-based authentication. If you use this approach, you must distribute a digital certificate to each client and map each certificate to the appropriate Windows account. Unfortunately, this technique is rife with administrative and deployment headaches. Additionally, IIS 6 supports Advanced Digest authentication (which works essentially the same way as Digest authentication but stores the passwords more securely) and Passport authentication, which allows a user to log in using a Passport account that maps to a Windows user account.

Basic Authentication

The most widely supported authentication protocol is Basic authentication. Almost all web browsers support it. When a website requests client authentication using Basic authentication, the web browser displays a login dialog box for user and password, like the one shown in Figure 22-2.

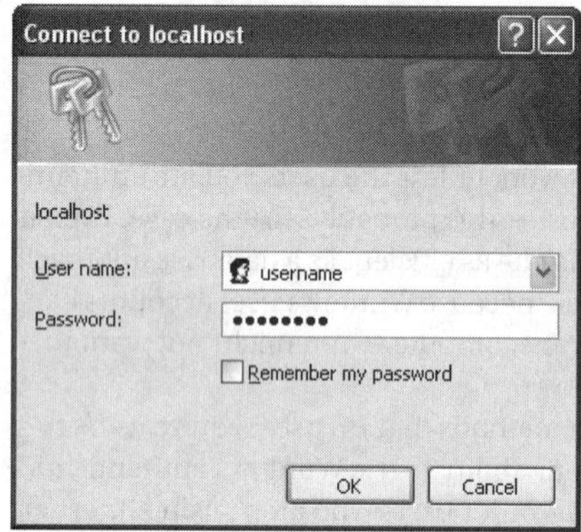

Figure 22-2. *A login box for Basic authentication*

After a user provides this information, the data itself is transmitted to the web server (in this case localhost). Once IIS receives the authentication data, it attempts to authenticate the user with the corresponding Windows account.

The key limitation of Basic authentication is that it isn't secure—at least not on its own. User name and password credentials obtained via Basic authentication are transmitted between the client and server as clear text. The data itself is encoded (not encrypted) into a Base64 string that eavesdroppers can easily read. For this reason, you should use Basic authentication only in situations where there's no need to protect user credentials or only in conjunction with an HTTP wire encryption protocol such as SSL. This way, the data that would otherwise be clearly visible to any network sniffing utility will be encrypted using complex algorithms. (You can find more information on SSL in Chapter 18.)

Digest Authentication

Digest authentication, like Basic authentication, requires the user to provide account information using a login dialog box that is displayed by the browser. Unlike Basic authentication, however, Digest authentication passes a hash of the password, rather than the password itself. (*Digest* is another name for *hash*, which explains the name of this authentication scheme.) Because a hash is used, the password itself is never sent across the network, thereby preventing it from being stolen even if you aren't using SSL.

The process of authenticating a user with Digest authentication works like this:

1. The unauthenticated client requests a restricted web page.
2. The server responds with an HTTP 401 response. This response includes a *nonce* value—a randomly generated series of bytes. The web server ensures that each nonce value is unique before it issues it.
3. The client uses the nonce, the password, the user name, and some other values to create a hash. This hash value, known as the *digest*, is sent back to the server along with the plain-text user name.
4. The server uses the nonce value, its stored password for the user name, and the other values to create a hash. It then compares this hash to the one provided by the client. If they match, then the authentication succeeds.

Since the nonce value changes with each authentication request, the digest is not very useful to an attacker. The original password cannot be extracted from it. Similarly, because it incorporates a random nonce, the digest cannot be used for *replay attacks*, in which an attacker attempts to gain access at a later time by resending a previously intercepted digest.

In theory, Digest authentication is a standard, and web servers and web browsers should all be able to use Digest authentication to exchange authentication information. Unfortunately, Microsoft interpreted a part of the Digest authentication specification in a slightly different way than other organizations, such as the Apache Foundation (which provides the Apache web server) and the Mozilla project (which provides the Mozilla web browser). Currently, IIS Digest authentication works only with Internet Explorer 5.0 and later.

Another limitation of Digest authentication in IIS is that it will function only when the virtual directory being authenticated is running on or controlled by a Windows Active Directory domain controller.

Integrated Windows Authentication

Integrated Windows authentication is the most convenient authentication standard for WAN-based/LAN-based intranet applications, because it performs authentication without requiring any client interaction. When IIS asks the client to authenticate itself, the browser sends a token that represents the Windows user account of the current user. If the web server fails to authenticate the user with this information, a login dialog box is shown where the user can enter a different user name and password.

For integrated Windows authentication to work, both the client and the web server must be on the same local network or intranet. That's because integrated Windows authentication doesn't actually transmit the user name and password information. Instead, it coordinates with the domain server or Active Directory instance where it is logged in and gets that computer to send the authentication information to the web server.

The protocol used for transmitting authentication information is either NTLM (NT LAN Manager) authentication or Kerberos 5—depending on the operating system version of the client and the server. If both are running Windows 2000 or higher and both machines are running in an Active Directory domain, Kerberos is used as the authentication protocol; otherwise, NTLM authentication will be used. Both protocols are extremely secure (Kerberos is the most secure protocol currently available), but they are limited. Therefore, in general, integrated authentication works only on Internet Explorer 2.0 or higher (integrated Windows authentication is not supported in non–Internet Explorer clients). Kerberos, of course, works only for machines running Windows 2000 or higher, and neither protocol can work across a proxy server. In addition, Kerberos requires some additional ports to be open on firewalls. In the following section, you will learn the basics of the authentication protocols used for integrated Windows authentication. These concepts will help you understand the configuration steps, especially for impersonation and delegation.

NT LAN Manager Authentication

NTLM authentication is integrated into the Windows operating system since it has built-in network support. NTLM authenticates clients through a challenge/response mechanism that is based on a three-way handshake between the client and the server. Everything you will learn about in this section takes place on the operating system automatically. Of course, this works only if the client and the server are running Windows.

Basically, the client starts the communication by sending a message to the server, which indicates that the client wants to talk to the server. The server generates a 64-bit random value called the *nonce*. The server responds to the client's request by returning this nonce. This response is called the *challenge*. Now the client operating system asks the user for a user name and password. Immediately after the user has entered this information, the system hashes the password. This password hash—called the *master key*—will then be used for encrypting the nonce. Together with the user name, the client transmits the encrypted nonce in his *response* to the server (completing the challenge/response mechanism).

The server now needs to validate the returned nonce. Depending on whether the user is a local user or a domain user, this validation takes place locally or remotely on the domain controller. In both cases, the user's master key, which is the hashed version of the password, is retrieved from the security account database. This master key then encrypts the clear-text nonce again on the server (of course, the server has cached the clear-text nonce before it transmits the data to the client). If the re-created encrypted version of the nonce matches the encrypted version returned from the client, the user is authenticated successfully, and a logon session is created on the server for the user. Figure 22-3 shows the process flow.

As you can see, the password is never transmitted across the wire. Even the hashed version of the password is never transmitted. This makes NTLM really secure. But there is even a more secure protocol with additional possibilities, as you will see in the next section.

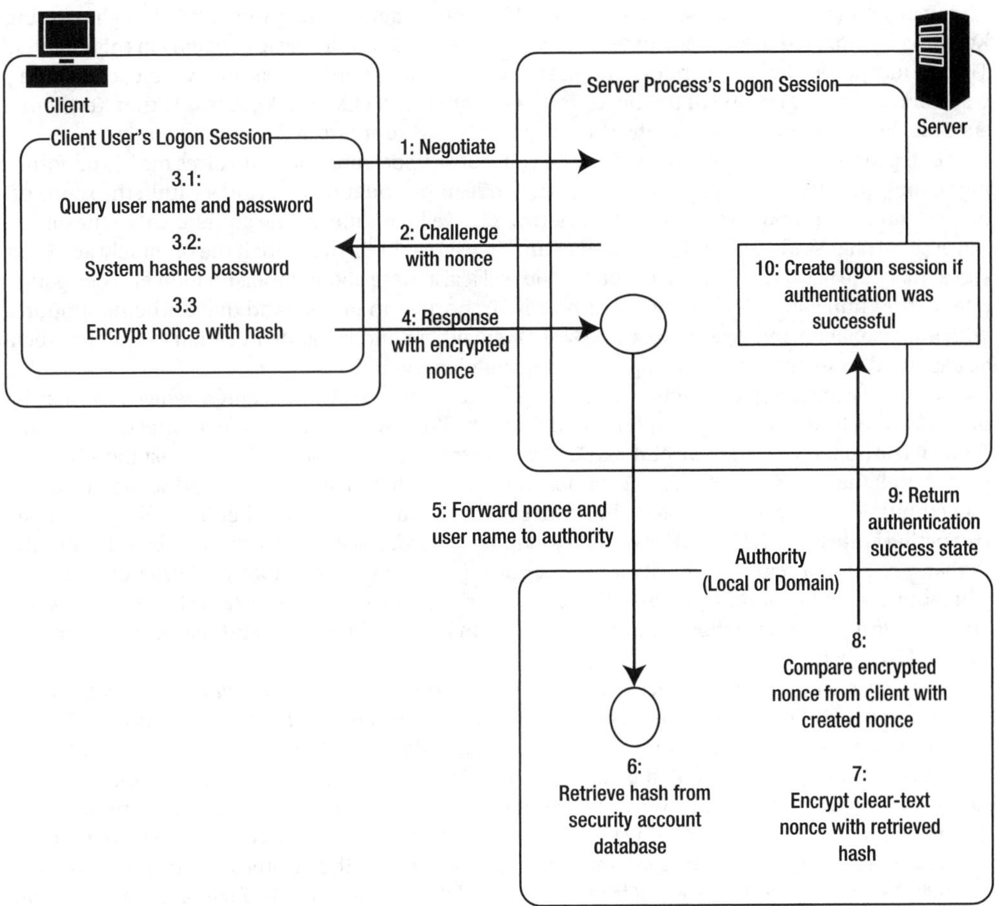

Figure 22-3. *The NTLM protocol at a glance*

Kerberos Authentication: A Short Introduction

Currently, Kerberos 5 is the most secure authentication protocol available. It is a well-known public standard created by the IETF (Internet Engineering Task Force), and it implements a ticket-based authentication protocol. On Windows operating systems, Kerberos has been available since Windows 2000. When activating integrated Windows authentication, Windows will use Kerberos automatically under the following circumstances:

- The client and the server are running Windows 2000 or higher.
- An Active Directory Domain with a primary domain controller (which automatically plays the role of the so-called key distribution center) is available in the network.

In any other case, Windows will select NTLM as the authentication protocol. Although covering Kerberos in detail requires a book of its own, you will learn about the basic concepts in this chapter. These concepts will help you understand the necessary configuration tasks and when each feature will work. For example, one of the big differences between NTLM and Kerberos is that Kerberos supports both impersonation and delegation, while NTLM supports impersonation only.

Delegation basically is based on the same concept as impersonation. It involves merely performing actions on behalf of the client's identity. But while impersonation just works within the scope of one machine, delegation works across the network as well. This means the authentication ticket of the original client's identity can be passed to another server in the network if the originally accessed server machine has the permission to do so. You will learn more about impersonation and delegation later in the "Impersonation" section. For now it's important to understand that Kerberos supports both impersonation and delegation, while NTLM and other Windows authentication techniques such as Basic or Digest authentication support impersonation only.

The core component of a Kerberos system is the KDC (key distribution center), which is responsible for issuing tickets and managing credentials. In the Windows world, an Active Directory primary domain controller plays the role of the KDC. Every actor, client, and server has to trust the KDC. It manages all the user and computer accounts and issues authentication tickets and session tickets for communication sessions between machines in the domain. This is another big difference when comparing Kerberos to NTLM: while NTLM works for workgroup scenarios without a central authority, Kerberos requires a central authority for issuing any type of ticket. Therefore, for Kerberos to work, you require a connection to an Active Directory domain controller. Figure 22-4 shows the flow for authenticating a user and then establishing a session between the client and the simple member server of a domain.

Every user authentication process starts with submitting a request to the *authentication service*, which runs on the KDC. This request contains the user name of the user to be authenticated. The KDC reads the user's master key from the security account database. Again, this is the hashed version of the user's password. Afterward, it creates a TGT (ticket-granting ticket). This ticket contains a session key for the user's session as well as an expiration date and time. Before the ticket is returned to the client, the server encrypts it using the user's master key. With only the correct password entered on the client, the client operating system can create the correct the master key (the hash) for successfully decrypting the TGT received from the server. If decryption of the TGT succeeds on the client, the user is authenticated successfully. Finally, the client caches the TGT locally.

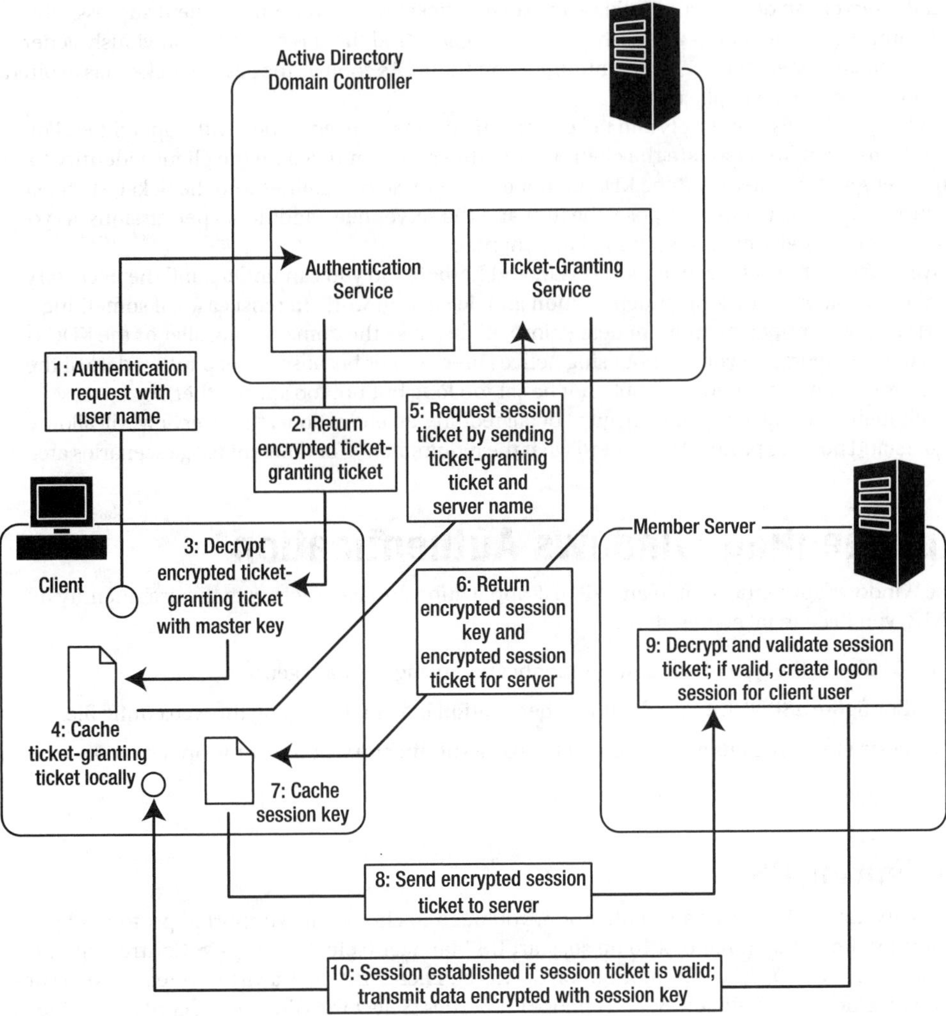

Figure 22-4. *Kerberos authentication and tickets*

When the client wants to communicate with another member server in the network, it first has to ask the KDC for a session ticket. For this purpose, it sends the locally cached TGT to a so-called ticket-granting service that runs on the KDC. This service validates the TGT, and if it's still valid (not expired, not tampered with, and so on), it generates a session key for the communication session between the client and the member server. This session key is then encrypted with the client's master key. In addition, the session key is packaged into an ST (session ticket), which contains additional expiration information for the server. This session ticket is encrypted with the member server's master key. Both the encrypted session key and the encrypted session ticket are forwarded to the client. The client decrypts the session key and forwards the session ticket to the server. Of course, both the server and the client are well known to the KDC, as somewhere in the past both have been *joined* to the domain (joining a machine to a domain means establishing a trust relationship between this machine and the KDC). Therefore, the KDC knows the client's and the member server's master keys.

If the server can decrypt and validate the session ticket received from the client successfully, the communication session is established. Both the client and the server use the previously generated session key for encrypting the communication traffic. As soon as the session ticket has expired, the whole operation takes place again.

Every ticket—session tickets and ticket-granting tickets—are equipped with capabilities. For example, they can impersonate the client user on the server or delegate the client's identity to another server. If the client and the KDC do not include these capabilities into the ticket, such features just don't work. For this purpose, the user and the server need additional permissions, as you will see in the "Impersonation" section of this chapter.

We'll discuss the basic concepts of NTLM and Kerberos so you can understand the necessary configuration steps for making impersonation and delegation work. In most cases, if something doesn't work with impersonation (or delegation), it's because the domain controller or the KDC is incorrectly configured (if you are not using Active Directory) or because the expiration date of the ticket is not set appropriately (it should not be set too long but not too short either).

Although covering these topics in great detail requires an entire book, this overview will allow you to understand how the protocol works and what the requirements for different usage scenarios are.

Implementing Windows Authentication

To use Windows authentication in an ASP.NET application and have access to the user identity in ASP.NET, you need to take three steps:

1. Configure the type of Windows authentication using IIS Manager.
2. Configure ASP.NET to use the IIS authentication information using the web.config file.
3. Restrict anonymous access for a web page, a subdirectory, or the entire application.

The following sections describe these steps.

Configuring IIS

Before you can use Windows authentication, you need to choose the supported protocols by configuring the virtual directory. To do so, start IIS Manager (select Settings ➤ Control Panel ➤ Administrative Tools ➤ Internet Information Services). Then right-click a virtual directory or a subdirectory inside a virtual directory, and choose Properties. Select the Directory Security tab, which is shown in Figure 22-5.

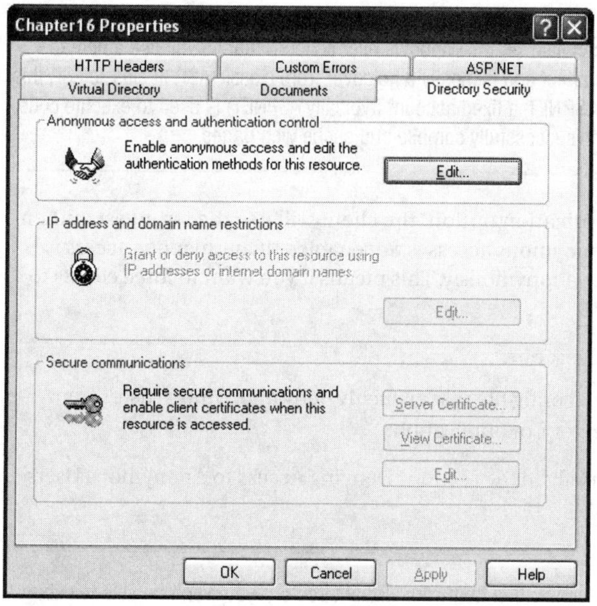

Figure 22-5. *Directory security settings*

Click the Edit button to modify the directory security settings. Enable the supported protocols in the Authenticated access box in the bottom half of the window. If you enable Basic authentication, you can also set a default domain to use when interpreting the user credentials. (The user can also log into a specific domain by supplying a user name in the format DomainName\UserName.) In the example in Figure 22-6, support is enabled for integrated Windows authentication and anonymous access.

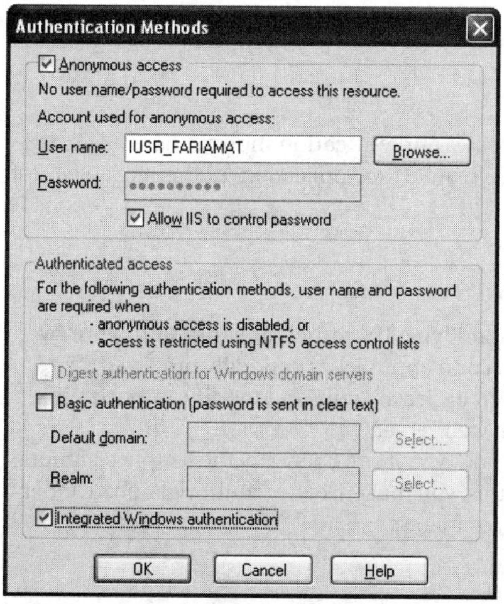

Figure 22-6. *Directory authentication methods*

Note If you allow anonymous access, you can also set the Windows user account that IIS will use automatically. However, this user account has very little effect and is mostly a holdover from classic ASP. In classic ASP, this account would be used to execute all code. In ASP.NET, a fixed account (typically ASPNET) is used to execute code, because more privileges are required in order to successfully compile and cache web pages.

If you enable more than one authentication option, the client will use the strongest authentication method it supports as long as anonymous access is *not* enabled. If anonymous access is enabled, the client will access the website anonymously. This means if you want to force clients to log in, you need to take one of two steps:

- Remove the Anonymous access check box.
- Add authorization rules to the web.config file that explicitly deny anonymous users from accessing a specific page, subdirectory, or application.

Authorization rules are described briefly in the section "Denying Access to Anonymous Users" and in more detail in Chapter 23.

Note If you remove integrated Windows authentication from your virtual directory, you won't be able to debug your web application. That's because Visual Studio .NET uses this protocol to authenticate you when you compile and run an application in the development environment.

Configuring ASP.NET

Once you've configured IIS, the authentication process happens automatically. However, if you want to be able to access the identity information for the authenticated user, you need to configure the web.config file to use Windows authentication, as shown here:

```
<configuration>
    <system.web>
        <!-- Other settings omitted. -->
        <authentication mode="Windows"/>
    </system.web>
</configuration>
```

This tells ASP.NET that you want to use the Windows authentication module. The WindowsAuthenticationModule HTTP module will then handle the Application_AuthenticateRequest event.

Denying Access to Anonymous Users

As described earlier, you can force users to log on by modifying IIS virtual directory settings or by using authorization rules in the web.config file. The second approach is generally preferred. Not only does it give you more flexibility, but it also makes it easier to verify and modify authorization rules after the application is deployed to a production web server.

Chapter 23 describes authorization in detail. For now, you'll consider only the simple technique of denying access to all unauthenticated users. To do this, you must use the <authorization> element of the web.config file to add a new authorization rule, as follows:

```
<configuration>
    <system.web>
        <!-- Other settings omitted. -->
```

```
        <authorization>
            <deny users="?" />
        </authorization>
    </system.web>
</configuration>
```

The question mark (?) is a wildcard character that matches all anonymous users. By including this rule in your web.config file, you're specifying that anonymous users are not allowed. Every user must be authenticated using one of the configured Windows authentication protocols.

Accessing Windows User Information

One of the nice things about Windows authentication is that no login page is required. When the user requests a page that requires authentication, the browser transmits the credentials to IIS. Your web application can then retrieve information directly from the User property of the web page.

Here's an example that displays the currently authenticated user:

```
If Request.IsAuthenticated Then
    ' Display generic identity information.
    lblInfo.Text = "<b>Name: </b>" & User.Identity.Name
    lblInfo.Text &= "<br/><b>Authenticated With: </b>"
    lblInfo.Text &= User.Identity.AuthenticationType
End If
```

This is the same code you can use to get information about the current identity when using forms authentication. However, you'll notice one slight difference. The user name is always in the form DomainName\UserName or ComputerName\UserName. Figure 22-7 shows an example with a user account named Matthew on the computer FARIAMAT.

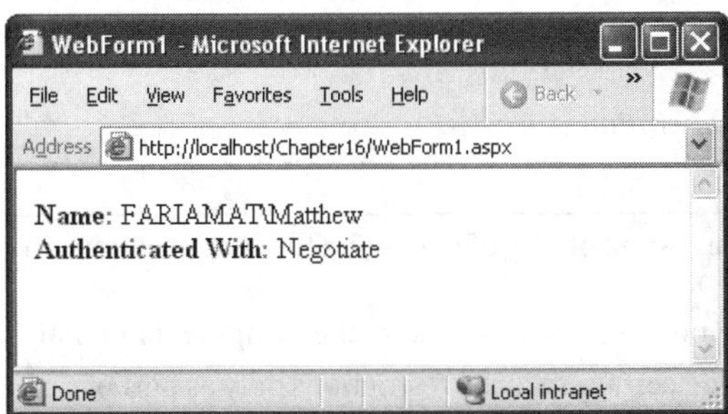

Figure 22-7. *Displaying user information*

The WindowsPrincipal Class

As you've learned in the past two chapters, the User property returns an IPrincipal object. When you use Windows authentication, this is an instance of the WindowsPrincipal class. The WindowsPrincipal class provides access to a WindowsIdentity object through the Identity property.

The WindowsPrincipal class implements three overloads of IsInRole() that all check whether the user is in a specified Windows user group. The required IsInRole(string) overload is implemented so that it accepts the name of the user group to be checked. IsInRole(int) expects an integer RID (role identifier) that refers to a user group. Finally, an overload is provided that expects a member of the WindowsBuiltInRole enumeration, which provides a list of predefined Windows account types (such as Guest, Administrator, and so on). You can find the WindowsPrincipal, WindowsIdentity, and WindowsBuiltInRole types in the System.Security.Principal namespace.

Here's a simple example that tests whether the user is in a predefined Windows role:

```
If Request.IsAuthenticated Then
    lblInfo.Text = "<b>Name: </b>" & User.Identity.Name
    Dim principal As WindowsIdentity = CType(User, WindowsPrincipal)
    lblInfo.Text &= "<br/><b>Power user? </b>"
    lblInfo.Text &= principal.IsInRole(WindowsBuiltInRole.PowerUser).ToString()
End If
```

Note that you must cast the User object to a WindowsPrincipal in order to access this Windows-specific functionality. Figure 22-8 shows the result.

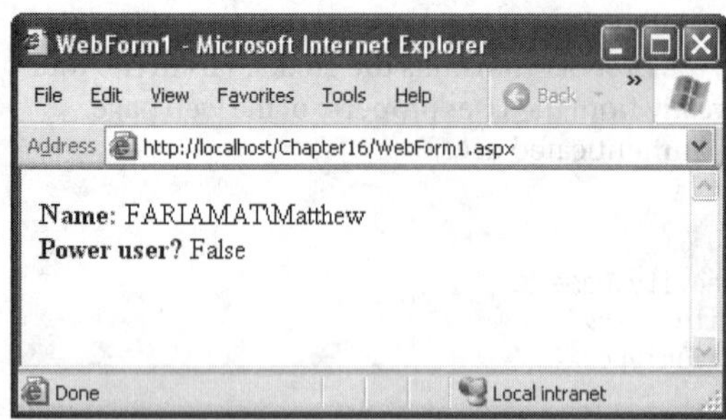

Figure 22-8. *Testing group membership*

Table 22-1 lists all the possible roles provided through the WindowsBuiltInRole enumeration. You can also test for membership with any arbitrary group you've created. Chapter 23 discusses this technique.

Table 22-1. *Values for the WindowsBuiltInRole Enumeration*

Role	Description
AccountOperator	Users with the special responsibility of managing the user accounts on a computer or domain.
Administrator	Users with complete and unrestricted access to the computer or domain.
BackupOperator	Users who can override certain security restrictions only as part of backing up or restoring operations.
Guest	Like the User role but even more restrictive.
PowerUser	Similar to Administrator but with some restrictions.
PrintOperator	Like a User but with additional privileges for taking control of a printer.
Replicator	Like a User but with additional privileges to support file replication in a domain.
SystemOperator	Similar to Administrator but with some restrictions. Generally, system operators manage a computer.
User	Users are restricted accounts that are prevented from making system-wide changes.

The WindowsIdentity Class

You can access some additional information about the currently authenticated user by casting the general identity object to a WindowsIdentity object. WindowsIdentity provides a number of additional members, as described in Table 22-2.

Table 22-2. *Additional Members of the WindowsIdentity*

Member	Description
IsAnonymous	This property returns True if the user is anonymous (has not been authenticated).
IsGuest	This property returns True if the user is using a Guest account. Guest accounts are designed for public access and do not confer many privileges.
IsSystem	Returns True if the user account has the Act As Part of the Operating System permission, which means it is a highly privileged system account.
Groups	Retrieves a collection that contains instances of SecurityIdentifier, which returns the SID values for the groups the user is in.
Token	Returns the operating system token for the identity.
Owner	Gets the SID for the token owner.
User	Gets the user's SID. For example, you can use this SID if you want to modify permissions for this user on ACLs through the classes provided in the System.Security.AccessControl namespace.
Impersonate()	This method instructs ASP.NET to run the following code under the corresponding Windows account. You'll learn much more about impersonation in the next section.
GetAnonymous()	This Shared method creates a WindowsIdentity that represents an anonymous user.
GetCurrent()	This Shared method creates a WindowsIdentity that represents the identity tied to the current security context (the user whose identity the current code is running under). If you use this method in an ASP.NET application, you'll retrieve the user account under which the code is running, *not* the user account that was authenticated by IIS and is provided in the User object.

The following code displays extra Windows-specific information about the user:

```
If Request.IsAuthenticated Then
    lblInfo.Text = "<b>Name: </b>" & User.Identity.Name

    Dim identity As WindowsIdentity = CType(User.Identity, WindowsIdentity)
    lblInfo.Text &= "<br/><b>Token: </b>"
    lblInfo.Text &= identity.Token.ToString()
    lblInfo.Text &= "<br/><b>Guest? </b>"
    lblInfo.Text &= identity.IsGuest.ToString()
    lblInfo.Text &= "<br/><b>System? </b>"
    lblInfo.Text &= identity.IsSystem.ToString()
End If
```

Figure 22-9 shows the result.

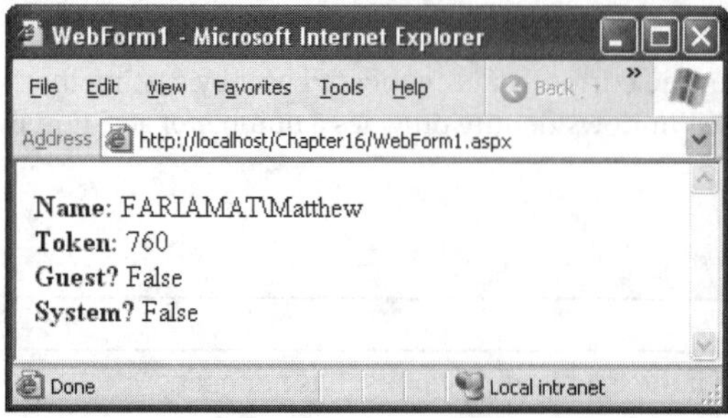

Figure 22-9. *Showing Windows-specific user information*

Impersonation

Everything that ASP.NET does is executed under a Windows account. By default, this identity is the account ASPNET (in IIS 5), but it can be configured through the machine.config file, as described in Chapter 2. As each page request is processed, the configured identity determines what ASP.NET can and cannot do.

Impersonation provides you with a way to make this system more flexible. Instead of using a fixed account for all users, web pages, and applications, you can temporarily change the identity that ASP.NET uses for certain tasks. This process of temporarily assuming the identity of another Windows account is *impersonation.*

One common reason to use impersonation is to differentiate the permissions given to different web applications on the same computer. In this case, you configure impersonation to use a specific, fixed account for each web application. Another potential reason to use impersonation is to use the permissions that are defined for the currently authenticated user. This means the actions ASP.NET performs will be limited according to the person who is using the application. For example, your web server might be set up with a number of personalized directories, one for each user. By impersonating the user in your web application, you ensure that your application cannot inadvertently give the user access to any files except the ones in that user's directory. If you attempt to access a restricted file, the Windows operating system will intervene, and an exception will be raised in your code.

■ **Note** Impersonation does not give you the ability to circumvent Windows security. You must still have the credentials for the user you want to impersonate, whether you write them into your code or a user provides them at runtime.

ASP.NET has two types of impersonation. *Configured* (web.config) impersonation allows you to specify that page requests should be run under the identity of the user who is making the request. *Programmatic* impersonation gives you the ability to switch to another identity within the code and switch back to the original identity when a specific task is finished. You'll learn about both of these techniques in the following sections.

Impersonation in Windows 2000

To impersonate other users when running on Windows 2000, the account that does the impersonation must have the Act As Part of the Operating System permission. This permission is not required on Windows XP and later.

To use impersonation, you must specifically add this permission to the ASPNET account. You can perform this administrative task using the Local Security Policy tool. Select Control Panel ➤ Administrative Tools, and select Local Security Policy. Then browse to the Local Policies ➤ User Rights Assignment node. You'll see a list of settings, as shown in Figure 22-10.

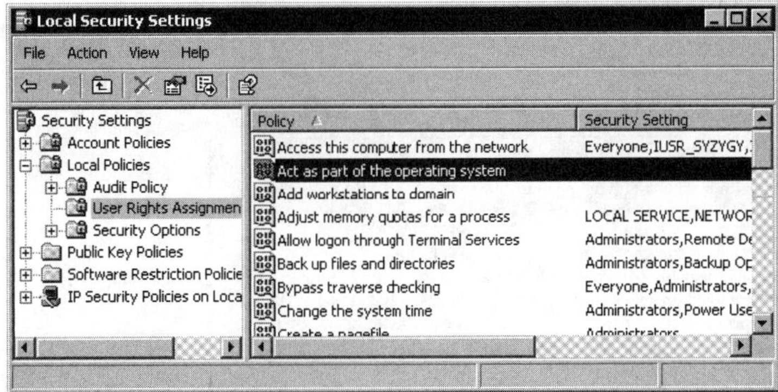

Figure 22-10. *Reviewing user rights assignments*

Double-click the Act As Part of the Operating System entry, and select Add User or Group. This displays a dialog box where you can explicitly give this permission to an account. In the text box at the bottom of the window, enter the account name ASPNET, as shown in Figure 22-11.

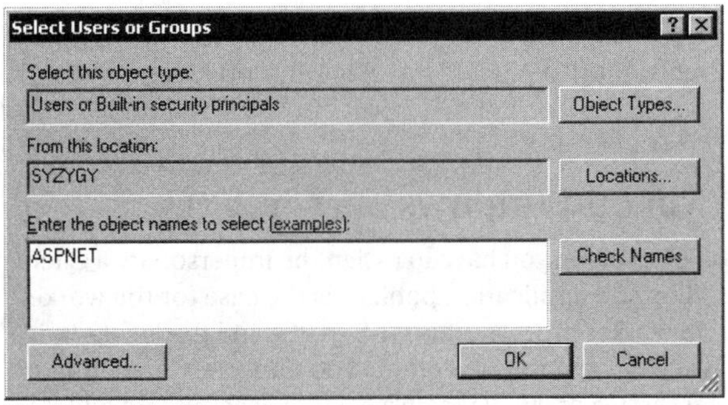

Select Users or Groups
Select this object type:
Users or Built-in security principals
Object Types...
From this location:
SYZYGY
Locations...
Enter the object names to select (examples):
ASPNET
Check Names
Advanced...
OK
Cancel

Figure 22-11. *Assigning the permission to ASPNET*

Finally, click OK to confirm your action and add this permission to the ASPNET account.

■ **Tip** This permission doesn't need to be assigned to the local system account, which always has it. As a result, if you've configured ASP.NET to use the local system account, you don't need to perform any additional configuration steps.

Impersonation on Windows XP

In its default configuration, impersonation works on Windows XP workstations. Fortunately, you even don't need to apply a high-level privilege such as the Act As Part of the Operating System privilege to a low-privileged account such as the ASP.NET user. Windows XP (and Windows Server 2003) supports a separate privilege for impersonation, as shown in Figure 22-12, which you have to assign to the account under which your worker process is running.

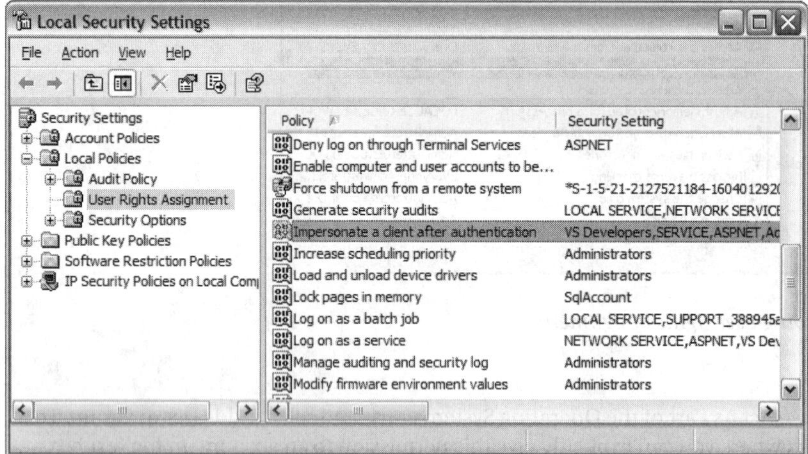

Figure 22-12. *The Impersonate a Client After Authentication privilege*

By default the ASP.NET worker process account (the ASPNET user) has this privilege, so you don't need to perform any extra configuration steps.

Impersonation and Delegation on Windows Server 2003

When using Windows Server 2003 as stand-alone server, you have to assign the Impersonate a Client After Authentication privilege to the account of the application pool, as is the case for the worker process account on Windows XP. The local IIS worker process group (IIS_WPG) and the local service and network service account have this privilege by default. Therefore, you don't need to configure anything if you use a network service or local service or if you create a custom account and add it to the IIS_WPG group.

But delegation is different. As mentioned previously, delegation means that a server that has authenticated the client can pass the client's authentication ticket to another server in this network. This means that this server (and therefore your application) acts on behalf of the client across the network. Figure 22-13 shows this in detail.

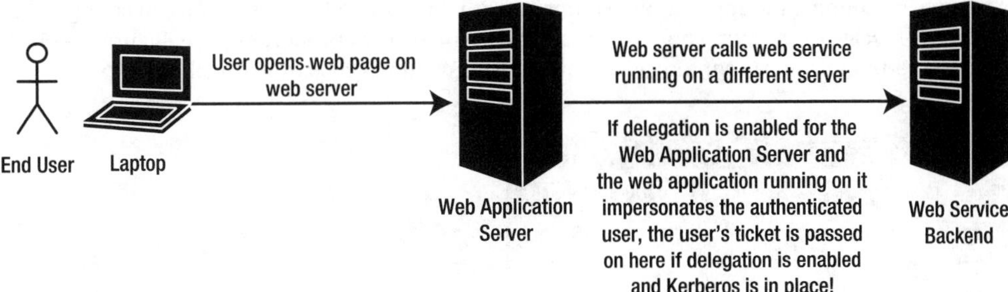

Figure 22-13. *Identity flows across network hops*

In Figure 22-13, you can see the big difference of impersonation. While impersonation takes place on the local machine only, delegation brings the concept of impersonation to calls across the network. Of course, if every server could do that in an uncontrolled fashion, this feature would definitely lead to a security risk. Therefore, Windows provides you with a way to specify which computer is trusted for delegation. By default no computer in the network except the domain controller is trusted for delegation. In Figure 22-13, the server you would configure for delegation would be the Web Application Server, as this is the one that needs to pass the credentials onto the next server.

You can configure delegation through the Active Directory Users and Computers management console on your domain controller. First, you have to open the Computers node, and then select the properties of the computer you want to configure for delegation. If you are running your domain with Windows Server 2003 at a functional level (which implies you don't have any Windows 2000 or older machines in your network), you can use constrained delegation, as shown in Figure 22-14.

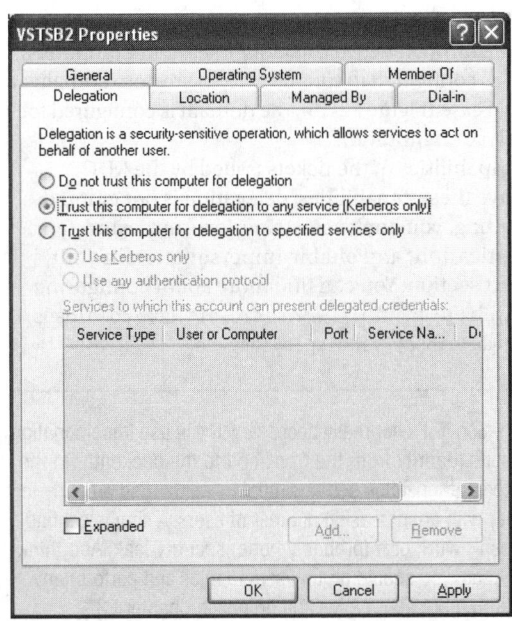

Figure 22-14. *Configuring delegation in Windows Server 2003 (functional level)*

If you are running the application in domains with Windows 2000 servers, you can configure the Trust for Delegation setting on the General tab of the server's properties page. Figure 22-15 shows the settings if you are running your domain with Windows 2000 (functional level).

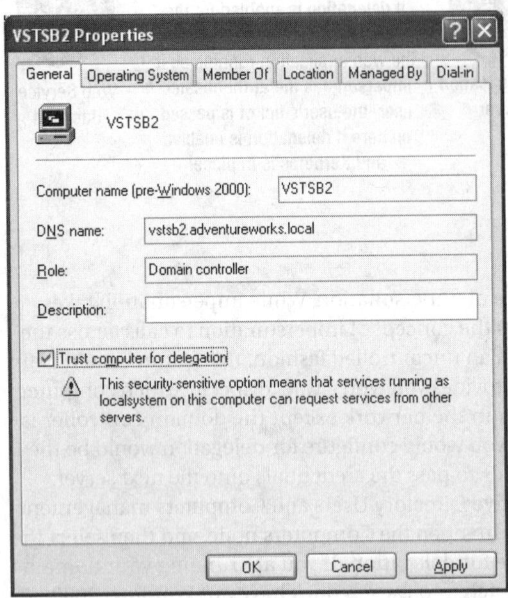

Figure 22-15. *Trusted for delegation for Windows 2000 (functional level)*

It's important to keep in mind that both Figure 22-14 and Figure 22-15 show the same dialog box (the properties of the computer you want to configure through Active Directory Users and Computers). In the first case (Figure 22-14), Windows Server 2003 is configured to run the Active Directory domain at a Windows Server 2003 functional level; in the second case (Figure 22-15), the domain is configured for Windows 2000 functional level (which is the default configuration).

With these settings you basically specify the capabilities of the tickets issued by the KDC (which is the domain controller). If tickets don't have these capabilities, delegation is not granted and not possible. After you have configured this setting, you don't need to perform any extra steps. Just configure IIS for integrated Windows authentication, and enable impersonation in your ASP.NET web application, as you will see in the next section. You can find more about configuring and troubleshooting delegation on the Microsoft website at `http://www.microsoft.com/downloads/details.aspx?FamilyID=7dfeb015-6043-47db-8238-dc7af89c93f1&displaylang=en`.

■ **Caution** We suggest *not* using impersonation or delegation if it's not really necessary. If you use impersonation or delegation, this includes flowing the original client user's identity from the front-end to the backend. On the backend, all the ACLs and operating system security-related authorization settings must be configured properly for every single user. This configuration gets harder and harder with an increasing number of users. A simple configuration mistake can lead to either an application that doesn't work or a (probably huge) security leak. And think about the additional security configurations necessary! Instead, you should group users to roles and perform any security configuration based on roles or groups. You will learn more about roles and groups in Chapter 23.

■ **Caution** Enabling delegation for a server is something you should do carefully. Thoroughly review applications running on such a server, because malicious applications can lead to repudiation attacks. Imagine a malicious application (or malicious part of an application that has not been reviewed) running on this server and performing some "illegal" actions under an impersonated/delegated user's identity. Applications (and therefore servers) should be allowed only for performing delegation if it's really necessary so that applications running on such servers cannot do any "illegal" things based on other, impersonated/delegated user identities.

Configured Impersonation

The simplest form of impersonation is configured impersonation, where you use the web.config file to define the impersonation behavior you want. You accomplish this by adding the <identity> element shown here:

```
<configuration>
    <system.web>
        <!-- Other settings omitted. -->
        <identity impersonate="true" />
    </system.web>
</configuration>
```

You can configure the identity element in more than one way, depending on the result you want. If you want to impersonate the IIS authenticated account, you should use this setting:

```
<identity impersonate="true"/>
```

Keep in mind that if you allow anonymous access, you can use the IUSR_[ComputerName] account. When using this approach, the impersonated account must have all the permissions required to run ASP.NET code, including read-write access to the c:\[WinDir]_Microsoft.NET\Framework\[Version]\Temporary ASP.NET Files directory where the compiled ASP.NET files are stored. Otherwise, an error will occur and the page will not be served.

ASP.NET also provides the option to specifically set an account that will be used for running code. This technique is useful if you want different ASP.NET applications to execute with different, but fixed, permissions. In this case, the user's authenticated identity isn't used by the ASP.NET code. It just sets a base level of permissions you want your application to have. Here's an example:

```
<identity impersonate="true" userName="matthew" password="secret" />
```

This approach is more flexible than changing the machine.config account setting. The machine.config setting determines the default account that will be used for all web applications on the computer. The impersonation settings, on the other hand, override the machine.config setting for individual websites. Unfortunately, the password for the impersonated account cannot be encrypted in the web.config file by default. This constitutes a security risk if other users have access to the computer and can read the password. The risk is especially severe if you are using impersonation with a highly privileged account.

Fortunately, you can encrypt such settings with a tool provided by Microsoft called aspnet_setreg.exe. Because the following configuration sections cannot be encrypted with the aspnet_regiis.exe utility, you can use aspnet_setreg.exe to secure the following information in your web.config file:

- The <processModel> user name and password in the machine.config file
- The user name and password in the <identity> element
- Session state connection strings in the <session> element if you are using SQL state

The aspnet_setreg.exe tool was originally created for .NET 1.0, but it can be used with .NET 1.1 and 2.0 as well. You can download the tool from Microsoft at `http://support.microsoft.com/default.aspx?scid=kb;en-us;329290`.

The aspnet_setreg.exe tool queries the information and stores it encrypted in the registry. Of course, the worker process user has to have permissions for this registry key, as the first action it performs is to read the identity information from the registry key for impersonating this identity. You can use aspnet_setreg.exe as follows for encrypting a user name and password for the <identity> element:

```
aspnet_setreg -k:Software\ProAspNet\Identity -u:Developer -p:pass@word1
```

This encrypts the specified user name and password and stores the encrypted version in the registry key HKLM\Software\ProAspNet\Identity. Next you have to grant the worker process or application pool's identity read access to this registry hive, as shown in Figure 22-16.

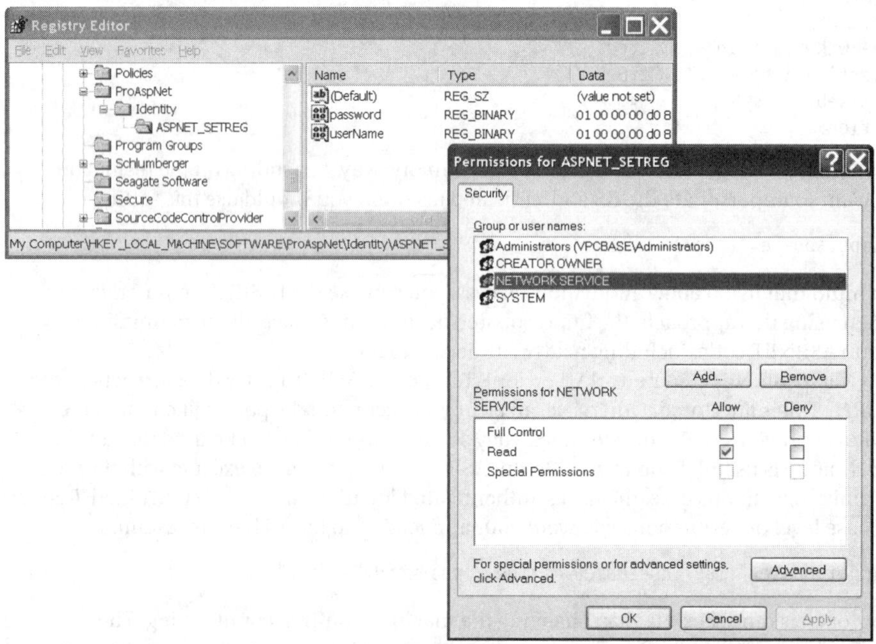

Figure 22-16. *Granting access to the registry hive*

Now you have to configure your <identity> element in the web.config file as follows:

```
<identity impersonate="true"
          userName=
             "registry:HKLM\Software\ProAspNet\Identity\ASPNET_SETREG,userName"
          password=
             "registry:HKLM\Software\ProAspNet\Identity\ASPNET_SETREG,password"
/>
```

When you now create a Default.aspx page as follows with the preceding <identity/> element configured, the result looks like Figure 22-17:

```
<%@ Page Language="VB" CodeFile="Default.aspx.vb" Inherits="_Default" %>
<html xmlns="http://www.w3.org/1999/xhtml" >
<head runat="server">
  <title>Untitled Page</title>
</head>
<body>
    <form id="form1" runat="server">
    <div>
    <b>Authenticated:</b> <%= User.Identity.Name %>
    <b>Impersonated:</b>
    <%= System.Security.Principal.WindowsIdentity.GetCurrent().Name %>
    </div>
    </form>
</body>
</html>
```

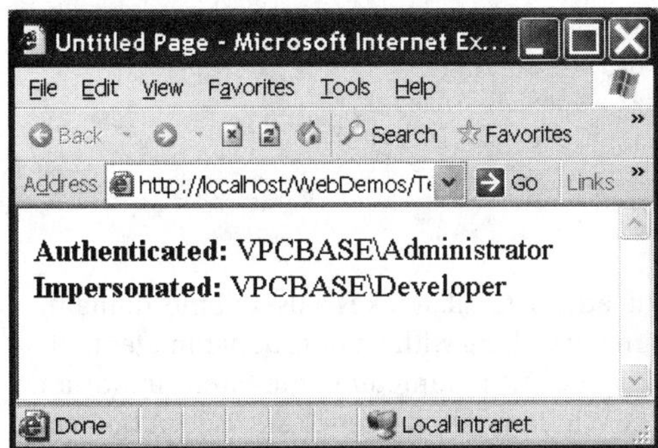

Figure 22-17. *Configured impersonation with fixed user name and password*

Programmatic Impersonation

Configured impersonation allows you to impersonate a user for the entire duration of a request. If you want more control, such as the ability to impersonate a user for only part of the page request, you have to do the impersonation yourself in your code.

The key to impersonating a user programmatically is the WindowsIdentity.Impersonate() method. This method sets up impersonation for a specific account. You identify the account you want to impersonate by using its *account token*. Account tokens are what Windows uses to track users once their credentials are approved. If you have the token for a user, you can impersonate that user.

The general process is as follows:

1. Obtain an account token for the account you want to impersonate.
2. Use WindowsIdentity.Impersonate() to start impersonation. This method returns a WindowsImpersonationContext object.
3. Call the Undo() method of the WindowsImpersonationContext object to revert to the original identity.

Getting a Token

You can get an account token in two main ways. The most common approach is to retrieve the token for the currently authenticated user. You can access this token through the current security context, using the WindowsIdentity.Token property. Tokens are represented in .NET as IntPtr objects, which are representations of pointers to unmanaged memory locations. However, you never need to interact with this directly. Instead, you simply need to pass the token to the WindowsIdentity.Impersonate() method.

Here's an example that extracts the token for the current user:

```
Dim token As IntPtr = (CType(User.Identity, WindowsIdentity)).Token
```

The only other way to get a user token is to programmatically log in with a specific user name and password. Unfortunately, .NET does not provide managed classes for logging a user in. Instead, you must use the LogonUser() function from the unmanaged Win32 security API.

To use the LogonUser() function, you must first declare it as shown here:

```
<DllImport("c:\Windows\System32\advapi32.dll")> _
Public Shared Function LogonUser(ByVal lpszUserName As String,
    ByVal lpszDomain As String, ByVal lpszPassword As String,
    ByVal dwLogonType As Integer, ByVal dwLogonProvider As Integer,
    <System.Runtime.InteropServices.Out()> ByRef phToken As Integer)
    As Boolean
...
End Function
```

As you can see, the LogonUser() function exists in advapi32.dll. It takes a user name, domain, password, logon type, and logon provider input parameters, along with an output parameter that allows you to access the token following a successful logon. The parameter names aren't important. In this example, the somewhat cryptic names from the Windows API reference are used. A Boolean result is returned to indicate whether the logon was successful.

■ **Note** Windows XP or later operating systems impose restrictions on the use of blank passwords to prevent network-based attacks. As a result of these restrictions, you won't be able to use the LogonUser() function to impersonate an account with a blank password.

Once you have imported the LogonUser() function, you can use it in your code to log the user in, as shown here:

```
' Define required variables.
Dim user As String = "matthew"
Dim password As String = "secret"
Dim machine As String = "FARIAMAT"
Dim returnedToken As Integer

' Try to log on.
If LogonUser(user, machine, password, 3, 0, returnedToken) Then
    ' The attempt was successful. Get the token.
    Dim token As New IntPtr(returnedToken)
End If
```

Note that you must convert the integer value returned by LogonUser() into an IntPtr in order to use it with the WindowsIdentity.Impersonate() method.

Performing the Impersonation

Once you have an account token, you can use the WindowsIdentity.Impersonate() method to start impersonating the corresponding identity. You can use the Impersonate() method in two ways. You can use the Shared version, which requires an account token. Alternatively, you can use the instance version, which impersonates the identity represented by the corresponding WindowsIdentity object. In either case, the Impersonate() method returns a WindowsImpersonationContext object that has a single function—it allows you to revert to the original identity by calling its Undo() method.

Here's an example of programmatic impersonation at its simplest, using the Shared version of the Impersonate() method:

```
Dim impersonateContext As WindowsImpersonationContext
impersonateContext = WindowsIdentity.Impersonate(token)

' (Now perform tasks under the impersonated ID.
' This code will not be able to perform any task
' that the user would not be allowed to do.)

impersonateContext.Undo()
```

At any time, you can determine the identity that your code is currently executing under by calling the WindowsIdentity.GetCurrent() method. Here's a function that uses this technique to determine the current identity and display the corresponding user name in a label on a web page:

```
Private Sub DisplayIdentity()
    ' Get the identity under which the code is currently executing.
    Dim identity As WindowsIdentity = WindowsIdentity.GetCurrent()
    lblInfo.Text &= "Executing as: " & identity.Name & "<br/>"
End Sub
```

Using the method, you can create a simple test that impersonates the authenticated IIS identity and then reverts to the standard identity:

```
Private Sub Page_Load(ByVal sender As Object, ByVal e As System.EventArgs)
    If TypeOf User Is WindowsPrincipal Then
        DisplayIdentity()

        ' Impersonate the IIS identity.
        Dim id As WindowsIdentity
        id = CType(User.Identity, WindowsIdentity)
        Dim impersonateContext As WindowsImpersonationContext
        impersonateContext = id.Impersonate()
        DisplayIdentity()

        ' Revert to the original ID as shown here.
        impersonateContext.Undo()
        DisplayIdentity()
    Else
        ' User isn't Windows authenticated.
        ' Throw an error or take other steps.
    End If
End Sub
```

Figure 22-18 shows the result.

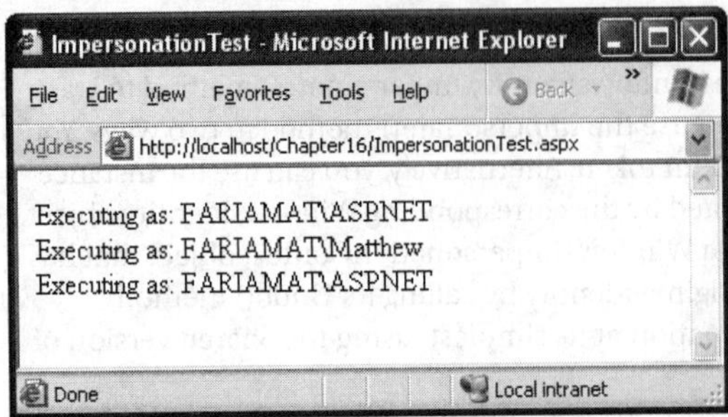

Figure 22-18. *Impersonating a user programmatically*

Summary

In this chapter, you learned how to use Windows authentication with ASP.NET to let IIS validate user identities. You also learned about the different types of authentication, how to retrieve user information, and how to impersonate users so your code runs under a different Windows account. In the next chapter, you'll learn about using advanced authorization rules that apply to Windows authentication and forms authentication.

CHAPTER 23

■ ■ ■

Authorization and Roles

So far, you've seen how to confirm that users are who they say they are and how to retrieve information about those authenticated identities. This gives your application the basic ability to distinguish between different users, but it's only a starting point. To create a truly secure web application, you need to act upon that identity at various points using *authorization*.

Authorization is the process of determining whether an authenticated user has sufficient permissions to perform a given action. This action could be requesting a web page, accessing a resource controlled by the operating system (such as a file or database), or performing an application-specific task (such as placing an order or assigning a project). Windows performs some of these checks automatically, and you can code others declaratively using the web.config file. You'll need to perform still others directly in your code using the IPrincipal object.

In this chapter, you'll learn how ASP.NET authorization works, how to protect different resources, and how to implement your own role-based security.

URL Authorization

The most straightforward way to set security permissions is on individual web pages, web services, and subdirectories. Ideally, a web application framework should support resource-specific authorization without requiring you to change code and recompile the application. ASP.NET supports this requirement with declarative *authorization rules*, which you can define in the web.config file.

The rules you define are acted upon by the UrlAuthorizationModule, a specific HTTP module. This module examines these rules and checks each request to make sure users can't access resources you've specifically restricted. This type of authorization is called *URL authorization* because it considers only two details—the security context of the user and the URL of the resource that the user is attempting to access. If the page is forbidden and you're using forms authentication, the user will be redirected to the login page. If the page is forbidden and you're using Windows authentication, the user will receive an "access denied" (HTTP 401) error page, as shown in Figure 23-1, or a more generic error message or custom error page, depending on the <customErrors> element.

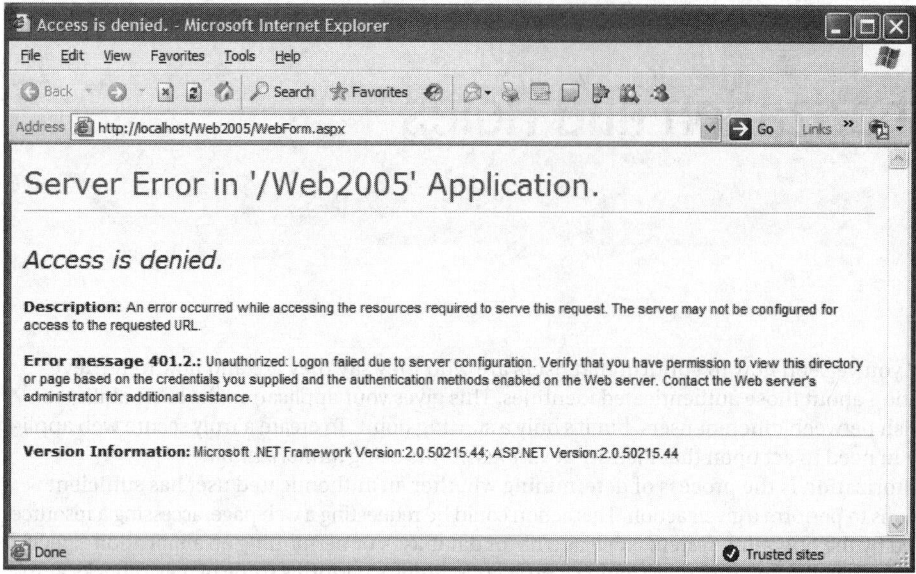

Figure 23-1. *Trying to request a forbidden web page*

Authorization Rules

You define the authorization rules in the <authorization> element of the web.config file. The basic structure is as follows:

```
<authorization>
  <allow users="comma-separated list of users"
         roles="comma-separated list of roles"
         verbs="comma-separated list of verbs" />
  <deny  users="comma-separated list of users"
         roles="comma-separated list of roles"
         verbs="comma-separated list of verbs" />
</authorization>
```

In other words, two types of rules exist: allow and deny. You can add as many allow and deny rules as you want. Each rule identifies one or more users or roles (groups of users). In addition, you can use the verbs attribute to create a rule that applies only to specific types of HTTP requests (GET, POST, HEAD, or DEBUG).

You've already seen the simplest example in the previous chapters. To deny access to all anonymous users, you can use a <deny> rule like this:

```
<authorization>
  <deny users="?" />
</authorization>
```

In this case, the question mark (?) is a wildcard that represents all users with unknown identities. This rule is almost always used in authentication scenarios. That's because you can't specifically deny other, known users unless you first force all users to authenticate themselves.

You can use an additional wildcard—the asterisk (*), which represents all users. For example, the following <authorization> section allows access by authenticated and anonymous users:

```
<authorization>
  <allow users="*" />
</authorization>
```

This rule is rarely required, because it's already present in the machine.config file. After ASP.NET applies all the rules in the web.config file, it applies rules from the machine.config file. As a result, any user who is explicitly denied access automatically gains access.

Now consider what happens if you add more than one rule in the authorization section:

```
<authorization>
    <allow users="*" />
    <deny users="?" />
</authorization>
```

When evaluating rules, ASP.NET scans through the list from top to bottom. As soon as it finds an applicable rule, it stops its search. Thus, in the previous case, it will determine that the rule <allow users="*"> applies to the current request and will not evaluate the second line. That means these rules will allow all users, including anonymous users. Reversing the order of these two lines, however, will deny anonymous users (by matching the first rule) and allow all other users (by matching the second rule).

```
<authorization>
    <deny users="?" />
    <allow users="*" />
</authorization>
```

When you add authorization rules to the web.config file in the root directory of the web application, the rules automatically apply to all the web resources that are part of the application. If you've denied anonymous users, ASP.NET will examine the authentication mode. If you've selected forms authentication, ASP.NET will direct the user to the login page. If you're using Windows authentication, IIS will request user credentials from the client browser, and a login dialog box may appear (depending on the protocols you've enabled).

In the following sections, you'll learn how to fine-tune authorization rules to give them a more carefully defined scope.

Controlling Access for Specific Users

The <allow> and <deny> rules don't need to use the asterisk or question mark wildcards. Instead, they can specifically identify a user name or a list of comma-separated user names. For example, the following authorization rule specifically restricts access from three users. These users will not be able to access the pages in this directory. All other authenticated users will be allowed.

```
<authorization>
  <deny users="?" />
  <deny users="dan" />
  <deny users="jenny" />
  <deny users="matthew" />
  <allow users="*" />
</authorization>
```

You can also use a comma-separated list to deny multiple users at once. Here's an equivalent version of the previous example that uses only two authorization rules:

```
<authorization>
  <deny users="?" />
  <deny users="dan,jenny,matthew" />
  <allow users="*" />
</authorization>
```

Note that in both these cases the order in which the three users are listed is unimportant. However, it is important that these users are denied before you include the <allow> rule. For example, the following authorization rules won't affect the user jenny, because ASP.NET matches the rule that allows all users and doesn't read any further:

```
<authorization>
  <deny users="?" />
  <deny users="dan,matthew" />
  <allow users="*" />
  <deny users="jenny" />
</authorization>
```

When creating secure applications, it's often a better approach to explicitly allow specific users or groups and then deny all others (rather than denying specific users, as in the examples so far). Here's an example of authorization rules that explicitly allow two users. All other user requests will be denied access, even if they are authenticated.

```
<authorization>
  <deny users="?" />
  <allow users="dan,matthew" />
  <deny users="*" />
</authorization>
```

You should consider one other detail. The format of user names in these examples assumes forms authentication. In forms authentication, you assign a user name when you call the RedirectFromLoginPage() method. At this point, the UrlAuthorizationModule will use that name and check it against the list of authorization rules. Windows authentication is a little different, because names are entered in the format DomainName\UserName or ComputerName\UserName. You need to use the same format when listing users in the authorization rules. For example, if you have the user accounts dan and matthew on a computer named FARIAMAT, you can use these authorization rules:

```
<authorization>
  <deny users="?" />
  <allow users="FARIAMAT\dan,FARIAMAT\matthew" />
  <deny users="*" />
</authorization>
```

■ **Note** Make sure you specify the computer or domain name in the users attribute when you use Windows authentication. You can't use an alias such as localhost, because this will not be successfully matched.

Controlling Access to Specific Directories

A common application design is to place files that require authentication into a separate directory. With ASP.NET configuration files, this approach is easy. Just leave the <authorization> element in the normal parent directory empty, and add a web.config file that specifies stricter settings in the secured directory.

Remember that when you add the web.config file in the subdirectory, it shouldn't contain any of the application-specific settings. In fact, it should contain only the authorization information, as shown here:

```
<configuration>
  <system.web>
    <authorization>
      <deny users="?" />
```

```
    </authorization>
  </system.web>
</configuration>
```

■Note You cannot change the <authentication> tag settings in the web.config file of a subdirectory in your application. Instead, all the directories in the application must use the same authentication system. However, each directory can have its own authorization rules.

When using authorization rules in a subdirectory, ASP.NET still reads the authorization rules from the parent directory. The difference is that it applies the rules in the subdirectory *first*. This is important, because ASP.NET stops as soon as it matches an authorization rule. For example, consider an example in which the root virtual directory contains this rule:

```
<allow users="dan" />
```

and a subdirectory contains this rule:

```
<deny users="dan" />
```

In this case, the user dan will be able to access any resource in the root directory but no resources in the subdirectory. If you reverse these two rules, dan will be able to access resources in the subdirectory but not the root directory.

To make life more interesting, ASP.NET allows an unlimited hierarchy of subdirectories and authorization rules. For example, it's quite possible to have a virtual directory with authorization rules, a subdirectory that defines additional rules, and then a subdirectory inside that subdirectory that applies even more rules. The easiest way to understand the authorization process in this case is to imagine all the rules as a single list, starting with the directory where the requested page is located. If all those rules are processed without a match, ASP.NET then begins reading the authorization rules in the parent directory, and then its parent directory, and so on, until it finds a match. If no authorization rules match, ASP.NET will ultimately match the <allow users="*"> rule in the machine.config file.

Controlling Access to Specific Files

Generally, setting file access permissions by directory is the cleanest and easiest approach. However, you also have the option of restricting specific files by adding <location> tags to your web.config file.

The location tags sit outside the main <system.web> tag and are nested directly in the base <configuration> tag, as shown here:

```
<configuration>
    <system.web>
        <!-- Other settings omitted. -->
        <authorization>
            <allow users="*" />
        </authorization>
    </system.web>

    <location path="SecuredPage.aspx">
        <system.web>
            <authorization>
                <deny users="?" />
            </authorization>
        </system.web>
    </location>
```

```
    <location path="AnotherSecuredPage.aspx">
        <system.web>
            <authorization>
                <deny users="?" />
            </authorization>
        </system.web>
    </location>

</configuration>
```

In this example, all files in the application are allowed, except SecuredPage.aspx and AnotherSecuredPage.aspx, which have an access rule that denies anonymous users.

Controlling Access for Specific Roles

To make website security easier to understand and maintain, users are often grouped into categories, called *roles*. If you need to manage an enterprise application that supports thousands of users, you can understand the value of roles. If you needed to define permissions for each individual user, it would be tiring, difficult to change, and nearly impossible to complete without error.

In Windows authentication, roles are automatically available and naturally integrated. In this case, roles are actually Windows groups. You might use built-in groups (such as Administrator, Guest, PowerUser, and so on), or you can create your own to represent application-specific categories (such as Manager, Contracter, Supervisor, and so on). Roles aren't provided intrinsically in forms authentication alone, but, together with membership, ASP.NET employs the roles service, which is an out-of-the-box implementation for supporting and managing roles in your application. Furthermore, if you don't want to use this infrastructure, it's fairly easy to create your own system that slots users into appropriate groups based on their credentials. You'll learn details about the two ways of supporting roles in the section "Using the Roles Service for Role-Based Authorization" in this chapter.

Once you have defined roles, you can create authorization rules that act on these roles. In fact, these rules look essentially the same as the user-specific rules you've seen already.

For example, the following authorization rules deny all anonymous users, allow two specific users (dan and matthew), and allow two specific groups (Manager and Supervisor). All other users are denied.

```
<authorization>
  <deny users="?" />
  <allow users="FARIAMAT\dan,FARIAMAT\matthew" />
  <allow roles="FARIAMAT\Manager,FARIAMAT\Supervisor" />
  <deny users="*" />
</authorization>
```

Using role-based authorization rules is simple conceptually, but it can become tricky in practice. The issue is that when you use roles, your authorization rules can overlap. For example, consider what happens if you allow a group that contains a specific user and then explicitly deny that user. Or consider the reverse—allowing a user by name but denying the group to which the user belongs. In these scenarios, you might expect the more fine-grained rule (the rule affecting the user) to take precedence over the more general rule (the rule affecting the group). Or, you might expect the more restrictive rules to always take precedence, as in the Windows operating system. However, neither of these approaches is used in ASP.NET. Instead, ASP.NET simply uses the first matching rule. As a result, rule ordering can become important.

Consider this example:

```
<authorization>
  <deny users="?" />
  <allow users="FARIAMAT\matthew" />
```

```
  <deny roles="FARIAMAT\Guest" />
  <allow roles="FARIAMAT\Manager" />
  <deny users="FARIAMAT\dan" />
  <allow roles="FARIAMAT\Supervisor" />
  <deny users="*" />
</authorization>
```

Here's how ASP.NET parses these rules:

- In this example, the user matthew is allowed, regardless of the group to which he belongs.
- All users in the Guest role are then denied. If matthew is in the Guest role, matthew is still allowed because the user-specific rule is matched first.
- Next, all users in the Manager group are allowed. The only exception is users who are in both the Manager and Guest groups. The Guest rule occurs earlier in the list, so those users would have already been denied.
- Next, the user dan is denied access. But if dan belongs to the allowed Manager group, dan will already have been allowed, because this rule won't be executed.
- Any users who are in the Supervisor group, and who haven't been explicitly allowed or denied by one of the preceding rules, are allowed.
- Finally, all other users are denied.

Keep in mind that these overlapping rules can also span multiple directories. For example, a subdirectory might deny a user, while a parent directory allows a user in that group. In this example, when accessing files in the subdirectory, the user-specific rule is matched first.

File Authorization

URL authorization is one of the cornerstones of ASP.NET authorization. However, ASP.NET also uses another type of authorization that's often not recognized. This is file-based authorization, and it's implemented by the FileAuthorizationModule. File-based authorization takes effect only if you're using Windows authentication. If you're using custom authentication or forms authentication, it's not used.

To understand file authorization, you need to understand how the Windows operating system enforces file system security. If your file system uses the NTFS format, you can set ACLs that specifically identify users and roles that are allowed or denied access to individual files. The FileAuthorizationModule simply checks the Windows permissions for the file you're requesting. For example, if you request a web page, the FileAuthorizationModule checks that the currently authenticated IIS user has the permissions required to access the underlying .aspx file. If the user doesn't, the page code is not executed, and the user receives an "access denied" message.

New ASP.NET users often wonder why file authorization needs to be implemented by a separate module—shouldn't it take place automatically at the hands of the operating system? To understand why the FileAuthorizationModule is required, you need to remember how ASP.NET executes code. Unless you've enabled impersonation, ASP.NET executes under a fixed user account, such as ASPNET. The Windows operating system will check that the ASPNET account has the permissions it needs to access the .aspx file, but it wouldn't perform the same check for a user authenticated by IIS. The FileAuthorizationModule fills the gap. It performs authorization checks using the security context of the current user. As a result, the system administrator can set permissions to files or folders and control access to portions of an ASP.NET application. Generally, it's clearer and more straightforward to use authorization rules in the web.config file. However, if you want to take advantage of existing Windows permissions in a local network or an intranet scenario, you can.

Authorization Checks in Code

With URL authorization and file authorization, you can control access only to individual web pages. The next step in ensuring a secure application is to build checks into your application before attempting specific tasks or allowing certain operations. To use these techniques, you'll need to write some code.

Using the IsInRole() Method

As you saw in earlier chapters, all IPrincipal objects provide an IsInRole() method, which lets you evaluate whether a user is a member of a group. This method accepts the role name as a string name and returns True if the user is a member of that role.

For example, here's how you can check if the current user is a member of the Supervisors role:

```
If User.IsInRole("Supervisors") Then
    ' Do nothing; the page should be accessed as normal because the
    ' user has administrator privileges.
Else
    ' Don't allow this page. Instead, redirect to the home page.
    Response.Redirect("Default.aspx")
End If
```

Remember that when using Windows authentication, you need to use the format DomainName\GroupName or ComputerName\GroupName. Here's an example:

```
If User.IsInRole("FARIAMAT\Supervisors") Then
    ...
End If
```

This approach works for custom groups you've created but not for built-in groups that are defined by the operating system. If you want to check whether a user is a member of one of the built-in groups, you use this syntax:

```
If User.IsInRole("BUILTIN\Administrators") Then
    ...
End If
```

Of course, you can also cast the User object to a WindowsPrincipal and use the overloaded version of IsInRole() that accepts the WindowsBuiltInRole enumeration, as described in Chapter 22.

Using the PrincipalPermission Class

.NET includes another way to enforce role and user rules. Instead of checking with the IsInRole() method, you can use the PrincipalPermission class from the System.Security.Permissions namespace.

The basic strategy is to create a PrincipalPermission object that represents the user or role information you require. Then, invoke the PrincipalPermission.Demand() method. If the current user doesn't meet the requirements, a SecurityException will be thrown, which you can catch (or deal with using a custom error page).

The Demand() method takes two parameters—one for the user name and one for the role name. You can omit either one of these parameters by supplying a null reference in its place. For example, the following code tests whether the user is a Windows administrator:

```
Try
    Dim pp As New PrincipalPermission(Nothing, "BUILTIN\Administrators")
    pp.Demand()
```

```
    ' If the code reaches this point, the demand succeeded.
    ' The current user is an administrator.
Catch err As SecurityException
    ' The demand failed. The current user isn't an administrator.
End Try
```

The advantage of this approach is that you don't need to write any conditional logic. Instead, you can simply demand all the permissions you need. This works particularly well if you need to verify that a user is a member of multiple groups. The disadvantage is that using exception handling to control the flow of your application is slower. Often, PrincipalPermission checks are used in addition to web.config rules as a failsafe. In other words, you can call Demand() to ensure that even if a web.config file has been inadvertently modified, users in the wrong groups won't be allowed.

Merging PrincipalPermission Objects

The PrincipalPermission approach also gives you the ability to evaluate more-complex authentication rules. For example, consider a situation where UserA and UserB, who belong to different groups, are both allowed to access certain functionality. If you use the IPrincipal object, you need to call IsInRole() twice. An alternate approach is to create multiple PrincipalPermission objects and merge them to get one PrincipalPermission object. Then you can call Demand() on just this object.

Here's an example that combines two roles:

```
Try
    Dim pp1 As New PrincipalPermission(Nothing, "BUILTIN\Administrators")
    Dim pp2 As New PrincipalPermission(Nothing, "BUILTIN\Guests")

    ' Combine these two permissions.
    Dim pp3 As PrincipalPermission = CType(pp1.Union(pp2), PrincipalPermission)
    pp3.Demand()

    ' If the code reaches this point, the demand succeeded.
    ' The current user is in one of these roles.
Catch err As SecurityException
    ' The demand failed. The current user is in none of these roles.
End Try
```

This example checks that a user is a member of either one of the two Windows groups, Administrators or Guests. You can also ensure that a user is a member of *both* groups. In this case, use the PrincipalPermission.Intersect() method instead of PrincipalPermission.Union().

Using the PrincipalPermission Attribute

The PrincipalPermission attribute provides another way of validating the current user's credentials. It serves the same purpose as the PrincipalPermission class, but it's used declaratively. In other words, you attach it to a given class or method, and the CLR checks it automatically when the corresponding code runs. The exception handling now works a little bit differently: this time you cannot catch the exception within the function on which the attribute has been applied. You have to catch the exception in the function that actually calls this function. If you apply the PrincipalPermission attribute on an event procedure (such as Button_Click), you have to catch the exception in the global Application_Error event, which you can find in the global.asax file.

When you use a PrincipalPermission attribute, you can restrict access to a specific user or a specific role. Here's an example that requires the user accessing the page to be in the server's Administrators group. If the user is not member of the web server's Administrators group, the ASP.NET runtime throws a security exception.

```
<PrincipalPermission(SecurityAction.Demand, Role:="BUILTIN\Administrators")> _
Public Class MyWebPage
      Private ...
End Class
```

Again, with the previous example you have to catch the exception in the global error handler (Application_Error) because your code is not the caller of this web page. Otherwise, ASP.NET would raise the exception and display the ASP.NET error page according to the web.config configuration. The following example restricts a particular method to a specific user:

```
<PrincipalPermission(SecurityAction.Demand, Name="FARIAMAT\matthew")> _
Private Sub DoSomething()
      ...
End Sub
```

The caller of this method, of course, can catch the SecurityException with a Try/Catch block.

PrincipalPermission attributes give you another way to safeguard your code. You won't use them to make decisions at runtime, but you might use them to ensure that even if web.config rules are modified or circumvented, a basic level of security remains.

■ **Note** Changing declarative permissions means that you need to recompile the application. But why use them if every change requires recompilation? Don't you want to have the possibility of managing roles in terms of adding, deleting, and changing them? Yes, and that requires more generic code, but it can't be done with declarative permissions. So, when is it helpful to use declarative permissions? Well, declarative permissions are especially suited for fixed roles in your application that cannot be deleted anyway. For example, an Administrators role is required in most applications and therefore cannot be deleted. So, you can secure functionality that should be accessible to only administrators with declarative permissions. Typical examples in Windows are all the built-in groups such as Administrators, Power Users, Backup Operators, and Users.

Using the Roles Service for Role-Based Authorization

ASP.NET 2.0 ships with a ready-to-use infrastructure for managing and using roles (as well as the membership service introduced in Chapter 21). This infrastructure—which is completely extensible through providers such as the membership service—includes prebuilt functionality for managing roles, assigning roles to users, and accessing all the role information from code. In more detail, the roles infrastructure includes the following:

- A provider-based extensible mechanism for including different types of role data stores.
- A ready-to-use implementation of a provider for SQL Server and the necessary database tables based on the membership database introduced in Chapter 21. These tables associate membership user entries with roles in a many-to-many relationship and are automatically created when calling the aspnet_regsql.exe tool (also introduced in Chapter 21).
- The prebuilt RolePrincipal class that is automatically initialized for authenticated users through the RoleManagerModule (also included with the roles infrastructure).
- Complete programmatic access to the roles through the Roles class.

To use this infrastructure, you have to first enable it. You can do this either by checking the Enable Roles for This Web Site box when running through the security wizard or by clicking the Enable Roles link in the Security tab of the WAT. Figure 23-2 shows both of these possibilities.

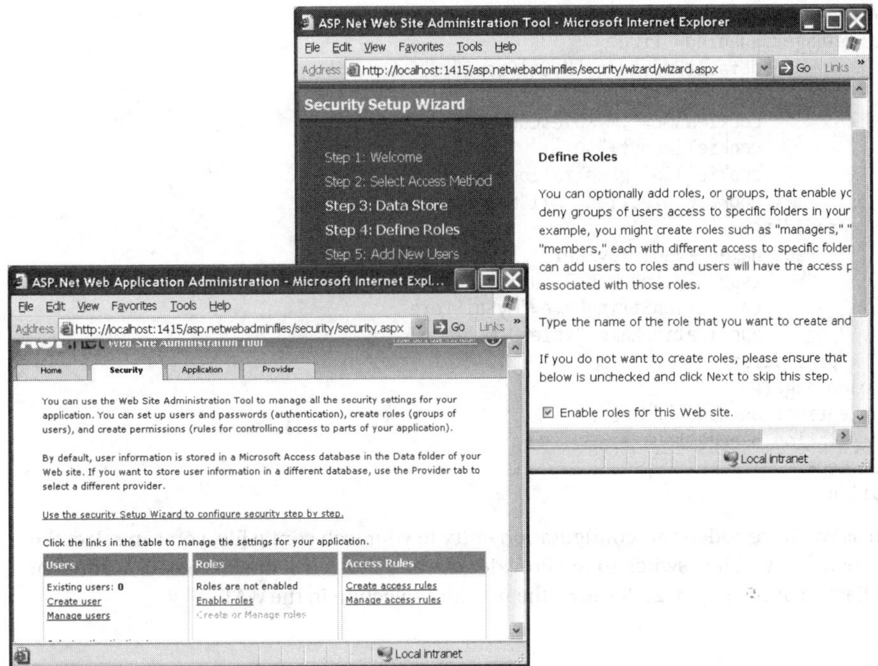

Figure 23-2. *Configuring the roles service*

In both cases, the tool adds a little configuration entry to the application's web.config file. You can do this manually, just as you can enable the roles service.

```
<configuration xmlns="http://schemas.microsoft.com/.NetConfiguration/v2.0">
    <system.web>
        <roleManager enabled="true" />
        <authentication mode="Forms" />
    </system.web>
</configuration>
```

With this configuration in place, ASP.NET automatically creates a file-based database, ASPNETDB.MDF, in the application's App_Data directory, as already described in Chapter 21. If you want to use a custom store, you have to complete the following steps:

1. Create the data store either by using aspnet_regsql.exe or by executing the TSQL command scripts included in the .NET Framework directory. Both were introduced in Chapter 21.
2. Configure the roles provider to use the previously created custom store.

You can configure the roles provider through the <roleManager> tag. You can either use a different database or use a completely different store if you want. In addition, you can configure certain properties through the <roleManager> tag that can't be configured in the WAT.

```
<configuration xmlns="http://schemas.microsoft.com/.NetConfiguration/v2.0">
    <connectionStrings>
        <add name="MySqlStore"
             connectionString="data source=(local);
                    Integrated Security=SSPI;initial catalog=MySqlDB"/>
    </connectionStrings>
```

```
    <system.web>
        <roleManager enabled="true"
                     defaultProvider="MySqlProvider"
                     cacheRolesInCookie="true"
                     cookieName=".MyRolesCookie"
                     cookieTimeout="30"
                     cookieSlidingExpiration="true"
                     cookieProtection="All">
            <providers>
                <add name="MySqlProvider"
                     type="System.Web.Security.SqlRoleProvider"
                     connectionStringName="MySqlStore"
                     applicationName="RolesDemo"/>
            </providers>
        </roleManager>
        <authentication mode="Forms"/>
        <compilation debug="true"/>
    </system.web>
</configuration>
```

As soon as you have added this configuration entry to your web.config file, you can select the provider through the WAT. Just switch to the Provider tab, and then click the link Select a Different Provider for Each Feature. Figure 23-3 shows the provider selection in the WAT.

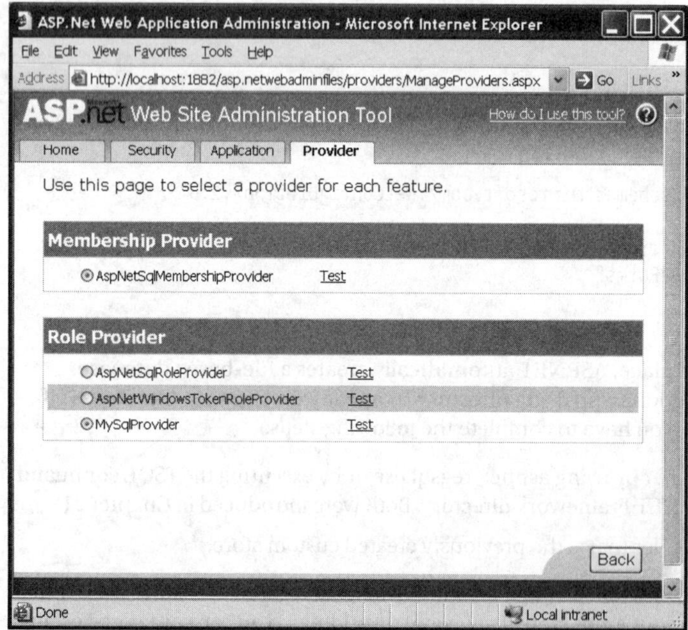

Figure 23-3. *The roles provider in the web-based configuration tool*

Table 23-1 lists the properties you can configure through the <roleManager> configuration tag.

Table 23-1. *Options for the <roleManager> Configuration*

Option	Description
Enabled	Indicates whether the roles service is enabled (True) or not (False).
defaultProvider	Optional attribute for specifying the currently active provider for storing role information. If you want to use a different provider, you have to configure it and set the defaultProvider attribute to the name of the provider you want to use.
cacheRolesInCookie	Instead of reading the roles every time from the back-end store, you can store roles in a cookie. This attribute indicates whether a cookie is used.
cookieName	If roles are cached in a cookie, you can specify a name for this cookie through this attribute.
cookiePath	Specifies the root path of the cookie. The default value is /.
cookieProtection	The roles cookie can be encrypted and signed. The level of protection is specified through this attribute. Valid values are All (encrypt and sign), Encryption, Validation, and None.
cookieRequireSSL	Specifies whether the cookie will be returned by ASP.NET only if SSL is enabled (True) or in any other case (False). If this attribute is set to True and SSL is not activated, the runtime simply doesn't return the cookie, and therefore role checks always happen against the underlying roles provider.
cookieTimeout	Gets or sets a timeout for the roles cookie in minutes with a default of 30 minutes.
createPersistentCookie	If set to True, the cookie will be stored persistently on the client machine. Otherwise, the cookie is just a session cookie that will be deleted when the user is closing the browser.
domain	Specifies the valid domain for the role cookie.
maxCachedResults	Specifies the maximum number of role names persisted in the cookie.

In the previous example, you configured the SqlRoleProvider. The provider includes a couple of additional settings you can configure through web.config, as shown in Table 23-2.

Table 23-2. *Additional Properties of the SqlRoleProvider*

Property	Description
name	Name of the provider. This name can be used in the defaultProvider attribute described in Table 23-1 for specifying the provider by the application.
applicationName	Name of the application for which the roles are managed.
description	Short, friendly description of the provider.
connectionStringName	Name of the connection string specified in the web.config file's <connectionStrings> section that will be used for connecting to the back-end roles store.

In addition to the SqlRoleProvider, ASP.NET ships with a provider that can be used on Windows Server 2003 with Authorization Manager. You can also create and use your own custom providers, as you will learn in Chapter 26. Table 23-3 shows the classes included in the roles service framework.

Table 23-3. *The Fundamental Roles Service Classes*

Class	Description
RoleManagerModule	This module ensures that roles will be assigned to the currently logged-on user for every request. It attaches to the Application_AuthenticateRequest event and creates an instance of RolePrincipal containing the roles the user is assigned to automatically if the roles service is enabled in web.config.
RoleProvider	Base class for every roles provider that defines the interface you must implement for a custom RoleProvider. Every custom provider must be inherited from this class.
RoleProviderCollection	A collection of roles providers. This collection allows you to iterate through the configured roles providers on your system and for your application.
SqlRoleProvider	Implementation of a roles provider for SQL Server–based databases.
WindowsTokenRoleProvider	Gets role information for an authenticated Windows user based on Windows group associations.
AuthorizationStoreRoleProvider	Implementation of a roles provider for storing roles in a Authorization Manager–based store. Authorization Manager ships with Windows Server 2003 and allows you to declaratively define application roles and permissions for this role. Your application can use Authorization Manager for programmatically authorizing users.
Roles	You use the Roles class as your primary interface to the roles store. This class includes methods for programmatically managing roles.
RolePrincipal	This is a IPrincipal implementation that connects the configured roles with the authenticated user. It is created automatically by the RoleManagerModule if the roles service is enabled.

As soon as you have configured the roles service, you can create users and roles and then assign users to these roles using either the WAT or the Roles class in your code. On the Security tab, just click the Create or Manage Roles link. Then you can create roles and add users to roles, as shown in Figure 23-4.

After you have configured users and roles, you need to configure the authorization rules for your application. You have already learned all the necessary details. Just configure the appropriate <authorization> sections in the different directories of your application. Fortunately, you even don't have to do this manually. When selecting the Security tab, you just need to click one of the links in the Access Rules section, as shown in Figure 23-5.

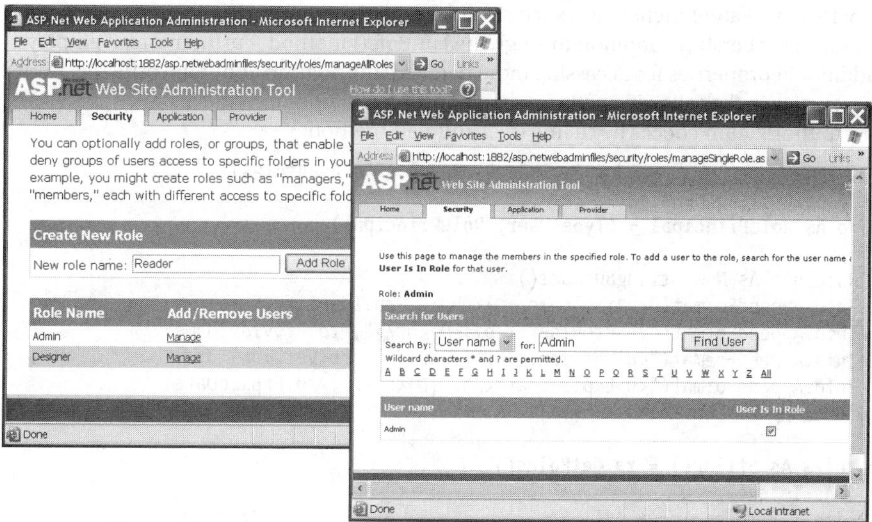

Figure 23-4. *Adding users to roles*

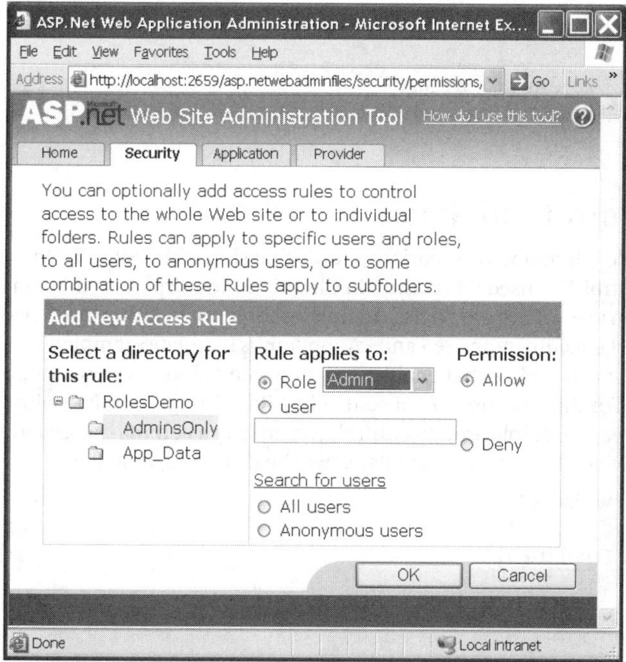

Figure 23-5. *Configuring access rules with the WAT*

When the roles service is enabled, the RoleManagerModule automatically creates a RolePrincipal instance containing both the authenticated user's identity and the roles of the user. The RolePrincipal is just a custom implementation of IPrincipal, which is the base interface for all principal classes. It therefore supports the default functionality, such as access to the authenticated identity and a method for verifying a role membership condition through the IsInRole() method. Furthermore, it employs a couple of additional properties for accessing more detailed information about the principal. You can use the properties in the following code for extracting information from the instance as well as for performing authorization checks by calling the IsInRole() method:

```
Protected Sub Page_Load(ByVal sender As Object, ByVal e As EventArgs)
    If User.Identity.IsAuthenticated Then
        Dim rp As RolePrincipal = CType(User, RolePrincipal)

        Dim RoleInfo As New StringBuilder()
        RoleInfo.AppendFormat("<h2>Welcome {0}</h2>", rp.Identity.Name)
        RoleInfo.AppendFormat("<b>Provider:</b> {0}<br/>", rp.ProviderName)
        RoleInfo.AppendFormat("<b>Version:</b> {0}<br/>", rp.Version)
        RoleInfo.AppendFormat("<b>Expires at:</b> {0}<br/>", rp.ExpireDate)
        RoleInfo.Append("<b>Roles:</b> ")

        Dim roles As String() = rp.GetRoles()
        Dim i As Integer = 0
        Do While i < roles.Length
            If i > 0 Then
                RoleInfo.Append(", ")
            End If
            RoleInfo.Append(roles(i))
            i += 1
        Loop

        LabelRoleInformation.Text = RoleInfo.ToString()
    End If
End Sub
```

Using the LoginView Control with Roles

In the previous chapter, you learned details about the security controls that ship with ASP.NET. One of these controls is the LoginView control. You used this control in Chapter 21 for displaying different controls for anonymous and logged-in users. The control uses templates for implementing this functionality. In Chapter 21 you used the <LoggedInTemplate> and <AnonymousTemplate> templates.

The control supports one additional template that enables you to create different views based on the roles to which a user belongs. For this purpose you need to add a RoleGroups template with <asp:RoleGroup> controls. Within every <asp:RoleGroup> control, you specify a comma-separated list of roles in the Roles attribute for which its <ContentTemplate> will be displayed, as follows:

```
<asp:LoginView runat="server" ID="MainView">
    <LoggedInTemplate>
        <h2>This is the logged in template</h2>
    </LoggedInTemplate>
    <RoleGroups>
        <asp:RoleGroup Roles="Admin">
            <ContentTemplate>
                <h2>Only Admins will see this</h2>
            </ContentTemplate>
        </asp:RoleGroup>
        <asp:RoleGroup Roles="Contributor">
            <ContentTemplate>
                <h2>This is for contributors!</h2>
            </ContentTemplate>
```

```
        </asp:RoleGroup>
        <asp:RoleGroup Roles="Reader, Designer">
            <ContentTemplate>
                <h2>This is for web designers and readers</h2>
            </ContentTemplate>
        </asp:RoleGroup>
    </RoleGroups>
</asp:LoginView>
```

The LoginView control in the previous code displays different content for logged-in users and for users assigned to specific roles. For example, for users in the Admin role the control displays the text "Only Admins will see this," while for users in the Contributor role it displays the text "This is for contributors!" Also, for users who are associated with the Reader or Designer role, it displays different content.

It's important to understand that just one of these templates will be displayed. The control simply displays the first template that fits the logged-in user. For example, if you have a user associated with the Contributor, Reader, and Designer roles, the first matching template is the <asp:RoleGroup> for contributors. The other role group will simply not be displayed. The LoggedInTemplate, for example, will be displayed only for authenticated users with no matching <asp:RoleGroup> element. As soon as a matching role group is found, the contents of the LoggedInTemplate will not be displayed.

Accessing Roles Programmatically

As is the case for the membership service introduced in Chapter 21, the roles service includes an API that allows you to perform all tasks from code. You can programmatically add new roles, read role information, and delete roles from your application. Furthermore, you can associate users with roles as well as get users associated with a specific role. You can do all this by calling methods of the Roles class.

Most of the properties included in the Roles class just map to the settings for the <roleManager> tag described in Table 23-1. Therefore, Table 23-4 includes the additional properties and the Roles class's methods that you can use for managing and accessing the roles service programmatically.

Table 23-4. *Members of the Roles Class*

Member	Description
Provider	Returns the provider currently used by your application.
Providers	Returns a collection of all the available providers on the system and for your application. It therefore returns the providers configured in machine.config and in web.config of your application.
AddUserToRole	Accepts a user name and a role name as a string parameter and adds the specified user to the specified role.
AddUserToRoles	Accepts a user name as a string parameter and role names as an array of strings and adds the specified user to all the roles specified in the role names parameter.
AddUsersToRole	Accepts a string array with user names and a string parameter that specifies a role name and adds all the specified users to the role specified in the second parameter.
AddUsersToRoles	Accepts a string array with user names and a second one with role names and adds all the users in the user names parameter to all the roles in the role names parameter.
CreateRole	Creates a new role.

(Continued)

Table 23-4. *Continued*

Member	Description
DeleteRole	Deletes an existing role.
FindUsersInRole	Accepts a string array with a list of role names and a string parameter with a list of user names. It returns every user specified in the user names array that is associated with one of the roles specified in the array of role names.
GetAllRoles	Returns a string array containing all the role names of the roles available in the role store of the configured provider.
GetRolesForUser	Returns a string array containing all the roles the specified user is associated with.
GetUsersInRole	Returns a list of users who are associated with the role passed in as a parameter.
IsUserInRole	Returns True if the specified user is a member of the specified role.
RemoveUserFromRole	Removes a single user from the specified role.
RemoveUserFromRoles	Removes the specified user from all roles specified.
RemoveUsersFromRole	Removes all the specified users from a single role.
RemoveUsersFromRoles	Removes all the specified users from all the specified roles.
RoleExists	Returns True if a role exists and otherwise False.

A good use for accessing roles programmatically is to associate users to roles automatically when they register themselves. Of course, this is useful only for specific roles. Imagine that your application supports a role called Everyone, and every single user should be a member of this role. If you register users on your own, you can enter this relationship manually. But if your application supports self-registration for Internet users, you can't do this. Therefore, you somehow have to make sure users will be associated with the Everyone role automatically.

With your first attempt, you might want to catch the CreatedUser event of the CreateUserWizard control, but that's not sufficient. Remember the existence of the ASP.NET WAT, where you can create users. In this case, catching the CreatedUser event of the control placed in your application won't help. Therefore, you have to find a different solution. You definitely need an application-wide event for this purpose, although this will not be raised by the configuration application because it is a different application. One possibility is to catch the Application_AuthenticateRequest event; within the event you verify whether the user is a member of the Everyone class. If not, you can add the user automatically. This shifts the task of adding a user automatically to the role to the point of authentication, which definitely affects every user. To do so, you just have to add a global application class to your project and add the following code.

■ Caution Of course, you should do something like this only for the lowest privileged roles such as Everyone. It's never a good idea to perform such an action for any other type of role.

```
Private Sub Application_AuthenticateRequest(ByVal sender As Object,
            ByVal e As System.EventArgs)
    If User IsNot Nothing Then
        If User.Identity.IsAuthenticated AndAlso Roles.Enabled Then
            Dim EveryoneRoleName As String =
                ConfigurationManager.AppSettings("EveryoneRoleName")
```

```
            If (Not Roles.IsUserInRole(EveryoneRoleName)) AndAlso
                    Roles.RoleExists(EveryoneRoleName) Then

                Roles.AddUserToRole(User.Identity.Name, EveryoneRoleName)
            End If
        End If
    End If
End Sub
```

The previous code reads the name of the Everyone role from the configuration file so that it is not hard-coded into the application. It then uses the Roles class to check whether the user is already associated with the role, and if not, it checks whether the role exists. If the user is not associated with the role, and the user exists in the system, it uses the Roles.AddUsersToRole method for programmatically adding the user to the Everyone role.

■ **Caution** You might want to use the User.IsInRole() in the previous code; however, this is not valid. When the application-wide Application_AuthenticateRequest is called, the RoleManagerModule itself has not been called yet. Therefore, the RolePrincipal with the association of the user and its roles has not been created yet, so a call such as User.IsInRole("Everyone") would return False. Later in your page code—for example, in a Page_Load routine—the RolePrincipal is already initialized, and the call to User.IsInRole("Everyone") will work appropriately.

Using the Roles Service with Windows Authentication

The roles service comes with a provider that integrates with Windows roles for Windows authentication: the WindowsTokenRoleProvider. This provider retrieves the Windows group membership information for the currently logged-on user and provides it in the same way for your application as you saw previously with the SqlRoleProvider. When using the WindowsTokenRoleProvider, you have to configure your application using Windows authentication and then configure the WindowsTokenRoleProvider as follows:

```
<configuration xmlns="http://schemas.microsoft.com/.NetConfiguration/v2.0">
    <system.web>
        <authentication mode="Windows"/>
        <authorization>
            <deny users="?" />
        </authorization>
        <roleManager enabled="true"
                     cacheRolesInCookie="false"
                     defaultProvider="WindowsRoles">
            <providers>
                <add name="WindowsRoles"
                     type="System.Web.Security.WindowsTokenRoleProvider" />
            </providers>
        </roleManager>
    </system.web>
</configuration>
```

With this configuration in place, the user is authenticated through Windows authentication. The RoleManagerModule automatically creates an instance of RolePrincipal and associates it with the HttpContext.Current.User property. Therefore, you can use the RolePrincipal as follows—there is no difference compared to other roles providers in terms of usage:

```
Protected Sub Page_Load(ByVal sender As Object, ByVal e As System.EventArgs)
    If (User IsNot Nothing) AndAlso (User.Identity.IsAuthenticated) Then
        Dim rp As RolePrincipal = CType(User, RolePrincipal)

        Dim Info As New StringBuilder()
        Info.AppendFormat("<h2>Welcome {0}!</h2>", User.Identity.Name)
        Info.AppendFormat("<b>Provider: </b>{0}<br/>", rp.ProviderName)
        Info.AppendFormat("<b>Version: </b>{0}<br/>", rp.Version)
        Info.AppendFormat("<b>Expiration: </b>{0}<br/>", rp.ExpireDate)
        Info.AppendFormat("<b>Roles: </b><br/>")

        Dim Roles As String() = rp.GetRoles()
        For Each role As String In Roles
            If (Not role.Equals(String.Empty)) Then
                Info.AppendFormat("-) {0}<br/>", role)
            End If
        Next

        LabelPrincipalInfo.Text = Info.ToString()
    End If
End Sub
```

You can see the result of the previous code in Figure 23-6.

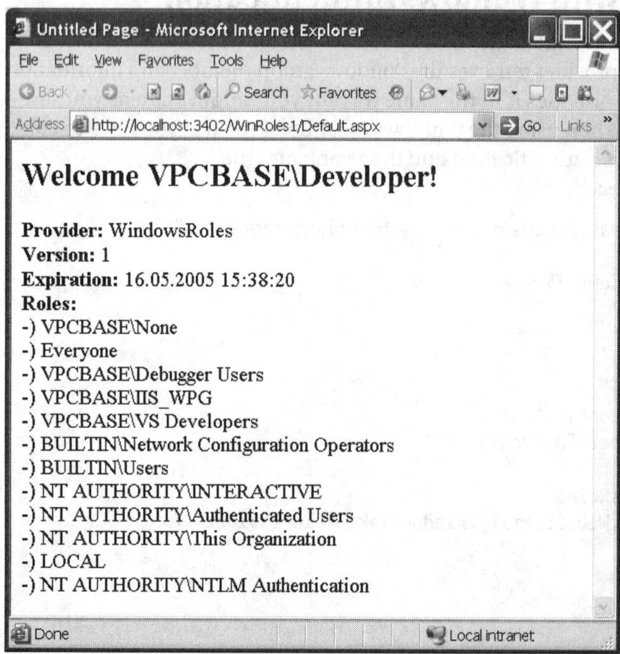

Figure 23-6. *Results of querying the RolePrincipal with Windows authentication*

The provider-based architecture enables you to use Windows authentication with Windows groups without changing the inner logic of your application. Everything works the same as with the SqlRoleProvider. The same is True for the membership service introduced in Chapter 21. When configuring another provider, you don't have to change your code; however, you should have some programmatic authorization checks with hard-coded role names in your code, because the Windows groups include the domain qualifier and the custom roles do not. To avoid this, you can add functionality to your application that allows you to associate roles with permissions in either a database or a configuration file. The way you do this depends on the requirements of your application.

We suggest not using Windows groups for authorization in your application directly except for a few of the built-in groups such as the Administrators group. In most cases, it's useful to define roles that are specific to your application. This is why:

- Windows groups other than the built-in groups depend on the name of the domain or machine on which they exist.
- In most cases, Windows groups in a domain are structured according to the organizational and network management requirements of the enterprise. Often these requirements do not map to the application requirements.
- Structuring application roles independently from the network groups makes your application more flexible and usable across multiple types of network structures.

A good example that introduces such a design is Windows SharePoint Services. SharePoint is a ready-to-use portal solution built on ASP.NET 1.*x* that can be used for free with Windows Server 2003. SharePoint includes prebuilt functionality for document libraries, meeting workspaces, and lists. You can use SharePoint for collaboratively working in teams—sharing documents, planning meetings and more.

The application defines application-specific roles that are typical for a collaborative portal solution. You can assign both Windows users and Windows groups to these roles. SharePoint by default includes the roles Administrator, Web Author, Designer, and Reader. All of these roles are optimized for performing authorization within the portal. For example, while a Web Author automatically gets permission to create new workspaces for meetings and structure contents displayed on the portal, a Reader is just able to view information on the portal. Every Windows user assigned to one of these roles, or every Windows user who is member of a Windows group assigned to one of these roles, automatically gets the appropriate permissions. Therefore, SharePoint is independent of the network structure deployed in the Windows network where it is used. You will learn more details about implementing such concepts in your own application in Chapter 26 where you will learn details about custom membership and roles providers.

Protecting Non–Web Page Resources

All the authorization and authentication systems you've about learned so far have one limitation—they work only on file types that ASP.NET handles. In other words, if a user requests a GIF file or HTML page from the same virtual directory, that user will completely bypass your authentication and authorization mechanisms. Depending on your security needs, this may be completely acceptable, simply irrelevant, or potentially dangerous.

This behavior is a result of the way IIS uses file mappings, which were first covered in Chapter 18. By default, ASP.NET is registered to deal with a small set of relevant files. These include files it needs to execute, such as web pages and web services, and files it wants to protect, such as source code files, configuration files, and project files. If you want requests for other file types to filter through the ASP.NET request processing architecture and security models, you have to map those file types to the ASP.NET ISAPI filter.

Mapping additional file types to ASP.NET gives you some extra features. For example, it gives you the ability to deny anonymous user requests for image files. However, it can also add overhead, because files that would normally be served directly now require ASP.NET to perform some work. This overhead is fairly minimal if you aren't expecting users to request non-ASP.NET file types and if you're simply using this technique to provide a higher level of security.

Furthermore, if you map a file type with the ASP.NET runtime, you have to tell the runtime how it should process this file type. You can do this by creating your own HTTP handler, as you will learn later in this chapter.

■**Note** If you're using Windows authentication, it is technically possible to force IIS to authenticate all requests, even those that are for non-ASP.NET files. To do so, you simply need to remove the Anonymous access option for the virtual directory. However, this option isn't as useful as it seems, because it doesn't allow you to enforce authentication for specific files or file types. As a result, you may find it more useful to allow anonymous access but use the techniques described in the following sections to protect specific resources.

Adding a File Type Mapping

To add a file type mapping to IIS 5, follow these steps:

1. Launch IIS Manager, and browse to the virtual directory in the tree.
2. Right-click the virtual directory, and select Properties.
3. Choose the Virtual Directory tab. Then click the Configuration button in the Application section of the Virtual Directory tab. The Application Configuration dialog box will appear, as shown in Figure 23-7.

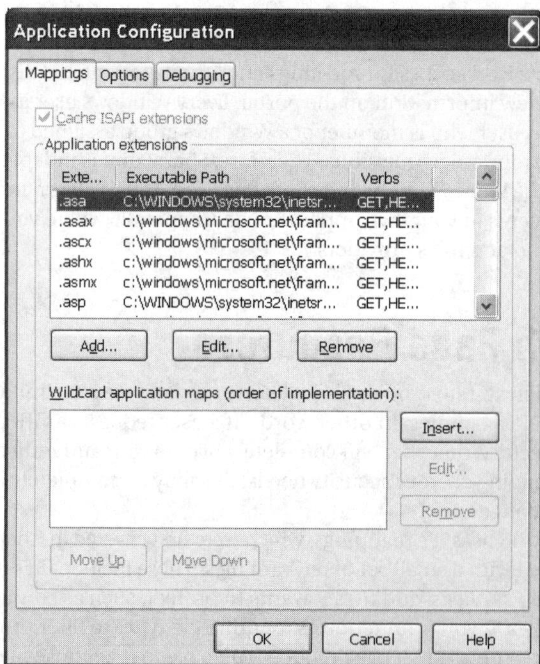

Figure 23-7. *Application mappings*

4. You need to add a new mapping for each file type you want to protect with forms authentication. This mapping will route requests for that file type to the ASP.NET ISAPI DLL. Click the Add button to create a new mapping. You'll see the dialog box shown in Figure 23-8.

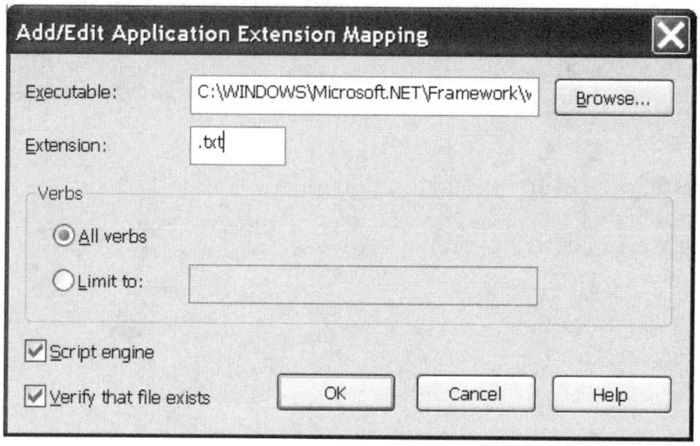

Figure 23-8. *Adding an application mapping*

5. The executable you want to use is aspnet_isapi.dll. The exact directory depends on the version of ASP.NET you have installed. In .NET 2.0, it's c:\[WinDir]\Microsoft.Net\Framework\v2.0.50215\aspnet_isapi.dll. You also need to enter the file extension you want to map. Finally, you should also specify that you want to perform this mapping for all verbs (a *verb* is a method for requesting the file from the server over HTTP, such as GET or POST).
6. Once you have taken these steps, click OK to add the extension.

Writing a Custom HTTP Handler

Every resource processed by ASP.NET is processed by an actor called an *HTTP handler*. For example, web pages with the extension .aspx are processed by a page handler, while web services with the extension .asmx are processed by a SOAP handler. All these classes are implementations of the IHttpHandler interface.

When you associate your custom file type with the ASP.NET runtime, as shown in the previous section, you have to tell ASP.NET how to process this resource. The way to do this is to write a custom HTTP handler class that implements this interface. A custom handler processing any type of binary file looks like this:

```
Namespace RolesDemo.Handlers

    Public Class GenericHandler
        Implements IHttpHandler

        Public ReadOnly Property IsReusable() As Boolean
           Implements IHttpHandler.IsReusable
           Get
                   Return True
           End Get
        End Property
```

```
        Public Sub ProcessRequest(ByVal context As HttpContext)
                Implements IHttpHandler.ProcessRequest
            Dim ret As Byte() = Nothing

            ' Open the file specified in the context
            Dim PhysicalPath As String = context.Server.MapPath(context.Request.Path)
            Using fs As New FileStream(PhysicalPath, FileMode.Open)
                ret = New Byte(fs.Length - 1) {}
                fs.Read(ret, 0, CInt(fs.Length))
            End Using

            ' If it is not Nothing, return the byte array
            If ret IsNot Nothing Then
                context.Response.BinaryWrite(ret)
            End If
        End Sub

    End Class

End Namespace
```

This handler simply determines the local physical path of the resource requested by calling Server.MapPath. Afterward it uses a FileStream for opening the resource and returning the bytes included for this resource. You have to configure this HTTP handler as well. For this purpose, you just add a <httpHandlers> section within the <system.web> section of your web.config application configuration, as follows:

```
<httpHandlers>
    <add verb="GET,POST"
         path="*.txt"
         type="RolesDemo.Handlers.GenericHandler"/>
</httpHandlers>
```

The type attribute includes the full namespace and class name of the IHttpHandler implementation, and optionally if it is placed in a different assembly, you have to specify the name of the assembly in the format "namespace.typename, assembly" within it. The additional attributes specify the HTTP verb (GET, PUT, POST, or * for all) as well as the path and file types for which the handler will be used.

PROBLEMS WITH SOME FILE TYPES

Developers have reported some problems when using forms authentication to protect Adobe Acrobat (PDF) files. It's possible that similar problems could affect other file types, especially if they require a web browser plug-in to be displayed.

With PDF files, the problems are caused by a combination of the ActiveX component that allows Internet Explorer to view Acrobat files and IIS. The problem is that PDF files are sent from the server to the client in chunks so that the user does not have to wait until the whole file has downloaded to start viewing it. For some reason, this system is adversely affected by redirections (for example, using the Response.Redirect() method). Redirecting to a PDF file causes the file to be reported as corrupted. This creates problems if you try to use forms authentication to protect PDF files. After the user logs in, the redirection back to the original PDF causes the file to be reported as corrupted or simply not displayed.

To solve this problem, you need to avoid using FormsAuthentication.RedirectFromLoginPage() or Response.Redirect() to send the user back to the PDF file. Fortunately, you simply need to write an HTML page that instructs the browser to redirect itself using the Response.AppendHeader() method. This header has the name *refresh* and takes the form 0;url=[originalUrl]. This causes the browser to immediately load the target URL (the 0 indicates a delay of 0 seconds).

Here's the code statement you need to use instead of the RedirectFromLoginPage() method:

```
Response.AppendHeader("refresh","0;url=" + url)
```

Remember that because you aren't using the RedirectFromLoginPage() method, you'll also need to create and attach the cookie before you perform the redirect.

Summary

Authorization provides an effective way to control access to resources. In this chapter, you learned how to safeguard different pages, directories, and code routines in your web application using authorization. You also saw how to use the roles service for managing and associating users with roles for simpler authorization.

In the next chapter, you'll take a look at a few advanced security techniques that you can use to extend ASP.NET authentication and authorization.

CHAPTER 24

Profiles

In previous chapters, you learned how to use a range of ASP.NET security features. Many of these features are geared to identifying individual users (authentication) and then determining what actions they should be able to perform (authorization). But you need to uniquely identify and authenticate users for another important reason—to keep track of user-specific information.

In ASP.NET 1.*x*, the only practical option to store user-specific information was to create your own data access component (a topic covered in Chapter 8). Your web page could call the methods of your data access component to retrieve the current user's data and then save any changes. As you'll see in this chapter, this approach still makes a lot of sense in many scenarios. However, ASP.NET 2.0 adds another option with a new *profiles* feature. When you use profiles, ASP.NET handles retrieving and updating user-specific data automatically by using a back-end data source (typically a database).

Conceptually, the profiles feature is a lot like creating your own database component. However, it adds some neat conveniences. Most impressively, it integrates with the ASP.NET authentication model in such a way that user information is automatically retrieved for the current user when needed and (if this information is changed) written back to the database at the end of the current request. Best of all, your web-page code can access the current user's profile data using strongly typed properties.

In this chapter, you'll learn how to use profiles, how the profiles system works, and when profiles make the most sense. You'll also learn how to extend the profiles API with a custom profiles provider.

Understanding Profiles

One of the most significant differences between profiles and other types of state management (as discussed in Chapter 6) is that profiles are designed to store information permanently by using a back-end data source such as a database. Most other types of state management are designed to maintain information for a series of requests that occur in a relatively short space of time (such as session state and caching) or in the current browser session (such as cookies and view state) or to transfer information from one page to another (such as cross-page posting and the query string). If you need to store information for the longer term in a database, profiles simply provide a convenient model that manages the retrieval and persistence of this information for you.

Before you begin using profiles, you need to assess them carefully. In the following sections, you'll learn how they stack up.

Profile Performance

The goal of ASP.NET's profiles feature is to provide a transparent way to manage user-specific information, without forcing you to write custom data access code using the ADO.NET data classes. Unfortunately, many features that seem convenient suffer from poor performance or scalability. This is particularly a concern with profiles, because they involve database access, and database access can easily become a scalability bottleneck for any distributed application.

So, do profiles suffer from scalability problems? This question has no simple answer. It all depends on how much data you need to store and how often you plan to access it. To make an informed decision, you need to know a little more about how profiles work.

Profiles plug into the page life cycle in two ways:

- The first time you access the Profile object in your code, ASP.NET retrieves the complete profile data for the current user from the database. From this point onward, you can read the profile information in your code without any database work.
- If you change any profile data, the update is deferred until the page processing is complete. At that point (after the PreRender, PreRenderComplete, and Unload events have fired for the page), the profile is written back to the database. This way, multiple changes are batched into one operation. If you don't change the profile data, no extra database work is incurred.

■ Note Profile reading and saving is implemented by a dedicated ProfileModule, which runs during each request. Chapter 5 discusses HTTP modules in more detail.

Overall, the profiles feature could result in two extra database trips for each request (in a read-write scenario) or one extra database trip (if you are simply reading profile data). The profiles feature doesn't integrate with caching, so every request that uses profile data requires a database connection.

From a performance standpoint, profiles work best when the following is true:

- You have a relatively small number of pages that access the profile data.
- You are storing small amounts of data.

They tend to work less well when the following is true:

- You have a large number of pages that need to use profile information.
- You are storing large amounts of data. This is particularly inefficient if you need to use only some of that data in a given request (because the profile model always retrieves the full block of profile data).

Of course, you can combine profiles with another type of state management. For example, imagine your website includes an order wizard that walks the user through several steps. At the beginning of this process, you could retrieve the profile information and store it in session state. You could then use the Session collection for the remainder of the process. Assuming you're using the in-process or out-of-process state server to maintain session data, this approach is more efficient because it saves you from needing to connect to the database repeatedly.

How Profiles Store Data

The most significant limitation with profiles doesn't have anything to do with performance—instead, it's a limitation of how the profiles are serialized. The default profiles provider included with ASP.NET serializes profile information into a block of data that's inserted into a single field in a database record. For example, if you serialize address information, you'll end up with something like this:

```
Marty Soren315 Southpart DriveLompocCalifornia93436U.S.A.
```

Another field indicates where each value starts and stops, using a format like this:

```
Name:S:0:11:Street:S:11:19:City:S:30:6:State:S:36:10:ZipCode:S:46:5:Country:S:51:6
```

Although this approach gives you the flexibility to store just about any type of data, it makes it more difficult to use this data in other applications. You can write custom code to parse the profile data in order to find the information you want, but depending on the amount of data and the data types you're using, this can be an extremely tedious process. And even if you do this, you're still limited in the ways you can reuse this information. For example, imagine you use profiles to store customer address information. Because of the proprietary format, it's no longer possible to generate customer lists in an application such as Microsoft Word or perform queries that filter or sort records using this profile data. (For example, you can't easily perform a query to get all the customers living in a specific city.)

This problem has two solutions:

- Use custom data access components instead of profiles to store and retrieve data in a database.
- Create a custom profiles provider that's designed to store information using your database schema.

Out of the two options, creating a custom data access component is easier, and it gives you more flexibility. You can design your data component to have any interface you want, and you can then reuse that component with other .NET applications. Currently, ASP.NET developers are more likely to use this approach because it has been around since .NET 1.0 and is well understood.

The second option is interesting because it allows your page to keep using the profile model. In fact, you could create an application that uses the standard profile serialization with the SqlProfileProvider and then switch it later to use a custom provider. To make this switch, you don't need to change any code. Instead, you simply modify the profile settings in the web.config file. As it becomes more common for websites to use profiles, custom profiles providers will become more attractive.

■ **Note** It's also important to consider the type of data that works best in a profile. As with many other types of state management, you can store any serializable types into a profile, including simple types and custom classes.

Profiles and Authentication

One significant difference between profiles and other types of state management is that profiles are stored as individual records, each of which is uniquely identified by user name. This means that profiles require you to use some sort of authentication system. It makes no difference what type of authentication system you use (Windows, forms, or a custom authentication system)—the only requirement is that authenticated users are assigned a unique user name. That user name is used to find the matching profile record in the database.

■ **Note** Later in this chapter (in the section "Anonymous Profiles"), you'll also learn how the anonymous identification feature lets you temporarily store profile information for users who haven't logged in.

Profiles vs. Custom Data Components

Profiles are a natural competitor with custom data components of the kind you saw in Chapter 8. Clearly, data components are far more flexible. They allow you not only to maintain user-specific information but also to store other types of information and perform more complex business tasks.

For example, an e-commerce website could realistically use profiles to maintain customer address information (with the limitations discussed in the previous section). However, you wouldn't use a profile to store information about previous orders. Not only is it far too much information to store efficiently, it's also awkward to manipulate.

■ **Tip** As a rule of thumb, use a profile to store only the same sort of information you'd place in the user table. Don't use it to store related data that you'd place in separate tables.

The standard profiles provider that's included with ASP.NET (named SqlProfileProvider) doesn't provide many additional features. The following list includes some features that you can easily add through a custom database component but aren't available if you're using the SqlProfileProvider. If you need any of these features, you'll need to abandon profiles and create your own data access component, or you'll need to design a custom profiles provider.

Encryption: Profile data can be serialized into a string, XML, or a binary representation. But no matter what you choose, you'll always end up storing the raw text. If you have sensitive information, your only option is to encrypt it manually before you store it, which has the undesirable result of putting encryption logic in your user interface code.

Validation: You can't restrict the type of information that can be placed in a profile. You need to use other tools (such as validator controls and custom data classes) to prevent invalid data.

Caching: If profile information is used in a page, it's always retrieved from the database. You can't keep profile information around in memory. Although you can copy profile information into the cache, it becomes more difficult to track this information.

Auditing: When you design a custom database component, you have the ability to add any logging or tracing code you want. You can use this to diagnose unexpected errors or monitor the performance of your web application. However, if you want these features with profiles, you'll need to build a custom profiles provider that has the logging code.

Now that you know the ins and outs of profiles, you're ready to try them.

Using the SqlProfileProvider

The SqlProfileProvider allows you to store profile information in a SQL Server 7.0 or later database. You can choose to create the profile tables in any database. However, you can't change any of the other database schema details, which means you're locked into specific table names, column names, and serialization formats.

From start to finish, you need to perform the following steps to use profiles:

1. Create the profile tables.
2. Configure the provider.
3. Define some profile properties.
4. Enable authentication for a portion of your website.
5. Use the profile properties in your web-page code.

You'll tackle these steps in the following sections.

Creating the Profile Tables

To create the profile tables, you use the aspnet_regsql.exe command-line utility, the same tool that allows you to generate databases for other ASP.NET features, such as SQL Server–based session state, membership, roles, database cache dependencies, and web parts personalization. You can find the aspnet_regsql.exe tool in the c:\[WinDir]\Microsoft.NET\Framework\[Version] folder.

To create the tables, views, and stored procedures required for profiles, you use the -A p command-line option. The only other detail you need to supply is the server location (-S), database name (-d), and authentication information for connecting to the database (use -U and -P to supply a password and user name, or use -E to use the current Windows account). If you leave the other server location and database name, aspnet_regsql.exe uses the default instance on the current computer and creates a database named aspnetdb.

Here's an example that creates the aspnetdb database with the default name on the current computer by logging into the database using the current Windows account:

```
aspnet_regsql.exe -A p -E
```

Table 24-1 shows the tables that aspnet_regsql.exe creates. (The rather unexciting views aren't included.)

■ **Note** Even if you don't use the default database name (aspnetdb), you should use a new, blank database that doesn't include any other custom tables. That's because aspnet_regsql.exe creates several tables for profiles (see Table 24-1), and you shouldn't risk confusing them with business data. The examples in the rest of this chapter assume you're using aspnetdb.

Table 24-1. *Database Tables Used for Profiles*

Table Name	Description
aspnet_Applications	Lists all the web applications that have records in this database. It's possible for several ASP.NET applications to use the same aspnetdb database. In this case, you have the option of separating the profile information so that it's distinct for each application (by giving each application a different application name when you register the profiles provider) or of sharing it (by giving each application the same application name).
aspnet_Profile	Stores the user-specific profile information. Each record contains the complete profile information for a single user. The PropertyNames field lists the property names, and the PropertyValuesString and PropertyValuesBinary fields list all the property data, although you'll need to go to some work if you want to parse this information for use in other non-ASP.NET programs. Each record also includes the last update date and time (LastUpdatedDate).
aspnet_SchemaVersions	Lists the supported schemas for storing profile information. In the future, this could allow new versions of ASP.NET to provide new ways of storing profile information without breaking support for old profile databases that are still in use.
aspnet_Users	Lists user names and maps them to one of the applications in aspnet_Applications. Also records the last request date and time (LastActivityDate) and whether the record was generated automatically for an anonymous user (IsAnonymous). Anonymous user support is discussed later in this chapter (in the section "Anonymous Profiles").

Figure 24-1 shows the relationships between the most important profile tables.

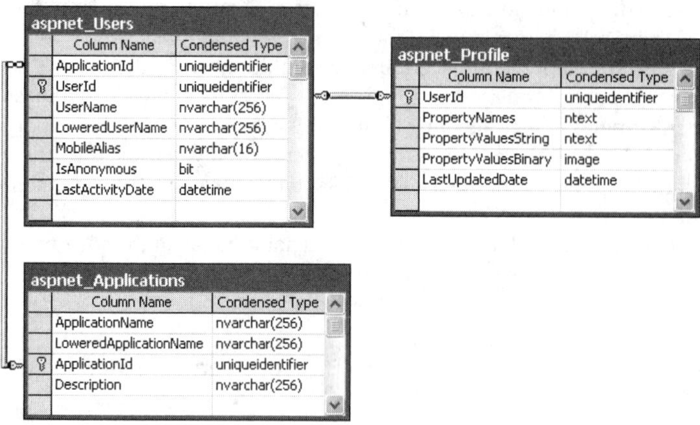

Figure 24-1. *The profile tables*

ASP.NET also creates several stored procedures that allow it to manage the information in these tables more easily. Table 24-2 lists the most noteworthy stored procedures.

Table 24-2. *Database Stored Procedures Used for Profiles*

Stored Procedure	Description
aspnet_Applications_CreateApplications	Checks whether a specific application name exists in the aspnet_Applications table and creates the record if needed.
aspnet_CheckSchemaVersion	Checks for support of a specific schema version for a specific feature (such as profiles) using the aspnet_SchemaVersions table.
aspnet_Profile_GetProfiles	Retrieves the user name and update times for all the profile records in the aspnet_Profile table for a specific web application. Doesn't return the actual profile data.
aspnet_Profile_GetProperties	Retrieves the profile information for a specific user (which you specify by user name). The information is not parsed in any way—instead, this stored procedure simply returns the underlying fields (PropertyNames, PropertyValuesString, PropertyValuesBinary).
aspnet_Profile_SetProperties	Sets the profile information for a specific user (which you specify by user name). This stored procedure requires values for the PropertyNames, PropertyValuesStrings, and PropertyValuesBinary fields. There's no way to update just a single property in a profile.
aspnet_Profile_GetNumberOfInactiveProfiles	Returns profile records that haven't been used within a time window you specify.
aspnet_Profile_DeleteInactiveProfiles	Removes profile records that haven't been used within a time window you specify.

Stored Procedure	Description
aspnet_Users_CreateUser	Creates a new record in the aspnet_Users table for a specific user. Checks whether the user exists (in which case no action is taken) and creates a GUID to use for the UserID field if none is specified.
aspnet_Users_DeleteUser	Removes a specific user record from the aspnet_Users table.

Configuring the Provider

Now that you have the database in place, you can register the SqlProfileProvider using the web.config file. First, define a connection string for the profile database. Then, use the <profile> section to remove any existing providers (with the <clear> element), and add a new instance of the System.Web.Profile.SqlProfileProvider class (with the <add> element). Here are the configuration settings you need:

```
<configuration xmlns="http://schemas.microsoft.com/.NetConfiguration/v2.0">
  <connectionStrings>
    <add name="SqlServices" connectionString=
      "Data Source=localhost;Integrated Security=SSPI;Initial Catalog=aspnetdb;" />
  </connectionStrings>

  <system.web>
    <profile defaultProvider="SqlProvider">
      <providers>
        <clear />
        <add name="SqlProvider"
          type="System.Web.Profile.SqlProfileProvider"
          connectionStringName="SqlServices"
          applicationName="TestApplication" />
      </providers>
    </profile>
    ...
  </system.web>
</configuration>
```

When you define a profiles provider, you need to supply a name (which the <profile> element can then reference as the default provider), the exact type name, a connection string, and a web application name. Use different application names to separate the profile information between web applications (or use the same application name to share it).

Defining Profile Properties

Before you can store anything in the aspnet_Profile table, you need to define it specifically. You do this by adding the <properties> element inside the <profile> section of the web.config file. Inside the <properties> element, you place one <add> tag for each user-specific piece of information you want to store. At a minimum, the <add> element supplies the name for the property, like this:

```
<profile defaultProvider="SqlProvider">
  <providers>
    ...
  </providers>
  <properties>
    <add name="FirstName"/>
    <add name="LastName"/>
```

```
  </properties>
</profile>
```

Usually, you'll also supply the data type. (If you don't, the property is treated as a string.) You can specify any serializable .NET class as the type, as shown here:

```
<add name="FirstName" type="String"/>
<add name="LastName" type="String"/>
<add name="DateOfBirth" type="DateTime"/>
```

You can set a few more property attributes to create the more advanced properties shown in Table 24-3.

Table 24-3. *Profile Property Attributes*

Attribute (for the <add> Element)	Description
name	The name of the property.
type	The fully qualified class name that represents the data type for this property. By default, this is String.
serializeAs	Indicates the format to use when serializing this value (String, Binary, Xml, or ProviderSpecific). You'll look more closely at the serialization model in the section "Profile Serialization."
readOnly	Add this attribute with a value of True to create a property that can be read but not changed. (Attempting to change the property will cause a compile-time error.) By default, this is False.
defaultValue	A default value that will be used if the profile doesn't exist or doesn't include this particular piece of information. The default value has no effect on serialization—if you set a profile property, the ProfileModule will commit the current values to the database, even if they match the default values.
allowAnonymous	A Boolean value that indicates whether this property can be used with the anonymous profiles feature discussed later in this chapter. By default, this is False.
Provider	The profiles provider that should be used to manage just this property. By default, all properties are managed using the provider specified in the <profile> element, but you can assign different properties to different providers.
Group	Allows you to organize profiles into groups of related properties. Profile groups are discussed in the section "Profile Groups."

Using Profile Properties

Because profiles are stored in a user-specific record, you need to authenticate the current user before you can read or write profile information. You can use any type of authentication system (Windows, forms, or custom). You simply need to add an authorization rule to prevent anonymous access for the page or folder where you plan to use the profile. Here's an example:

```
<configuration xmlns="http://schemas.microsoft.com/.NetConfiguration/v2.0">
  ...
  <system.web>
    <authentication mode="Windows"/>
    <authorization>
      <deny users="?"/>
    </authorization>
    ...
  </system.web>
</configuration>
```

Chapter 23 has much more information about authorization rules.

With these details in place, you're ready to access the profile information using the Profile property of the current page. When you run your application, ASP.NET creates a new class to represent the profile by deriving from System.Web.Profile.ProfileBase, which wraps a collection of profile settings. ASP.NET adds a strongly typed property to this class for each profile property you've defined in the web.config file. These strongly typed properties simply call the GetPropertyValue() and SetPropertyValue() methods of the ProfileBase base class to retrieve and set the corresponding profile values.

For example, if you've defined a string property named FirstName, you can set it in your page like this:

```
Profile.FirstName = "..."
```

Figure 24-2 presents a complete test page that allows the user to display the profile information for the current user or set new profile information.

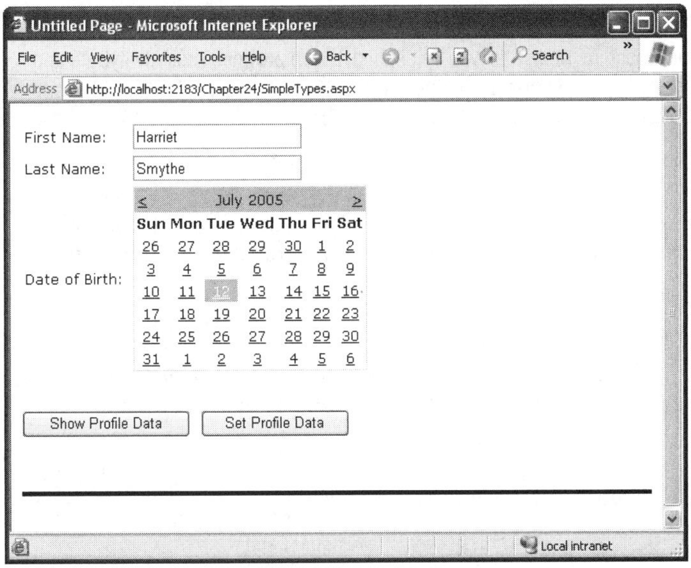

Figure 24-2. *Testing profiles*

The first time this page runs, no profile information is retrieved, and no database connection is used. However, if you click the Show Profile Data button, the profile information is retrieved and displayed on the page:

```
Protected Sub cmdShow_Click(ByVal sender As Object, ByVal e As EventArgs)
    lbl.Text = "First Name: " & Profile.FirstName _
        & "<br />" & "Last Name: " & Profile.LastName _
        & "<br />" & "Date of Birth: " & Profile.DateOfBirth.ToString()
End Sub
```

At this point, an error will occur if the profile database is missing or the connection can't be opened. Otherwise, your page will run without a hitch, and you'll see the newly retrieved profile information. Technically, the complete profile is retrieved when your code accesses the Profile.FirstName property in the first line and is used for the subsequent code statements.

Note Profile properties behave like any other class member variable. That means if you read a profile value that hasn't been set, you'll get a default initialized value (like an empty string or the number 0).

If you click the Set Profile Data button, the profile information is set based on the current control values:

```
Protected Sub cmdSet_Click(ByVal sender As Object, ByVal e As EventArgs)
    Profile.FirstName = txtFirst.Text
    Profile.LastName = txtLast.Text
    Profile.DateOfBirth = Calendar1.SelectedDate
End Sub
```

Now the profile information is committed to the database when the page request finishes. If you want to commit some or all of the information earlier (and possibly incur multiple database trips), just call the Profile.Save() method. As you can see, the profiles feature is unmatched for simplicity.

Tip The Profile object doesn't include just the properties you've defined. It also provides LastActivityDate and LastUpdatedDate properties with information drawn from the database.

Profile Serialization

Earlier, you learned how properties are serialized into a single string. For example, if you save a FirstName of Harriet and a LastName of Smythe, both values are crowded together in the PropertyValuesString field, saving space:

```
HarrietSmythe
```

The PropertyNames field gives the information you need to parse each value from the PropertyValuesString field. Here's what you'll see in the PropertyNames field in this example:

```
FirstName:S:0:7:LastName:S:7:6:
```

The colons (:) are used as delimiters. The basic format is as follows:

```
PropertyName:StringOrBinarySerialization:StartingCharacterIndex:Length:
```

Something interesting happens if you create a profile with a DateTime data type. When you look at the PropertyValuesString field, you'll see something like this:

```
<?xml version="1.0" encoding="utf-16"?><dateTime>2005-07-12T00:00:00-04:00
</dateTime>HarrietSmythe
```

Initially, it looks like the profile data is serialized as XML, but the PropertyValuesString clearly doesn't contain a valid XML document (because of the text at the end). What has actually happened is that the first piece of information, the DateTime, is serialized (by default) as XML. The following two profile properties are serialized as ordinary strings.

The ProperyNames field makes it slightly clearer:

```
DateOfBirth:S:0:87:FirstName:S:87:7:LastName:S:94:6:
```

Interestingly, you have the ability to change the serialization format of any profile property by adding the serializeAs attribute to its declaration in the web.config file. Table 24-4 lists your choices.

Table 24-4. *Serialization Options*

SerializeAs	Description
String	Converts the type to a string representation. Requires a type converter that can handle the job. (See Chapter 28 for more information about type converters.)
Xml	Converts the type to an XML representation, which is stored in a string, using the System.Xml.XmlSerialization.XmlSerializer (the same class that's used with web services).
Binary	Converts the type to a proprietary binary representation that only .NET understands using the System.Runtime.Serialization.Formatters.Binary.➥ BinaryFormatter. This is the most compact option but the least flexible. Binary data is stored in the PropertyValuesBinary field instead of the PropertyValues.
ProviderSpecific	Performs customized serialization that's implement in a custom provider.

For example, here's how you can change the serialization for the profile settings:

```
<add name="FirstName" type="String" serializeAs="Xml"/>
<add name="LastName" type="String" serializeAs="Xml"/>
<add name="DateOfBirth" type="DateTime" serializeAs="String"/>
```

Now the next time you set the profile, the serialized representation in the PropertyValuesString field will take this form:

```
7/12/2005<?xml version="1.0" encoding="utf-16"?><string>Harriet</string>
<?xml version="1.0" encoding="utf-16"?><string>Smythe</string>
```

If you use the binary serialization mode, the property value will be placed in the PropertyValuesBinary field instead of the PropertyValuesString field. The only indication of this shift is the use of the letter *B* instead of *S* in the PropertyNames field. Here's an example where the FirstName property is serialized in the PropertyValuesBinary field:

```
DateOfBirth:S:0:9:FirstName:B:0:31:LastName:S:9:64:
```

All of these serialization details raise an important question—what happens when you change profile properties or the way they are serialized? Profile properties don't have any support for versioning. However, you can add or remove properties with relatively minor consequences. For example, the ProfileModule will ignore properties that are present in the aspnet_Profile table but not defined in the web.config file. The next time you modify part of the profile, these properties will be replaced with the new profile information. Similarly, if you define a profile in the web.config file that doesn't exist in the serialized profile information, the ProfileModule will just use the default value. However, more dramatic changes—such as renaming a property, changing its data type, and so on, are likely to cause an exception when you attempt to read the profile information. Even worse, because the serialized format of the profile information is proprietary, you have no easy way to migrate existing profile data to a new profile structure.

■ Tip Not all types are serializable in all ways. For example, classes that don't provide a parameterless constructor can't be serialized in Xml mode. Classes that don't have the Serializable attribute can't be serialized in Binary mode. You'll consider this distinction when you learn how to use custom types with profiles, but for now just keep in mind that you may run across types that can be serialized only if you choose a different serialization mode.

Profile Groups

If you have a large number of profile settings, and some settings are logically related to each other, you may want to use profile groups to achieve better organization.

For example, you may have some properties that deal with user preferences and others that deal with shipping information. Here's how you could organize these profile properties using the <group> element:

```
<profile defaultProvider="SqlProvider">
  <properties>
    <group name="Preferences">
      <add name="LongDisplayMode" defaultValue="True" type="Boolean" />
      <add name="ShowSummary" defaultValue="True" type="Boolean" />
    </group>
    <group name="Address">
      <add name="Name" type="String" />
      <add name="Street" type="String" />
      <add name="City" type="String" />
      <add name="ZipCode" type="String" />
      <add name="State" type="String" />
      <add name="Country" type="String" />
    </group>
  </properties>
</profile>
```

Now you can access the properties through the group name in your code. For example, here's how you retrieve the country information:

```
lblCountry.Text = Profile.Address.Country
```

Groups are really just a poor man's substitute for a full-fledged custom structure or class. For example, you could achieve the same effect as in the previous example by declaring a custom Address class. You'd also have the ability to add other features (such as validation in the property procedures). The next section shows how.

Profiles and Custom Data Types

Using a custom class with profiles is easy. You need to begin by creating the class that wraps the information you need. In your class, you can use public member variables or full-fledged property procedures. The latter choice, though longer, is the preferred option because it ensures your class will support data binding and gives you the flexibility to add property procedure code later.

Here's a slightly abbreviated Address class that ties together the same information you saw in the previous example:

```
<Serializable()> _
Public Class Address
    Private strName As String
    Public Property Name() As String
        ...
    End Property

    Private strStreet As String
    Public Property Street() As String
        ...
    End Property
```

```
    Private strCity As String
    Public Property City() As String
        ...
    End Property

    Private strZipCode As String
    Public Property ZipCode() As String
        ...
    End Property

    Private strState As String
    Public Property State() As String
        ...
    End Property

    Private strCountry As String
    Public Property Country() As String
        ...
    End Property

    Public Sub New(ByVal strName As String, ByVal strStreet As String,
                          ByVal strCity As String, ByVal strZipCode As String,
                          ByVal strState As String, ByVal strCountry As String)
        Name = strName
        Street = strStreet
        City = strCity
        ZipCode = strZipCode
        State = strState
        Country = strCountry
    End Sub
    Public Sub New()
    End Sub
End Class
```

You can place this class in the App_Code directory (or compile it and place the DLL assembly in the Bin directory). The final step is to add a property that uses it:

```
<properties>
  <add name="Address" type="Address" />
  ...
</properties>
```

Now you can manipulate it in your code like this:

```
Profile.Address = New Address("Name", "Street", "City", "Zip", "State", "Country")
lbl.Text = "You are in " & Profile.Address.Country
```

Custom Type Serialization

You need to keep in mind a few points, depending on how you decide to serialize your custom class. By default, all custom data types use XML serialization with the XmlSerializer. This class is relatively limited in its serialization ability. It simply copies the value from every public property or member variable into a straightforward XML format like this:

```
<Address>
  <Name>...</Name>
  <Street>...</Street>
  <City>...</City>
```

```
  <ZipCode>...</ZipCode>
  <State>...</State>
  <Country>...</Country>
</Address>
```

You do have the ability to shape this XML representation by adding attributes to your class. For example, you can rename elements or tell .NET to serialize a property as an attribute instead of an element. The XML elements are described with web services in Chapter 32, because web services use the same XmlSerializer.

When deserializing your class, the XmlSerializer needs to be able to find a parameterless public constructor. In addition, none of your properties can be read-only. If you violate either of these rules, the deserialization process will fail.

If you decide to use binary serialization instead of XmlSerialization, .NET uses a completely different approach.

```
<add name="Address" type="Address" serializeAs="Binary"/>
```

In this case, the ProfileModule enlists the help of the BinaryFormatter. The BinaryFormatter can serialize the full public and private contents of any class, provided the class is decorated with the Serializable attributes. (Additionally, any class it derives from or references must also be serializable.) You can learn much more about the binary formatter in Chapter 13.

Finally, you can decide to use string serialization:

```
<add name="Address" type="Address" serializeAs="String"/>
```

In this case, you need a type converter that can translate between an instance of your class and its string representation. Chapter 28 shows you how to create type converters.

Automatic Saves

The ProfileModule that saves profile information isn't able to detect changes in complex data types (anything other than strings, simple numeric types, Boolean values, and so on). This means if your profile includes complex data types, the ProfileModule saves the profile information at the end of every request that accesses the Profile object.

This behavior obviously adds unnecessary overhead. To optimize performance when working with complex types, you have several choices. One option is to set the corresponding profile property to be read-only (if you know it never changes). Another approach is to disable the autosave behavior completely by adding the automaticSaveEnabled attribute on the <profile> element and setting it to False, as shown here:

```
<profile defaultProvider="SqlProvider" automaticSaveEnabled="False">
...
</profile>
```

If you choose this approach, it's up to you to call Profile.Save() to explicitly commit changes. Generally, this approach is the most convenient, because it's easy to spot the places in your code where you modify the profile. Just add the Profile.Save() call at the end:

```
Profile.Address = New Address(txtName.Text, txtStreet.Text,
                              txtCity.Text, txtZip.Text, txtState.Text, txtCountry.Text)
Profile.Save()
```

One final option is to handle the ProfileModule.ProfileAutoSaving event in the global.asax file. At this point, you can check to see if a save is really necessary and cancel the save if it isn't.

With this technique, the obvious problem is determining whether the automatic save should be cancelled. You could store the original profile data in memory and then compare these objects with the current objects when the ProfileAutoSaving event fires. However, this approach would be awkward and slow. A better option is to make the page keep track of whether a change has been made. If a change has been made, your code can then set a flag to indicate that the update should go ahead.

For example, consider the test page shown in Figure 24-3 that allows you to retrieve and modify address information.

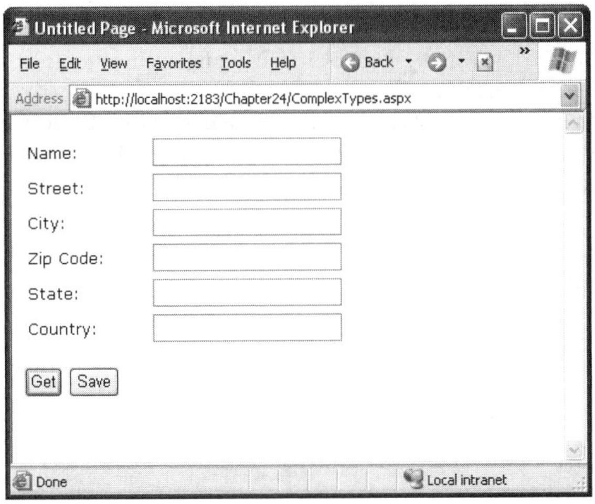

Figure 24-3. *Modifying a complex type in a profile*

All the text boxes on this page use the same event handler for their TextChanged event. This event handler indicates that a change has been made by storing a Boolean value in the context for the current request:

```
Protected Sub txt_TextChanged(ByVal sender As Object, ByVal e As EventArgs)
    Context.Items("AddressDirtyFlag") = True
End Sub
```

Keep in mind that a value stored in this way lasts only for the duration of the current request. In this example, that's not a problem because the user has only two options after making a change—rejecting the change (by clicking Get) or applying the change (by clicking Save). However, if you create a page where the user can make changes over several steps and then apply them later, you would need to go to more work to maintain the flag. Storing the flag in other locations such as session state or view state won't work, because they aren't available when the AutoSaving event fires in the global.asax file.

Finally, here's the event handler you need that allows the autosave to carry on only if a change has been made:

```
Private Sub Profile_ProfileAutoSaving(ByVal sender As Object,
                ByVal e As ProfileAutoSaveEventArgs)
    If (e.Context.Items("AddressDirtyFlag") Is Nothing)
    OrElse (CBool(e.Context.Items("AddressDirtyFlag")) = False) Then
        e.ContinueWithProfileAutoSave = False
    End If
End Sub
```

Remember, the Profile.AutoSaving event fires for any change. If you have more than one page that modifies different profile details, you might need to write conditional code that checks which page was requested and restricts or permits the save accordingly. In this situation, it's usually easier to turn off automatic saving altogether and force the page to use the Profile.Save() method.

The Profiles API

Although your page automatically gets the profile information for the current user, that doesn't prevent you from retrieving and modifying the profiles of other users. In fact, you have two tools to help you—the ProfileBase class and the ProfileManager class.

The ProfileBase object (provided by the Page.Profile property) includes a useful GetProfile() function that retrieves, by user name, the profile information for a specific user. Figure 24-4 shows an example with a Windows authenticated user.

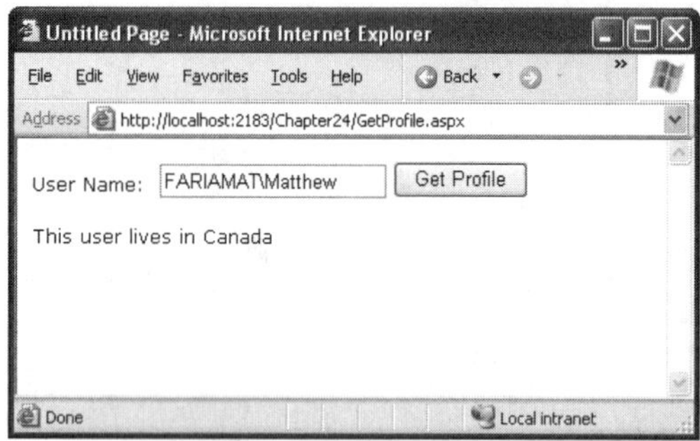

Figure 24-4. *Retrieving a profile manually*

Here's the code that gets the profile:

```
Protected Sub cmdGet_Click(ByVal sender As Object, ByVal e As EventArgs)
    Dim profile As ProfileCommon = Profile.GetProfile(txtUserName.Text)
    lbl.Text = "This user lives in " & profile.Address.Country
End Sub
```

Notice that once you have a Profile object, you can interact with it in the same way as you interact with the profile for the current user. You can even make changes. The only difference is that changes aren't saved automatically. If you want to save a change, you need to call the Save() method of the Profile object.

■ Note If you try to retrieve a profile that doesn't exist, you won't get an error. Instead, you'll simply end up with blank data. If you change and save the profile, a new profile record will be created.

If you need to perform other tasks with profiles, you can use the ProfileManager class in the System.Web.Profile namespace, which exposes the useful Shared methods described in Table 24-5. Many of these methods work with a ProfileInfo class, which provides information about a profile. The ProfileInfo includes the user name (UserName), last update and last activity dates (LastActivityDate and LastUpdateDate), the size of the profile in bytes (Size), and whether the profile is for an anonymous user (IsAnonymous). It doesn't provide the actual profile values.

Table 24-5. *ProfileManager Methods*

Method	Description
DeleteProfile()	Deletes the profile for the user you specify.
DeleteProfiles()	Deletes multiple profiles at once. You supply an array of user names.
DeleteInactiveProfiles()	Deletes profiles that haven't been used since a time you specify. You also must supply a value from the ProfileAuthenticationOption enumeration to indicate what type of profiles you want to remove (All, Anonymous, or Authenticated).
GetNumberOfProfiles()	Returns the number of profile records in the data source.
GetNumberOfInactiveProfiles()	Returns the number of profiles that haven't been used since the time you specify.
GetAllInactiveProfiles()	Retrieves profile information for profiles that haven't been used since the time you specify. The profiles are returned as ProfileInfo objects.
GetAllProfiles()	Retrieves all the profile data from the data source as a collection of ProfileInfo objects. You can choose what type of profiles you want to retrieve (All, Anonymous, or Authenticated). You can also use an overloaded version of this method that uses paging and retrieves only a portion of the full set of records based on the starting index and page size you request.
FindProfilesByUserName()	Retrieves a collection of ProfileInfo objects that match a specific user name. The SqlProfileProvider uses a LIKE clause when it attempts to match user names. That means you can use wildcards such as the % symbol. For example, if you search for the user name user%, you'll return values like user1, user2, user_guest, and so on. You can use an overloaded version of this method that uses paging.
FindInactiveProfilesByUserName()	Retrieves profile information for profiles that haven't been used since the time you specify. You can also filter out certain types of profiles (All, Anonymous, or Authenticated) or look for a specific user name (with wildcard matching). The return value is a collection of ProfileInfo objects.

For example, if you want to remove the profile for the current user, you need only a single line of code:

```
ProfileManager.DeleteProfile(User.Identity.Name)
```

And if you want to display the full list of users in a web page (not including anonymous users), just add a GridView with AutoGenerateColumns set to True and use this code:

```
Protected Sub Page_Load(ByVal sender As Object, ByVal e As EventArgs)
    GridView1.DataSource =
        ProfileManager.GetAllProfiles(ProfileAuthenticationOption.Authenticated)
    GridView1.DataBind()
End Sub
```

Figure 24-5 shows the result.

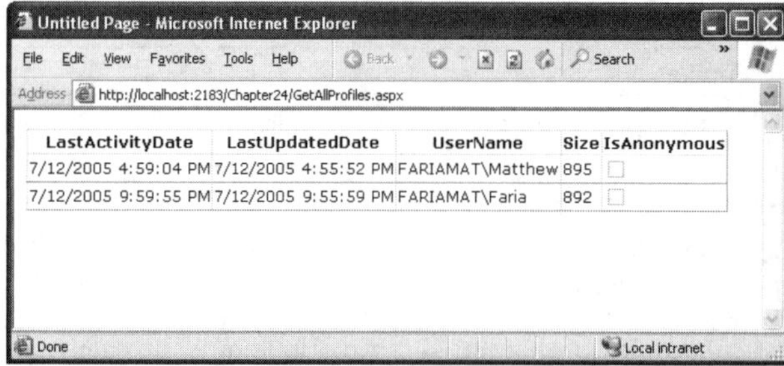

Figure 24-5. *Retrieving information about all the profiles in the data source*

Anonymous Profiles

So far, all the examples have assumed that the user is authenticated before any profile information is accessed or stored. Usually, this is the case. However, sometimes it's useful to create a temporary profile for a new, unknown user. For example, most e-commerce websites allow new users to begin adding items to a shopping cart before registering. If you want to provide this type of behavior and you choose to store shopping cart items in a profile, you'll need some way to uniquely identify anonymous users.

ASP.NET provides an anonymous identification feature that fills this gap. The basic idea is that the anonymous identification feature automatically generates a random identifier for any anonymous user. This random identifier stores the profile information in the database, even though no user ID is available. The user ID is tracked on the client side using a cookie (or in the URL, if you've enable cookieless mode). Once this cookie disappears (for example, if the anonymous user closes and reopens the browser), the anonymous session is lost and a new anonymous session is created.

Anonymous identification has the potential to leave a lot of abandoned profiles, which wastes space in the database. For that reason, anonymous identification is disabled by default. However, you can enable it using the <anonymousIdentification> element in the web.config file, as shown here:

```
<configuration xmlns="http://schemas.microsoft.com/.NetConfiguration/v2.0">
  ...
  <system.web>
    <anonymousIdentification enabled="True" />
    ...
  </system.web>
</configuration>
```

You also need to flag each profile property that will be retained for anonymous users by adding the allowAnonymous attribute and setting it to True. This allows you to store just some basic information and restrict larger objects to authenticated users.

```
<properties>
  <add name="Address" type="Address" allowAnonymous="True" />
  ...
</properties>
```

The <anonymousIdentification> element also supports numerous optional attributes that let you set the cookie name and timeout, specify whether the cookie will be issued only over an SSL connection, control whether cookie protection (validation and encryption) is used to prevent tampering and eavesdropping, and configure support for cookieless ID tracking. Here's an example:

```
<anonymousIdentification enabled="true" cookieName=".ASPXANONYMOUS"
  cookieTimeout="43200" cookiePath="/" cookieRequireSSL="False"
  cookieSlidingExpiration="True" cookieProtection="All"
  cookieless="UseCookies"/>
```

For more information, refer to the configuration settings for forms authentication (Chapter 20) and role management (Chapter 23), which use the same settings.

Tip If you use anonymous identification, it's a good idea to delete old anonymous sessions regularly using the aspnet_Profile_DeleteInactiveProfiles stored procedure, which you can run at scheduled intervals using the SQL Server Agent. You can also delete old profiles using the ProfileManager class, as described in the previous section.

Migrating Anonymous Profiles

A challenge that occurs with anonymous profiles is what to do with the profile information when a previously anonymous user logs in. For example, in an e-commerce website a user might select several items and then register or log in to complete the transaction. At this point, you need to make sure the shopping cart information is copied from the anonymous user's profile to the appropriate authenticated (user) profile.

Fortunately, ASP.NET provides a solution through the ProfileModule.MigrateAnonymous event. This event (which can be handled in the global.asax file) fires whenever an anonymous identifier is available (either as a cookie or in the URL if you're using cookieless mode) *and* the current user is authenticated.

The basic technique when handling the MigrateAnonymous event is to load the profile for the anonymous user by calling Profile.GetProfile() and passing in the anonymous ID, which is provided to your event handler through the ProfileMigrateEventArgs.

Once you've loaded this data, you can then transfer the settings to the new profile manually. You can choose to transfer as few or as many settings as you want, and you can perform any other processing that's required. Finally, your code should remove the anonymous profile data from the database and clear the anonymous identifier so the MigrateAnonymous event won't fire again.

```
Private Sub Profile_MigrateAnonymous(ByVal sender As Object,
       ByVal pe As ProfileMigrateEventArgs)
    ' Get the anonymous profile.
    Dim anonProfile As ProfileCommon = Profile.GetProfile(pe.AnonymousID)

    ' Copy information to the authenticated profile
    ' (but only if there's information there).
    If (anonProfile.Address.Name IsNot Nothing)
         OrElse (anonProfile.Address.Name <> "") Then
        Profile.Address = anonProfile.Address
    End If

    ' Delete the anonymous profile from the database.
    ' (You could decide to skip this step to increase performance
    '  if you have a dedicated job scheduled on the database server
    '  to remove old anonymous profiles.)
    System.Web.Profile.ProfileManager.DeleteProfile(pe.AnonymousID)

    ' Remove the anonymous identifier.
    AnonymousIdentificationModule.ClearAnonymousIdentifier()
End Sub
```

You need to handle this task with some caution. If you've enabled anonymous identification, every time a user logs in, the MigrateAnonymous event fires, even if the user hasn't entered any information into the anonymous profile. That's a problem, because if you're not careful, you could easily overwrite the real (saved) profile for the user with the blank anonymous profile. The problem is further complicated because complex types (such as the Address object) are created automatically by the

ProfileModule, so you can't just check for a null reference to determine whether the user has anonymous address information.

In the previous example, the code tests for a missing Name property in the Address object. If this information isn't a part of the anonymous profile, no information is migrated. A more sophisticated example might test for individual properties separately or might migrate an anonymous profile only if the information in the user profile is missing or out-of-date.

Building a Shopping Cart

Now that you've learned how to use profiles, it's worth considering an end-to-end example that uses the GridView and the profiles feature to build a basic shopping cart.

Shopping carts are a hallmark of e-commerce websites. They allow users to select a batch of items for an upcoming purchase. Using profiles, you can store shopping cart information in a user's profile so that it's stored permanently for repeat visits. When the user makes the purchase, you can remove the profile information and use a database component to commit the corresponding order records.

In the following sections, you'll go through the steps needed to build a complete shopping cart framework that revolves around a single test page (see Figure 24-6). This test pages uses two data-bound controls—one to show the product catalog and one to show the shopping cart items. To add items from the catalog, the user must click a link in the product catalog.

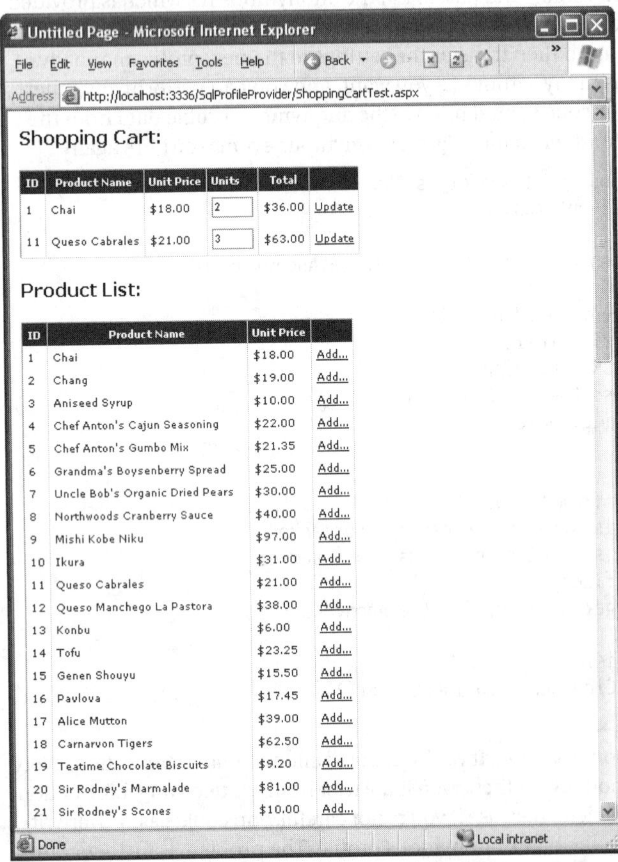

Figure 24-6. *A shopping cart*

■ **Note** You can also use the following model if you want to store shopping cart information in session state. You still set up the grid controls in the same way and use the same shopping cart classes. The only difference is that the shopping cart is stored temporarily in the Session collection instead of in the database through the Page.Profile property.

The Shopping Cart Classes

In theory, you could use the DataRow and DataTable objects to represent a shopping cart. However, because the shopping cart information doesn't directly correspond to a table in the database, the process would be awkward and counterintuitive. A better approach is to design your own classes to represent the shopping cart and its items.

The first ingredient you need is a class to represent individual shopping cart items. This class needs to track the product information, along with the number of units the user wants to order. Here's a ShoppingCartItem class that fills this role:

```
<Serializable()> _
Public Class ShoppingCartItem
    Private m_productID As Integer
    Public ReadOnly Property ProductID() As Integer
        Get
                Return m_productID
        End Get
    End Property

    Private m_productName As String
    Public ReadOnly Property ProductName() As String
        Get
                Return m_productName
        End Get
    End Property

    Private m_unitPrice As Decimal
    Public ReadOnly Property UnitPrice() As Decimal
        Get
                Return m_unitPrice
        End Get
    End Property

    Private m_units As Integer
    Public Property Units() As Integer
        Get
                Return m_units
        End Get
        Set
                m_units = Value
        End Set
    End Property

    Public ReadOnly Property Total() As Decimal
        Get
                Return Units * UnitPrice
        End Get
    End Property
```

```
    Public Sub New(ByVal p_productID As Integer, ByVal p_productName As String,
          ByVal p_unitPrice As Decimal, ByVal p_units As Integer)
        Me.m_productID = p_productID
        Me.m_productName = p_productName
        Me.m_unitPrice = p_unitPrice
        Me.m_units = p_units
    End Sub
End Class
```

You'll notice a few interesting details about this class. First, its properties are almost all read-only. None of the shopping cart item information can be changed once the item is created, with the exception of the number of desired units. The second interesting detail is the Total property. This property doesn't map to a private member variable—instead it's calculated based on the unit price and the number of desired units. It's the class equivalent of a calculated column. This property is a great help when you bind a ShoppingCartItem to a control, because it allows you to easily show the total price of each line.

■ **Note** When designing a class that you intend to use with a data-bound control, you *must* use property procedures rather than public member variables. For example, if you implemented the UnitPrice information using a public member variable instead of a property procedure, you wouldn't be able to bind to it and display that information in a data-bound control.

Finally, note that the ShoppingCartItem class is decorated with the Serializable attribute but doesn't include a default parameterless constructor. This is because it's intended for use with binary serialization, as discussed earlier.

Of course, a shopping cart is a *collection* of zero or more shopping cart items. To create the shopping cart, you can use a standard .NET collection class. However, it's often useful to create your own strongly typed collection class. This way, you can add your own helper methods and control the serialization process.

Creating a strongly typed collection is easy because you can derive from the System.Collections.CollectionBase class to acquire the basic functionality you need. Essentially, the CollectionBase wraps an ordinary ArrayList, which is exposed through the protected variable List. However, this ArrayList isn't directly accessible to other classes. Instead, your custom class must add methods such as Add(), Remove(), Insert(), and so on, which allow other classes to use the collection. Here's the trick—even though the internal ArrayList isn't type-safe, the collection methods that you create are, which prevents errors and ensures that the collection contains the correct type of object.

Here's a strongly typed ShoppingCart collection that accepts only ShoppingCartItem instances:

```
<Serializable()> _
Public Class ShoppingCart : Inherits CollectionBase
    Public Default Property Item(ByVal index As Integer) As ShoppingCartItem
        Get
                Return(CType(List(index), ShoppingCartItem))
        End Get
        Set
                List(index) = Value
        End Set
    End Property

    Public Function Add(ByVal value As ShoppingCartItem) As Integer
        Return(List.Add(value))
    End Function
```

```
    Public Function IndexOf(ByVal value As ShoppingCartItem) As Integer
        Return(List.IndexOf(value))
    End Function

    Public Sub Insert(ByVal index As Integer, ByVal value As ShoppingCartItem)
        List.Insert(index, value)
    End Sub

    Public Sub Remove(ByVal value As ShoppingCartItem)
        List.Remove(value)
    End Sub

    Public Function Contains(ByVal value As ShoppingCartItem) As Boolean
        Return(List.Contains(value))
    End Function
End Class
```

Notice that the ShoppingCart doesn't implement ICollection, which is a requirement for data binding. It doesn't need to, because the CollectionBase class it inherits from already does.

At this point, you're ready to use the ShoppingCart and ShoppingCartItem classes in an ASP.NET web page. To make them available, simply add the following profile property:

```
<add name="Cart" type="ShoppingCart" serializeAs="Binary"/>
```

The Test Page

The next step is to create and configure the GridView controls for showing the product and shopping cart information. This example has two separate GridView controls—one for showing the product catalog and another for showing the current contents of the shopping cart. The GridView for the product information has a fairly straightforward structure. It uses several BoundField tags that display fields from the bound table (with the correct numeric formatting) and one ButtonField that allows the user to select the row. The ButtonField is displayed as a hyperlink with the text *Add*.

Here are the definitions for all the GridView columns used to display the product catalog:

```
<Columns>
  <asp:BoundField DataField="ProductID" HeaderText="ID"></asp:BoundField>
  <asp:BoundField DataField="ProductName"
   HeaderText="Product Name"></asp:BoundField>
  <asp:BoundField DataField="UnitPrice" HeaderText="Unit Price"
      DataFormatString="{0:C}"></asp:BoundField>
  <asp:CommandField ShowSelectButton="True" ButtonType="Link" SelectText="Add..." />
</Columns>
```

When this page first loads, it queries the database component to get the full list of products. Then it binds the product list to the GridView. The code that performs this work is as follows:

```
Private db As New NorthwindDB()
Private ds As DataSet

Protected Sub Page_Load(ByVal sender As Object, ByVal e As System.EventArgs)
    ' Update the product list.
    ds = db.GetCategoriesProductsDataSet()
    gridProducts.DataSource = ds.Tables("Products")
    gridProducts.DataBind()
End Sub
```

No matter what other events happen, the shopping cart is bound just before the page is rendered. That's because the shopping cart may be modified as a result of other event handlers. By binding it at the end of the page life cycle, you ensure that the GridView shows the most up-to-date information.

```
Protected Sub Page_PreRender(ByVal sender As Object, ByVal e As System.EventArgs)
    ' Show the shopping cart in the grid.
    gridCart.DataSource = Profile.Cart
    gridCart.DataBind()
End Sub
```

So, what can happen in the meantime between the Page.Load and Page.PreRender events? One possibility is that the user clicks one of the Add links in the GridView of the product catalog. In this case, the SelectedIndexChanged event fires, and a series of steps take place.

First, the code retrieves the DataRow for the selected product using the in-memory copy of the DataSet:

```
Protected Sub gridProducts_SelectedIndexChanged(ByVal sender As Object,
        ByVal e As System.EventArgs)
    ' Get the full record for the one selected row.
    Dim rows As DataRow() = ds.Tables("Products").Select("ProductID=" &
        gridProducts.SelectedDataKey.Values("ProductID").ToString())
    Dim row As DataRow = rows(0)
 ...
```

Next, the code searches to see if this product is already in the cart. If it is, the Units property of the corresponding ShoppingCartItem is incremented by 1, as shown here:

```
...
' Search to see whether an item of this type is already in the cart.
Dim inCart As Boolean = False
For Each item As ShoppingCartItem In Profile.Cart
    ' Increment the number count.
    If item.ProductID = CInt(row("ProductID")) Then
        item.Units += 1
        inCart = True
        Exit For
    End If
Next item
...
```

If the item isn't in the cart, a new ShoppingCartItem object is created and added to the collection, as follows:

```
...
' If the item isn't in the cart, add it.
If (Not inCart) Then
    Dim item As New ShoppingCartItem(CInt(row("ProductID")),
        CStr(row("ProductName")), CDec(row("UnitPrice")), 1)
    Profile.Cart.Add(item)
End If
...
```

Finally, the selected index is cleared so that the product row doesn't become highlighted. (You could also set the selection style so that the selected row doesn't appear to the user.) The act of selection is now complete.

```
    ...
' Don't keep the item selected in the product list.
    gridProducts.SelectedIndex = -1
End Sub
```

Notice that the GridView that displays the shopping cart information binds directly to the ShoppingCart collection. Creating this GridView is fairly straightforward. You can use BoundField tags in the same way that you would with a table, except now the DataField identifies the name of one of the properties in the ShoppingCartItem class. Here are the bound columns used in the GridView for the shopping cart details:

```
<asp:BoundField DataField="ProductID" HeaderText="ID"></asp:BoundField>
<asp:BoundField DataField="ProductName" HeaderText="Product Name">
  </asp:BoundField>
<asp:BoundField DataField="UnitPrice" HeaderText="Unit Price"
  DataFormatString="{0:C}"></asp:BoundField>
<asp:BoundField DataField="Total" HeaderText="Total"
  DataFormatString="{0:C}"></asp:BoundField>
```

The column for displaying the Units property is slightly different. It uses a TemplateField. The template uses a text box, which displays the number of desired units, and allows the user to edit this number.

```
<asp:TemplateField HeaderText="Units">
  <HeaderStyle Width="5px"></HeaderStyle>
  <ItemTemplate>
    <asp:TextBox runat="server" Font-Size="XX-Small" Width="31px"
      Text='<%# DataBinder.Eval(Container, "DataItem.Units") %>'>
    </asp:TextBox>
  </ItemTemplate>
</asp:TemplateField>
```

If a user does decide to change the number of units for an item, the change must be committed by clicking an Update link in another column:

```
<asp:CommandField ShowSelectButton="True" SelectText="Update" />
```

For simplicity, this link is also treated as a select command. However, with slightly more code you could use the RowCommand event instead (as discussed in Chapter 10).

When the user clicks the Update link, the GridView.RowCommand event fires. At this point, the code finds the corresponding ShoppingCartItem instance and updates the Units property (or removes the item entirely if the count has reached 0). Here's the code that performs this task:

```
Protected Sub gridCart_SelectedIndexChanged(ByVal sender As Object,
    ByVal e As EventArgs)
    ' The first control in a template column is always a blank LiteralControl.
    ' The text box is the second control.
    Dim txt As TextBox =
        CType(gridCart.Rows(gridCart.SelectedIndex).Cells(3).Controls(1), TextBox)
    Try
        ' Update the appropriate cart item.
        Dim newCount As Integer = Integer.Parse(txt.Text)
        If newCount > 0 Then
            Profile.Cart(gridCart.SelectedIndex).Units = newCount
        ElseIf newCount = 0 Then
            Profile.Cart.RemoveAt(gridCart.SelectedIndex)
        End If
    Catch
        ' Ignore invalid (nonnumeric) entries.
    End Try
    gridCart.SelectedIndex = -1
End Sub
```

Invalid entries are simply ignored using an exception handler. Another option is to use a CompareValidator validation control to prevent the user from entering negative numbers or text.

As written, this example is fairly powerful, and it's a reasonable starting point for creating a shopping cart for a highly professional application. All you need to do is implement the checkout logic, which would commit the order to the database and clear the Profile.Cart by replacing it with a new, empty shopping cart.

Multiple Selection

Another refinement you might want to add to this example is to allow the product list to support multiple selection (similar to the way files are selected in a Hotmail inbox). The basic approach is to create a template column that includes a CheckBox control. When the user clicks another button (such as submit), you can loop over all the items in the GridView and check the state of the check box in each item. If the state is checked, you would then add that item to the shopping cart.

Custom Profiles Providers

The profile model plugs neatly into ASP.NET web pages. However, it isn't very configurable. You might decide you need to create a custom profiles provider for a number of reasons:

- You need to store profile information in a data source other than a SQL Server database, such as an Oracle database.
- You need your profile data to be available to other applications. Parsing the information in the PropertyValuesString and PropertyValuesBinary fields is tedious, error-prone, and inflexible. If you need to use this information in other queries or applications, you need to store your profile information in a database table that's split into distinct fields.
- You need to implement additional logic when storing or retrieving profile data. For example, you could apply validation, caching, logging, encryption, or compression. (In some cases, you can get these features by simply extending the ProfileBase class that wraps profile settings, rather than creating an entirely new ProfileProvider.)

In the following sections, you'll focus on the second scenario. You'll see how to build a custom provider that keeps its property values in separate fields and can be adapted to fit any existing database.

The Custom Profiles Provider Classes

To implement a profiles provider, you need to create a class that derives from the ProfileProvider abstract class from the System.Web.Profile namespace. The ProfileProvider abstract class itself inherits the SettingsProvider abstract class from the System.Configuration namespace, which inherits from the ProviderBase abstract class from the System.Configuration.Provider namespace. As a result, you also need to implement members from the SettingsProvider and ProviderBase classes. Altogether, more than a dozen members must be implemented before you can compile your custom profiles provider.

However, these methods aren't all of equal importance. For example, you can create a basic provider that saves and retrieves profile information by implementing two or three of these methods. Many of the other methods support functionality that's exposed by the ProfileManager class, such as the ability to delete profiles or find inactive profiles.

In the following example, you'll consider a simple profiles provider that includes the core logic that's needed to plug into a page but doesn't support most other parts of the profiles API. Methods that aren't supported simply throw a NotImplementedException, like this:

```
Public Overrides Function DeleteProfiles(ByVal usernames As String()) As Integer
    Throw New Exception("The method or operation is not implemented.")
End Function
```

All of these methods are conceptually easy to implement (all you need is some basic ADO.NET code). However, properly coding each method requires a fairly substantial amount of code.

Table 24-6 lists all the overridable properties and methods and indicates which class defines them. Those that are implemented in the following example are marked with an asterisk. To be considered truly complete, a provider must implement all of these members.

Table 24-6. *Abstract Methods for Profiles Providers*

Class	Member	Description
*ProviderBase	Name	A read-only property that returns the name (set in the web.config file) for the current provider.
*ProviderBase	Initialize()	Gets the configuration element from the web.config file that initializes this provider. Gives you the chance to read custom settings and store the information in member variables.
SettingsProvider	ApplicationName	A name (set in the web.config file) that allows you to separate the users of different applications that are stored in the same database.
*SettingsProvider	GetPropertyValues()	Retrieves the profile information for a single user. This method is called automatically when a web page accesses the Page.Profile property. This method is provided with a list of all the profile properties that are defined in the application. You must return a value for each of these properties.
*SettingsProvider	SetPropertyValues()	Updates the profile information for a single user. This method is called automatically at the end of a request when profile information is changed. This method is provided with a list of all the profile properties that are defined in the application and their current values.
ProfileProvider	DeleteProfiles()	Deletes one or more user profile records from the database. This method has two overloads, which take different parameters.
ProfileProvider	DeleteInactiveProfiles()	Similar to DeleteProfiles() but looks for profiles that haven't been accessed since a specific time. To support this method, you must keep track of when profiles are accessed or updated in your database.

(Continued)

Table 24-6. *Continued*

Class	Member	Description
ProfileProvider	GetAllProfiles()	Returns information about a group of profile records. This method must support paging so that it returns only a subset of the total records. Refer to the aspnet_Profile_GetProfiles stored procedure that aspnet_regsql creates for a sample paging implementation.
ProfileProvider	GetAllInactiveProfiles()	Similar to GetAllProfiles() but looks for profiles that haven't been accessed since a specific time. To support this method, you must keep track of when profiles are accessed or updated in your database.
ProfileProvider	FindProfilesByUserName()	Retrieves profile information based on the user name of one or more (if you support wildcard matching) users. The actual profile information isn't returned—only some standard information such as the last activity date is returned.
ProfileProvider	FindInactiveProfilesByUserName()	Similar to FindProfilesByUserName () but looks for profiles that haven't been accessed since a specific time.
ProfileProvider	GetNumberOfInactiveProfiles()	Counts the number of profiles that haven't been accessed since a specific time.

* *Implemented in the following example*

Designing the FactoredProfileProvider

The FactoredProfileProvider stores property values in a series of fields in a database table, rather than in a single block. This makes the values easier to use in different applications and with different queries. Essentially, the FactoredProfileProvider unlocks the profiles table so that it's no longer using a proprietary schema. The only disadvantage to this approach is that it's no longer possible to change the profile or add information to it without modifying the schema of your database.

When implementing a custom profiles provider, you need to determine how generic you want your solution to be. For example, if you decide to implement compression using the classes in the System.IO.Compression namespace (see Chapter 13) or encryption with the classes in the System.Security.Cryptography namespace (see Chapter 25), you'll also need to decide whether you want to create an all-purpose solution or a more limited provider that's fine-tuned for your specific scenario.

Similarly, the FactoredProfileProvider has two possible designs:

- You can create a provider that's designed specifically for your database schema.
- You can create a generic provider that can work with any database table by making certain assumptions. For example, you can simply assume that profile properties match field names.

The first approach is the most straightforward and in some cases will be the easiest to secure and optimize. However, it also limits your ability to reuse your provider or change your database schema later. The second approach is the one you'll see in the following example.

The basic idea behind the FactoredProfileProvider is that it will perform its two key tasks (retrieving and updating profile information) through two stored procedures. That gives you a powerful layer of flexibility, because you can modify the stored procedures at any time to use different tables, field names, data types, and even serialization choices.

The critical detail in this example is that the web application chooses which stored procedures to use by using the provider declaration in the web.config file. Here's an example of how you might use the FactoredProfileProvider in an application:

```
<profile defaultProvider="FactoredProfileProvider">
  <providers >
    <clear />
    <add name="FactoredProfileProvider"
         type="FactoredProfileProvider"
         connectionStringName="SqlServices"
         updateUserProcedure="Users_Update"
         getUserProcedure="Users_GetByUserName"/>
  </providers>
  <properties>...</properties>
</profile>
```

Along with the expected attributes (name, type, and connectionStringName), the <add> tag includes two new attributes: updateUserProcedure and getUserProcedure. The updateUserProcedure indicates the name of the stored procedure that's used to insert and update profile information. The getUserProcedure indicates the name of the stored procedure that's used to retrieve profile information.

This design allows you to use the FactoredProfileProvider with any database table. But what about mapping the properties to the appropriate columns? You could take a variety of approaches to make this possible, but the FactoredProfileProvider takes a convenient shortcut. When updating, it simply assumes that every profile property you define corresponds to the name of a stored procedure parameter. So, if you define the following properties:

```
<properties>
  <add name="FirstName"/>
  <add name="LastName"/>
</properties>
```

the FactoredProfileProvider will call the update stored procedure you've specified and pass the value in for parameters named @FirstName and @LastName. When querying profile information, the FactoredProfileProvider will look for the field names FirstName and LastName.

This is similar to the design used by the SqlDataSource and ObjectDataSource controls. Although it forces you to follow certain conventions in your two stored procedures, it imposes no other restrictions on the rest of your database. For example, the update stored procedure can insert the information into any series of fields in any table, and the stored procedure used to query profile information can use aliases or joins to construct the expected table.

Coding the FactoredProfileProvider

The first step of creating the FactoredProfileProvider is to derive the class from ProfileProvider:

```
Public Class FactoredProfileProvider
    Inherits ProfileProvider

    Private ...

End Class
```

All the methods that you choose not to implement (see Table 24-6) are simply filled with a single line of code that throws an exception.

■ **Tip** One quick way to fill all the methods with exception-throwing logic is to right-click ProfileProvider in the class declaration and choose Refactor ➤ Implement Abstract Class.

Initialization

The FactoredProfileProvider needs to keep track of a few basic details, such as the provider name, the connection string, and the two stored procedures. These details are all exposed through read-only properties, as shown here:

```
Private strName As String
Public Overrides ReadOnly Property Name() As String
    Get
        Return strName
    End Get
End Property

Private strConnectionString As String
Public ReadOnly Property ConnectionString() As String
    Get
        Return strConnectionString
    End Get
End Property

Private updateProcedure As String
Public ReadOnly Property UpdateUserProcedure() As String
    Get
        Return updateProcedure
    End Get
End Property

Private getProcedure As String
Public ReadOnly Property GetUserProcedure() As String
    Get
            Return getProcedure
    End Get
End Property
```

To set these details, you need to override the Initialize() method. At this point, you receive a collection that contains all the attributes of the <add> element that registered the provider. If any of the necessary details are absent, you should raise an exception.

```
Public Overrides Sub Initialize(ByVal name As String,
        ByVal config As NameValueCollection)
    Me.name = name

    ' Initialize values from web.config.
    Dim cString As String
    Dim cStringSettings As ConnectionStringSettings =
      ConfigurationManager.ConnectionStrings(config("connectionStringName"))
    If (cStringSettings Is Nothing)
    OrElse cStringSettings.ConnectionString.Trim() = String.Empty Then

        Throw New HttpException("You must supply a connection string.")
    Else
        cString = cStringSettings.ConnectionString
    End If
```

```
    updateProcedure = config("updateUserProcedure")
    If updateProcedure.Trim() = String.Empty Then
      Throw New HttpException("You must specify a stored procedure for updates.")
    End If

    getProcedure = config("getUserProcedure")
    If getProcedure.Trim() = String.Empty Then
      Throw New HttpException(
          "You must specify a stored procedure to use for retrieving user records.")
    End If
End Sub
```

Reading Profile Information

When the web page accesses any profile information, ASP.NET calls the GetPropertyValues() method. It passes in two parameters—a SettingsContext object that includes information such as the current user name and a SettingsPropertyCollection object that contains a collection of all the profile properties that the application has defined (and expects to be able to access). You need to return a SettingsPropertyValueCollection with the corresponding values.

Before doing anything, you should create a new SettingsPropertyValueCollection:

```
Public Overrides Function GetPropertyValues(ByVal context As SettingsContext,
      ByVal properties As SettingsPropertyCollection)
      As SettingsPropertyValueCollection
    ' This collection will store the retrieved values.
    Dim values As New SettingsPropertyValueCollection()
    ...
```

Now create the ADO.NET objects that you need in order to execute the stored procedure that retrieves the profile information. The connection string and stored procedure name are specified through the configuration attributes that were retrieved in the Initialize() method.

```
...
Dim con As New SqlConnection(connectionString)
Dim cmd As New SqlCommand(getProcedure, con)
cmd.CommandType = CommandType.StoredProcedure
...
```

The only nonconfigurable assumption in this code is that the stored procedure accepts a parameter named @UserName. You could add other configuration attributes to make this parameter name configurable.

```
...
cmd.Parameters.Add(New SqlParameter("@UserName", CStr(Context("UserName"))))
...
```

Now you're ready to execute the command and retrieve the matching record. Depending on the design of the database, this record may actually represent the joining of two tables (one with a list of users and one with profile information), or all the information may come from a single table.

```
...
Try
    con.Open()
    Dim reader As SqlDataReader = cmd.ExecuteReader(CommandBehavior.SingleRow)

    ' Get the first row.
    reader.Read()
    ...
```

Once you have the row, the next task is to loop through the SettingsPropertyCollection. For each defined property, you should retrieve the value from the corresponding field. However, it's perfectly valid for a user to exist without any profile information. In this case (when reader.HasRows is False), you should still create the SettingsPropertyValue objects for each requested property, but don't bother setting the property values. They'll simply keep their defaults.

```
...
For Each theproperty As SettingsProperty In properties
    Dim value New SettingsPropertyValue(theproperty)

    If reader.HasRows Then
        value.PropertyValue = reader(theproperty.Name)
    End If
    values.Add(value)
Next theproperty
...
```

The final step is to close the reader and connection and to return the collection of values.

```
        ...
        reader.Close()
    Finally
        con.Close()
    End Try
    Return values
End Function
```

Note If you want to mimic the behavior of the SqlProfileProvider, you should also update the database with the last activity time whenever the GetPropertyValues() method is called.

Updating Profile Information

The job of updating profile properties in the SetPropertyValues() is just as straightforward as reading property values. This time, the update stored procedure is used, and every supplied value is translated into a parameter with the same name.

Here's the complete code:

```
Public Overrides Sub SetPropertyValues(ByVal context As SettingsContext,
        ByVal values As SettingsPropertyValueCollection)
    ' Prepare the command.
    Dim con As New SqlConnection(connectionString)
    Dim cmd As New SqlCommand(updateProcedure, con)
    cmd.CommandType = CommandType.StoredProcedure

    ' Add the parameters.
    ' The assumption is that every property maps exactly
    ' to a single stored procedure parameter name.
    For Each value As SettingsPropertyValue In values
        cmd.Parameters.Add(New SqlParameter(value.Name, value.PropertyValue))
    Next
    ' Again, this provider assumes the stored procedure accepts a parameter named
    ' @UserName.
    cmd.Parameters.Add(New SqlParameter("@UserName", CStr(context("UserName"))))

    ' Execute the command.
    Try
```

```
        con.Open()
        cmd.ExecuteNonQuery()
    Finally
        con.Close()
    End Try
End Sub
```

This completes the code you need for the simple implementation of the FactoredProfileProvider.

Note If you want to mimic the behavior of the SqlProfileProvider, you should also update the database with the last update time whenever the SetPropertyValues() method is called.

Testing the FactoredProfileProvider

To try this example, you need to create, at a bare minimum, a database with a Users table and the two stored procedures. The following example demonstrates an example with a Users table that provides address information (see Figure 24-7).

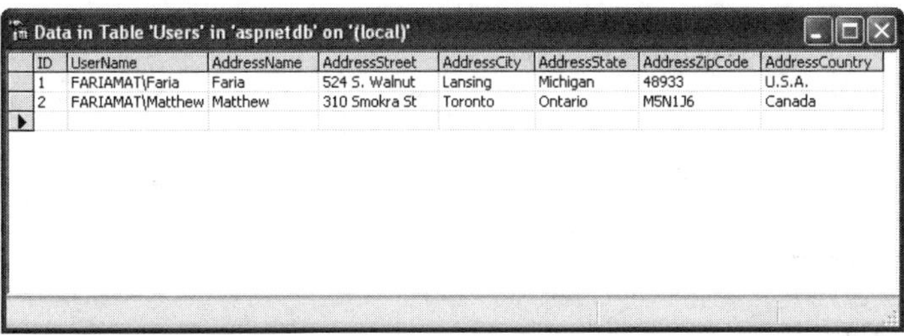
Data in Table 'Users' in 'aspnetdb' on '(local)'

ID	UserName	AddressName	AddressStreet	AddressCity	AddressState	AddressZipCode	AddressCountry
1	FARIAMAT\Faria	Faria	524 S. Walnut	Lansing	Michigan	48933	U.S.A.
2	FARIAMAT\Matthew	Matthew	310 Smokra St	Toronto	Ontario	M5N1J6	Canada

Figure 24-7. *A custom Users table*

A straightforward procedure named Users_GetByUserName queries the profile information from the table:

```
CREATE PROCEDURE Users_GetByUserName
(
  @UserName varchar(50)
)
AS
  SELECT * FROM Users WHERE UserName = @UserName
GO
```

The Users_Update stored procedure is a little more interesting. It begins by checking for the existence of the specified user. If the user doesn't exist, a record is created with the profile information. If the user does exist, that record is updated. This design meshes with the behavior of the SqlProfileProvider.

Note Remember, all profiles providers assume the user has already been authenticated. If you're using the same table to store user authentication information and profile information, an unauthenticated user must have a record in this table. However, this isn't the case if you use separate tables or Windows authentication.

Here's the complete code for the Users_Update stored procedure:

```
CREATE PROCEDURE [Users_Update]
(
   @UserName       varchar(50),
   @AddressName    varchar(50),
   @AddressStreet  varchar(50),
   @AddressCity   varchar(50),
   @AddressState   varchar(50),
   @AddressZipCode varchar(50),
   @AddressCountry varchar(50)
)
AS
  DECLARE @Match int
  SELECT @Match = COUNT(*) FROM Users
    WHERE  UserName = @UserName

  IF (@Match = 0)
    INSERT INTO Users
      (UserName, AddressName, AddressStreet, AddressCity,
       AddressState, AddressZipCode, AddressCountry)
    VALUES
      (@UserName, @AddressName, @AddressStreet, @AddressCity,
       @AddressState, @AddressZipCode, @AddressCountry)

  IF (@Match = 1)
    UPDATE Users SET
      UserName = @UserName,
      AddressName = @AddressName,
      AddressStreet = @AddressStreet,
      AddressCity = @AddressCity,
      AddressState = @AddressState,
      AddressZipCode = @AddressZipCode,
      AddressCountry = @AddressCountry
    WHERE
      (UserName = @UserName)
GO
```

■ **Note** You can download a script to create this table and the corresponding stored procedures with the sample code for this chapter.

To use this table, you simply need to configure the FactoredProfileProvider, identify the stored procedures you're using, and define all the fields of the Users table that you need to access. Here are the complete web.config configuration details:

```
<profile defaultProvider="FactoredProfileProvider">
  <providers >
    <clear />
    <add name="FactoredProfileProvider"
         type="FactoredProfileProvider"
         connectionStringName="SqlServices"
         updateUserProcedure="Users_Update"
         getUserProcedure="Users_GetByUserName"/>
  </providers>
  <properties>
```

```
    <add name="AddressName"/>
    <add name="AddressStreet"/>
    <add name="AddressCity"/>
    <add name="AddressState"/>
    <add name="AddressZipCode"/>
    <add name="AddressCountry"/>
  </properties>
</profile>
```

From this point, you can access the profile details exactly as you would with the SqlProfileProvider. For example, here's the code you need to copy the address information into a series of text boxes:

```
Protected Sub cmdGet_Click(ByVal sender As Object, ByVal e As EventArgs)
    txtName.Text = Profile.AddressName
    txtStreet.Text = Profile.AddressStreet
    txtCity.Text = Profile.AddressCity
    txtZip.Text = Profile.AddressZipCode
    txtState.Text = Profile.AddressState
    txtCountry.Text = Profile.AddressCountry
End Sub
```

Figure 24-8 shows the test page.

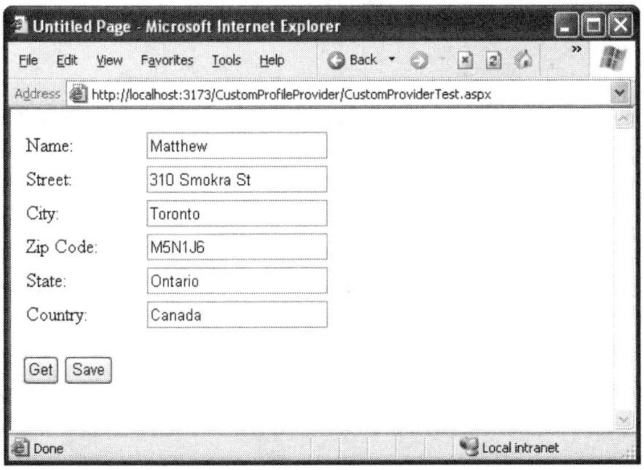

Figure 24-8. *Testing a custom profiles provider*

Summary

In this chapter, you took a detailed look at the new profiles feature in ASP.NET 2.0. You considered how it works behind the scenes, when it makes the most sense, and how to configure its behavior. Next, you tried out profiles with a full-scale example that stores a user-specific shopping cart.

The final part of this chapter explored how to create a simple profiles provider of your own. Using these techniques, you can overcome many of the limitations of the profiles feature (such as the way it serializes all information into a single, opaque field). The ultimate decision of whether to use profiles or a custom database component still depends on several factors, but with this ability profiles become a valid alternative.

CHAPTER 25

■ ■ ■

Cryptography

Over the past four chapters, you learned how to identify users through several supported authentication mechanisms and how to implement authorization for those users in your applications. ASP.NET supports rich services such as the membership and roles APIs that help you implement this functionality. However, although authentication and authorization are two important factors for securing applications, you have to keep much more in mind. Therefore, .NET has a bit more functionality in store. One of the most important examples is .NET's support for *cryptography*—the science of scrambling data to ensure confidentiality and adding hash codes to detect tampering.

.NET includes the rich CryptoAPI for a wide range of cryptographic tasks, such as creating hashes of different types (MD5, SHA1, and so on) and implementing the most important symmetric and asymmetric encryption algorithms. And if that's not enough, .NET 2.0 comes with separate functions for protecting secrets on the local machine or on a per-user basis through a completely managed wrapper for the Windows data protection API (DPAPI). In this chapter, you'll learn when to use these APIs and how to use them correctly.

Encrypting Data: Confidentiality Matters

In Chapter 20, you learned how to use hashing to protect passwords. With hashing, you store a digital fingerprint of the original data, not the data itself. As a result, you have no way to reverse the hashing process to retrieve the original data. All you can do is hash new data and perform a comparison.

The hashing approach is the most secure practice for validating passwords. However, it's not much help when you want to protect sensitive data that you need to decrypt later. For example, if you're creating an e-commerce application, you probably want to store a user's credit card information so it can be reused in later orders. In this scenario, your application needs to be able to retrieve the credit card details on its own. Hashing doesn't apply.

Often developers deal with this situation by storing sensitive data in clear text. They assume that because the data is kept in a secure server-side storage location, they don't need to go to the additional work of encrypting it. However, security experts know this is not true. Without encryption, a malicious user needs to gain access to the server for only a matter of minutes or even seconds to retrieve passwords or credit card numbers for every customer. Security breaches can occur because of poor administrative policies, weak administrator passwords, or other exploitable software on the server. Problems can even occur because of hardware maintenance; in fact, dozens of companies have reported selling or discarding old server hard drives without properly erasing the sensitive customer data they contained. Finally, many organizations have a privacy policy that explicitly pledges to keep customer information confidential and encrypted at all times. If a security breach occurs and the company is forced to notify users that their data is at risk because it wasn't properly encrypted, the company can face significant embarrassment and loss of trust. To avoid these problems and ensure that data is safe, you need to encrypt sensitive information stored by your application.

The .NET Cryptography Namespace

In the System.Security.Cryptography namespace, you can find the necessary classes for encrypting and decrypting information in your application. Furthermore, you find all the fundamental classes for creating different types of hashes. If you then reference the additional assembly System.Security.dll, you even have access to more advanced security functionality such as an API for modifying Windows ACLs (the System.Security.AccessControl namespace), the DPAPI, and classes for creating key-hashed message authentication codes (HMAC). Table 25-1 shows the categories of classes.

Table 25-1. *Categories of Security Classes in the System.Security.Cryptography Namespace*

Category	Description
Encryption algorithms	The namespace includes the most important hashing and encryption algorithms and classes for creating digital signatures. You will learn more about the details of these classes in the section "Understanding the .NET Cryptography Classes."
Helper classes	If you need to create true cryptographic random numbers, you will find helper classes in the System.Security.Cryptography namespace. The helper classes are for interacting with the underlying Windows cryptography system (the CryptoAPI).
X509 certificates	In the namespace System.Security.Cryptography.X509Certificates, you will find all the necessary classes for working with X509 certificates and (since .NET 2.0) classes for accessing the Windows certificate store.
XML signature and encryption	You can find complete support of the XML signature and encryption standards in the System.Security.Cryptography.Xml namespace. The classes in this namespace are used for encrypting and signing XML documents according to the standards published by the W3C.
CMS/PKCS#7	Since .NET 2.0, the framework has managed support for creating CMS/PKCS-enveloped messages directly without unmanaged calls. (CMS stands for Cryptographic Message Syntax and PKCS stands for Public-Key Cryptography Standard.)

In the world of the Web, X509 certificates play an important role. They establish SSL communications and perform certificate authentication. An X509 certificate is a binary standard for encapsulating keys for asymmetric encryption algorithms together with a signature of a special organization that has issued the certificate (usually such organizations are called *certificate authorities*).

For simple SSL connections, you don't need access to the certificate store, but if you want to call web services or web applications in your code hosted on a different server that requires you to authenticate with an X509 certificate, your application has to read the certificate from the Windows certificate store and then add the certificate to the web request (or the web service proxy) before actually sending the request. You can read a certificate from the store and assign it to a web request as follows:

```
Dim Certificate As X509Certificate2 = Nothing

' Read the certificate from the store
Dim store As New X509Store(StoreName.My, StoreLocation.LocalMachine)
store.Open(OpenFlags.ReadOnly)
Try
    ' Try to find the certificate
    ' based on its common name
    Dim Results As X509Certificate2Collection =
        store.Certificates.Find(X509FindType.FindBySubjectDistinguishedName,
                                "CN=Mario, CN=Szpuszta", False)

    If Results.Count = 0 Then
        Throw New Exception("Unable to find certificate!")
    Else
        Certificate = Results(0)
    End If
Finally
    store.Close()
End Try
```

Windows supports several types of certificate stores that are called *store locations*. The local machine store, for example, is accessible to all applications running on the local machine with the appropriate permissions. You can create a separate store for each Windows service of a machine, and every user has a separate certificate store. Certificates are stored securely in those stores. While the local machine store is encrypted with a key managed by the local security authority of the machine, the user store is encrypted with a key stored in the user's profile. Within a store location, Windows differentiates between stores used for different purposes. The most important stores are the Personal ("my") store and the Trusted Root Certification Authorities. Usually, the "my" store contains all the certificates used by applications (and users if it's a user store), while the Trusted Root Certification Authorities store contains certificates of authorities issuing certificates. VeriSign is an example of a well-known authority from which you can buy certificates. If you place a certificate into the Trusted Root Certification Authorities store, you indicate that any certificates issued by this authority are trusted by the system and therefore can be used by any application without any fear. Other certificates by default are not trusted and therefore marked with a special flag. Of course, you should use only valid certificates issued by a trusted authority for critical operations such as authenticating or setting up SSL on the server, because any other certificate could lead to a potential security risk.

In ASP.NET web applications, you have to use either the local machine store or a service account's store (which is nothing more than the user store of the service account under which a Windows service is executed). Therefore, the code introduced previously opens the store with the flag StoreLocation.LocalMachine. The second possible flag for this option is StoreLocation.CurrentUser, which opens a current user's or service account's store. As the certificate is a "usage" certificate, you will read it from the personal store. You can view the certificates of a store by opening a Microsoft Management Console and then adding the Certificates snap-in, as shown in Figure 25-1.

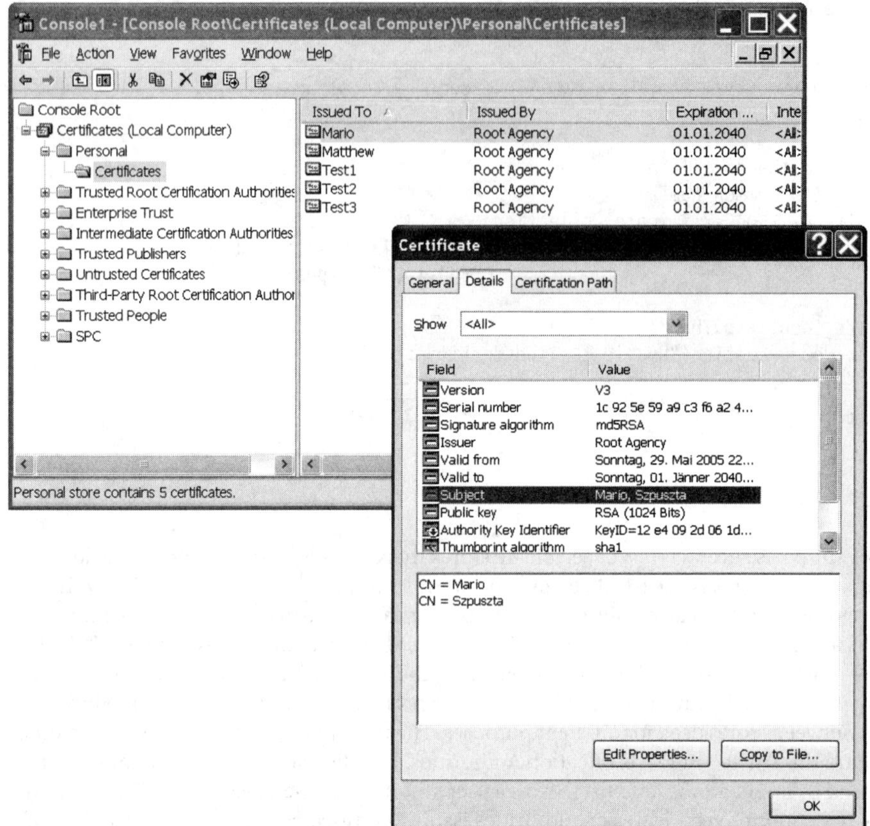

Figure 25-1. *The Windows Certificates snap-in*

You can create test certificates through the makecert.exe command. This command creates a certificate in the personal store of the local machine:

```
makecert -ss my -sr LocalMachine -n "CN=Mario, CN=Szpuszta"
```

You have to import the System.Security.Cryptography.X509Certificates namespace when using the classes shown previously. As soon as you have the certificate from the store in place, you can use it when sending requests through SSL to a server that requires certificate authentication, as follows:

```
' Now create the web request
Dim Request As HttpWebRequest = CType(WebRequest.Create(url), HttpWebRequest)
Request.ClientCertificates.Add(Certificate)
Dim Response As HttpWebResponse = CType(Request.GetResponse(), HttpWebResponse)
' ...
```

Another useful example of security is a class for generating cryptographically strong random numbers. This class is important for generating random key values or salt values when you want to store salted password hashes. A *salted password hash* is a hash created from a password and a so-called salt. A salt is a random value. This ensures that even if two users select the same passwords, the results stored in the back-end store will look different, as the random salt value is hashed with the password. It also requires you to store the salt value in a separate field together with the password, because you will need it for password validation. You will learn more about salted hash values when creating a custom membership provider in Chapter 26. For now, this shows how you can create random number values with the System.Security.Cryptography.RandomNumberGenerator class:

```
Dim RandomValue As New Byte(15) {}
Dim RndGen As RandomNumberGenerator = RandomNumberGenerator.Create()
RndGen.GetBytes(RandomValue)
ResultLabel.Text = Convert.ToBase64String(RandomValue)
```

For more information about the random number generator, refer to the Cryptographic Service Provider documentation of Windows, as this class is just a wrapper around the native implementation (`http://msdn.microsoft.com/library/default.asp?url=/library/en-us/seccrypto/security/cryptographic_service_providers.asp`).

Understanding the .NET Cryptography Classes

Before you can perform cryptography in .NET, you need to understand a little more about the underlying plumbing. The .NET encryption classes are divided into three layers. The first layer is a set of abstract base classes; these classes represent an encryption task. These include the following:

AsymmetricAlgorithm: This class represents asymmetric encryption, which uses a public/private key pair. Data encrypted with one key can be decrypted only with the other key.

SymmetricAlgorithm: This class represents symmetric encryption, which uses a shared secret value. Data encrypted with the key can be decrypted using only the same key.

HashAlgorithm: This class represents hash generation and verification. Hashes are also known as *one-way encryption algorithms*, as you can only encrypt but not decrypt data. You can use hashes to ensure that data is not tampered with.

The second level includes classes that represent a specific encryption algorithm. They derive from the encryption base classes, but they are also abstract classes. For example, the DES algorithm class, which represents the DES (Data Encryption Standard) algorithm, derives from SymmetricAlgorithm.

The third level of classes is a set of encryption implementations. Each implementation class derives from an algorithm class. This means a specific encryption algorithm such as DES could have multiple implementation classes. While some .NET Framework encryption classes are implemented entirely in managed code, most are actually thin wrappers over the CryptoAPI library. The classes that wrap the CryptoAPI functions have *CryptoServiceProvider* in their name (for example, DESCryptoServiceProvider), while the managed classes typically have *Managed* in their name (for example, RijndaelManaged). Essentially, the managed classes perform all their work in the .NET world under the supervision of the CLR, while the unmanaged classes use calls to the unmanaged CryptoAPI library. This might seem like a limitation, but it's actually an efficient reuse of existing technology.

The CryptoAPI has never been faulted for its technology, just its awkward programming interface. Figure 25-2 shows the classes in the System.Security.Cryptography namespace. This three-layer organization allows almost unlimited extensibility. You can create a new implementation for an existing cryptography class by deriving from an existing algorithm class. For example, you could create a class that implements the DES algorithm entirely in managed code by creating a new DESManaged class and inheriting from DESCryptoServiceProvider. Similarly, you can add support for a new encryption algorithm by adding an abstract algorithm class (for example, CAST128, which is similar to DES but is not provided in the framework) and a concrete implementation class (such as CAST128Managed).

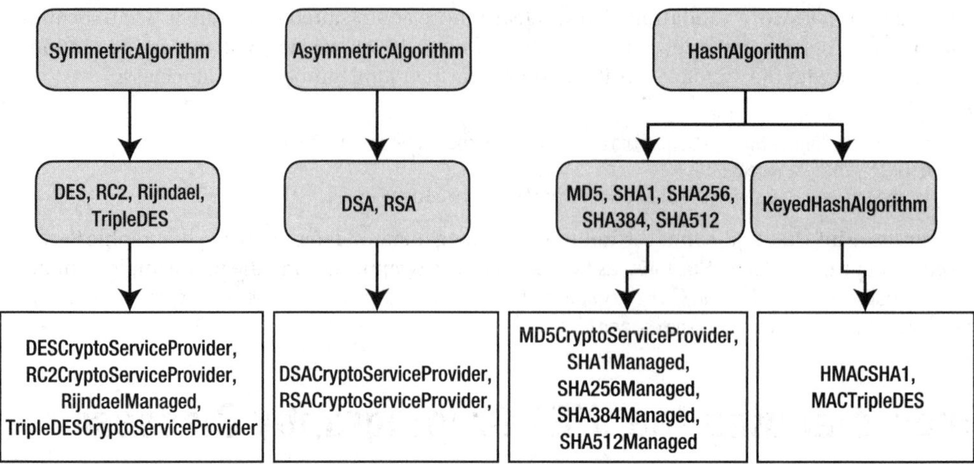

Figure 25-2. *The cryptographic class hierarchy*

■ **Note** The encryption classes are one of the few examples in the .NET class library where the standard naming and case rules are not followed. For example, you'll find classes such as TripleDES and RSA rather than TripleDes and Rsa.

Symmetric Encryption Algorithms

As mentioned earlier in this chapter, the .NET Framework supports three types of encryption: symmetric, asymmetric, and one-way encryption (hashes). Symmetric algorithms always use the same key for encryption and decryption. Symmetric algorithms are fast for encryption and decryption. Table 25-2 lists the most important symmetric algorithms supported by the .NET Framework.

Table 25-2. *Symmetric Algorithms Supported by .NET*

	Abstract Algorithm	Default Implementation	Valid Key Size	Maximum Key Size
DES	DES	DESCryptoServiceProvider	64	64
TripleDES	TripleDES	TripleDESCryptoServiceProvider	128, 192	192
RC2	RC2	RC2CryptServiceProvider	40–128	128
Rijndael	Rijndael	RijndaelManaged	128, 192, 256	256

The strength of the encryption corresponds to the length of the key. Keep in mind that the greater the key size, the harder it is for a brute-force attack to succeed, because there are far more possible key values to test. Of course, greater symmetric key sizes also lead to larger messages and slower encryption times. For most purposes, a good standard choice is Rijndael. It offers solid performance and support for large key sizes.

■ Note DES, TripleDES, and RC2 are all implemented using the CryptoAPI and thus need the high encryption pack on Windows 2000. Note also that the key length for DES and TripleDES include parity bits that don't contribute to the strength of the encryption. TripleDES with a 192-bit key uses only 168 bits, while a 128-bit key uses 112 bits. In DES, the 64-bit key uses only 56 bits. For that reason, it's considered fairly weak, and you should use other key algorithms instead. For additional information about the relative strengths of these algorithms, consult a dedicated book or Internet resource about encryption theory, such as Bruce Schneier's *Applied Cryptography: Protocols, Algorithms, and Source Code in C, Second Edition* (Wiley, 1995).

As mentioned, the big advantage of symmetric algorithms is performance. Conversely, the major problems with symmetric algorithms are as follows:

Key exchange: If you are using symmetric algorithms to exchange data between two applications hosted by different parties, you have to exchange the key in a secure way.

Brute-force attacks: If you use the symmetric key for a longer period of time, attackers might have enough time to decrypt traffic by just trying any valid combination of bits in a key. Therefore, with an increasing bit size, the strength of the key increases, as explained previously. But generally this means you should use a different key in regular intervals anyway.

Long-term key management: If you have to update keys in regular intervals, you have to exchange them in regular intervals, which might lead to additional security risks. Furthermore, you have to store the key in a secure place.

Symmetric algorithms are not enough for secure systems, and that's why asymmetric algorithms exist.

Asymmetric Encryption

Asymmetric algorithms try to solve some of the problems of symmetric algorithms. They are based on mathematical methods that require different keys for encryption and decryption. Usually the key used for encryption is called a *public key*. You can give this key to anyone who wants to send encrypted information to you. On the other hand, the private key is the only key that can be used for decryption. Therefore, if you are the only one with access to the private key, you are the only person who is able to decrypt the information. This fact makes key exchange between parties definitely easier, because you don't need to transmit the key that can decrypt sensitive data. Table 25-3 lists the asymmetric algorithms supported by the .NET Framework.

Table 25-3. *Asymmetric Algorithms Supported by .NET*

	Abstract Algorithm	Default Implementation	Valid Key Size	Maximum Key Size
RSA	RSA	RSACryptoServiceProvider	384–16384 (8-bit increments)	1024
DSA	DSA	DSACryptoServiceProvider	512–1024 (64-bit increments)	1024

When you use RSA and DSA, you will recognize that only RSA supports the direct encryption and decryption of values. The DSA algorithm—as its name Digital Signature Algorithm implies—can be used only for signing information and verifying signatures.

The big problem is that asymmetric algorithms are much slower (depending on the size of the data you want to encrypt) than symmetric algorithms. This will affect the performance of your application if you need to exchange data through lots of requests. Therefore, technologies such as SSL use asymmetric algorithms at the beginning when establishing a connection session. Through the first communication steps, traffic between the client and the server is secured through asymmetric encryption (the client encrypts with a public key, and the server decrypts with a private key). With these steps the client and the server can exchange a symmetric key securely. This symmetric key then secures traffic for any subsequent communication through symmetric encryption. This combines the advantages of symmetric and asymmetric encryption. Of course, you have to find a way to securely store the private key so that unauthorized people don't have a chance to access it.

■ **Note** If you don't store the private key on an external device such as a smart card, you create a chance of someone gaining unauthorized access (and even the smart card is not completely secure, because you can lose it), especially if actors are administrators of machines. But you should always make your solution as secure as possible and "raise the bar" for attackers. Therefore, any additional security mechanism (gatekeeper) will make life for a potential attacker harder.

The Abstract Encryption Classes

The abstract encryption classes actually serve two purposes. First, they define the basic members that encryption implementations need to support. Second, they provide some functionality, through the Shared Create() method, that you can use directly without creating a class instance. This method allows you to create one of the concrete implementation classes without needing to know how it is implemented.

For example, consider the following line of code:

```
Dim crypt As DES = DES.Create()
```

The Shared Create() method returns an instance of the default DES implementation class. In this case, the class is DESCryptoServiceProvider. The advantage of this technique is that you can code generically, without creating a dependency on a specific implementation. Best of all, if Microsoft updates the framework and the default DES implementation class changes, your code will pick up the change seamlessly. This is particularly useful if you are using a CryptoAPI class, which could be replaced with a managed class equivalent in the future.

In fact, you can work at even higher level if you want by using the Shared Create() method in one of the cryptographic task classes. For example, consider this code:

```
Dim crypt As SymmetricAlgorithm = SymmetricAlgorithm.Create()
```

This creates an instance of whatever cryptography class is defined as the default symmetric algorithm. In this case, it isn't DES but is Rijndael. The object returned is an instance of the RijndaelManaged implementation class.

■ **Tip** It is good practice to code generically using the abstract algorithm classes. This allows you to know which type of algorithm you are using (and any limitations it may have) without worrying about the underlying implementation.

The ICryptoTransform Interface

.NET uses a stream-based architecture for encryption and decryption, which makes it easy to encrypt and decrypt different types of data from different types of sources. This architecture also makes it easy to perform multiple cryptographic operations in succession, on the fly, independent of the low-level details of the actual cryptography algorithm you're using (such as the block size).

To understand how all this works, you need to consider the core types—the ICryptoTransform interface and the CryptoStream class. The ICryptoTransform interface represents blockwise cryptographic transformation. This could be an encryption, decryption, hashing, Base64 encoding/decoding, or formatting operation. To create an ICryptoTransform object for a given algorithm, you use the CreateEncryptor() and CreateDecryptor() methods (depending on whether you want to encrypt or decrypt data).

Here's a code snippet that creates an ICryptoTransform for encrypting with the DES algorithm:

```
Dim crypt As DES = DES.Create()
Dim transform As ICryptoTransform = crypt.CreateEncryptor()
```

Various cryptographic tasks execute in the same way, even though the actual cryptographic function performing the transformation may be different. Every cryptographic operation requires that data be subdivided into blocks of a fixed size before it can be processed. You can use an ICryptoTransform instance directly, but in most cases you'll take an easier approach and simply pass it to another class: the CryptoStream.

The CryptoStream Class

The CryptoStream wraps an ordinary stream and uses an ICryptoTransform to perform its work behind the scenes. The key advantage is that the CryptoStream uses buffered access, thereby allowing you to perform automatic encryption without worrying about the block size required by the algorithm. The other advantage of the CryptoStream is that, because it wraps an ordinary .NET stream-derived class, it can easily "piggyback" on another operation, such as file access (through a FileStream), memory access (through a MemoryStream), a low-level network call (through a NetworkStream), and so on.

To create a CryptoStream, you need three pieces of information: the underlying stream, the mode, and the ICryptoTransform you want to use. For example, the following code snippet creates an ICryptoTransform using the DES algorithm implementation class and then uses it with an existing stream to create a CryptoStream:

```
Dim crypt As DES = DES.Create()
Dim transform As ICryptoTransform = crypt.CreateEncryptor()
Dim cs New CryptoStream(fileStream, transform, CryptoStreamMode.Write)

' (Now you can use cs to write encrypted information to the file.)
```

Note that the CryptoStream can be in one of two modes: read mode or write mode, as defined by the CryptoStreamMode enumeration. In read mode, the transformation is performed as it is retrieved from the underlying stream (as shown in Figure 25-3).

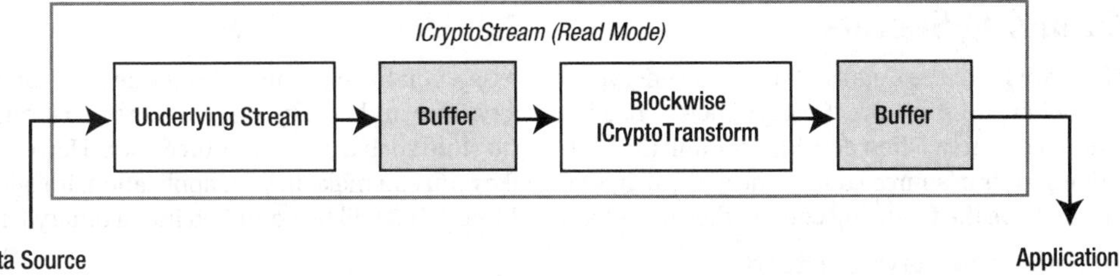

Figure 25-3. *Reading and decrypting data*

In write mode, the transformation is performed before the data is written to the underlying stream (as shown in Figure 25-4).

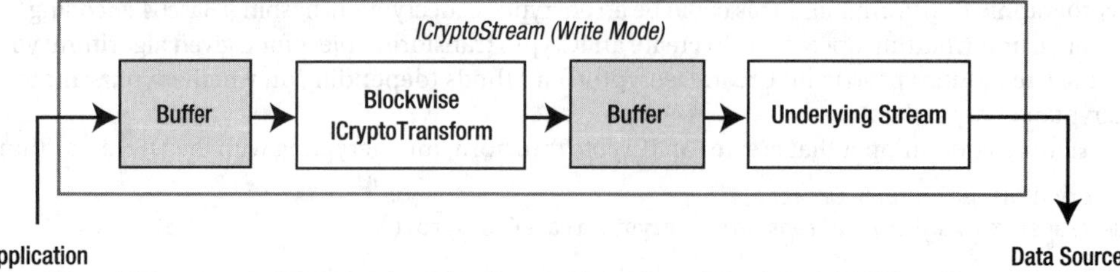

Figure 25-4. *Writing and encrypting data*

You cannot combine both modes to make a readable and writable CryptoStream (which would have no meaning anyway). Similarly, the Seek() method and the Position property, which are used to move to different positions in a stream, are not supported for the CryptoStream() and will throw a NotSupportedException if called. However, you can often use these members with the underlying stream.

Encrypting Sensitive Data

Now that you've taken an in-depth look at .NET cryptography, it's time to put it all together. In the following sections, you will create two utility classes that use symmetric and asymmetric algorithms. In the "Encrypting Sensitive Data in a Database" section, you will use one of these classes to encrypt sensitive information such as a credit card number stored in a database and to encrypt the query string. You need to perform the following steps to encrypt and decrypt information:

1. Choose and create an algorithm.
2. Generate and store the secret key.
3. Encrypt or decrypt information through a CryptoStream.
4. Close the source and target streams appropriately.

After you have created and tested your encryption utility classes, you will prepare a database to store secret information and then write the code for encrypting and decrypting this secret information in the database.

Managing Secrets

Before you learn the details of using the encryption classes, you have to think about one additional thing: where do you store the key? The key used for encryption and decryption is a secret, so it must be stored securely. Often developers think the best way to store such a key is in source code. However, storing secrets in source code is one of the biggest mistakes you can make in your application. Imagine that you have the following code in the code of a class library that will be compiled into a binary DLL:

```
Public Class MyEncryptionUtility
    ' Shhh!!! Don't tell anybody!
    Private Const MyKey As String = "m$%&kljasldk$%/65asjdl"

    Private Sub New()

    End Sub
    Public Shared Function Encrypt(ByVal data As String) As Byte()
        ' Use "MyKey" to encrypt data
```

```
        Return Nothing
    End Function
End Class
```

Keys such as this can easily be revealed through disassembling tools. You just need to open ILDASM and analyze your class. Of course, you definitely will be able to find this secret, as shown in Figure 25-5.

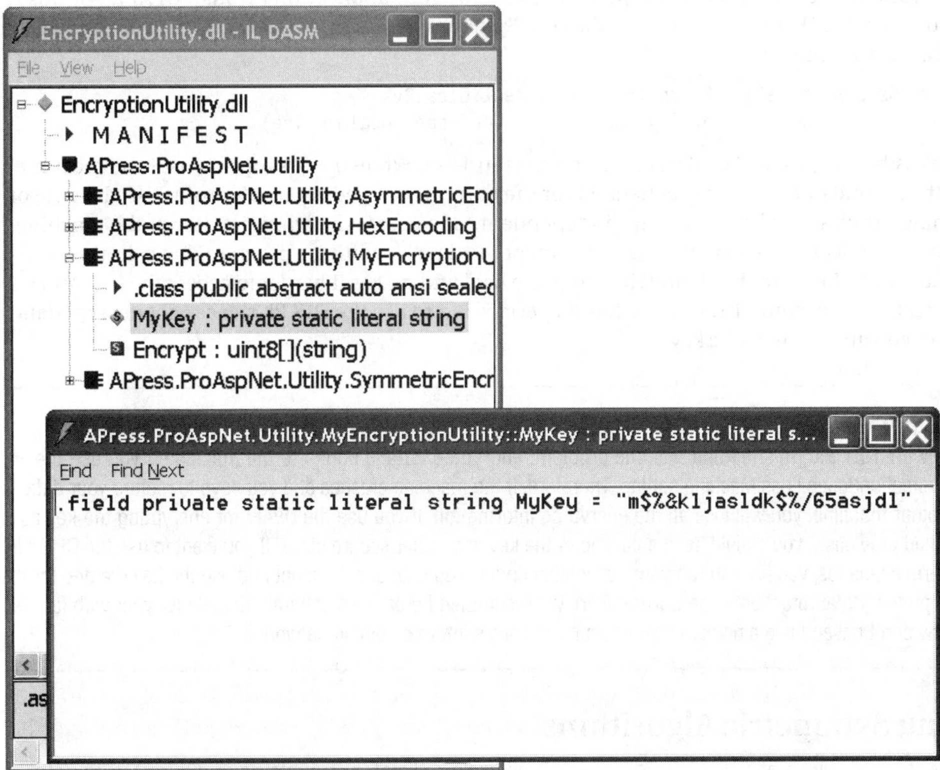

Figure 25-5. *ILDASM with the previous class and the secret*

If you think this is a problem in the managed world only, try something similar with an unmanaged C++ application. Create a class, and include the secret as a constant value in your application. Because constant values are stored in a special section of native executables, perform the following steps:

1. Install the Microsoft platform SDK.
2. Open a command shell, and execute the following command:

   ```
   dumpbin /all BadProtectCPlus.exe /out:test.txt
   ```

3. Open the generated file test.txt with Notepad, and scroll to the .rdata section. Somewhere in this section you will find your hard-coded secret.

So, you definitely have to protect the key somehow. You might want to encrypt the key on its own, but then you need another encryption key.

Windows supports a built-in mechanism for storing and protecting secrets. This mechanism uses a machine key generated with the system installation for encrypting data. Only the local operating system (the system's local security authority) has access to this machine key. Of course, the machine key is unique for every installation. Windows supports the Data Protection API for protecting data with this key. You don't have direct access to the key when using this API; you just tell the system to encrypt or decrypt something with the machine's key. So, this solves the problem of key management: your application could encrypt the key used by your application through DPAPI. For this purpose, the .NET Framework supports the class System.Security.Cryptography.ProtectedData, which you can use as follows:

```
Dim ProtData As Byte() = ProtectedData.Protect(ClearBytes,
                         Nothing, DataProtectionScope.LocalMachine)
```

Possible scopes are LocalMachine and CurrentUser. While the first option uses the machine key, the second one uses a key generated for the currently logged-on user's profile. (In the case of roaming profiles, this key is machine independent.) If a user is the administrator of the machine and has the necessary know-how, he can decrypt the data by writing a program that calls the previous function. However, this definitely "raises the bar" and makes it harder to access the key. And if the user is not the administrator and has no permission to use the DPAPI, she cannot decrypt data encrypted with the machine key.

■ **Caution** Don't use the DPAPI to encrypt information in your database. Although it is easy to use the DPAPI with .NET 2.0, this method has one problem: encrypted data is bound to the machine if you use the DataProtectionScope.LocalMachine setting. Therefore, if the machine crashes and you have to restore your data on another machine, you will lose all the encrypted information. If you use the DPAPI for encrypting the key as described previously, you should have a backup of the key in another secure place. If you want to use the DPAPI in web farm scenarios, you have to run your application under a domain user account and use the key created for the user's profile (DataProtectionScope.CurrentUser). We recommend creating a separate domain for your web farm so that you don't have to use a domain user of your company's internal domain network.

Using Symmetric Algorithms

As mentioned, symmetric encryption algorithms use one key for encrypting and decrypting data. The class you will create basically has the following structure and can be used for encrypting and decrypting string data:

```
Public Class SymmetricEncryptionUtility
    Dim Shared _ProtectKey As Boolean
    Dim Shared _AlgorithmName As String

    Private Sub New()

    End Sub

    Private Shared Property AlgorithmName() As String
        Get
                Return _AlgorithmName
        End Get
        Set
                _AlgorithmName = Value
        End Set
    End Property
```

```
    Public Shared Property ProtectKey() As Boolean
        Get
                Return _ProtectKey
        End Get
        Set
                _ProtectKey = Value
        End Set
    End Property

    Public Shared Sub GenerateKey(ByVal targetFile As String)

    End Sub

    Public Shared Sub ReadKey(ByVal algorithm As SymmetricAlgorithm,
            ByVal file As String)

    End Sub

    Public Shared Function EncryptData(ByVal data As String,
            ByVal keyFile As String) As Byte()

    End Function

    Public Shared Function DecryptData(ByVal data As Byte(),
            ByVal keyFile As String) As String

    End Function

End Class
```

The class offers a possibility for specifying the name of the algorithm (DES, TripleDES, RijnDael, or RC2) through the AlgorithmName property. It also supports operations for generating a new key, reading this key from the file specified directly into the key property of an algorithm instance, and encrypting and decrypting data. For using this class, you must set the algorithm name appropriately and then generate a key if none exists already. Then you just need to call the EncryptData and DecryptData methods, which internally will call the ReadKey method for initializing the algorithm. The ProtectKey property allows the user of the class to specify whether the key should be protected through the DPAPI.

You can generate encryption keys through the algorithm classes. The GenerateKey method looks like this:

```
Public Shared Sub GenerateKey(ByVal targetFile As String)
    ' Create the algorithm
    Dim Algorithm As SymmetricAlgorithm =
        SymmetricAlgorithm.Create(AlgorithmName)
    Algorithm.GenerateKey()

    ' Now get the key
    Dim Key As Byte() = Algorithm.Key

    If ProtectKey Then
        ' Use DPAPI to encrypt key
        Key = ProtectedData.Protect(Key, Nothing, DataProtectionScope.LocalMachine)
    End If

    ' Store the key in a file called key.config
    Using fs As New FileStream(targetFile, FileMode.Create)
```

```
        fs.Write(Key, 0, Key.Length)
    End Using

End Sub
```

The GenerateKey() method of the SymmetricAlgorithm class generates a new key through cryptographically strong random number algorithms and initializes the Key property with this new key. If configured appropriately, it encrypts the key using the DPAPI. The ReadKey method reads the key from the file created by the GenerateKey method, as follows:

```
Public Shared Sub ReadKey(ByVal algorithm As SymmetricAlgorithm,
                ByVal keyFile As String)
    Dim Key As Byte()

    Using fs As New FileStream(keyFile, FileMode.Open)

        Key = New Byte(fs.Length - 1) {}
        fs.Read(Key, 0, CInt(fs.Length))
    End Using

    If ProtectKey Then
        algorithm.Key = ProtectedData.Unprotect(Key,
                Nothing, DataProtectionScope.LocalMachine)
    Else
        algorithm.Key = Key
    End If
End Sub
```

If the key was protected previously, the ReadKey method uses the DPAPI for unprotecting the encrypted key when reading it from the file. The method furthermore requires passing in an existing instance of a symmetric algorithm. It directly initializes the key property of the algorithm so that this key will be used automatically for all subsequent operations. The function itself is used by both the EncryptData and DecryptData functions.

```
Public Shared Function EncryptData(ByVal data As String,
                       ByVal keyFile As String) As Byte()
End Function

Public Shared Function DecryptData(ByVal data As Byte(),
                       ByVal keyFile As String) As String

End Function
```

As you can see, both methods require a keyFile parameter with the path to the file that stores the key. They subsequently call the ReadKey method for initializing their algorithm instance with the key. While the EncryptData method accepts a string and returns a byte array with the encrypted representation, the DecryptData accepts the encrypted byte array and returns the clear-text string.

Let's get started with the EncryptData method:

```
Public Shared Function EncryptData(ByVal data As String,
                ByVal keyFile As String) As Byte()
    ' Convert string data to byte array
    Dim ClearData As Byte() = Encoding.UTF8.GetBytes(data)

    ' Now create the algorithm
    Dim Algorithm As SymmetricAlgorithm = SymmetricAlgorithm.Create(AlgorithmName)
    ReadKey(Algorithm, keyFile)
```

```
    ' Encrypt information
    Dim Target As New MemoryStream()

    ' Append Initialization Vector (IV)
    Algorithm.GenerateIV()
    Target.Write(Algorithm.IV, 0, Algorithm.IV.Length)

    ' Encrypt actual data
    Dim cs As New CryptoStream(Target, Algorithm.CreateEncryptor(),
                CryptoStreamMode.Write)
    cs.Write(ClearData, 0, ClearData.Length)
    cs.FlushFinalBlock()

    ' Output the bytes of the encrypted array to the text box
    Return Target.ToArray()
End Function
```

First, the method converts the string value into a byte array because all the encryption functions of the algorithms require byte arrays as input parameters. You can use the Encoding class of the System.Text namespace to do this easily. Next, the method creates the algorithm according to the AlgorithmName property of the class. This value can be one of the names RC2, Rijndael, DES, or TripleDES. The factory method of the SymmetricAlgorithm creates the appropriate instance, while additional cryptography classes can be registered through the <cryptographySettings> section in the machine.config file.

Afterward, the method creates a memory stream that will be the target of your encryption operation in this case. Before the class starts with the encryption operation through the CryptoStream class, it generates an initialization vector (IV) and writes the IV to the target stream on the first position. The IV adds random data to the encrypted stream of data.

Imagine the following situation: if your application exchanges the same information multiple times with actors, simple encryption will always result in the same encrypted representation of the information. This makes brute-force attacks easier. To add some sort of random information, symmetric algorithms support IV. These IVs are not only added to the encrypted stream of bytes themselves but they are also used as input for encrypting the first block of data. When using the CryptoStream for encrypting information, don't forget to call the FlushFinalBlock() method to make sure the last block of encrypted data is written appropriately to the target.

Furthermore, you have to add initialization vectors to the encrypted set of bytes because you need the vector for decryption later, as follows:

```
Public Shared Function DecryptData(ByVal data As Byte(),
            ByVal keyFile As String) As String
    ' Now create the algorithm
    Dim Algorithm As SymmetricAlgorithm =
        SymmetricAlgorithm.Create(AlgorithmName)
    ReadKey(Algorithm, keyFile)

    ' Decrypt information
    Dim Target As New MemoryStream()

    ' Read IV, and initialize the algorithm with it
    Dim ReadPos As Integer = 0
    Dim IV As Byte() = New Byte(Algorithm.IV.Length - 1) {}
    Array.Copy(data, IV, IV.Length)
    Algorithm.IV = IV
    ReadPos += Algorithm.IV.Length

    Dim cs As New CryptoStream(Target,
```

```
                        Algorithm.CreateDecryptor(), CryptoStreamMode.Write)
    cs.Write(data, ReadPos, data.Length - ReadPos)
    cs.FlushFinalBlock()

    ' Get the bytes from the memory stream, and convert them to text
    Return Encoding.UTF8.GetString(Target.ToArray())
End Function
```

The decryption function is structured the other way around. It creates the algorithm and creates a stream for the decrypted target information. Before you can start decrypting the data, you have to read the IV from the encrypted stream, because it is used by the algorithm for the last transformation. You then use the CryptoStream as you did previously, except you create a decryptor transformer this time. Finally, you get the decrypted byte representation of the string you have created through Encoding.UTF8.GetBytes(). To reverse this operation, you need to call the GetString() method of the UTF-8 encoding class for getting the clear-text representation of the string.

Using the SymmetricEncryptionUtility Class

Now you can create a Web page for testing the class you created previously. Just create a page that allows you to generate a key and enter clear-text data through a text box. You can output the encrypted data through Convert.ToBase64String() easily. For decryption, you just need to revert the operation through Convert.FromBase64String() to get the encrypted bytes back and pass them into the DecryptData method.

```
Dim KeyFileName As String
Dim AlgorithmName As String = "DES"

Protected Sub Page_Load(ByVal sender As Object, ByVal e As EventArgs)
        SymmetricEncryptionUtility.AlgorithmName = AlgorithmName
        KeyFileName = Server.MapPath("~/") & "\symmetric_key.config"
End Sub

Protected Sub GenerateKeyCommand_Click(ByVal sender As Object, ByVal e As EventArgs)
        SymmetricEncryptionUtility.ProtectKey = EncryptKeyCheck.Checked
        SymmetricEncryptionUtility.GenerateKey(KeyFileName)
        Response.Write("Key generated successfully!")
End Sub

Protected Sub EncryptCommand_Click(ByVal sender As Object, ByVal e As EventArgs)
        ' Check for encryption key
        If (Not File.Exists(KeyFileName)) Then
                Response.Write("Missing encryption key. Please generate key!")
        End If

    Dim data As Byte() =
        SymmetricEncryptionUtility.EncryptData(ClearDataText.Text, KeyFileName)
    EncryptedDataText.Text = Convert.ToBase64String(data)
End Sub

Protected Sub DecryptCommand_Click(ByVal sender As Object, ByVal e As EventArgs)
        ' Check for encryption key
        If (Not File.Exists(KeyFileName)) Then
                Response.Write("Missing encryption key. Please generate key!")
        End If

        Dim data As Byte() =
                Convert.FromBase64String(EncryptedDataText.Text)
```

```
        ClearDataText.Text =
                SymmetricEncryptionUtility.DecryptData(data, KeyFileName)

End Sub
```

The previous page uses the DES algorithm because you set the AlgorithmName of your utility class appropriately. Within the Click event of the GenerateKeyCommand button, it calls the GenerateKey() method. Depending on the check box of the page, it encrypts the key itself through the DPAPI or not. After the data has been encrypted through your utility class within the Click event of the EncryptCommand button, it converts the encrypted bytes to a Base64 string and then writes it to the EncryptedDataText text box. Therefore, if you want to decrypt information again, you have to create a byte array based on this Base64 string representation and then call the method for decryption. You can see the result in Figure 25-6.

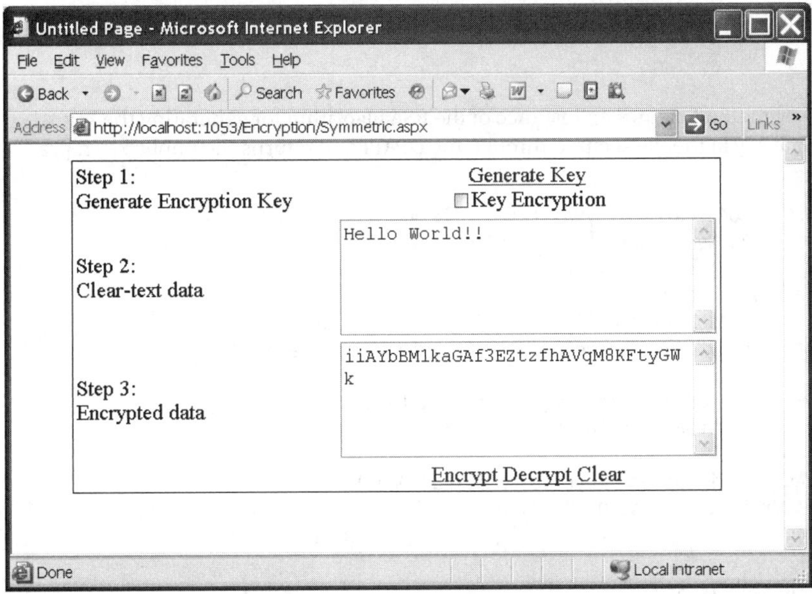

Figure 25-6. *The resulting test page for symmetric algorithms*

Using Asymmetric Algorithms

Using asymmetric algorithms is similar to using symmetric algorithms. You will see just a handful of differences. The major difference has to do with key management. Symmetric algorithms just have one key, and asymmetric algorithms have two keys: one for encrypting data (public key) and one for decrypting data (private key). While the public key can be available to everyone who wants to encrypt data, the private key should be available only to those decrypting information. In this section, you will create a utility class similar to the previous one.

Because the .NET Framework ships with only one asymmetric algorithm for real data encryption (RSA; remember, DSA is used for digital signatures only), you don't need to include a way to select the algorithm (for a while).

```
Public Class AsymmetricEncryptionUtility
        Private Sub New()
```

```
        End Sub
        Public Shared Function GenerateKey(ByVal targetFile As String) As String

        End Function
        Private Shared Sub ReadKey(ByVal algorithm As RSACryptoServiceProvider,
                        ByVal keyFile As String)

        End Sub
        Public Shared Function EncryptData(ByVal data As String,
                        ByVal publicKey As String) As Byte()
        End Function

        Public Shared Function DecryptData(ByVal data As Byte(),
                        ByVal keyFile As String) As String

        End Function

End Class
```

The GenerateKey method creates an instance of the RSA algorithm for generating the key. It stores only the private key in the file secured through the DPAPI and returns the public key representation as a string.

```
Public Shared Function GenerateKey(ByVal targetFile As String) As String
        Dim Algorithm As New RSACryptoServiceProvider()

        ' Save the private key
        Dim CompleteKey As String = Algorithm.ToXmlString(True)
        Dim KeyBytes As Byte() = Encoding.UTF8.GetBytes(CompleteKey)

        KeyBytes = ProtectedData.Protect(KeyBytes, Nothing,
                        DataProtectionScope.LocalMachine)

        Using fs As New FileStream(keyFile, FileMode.Open)
                fs.Write(KeyBytes, 0, KeyBytes.Length)
        End Using

        ' Return the public key
        Return Algorithm.ToXmlString(False)
End Function
```

The caller of the function needs to store the public key somewhere; this is necessary for encrypting information. You can retrieve the key as an XML representation through a method called ToXmlString(). The parameter specifies whether private key information is included (True) or not (False). Therefore, the GenerateKey function first calls the function with the True parameter to store the complete key information in the file and then calls it with the False parameter to include the public key only. Subsequently, the ReadKey() method just reads the key from the file and then initializes the passed algorithm instance through FromXmlString(), the opposite of the ToXmlString() method:

```
Private Shared Sub ReadKey(ByVal algorithm As RSACryptoServiceProvider,
                        ByVal keyFile As String)
        Dim KeyBytes As Byte()

        Using fs As New FileStream(keyFile, FileMode.Open)
                KeyBytes = New Byte(fs.Length - 1) {}
                fs.Read(KeyBytes, 0, CInt(fs.Length))
        End Using

        KeyBytes = ProtectedData.Unprotect(KeyBytes,
                Nothing, DataProtectionScope.LocalMachine)

        algorithm.FromXmlString(Encoding.UTF8.GetString(KeyBytes))

End Sub
```

This time the ReadKey method is used by the decryption function only. The EncryptData() function requires the caller to pass in the XML string representation of the public key returned by the GenerateKey method, because the private key is not required for encryption. Encryption and decryption with RSA takes place as follows:

```
Public Shared Function EncryptData(ByVal data As String,
                ByVal publicKey As String) As Byte()
        ' Create the algorithm based on the public key
        Dim Algorithm As New RSACryptoServiceProvider()
        Algorithm.FromXmlString(publicKey)

        ' Now encrypt the data
        Return Algorithm.Encrypt(Encoding.UTF8.GetBytes(data), True)
End Function

Public Shared Function DecryptData(ByVal data As Byte(),
                ByVal keyFile As String) As String
        Dim Algorithm As New RSACryptoServiceProvider()
        ReadKey(Algorithm, keyFile)

        Dim ClearData As Byte() = Algorithm.Decrypt(data, True)
        Return Convert.ToString(Encoding.UTF8.GetString(ClearData))
End Function
```

Now you can build a test page, as shown in Figure 25-7. (You can find the source code of this page in the book's downloads at www.apress.com.)

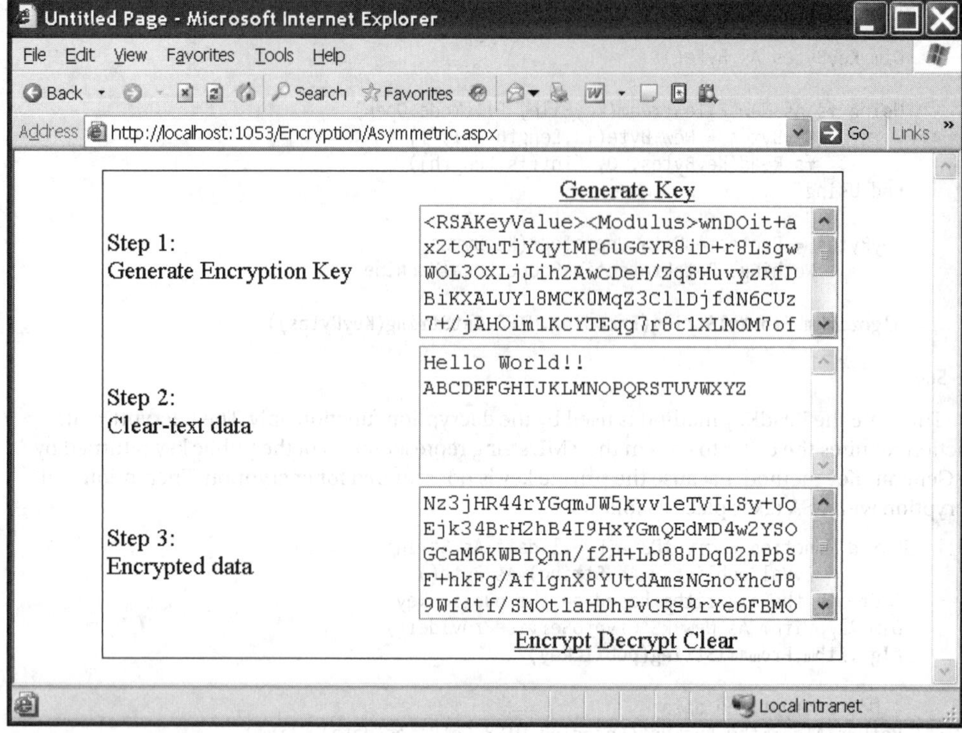

Figure 25-7. *A sample test page for asymmetric algorithms*

Encrypting Sensitive Data in a Database

In this section, you will learn how to create a simple test page for encrypting information stored in a database table. This table will be connected to a user registered in the membership service. We suggest not creating a custom membership provider with custom implementations of MembershipUser that support additional properties. As long as you stay loosely coupled with your own logic, you can use it with multiple membership providers. In this sample, you will create a database table that stores additional information for a MembershipUser without creating a custom provider. It just connects to the MembershipUser through the ProviderUserKey—this means the actual primary key of the underlying data store. Therefore, you have to create a table on your SQL Server as follows:

```
CREATE DATABASE ExtendedUser
GO
USE ExtendedUser
GO
CREATE TABLE ShopInfo
(
  UserId UNIQUEIDENTIFIER PRIMARY KEY,
  CreditCard VARBINARY(60),
  Street VARCHAR(80),
  ZipCode VARCHAR(6),
  City VARCHAR(60)
)
```

The primary key, UserId, will contain the same key as the MembershipUser for which this information is created. That's the only connection to the underlying membership service. As mentioned, the advantage of not creating a custom provider for just these additional fields is that you can use it for other providers. We suggest creating custom providers only for supporting additional types of data stores for the membership service. The sensitive information is the CreditCard field, which now is not stored as VARCHAR but as VARBINARY instead. Now you can create a page that looks like this:

```
<form id="form1" runat="server">
<div>
<asp:LoginView runat="server" ID="MainLoginView">
    <AnonymousTemplate>
        <asp:Login ID="MainLogin" runat="server" />
    </AnonymousTemplate>
    <LoggedInTemplate>
        Credit Card: <asp:TextBox ID="CreditCardText" runat="server" /><br />
        Street: <asp:TextBox ID="StreetText" runat="server" /><br />
        Zip Code: <asp:TextBox ID="ZipCodeText" runat="server" /><br />
        City: <asp:TextBox ID="CityText" runat="server" /><br />
        <asp:Button runat="server" ID="LoadCommand" Text="Load"
                    OnClick="LoadCommand_Click" /> 
        <asp:Button runat="server" ID="SaveCommand" Text="Save"
                    OnClick="SaveCommand_Click" />
    </LoggedInTemplate>
</asp:LoginView>
</div>
</form>
```

The page includes a LoginView control to display the Login control for anonymous users and display some text fields for the information introduced with the CREATE TABLE statement. Within the Load button's Click event handler, you will write code for retrieving and decrypting information from the database, and within the Save button's Click event handler, you will obviously do the opposite. Before doing that, though, don't forget to configure the connection string appropriately.

```
<configuration xmlns="http://schemas.microsoft.com/.NetConfiguration/v2.0">
    <connectionStrings>
        <add name="DemoSql"
             connectionString="data source=(local);
                               Integrated Security=SSPI;
                               initial catalog=ExtendedUser"/>
    </connectionStrings>
    <system.web>
        <authentication mode="Forms" />
    </system.web>
</configuration>
```

Now you should use the ASP.NET WAT to create a couple of users in your membership store. After you have done that, you can start writing the actual code for reading and writing data to the database. The code doesn't include anything special. It just uses the previously created encryption utility class for encrypting the data before updating the database and decrypting the data stored on the database.

Let's take a look at the update method first:

```
Protected Sub SaveCommand_Click(ByVal sender As Object,
                ByVal e As EventArgs)
        DemoDb.Open()
```

```
        Try
        Dim SqlText As String = "UPDATE ShopInfo " _
                        & "SET Street=@street, ZipCode=@zip, " _
                        & "City=@city, CreditCard=@card " _
                        & "WHERE UserId=@key"

        Dim Cmd As New SqlCommand(SqlText, DemoDb)

        ' Add simple values
        Cmd.Parameters.AddWithValue("@street", StreetText.Text)
        Cmd.Parameters.AddWithValue("@zip", ZipCodeText.Text)
        Cmd.Parameters.AddWithValue("@city", CityText.Text)
        Cmd.Parameters.AddWithValue("@key", Membership.GetUser().ProviderUserKey)

        ' Now add the encrypted value
        Dim EncryptedData As Byte() =
                SymmetricEncryptionUtility.EncryptData
                        (CreditCardText.Text, EncryptionKeyFile)
        Cmd.Parameters.AddWithValue("@card", EncryptedData)

        ' Execute the command
        Dim results As Integer = Cmd.ExecuteNonQuery()
        If results = 0 Then
                Cmd.CommandText = "INSERT INTO ShopInfo VALUES " _
                        & "(@key, @card, @street, @zip, @city)"
                Cmd.ExecuteNonQuery()
        End If
    Finally
        DemoDb.Close()
    End Try
End Sub
```

The two key parts of the previous code are the part that retrieves the ProviderUserKey from the currently logged-on MembershipUser for connecting the information to a membership user and the position where the credit card information is encrypted through the previously created encryption utility class. Only the encrypted byte array is passed as a parameter to the SQL command. Therefore, the data is stored encrypted in the database.

The opposite of this function, reading data, looks quite similar, as shown here:

```
Protected Sub LoadCommand_Click(ByVal sender As Object,
                        ByVal e As EventArgs)

        DemoDb.Open()

        Try
                Dim SqlText As String = "SELECT * FROM ShopInfo WHERE UserId=@key"
                Dim Cmd As New SqlCommand(SqlText, DemoDb)
                Cmd.Parameters.AddWithValue("@key",
                        Membership.GetUser().ProviderUserKey)

        Using fs As Reader As SqlDataReader = Cmd.ExecuteReader()
            If Reader.Read() Then
                ' Cleartext Data
                StreetText.Text = Reader("Street”).ToString()
                ZipCodeText.Text = Reader("ZipCode").ToString()
                CityText.Text = Reader("City").ToString()
```

```
            ' Encrypted Data
            Dim SecretCard As Byte() =
                      CType(Reader("CreditCard"), Byte())
            CreditCardText.Text =
                      SymmetricEncryptionUtility.DecryptData
                       (SecretCard, EncryptionKeyFile)
            End If
        End Using

        Finally
            DemoDb.Close()
        End Try
End Sub
```

Again, the function uses the currently logged-on MembershipUser's ProviderUserKey property for retrieving the information. If successfully retrieved, it reads the clear-text data and then retrieves the encrypted bytes from the database table. These bytes are then decrypted and displayed in the credit card text box. You can see the results in Figure 25-8.

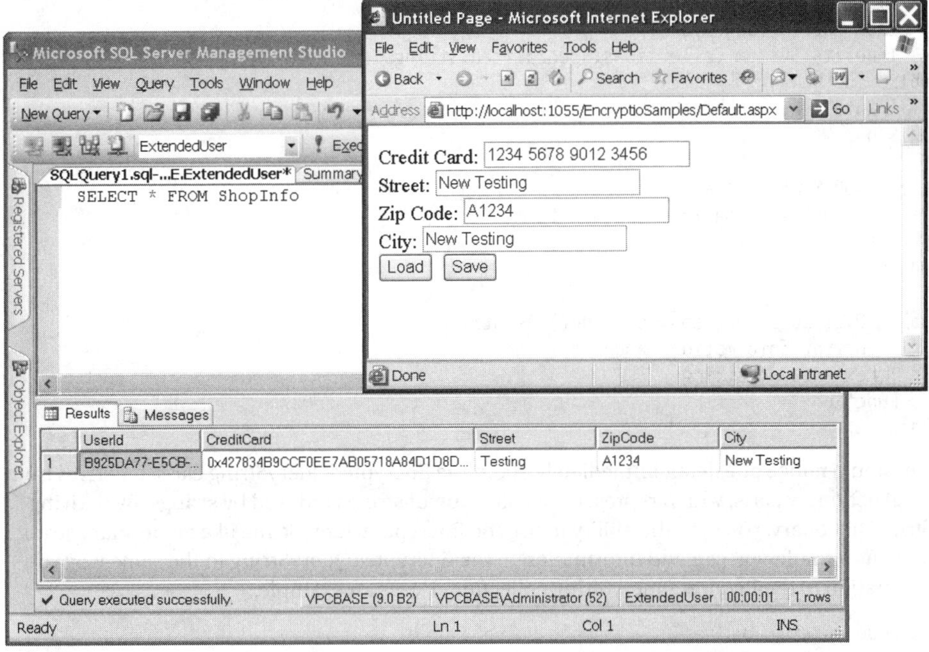

Figure 25-8. *Encrypting sensitive information on the database*

Encrypting the Query String

In this book, you've seen several examples in which ASP.NET security works behind the scenes to protect your data. For example, in Chapter 20 you learned how ASP.NET uses encryption and hash codes to ensure that the data in the form cookie is always protected. You have also learned how you can use the same tools to protect view state. Unfortunately, ASP.NET doesn't provide a similar way to enable automatic encryption for the query string (which is the extra bit of information you add to URLs to transmit information from one page to another). In many cases, the URL query information corresponds to user-supplied data, and it doesn't matter whether the user can see or modify it. In other cases, however, the query string contains information that should remain hidden from the user. In this case, the only option is to switch to another form of state management (which may have other limitations) or devise a system to encrypt the query string.

In the next example, you'll see a simple way to tighten security by scrambling data before you place it in the query string. Once again, you can rely on the cryptography classes provided with .NET. In fact, you can leverage the DPAPI. (Of course, you can do this only if you are not in a server farm environment. In that case, you could use the previously created encryption classes and deploy the same key file to any machine in the server farm.)

Wrapping the Query String

The starting point is to build an EncryptedQueryString class. This class should accept a collection of string-based information (just like the query string) and allow you to retrieve it in another page. Behind the scenes, the EncryptedQueryString class needs to encrypt the data before it's placed in the query string and decrypt it seamlessly on the way out.

Here's the starting point for the EncryptedQueryString class you need:

```
Public Class EncryptedQueryString
        Inherits System.Collections.Specialized.StringDictionary
    Public Sub New()
        ' Nothing to do here
    End Sub

    Public Sub New(ByVal encryptedData As String)
        ' Decrypt information, and add to
        ' the dictionary
    End Sub

    Public Overrides Function ToString() As String
        ' Encrypt information, and return as
        ' hex-encoded string
    End Function
End Class
```

You should notice one detail immediately about the EncryptedQueryString class: it derives from the StringDictionary class, which represents a collection of strings indexed by strings. By deriving from StringDictionary, you gain the ability to use the EncryptedQueryString like an ordinary string collection. As a result, you can add information to the EncryptedQueryString in the same way you add information to the Request.QueryString collection. Here's an example:

```
encryptedQueryString("value1") = "Sample Value"
```

Best of all, you get this functionality for free, without needing to write any additional code. So, with just this rudimentary class, you have the ability to store a collection of name/value strings. But how do you actually place this information into the query string? The EncryptedQueryString class provides a ToString() method that examines all the collection data and combines it in a single encrypted string.

First, the EncryptedQueryString class needs to combine the separate collection values into a delimited string so that it's easy to split the string back into a collection on the destination page. In this case, the ToString() method uses the conventions of the query string, separating each value from the name with an equal sign (=) and separating each subsequent name/value pair with the ampersand (&). However, for this to work, you need to make sure the names and values of the actual item in the collection don't include these special characters. To solve this problem, the ToString() method uses the HttpServerUtility.UrlEncode() method to escape the strings before joining them.

Here's the first portion of the ToString() method, which escapes and joins the collection settings into one string:

```
Public Overrides Function ToString() As String
    Dim Content As New StringBuilder()

    ' Go through the contents, and build a
    ' typical query string
    For Each key As String In MyBase.Keys
        Content.Append(HttpUtility.UrlEncode(key))
        Content.Append("=")
        Content.Append(HttpUtility.UrlEncode(MyBase.Item(key)))
        Content.Append("&")
    Next
    ' Remove the last '&'
    Content.Remove(Content.Length-1, 1)
    ...
```

The next step is to use the ProtectedData class to encrypt the data. This class uses the DPAPI to encrypt the information and its Protect method to return a byte array, so you need to take additional steps to convert the byte array to a string form that's suitable for the query string. One approach that seems reasonable is the Shared Convert.ToBase64String() method, which creates a Base64-encoded string. Unfortunately, Base64 strings can include symbols that aren't allowed in the query string (namely, the equal sign). Although you could create a Base64 string and then URL-encode it, this further complicates the decoding stage. The problem is that the ToBase64String() method may also introduce a series of characters that look like URL-encoded character sequences. These character sequences will then be incorrectly replaced when you decode the string.

A simpler approach is to use a different form of encoding. This example uses hex encoding, which replaces each character with an alphanumeric code. The methods for hex encoding aren't shown in this example, but they are available with the downloadable code.

```
    ...
' Now encrypt the contents using DPAPI
    Dim EncryptedData As Byte() =
        ProtectedData.Protect(Encoding.UTF8.GetBytes(Content.ToString()),
                Nothing, DataProtectionScope.LocalMachine)

    ' Convert encrypted byte array to a URL-legal string
    ' This would also be a good place to check that data
    ' is not larger than typical 4 KB query string
    Return HexEncoding.GetString(EncryptedData)
End Function
```

You can place the string returned from EncryptedQueryString.ToString() directly into a query string using the Response.Redirect() method.

The destination page that receives the query data needs a way to deserialize and decrypt the string. The first step is to create a new EncryptedQueryString object and supply the encrypted data. To make this step easier, it makes sense to add a new constructor to the EncryptedQueryString class that accepts the encrypted string, as follows:

```
Public Sub New(ByVal encryptedData As String)
    ' Decrypt data passed in using DPAPI
    Dim RawData As Byte() = HexEncoding.GetBytes(encryptedData)
```

```
    Dim ClearRawData As Byte() = ProtectedData.Unprotect(RawData, Nothing,
                     DataProtectionScope.LocalMachine)
    Dim StringData As String = Encoding.UTF8.GetString(ClearRawData)

    ' Split the data, and add the contents
    Dim Index As Integer
    Dim SplittedData As String() = StringData.Split(New Char() { "&"c })
    For Each SingleData As String In SplittedData
        Index = SingleData.IndexOf("="c)
        MyBase.Add(HttpUtility.UrlDecode
                (SingleData.Substring(0, Index)),
               HttpUtility.UrlDecode(SingleData.Substring(Index + 1)))
    Next
End Sub
```

This constructor first decodes the hexadecimal information from the string passed in and uses the DPAPI to decrypt information stored in the query string. It then splits the information back into its parts and adds the key/value pairs to the base StringCollection.

Now you have the entire infrastructure in place to create a simple test page and transmit information from one page to another in a secure fashion.

Creating a Test Page

To try the EncryptedQueryString class, you need two pages—one that sets the query string and redirects the user and another that retrieves the query string. The first one contains a text box for entering information, as follows:

```
<form id="form1" runat="server">
<div>
Enter some data here: <asp:TextBox runat="server" ID="MyData" />
<br />
<br />
<asp:Button ID="SendCommand" runat="server" Text="Send Info"
         OnClick="SendCommand_Click" />
</div>
</form>
```

When the user clicks the SendCommand button, the page sends the encrypted query string to the receiving page, as follows:

```
Protected Sub SendCommand_Click(ByVal sender As Object, ByVal e As EventArgs)
    Dim QueryString As New EncryptedQueryString()

    QueryString.Add("MyData", MyData.Text)
    QueryString.Add("MyTime", DateTime.Now.ToLongTimeString())
    QueryString.Add("MyDate", DateTime.Now.ToLongDateString())

    Response.Redirect("QueryStringRecipient.aspx?data=" & QueryString.ToString())
End Sub
```

Notice that the page enters the complete encrypted data string as one parameter called *data* into the query string for the destination page. Figure 25-9 shows the page in action.

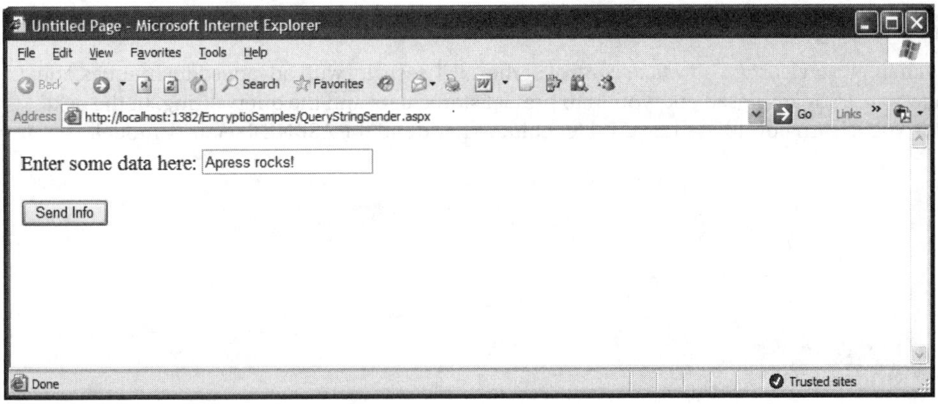

Figure 25-9. *The source page in action*

The destination page deserializes the query string passed in through the data query string parameter with the previously created class, as follows:

```
Protected Sub Page_Load(ByVal sender As Object, ByVal e As EventArgs)
    ' Deserialize the encrypted query string
    Dim QueryString As New EncryptedQueryString(Request.QueryString("data"))

    ' Write information to the screen
    Dim Info As New StringBuilder()
    For Each key As String In QueryString.Keys
        Info.AppendFormat("{0} = {1}<br>", key, QueryString(key))
    Next
    QueryStringLabel.Text = Info.ToString()
End Sub
```

This code adds the information to a label on the page. You can see the result of the previously posted information in Figure 25-10.

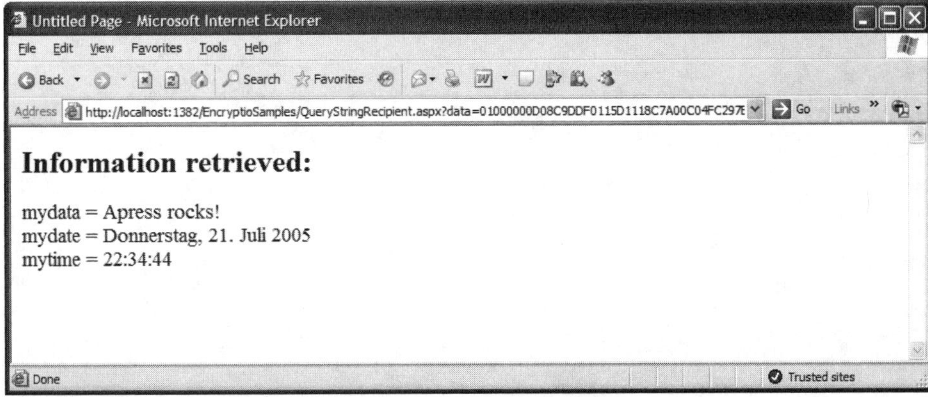

Figure 25-10. *The results of the received query string information*

Summary

In this chapter, you learned how take control of the .NET security with advanced techniques. You saw how to use stream-based encryption to protect stored data and the query string. In the next chapter, you'll learn how to use powerful techniques to extend the ASP.NET security model.

CHAPTER 26

Custom Membership Providers

In the previous chapters, you learned all the necessary details for authenticating and authorizing users with ASP.NET through both forms authentication and Windows authentication. You learned that with forms authentication on its own, you are responsible for managing users (and roles if you want to implement role-based authorization in your application) in a custom store.

Fortunately, ASP.NET 2.0 ships with the membership API and the roles API, which provide you with a framework for user and roles management. You learned the details about the membership API in Chapter 21, and you learned about the roles API in Chapter 23. You can extend the framework through providers that implement the actual access to the underlying data store. In both of those chapters, you used the default provider for SQL Server that ships with ASP.NET 2.0.

Of course, you can exchange the default implementation that works with SQL Server by implementing custom membership and roles providers. This gives you the possibility of exchanging the underlying storage used for user and role information, without affecting your web application.

In this chapter, you will learn how you can extend the membership API and the roles API by implementing custom membership and roles providers. Furthermore, you will learn how you can configure and debug your custom provider for web applications. With the information in this chapter, you will also be equipped to create other custom providers—for example, providers for the profiles API and the personalization engine of web parts—because the creation process is always the same.

Note Because the provider model was introduced in ASP.NET 2.0, most of the information in this chapter is new. Of course, for developing a custom membership and roles provider, you need in-depth know-how of ADO.NET, System.Xml, and the basic ASP.NET infrastructure. If you are coming from ASP.NET 1.1, you should read Chapters 21 and 23 before digging into this chapter. If you are new to ASP.NET, you should read Chapters 19, 20, 21, 23, and 25 as well as Chapters 7, 8, 12, and 13 before you start reading this chapter.

Architecture of Custom Providers

In Chapters 21 and 23 you learned many details of the integrated membership and roles services. These services provide you with an out-of-the-box solution for managing users and roles with forms authentication. As explained earlier, you can extend the model through providers, as shown in Figure 26-1. When implementing custom providers, you should always keep the architecture shown in Figure 26-1 in mind. A custom provider is always based on the lowest level in the layered model introduced by the ASP.NET 2.0 membership and roles framework. It's important to know that every other provider-based API in ASP.NET 2.0 is structured in the same way. Therefore, implementing custom providers for the profiles API or the personalization engine of ASP.NET 2.0 is similar.

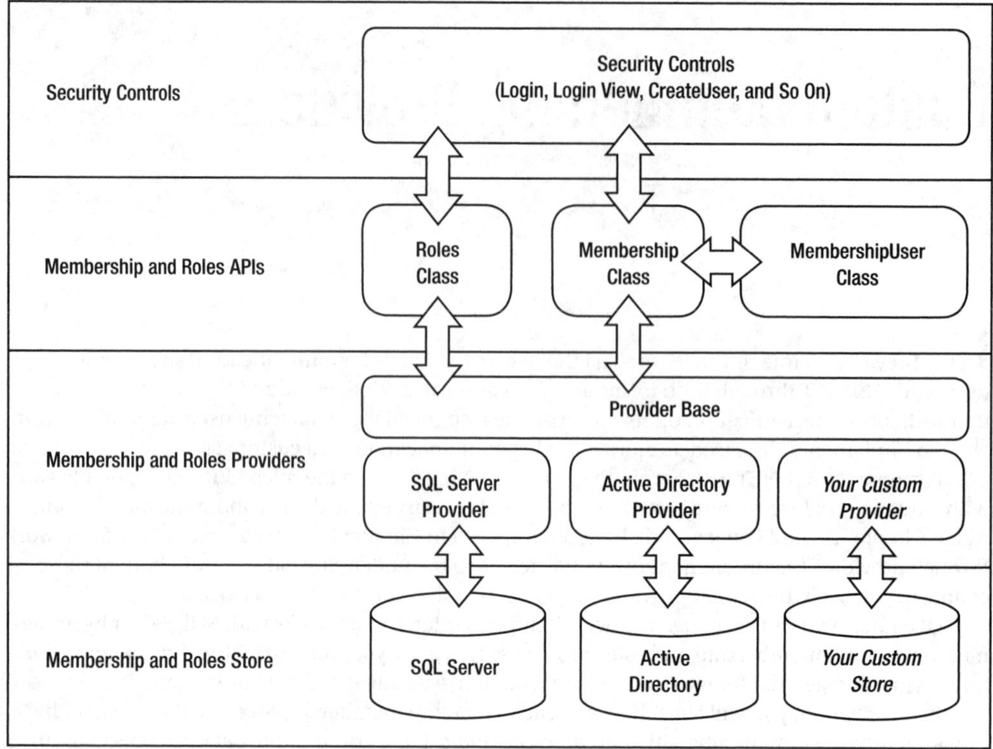

Figure 26-1. *The membership and roles framework*

As you can see from their basic architectures, the membership and roles services are independent from each other. Therefore, membership providers and Role providers have separate base classes; in addition, you can store membership users and roles in different back-end systems. A good example is when using the roles service with Windows authentication. Remember what you learned in Chapter 23 about application-specific roles that are used for authorization within the application instead of within Windows groups: This provides you with a way to decouple your application from an underlying Active Directory infrastructure.

Before you learn about the details of implementing custom providers, it's important to understand why you might want to create a custom membership provider. Some common reasons include the following:

- You want to use an existing user and roles database that has a different schema than the ASP.NET standard.
- You want to use a database other than Microsoft SQL Server.
- You want to use an unusual data store (such as an XML file, web service, or Active Directory).
- You want implement additional authentication logic. A good example of this is often implemented for governmental websites where users have to authenticate by specifying three values: a user name, a subscription ID, and a password.

If you just want to store your own information in addition to the information stored by the default implementation, we recommend not implementing a custom provider. Because the membership API gives you access to a key that uniquely identifies a user in the store, we recommend adding your own tables for storing your additional information and connecting information stored in your tables through the user's unique key with the actual user of the membership provider's storage; alternatively, you could implement user profiles for these additional properties. This is far easier than implementing a custom provider for adding a few extra values.

From within the application, you can access the user's unique key through the ProviderUserKey property of the MembershipUser class. In this chapter, you will learn how the unique key is propagated to the ProviderUserKey of the MembershipUser class.

Basic Steps for Creating Custom Providers

You will now learn how to implement your custom provider for the membership and roles services. Creating a custom provider involves the following steps:

1. Design and create the underlying data store.
2. Create utility classes for accessing the underlying data store.
3. Create a class that inherits from the MembershipProvider.
4. Create a class that inherits from the RoleProvider.
5. Create a provider test application.
6. Configure the custom providers in your test application.
7. Use the custom providers in your custom application.

Implementing custom providers is fairly straightforward but will require some time, as you have to implement lots of methods and properties. In the following sections, you will create a custom membership and roles provider that uses an XML file as the underlying data store. XML files are not a good solution for highly scalable applications but may be a nice alternative if you write a simple application and need to host this application on a provider site and don't have access to a database such as SQL Server.

Overall Design of the Custom Provider

Before creating a custom provider, you have to think about the overall design of the solution. Your goal is to keep the underlying functionality as simple as possible so that you can concentrate on the actual membership and roles provider implementation. In terms of XML, the easiest way to load and save data to XML files is XML serialization. This allows you to store a complete object graph with just one function call in a file and to read it with one function call.

```
Dim Serializer As New XmlSerializer(GetType(List(Of SimpleUser)))
Using reader As New XmlTextReader(fileName)
    Users = CType(Serializer.Deserialize(reader), (List(Of SimpleUser)))
End Using
```

Because classes such as MembershipUser don't allow you to access some information—for example, the password—you cannot use them with XML serialization directly; XML serialization requires all properties and members that need to be stored as public properties or members. Therefore, you will create your own representation of users and roles as utility classes for the back-end store. These classes will never be passed to the application, which simply relies on the existing membership classes. (You will include some mapping logic, which is fairly simple, between this internal user representation and the MembershipUser class.) Figure 26-2 shows the overall design of the custom provider solution.

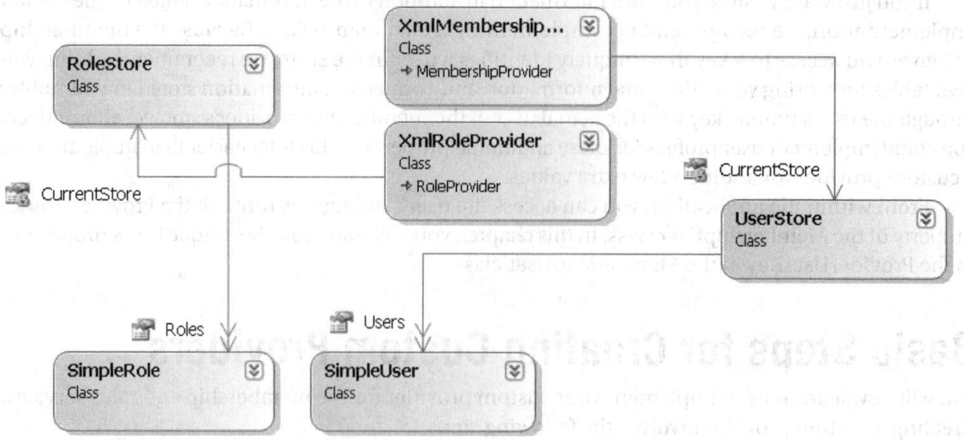

Figure 26-2. *The design of your custom provider solution*

As mentioned, the SimpleUser and SimpleRole classes make XML serialization possible. Although this requires some mapping logic for supporting MembershipUser, this makes the whole implementation much easier. UserStore and RoleStore are both utility classes for encapsulating the access to the XML file. These classes include functions for loading and saving XML files as well as some basic utility functions for searching information in the store.

Finally, the model includes the XmlMembershipProvider and XmlRoleProvider classes. XmlMembershipProvider inherits basic functionality from MembershipProvider, while XmlRoleProvider is inherited from RoleProvider. Both base classes are defined in the System.Web.Security namespace.

Designing and Implementing the Custom Store

After you have designed your overall architecture, you can start thinking about the underlying data store. In the example, the data store will consist of an XML file for the users and an XML file for the roles. To make access to these files as simple as possible, you will use XML serialization as the primary mechanism for reading from and writing to these files. Therefore, you need some classes to hold the data stored to the XML files either as public fields or as properties, as follows:

```
Public Class SimpleUser
    Public UserKey As Guid = Guid.Empty

    Public UserName As String.Empty
    Public Password As String.Empty

    Public Email As String.Empty
    Public CreationDate As DateTime = DateTime.Now
    Public LastActivityDate As DateTime = DateTime.MinValue
    Public LastLoginDate As DateTime = DateTime.MinValue
    Public LastPasswordChangeDate As DateTime = DateTime.MinValue
    Public PasswordQuestion As String.Empty
    Public PasswordAnswer As String.Empty
    Public Comment As String
End Class
```

```
Public Class SimpleRole
    Public RoleName As String.Empty
    Public AssignedUsers As New StringCollection()
End Class
```

In this example, you will use a GUID as ProviderUserKey for uniquely identifying users in your store. For every user you will then store a user name, a password (hashed), an e-mail, some date information, a password question and answer, and some comments. For the roles, you will store a name as well as the association to the users. For simplicity, every role will contain an array of user names (which are strings) that are associated with this role. The serialized version of an array of users will be the user store, while the serialized version of an array of roles will be the roles store, as shown in Figure 26-3.

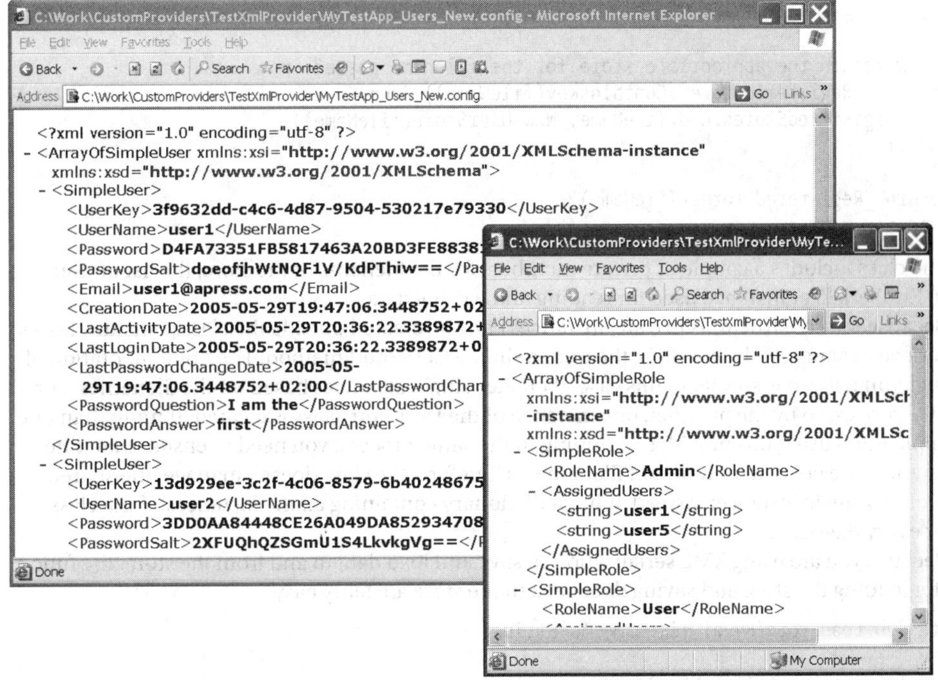

Figure 26-3. *Serialized versions of the SimpleUser/SimpleRole arrays*

Another design aspect you have to think about is how to access the store. Basically, for every store, you need only one instance in memory in order to save resources and avoid loading the XML files too often. You can implement this through the Singleton pattern, which is a solution for ensuring that only one instance of a class exists within a process. It does this by making the constructor private and providing a public Shared method for retrieving an instance. This public method verifies whether the instance already exists, and if not, it automatically creates an instance of its own, which is then returned.

Let's examine all these aspects based on the UserStore class introduced in Figure 26-3:

```
Private _FileName As String
Private _Users As List(Of SimpleUser)
Private _Serializer As XmlSerializer
```

```
Private Shared _RegisteredStores As Dictionary(Of String, UserStore)

Private Sub New(ByVal fileName As String)
    _FileName = fileName
    _Users = New List(Of SimpleUser)()
    _Serializer = New XmlSerializer(GetType(List(Of SimpleUser)))

    LoadStore(_FileName)
End Sub

Public Shared Function GetStore(ByVal fileName As String) As UserStore
    ' Create the registered store if it does not exist yet
    If _RegisteredStores Is Nothing Then
        _RegisteredStores = New Dictionary(Of String, UserStore)()
    End If

    ' Now return the appropriate store for the filename passed in
    If (Not _RegisteredStores.ContainsKey(fileName)) Then
        _RegisteredStores.Add(fileName, New UserStore(fileName))
    End If

    Return _RegisteredStores(fileName)
End Function
```

The class includes a couple of private members for the filename of the store, the list of users, and an XmlSerializer instance used for reading and writing data.

Because the constructor is private, instances can't be created outside the class. Outside classes can retrieve instances only by calling the public shared GetStore() method. The implementation of the Singleton pattern is special in this case. It creates single instances based on the filenames. For every file processed by the provider, one instance of the UserStore class is created. If more than one web application using this provider is running in the same process, you need to ensure that different instances are created for different filenames. Therefore, the class doesn't manage one shared variable for a single instance; instead, it has a dictionary containing all the instances of the class, one for every filename.

Because you are using XML serialization to save and load data to and from the store, the functions for loading the store and saving data back to the store are fairly easy:

```
Private Sub LoadStore(ByVal fileName As String)
    Try
        If File.Exists(fileName) Then
            Using reader As New XmlTextReader(fileName)
              _Users = CType(_Serializer.Deserialize(reader), List(Of SimpleUser))
            End Using
        End If
    Catch ex As Exception
        Throw New Exception(String.Format("Unable to load file {0}", fileName), ex)
    End Try
End Sub

Private Sub SaveStore(ByVal fileName As String)
    Try
        If System.IO.File.Exists(fileName) Then
            System.IO.File.Delete(fileName)
        End If

        Using writer As New XmlTextWriter(fileName, Encoding.UTF8)
                _Serializer.Serialize(writer, _Users)
```

```
        End Using
    Catch ex As Exception
        Throw New Exception(String.Format("Unable to save file {0}", fileName), ex)
    End Try
End Sub
```

Both functions are private, as they are called only within the class itself. The LoadStore() method is called within the constructor of the UserStore class. Within the method, the private variable _Users is initialized. Every subsequent query happens based on querying the _Users collection of the store class. The SaveStore() method, on the other hand, just serializes the _Users collection to the file specified in the private _FileName member, which is passed in through the constructor (and indirectly through the static GetStore() method). Finally, the class supports a couple of methods for querying information in the _Users collection.

```
Public ReadOnly Property Users() As List(Of SimpleUser)
    Get
        Return _Users
    End Get
End Property

Public Sub Save()
    SaveStore(_FileName)
End Sub

Public Function GetUserByName(ByVal name As String) As SimpleUser
            Dim theUser As New SimpleUser
            Dim nUserItem As Integer
            For nUserItem = 0 To Users.Count - 1
                If Users.Item(nUserItem).UserName = name Then
                    theUser = Users.Item(nUserItem)
                    Exit For
                End If
            Next
            Return theUser
End Function


Public Function GetUserByEmail(ByVal email As String) As SimpleUser
            Dim theUser As New SimpleUser
            Dim nUserItem As Integer
            For nUserItem = 0 To Users.Count - 1
                If Users.Item(nUserItem).Email = email Then
                    theUser = Users.Item(nUserItem)
                    Exit For
                End If
            Next
            Return theUser
End Function

Public Function GetUserByKey(ByVal key As Guid) As SimpleUser
            Dim theUser As New SimpleUser
            Dim nUserItem As Integer
            For nUserItem = 0 To Users.Count - 1
                If Users.Item(nUserItem).UserKey = key Then
                    theUser = Users.Item(nUserItem)
                    Exit For
                End If
            Next
```

```
        Return theUser
End Function
```

The Users property is a simple property that allows the actual provider (XmlMembershipProvider) to access users of the store. After the provider implementation has changed something within the store (has changed properties of a user, for example), it calls the public Save() method, which internally calls the SaveStore() to serialize information back to the file specified in the private _FileName variable of this instance. The remaining methods are for searching users based on different criteria.

The UserStore includes the implementation for saving user information only. Roles are not included. For this purpose, you have to implement the RoleStore class (which is similar to the UserStore class), as shown here:

```
Public Class RoleStore
    Private _Serializer As XmlSerializer
    Private _FileName As String
    Private _Roles As List(Of SimpleRole)

    #Region "Singleton Implementation"

    Private Shared _RegisteredStores As Dictionary(Of String, RoleStore)

    Public Shared Function GetStore(ByVal fileName As String) As RoleStore
        ' Create the registered stores
        If _RegisteredStores Is Nothing Then
            _RegisteredStores = New Dictionary(Of String, RoleStore)()
        End If

        ' Now return the appropriate store
        If (Not _RegisteredStores.ContainsKey(fileName)) Then
            _RegisteredStores.Add(fileName, New RoleStore(fileName))
        End If

        Return _RegisteredStores(fileName)
    End Function

    Private Sub New(ByVal fileName As String)
        _Roles = New List(Of SimpleRole)()
        _FileName = fileName
        _Serializer = New XmlSerializer(GetType(List(Of SimpleRole)))

        LoadStore(_FileName)
    End Sub

    #End Region

    #Region "Private Helper Methods"

    Private Sub LoadStore(ByVal fileName As String)
        Try
                If File.Exists(fileName) Then
                        Using reader As New XmlTextReader(fileName)
                            _Roles = CType(_Serializer.Deserialize(reader),
                                (List(Of SimpleRole)))
                        End Using
                End If
        Catch ex As Exception
            Throw New Exception(
```

```
                    String.Format("Unable to load file {0}", fileName), ex)
        End Try
    End Sub

    Private Sub SaveStore(ByVal fileName As String)
        Try
            If File.Exists(fileName) Then
                File.Delete(fileName)
            End If

            Using writer As New XmlTextWriter(fileName, Encoding.UTF8)
                _Serializer.Serialize(writer, _Roles)
            End Using
        Catch ex As Exception
            Throw New Exception(
                String.Format("Unable to save file {0}", fileName), ex)
        End Try
    End Sub

    #End Region

    Public ReadOnly Property Roles() As List(Of SimpleRole)
        Get
                Return _Roles
        End Get
    End Property

    Public Sub Save()
        SaveStore(_FileName)
    End Sub

    Public Function GetRolesForUser(
                ByVal userName As String) as List(Of SimpleRole)()
        Dim Results As List(Of SimpleRole) = New List(Of SimpleRole)()
        For Each r As SimpleRole In Roles
            If r.AssignedUsers.Contains(userName) Then
                Results.Add(r)
            End If
        Next
        Return Results
    End Function

    Public Function GetUsersInRole(ByVal roleName As String) As String()
        Dim Role As SimpleRole = GetRole(roleName)
        If Role IsNot Nothing Then
            Dim Results As String() = New String(Role.AssignedUsers.Count - 1) {}
            Role.AssignedUsers.CopyTo(Results, 0)
            Return Results
        Else
            Throw New Exception(
                String.Format("Role with name {0} does not exist!", roleName))
        End If
    End Function

Public Function GetRole(ByVal roleName As String) As SimpleRole
```

```
        Dim theRole As New SimpleRole
        Dim nRoleItem As Integer
        For nRoleItem = 0 To Roles.Count - 1
            If Roles.Item(nRoleItem).RoleName = roleName Then
                theRole = Roles.Item(nRoleItem)
                Exit For
            End If
        Next
        Return theRole
    End Function
End Class
```

This implementation looks fairly similar to the UserStore. The major difference is that it uses the SimpleRole class instead of the SimpleUser class, and it initializes the XmlSerializer class with a different type. Also, the functions for querying the store are different.

Now the classes for accessing the underlying stores are complete, which means you can start implementing the custom provider classes.

Implementing the Provider Classes

In this section, you will create the XmlMembershipProvider class, which actually fulfills the role of an adapter between your custom store and the requirements of the membership API. (The code for the complete provider implementation is included in this book's downloads.) In this section you will go through the most important parts of creating a membership provider.

Every custom membership provider must be inherited from System.Web.Security.Membership provider, as follows:

```
Public Class XmlMembershipProvider
       Inherits MembershipProvider
    ' ...
End Class
```

When inheriting from MembershipProvider, you have to implement lots of properties and methods to fulfill the requirements of the membership API. These properties and methods are used for querying, creating, updating, and deleting users as well as retrieving specific information about the provider such as password requirements. These types of properties are queried by the security controls introduced in Chapter 21. (For example, the RequirePasswordQuestionAndAnswer property is queried by the CreateUserWizard to decide whether to display the text boxes for entering password questions and answers.) You should start by implementing the properties of the provider, as this is the easiest part of the whole task. For every property, you should provide one private variable that contains the state of the appropriate property.

```
Public Overrides Property ApplicationName() As String
End Property

Public Overrides Property EnablePasswordReset() As Boolean
End Property

Public Overrides Property EnablePasswordRetrieval() As Boolean
End Property

Public Overrides Property MaxInvalidPasswordAttempts() As Integer
End Property

Public Overrides Property MinRequiredNonAlphanumericCharacters() As Integer
End Property
```

```
Public Overrides Property MinRequiredPasswordLength() As Integer
End Property

Public Overrides Property PasswordAttemptWindow() As Integer
End Property

Public Overrides Property PasswordFormat() As MembershipPasswordFormat
End Property

Public Overrides Property PasswordStrengthRegularExpression() As String
End Property

Public Overrides Property RequiresQuestionAndAnswer() As Boolean
End Property

Public Overrides Property RequiresUniqueEmail() As Boolean
End Property
```

For a detailed description of these properties, you can refer to Chapter 21. The properties of providers are described there, and they have the same meaning as in the underlying provider implementation. Many of these properties just have get accessors and no setters. So, how can the ASP.NET infrastructure initialize these properties with values configured in web.config? You can find the answer in the original base class for all providers, which is in the System.Configuration.Provider.ProviderBase class. The ProviderBase class in turn is the base class for the MembershipProvider class, and therefore all classes that inherit from MembershipProvider are indirectly inherited from ProviderBase and have the basic properties of ProviderBase. All you have to do is override the Initialize method. This method accepts two parameters: a name (which is configured through the name attribute in web.config) and a NameValueCollection (which contains keys and their appropriate values for all settings configured through web.config). Within this method you can initialize the private members of the properties shown previously.

Let's examine the contents of this function for the XmlMembershipProvider step by step:

```
Public Overrides Sub Initialize(ByVal name As String, ByVal config As
                System.Collections.Specialized.NameValueCollection)
    If config Is Nothing Then
        Throw New ArgumentNullException("config")
    End If
    If String.IsNullOrEmpty(name) Then
        name = "XmlMembershipProvider"
    End If
    If String.IsNullOrEmpty(config("description")) Then
        config.Remove("description")
        config.Add("description", "XML Membership Provider")
    End If

    ' Initialize the base class
    MyBase.Initialize(name, config)
    ...
```

First, you have to verify whether any configuration is passed in. If nothing is configured for the provider, it won't work. Second, if no name is specified, you have to initialize a default name, which is required by the configuration tool for displaying the provider in the list of providers. Finally, you have to add a default description if no description is configured for the provider. This final step is optional but useful for configuration tools that query provider information.

Don't forget to call the base class's Initialize implementation for initializing basic properties properly. You do this in the last line of code in the previous code.

Next, you can start initializing your properties:

```
...
' Initialize default values
_ApplicationName = "DefaultApp"
_EnablePasswordReset = False
_PasswordStrengthRegEx = "[\w| !§$%&/()=\-?\*]*"
_MaxInvalidPasswordAttempts = 3
_MinRequiredNonAlphanumericChars = 1
_MinRequiredPasswordLength = 5
_RequiresQuestionAndAnswer = False
_PasswordFormat = MembershipPasswordFormat.Hashed

' Now go through the properties, and initialize custom values
For Each key As String In config.Keys
    Select Case key.ToLower()
        Case "name"
            _Name = config(key)
        Case "applicationname"
            _ApplicationName = config(key)
        Case "filename"
            _FileName = config(key)
        Case "enablepasswordreset"
            _EnablePasswordReset = Boolean.Parse(config(key))
        Case "passwordstrengthregex"
            _PasswordStrengthRegEx = config(key)
        Case "maxinvalidpasswordattempts"
            _MaxInvalidPasswordAttempts = Integer.Parse(config(key))
        Case "minrequirednonalphanumericchars"
            _MinRequiredNonAlphanumericChars = Integer.Parse(config(key))
        Case "minrequiredpasswordlength"
            _MinRequiredPasswordLength = Integer.Parse(config(key))
        Case "passwordformat"
            _PasswordFormat = CType(System.Enum.Parse(GetType
                (MembershipPasswordFormat), config(key)), MembershipPasswordFormat)
        Case "requiresquestionandanswer"
            _RequiresQuestionAndAnswer = Boolean.Parse(config(key))
    End Select
```

■ Caution In our first implementation, we tried to derive the default application name from the current HTTP context automatically based on the virtual root directory. The effect was that our provider worked properly as long as we used the management functions from within the application. As soon as we tried to use it from the ASP.NET WAT, though, it failed with an exception. When debugging, we discovered that in this case the provider doesn't have access to members of the application's HTTP context. Therefore, you should avoid using the HttpContext.Current in your membership provider and instead keep it as simple as possible.

The previous code starts by initializing some default values for your options, just in case they are not included in the web.config configuration file. After initializing these default values, you can go through the entries of the config parameter passed into the method (which is a simple NameValueCollection). As you can see, you even can include custom settings such as the filename setting, which is not included in the default set of properties of the membership provider. This filename property is a custom property for your specific provider that points to the XML file that contains the user information. You will pass this filename to the UserStore class in a separate property that you will use in the remaining functions of the implementation.

```
Private ReadOnly Property CurrentStore() As UserStore
    Get
        If _CurrentStore Is Nothing Then
            _CurrentStore = UserStore.GetStore(_FileName)
        End If
        Return _CurrentStore
    End Get
End Property
```

Next, you have a large number of methods in your provider. These methods are for creating, updating, and deleting users as well as for accessing and retrieving user details. The methods basically access the information through the previously created store classes.

Within those methods, you just have to call the appropriate methods of the UserStore class through the previously introduced CurrentStore property. These are the only methods defined by the provider. Any additional method introduced in this chapter is a helper method that you have to include on your own. (In this book, you will see the most important implementations of these methods but not all of them. The complete code is available with the book's download.)

Let's get started with the CreateUser method.

Creating Users and Adding Them to the Store

The CreateUser method is interesting because it needs to make sure that the user name and e-mail are unique and that the password is valid and adheres to the password strength requirements.

```
Public Overrides Function CreateUser(ByVal username As String, _
         ByVal password As String, ByVal email As String, _
         ByVal passwordQuestion As String, ByVal passwordAnswer As String, _
         ByVal isApproved As Boolean, ByVal providerUserKey As Object, _
         <System.Runtime.InteropServices.Out()>
        ByRef status As MembershipCreateStatus) As MembershipUser
    Try
        ' Validate the user name and e-mail
        If (Not ValidateUsername(username, email, Guid.Empty)) Then
            status = MembershipCreateStatus.InvalidUserName
            Return Nothing
        End If

        ' Raise the event before validating the password
        MyBase.OnValidatingPassword(New ValidatePasswordEventArgs(
                username, password, True))

        ' Validate the password
        If (Not ValidatePassword(password)) Then
            status = MembershipCreateStatus.InvalidPassword
            Return Nothing
        End If
...
```

In the first section, the function calls the Private methods ValidateUserName and ValilldatePassword. These methods make sure the user name and e-mail are unique in the store and the password adheres to the password strength requirements. After these checks succeed, you can create the user for the underlying store (SimpleUser), add the user to the store, and then save the store.

```
...
' Everything is valid; create the user
        Dim user As New SimpleUser()
        user.UserKey = Guid.NewGuid()
```

```
        user.UserName = username
        user.Password = Me.TransformPassword(password)
        user.Email = email
        user.PasswordQuestion = passwordQuestion
        user.PasswordAnswer = passwordAnswer
        user.CreationDate = DateTime.Now
        user.LastActivityDate = DateTime.Now
        user.LastPasswordChangeDate = DateTime.Now

        ' Add the user to the store
        CurrentStore.Users.Add(user)
        CurrentStore.Save()

        status = MembershipCreateStatus.Success
        Return CreateMembershipFromInternalUser(user)
    Catch
        ' Do some local error handling
        Throw
    End Try
End Function
```

Finally, the method needs to return an instance of MembershipUser to the calling Membership class with the details of the created user. For this purpose, you just need to match the properties of your SimpleUser instance to the properties of the MembershipUser, as shown in the following function:

```
Private Function CreateMembershipFromInternalUser(ByVal user As SimpleUser)
        As MembershipUser
    Dim muser As New MembershipUser(MyBase.Name, user.UserName, user.UserKey,
        user.Email, user.PasswordQuestion, String.Empty, True, False,
        user.CreationDate, user.LastLoginDate, user.LastActivityDate,
        user.LastPasswordChangeDate, DateTime.MaxValue)

    Return muser
End Function
```

As you can see, this mapping creates an instance of MembershipUser and passes the appropriate properties from your own SimpleUser as constructor parameters.

Next, take a look at the validation functions for validating the user name, e-mail, and password:

```
Private Function ValidatePassword(ByVal password As String) As Boolean
    Dim IsValid As Boolean = True
    Dim HelpExpression As Regex

    ' Validate simple properties
    IsValid = IsValid AndAlso (password.Length >= Me.MinRequiredPasswordLength)

    ' Validate nonalphanumeric characters
    HelpExpression = New Regex("\W")
    IsValid = IsValid AndAlso
              (HelpExpression.Matches(password).Count >=
                  Me.MinRequiredNonAlphanumericCharacters)

    ' Validate regular expression
    HelpExpression = New Regex(Me.PasswordStrengthRegularExpression)
    IsValid = IsValid AndAlso (HelpExpression.Matches(password).Count > 0)

    Return IsValid
End Function
```

The password validation first verifies the length of the password. If the password is too short, it returns False. It then verifies through the .NET Framework regular expression classes whether the number of nonalphanumeric characters in the password is high enough according to the MinRequiredNonAlphanumericCharacters and then validates the password again through regular expressions against the PasswordStrengthRegularExpression. If all these checks pass, the function returns True. If these checks don't pass, it returns False.

Now let's take a closer look at the method for validating the user name and the e-mail. Both need to be unique in the underlying store.

```
Private Function ValidateUsername(ByVal userName As String, _
        ByVal email As String, ByVal excludeKey As Guid) As Boolean
    Dim IsValid As Boolean = True

    Dim store As UserStore = UserStore.GetStore(_FileName)
    For Each user As SimpleUser In store.Users
        If user.UserKey.CompareTo(excludeKey) <> 0 Then
            If String.Equals(user.UserName, userName,
                                        StringComparison.OrdinalIgnoreCase) Then
                IsValid = False
                Exit For
            End If

            If String.Equals(user.Email, email,
                                        StringComparison.OrdinalIgnoreCase) Then
                IsValid = False
                Exit For
            End If
        End If
    Next
    Return IsValid
End Function
```

As you can see in the previous snippet, user validation is fairly simple. The code goes through the users in the CurrentStore and verifies whether there is any user with the same user name or e-mail. If that's the case, the function returns False or otherwise True. The last interesting part in the CreateUser method is how the password is set for the user. Through the PasswordFormat property, every provider has three types for storing the password: clear, hashed, and encrypted. The CreateUser method uses a private helper method of the XmlMembershipProvider class called TransformPassword, as follows:

```
user.Password = Me.TransformPassword(password)
```

This method queries the current setting for the PasswordFormat property, and according to the setting it leaves the password as clear text, creates a hash for the password, or encrypts the password, as follows:

```
Private Function TransformPassword(ByVal password As String) As String
    Dim ret As String = String.Empty

    Select Case PasswordFormat
        Case MembershipPasswordFormat.Clear
            ret = password
        Case MembershipPasswordFormat.Hashed
            ret = FormsAuthentication.HashPasswordForStoringInConfigFile(
                    password, "SHA1")
        Case MembershipPasswordFormat.Encrypted
            Dim ClearText As Byte() = Encoding.UTF8.GetBytes(password)
            Dim EncryptedText As Byte() = MyBase.EncryptPassword(ClearText)
```

```
            ret = Convert.ToBase64String(EncryptedText)
    End Select

    Return ret
End Function
```

If the password format is set to Clear, it just returns the clear-text password. In the case of the Hashed setting, it creates the simple hash through the forms authentication utility method and then returns the hash for the password. The last possible option stores the password encrypted in the database, which has the advantage that the password can be retrieved from the database through decryption. In that case, the method uses the EncryptPassword method from the base class implementation for encrypting the password. This method uses a key stored in machine.config for encrypting the password. If you are using this in a web farm environment, you have to sync the key stored in machine.config on every machine so that a password encrypted on one machine of the farm can be decrypted on another machine on the web farm properly.

Validating Users on Login

The Membership class supports a method for programmatically validating a password entered by a user. This method is used by the Login control as well. This means every time the user tries to log in, the ValidateUser method of the Membership class is involved. This method on its own calls the ValidateUser method of the underlying membership provider. According to the settings of the PasswordFormat property, it has to retrieve the user from the store based on the user name and then somehow validate the password. If the password is clear text, validating the password involves a simple string comparison. Encrypted passwords have to be decrypted and compared afterward, while last but not least validating hashed passwords means re-creating the hash and then comparing the hash values.

```
Public Overrides Function ValidateUser(ByVal username As String,
        ByVal password As String) As Boolean
    Try
        Dim user As SimpleUser = CurrentStore.GetUserByName(username)
        If user Is Nothing Then
            Return False
        End If

        If ValidateUserInternal(user, password) Then
            user.LastLoginDate = DateTime.Now
            user.LastActivityDate = DateTime.Now
            CurrentStore.Save()
            Return True
        Else
            Return False
        End If
    Catch
          ' Do some local error handling
        Throw
    End Try
End Function
```

This method retrieves the user from the store. It then validates the password against the password passed in (which is the one entered by the user for login) through a private helper method called ValidateUserInternal. Finally, if the user name and password are fine, it updates the LastLoginDate and the LastActivityDate for the user and then returns True. It's always useful to encapsulate password validation functionality into a separate function, because it may be used more than once in your provider. A typical example for reusing this functionality is the ChangePassword method where the user has to enter the old password and the new password. If validation of the old password fails, the provider should not change the password, as shown here:

```
Public Overrides Function ChangePassword(ByVal username As String, _
        ByVal oldPassword As String, ByVal newPassword As String) As Boolean
    Try
        ' Get the user from the store
        Dim user As SimpleUser = CurrentStore.GetUserByName(username)
        If user Is Nothing Then
            Throw New Exception("User does not exist!")

            If ValidateUserInternal(user, oldPassword) Then
                '  Raise the event before validating the password
                MyBase.OnValidatingPassword(
                    New ValidatePasswordEventArgs(username, newPassword, False))

                If (Not ValidatePassword(newPassword)) Then
                    Throw New ArgumentException(
                                "Password doesn't meet requirements!")
                End If

                user.Password = TransformPassword(newPassword)
                user.LastPasswordChangeDate = DateTime.Now
                CurrentStore.Save()

                Return True
            End If
        End If

        Return False
    Catch
        ' Do some local error handling.
        Throw
    End Try
End Function
```

Only if the old password is entered correctly by the user does the change take place. The ChangePassword method again uses the TransformPassword method to generate the protected version (hashed, encrypted) of the password if necessary. You can reuse the function introduced previously with the CreateUser method. But now let's take a look at the password validation functionality:

```
Private Function ValidateUserInternal(
        ByVal user As SimpleUser, ByVal password As String) As Boolean
    If user IsNot Nothing Then
        Dim passwordValidate As String = TransformPassword(password)
        If passwordValidate = user.Password Then
            Return True
        End If
    End If

    Return False
End Function
```

This method uses the TransformPassword method for creating the protected version of the password (hashed, encrypted) if necessary. The results are then compared through simple string comparison. (Even the encrypted version returns a Base64-encoded string that will be stored in the XML file; therefore, string comparison is fine.) This is why validating hashed passwords works at all, for example. Just re-create the hash, and then compare the hashed version of the password.

Using Salted Password Hashes

If you want to change this to include a salt value as mentioned, you have to complete the following steps:

1. Add a new field to your SimpleUser class called PasswordSalt.
2. Extend your TransformPassword method to accept a salt value. This salt is necessary for re-creating the hash, which actually will be based on both the password and the salt.
3. When creating a new password, you simply have to create the random salt value and then store it with your user. For any validation, pass the previously generated salt value to the TransformPassword function for validation.

The best way to do this is to extend the TransformPassword so that it generates the salt value automatically if necessary. Therefore, it accepts the salt as a second parameter. This parameter is not just a simple parameter—it's a reference parameter, as shown here:

```
Private Function TransformPassword(
        ByVal password As String, ByRef salt As String) As String
   ...
End Function
```

Whenever you pass in String.Empty or Nothing for the salt value, the function automatically generates a new salt. The method therefore is called as follows from other methods that create the new password hash. These methods are CreateUser, ChangePassword, and ResetPassword, as they all update the password value of your SimpleUser class.

```
Dim user As SimpleUser =...
user.PasswordSalt = String.Empty
user.Password = Me.TransformPassword(password, user.PasswordSalt)

...
```

This means every method that updates the password field of your user store sets the PasswordSalt value to String.Empty before it calls TransformPassword and passes in a reference to the user.PasswordSalt field. When validating the password, you don't want the method to regenerate a new salt value. Therefore, you have to pass in the salt value stored with the hashed version of the password in the data store. Having said that, the previously introduced ValidateUserInternal() method now looks like this:

```
Private Function ValidateUserInternal(ByVal user As SimpleUser, _
            ByVal password As String) As Boolean
    If user IsNot Nothing Then
        Dim passwordValidate As String =
                TransformPassword(password, user.PasswordSalt)
        If passwordValidate = user.Password Then
            Return True
        End If
    End If

    Return False
End Function
```

The only thing that changes compared to the original version is that the method now passes in an initialized version of the salt value that will be used by the TransformPassword method to regenerate the password hash based on the existing salt and the password entered by the user. Therefore, internally the TransformPassword method now looks as follows for validating and optionally generating a salt value:

```
Private Function TransformPassword(ByVal password As String,
                ByRef salt As String) As String
    Dim ret As String = String.Empty

    Select Case PasswordFormat
        Case MembershipPasswordFormat.Clear
            ret = password

        Case MembershipPasswordFormat.Hashed

            ' Generate the salt if not passed in
            If String.IsNullOrEmpty(salt) Then
                Dim saltBytes As Byte() = New Byte(15) {}
                Dim rng As RandomNumberGenerator = RandomNumberGenerator.Create()
                rng.GetBytes(saltBytes)
                salt = Convert.ToBase64String(saltBytes)
            End If
            ret = FormsAuthentication.HashPasswordForStoringInConfigFile((
                salt And password), "SHA1")

        Case MembershipPasswordFormat.Encrypted
            Dim ClearText As Byte() = Encoding.UTF8.GetBytes(password)
            Dim EncryptedText As Byte() = MyBase.EncryptPassword(ClearText)
            ret = Convert.ToBase64String(EncryptedText)
    End Select

    Return ret
End Function
```

When the provider is configured for storing the passwords as salted hashes, it verifies whether the passed-in salt value is empty or Nothing. If the provider is configured for using salted hashes, it generates a new salt value using the cryptographic random number generator of the System.Security.Cryptography namespace to generate a real random number. The functions CreateUser, ChangePassword, and ResetPassword will pass in Nothing or String.Empty to generate a new salt value, while the ValidateUserInternal method passes in the already initialized salt value from the underlying data store of the provider. Afterward, the method again uses the HashPasswordForStoringInConfigFile method, but this time it passes a combination of the random salt value and the actual password. The result is returned to the caller.

The Remaining Functions of the Provider

Initializing the provider and creating and validating users are the most important and hardest functions to implement in the provider. The rest of the functions are just for reading information from the store and for updating the users in the store. Basically, these functions call the underlying methods of the UserStore class or try to find users in the UserStore.Users collection. A typical example is the GetUser() method, which retrieves a single user from the data store based on its user name or key:

```
Public Overrides Function GetUser(ByVal username As String,
        ByVal userIsOnline As Boolean) As MembershipUser
    Try
        Dim user As SimpleUser = CurrentStore.GetUserByName(username)
        If user IsNot Nothing Then
            If userIsOnline Then
                user.LastActivityDate = DateTime.Now
                CurrentStore.Save()
            End If
            Return CreateMembershipFromInternalUser(user)
```

```
            Else
                Return Nothing
            End If
        Catch
            ' Do some local error handling.
            Throw
        End Try
    End Function
```

This example accepts the name of the user as a parameter and another parameter that indicates whether the user is online. This parameter is automatically initialized by the Membership class when it calls your provider's method. In your method, you can query this parameter; if it is set to True, you must update the LastActivityDate of your user in the store. The function does nothing other than find the user in the underlying store by calling the UserStore's GetUserByName method. It then creates an instance of MembershipUser based on the information of the store by calling the private CreateMembershipFromInternalUser utility method. The provider implementation requires you to implement a couple of methods that work this way. You just need to call the methods of the UserStore appropriately. Some of the methods require you to not return just a MembershipUser but a whole MembershipUserCollection, as follows:

```
Public Overrides Function FindUsersByEmail(ByVal emailToMatch As String,
                        ByVal pageIndex As Integer, ByVal pageSize As Integer,
                        <System.Runtime.InteropServices.Out()>
                         ByRef totalRecords As Integer)
                         As MembershipUserCollection
        Try
            Dim matchingUsers As New List(Of SimpleUser)
            Dim nUserItem As Integer
            For nUserItem = 0 To CurrentStore.Users.Count - 1
                If CurrentStore.Users.Item(nUserItem).Email = emailToMatch Then
                    matchingUsers.Add(CurrentStore.Users.Item(nUserItem))
                End If
            Next
            Return CreateMembershipCollectionFromInternalList(matchingUsers)
        Catch
            ' Do some local error handling
            Throw
        End Try

    End Function
```

For example, the FindUsersByEmail method finds all users with a specific e-mail (which is possible only if you have configured the provider to not require the e-mail to be unique or if you use pattern matching for e-mails through regular expressions). It returns a collection of membership users. Therefore, the collection returned from this method is a collection of SimpleUser instances that you use in the back-end store. You can create another helper method for mapping this type of collection to a MembershipUserCollection, as follows:

```
Private Function CreateMembershipCollectionFromInternalList(
        ByVal users As List(Of SimpleUser))
              As MembershipUserCollection

    Dim ReturnCollection As New MembershipUserCollection()

    For Each user As SimpleUser In users
        ReturnCollection.Add(CreateMembershipFromInternalUser(user))
    Next
```

```
    Return ReturnCollection
End Function
```

Finally, the LastActivityDate property stored for every user is used by membership to determine the number of current users online in the application. You have to implement this method in your custom provider through the GetNumberOfUsersOnline method, as follows:

```
Public Overrides Function GetNumberOfUsersOnline() As Integer
    Dim ret As Integer = 0

    For Each user As SimpleUser In CurrentStore.Users
        If user.LastActivityDate.AddMinutes(Membership.UserIsOnlineTimeWindow)
                >= DateTime.Now Then
            ret += 1
        End If
    Next
    Return ret
End Function
```

This method just goes through all users in the store and uses the UserIsOnlineTimeWindow property, which is a property managed through the Membership class and specifies the number of minutes a user is online without any activity. As long as the LastActivityDate with this number of minutes is larger than the current date and time, the user is considered to be online. The LastActivityDate is updated automatically by the different overloads of the GetUser method and the ValidateUser method.

Implementing the remaining functions of the provider does not involve any new concepts, and therefore we will skip them. They merely update some values on users and then call the CurrentStore.Save method to save it to the XML file on the file system. You can download the complete implementation of this provider with the source code for the book.

Implementing the XmlRoleProvider

Implementing the roles provider is much easier than implementing the membership provider, because the structures are much simpler for managing roles. Implementing the roles provider does not introduce any new concepts. It merely requires calling the appropriate methods of the previously introduced RoleStore class for creating roles, deleting roles, assigning users to roles, and deleting users from roles. The complete signature of the roles provider looks like this:

```
Public Class XmlRoleProvider
        Inherits RoleProvider

    Public Overrides Initialize(name As String, config As NameValueCollection)
    Public Overrides CreateRole(roleName As String)
    Public Overrides DeleteRole(roleName As String,
              throwOnPopulatedRole As Boolean) As Boolean
    Public Overrides RoleExists(roleName As String) As Boolean
    Public Overrides AddUsersToRoles(usernames As String(),roleNames As String())
    Public Overrides RemoveUsersFromRoles(usernames As String(),
        roleNames As String())
    Public Overrides GetAllRoles() As String()
    Public Overrides GetRolesForUser(username As String) As String()
    Public Overrides GetUsersInRole(roleName As String) As String()
    Public Overrides IsUserInRole(username As String, roleName As String) As Boolean
    Public Overrides FindUsersInRole(roleName As String,
              usernameToMatch As String) As String()

End Class
```

As you can see, the class derives from the base class RoleProvider. Again, it overrides the Initialize method for initializing custom properties. But this time initialization of the provider is much simpler because the roles provider supports only a handful of properties. The only property provided by the base class is the ApplicationName property. Everything else is up to you. Therefore, initialization is fairly simple here:

```
Public Overrides Sub Initialize(ByVal name As String,
        ByVal config As NameValueCollection)
    If config Is Nothing Then
        Throw New ArgumentNullException("config")
    End If
    If String.IsNullOrEmpty(name) Then
        name = "XmlRoleProvider"
    End If
    If String.IsNullOrEmpty(config("description")) Then
        config.Remove("description")
        config.Add("description", "XML Role Provider")
    End If

    ' Base initialization
    MyBase.Initialize(name, config)

    ' Initialize properties
    _ApplicationName = "DefaultApp"
    For Each key As String In config.Keys
        If key.ToLower()="applicationname" Then
            ApplicationName = config(key)
        Else If key.ToLower() ="filename" Then
            _FileName = config(key)
        End If
    Next
End Sub
```

Again, the initialization routine checks the name and description configuration parameters and initializes them with default values if they are not configured. It then calls the base class's Initialize implementation. Do not forget to call the base class's Initialize method; otherwise, the default configuration values managed by the base class will not be initialized. Next it initializes the properties while your implementation of the XmlRoleProvider just knows about the ApplicationName and FileName settings. Again, the FileName specifies the name of the XML file where role information is stored.

Next, the class supports a few methods for managing the roles: CreateRole, DeleteRole, and RoleExists. Within these methods, you have to access the underlying RoleStore's methods, as you can see in this example of CreateRole:

```
Public Overrides Sub CreateRole(ByVal roleName As String)
    Try
        Dim NewRole As New SimpleRole()
        NewRole.RoleName = roleName
        NewRole.AssignedUsers = New StringCollection()

        CurrentStore.Roles.Add(NewRole)
        CurrentStore.Save()
    Catch
        ' Do some local error handling.
        Throw
    End Try
End Sub
```

Compared to the CreateUser method introduced previously, this method is fairly simple. It creates a new instance of SimpleRole and then adds this new role to the underlying RoleStore. Again, you use the CurrentRole property for easy access to the underlying store with the membership provider's implementation. You just need to add a property as follows to your class:

```
Private ReadOnly Property CurrentStore() As RoleStore
    Get
        If _CurrentStore Is Nothing Then
            _CurrentStore = RoleStore.GetStore(_FileName)
        End If
        Return _CurrentStore
    End Get
End Property
```

The RoleExists method goes through the CurrentStore.Roles list and verifies whether the role with the name passed in through its parameter exists in the list. The DeleteRole tries to find the role in the roles list of the underlying role store, and if it exists, it deletes the role from the store and then saves the store back to the file system by calling CurrentStore.Save. Most of the methods for your custom roles provider are that simple. The most complex operations are adding a user to a role and removing the user from the role. The following is the first method—adding users to roles:

```
Public Overrides Sub AddUsersToRoles(ByVal usernames As String(),
    ByVal roleNames As String())
    Try
        ' Get the roles to be modified
        For Each roleName As String In roleNames
                    Dim Role As SimpleRole = CurrentStore.GetRole(roleName)
                    If Role IsNotNothing Then
                        For Each userName As String In usernames
                            If (Not Role.AssignedUsers.Contains(userName)) Then
                                Role.AssignedUsers.Add(userName)
                            End If
                        Next
                    End If
            Next

            CurrentStore.Save()
    Catch
         ' Do some local error handling.
        Throw
    End Try
End Sub
```

Although the Roles class you used in Chapter 23 provides more overloads for this type of method, your provider has to implement the most flexible one: adding all users specified in the first parameter array to all roles specified in the second parameter array. Therefore, you have go through the list of supported roles stored in your XML file, and for every role specified in the roleNames parameter you have to add all users specified in the usernames parameter to the corresponding role. That's what this method is doing. Within the first For Each loop it iterates through the array of role names passed in. It retrieves the role from the store by calling the RoleStore's GetRole method and then adds all the users specified in the usernames parameter to this role. Finally, it calls CurrentStore.Save() for serializing the roles back to the XML file. The RemoveUsersFromRoles is doing the opposite, as follows:

```
Public Overrides Sub RemoveUsersFromRoles(ByVal usernames As String(),
            ByVal roleNames As String())
    Try
        ' Get the roles to be modified
        Dim TargetRoles As New List(Of SimpleRole)()
```

```
        For Each roleName As String In roleNames
            Dim Role As SimpleRole = CurrentStore.GetRole(roleName)
            If Role IsNot Nothing Then
                For Each userName As String In usernames
                    If Role.AssignedUsers.Contains(userName) Then
                        Role.AssignedUsers.Remove(userName)
                    End If
                Next
            End If
        Next
        CurrentStore.Save()
    Catch
        ' Do some local error handling.
        Throw
    End Try
End Sub
```

The only difference in this method from the one introduced previously is that it removes the users specified in the usernames parameter from all the roles specified in the roleNames parameter. The remaining logic of the method is the same. The remaining methods of the custom roles provider are easy to implement; in most cases, they just iterate through the roles that exist in the store and return some information, in most cases arrays of strings with user names or role names, as shown here:

```
Public Overrides Function GetRolesForUser( _
       ByVal username As String) As String()
    Try
        Dim RolesForUser As List(Of SimpleRole) =
                CurrentStore.GetRolesForUser(username)
        Dim Results As String() = New String(RolesForUser.Count - 1) {}
        Dim i As Integer = 0
        Do While i < Results.Length
            Results(i) = RolesForUser(i).RoleName
            i += 1
        Loop
        Return Results
    Catch
        ' Do some local error handling
        Throw
    End Try
End Function

Public Overrides Function GetUsersInRole(ByVal roleName As String) As String()
    Try
        Return CurrentStore.GetUsersInRole(roleName)
    Catch
        ' Do some local error handling
        Throw
    End Try
End Function

Public Overrides Function IsUserInRole(ByVal username As String,
        ByVal roleName As String) As Boolean
    Try
        Dim Role As SimpleRole = CurrentStore.GetRole(roleName)
        If  Role Is Not Nothing Then
            Return Role.AssignedUsers.Contains(username)
```

```
        Else
            Throw New ProviderException("Role does not exist!")
        End If
    Catch
        ' Do some local error handling
        Throw
    End Try
End Function
```

The first method returns all roles for a single user. It therefore calls the RoleStore's GetRolesForUsers method, which returns a list of SimpleRole objects. The result is then mapped to an array of strings and returned to the caller. Retrieving users for one role is even simpler, as the functionality is provided by the RoleStore class. Finally, the IsUserInRole verifies whether a user is assigned to a role by retrieving the role and then calling the StringCollection's Contains method to verify whether the user exists in the SimpleRole's AssignedUsers collection.

You should take a look at one last method—FindUsersInRoles:

```
Public Overrides Function FindUsersInRole(ByVal roleName As String, _
      ByVal usernameToMatch As String) As String()
    Try
        Dim Results As New List(Of String)()
        Dim Expression As New Regex(usernameToMatch.Replace("%", "\w*"))
        Dim Role As SimpleRole = CurrentStore.GetRole(roleName)
        If  Role IsNot Nothing Then
            For Each userName As String In Role.AssignedUsers
                    If Expression.IsMatch(userName) Then
                        Results.Add(userName)
                    End If
                Next
        Else
            Throw New ProviderException("Role does not exist!")
        End If

        Return Results.ToArray()
    Catch
        ' Do some local error handling
        Throw
    End Try
End Function
```

This method tries to find users based on pattern matching in the role specified through the roleName parameter. For this purpose, it retrieves the role from the store and then creates a regular expression. The % character is used by the SQL membership provider for pattern matching, and because it is a good idea to have a provider that is compatible to existing implementations, you will use it for pattern matching again in your provider. But regular expressions don't understand the % as a placeholder for any characters in the string; therefore, you need to replace it with a representation that regular expressions understand: \w*. When the Membership class now passes in this character as a placeholder, your pattern-matching function will still work, and therefore this function is compatible to the SqlMembershipProvider's implementation. The remaining part of the function goes through the users assigned to the role; if the user name matches the pattern, it is added to the resulting list of strings that will be returned as a simple string array.

As you can see, implementing the custom roles provider is easy if you have previously implemented the custom membership provider. The process does not require you to understand any new concepts. In general, when you know how to implement one provider, you know how to implement another provider. Therefore, it should be easy for you to implement custom profile and personalization providers. Again, you can download the complete source code for the roles provider from this book's website. Now it's time to discuss how you can use these providers.

Using the Custom Provider Classes

Using providers in a custom web application is fairly easy. The steps for using custom providers are as follows (besides the typical ones such as configuring forms authentication):

1. If you have encapsulated the custom provider in a separate class library (which is definitely useful, as you want to use it in several web applications), you need to add a reference to this class library through the Visual Studio Add References dialog box.
2. Afterward, you must configure the custom provider appropriately in your web.config file.
3. Next you have to select your custom provider as the default provider either through the ASP.NET WAT or through web.config manually.
4. After you have completed these configuration steps, you are ready to use the provider. If you have not added any special functionality and have just implemented the inherited classes straightforwardly as shown in this chapter, you even don't need to change any code in your application.

The configuration of the previously created XmlMembershipProvider and XmlRoleProvider looks like this:

```
<membership defaultProvider="XmlMembership">
    <providers>
        <add name="XmlMembership"
                applicationName="MyTestApp"
                fileName="C:\Work\MyTestApp_Users.config"
                type="Apress.ProAspNet.Providers.XmlMembershipProvider,
                      Apress.ProAspNet.Providers"
                requiresQuestionAndAnswer="true"/>
    </providers>
</membership>

<roleManager enabled="true"
                defaultProvider="XmlRoles">
    <providers>
        <add name="XmlRoles"
                applicationName="MyTestApp"
                fileName="C:\Work\MyTestApp_Roles.config"
                type="Apress.ProAspNet.Providers.XmlRoleProvider,
                      Apress.ProAspNet.Providers" />
    </providers>
</roleManager>
```

In the previous example, the providers will be configured to use files stored on c:\Work for saving user and role information appropriately. With this configuration, you will find the providers in the ASP.NET WAT (under Providers/Advanced Configuration), as shown in Figure 26-4.

Don't try to test the provider; it will fail in this case. Testing providers is just supported for providers that are using database connection strings to connect to the underlying back-end store. Because you are using XML files, testing will not work for the custom provider in this case.

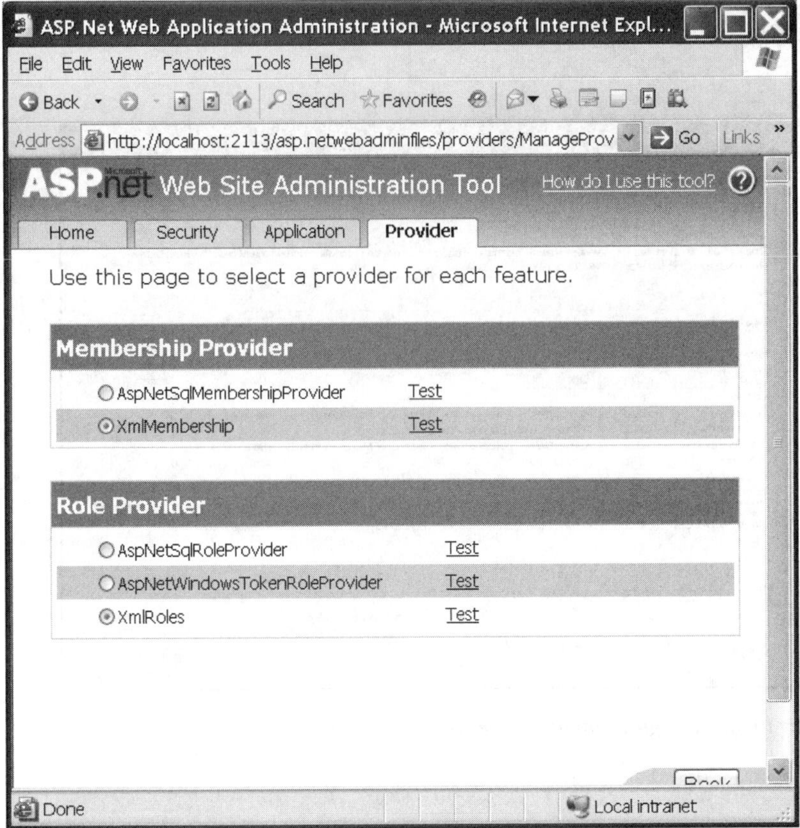

Figure 26-4. *Custom providers in the ASP.NET WAT*

Debugging Using the WAT

The ASP.NET WAT uses the Membership and Role classes for retrieving and updating data stored through the membership provider. Although we suggest building your own test driver classes by calling all the methods of the membership and Role classes, it is definitely useful to have the possibility of debugging from within the ASP.NET WAT, especially if you experience any problems you did not encounter while testing with your own applications.

For debugging through the WAT, you just need to launch the configuration utility through the Website ➤ ASP.NET Configuration menu and then attach to the web server process hosting the configuration tool. If you are using the file-based web server for development purposes, launch Visual Studio's Attach to Process dialog box by selecting Debug ➤ Attach to Process. Next, find the appropriate web server process. As in most cases, two of these processes will run when using the file-based web server, so you have to attach to the one with the right port number. Match the port number displayed in the address bar of the browser using the ASP.NET WAT with the one displayed in the Attach to Process dialog box. Then your breakpoints in the provider classes will be hit appropriately. Figure 26-5 shows how to attach to the web service process that hosts the ASP.NET WAT.

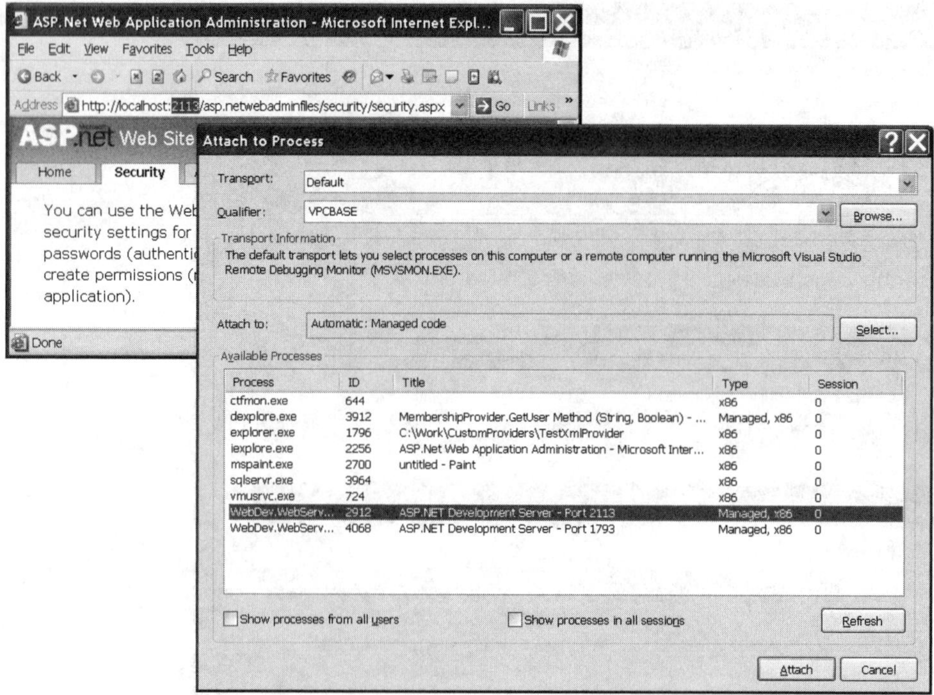

Figure 26-5. *Attaching to the Configuration utility web server process*

Summary

In this chapter, you saw how to extend the ASP.NET membership API and roles API through custom membership providers and roles providers. As an example, you developed a custom, XML-based provider for the membership and roles services. An XML-based provider is appropriate for simple applications only, but you learned the most important concepts for developing a custom membership and roles provider. These providers should conform as much as possible to the suggested interfaces so that you don't have to change your application when using a different provider.

PART 5

Advanced User Interface

CHAPTER 27

Custom Server Controls

Each type of custom control has its own advantages and disadvantages. In Chapter 14, you learned about user controls. User controls are easier to create than custom server controls, but server controls are far more powerful. Server controls beat user controls in two key areas:

Server controls give you complete control over the HTML you generate: In other words, you can create a control such as the ASP.NET Calendar, which provides a single object interface but renders itself as a complex combination of elements.

Server controls provide better design-time support: You can add them to the Toolbox in Visual Studio and set properties and add event handlers at design time. You can even configure the description that Visual Studio will show for each property, along with other design-time niceties.

All of ASP.NET's web controls are server controls. In this chapter, you'll learn how you can build your own.

CUSTOM CONTROL CHANGES IN .NET 2.0

Creating custom controls is a complex, detailed topic that's well-suited to a chapter of its own. ASP.NET 2.0 keeps the underlying control creation model from ASP.NET 1.*x*, but adds a number of important refinements. They include the following:

- *Control adapters*: ASP.NET 1.*x* makes a distinction between up-level and down-level clients. However, it's up to you to implement adaptive rendering by checking the properties of the current browser and writing conditional rendering code. In ASP.NET 2.0, a new model adds to the existing control model—*adaptive rendering*. Using this model, you can create an adapter that customizes a single control for a single type of browser, potentially allowing you to support different devices without rewriting your web forms.
- *Control state*: In ASP.NET 1.*x*, controls stored all their information in view state, which could be disabled through the EnableViewState property. ASP.NET 2.0 adds control state, a protected section of view state that can't ever be disabled.
- *Composite controls*: These controls, which wrap a combination of existing server controls in a higher-level abstraction, were fairly easy to create in ASP.NET 1.*x*. In ASP.NET 2.0 they get even easier with a new CompositeControl base class.
- *Client callbacks*: Rather than posting back the entire page, your custom control can send a request to the server to get just the additional information it needs. Client callbacks aren't discussed in this chapter—instead, you'll learn how to use them in Chapter 29.

The design-time support for controls also has a number of enhancements. You'll learn about these in the next chapter.

Custom Server Control Basics

Server controls are .NET classes that derive from System.Web.UI.WebControls.WebControl (which itself derives from Control) or System.Web.UI.Control. The Control class provides properties and methods that are common across all server controls (such as ID, ViewState, and the Controls collection). The WebControl class adds a few features that help you implement standard styles. These include properties such as Font, ForeColor, and BackColor.

Ideally, you'll create your server controls in a separate class library project and compile the project into a separate DLL assembly. Although you can create a custom control and place the source code directly in the App_Code directory, this limits your ability to reuse the control in pages written in different languages. If you place controls in a separate assembly, you'll also have better design-time support when you use them in pages.

To get a better idea of how custom controls work, the following sections demonstrate a couple of simple examples.

Creating a Bare-Bones Custom Control

To create a basic custom control, you need to derive from the Control class and override the Render() method. The Render() method provides an HtmlTextWriter object that you use to generate the HTML for the control. The simplest approach is to call HtmlTextWriter.Write() to write a string of raw HTML to the page. (ASP.NET tags and other server-side content obviously won't work here.)

Here's an example control that generates a simple hyperlink using the HtmlTextWriter in the Render() method:

```
Public Class LinkControl
      Inherits Control
    Protected Overrides Sub Render(ByVal output As HtmlTextWriter)
        output.Write("<a href='http://www.apress.com'>Click to visit Apress</a>")
    End Sub
End Class
```

The HtmlTextWriter class not only lets you write raw HTML but it also provides some helpful methods to help you manage style attributes and tags. Table 27-1 describes the key methods.

Table 27-1. *HtmlTextWriter Methods*

Method	Description
AddAttribute()	Adds any HTML attribute and its value to an HtmlTextWriter output stream. This attribute is automatically used for the next tag you create by calling RenderBeginTag(). Instead of using the exact attribute name, you can choose a value from the HtmlTextWriterAttribute enumeration.
AddStyleAttribute()	Adds an HTML style attribute and its value to an HtmlTextWriter output stream. This attribute is automatically used for the next tag you create by calling RenderBeginTag(). Instead of using the exact style name, you can choose a value from the HtmlTextWriterStyle enumeration, and it will be rendered appropriately depending on whether the browser is an up-level or down-level client.
RenderBeginTag()	Writes the start tag for the HTML element. For example, if you are writing an anchor tag, this writes <a>. Instead of using the exact tag name, you can choose a value from the HtmlTextWriterTag enumeration.
RenderEndTag()	Writes the end tag for the HTML element. For example, if you are in the process of writing an anchor tag, this writes the closing </a>. You don't need to specify the tag name.

Method	Description
WriteBeginTag()	This method is similar to the RenderBeginTag() method, except it doesn't write the closing > character for the start tag. That means you can call WriteAttribute() to add more attributes to the tag.
WriteAttribute()	Writes an HTML attribute to the output stream. This must follow the WriteBeginTag() method.
WriteEndTag()	Writes the closing > character for the current HTML tag (the one that was last opened using the WriteBeginTag() method).

Using the HtmlTextWriter methods, you can modify the rendering code. The next example presents the same control, with a couple of minor differences. First, it renders the start tag and the end tag for the anchor separately, using the RenderBeginTag() and RenderEndTag() methods. Second, it adds style attributes that configure how the control will appear. Here's the complete code:

```
Public Class LinkControl
      Inherits Control
    Protected Overrides Sub Render(ByVal output As HtmlTextWriter)
        ' Specify the URL for the upcoming anchor tag.
        output.AddAttribute(HtmlTextWriterAttribute.Href, "http://www.apress.com")

        ' Add the style attributes.
        output.AddStyleAttribute(HtmlTextWriterStyle.FontSize, "20")
        output.AddStyleAttribute(HtmlTextWriterStyle.Color, "Blue")

        ' Create the anchor tag.
        output.RenderBeginTag(HtmlTextWriterTag.A)

        ' Write the text inside the tag.
        output.Write("Click to visit Apress")

        ' Close the tag.
        output.RenderEndTag()

        ' (At this point, you could continue writing more tags and attributes.)
    End Sub
End Class
```

You should note a few important points in this example. First, to make life easier, the example uses several enumerations. These enumerations help avoid minor typographic mistakes that would cause unexpected problems. The enumerations include the following:

HtmlTextWriterTag: This enumeration defines a large set of common HTML tag attributes such as onClick, href, align, alt, and more.

HtmlTextWriterAttribute: This enumeration defines dozens of HTML tags, such as <a>, <p>, <font>, and many more.

HtmlTextWriterStyle: This enumeration defines 14 style attributes, including BackgroundColor, BackgroundImage, BorderColor, BorderStyle, BorderWidth, Color, FontFamily, FontSize, FontStyle, FontWeight, Height, and Width. All these pieces of information are joined in a semicolon-delimited list, which is the style attribute.

When the Render() method executes, it begins by defining all the attributes that will be added to the upcoming tag. Then when the start tag is created (using the RenderBeginTag() method), all of these attributes are placed into the tag. The final rendered tag looks like this:

```
<a href="http://www.apress.com" style="font-size:20;color:Blue;">
Click to visit Apress</a>
```

Using a Custom Control

To use a custom control, you need to make it available to your web application. You have two choices—you can copy the source code to the App_Code directory, or you can add the compiled assembly to the Bin directory (using Visual Studio's Add Reference command).

For the page to have access to a custom control, you must use the Register directive, just as you did with user controls in Chapter 14. However, this time you need to indicate slightly different information. Not only must you include a TagPrefix but you also need to specify the assembly file (without the DLL extension) and the namespace where the control class is located. You don't need to specify the TagName, because the server control's class name is used automatically.

Here's an example of the Register directive:

```
<%@ Register TagPrefix="apress" Namespace="CustomServerControlsLibrary"
  Assembly="CustomServerControlsLibrary" %>
```

You can reuse tag prefixes. In other words, it's completely valid to map two different namespaces or two completely different assemblies to the same tag prefix.

■ **Tip** If the control is in the App_Code directory of the current web application, you don't need to include the Assembly attribute.

If you want to use a control in several pages of the same web application, ASP.NET 2.0 adds a helpful shortcut—you can register the tag prefix in the web.config file like this:

```
<configuration xmlns="http://schemas.microsoft.com/.NetConfiguration/v2.0">
  <system.web>
    <pages>
      <controls>
        <add tagPrefix="apress" namespace="CustomServerControlsLibrary"
             assembly="CustomServerControlsLibrary" />
      </controls>
    </pages>
    ...
  </system.web>
</configuration>
```

This is particularly handy if you want to standardize on a specific tag prefix. Otherwise, Visual Studio chooses a default prefix (such as `cc1` for custom control 1) when you drop a control from the Toolbox.

Once you've registered the control, you can declare it with a standard control tag, as shown here:

```
<apress:LinkControl id="LinkControl1" runat="server"/>
```

Figure 27-1 shows the custom LinkControl in action.

Figure 27-1. *A bare-bones server control*

Custom Controls in the Toolbox

To make it easier to use your custom control, you probably want to allow it to appear in the Toolbox. Impressively, Visual Studio 2005 has built-in Toolbox support for custom controls, provided you create them in a separate assembly.

To try this, add a Web Control project to your website solution by choosing File ➤ Add ➤ New Project. (Alternatively, you can add a class library project—the only difference is that you'll need to add the assembly references and namespace imports needed for web development.

■ **Note** Remember, Visual Studio supports projectless development, which means it hides solution files away in a user-specific directory. This means that it's fairly easy to lose the solution file (for example, by moving the website to another computer or renaming the website directory outside of Visual Studio). If you take this step, you won't cause an error, but the next time you load your website, the custom control project won't be appear in the design environment—instead, you'll need to use Add ➤ Existing Project to get it back.

Once you've created your project, you can define your controls. You develop your control library project in the same way you work with any other DLL component. You can build the project at any time, but you can't start it directly because it isn't an actual application.

To test your controls, you need to use them in another application. You can use two approaches. First, you can add a reference in the same way that you add a reference to any other .NET assembly. Just right-click your website in the Solution Explorer, and choose Add Reference. Choose the Project tab, pick the custom control project you've created, and click OK. This copies the compiled control assembly to your Bin directory, making it available to your pages.

An easier approach is to use the new automatic Toolbox support in Visual Studio 2005. When you compile a project that contains custom server controls, Visual Studio examines each control and adds it dynamically to a temporary, project-specific section of the Toolbox at the top (see Figure 27-2). That means you can easily add controls to any page. When you drop the control on the page, Visual Studio automatically copies the assembly over to the Bin directory if you haven't already created a reference, adds the Register directive if it's not already present in the page, and then adds the control tag.

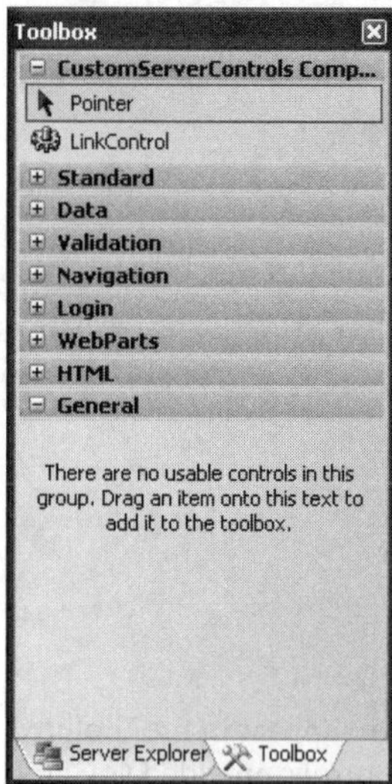

Figure 27-2. *A custom control in the Toolbox*

■ **Tip** As with any other type of reference in Visual Studio, every time you compile your project, the most recent version of the referenced assembly is copied into your web application's Bin directory. This means that if you change and recompile a custom control after adding it to the Toolbox, you have no reason to remove and re-add it.

The only limitation of the automatic Toolbox support is that your custom controls will appear in the Toolbox only when the custom control project is loaded in the design environment. If you want to make a control available to any web application but you don't want the web application developers to be able to change your custom control code, you need another approach. In this case, it makes sense to deploy just the compiled assembly. You can then add the controls to the Toolbox permanently so the application developers don't need to worry about finding the control.

To do this, right-click the Toolbox, and select Choose Items. Next, click the .NET Framework Components tab, and then click the Browse button. Then choose the custom control assembly from the file browser. The controls will be added to the list of available .NET controls, as shown in Figure 27-3.

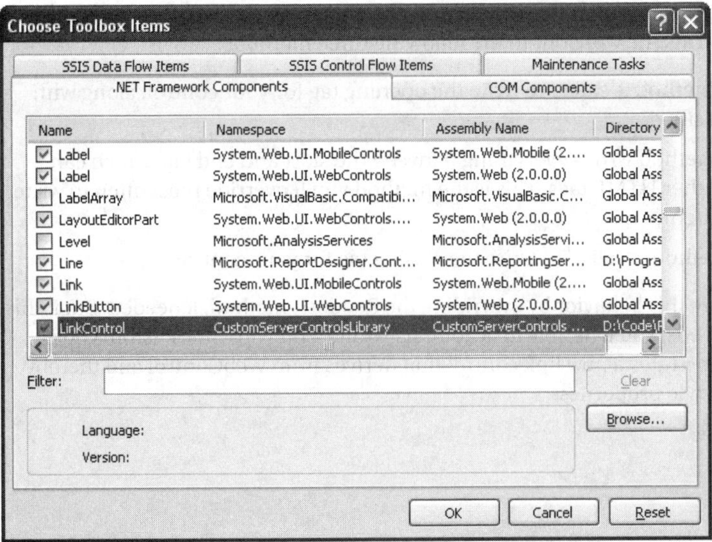

Figure 27-3. *Adding a custom control to the Toolbox*

All checked controls will appear in the Toolbox. Note that controls aren't added on a per-project basis. Instead, they will remain in the Toolbox until you delete them. To remove a control, right-click it, and select Delete. This action removes the icon only, not the referenced assembly.

Visual Studio gives you quite a bit of basic design-time support. For example, after you add a custom control to a web page, you can modify its properties in the Properties window (they will appear under the Misc group) and attach event handlers. In Chapter 28, you'll learn how you can further customize the design-time behavior and appearance of your control.

Creating a WebControl That Supports Style Properties

The previous custom control example doesn't allow the web page to customize the control's appearance. The custom control doesn't provide any properties for setting foreground or background colors, the font, or other attributes of the HTML tag that you generate. To add support for these features, you need to explicitly add public properties that represent these values. You then need to read these properties in the Render() method and generate the appropriate HTML code.

Of course, style properties are a basic part of infrastructure that many HTML controls need to use. Ideally, all controls should follow a single, streamlined model for style information and not force custom control developers to write this generic functionality themselves. ASP.NET does this with the WebControl base class (in the System.Web.UI.WebControls namespace). Every web control that's included with ASP.NET derives from WebControl, and you can derive your custom controls from it as well.

Not only does the WebControl class include basic style-related properties such as Font, ForeColor, BackColor, and so on, but it also renders them automatically in the control tag. Here's how it works: The WebControl assumes that it should add the attributes to a single HTML tag, called the *base tag*. If you're writing multiple elements, the attributes are added to the outermost element that contains the other elements. You specify the base tag for your web control in the constructor.

Finally, you don't override the Render() method. The WebControl already includes an implementation of Render() that farms the work out to the following three methods:

RenderBeginTag(): This method is called to write the opening tag for your control, along with the attributes you've specified.

RenderContents(): This method writes everything between the start and end tag, which can include text content or other HTML tags. This is the method you'll override most often to write your custom control content.

RenderEndTag(): This method is called to write the closing tag for your control.

Of course, you can change this behavior by overriding the Render() method, if needed. But if this basic framework suits your needs, you'll be able to accomplish quite a bit with little custom code.

The next example demonstrates a new link control that derives from WebControl and thereby gains automatic support for style properties.

```
Public Class LinkWebControl
    Inherits WebControl
        Private ...
End Class
```

The default constructor calls the WebControl constructor. More than one version of WebControl constructor exists—this code uses the version that allows you to specify a base control tag. In this example, the base control tag is the <a> anchor, as shown here:

```
Public Sub New()
        MyBase.New(HtmlTextWriterTag.A)
End Sub
```

The LinkWebControl constructor doesn't require any actual code. It's just important that you use this opportunity to call the WebControl constructor to set the base control tag. If you use the default (zero-parameter) WebControl constructor, a <span> tag is used automatically. You can then render additional HTML inside this <span> tag, which ensures that all elements will have the same style attributes.

The LinkWebControl also defines two properties, which allow the web page to set the text and the target URL:

```
Dim m_text As String
Public Property Text() As String
    Get
        Return m_text
    End Get
    Set
        m_text = Value
    End Set
End Property

Dim m_hyperLink As String
Public Property HyperLink() As String
    Get
        Return m_hyperLink
    End Get
    Set
        If Value.IndexOf("http://") = -1 Then
            Throw New ApplicationException("Specify HTTP as the protocol.")
        Else
```

```
            m_hyperLink = Value
        End If
    End Set
End Property
```

You could set the text and hyperLink variables to empty strings when you define them. However, this example overrides the OnInit() method to demonstrate how you can initialize a control programmatically:

```
Protected Overrides Sub OnInit(ByVal e As EventArgs)
    MyBase.OnInit(e)
    If HyperLink Is Nothing Then
        HyperLink = "http://www.apress.com"
    End If

    If Text Is Nothing Then
        Text = "Click here to visit Apress"
    End If
End Sub
```

The LinkWebControl presents a minor challenge. To successfully create an <a> tag, you need to specify a target URL and some text. The text is placed between the start and end tags. However, the URL is added as an attribute (named href) to the start tag. As you've already learned, the WebControl manages the attributes for the start tag automatically. Fortunately, the WebControl class gives you the ability to add extra tags by overriding the method AddAttributesToRender(), as shown here:

```
Protected Overrides Sub AddAttributesToRender(ByVal output As HtmlTextWriter)
    output.AddAttribute(HtmlTextWriterAttribute.Href, HyperLink)
    MyBase.AddAttributesToRender(output)
End Sub
```

Note that whenever a custom control overrides a method, it should call the base class implementation using the base keyword. This ensures that you don't inadvertently suppress any code that needs to run. Often, all the base method does is fire a related event, but that's not always the case. For example, if you override RenderBeginTag() and don't call the base implementation, the rendering code will fail with an unhandled exception because the tag isn't opened.

Finally, the RenderContents() method adds the text inside the anchor:

```
Protected Overrides Sub RenderContents(ByVal output As HtmlTextWriter)
    output.Write(Text)
    MyBase.RenderContents(output)
End Sub
```

Note that the code doesn't use the style properties. Instead, ASP.NET applies these automatically when it renders the base tag.

Now that you have created the control, you can use it in any ASP.NET web page. You can set the style properties in code or in the control tag. You can even use the Properties window. Here's an example:

```
<apress:LinkWebControl id="LinkWebControl1" runat="server"
  BackColor="#FFFF80" Font-Names="Verdana" Font-Size="Large"
  ForeColor="#C00000" Text="Click to visit Apress"
  HyperLink="http://www.apress.com"></apress:LinkWebControl>
```

The HyperLink and Text attributes are automatically mapped to the corresponding public properties of the custom control. The same is true of the style-related properties, which are defined in the base WebControl class.

Figure 27-4 shows this control in a web browser.

Figure 27-4. *A custom control that supports style properties*

■ **Tip** As a general guideline, you should derive from the WebControl class if your control needs to create any type of user interface. Of course, exceptions exist. For example, if you know you want only a subset of the UI features, or you want to combine multiple controls, which will each have their own specific style properties, you might want to derive from Control instead of WebControl. However, the basic rule of thumb that the .NET class library follows is always to derive from WebControl, even if some of the properties aren't relevant.

The Rendering Process

The previous example introduced several new rendering methods. Before going any further, it's a good idea to look at how they all work together.

The starting point for the rendering process is the RenderControl() method. The RenderControl() method is the public rendering method that ASP.NET uses to render each control on a web page to HTML. You can't override RenderControl(). Instead, RenderControl() calls the protected Render() method that starts the rendering process. You *can* override Render(), as demonstrated in the first example in this chapter. However, if you override Render() and don't call the base implementation of the Render() method, none of the other rendering methods will fire.

The base implementation of the Render() method calls RenderBeginTag(), RenderContents(), and then RenderEndTag(), as you saw in the previous example. However, this has one more twist. The base implementation of the RenderContents() method calls another rendering method—RenderChildren(). This method loops through the collection of child controls in the Controls collection and calls the RenderControl() method for each individual control. By taking advantage of this behavior, you can easily build a control from other controls. This approach is demonstrated later in this chapter with composite controls (see the section "Composite Controls").

So, which rendering method should you override? If you want to replace the entire rendering process with something new, or if you want to add HTML content *before* your base control tag (such as a block of JavaScript code), you can override Render(). If you want to take advantage of the automatic style attributes, you should define a base tag and override RenderContents(). If you want to prevent child controls from being displayed or customize how they are rendered (for example, by rendering them in the reverse order), you can override RenderChildren().

Figure 27-5 summarizes the rendering process.

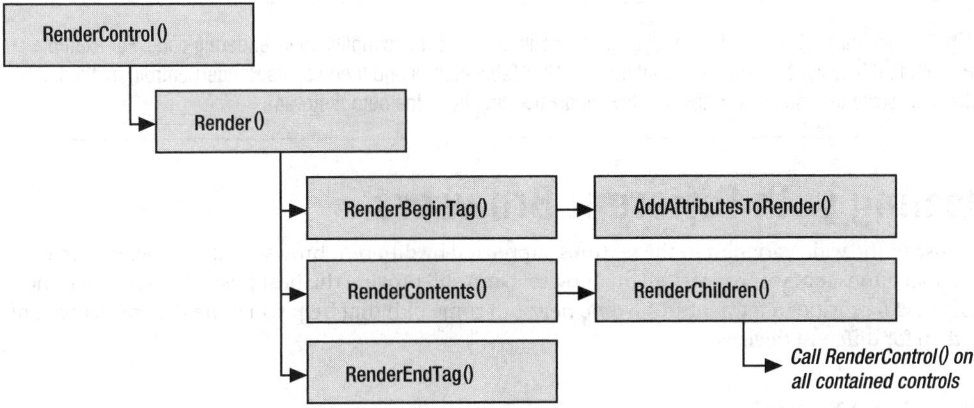

Figure 27-5. *The control rendering methods*

It's worth noting that you can call RenderControl() yourself to examine the HTML output for a control. In fact, this technique can be a convenient shortcut when debugging. Here's an example that gets the rendered HTML for a control and displays it in a label on a web page:

```
' Create the in-memory objects that will catch the rendered output.
Dim writer As New StringWriter()
Dim output As New HtmlTextWriter(writer)

' Render the control.
LinkWebControl1.RenderControl(output)

' Display the HTML (and encode it properly so that
' it appears as text in the browser).
lblHtml.Text = "The HTML for LinkWebControl1 is<br /><blockquote>" _
    & Server.HtmlEncode(writer.ToString()) & "</blockquote>"
```

Figure 27-6 shows the page with the control and its HTML.

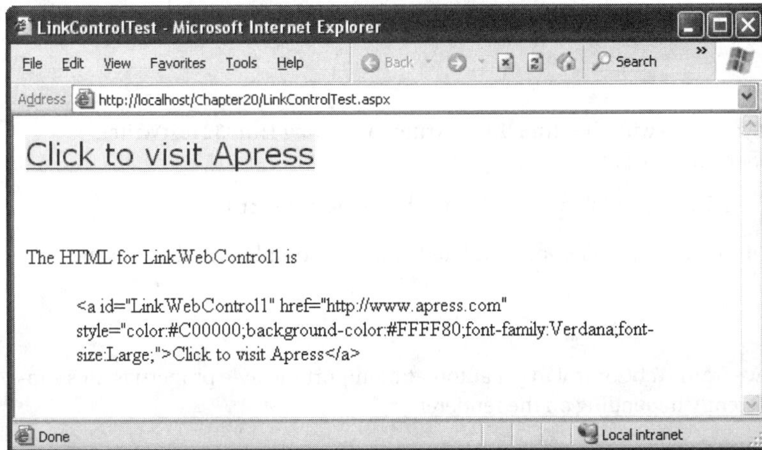

Figure 27-6. *Getting the HTML representation of a control*

■ **Tip** This technique isn't just for debugging. You could also use it to simplify your rendering code. For example, you might find it easier to create and configure an HtmlTable control and then call its RenderControl() method, rather than write tags such as <table>, <td>, and <tr> directly to the output stream.

Dealing with Different Browsers

Because of the wide variation in the features supported by different browsers, it's a challenge to create applications that work across all the browsers and still provide the best possible user experience. ASP.NET 2.0 provides a few features (some new and some old) that help you write the correct type of markup for different devices.

The HtmlTextWriter

First, ASP.NET makes a broad distinction in the type of markup that a client sees so that some clients get HTML 3.2, others get HTML 4.0, and others get XHTML 1.1. You might not even realize that this differentiation is taking place.

It all works through the HtmlTextWriter class, which has several derived classes. HtmlTextWriter itself is designed to write HTML 4.0 markup. But its derived classes are different—so, the Html32TextWriter writes HTML 3.2 markup for down-level clients, the ChtmlTextWriter can write compact HTML (cHTML) for mobile devices, and the XhtmlTextWriter writes XHTML 1.1. Because all these classes derive from HtmlTextWriter, you're free to use the same basic set of HtmlTextWriter methods in your rendering code. However, the implementations of many of these methods differ, so depending on which object you get, the output might not be the same.

For example, the Html32TextWriter doesn't support CSS (Cascading Style Sheets). This means that certain details that can't be easily faked through other means (such as background colors) are simply ignored.

However, it all depends on how high-level your rendering code is. If you write raw HTML text using the HtmlTextWriter.Write() method, it doesn't matter what text writer you're using—none of them will change your text. That's why it's dangerous to use this approach. On the other hand, if you use the HtmlTextWriter.RenderBeginTag() method, different text writers may substitute another tag.

For example, if you use this rendering code:

```
output.RenderBeginTag(HtmlTextWriterTag.Div)
```

You expect this:

```
<div>
```

But here's the result you'll see with the Html32TextWriter (assuming Html32TextWriter.ShouldPerformDivTableSubstitution is True):

```
<table cellpadding="0" cellspacing="0" border="0" width="100%"><tr><td>
```

On the other hand, if you use this code, your rendered output is completely inflexible and never changes:

```
output.Write("<div>")
```

Similarly, if you derive from WebControl to get automatic support for style properties, this support is implemented differently depending on the renderer.

■ **Tip** You can try different rendering behaviors by creating a console application that creates the appropriate text writer and uses it directly.

Browser Detection

So, how does ASP.NET decide which type of text writer suits a particular client? It's all based on the user-agent string that the client supplies when it makes a request. ASP.NET tries to match this string against a large catalog of known browsers. You can find this catalog in c:\[WinDir]\Microsoft.NET\Framework\[Version]\Config\Browsers. There you'll see a number of .browser files. Each one is an XML file that maps a user-agent string to a set of capabilities and a text writer.

Every .browser file has this basic structure:

```
<browsers>
  <browser id="..." parentID="...">
    <identification>
      <!-- Here is one regular expression that attempts to match the
           user-agent string.
           There may also be multiple nonmatches, which disqualify
           user-agent strings that otherwise match the desired pattern. -->
      <userAgent match="..." />
      <userAgent nonMatch="..." />
    </identification>

    <capabilities>
      <!-- Assuming the user-agent string matches, here are the
           capabilities ASP.NET should assume that the client has. -->
    </capabilities>

    <controlAdapters>
      <!-- For this client, some controls may need nondefault rendering
           of specific controls. This is made possible through adapters.
           Here is a list of all the control-specific adapters ASP.NET
           should use. -->
    </controlAdapters>
  </browser>

  <!-- More browsers can be defined here. -->
</browsers>
```

Further complicating the model is that you can create subcategories of browsers. To do this, the <browser> element includes the parentID attribute, which refers to another <browser> definition from which it should inherit settings.

For example, if you look at the opera.browser file, you'll find information like this:

```
<browser id="Opera" parentID="Default">
  <identification>
    <userAgent match=
     "Opera[ /](?'version'(?'major'\d+)(?'minor'\.\d+)(?'letters'\w*))" />
  </identification>

  <capabilities>
    <capability name="browser" value="Opera" />
    <capability name="cookies" value="true" />
    <capability name="css1" value="true" />
```

```
    <capability name="css2" value="true" />
    <capability name="ecmascriptversion" value="1.1" />
    <capability name="frames" value="true" />
    <capability name="javascript" value="true" />
    ...
    <capability name="tagwriter"   value="System.Web.UI.HtmlTextWriter" />
  </capabilities>

  <controlAdapters>
    <adapter controlType="System.Web.UI.WebControls.CheckBox" adapterType=
     "System.Web.UI.WebControls.Adapters.HideDisabledControlAdapter"/>
    <adapter controlType="System.Web.UI.WebControls.RadioButton" adapterType=
     "System.Web.UI.WebControls.Adapters.HideDisabledControlAdapter"/>
    <adapter controlType="System.Web.UI.WebControls.Menu" adapterType=
     "System.Web.UI.WebControls.Adapters.MenuAdapter"/>
  </controlAdapters>
</browser>
```

Here the Opera browser is given a set of basic settings and specifically associated with the HtmlTextWriter for HTML 4.0 rendering. In addition, several control adapters are defined to give Opera-specific rendering for these elements (more on that in the "Adaptive Rendering" section).

You probably think this is a somewhat brittle system—and unfortunately, it is. You have no guarantee that a browser won't appear with a browser string that doesn't match any of the known patterns or that a browser won't submit the wrong string. However, this is a necessary compromise in the loosely coupled world of the Web, and the ASP.NET team has worked hard to make sure the browser information that ships with ASP.NET 2.0 is much more reliable and up-to-date than the information with ASP.NET 1.1. You're also free to customize the browser presets completely or even add new definitions for different user-agent strings.

Browser Properties

You can detect the current browser configuration using the Browser property of the HttpRequest object, which returns a reference to an HttpBrowserCapabilities object. (You can also get the user-agent string from the UserAgent property.) When a client makes an HTTP request, an HttpBrowserCapabilities object is created and filled with information about the capabilities of the browser based on the corresponding .browser file. The information provided in the HttpBrowserCapabilities class includes the kind of browser and its version, whether scripting support is available on the client side, and so on. By detecting the capabilities of the browser, you can choose to customize your output to provide different behaviors on different browsers. This way, you can fully exploit the potential capabilities of up-level clients, without breaking down-level clients.

Table 27-2 summarizes the properties of HttpBrowserCapabilities class.

Table 27-2. *HttpBrowserCapabilities Properties*

Property	Description
Browser	Gets the browser string that was sent with the request in the user-agent header.
MajorVersion	Gets the major version number of the client browser. (For example, this returns 4 for version 4.5.)
MinorVersion	Gets the minor version number of the client browser. (For example, this returns 5 for version 4.5.)
Type	Gets the name and the major version number of the client browser.

Property	Description
Version	Gets the full version number of the client browser.
Beta	Returns True if the client browser is a beta release.
AOL	Returns True if the client is an AOL (America Online) browser.
Platform	Provides the name of the operating system platform that the client uses.
Win16	Returns True if the client is a Win16-based computer.
Win32	Returns True if the client is a Win32-based computer.
ClrVersion	Provides the highest version number of the .NET CLR installed on the client computer. You can also use the GetClrVersions() method to retrieve information about all the installed CLR versions. This setting is significant only if you have embedded .NET Windows Forms controls in your web page. Client browsers don't need the CLR to run ordinary ASP.NET web pages.
ActiveXControls	Returns True if the client browser supports ActiveX controls.
BackgroundSounds	Returns True if the client browser supports background sounds.
Cookies	Returns True if the client browser supports cookies.
Frames	Returns True if the client browser supports frames.
Tables	Returns True if the client browser supports HTML tables.
JavaScript	Indicates whether the client browser supports JavaScript.
VBScript	Returns True if the client browser supports VBScript.
JavaApplets	Returns True if the client browser supports embedded Java applets.
EcmaScriptVersion	Gets the version number of the ECMA script that the client browser supports.
MSDomVersion	Gets the version of Microsoft HTML DOM that the client browser supports.
Crawler	Returns True if the client browser is a web crawler search engine.

The following code snippet shows how you could dynamically tailor rendered output based on the capabilities of the requesting browser. In this example, the code simply outputs different strings to indicate what it has detected. In a more realistic example, you would render different HTML or JavaScript based on the same information.

```
Protected Overrides Sub RenderContents(ByVal writer As HtmlTextWriter)
    MyBase.RenderContents(writer)

    If Page.Request.Browser.JavaScript Then
        writer.Write("<i>You support JavaScript.</i><br>")
    End If

    If Page.Request.Browser.Browser = "IE" Then
        writer.Write("<i>Output configured for IE.</i><br>")
    ElseIf Page.Request.Browser.Browser = "Netscape" Then
        writer.Write("<i>Output configured for Netscape.</i><br>")
    End If
End Sub
```

The HttpBrowserCapabilities class has one glaring limitation—it's limited to evaluating the *expected* built-in functionality of the browser. It does *not* evaluate the current state of a browser's functionality. For example, imagine you are evaluating the client-side JavaScript support provided by the browser. If the requesting browser is Internet Explorer 5.5, this will return True since the browser supports client-side JavaScript support. However, if the user has the scripting capabilities turned off, the JavaScript property still returns True. In other words, you don't learn what the browser is capable of doing, just what it *should* be capable of doing. In fact, all ASP.NET really does is read the user-agent information that's passed from the browser to the server during the request and compare this string against the predefined user-agent information in the machine.config file. It's the machine.config file that lists the corresponding browser capabilities, such as whether the browser supports scripting, styles, frames, and so on. Unfortunately, the client just doesn't send any information about how the browser is configured.

This situation leaves you with two options. You can rely on the HttpBrowserCapabilities class to tell you whether certain browser features should be available and base your programming logic on that information. In this case, you may need to tolerate the occasional error. If you need a more robust approach, you need to write your own code to actually test the support for the features you need. For example, with cookies you could (over two web pages) attempt to set a cookie and then attempt to read it. If the second test doesn't succeed, cookie support isn't enabled. You could use similar workarounds to check for other features such as JavaScript support. For example, you could add a piece of JavaScript code to the page that writes to a hidden form variable and then check it on the server. These steps are awkward and messy, but they're the only way to be absolutely certain of specific browser features. Unfortunately, when creating custom controls, you usually don't have the luxury of performing these tests.

Table 27-3 shows how some common browsers stack up with the HttpBrowserCapabilities class.

Table 27-3. *HttpBrowserCapabilities Properties for Common Browsers*

Browser	EcmaScriptVersion	MSDomVersion	W3CDomVersion	ClrVersion
IE6+	1.2	6.0	1.0	1.0.3705
NS6+	1.5	0.0	1.0	0.0
Opera6+	1.3	0.0	1.0	0.0

Adaptive Rendering

In ASP.NET 1.*x*, every control needed to have the built-in smarts to tailor itself for different browsers. If you needed to support different devices and different types of markup, you needed to develop an entirely separate control.

ASP.NET 2.0 improves this situation dramatically with a new adaptive rendering model that's based on *control adapters*. This model makes it possible to create a single control that can be adapted for multiple types of devices. Best of all, because of the separation between controls and control adapters, third-party developers can write adapters for existing controls, allowing them to work with other platforms.

You can link any control to an adapter through the .browser file. For example, you could create a FirefoxSlideMenuAdapter that changes the rendered code for your SlideMenu control so that it better works with Firefox. You would then edit the mozilla.browser file to specifically indicate that this adapter should be used for your control with all Firefox browsers.

The control adapter works by plugging into the rendering process. ASP.NET calls the adapter at each state of the web control's life cycle, which allows the adapter to adjust the rendering process and handle other details, such as device-specific view state logic.

To create an adapter, derive a new class from System.Web.UI.Adapters.ControlAdapter (if your custom control derives from Control) or System.Web.UI.WebControls.Adapters.WebControlAdapter (if your custom control derives from WebControl). You can then implement the functionality you want by overriding methods. Each method corresponds to a method in the custom control class, and when you override the method in a control adapter, the control adapter method is used *instead* of the control method.

For example, in the ControlAdapter you can override methods such as OnInit(),Render(), and RenderChildren(). In the WebControlAdapter you can also override RenderBeginTag(), RenderEndTag(), and RenderContents(). Here's an example:

```
Public Class LinkControlAdapter
        Inherits ControlAdapter
    ' Replace the ordinary rendering logic so it uses different color
    ' and doesn't change the font.
    Protected Overrides Sub Render(ByVal output As HtmlTextWriter)
        ' Specify the URL for the upcoming anchor tag.
        output.AddAttribute(HtmlTextWriterAttribute.Href, "http://www.apress.com")

        ' Add the style attributes.
        output.AddStyleAttribute(HtmlTextWriterStyle.Color, "Red")

        ' Create the anchor tag.
        output.RenderBeginTag(HtmlTextWriterTag.A)
        output.Write("Click to visit Apress")
        output.RenderEndTag()
    End Sub
End Class
```

If you want to perform the normal control rendering *and* add your custom rendering steps, simply call the base ControlAdapter.Render() implementation, which calls the Render() method of the corresponding control. This technique works for all the rendering methods.

```
Protected Overrides Sub Render(ByVal output As HtmlTextWriter)
    ' (Custom rendering code here.)
    MyBase.Render(output)
    ' (More custom rendering code here.)
End Sub
```

You can also access the linked control through the ControlAdapter.Control property if you need to examine additional details.

The adaptive rendering model is a major shift in ASP.NET 2.0, and it allows endlessly customizable controls and cross-device integration. You can do quite a bit more with a custom control adapter. For example, you could hook to events in the underlying control and then use that to customize event behavior on different devices.

■ **Note** The implications of the adaptive rendering model haven't appeared yet, because it's quite new. Originally, Microsoft planned to remove all its mobile controls and allow the standard web controls to support mobile devices through specialized adapters. Unfortunately, this feature was cut during the beta cycle because of time constraints.

Control State and Events

ASP.NET uses web controls to create an object-oriented layer of abstraction over the lower-level details of HTML and HTTP. Two cornerstones of this abstraction are view state (the mechanism that lets you store information between requests) and postback (the technique wherein a web page posts back to the same URL with a collection of form data). To create realistic server controls, you need to know how to create classes that plug into both of these parts of the web-page infrastructure.

View State

Controls need to store information in state just like your web pages. Fortunately, all controls provide a ViewState property that you can use to store and retrieve information just as you do with a web page. You'll need to use the ViewState collection to restore private information after a postback.

A common design pattern with web controls is to access the ViewState collection in your property procedures. For example, consider the LinkWebControl presented earlier. Currently, this control doesn't use view state, which means that if you change its Text and HyperLink properties programmatically, the changes will be lost in subsequent postbacks. (This isn't True of the style properties such as Font, ForeColor, and BackColor, which are stored in view state automatically.) To change the LinkWebControl to ensure that state information is retained for the Text and HyperLink properties, you need to rewrite the property procedure code, as shown here:

```
Public Property Text() As String
    Get
        Return CStr(ViewState("Text"))
    End Get
    Set
        ViewState("Text") = Value
    End Set
End Property

Public Property HyperLink() As String
    Get
        Return CStr(ViewState("HyperLink"))
    End Get
    Set
        If Value.IndexOf("http://") = -1 Then
            Throw New ApplicationException("Specify HTTP as the protocol.")
        Else
            ViewState("HyperLink") = Value
        End If
    End Set
End Property

Protected Overrides Sub OnInit(ByVal e As EventArgs)
    MyBase.OnInit(e)
    If ViewState("HyperLink") Is Nothing Then
        ViewState("HyperLink") = "http://www.apress.com"
    End If

    If ViewState("Text") Is Nothing Then
        ViewState("Text") = "Click here to visit Apress"
    End If
End Sub
```

You can also request that the page encrypt the view state information by calling Page.RegisterRequiresViewStateEncryption() when your control initializes. This is useful if you need to store potentially sensitive data.

```
Protected Overrides Sub OnInit(ByVal e As EventArgs)
    MyBase.OnInit(e)
    Page.RegisterRequiresViewStateEncryption()
End Sub
```

It's important to realize that the ViewState property of a control is separate from the ViewState property of the page. In other words, if you add an item in your control code, you can't access it in your web page, and vice versa. When the page is rendered to HTML, ASP.NET takes the view state of the page and all the combined controls and then merges it into a special tree structure.

Although view state is easy to use in a control, you have to consider a couple of issues. First, you shouldn't store large objects because they will reduce page transmission times. For example, the ASP.NET controls that support data binding don't store the DataSource property in view state. They simply hold it in memory until you call the DataBind() method. This makes programming a little more awkward—for example, it forces you to rebind data controls after every postback—but it ensures that pages don't become ridiculously bloated.

Another consideration with view state is that it's at the mercy of the containing page. If the page sets the EnableViewState property of your control to False, all your view state information will be lost after each postback. If you have critical information that you require in order for your control to work, you should store it in control state instead (see the next section).

■ **Note** Even if the EnableViewState property is set to False, the ViewState collection will still work. The only difference is that the information you place in that collection will be discarded once the control is finished processing and the page is rendered.

Finally, keep in mind that you can't assume data is in the ViewState collection. If you try to retrieve an item that doesn't exist, you'll run into a NullReferenceException. To prevent this problem, you should check for null values or set default view state information in the OnInit() method or the custom control constructor. For example, the LinkWebControl won't run into null references because it uses OnInit() to set initial view state values.

■ **Note** Although the WebControl provides a ViewState property, it doesn't provide properties such as Cache, Session, and Application. However, if you need to use these objects to store or retrieve data, you can access them through the static HttpContext.Current property.

Occasionally, you might want more flexibility to customize how view state information is stored. You can take control by overriding the LoadViewState() and SaveViewState() methods. The SaveViewState() method is always called before a control is rendered to HTML. You can return a single serializable object from this method, which will be stored in view state. Similarly, the LoadViewState() is called when your control is re-created on subsequent postbacks. You receive the object you stored as a parameter, and you can now use it to configure control properties. In most simple controls, you'll have no reason to override these methods. However, sometimes it does become useful, such as when you've developed a more compact way of storing multiple pieces of information in view state using a single object or when you're deriving from an existing control and you want to prevent it from saving its state. You also need this method when you're managing how a complex control saves the state of nested child controls. You'll see an example of this last technique at the end of this chapter. For more information about advanced control programming, you may want to consult a dedicated book about ASP.NET control programming, such as *Developing Microsoft ASP.NET Server Controls and Components* (Microsoft Press, 2002).

Control State

ASP.NET 2.0 adds a new feature called *control state*. Technically, control state works in the same way as view state—it stores serializable information that's stuffed into a hidden field when the page is rendered. In fact, ASP.NET puts the view state information and the control state information into the same hidden field. The difference is that control state is not affected by the EnableViewState property. Even if this is set to False, your control can still store and retrieve information from control state.

■ **Note** The LinkWebControl doesn't require control state. If the developer sets EnableViewState to True, it's probably because the developer expects to set the HyperLink and Text properties in every postback.

Because control state cannot be disabled, you should carefully restrict the amount of information you store. Usually, it should be limited to something critical such as a current page index or a data key value. To use control state, you must begin by overriding the OnInit() method and call Page.RegisterRequiresControlState() to signal that your control needs to access control state.

```
Protected Overrides Sub OnInit(ByVal e As EventArgs)
    MyBase.OnInit(e)
    Page.RegisterRequiresControlState(Me)
End Sub
```

Unlike view state, you can't access control state directly through a collection. (This limitation is likely in place to prevent developers from overusing control state when view state is better suited.) Instead, you must override two methods—SaveControlState() and LoadControlState().

These methods use a slightly unusual pattern. The basic idea is that you want take any control state that has been serialized by the base class and combine that with an object that contains your new serializable object. You can accomplish this with the System.Web.Pair class, as shown here:

```
Dim someData As String

Protected Overrides Function SaveControlState() As Object
    ' Get the state from the base class.
    Dim baseState As Object = MyBase.SaveControlState()

    ' Combine it with the state object you want to store,
    ' and return final object.
    Return New Pair(baseState, someData)
End Function
```

This technique allows you to store only a single object. If you need to store several pieces of information, consider making a custom class that encapsulates all these details (and make sure it includes the Serializable attribute, as discussed in Chapter 6). Alternatively, you can create a chain of Pair objects:

```
Dim someData As String
Dim moreData As Integer

Protected Overrides Function SaveControlState() As Object
    ' Get the state from the base class.
    Dim baseState As Object = MyBase.SaveControlState()

    ' Combine it with the state objects you want to store,
    ' and return final object.
    Dim pair1 As New Pair(baseState, someData)
    Dim pair2 As New Pair(pair1, moreData)
    Return pair2
End Function
```

Unfortunately, this approach quickly becomes confusing.

In the LoadControlState(), you pass on the base class control state and then cast your part of the Pair object to the appropriate type:

```
Protected Overrides Sub LoadControlState(ByVal state As Object)
    Dim p As Pair = CType(IIf(TypeOf state Is Pair, state, Nothing), Pair)
    If p IsNot Nothing Then
```

```
        MyBase.LoadControlState(p.First)
        someData = CStr(p.Second)
    End If
End Sub
```

Postback Data and Change Events

View state and control state helps you keep track of your control's contents, but they're not enough for input controls. That's because input controls have an additional ability—they allow users to change their data. For example, consider a text box that's represented as an <input> tag in a form. When the page posts back, the data from the <input> tag is part of the information in the control collection. The TextBox control needs to retrieve this information and update its state accordingly.

To process the data that's posted to the page in your custom control, you need to implement the IPostBackDataHandler interface. By implementing this interface, you indicate to ASP.NET that when a postback occurs, your control needs a chance to examine the postback data. Your control will get this opportunity, regardless of which control actually triggers the postback.

The IPostBackDataHandler interface defines two methods:

LoadPostData(): ASP.NET calls this method when the page is posted back, before any control events are raised. It allows you to examine the data that's been posted back and update the state of the control accordingly. However, you shouldn't fire change events at this point, because other controls won't be updated yet.

RaisePostDataChangedEvent(): After all the input controls on a page have been initialized, ASP.NET gives you the chance to fire a change event, if necessary, by calling the RaisePostDataChangedEvent() method.

The best way to understand how these methods work is to examine a basic example. The next control emulates the basic TextBox control. Here's the basic control definition:

```
Public Class CustomTextBox
    Inherits WebControl
    Implements IPostBackDataHandler
       Private ...
End Class
```

As you can see, the control inherits from WebControl and implements IPostBackDataHandler.

The control requires only a single property, Text. The Text is stored in view state and initialized to an empty string in the control constructor. The constructor also sets the base tag to <input>.

```
Public Sub New()
    MyBase.New(HtmlTextWriterTag.Input)
    Text = String.Empty
End Sub

Public Property Text() As String
    Get
            Return CStr(ViewState("Text"))
    End Get
    Set
            ViewState("Text") = Value
    End Set
End Property
```

Because the base tag is already set to <input>, there's little extra rendering work required. You can handle everything by overriding the AddAttributesToRender() method and adding a type attribute that indicates the <input> control represents a text box and a value attribute that contains the text you want to display in the text box, as follows:

```
Protected Overrides Sub AddAttributesToRender(ByVal output As HtmlTextWriter)
    output.AddAttribute(HtmlTextWriterAttribute.Type, "text")
    output.AddAttribute(HtmlTextWriterAttribute.Value, Text)
    output.AddAttribute("name", Me.UniqueID)
    MyBase.AddAttributesToRender(output)
End Sub
```

You must also add the UniqueID for the control using the name attribute. That's because ASP.NET matches this string against the posted data. If you don't add the UniqueID, the LoadPostData() method will never be called, and you won't be able to retrieve posted data.

■Tip Alternatively, you can call the Page.RegisterRequiresPostback() method in the OnInit() method of your custom control. In this case, ASP.NET will add the unique ID if you don't explicitly render it, ensuring that you can still receive the postback.

All that's left is to implement the IPostBackDataHandler methods to give the control the ability to respond to user changes.

The first step is to implement the LoadPostData() method. This method uses two parameters. The second parameter is a collection of values posted to the page. The first parameter is the key value that identifies the data for the current control. Thus, you can access the data for your control using syntax like this:

```
Dim newData As String = postData(postDataKey)
```

The LoadPostData() also needs to tell ASP.NET whether a change event is required. You can't fire an event at this point, because the other controls may not be properly updated with the posted data. However, you can tell ASP.NET that a change has occurred by returning True. If you return True, ASP.NET will call the RaisePostDataChangedEvent() method after all the controls are initialized. If you return False, ASP.NET will not call this method.

Here's the complete code for the LoadPostData() method in the CustomTextBox:

```
Public Function LoadPostData(ByVal postDataKey As String,
      ByVal postData As NameValueCollection) As Boolean
    ' Get the value posted and the past value.
    Dim postedValue As String = postData(postDataKey)
    Dim val As String = Text

    ' If the value changed, then reset the value of the text property
    ' and return true so the RaisePostDataChangedEvent will be fired.
    If val <> postedValue Then
        Text = postedValue
        Return True
    Else
        Return False
    End If
End Function
```

The RaisePostDataChangedEvent() has the relatively simple task of firing the event. However, most ASP.NET controls use an extra layer, whereby the RaisePostDataChangedEvent() calls an OnXxx() method and the OnXxx() method actually raises the event. This extra layer gives other developers the ability to derive a new control from your control and alter its behavior by overriding the OnXxx() method.

Here's the remaining code:

```
Public Event TextChanged As EventHandler
```

```
Public Sub RaisePostDataChangedEvent()
    ' Call the method to raise the change event.
    OnTextChanged(New EventArgs())
End Sub

Protected Overridable Sub OnTextChanged(ByVal e As EventArgs)
    ' Check for at least one listener, and then raise the event.
    If TextChangedEvent IsNot Nothing Then
        RaiseEvent TextChanged(Me, e)
    End If
End Sub
```

Figure 27-7 shows a sample page that tests the CustomTextBox control and responds to its event.

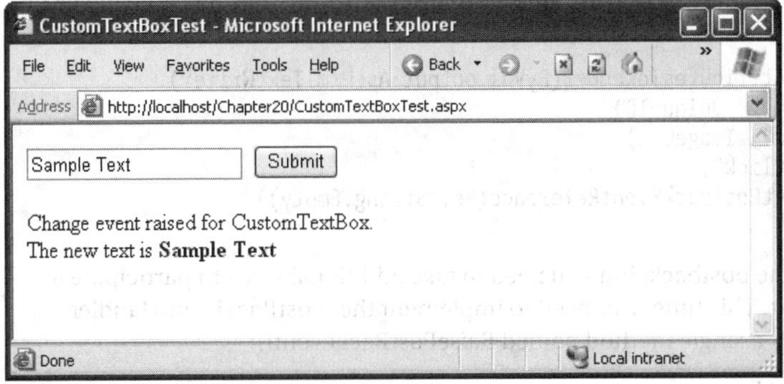

Figure 27-7. *Retrieving posted data in a custom control*

Triggering a Postback

By implementing IPostBackDataHandler, you're able to participate in every postback and retrieve the posted data that belongs to your control. But what if you want to *trigger* a postback? The simplest example of such a control is the Button control, but many other rich web controls—including the Calendar and GridView—allow you to trigger a postback by clicking an element or a link somewhere in the rendered HTML.

You can trigger a postback in two ways. First, you can render an <input> tag for a submit button, which always posts back the form. Your other option is to call the JavaScript function called __doPostBack() that ASP.NET automatically adds to the page. The __doPostBack() function accepts two parameters: the name of the control that's triggering the postback and a string representing additional postback data.

ASP.NET makes it easy to access the __doPostBack() function with the Page.ClientScript.GetPostBackEventReference() method. This method creates a reference to the client-side __doPostBack() function, which you can then render into your control. Usually, you'll place this reference in the onClick attribute of one of HTML elements in your control. That way, when that HTML element is clicked, the __doPostBack() function is triggered. Of course, JavaScript provides other attributes that you can use, some of which you'll see in Chapter 29.

The best way to see postbacks in action is to create a simple control. The following example demonstrates a clickable image. When clicked, the page is posted back, without any additional data.

This control is based on the <img> tag and requires just a single property:

```
Public Sub New()
    MyBase.New(HtmlTextWriterTag.Img)
    ImageUrl = String.Empty
End Sub

Public Property ImageUrl() As String
    Get
            Return CStr(ViewState("ImageUrl"))
    End Get
    Set
            ViewState("ImageUrl") = Value
    End Set
End Property
```

The only customization you need to do is add a few additional attributes to render. These include the unique control name, the image URL, and the onClick attribute that wires the image up to the __doPostBack() function, as follows:

```
Protected Overrides Sub AddAttributesToRender(ByVal output As HtmlTextWriter)
    output.AddAttribute("name", UniqueID)
    output.AddAttribute("src", ImageUrl)
    output.AddAttribute("onClick",
        Page.ClientScript.GetPostBackEventReference(Me, String.Empty))
End Sub
```

This is enough to trigger the postback, but you need to take additional steps to participate in the postback and raise an event. This time, you need to implement the IPostBackEventHandler interface. This interface defines a single method named RaisePostBackEvent():

```
Public Class CustomImageButton
    Inherits WebControl
    Implements IPostBackEventHandler
       Private ...
End Class
```

When the page is posted back, ASP.NET determines which control triggered the postback (by looking at each control's UniqueID property), and, if that control implements IPostBackEventHandler, ASP.NET then calls the RaisePostBackEvent() method with the event data. At this point, all the controls on the page have been initialized, and it's safe to fire an event, as shown here:

```
Public Event ImageClicked As EventHandler

Public Sub RaisePostBackEvent(ByVal eventArgument As String)
    OnImageClicked(New EventArgs())
End Sub

Protected Overridable Sub OnImageClicked(ByVal e As EventArgs)
    ' Check for at least one listener, and then raise the event.
    If ImageClickedEvent IsNot Nothing Then
       RaiseEvent ImageClicked(Me, e)
    End If
End Sub
```

Figure 27-8 shows a sample page that tests the CustomImageButton control and responds to its event.

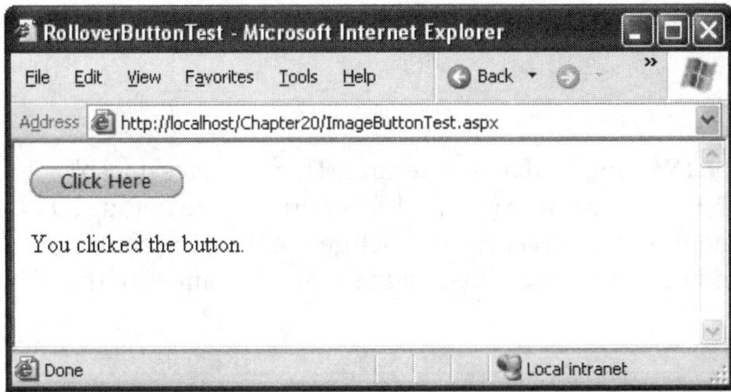

Figure 27-8. *Triggering a postback in a custom control*

This control doesn't offer any functionality you can't already get with existing ASP.NET web controls, such as the ImageButton. However, it's a great starting point for building something that's much more useful. In Chapter 29, you'll see how to extend this control with JavaScript code to create a rollover button—something with no equivalent in the .NET class library.

■ **Note** Rather than posting back the entire page, you can use a callback to fetch some specific information from the server. Callbacks are a new ASP.NET 2.0 feature, and we discuss them in Chapter 29.

Extending Existing Web Controls

In many situations, you don't need to create a new control from scratch. Some of the functionality might already exist in the basic set of ASP.NET web controls. Because all ASP.NET controls are ordinary classes, you can use their functionality with basic object-oriented practices such as composition (creating a class that uses instances of other classes) and inheritance (creating a class that extends an existing class to change its functionality). In the following sections, you'll see how both tasks apply to custom control design.

Composite Controls

So far you've seen a few custom controls that programmatically generate all the HTML code they need (except for the style properties, which can be inherited from the WebControl class). If you want to write a series of controls, you need to output all the HTML tags, one after the other. Fortunately, ASP.NET includes a feature that can save you this work by allowing you to build your control class out of other, existing web controls.

The basic technique is to create a control class that derives from System.Web.UI.WebControls.CompositeControl (which itself derives from WebControl). Then, you must override the CreateChildControls() method. At this point, you can create one or more control objects, set their properties and event handlers, and finally add them to the Controls collection of the current control. The best part about this approach is that you don't need to customize the rendering code at all. Instead, the rendering work is delegated to the constituent server controls. You also don't need to worry about details such as triggering postbacks and getting postback data, because the child controls will handle these details themselves.

The following example creates a TitledTextBox control that pairs a label (on the left) with a text box (on the right). Here's the class definition for the control:

```
Public Class TitledTextBox
    Inherits CompositeControl
      Private ...
End Class
```

The CompositeControl implements the INamingContainer interface. This interface doesn't have any methods. It simply instructs ASP.NET to make sure all the child controls have unique ID values. ASP.NET does this by prepending the ID of the server control before the ID of the control. This ensures that there won't be any naming conflict, even if you add several instances of the TitleTextBox control to a web form.

■ **Note** In ASP.NET 1.*x*, the process for creating a composite control was subtly different. No CompositeControl class existed, so you had to derive from the WebControl class yourself. However, there are only two differences between CompositeControl and WebControl. First, CompositeControl implements INamingContainer so all the child controls are uniquely scoped and their IDs won't conflict with page controls or other instances of your composite control. Second, CompositeControl calls the EnsureChildControls() method automatically when you access the Controls collection, which makes sure child controls are created before you try to manipulate them.

To make life easier, you should track the constituent controls with member variables. This allows you to access them in any method in your control. However, you shouldn't create these controls yet, because that's the function of the CreateChildControls() method.

```
Private m_label As Label
Private m_textBox As TextBox
```

The web page won't be able to directly access either of these controls. If you want to allow access to certain properties, you need to add property procedures to your custom control class, as follows:

```
Public Property Title() As String
    Get
        Return CStr(ViewState("Title"))
    End Get
    Set
        ViewState("Title") = Value
    End Set
End Property


Public Property Text() As String
    Get
        Return CStr(ViewState("Text"))
    End Get
    Set
        ViewState("Text") = Value
    End Set
End Property
```

Note that these properties simply store information in view state—they don't directly access the child controls. That's because the child controls might not yet exist. These properties will be applied to the child controls in the CreateChildControls() method. All the controls are rendered in a <span>, which works well. It ensures that if the web page applies font, color, or position attributes to the TitledTextBox control, it will have the desired effect on all the child controls.

Now you can override the CreateChildControls() method to create the Label and TextBox control objects. These objects are separated with one additional control object—a LiteralControl, which simply represents a scrap of HTML. In this example, the LiteralControl wraps two nonbreaking spaces. Here's the complete code for the CreateChildControls() method:

```
Protected Overrides Sub CreateChildControls()
    ' Add the label.
    m_label = New Label()
    m_label.EnableViewState = False
    m_label.Text = Title
    Controls.Add(m_label)

    ' Add a space.
    Controls.Add(New LiteralControl("  "))

    ' Add the text box.
    m_textBox = New TextBox()
    m_textBox.EnableViewState = False
    m_textBox.Text = Text
    AddHandler m_textBox.TextChanged, AddressOf OnTextChanged
    Controls.Add(m_textBox)
End Sub
```

The CreateChildControls() code attaches an event handler to the TextBox.TextChanged event. When this event fires, your TitledTextBox should pass it along to the web page as the TitledTextBox.TextChanged event. Here's the code you need to implement the rest of this design:

```
Public Event TextChanged As EventHandler

Protected Overridable Sub OnTextChanged(ByVal sender As Object,
        ByVal e As EventArgs)
    If TextChangedEvent IsNot Nothing Then
        RaiseEvent TextChanged(Me, e)
    End If
End Sub
```

Figure 27-9 shows a sample page that tests the TitledTextBox control and responds to its event.

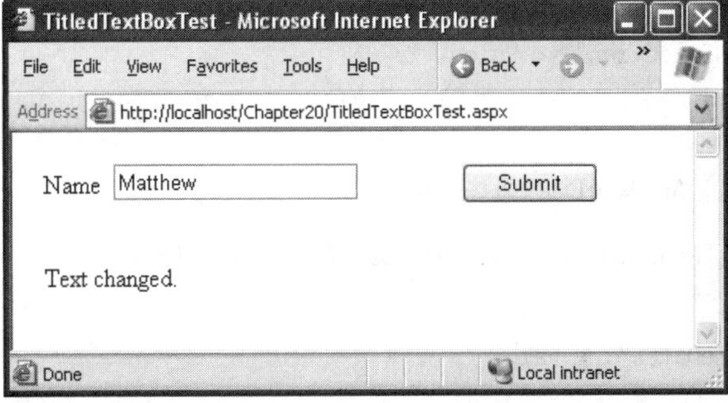

Figure 27-9. *Creating a composite control with a label and text box*

You may prefer to follow the earlier approach and use an HtmlTextWriter to get full control over the HTML markup you render. But if you want to handle postbacks and events and create complex controls (such as an extended GridView or a navigational aid), using composite controls can simplify your life dramatically.

Derived Controls

Another approach to creating controls is to derive a more specialized control from one of the existing control classes. You can then override or add just the functionality you need, rather than re-creating the whole control. This approach isn't always possible, because some controls keep key pieces of their infrastructure out of sight in private methods you can't override. However, when it does work, it can save a lot of work.

Sometimes, you might create a derived control so that you can preinitialize an existing control with certain styles or formatting properties. For example, you could create a custom Calendar or GridView that sets styles in the OnInit() method. That way, when you add this Calendar control, it's already formatted with the look you need. In other cases, you might add entirely new functionality in the form of new methods or properties, as demonstrated in the following examples.

Creating a Higher-Level Calendar

In previous chapters, you learned how to customize the GridView to add niceties such as a summary row. You also learned how to use day-specific formatting in the Calendar. To implement either one of these changes, you need to handle a generic control event and wait for the element you want to format. A more elegant solution would be to simply set a property and let the control handle the task. You can add this extra layer of abstraction with a custom control.

For example, imagine you want to provide an easy way to designate nonselectable days in a calendar. To accomplish this, you could create a custom calendar control that adds two properties, as shown here:

```
Public Class RestrictedCalendar
    Inherits Calendar

    Public Property AllowWeekendSelection() As Boolean
        Get
                Return CBool(ViewState("AllowWeekendSelection"))
        End Get
        Set
                ViewState("AllowWeekendSelection") = Value
        End Set
    End Property

    Public Property NonSelectableDates() As DateTimeCollection
        Get
                Return CType(ViewState("NonSelectableDates"), DateTimeCollection)
        End Get
        Set
                ViewState("NonSelectableDates") = Value
        End Set
    End Property

    ' (Other code omitted.)
End Class
```

The AllowWeekendSelection property indicates whether Saturday and Sunday should be selectable. The NonSelectableDates property provides a collection of exact dates that won't be selectable. The DateTimeCollection is a custom collection class defined in the control project. It works the same as an ordinary ArrayList, except that it's strongly typed to accept only DateTime values. You could use a List(Of Type) generic class, but it's better to design a custom collection because that makes it easier to add design-time support for the collection (as discussed Chapter 28). You can see the full collection code with the downloadable code sample.

Now when the calendar is rendered, you can take this information into account and automatically adjust any matching dates. This means you don't need to handle the DayRender event in your code. Instead, you can specify the restricted dates declaratively using the Properties window.

Here's the control code that handles the process:

```
Protected Overrides Sub OnDayRender(ByVal cell As TableCell,
      ByVal day As CalendarDay)
    If day.IsWeekend AndAlso (Not AllowWeekendSelection) Then
        day.IsSelectable = False
    Else If NonSelectableDates.Contains(day.Date) Then
        day.IsSelectable = False
    End If

    ' Let the base class raise this event.
    ' The web page can respond to this event to perform further processing
    ' (or even reverse the changes made here).
    MyBase.OnDayRender(cell, day)
End Sub
```

Note that your custom control doesn't handle the DayRender event. Instead, it overrides the corresponding OnDayRender() method. This gives a similar result without worrying about delegate code and event handlers. Although controls don't need to provide OnXxx() methods for every event, most do as a matter of convention. That makes it easier for you to customize the control.

The RestrictedCalendar control also uses the constructor to initialize some formatting-related properties:

```
Public Sub New()
    ' Set default properties.
    AllowWeekendSelection = True
    NonSelectableDates = New DateTimeCollection()

    ' Configure the default appearance of the calendar.
    CellPadding = 8
    CellSpacing = 8
    BackColor = Color.LightYellow
    BorderStyle = BorderStyle.Groove
    BorderWidth = Unit.Pixel(2)
    ShowGridLines = True

    ' Configure the font.
    Font.Name = "Verdana"
    Font.Size = FontUnit.XXSmall

    ' Set calendar settings.
    FirstDayOfWeek = FirstDayOfWeek.Monday
    PrevMonthText = "<--"
    NextMonthText = "-->"
```

```
    ' Select the current date by default.
    SelectedDate = DateTime.Today
End Sub
```

This code also demonstrates how you can access the inherited properties of the Calendar control (such as CellPadding and CellSpacing) just as easily as you access the new properties you've added (such as AllowWeekendSelection).

This example allows the user to designate specific restricted dates in a specific month and year. You could also use a similar approach to allow the user to restrict specific years, months in any year, days in any month, and so on. In a sense, adding these sorts of properties complicates the Calendar control and makes it less flexible. However, this isn't a problem if you want to tailor the control for a specific scenario.

■ **Note** The online code for the RestrictedCalendar adds quite a bit more logic to improve design-time support. This code ensures that you can set the restricted dates using the Properties window. You'll learn more about design-time support in Chapter 28.

Creating a Label for Specific Data

One common reason for creating customized controls is to fine-tune a control for specific types of data. For example, consider the Label control. In its standard form, it's a flexible all-purpose tool that you can use to render text content and insert arbitrary HTML. However, in many situations it would be nice to have a higher-level way to output text that takes care of some of the encoding. The following example is designed for one of these scenarios. It shows how you can customize the rendering of a derived Label control for a specific type of content.

In Chapter 12, you learned about the Xml control, which allows you to display XML content in a page using an XSLT stylesheet. However, the Xml control doesn't give you any way to show arbitrary XML. So, what should you do if you want to duplicate the Internet Explorer behavior, which shows a color-coded tree of XML tags? You could implement this approach using an XSLT stylesheet. However, another interesting choice is to create a custom Label control that's designed for XML content. This Label control can apply the formatting you want automatically.

First, consider what happens if you try to display XML content *without* taking any extra steps? In this case, all the XML tags will be interpreted as meaningless HTML tags, and they won't be shown. The display will simply show a jumbled block of text that represents all the content of all elements from start to finish. You can improve upon this situation slightly by using the HttpServerUtility.HtmlEncode() method, which replaces all special HTML characters with the equivalent character entities. However, the XML display you'll create with this approach is still far from ideal. For one thing, all the whitespace will be collapsed, and all the line breaks will be ignored, leading to a long string of text that's not easy to interpret. Figure 27-10 shows this approach with the DvdList.xml document used in Chapter 12.

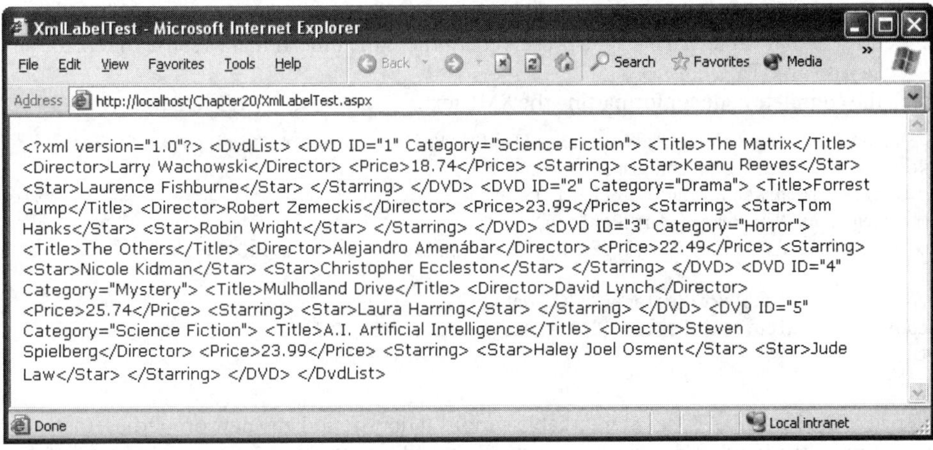

Figure 27-10. *Displaying XML data with HTML escaping*

The custom XmlLabel control solves this problem by applying formatting to XML start and end tags. This functionality is wrapped into a static method called ConvertXmlTextToHtmlText(), which accepts a string with XML content and returns a string with formatted HTML content. This functionality is implemented as a static method rather than an instance method so that you can call it to format text for display in other controls.

The ConvertXmlTextToHtmlText() method uses a regular expression to find all the XML tags in the string. Here's the expression you need:

```
<([^>]+)>
```

This expression matches the less-than sign (<) that starts the tag, followed by a sequence of one or more characters that aren't greater-than signs (>). The match ends as soon as a greater-than (>) sign is found. This expression matches both start tags (such as <DvdList>) and end tags (such as </DvdList>).

■ **Tip** You might think you could use a simpler regular expression such as <.+> to match a tag. The problem is that regular expressions use *greedy matching*, which means they often match as much as possible. As a result, an expression such as <.+> will match everything between the less-than (<) sign of the first tag to the greater-than sign (>) in the last tag at the end of document. In other words, you'll end up with a single match that obscures other embedded matches. To prevent this behavior, you need to create a regular expression that explicitly specifies what characters you *don't* want to match.

Once you have a match, the next step is to replace this text with the text you really want. The replacement expression is as follows:

```
&lt;<b>$1&gt;</b>
```

This replacement uses the HTML entities for the less-than and greater-than signs (< and >), and it adds an HTML <b> tag to format the text in bold. The $1 is a *back reference* that refers to the bracketed text in the search expression. In this example, the bracketed text includes the full tag name—everything between the opening < and the closing >.

Once the tags are in bold, the last step is to replace the spaces in the string with the   character entity so that whitespace will be preserved. At the same time, it makes sense to replace all the line feeds with an HTML <br />.

Here's the complete code for formatting the XML text:

```
Public Shared Function ConvertXmlTextToHtmlText(ByVal inputText As String) As String
    ' Replace all start and end tags.
    Dim startPattern As String = "<([^>]+)>"
    Dim myRegEx As New Regex(startPattern)
    Dim outputText As String = myRegEx.Replace(inputText, "&lt;<b>$1&gt;</b>")

    outputText = outputText.Replace(" ", " ")
    outputText = outputText.Replace(Constants.vbCrLf, "<br />")
    Return outputText
End Function
```

The rest of the XmlLabel code is remarkably simple. It doesn't add any new properties. Instead, it simply overrides the RenderContents() to ensure that the formatted text is rendered instead of the ordinary text:

```
Protected Overrides Sub RenderContents(ByVal output As HtmlTextWriter)
    Dim xmlText As String = XmlLabel.ConvertXmlTextToHtmlText(Text)
    output.Write(xmlText)
End Sub
```

Note that this code doesn't call the base implementation of RenderContents(). That's because the goal of the XmlLabel control is to *replace* the rendering logic for the label text, not to supplement it.

Figure 27-11 shows what ordinary XML data looks like when displayed in the XmlLabel control. Of course, now that you have the basic framework in place, you could do a lot more to perfect this output, including color-coding and automatic indenting.

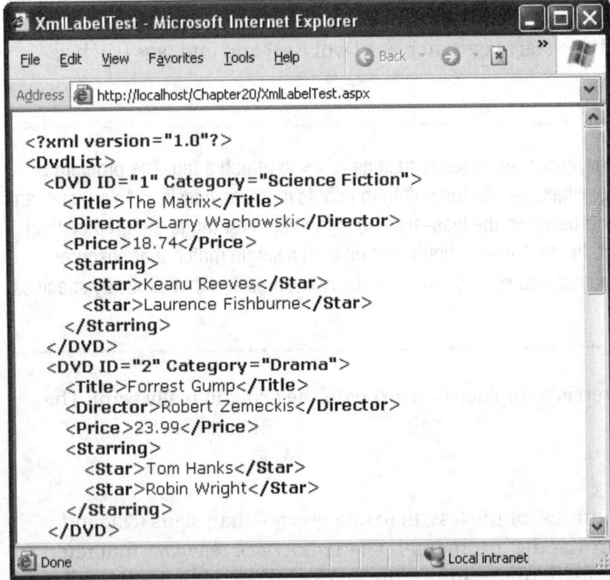

Figure 27-11. *Displaying formatted XML data*

Tip You could use a similar technique to create a label that automatically converts mail addresses and URLs to links (wrapped by the <a> tag), formats multiple lines of text into a bulleted list, and so on.

Templated Controls

Up to this point, the controls you've seen have rendered themselves based on the logic and code within the control. The consumers of the control (the web pages that use it) do not have the ability to directly define the layout and style of the control's content.

Templated controls and styles allow you to create controls and add functionality without needing to lock users into a fixed layout. With templates, the control consumer provides a set of HTML tags that define the information and formatting used by the control. The templated control uses one or more templates to render portions of its interface. As a result, templated controls can be much more flexible than ordinary controls.

ASP.NET includes several controls that support templates, including the Repeater, DataList, GridView, and FormView. In the following sections, you'll learn how to support templates in your own controls.

Creating a Templated Control

It's surprisingly easy to create a basic templated control. You start by creating a composite control. This control should derive from WebControl and implement the INamingContainer interface to make sure that every child control has a unique name.

The next step is to create one or more template containers. A template container allows the user to specify the template declaratively in the .aspx portion of the web page. To support a template, you just need a control property that accepts an ITemplate object, as shown here:

```
Private MyItemTemplate As ITemplate

Public Property ItemTemplate() As ITemplate
    Get
        Return MyItemTemplate
    End Get
    Set
        MyItemTemplate = Value
    End Set
End Property
```

Note that the template isn't stored in view state, because it's always retrieved from the .aspx file, and it doesn't change programmatically. That means you can store it in a private variable and re-create it with each postback.

The ITemplate interface defines a single method, InstantiateIn(), which creates an instance of a template inside an existing control. Essentially, when the InstantiateIn() method is called, ASP.NET parses the template and creates controls based on the tags and code in the template. These controls are then added to the control container that's passed into the method. For example, if a template contains a single Label tag, then calling InstantiateIn() creates a Label control and adds it to the Controls collection of the specified container. Your control uses the InstantiateIn() method to render its templates.

The final ingredient is the CreateChildControls() method. This is the place where you create the template using the InstantiateIn() method and add it to the Controls collection.

To understand how this all works together, consider the following extremely simple templated control. It defines a single template and an additional property that lets the user choose how many times the template should be repeated in the web page. Overall, it works more or less the same as the simple Repeater control (without any support for data binding). Here's the complete code:

```
Public Class SuperSimpleRepeater
        Inherits WebControl
        Implements INamingContainer

    Public Sub New()
        MyBase.New()
        RepeatCount = 1
    End Sub

    Public Property RepeatCount() As Integer
        Get
                Return CInt(ViewState("RepeatCount"))
        End Get
        Set
                ViewState("RepeatCount") = Value
        End Set
    End Property

    Private MyItemTemplate As ITemplate
    Public Property ItemTemplate() As ITemplate
        Get
                Return MyItemTemplate
        End Get
        Set
                MyItemTemplate=Value
        End Set
    End Property

    Protected Overrides Sub CreateChildControls()
        ' Clear out the control collection before starting.
        Controls.Clear()

        If (RepeatCount > 0) AndAlso (MyItemTemplate IsNot Nothing) Then
            ' Instantiate the template in a panel multiple times.
            Dim i As Integer = 0
            Do While i<RepeatCount
                Dim container As New Panel()
                MyItemTemplate.InstantiateIn(container)
                Controls.Add(container)
                i += 1
            Loop
        Else
                ' Show an error message.
                Controls.Add(
                New LiteralControl("Specify the record count and an item template"))
        End If
    End Sub
End Class
```

To use this control, you need to provide a template for the ItemTemplate property. You can do this declaratively by adding the HTML and control tags in an <ItemTemplate> tag. Here's an example:

```
<apress:SuperSimpleRepeater id="sample" runat="server" RepeatCount="10">
  <ItemTemplate>
    <div align="center">
```

```
      <hr />Creating templated controls is <b>easy</b> and <i>fun</i>.<br /><hr />
    </div>
  </ItemTemplate>
</apress:SuperSimpleRepeater>
```

Figure 27-12 shows the rendered content, which copies the template HTML into the page ten times.

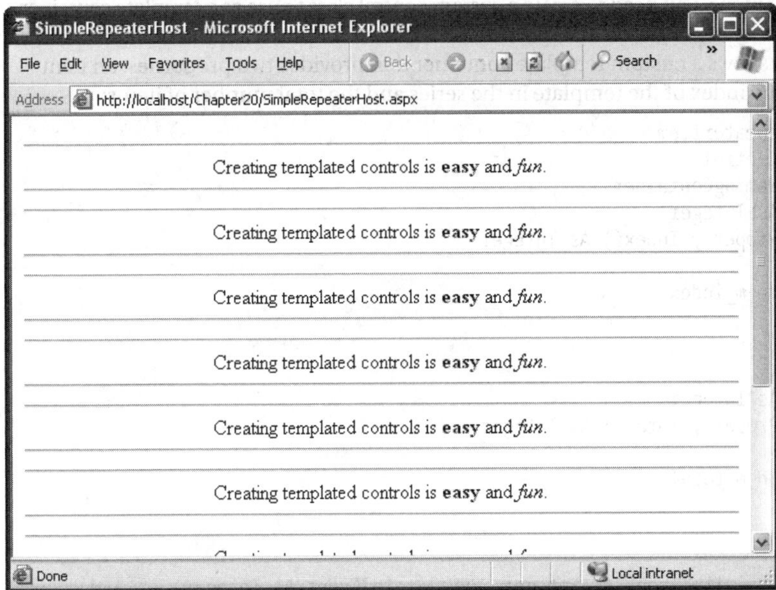

Figure 27-12. *Repeating a template*

This example has neglected one detail. All template controls should use the PersistChildren attribute, as shown here:

```
<PersistChildren(True)> _
Public Class SuperSimpleRepeater
    Inherits WebControl
    Implements INamingContainer
      Private ...
End Class
```

This tag indicates that all child elements in the control tag should be interpreted as properties. As a result, if you add an <ItemTemplate> tag inside the <SuperSimpleRepeater> tag, the ASP.NET parser will assume the <ItemTemplate> tag defines the content for the SuperSimpleRepeater. ItemTemplate property. If your control derives from WebControl, this is already the default behavior, so you don't need to take this step. However, it's still a good practice to include this attribute to explicitly indicate how the control deals with nested tags.

If you apply the PersistChildren with an argument of False, the ASP.NET parser assumes that any nested tags are child controls. It then creates the corresponding control object and passes it your control by calling the AddParsedSubObject() method. The default implementation of this method simply adds the child control to the Controls collection of the current control, although you can change this behavior by overriding this method.

Using Customized Templates

As you can see, creating a basic templated control isn't difficult and doesn't require much code. However, the previous example still lacks a few key features. For one thing, it doesn't allow you to access any information from the templated items. It would be much more useful if there were a way to access some basic information about each item. Using this information, you could write data-binding expressions in your template, as you can with templated controls such as the Repeater and DataList.

To support this technique, you need to create a custom control class to use as a template container. This control needs to include properties that provide the information in which you're interested. The following example shows a custom template container that provides two properties: an item number representing the index of the template in the series and the total number of items:

```
Public Class SimpleRepeaterItem
        Inherits WebControl
        Implements INamingContainer
    Private m_index As Integer
    Public ReadOnly Property Index() As Integer
        Get
                Return m_index
        End Get
    End Property

    Private m_total As Integer
    Public ReadOnly Property Total() As Integer
        Get
                Return m_total
        End Get
    End Property

    Public Sub New(ByVal itemIndex As Integer, ByVal totalCount As Integer)
        m_index = itemIndex
        m_total = totalCount
    End Sub
End Class
```

Note that because this control acts as a template container, it needs to implement the INamingContainer interface.

Now you need to adjust the CreateChildControls() method so that it creates instances of the SimpleRepeaterItem control, instead of an ordinary Panel control. Each instance of the SimpleRepeaterItem will then hold a single instance of the item template.

But before you get to this point, it's worth making the templated control a little more sophisticated. The next example adds a header and footer template and an alternating item template. With these four templates, the programmer will have much more control over the layout of the content. Here's the template code you need:

```
Private m_itemTemplate As ITemplate
<TemplateContainer(GetType(SimpleRepeaterItem))> _
Public Property ItemTemplate() As ITemplate
    Get
                Return m_itemTemplate
    End Get
    Set
                m_itemTemplate=Value
    End Set
End Property
```

```
Private m_alternatingItemTemplate As ITemplate
<TemplateContainer(GetType(SimpleRepeaterItem))> _
Public Property AlternatingItemTemplate() As ITemplate
    Get
        Return m_alternatingItemTemplate
    End Get
    Set
        m_alternatingItemTemplate=Value
    End Set
End Property

Private m_headerTemplate As ITemplate
<TemplateContainer(GetType(SimpleRepeaterItem))> _
Public Property HeaderTemplate() As ITemplate
    Get
        Return m_headerTemplate
    End Get
    Set
        m_headerTemplate=Value
    End Set
End Property

Private m_footerTemplate As ITemplate
<TemplateContainer(GetType(SimpleRepeaterItem))> _
Public Property FooterTemplate() As ITemplate
    Get
        Return m_footerTemplate
    End Get
    Set
        m_footerTemplate=Value
    End Set
End Property
```

Note that each template property uses the TemplateContainer attribute to indicate what type of container your control will use when it instantiates the template.

Now you can revise the CreateChildControls() method. The CreateChildControls() will create instances of the SimpleRepeaterItem container and pass the current index and the total item count as constructor arguments. Then, it will add the SimpleRepeaterItem as a child control of the SuperSimpleRepeater.

```
Protected Overrides Sub CreateChildControls()
    Controls.Clear()

    If (RepeatCount > 0) AndAlso (itemTemplate IsNot Nothing) Then
        ' Start by outputing the header template (if supplied).
        If headerTemplate IsNot Nothing Then
            Dim headerContainer As New SimpleRepeaterItem(0, RepeatCount)
            headerTemplate.InstantiateIn(headerContainer)
            Controls.Add(headerContainer)
        End If

        ' Output the content the specified number of times.
        Dim i As Integer = 0
        Do While i<RepeatCount
            Dim container As New SimpleRepeaterItem(i+1, RepeatCount)

            If (i Mod 2 = 0) AndAlso (alternatingItemTemplate IsNot Nothing) Then
                ' This is an alternating item, and there is an
```

```
                ' alternating template.
                alternatingItemTemplate.InstantiateIn(container)
            Else
                itemTemplate.InstantiateIn(container)
            End If
            Controls.Add(container)
             i += 1
        Loop

        ' Once all of the items have been rendered,
        ' add the footer template if specified.
        If footerTemplate IsNot Nothing Then
            Dim footerContainer As New SimpleRepeaterItem(RepeatCount, RepeatCount)
            footerTemplate.InstantiateIn(footerContainer)
            Controls.Add(footerContainer)
        End If
    Else
        ' Show an error message.
        Controls.Add(
            New LiteralControl("Specify the record count and an item template"))
    End If
End Sub
```

This has one additional caveat. For data binding to work with the new SuperSimpleRepeater control, you need to call the DataBind() method of the header, footer, and item containers. To make sure this critical step takes place, you need to override the DataBind() method. By default, the DataBind() method binds all the child controls in the Controls collection. However, your overridden implementation needs to call EnsureChildControls() first to make sure all the template containers have been created before the control is bound. Here's the code you need:

```
Public Overrides Sub DataBind()
    ' Make sure the template containers have been created.
    EnsureChildControls()

    ' Bind all the child controls.
    MyBase.DataBind()
End Sub
```

You can now test the new SuperSimpleRepeater with the following control tag and templates:

```
<apress:SuperSimpleRepeater2 id="sample" runat="server" RepeatCount="10">
  <HeaderTemplate>
    <h2 style="Color:Red">Super Simple Repeater Strikes Again!</h2>
    Now showing <%# Container.Total %> Items for your viewing pleasure.
  </HeaderTemplate>
  <ItemTemplate>
    <div align="center">
    <hr />Item <%# Container.Index %> of <%# Container.Total%><br /><hr />
    </div>
  </ItemTemplate>

  <AlternatingItemTemplate>
   <div align="center" style="border-right: fuchsia double; border-top: fuchsia
double; border-left: fuchsia double; border-bottom: fuchsia double">
   Item <%# Container.Index %> of <%# Container.Total%>
   </div>
  </AlternatingItemTemplate>
  <FooterTemplate>
```

```
    <i>This presentation of the Simple Repeater Control brought to you by the
    letter <b>W</b></i>
  </FooterTemplate>
</apress:SuperSimpleRepeater2>
```

Note how the <ItemTemplate> and <AlternatingItemTemplate> sections use data binding expressions that refer to Container. These expressions are evaluated against the properties of the container object, which in this example is an instance of the SimpleRepeaterItem class. All your web page needs to do is call the SuperSimpleReader.DataBind() method when the page loads. You can call SuperSimpleReader.DataBind() directly, or you can call it indirectly through the Page.DataBind() method, as shown here:

```
Private Sub Page_Load(ByVal sender As Object, ByVal e As System.EventArgs)
    Page.DataBind()
End Sub
```

Figure 27-13 shows the new repeater control in action. Odd items (1, 3, 5, and so on) use the normal item template, while even items (2, 4, 6, and so on) use the alternative item template with the double border.

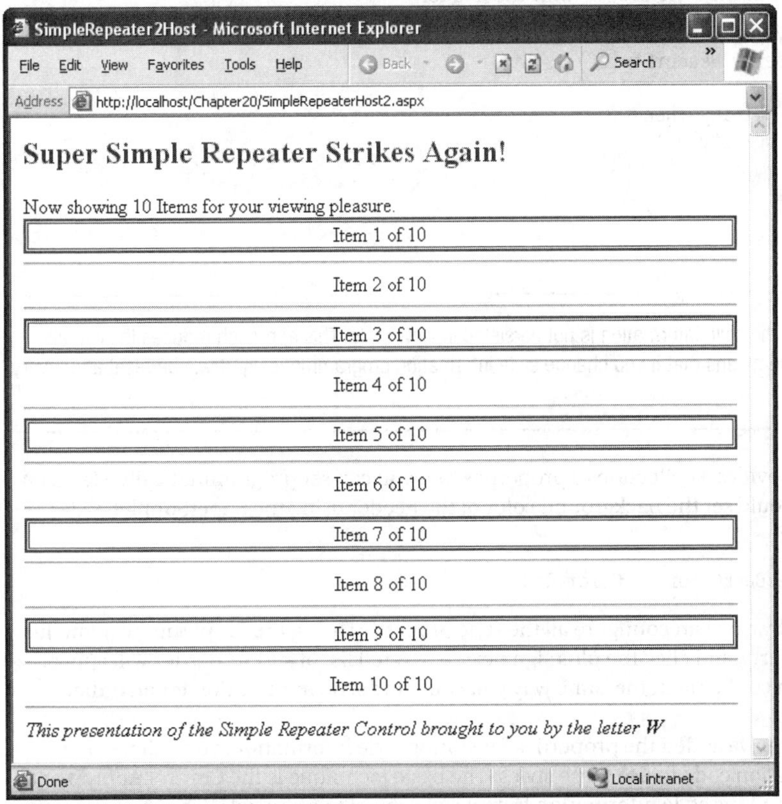

Figure 27-13. *Repeating more-advanced templates*

■ **Tip** As you saw with templated controls such as the Repeater and DataList, it is common practice to extend the container control to provide a DataItem property. When a data item is read from the data source, the data item is passed to the container, which then exposes it and allows the web page to bind to it. In this way, the templated control becomes ultimately flexible, because it doesn't need to know anything about the type or structure of the data it's displaying.

Styles

In the templated examples that you've seen so far, it's up to the web page to supply HTML elements for the template and the style attributes that tailor their appearance. Many templated controls simplify this process through style objects. In ASP.NET, the System.Web.UI.WebControls.Style class represents the complete collection of style information including colors, fonts, alignment, borders, and spacing. Using this class, you can easily add style support to your templated controls.

For example, consider the SuperSimpleRepeater presented in the previous example, which uses four templates (item, alternating item, header, and footer). Using the Style class, you can define four corresponding style properties, one for each template.

Here's an example of the style property for the header:

```
Private hstyl As Style
Public ReadOnly Property HeaderStyle() As Style
    Get
        If hStyl Is Nothing Then
            hStyl = New Style()
        End If
        Return hStyl
    End Get
End Property
```

■ **Note** In this example, the style information is not persisted in view state. This approach reduces the overall page size. However, it also means that if you change style information programmatically, it will be reset after every postback.

The Style class provides a collection of properties that you can set programmatically. Here's an example of how you could set the background color of the header using the SuperSimpleReader. HeaderStyle property:

```
repeater.HeaderStyle.BackColor  = Color.Red
```

Even more usefully, you can configure all the style properties using the Properties window. Just look for the style property, and click the plus sign next to it. A full list of subproperties will appear, each of which you can configure in the same way you configure style information for an ordinary web control.

Of course, once you've added the properties for storing style information, you still need to adjust the control creation code to use these styles. The basic technique is the Control.ApplyStyle() method, which copies all the style information from a style object to a control. Here's how you can use this technique to set the style attributes for the header:

```
if (headerStyle != null)
{
    headerContainer.ApplyStyle(headerStyle);
}
```

The alternating item template is a special case. Usually, the alternating item will use the item style plus any styles that are redefined in the alternating item style. In this way, the user can just add a few style settings for the alternating item, rather than redefining all the style settings from the item style.

To accomplish this behavior, you need the help of the CopyFrom() and MergeWith() methods of the Style class. The CopyFrom() method copies the styles from one style object to the calling style object, overwriting current values if they exist. The MergeWith() method combines the two styles so that if a value exists for the style attribute in the first style, this value will not be overwritten by the style value from the second style object.

Table 27-4 demonstrates how this works. The first two columns show the values for several style properties on two instances of the style class. The third column shows the updated values for the first style after calling CopyFrom() and passing in the second style. The last column shows the same values in Style1 after calling MergeWith() and passing Style2 as a parameter. Note that Style2 is not changed by either of these operations.

Table 27-4. *How Styles Are Copied and Merged*

	Style1 Before	Style2 Before	Style1 After CopyFrom(Style2)	Style1 After MergeWith(Style2)
BackColor	Black	White	White	Black
ForeColor	White	Black	Black	White
Height	25	[Not set]	25	25
Width	[Not set]	25	25	25

Here's how you can use the CopyFrom() and MergeWith() methods to create a style for alternating items:

```
Dim altStyle As New Style()
altStyle.MergeWith(itemStyle)
altStyle.CopyFrom(alternatingItemStyle)
```

You can now apply that style when needed, just as with any other style:

```
container.ApplyStyle(altStyle)
```

With this revised version of the control, you can add style tags to the repeater. Here's an example of the style information that might be created after configuring the style properties in Visual Studio:

```
<apress:SimpleStyledRepeater id="sample" runat="server" repeatcount="10">
  <AlternatingItemStyle Font-Bold="True" BorderStyle="Solid" BorderWidth="1px"
   ForeColor="White" BackColor="Red"></AlternatingItemStyle>
  <HeaderStyle Font-Italic="True" BackColor="#FFFFC0"></HeaderStyle>
  <AlternatingItemTemplate>
    Item <%# Container.Index %> of <%# Container.Total%>
  </AlternatingItemTemplate>

  <ItemTemplate>
    <hr />Item <%# Container.Index %> of <%# Container.Total%><br /><hr />
  </ItemTemplate>
  <HeaderTemplate>
    Now showing <%# Container.Total %> Items for your viewing pleasure.
  </HeaderTemplate>
</apress:SimpleStyledRepeater>
```

Notice that the templates in this example are pared down so that they no longer apply formatting directly through HTML tags and style attributes. Instead, all the formatting is set using the styles. Figure 27-14 shows the result when you bind the SimpleStyledRepeater and show the page.

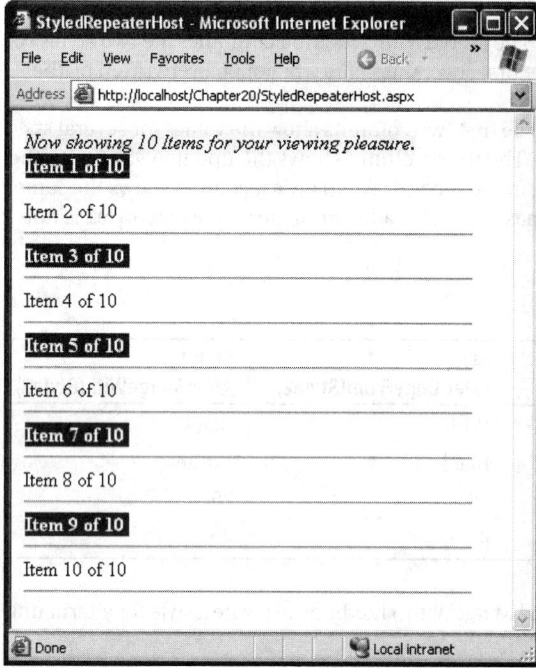

Figure 27-14. *Using styles with templates*

You can accomplish quite a bit more with templated controls, and it would take a significant amount of code (and a major investment of time) to duplicate a control such as the GridView. However, these examples show what you need to get started. Using them, you can create templated controls that are fine-tuned for your own custom data.

Summary

In this chapter, you learned how to use a variety of techniques to create custom controls. In the next chapter, you'll continue your exploration by learning how to take control of the design-time representation of a control. In Chapter 29 and Chapter 29, you'll see examples of custom controls that use JavaScript and GDI+ for advanced solutions.

Even after you've read all these chapters, you still will not have learned everything there is to know about ASP.NET custom control creation. If you want to continue your exploration into the tricks, techniques, and idiosyncrasies of custom control programming, you might be interested in a dedicated book about the topic. A good resource is *Developing Microsoft ASP.NET Server Controls and Components* (Microsoft Press, 2002).

CHAPTER 28

Design-Time Support

Custom controls have two requirements. They need to interact with a web page (and your code) at runtime, and they need to interact with Visual Studio at design time. These two tasks are related, but they can be refined and customized separately. Some of ASP.NET's most advanced controls (such as the Calendar and DataList) include an impressive degree of design-time smarts, including the ability to configure complex properties and apply themes with the click of a mouse.

You've probably already noticed that Visual Studio gives custom controls a high degree of design-time support automatically. For example, every custom control can be added to the Toolbox, dragged onto a form, and moved and repositioned. Additionally, you can configure the properties of the control in the Properties window, and depending on how you've implemented the rendering logic, you may even see a design-time representation of the control's HTML. In this chapter, you'll learn how to extend this level of design-time support.

Many of the techniques you'll see are frills and niceties that make it easier to work with custom controls. For example, you might use design-time support to add descriptions that appear in the Properties window or render a more representative appearance for your control on the design surface. However, other times design-time support is required. For example, if you create a control that exposes complex objects as properties and you don't take any extra steps to add design-time support, the control will work erratically in the design-time environment. You might find that properties you set using the Properties window are reset sporadically or cause nested child control tags to disappear. These quirks are a result of how ASP.NET serializes your control properties, and you'll learn how to tackle these issues in this chapter.

DESIGN-TIME SUPPORT CHANGES IN .NET 2.0

ASP.NET 2.0 continues to increase the design-time features for .NET controls. Many of these features will appeal to hard-core control developers, and they're out of the scope of this book. However, you will see the following enhancements:

- *New attributes*: ASP.NET 2.0 introduces new features, such as themes and better localization, and you can use new attributes to tailor whether your control supports them.
- *Web resources*: Using this feature, you can embed images, scripts, and other support files that your custom controls need directly in the compiled assembly. Best of all, you can still access these resources through a special URL format that uses the WebResource.axd handler.
- *Smart tags*: Many ASP.NET controls offer convenient smart tags that group common tasks. With a custom designer, you can create your own smart tags that bring together static information, property-style edit boxes, and links.

Design-Time Attributes

The first level of design-time support consists of control *attributes*—declarative flags that are compiled into the metadata of your custom control assembly. Attributes give you a way to add information that's related to a piece of code without forcing you to change the code or create a separate file in an entirely different format.

You always place attributes in angle brackets before the code element they modify. For example, here's how you can add an attribute that provides a description for the Text property of a control:

```
<Description("The text to be shown in the control")> _
Public Property Text() As String
    ...
End Property
```

In this case, the Description attribute *decorates* the Text property.

■ Note All attributes are actually classes. By convention, the class name ends in *Attribute*. For example, the Description attribute is actually represented by the DescriptionAttribute class. Although you can use the full class name, the Visual Basic .NET compiler allows you to use a handy shortcut and omit the final *Attribute* word.

In .NET, you can use attributes for a range of tasks. The key detail to understand about attributes is that they can be read and interpreted by different agents. For example, you can add attributes that give information to the CLR, the compiler, or a custom tool. This chapter focuses primarily on attributes that provide information to Visual Studio and tell it how to work with a control at design time. Later in the "Code Serialization" section, you'll also learn about some attributes that influence how the ASP.NET parser interprets control tags in the .aspx file.

■ Tip Like many of the classes for design-time support, most of the attributes you'll learn about in this chapter are found in the System.ComponentModel namespace. Before applying these attributes, you should import this namespace into the code files for your custom controls.

The Properties Window

The simplest attributes influence how the properties of your control appear in the Properties window. For example, you've probably noticed that the core set of ASP.NET web controls group their properties into several categories. When you select a property, the Properties window shows a brief description. To add this information to your own control, you need to decorate each property with the Category and Description attributes, as shown here:

```
<Category("Appearance"), Description("The text to be shown in the control")> _
Public Property Text() As String
    Get
        Return CStr(ViewState("Text"))
    End Get
    Set
        ViewState("Text") = Value
    End Set
End Property
```

As you can see, both the Category and Description attributes accept a single string as an argument. Figure 28-1 shows the resulting display if you select the Text property in the Properties window.

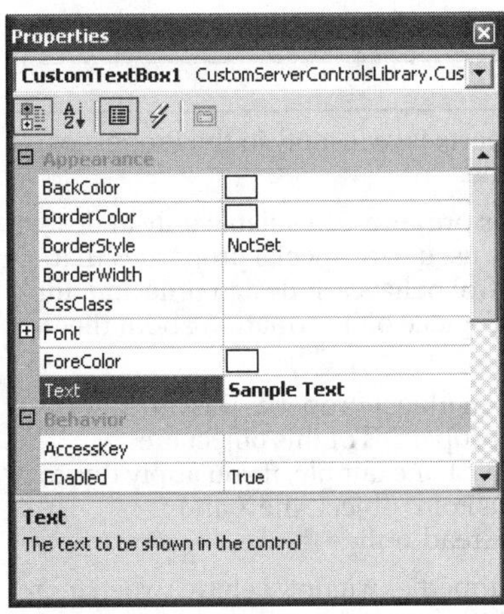

Figure 28-1. *A property with a description*

Table 28-1 lists the key attributes that influence the way a property appears in the Properties window.

Table 28-1. *Attributes for Control Properties*

Attribute	Description
Browsable(Boolean)	If False, this property will not appear in the Properties window. (However, the programmer can still modify it by altering the code or by manually adding the control tag attribute, as long as you include a Set property procedure.) One reason you might use this attribute is to hide calculated or runtime properties that can't be changed at design time.
Category(string)	A string that indicates the category under which the property will appear in the Properties window.
Description(string)	A string that indicates the description the property will have when selected in the Properties window.
DefaultValue()	Sets the default value that will be displayed for the property in the Properties window. The default value is typically the initial value, in which case you don't need to use the DefaultValue attribute. However, using this attribute can sometimes allow the code generator to optimize the tags it generates by omitting information if it matches the default.
Themeable(Boolean)	All custom controls automatically support theming (see Chapter 15). However, if you don't want a specific property to be configurable as part of a skin, apply the Themeable attribute with a value of False.
Localizable(Boolean)	Localization is enabled for all controls and objects. If a property is localizable, Visual Studio will allow its values to be persisted in a satellite assembly. If you don't want this to be possible, or you have a property that shouldn't vary based on locale, set this to False.

(Continued)

Table 28-1. *Continued*

Attribute	Description
ReadOnly(Boolean)	When True, this property is read-only in the Properties window at design time.
DesignOnly(Boolean)	When set to True, this property is available only at design time. This is typically used with special properties that configure how a control behaves at design time and don't correspond to a "real" piece of information about the control.
ImmutableObject(Boolean)	When set to True on an object property, this attribute ensures that the subproperties of this object are displayed as read-only. For example, if you apply this to a property that uses a Point object, the X and Y subproperties will be read-only.
MergableProperty(Boolean)	Configures how the Properties window behaves when more than one instance of this control is selected at once. If False, the property is not shown. If True (the default), the property can be set for all selected controls at once.
ParenthesizePropertyName(Boolean)	If True, Visual Studio will display parentheses around this property in the Properties window (as it does with the ID property).
Bindable(Boolean)	If True, Visual Studio will display this property in the Data Bindings dialog box and allow it to be bound to a field in a data source.
RefreshProperties()	You use this attribute with a value from the RefreshProperties enumeration. It specifies whether the rest of the Properties window must be updated when this property is changed (for example, if one property procedure could change another property).

You can apply two attributes, DefaultEvent and DefaultProperty, to your custom control class declaration, rather than a specific property. Additionally, the TagPrefix attribute is used at the assembly level and isn't attached to any code construct. Table 28-2 describes these attributes.

Table 28-2. *Attributes for Control Classes and Assemblies*

Attribute	Description
DefaultEvent(string)	Indicates the name of the default event. When you double-click the control in the design environment, Visual Studio automatically adds an event handler for the default event.
DefaultProperty(string)	Indicates the name of the default property. The DefaultProperty is the property that is highlighted in the Properties window by default, the first time the control is selected.
TagPrefix(string, string)	Associates a namespace with a prefix, which will be used when adding control tags to an .aspx page.

As you learned in Chapter 27, every custom control has a prefix that's registered with the Register directive in the .aspx page. Visual Studio adds this directive automatically when you insert the control. If you want to customize the prefix, you can use the TagPrefix attribute, which accepts two string parameters. The first string is the namespace your controls are in, and the second string is the tag prefix you want to use.

The following example specifies that controls in the CustomServerControlsLibrary should use the apress tag prefix:

```
<assembly: System.Web.UI.TagPrefix("CustomServerControlsLibrary", "apress")>
```

Now, if you add a control with the class name CustomTextBox from the CustomServerControlsLibrary namespace, this is the tag Visual Studio uses:

```
<apress:CustomTextBox ... />
```

If you have controls in multiple namespaces, you need to use TagPrefix multiple times, once for each namespace. You can use the same prefix or different prefixes. Often, the TagPrefix attribute is placed in the AssemblyInfo.vb file.

The following is the simple CustomTextBox control from the previous chapter, with a full complement of attributes.

```
<Assembly: System.Web.UI.TagPrefix("CustomServerControlsLibrary", "apress")>
Namespace CustomServerControlsLibrary
    <DefaultProperty("Text"), DefaultEvent("TextChanged")> _
    Public Class CustomTextBox
        Inherits WebControl
        Implements IPostBackDataHandler
        Public Sub New()
                MyBase.New(HtmlTextWriterTag.Input)
                ...
        End Sub

<Category("Appearance"), Description("The text to be shown in the control"),
  DefaultValue(""), MergableProperty(True)> _
        Public Property Text() As String
               ...
        End Property

        Protected Overrides Sub AddAttributesToRender(
                ByVal output As HtmlTextWriter)
               ...
        End Sub

        Public Function LoadPostData(ByVal postDataKey As String, _
                ByVal postData As NameValueCollection) As Boolean _
                Implements IPostBackDataHandler.LoadPostData
               ...
        End Function

        Public Sub RaisePostDataChangedEvent() _
                Implements IPostBackDataHandler.RaisePostDataChangedEvent
               ...
        End Sub

        Public Event TextChanged As EventHandler
        Protected Overridable Sub OnTextChanged(ByVal e As EventArgs)
               ...
        End Sub
    End Class
End Namespace
```

Attributes and Inheritance

When you derive a control from a base class that has design-time attributes, the control inherits the design-time functionality of its parent, just like it inherits the methods and properties. If the parent class's implementation of the design-time attributes is sufficient for your control, you do not need to reapply them.

However, in some cases you might want to change the design-time behavior of an existing property. In this case, you must first override the property and then reapply the changed attributes or add the new ones.

Most of the properties in the base classes WebControl and Control are marked as virtual, which allows you to change their behaviors. For example, if you wanted to hide the Height property of a custom control that derives from WebControl (maybe because it is calculated from the content rather than set by the developer), you could override the Height property and apply the Browsable attribute, as shown here:

```
<Browsable(False)> _
Public Overrides Property Height() As Unit
  Get
        Return MyBase.Height
  End Get
  Set
        MyBase.Height = Value
  End Set
End Property
```

The Toolbox Icon

Adding a Toolbox icon is refreshingly easy. All you need to do is add a bitmap to your project and ensure that it has the same filename as your custom control class. This bitmap must meet a few basic criteria:

- It must be 16×16 pixels. Otherwise, it will be mangled when Visual Studio attempts to scale it.
- It must use only 16 colors.

Once you add the file, use the Properties window to set the Build Action option for it to Embedded Resource. Then recompile the control project. Figure 28-2 shows the required image for the CustomTextBox control.

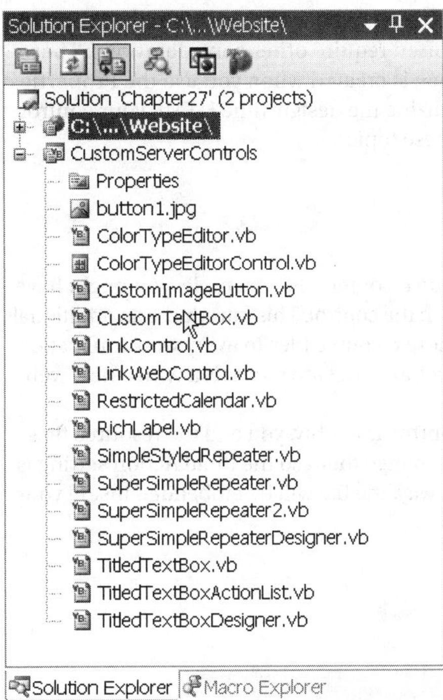

Figure 28-2. *Adding a Toolbox bitmap*

When you add the control to a client project, the embedded bitmap appears in the Toolbox. Figure 28-3 shows an example with two custom controls. One has the generic gear icon, and the CustomTextBox uses the bitmap added to the control project.

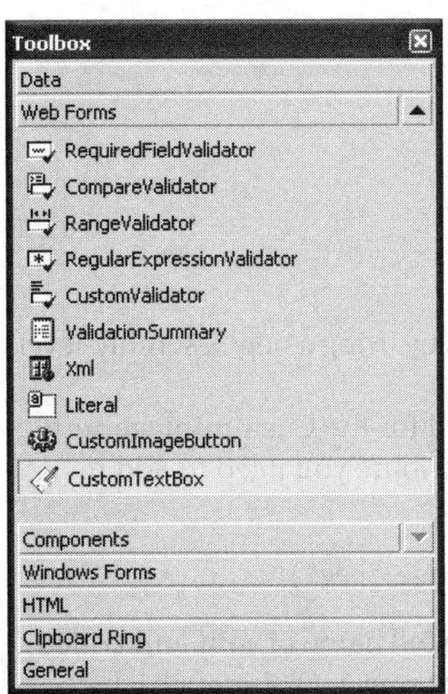

Figure 28-3. *A custom Toolbox bitmap*

If you're creating a simple control, all you may need to do is add a set of descriptive properties and a Toolbox icon. However, more-complex controls often require other considerations. These range from code-serialization issues (how the control tag is created when you use the Properties window) to control designers (advanced tools for customizing the design-time HTML your control renders). In the rest of the chapter, you'll take a look at these topics.

Web Resources

Often, custom controls will have other associated noncode resources. For example, you might have script files, stylesheets, and images that you need to use with the control. This introduces an additional deployment headache, because you now need to copy these resource files to every web application that uses your control. Fortunately, ASP.NET 2.0 introduces an innovative solution with a new web resources model.

Here's how it works: When you create the custom control assembly, you add the resource files directly to your project. Using the Solution Explorer, you change them so the Build Action setting is Embedded Resource, not Content (see Figure 28-4). This way, the file will be embedded inside your compiled assembly.

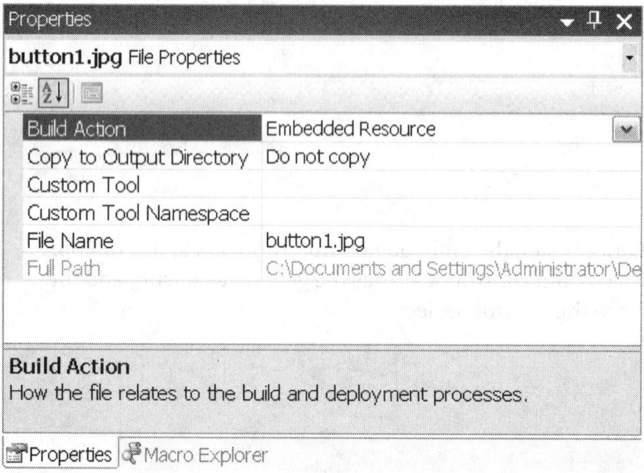

Figure 28-4. *An embedded resource*

The next step is to make the resource URL-accessible. This works by using a new assembly-level WebResource attribute.

For example, imagine you want to access the button image used for the CustomImageButton control. Once you've changed the Build Action setting, here's the attribute you need to add to your code:

```
<assembly: WebResource("CustomServerControls.button1.jpg", "image/jpeg")>
```

The WebResource attribute takes two parameters. The first is the full name of your embedded resource, which *must* be prefixed with the default namespace of your project. (This detail, which you can see by right-clicking your project in the Solution Explorer and choosing Properties, is automatically added to the beginning of the resource name). The second parameter is the content type.

Once you've taken these steps, the last bit of work you need to do is get the URL for your embedded resource. ASP.NET supports this through a new WebResource.axd handler. This handler accepts URL requests, extracts the corresponding resource from the appropriate assembly, and then returns the content. In other words, you don't need a clutter of images and scripts, because the WebResource.axd file can serve them as needed, right from your custom control assembly.

To get your resource, you need to tell the WebResource.axd handler what resource you need and what assembly contains it. You can generate the right URL using the Page.ClientScript.GetWebResourceUrl() method, as shown here:

```
Protected Overrides Sub OnInit(ByVal e As EventArgs)
    ImageUrl = Page.ClientScript.GetWebResourceUrl(
        GetType(CustomImageButton), "CustomServerControls.button1.jpg")
End Sub
```

Note Incidentally, web resources automatically take localization into account. If you have a satellite resource assembly with a locale-specific version of this image file, that version would be used instead. For more information, refer to Chapter 17.

The actual URL looks something like this:

```
WebResource.axd?a=CustomServerControls&r=button.jpg&t=632059604175183419
```

The *a* and *r* query string parameters specify the assembly and resource names, respectively. The *t* is a workaround to support caching. Essentially, WebResource.axd caches every requested resource. That way, you can request the same image hundreds of times without incurring extra work digging up the resource from the assembly. (This is particularly important to ensure performance if you have an assembly that's packed with a large number of resources.) However, caching introduces its own problem—namely, you don't want to reuse a cached resource if the assembly contains a newer version. The *t* parameter defends against this. It's an assembly timestamp. When the custom control assembly is rebuilt, the generated URLs will have a different *t* value; as a result, the browser will make a new request, and the WebResource.axd file will get the latest content.

Note You can find an example of this technique in the ImageButton control with the downloadable code for this chapter.

The WebResource.axd handler has one other trick in store. You can supply a Boolean third parameter in the WebResource attribute constructor to tell it to perform automatic substitution. This allows you to create an embedded resource that points to *other* embedded resources.

This trick works only for text-based resources (think of an HTML Help file, for example). Here's what the attribute looks like:

```
<assembly: WebResource("CustomServerControls.Help.htm", "text/html", True)>
```

Now WebResource.axd will scan through the resource and look for expressions in this format:

```
<%= WebResource(HelpTitle.gif) %>
```

Every time it finds one of these, it will replace it with another automatically generated WebResource.axd URL. So, if you write this in your HTML resource:

```
<img src="WebResource(HelpTitle.gif)" />
```

then it's automatically converted into something like this before it's served:

```
<img src=
"WebResource.axd?a=CustomServerControls&r=HelpTitle.gif&t=632059604175183419" />
```

Code Serialization

When you configure control properties in the Properties window, Visual Studio needs to be able to create and modify the corresponding control tag in the .aspx file. This process is called *code serialization*, and it often works automatically. However, you can run into trouble if you use properties that are themselves complex types or if you create a templated control or a control that supports child controls.

In the following sections, you'll learn about the ingredients that affect control serialization and what changes you need to make in order to resolve common problems.

Type Converters

The Properties window deals seamlessly with common data types. String data doesn't present a problem, but the Properties window can also convert strings to numeric types. For example, if you look at the Width property of a control, you'll see a value such as 50 px. You can enter any characters in this field, but if you try to commit the change (by pressing Enter or moving to another field) and you've included characters that can't be interpreted as a unit, the change will be rejected.

This behavior is made possible by *type converters*, specialized classes that are designed for the sole purpose of converting a specialized data type to a string representation and back. Most of the core .NET data types have default type converters that work perfectly well. (You can find these type converters in the System.ComponentModel.TypeConverter namespace.) However, if you create your own structures or classes and use them as properties, you may also want to create custom type converters that allow them to work in the Properties window.

A Control with Object Properties

The next example uses a RichLabel control that's a slightly revised version of the XmlLabel control presented in Chapter 27. The difference is that although the XmlLabel is designed to show XML documents, the RichLabel control is designed to support different types of content.

Essentially, the RichLabel control can support any type of content that's defined in the following RichLabelTextType enumeration. In this simple example, the RichLabelTextType enumeration includes only two options: Xml (which uses the same code as the XmlLabel) and Html (which treats the text as is and doesn't perform any additional processing). However, you could easily add the rendering code for different types of text.

```
Public Enum RichLabelTextType
    Xml
    Html
End Enum
```

The RichLabel also allows you to choose what tag you want to use to format important details (such as the XML tags in XML-rendering mode). The way this works is through another class, named RichLabelFormattingOptions. The RichLabelFormattingOptions class defines two properties: Type (which holds a value from the RichLabelTextType enumeration) and HighlightTag (which stores a tag name as a string, such as b for the <b> tag, which applies bold formatting).

```
<Serializable()> _
Public Class RichLabelFormattingOptions
    Private typType As RichLabelTextType
    Public Property Type() As RichLabelTextType
        Get
                    Return typType
        End Get
        Set
```

```
            typType= Value
        End Set
    End Property

    Private hltTag As String
    Public Property HighlightTag() As String
        Get
            Return hltTag
        End Get
        Set
            hltTag = Value
        End Set
    End Property
    Public Sub New(ByVal typType As RichLabelTextType, ByVal hltTag As String)
        Me.highlightTag = hltTag
        Me.type = typType
    End Sub
End Class
```

The RichLabel class includes a Format property, which exposes an instance of the custom RichLabelFormattingOptions class. The rendering logic in the RichLabel control uses this information to customize the HTML it generates.

Here's the code for the RichLabel control:

```
<DefaultProperty("RichText")> _
Public Class RichLabel
    Inherits WebControl
    Public Sub New()
        MyBase.New()
        Text = String.Empty
        ' Default to XML text with tags formatted in bold.
        Format = New RichLabelFormattingOptions(RichLabelTextType.Xml, "b")
    End Sub

    <Category("Appearance"), Description("The content that will be displayed.")> _
    Public Property Text() As String
        Get
            Return CStr(ViewState("Text"))
        End Get
        Set
            ViewState("Text") = Value
        End Set
    End Property

    <Category("Appearance"),
        Description("Options for configuring how text is rendered.")> _
    Public Property Format() As RichLabelFormattingOptions
        Get
            Return CType(ViewState("Format"), RichLabelFormattingOptions)
        End Get
        Set
            ViewState("Format") = Value
        End Set
    End Property

    Protected Overrides Sub RenderContents(ByVal output As HtmlTextWriter)
        Dim convertedText As String = String.Empty
```

```
        Select Case Format.Type
            Case RichLabelTextType.Xml
                ' Find and highlight the XML tags.
                convertedText =
                    RichLabel.ConvertXmlTextToHtmlText(Text, Format.HighlightTag)
            Case RichLabelTextType.Html
                ' Keep the text as is.
                convertedText = Text
        End Select
        output.Write(convertedText)
    End Sub

Public Shared Function ConvertXmlTextToHtmlText(ByVal inputText As String, _
         ByVal highlightTag As String) As String
        ' (Code omitted.)
    End Function
End Class
```

Alternative designs are possible. For example, you could add these two pieces of information (Type and HighlightTag) as separate properties in the RichLabel class, in which case you wouldn't need to take any extra steps to ensure proper serialization. However, you might decide to group related properties together using a custom class for a number of reasons. Perhaps you want the ability to reuse the RichLabelFormattingOptions class in order to specify text-formatting options for other controls. Or maybe you need to create a more complex control that accepts several different pieces of text and can convert all of them using independent RichLabelFormattingOptions settings. In both of these situations, it becomes useful to group the properties using the RichLabelFormattingOptions class.

However, the RichLabel control doesn't work well with Visual Studio. When you try to modify this control at design time, you'll immediately notice the problem. The Properties window doesn't allow you to edit the RichLabel.Format property. Instead, it shows an empty edit box where you can't type anything. To solve this problem, you need to create a custom type converter, as explained in the next section.

Creating a Custom Type Converter

A custom type converter is a class that can convert from your proprietary data type (in this case, the RichLabelFormattingOptions class) to a string and back. In the following example, you'll see such a class, named RichLabelFormattingOptionsConverter.

The first step is to create a custom class that derives from the base class TypeConverter, as shown here:

```
Public Class RichLabelFormattingOptionsConverter
    Inherits TypeConverter
    ...
End Class
```

By convention, the name of a type converter class consists of the class type it converts, followed by the word *Converter*.

Once you create the type converter, you have several methods to override:

CanConvertFrom(): This method examines a data type and returns True if the type converter can make the conversion from this data type to the custom data type.

ConvertFrom(): This method performs the conversion from the supplied data type to the custom data type.

CanConvertTo(): This method examines a data type and returns True if the type converter can make the conversion from the custom object to this data type.

ConvertTo(): This method performs the conversion from the custom data type to the requested data type.

Remember that the key task of a type converter is to convert from your custom data type to a string representation. This example uses a string representation that includes both values from the RichLabelFormattingOptions object, separated by a comma and a space and with angled brackets around the tag name. Here's what the string format looks like:

```
Type Name, <HighlightTag>
```

Here's an example with XML formatting and a <b> tag:

```
Xml, <b>
```

With that in mind, you can create two helper methods in the converter class to perform this conversion. The first is a ToString() method that builds the required string representation:

```
Private Function ToString(ByVal value As Object) As String
    Dim format As RichLabelFormattingOptions =
             CType(value, RichLabelFormattingOptions)
    Return String.Format("{0}, <{1}>", format.Type, format.HighlightTag)
End Function
```

The second part is a FromString() method that decodes the string representation. If the string isn't in the format you need, the FromString() code raises an exception. Otherwise, it returns the new object instance.

```
Private Function FromString(ByVal value As Object) As RichLabelFormattingOptions
    Dim values As String() = (CStr(value)).Split(","c)
    If values.Length <> 2 Then
        Throw New ArgumentException("Could not convert the value")
    End If

    Try
        ' Convert the name of the enumerated value into the corresponding
        ' enumerated value (which is actually an integer constant).
        Dim type As RichLabelTextType = _
              CType(System.Enum.Parse(GetType(RichLabelTextType), _
                        values(0), True), RichLabelTextType)

        ' Get rid of the spaces and angle brackets around the tag name.
        Dim tag As String = values(1).Trim(New Char(){" "c,"<"c,">"c})
        Return New RichLabelFormattingOptions(type, tag)
    Catch
        Throw New ArgumentException("Could not convert the value")
    End Try
End Function
```

Before attempting a conversion from a string to a RichLabelFormattingOptions object, the Properties window will first query the CanConvertFrom() method. If it receives a True value, it will call the actual ConvertFrom() method. All the CanConvertFrom() method needs to do is check that the supplied type is a string, as follows:

```
Public Overrides Function CanConvertFrom(ByVal context As ITypeDescriptorContext, _
      ByVal sourceType As Type) As Boolean
```

```
    If sourceType Is GetType(String) Then
        Return True
    Else
        Return MyBase.CanConvertFrom(context, sourceType)
    End If
End Function
```

The ConvertFrom() method calls the conversion by calling the FromString() method shown earlier:

```
Public Overrides Function ConvertFrom(ByVal context As ITypeDescriptorContext,
        ByVal culture As CultureInfo, ByVal value As Object) As Object
    If TypeOf value Is String Then
        Return FromString(value)
    Else
        Return MyBase.ConvertFrom(context, culture, value)
    End If
End Function
```

■ **Note** It is good object-oriented programming practice to always give the base classes from which you inherit a chance to handle a message you are not going to support. In this case, any requests to perform a conversion from an unrecognized type are passed to the base class.

The same process occurs in reverse when converting a RichLabelFormattingOptions object to a string. First, the Properties window calls CanConvertTo(). If it returns True, the next step is to call the ConvertTo() method. Here's the code you need:

```
Public Overrides Function CanConvertTo(ByVal context As ITypeDescriptorContext, _
        ByVal destinationType As Type) As Boolean
    If destinationType Is GetType(String) Then
        Return True
    Else
        Return MyBase.CanConvertTo(context, destinationType)
    End If
End Function

Public Overrides Function ConvertTo(ByVal context As ITypeDescriptorContext, _
        ByVal culture As CultureInfo, ByVal theValue As Object,
        ByVal destinationType As Type) As Object
    If destinationType Is GetType(String) Then
        Return ToString(value)
    Else
        Return MyBase.ConvertTo(context, culture, theValue, destinationType)
    End If
End Function
```

Now that you have a fully functioning type converter, the next step is to attach it to the corresponding property.

Attaching a Type Converter

You can attach a type converter in two ways. You can add the TypeConverter attribute to the related class (in this case, RichLabelFormattingOptions), as shown here:

```
<TypeConverter(GetType(RichLabelFormattingOptionsConverter))> _
Public Class RichLabelFormattingOptions
```

```
    ...
End Class
```

This way, whenever an instance of this class is used for a control, Visual Studio knows to use your type converter.

Alternatively, you can attach the type converter directly to the property in your custom control that uses it, as shown here:

```
<TypeConverter(GetType(RichLabelFormattingOptionsConverter))> _
 Public Property Format() As RichLabelFormattingOptions
    ...
 End Property
```

This approach makes the most sense if you are using a generic data type (such as a string) and you want to customize its behavior in only this case.

Now you can recompile the code and try using the RichLabel control in a sample web page. When you select a RichLabel, you'll see the current value of the RichLabel.Format property in the Properties window (shown in Figure 28-5), and you can edit it by hand.

■ **Note** When changing details such as type converter, control designer, and control builders, your changes will not appear immediately in the design environment after a recompile. Instead, you may need to close the solution with the test web pages and then reopen it.

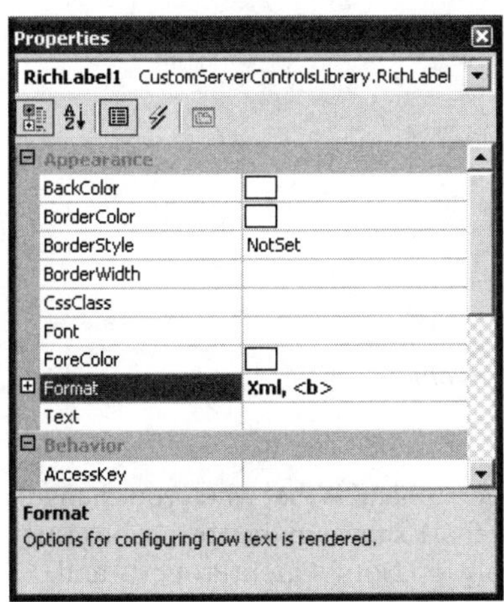

Figure 28-5. *A string representation of the RichLabelFormattingOptions object*

Of course, unless you enter the correct string representation, you'll receive an error message, and your change will be rejected. In other words, the custom type converter shown here gives you the ability to specify a RichLabelFormattingOptions object as a string, but the process certainly isn't user-friendly. The next section shows you how to improve this level of support.

The ExpandableObjectConverter

ASP.NET web controls support a number of object properties. The best example is Font, which refers to a FontInfo object with properties such as Bold, Italic, Name, and so on. When you set the

Font property in the Properties window, you don't need to type all this information in a single, correctly formatted string. Instead, you can expand the Font property by clicking the plus (+) sign and edit the FontInfo properties individually.

You can enable the same type of editing with your own custom object types—you simply need to create a custom type converter that derives from the ExpandableObjectConverter class instead of the base TypeConverter class. For example, you could take the RichLabelFormattingOptionsConverter developed in the previous section and change it as shown here:

```
Public Class RichLabelFormattingOptionsConverter
    Inherits ExpandableObjectConverter
    ...
End Class
```

Now you can specify the Format property by typing a string or by expanding the property and modifying one of the two subproperties. Figure 28-6 shows the much more convenient interface you'll see in the Properties window.

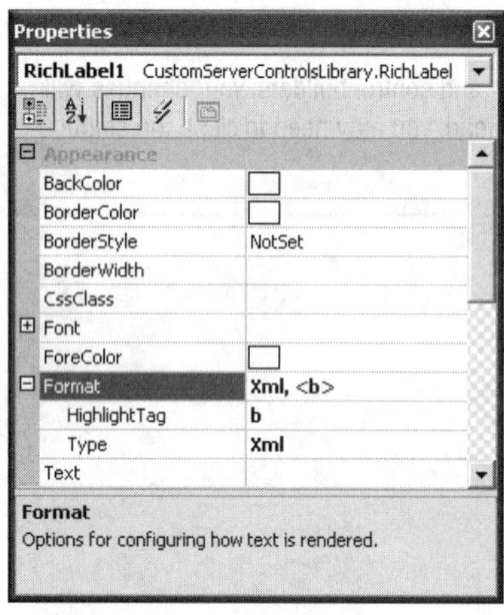

Figure 28-6. *Editing properties of the RichLabelFormattingOptions object*

This looks good at first pass, but it has still a few quirks. One problem is that when you change a subproperty (Type or HighlightTag), the string representation that's shown in the Format box isn't immediately updated. To solve this problem, you need to apply the NotifyParentProperty and RefreshProperties attributes to the properties of the RichLabelFormattingOptions class. At the same time, you might also want to add a Description attribute to configure the text that will appear in the Properties window for this subproperty.

Here's the revised code for the RichLabelFormattingOptions class:

```
Public Class RichLabelFormattingOptions
    Private typType As RichLabelTextType

    <RefreshProperties(RefreshProperties.Repaint), _
        NotifyParentProperty(True), _
        Description("Type of content supplied in the text property")> _
    Public Property Type() As RichLabelTextType
        Get
            Return typType
```

```
        End Get
        Set
                typType= Value
        End Set
    End Property

    Private hltTag As String

    <RefreshProperties(RefreshProperties.Repaint), _
        NotifyParentProperty(True), _
        Description("The HTML tag to mark up highlighted portions.")> _
    Public Property HighlightTag() As String
        Get
                Return hltTag
        End Get
        Set
                hltTag = Value
        End Set
    End Property

    Public Sub New(ByVal typType As RichLabelTextType, ByVal hltTag As String)
        Me.hltTag = hltTag
        Me.typType= typType
    End Sub
End Class
```

This solves the synchronization and editing problems, but all the quirks *still* aren't fixed. The problem is that although you can edit the RichLabel.Format property, the information you set isn't persisted to the control tag. This means the changes you make at design time are essentially ignored. To resolve this problem, you need to dig a little deeper into how .NET serializes control properties, as described in the next section.

Serialization Attributes

You can control how control properties are serialized into the .aspx file using attributes. You need to consider two key attributes—DesignerSerializationVisibility and PersistenceMode.

The DesignerSerializationVisibility attribute determines whether a property will be serialized. You have three choices:

Visible: This is the default value. It specifies the property should be serialized, and it works for simple data types (such as strings, dates, and enumerations) and the numeric data types.

Content: This serializes the entire content of an object. You can use this value to serialize complex types with multiple properties, such as a collection.

Hidden: This specifies a property shouldn't be serialized at all. For example, you might use this to prevent a calculated value from being serialized.

The PersistenceMode attribute allows you to specify *how* a property is serialized. You have the following choices:

Attribute: This is the default option. The property will be serialized as an HTML attribute of the control.

InnerProperty: The property will be persisted as a nested tag inside the control. This is the preferred setting to generate complex nested hierarchies of objects. Examples are the Calendar and DataList controls.

InnerDefaultProperty: The property will be persisted inside the control tag. It will be the only content of the control tag. An example is the Text property of the Label control. When using a default property, the property name doesn't appear in the nested content.

EncodedInnerDefaultProperty: This is the same as InnerDefaultProperty, except that the content will be HTML encoded before it is persisted.

To understand how these different options work, it's worth considering a few examples. The PersistenceMode.Attribute choice is the default option you've seen with the core set of ASP.NET control tags. If you combine this attribute with DesignerSerializationVisibility.Content in a property whose type contains subproperties, ASP.NET uses the object-walker syntax, in the form of Property-SubProperty="Value". You can see an example with the Font property, as shown here:

```
<apress:ctrl Font-Size="8pt" Font-Names="Tahoma" Bold="True" ... />
```

On the other hand, consider what happens if you create a custom control that overrides the persistence behavior of the Font property to use PersistenceMode.InnerProperty, as shown here:

```
<PersistenceMode(PersistenceMode.InnerProperty)> _
Public Overrides ReadOnly Property Font() As FontInfo
    Get
            Return MyBase.Font
    End Get
End Property
```

Now the persisted code for the Font property takes this form:

```
<apress:ctrl ... >
  <Font Size="8pt" Names="Tahoma" Bold="True"></Font>
</apress:ctrl>
```

To allow the RichLabel to serialize its Format property correctly, you need to apply both the PersistenceMode and DesignerSerializationVisibility attributes. The DesignerSerializationVisibility attribute will specify Content, because the Format property is a complex object. The PersistenceMode attribute will specify InnerProperty, which stores the Format property information as a separate, nested tag. Here's how you need to apply these two attributes:

```
<TypeConverter(GetType(RichLabelFormattingOptionsConverter)), _
DesignerSerializationVisibility(DesignerSerializationVisibility.Content), _
PersistenceMode(PersistenceMode.InnerProperty)> _
Public Property Format() As RichLabelFormattingOptions
    Get
            Return CType(ViewState("Format"), RichLabelFormattingOptions)
    End Get
    Set
            ViewState("Format") = Value
    End Set
End Property
```

Now when you configure the Format property in the Properties window, ASP.NET will create a tag in this form:

```
<apress:RichLabel id="RichLabel1" runat="server">
  <Format Type="Xml" HighlightTag="b"></Format>
</apress:RichLabel>
```

The end result is that the RichLabel control works perfectly when inserted into a web page at runtime as well as when a developer is using it at design time.

You apply two other related serialization properties at the class level—PersistChildren and ParseChildren. Both attributes control how ASP.NET deals with nested tags and whether it supports child controls. When PersistChildren is True, child controls are persisted as contained tags. When PersistChildren is False, any nested tags designate properties. ParseChildren plays the same role when reading control tags. When ParseChildren is True, the ASP.NET parser interprets all nested tags as properties rather than controls.

When deriving from the WebControl class, the default is that PersistChildren is False and ParseChildren is True, in which case any nested tags are treated as property values. If you want child content to be treated as child controls in the control hierarchy, you need to explicitly set PersistChildren to True and ParseChildren to False. Because the RichLabel control isn't designed to hold other controls, this step isn't needed—the defaults are what you want.

Templated Controls

The RichLabel isn't the only control that needs the serialization attributes. To successfully use the templated controls described in Chapter 27 (such as the SuperSimpleRepeater), all the template properties need to use PersistenceMode.InnerProperty serialization.

Here's an example of a templated property that's correctly configured:

```
<PersistenceMode(PersistenceMode.InnerProperty), _
TemplateContainer(GetType(SimpleRepeaterItem))> _
Public Property ItemTemplate() As ITemplate
    Get
        Return itemTemplate
    End Get
    Set
        itemTemplate=Value
    End Set
End Property
```

Otherwise, when you set other properties in the control, the template content will be erased.

Controls with Collections

Unfortunately, serialization can become a fair bit more complicated than the RichLabel example. One such case is the RestrictedCalendar control demonstrated in the previous chapter. The RestrictedCalendar stores a collection of dates the user isn't allowed to select in a NonSelectableDates property. Ordinarily, you would deal with the serialization of the NonSelectableDates property by adding the attributes shown here:

```
<DesignerSerializationVisibility(DesignerSerializationVisibility.Content), _
PersistenceMode(PersistenceMode.InnerProperty)> _
Public Property NonSelectableDates() As DateTimeCollection
    Get
        Return CType(ViewState("NonSelectableDates"), DateTimeCollection)
    End Get
    Set
        ViewState("NonSelectableDates") = Value
    End Set
End Property
```

Everything seems fine at first. In fact, you don't even need to create a type converter for the NonSelectableDates property. That's because .NET automatically recognizes it as a collection and uses the CollectionConverter. The CollectionConverter simply displays the text (Collection), as shown in Figure 28-7.

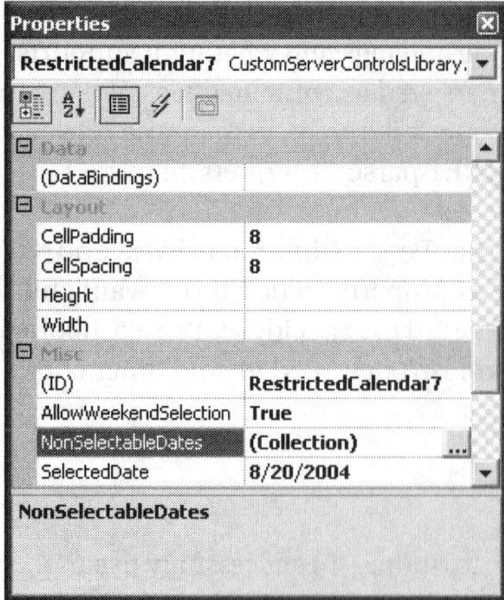

Figure 28-7. *A collection property*

You can click the ellipsis next to the property name to open a designer where you can add DateTime objects. You can even choose values for each date using a drop-down calendar, as shown in Figure 28-8. This graphical functionality is actually the work of another component, called a *type editor*. (You'll learn about type editors in the next section.)

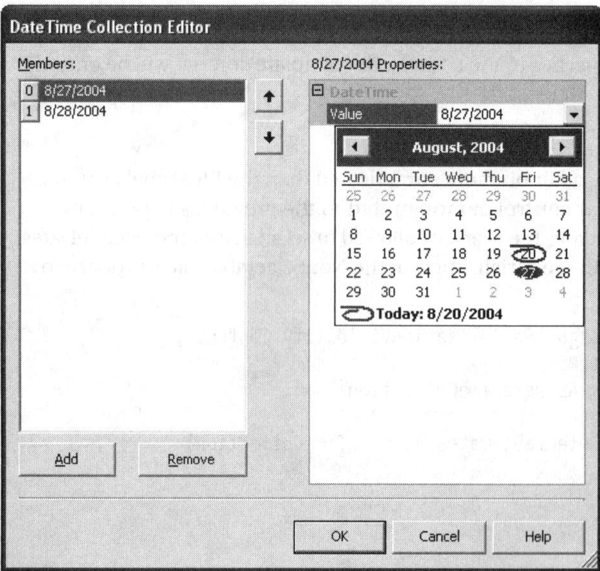

Figure 28-8. *Adding dates to a collection property*

This all works well enough. If you look at the generated HTML for the RestrictedCalendar after you add two dates, you'll see something like this:

```
<cc1:RestrictedCalendar id="RestrictedCalendar8" runat="server">
  <NonSelectableDates>
    <System.DateTime Year="2004" DayOfWeek="Friday" Second="0" Minute="0"
     TimeOfDay="00:00:00" Day="20" Millisecond="0" Date="2004-08-20" Hour="0"
     DayOfYear="233" Ticks="632285568000000000" Month="8"></System.DateTime>
    <System.DateTime Year="2004" DayOfWeek="Saturday" Second="0" Minute="0"
     TimeOfDay="00:00:00" Day="21" Millisecond="0" Date="2004-08-21" Hour="0"
     DayOfYear="234" Ticks="632286432000000000" Month="8"></System.DateTime>
  </NonSelectableDates>
</cc1:RestrictedCalendar>
```

This code raises two problems. First, there's more information there than you really need to store. The RestrictedCalendar is interested only in the date portion of the DateTime object, and the time information is wasted space. A more serious problem is that when you request this page, ASP.NET won't be able to re-create the DateTimeCollection that's exposed by the NonSelectableDates property. Instead, it will raise an error when attempting to deserialize the nested tags and set read-only properties such as Year, Month, and Ticks.

To solve this problem, you need to plug into the serialization and parsing infrastructure for your control. The first step is to customize the code that's serialized for each DateTime object in the NonSelectableDates collection. To accomplish this, you need to create a new class called a *control designer*. Control designers are complex components that can perform a whole variety of design-time services, including generating HTML for a design-time representation and providing services for entering and editing templates at design time.

In this case, you're interested in only one aspect of the control designer—its ability to control how the content inside the control tag is serialized. To accomplish this, you create a class that inherits from ControlDesigner, and you override the GetPersistenceContent() method. This method will read the list of restricted dates and create a new tag for each DateTime object. This tag will then be added to the RestrictedCalendar control tag.

Here's the complete code:

```
Public Class RestrictedCalendarDesigner
        Inherits ControlDesigner
    Public Overrides Function GetPersistenceContent() As String
        Dim sw As New StringWriter()
        Dim html As New HtmlTextWriter(sw)

        Dim MyCalendar As RestrictedCalendar =
            TryCast(Me.Component, RestrictedCalendar)
        If MyCalendar IsNot Nothing Then
            ' Create tags in this format:
            '   <DateTime Value='xxx' />
            For Each dteDate As DateTime In MyCalendar.NonSelectableDates
                html.WriteBeginTag("DateTime")
                html.WriteAttribute("Value", dteDate.ToString())
                html.WriteLine(HtmlTextWriter.SelfClosingTagEnd)
            Next
        End If
        Return sw.ToString()
    End Function
End Class
```

To tell the control to use this control designer, you need to apply a Designer attribute to the RestrictedCalendar class declaration. At the same time, you should also set ParseChildren to False so that the nested tags the ControlDesigner creates aren't treated as control properties.

```
<ControlBuilder(GetType(RestrictedCalendarDesigner)), ParseChildren(False)> _
Public Class RestrictedCalendar
    Inherits Calendar
      ...
End Class
```

This accomplishes half the process. Now when you add restricted dates at design time, the control tag markup will be created in this format:

```
<cc1:RestrictedCalendar id="RestrictedCalendar1" runat="server">
  <DateTime Value="8/27/2004 " />
  <DateTime Value="8/28/2004 " />
</cc1:RestrictedCalendar>
```

The next step is to enable your control to read this custom HTML and regenerate the RestrictedDates collection at runtime. To make deserialization easier, you need to create a class that models the <DateTime> tag. In this case, the <DateTime> tag has only a single attribute named value. As a result, the following class works perfectly well:

```
Public Class DateTimeHelper
    Private val As String
    Public Property Value() As String
        Get
                Return val
        End Get
        Set
                val = Value
        End Set
    End Property
End Class
```

Note how the public property of this class matches the serialized tag exactly. That means ASP.NET will be able to deserialize the tag into a DateTimeHelper without needing any extra help. However, you still need to take extra steps to instruct the ASP.NET parser to use the DateTimeHelper class for deserialization. Finally, you also need to write code that can examine the DateTimeHelper and use it to configure a RestrictedCalendar instance.

To perform the first task of these two tasks, you need the help of a *control builder*. When ASP.NET parses a page, it enlists the help of a control builder to interpret the HTML and generate the control objects. The default control builder simply examines the ParseChildren attribute for the control and then tries to interpret the nested tags as properties (if ParseChildren is True) or as child controls (if ParseChildren is False). The custom control builder that the RestrictedCalendar will use overrides the GetChildControlType(), which is called every time the parser finds a nested tag.

The GetChildControlType() method examines a nested tag and then returns a Type object that tells the parser what type of child object to create. In this case, your custom control builder should find a <DateTime> tag and then inform the runtime to create a DateTimeHelper object.

Here's the complete control builder code:

```
Public Class RestrictedCalendarBuilder
        Inherits ControlBuilder
    Public Overrides Function GetChildControlType(ByVal tagName As String, _
                ByVal attribs As IDictionary) As Type
        If tagName = "DateTime" Then
             Return GetType(DateTimeHelper)
        End If
        Return MyBase.GetChildControlType (tagName, attribs)
    End Function
End Class
```

To associate this builder with the RestrictedCalendar control, you need to add a Designer attribute to the class declaration:

```
<ControlBuilder(GetType(RestrictedCalendarBuilder)), _
ParseChildren(False), _
Designer(GetType(RestrictedCalendarDesigner))> _
Public Class RestrictedCalendar
    Inherits Calendar
    ...
End Class
```

Your odyssey still isn't quite complete. Now the ASP.NET parser can successfully create the DateTimeHelper object, but it doesn't know what to do with it. Because you've set ParseChildren to False, the parser won't attempt to recognize it as a property. Instead, it will call the AddParsedSubObject() method of your control class, which will fail because the DateTimeHelper isn't a control and can't be added to the Controls collection. Fortunately, you can override the AddParsedSubObject() method to provide more suitable functionality. In this case, you need to take the supplied DataTimeHelper object and use it to add a new DateTime to the NonSelectableDates collection, as shown here:

```
Protected Overrides Sub AddParsedSubObject(ByVal obj As Object)
    If TypeOf obj Is DateTimeHelper Then
        Dim dteDate As DateTimeHelper = CType(obj, DateTimeHelper)
        NonSelectableDates.Add(DateTime.Parse(dteDate.Value))
    End If
End Sub
```

Now you've finished all the code required to both serialize and parse the custom HTML content. This process clearly wasn't easy, and it demonstrates that though basic design-time support is easy, advanced custom control design is a highly complex topic. To become an expert, you'll need to study the MSDN documentation or continue your exploration with a dedicated book about server controls.

Type Editors

So far you've seen how type converters can convert various data types to strings for representation in the Properties window. But some data types don't rely on string editing at all. For example, if you need to set an enumerated value (such as BorderStyle), you can choose from a drop-down list of all the values in the enumeration. More impressively, if you need to set a color, you can choose from a drop-down color picker. And some properties have the ability to break out of the Properties window altogether. One example is the Columns property of the DataGrid. If you click the ellipsis next to the property name, a dialog box will appear where you can configure the column collection using a rich user interface. The RestrictedCalendar in the previous example showed a similar but less-impressive example with the collection editor for editing restricted dates.

These properties all rely on *UI type editors*. Type editors have a single task in life—they generate user interfaces that allow you to set control properties more conveniently. Certain data types (such as collections, enumerations, and colors) are automatically associated with advanced type editors. In other cases, you might want to create your own type editor classes from scratch. All UI type editors are located in the System.Drawing.Design namespace.

Just as with type converters (and almost everything in the extensible architecture of .NET design-time support), creating a new type editor involves inheriting a base class (in this case UITypeEditor) and overriding desired members. The methods you can override include the following:

GetEditStyle(): Specifies whether the type editor is a DropDown (provides a list of specially drawn choices), Modal (provides a dialog box for property selection), or None (no editing supported).

EditValue(): This method is invoked when property is edited (for example, the ellipsis next to the property name is clicked in the Properties window). Generally, this is where you would create a special dialog box for property editing.

GetPaintValueSupported(): Use this to return True if you are providing a PaintValue() implementation.

PaintValue(): Invoked to paint a graphical thumbnail that represents the value in the property grid. For example, this is used to create the color box for color properties.

The code for UI type editors isn't overly complicated, but it can take a bit of getting used to for web developers. That's because it involves using the other user interface platform in .NET—Windows Forms. Although the topic of Windows Forms is outside the scope of this book, you can learn a lot from a basic example. Figure 28-9 shows a custom color-editing control that allows you to set various components of a color independently using sliders. As you do, it displays the color in a box at the bottom of the control.

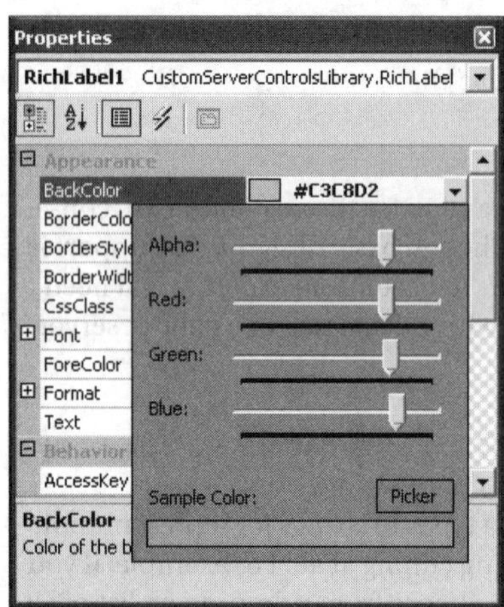

Figure 28-9. *Using a custom type editor*

The code for the actual control isn't shown here, but you can refer to the downloadable examples for this chapter to take a closer look. However, the full code for the type editor that uses this control is as follows:

```
Public Class ColorTypeEditor
    Inherits UITypeEditor
  Public Overrides Function GetEditStyle(ByVal context As ITypeDescriptorContext)
      As UITypeEditorEditStyle
    ' This editor appears when you click a drop-down arrow.
    Return UITypeEditorEditStyle.DropDown
  End Function

  Public Overrides Function EditValue(
            ByVal context As ITypeDescriptorContext,
            ByVal provider As IServiceProvider,
            ByVal value As Object) As Object
```

```
        Dim srv As IWindowsFormsEditorService = Nothing

        ' Get the editor service from the provider,
        ' which you need to create the drop-down window.
        If provider IsNot Nothing Then
                srv = CType(provider.GetService(
                        GetType(IWindowsFormsEditorService)),
                        IWindowsFormsEditorService)
        End If

        If srv IsNot Nothing Then
            ' Create an instance of the custom Windows Forms
            ' color-picking control.
            ' Pass the current value of the color.
            Dim editor As New ColorTypeEditorControl(
                                CType(value, System.Drawing.Color),
                                TryCast(context.Instance, WebControl))

            ' Show the control.
            srv.DropDownControl(editor)

            ' Return the selected color information.
            Return editor.SelectedColor
        Else
            ' Return the current value.
            Return value
        End If
    End Function

    Public Overrides Function GetPaintValueSupported(
            ByVal context As ITypeDescriptorContext) As Boolean
        ' This type editor will generate a color box thumbnail.
        Return True
    End Function

    Public Overrides Sub PaintValue(ByVal e As PaintValueEventArgs)
        ' Fills the left rectangle with a color.
        Dim control As WebControl = TryCast(e.Context.Instance, WebControl)
        e.Graphics.FillRegion(
           New SolidBrush(control.BackColor), New Region(e.Bounds))
    End Sub
End Class
```

To use this type editor, you need to attach it to a property that uses the Color data type. Most web controls already include color properties, but you can override one of them and apply a new Editor attribute.

Here's an example that does exactly that to attach the type editor to the BackColor property of the RichLabel control:

```
<Editor(GetType(ColorTypeEditor), GetType(UITypeEditor))> _
Public Overrides Property BackColor() As Color
    Get
        Return MyBase.BackColor
    End Get
    Set
        MyBase.BackColor = Value
    End Set
End Property
```

Control Designers

You've probably noticed that custom controls aren't all treated the same on the design surface. ASP.NET tries to show a realistic design-time representation by running the rendering logic, but exceptions exist. For example, composite and templated controls aren't rendered at all in the design-time environment, which means you're left with nothing but a blank rectangle on your design surface.

To deal with these issues, controls often use custom control designers that produce basic HTML that's intended only for design-time display. This display can be a sophisticated block of HTML that's designed to reflect the real appearance of the control, a basic snapshot that shows a typical example of the control (as you'll see for a DataGrid that doesn't have any configured columns), or just a gray placeholder box with a message (as shown for the Repeater and DataList when they don't have any templates).

If you want to customize the design-time HTML for your control, you can derive a custom designer from the ControlDesigner base class and override one of the following three methods:

GetDesignTimeHtml(): Returns the HTML that's used to represent the current state of the control at design time. The default implementation of this method simply returns the result of calling the RenderControl() method.

GetEmptyDesignTimeHtml(): Returns the HTML that's used to represent an empty control. The default implementation simply returns a string that contains the name of the control class and the ID.

GetErrorDesignTimeHtml(): Returns the HTML that's used if a design-time error occurs in the control. This HTML can provide information about the exception (which is passed as an argument to this method).

Of course, these methods reflect only a small portion of the functionality that's available through the ControlDesigner. You can override many more methods to configure different aspects of design-time behavior. In the following section, you'll see how to create a control designer that adds enhanced support for the SuperSimpleRepeater.

■ **Tip** ASP.NET 2.0 adds some new control designer base classes, including CompositeControlDesigner and ContainerControlDesigner, that are useful in many common scenarios (in this case, designing composite and container controls).

A Basic Control Designer

The next example develops a control designer that generates a reasonable representation for the SuperSimpleRepeater developed in the previous chapter. Without a custom control designer, the design-time content of the SuperSimpleRepeater is an empty string.

The first step in creating a designer is to build a class that derives from the ControlDesigner namespace in the System.Web.UI.Design namespace, as shown here:

```
Public Class SuperSimpleRepeaterDesigner
      Inherits ControlDesigner
      ...
End Class
```

You can apply the designer to the control using the Designer attribute, as shown here:

```
<Designer(GetType(SuperSimpleRepeaterDesigner))> _
Public Class SuperSimpleRepeater
        Inherits WebControl
        Implements INamingContainer
        ...
End Class
```

When creating a control designer, the first step is to create the GetEmptyDesignTimeHtml() method. This method simply needs to return a static piece of text. The ControlDesigner includes a helper method named CreatePlaceHolderDesignTimeHtml(), which generates a gray HTML box with a message you specify (just like the Repeater control without any templates). You can use this method to simplify your rendering code, as shown here:

```
Protected Overrides Function GetEmptyDesignTimeHtml() As String
    Dim text As String = "Switch to design view to add a template to this control."
    Return CreatePlaceHolderDesignTimeHtml(text)
End Function
```

Figure 28-10 shows the empty design-time view of the SuperSimpleRepeater control.

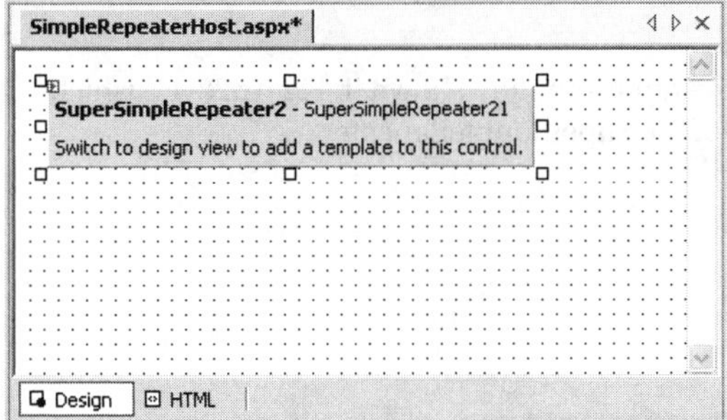

Figure 28-10. *The empty design-time HTML*

■Note Keep in mind that ASP.NET isn't able to decide when your control is empty. Instead, you'll need to call the GetEmptyDesignTimeHtml() method when necessary. As you'll see in this example, the GetDesignTimeHtml() method calls GetEmptyDesignTimeHtml() if a template isn't present.

Coding the GetErrorDesignTimeHtml() method is just as easy. Once again, you can use the CreatePlaceHolderDesignTimeHtml() method, but this time you should supply the details about the exception that occurred.

```
Protected Overrides Function GetErrorDesignTimeHtml(ByVal e As Exception) As String

        Dim text As String = String.Format("{0}{1}{2}{3}", _
                "There was an error and the control can't be displayed.", _
                "<br />", "Exception: ", e.Message)
        Return CreatePlaceHolderDesignTimeHtml(text)
End Function
```

The final step is to build the GetDesignTimeHtml() method. This code retrieves the current instance of the SuperSimpleRepeater control from the ControlDesigner.Component property. It then checks for an item template. If no template is present, the empty HTML is shown. If a template is present, the control is data-bound, and *then* the design-time HTML is displayed, as follows:

```
Public Overrides Function GetDesignTimeHtml() As String
    Try
        Dim repeater As SuperSimpleRepeater =
            CType(MyBase.Component, SuperSimpleRepeater1)
        If repeater.ItemTemplate Is Nothing Then
            Return GetEmptyDesignTimeHtml()
        Else
            Dim designTimeHtml As String = String.Empty
            repeater.DataBind()
            designTimeHtml = MyBase.GetDesignTimeHtml()
            Return designTimeHtml
        End If
        Return MyBase.GetDesignTimeHtml()
    Catch e As Exception
        Return GetErrorDesignTimeHtml(e)
    End Try
End Function
```

This produces the vastly improved design-time representation shown in Figure 28-11, which closely resembles the actual runtime appearance of the SuperSimpleRepeater.

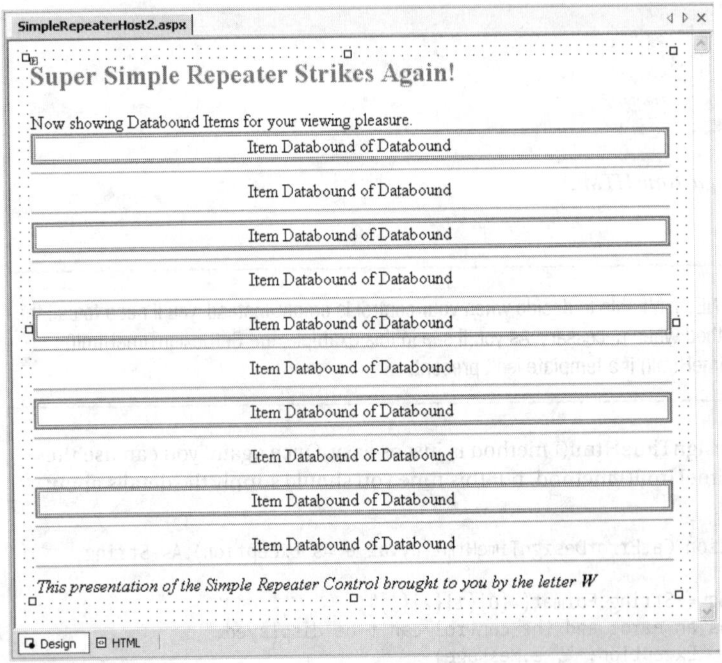

Figure 28-11. *The improved design-time representation*

Smart Tags

Visual Studio 2005 includes a new feature for creating a rich design-time experience—*smart tags*. These are the pop-up windows that appear next to a control when you click the tiny arrow in the corner.

Smart tags are similar to menus in that they have a list of items. However, these items can be commands (which are rendered like hyperlinks) or other controls such as check boxes, drop-down lists, and more. They can also include static descriptive text. In this way, a smart tag can act like a mini–Properties window.

Figure 28-12 shows an example of the custom smart tag that's created in the next example. It allows the developer to set a combination of TitledTextBox properties. It includes two text boxes that let you set the text, a See Website Information link that launches a browser for a specific URL, and some static information that indicates the control's name.

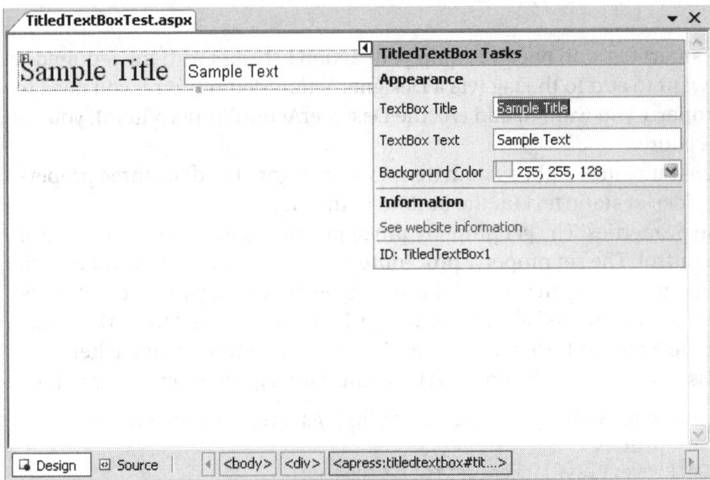

Figure 28-12. *A custom smart tag*

To create this smart tag, you need the following ingredients:

A collection of DesignerActionItem objects: Each DesignerActionItem represents a single item in the smart tag.

An action list class: This class has two roles—it configures the collection of DesignerActionItem instances for the smart tag, and, when a command or change is made, it performs the corresponding operation on the linked control.

A control designer: This hooks your action list up to the control so the smart tag appears at design time.

In the following sections, you'll build this solution piece by piece.

The Action List

Smart tags allow a number of options. To keep it all well-organized, it's a good idea to separate your code by creating a custom class that encapsulates your action list. This custom class should derive from DesignerActionList (in the System.ComponentModel.Design namespace).

Here's an example that creates an action list that's intended for use with the TitledTextBox:

```
Public Class TitledTextBoxActionList
    Inherits DesignerActionList
        ...
End Class
```

You should add a single constructor to the action list that requires the matching control type. You can then store the reference to the control in a member variable. This isn't required, because the base ActionList class does have a Component property that provides access to your control. However, by using this approach, you gain the convenience of strongly typed access to your control.

```
Private linkedControl As TitledTextBox

Public Sub New(ByVal ctrl As TitledTextBox)
    MyBase.New(ctrl)
    linkedControl = ctrl
End Sub
```

Before you can build the smart tag, you need to equip your action list class with the required members. For every link you want to add to the tag (via a DesignerActionMethodItem), you need to create a method. For every property you want to add (via the DesignerActionPropertyItem), you need to create a property procedure.

The smart tag in Figure 28-4 includes eight custom items: two category headers, three properties, one action link, and one piece of static text (at the bottom of the tag).

The first step is to add the properties. The get property procedure needs to retrieve the value of the property from the linked control. The set property procedure needs to apply the new value to the linked control. However, this has a catch—you can't set the new value directly. If you do, other parts of the designer infrastructure won't be notified about the change. Instead, you need to work through the PropertyDescriptor.SetValue() method. To make this easier, you can define a private helper method in your action list class that retrieves the PropertyDescriptor for a given property by name:

```
Private Function GetPropertyByName(ByVal propName As String) As PropertyDescriptor
    Dim prop As PropertyDescriptor
    prop = TypeDescriptor.GetProperties(linkedControl)(propName)

    If prop Is Nothing Then
        Throw New ArgumentException("Matching property not found.", propName)
    Else
        Return prop
    End If
End Function
```

Now you can create the three properties that wrap the properties in the TitledTextBox control:

```
Public Property Text() As String
    Get
        Return linkedControl.Text
    End Get
    Set
        GetPropertyByName("Text").SetValue(linkedControl, Value)
    End Set
End Property

Public Property Title() As String
    Get
        Return linkedControl.Title
    End Get
    Set
```

```
            GetPropertyByName("Title").SetValue(linkedControl, Value)
        End Set
    End Property

    Public Property BackColor() As Color
        Get
            Return linkedControl.BackColor
        End Get
        Set
            GetPropertyByName("BackColor").SetValue(linkedControl, Value)
        End Set
    End Property
```

■ **Note** Not all properties can be edited natively in a smart tag—it all depends on the data type. If the data type has an associated UITypeEditor (for graphically editing the property) or a TypeConverter (for converting the data type to and from a string representation), editing will work. Most common data types have these ingredients, but your custom objects won't (and as a result, all you'll see is a read-only string generated by calling ToString() on the object). For more information, refer to the next chapter, which looks at type conversion in detail.

The next step is to build the functionality for the See Website Information link. To do this, create a method in the action list class. Here's the code, which uses the Process class to launch the default browser:

```
Public Sub LaunchSite()
    Try
        System.Diagnostics.Process.Start("http://www.prosetech.com")
    Catch
    End Try
End Sub
```

The DesignerActionItem Collection

The individual items in a smart tag are represented by the DesignerActionItem class. The .NET Framework provides four basic classes that derive from DesignerActionItem, as described in Table 28-3.

Table 28-3. *Classes Derived from DesignerActionItem*

Method	Description
DesignerActionMethodItem	This item is rendered as a link. When you click it, it triggers an action by calling a method in your DesignerActionList class.
DesignerActionPropertyItem	This item is rendered as an edit control and uses logic that's similar to the Properties window. Strings are given edit boxes, enumerated values become drop-down lists, and Boolean values are turned into check boxes. When you change the value, the underlying property is modified.
DesignerActionTextItem	This item is rendered as a static piece of text. Usually, it provides additional information about the control. It's not clickable.
DesignerActionHeaderItem	This item derives from DesignerActionTextItem. It's a static piece of text that's styled as a heading. Using one or more header items, you can divide the smart tag into separate categories and group your other properties accordingly. It's not clickable.

To create your smart tag, you need to build a DesignerActionItemCollection that combines your group of DesignerActionItem objects. Order is important in this collection, because Visual Studio will add the DesignerActionItem objects to the smart tag from top to bottom in the order they appear.

To build your action list, you override the DesignerActionList.GetSortedActionItems() method, create the DesignerActionItemCollection, add each DesignerActionItem to it, and then return the collection. Depending on the complexity of your smart tag, this may take several steps.

The first step is to create the headers that divide the smart tag into separate regions. You can then add other items to these categories. This example uses two headers:

```
Public Overrides Function GetSortedActionItems() As DesignerActionItemCollection

    ' Create eight items.
    Dim items As New DesignerActionItemCollection()

    ' Begin by creating the headers.
    items.Add(New DesignerActionHeaderItem("Appearance"))
    items.Add(New DesignerActionHeaderItem("Information"))
    ...
```

Next, you can add the properties. You specify the name of the property of the class, followed by the name that should appear in the smart tag. The last two items include the category where the item should be placed (corresponding to one of the DesignerActionHeaderItems you just created) and a description (which appears as a tooltip when you hover over that item).

```
    ...
' Add items that wrap the properties.
    items.Add(New DesignerActionPropertyItem(
        "Title", "TextBox Title", "Appearance",
        "The heading for this control."))

    items.Add(New DesignerActionPropertyItem(
        "Text", "TextBox Text", "Appearance",
        "The content in the TextBox."))

    items.Add(New DesignerActionPropertyItem(
        "BackColor", "Background Color",
        "Appearance", "The color shown behind the control as a background."))

    ...
```

Visual Studio connects the action item to the property in the action item class by using reflection with the property name you supply. If you add more than one property to the same category, they're ordered based on the order in which you add them. If you add more than one category header, the categories are also ordered according to their positions.

The next step is to create a DesignerActionMethodItem(), which binds a smart tag item to a method. In this case, you specify the object where the callback method is implemented, the name of the method, the name that should appear in the smart tag display, the category where it will appear, and the tooltip description. The last parameter is a Boolean value. If True, the item will be added to the context menu for the control as well as to the smart tag.

```
...
items.Add(New DesignerActionMethodItem(
    Me, "LaunchSite", "See website information",
    "Information", "Opens a web browser with the company site.", True))
...
```

Finally, you can create new DesignerActionTextItem objects with the static text you want to show and return the complete collection of items, like so:

```
    ...
    items.Add(New DesignerActionTextItem("ID: " & linkedControl.ID, "ID"))

    Return items
End Function
```

The Control Designer

Once you've perfected your smart tag action list, you still need to connect it to your control. You do this by creating a custom designer and overriding the ActionLists property so that it returns an instance of your custom action list class. The following control designer demonstrates this. Notice that the action list isn't created each time ActionList is called—instead, it's cached in a private member variable to optimize performance.

```
Public Class TitledTextBoxDesigner
        Inherits ControlDesigner
    Private lstActions As DesignerActionListCollection

    Public Overrides ReadOnly Property ActionLists() As DesignerActionListCollection
        Get
            If lstActions Is Nothing Then
                lstActions = New DesignerActionListCollection()
                lstActions.Add(
                   New TitledTextBoxActionList(CType(Control, TitledTextBox)))
            End If
            Return lstActions
        End Get
    End Property
End Class
```

Summary

In this chapter, you took a tour through some of the simple and complex aspects of the .NET design-time architecture. You learned how to configure the way control properties are displayed in the Properties window and how to take charge of control serialization and parsing. For many more advanced topics, such as custom control designers, you can consult the MSDN documentation.

CHAPTER 29

Dynamic Graphics and GDI+

In Chapter 4, you learned about basic web controls for displaying graphics, such as the Image and ImageButton. Both allow you to display an image, and the ImageButton also fires a Click event that gives you the mouse coordinates. But in a modern web application you'll often want much more.

In this chapter, you'll learn about two .NET innovations that give you greater control over the look and feel of your website. First, you'll learn about the ImageMap control, which allows you to define invisible shaped regions over an image and react when they're clicked. Next you'll tackle GDI+, a .NET model for rendering dynamic graphics. You'll learn how to create render custom graphics with GDI+, how to embed these graphics in a web page, and how to create custom controls that use GDI+.

Note Almost all the techniques discussed in this chapter are equally well-supported in ASP.NET 1.*x*. The key addition is the ImageMap control, which provides a server control wrapper for the <map> and <area> tags.

The ImageMap Control

Web pages commonly include complex graphics where different actions are taken depending on what part of the graphic is clicked. ASP.NET developers can use several tricks to implement this design:

Using stacked Image controls: Multiple borderless pictures will look like one graphic when carefully positioned next to each other. You can then handle the clicks of each control separately. This approach works well for buttons and navigational controls that have defined, rectangular edges.

Using the ImageButton control: When an ImageButton control is clicked, it provides the coordinates where the click was made. You can examine these coordinates in your server-side code and determine what region was clicked programmatically. This technique is very flexible but tedious and error-prone to code.

Using the ImageMap control: With the ImageMap control, you can define separate regions and give each one a unique name. One advantage of this approach is that as the user moves the mouse pointer over the image, it changes to a hand only when the user is positioned over a defined region. Thus, this approach works particularly well for detailed images that have small hotspots.

The ImageMap control is new in ASP.NET 2.0. It provides a server-side abstraction over the HTML <map> and <area> tags, which define an image map. The ImageMap renders itself as a <map> tag. You define regions by adding HotSpot objects to the ImageMap.HotSpots collection, and each region is rendered as an <area> tag inside the <map> tag. Just before the <map> tag, ASP.NET renders the linked <img> tag that shows the picture and uses the image map.

For example, if you create a map named ImageMap1 with three circular hotspots, the ImageMap control will render markup like this:

```
<img id="ImageMap1" src="cds.jpg" usemap="#ImageMapImageMap1"
 style="border-width:0px;" />
<map name="ImageMapImageMap1">
  <area shape="circle" coords="272,83,83"
   href="javascript:__doPostBack('ImageMap1','0')" title="DVDs" alt="DVDs" />
  <area shape="circle" coords="217,221,83"
   href="javascript:__doPostBack('ImageMap1','1')" title="Media" alt="Media" />
  <area shape="circle" coords="92,173,83"
   href="javascript:__doPostBack('ImageMap1','2')" title="CDs" alt="CDs" />
</map>
```

Creating Hotspots

You can add an ImageMap control to a form in much the same way as an Image control. Just drop it onto the page, and set the ImageUrl property to the name of the image file you want to use. You also have the usual ImageAlign, BorderStyle, BorderWidth, and BorderColor properties.

To define the clickable regions, you need to add HotSpot objects to the ImageMap.HotSpots property. You can use three classes: CircleHotSpot, RectangleHotSpot, and PolygonHotSpot. These choices aren't arbitrary—they match the three shape types defined in the HTML standard.

Before you can tackle this task, you need to know the exact coordinates of the hotspot you want to create. Unfortunately, the ImageMap designer isn't much help, so you'll probably rely on a dedicated HTML-authoring program. For example, Figure 29-1 shows three circle hotspots being adjusted with Microsoft FrontPage.

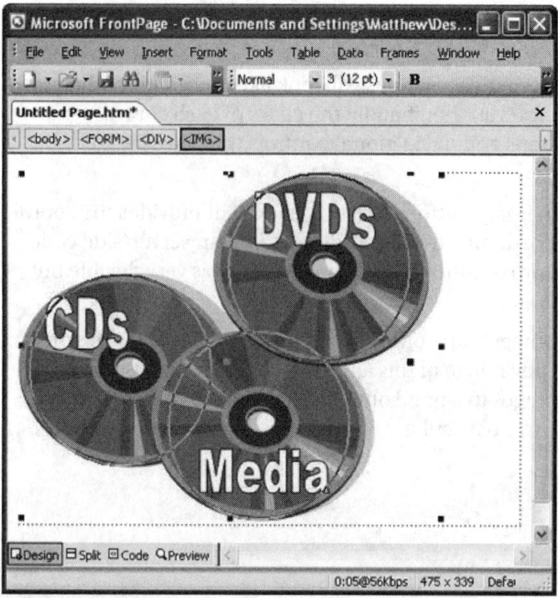

Figure 29-1. *Configuring hotspots in FrontPage*

Tip It's acceptable to have overlapping hotspots, but the hotspot that is defined first will handle the click. In the example shown in Figure 29-1, it makes sense to define the hotspots in this order: DVDs, Media, CDs.

Once you've tweaked the hotspots to perfection, you can look at the source code to find the coordinates. In the case of a circle, three details are important: the X coordinate, Y coordinate, and radius. They appear in this order in the <area> tag:

```
<area shape="circle" coords="272, 83, 83" ...>
```

This tag defines the hotspot around the DVD region. The circle's center is at (272, 83), and the radius is 83 pixels.

When defining a rectangle, you define the top-left and bottom-right corners. The order of coordinates is left X, top Y, right X, and bottom Y. When defining a polygon, you can have as many points as you like. The browser draws a line from one point to another to create the shape. You list the X and Y coordinate for your points in pairs like this: X1, Y1, X2, Y2, X3, Y3, and so on. It's recommended (according to the HTML standard) that you end with the same point with which you started.

Once you've determined your hotspots, you can add the corresponding HotSpot objects. Here's the ImageMap for Figure 29-1, with three hotspots:

```
<asp:ImageMap ID="ImageMap1" runat="server" ImageUrl="~/cds.jpg">
  <asp:CircleHotSpot AlternateText="DVDs"
   Radius="83" X="272" Y="83" />
  <asp:CircleHotSpot AlternateText="Media"
   Radius="83" X="217" Y="221" />
  <asp:CircleHotSpot AlternateText="CDs"
   Radius="83" X="92" Y="173" />
</asp:ImageMap>
```

Rather than coding this by hand, you can select your ImageMap and click the ellipsis next to the HotSpots property in the Properties window. This opens a collection editor where you can add and modify each hotspot.

Once you've defined the hotspots, you can test them in a browser. When you move the mouse pointer over a hotspot, it changes into a hand. You'll also see the alternate text that you've defined for the hotspot appear in a tooltip.

Handling Hotspot Clicks

The next step is to make the hotspots clickable. A hotspot can trigger one of two actions—it can navigate to a new page, or it can post back your page (and fire the ImageMap.Click event). To choose which option you prefer, simply set the ImageMap.HotSpotMode property.

Tip When you set the ImageMap.HotSpotMode property, it applies to all hotspots. You can also override this setting for individual hotspots by setting the HotSpot.HotSpotMode property. This allows you to have some hotspots that post back the page and others that trigger page navigation.

To disable hotspots completely, use HotSpotMode.Inactive. If you use HotSpotMode.Navigate, you need to set the URL for each hotspot using the HotSpot.NavigateUrl property. If you use HotSpotMode.PostBack, you should give each hotspot a unique HotSpot.PostBackValue. This allows you to identify which hotspot triggered the postback in the Click event.

Here's the revised ImageMap control declaration that adds these details:

```
<asp:ImageMap ID="ImageMap1" runat="server" ImageUrl="~/cds.jpg"
 HotSpotMode="PostBack" OnClick="ImageMap1_Click">
  <asp:CircleHotSpot AlternateText="DVDs" PostBackValue="DVDs"
   Radius="83" X="272" Y="83" />
  <asp:CircleHotSpot AlternateText="Media" PostBackValue="Media"
   Radius="83" X="217" Y="221" />
  <asp:CircleHotSpot AlternateText="CDs" PostBackValue="CDs"
   Radius="83" X="92" Y="173" />
</asp:ImageMap>
```

Here's the Click event handler, which simply displays the name of the clicked hotspot:

```
Protected Sub ImageMap1_Click(ByVal sender As Object, ByVal e As ImageMapEventArgs)
    lblInfo.Text = "You clicked " & e.PostBackValue
End Sub
```

Figure 29-2 shows the resulting page.

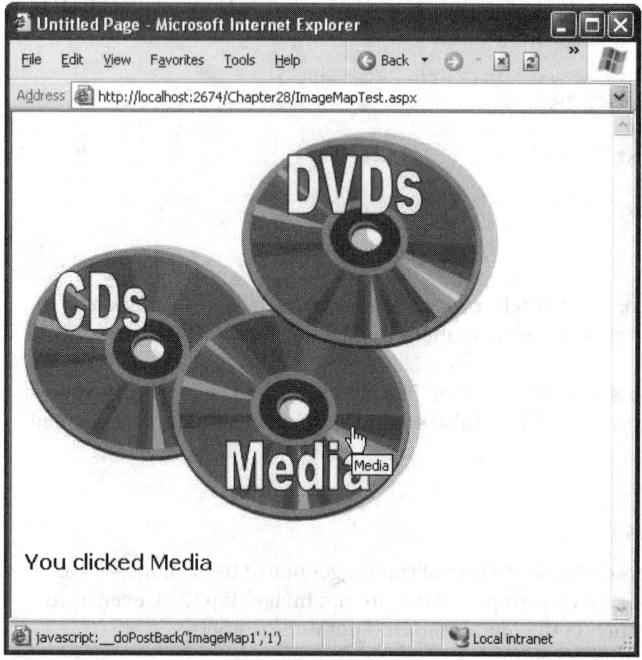

Figure 29-2. *Handling a hotspot click*

A Custom Hotspot

The ImageMap control supports any HotSpot-derived hotspot class. ASP.NET includes exactly three, which correspond to the three basic types of <area> shapes defined in the HTML standard. However, you can create your own hotspots by deriving your own custom class from HotSpot.

Obviously, a custom hotspot class can't do anything that falls outside the HTML standard. For example, it would be nice to have an ellipse and other curved shapes, but that just isn't available. However, you can create a variety of complex multisided shapes, such as triangles, octagons, diamonds, and so on, using the polygon type. By deriving a custom HotSpot, you can create a higher-level model that generates the appropriate polygon based on a few basic pieces of information (such as the center coordinate and the radius).

For example, the following class presents a simple custom triangle. This triangle is created based on a center point, width, and height:

```
Public Class TriangleHotSpot
    Inherits HotSpot

    Public Sub New()
        Width = 0
        Height = 0
        X = 0
        Y = 0
    End Sub

    Public Property Width() As Integer
        Get
                Return CInt(ViewState("Width"))
        End Get
        Set
                ViewState("Width") = Value
        End Set
    End Property

    Public Property Height() As Integer
        Get
                Return CInt(ViewState("Height"))
        End Get
        Set
                ViewState("Height") = Value
        End Set
    End Property

    ' X and Y are the coordinates of the center point.
    Public Property X() As Integer
        Get
                Return CInt(ViewState("X"))
        End Get
        Set
                ViewState("X") = Value
        End Set
    End Property

    Public Property Y() As Integer
        Get
                Return CInt(ViewState("Y"))
        End Get
        Set
                ViewState("Y") = Value
        End Set
    End Property
...
```

When creating a custom HotSpot, you must override the MarkupName property to return the type of shape you are creating. Remember, the only valid choices are circle, rectangle, and polygon. Place this information in the shape attribute of the <area> tag:

```
....
 Protected Overrides ReadOnly Property MarkupName() As String
        Get
                Return "polygon"
        End Get
End Property
  ...
```

Finally, you need to override the GetCoordinates() method to return the string for the cords attribute. For a polygon, this must be a comma-separated series of points in X, Y pairs. Here's the code that creates a simple triangle, with a bottom edge and a single point in the top center:

```
...
Public Overrides Function GetCoordinates() As String
        ' Top coordinate.
        Dim topX As Integer = X
        Dim topY As Integer = CInt(Y - Height / 2)

        ' Bottom-left coordinate.
        Dim btmLeftX As Integer = CInt(X - Width / 2)
        Dim btmLeftY As Integer = CInt(Y + Height / 2)

        ' Bottom-right coordinate.
        Dim btmRightX As Integer = CInt(X + Width / 2)
        Dim btmRightY As Integer = CInt(Y + Height / 2)

        Return topX.ToString() & "," & topY.ToString() & "," & _
              btmLeftX.ToString() & "," & btmLeftY.ToString() & _
              "," & btmRightX.ToString() & "," & btmRightY.ToString()
  End Function
End Class
```

Now you can use your custom hotspot like you would use a custom control. The first step is to register a tag prefix for your namespace, as shown here:

```
<%@ Register TagPrefix="chs" Namespace="CustomHotSpots" %>
```

And here's an ImageMap that uses the TriangleHotSpot:

```
<asp:ImageMap ID="ImageMap1" runat="server" ImageUrl="~/triangle.gif">
  <chs:TriangleHotSpot AlternateText="Triangle"
   X="140" Y="50" Height="75" Width="85" />
</asp:ImageMap>
```

Drawing with GDI+

GDI+ is an all-purpose drawing model for .NET applications. GDI+ has a number of uses in .NET, including writing documents to the printer, displaying graphics in a Windows application, and rendering graphics in a web page.

Using GDI+ code to draw a graphic is slower than using a static image file. However, it gives you much more freedom and enables several possibilities that weren't possible (or were prohibitively difficult) in earlier web development platforms, such as classic ASP. For example, you can create rich graphics that incorporate user-specific information and render charts and graphs on the fly based on the records in a database.

The heart of GDI+ programming is the System.Drawing.Graphics class. The Graphics class encapsulates a GDI+ drawing surface, whether it is a window, a print document, or an in-memory bitmap. ASP.NET developers rarely have the need to paint windows or print documents, so it's the last option that is the most practical.

To use GDI+ in ASP.NET, you need to follow four steps:

1. Create the in-memory bitmap where you'll perform all your drawing.
2. Create a GDI+ graphics context for the image. This gives you the System.Drawing.Graphics object you need.
3. Perform the drawing using the methods of the Graphics object. You can draw and fill lines and shapes, and you can even copy bitmap content from existing files.
4. Write the binary data for the image to the browser by using the Response.OutputStream property.

In the following sections, you'll see several examples of web pages that use GDI+. Before continuing, you may want to ensure that the following namespaces are imported:

```
Imports System.Drawing
Imports System.Drawing.Drawing2D
Imports System.Drawing.Imaging
```

The System.Drawing namespace defines many of the fundamental ingredients for drawing, including pens, brushes, and bitmaps. Visual Studio adds this namespace import to all your web pages by default. The System.Drawing.Drawing2D namespace adds other useful details such as the flexible GraphicsPath class, and System.Drawing.Imaging includes the ImageFormat namespace that lets you choose the graphics format in which your bitmap will be rendered when it's sent to the client.

Simple Drawing

The following example demonstrates the simplest possible GDI+ page. All the work is performed in the event handler for the Page.Load event.

The first step is to create the in-memory bitmap by creating an instance of the System.Drawing.Bitmap class. When you create this object, you need to specify the height and width of the image in pixels as constructor arguments. You should make the size as small as possible. Not only will a larger bitmap consume additional server memory while your code is executing, but the size of the rendered content you send to the client will also increase, slowing down the transmission time.

```
' Create the in-memory bitmap where you will draw the image.
' This bitmap is 300 pixels wide and 50 pixels high.
Dim theImage As New Bitmap(300, 50)
```

The next step is to create a GDI+ graphics context for the image, which is represented by the System.Drawing.Graphics object. This object provides the methods that allow you to draw content on the in-memory bitmap. To create a Graphics object from an existing Bitmap object, you just use the static Graphics.FromImage() method, as shown here:

```
Dim g As Graphics = Graphics.FromImage(theImage)
```

Now comes the interesting part. Using the methods of the Graphics class, you can draw text, shapes, and image on the bitmap. In this example, the drawing code is exceedingly simple. First, it fills the graphic with a solid white background using the FillRectangle() method of the Graphics object.

```
' Draw a solid white rectangle.
' Start from point (1, 1).
' Make it 298 pixels wide and 48 pixels high.
g.FillRectangle(Brushes.White, 1, 1, 298, 48)
```

The FillRectangle() method requires several arguments. The first argument sets the color, the next two parameters set the starting point, and the final two parameters set the width and height. When measuring pixels, the point (0, 0) is the top-left corner of your image in (x, y) coordinates. The X coordinate increases as you go further to the right, and the Y coordinate increases as you go further down. In the current example, the image is 300 pixels wide and 50 pixels high, which means the point (300, 50) is the bottom-right corner.

In this example, the FillRectangle() method doesn't quite fill the entire bitmap. Instead, it leaves a border 1-pixel wide all around. Because you haven't painted any content to this area, these pixels will have the default color (which, for a bitmap you render to GIF, is black).

The next portion of the drawing code renders a static label message. To do this, you need to create a System.Drawing.Font object that represents the font you want to use. This shouldn't be confused with the FontInfo object you use with ASP.NET controls to specify the requested font for a web page. Unlike FontInfo, Font represents a single, specific font (including typeface, size, and style) that's installed on the current computer. When you create a Font object, you specify the font name, point size, and style, as shown here:

```
Dim theFont As New Font("Impact", 20, FontStyle.Regular)
```

■ **Tip** Because this image is generated on the server, you can use any font that the server has installed when creating the graphic. The client won't need to have the same font, because the client receives the text as a rendered image.

To render the text, you use the DrawString() method of the Graphics object. As with the FillRectangle() object, you need to specify the coordinates where the drawing should begin. This point represents the top-left corner of the text block. In this case, the point (10, 5) is used, which gives a distance of 10 pixels from the left and 5 pixels from the top:

```
g.DrawString("This is a test.", theFont, Brushes.Blue, 10, 5)
```

Once the image is complete, you can send it to the browser using the Image.Save() method. Conceptually, you "save" the image to the browser's response stream. It then gets sent to the client and is displayed in the browser. When you use this technique, your image replaces any other web-page data and bypasses the web control model.

```
' Render the image to the output stream.
theImage.Save(Response.OutputStream, _
    System.Drawing.Imaging.ImageFormat.Gif)
```

■ **Tip** You can save an image to any valid stream, including a FileStream. This technique allows you to save dynamically generated images to disk so you can use them later in other web pages.

Finally, you should explicitly release your image and graphics context when you're finished, because both hold onto some unmanaged resources that won't be released right away if you don't. You release resources by calling the Dispose() method, as shown here:

```
g.Dispose()
theImage.Dispose()
```

Figure 29-3 shows the completed web page created by this code.

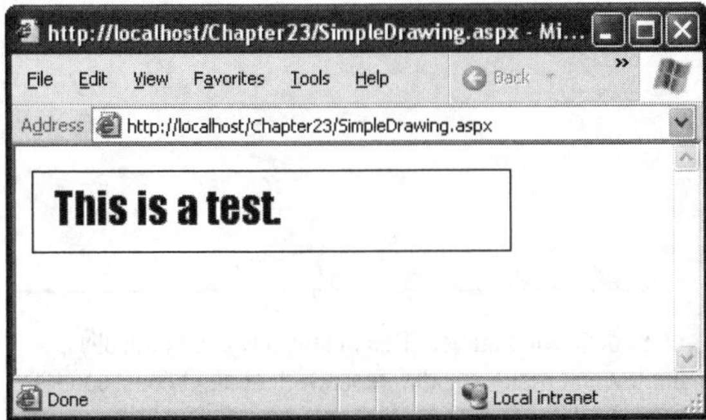

Figure 29-3. *A graphical label*

Image Format and Quality

When you save the image, you can also choose the format you want to use. JPEG offers the best color support and graphics, although it uses compression that can lose detail and make text look fuzzy. GIF is often a better choice for graphics containing text, but it doesn't offer good support for color. In .NET, every GIF uses a fixed palette with 256 generic colors. If you use a color that doesn't map to one of these presets, the color will be dithered, leading to a less-than-optimal graphic.

■ Tip Another choice is the PNG format, which gives you the best of both JPEG and GIF. However, the PNG format doesn't work directly in a web page—instead, you need to wrap it in an <img> tag. Later, in the section "Embedding Graphics in a Web Page," you'll see how to take this step.

Quality isn't just determined by the image format. It also depends on the way you render the original bitmap. GDI+ allows you to choose between optimizing your drawing code for appearance or speed. When you choose to optimize for the best appearance, .NET uses extra rendering techniques such as antialiasing to improve the drawing.

Antialiasing is a technique used to smooth out jagged edges in shapes and text. It works by adding shading at the border of an edge. For example, gray shading might be added to the edge of a black curve to make a corner look smoother. Technically, antialiasing blends a curve with its background. Figure 29-4 shows a close-up of an antialiased ellipse.

To use smoothing in your applications, you set the SmoothingQuality property of the Graphics object. You can choose between None, HighSpeed (the default), AntiAlias, and HighQuality (which is similar to AntiAlias but uses other, slower optimizations that improve the display on LCD screens). The Graphics.SmoothingQuality property is one of the few stateful Graphics class members. This means you set it before you begin drawing, and it applies to any text or shapes you draw in the rest of the paint session (until the Graphics object is disposed of).

```
g.SmoothingMode = SmoothingMode.AntiAlias
```

Figure 29-4. *Antialiasing with an ellipse*

■ **Tip** Antialiasing makes the most difference when you're displaying curves. This means it will dramatically improve the appearance of ellipses, circles, and arcs, but it won't make any difference with straight lines, squares, and rectangles.

You can also use antialiasing with fonts to soften jagged edges on text. You can set the Graphics.TextRenderingHint property to ensure optimized text. You can choose between SingleBitPerPixelGridFit (fastest performance and lowest quality), AntiAliasGridFit (better quality but slower performance), and ClearTypeGridFit (the best quality on an LCD display). Or you can use the SystemDefault value to use whatever font-smoothing settings the user has configured. SystemDefault is the default setting, and the default system settings for most computers enable text antialiasing. Even if you don't set this setting, your dynamically rendered text will probably be drawn in high quality. However, because you can't necessarily control the system settings of the web server, it's a good practice to specify this setting explicitly if you need to draw text in an image.

The Graphics Class

The majority of the GDI+ drawing smarts are concentrated in the Graphics class. The Graphics class also provides a slew of methods for drawing specific shapes, images, and text. Table 29-1 describes these methods, many of which are used in the examples in this chapter.

Table 29-1. *Graphics Class Methods for Drawing*

Method	Description
DrawArc()	Draws an arc representing a portion of an ellipse specified by a pair of coordinates, a width, and a height.
DrawBezier() and DrawBeziers()	Draws the infamous and attractive Bezier curve, which is defined by four control points.
DrawClosedCurve()	Draws a curve and then closes it off by connecting the endpoints.
DrawCurve()	Draws a curve (technically, a cardinal spline).
DrawEllipse()	Draws an ellipse defined by a bounding rectangle specified by a pair of coordinates, a height, and a width.
DrawIcon() and DrawIconUnstreched()	Draws the icon represented by an Icon object and (optionally) stretches it to fit a given rectangle.
DrawImage and DrawImageUnscaled()	Draws the image represented by an Image-derived object and (optionally) stretches it to fit a given rectangle.

Method	Description
DrawLine() and DrawLines()	Draws a line connecting the two points specified by coordinate pairs.
DrawPath()	Draws a GraphicsPath object, which can represent a combination of curves and shapes.
DrawPie()	Draws a "piece-of-pie" shape defined by an ellipse specified by a coordinate pair, a width, a height, two radial lines.
DrawPolygon()	Draws a multisided polygon defined by an array of points.
DrawRectangle() and DrawRectangles()	Draws an ordinary rectangle specified by a starting coordinate pair and width and height.
DrawString()	Draws a string of text in a given font.
FillClosedCurve()	Draws a curve, closes it off by connecting the endpoints, and fills it.
FillEllipse()	Fills the interior of an ellipse.
FillPath()	Fills the shape represented by a GraphicsPath object.
FillPie()	Fills the interior of a "piece-of-pie" shape.
FillPolygon()	Fills the interior of a polygon.
FillRectangle() and FillRectangles()	Fills the interior of a rectangle.
FillRegion()	Fills the interior of a Region object.

The DrawXxx() methods draw outlines (for example, the edge around a rectangle). The FillXxx() methods paint solid regions (for example, the actual surface inside the borders of a rectangle). The only exceptions are the DrawString() method, which draws filled-in text using a font you specify, and the DrawIcon() and DrawImage() methods, which copy bitmap images onto the drawing surface.

If you want to create a shape that has both an outline in one color and a fill in another color, you need to combine both a draw and a fill method. Here's an example that first paints a white rectangle and then adds a green border around it:

```
g.FillRectangle(Brushes.White, 0, 0, 300, 50)
g.DrawRectangle(Pens.Green, 0, 0, 299, 49)
```

■Note If you specify coordinates that are not in the drawing area, you won't receive an exception. However, the content you draw that's off the edge won't appear in the final image. In some cases, this means a partial shape may appear (which might be exactly the effect you want).

You'll notice that when you use a fill method, you need to specify a Brush object. When you use a draw method, you need to specify a Pen object. In this example, the code uses a prebuilt Pen and Brush object, which can be retrieved from the Pens and Brushes classes, respectively. Brushes retrieved in this way always correspond to solid colors. Pens retrieved in this way are always 1-pixel wide. Later in this chapter (in the "Pens" and "Brushes" sections), you'll learn how to create your own custom pens and brushes for more exotic patterns.

Using the techniques you've learned, it's easy to create a simple web page that draws a more complex GDI+ image. The next example uses the Graphics class to draw an ellipse, a text message, and an image from a file.

Here's the code you'll need:

```
Protected Sub Page_Load(ByVal sender As Object, ByVal e As EventArgs)
    ' Create the in-memory bitmap where you will draw the image.
    ' This bitmap is 450 pixels wide and 100 pixels high.
    Dim theImage As New Bitmap(450, 100)
    Dim g As Graphics = Graphics.FromImage(theImage)

    ' Ensure high-quality curves.
    g.SmoothingMode = SmoothingMode.AntiAlias

    ' Paint the background.
    g.FillRectangle(Brushes.White, 0, 0, 450, 100)

    ' Add an ellipse.
    g.FillEllipse(Brushes.PaleGoldenrod, 120, 13, 300, 50)
    g.DrawEllipse(Pens.Green, 120, 13, 299, 49)

    ' Draw some text using a fancy font.
    Dim font As New Font("Harrington", 20, FontStyle.Bold)
    g.DrawString("Oranges are tasty!", font, Brushes.DarkOrange, 150, 20)

    ' Add a graphic from a file.
    Dim orangeImage As Image = Image.FromFile(Server.MapPath("oranges.gif"))
    g.DrawImageUnscaled(orangeImage, 0, 0)

    ' Render the image to the output stream.
    theImage.Save(Response.OutputStream, ImageFormat.Jpeg)
    ' Clean up.
    g.Dispose()
    theImage.Dispose()
End Sub
```

Figure 29-5 shows the resulting web page.

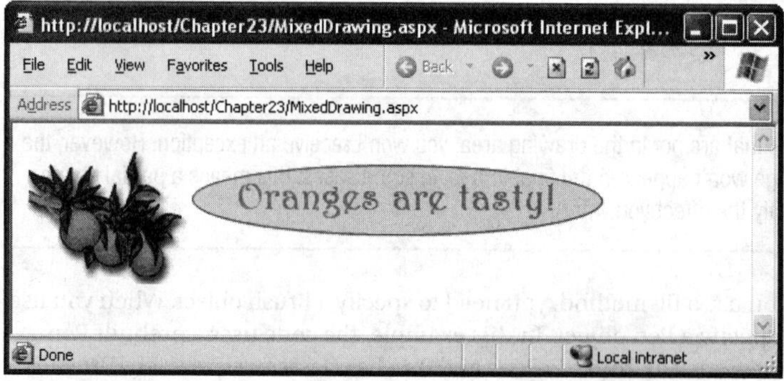

Figure 29-5. *Using multiple elements in a drawing*

Using a GraphicsPath

Two interesting methods that you haven't seen yet include DrawPath() and FillPath(), which work with the GraphicsPath class in the System.Drawing.Drawing2D namespace.

The GraphicsPath class encapsulates a series of connected lines, curves, and text. To build a 3GraphicsPath object, you simply create a new instance and use the methods in Table 29-2 to add all the required elements:

```
Dim path As New GraphicsPath()
path.AddEllipse(0, 0, 100, 50)
path.AddRectangle(New Rectangle(100, 50, 100, 50))
```

Optionally, you can also create a solid, filled figure from separate line segments. To do this, you first call the StartFigure() method. Then you add the required curves and lines using the appropriate methods. When finished, you call the CloseFigure() method to close off the shape by drawing a line from the endpoint to the starting point. You can use these methods multiple times to add several closed figures to a single GraphicsPath object. Here's an example that draws a single figure based on an arc and a line:

```
Dim path As New GraphicsPath()
path.StartFigure()
path.AddArc(10, 10, 100, 100, 20, 50)
path.AddLine(20, 100, 70, 230)
path.CloseFigure()
```

Table 29-2. *GraphicsPath Methods*

Method	Description
AddArc()	Draws an arc representing a portion of an ellipse specified by a pair of coordinates, a width, and a height.
AddBezier() and AddBeziers()	Draws the infamous and attractive Bezier curve, which is defined by four control points.
AddClosedCurve()	Draws a curve and then closes if off by connecting the endpoints.
AddCurve()	Draws a curve (technically, a cardinal spline).
AddEllipse()	Draws an ellipse defined by a bounding rectangle specified by a pair of coordinates, a height, and a width.
AddLine() and AddLines()	Draws a line connecting the two points specified by coordinate pairs.
AddPath()	Adds another GraphicsPath object to this GraphicsPath object.
AddPie()	Draws a "piece-of-pie" shape defined by an ellipse specified by a coordinate pair, a width, a height, and two radial lines.
AddPolygon()	Draws a multisided polygon defined by an array of points.
AddRectangle() and AddRectangles()	Draws an ordinary rectangle specified by a starting coordinate pair and width and height.
AddString()	Draws a string of text in a given font.
StartFigure() and CloseFigure()	StartFigure() defines the start of a new closed figure. When you use CloseFigure(), the starting point will be joined to the endpoint by an additional line.
Transform(), Warp(), and Widen()	Applies a matrix transform, a warp transform (defined by a rectangle and parallelogram), or an expansion, respectively.

Pens

When you use the DrawXxx() methods from the Graphics class, the border of the shape or curve is drawn with the Pen object you supply. You can retrieve a standard pen using one of the static properties from the System.Drawing.Pens class. These pens all have a width of 1 pixel. They only differ in their color.

```
Pen myPen = Pens.Black
```

You can also create a Pen object on your own and configure all the properties described in Table 29-3. Here's an example:

```
Dim myPen As New Pen(Color.Red)
myPen.DashCap = DashCap.Triangle
myPen.DashStyle = DashStyle.DashDotDot
g.DrawLine(myPen, 0, 0, 10, 0)
```

Table 29-3. *Pen Members*

Member	Description
DashPattern	Defines a dash style for broken lines using an array of dashes and spaces.
DashStyle	Defines a dash style for broken lines using the DashStyle enumeration.
LineJoin	Defines how overlapping lines in a shape will be joined together.
PenType	The type of fill that will be used for the line. Typically this will be SolidColor, but you can also use a gradient, bitmap texture, or hatch pattern by supplying a brush object when you create the pen. You cannot set the PenType through this property, however, because it is read-only.
StartCap and EndCap	Determines how the beginning and ends of lines will be rendered. You can also define a custom line cap by creating a CustomLineCap object (typically by using a GraphicsPath) and then assigning it to the CustomStartCap or CustomEndCap property.
Width	The pixel width of lines drawn by this pen.

The easiest way to understand the different LineCap and DashStyle properties is to create a simple test page that loops through all the options and displays a short line segment of each. The following web-page code creates a drawing that does exactly that:

```
Protected Sub Page_Load(ByVal sender As Object, ByVal e As System.EventArgs)
    ' Create the in-memory bitmap where you will draw the image.
    ' This bitmap is 300 pixels wide and 50 pixels high.
    Dim theImage As New Bitmap(500, 400)
    Dim g As Graphics = Graphics.FromImage(theImage)

    ' Paint the background.
    g.FillRectangle(Brushes.White, 0, 0, 500, 400)
```

```
    ' Create a pen to use for all the examples.
    Dim myPen As New Pen(Color.Blue, 10)

    ' The y variable tracks the current y (up/down) position
    ' in the image.
    Dim y As Integer = 60

    ' Draw an example of each LineCap style in the first column (left).
    g.DrawString("LineCap Choices", New Font("Tahoma",
      15, FontStyle.Bold), Brushes.Blue, 0, 10)
    For Each cap As LineCap In System.Enum.GetValues(GetType(LineCap))
        myPen.StartCap = cap
        myPen.EndCap = cap
        g.DrawLine(myPen, 20, y, 100, y)
        g.DrawString(cap.ToString(), New Font("Tahoma", 8),
          Brushes.Black, 120, y - 10)
        y += 30
    Next

    ' Draw an example of each DashStyle in the second column (right).
    y = 60
    g.DrawString("DashStyle Choices", New Font("Tahoma", 15, FontStyle.Bold),
      Brushes.Blue, 200, 10)
    For Each dash As DashStyle In System.Enum.GetValues(GetType(DashStyle))
        ' Configure the pen.
        myPen.DashStyle = dash

        ' Draw a short line segment.
        g.DrawLine(myPen, 220, y, 300, y)

        ' Add a text label.
        g.DrawString(dash.ToString(), New Font("Tahoma", 8),
          Brushes.Black, 320, y - 10)

        ' Move down one line.
        y += 30
    Next

    ' Render the image to the output stream.
    theImage.Save(Response.OutputStream, System.Drawing.Imaging.ImageFormat.Gif)

    g.Dispose()
    theImage.Dispose()
End Sub
```

Figure 29-6 shows the resulting web page.

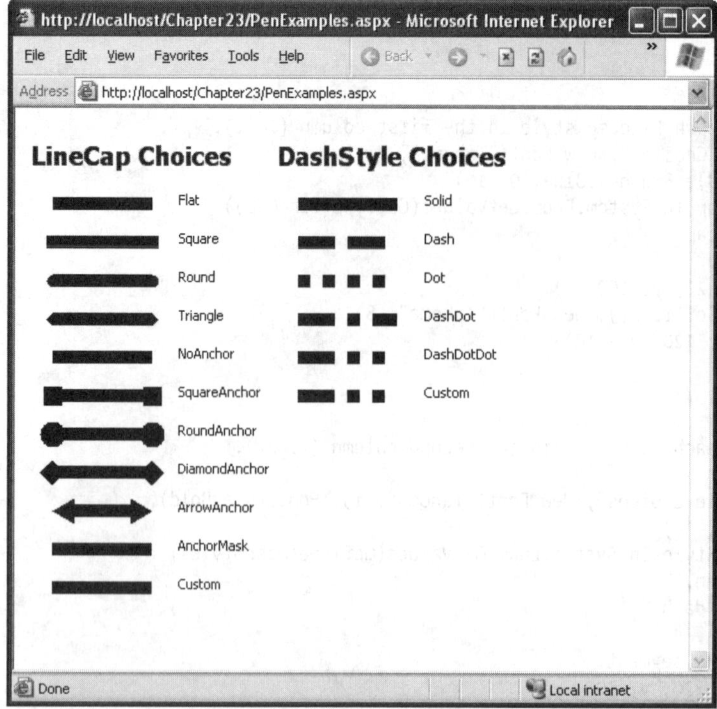

Figure 29-6. *Different pen options*

Brushes

Brushes fill the space between lines. You'll use brushes when drawing text or when using any of the FillXxx() methods of the Graphics class for painting the inside of a shape.

You can quickly retrieve a predefined solid brush using a static property from the Brushes class, as shown here:

```
Brush myBrush = Brushes.White;
```

You can also create a custom brush. You need to decide what type of brush you are creating. Solid brushes are created from the SolidBrush class, and other classes allow fancier options:

HatchBrush: A HatchBrush has a foreground color, a background color, and a hatch style that determines how these colors are combined. Typically, colors are interspersed using stripes, grids, or dots, but you can even select unusual pattern styles such as bricks, confetti, weave, and shingles.

LinearGradientBrush: The LinearGradientBrush allows you to blend two colors in a gradient pattern. You can choose any two colors (as with the hatch brush) and then choose to blend horizontally (from left to right), vertically (from top to bottom), diagonally (from the top-left corner to the bottom-right), or diagonally backward (from the top-right to the bottom-left). You can also specify the origin point for either side of the gradient.

TextureBrush: The TextureBrush attaches a bitmap to a brush. The image is tiled in the painted portion of the brush, whether it is text or a simple rectangle.

You can experiment with all these brush types in your applications. Here's an example of the drawing logic you need to test all the styles of LinearGradientBrush:

```
Protected Sub Page_Load(ByVal sender As Object, ByVal e As System.EventArgs)
    ' Create the in-memory bitmap.
    Dim theImage As New Bitmap(300, 300)
    Dim g As Graphics = Graphics.FromImage(theImage)

    ' Paint the background.
    g.FillRectangle(Brushes.White, 0, 0, 300, 300)

    ' Show a rectangle with each type of gradient.
    Dim myBrush As LinearGradientBrush
    Dim y As Integer = 20
    For Each gradientStyle As LinearGradientMode
        In System.Enum.GetValues(GetType(LinearGradientMode))
        ' Configure the brush.
        myBrush = New LinearGradientBrush(New Rectangle(20, y, 100, 60),
            Color.Violet, Color.White, gradientStyle)

        ' Draw a small rectangle and add a text label.
        g.FillRectangle(myBrush, 20, y, 100, 60)
        g.DrawString(gradientStyle.ToString(), New Font("Tahoma", 8),
            Brushes.Black, 130, y + 20)

        ' Move to the next line.
        y += 70
    Next

    ' Render the image to the output stream.
    theImage.Save(Response.OutputStream, System.Drawing.Imaging.ImageFormat.Jpeg)

    g.Dispose()
    theImage.Dispose()
End Sub
```

Figure 29-7 shows the result.

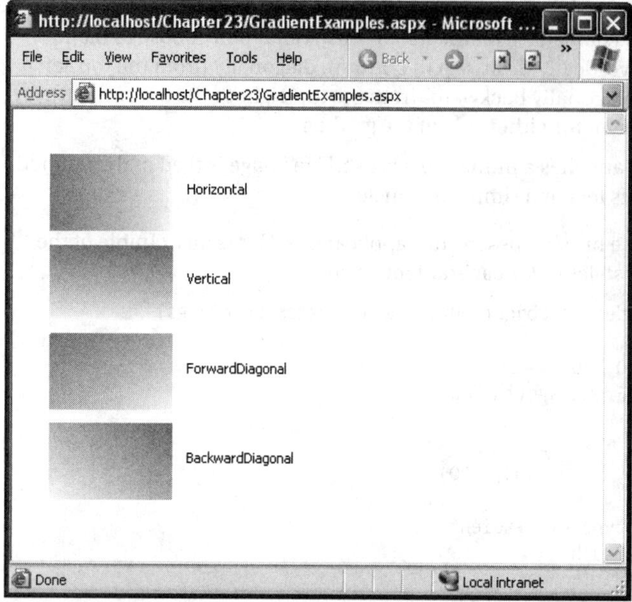

Figure 29-7. *Testing different gradient styles*

Tip You can also create a pen that draws using the fill style of a brush. This allows you to draw lines that are filled with gradients and textures. To do so, begin by creating the appropriate brush, and then create a new pen. One of the overloaded pen constructor methods accepts a reference to a brush—that's the one you need to use for a brush-based pen.

Embedding Dynamic Graphics in a Web Page

The Image.Save() approach has one problem that has been used in all the examples so far. When you save an image to the response stream, you overwrite whatever information ASP.NET would otherwise use. If you have a web page that includes other static content and controls, this content won't appear at all in the final web page. Instead, the dynamically rendered graphics will replace it.

Fortunately, you can solve this in a simple. You can link to a dynamically generated image using the HTML <img> tag or the Image web control. But instead of linking your image to a static image file, link it to the .aspx file that generates the picture.

For example, consider the earlier Figure 29-1. It's stored in a file named SimpleDrawing.aspx, and it writes a dynamically generated image to the response stream. In another page, you could show the dynamic image by adding an Image web control and setting the ImageUrl property to SimpleDrawing.aspx. You could then add other controls or even multiple Image controls that link to the same content.

Figure 29-8 shows an example that uses two <img> tags that point to SimpleDrawing.aspx, along with additional ASP.NET web controls in between.

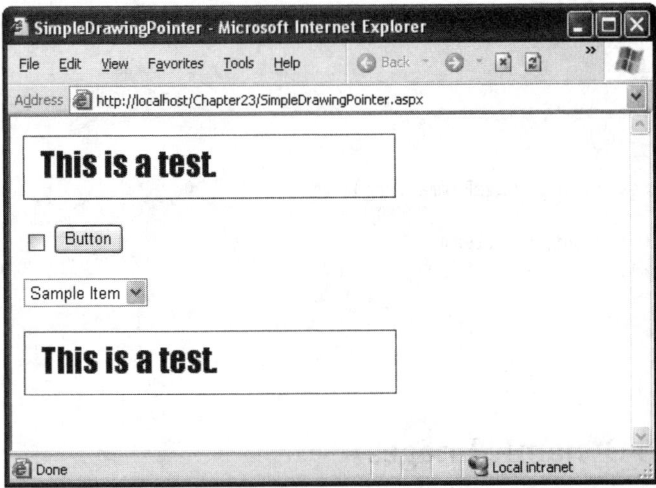

Figure 29-8. *Mixing dynamically drawn content and ordinary web controls*

Tip Remember that creating a GDI+ drawing is usually an order of magnitude slower than serving a static image. As a result, it's probably not a good idea to implement graphical buttons and other elements that you'll repeat multiple times on a page using GDI+. (If you do, consider caching or saving the image file once you've generated it to increase performance.)

Using the PNG Format

Once you start using this technique, you gain the ability to use the PNG format. PNG is an all-purpose format that always provides high quality by combining the lossless compression of GIFs with the rich color support of JPEGs. However, browsers such as Internet Explorer often don't handle it correctly when you return PNG content directly from a page. Instead of seeing the picture content, you'll receive a message prompting you to download the picture content and open it in another program. However, the <img> tag approach effectively sidesteps this problem.

You need to be aware of two more quirks when using PNG. First, some older browsers (including Netscape 4.*x*) don't support PNG. Second, you can't use the Bitmap.Save() method shown in earlier examples.

Technically speaking, the problem is that you can't use the Save() method with a nonseekable stream. Response.OutputStream is a nonseekable stream, which means data must be written from beginning to end. Unfortunately, to create a PNG file, .NET needs to be able to move back and forth in file, which means it requires a seekable stream. The solution is fairly simple. Instead of saving directly to Response.OutputStream, you can create a System.IO.MemoryStream object, which represents an in-memory buffer of data. The MemoryStream is always seekable, so you can save the image to this object. Once you've performed this step, you can easily copy the data from the MemoryStream to the Response.OutputStream. The only disadvantage is that this technique requires more memory because the whole graphic needs to be helped in memory at once. However, the graphics you use in web pages generally aren't that large, so you probably won't observe any reduction in performance.

Here's the code you need to implement this solution, assuming you've imported the System.IO namespace:

```
Response.ContentType = "image/png"

' Create the PNG in memory.
Dim mem As New MemoryStream()
theImage.Save(mem, System.Drawing.Imaging.ImageFormat.Png)

' Write the MemoryStream data to the output stream.
mem.WriteTo(Response.OutputStream)

' Clean up.
g.Dispose()
theImage.Dispose()
```

Passing Information to Dynamic Images

When you use this technique to embed dynamic graphics in web pages, you also need to think about how the web page can send information to the code that generates the dynamic graphic. For example, what if you don't want to show a fixed piece of text but you want to generate a dynamic label that incorporates the name of the current user? (In fact, if you do want to show a static piece of text, it's probably better to create the graphic ahead of time and store it in a file, rather than generating it using GDI+ code each time the user requests the page.) One solution is to pass the information using the query string. The page that renders the graphic can then check for the query string information it needs.

The following example uses this technique to create a data-bound list that shows a thumbnail of every bitmap in a given directory. Figure 29-9 shows the final result.

This page needs to be designed in two parts: the page that contains the GridView and the page that dynamically renders a single thumbnail. The GridView page will call the thumbnail page multiple times (using <img> tags) to fill the list.

It makes sense to design the page that creates the thumbnail first. To make this component as generic as possible, you shouldn't hard-code any information about the directory to use or the size of thumbnail. Instead, this information will be retrieved through three query string arguments. The first step you need to perform is to check that all this information is supplied when the page first loads, as shown here:

```
Protected Sub Page_Load(ByVal sender As Object, ByVal e As System.EventArgs)
    If (Request.QueryString("X") Is Nothing)
        OrElse (Request.QueryString("Y") Is Nothing)
        OrElse (Request.QueryString("FilePath") Is Nothing) Then
        ' There is missing data, so don't display anything.
        ' Other options include choosing reasonable defaults
        ' or returning an image with some static error text.
    Else
        Dim x As Integer = Integer.Parse(Request.QueryString("X"))
        Dim y As Integer = Integer.Parse(Request.QueryString("Y"))
        Dim file As String = Server.UrlDecode(Request.QueryString("FilePath"))
        ...
```

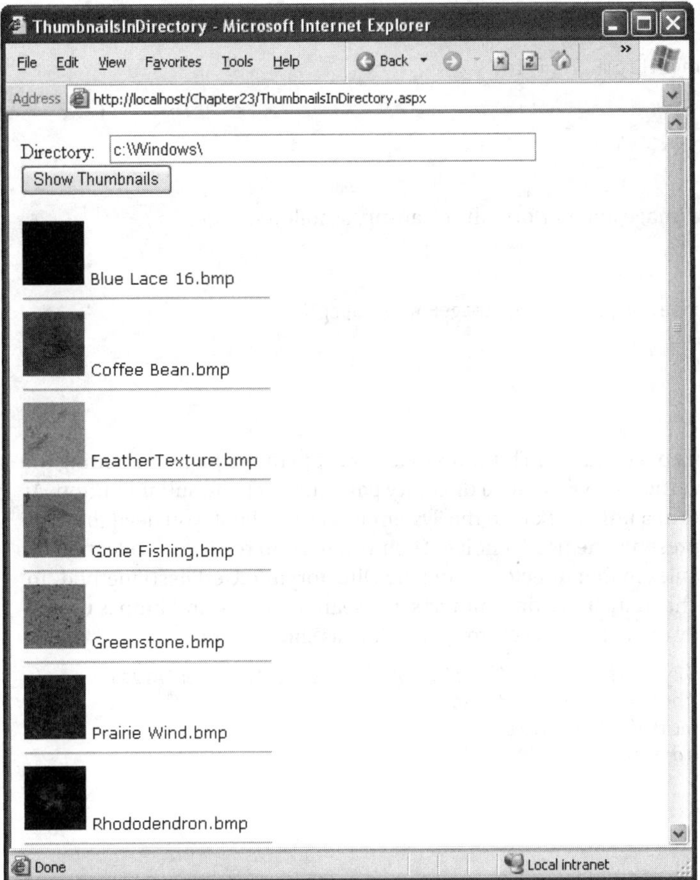

Figure 29-9. *A data-bound thumbnail list*

Once you have the basic set of data, you can create your Bitmap and Graphics object as always. In this case, the Bitmap dimensions should correspond to the size of the thumbnail, because you don't want to add any content:

```
...
' Create the in-memory bitmap where you will draw the image.
Dim theImage As New Bitmap(x, y)
Dim g As Graphics = Graphics.FromImage(theImage)
...
```

Creating the thumbnail is easy. All you need to do is load the image (using the static Image.FromFile() method) and then draw it on the drawing surface. When you draw the image, you specify the starting point (0, 0) and the height and width. The height and width correspond to the size of the Bitmap object. The Graphics class will automatically scale your image to fit these dimensions, using antialiasing to create a high-quality thumbnail:

```
...
' Load the file data.
Dim thumbnail As Image = Image.FromFile(file)

' Draw the thumbnail.
g.DrawImage(thumbnail, 0, 0, x, y)
...
```

Lastly, you can render the image and perform the clean-up, as follows:

```
        ...
        ' Render the Image.
        theImage.Save(Response.OutputStream, ImageFormat.Jpeg)
        g.Dispose()
        theImage.Dispose()
    End If
End Sub
```

The next step is to use this page (named ThumbnailViewer.aspx) in the page containing the GridView. The basic idea is that the user will enter a directory path and click the submit button. At this point, your code can perform a little work with the System.IO classes. First, you need to create a DirectoryInfo object that represents the user's choice. Then you need to retrieve a collection of FileInfo objects that represent files in that directory using the DirectoryInfo.GetFiles() method. To narrow the selection down so that it includes only bitmaps, the search expression *.bmp is used. Finally, the code binds the array of FileInfo objects to a GridView, as shown here:

```
Protected Sub cmdShow_Click(ByVal sender As Object, ByVal e As System.EventArgs)
    ' Get a string array with all the image files.
    Dim dir As New DirectoryInfo(txtDir.Text)
    gridThumbs.DataSource = dir.GetFiles("*.bmp")

    ' Bind the string array.
    gridThumbs.DataBind()
End Sub
```

It's up to the GridView template to determine how the bound FileInfo objects are displayed. In this example, you need to show two pieces of information—the short name of the file and the corresponding thumbnail. Showing the short name is straightforward. You simply need to bind to the FileInfo.Name property. Showing the thumbnail requires using an <img> tag to invoke the ThumbnailViewer.aspx page. However, constructing the right URL can be a little tricky, so the best solution is to hand the work off to a method in the web-page class called GetImageUrl().

Here's the complete GridView declaration with the template:

```
<asp:GridView ID="gridThumbs" runat="server"
 AutoGenerateColumns="False" Font-Names="Verdana"
 Font-Size="X-Small" GridLines="None">
  <Columns>
    <asp:TemplateField>
      <ItemTemplate>
        <img src='<%# GetImageUrl(Eval("FullName")) %>' />
        <%# Eval("Name") %>
        <hr/>
      </ItemTemplate>
    </asp:TemplateField>
  </Columns>
</asp:GridView>
```

The GetImageUrl() method examines the full file path, encodes it, and adds it to the query string so ThumbnailViewer.aspx can find the required file. At the same time, the GetImageUrl() method also chooses a thumbnail size of 50 pixels by 50 pixels. Note that the file path is URL-encoded. That's because filenames commonly include characters that aren't allowed in URLs, such as the space:

```
Protected Function GetImageUrl(ByVal path As Object) As String
    Return "ThumbnailViewer.aspx?x=50&y=50&FilePath=" & Server.UrlEncode(CStr(path))
End Function
```

All in all, this solution demonstrates a fairly impressive result without much code required.

Custom Controls That Use GDI+

Based on everything you learned in Chapter 27, you're probably eager to use GDI+ to create your own well-encapsulated custom controls. Unfortunately, ASP.NET doesn't make it easy because of the way you need to embed GDI+ images in a page.

As you've seen, if you want to use GDI+, you need to create a separate web page. You can then embed the content of this page in another page by using an <img> tag. As a result, you can't just drop a custom control that uses GDI+ onto a web page. What you *can* do is create a custom control that wraps an <img> tag. This control can provide a convenient programming interface, complete with properties, methods, and events. However, the custom control won't actually generate the image. Instead, it will collect the data from its properties and use it to build the query string portion of a URL. The custom control will then render itself on the page as an <img> tag, which points to the page that performs the real work.

■ **Tip** If you want, the custom control can also render other HTML elements above or below the <img> tag, such as a separating line, a title, and so on.

Essentially, the custom control provides a higher-level wrapper that abstracts the process of transferring information to your GDI+ page. Figure 29-10 shows how this process works with the example you'll consider next, which uses the custom control approach to create a simple label that renders with a gradient background. In this example, the custom control is named GradientLabel. You can find the GDI+ code in a separate web page named GradientLabel.aspx. To see this example at work, you can request the GradientTest.aspx web page, which hosts a single instance of the GradientLabel control.

■ **Tip** If you're worried about confusing your real web pages with the web pages you use to supply GDI+ drawing, consider using a custom HTTP handler to generate the image. With an HTTP handler, your image generators can have a custom extension and use essentially the same code in the ProcessRequest() method. HTTP handlers were first demonstrated in Chapter 5

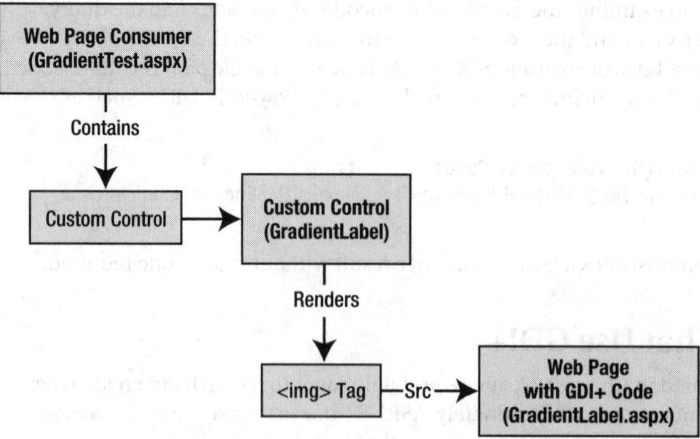

Figure 29-10. *Using custom controls with GDI+*

The Custom Control Class

The first step is to create the control class. This class (named GradientLabel) derives from Control rather than WebControl. That's because it won't be able to support the rich set of style properties because it renders a dynamic graphic, not an HTML tag.

```
Public Class GradientLabel
        Inherits Control
    ...
End Class
```

The GradientLabel class provides five properties, which allow the user to specify the text, the font size, and the colors used for the gradient and text, as follows:

```
Public Property Text() As String
    Get
            Return CStr(ViewState("Text"))
    End Get
    Set
            ViewState("Text") = Value
    End Set
End Property

Public Property TextSize() As Integer
    Get
            Return CInt(ViewState("TextSize"))
    End Get
    Set
            ViewState("TextSize") = Value
    End Set
End Property

Public Property GradientColorA() As Color
    Get
            Return CType(ViewState("ColorA"), Color)
    End Get
    Set
```

```
            ViewState("ColorA") = Value
        End Set
    End Property

    Public Property GradientColorB() As Color
        Get
            Return CType(ViewState("ColorB"), Color)
        End Get
        Set
            ViewState("ColorB") = Value
        End Set
    End Property

    Public Property TextColor() As Color
        Get
            Return CType(ViewState("TextColor"), Color)
        End Get
        Set
            ViewState("TextColor") = Value
        End Set
    End Property
```

The properties are set to some sensible defaults in the GradientLabel constructor, as shown here:

```
Public Sub New()
    Text = String.Empty
    TextColor = Color.White
    GradientColorA = Color.Blue
    GradientColorB = Color.DarkBlue
    TextSize = 14
End Sub
```

The GradientLabel renders itself as an <img> tag that points to the GradientLabel.aspx page. It's the GradientLabel.aspx page that contains the actual GDI+ drawing code. When the GradientLabel is rendered, it reads the information from all the properties and supplies the information in the query string.

```
Protected Overrides Sub Render(ByVal writer As HtmlTextWriter)
    Dim context As HttpContext = HttpContext.Current
    writer.Write("<img src='" & "GradientLabel.aspx?" & _
            "Text=" & context.Server.UrlEncode(Text) & _
            "&TextSize=" & TextSize.ToString() & "&TextColor=" & _
            TextColor.ToArgb() & "&GradientColorA=" & _
            GradientColorA.ToArgb() & "&GradientColorB=" & _
            GradientColorB.ToArgb() & "'>")
End Sub
```

The Rendering Page

The first step for the GradientLabel.aspx page is to retrieve the properties from the query string, as follows:

```
Protected Sub Page_Load(ByVal sender As Object, ByVal e As System.EventArgs)
    Dim text As String = Server.UrlDecode(Request.QueryString("Text"))
    Dim textSize As Integer = Integer.Parse(Request.QueryString("TextSize"))
    Dim textColor As Color =
        Color.FromArgb(Int32.Parse(Request.QueryString("TextColor")))
    Dim gradientColorA As Color =
```

```
        Color.FromArgb(Int32.Parse(Request.QueryString("GradientColorA")))
    Dim gradientColorB As Color =
        Color.FromArgb(Int32.Parse(Request.QueryString("GradientColorB")))
    ...
```

The GradientLabel.aspx has an interesting challenge. The text and font size are supplied dynamically, so it's impossible to use a fixed bitmap size without the risk of creating it too small (so that some text content is cut off) or too large (so that extra server memory is wasted and the image takes longer to send to the client). One way to try to resolve this problem is to create the Font object you want to use and then invoke the Graphics.MeasureString() argument to determine how many pixels are required to display the desired text. The only caveat is that you need to be careful not to allow the bitmap to become too large. For example, if the user submits a string with hundreds of characters, you don't want to create a bitmap that's dozens of megabytes in size! To avoid this risk, the rendering code imposes a maximum height and width of 800 pixels.

■Tip You can also use an alternative version of the DrawString() method that accepts a rectangle in which you want to place the text. This version of DrawString() automatically wraps the text if there's room for more than one line. You could use this approach to allow the display of large amounts of text over several lines.

Here's the portion of the drawing code that retrieves the query string information and measures the text:

```
...
' Define the font.
Dim font As New Font("Tahoma", textSize, FontStyle.Bold)

' Use a test image to measure the text.
Dim theImage As New Bitmap(1, 1)
Dim g As Graphics = Graphics.FromImage(theImage)
Dim size As SizeF = g.MeasureString(text, font)
g.Dispose()
theImage.Dispose()

' Using these measurements, try to choose a reasonable bitmap size.
' Even if the text is large, cap the size at some maximum to
' prevent causing a serious server slowdown!
Dim width As Integer = CInt(Math.Min(size.Width + 20, 800))
Dim height As Integer = CInt(Math.Min(size.Height + 20, 800))
theImage = New Bitmap(width, height)
g = Graphics.FromImage(theImage)
...
```

You'll see that in addition to the size needed for the text, an extra 20 pixels are added to each dimension. This allows for a padding of 10 pixels on each side.

Finally, you can create the LinearGradientBrush, paint the drawing surface, and then add the text, as follows:

```
    ...
    Dim brush As New LinearGradientBrush(
      New Rectangle(New Point(0,0), theImage.Size),
        gradientColorA, gradientColorB,
        LinearGradientMode.ForwardDiagonal)

    ' Draw the gradient background.
    g.FillRectangle(brush, 0, 0, 300, 300)
```

```
    ' Draw the label text.
    g.DrawString(text, font, New SolidBrush(textColor), 10, 10)

    ' Render the image to the output stream.
    theImage.Save(Response.OutputStream, System.Drawing.Imaging.ImageFormat.Jpeg)

    g.Dispose()
    theImage.Dispose()
End Sub
```

To test the label, you can create a control tag like this:

```
<cc1:gradientlabel id="GradientLabel1" runat="server"
  Text="Test String" GradientColorA="MediumSpringGreen"
  GradientColorB="RoyalBlue"></cc1:gradientlabel>
```

Figure 29-11 shows the rendered result.

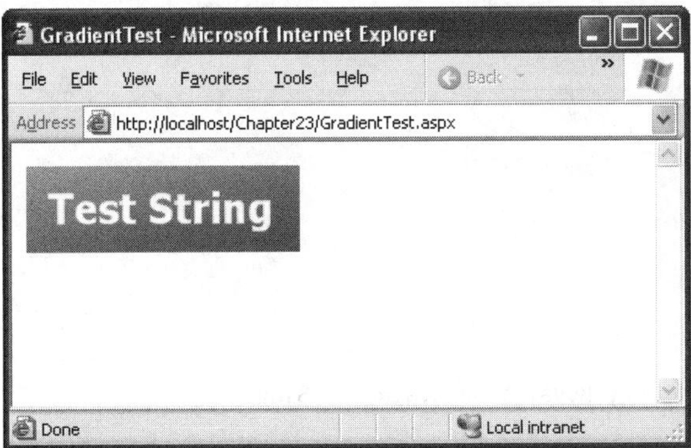

Figure 29-11. *A GDI+ label custom control*

This control still has many shortcomings. Notably, it can't size the drawing surface or wrap its text dynamically, and it doesn't allow the user to set the text font or the spacing between the text and the border. To complete the control, you would need to find a way to pass this extra information in the query string. Clearly, if you want to create a practical web control using GDI+, you have a significant amount of work to do.

Charting with GDI+

When the query approach works, it's a great logical way to solve the problem of sending information from an ordinary page to a page that creates a dynamic graphic. However, it won't always work. One of the problems with the query string is that it's limited to a relatively small amount of string data. If you need to send something more complex, such as an object or a block of binary data, you need to find another technique.

One realistic solution is to use the Session collection. This has more overhead, because everything you put in the Session collection uses server memory, but it allows you to transmit any serializable type of data, including custom objects. To get a feel for why you might want to use the Session collection, it helps to consider a more advanced example.

The next example uses GDI+ to create a graphical pie chart. Because the pie chart is drawn dynamically, your code can build it according to information in a database or information supplied by the user. In this example, the user adds each slice of the pie using the web page, and the image is redrawn automatically. The slices are sent to the dynamic image page through the Session collection as special PieSlice objects.

To create this example, the first step is to create the PieSlice object. Each PieSlice includes a text label and a numeric value, as shown here:

```
Public Class PieSlice
    Dim p_dataValue As Single
    Public Property DataValue() As Single
        Get
                Return p_dataValue
        End Get
        Set
                p_dataValue = Value
        End Set
    End Property

    Dim p_caption As String
    Public Property Caption() As String
        Get
                Return p_caption
        End Get
        Set
                p_caption = Value
        End Set
    End Property

    Public Sub New(ByVal m_caption As String, ByVal m_dataValue As Single)
        Caption = m_caption
        DataValue = m_dataValue
    End Sub

    Public Overrides Function ToString() As String
        Return Caption & " (" & DataValue.ToString() & ")"
    End Function
End Class
```

The PieSlice class overrides the ToString() method to facilitate display in a data-bound ListBox. When a ListBox contains custom objects, it calls the ToString() method to get the text to show. (Another approach would be to use a GridView with a custom template.)

The test page (shown in Figure 29-12) has the responsibility of letting the user create pie slices. Essentially, the user enters a label and a numeric value for the slice and then clicks the Add button. The PieSlice object is then created and shown in a ListBox.

The amount of code required is fairly small. The trick is that every time the page is finished processing (and the Page.PreRender event fires), all the PieSlice objects in the ListBox are stored in session state. Every time the page is requested (and the Page.Load event fires), any available PieSlice objects are retrieved from session state.

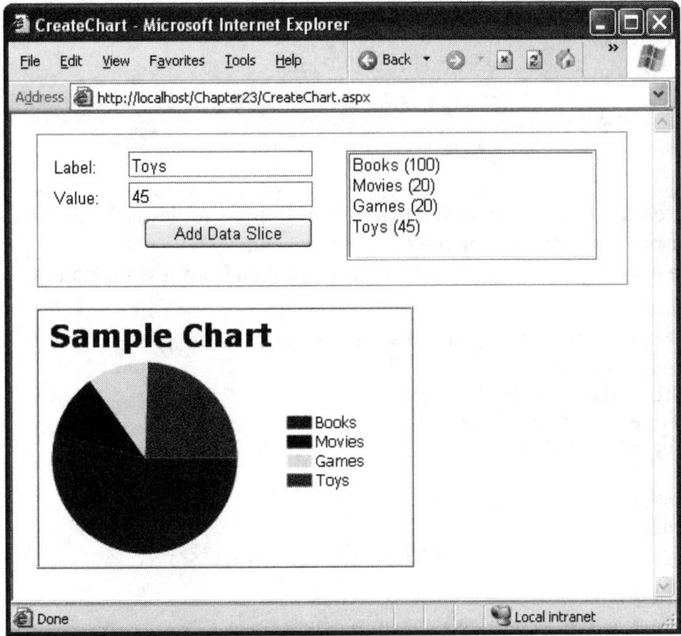

Figure 29-12. *A dynamic pie chart page*

Here's the complete code for the test page:

```
Public Class CreateChart
    Inherits System.Web.UI.Page

    Protected lstPieSlices As ListBox
    Protected cmdAdd As Button
    Protected txtLabel As TextBox
    Protected txtValue As TextBox

    ' The data that will be used to create the pie chart.
    Dim pieSlices As New ArrayList()

    Protected Sub Page_Load(ByVal sender As Object, ByVal e As System.EventArgs)
        ' Retrieve the pie slices that are defined so far.
        If Session("ChartData") IsNot Nothing Then
            pieSlices = CType(Session("ChartData"), ArrayList)
        End If
    End Sub

    Protected Sub cmdAdd_Click(ByVal sender As Object, ByVal e As System.EventArgs)
        ' Create a new pie slice.
        Dim pieSlice As New PieSlice(txtLabel.Text, Single.Parse(txtValue.Text))
        pieSlices.Add(pieSlice)

        ' Bind the list box to the new data.
        lstPieSlices.DataSource = pieSlices
        lstPieSlices.DataBind()
    End Sub
```

```
    Protected Sub CreateChart_PreRender(ByVal sender As Object,
        ByVal e As System.EventArgs)
        ' Before rendering the page, store the current collection
        ' of pie slices.
        Session("ChartData") = pieSlices
    End Sub
End Class
```

The pie-drawing code is quite a bit more involved. It creates a new bitmap, retrieves the PieSlice objects, examines them, and draws the corresponding pie slices and legend.

The first step is to create the drawing surface and retrieve the chart data from session state, as follows:

```
Protected Sub Page_Load(ByVal sender As Object, ByVal e As System.EventArgs)
    Dim theImage As New Bitmap(300, 200)
    Dim g As Graphics = Graphics.FromImage(theImage)
    g.FillRectangle(Brushes.White, 0, 0, 300, 200)
    g.SmoothingMode = SmoothingMode.AntiAlias

    If Session("ChartData") IsNot Nothing Then
        ' Retrieve the chart data.
        Dim chartData As ArrayList = CType(Session("ChartData"), ArrayList)
        ...
```

Next, the drawing code adds a title to the chart, as you can see here:

```
...
' Write some text to the image.
g.DrawString("Sample Chart", New Font("Verdana", 18, FontStyle.Bold), _
        Brushes.Black, New PointF(5, 5))
...
```

The next step is to calculate the total of all the data points, as follows. This allows you to size each slice proportionately in the pie.

```
...
' Calculate the total of all data values.
Dim total As Single = 0
    For Each item As PieSlice In chartData
        total += item.DataValue
    Next
...
```

Once you know the total, you can calculate the percentage of the pie that each slice occupies. Finally, you can multiply this percentage by the total angle width of a circle (360 degrees) to find the angle width required for that slice.

To draw each slice, you can use the Graphics.FillPie() method and specify the starting and ending angle. When you draw each slice, you also need to ensure that you choose a new color that hasn't been used for a previous slice. This task is handled by a GetColor() helper method, which chooses the color from a short list based on the slice's index number:

```
...
 ' Draw the pie slices.
Dim currentAngle As Single = 0, totalAngle As Single = 0
Dim i As Integer = 0
For Each item As PieSlice In chartData
    currentAngle = item.DataValue / total * 360
    g.FillPie(New SolidBrush
          (GetColor(i)), 10, 40, 150, 150,
          CSng(Math.Round(totalAngle)),
```

```
            CSng(Math.Round(currentAngle)))
        totalAngle += currentAngle
        i += 1
    Next
    ...
```

The last drawing step is to render the legend. To create the legend, you need a rectangle that shows the slice color, followed by the pie slice label. Once again, the GetColor() method returns the correct color for the slice:

```
...
     ' Create a legend for the chart.
Dim colorBoxPoint As New PointF(200, 83)
Dim textPoint As New PointF(222, 80)

i = 0
For Each item As PieSlice In chartData
    g.FillRectangle(New SolidBrush(GetColor(i)),
        colorBoxPoint.X, colorBoxPoint.Y, 20, 10)
    g.DrawString(item.Caption, New Font("Tahoma", 10), Brushes.Black, textPoint)
    colorBoxPoint.Y += 15
    textPoint.Y += 15
    i += 1
Next item
...
```

Finally, you can render the image. In this case, GIF is acceptable because the drawing code uses a fixed set of colors that are all in the basic 256-color GIF palette, as follows:

```
        theImage.Save(Response.OutputStream, ImageFormat.Gif)
    End If
End Sub
```

The only detail that has been omitted so far is the GetColor() method, which returns a color for each pie slice, as shown here:

```
Private Function GetColor(ByVal index As Integer) As Color
    ' Support six different colors. This could be enhanced.
    If index > 5 Then
        index = index Mod 5
    End If

    Select Case index
        Case 0
            Return Color.Red
        Case 1
            Return Color.Blue
        Case 2
            Return Color.Yellow
        Case 3
            Return Color.Green
        Case 4
            Return Color.Orange
        Case 5
            Return Color.Purple
        Case Else
            Return Color.Black
    End Select
End Function
```

In its current implementation, GetColor() starts to return the same set of colors as soon as you reach the seventh slice, although you could easily change this behavior.

The end result is that both pages work together without a hitch. Every time a new slice is added, the image is redrawn seamlessly.

You could do a fair bit to improve this chart. For example, you could make it more generic so that it could render to different sizes, display larger amounts of data in the legend, and provide different labeling options. You could also render different types of charts, such as line charts and bar graphs.

■ **Tip** To take a look at a more ambitious pie-chart/bar-chart renderer, you can download a free starter kit sample from Microsoft's ASP.NET website at `http://www.asp.net/ReportsStarterKit`. This sample is available in C# and VB .NET and is free to customize as you desire. Although it sports improved drawing logic, the mechanism used to transfer information is somewhat limited. Because it uses the query string, there's a limit to how much chart data you can specify. Of course, nothing is stopping you from improving the example to support other options, such as session state.

Summary

In this chapter, you learned how to master basic and advanced GDI+. Although these techniques aren't right for every web page, they give you a set of features that can't be matched by many other web application programming frameworks. You also explored how to create server-side image maps with the ImageMap control. For even more detailed information about how GDI+ works and how to optimize it, you may be interested to check out *Pro .NET 2.0 Graphics Programming* (Apress, 2005).

CHAPTER 30

Portals with WebPart Pages

Websites are more sophisticated than ever. Nowadays it's not enough if a website has a great look and feel. It has to be easy to use and must present exactly the information that users want to see. In addition, users want websites to present this information in a specific way—based on their individual preferences. Therefore, personalization and user profiles have become more important in web development.

But users want to be able to customize more than simple profile information. They want to be able to customize the website's user interface to fit their requirements with the goal of accessing the information they need for their daily business as soon as they are logged in. So, in this chapter, you will learn how you can create modular and dynamically configurable web pages to fulfill these sorts of requirements using the ASP.NET 2.0 WebParts Framework and personalization features.

Typical Portal Pages

In a personalized environment, users want specific information stored in a profile, as you learned in Chapter 24. Furthermore, users want to be able to customize most of a website's appearance and the information it displays.

A good example of a personalized website is Microsoft's MSN. As soon as you log into MSN, you can configure the information displayed on your personal home page. For example, MSN allows you to select the types of information items you can see and then displays those pieces of information on your personal home page, as shown in Figure 30-1.

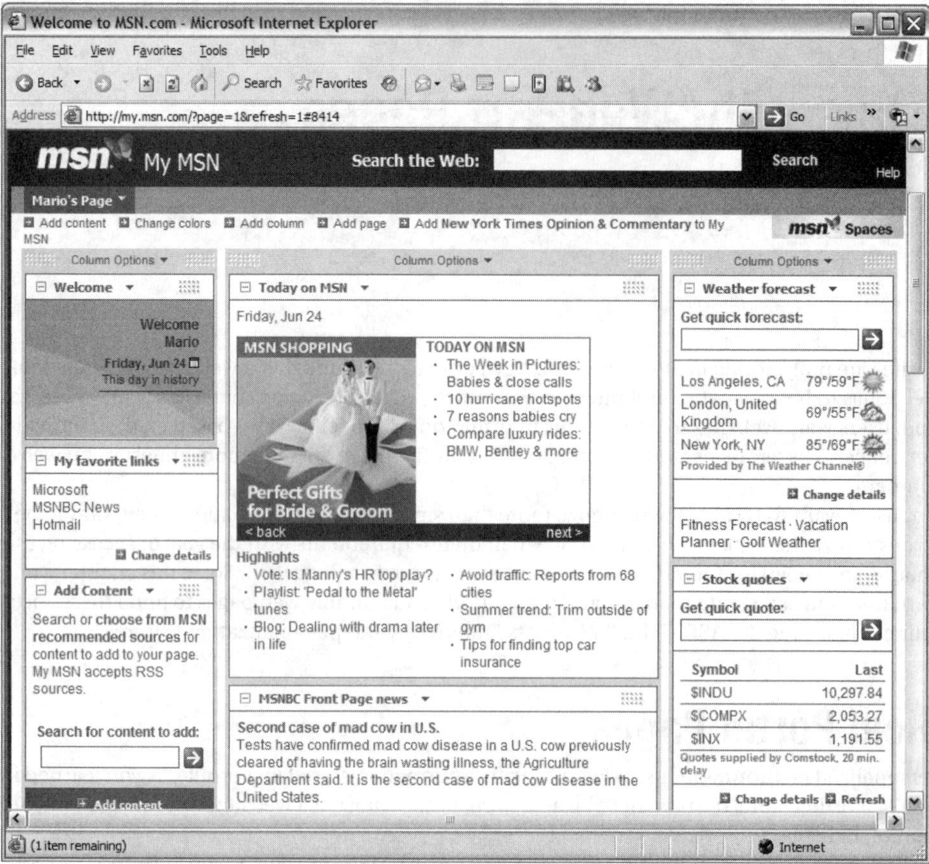

Figure 30-1. *MSN: A good example of a personalized home page*

Some of the information items you can select are simple, such as the search item displayed in the upper-right corner of Figure 30-1, and others are more complex, such as the stock quotes listed in the bottom-right corner. Interestingly, you have many more possibilities than just selecting information items. You can specify where the information is displayed on the page by dragging items into different positions on the web page. When you log off and then later return to the page and log in, all the changes you have made will be present—the page design will appear exactly how you left it.

These types of pages define content areas where the user can add or remove information items. The user can select the information items from a list of available items, which are nothing more than reusable user interface elements (or controls in ASP.NET), and add them to the specified content areas of the web page. In most cases, a portal page defines multiple content areas: a main area in the center of the page for displaying the most important information, a navigational area in the left or right section of the page, and optionally another area (either on the left or right side of the page) for small items (such as a weather item or a quick-links list). Of course, most web pages also include a header and footer (which you can create easily with master pages).

With the ASP.NET 2.0 WebParts Framework, you can create customizable web pages on your own easily. The framework consists of controls and components that perform the following work for you:

Defining customizable sections: The framework allows you to structure your page and specify customizable sections of the page through WebPartZones.

Offering components for item selection: In addition to customizable sections, the framework ships with special sections that allow you to edit properties for information items displayed on the page or to add and remove information items to/from the page.

Customizing the web page: As soon as the user is logged into your application, she can customize the web page by dragging and dropping items displayed on the web page onto different customizable sections. The user can even close or minimize content to create more space for other, more interesting content.

Saving the customized appearance: ASP.NET automatically saves the user's personalized appearance of the web page through its personalization infrastructure.

A page that uses this framework is called a *WebPart page*, and the information items that can be displayed on the page are called *WebParts*. All the pieces you put together to display on the page are controls, as you will see in the next section. Therefore, to create WebPart pages, you just need to know how to put all your custom and prebuilt controls together to create a customizable page. You will learn the details of how to do this in this chapter.

Basic WebPart Pages

The first thing you need to know is how to create a basic WebPart page. In the following sections, you will learn the major steps for creating such a page. After that, you will learn how to create WebParts, which are the information items that go on the WebPart page.

The steps for creating a WebPart page are as follows:

1. *Create the page*: Create a simple ASP.NET page as usual with Visual Studio .NET. You don't need any special type of page—this is an .aspx page just as any other page. Before you continue, you can structure the layout of your page using HTML tables to create, for example, a page with a navigation area, a main area, and a side panel for additional information (similar to the MSN page presented in Figure 30-1).
2. *Add a WebPartManager*: Next, you need to add a WebPartManager control to your page. This is an invisible control that knows about all the available WebParts on a page and manages personalization. The WebPartManager needs to be the first control created on a WebPart page, because every other WebPart-related control depends on it.
3. *Add WebPartZones*: Every section on the page that should display your custom WebParts is encapsulated in an instance of the WebPartZone. Add a WebPartZone on every section of your page that should contain WebParts and should be customizable.
4. *Add WebParts*: You can use simple user controls, prebuilt user controls, custom server controls, or controls directly inherited from WebPart. You can place all these controls into a WebPartZone using the Visual Studio designer or using the code. The ASP.NET infrastructure does the rest automatically.
5. *Add prebuilt zones and parts*: If the user wants to add or remove WebParts at runtime or edit properties of WebParts, you need to add prebuilt zones to your web page, such as the CatalogZone (which allows the user to add WebParts to the page).

After you have completed these steps, your WebPart page is ready to use. Remember that you need to include authentication (either Windows or forms authentication) to your application so that the framework can store personalized information on a per-user basis. By default this information is stored in the SQL Server 2005 file-based database ASPNETDB.MDF, which is automatically created in the App_Data directory if you have SQL Server 2005 installed. Otherwise, you need to create the database on SQL Server using aspnet_regsql.exe, as described in Chapter 21 (personalization information is stored in the same database as user information). Of course, as is the case with any other part of the framework, and as you have learned for the membership and roles APIs, your custom provider can replace the personalization infrastructure without affecting the application.

Creating the Page Design

The first step of creating a WebPart page is to create an .aspx page in your solution. You don't have to add a special item—just add a simple web form to your project. Afterward, you can structure the basic layout of your page as you'd like.

The following example uses a simple HTML table to structure the page with a main center area, a configuration area on the left, and a simple information area on the right:

```
<form id="form1" runat="server">
<div>
<table width="100%">
    <tr valign="middle" bgcolor="#00ccff">
        <td colspan="2">
            <span style="font-size: 16pt; font-family: Verdana">
            <strong>Welcome to web part pages!</strong>
            </span>
        </td>
        <td>Menu</td>
    </tr>
    <tr valign="top">
        <td width="20%">
        </td>
        <td style="width: 60%">
        </td>
        <td width="20%">
        </td>
    </tr>
</table>
</div>
</form>
```

The first table row is just a simple header for the application. Within the second row, the table contains three columns: the left one will be used as a column for configuration controls (such as a control for selecting available WebParts), the center column will be used for displaying the main information, and the right column will be used for little WebParts with additional information. Notice that the first row includes a second column for a menu; you will use this menu later for switching between the modes of the page (for example, from the Browse mode that merely displays information to the Design mode that allows the user to move WebParts from one zone to another). You can see the page layout in Figure 30-2.

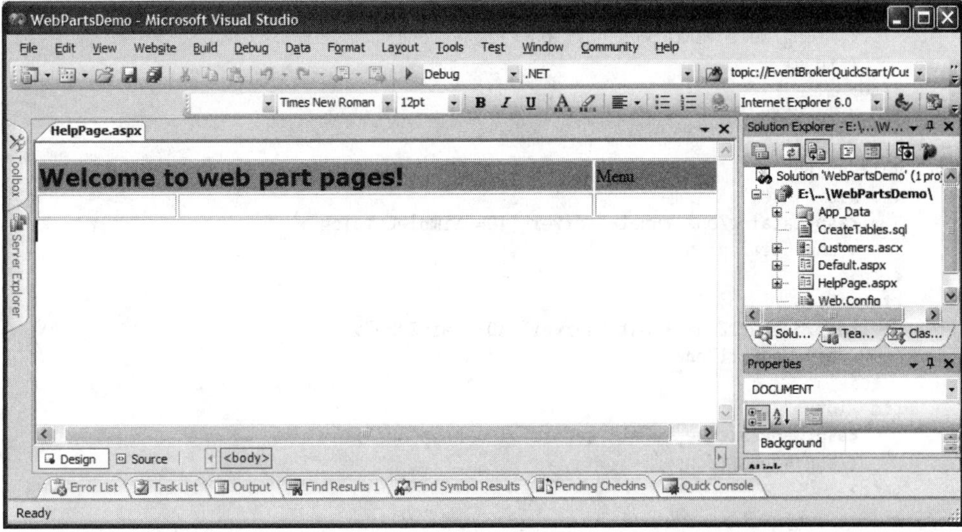

Figure 30-2. *The basic layout of the page*

WebPartManager and WebPartZones

After you have created the web page's design, you can continue adding the first WebPart controls to your page. These controls are summarized in the WebParts section of Visual Studio's Toolbox. For this example, the first control to add at the bottom of your page is the WebPartManager control. The WebPartManager works with all the zones added to the web page and knows about all the WebParts available for the page. It furthermore manages the personalization and makes sure the web page is customized for the currently logged-on user. The following code snippet shows the modified portion of the page code:

```
<form id="form1" runat="server">
<div>
<asp:WebPartManager runat="server" ID="MyPartManager" />
<table width="100%">
    ...
</table>
</div>
</form>
```

The WebPartManager also throws events you can catch in your application to perform actions when the user adds or deletes a WebPart or when a WebPart communicates with another WebPart. (You will learn more about WebPart communication later in the "Connecting WebParts" section.)

After you have added the WebPartManager to the page, you can add customizable sections to your WebPart. These sections are called *WebPartZones,* and every zone can contain as much WebParts as the user wants. With the WebPartZone controls added, the complete code looks as follows:

```
<form id="form1" runat="server">
<div>
<asp:WebPartManager runat="server" ID="MyPartManager" />
<table width="100%">
    <tr valign="middle" bgcolor="#00ccff">
        <td colspan="2">
```

```
            <span style="font-size: 16pt; font-family: Verdana">
            <strong>Welcome to web part pages!</strong>
            </span>
        </td>
        <td>Menu</td>
    </tr>
    <tr valign="top">
        <td width="20%">
            <asp:CatalogZone runat="server" ID="SimpleCatalog">
            </asp:CatalogZone>
        </td>
        <td style="width: 60%">
            <asp:WebPartZone runat="server" ID="MainZone">
            </asp:WebPartZone>
        </td>
        <td width="20%">
            <asp:WebPartZone runat="server" ID="HelpZone">
            </asp:WebPartZone>
        </td>
    </tr>
</table>
</div>
</form>
```

As you can see, the page now contains three zones: two zones for adding custom WebParts to the page and one special zone. The special zone is a CatalogZone, which displays every WebPart that is available for the current page. It displays the list of available WebParts and allows the user to select WebParts from this list and add them to the page. In the designer, the previous code looks like Figure 30-3.

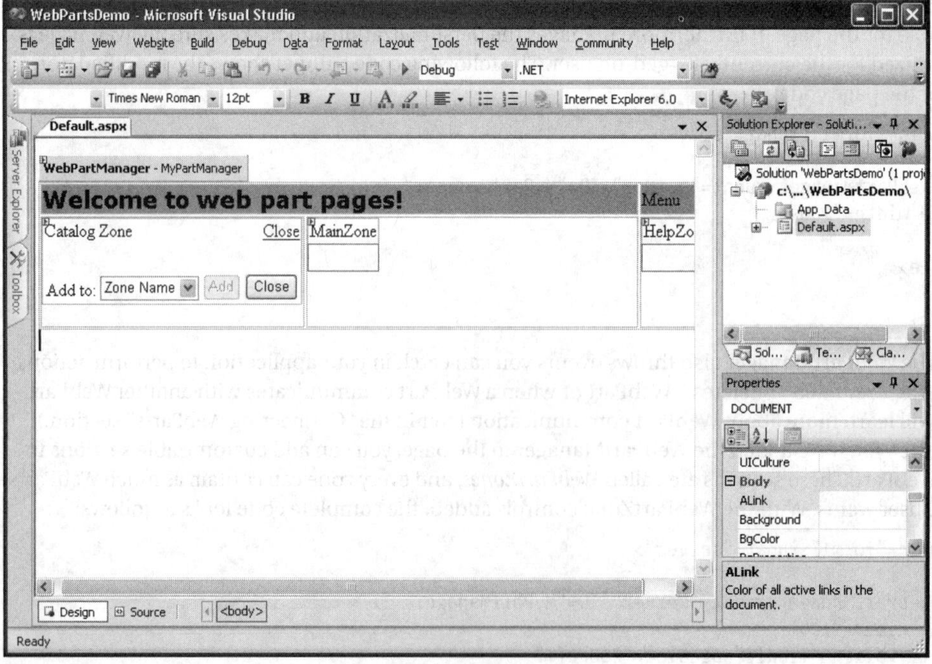

Figure 30-3. *WebPart pages in the Visual Studio designer*

Adding WebParts to the Page

Now you can start adding WebParts to the web page. A *WebPart* is basically an ASP.NET control. You can use any type of control, including existing server controls, existing user controls, and custom server controls you have created on your own. You don't even need to implement any special interfaces if you don't need to interact with the WebParts infrastructure or with other WebParts on the page. Adding controls to a WebPart page is as simple as adding controls to a basic page. The only difference is that you add the controls to one of the previously added WebPartZone controls instead of to the page directly. For this purpose, WebPartZones use templates. The concept is the same as with grid controls, where you can specify a template that is created for every row in the grid. The template just defines the appearance of the WebPart. You can add existing server controls to a zone as follows:

```
<asp:WebPartZone runat="server" ID="HelpZone">
    <ZoneTemplate>
        <asp:Calendar runat="server" ID="MyCalendar" />
        <asp:FileUpload ID="FileUpload1" runat="server" />
    </ZoneTemplate>
</asp:WebPartZone>
```

The previous example shows the WebPartZone control you added earlier in this chapter for the right section of your page. This zone now contains two controls: the standard Calendar control as well as a FileUpload control. Figure 30-4 shows the page in the Visual Studio designer after you have added this zone template.

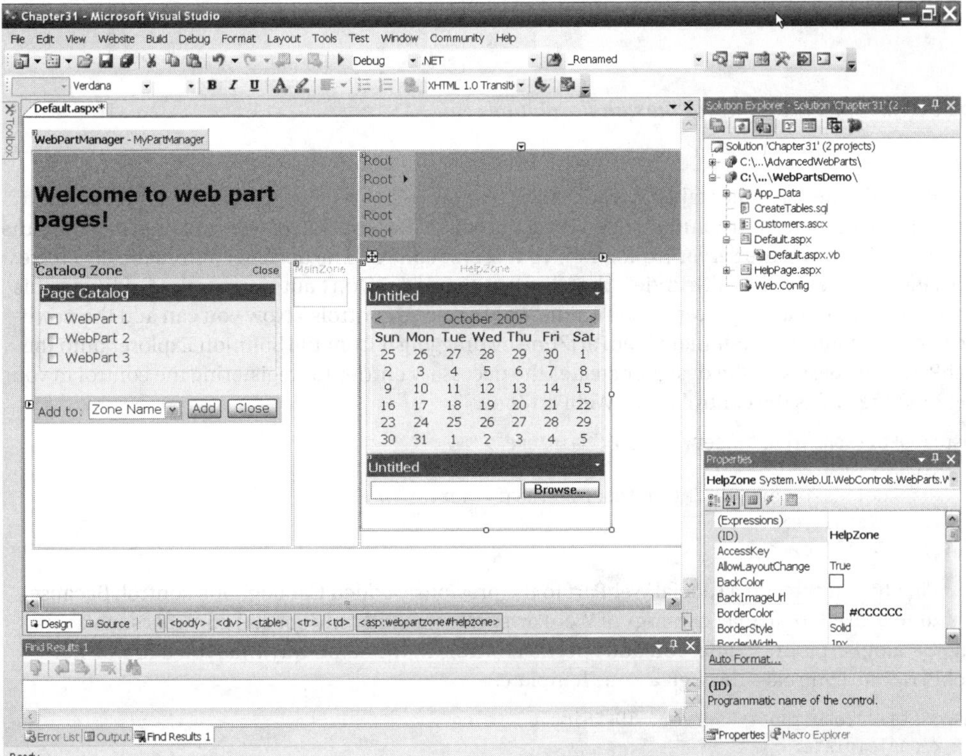

Figure 30-4. *A WebPartZone with controls added*

Of course, you can create one or more user controls and add them to one of the WebPartZones. For example, create the database tables shown in Figure 30-5, and fill in some test records so that you can use them for extending the sample later.

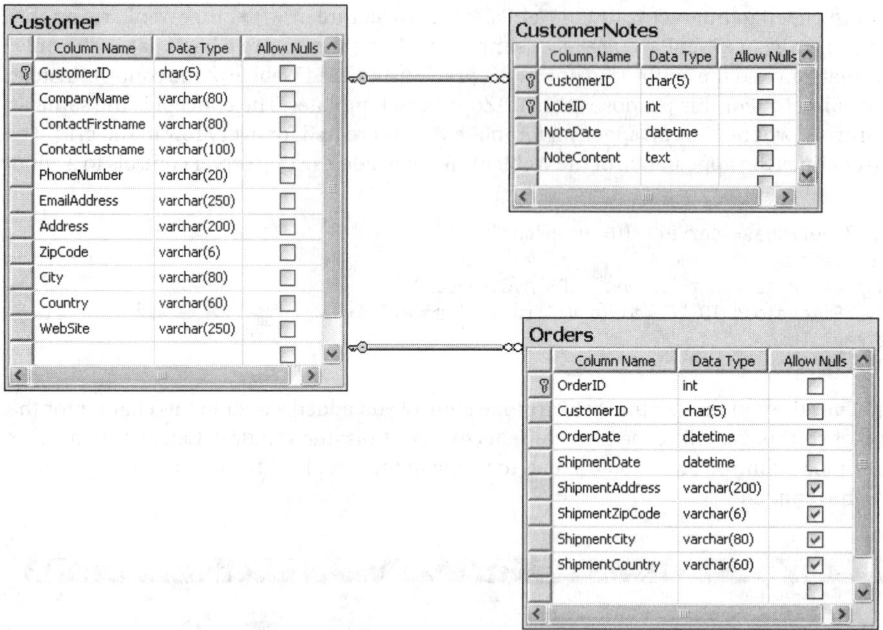

Figure 30-5. *Database tables for the sample solution*

Based on the Customer table, we will show you how to create your first WebPart now. Just add a new user control to your solution, open the database in the Server Explorer, and drag and drop the Customer table from the Server Explorer on your server control. The designer automatically creates the data source as well as a GridView that displays the data. (Don't autoformat the GridView; this will happen automatically later, based on the WebPartZone controls.) Now you can add the newly created user control to your main WebPartZone by dragging it from the Solution Explorer onto the WebPartZone. Basically, the designer creates the necessary entries for registering the control in your page and then adds the control to the WebPartZone.

```
<asp:WebPartZone runat="server" ID="MainZone">
    <ZoneTemplate>
        <uc1:Customers ID="MyCustomers" runat="server" />
    </ZoneTemplate>
</asp:WebPartZone>
```

Finally, you can add a special WebPart to the previously added CatalogZone control. Because this zone is used to display catalogs of WebParts, you can add only special controls such as the PageCatalogPart to this zone. You add special controls in the same way that you add normal WebPartZone controls—through a ZoneTemplate.

```
<asp:CatalogZone runat="server" ID="SimpleCatalog">
    <ZoneTemplate>
        <asp:PageCatalogPart runat="server" ID="MyCatalog" />
    </ZoneTemplate>
</asp:CatalogZone>
```

Before you start the web application, you can autoformat WebPartZone controls by opening the smart tag for the corresponding zone. You will see that formatting applies automatically to every control that is placed directly into a zone. Next, test the application by running your created WebPart page, and then you can debug the page. When you start the solution for debugging the page, you will see the screen in Figure 30-6 (depending on your autoformat selections).

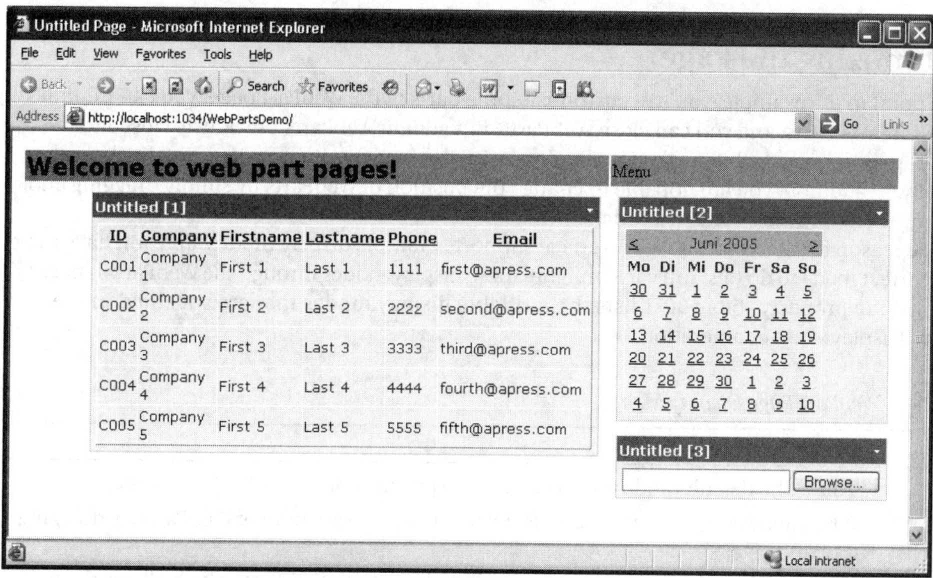

Figure 30-6. *The WebPart page displayed in the browser*

You may notice that for every WebPart a title and a box for minimizing and restoring the WebPart is displayed with default captions. Later in the "Customizing the Page" section, you will learn how to customize these captions.

Because you have not configured any authentication method yet, by default the application uses Windows authentication. Therefore, you can customize the WebPart page in terms of minimizing single parts and closing single parts. Without any additional effort, the same is True when you authenticate your users through forms authentication (either with or without using the membership API introduced in Chapter 21). So far, you cannot move WebParts from one zone to another. To do this, you have to switch to a special page mode that you will learn about in the next section. When you close the browser and start another browser session, the page appears in the same layout as when you left it. That's because the WebPartManager stores your changes in the personalization store.

Again, by default these settings are stored in the SQL Server 2005–based ASPNETDB.MDF database that is stored in the App_Data directory if you have not changed any configuration settings. You can change this default behavior by creating a database on the server of your choice using aspnet_regsql.exe. (This tool works with SQL Server only; for other databases, you have to create your own provider.) You can configure the provider with this database as follows:

```
<webParts>
<personalization defaultProvider="MyProvider">
    <providers>
        <add name="MyProvider"
           type="System.Web.UI.WebControls.WebParts.SqlPersonalizationProvider"
           connectionStringName="CustomSqlConnection" />
```

```
    </providers>
</personalization>
</webParts>
```

You have to add the connection string (CustomSqlConnection in this example) to the <connectionStrings> section of the configuration file, and it should point to the database created with aspnet_regsql.exe.

Customizing the Page

At this point in the example, you can customize some parts of the WebPart page; you can minimize and restore WebParts, and you can close WebParts. But adding WebParts previously closed to the WebPart page is not possible, as the CatalogZone with the PageCatalogPart does not display automatically. In addition, you are not able to change the position of WebParts by simply dragging and dropping them from one zone to another.

The reason for this is that a WebPart page supports multiple display modes, and you have to be in the correct mode to do this. You can configure these display modes through the WebPartManager's DisplayMode property. Table 30-1 lists the available display modes that are specified in the WebPartDisplayMode enumeration.

Table 30-1. *WebPart Page Display Modes*

Mode	Description
Browse	This is the default mode and is used for displaying contents of a WebPart page.
Design	When activating this mode, the user can change the position of WebParts by dragging and dropping.
Catalog	If activated, the WebPartManager displays the catalog WebPart, which allows the user to add WebParts to the WebPart page.
Connect	When activated, the user can configure connections between connectable WebParts (more about this later in this section).
Edit	Allows the user to edit properties of WebParts. This mode displays WebParts of an editor. The EditorZone control is one of the prebuilt WebPartZones that you can use to display WebPart editor controls, which allow the user to modify settings for WebParts.

Now, add a Menu control to the first row of your layout table, as follows:

```
<table width="100%">
    <tr valign="middle" bgcolor="#00ccff">
        <td colspan="2" style="height: 104px">
            <span style="font-size: 16pt; font-family: Verdana">
            <strong>Welcome to web part pages!</strong>
            </span>
        </td>
        <td style="height: 104px">
            <asp:Menu ID="PartsMenu" runat="server"
                    OnMenuItemClick="PartsMenu_MenuItemClick">
            </asp:Menu>
        </td>
    </tr>
...
</table>
```

Next, you can create code in your page that populates the menu with all the available display modes for the WebPartManager. To do this, you just need to iterate through the DisplayModes property, which actually is a collection of WebPartDisplayMode items, and verify whether the mode is available. If it is available, just add it to the menu.

```
Protected Sub Page_Load(ByVal sender As Object, ByVal e As EventArgs)
   If (Not Me.IsPostBack) Then
      Dim Root As MenuItem = New MenuItem("Select Mode")

      For Each mode As WebPartDisplayMode In MyPartManager.DisplayModes
         If mode.IsEnabled(MyPartManager) Then
            Root.ChildItems.Add(New MenuItem(mode.Name))
         End If
      Next

      PartsMenu.Items.Add(Root)
   End If
End Sub
```

Remember that you need to populate the menu only on the first request, because with view state enabled, it remembers its state and therefore its child menu items. When the user clicks the menu item, you have to switch to the appropriate WebPart page mode. You can do this by setting the WebPartManager's DisplayMode property to the selected WebPartDisplayMode, as follows:

```
Protected Sub PartsMenu_MenuItemClick(ByVal sender As Object,
          ByVal e As MenuEventArgs)
   For Each mode As WebPartDisplayMode In MyPartManager.DisplayModes
      If mode.Name = e.Item.Text Then
         MyPartManager.DisplayMode = mode
      End If
   Next
End Sub
```

Now when the user selects the Catalog mode from the menu, the CatalogZone with the PageCatalogPart will be visible, and you can add WebParts you closed previously to the WebPart page again (see Figure 30-7).

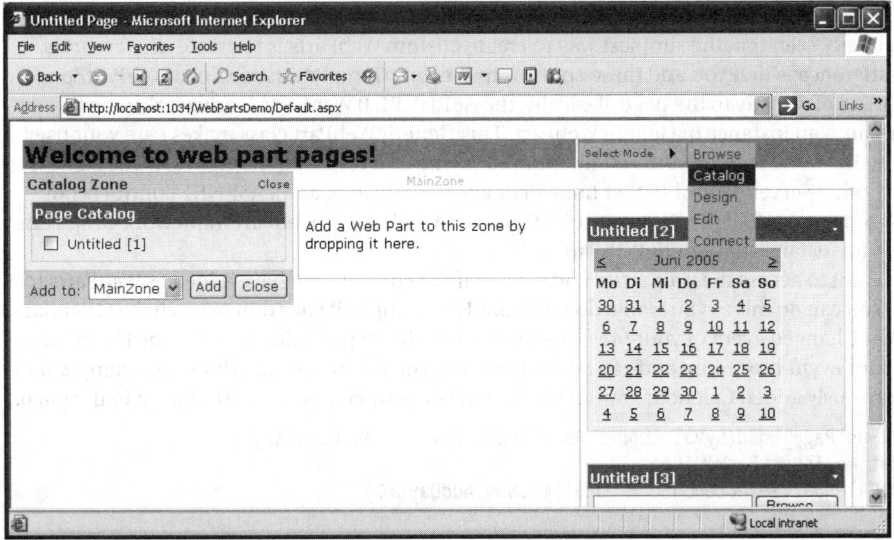

Figure 30-7. *The CatalogZone displayed in the Catalog mode*

■ **Note** Customizing the page via dragging and dropping uses special DHTML features of Internet Explorer and therefore works only for Internet Explorer. All the other features such as adding personalization, minimizing and maximizing windows, and adding WebParts from the catalog to specific zones work with any browser of your choice.

All the changes you make will be stored persistently in the personalization store based on the personalization provider. Later in the "Final Tasks for Personalization" section, you will learn how you can enable and disable personalization at a per-page level. Furthermore, if you are developing a custom WebPart from scratch, you can define properties on the class that are stored in the personalization store. By doing this you can specify whether personalization happens on a per-user basis or is shared across authenticated users. You will learn how to do this in the next section.

Creating WebParts

Now that you know the steps for creating WebPart pages with ASP.NET 2.0, it's time to take a closer look at WebPart development. As you know, a WebPart can be any type of ASP.NET control, including user controls, built-in or custom server controls, and ASP.NET controls directly inherited from the WebPart base class of the new namespace System.Web.UI.WebControls.WebParts.

You have seen that every WebPart on your page automatically gets a default caption and default menus for minimizing and restoring the WebPart. Now it's time to learn how you can customize this text and add menu entries (called *verbs*) to your custom WebPart. Any WebPart can provide custom public properties that the user can modify through an editor WebPart, which can be added to a WebPart called EditorZone. This EditorZone is displayed when the WebPart page is switched to the Edit mode, as introduced in Table 30-1. To do this, you have to create a separate editor part for your WebPart and somehow connect them. The next section shows how to do this.

Finally, WebParts can communicate with other WebParts through a well-defined mechanism. Therefore, these WebParts exchange data and display information based on events that happen in other WebParts. You will learn how to connect WebParts in the "Connecting WebParts" section.

Simple WebPart Tasks

You have already seen that the simplest way to create custom WebParts is to create user controls. The only difference is that you add these controls to the ZoneTemplate section of a WebPartZone control instead of directly to the page. Basically, the ASP.NET 2.0 WebParts Framework wraps your user control into an instance of GenericWebPart. This GenericWebPart class makes sure your user control gets the frame and the verbs menu for minimizing and restoring the WebPart. The same is true for any other server control (either built-in or custom): As long as an ASP.NET control is not inherited from System.Web.UI.WebControls.WebParts.WebPart, the WebPart framework wraps this control into an instance of GenericWebPart.

If you want to access the properties and events of the controls you have added as WebParts to your page, you can do this as you would do normally. For example, if you want to catch the Calendar's SelectedDateChanged event of your previously created WebPart page, double-click the Calendar. You'll see your event procedure and can add some code. The following code shows an example that sets the previously added Calendar control's SelectedDate property on the first request to the page:

```
Protected Sub Page_Load(ByVal sender As Object, ByVal e As EventArgs)
    If (Not Me.IsPostBack) Then
        MyCalendar.SelectedDate = DateTime.Now.AddDays(7)
    End If
  ...
End Sub
```

So, you have complete access to the controls added as WebParts and don't have to do anything special here. But what if you want to access WebPart-specific properties such as the title of the WebPart or WebPart-specific events? As mentioned, every WebPart that is not inherited from System.Web.UI.WebControls.WebParts.WebPart is wrapped automatically into an instance of GenericWebPart. If you want to access WebPart-specific properties, you somehow have to retrieve the WebPart and then set or get the properties you need. Fortunately, the WebPartManager class includes a WebParts collection property that contains all the WebParts available for the page. The advantage of accessing WebParts directly through the WebPartManager is that you don't have to know which WebPartZone control they have been added to (remember that the user can change this as she wants).

The following example uses the WebPartManager's WebParts collection to iterate through the WebPart and assign a default title for every WebPart that has been wrapped into a GenericWebPart class by the framework:

```
Protected Sub Page_Load(ByVal sender As Object, ByVal e As EventArgs)
    If (Not Me.IsPostBack) Then
        Dim i As Integer = 1
        For Each part As WebPart In MyPartManager.WebParts
            If TypeOf part Is GenericWebPart Then
                part.Title = String.Format("Web Part Nr. {0}", i)
                i += 1
            End If
        Next
    End If

  ...
End Sub
```

You can also modify other aspects through the WebPart properties. Table 30-2 shows some typical examples and gives you an overview of the most important properties of a WebPart control.

Table 30-2. *Important Properties of the WebPart Class*

Property	Description
AllowClose	Specifies whether the WebPart can be closed by the user. If set to False, the close menu verb is not displayed in the WebPart's verbs menu.
AllowConnect	Enables or disables connecting functionality of the WebPart.
AllowEdit	Enables or disables editing properties of the WebPart through a custom EditorPart.
AllowHide	If set to True, the user can hide the WebPart on the page.
AllowMinimize	If set to True, the user can minimize the WebPart through the WebPart's minimize menu entry.
AllowZoneChange	When the user should be able to change the position of the WebPart by dragging it from one WebPartZone control to another, you have to set this property to True and otherwise to False (the default is True).
CatalogIconImageUrl	As you have seen previously, the PageCatalogPart displays a list of WebParts available for a page. If you want to add a special icon to be displayed in the PageCatalogPart in the CatalogZone, you can set the CatalogIconImageUrl to a valid image.
ChromeType	Customizes the appearance. You can specify whether the WebPart should have a border, a title bar, and the verbs menu that contains the menu actions for minimizing or closing your WebPart. This property is of type PartChromeType, which supports the values None, BorderOnly, TitleOnly, TitleAndBorder, and Default.

(Continued)

Table 30-2. *Continued*

Property	Description
ChromeState	Defines the WebPart's initial appearance state. This property is of type PartChromeState and can have the values Minimized or Normal so that the WebPart initially is minimized or displayed.
ConnectErrorMessage	Specifies the error message that is displayed if an error occurs when connecting one WebPart to another.
Controls	This important collection gives you access to all the controls that are contained in the WebPart. You'll learn more about this immediately following this table.
Description	Specifies a friendly, user-ready description for the WebPart.
Direction	Specifies the content flow direction (LeftToRight or RightToLeft) within the WebPart.
DisplayTitle	Gets a string that returns the title that is actually displayed in the WebPart. If you haven't set the Title property, it returns the either automatically generated title or the title specified from the containing control.
ExportMode	As you will see later in this chapter, information and settings from WebParts can be exported and imported. This property specifies which parts of a WebPart can be exported or imported.
HasSharedData	Specifies whether the WebPart contains personalized properties that are persisted for multiple users.
HasUserData	Specifies whether the WebPart contains personalized properties that are persisted on a per-user basis.
HelpUrl	Through the HelpUrl property you can specify a URL that returns contents to be displayed as help for the WebPart. This can point to a static HTML page or to any other type of page, including an .aspx page. As soon as this URL is specified, the WebPart displays an additional verb menu for opening the help of this WebPart.
HelpMode	When a HelpUrl is specified, you can determine where the help is displayed. The help can be displayed in a modal or modeless pop-up window, or you can specify to directly navigate to the help page.
Hidden	Gets or sets a value that determines whether the WebPart is hidden on the page.
IsClosed	Gets or sets a value that determines whether the WebPart is closed.
IsShared	Gets or sets a value that determines whether the WebPart is visible for all users or for specific users only. You will learn more about this in the "Authorizing WebParts" section.
IsStandalone	Determines whether the WebPart is visible only to a particular user (True) or to all users (False).
IsStatic	Gets or sets a value that determines whether the WebPage is statically added to the web page through the designer (True) or dynamically imported to the WebPage.
Title	Gets or sets the title to be displayed in the title bar of the WebPart.

Property	Description
TitleUrl	The title can be displayed as URL to point to a details page for the WebPart. If this URL is specified, the WebPart renders the title as a link that points to this URL instead of static text.
Verbs	Returns the entries in the WebPart's menu that typically contains the Minimize, Close, or Help verb. You can customize the verbs by modifying this collection.
Zone	Returns a reference to the WebPartZone control to which the WebPart is currently added.
ZoneIndex	Returns the WebPartZone control's index to which the WebPart is currently added.

As mentioned in Table 30-2, the Controls collection of the WebPart control contains all the controls hosted within the WebPart. When it comes to the GenericWebPart, this collection contains the controls you have added to the WebPartZone control. So, you can iterate through the WebPart controls stored in the Controls collection to find your control and do something with it. The following example shows how you can access the controls of the WebPartPage to set properties of the WebPart that contains the Calendar control added earlier in this chapter:

```
For Each part As WebPart In MyPartManager.WebParts
    If part.Controls.Contains(MyCalendar) Then
        part.AllowClose = False
        part.HelpMode = WebPartHelpMode.Modeless
        part.HelpUrl = "CalendarHelp.htm"
    End If
Next
```

The control added to the WebPartZone control is available directly from within the page. Therefore, if you want to set any WebPart-specific properties when loading the page, you can do this the other way around as well. Instead of iterating through the WebPartManager's WebParts and then accessing every WebPart's Controls collection, it might be faster to catch the control's events and then access the WebPart's properties through the control's parent property, as follows:

```
Protected Sub MyCalendar_Load(ByVal sender As Object, ByVal e As EventArgs)
    Dim part As GenericWebPart = CType(MyCalendar.Parent, GenericWebPart)
    part.AllowClose = False
    part.HelpMode = WebPartHelpMode.Modeless
    part.HelpUrl = "CalendarHelp.htm"
End Sub
```

This is definitely faster than searching controls in collections of controls as shown previously. The previous example is doing the same initialization work as shown in the other example: It disables the close function for the WebPart that contains the calendar MyCalendar and then specifies a help page for the calendar that can be displayed in a modeless pop-up browser window. Figure 30-8 shows the result of these modifications. Take a close look at the menu displayed for the WebPart. Because you have initialized the HelpUrl, it now displays an additional Help menu entry. On the other hand, because you have set the AllowClose property to False, it doesn't contain a Close menu entry anymore.

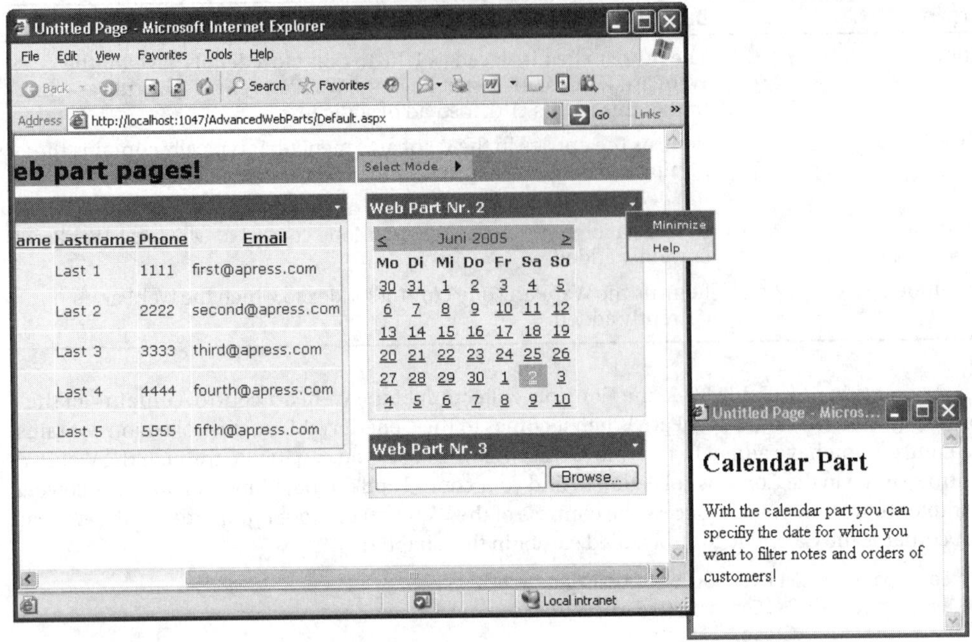

Figure 30-8. *The previously made changes in action*

Implementing the IWebPart Interface

Until now you have accessed WebParts from the outside only. But when creating a user control that will be used as a WebPart on a WebPart page, you can access properties of the WebPart from inside the user control as well. To a certain degree, you can control the WebPart's appearance and behavior in a more detailed manner by implementing the IWebPart interface.

The IWebPart interface defines a contract between your control (a server control or user control), which is used by the GenericWebPart wrapper class to communicate with your control for specific things such as automatically retrieving a control's title so that you don't need to set it from outside every page where you are going to use this WebPart. Table 30-3 lists the members you have to provide in your WebPart when implementing the IWebPart interface.

Table 30-3. *The Members of the IWebPart Interface*

Member	Description
CatalogImageUrl	Gets or sets the URL to an image displayed for the WebPart in the PageCatalogPart of a CatalogZone.
Description	Gets or sets a string that contains a user-friendly description of the WebPart.
Subtitle	Specifies the user-friendly subtitle of the WebPart.
Title	Specifies a title displayed for the WebPart. With this property specified, you don't need to set the title from outside as previously described.
TitleIconImageUrl	URL that points to an image displayed as an icon within the title bar of the WebPart.
TitleUrl	Specifies the URL to which the browser should navigate when the user clicks the title of the WebPart. If this URL is set, the title renders as a link; otherwise, the title renders as static text.

As you can see, implementing this interface is not too much work. You can now implement the interface in the previously created Customers WebPart as follows:

```
Public Partial Class Customers
        Inherits System.Web.UI.UserControl
        Implements IWebPart
    Private _CatalogImageUrl As String
    Public Property CatalogIconImageUrl() As String
        Implements IWebPart.CatalaogIconImageUrl
        Get
            Return _CatalogImageUrl
        End Get
        Set
            _CatalogImageUrl = Value
        End Set
    End Property

    Private _Description As String
    Public Property Description() As String Implements IWebPart.Description
        Get
            Return _Description
        End Get
        Set
            _Description = Value
        End Set
    End Property

    Public ReadOnly Property Subtitle() As String Implements IWebPart.Subtitle
        Get
                Return "Internal Customer List"
        End Get
    End Property

    Private _TitleImage As String
    Public Property TitleIconImageUrl() As String
        Implements IWebPart.TItleIconImageUrl
        Get
            If _TitleImage Is Nothing Then
                Return "CustomersSmall.jpg"
            Else
                Return _TitleImage
            End If
        End Get
        Set
            _TitleImage = Value
        End Set
    End Property

    Private _TitleUrl As String
    Public Property TitleUrl() As String Implements IWebPart.TitleUrl
        Get
            Return _TitleUrl
        End Get
        Set
            _TitleUrl = Value
        End Set
    End Property
```

```
    Public Property Title() As String Implements IWebPart.Title
        Get
            If ViewState("Title") Is Nothing Then
                Return String.Empty
            Else
                Return CStr(ViewState("Title"))
            End If
        End Get
        Set
            ViewState("Title") = Value
        End Set
    End Property
End Class
```

When implementing the IWebPart interface, you should think about which property values you want to put into view state and which values are sufficient as private members. Basically, for saving bytes sent across the wire with the page, you should add as little information as possible to the view state. You should use view state only for information that can be edited by the user while browsing and that you don't want to lose between page postbacks. In the previous example, you used private members for every property of the WebPart but not for the title property because it might change while browsing (for example, if you want to display the current page of the GridView in the title bar as well). When implementing this interface, the information (which is set from outside) is automatically passed in by the GenericWebPart to your control's implementation. Consider the following code in your Default.aspx page:

```
Protected Sub MyCustomers_Load(ByVal sender As Object, ByVal e As EventArgs)
    ' Some of the properties are set; others such as the TitleImageUrl are not!
    Dim part As GenericWebPart = CType(MyCustomers.Parent, GenericWebPart)
    part.Title = "Customers"
    part.TitleUrl = "http://www.apress.com"
    part.Description = "Displays all customers in the database!"
End Sub
```

When someone sets the WebPart's title this way from outside, the GenericWebPart class passes the value to the interface implementation of the Title property so that you can handle the information. On the other hand, if someone queries information such as the Title or TitleUrl, the GenericWebPart retrieves the information from your control by calling the appropriate property in your IWebPart implementation. This way your control can return default values even for properties that have not been explicitly set. Your implementation of the TitleIconImageUrl is doing this. To reiterate, here is the fragment of the previous IWebPart implementation:

```
...
Private _TitleImage As String
Public Property TitleIconImageUrl() As String
     Implements IWebPart.TitleIconImageUrl
    Get
        If _TitleImage Is Nothing Then
            Return "CustomersSmall.jpg"
        Else
            Return _TitleImage
        End If
    End Get
    Set
        _TitleImage = Value
    End Set
End Property
...
```

This property returns a default image URL if no TitleImage has been set. This means even if you don't set this property in the previously shown Load event procedure of your WebPart page, the WebPart displays the CustomersSmall.jpg image as a title image (see Figure 30-9). Although you have not set the TitleImageUrl in the MyCustomers_Load event procedure in the WebPart page, the icon for the title is displayed because of its default value provided through your implementation of IWebPart.

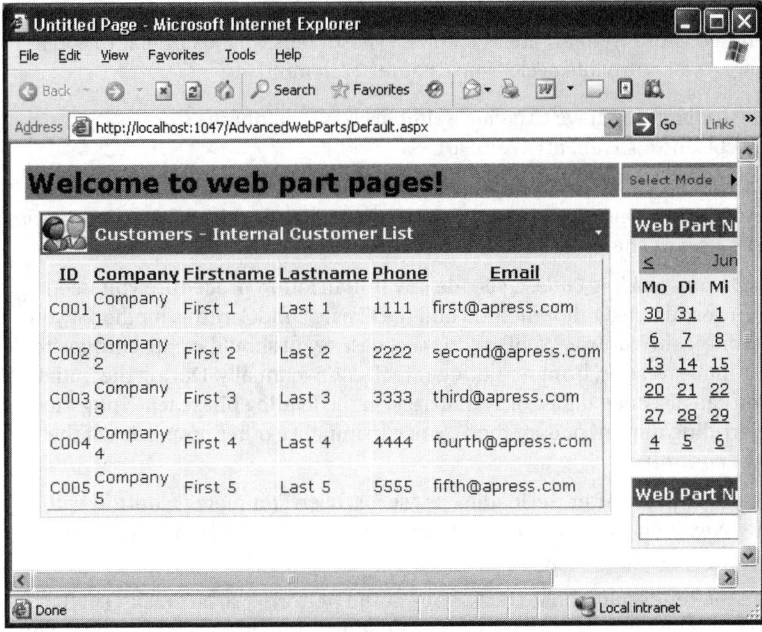

Figure 30-9. *Customized Customers WebPart through the interface implementation*

Developing Advanced WebParts

Implementing WebParts through user controls is a fairly easy way to create WebParts. But user controls have some disadvantages as well:

Restricted reusability: You cannot add them dynamically to WebPart pages of other web applications without manually copying the .ascx file to the directories of the other web application. Manually implemented WebParts can be encapsulated in separate assembly DLLs and therefore can be reused in multiple web applications by referencing them through Add References or by copying the DLL into the target web application's Bin directory.

Restricted personalization: Personalization with user controls is restricted to common properties such as title, title URL, and so on. You cannot have custom properties in the user control that are stored in the personalization store. Only classes that inherit from WebPart can have this sort of functionality.

Therefore, sometimes implementing advanced WebParts as server controls inherited from System.Web.UI.WebControls.WebParts.WebPart is useful. With the basic know-how for creating custom ASP.NET server controls, you are definitely ready to create this sort of WebPart. All you have to keep in mind when creating a custom WebPart this way is that ASP.NET pages and ASP.NET controls are processed by the runtime (which determines the order of control and page events and what to do in each of these events). This makes it much easier because you always have the steps for the implementation in mind. For more information about creating custom server controls, refer to Chapter 27.

The steps for creating a custom WebPart are as follows. (These steps will be familiar to you if you keep the ASP.NET page and control life cycle from Chapter 27 in mind.)

1. *Inherit from WebPart*: First you have to create a simple class that inherits from System.Web.UI.WebControls.WebParts.WebPart.
2. *Add custom properties*: Next, add custom properties of your WebPart and specify through attributes which of those properties can be edited by the user and which of these properties are stored on a per-user or shared basis in the personalization store.
3. *Write initialization and loading code*: Override any initialization procedure you need. Typically you will override the OnInit method and the CreateChildControls method if you want to create a composite control/WebPart. In most cases, you should create composite controls, because that saves you from rendering HTML code manually. During the initialization phase, you can also load data from databases; in the loading phase (catching the Load event or overriding the OnLoad method), you can initialize other properties of the WebPart (or server control).
4. *Catch events of child controls*: After the loading phase has been completed, controls will raise their events. Next you can add the event handlers for your child controls to your custom WebPart.
5. *Prerender*: Before the rendering phase starts, you should perform the last tasks, such as setting the properties of your controls and actually building the control structure based on data sources they are bound to (for example, calling the DataBind method if you don't use the new DataSources programming model).
6. *Render the HTML*: Finally, you have to write code to render your WebPart. This time you don't override the RenderControl method (as is the case for server controls). You have to override the RenderContents method that is called from the base class in between rendering the border, title bar, and title menu with the appropriate verbs.

Keeping these steps in mind, creating a custom WebPart is easy (although it's not as easy as creating WebParts based on user controls). Let's create a simple WebPart using this technique. The WebPart allows customers to add notes to the CustomerNotes table presented in Figure 30-4.

Before You Start: Create Typed DataSets

Before you dig into the details of developing the WebPart, you have to add special components for easily accessing the data stored in the database. (You also need these components to complete the code samples shown in this chapter.)

In the WebParts that you will develop in this chapter, you need to access data from the Customers table and the CustomerNotes table shown in Figure 30-5. For both tables you need to add a typed DataSet (you can find more information about DataSets in Chapter 7 and Chapter 8) to your web application project, as shown in Figure 30-10.

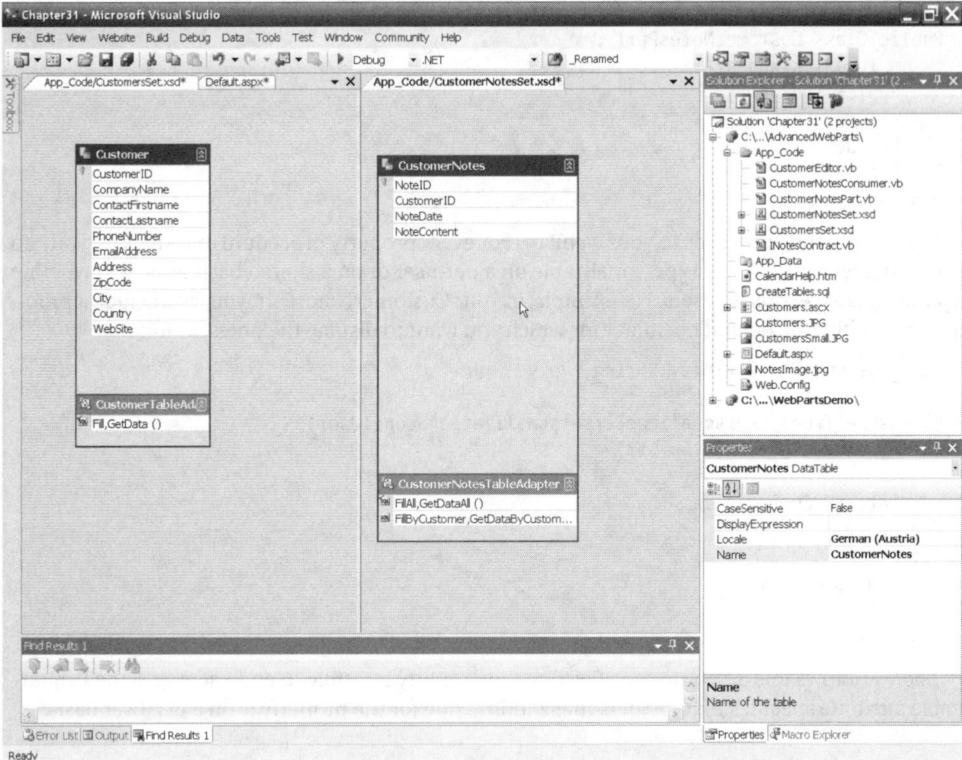

Figure 30-10. *The typed DataSets necessary for the solution*

Both typed DataSets create the DataSet class and typed table adapters that you will use to develop the remaining parts of the web application in this chapter. In general, you should always create the business layer and data access layer before you start creating the actual user interface components—and WebParts are definitely user interface components. Although this step dramatically simplifies the process, it demonstrates that you should always create the business layer and/or data access layer before you start with the actual WebPart implementation. Of course, components in the business layer and data access layer are reusable across different applications just as these two typed DataSets are.

The Custom WebPart's Skeleton

First, you have to create a custom class that inherits from WebPart. Also, you need to include the System.Web.UI.WebControls.WebParts namespace so you have easy access to the WebParts framework classes.

```
Imports System
Imports System.Web.UI
Imports System.Web.UI.WebControls
Imports System.Web.UI.WebControls.WebParts
```

```
Namespace APress.WebParts.Samples
    Public Class CustomerNotesPart
          Inherits WebPart
        Public Sub New()

        End Sub
    End Class
End Namespace
```

Next, add some properties to your WebPart. For every property procedure in your class, you can specify whether the property is personalizable on a per-user or on a shared basis as well as whether the property is accessible to users. For example, in your CustomerNotesPart, you can include a property that specifies the default customer for which you want to display the notes, as follows:

```
Private _Customer As String = String.Empty

<WebBrowsable(True), Personalizable(PersonalizationScope.User)> _
Public Property Customer() As String
    Get
        Return _Customer
    End Get
    Set
        _Customer = Value
    End Set
End Property
```

The WebBrowsable attribute specifies that the property is visible to end users, and the Personalizable attribute specifies that the personalization scope for the property is on a per-user basis.

Initializing the WebPart

To write the initialization code, you can optionally create child controls; you do this just as you would create a composite WebPart. You can render the WebPart on your own if you don't want to use prebuilt controls in the RenderContents method; however, using composite controls makes life much easier, because you don't have to worry about the HTML details. For creating controls, you have to override the CreateChildControls method as follows. Don't forget to keep members for every control you are going to create in your WebPart class.

```
Dim NewNoteText As TextBox
Dim InsertNewNote As Button
Dim CustomerNotesGrid As GridView

Protected Overrides Sub CreateChildControls()
    ' Create a text box for adding new notes
    NewNoteText = New TextBox()

    ' Create a button for submitting new notes
    InsertNewNote = New Button()
    InsertNewNote.Text = "Insert..."
    AddHandler InsertNewNote.Click, AddressOf InsertNewNote_Click

    ' Create the grid for displaying customer notes
    CustomerNotesGrid = New GridView()
    CustomerNotesGrid.HeaderStyle.BackColor = System.Drawing.Color.LightBlue
    CustomerNotesGrid.RowStyle.BackColor = System.Drawing.Color.LightGreen
    CustomerNotesGrid.AlternatingRowStyle.BackColor = System.Drawing.Color.LightGray
    CustomerNotesGrid.AllowPaging = True
    CustomerNotesGrid.PageSize = 5
```

```
    AddHandler CustomerNotesGrid.PageIndexChanging, AddressOf
               CustomerNotesGrid_PageIndexChanging

    ' Add all controls to the controls collection
    Controls.Add(NewNoteText)
    Controls.Add(InsertNewNote)
    Controls.Add(CustomerNotesGrid)
End Sub

Private Sub CustomerNotesGrid_PageIndexChanging(ByVal sender As Object,
               ByVal e As GridViewPageEventArgs)
    ' Insert page change logic
    ' ...
End Sub

Private Sub InsertNewNote_Click(ByVal sender As Object,
               ByVal e As EventArgs)
    ' Insert new note here
    ' ...
End Sub
```

Within the CreateChildControls method, all controls used by the custom WebPart are created. Don't forget to add them to the Controls collection of the WebPart so that the ASP.NET runtime is aware of these controls and can manage view state and all the other things that happen in the life cycle of the page (as described in Chapter 27). Furthermore, the method sets up the event-handling routines as shown with the InsertNewNote button or the CustomerNotesGrid GridView control.

Loading Data and Processing Events

The next phase in the control's (WebPart's) life cycle is the loading phase. Here you can connect to your database and load data into your control. To do this, you have to override the OnInit and OnLoad methods or catch the Init and Load events of the WebPart. Both ways have the same effect. But when overriding the OnLoad method, for example, don't forget to call base.Onload() so that the base class's loading functionality is executed as well. Therefore, it makes sense to set up event handlers once and catch the events of your custom control so that you can't forget this, as follows:

```
Public Sub New()
    AddHandler Init, AddressOf CustomerNotesPart_Init
    AddHandler Load, AddressOf CustomerNotesPart_Load
    AddHandler PreRender, AddressOf CustomerNotesPart_PreRender
End Sub

Private Sub CustomerNotesPart_Load(ByVal sender As Object, ByVal e As EventArgs)
    ' Initialize other properties ...
End Sub

Private Sub CustomerNotesPart_Init(ByVal sender As Object, ByVal e As EventArgs)
    ' Load data from the database...
End Sub
```

You will use the PreRender event later.

Now you can write functionality for loading the data from the database. Let's assume that you have already created a typed DataSet for your CustomerNotes table. You can create a helper method for binding the previously created GridView to the data from the database and then call this method in the Load event as follows. For simplicity the method binds the information directly to the GridView and doesn't use caching for optimizing data access, because you should concentrate on WebPart creation now.

```
Private Sub BindGrid()
    EnsureChildControls()

    Dim adapter As New CustomerNotesTableAdapter()

    If Customer.Equals(String.Empty) Then
        CustomerNotesGrid.DataSource = adapter.GetDataAll()
    Else
        CustomerNotesGrid.DataSource =
                adapter.GetDataByCustomer(Customer)
    End If
End Sub

Private Sub CustomerNotesPart_Load(ByVal sender As Object, ByVal e As EventArgs)
    ' Initialize web part properties
    Me.Title = "Customer Notes"
    Me.TitleIconImageUrl = "NotesImage.jpg"
End Sub

Private Sub CustomerNotesPart_Init(ByVal sender As Object, ByVal e As EventArgs)
    ' Don't try to load data in Design mode
    If (Not Me.DesignMode) Then
        BindGrid()
    End If
End Sub
```

Remember the call of EnsureChildControls: because you don't know when ASP.NET creates the controls (because it creates them as they are needed), you need to make sure controls are available from within this method by calling EnsureChildControls. (You can find more information about this in Chapter 27.)

Now you have loaded the data into the grid. During the next phase of the life cycle, events are processed by the ASP.NET runtime. Your custom WebPart has to catch the event for the previously added InsertNewNote button that submits a new note to the database and the CustomerNotesGrid that changes the page, as follows:

```
Private Sub InsertNewNote_Click(ByVal sender As Object,
            ByVal e As System.EventArgs)
    Dim adapter As New CustomerNotesTableAdapter()

    adapter.Insert(Customer, DateTime.Now, NewNoteText.Text)

    ' Refresh the Grid with the new row as well
    BindGrid()
End Sub

Private Sub CustomerNotesGrid_PageIndexChanging(ByVal sender As Object,
            ByVal e As GridViewPageEventArgs)
    CustomerNotesGrid.PageIndex = e.NewPageIndex
End Sub
```

Finally, you have to load the data into the GridView in one more place in your code. As soon as someone changes the value for the Customer property, you want your WebPart to display information associated with a single customer. Therefore, you have to modify the property's code as follows:

```
<WebBrowsable(True), Personalizable(PersonalizationScope.User)> _
Public Property Customer() As String
    Get
        Return _Customer
```

```
        End Get
        Set
            _Customer = Value

            ' Don't try to load data in Design mode
            If (Not Me.DesignMode) Then
                EnsureChildControls()
                CustomerNotesGrid.PageIndex = 0
                CustomerNotesGrid.SelectedIndex = -1
                BindGrid()
            End If
        End Set
    End Property
```

You should reset the page index in case the new data displayed will not fill as many pages as the previous data source filled.

The Final Rendering

You have now initialized the WebPart, created controls, wrote code for loading data, and caught control events. So, it's time to render the WebPart. Immediately before you render the WebPart, you can set final property values on your controls that affect rendering. For example, you should disable the InsertNewNote button if the user has not initialized the Customer property. And of course the GridView can now create the necessary HTML controls for displaying the data to which it is bound. To do this, you need to call the DataBind method as follows:

```
Private Sub CustomerNotesPart_PreRender(ByVal sender As Object,
                ByVal e As System.EventArgs)
    If Customer = String.Empty Then
        InsertNewNote.Enabled = False
    Else
        InsertNewNote.Enabled = True
    End If

    CustomerNotesGrid.DataBind()
End Sub
```

In the RenderContents method, you can create the HTML code to lay out your WebPart. If you don't override the method, the WebPart automatically renders the previously added controls in the order they have been inserted into the WebPart's Controls collection within the CreateChildControls method. Because this layout is simple (just a sequence of the controls), you will now override the RenderContents method to create a better, table-based layout, as follows:

```
Protected Overrides Sub RenderContents(ByVal writer As HtmlTextWriter)
    writer.Write("<table>")

    writer.Write("<tr>")
    writer.Write("<td>")
    NewNoteText.RenderControl(writer)
    InsertNewNote.RenderControl(writer)
    writer.Write("</td>")
    writer.Write("</tr>")

    writer.Write("<tr>")
    writer.Write("<td>")
    CustomerNotesGrid.RenderControl(writer)
    writer.Write("</td>")
    writer.Write("</tr>")
```

```
    writer.Write("</table>")
End Sub
```

This code renders an HTML table through the HtmlTextWriter with two rows and one column. The first row contains the text box and the button, and the second row contains the GridView with the notes. Finally, the method uses the RenderControl method of the child controls to render the text box, button, and grid in a specific position within the table. Therefore, you have easily overridden the default rendering of the WebPart base class.

More Customization Steps

As previously shown, with the IWebPart interface a custom WebPart implemented this way can override properties such as the title or description. Furthermore, you can specify default values for other properties of the WebPart by just setting the values for them (which works best in the Load method). You can even override the implementations of default properties and methods from the WebPart. The following example shows how you can initialize the WebPart and override WebPart properties:

```
Private Sub CustomerNotesPart_Load(ByVal sender As Object,
                ByVal e As EventArgs)
    ' Initialize web part properties
    Me.Title = "Customer Notes"
    Me.TitleIconImageUrl = "NotesImage.jpg"
End Sub

Public Overrides Property AllowClose() As Boolean
    Get
        Return False
    End Get
    Set
        ' Don't want this to be set
    End Set
End Property
```

This code initializes some of the WebPart's properties in the Load event with default values. It then overrides the AllowClose property to always return False, and it ignores any set operation by just leaving the logic here. This way, you have created a WebPart where the caller cannot override this behavior by just setting this property from outside. You really have complete customization and control over what can and can't be done with your WebPart. This is the sort of power you can never get when working with user controls.

Using the WebPart

Now you can take a close look at the details of your WebPart. To do this, register the WebPart on your WebPart page using the <%@ Register%> directive at the top of the web page, as follows:

```
<%@ Register TagPrefix="apress" Namespace="Apress.WebParts.Samples" %>
```

Remember that you used the namespace Apress.WebParts.Samples in the class file of the custom WebPart. The <%@ Register %> directive assigns the prefix *Apress* to this namespace. Therefore, you can use the WebPart in one of the previously created WebPartZone controls, as follows:

```
<asp:WebPartZone runat="server" ID="MainZone">
    <ZoneTemplate>
        <uc1:Customers ID="MyCustomers"
                       runat="server" OnLoad="MyCustomers_Load" />
        <apress:CustomerNotesPart ID="MyCustomerNotes" runat="server" />
```

```
    </ZoneTemplate>
</asp:WebPartZone>
```

Now you can test your newly created WebPart by starting your web application. Figure 30-11 shows the results of your work.

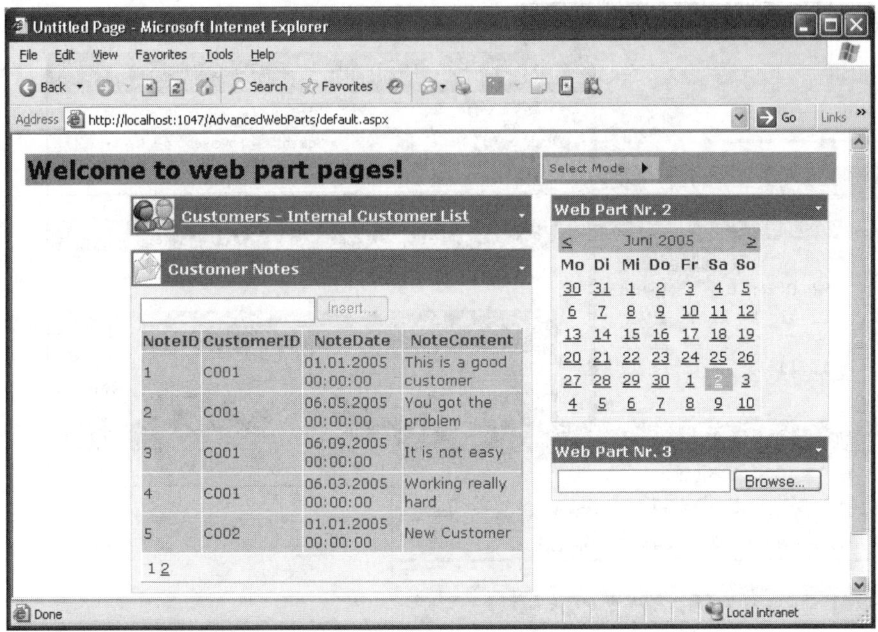

Figure 30-11. *The custom WebPart in action with the other WebParts*

WebPart Editors

In the previous example, you created a custom WebPart with a personalizable property called Customer. This property determined whether the content of the GridView in the WebPart displays information for just one customer or for all customers. You were not able to change this property through the WebPart page's user interface, so you will now see how you can accomplish this.

Basically, the ASP.NET 2.0 WebParts Framework provides functionality for editing properties of WebParts. As you saw when creating the Menu control for switching the page's DisplayMode, it includes an Edit mode. However, if you try to activate it now, you will get an exception about missing controls on the page. The missing pieces for the Edit mode are the EditorWebZone and some appropriate editor parts. Both are prebuilt; the WebPartZone control hosts editor parts. You can use them by adding an EditorZone and one of the prebuilt editor parts to your page, as follows:

```
<asp:EditorZone runat="server" ID="SimpleEditor">
    <ZoneTemplate>
        <asp:AppearanceEditorPart ID="MyMainEditor" runat="server" />
    </ZoneTemplate>
</asp:EditorZone>
```

This code adds an AppearanceEditorPart to the zone, which allows you to configure the appearance of the WebPart including its title and chrome settings (see Table 30-2). Now you can switch to the Edit mode on your page; Figure 30-12 shows the steps required for opening an appropriate editor on your page.

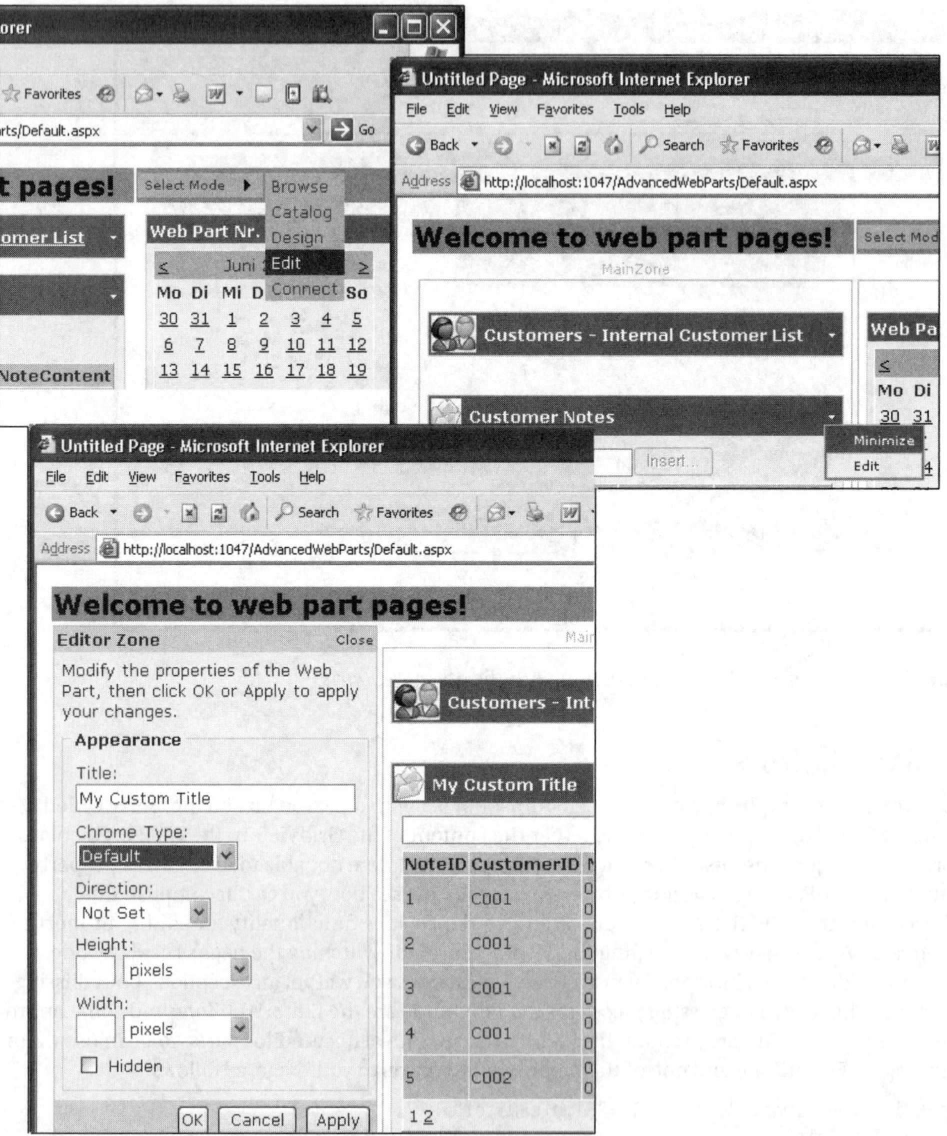

Figure 30-12. *Editing properties of your WebParts*

Table 30-4 lists the available editor WebParts of the framework.

Table 30-4. *Editor WebParts Shipping with ASP.NET 2.0*

Editor Part	Description
AppearanceEditorPart	Allows you to configure basic properties of the WebPart including its title and its ChromeStyle.
BehaviorEditorPart	Includes editors for modifying properties that affect the behavior of the WebPart. Typical examples of such properties are the AllowClose or AllowMinimize properties as well as properties such as TitleUrl, HelpMode, and HelpUrl. Every property modifies behavior such as whether the WebPart can be minimized.
LayoutEditorPart	Allows the user to change the WebPart's zone as well as its ChromeState. By the way, this editor enables browsers where changing a WebPart's zone through dragging and dropping doesn't work manually through the controls of this editor part.
PropertyGridEditorPart	Displays a text box for every public property of your custom WebPart that includes the attribute <WebBrowsable(True)>.

The PropertyGridEditorPart editor part is a suitable way to enable the user to modify the previously implemented Customer property of your WebPart. Just add the editor part to your page as follows, and edit your custom WebPart:

```
<asp:EditorZone runat="server" ID="SimpleEditor">
    <ZoneTemplate>
        <asp:PropertyGridEditorPart ID="MyPropertyEditor" runat="server" />
        <asp:AppearanceEditorPart ID="MyMainEditor" runat="server" />
    </ZoneTemplate>
</asp:EditorZone>
```

Figure 30-13 shows the results. As soon as you switch to the Edit mode and edit your custom WebPart, you can change the value for the Customer property.

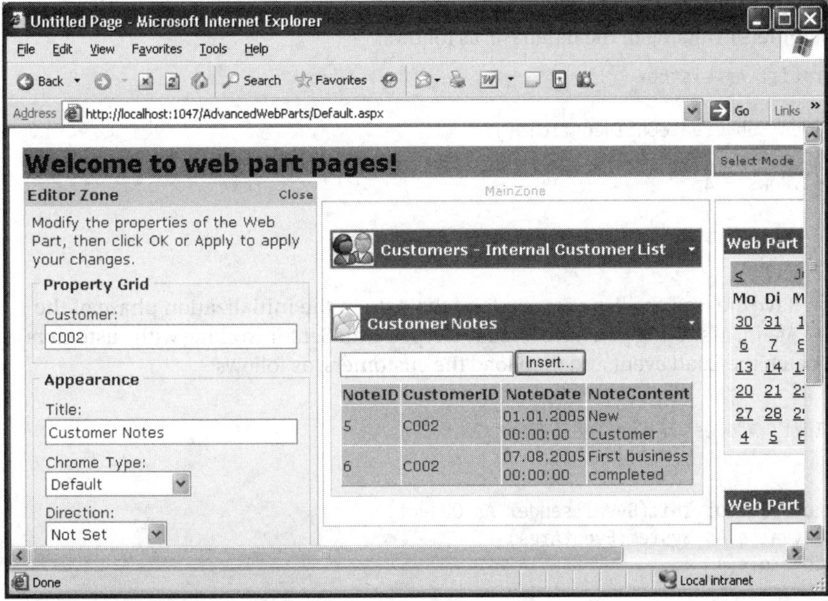

Figure 30-13. *The PropertyGridEditorPart in action*

Because you have called BindGrid in the property's set method previously, the appearance of the WebPart changes as soon as you hit the Apply button of the EditorZone. Additionally, if you add a <WebDisplayName> in addition to the <WebBrowsable> attribute to your custom property, you can control the name of the property that the editor will display.

Creating a Custom Editor

Displaying a text box (where the user has to manually enter the customer ID) to select a customer is not a great ergonomic solution. Creating a custom editor that enables the user to select the customer from a list would be more helpful. That's what you'll learn in this section.

Creating a custom editor for a WebPart page is as easy as creating a custom WebPart or a custom server control. The only difference is that you need to inherit from EditorPart instead of WebPart or WebControl, as follows:

```
Public Class CustomerEditor
    Inherits EditorPart

    Public Sub New()
        '
        ' TODO: Add constructor logic here
        '
    End Sub

    Public Overrides Function ApplyChanges() As Boolean
        ' Apply changes to the WebPart's property
    End Function

    Public Overrides Sub SyncChanges()
        ' Initialize EditorPart with values from WebPart
    End Sub
End Class
```

Again, because the custom editor is nothing more than a composite control, you can add child controls by overriding the CreateChildControls method. In this case, you need to create a list for displaying the customers available in the database, as follows:

```
Private CustomersList As ListBox

Protected Overrides Sub CreateChildControls()
    CustomersList = New ListBox()
    CustomersList.Rows = 4

    Controls.Add(CustomersList)
End Sub
```

Now that you have created the list, you can load the data in the initialization phase of the EditorPart control. Again, assuming you have already a typed DataSet for working with customers in place, you can catch the Load event and then load the customers, as follows:

```
Public Sub New()
    AddHandler Init, AddressOf CustomerEditor_Init
End Sub

Private Sub CustomerEditor_Init(ByVal sender As Object,
            ByVal e As System.EventArgs)
    EnsureChildControls()

    Dim adapter As CustomerTableAdapter = New CustomerTableAdapter()
    CustomersList.DataSource = adapter.GetData()
```

```
    CustomersList.DataTextField = "CompanyName"
    CustomersList.DataValueField = "CustomerID"
    CustomersList.DataBind()

    ' Empty selection to show all notes
    CustomersList.Items.Insert(0, "")
End Sub
```

Finally, you have to synchronize changes between the EditorPart and the actual WebPart. You'll learn how to retrieve information from the WebPart. To do this, you need to add code to your SyncChanges method, which you have to override when inheriting from EditorPart. Within this method, you get access to the WebPart that will be edited through the base class's WebPartToEdit property. Of course, then you have access to all the properties of your WebPart as usual.

```
Public Overrides Sub SyncChanges()
    ' Make sure all controls are available
    EnsureChildControls()

    ' Get the property from the WebPart
    Dim part As CustomerNotesPart =
             CType(WebPartToEdit, CustomerNotesPart)
    If part IsNot Nothing Then
        CustomersList.SelectedValue = part.Customer
    End If
End Sub
```

When the user updates the value in the editor by clicking Apply, you have to update the WebPart's property. You can do this in the ApplyChanges method, where again you can access the WebPart through the base class's WebPartToEdit property, as follows:

```
Public Overrides Function ApplyChanges() As Boolean
    ' Make sure all controls are available
    EnsureChildControls()

    ' Get the property from the WebPart
    Dim part As CustomerNotesPart =
             CType(WebPartToEdit, CustomerNotesPart)
    If part IsNot Nothing Then
        If CustomersList.SelectedIndex >= 0 Then
            part.Customer = CustomersList.SelectedValue
        Else
            part.Customer = String.Empty
        End If
    Else
        Return False
    End If

    Return True
End Function
```

The method returns True if the value has been updated successfully, and returns False otherwise. Basically, that's it—you have created a custom editor. But how can you use it? Somehow the infrastructure has to know that this editor has to be used with only specific WebParts—in this case with the CustomerNotesPart. To do this, modify the originally created WebPart. It has to implement the IWebEditable interface as follows:

```
Public Class CustomerNotesPart
        Inherits WebPart
```

```
    Implements IWebEditable
#Region "IWebEditable Members"

Private Function CreateEditorParts() As EditorPartCollection
    Implements IWebEditable.CreateEditorParts
    ' Create editor parts
    Dim Editors As New List(Of EditorPart)()
    Editors.Add(New CustomerEditor())
    Return New EditorPartCollection(Editors)
End Function

Private ReadOnly Property WebBrowsableObject() As Object
    Implements IWebEditable.WebBrowsableObject
    Get
            Return Me
    End Get
End Property

#End Region

' Rest of the implementation
...
```

This method works for user controls and server controls. The GenericWebPart that wraps user controls and server controls verifies whether the wrapped control implements the IWebEditable interface. If the control implements the interface, it calls the control's implementation of the interface for providing the custom editors. The CreateEditorParts just returns a collection of EditorParts to be displayed for this WebPart, and the WebBrowsableObject returns the class that contains the personalizable properties. Figure 30-14 shows the results.

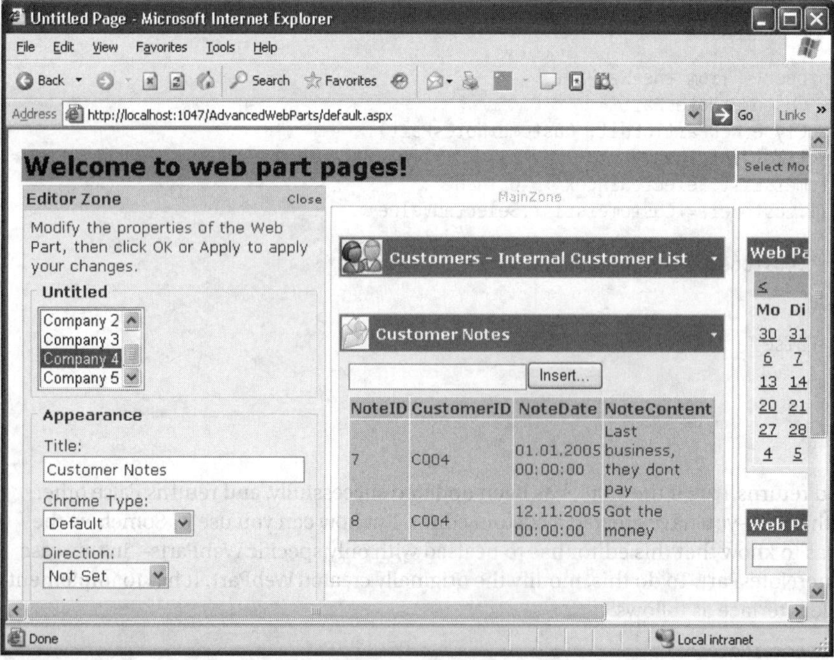

Figure 30-14. *The custom editor part in action*

Connecting WebParts

WebParts can also exchange information in a well-defined manner. For example, a WebPart that displays a list of customers could notify another WebPart (or many other WebParts) if a specific customer has been selected so that this other WebPart can display information according to the selection in the customer WebPart. The ASP.NET framework lets you create such "connectable" WebParts and offers the possibility of statically or dynamically connecting WebParts. For creating connectable WebParts, you have to create and combine several pieces. Figure 30-15 shows these pieces and how they relate to each other.

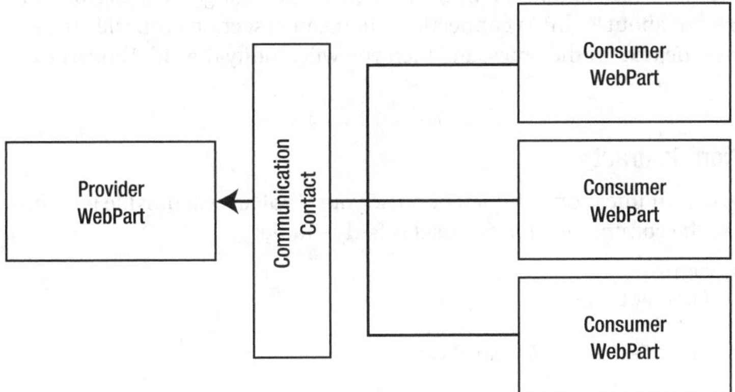

Figure 30-15. *The pieces for creating connectable WebParts*

You can see that Figure 30-15 has two primary types of WebParts: *Providers* make information available to other WebParts, and every WebPart that requires information from a provider WebPart is a *consumer* WebPart. Finally, you have to establish a standardized way for exchanging the information, which leads to the final missing piece, the communication contract. Technically, the communication contract is an interface that has to be implemented by the provider WebPart. This interface defines how a consumer WebPart can access information from the provider WebPart. In other words, the provider WebPart makes its data available through this interface. The steps for creating and connecting WebParts are as follows:

1. *Create a communication contract*: The first thing you should think about is, which information needs to be exchanged? Based on the response to this question, you can design an interface for data exchange that has to be implemented by the provider WebPart.
2. *Create a provider WebPart*: Next you can create the provider WebPart. This WebPart has to perform two tasks: It needs to implement the previously defined communication contract interface or know a class implementing this interface, and it needs to provide a method that returns an instance of a class implementing the interface. This method must be marked with the <ConnectionProvider> attribute.
3. *Create a consumer WebPart*: Next, you can create a consumer WebPart. The consumer WebPart does not need to implement any interfaces, but it needs to know how to communicate to the provider. Therefore, it needs to know about the interface (which means if you have the consumer in a separate DLL, it needs to reference an assembly that defines this interface). A consumer WebPart then needs to implement a method that is marked with the <ConnectionConsumer> attribute. This method accepts a variable as a parameter that implements the previously defined communication contract interface.

4. *Configure the connection*: Finally, you have to configure the connection between the consumer and the provider WebPart. You can do that statically through the <StaticConnections> section within the WebPartManager, or the user can configure connections at runtime. You will learn more details about how to implement both ways later in the "Static Connections Between WebParts" section.

You can connect only WebParts inherited from WebPart; because user controls and custom server controls are wrapped by the GenericWebPart, the framework has no direct access to the methods marked with the <ConnectionProvider> and <ConnectionConsumer> attributes.

Previously you created a WebPart for displaying customer notes in a grid. Because notes can get long (remember, the column is a text column), it might be nice to have a larger text box for editing the value of this field. To learn about WebPart connections, in the next sections you will create a simple WebPart that displays the text for the notes, and then you will modify the old WebPart to become a provider WebPart.

Defining the Communication Contract

The first step is to design the communication contract. Because your WebPart will provide just simple text and date information, the communication contract is fairly simple:

```
Namespace Apress.WebParts.Samples
    Public Interface INotesContract
        Property Notes() As String
        ReadOnly Property SubmittedDate() As DateTime
    End Interface
End Namespace
```

This contract defines two properties: one for retrieving and updating the notes text for a customer and the second for retrieving the date of a submitted entry. Now the provider has to implement this interface, while the consumer has just to know about the interface.

Implementing the Provider

As the provider WebPart will be the previously created CustomerNotesPart, you need to modify this one so it implements the INotesContract communication contract interface and contains a public method with the <ConnectionProvider> attribute. Basically, the code is as follows:

```
Public Class CustomerNotesPart
        Inherits WebPart
        Implements IWebEditable, INotesContract
    #Region "INotesContract Members"

    Public Property Notes() As String
        Get
                ' Get the NoteContent value from the grid's data source
                ' ...
        End Get
        Set
            ' Update value to the grid's data source
            ' ...
        End Set
    End Property

    Public ReadOnly Property SubmittedDate() As DateTime
        Get
            ' Get the NoteDate value from the grid's data source
```

```
            ' ...
        End Get
    End Property

    #End Region

' Rest of the implementation
...
```

Within the property procedures, you need to add the appropriate code for retrieving the values from the data source you have bound to the GridView in the WebPart's original version. Updating the data in the property's set procedure means updating the value in the GridView's data source and then using, for example, a SqlCommand or a SqlDataAdapter for updating the values on the database. Retrieving the SubmittedDate from the GridView's data source might look like this:

```
Public ReadOnly Property SubmittedDate() As DateTime
    Get
        EnsureChildControls()

        If CustomerNotesGrid.SelectedIndex >= 0 Then
            Dim RowIndex As Integer =
                        CustomerNotesGrid.SelectedRow.DataItemIndex

            Dim dt As DataTable =
                        CType(CustomerNotesGrid.DataSource, DataTable)
            Return CDate(dt.Rows(RowIndex)("NoteDate"))
        Else
            Return DateTime.MinValue
        End If
    End Get
End Property
```

You can verify whether an item has been selected in the GridView. (To do this, you need to enable selection on the GridView.) If an item is selected, you retrieve the DataItemIndex, which then can be used as an index for accessing the DataRow of the DataTable, which is bound to the GridView. You can read the value from the DataRow and return it.

The next thing your provider WebPart has to support is a method marked with the <ConnectionProvider> attribute. This method returns the actual implementation of the communication contract interface, which is the WebPart in this case. Therefore, you need to implement it as follows:

```
<ConnectionProvider("Notes Text")> _
Public Function GetNotesCommunicationPoint() As INotesContract
    Return CType(Me, INotesContract)
End Function
```

That's it! Your provider WebPart is ready to use. Next you need to implement the consumer WebPart, which is much easier.

Creating the Consumer WebPart

The consumer WebPart retrieves information from the provider WebParts for its own purposes. In this example, you just display the text for the currently selected note in the CustomerNotesPart that you have implemented as the provider.

Because this solution does not contain this WebPart yet, you have to start from scratch. Just add a new class that inherits from WebPart. The WebPart uses the CreateChildControls for creating a label that displays the date, a text box that displays the notes text, and a button that updates the notes text.

```
Public Class CustomerNotesConsumer
    Inherits WebPart

    Private NotesTextLabel As Label
    Private NotesContentText As TextBox
    Private UpdateNotesContent As Button

    Protected Overrides Sub CreateChildControls()
        NotesTextLabel = New Label()
        NotesTextLabel.Text = DateTime.Now.ToString()

        NotesContentText = New TextBox()
        NotesContentText.TextMode = TextBoxMode.MultiLine
        NotesContentText.Rows = 5
        NotesContentText.Columns = 20

        UpdateNotesContent = New Button()
        UpdateNotesContent.Text = "Update"
        AddHandler UpdateNotesContent.Click,
                        AddressOf UpdateNotesContent_Click

        Controls.Add(NotesTextLabel)
        Controls.Add(NotesContentText)
        Controls.Add(UpdateNotesContent)
    End Sub
End Class
```

Next, you have to add a simple method that is called by the ASP.NET WebParts framework automatically if the WebPart is connected to another WebPart. This method accepts the other connection point (which is the provider) as a parameter and needs to be marked with the <ConnectionConsumer> attribute so that the runtime knows this is the method to be called for passing in the provider.

```
Private _NotesProvider As INotesContract = Nothing

<ConnectionConsumer("Customer Notes")> _
Public Sub InitializeProvider(ByVal provider As INotesContract)
    _NotesProvider = provider
End Sub
```

With the provider initialized, the WebPart of course can consume information from the provider by just calling properties (or methods) defined in the communication contract. For example, in the PreRender event you can initialize your controls, whereas in the button's event procedure you can update the notes content by setting the Notes property appropriately:

```
Private Sub UpdateNotesContent_Click(ByVal sender As Object, ByVal e As EventArgs)
    If _NotesProvider IsNot Nothing Then
        _NotesProvider.Notes = NotesContentText.Text
    End If
End Sub

Protected Overrides Sub OnPreRender(ByVal e As EventArgs)
    ' Don't forget to call base implementation
    MyBase.OnPreRender(e)

    ' Initialize control
    If _NotesProvider IsNot Nothing Then
        NotesContentText.Text = _NotesProvider.Notes
```

```
        NotesTextLabel.Text = _NotesProvider.SubmittedDate. ToShortDateString ()
    End If
End Sub
```

Of course, you have to validate whether the provider has been initialized. If it hasn't been, the WebPart is not connected with any other WebPart, and therefore you cannot access any information. However, with this code in place you are basically finished. You have created a consumer WebPart and a provider WebPart, and communication between those two takes place through the communication contract interface. Next you can connect these WebParts either manually or dynamically at runtime.

Static Connections Between WebParts

The simple way to connect WebParts is through static connections. How can you do that? Well, let's think about the roles of the different controls involved in WebPart pages again. The WebPartManager knows about all the WebParts and manages features such as personalization. WebPartZones are areas on your web page that can contain WebParts, while the WebParts are independent controls. If you think about it one moment, you definitely will recognize that the WebPartManager might be a good starting point for taking a closer look at connection points. You are right: Static connection points are configured through the WebPartManager as follows:

```
<asp:WebPartManager runat="server" ID="MyPartManager">
    <StaticConnections>
        <asp:WebPartConnection ID="SimpleConnection"
                               ProviderID="MyCustomerNotes"
                               ConsumerID="MyNotesConsumer" />
    </StaticConnections>
</asp:WebPartManager>
```

The ID values used for the ProviderID and ConsumerID are just the ID values of the WebParts as they have been added to the WebPartZone. You can find these WebParts in the zones of your WebPart page, as you can see in the following code fragment:

```
<table width="100%">
...
    <asp:WebPartZone runat="server" ID="MainZone" >
        <ZoneTemplate>
            <uc1:Customers ID="MyCustomers"
                          runat="server"
                          OnLoad="MyCustomers_Load" />
            <apress:CustomerNotesPart
                          ID="MyCustomerNotes" runat="server" />
        </ZoneTemplate>
    </asp:WebPartZone>
...
    <asp:WebPartZone runat="server" ID="HelpZone>
        <ZoneTemplate>
            <apress:CustomerNotesConsumer
                    ID="MyNotesConsumer" runat="server" />
            <asp:Calendar runat="server" ID="MyCalendar"
                         OnLoad="MyCalendar_Load" />
            <asp:FileUpload ID="MyUpload" runat="server" />
        </ZoneTemplate>
    </asp:WebPartZone>
...
</table>
```

When configuring this connection point, you will recognize that the consumer WebPart always displays information from the selected entry of the CustomerNotes WebPart.

Dynamically Configuring Connection Points

If you don't want to connect WebParts statically but want the user to have the possibility of connecting WebParts at runtime, you cannot use the WebPartManager's StaticConnections configuration. But providing dynamic configuration of connection points is nearly as simple as configuring static connection points. All you need to add to your page is a special zone called ConnectionsZone, as follows:

```
<asp:ConnectionsZone ID="MyConnections" runat="server">
    <ConnectVerb Text="Connect Now..." />
    <CancelVerb Text="Don't connect" />
    <DisconnectVerb Text="Release connection" />
</asp:ConnectionsZone>
```

The child tags of the ConnectionsZone are optional and allow you to customize the default user interface created for editing the connections. After adding such a zone to your WebPart page, you can switch to the Connect mode (what is not possible otherwise). If you want to edit connections for a WebPart in the running web application at runtime, you need to perform the following tasks as the user of the web page:

1. Switch to the Connect mode.
2. Select the consumer WebPart, and select Connect from the WebPart's menu.
3. Now the connection editor appears in the previously added ConnectionsZone. Here you can select a provider and click the Connect button.
4. The WebParts are connected now. You can release the connection by clicking the Release button.

Figure 30-16 shows the ConnectionsZone in action.

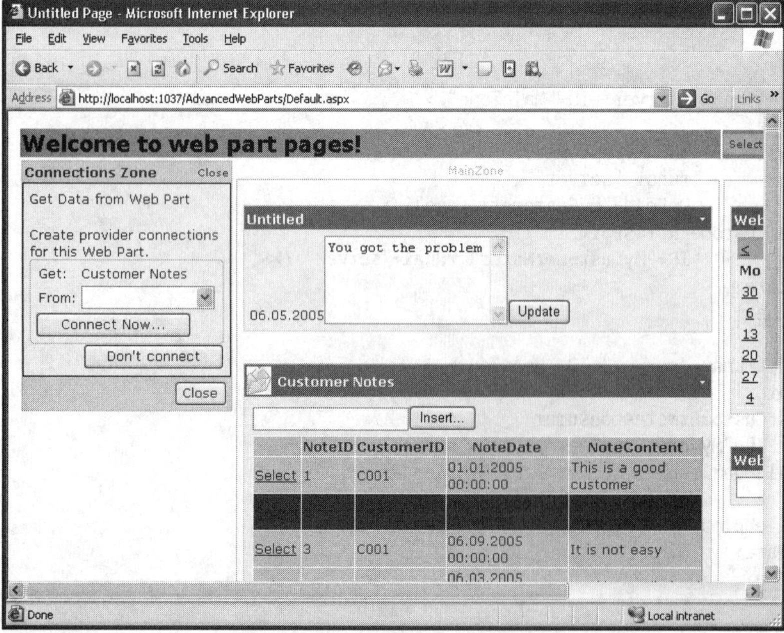

Figure 30-16. *ConnectionsZone in action*

Multiple Connection Points

A WebPart provider can make multiple connection points available, while a WebPart consumer can consume multiple provider connection points. In that case, every connection point requires a unique ID on both the consumer side and the provider side. On the provider side, you specify the connection point ID in the <ConnectionProvider> attribute, as follows:

```
<ConnectionProvider("Notes Text", "MyProviderID")> _
Public Function GetNotesCommunicationPoint() As INotesContract
    Return CType(Me, INotesContract)
End Function
```

You can specify an ID for consumer endpoints in the same way if a WebPart is a consumer of multiple providers, as follows:

```
<ConnectionConsumer("Customer Notes", "MyConsumerID")> _
Public Sub InitializeProvider(ByVal provider As INotesContract)
    _NotesProvider = provider
End Sub
```

These IDs have to be unique within the WebPart. This means other WebParts can define connection points with the same ID. When configuring static connections for WebParts that support multiple connection points, you have to specify those through additional ProviderConnectionPointID and ConsumerConnectionPointID parameters, as follows:

```
<asp:WebPartManager runat="server" ID="MyPartManager">
    <StaticConnections>
        <asp:WebPartConnection ProviderID="MyCustomerNotes"
                               ProviderConnectionPointID="MyProviderID"
                               ConsumerID="MyCustomerNotesConsumer"
                               ConsumerConnectionPointID="MyConsumerID" />
    </StaticConnections>
</asp:WebPartManager>
```

In the case of dynamic configuration, the user can select the point to connect to based on the name specified as the first parameter in the previously used <ConnectionProvider> and <ConnectionConsumer> attributes.

Authorizing WebParts

When you have all your WebPart controls on your page, you might want to make some available to specific groups of users. Fortunately, the ASP.NET 2.0 WebParts Framework includes a way to specify such authorization information for WebParts. All you need to do is catch one specific event of the WebPartManager class called AuthorizeWebPart. Within this event procedure, you can encapsulate logic for deciding whether a user is authorized to view a WebPart control.

The following example shows how to display the CustomerNotes WebPart only if the user browsing to the page is member of the local Administrators group:

```
Protected Sub MyPartManager_AuthorizeWebPart(ByVal sender As Object,
                ByVal e As WebPartAuthorizationEventArgs)
    ' Ignore authorization in Visual Studio Design mode
    If Me.DesignMode Then
        Return
    End If

    ' Authorize a web part or not
    Dim PartType As Type = e.Type
    If PartType Is GetType(CustomerNotesPart) Then
```

```
        If User.Identity.IsAuthenticated Then
            If User.IsInRole("BUILTIN\Administrators") Then
                e.IsAuthorized = True
            Else
                e.IsAuthorized = False
            End If
        Else
            e.IsAuthorized = False
        End If
    End If
End Sub
```

Because authorization takes place on types of WebParts and not on individual instances of WebParts, you get the type of the WebPart to be authorized from the WebPartManager in the event arguments. You then can make authorization decisions based on the type of the WebPart as demonstrated previously. As soon as you set the IsAuthorized property of the WebPartAuthorizationEventArgs structure passed in to False, the WebPartManager will not display WebParts of this type—neither on the page nor in other situations such as a PageCatalogPart of a CatalogZone.

Final Tasks for Personalization

Finally, you should keep in mind a couple of final tasks for personalization. You can configure personalization properties on a per-page level through the WebPartManager, as follows:

```
<asp:WebPartManager runat="server" ID="MyPartManager">
    <Personalization Enabled="True" ProviderName="YourProvider" />
</asp:WebPartManager>
```

If you want to configure personalization settings for the whole application, you have to do that through the <webParts> configuration element in the web.config application configuration, as follows:

```
<webParts>
<personalization defaultProvider="MyProvider">
    <authorization>
        <allow roles="BUILTIN\Administrators"/>
        <deny roles="BUILTIN\Guests" />
    </authorization>
    <providers>
        <add name="MyProvider"
            type="System.Web.UI.WebControls.WebParts.SqlPersonalizationProvider"
            connectionStringName="CustomSqlConnection" />
    </providers>
</personalization>
</webParts>
```

This code also shows that you can even configure the specific users for which personalization is enabled or disabled. You do this through the <authorization> element; this element works the same way as the <authorization> element you learned about in Chapter 23.

Clearing Personalization

How can you delete personalization information from the store? To do this, you can use the Personalization property of the WebPartManager class; this gives you access to the personalization provider, the settings, and the functions for resetting personalization information. You can do this as follows:

```
If MyPartManager.Personalization.HasPersonalizationState Then
    MyPartManager.Personalization.ResetPersonalizationState()
End If
```

You can then include functionality in your application for resetting personalization in this way. This could be an administration page, for example.

Summary

In this chapter, you learned how to create real-world WebPart pages. Such pages include requirements such as personalization as well as a modularized structure through WebParts that enable the user to select exactly the information that should be displayed. You also learned what WebPartManagers, WebPartZones, and WebParts are and what their tasks are.

Then you learned about important advanced features such as connecting WebParts and authorizing WebParts. You also know how to add custom properties to WebParts that will be stored on a per-user or shared basis, and you created custom editors for editing those properties.

The ASP.NET 2.0 WebParts Framework provides you with a huge set of functionality. You never have to implement your own portal framework, as it is already included with the framework. And, as it is part of the .NET Framework, you get this all for free!

PART 6

Web Services

CHAPTER 31

■ ■ ■

Creating Web Services

For years, software developers and architects have struggled to create software components that can be called remotely over local networks and the Internet. In the process, many new technologies and patched-together proprietary solutions have been created. Although some of these technologies have been quite successful running back-end systems on internal networks, none has met the challenges of the Internet—a wide (sometimes unreliable) network of computers running on every type of hardware and operating system possible.

This is where XML web services enter the scene. To interact with a web service, you simply need to send an XML message over HTTP. Because every Internet-enabled device supports HTTP, and virtually every programming language has access to an XML parser, few limits exist on what types of applications can use web services. In fact, most programming frameworks include higher-level toolkits that make communicating with a web service as easy as calling a local function.

This chapter provides an overview of web services and the problems they solve. If you're new to web services, you'll learn how to create and consume them in ASP.NET. However, you won't dive into the lower-level details of the underlying protocols just yet. Instead, you'll get started using a web service and then learn to extend it in the next chapter.

WEB SERVICE CHANGES IN .NET 2.0

If you've programmed with web services in .NET 1.*x*, you're probably wondering what has changed in .NET 2.0. From a practical point of view, surprisingly little is new—in fact, the underlying infrastructure is the same. But you'll see several useful refinements, many of which deal with how web services work with complex types (custom data classes used to send or retrieve information to a web method). The changes include the following:

- *Support for property procedures*: If you have a web service that uses a custom type, .NET creates a copy of that class in the client. In .NET 1.*x*, this automatically generated class is built from public properties. In .NET 2.0, it uses property procedures instead. This minor switch doesn't change how the web service works, but it allows you to use the class in data binding scenarios.
- *Type sharing*: .NET now recognizes when two web services use the same complex type and generates only one client-side class. Best of all, because both proxy classes use the same types, you can easily retrieve an object from one web service and send it directly to another.
- *Custom serialization*: You can now plug into the serialization process for custom classes to take complete control over their XML representation.
- *Rich objects*: Need to exchange complex objects, complete with methods and constructors intact? It's possible if you build a new component called a *schema importer*. The schema importer checks the schema of the web service and tells the proxy class what types to use.
- *Contract-first development*: You can now build a .NET web service that conforms to an existing WSDL (Web Service Description Language) contract.

Chapter 30 describes all these improvements.

Many more dramatic changes are just around the corner. Microsoft developers are readying the Windows Communication Foundation (a.k.a. Indigo), a new model for distributed messaging that incorporates the functionality of web services and other .NET technologies, such as remoting. Although you'll get a natural upgrade path from ASP.NET web services to Indigo, many of the implementation details will change. Indigo isn't part of .NET 2.0—instead, it's slated to ship with the next version of Windows (and won't arrive any sooner than late 2006). However, Microsoft has hinted it could release an Indigo toolkit for other versions of Windows earlier. For more information, refer to the Microsoft Indigo developer center at `http://msdn.microsoft.com/Longhorn/understanding/pillars/Indigo`.

Web Services Overview

While HTML pages (or the HTML output generated by ASP.NET web forms) are meant to be read by the end user, web services are used by other applications. They are pieces of business logic that can be accessed over the Internet. For example, e-commerce sites can use the web service of a shipping and packaging company to calculate the cost of the shipment. A news site can retrieve the news headlines and articles produced by external news providers and expose them on its own pages in real time. A company can even provide the real-time value of their stock options, reading it from a specialized financial or investment site. All these scenarios are already taking place on the Web, and major Internet companies such as Amazon, Google, and eBay are providing their own web service offerings to third-party developers.

With web services, you can reuse someone else's business logic, instead of replicating it yourself, using just a few lines of code. This technique is similar to what programmers currently do with libraries of APIs, classes, and components. The main difference is that web services can be located remotely on another server and managed by another company.

The History of Web Services

Even though web services are a relatively new technology, you can learn a lot from recent history. Two of the major shifts in software development over the last couple of decades have been the development of object-oriented programming and component-based technology.

Object-oriented programming joined the mainstream in the early 1980s. Many saw object-oriented programming as the solution to the software crisis that resulted from the increasing complexity and size of software applications. Many projects were late and over budget, and the end result was often unreliable. The promise of object-oriented code was that by structuring code into objects, developers could create software units that were more reusable, extensible, and maintainable.

The 1990s saw the birth of component technology, which made it possible to build applications by assembling components. Component technology is really an extension of object-oriented principles outside the boundaries of any one particular language so that the technology becomes a core piece of infrastructure everyone can use. While object-oriented languages allowed developers to reuse objects in their applications, component-based technologies allowed developers to easily share compiled objects *between* applications. Two dominant component-based technologies emerged: COM (Component Object Model) and CORBA (Common Object Request Broker Architecture). Since that time, other component technologies have appeared (such as Enterprise JavaBeans and .NET), but these are proprietary solutions for specific programming frameworks.

Soon after COM and CORBA were created, these standards were applied to distributed components so that an application could interact between components hosted on different computers in a network. COM and CORBA have a great deal of technical sophistication, they are often difficult to set up and support in network environments, and they can't work together without using specialized bridging software. These headaches became dramatically worse when the Internet appeared and developers began to apply these technologies to create distributed applications that spanned slower, less-reliable WANs (wide area networks). Because of their inherent complexity and proprietary nature, neither COM nor CORBA became truly successful in this environment. Furthermore, companies started to install firewalls to protect their Internet-facing networks, which made it impossible for external clients to access COM and CORBA components located behind the firewall.

Web services aim to answer these problems by extending object technology to the Web. Essentially, a *web service* is a unit of application logic (a component) that can be remotely invoked over the Internet. Many of the promises of web services are the same as those of component technology—the aim is to make it easier to assemble applications from prebuilt application logic, share functionality between organizations and partners, and create more modular applications. Unlike earlier component technologies, web services are designed *exclusively* for this purpose. This means as a .NET developer, you will still use the .NET component model to share compiled assemblies between .NET applications. However, if you want to share functionality between applications running on different platforms or hosted by different companies, web services fit perfectly.

Web services also place a much greater emphasis on interoperability. All software development platforms that allow programmers to create web services use the same bedrock of open XML-based standards. This ensures you can create a web service using .NET and call it from a Java client and you can create a Java web service and call it from a .NET application.

■ **Note** Web services are not limited to the .NET Framework. The standards were defined before .NET was released, and they are exposed, used, and supported by vendors other than Microsoft. Visual Studio .NET and the .NET Framework make it easy to create and consume Web services, and this makes it far easier to expose your own services over the Internet or to access the services provided by other companies. As you'll see, you don't need to know all the details of XML and SOAP to successfully program web services (although, of course, some knowledge helps). ASP.NET abstracts the nitty-gritty stuff and generates wrapper classes that expose a simple object-oriented model to send, receive, and interpret the SOAP messages easily.

Distributed Computing and Web Services

To fully understand the importance of web services, you need to understand the requirements of *distributed computing*. Distributed computing is the partitioning of application logic into units that are executed on two or more computers in a network. The idea of distributed computing has been around a long time, and numerous communication technologies have been developed to allow the distribution and reuse of application logic.

Distributing application logic has several benefits:

High scalability: By distributing the application logic, the load is spread out to different machines. This usually won't improve the performance of the application for individual users (in fact, it may slow it down), but it will almost always improve the scalability, thereby allowing the application to serve a much larger number of users at the same time.

Easy deployment: Pieces of a distributed application may be upgraded without upgrading the whole application. You can update a centrally located component without needing to update hundreds (or event thousands) of clients.

Improved security: Distributed applications often span company or organization boundaries. For example, you might use distributed components to let a trading partner query your company's product catalog. It wouldn't be secure to let the trading partner connect directly to your company database. Instead, the trading partner needs to use a component running on your servers, which you can control and restrict appropriately.

The Internet has increased the importance and applicability of distributed computing. The simplicity and ubiquity of the Internet makes it a logical choice as the backbone for distributed applications.

Before web services, the dominant protocols were COM (which is called DCOM, or Distributed COM, when used on a network), EJB, and CORBA. Although CORBA and DCOM have a lot in common, they differ in the details, making it hard to get the protocols to interoperate. Table 31-1 summarizes some similarities and differences between CORBA, DCOM, and web services. It also introduces a slew of acronyms.

Table 31-1. *Comparing Different Distributed Technologies*

Characteristic	CORBA	DCOM	Web Services
RPC (Remote Procedure Call) mechanism	IIOP (Internet Inter-ORB Protocol)	DCE-RPC (Distributed Computing Environment Remote Procedure Call)	HTTP (Hypertext Transfer Protocol)
Encoding	CDR (Common Data Representation)	NDR (Network Data Representation)	XML (Extensible Markup Language) /SOAP
Interface description	IDL (Interface Definition Language)	IDL (Interface Definition Language)	WSDL (Web Service Description Language)
Discovery	Naming service and trading service	Registry	UDDI (Universal Description, Discovery, and Integration)
Firewall-friendly	No	No	Yes
Complexity of protocols	High	High	Low
Cross-platform	Yes	No	Yes

Both CORBA and DCOM allow for the invocation of methods on remote objects. CORBA uses a standard called IIOP (Internet Inter-ORB Protocol), and DCOM uses a variation of a standard named DCE-RPC (Distributed Computing Environment Remote Procedure Call). The encoding of data in CORBA is based on a format named CDR (Common Data Representation). In DCOM, the encoding of data is based on a similar but incompatible format named NDR (Network Data Representation). These layers of standards make for significant complexity!

Also, differences exist between the languages that both protocols support. DCOM supports a wide range of languages (C++, Visual Basic, and so on) but was used primarily on Microsoft operating systems. CORBA supports different platforms but mostly gained traction with Java-based applications (though it is supported by other languages). As a result, developers had two platforms that had the technical ability to support systems of distributed objects but in many cases couldn't work together.

The Problems with Distributed Component Technologies

Interoperability is only part of the problem with CORBA and DCOM. Other technical challenges exist. Both protocols were developed before the Internet, and as such they aren't designed with the needs of a loosely coupled (sometimes unreliable) heavily trafficked network in mind. For example, both protocols are connection-oriented. This means a DCOM client holds onto a connection to the DCOM server to make multiple calls. The server-side DCOM component can also retain information about the client in memory. This provides a rich, flexible programming model, but it's a poor way to design large-scale applications that use the stateless protocols of the Internet. If the client simply disappears without properly cleaning up the connection, unnecessary resources are wasted. Similarly, if thousands of clients try to connect at once, the server can easily become swamped, running out of memory or connections.

Another problem is that both protocols are exceedingly complex. They combine distributed-object technology with features for network security and lifetime management. Web services are so much easier to use in large part because they don't include this level of sophistication. However, this doesn't mean you can't create a secure web service. It just means that if you do, you'll need to rely on web services *and* another standard, such as SSL (Secure Sockets Layer) (as implemented by the web server), or WS-Security and XML Encryption (as implemented by the programming framework).

■ **Note** The danger here is that developers could be swamped by a proliferation of standards that aren't required for basic web services but are required for sophisticated web service applications. However, this model still represents the best trade-off between complexity and simplicity. The advantage is that architects can develop new innovations for web services (such as transactional support) without compromising the basic level of interoperability provided by the core web service standards.

The Benefits of Web Services

Web services are interesting from several perspectives. From a technological perspective, web services try to solve some of the problems faced when using tightly coupled technologies such as CORBA and DCOM. These are problems such as getting through firewalls, dealing with the complexities of lower-level transport protocols, and integrating heterogeneous platforms. Web services are also interesting from an organizational and economic perspective, because they open doors for new ways of doing business and integrating systems between organizations.

DCOM and CORBA are fine for building enterprise applications with software running on the same platform and in the same closely administered local network. They are not fine, however, for building applications that span platforms, span the Internet, and need to achieve Internet scalability. They were simply not designed for this purpose.

This is where web services come in. Web services represent the next logical step in the evolution of component-based distributed technologies. Some key advantages include the following:

Web services are simple: This simplicity means they can be easily supported on a wide range of platforms.

Web services are loosely coupled: The web service may extend its interface and add new methods without affecting the clients as long as it still provides the old methods and parameters.

Web services are stateless: A client makes a request to a web service, the web service returns the result, and the connection is closed. No permanent connection exists. This makes it easy to scale up and out to many clients and use a server farm to serve the web services. The underlying HTTP used by web services is also stateless. Of course, it is possible to provide some state by using additional techniques such as the ones you use in ASP.NET web pages, including cookies and session state. However, these techniques aren't standardized.

Web services are firewall-friendly: Firewalls can pose a challenge for distributed object technologies. The only thing that almost always gets through firewalls is HTTP traffic on ports 80 and 443. Because web services use HTTP, they can pass through firewalls without explicit configuration.

■ **Note** It is still possible to use the firewall to block SOAP traffic. This is possible because the HTTP header of a web service message identifies it as a SOAP message and because an administrator may configure the firewall to stop SOAP traffic. For business-to-business scenarios, the firewall may allow SOAP traffic only from selected ranges of IP addresses.

Of course, the simplicity of web services comes with a cost. Namely, web services don't have all the features of more-complex distributed component technologies. For example, they don't support bidirectional communication, which means the web server cannot call a client after the client disconnects. In this respect, tightly coupled protocols such as DCOM and CORBA are more powerful than web services. The .NET Framework also has a technology called *remoting*, which is ideal for communicating between distributed .NET applications in an internal network. Remoting is the successor to DCOM on the .NET platform. If you want to know more, you can read *Advanced .NET Remoting*, Second Edition by Ingo Rammer and Mario Szpuszta (Apress, 2004). For information about whether you should use remoting instead of web services, refer to the sidebar "When to Use Web Services."

WHEN TO USE WEB SERVICES

Microsoft suggests two rules of thumb for deciding whether to use web services. If you need to cross platform boundaries (for example, to communicate between a .NET and a Java application) or trust boundaries (for example, to communicate between two different companies), web services make great sense. Web services are also a good choice if you want to use built-in ASP.NET features such as caching or IIS features such as SSL security or Windows authentication. They also make sense if you want to leave yourself open to third-party integration in the future.

However, if you simply want to share functionality between two .NET applications, web services can be overkill—and they may introduce unnecessary overhead. For example, if you simply want web applications to have access to specific business logic, a much better approach is to create a class library assembly (which is compiled to a DLL) and use it in both applications. This avoids the overhead of out-of-process or network communication, which can be significant.

Finally, if you want to distribute functionality so it can be accessed remotely but both the client and server are built using the .NET Framework, you might want to consider using .NET remoting instead. Remoting gives you the freedom to use different types of communication, proprietary .NET data types, stateful objects, and faster TCP/IP communication. In short, remoting offers more features and the possibility to enhance performance for .NET-only solutions, but it is still recommended only for cross-application-domain communication on the same machine.

Making Money with Web Services

A new technology is doomed if it does not give new opportunities for the people concerned with making money. From a businessperson's perspective, web services open new possibilities for the following reasons:

New payment structures: The user of a web service can pay a subscription fee for using the service. One example may be the news feed from the Associated Press. Another possibility is a pay-per-view, or *micro payment*, model. A provider of a credit verification service, for instance, may charge per request.

Real-time interaction and collaboration: Today, data is typically replicated and used locally. Web services enable real-time queries to remote data. An example is an e-commerce site selling computer games. The e-commerce site may hook up to a warehouse to get the number of items in stock in real time. This enables the e-commerce site to provide a better service. Nothing is more frustrating than buying something over the Internet just to learn the next day the product you wanted is out of stock.

Aggregated services: A web service may aggregate other web services, screen-scraped websites, legacy components exposed using proprietary protocols, and so on. A typical example of an aggregated service is a comparative service giving you the best deal on products. Another type of service is one that groups related services. For example, imagine you're moving to a new home. Someone could provide you with a service that can update your address at the post office, find the transportation company to move all your possessions, and so on.

Web services are by no means the only technology that can provide these solutions. Many similar solutions are available today using existing technology. However, web services have the momentum and standards to make these kinds of services generally available.

The Web Service Stack

The key to the success of web services is that they are based on open standards *and* that major vendors such as Microsoft, IBM, and Sun are behind these standards. Still, open standards do not automatically lead to interoperability. First, the vendors must implement all the standards. Furthermore, they must implement the standards in a compatible way, as defined by the WS-I Base Profile (see `http://www.ws-i.org`).

Several specifications are used when building web services. Figure 31-1 shows the web service stack as it exists today.

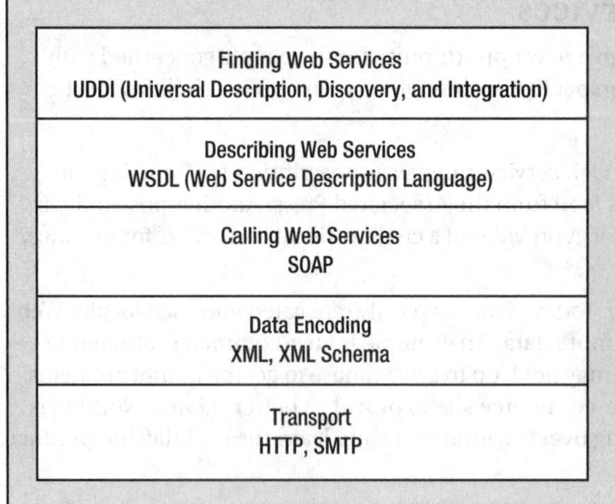

Figure 31-1. *The web service technology stack*

You'll learn much more about the SOAP, WSDL, and UDDI protocols that support web services in the next chapter. However, before you get started creating and using web services, it's important to get a basic understanding of the role these standards play. Table 31-2 summarizes these standards, and the next few sections fill in some of the details. You'll get into much more detail in the next chapter.

Table 31-2. *Web Service Standards*

Standard	Description
WSDL	Used to create an interface definition for a web service. The WSDL document tells a client what methods are present in a web service, what parameters and return values each method uses, and how to communicate with them.
SOAP	The message format used to encode information (such as data values) when communicating with a web service.
HTTP	The protocol over which all web service communication takes place. For example, SOAP messages are sent over HTTP channels.
DISCO	Used to create discovery documents that provide links to multiple web service endpoints. This standard is Microsoft-specific and will eventually be replaced by a similar standard named WS-Inspection.
UDDI	A standard for creating business registries that catalog companies, the web services they provide, and the corresponding URLs for their WSDL contracts.

Finding Web Services

In a simple application, you may already know the URL of the web service you want to use. If so, you can hardcode it or place it in a configuration file. No other steps are required.

In other situations, you might want to search for the web service you need at runtime. For example, you might use a standardized service that's provided by different hosting companies and is not always available at the same URL. Or, you may just want an easy way to find all the web services provided by a trading partner. In both of these situations, you need to use *discovery* to programmatically locate the web services you need.

Two specifications help in the discovery of a web service:

DISCO (an abbreviation of discovery): The DISCO standard is used to create a single file that groups a list of related web services. A company can publish a DISCO file on its server that contains links to all the web services it provides. Then clients simply need to request this file to find all the available web services. This is useful when the client already knows the company, and that it's offering services, and wants to see what web services it exposes and find links to the details of its services. It's not useful for searching for new web services over the Internet, but it may be helpful for local networks where a client connects to the server and can see what and where services are available.

UDDI (Universal Description, Discovery, and Integration): UDDI is a centralized directory where web services are published by a group of companies. It's also the place where potential clients can go to search for their specific needs. Different organizations and groups of companies may use different UDDI registries. To retrieve information from a UDDI directory or register your components, you use a web service interface.

Discovery is one of the newest and least-mature parts of the web service protocol stack. DISCO is only supported by Microsoft and is slated to be replaced by a similar more general standard named WS-Inspection in future .NET releases. UDDI is designed for web services that are intended to be shared publicly or among a consortium of companies or organizations. It's not incorporated into the .NET Framework, although you can download a separate .NET component to search UDDI directories and register your components (see `http://msdn.microsoft.com/library/en-us/uddi/uddi/portal.asp`). Because there aren't yet any well-established UDDI directories, and because many web services are simply designed for use in a single company or between a small set of known trading partners, it's likely that most web services will not be published in UDDI.

Describing a Web Service

For a client to know how to access a web service, it must know what methods are available, what parameters each method uses, and what the data type of each parameter is. WSDL is an XML-based language that describes all these details. It describes the request message a client needs to submit to the web service and the response message the web service returns. It also defines the transport protocol you need to use (typically HTTP) and the location of the web service.

WSDL is a complex standard. But as you'll see in this chapter, certain tools consume WSDL information and automatically generate helper classes that hide the low-level plumbing required to interact with web services.

The Wire Format

To communicate with a web service, you need a way to create request and response messages that can be parsed and understood on any platform. SOAP (formerly Simple Object Access Protocol but no longer considered an acronym) is the XML-based language you use to create these messages. (Similarly, SOA [Service Oriented Architecture] is no longer considered an acronym.)

It's important to understand that SOAP defines the messages you use to exchange data (the message format), but it doesn't describe how you send the message (the transport protocol). With ASP.NET web services, the transport protocol is HTTP. In other words, to communicate with a web service, a client opens an HTTP connection and sends a SOAP message.

.NET also supports HTTP GET and HTTP POST, two simpler approaches for interacting with web services that aren't as standardized and don't offer the same rich set of features. In both cases, an HTTP channel is used for communication, and data is sent as a simple collection of name/value pairs, not as a full-blown SOAP message. The only place you're likely to see this simpler approach used in the .NET environment is in the simple browser-based test page ASP.NET provides for testing your web services. In fact, by default the ASP.NET 1.1 machine.config file allows only HTTP POST requests from the local computer and disables HTTP GET support entirely.

Figure 31-2 summarizes the web service life cycle. First, the web service consumer finds the web service, either by going directly to the web service URL or by using a UDDI server or DISCO file. Next, the client retrieves the web service WSDL document, which describes how to interact with the web service. Both of these tasks are performed at design time. When you run the application and actually interact with the web service, the client sends a SOAP message to trigger to the appropriate web method.

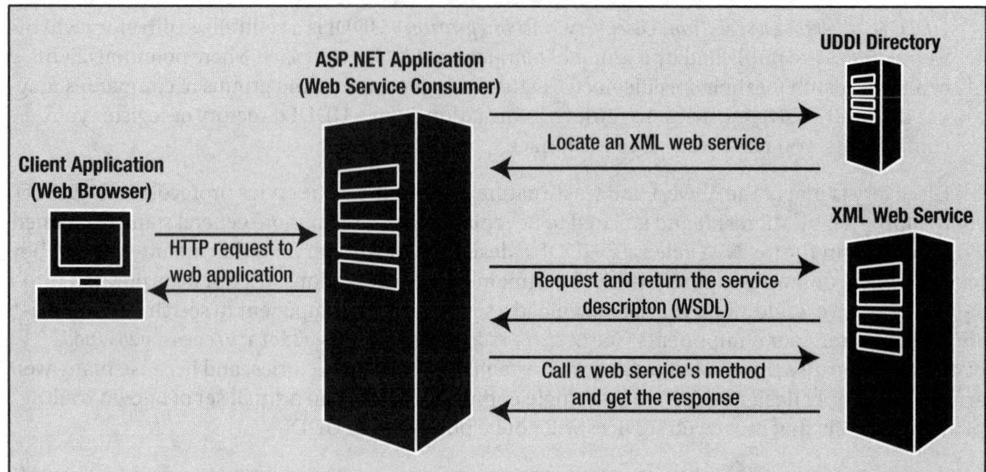

Figure 31-2. *The web service life cycle*

Building a Basic Web Service

You'll now see how to build a web service with ASP.NET and how to test it in a browser. In this example, you'll develop a web service called EmployeesService, which will count and return the number of employees for a specific city (or the total of all employees) by querying the Employees table in SQL Server's sample Northwind database.

The Web Service Class

A web service begins as a stateless class with one or more methods. It's these methods that the remote clients call to invoke your code.

The EmployeesService allows remote clients to retrieve information about the employees in a company. It provides a GetEmployees() method that returns a DataSet with the full set of employee information. It also provides a GetEmployeesCount() method, which simply returns the number of employees in the database. To provide these methods, you need nothing more than some basic ADO.NET code. Here's the full class listing:

```
Public Class EmployeesService
    Private connectionString As String
    Public Sub New()
    Dim connectionString As String =
        WebConfigurationManager.ConnectionStrings("Northwind").ConnectionString
    End Sub
```

```
    Public Function GetEmployeesCount() As Integer
        Dim con As New SqlConnection(connectionString)
        Dim sql As String = "SELECT COUNT(*) FROM Employees"
        Dim cmd As New SqlCommand(sql, con)
        Try

            ' Open the connection and get the value.
            con.Open()
            Dim numEmployees As Integer = -1
            numEmployees = CInt(cmd.ExecuteScalar())
        Finally
            con.Close()
        End Try
        Return numEmployees
    End Function

    Public Function GetEmployees() As DataSet
        ' Create the command and the connection.
        Dim sql As String = "SELECT EmployeeID, LastName, FirstName, Title, " _
              & "TitleOfCourtesy, HomePhone FROM Employees"
        Dim con As New SqlConnection(connectionString)
        Dim da As New SqlDataAdapter(sql, con)
        Dim ds As New DataSet()

        ' Fill the DataSet.
        da.Fill(ds, "Employees")
        Return ds
    End Function
End Class
```

Both GetEmployees() and GetEmployeesCount() are public methods, which means the class can be used from any web page in the same project (or, if you compile this class into a separate DLL, in any project that references this assembly). However, you need to take a few extra steps to make this class ready for a web service.

Web Service Requirements

Before you transform your class into a web service, you need to make sure it's compatible with the requirements of the underlying XML-based standards (which you'll learn more about in the next chapter). Because web services are executed by ASP.NET, which hosts the CLR (common language runtime), you can use any valid .NET code. This means you can use .NET classes to access data with ADO.NET or validate data with regular expressions. As with any back-end business component, you can't show any user interface, but other than that your code has no restrictions.

However, limitations do exist for what information your code can accept (in the form of parameters) and return (in the form of a return value). That's because web services are built on XML-based standards for exchanging data. As a result, the set of data types they can use is limited to the set of data types recognized by the XML Schema standard. Therefore, you can use simple data types such as strings and numbers, but you don't have any automatic way to send proprietary .NET objects such as a FileStream, an Image, or an EventLog. This restriction makes a lot of sense. Clearly, other programming languages have no way to interpret these more complex classes, so even if you could devise a way to send them over the wire, the client might not be able to interpret them, which would thwart interoperability. (.NET remoting is an example of a distributed component technology that *does* allow you to use .NET-specific types. However, the cost of this convenience is it won't support non-.NET clients.)

Table 31-3 lists the supported web service data types.

Table 31-3. *Web Service Data Types for Parameters and Return Values*

Data Type	Description
The basics	Simple data types such as integers (Short, Integer, Long), unsigned integers (UShort, UInteger, ULong), nonintegral numeric types (Single, Double, Decimal), and a few other miscellaneous types (Boolean, String, Character, Byte, and DateTime).
Arrays	You can use arrays of any supported type. You can also use an ArrayList (which is simply converted into an array), but you can't use more-specialized collections such as the Hashtable. You can also use binary data through byte arrays. Binary data is automatically Base64 encoded so that it can be inserted into an XML web service message.
Custom Objects	You can pass any object you create based on a custom class or structure. The limitation is that only public data members are transmitted, and all public members and properties must use one of the other supported data types. If you use a class that includes custom methods, these methods will not be transmitted to the client, and they will not be accessible to the client.
Enumerations	Enumerations types are supported. However, the web service uses the string name of the enumeration value (not the underlying integer).
XmlNode	Objects based on System.Xml.XmlNode are representations of a portion of an XML document. You can use this to send arbitrary XML.
DataSet and DataTable	You can use the DataSet and DataTable to return information from a relational database. Other ADO.NET data objects, like DataColumns and DataRows, aren't supported. When you use a DataSet or DataTable, it's automatically serialized to XML in a similar way as if you used the GetXml() or WriteXml() methods.

■**Note** The supported web service data types are based on the types defined by the XML Schema standard. These map fairly well to the basic set of .NET data types.

The EmployeesServices class follows these rules:

- The only data types it uses for parameters and return values are int and DataSet, both of which are supported. Of course, some web service programmers prefer to steer clear of the DataSet (see the sidebar in this section), but it's still a reasonable, widely used approach.
- One other requirement is that your web services should be stateless. In fact, the web service architecture works in the same way as the web-page architecture—a new web service object is created at the beginning of the request, and the web service object is destroyed as soon as the request has been processed and the response has been returned. The EmployeesServices class fits well with this model, because it doesn't retain any state in class member variables. The only exception is the connectionString variable, which is initialized with the required value every time the class is instantiated.

THE DATASET AND XML WEB SERVICES

You'll notice that the DataSet is one of the few specialized .NET classes supported by web services. That's because the DataSet has the ability to automatically serialize itself to XML. However, this support comes with a significant caveat—even though non-.NET clients can use a web service that returns a DataSet, they might not be able to do anything useful with the DataSet XML! That's because other languages won't be able to automatically convert the DataSet into a manageable object. Instead, they will be forced to use their own XML programming APIs. Although these work in theory, they can be tedious in practice, especially with complex, proprietary XML. For that reason, developers usually avoid the DataSet when creating web services that need to support clients on a wide range of different platforms.

It's worth noting that Microsoft could have used the DataSet approach with many other .NET classes in order to allow them to automatically serialize themselves as XML. However, Microsoft wisely restrained itself from adding these features, realizing that this would make it far too easy for programmers to create applications that used web service standards but weren't practical in cross-platform scenarios. (Not so long ago, Microsoft might have pursued exactly this "embrace and extend" philosophy, but fortunately it has recognized the need to foster integration and broad compatibility between applications.)

So that still leaves the question of why Microsoft decided to support the DataSet in the web services toolkit. Well, the DataSet enables one of the most common uses of web services—returning a snapshot of information from a relational database. The benefit of adding this feature seemed worth the cost of potential interoperability headaches for developers who don't consider their web service architecture carefully.

Support for Generics

Web services support generics. However, this support might not be exactly what you expect.

It's completely acceptable to create a web service method that accepts or returns a generic type. For example, if you want to return a collection of EmployeeDetails objects, you could use the generic List class, as shown here:

```
Public Function GetEmployees() As List(Of EmployeeDetails)()
    ...
End Function
```

In this case, .NET treats your collection of EmployeeDetails objects in the same way as an array of EmployeeDetails objects:

```
Public Function GetEmployees() As EmployeeDetails()
    ...
End Function
```

Of course, for this to work, nothing can break the serialization rules in the EmployeeDetails class or the List class. For example, if these classes have a nonserializable property, the entire object can't be serialized.

The reason .NET supports generics in this example is because it's quite easy for .NET to determine the real class types at compile time. That allows it to determine the structure of the XML messages this method will use and add the information to the WSDL document (as you'll see in the next chapter).

However, .NET doesn't support generic methods. For example, this method isn't allowed:

```
Public Function(Of T) GetEmployees () As List(Of T)
...
End Function
```

Here the GetEmployees() method is itself generic. It allows the caller to choose a type that will be used by the method. Because this method could in theory be used with absolute any type of document, you have way to document it properly and determine the appropriate XML message format in advance.

Exposing a Web Service

Now that you've verified the EmployeesService class is ready for the Web, it's time to convert it to a web service. The crucial first step is to add the System.Web.Services.WebMethod attribute to each method you want to expose as part of your web service. This attribute instructs ASP.NET to make this method available for inspection and remote invocation.

Here's the revised class with two web methods:

```
Public Class EmployeesService
    <WebMethod()> _
    Public Function GetEmployeesCount() As Integer
        ...
    End Function

    <WebMethod()> _
    Public Function GetEmployees() As DataSet
        ...
    End Function
End Class
```

These two simple changes complete the transformation from your class into a web service. However, the client still has no entry point into your web service—in other words, another application has no way to trigger your web methods. To allow this, you need to create an .asmx file that exposes the web service.

■ **Note** In this example, the web service contains the data access code. However, if you plan to use the same code in a web application, it's worth adding an extra layer using database components. To implement this design, you would first create a separate database component (as described in Part 2) and then use that database component directly in your web pages and your web service.

ASP.NET implements web services as files with the .asmx extension. As with a web page, you can place the code for a web service directly in the .asmx or in a class in a code-behind file that the .asmx file references (which is the Visual Studio approach).

For example, you could create a file named EmployeesService.asmx and link it to your EmployeesService class. Every .asmx file begins with a WebService directive that declares the server-side language used in the file and the class. It can optionally declare other information, such as the code-behind file and whether you want to generate debug symbols during the compilation. In this respect, it is similar to the Page directive for .aspx files.

Here's an example .asmx file with the EmployeesService:

```
<%@ WebService Language="vb" Class="EmployeesService" %>
```

In this case, you have two choices. You can insert the class code immediately after the WebService attribute, or you can compile it into one of the assemblies in the Bin directory. If you've added the EmployeesService class to a Visual Studio project, it will automatically be compiled as part of the web application DLL, so you don't need to include anything else in the .asmx file.

At this point, you're finished. Your web service is complete, available, and ready to be used in other applications.

■ **Tip** You can add as many web services as you want to a single web application, and you can freely mingle web services and web pages.

Web Services in Visual Studio

If you're using Visual Studio, you probably won't go through the process of creating a class, converting it to a web service, and then adding an .asmx file. Instead, you'll create the .asmx file and the code-behind in one step (by selecting Website ➤ Add New Item from the menu). You can choose to put the web service code directly in the .asmx file or in a separate code-behind file, just as you can with a web page.

Also, you haven't used two additional details in the web service. First, the web service class inherits from System.Web.Services.WebService, and second, a WebService attribute is applied to the class declaration. Neither of these details is required, but you'll consider their roles in the following sections.

Deriving from the WebService Class

When you create a web service in Visual Studio, your web service class automatically derives from the base WebService class, as shown here:

```
Public Class EmployeesService : Inherits System.Web.Services.WebService
    ...
End Class
```

Inheriting from the WebService class is a convenience that allows you to access the built-in ASP.NET objects (such as Application, Session, and User) just as easily as you can in a web form. These objects are provided as properties of the WebService class, which your web service acquires through inheritance. If you don't need to use any of these objects (or if you're willing to go through the static HttpContext.Current property to access them), you don't need to inherit.

Here's how you would access session state in a web service if you derive from the base WebService class:

```
' Store a number in session state.
Session("Counter") = 10
```

Here's the equivalent code you would need to use if your web service class doesn't derive from WebService:

```
' Store a number in session state.
HttpContext.Current.Session("Counter") = 10
```

This technique won't actually work as intended (in other words, the client won't keep the same session across multiple web method calls) unless you take some extra steps, as described later in this chapter (in the "EnableSession" section).

Table 31-4 lists the properties you receive by inheriting from WebService.

Table 31-4. *WebService Properties*

Property	Description
Application	An instance of the HttpApplicationState class that provides access to the global application state of the web application
Context	An instance of the HttpContext class for the current request
Server	An instance of the HttpServerUtility class
Session	An instance of the HttpSessionState class that provides access to the current session state
User	An IPrincipal object that allows you to examine user credentials and roles, if the user has been authenticated

Since the .NET Framework supports only single inheritance, inheriting from WebService means your web service class cannot inherit from other classes. This is really the only reason not to inherit from WebService.

■ **Note** An interesting point with inheriting from WebService is that WebService is derived from the System.MarshalByRefObject class. This class is the base class used for .NET remoting. As a result, when you create a class that derives from WebService, you gain the ability to use your class in several ways. You can use it as any other local class (and access it directly in your web pages), you can expose it as part of a web service, or you can expose it as a distributed object in a .NET remoting host. To learn more about .NET remoting, refer to *Advanced .NET Remoting*, Second Edition by Ingo Rammer and Mario Szpuszta (Apress, 2004).

Documenting a Web Service

Web services are self-describing, which means ASP.NET automatically provides all the information the client needs about what methods are available and what parameters they require. This is provided by the XML-based standard called WSDL, which you'll explore in the next chapter. However, although a WSDL document describes the mechanics of the web service, it doesn't describe its purpose or the meaning of the information supplied to and returned from each method. Most web services will provide this information in separate developer documents. However, you can (and should) include a bare minimum of information with your web service by using the WebMethod and WebService attributes.

You can add descriptions to each method through the Description property of the WebMethod attribute and to the entire web service as a whole using the Description property of the WebService attribute. You can also apply a descriptive name to the web service using the Name property of the WebService attribute. Here's an example of how you might insert this information in the EmployeesService:

```
<WebService(Name:="Employees Service",
      Description:="Retrieve the Northwind Employees")> _
Public Class EmployeesService : Inherits System.Web.Services.WebService
    <WebMethod(Description:="Returns the total number of employees.")> _
    Public Function GetEmployeesCount() As Integer
        ...
    End Function
```

```
    <WebMethod(Description:="Returns the full list of employees.")> _
    Public Function GetEmployees() As DataSet
        ...
    End Function
End Class
```

These custom descriptions are added to the WSDL document that describes your service. It's also shown in the automatically generated test page you'll use in the next section.

Also, you should supply on other detail for your web service—a unique XML namespace. This allows your web service (and the XML messages it generates) to be uniquely identified. (Chapter 12 introduced XML namespaces.) By default, ASP.NET web services use the default XML namespace `http://tempuri.org/`, which is suitable only for testing. If you don't set a custom namespace, you'll see a warning message in the test page advising you to use something more distinctive. Note that the XML namespace has no relationship to the concept of .NET namespaces. It doesn't affect how your code works or the code for your client using your web service. It may affect the SOAP message that is generated by the client proxy. Instead, the XML namespace is simply used to identify your web service. XML namespaces usually look like URLs or URNs. However, they don't need to correspond to a valid Internet location.

Ideally, the namespace you use will refer to a URL address you control. Often, this will incorporate your company's Internet domain name as part of the namespace. For example, if your company uses the website `http://www.mycompany.com`, you might give the Employees web service a namespace such as `http://www.mycompany.com/EmployeesService`.

You specify the namespace through the WebService attribute, as shown here:

```
<WebService (Name:="Employees Service",
        Description:="Retrieve the Northwind Employees",
        Namespace:="http://www.apress.com/ProASP.NET/")> _
Public Class EmployeesService : Inherits System.Web.Services.WebService
       Private ...
End Class
```

Testing a Web Service

Now that you've seen how to create a simple web service, you're ready to test it. Fortunately, you don't need to write a client application to test it because .NET includes a test web page that ASP.NET uses automatically when you request the URL of an .asmx file in a browser. This page uses reflection to read and show information about the web services, such as the names of the methods it provides.

To try the test page, request the EmployeesService.asmx file in your browser. (In Visual Studio, you simply need to set this as the start page for your application and then run it.) Figure 31-3 shows the test page you'll see.

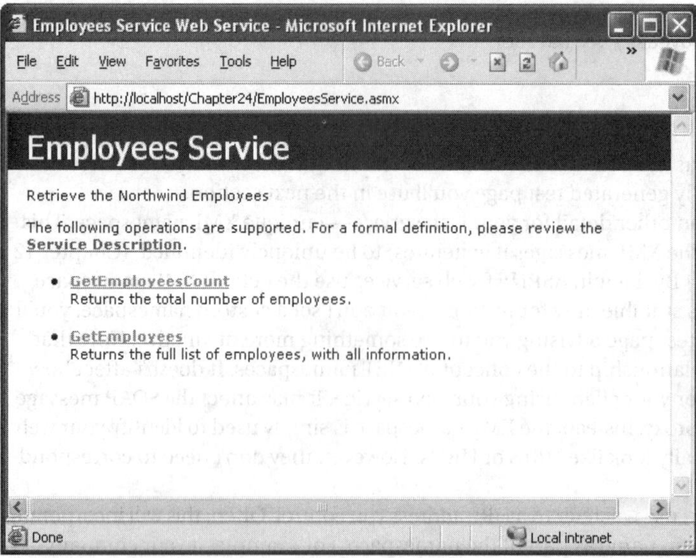

Figure 31-3. *The web service test page*

Note that the page displays the two web methods with their descriptions, and the page's title is the name of the web service. If you click one of the methods, you'll see a page that allows you to test the method (and supply the data for any method parameters). Figure 31-4 shows the page that allows you to test the GetEmployeesCount() method.

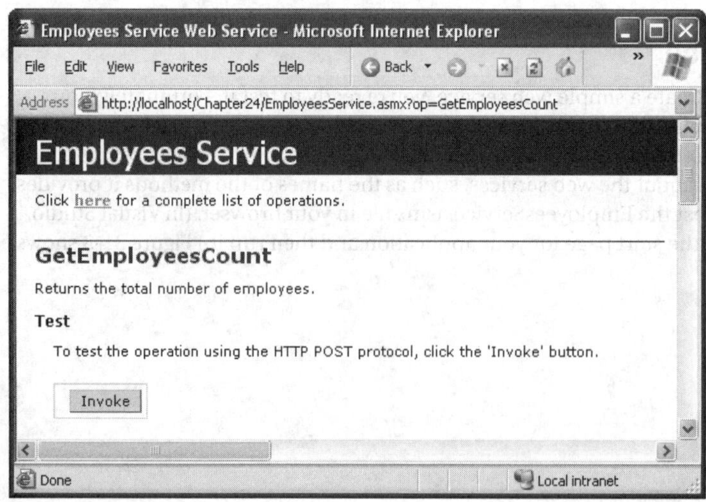

Figure 31-4. *Testing a web method*

When you click the Invoke button, a new web page appears with an XML document that contains the requested data. Looking at Figure 31-5, you can see nine employee records. If you look at the URL, you'll see that it incorporates the .asmx file, followed by the web service method name.

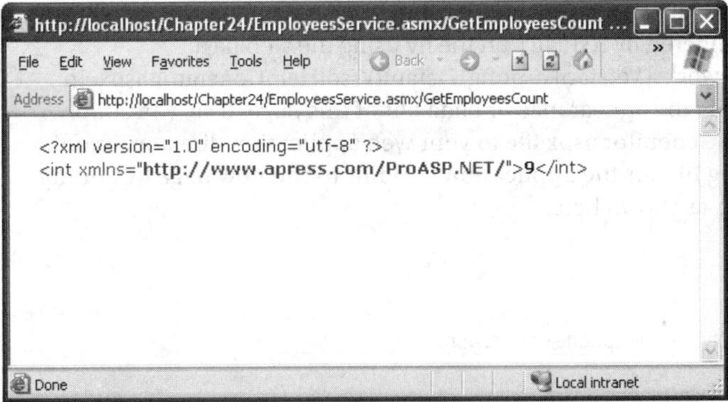

Figure 31-5. *The results for GetEmployeesCount()*

You can repeat this process to invoke GetEmployees(), in which case you'll see the much more detailed XML that represents the entire DataSet contents (as shown in Figure 31-6).

As you can see, thanks to this helper page, testing a basic web service is quite straightforward and doesn't require you to build a client.

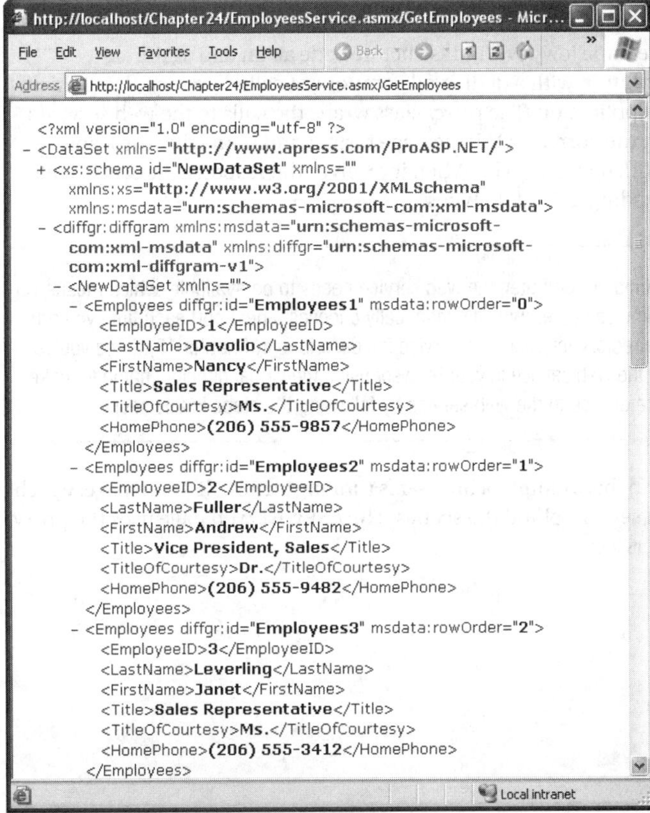

Figure 31-6. *The results for GetEmployees()*

The test pages aren't part of the web services standards; they're just a frill ASP.NET provides. In fact, the test page is rendered by ASP.NET on the fly using the web page c:\[WinDir]\Microsoft.NET\Framework\[Version]\Config\DefaultWsdlHelpGenerator.aspx. In some cases, you may want to modify the appearance or behavior of this page. If so, you simply need to copy the DefaultWsdlHelpGenerator.aspx file to your web application directory, modify it, and then change the web.config file for the application to point to the new page by adding the <wsdlHelpGenerator> element, as shown here:

```
<configuration>
  <system.web>
    <webServices>
      <wsdlHelpGenerator href="MyWsdlHelpGenerator.aspx"/>
    </webServices>
    <!-- Other settings omitted. -->
  </system.web>
</configuration>
```

This technique is most commonly used to change the look of the test page. For example, you might use this technique to substitute a version of the page that has a company logo or copyright notice.

Consuming a Web Service

For a client to use the web service, it has to be able to create, send, receive, and understand XML-based messages. This process is easy in principle but fairly tedious in practice. If you had to implement it yourself, you would need to write the same low-level infrastructure code again and again.

Fortunately, .NET provides a solution with a dedicated component called a *proxy class*, which performs the heavy lifting for your application. The proxy class wraps the calls to the web service's methods. It takes care of generating the correct SOAP message format and managing the transmission of the messages over the network (using HTTP). When it receives the response message, it also converts the results to the corresponding .NET data types.

■ **Note** To access a web service from another computer, the web service needs to be available, which means you can't rely on just the built-in Visual Studio web server (which dynamically chooses a new port each time you run it). Instead, you need to create a virtual directory for your web service (as described in Chapter 18). Once you've taken this step, you should try requesting the web service in your browser using the virtual directory name to make sure it's accessible. You can then add a reference to the web service by following the steps in this section.

Figure 31-7 shows this process. In this example, a browser is running an ASP.NET web page, which is using a web service from another server behind the scenes. The ASP.NET web page uses the proxy class to contact this external web service.

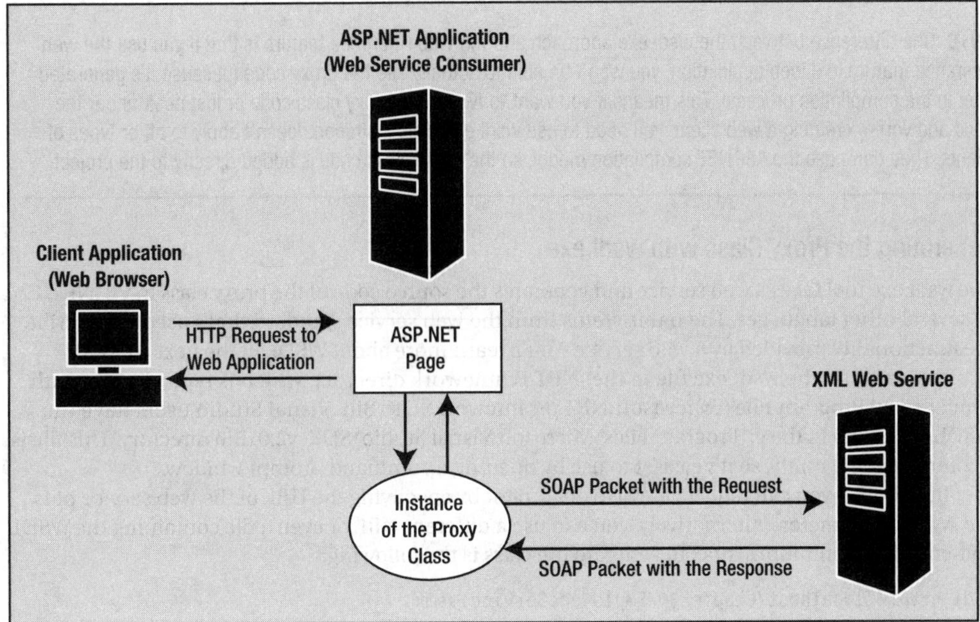

Figure 31-7. *The web service proxy class*

Note Thanks to the proxy class, you can call a method in a web service as easily as you call a method in a local component. Of course, this behavior isn't always a benefit. Web services have different characteristics than local components do. For example, it takes a nontrivial amount of time to call a web method because every call needs to be converted to XML and sent over the network. The danger is that the more this reality is hidden from developers, the less likely they are to take it into account and design their applications accordingly.

You have two ways to create a proxy class in .NET:

- You can use the wsdl.exe command-line tool.
- You can use the Visual Studio web reference feature.

Both of these approaches produce essentially the same result, because they use the same classes in the .NET Framework to perform the actual work. In fact, you can even harness these classes (which are found in the System.Web.Services namespaces) to generate your own proxy classes programmatically, although this approach isn't terribly practical.

In the following sections, you'll learn how to use wsdl.exe and Visual Studio to create proxy classes. You'll learn how to consume a web service in three types of clients—an ASP.NET web page, a Windows application, and a classic ASP page.

Tip One difference between the wsdl.exe approach and the web reference feature is that if you use the web reference feature in a web application, you won't be able to actually see the proxy code (because it's generated later in the compilation process). This means if you want to tweak the proxy class code or just peek under the hood and you're creating a web client, you need to use wsdl.exe. This limitation doesn't apply to other types of clients. They don't use the ASP.NET compilation model, so the proxy class code is added directly to the project.

Generating the Proxy Class with wsdl.exe

The wsdl.exe tool takes a web service and generates the source code of the proxy class in VB .NET, C#, or several other languages. The name stems from the web service standard that's used to describe the functionality provided by a web service. You'll learn more about WSDL in the next chapter.

You can find the wsdl.exe file in the .NET Framework directory, which is typically in a path similar to c:\Program Files\Microsoft.NET\FrameworkSDK\Bin. Visual Studio users have the WSDL.exe utility in the c:\Program Files\Microsoft Visual Studio\SDK\v2.0\Bin directory. This file is a command-line utility, so it's easiest to use by opening a command prompt window.

In ASP.NET, you can request a WSDL document by specifying the URL of the web service plus the ?WSDL parameter. (Alternatively, you can use a different URL or even a file containing the WSDL content.) The minimum syntax to generate the class is the following:

```
wsdl http://localhost/Chapter30/EmployeesService.asmx
```

By default the generated class is in the C# language, but you can change it by adding the /language parameter, as follows:

```
wsdl /language:VB http://localhost/Chapter30/EmployeesService.asmx
```

By default the generated file also has the same name as the web service (specified in the Name property of the WebService attribute). You can change it by adding an /out parameter to the wsdl.exe command, and you can use a /namespace parameter to change the namespace for the generated class. Here's an example (split over two lines to fit the page margins):

```
wsdl /namespace:ApressServices /out:EmployeesProxy.vb /language:VB
  http://localhost/Chapter30/EmployeesService.asmx
```

Table 31-5 shows the list of supported parameters.

Table 31-5. *Wsdl.exe Parameters*

Parameter	Description
<url or path>	Specifies a URL or path to a WSDL contract, an XSD schema, or a .discomap document.
/nologo	Suppresses the banner.
/language:<language>	Specifies the language to use for the generated proxy class. Choose from CS, VB, JS, VJS, or CPP provide a fully qualified name for a class implementing System.CodeDom.Compiler.CodeDomProvider. The default is C#. The short form is /l.
/server	Generates an abstract class for a web service implementation based on the contracts. The default is to generate client proxy classes.
/namespace:<namespace>	Specifies the .NET namespace for the generated proxy or template. The default namespace is the global namespace. The short form is /n.

Parameter	Description
/out:<fileName>	Specifies the filename for the generated proxy code. The default name is derived from the service name. The short form is /o.
/protocol:<protocol>	Overrides the default protocol to implement. Choose from SOAP (for SOAP 1.1), SOAP12 (for SOAP 1.2), HTTP-GET, HTTP-POST, or a custom protocol as specified in the configuration file.
/username:<username> /password:<password> /domain:<domain>	Specifies the credentials to use when connecting to a server that requires authentication. The short forms are /u, /p, and /d.
/proxy:<URL>	Specifies the URL of the proxy server to use for HTTP requests. The default is to use the system proxy setting.
/proxyusername:<username> /proxypassword:<password> /proxydomain:<domain>	Specifies the credentials to use when connecting to a proxy server that requires authentication. The short forms are /pu, /pp, and /pd.
/appsettingurkey:<key>	Specifies the configuration key to use in the code generation to read the default value for the URL property. The default is to not read from the config file. The short form is /urlkey.
/appsettingbaseurl:<baseURL>	Specifies the base URL to use when calculating the URL fragment. You must also specify the appsettingurlkey option. The URL fragment is the result of calculating the relative URL from the appsettingbaseurl to the URL in the WSDL document. The short form is /baseurl.
/fields	If set, any complex types used by the web service will consist of public fields instead of public properties. Chapter 30 discusses how complex types work with web services in much more detail.
/sharetypes	Allows you to add a reference to two or more web services that use the same complex types. Chapter 32 describes this technique.
/serverinterface	Generates an interface with just the methods of the WSDL document. You can implement this interface to create your web service. Chapter 32 describes this technique.

Once you've created this file, you need to copy it to the App_Code directory so the class is available to the pages in your web application. If you're creating a rich client application (such as a Windows Forms application), you would instead add this file directly to the project so it is compiled into the final EXE.

Generating the Proxy Class with Visual Studio

In Visual Studio, you create the proxy class by adding a web reference in the client project.

To create a web reference, follow these steps:

1. Right-click the client project in the Solution Explorer, and select Add Web Reference. The Add Web Reference window opens, as shown in Figure 31-8. This window provides options for searching web registries or entering a URL directly. Another link allows you to browse all the web services on the local computer or search a UDDI registry.

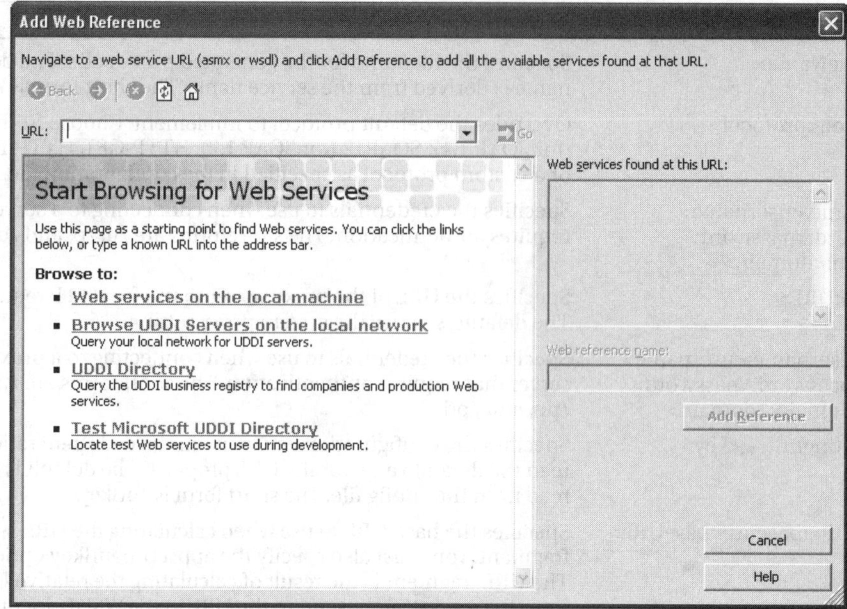

Figure 31-8. *The Add Web Reference window*

2. You can browse directly to your web service by entering a URL that points to the .asmx file. The test page will appear in the window (as shown in Figure 31-9), and the Add Reference button will be enabled.

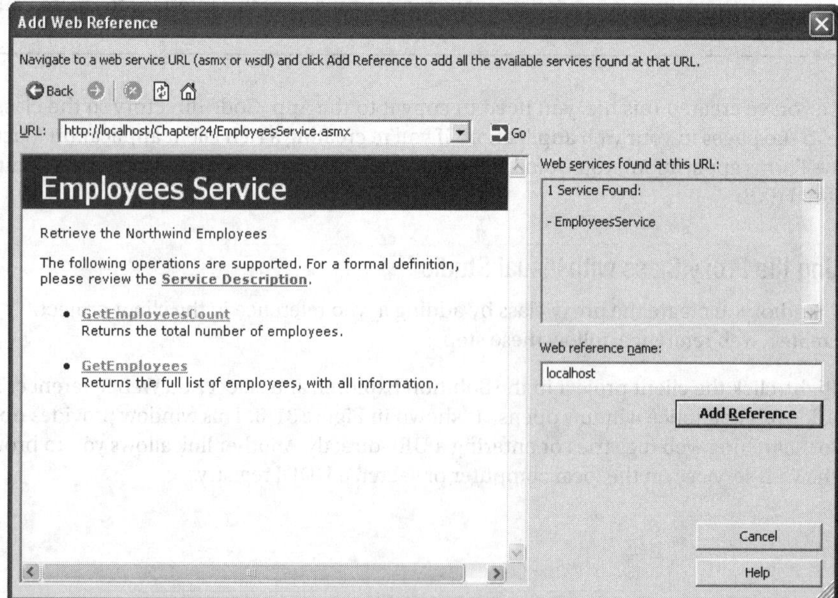

Figure 31-9. *Adding a web reference*

3. In the Web Reference Name text box, you can change the .NET namespace in which the proxy class will be generated.
4. To add the reference to this web service, click Add Reference at the bottom of the window.
5. Now the web reference will appear in the Web References group for your project in the Solution Explorer window.

The web reference you create uses the WSDL contract and information that exists at the time you add the reference. If the web service changes, you'll need to update your proxy class by right-clicking the web reference and choosing Update Web Reference. Unlike local components, web references aren't updated automatically when you recompile the application.

Tip When developing and testing a web service in Visual Studio, it's often easiest to add both the web service and the client application to the same solution. This allows you to test and change both pieces at the same time. You can even use the integrated debugger to set breakpoints and step through the code in both the client and the server, as though they were really a single application. To choose which application you want Visual Studio to launch when you click Start, right-click the appropriate project name in the Solution Explorer, and select Set As StartUp Project.

When you add a web reference, Visual Studio saves a copy of the WSDL document in your project. Where it stores this information depends on the type of project.

In a web application, Visual Studio creates the App_WebReferences folder (if it doesn't already exist) and then creates a folder inside it with the web reference name (which you chose in the Add Web Reference dialog box). Finally, Visual Studio places the web service files in that folder. However, Visual Studio *doesn't* generate the proxy class. Instead, it's built and cached as part of the ASP.NET compilation process. This is a change in the behavior from ASP.NET 1.*x*.

In any other type of application, Visual Studio creates a Web References folder and then creates a folder inside it with the web reference name. Inside that folder it places all the support files you see in a web application (most important, a copy of the WSDL document). It also creates a file named Reference.vb (assuming it's a Visual Basic application) with the proxy class source code. By default, this class is hidden from view. To see it, select Project ➤ Show All Files, as shown in Figure 31-10.

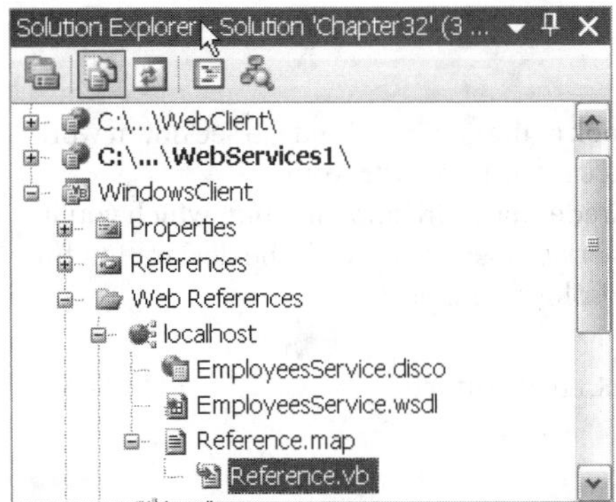

Figure 31-10. *The WSDL contract and proxy class*

Dynamic URLs

In previous versions of .NET, the web service URL was (by default) hard-coded in the class constructor. However, when you create a web reference with Visual Studio 2005, the location is always stored in a configuration file. This is useful, because it allows you to change the location of the web service when you deploy the application, without forcing you to regenerate the proxy class.

The location of this setting depends on the type of application. If the client is a web application, this information will be added to the web.config file, as shown here:

```
<?xml version="1.0" encoding="utf-8"?>
<configuration>
  <appSettings>
    <add key="localhost.EmployeesService"
     value="http://localhost/EmployeesService/EmployeesService.asmx"/>
  </appSettings>
  ...
</configuration>
```

If you're creating a different type of client application, such as a Windows application, the configuration file will have a name in the format [AppName].exe.config. For example, if your application is named SimpleClient.exe, the configuration file will be SimpleClient.exe.config. You must follow this naming convention.

Tip Visual Studio uses a little sleight of hand with named configuration files. In the design environment, the configuration file will have the name App.config. However, when you build the application, this file will be copied to the build directory and given the appropriate name (to match the executable file). The only exception is if the client application is a web application. All web applications use a configuration file named web.config, no matter what filenames you use. That's what you'll see in the design environment as well.

If you want to control the name of the setting, you need to use the wsdl.exe utility with /appsettingurlkey. For example, you could use this command line:

```
wsdl http://localhost/Chapter30/EmployeesService.asmx /appsettingurlkey:WsUrl
      /language:VB
```

In this case, the key is stored with the key WsUrl in the <appSettings> section.

The Proxy Class

Once you create the proxy class, it's worth taking a closer look at the generated code to see how it works.

The proxy class has the same name as the web service class. It inherits from SoapHttpClientProtocol, which has properties such as Credentials, Url, and Timeout, which you'll learn about later in this chapter (in the "Refining a Web Service" section). Here's the declaration for the proxy class that provides communication with the EmployeesService:

```
Public Class EmployeesService
    Inherits System.Web.Services.Protocols.SoapHttpClientProtocol
        ...
End Class
```

The proxy class contains a copy of each method in the web service. However, the version in the proxy class doesn't contain the business code. (In fact, the client has no way to get any information about the internal workings of your web service code—if it could, that would constitute a serious security breach.) Instead, the proxy class contains the code needed to query the remote web service and convert the results. For example, here's a snippet from the GetEmployeesCount() method in the proxy class:

```
<System.Web.Services.Protocols.SoapDocumentMethodAttribute()> _
Public Function GetEmployeesCount() As Integer
    Dim results As Object() = Me.Invoke("GetEmployeesCount", New Object(){})
    Return (CInt(results(0)))
End Function
```

This method calls the base SoapHttpClientProcotol.Invoke() to actually create the SOAP message and start waiting for the response. The second line of code converts the returned object into an integer.

Note The proxy also has other methods used to support asynchronous calls to the web methods. You'll learn more about asynchronous calls and see practical examples of how to use them in Chapter 30.

The proxy class concludes with the proxy code for the GetEmployees() method. You'll notice that this code is nearly identical to the code used for the GetEmployeesCount() method—the only difference is the method name that's passed to the Invoke() method and that the return value is converted to a DataSet rather than an integer.

```
<System.Web.Services.Protocols.SoapDocumentMethodAttribute()> _
Public Function GetEmployees() As System.Data.DataSet
    Dim results As Object() = Me.Invoke("GetEmployees", New Object(){})
    Return (CType(results(0), System.Data.DataSet))
End Function
```

Creating an ASP.NET Client

Now that you have a web service and proxy class, it's quite easy to develop a simple web-page client. If you're using Visual Studio, the first step is to create a new web project and add a web reference to the web service. If you're using another tool, you'll need to generate a proxy class first using wsdl.exe and then place it in the new web application Bin directory.

The following example uses a simple web page with a button and a DataGrid. When the user clicks the button, the web page posts back, instantiates the proxy class, retrieves the DataSet of employees from the web service, and then displays the result by binding it to the grid.

Before you add this code, it helps to import the proxy class namespace. In Visual Studio, the namespace is automatically the namespace of the current project, plus the .NET namespace you specified in the Add Web Reference dialog box (which is localhost by default). Assuming your project is named WebClient, the web service is on the local computer, and you didn't make any changes in the Add Web Reference dialog box, you'll use this namespace:

```
Imports WebClient.localhost
```

Now you can add the code that uses the proxy class to retrieve the data:

```
Private Sub cmdGetData_Click(ByVal sender As Object, ByVal e As System.EventArgs)
    ' Create the proxy.
    Dim proxy As New EmployeesService()

    ' Call the web service and get the results.
    Dim ds As DataSet = proxy.GetEmployees()

    ' Bind the results.
    DataGrid1.DataSource = ds.Tables(0)
    DataGrid1.DataBind()
End Sub
```

Because the proxy class has the same name as the web service class, when the client instantiates the proxy class, it seems as though the client is actually instantiating the web service. To help emphasize the difference, this code-names the object variable *proxy*.

If you run the page, you'll see the page shown in Figure 31-11.

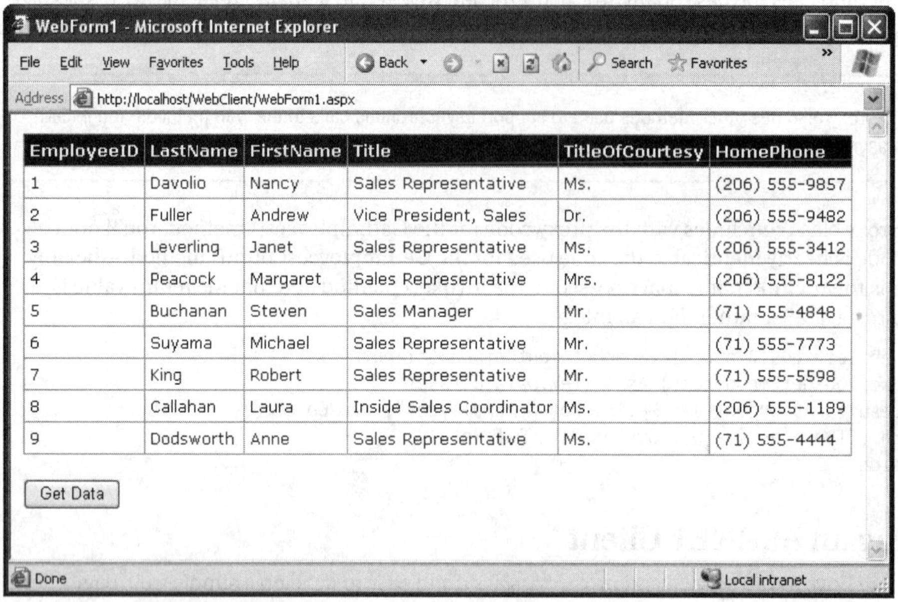

EmployeeID	LastName	FirstName	Title	TitleOfCourtesy	HomePhone
1	Davolio	Nancy	Sales Representative	Ms.	(206) 555-9857
2	Fuller	Andrew	Vice President, Sales	Dr.	(206) 555-9482
3	Leverling	Janet	Sales Representative	Ms.	(206) 555-3412
4	Peacock	Margaret	Sales Representative	Mrs.	(206) 555-8122
5	Buchanan	Steven	Sales Manager	Mr.	(71) 555-4848
6	Suyama	Michael	Sales Representative	Mr.	(71) 555-7773
7	King	Robert	Sales Representative	Mr.	(71) 555-5598
8	Callahan	Laura	Inside Sales Coordinator	Ms.	(206) 555-1189
9	Dodsworth	Anne	Sales Representative	Ms.	(71) 555-4444

Figure 31-11. *Displaying data from a web service in a web page*

From the point of view of your web-page code, calling a web service and using an ordinary stateless class are not different. However, you must remember that the web service actually implementing the business logic could be on a web server on the other side of the world. As a result, you need to reduce the number of times you call it and be prepared to handle exceptions resulting from network problems and connectivity errors.

Timeouts

The proxy class includes a Timeout property that allows you to specify the maximum amount of time you're willing to wait, in milliseconds. By default, the timeout is 100,000 milliseconds (100 seconds).

When using the Timeout property, you need to include error handling. If the Timeout period expires without a response, an exception will be thrown, giving you the chance to notify the user about the problem.

Here's how you could rewrite the ASP.NET web-page client to use a timeout of three seconds:

```
Private Sub cmdGetData_Click(ByVal sender As Object, ByVal e As System.EventArgs)
    ' Create the proxy object.
    Dim proxy As New EmployeesService()

    ' This timeout will apply to all web service method calls.
    proxy.Timeout = 3000 ' 3,000 milliseconds is 3 seconds.
```

```
    Dim ds As DataSet = Nothing
    Try
        ' Call the web service and get the results.
        ds = proxy.GetEmployees()
    Catch err As System.Net.WebException
        If err.Status = WebExceptionStatus.Timeout Then
            lblResult.Text = "Web service timed out after 3 seconds."
        Else
            lblResult.Text = "Another type of problem occurred."
        End If
    End Try

    ' Bind the results.
    If Not ds Is Nothing Then
        DataGrid1.DataSource = ds.Tables(0)
        DataGrid1.DataBind()
    End If
End Sub
```

You can also set the timeout to -1 to indicate that you'll wait as long as it takes. However, this will make your web application unacceptably slow if you attempt to perform a number of operations with an unresponsive web service.

Connecting Through a Proxy

The proxy class also has some built-in intelligence that allows you to reroute its HTTP communication with special Internet settings. By default the proxy class uses the Internet settings on the current computer. In some networks, this may not be the best approach. You can override these settings by using the Proxy property of the web service proxy class.

■Tip In this case, *proxy* is being used in two different ways: as a proxy that manages communication between a client and a web service and as a proxy server in your organization that manages communication between a computer and the Internet.

For example, if you need to connect through a computer called ProxyServer using port 80, you could use the following code before you call any web service methods:

```
' Create the web service proxy.
Dim proxy As New EmployeesService()

' Specify a proxy server for network communication.
Dim connectionProxy As New WebProxy("ProxyServer", 80)
proxy.Proxy = connectionProxy
```

Many other options for the WebProxy class allow you to configure connections and set authentication information in more complicated scenarios.

Creating a Windows Forms Client

One of the main advantages of web services is the way they allow you to web-enable local applications, such as rich client applications. Using a web service, you can create a desktop application that gets up-to-the-minute data from a web server. The process is almost entirely transparent. In fact, as high-speed access becomes more common, you may not even be aware of which portions of functionality depend on the Internet and which ones don't.

You can use web service functionality in a Windows application in the same way that you would use it in an ASP.NET application. First, you create the proxy class using Visual Studio or the wsdl.exe utility. Second, you add code to create an instance of the proxy class and call a web method. The only difference is the user interface the application uses.

If you haven't explored desktop programming with .NET yet, you'll be happy to know that you can reuse much of what you've learned in ASP.NET development. Many web controls (including labels, buttons, text boxes, and lists) closely parallel their .NET desktop equivalents. In fact, the most significant difference between desktop programming and web programming in .NET is the extra steps you need to take in web applications to preserve information between postbacks and when transferring the user from one page to another.

To begin creating your Windows client in Visual Studio, create a new Windows Application project, and then add the web reference. Windows Application projects start with a single startup form, which you can design in much the same way you design a web page. For this example, you simply need to drag and drop a button and a DataGrid from the Toolbox. (Keep in mind the Button and DataGrid classes used in a Windows application aren't the same as their ASP.NET counterparts. Even though they use the same class name and expose a similar programming, they're stored in different .NET namespaces, and their plumbing is completely different.)

To consume a web service in a Windows application, begin by importing the namespace you need at the top of the form class file, as you did in the ASP.NET page:

```
Imports WindowsClient.localhost
```

Next, add the event-handling code for the button. This code retrieves the DataSet and displays it in the form. Data binding works slightly differently in a Windows application—for example, you don't need to call an explicit DataBind() method after you set the data source. This code also introduces one refinement—it explicitly sets the application to use an hourglass cursor while the web service call is underway so the user knows the operation is in progress. Other than that, the code is identical.

```
Private Sub cmdGetData_Click(ByVal sender As Object, ByVal e As System.EventArgs)
    Me.Cursor = Cursors.WaitCursor

    ' Create the proxy.
    Dim proxy As New EmployeesService()

    ' Call the web service and get the results.
    Dim ds As DataSet = proxy.GetEmployees()

    ' Bind the results.
    DataGrid1.DataSource = ds.Tables(0)

    Me.Cursor = Cursors.Default
End Sub
```

Figure 31-12 shows what you'll see when you run the Windows client and click the button to retrieve the web service data.

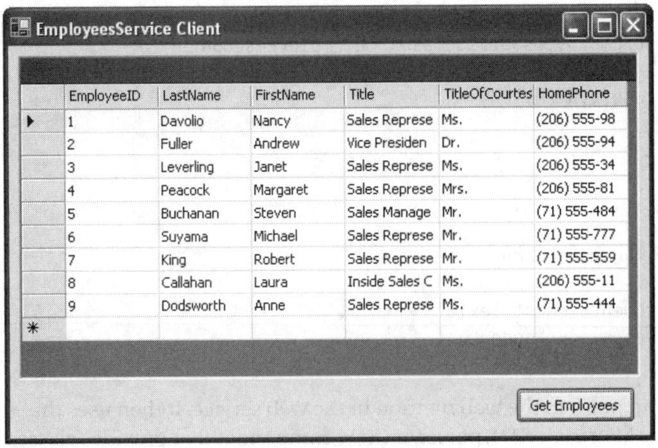

EmployeesService Client

	EmployeeID	LastName	FirstName	Title	TitleOfCourtes	HomePhone
▶	1	Davolio	Nancy	Sales Represe	Ms.	(206) 555-98
	2	Fuller	Andrew	Vice Presiden	Dr.	(206) 555-94
	3	Leverling	Janet	Sales Represe	Ms.	(206) 555-34
	4	Peacock	Margaret	Sales Represe	Mrs.	(206) 555-81
	5	Buchanan	Steven	Sales Manage	Mr.	(71) 555-484
	6	Suyama	Michael	Sales Represe	Mr.	(71) 555-777
	7	King	Robert	Sales Represe	Mr.	(71) 555-559
	8	Callahan	Laura	Inside Sales C	Ms.	(206) 555-11
	9	Dodsworth	Anne	Sales Represe	Ms.	(71) 555-444
*						

Get Employees

Figure 31-12. *Displaying data from a web service in a Windows form*

Of course, Windows development contains many other possibilities, which are covered in many other excellent books. The interesting part from your vantage point is the way a Windows client can interact with a web service just like an ASP.NET application does. This raises a world of new possibilities for integrated Windows and web applications. For example, you could extend this Windows application so it allows the user to modify the employee data. You could then add methods to the EmployeesService that allow the client to submit the changed data and commit the changes to the back-end database.

It's important to understand that what you do to consume your sample web service is exactly what you would do to consume any other third-party web service. Web service providers don't need to distribute their proxy classes, because programming platforms such as .NET include the tools to generate them automatically.

■ **Tip** If you'd like to try consuming some non-.NET web services, you can search the web service catalog at XMethods (`http://www.xmethods.com`). Or, for more practice with genuinely useful web services, Microsoft's MapPoint (`http://msdn.microsoft.com/library/en-us/dnanchor/html/anch_mappointmain.asp`) is an interesting example that enables you to access high-quality maps and geographical information. You can also check out Microsoft's TerraService (`http://terraservice.net/webservices.aspx`), which is based on the hugely popular TerraServer site where web surfers can view topographic maps and satellite photographs of the globe. Using TerraService you can query information about different locations on the globe and even download tiles with satellite photography of specific regions.

Creating an ASP Client with MSXML

It's also interesting to demonstrate how a web service can be called by a legacy application of any type and platform. The following example shows a bare-bones approach to displaying data in a legacy ASP page:

```
<script language="VBScript" runat="Server">
Option Explicit
```

```
Dim URL
URL = "http://localhost/Chapter30/EmployeesService.asmx/GetEmployeesCount"
Dim objHTTP
Set objHTTP = CreateObject("Microsoft.XMLHTTP")

' Send an HTTP_POST command to the URL.
objHTTP.Open "POST", URL, False
objHTTP.Send

' Read and display the value of the root node.
Dim numEmp
numEmp = objHTTP.responseXML.documentElement.Text
Response.Write(numEmp & " employee(s) in London")
</script>
```

This code simply sets the URL to point to the web method in the web service. It then uses the Microsoft.XMLHTTP class (from the Microsoft XML parser, a COM component that provides classes to manipulate XML data, send HTTP commands, and receive the respective responses) to open an HTTP connection and to send the command in a synchronous manner. In this case, the code is accessing the service through an HTTP POST command, which ASP.NET web services support only on the local computer. When the send method returns, the response text is saved in the responseXML property. It's provided as an MSXML2.DOMDocument object with a documentElement property that points to the root element of the returned XML data. Using this object, you can navigate the XML of the response. In this case, because the data simply contains an integer result, you can use the text property to read the value of that element. Figure 31-13 shows the result.

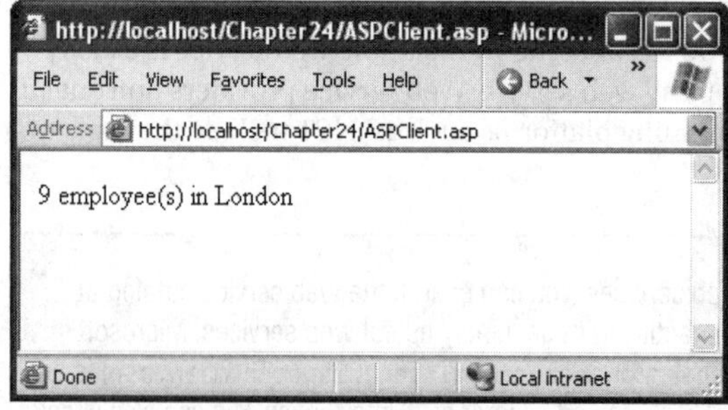

Figure 31-13. *Displaying data from a web service in an ASP page*

The interesting part of this example is that it uses the Microsoft XML library, which has classes to send commands via HTTP, receive the response text, and parse XML. That's all you need. If you don't already have this common component, you can download it from `http://msdn.microsoft.com/library/en-us/xmlsdk/html/xmmscxmlinstallregister.asp`. Note that you can use the previous code, with minor modifications, in any VBScript or VBA application, including a Microsoft Office macro or a WSH (Windows Scripting Host) client. Newer versions of Microsoft Office also support Web services explicitly.

Now consider a more complex example—the GetEmployees() web method that returns a complete DataSet. To interact with this data, you need to dig through the XML response. Here's the code that loops through the <Employees> tags and extracts several pieces of information about each employee to create a list:

```
<script language="VBScript" runat="Server">
Option Explicit

Dim URL
URL = "http://localhost/Chapter30/EmployeesService.asmx/GetEmployeesCount"
Dim objHTTP
Set objHTTP = CreateObject("Microsoft.XMLHTTP")

' Send an HTTP_POST command to the URL.
objHTTP.Open "POST", URL, False
objHTTP.Send

' Retrieve the XML response.
Dim Doc
Set Doc = objHTTP.responseXML

' Dig into the XML DataSet structure.
' Skip down one node to get past the schema. Then go one level deeper
' to the root DataSet element.
' Finally, loop through the contained tags, each of which
' represents an employee.
Dim Child
For Each Child In Doc.documentElement.childNodes(1).childNodes(0).childNodes
    ' The first node is the ID.
    Response.Write(Child.childNodes(0).Text + "<br>")
    ' The second node is the first name.
    Response.Write(Child.childNodes(1).Text)
    ' The third node is the last name.
    Response.Write(Child.childNodes(2).Text + "<br><br>")
Next
</script>
```

Creating an ASP Client with the SOAP Toolkit

The previous example showed the lowest common denominator for web service invocation—posting a message over HTTP and parsing the returned XML by hand. Most clients have access to more robust toolkits that directly support SOAP. One example is the Microsoft SOAP Toolkit, which is a COM component you can use to call any type of web service that provides a valid WSDL document. Thus, the SOAP Toolkit supports .NET web services and web services created on other platforms. You can use the SOAP Toolkit to use web services in COM-based applications such as those created in Visual Basic 6, Visual C++ 6, and ASP. To download the latest version of the Microsoft SOAP Toolkit, refer to `http://msdn.microsoft.com/webservices/_building/soaptk`.

To use the Microsoft SOAP Toolkit, you need to know the location of the WSDL for the service you want to use. Using this WSDL document, the SOAP Toolkit will dynamically generate a proxy. You can't see the proxy (because it's created at runtime), but you can use it to have access the same higher-level web services model.

The following example rewrites the ASP page to use the SOAP Toolkit. In this case, the WSDL document is retrieved directly from the web server. To improve performance, it's recommended you save a local copy of the WSDL file and use that to configure the SoapClient object.

```
<script language="VBScript" runat="Server">
Option Explicit

Dim SoapClient
Set SoapClient = CreateObject("MSSOAP.SoapClient")
```

```
' Generate a proxy.
Dim WSDLPath
WSDLPath = "http://localhost/Chapter30/EmployeesService.asmx?WSDL"
SoapClient.MSSoapInit WSDLPath

' Read the number of employees.
Dim numEmp
numEmp = SoapClient.GetEmployeesCount()
Response.Write(numEmp & " employee(s) in London")
</script>
```

Notice that in this example, you don't need to read any XML. Instead, the client calls the GetEmployeesCount() method directly using the SoapClient object. However, this approach still won't help you manipulate a DataSet, because COM have no equivalent class. Instead, you'll need to fall back on parsing XML, as shown in the previous example.

Of course Java, C++, Delphi, and so on, have their own components, libraries, and APIs to establish HTTP connections, send commands, and parse XML text, but the essential approach is the same.

Refining a Web Service

So far you've seen how to create a basic web service with a couple of methods and create a web page and Windows application that use it. However, you haven't see several other web service features. For example, a web method can cache data, use session state, and perform transactions. In the remainder of this chapter, you'll see how you can use these techniques.

The secret to applying these features is the WebMethod attribute. So far the examples have used the WebMethod attribute to mark the methods you want to expose as part of a web service and to attach a description (using the Description property). However, several additional WebMethod properties exist, as described in Table 31-6.

Table 31-6. *Properties of the WebMethod Attribute*

Argument	Description
Description	The method's description.
MessageName	The alias name for the method, which is used if you have overloaded versions of the method or if you want to expose the method with a different name. This technique is deprecated.
CacheDuration	This is the number of seconds that the method's response will be maintained in cache. The default is zero, meaning it's not cached.
EnableSession	Gets or sets whether the method can access information in the Session collection.
BufferResponse	Gets or sets whether the method's response is buffered. It is True by default, and it should be set to False only if you know that the request will take long to complete and you want to send sections of data earlier.
TransactionOption	Gets or sets whether the method supports transactions and of what type. Allowed values are disabled, NotSupported, Supported, Required, RequiresNew. Because of the stateless nature of web services, they can participate only as the root object of a transaction.

CacheDuration

As you learned in Chapter 11, ASP.NET has built-in support for two types of caching: output caching and data caching. Web services can use both these forms of caching, as you'll see in the following sections.

Output Caching

The simplest kind of web service caching is output caching, which works with web services in the same way it does with web pages: Identical requests (in this case, requests for the same method and with the same parameters) will receive identical responses from the cache, until the cached information expires. This can greatly increase performance in heavily trafficked sites, even if you store a response only for a few seconds.

You should use output caching only for straightforward information retrieval or data-processing functions. You should not use it in a method that needs to perform other work, such as changing session items, logging usage, or modifying a database. This is because subsequent calls to a cached method will receive the cached result, and the web method code will not be executed.

To enable caching for a web method, you use the CacheDuration property of the WebMethod attribute. Here's an example with the GetEmployees() method:

```
<WebMethod(CacheDuration:=30)> _
Public Function GetEmployees() As DataSet
    ...
End Function
```

This example caches the employee DataSet for 30 seconds. Any user who calls the GetEmployees() method in this time span will receive the same DataSet directly from the ASP.NET output cache.

Output caching becomes more interesting when you consider how it works with methods that require parameters. Here's an example that caches a GetEmployeesByCity() web method for ten minutes:

```
<WebMethod(CacheDuration:=600)> _
Public Function GetEmployeesByCity(ByVal city As String) As DataSet
    ...
End Function
```

In this case, ASP.NET is a little more intelligent. It reuses only those requests that supply the same city value. For example, here's how three web service requests might unfold:

1. A client calls GetEmployeesByCity() with the city parameter of London. The web method calls, contacts the database, and stores the result in the web service cache.
2. A client calls GetEmployeesByCity() with the city parameter of Kirkland. The web method calls, contacts the database, and stores the result in the web service cache. The previously cached DataSet is not reused, because the city parameter differs.
3. A client calls GetEmployeesByCity() with the city parameter of London. Assuming ten minutes haven't elapsed since the request in step 1, ASP.NET automatically reuses the first cached result. No code is executed.

Whether it makes sense to cache this version of GetEmployeesByCity() really depends on how much traffic your web service receives and on how many different cities there are. You'll also need to address the data going "stale" and how that may affect your application. If you have only a few city values, this approach may make sense. If you have dozens and your web server memory is limited, it's guaranteed to be inefficient.

Data Caching

ASP.NET also supports data caching, which allows you to store full-fledged objects in the cache. As with all ASP.NET code, you can use data caching through the Cache object (which is available through the Context.Cache property in your web service code). This object can temporarily store information that is expensive to create so the web method can reuse it for other calls by other clients. In fact, you can even reuse the data in other web services or web pages in the same application.

Data caching makes a lot of sense in the version of the EmployeesService that provides two GetEmployees() methods, one of which accepts a city parameter. To ensure optimum performance but reduce the amount of data in the cache, you can store a single object in the cache: the full employee DataSet. Then, when a client calls the version of GetEmployees() that requires a city parameter, you simply need to filter out the rows for the city the client requested.

The following code shows this pattern at work. The first step is to create a private method that uses the cache, called GetEmployeesDataSet(). If the DataSet is available in the cache, GetEmployeesDataSet() uses that version and bypasses the database. Otherwise, it creates a new DataSet and fills it with the full set of employee records. Here's the complete code:

```
Private Function GetEmployeesDataSet() As DataSet
    Dim ds As DataSet

    If Not Context.Cache("EmployeesDataSet") Is Nothing Then
        ' Retrieve it from the cache
        ds = CType(Context.Cache("EmployeesDataSet"), DataSet)
    Else
        ' Retrieve it from the database.
        Dim sql As String = "SELECT EmployeeID, LastName, FirstName, Title, " _
                & "TitleOfCourtesy, HomePhone, City FROM Employees"
        Dim con As New SqlConnection(connectionString)
        Dim da As New SqlDataAdapter(sql, con)
        ds = New DataSet()
        da.Fill(ds, "Employees")

        ' Track when the DataSet was created. You can
        ' retrieve this information in your client to test
        ' that caching is working.
        ds.ExtendedProperties.Add("CreatedDate", DateTime.Now)

        ' Store it in the cache for ten minutes.
        Context.Cache.Insert("EmployeesDataSet", ds, Nothing, _
               DateTime.Now.AddMinutes(10), TimeSpan.Zero)
    End If
    Return ds
End Function
```

Both the GetEmployees() and GetEmployeesByCity() methods can use the private GetEmployeesDataSet() method. The difference is that GetEmployeesByCity() loops through the records and manually removes each record that doesn't match the supplied city name. Here are both versions:

```
<WebMethod(Description:="Returns the full list of employees.")> _
Public Function GetEmployees() As DataSet
    Return GetEmployeesDataSet()
End Function
```

```
<WebMethod(Description:="Returns the full list of employees by city.")> _
Public Function GetEmployeesByCity(ByVal city As String) As DataSet
    ' Copy the DataSet.
    Dim dsFiltered As DataSet = GetEmployeesDataSet().Copy()

    ' Remove the rows manually.
    ' This is a good approach (rather than using the
    ' DataTable.Select() method) because it is impervious
    ' to SQL injection attacks.
    For Each row As DataRow In dsFiltered.Tables(0).Rows
        ' Perform a case-insensitive compare.
        If CStr(row("City"))=city Then
            row.Delete()
        End If
    Next row

    ' Remove these rows permanently.
    dsFiltered.AcceptChanges()

    Return dsFiltered
End Function
```

Generally, you should determine the amount of time to cache information depending on how long the underlying data will remain valid. For example, if a stock quote were being retrieved, you would use a much smaller number of seconds than you might for a weather forecast. If you were storing a piece of information that seldom changes, such as the results of a yearly census poll, your considerations would be entirely different. In this case, the information is almost permanent, but the amount of returned information will be larger than the capacity of ASP.NET's output cache. Your goal in this situation would be to limit the cache duration enough to ensure that only the most popular requests are stored.

Of course, caching decisions should also be based on how long it will take to re-create the information and how many clients will be using the web service. You may need to perform substantial real-world testing and tuning to achieve perfection. For more information on data caching, refer to Chapter 11.

Tip The data cache is global to an entire application (on a single web server). This means you can store information in the cache in a web service and retrieve it in a web page in the same web application, and vice versa.

EnableSession

The best practice for ASP.NET web services is to disable session state. In fact, by default, web services do not support session state. Most web services should be designed to be stateless in order to achieve high scalability. Sometimes, however, you might decide to use state management to retain user-specific information or optimize performance in a specialized scenario. In this case, you need to use the EnableSession property, as shown here:

```
<WebMethod(EnableSession:=True)> _
Public Function StatefulMethod() As DataSet
    ...
End Function
```

What happens when you have a web service that enables session state management for some methods but disables it for others? Essentially, disabling session management just tells ASP.NET to ignore any in-memory session information and withhold the Session collection from the current method. It doesn't cause existing information to be cleared from the collection (that will happen only when the session times out). The only performance benefit you're receiving is not having to look up session information when it isn't required. You don't need to take the same steps to allow your code to use Application state—this global state collection is always available.

Session state handling is not a part of the SOAP specification. As a result, you must rely on the support of the underlying infrastructure. ASP.NET relies on HTTP cookies to support session state. The session cookie stores a session ID, and ASP.NET uses the session ID to associate the client with the session state on the server. However, when you use a stateful web service, you have no guarantee the client will support cookies. In fact, many will not. If the client doesn't support cookies, ASP.NET state management won't work, and a new session will be created with each new request. Unfortunately, your code has no way to identify this error condition.

To try session state (and observe the potential problems), you can create the simple web service shown here. It stores a single piece of personalized information (the user name) and allows you to retrieve it later.

```
Public Class StatefulService : Inherits System.Web.Services.WebService
    <WebMethod(EnableSession:=True)> _
    Public Sub StoreName(ByVal name As String)
        Session("Name") = name
    End Sub

    <WebMethod(EnableSession:=True)> _
    Public Function GetName() As String
        If Session("Name") Is Nothing Then
            Return String.Empty
        Else
            Return CStr(Session("Name"))
        End If
    End Function
End Class
```

When you test the StoreName() and GetName() web methods using the ASP.NET test page, you get the expected behavior. When you call GetName(), you receive whatever string you supplied the last time you called StoreName(). That's because web browsers can support cookies without a hitch.

By default, the proxy class doesn't share this ability. To see this problem in action, add a reference to the StatefulService in the Windows client. Then add a new button with the following event-handling code:

```
Private Sub cmdTestState_Click(ByVal sender As Object, ByVal e As System.EventArgs)
    ' Create the proxy.
    Dim proxy As New StatefulService()


    ' Set a name.
    proxy.StoreName("John Smith")

    ' Try to retrieve the name.
    MessageBox.Show("You set: " & proxy.GetName())
End Sub
```

Unfortunately, this code doesn't work as you might expect. When you run it, you'll see the empty string shown in Figure 31-14.

Figure 31-14. *A failed stateful service*

To resolve this problem, you need to explicitly prepare the web service proxy to accept the session cookie by creating a cookie container (an instance of the System.Net.CookieContainer class).

To correct this code, you can create the cookie container as a form-level variable, as shown next. This ensures it lives as long as the enclosing class (the form object) and can be reused in multiple methods in the same form, without losing the current web service session.

```
Public Class Form1
    Inherits System.Windows.Forms.Form

    Private cookieContainer As New System.Net.CookieContainer()
    ...
End Class
```

Now you simply need to attach this cookie container to the proxy class before you call any web method:

```
Private Sub cmdTestState_Click(ByVal sender As Object, ByVal e As System.EventArgs)
    Dim proxy As New StatefulService()
    proxy.CookieContainer = Me

    proxy.StoreName("John Smith")
    MessageBox.Show("You set: " & proxy.GetName())
End Sub
```

Now both web method calls use the same session, and the user name appears in the message box, as shown in Figure 31-15.

Figure 31-15. *A successful stateful service*

You need to keep the cookie container around as long as you need to keep the session cookie. For example, if your client is a web application and you want to be able to perform web service operations after every postback without losing the session, you'll need to store the session cookie in the session state of the current page. Note that the session state of the web application is different from the session state of the web service. Not only are they separate applications, but they may also run on completely separate web servers.

By now, you're probably seeing a hint of the complexity of trying to use sessions with web services. Web services are stateless; they don't provide a natural mechanism for storing state information. You can use the Session collection to compensate for this limitation, but this approach raises the following complications:

- Session state will disappear when the session times out. The client will have no way of knowing when the session times out, which means the web service may behave unpredictably.
- Session state is tied to a specific user, not to a specific class or object. This can cause problems if the same client wants to use the same web service in two different ways or creates two instances of the proxy class at once.
- Session state is maintained only if the client preserves the session cookie. The state management you use in a web service won't work if the client fails to take these steps.

For these reasons, web services and state management don't offer a natural fit. So, you should avoid creating stateful web services.

BufferResponse

The BufferResponse property allows you to control when the data returned from the web service is sent to the client. By default the BufferResponse property is set to True. This means the entire result is serialized before it is sent to the client. By setting this property to False (as follows), ASP.NET will start outputting the content straight away, without waiting for all the data to be serialized:

```
<WebMethod(BufferResponse:=False)> _
Public Function GetLargeStreamOfData() As Byte()
    ...
End Function
```

The web service method will always finish executing before anything is returned. The BufferResponse setting applies to the serialization that takes place *after* the method has executed. With buffering turned off, the first part of the result is serialized and sent. Then the next part of the result is serialized and sent, and so on.

Setting BufferResponse to False makes sense only when the web service returns a large amount of data. Even then, it rarely makes any difference, because the automatically generated .NET proxy class doesn't have the ability to start processing the returned data piece by piece. This means the proxy class will still wait for all the information to be received before it passes it back to your application. However, you can change this behavior by taking direct control over the XML message processing with the IXmlSerializable interface, as described in the next chapter.

TransactionOption

Web services, like any other piece of .NET code, can initiate ADO.NET transactions. Additionally, web services can easily participate in COM+ transactions. COM+ transactions are interesting because they allow you to perform a transaction that spans different resources (for example, a SQL Server database, a Microsoft Messaging message queue, and an Oracle database). COM+ transactions also commit or roll back automatically. However, you must pay a price for these added features and convenience—because COM+ transactions use a two-stage commit protocol, they are always slower than using ADO.NET client-initiated transactions or stored procedure transactions.

The support for COM+ transactions in a web service is also somewhat limited. Because of the stateless nature of HTTP, web service methods can act only as the root object in a transaction. This means a web service method can start a transaction and use it to perform a series of related tasks, but multiple web services cannot be grouped into one transaction. As a result, you may have to put in some extra thought when you're creating a transactional web service. For example, it won't make sense to create a financial web service with separate DebitAccount() and CreditAccount() methods, because they won't be able to be grouped into a transaction. Instead, you can make sure both tasks execute as a single unit using a transactional TransferFunds() method.

To use a transaction in a web service, you first have to add a reference to the System.EnterpriseServices assembly. To do this in Visual Studio, right-click References in the Solution Explorer, select Add Reference, and choose System.EnterpriseServices. You should then import the corresponding namespace so that the types you need (TransactionOption and ContextUtil) are at your fingertips:

```
Imports System.EnterpriseServices
```

To start a transaction in a web service method, set the TransactionOption property of the WebMethod attribute. TransactionOption is an enumeration that provides several values that allow you to specify whether a code component uses or requires transactions. Because web services must be the root of a transaction, most of these options don't apply. To create a web service method that starts a transaction automatically, use the following attribute:

```
<WebMethod(TransactionOption:=TransactionOption.RequiresNew)> _
Public Function TransactionMethod() As DataSet
    ...
End Function
```

The transaction is automatically committed when the web method completes. The transaction is rolled back if any unhandled exception occurs or if you explicitly instruct the transaction to fail using the following code:

```
ContextUtil.SetAbort()
```

Most databases support COM+ transactions. The moment you use these databases in a transactional web method, they will automatically be enlisted in the current transaction. If the transaction is rolled back, the operations you perform with these databases (such as adding, modifying, or removing records) will be automatically reversed. However, some operations (such as writing a file to disk) aren't inherently transactional. This means these operations will not be rolled back if the transaction fails.

Now consider the following web method, which takes two actions. It deletes records in a database and then tries to read from a file. However, if the file operation fails and the exception isn't handled, the entire transaction will be rolled back, and the deleted records will be restored. Here's the transactional code:

```
<WebMethod(TransactionOption:=TransactionOption.RequiresNew)> _
Public Sub UpdateDatabase()
    ' Create ADO.NET objects.
    Dim con As New SqlConnection(connectionString)
    Dim cmd As New SqlCommand("DELETE * FROM Employees", con)

    ' Apply the update. This will be registered as part of the transaction.
    Try
        con.Open()
        cmd.ExecuteNonQuery()
    Finally
        con.Close()
    End Try

    ' Try to access a file. This generates an exception that isn't handled.
    ' The web method will be aborted and the changes will be rolled back.
    Dim fs As New FileStream("does_not_exist.bin", IO.FileMode.Open)

    ' (If no errors have occurred, the database changes
    ' are committed here when the method ends).
End Sub
```

Another way to handle this code is to catch the error, perform any cleanup that's required, and then explicitly roll back the transaction, if necessary:

```
<WebMethod(TransactionOption:=TransactionOption.RequiresNew)> _
Public Sub UpdateDatabase()
    ' Create ADO.NET objects.
    Dim con As New SqlConnection(connectionString)
    Dim cmd As New SqlCommand("DELETE * FROM Employees", con)

    ' Apply the update.
    Try
        con.Open()
        cmd.ExecuteNonQuery()

        Dim fs As New FileStream("does_not_exist.bin", IO.FileMode.Open)
    Catch
        ContextUtil.SetAbort()
    Finally
        con.Close()
    End Try
End Sub
```

Does a web service need to use COM+ transactions? It all depends on the situation. If multiple updates are required in separate data stores, you may need to use transactions to ensure your data's integrity. If, on the other hand, you're modifying values only in a single database (such as SQL Server 2000), you can probably use the data provider's built-in transaction features instead, as described in Chapter 7.

■ **Note** In the future, other emerging standards, such as XLANG and WS-Transactions, may fill in the gaps by defining a cross-platform standard that will let different web services participate in a single transaction. However, this goal is still a long way from being realized.

Summary

In this chapter, you learned what web services are and why they are important for businesses. You also took your first look at how to create and consume web services in .NET and test web services with nothing but a browser. In the next two chapters, you'll dig into the underlying standards and learn how to extend the web service infrastructure.

CHAPTER 32

Web Service Standards and Extensions

In the previous chapter, you learned how .NET hides the low-level plumbing of web services, allowing you to create and consume sophisticated web services without needing to know anything about the low-level details of the protocols you're using. This higher-level abstraction is a general theme of modern programming—for example, few Windows developers worry about the individual pixels in their business applications, and ASP.NET developers rarely need to write raw markup to the output stream. Of course, sometimes high-level frameworks aren't quite enough. For example, Windows developers creating real-time games just might need to work with low-level video hardware, and web developers creating custom controls will probably need to immerse themselves in a thorny tangle of JavaScript and HTML.

The same principle is true of web services. In most cases, the high-level web services model in .NET is all you need. It ensures fast, productive, error-proof coding. Sometimes, however, you need to dig a little deeper. This is particularly true if you need to send complex objects to non-.NET clients or build extensions that plug into the .NET web services model. In this chapter, you'll take a look at this lower level, and learn more about the underlying SOAP and WSDL protocols.

Tip If you're a web service expert looking for new .NET 2.0 features, pay special attention to the "Customizing SOAP Messages" section toward the end of this chapter. It describes how to control the serialization process with IXmlSerializable and how to create schema importer extensions to allow types that web services wouldn't ordinarily support. Also, look for the "Implementing an Existing Contract" section that describes how to perform contract-first development with WSDL.

WS-Interoperability

Web services have developed rapidly, and standards such as SOAP and WSDL are still evolving. In early web service toolkits, different vendors interpreted parts of these standards in different ways, leading to interoperability headaches. Further, some features from the original standards are now considered obsolete.

Negotiating these subtle differences is a small minefield, especially if you need to create web services that will be accessed by clients using other programming platforms and web service toolkits. Fortunately, another standard has appeared recently that sets out a broad range of rules and recommendations and is designed to guarantee interoperability across the web service implementations of different vendors. This document is the WS-Interoperability Basic Profile (see `http://www.ws-i.org`). It specifies a recommended subset of the full SOAP 1.1 and WSDL 1.1 specifications, and it lays out a few ground rules. WS-Interoperability is strongly backed by all web service vendors (including Microsoft, IBM, Sun, and Oracle).

Ideally, as a developer you shouldn't need to worry about the specifics of WS-Interoperability. Instead, .NET should respect its rules implicitly. The way .NET 2.0 handles this is with a new WebServiceBinding attribute that is automatically added to your web service class when you create it in Visual Studio:

```
<WebServiceBinding(ConformsTo := WsiProfiles.BasicProfile1_1)> _
Public Class MyService
    Inherits WebService
        Private ...
End Class
```

The WebServiceBinding attribute indicates the level of compatibility you're targeting. Currently, the only option is WsiProfiles.BasicProfile1_1, which represents the WS-Interoperability Basic Profile 1.1. However, as standards evolve there will be newer versions of SOAP and WSDL, as well as newer versions of the WS-Interoperability profile that go along with them.

Once you have the WebServiceBinding attribute in place, .NET will warn you with a compile error if your web service strays outside the bounds of allowed behavior. By default, all .NET web services are compliant, but you can inadvertently create a noncompliant service by adding certain attributes. For example, it's possible to create two web methods with the same name, as long as their signatures differ and you give them different message names using the MessageName property of the WebMethod attribute. However, this behavior isn't allowed according to the WS-Interoperability profile; it generates the error page shown in Figure 32-1 when you try to run the web service.

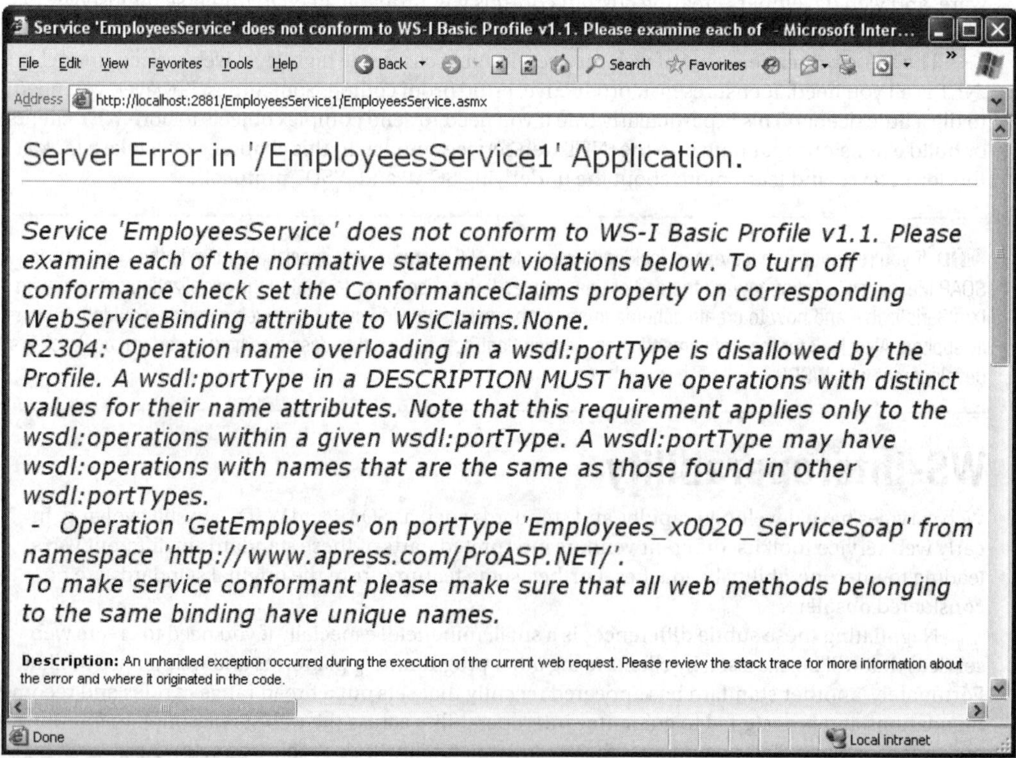

Figure 32-1. *The SOAP message*

You can also choose to advertise your conformance with the EmitConformanceClaims property, as shown here:

```
<WebServiceBinding(ConformsTo := WsiProfiles.BasicProfile1_1,
      EmitConformanceClaims:=True)> _
Public Class MyService
    Inherits WebService
       Private ...
End Class
```

In this case, additional information is inserted into the WSDL document to indicate that your web service is conformant. It's important to understand that this is for informational purposes only—your web service can be conformant without explicitly stating that it is.

In rare cases you might choose to violate one of the WS-Interoperability rules in order to create a web service that can be consumed by an older, noncompliant application. In this situation, your first step is to turn off compliance by removing the WebServiceBinding attribute. Alternatively, you can disable compliance checking and document that fact by using the WebServiceBinding attribute without a profile:

```
<WebServiceBinding(ConformsTo := WsiProfiles.None)> _
Public Class MyService
    Inherits WebService
       Private ...
End Class
```

SOAP

SOAP is a cross-platform standard used to format the messages sent between web services and client applications. The beauty of SOAP is its flexibility. Not only can you use SOAP to send any type of XML data (including your own proprietary XML documents); you can also use SOAP with transport protocols other than HTTP. For example, you could send SOAP messages over a direct TCP/IP connection.

■ **Note** The .NET Framework includes support only for the most common use of SOAP, which is SOAP over HTTP. If you want more flexibility, you might want to consider the WSE (Web Services Enhancements) toolkit available from Microsoft, which is introduced in the next chapter.

SOAP is a fairly straightforward standard. The first principle is that every SOAP message is an XML document. This XML document has a single root element that is the SOAP envelope. The rest of the data for the message is stored inside the envelope, which includes a header section and a body.

■ **Note** SOAP was originally considered an acronym (Simple Object Access Protocol). However, in the current versions of the SOAP standard, this is no longer the case. For the detailed SOAP specifications, surf to `http://www.w3.org/TR/soap`.

Essentially, .NET web services use two types of SOAP messages. The client sends a *request message* to a web service to trigger a web method. When processing is complete, the web service sends back a *response message*. Both of these messages have the same format, which is shown in Figure 32-2.

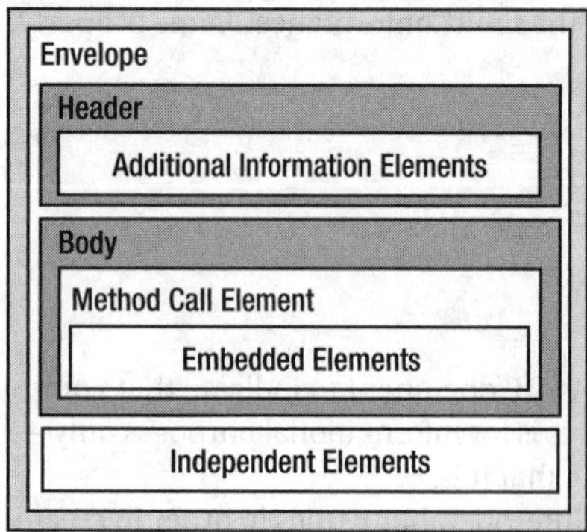

Figure 32-2. *The SOAP message*

SOAP Encoding

Two different (but closely related) styles of SOAP exist. *Document-style* SOAP views the data exchanged as documents. In other words, each SOAP message you send or receive contains an XML document in its body. *RPC-style* SOAP views the data exchange as method calls on remote objects. The remote object may be a Java object, a COM component, a .NET object, or something else entirely. In RPC-style SOAP, the outermost element in the request is always named after the method, and there is an element for each parameter on that method. In the response, the outermost element has the same name as the method with the text *Response* appended.

Seeing as .NET web services embrace the object-oriented RPC model, you might assume that .NET web services use RPC-style SOAP. However, this isn't the case. The simple reason is that document-style SOAP is more flexible—it gives you the ability to exchange arbitrary XML documents between the web service and the web service consumer. However, even though .NET uses document-style SOAP, it formats messages in a similar way to RPC-style SOAP, using many of the same conventions.

To make life even more interesting, data in a SOAP message can be encoded in two ways—literal and SOAP section 5. *Literal encoding* means that the data is encoded according to a specific XML schema. *SOAP section 5 encoding* means the data is encoded according to the similar, but more restricted, rules set out in section 5 of the SOAP specification. The section 5 rules are a bit of a throwback. The underlying reason they exist is because SOAP was developed before the XML Schema standard was finalized.

■ **Note** By default, all .NET web services use document-style SOAP with literal encoding. You should consider changing this behavior only if you need to be compatible with a legacy application.

At this point, you might wonder why you need to know any of these lower-level SOAP details. In most cases, you don't. However, sometimes you might want to change the overall encoding of your web service. One reason might be that you need to expose a web method that needs to be called by a client that supports only RPC-style SOAP. Although this scenario is becoming less and less common (and it violates WS-Interoperabiltiy), it can still occur.

ASP.NET has two attributes (both of which are found in the System.Web.Services.Protocols namespace) that you can use to control the overall encoding of all methods in a web service:

SoapDocumentService: Use this to make every web service use document-style SOAP (which is already the default). However, you can use the SoapBindingUse parameter to specify SOAP section 5 encoding instead of document encoding.

SoapRpcService: Use this to make every web service use RCP style SOAP with SOAP section 5 encoding.

You can also use the following two attributes on individual web methods:

SoapDocumentMethod: Add this attribute to use document-style SOAP for a single web method. You can specify the encoding to use.

SoapRpcMethod: Add this attribute to use RPC-style SOAP for a single web method.

This is useful if you want to expose two methods in a web service that perform a similar function but support a different type of SOAP encoding. However, in this chapter you'll focus on understanding the SOAP message style that .NET uses by default (document/literal).

SOAP Versions

The most common version of SOAP in use today is SOAP 1.1. The only other variant is the more recent SOAP 1.2, which clarifies many aspects of the SOAP standard, introduces some minor refinements, and formalizes the extensibility model.

■Note No matter which version of SOAP you use, the capabilities of a .NET web service are the same. In fact, the only reason you would pay particular attention to which version is being used is when you need to ensure compatibility with non-.NET clients. The examples in this chapter use SOAP 1.1.

.NET 1.*x* supported SOAP 1.1 only. However, a web service created in .NET 2.0 automatically supports both SOAP 1.1 and SOAP 1.2. If you want to change this, you can disable either one through the web.config file:

```
<configuration>
  <system.web>
    <webServices>
      <Protocols>
        <!-- Use this to disable SOAP 1.2 -->
        <remove name="HttpSoap12"/>

        <!-- Use this to disable SOAP 1.1 -->
        <remove name="HttpSoap"/>
      </Protocols>
    </webServices>
  ...
  </system.web>
</configuration>
```

When you create a proxy class with .NET, it uses SOAP 1.1 by default, unless only SOAP 1.2 is available. You can override this behavior programmatically by setting the SoapVersion property of the proxy class before you call any web methods:

```
proxy.SoapVersion = System.Web.Services.Protocols.SoapProtocolVersion.Soap12;
```

Alternatively, you can build a proxy class that always uses SOAP 1.2 by default by using the /protocol:SOAP12 command-line switch with wsdl.exe.

Tracing SOAP Messages

Before looking at the SOAP standard in detail, it's worth exploring how you can look at the SOAP messages sent to and from a .NET web service. Unfortunately, .NET doesn't include any tools for tracing or debugging SOAP messages. However, it's fairly easy to look at the underlying SOAP using other tools.

The first approach is to use the browser test page. As you know, the browser test page doesn't use SOAP—instead, it uses the scaled-down HTTP POST protocol that encodes data as name/value pairs. However, the test page does include an example of what a SOAP message should look like for a particular web method.

For example, consider the EmployeesService developed in the previous chapter. If you load the test page, click the link for the GetEmployeesCount() method, and scroll down the page, you'll see a sample request and response message with placeholders where the data values should go. Figure 32-3 shows part of this data example. You can also scroll farther down the page to see the format of the simpler HTTP POST messages.

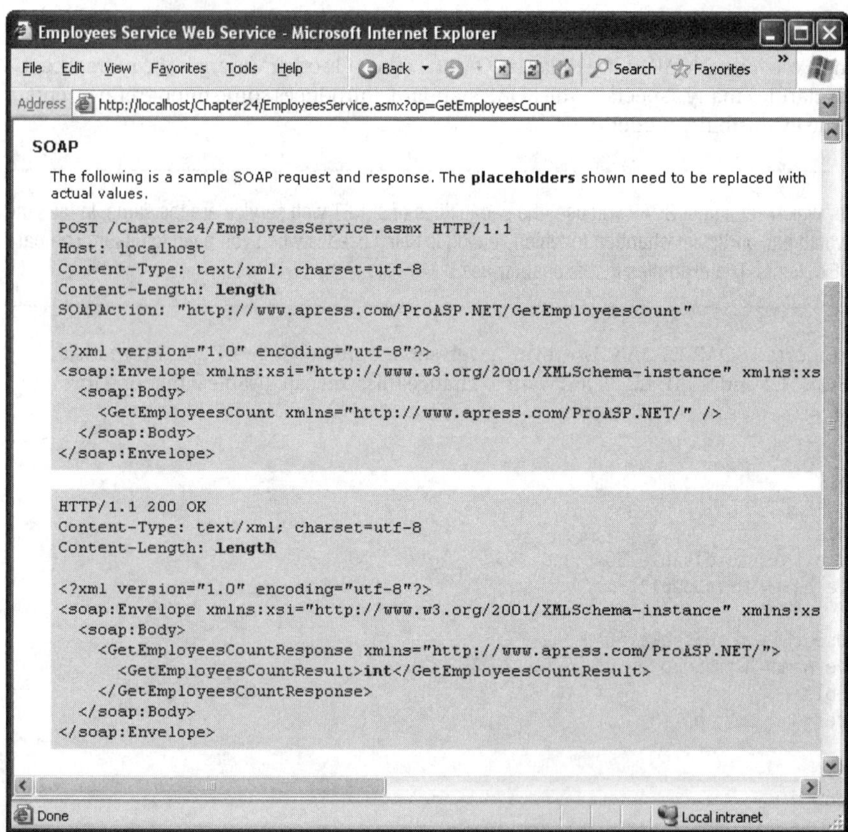

Figure 32-3. *Sample SOAP messages for GetEmployeesCount()*

These examples can help you understand the SOAP standard, but they aren't as useful if you want to see live SOAP messages, perhaps to troubleshoot an unexpected compatibility problem between a .NET web service and another client. Fortunately, there is an easy way to capture real SOAP messages as they flow across the wire, but you need to use another tool. This is the Microsoft

SOAP Toolkit, a COM library that includes objects that allow you to consume web services in COM-based languages such as Visual Basic 6 and Visual C++ 6. Along with these tools, the SOAP Toolkit also includes an indispensable tracing tool for peeking under the covers at SOAP communication.

To download the SOAP Toolkit, surf to `http://msdn.microsoft.com/webservices/_building/soaptk`. Once you've installed the SOAP Toolkit, you can run the trace utility by selecting Microsoft SOAP Toolkit ➤ Trace Utility from the Start menu. Once the trace utility loads, select File ➤ New ➤ Formatted Trace. You'll see the window shown in Figure 32-4.

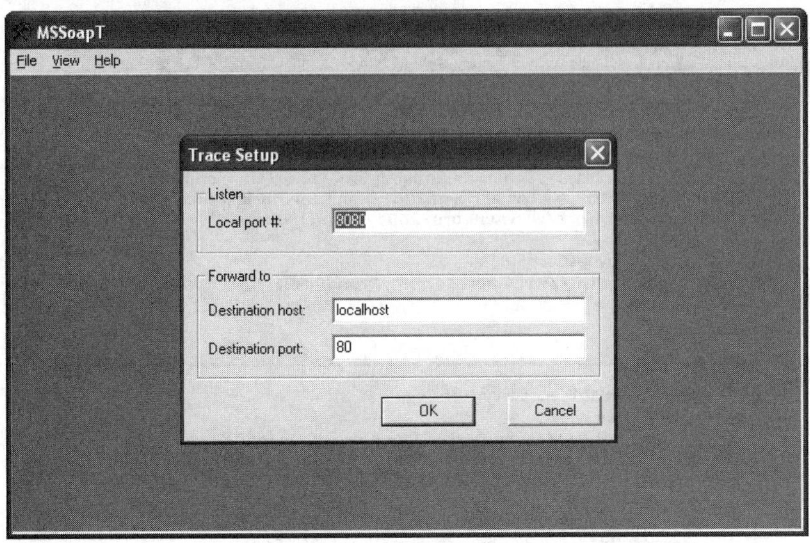

Figure 32-4. *Starting a new SOAP trace*

The default settings indicate that the trace utility will listen for communication on port 8080 and forward all messages to port 80 (which is where the IIS web server is listening for unencrypted HTTP traffic, including GET and POST requests and SOAP messages). Click OK to accept these settings.

You need one additional detail. By default, your web service clients will bypass the tracing tool by sending their SOAP messages directly to port 80, not 8080. You need to tweak your client code so that it sends the SOAP messages to port 8080 instead. To do this, you simply need to use a URL that specifies the port, as shown here:

```
http://localhost:8080/MyWebSite/MyWebService.asmx
```

To change the URL, you need to modify the Url property of the proxy class before you invoke any of its methods. Rather than hard-coding a new URL, you can use the code shown here, which uses the System.Uri class to generically redirect any URL to port 8080:

```
' Create the proxy.
Dim proxy As New EmployeesService()

Dim newUrl As New Uri(proxy.Url)
proxy.Url = newUrl.Scheme & "://" & newUrl.Host & ":8080" & newUrl.AbsolutePath

' Call the web service, and get the results.
Dim ds As DataSet = proxy.GetEmployeesCount()
```

You don't need to make a similar change to the web service, because it automatically sends its response message back to the port where the request message originated—in this case 8080. The trace utility will then log the response message and forward it back to the client application.

Once you've finished calling the web service, you can expand the tree in the trace utility to look at the request and response messages. Figure 32-5 shows the result of running the previous code snippet. In the top window is the request message for the GetEmployeesCount() method. In the bottom window is the response with the current number of employees in the table (nine). As you invoke more web methods, additional nodes will be added to the tree.

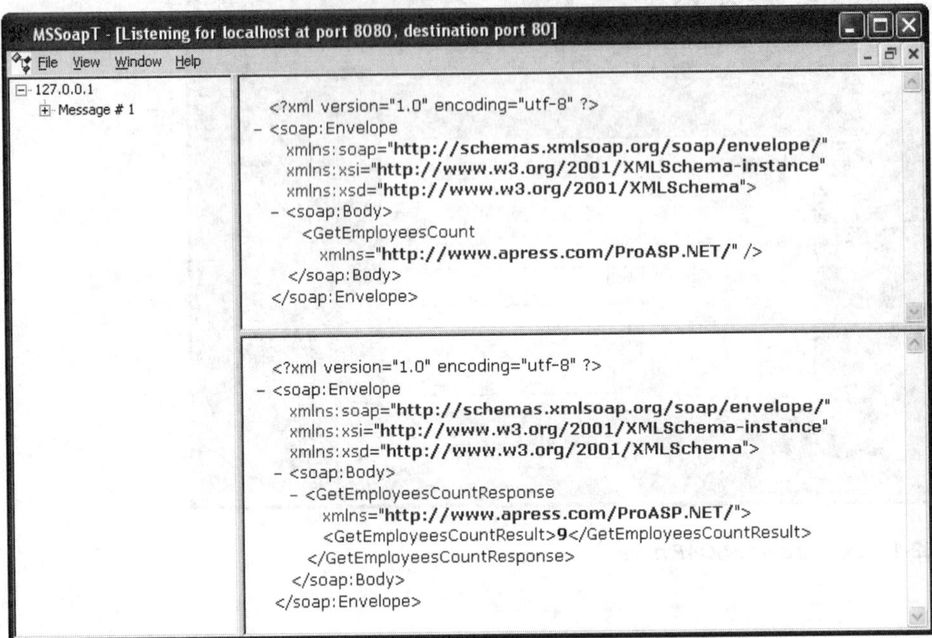

Figure 32-5. *Capturing SOAP messages*

The SOAP trace tool is a powerful tool for looking at SOAP messages, particularly if you want to see how an unusual data type is serialized, test a custom extension, or troubleshoot an interoperability problem. Best of all, you don't need to install any special software on the web server. Instead, you simply need to forward the client's messages to the local trace utility.

In the following sections, you'll take a closer look at the SOAP format. You may want to use the SOAP trace utility to test these examples and take a look at the underlying SOAP messages for yourself.

The SOAP Envelope

Every SOAP message is enclosed in a root <Envelope> element. Inside the envelope, there is an optional <Header> element and a required <Body> element. Here's the basic skeleton:

```
<soap:Envelope xmlns:soap="http://schemas.xmlsoap.org/soap/envelope/" >
  <soap:Header>
  </soap:Header>
  <soap:Body>
  </soap:Body>
</soap:Envelope>
```

Notice that the <Envelope>, <Body>, and <Header> elements all exist in the SOAP envelope namespace. This is a requirement.

The <Body> element contains the message payload. It's here that you place the actual data, such as the parameters in a request message or the return value in the response message. You can also specify fault information to indicate an error condition and *independent elements*, which define the serialization of complex types.

Request Messages

With automatically generated .NET web services, the first element in the <Body> element identifies the name of the method you are invoking. For example, here's a complete SOAP message for calling the GetEmployeesCount() method:

```
<soap:Envelope xmlns:soap="http://schemas.xmlsoap.org/soap/envelope/" >
  <soap:Body>
    <GetEmployeesCount xmlns="http://www.apress.com/ProASP.NET/" />
  </soap:Body>
</soap:Envelope>
```

In this example, all you need is an empty <GetEmployeesCount> element. However, if the method requires any information (in the form of parameters), these are encoded in the <GetEmployeesCount> element with the appropriate parameter name. For example, the following SOAP represents a call to GetEmployeesByCity() that specifies a city name of London:

```
<soap:Envelope xmlns:soap="http://schemas.xmlsoap.org/soap/envelope/" >
  <soap:Body>
     <GetEmployeesByCity xmlns="http://www.apress.com/ProASP.NET/">
      <city>London</city>
    </GetEmployeesByCity>
  </soap:Body>
</soap:Envelope>
```

You'll notice that in both these examples, the data inside the <Body> element is given the namespace of the web service (in this example, `http://www.apress.com/ProASP.NET`). The SOAP protocol is actually flexible enough to allow any XML markup in the <Body> element. This means that rather than treating SOAP as a protocol for remote method invocation, you can also use it as a way to exchange complex XML documents. In a business-to-business scenario, different parts of this document might be created by different companies in an automated workflow, and they might even include digital signatures. Unfortunately, the .NET programming model makes it hard to work in this way, because it wraps the SOAP and WSDL details with an object-oriented abstraction. However, leading web service developers are challenging this approach, and it's likely that future versions of ASP.NET will include increased flexibility.

■ Note At this point, you may be wondering if there's the possibility to create incompatible SOAP messages. For example, .NET web services use the name of a method for the first element in the <Body>, but other web service implementations may not follow this convention. The solution to these challenges is WSDL, a standard you'll consider in the "WSDL" section later in this chapter. It allows .NET to define the message format for your web services in great detail. In other words, it doesn't matter if the naming and organization of a .NET SOAP message is slightly different from that of a competitor's platform, because the non-.NET platform will read the rules in the WSDL document to determine how it should interact with the web service.

Response Messages

After sending a request message, the client waits to receive the response from the web server (as with any HTTP request). This response message uses a similar format to the request message. By .NET convention (again, not a requirement of the SOAP specification), the first child element in the <Body> element has the name of the method with the suffix *Response* appended. For example, after calling the GetEmployeesCount() method, you might receive a response like this:

```
<soap:Envelope xmlns:soap="http://schemas.xmlsoap.org/soap/envelope/" >
  <soap:Body>
    <GetEmployeesCountResponse xmlns="http://www.apress.com/ProASP.NET/">
      <GetEmployeesCountResult>9</GetEmployeesCountResult>
    </GetEmployeesCountResponse>
  </soap:Body>
</soap:Envelope>
```

As with the request message, the response message is namespace-qualified using the namespace of the web service. Inside the <GetEmployeesCountResponse> element is an element with the return value named <GetEmployeesCountResult>. By .NET convention, this has the name of the web method, followed by the suffix *Result*. Interestingly, this isn't the only piece of information you can find in the <XxxResponse> element. If the method uses ref or out parameters, the data for those parameters will also be included. This allows the client to update its parameter values after the method call completes, which gives the same behavior as when you use out or ref parameters with a local method call.

Fault Messages

The SOAP standard also defines a way to represent error conditions. If an error occurs on the server, a message is sent with a <Fault> element as the first element inside the <Body> element. Fortunately, .NET follows this standard and applies it automatically. If an unhandled exception occurs while a web method is running, .NET sends a SOAP fault message back to the client. When the proxy class receives the fault message, it throws a client-side exception to notify the client application. However, as you'll see, this process of converting a web service exception to a client application exception isn't entirely seamless.

Consider, for example, what happens if you call the GetEmployeesCount() method when the database server isn't available. A SqlException is thrown on the web server side and caught by ASP.NET, which returns the following (somewhat abbreviated) fault message:

```
<soap:Envelope xmlns:soap="http://schemas.xmlsoap.org/soap/envelope/" >
  <soap:Body>
    <soap:Fault>
      <faultcode>soap:Server</faultcode>
      <faultstring>System.Web.Services.Protocols.SoapException: Server was unable
to process request. ---> System.Data.SqlClient.SqlException: SQL Server does not
exist or access denied. at ... </faultstring>
      <detail />
    </soap:Fault>
  </soap:Body>
</soap:Envelope>
```

In general, the Fault element contains a <faultcode>, <faultstring>, and <detail> elements. The <faultcode> takes one of several predefined values, including ClientFaultCode (there was a problem with the client's SOAP request), MustUnderstandFaultCode (a required part of the SOAP message was not recognized), ServerFaultCode (an error occurred on the server), and VersionMismatchFaultCode (an invalid namespace was found). The <faultstring> element contains a full description of the problem. You can use the optional <detail> element to store additional information about the error that occurred (although it's empty in this example).

The problem is that the <Fault> element doesn't map directly to the .NET exception class. When the proxy receives this message, it can't identify the original exception object (and it has no way of knowing if that exception class is even available on the client). As a result, the proxy class simply throws a generic SoapException with the full <faultstring> details.

To understand how this works, consider what happens if you write the following code in your client:

```
Dim proxy As New EmployeesService()

Dim count As Integer = -1
Try
    count = proxy.GetEmployeesCount()
Catch err As SqlException
    ...
End Try
```

In this case, the exception will never be caught, because it's a SoapException, not a SqlException (even though the root cause of the problem and the original exception object *is* a SqlException). Even if you catch the SqlException in the web method and manually throw a different exception object, it will still be converted into a SoapException on the client. That makes it difficult for the client to distinguish between different types of error conditions. The client can catch only a System.Net.WebException (which represents a timeout or a general network problem) or a System.Web.Services.Protocols.SoapException (which represents any .NET exception that occurred in the web service).

You have one other option. You can catch the exception in the web method on the server side and throw the supported SoapException yourself. The advantage of this approach is that before your web service throws the SoapException object, you can configure it by inserting additional XML in the <detail> element. The client can then read the content and use it to programmatically determine what really happened.

For example, here's a faulty version of the GetEmployeesCount() method that uses this approach to add the original exception type name to the SoapException using a custom <ExceptionType> element. You could extend this approach to add any combination of elements, attributes, and data.

```
<WebMethod()> _
Public Function GetEmployeesCountError() As Integer
    Dim con As SqlConnection = Nothing
    Try
        con = New SqlConnection(connectionString)

        ' Make a deliberately faulty SQL string
        Dim sql As String = "INVALID_SQL COUNT(*) FROM Employees"
        Dim cmd As New SqlCommand(sql, con)

        con.Open()
        Return CInt(cmd.ExecuteScalar())
    Catch err As Exception
        ' Create the detail information
        ' an <ExceptionType> element with the type name.
        Dim doc As New XmlDocument()
        Dim node As XmlNode = doc.CreateNode(XmlNodeType.Element, _
                SoapException.DetailElementName.Name, _
                SoapException.DetailElementName.Namespace)
        Dim child As XmlNode = doc.CreateNode(XmlNodeType.Element, _
                "ExceptionType", SoapException.DetailElementName.Namespace)
        child.InnerText = err.GetType().ToString()
        node.AppendChild(child)
```

```
            ' Create the custom SoapException.
            ' Use the message from the original exception,
            ' and add the detail information.
            Dim soapErr As New SoapException(err.Message, _
                SoapException.ServerFaultCode, Context.Request.Url.AbsoluteUri, node)

            ' Throw the revised SoapException.
            Throw soapErr
        Finally
            con.Close()
        End Try
    End Function
```

The client application can read the <ExceptionType> element to get the additional information you've added. Here's an example that displays the exception name in a Windows message box (see Figure 32-6):

```
Dim proxy As New EmployeesService()
Try
    Dim count As Integer = proxy.GetEmployeesCountError()
Catch err As SoapException
    MessageBox.Show("Original error was: " & err.Detail.InnerText)
End Try
```

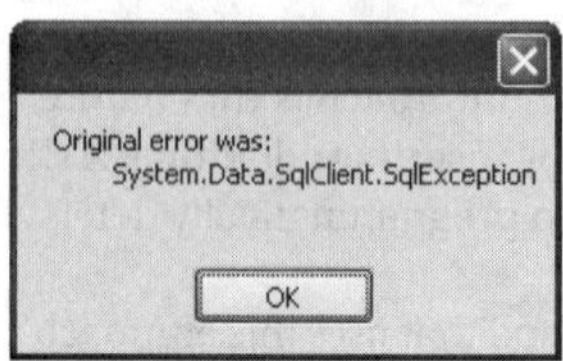

Figure 32-6. *Retrieving additional SOAP fault information*

The SOAP Header

SOAP also defines a <Header> section where you can place out-of-band information. This is typically information that doesn't belong in the message payload. For example, a SOAP header might contain user authentication credentials or a session ID. These details might be required for processing the request, but they aren't directly related to the method you're calling. By separating these two portions, you achieve two improvements:

> *The method interface is simpler*: For example, you don't need to create a version of the GetEmployees() method that accepts a user name and password as parameters. Instead, that information is passed in the header, keeping the method less cluttered.
>
> *The service is more flexible*: For example, if you add an authentication service using a SOAP header, you have the freedom to change how that service works and what information it requires without changing the interface of your web methods. As in all types of programming, loosely coupled solutions are almost always preferable.

The <Header> element is optional, and it allows for an unlimited number of child elements to be placed within the header. To define new headers for use with a .NET web service, you create classes that derive from System.Web.Services.Protocols.SoapHeader.

For example, imagine you want to design a better way to support state in a web service. Instead of trying to use the session cookie (which requires an HTTP cookie and can't be defined in the WSDL document), you could pass the session ID as a header with every SOAP message. The following sections implement this design.

The Custom Header

The first step to implement this design is to create a custom class that derives from SoapHeader and includes the information you want to transmit as public properties.

Here's an example:

```
Public Class SessionHeader
    Inherits SoapHeader

    Public SessionID As String

    Public Sub New(ByVal sessionID As String)
        SessionID = sessionID
    End Sub

    ' A default constructor is required for automatic deserialization.
    Public Sub New()
    End Sub

End Class
```

The SoapHeader class is really nothing more than a data container that can be serialized in and out of the <Header> element in a SOAP message. The custom SessionHeader adds a string SessionID variable with the session key.

Linking the Header to a Web Service

To use the SessionHeader in the web service, you need to create a public member variable in the web service for the header, as shown here:

```
Public Class SessionHeaderService
    Inherits WebService

    Public CurrentSessionHeader As SessionHeader
   Private ...
End Class
```

When you build a proxy class for this web service, it automatically includes a CurrentSessionHeader property. You can read or set the session header using this property. The definition for the custom SessionHeader class is also added to the proxy class file.

Headers are linked to individual methods using the SoapHeader attribute. For example, if you want to use the SessionHeader service in a web method named DoSomething(), you would apply the WebMethod and SoapHeader attributes like this:

```
<WebMethod(), SoapHeader("CurrentSessionHeader")> _
Public Sub DoSomething()
End Sub
```

Note that the SoapHeader attribute takes the name of the public member variable where you want .NET to store the SOAP header. In the DoSomething() method, the SoapHeader attributes tells ASP.NET to create a new SessionHeader object using the header information that's been received from the client and store it in the public CurrentSessionHeader member variable of the web service. ASP.NET uses reflection to find this member variable at runtime. If it's not present, an error will occur. The SoapHeader attribute can also accept a named Direction property. Direction specifies whether the SOAP header will be sent from the client to the web service, from the web service to the web client, or both.

The following example shows how you can use the session header to create a simple system for storing state. First, a CreateSession() web method allows the client to initiate a new session. At this point, a new session ID is generated for a new SessionHeader object. Next, a new Hashtable collection is created in the Application collection, indexed under the session ID. Because the session ID uses a GUID, it's statistically guaranteed to be unique among all users.

```
<WebMethod(), SoapHeader("CurrentSessionHeader",
      Direction:=SoapHeaderDirection.Out)> _
Public Sub CreateSession()
    ' Create the header.
    CurrentSessionHeader = New SessionHeader(Guid.NewGuid().ToString())

    ' From now on, all session data will be indexed under that key.
    Application(CurrentSessionHeader.SessionID) = New Hashtable()
End Sub
```

This Hashtable will be used to store the additional session information. This isn't the best approach (for example, the Application collection isn't shared between computers in a web farm, doesn't persist if the web application restarts, and isn't scalable with large numbers of users). However, you could easily extend this approach to use a combination of a back-end database and caching. That solution would be much more scalable, and it would use the same system of session headers that you see in this example.

You'll also notice that the CreateSession() method uses the direction SoapHeaderDirection.Out, because it creates the header and sends it back to the client. Here's the interesting part: When the client receives the custom header, it's stored in the CurrentSessionHeader property of the proxy class. The best part is that from that point on, whenever the client application calls a method in the web service that requires the header, it's submitted with the request. In fact, as long as the client uses the same proxy class, the headers are automatically transmitted and the session management system is completely transparent.

To test this, you need to add two more methods to the web service. The first method, SetSessionData(), accepts a DataSet and stores it in the Application slot for the current user's session.

```
<WebMethod(), SoapHeader("CurrentSessionHeader",
    Direction:=SoapHeaderDirection.In)> _
Public Sub SetSessionData(ByVal ds As DataSet)
    Dim session As Hashtable =
        CType(Application(CurrentSessionHeader.SessionID), Hashtable)
    session.Add("DataSet", ds)
End Sub
```

■ **Note** You don't need to lock the Application collection in this example. That's because no two clients use the same session ID, so there's no possibility for two users to attempt to change that slot of the Application collection at the same time.

Next, you can use a GetSessionData() method to retrieve the DataSet for the current user's session and return it:

```
<WebMethod(), SoapHeader("CurrentSessionHeader",
      Direction:=SoapHeaderDirection.In)> _
Public Function GetSessionData() As DataSet
    Dim session As Hashtable =
        CType(Application(CurrentSessionHeader.SessionID), Hashtable)
```

```
    Return CType(session("DataSet"), DataSet)
End Function
```

Of course, if you were creating a real-world implementation of this model, you wouldn't store the session information in application state, because it isn't robust or scalable enough. (For a rehash of the problems with application state, refer to Chapter 6.) Instead, you'd probably choose to store the information in a back-end database and cache it in the data cache (see Chapter 11) for quick retrieval.

Consuming a Web Service That Uses a Custom Header

When a web method requires a SOAP header, there's no way to test it using the simpler HTTP GET or HTTP POST protocols. As a result, you can't test the code in the browser test page. (In fact, the Invoke button won't even appear on this page.) Instead, you need to create a simple client.

The following code shows an example test. It creates the session (at which point it receives the SOAP header), stores a new, empty DataSet on the server, and then retrieves it.

```
Dim proxy As New SessionHeaderService()
proxy.CreateSession()
proxy.SetSessionData(New DataSet("TestDataSet"))
Dim ds As DataSet = proxy.GetSessionData()
```

The SOAP message used for the call to CreateSession() is similar to the previous examples:

```
<soap:Envelope xmlns:soap="http://schemas.xmlsoap.org/soap/envelope/" >
  <soap:Body>
    <CreateSession xmlns="http://www.apress.com/ProASP.NET/" />
  </soap:Body>
</soap:Envelope>
```

The response message includes the SOAP header:

```
<soap:Envelope xmlns:soap="http://schemas.xmlsoap.org/soap/envelope/" >
  <soap:Header>
    <SessionHeader xmlns="http://tempuri.org/">
      <SessionID>bbc0bfed-c3c2-4552-b70e-dfa5564447fd</SessionID>
    </SessionHeader>
  </soap:Header>
  <soap:Body>
    <CreateSessionResponse xmlns="http://www.apress.com/ProASP.NET/" />
  </soap:Body>
</soap:Envelope>
```

Now, subsequent method invocations also have the SOAP header automatically included, as shown here:

```
<soap:Envelope xmlns:soap="http://schemas.xmlsoap.org/soap/envelope/" >
  <soap:Header>
    <SessionHeader xmlns="http://tempuri.org/">
      <SessionID>bbc0bfed-c3c2-4552-b70e-dfa5564447fd</SessionID>
    </SessionHeader>
  </soap:Header>
  <soap:Body>
    <GetSessionData xmlns="http://www.apress.com/ProASP.NET/" />
  </soap:Body>
</soap:Envelope>
```

The result, in this example, is a web service that provides an alternate session state mechanism that uses SOAP headers instead of less reliable HTTP cookies. However, you can also use SOAP headers for many more web service extensions. In fact, in the next chapter you'll see how they allow you to leverage new and emerging web service standards with Microsoft's Web Services Enhancements component.

WSDL

WSDL (Web Service Description Language) is an XML-based language used to describe the public interface of a web service and the communication protocols it supports. A WSDL document is essentially a contract that tells the client what it needs to know in order to interact with a web service. Essentially, a WSDL document plays the same role as a type library for a COM component. (There's no direct analog to a type library in the .NET world, because all the descriptive type information you need is embedded into the compiled assembly as metadata.)

SOAP provides the ability to communicate with a web service. However, it doesn't tell you how to format your messages. Without WSDL, it would be up to you to document and explain the XML format your web services expect in the SOAP envelope. After locating a web service, the client developers would need to understand this information and handcraft the SOAP request and response messages accordingly. If this sort of human intervention were required in order to access every new service, the move toward web services would certainly be inhibited.

WSDL fills in the gaps by describing the supported protocols and expected message formats used by a web service. The power of WSDL is that it is not tied to any particular platform or object model. It is an XML language that provides an interface to web services across all platforms.

You can find the full WSDL standard at `http://www.w3.org/TR/wsdl`. The standard is fairly complex, but its underlying logic is hidden from the developer in ASP.NET programming, just as ASP.NET web controls abstract away the messy details of HTML tags and attributes.

■ Tip Depending on the type of web services you create, you may not need to view the WSDL information—instead, you may be content to let .NET generate it for you automatically. However, if you need to support third-party clients or you plan to use contract-first development techniques (described in the section "Implementing an Existing Contract"), you'll need a solid understanding.

Viewing the WSDL for a Web Service

Once you've created a web service, you can easily get ASP.NET to generate the corresponding WSDL document. All you need to do is request the web service .asmx file, and add ?WSDL to the end of the URL. (Another option is to click the Service Description link on the browser test page, which requests this URL.) Figure 32-7 shows part of the WSDL document you'll see for the EmployeesService developed in the previous chapter.

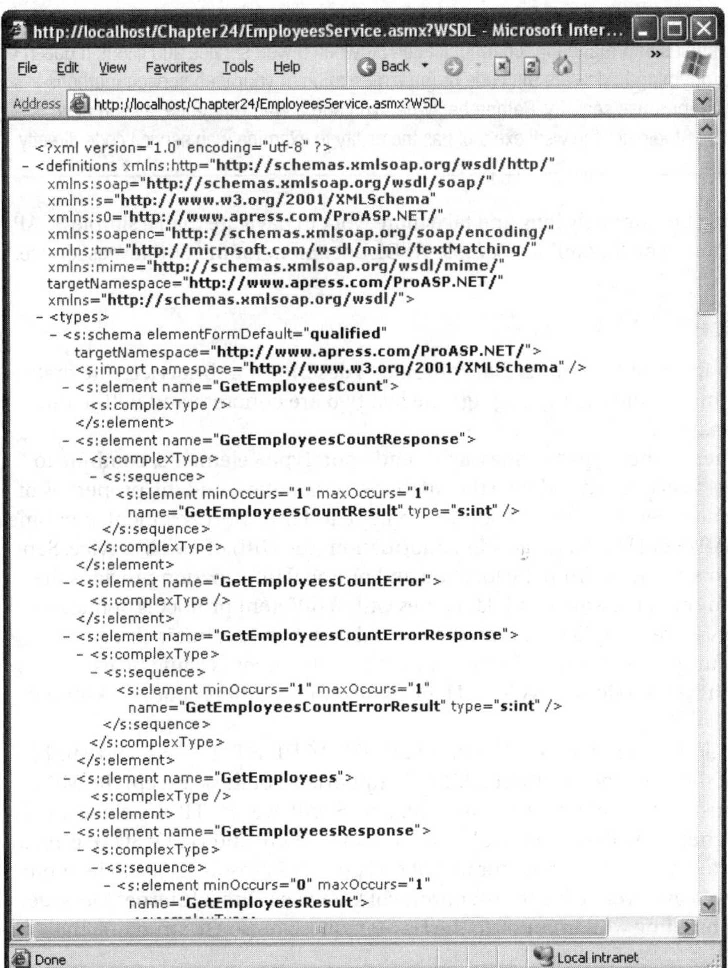

Figure 32-7. *A WSDL document for the EmployeesService*

WSDL is keenly important because it allows the designers of programming frameworks such as .NET to create tools that can create proxy classes programmatically. When you add a web reference in Visual Studio (or use wsdl.exe), you point it to the WSDL document for the web service. (If it's a .NET web service, you can save a step by pointing it to the .asmx web service file, because both tools are smart enough to add the ?WSDL to the end of the query string to get a WSDL document for a .NET web service.) The tool then scans the WSDL document and creates a proxy class that uses the same methods, parameters, and data types. Other languages and programming platforms provide tools that work similar magic.

■ **Note** The WSDL document contains information for communication between a web service and client. It doesn't contain any information that has anything to do with the code or implementation of your web service methods—that is unnecessary and would compromise security. Remember, when you add a web reference, all you need is the WSDL document. Neither Visual Studio nor the wsdl.exe tool has the ability to examine web service code directly.

WSDL documents tend to be extremely long and take more work to navigate than a simple SOAP message. In the next few sections, you'll examine a sample WSDL document for the EmployeesService.

The Basic Structure

WSDL documents consist of five main elements that combine to describe a web service. The first three of these are abstract and define the messaging. The last two are concrete and define the protocol and address information.

The three abstract elements, the <types>, <message>, and <portType> elements, combine to define the interface of the web service. They define the methods, parameters, and the properties of a web service. The two concrete elements, the <binding> element and the <port> element, combine to provide the protocol (SOAP over HTTP) and address information (the URI) of a web service. Separating the message definition elements from the location and protocol information provides the flexibility to reuse a common set of messages and data types within different protocols. It makes WSDL documents quite a bit more complicated than they would be otherwise, but it also gives unlimited flexibility for the future. For example, in the future WSDL documents could be used to describe how to interact with web services of SMTP, FTP, or some entirely different network-based protocol.

The WSDL 1.1 specification comes with SOAP over HTTP, HTTP GET, HTTP POST, and MIME extensions layered on top of the base specification. ASP.NET supports all of these except the MIME extension. Since WSDL is most commonly implemented utilizing SOAP over HTTP and since that is the default in ASP.NET, this chapter will focus on WSDL in relation to SOAP and HTTP. SOAP is really dominant, and there seems to be no real competitor to it at this point. Microsoft seems to be more interested in supporting raw SOAP over TCP, a transfer protocol known as Direct Internet Message Encapsulation (DIME), and building workarounds to the HTTP request-response structure, than they are in supporting MIME.

The <definitions> element is the root element of a WSDL document. It is where most of the namespaces are defined. Inside the <definitions> element are five main elements—one of which, <message>, commonly occurs multiple times.

Here's the basic structure of a WSDL document:

```
<?xml version="1.0" encoding="utf-8" ?>
<definitions>
  <types></types>
  <message></message>
  <message></message>
  <portType></portType>
  <binding></binding>
  <service></service>
</definitions>
```

Here is an overview of the main elements of a WSDL document:

Types: This section is where all the web service data types are defined. This includes custom data types and the message formats.

Messages: This section provides details about the request and response messages used to communicate with the web service.

PortType: This section groups messages in input/output pairs. Each pair represents a method.

Binding: This section provides information about the transport protocols supported by the web service.

Service: This section provides the endpoint (URI address) for the web service.

The following sections examine these elements.

Types Section

The <types> section is where the web service data types are defined. The <types> element is actually an embedded XML schema, and all data types defined in the XML Schema standard are valid. You can add other type systems through extensibility if required.

In a .NET web service, every message is defined as a complex type. The complex type definition describes the method name, its parameters, the minimum and maximum times the element can occur, and the data types. For example, consider the GetEmployeesCount() method. The request message needs no data and is defined using XML schema syntax, like this:

```
<s:element name="GetEmployeesCount">
  <s:complexType />
</s:element>
```

The response message returns an integer (the int type from the XML Schema standard). It's defined like this:

```
<s:element name="GetEmployeesCountResponse">
  <s:complexType>
    <s:sequence>
      <s:element minOccurs="1" maxOccurs="1" name="GetEmployeesCountResult"
       type="s:int" />
    </s:sequence>
  </s:complexType>
</s:element>
```

The <types> section will typically be quite lengthy, because it defines two complex types for each web method.

A more interesting example is the web service that returns a custom object. For example, consider this version of the GetEmployees() method, which returns an array of EmployeeDetails objects:

```
<WebMethod()> _
Public Function GetEmployees() As EmployeeDetails()
    ...
End Function
```

If you look in the <types> section for this web service, you'll find that the request message is unchanged:

```
<s:element name="GetEmployees">
  <s:complexType />
</s:element>
```

However, the response refers to another complex type, named ArrayOfEmployeeDetails:

```
<s:element name="GetEmployeesResponse">
  <s:complexType>
    <s:sequence>
      <s:element minOccurs="0" maxOccurs="1" name="GetEmployeesResult"
       type="s0:ArrayOfEmployeeDetails" />
    </s:sequence>
  </s:complexType>
</s:element>
```

This ArrayOfEmployeeDetails is a complex type that's generated automatically. It represents a list of zero or more EmployeeDetails objects, as shown here:

```
<s:complexType name="ArrayOfEmployeeDetails">
  <s:sequence>
    <s:element minOccurs="0" maxOccurs="unbounded" name="EmployeeDetails"
     nillable="true" type="s0:EmployeeDetails" />
  </s:sequence>
</s:complexType>
```

The EmployeeDetails data class is also defined as a complex type in the <types> section. It's made up of an EmployeeID, FirstName, LastName, and TitleOfCourtesy, as shown here:

```
<s:complexType name="EmployeeDetails">
  <s:sequence>
    <s:element minOccurs="1" maxOccurs="1" name="EmployeeID" type="s:int" />
    <s:element minOccurs="0" maxOccurs="1" name="FirstName" type="s:string" />
    <s:element minOccurs="0" maxOccurs="1" name="LastName" type="s:string" />
    <s:element minOccurs="0" maxOccurs="1" name="TitleOfCourtesy"
     type="s:string" />
  </s:sequence>
</s:complexType>
```

You'll learn more about how complex types work in web services later in this chapter (in the "Customizing SOAP Messages" section).

Another ingredient that will turn up in the <types> section is the definition for any SOAP headers you use. For example, the stateful web service test developed earlier in this chapter defines the following type to represent the data in the session header:

```
<s:element name="SessionHeader" type="s0:SessionHeader" />
<s:complexType name="SessionHeader">
  <s:sequence>
    <s:element minOccurs="0" maxOccurs="1" name="SessionID" type="s:string" />
  </s:sequence>
</s:complexType>
```

Message Section

Messages represent the information exchanged between a web service method and a client. When you request a stock quote from the simple web service, ASP.NET sends a message, and the web service returns a different message. You can find the definition for these messages in the <message> section of the WSDL document. Here's an example:

```
<message name="GetEmployeesCountSoapIn">
  <part name="parameters" element="s0:GetEmployeesCount" />
</message>
<message name="GetEmployeesCountSoapOut">
  <part name="parameters" element="s0:GetEmployeesCountResponse" />
</message>
```

In this example, you'll notice that ASP.NET creates both a GetEmployeesCountSoapIn and a GetEmployeesCountSoapOut message. The naming is a matter of convention, but it underscores that a separate message is required for input (sending parameters and invoking a web service method) and output (retrieving a return value from a web service method).

The data used in these messages is defined in terms of the information in the <types> section. For example, the GetEmployeesCountSoapIn request message uses the GetEmployeesCount message, which is defined as an empty complex type in the <types> section.

PortType Section

The information in the <portType> section of the WSDL document provides a catalog of the functionality available in a web service. Unlike the <message> element just discussed, which contained independent elements for the input and output messages, these operations are tied together in a request-response grouping. The operation name is the name of the method. The <portType> is a collection of operations, as shown here:

```
<portType name="EmployeesServiceSoap">
  <operation name="GetEmployeesCount">
    <documentation>Returns the total number of employees.</documentation>
    <input message="s0:GetEmployeesCountSoapIn" />
    <output message="s0:GetEmployeesCountSoapOut" />
  </operation>
  <operation name="GetEmployees">
    <documentation>Returns the full list of employees.</documentation>
    <input message="s0:GetEmployeesSoapIn" />
    <output message="s0:GetEmployeesSoapOut" />
  </operation>
</portType>
```

Additionally, you'll see a <documentation> tag with the information added through the Description property of the WebMethod attribute.

■ **Note** Four types of operations exist: one-way, request-response, solicit-response, and notification. The current WSDL specification defines bindings only for the one-way and request-response operation types. The other two can have bindings defined via binding extensions. The latter two are simply the inverse of the first two; the only difference is whether the endpoint in question is on the receiving or sending end of the initial message. HTTP is a two-way protocol, so the one-way operations will work only with MIME (which is not supported by ASP.NET) or with another custom extension.

Binding Section

The <binding> elements link the abstract data format to the concrete protocol used for transmission over an Internet connection. So far, the WSDL document has specified the data type used for various pieces of information, the required messages used for an operation, and the structure of each message. With the <binding> element, the WSDL document specifies the low-level communication protocol that you can use to communicate with a web service. It links this to an <operation> from the <portType> section.

Although we won't go into all the details of SOAP encoding, here's an example that defines how SOAP communication should work with the GetEmployeesCount() method of the EmployeesService:

```
<binding name="EmployeesServiceSoap" type="s0:EmployeesServiceSoap">
  <soap:binding transport="http://schemas.xmlsoap.org/soap/http"
   style="document" />
  <operation name="GetEmployeesCount">
    <soap:operation
    soapAction="http://www.apress.com/ProASP.NET/GetEmployeesCount"
    style="document" />
    <input>
      <soap:body use="literal" />
    </input>
    <output>
      <soap:body use="literal" />
```

```
    </output>
  </operation>
```

If your method uses a SOAP header, that information is added as a <header> element. Here's an example with the CreateSession() method from the custom state web service developed earlier in this chapter. The CreateSession() method doesn't require the client to submit a header, but it does return one. As a result, only the output message references the header:

```
<operation name="CreateSession">
  <soap:operation soapAction="http://tempuri.org/CreateSession"
   style="document" />
  <input>
    <soap:body use="literal" />
  </input>
  <output>
    <soap:body use="literal" />
    <soap:header message="s0:CreateSessionSessionHeader"
     part="SessionHeader" use="literal" />
  </output>
</operation>
```

In addition, if your web service supports SOAP 1.2, you'll find a duplicate <binding> section with similar information:

```
<binding name="EmployeesServiceSoap12" type="s0:EmployeesServiceSoap">
  ...
</binding>
```

Remember, .NET web services support both SOAP 1.1 and SOAP 1.2 by default, but you can change this using configuration files, as shown earlier in this chapter.

Service Section

The <service> section defines the entry points into your web service, as one or more <port> elements. Each <port> provides address information or a URI. Here's an example from the WSDL for the EmployeesService:

```
<service name="EmployeesService">
  <documentation>Retrieve the Northwind Employees</documentation>
  <port name="EmployeesServiceSoap" binding="s0:EmployeesServiceSoap">
    <soap:address location="http://localhost/Chapter32/EmployeesService.asmx" />
  </port>
</service>
```

The <service> section also includes a <documentation> element with the Description property of the WebService attribute, if it's set.

Implementing an Existing Contract

Since web services first appeared, a fair bit of controversy has existed about the right way to develop them. Some developers argue that the best approach is to use platforms such as .NET that abstract away the underlying details. They want to work with a higher-level framework of *remote procedure calls*. But XML gurus argue that you should look at the whole system in terms of *XML message passing*. They believe the first step in any web service application should be to develop a WSDL contract by hand.

As with many controversies, the ultimate solution probably lies somewhere in between. Application developers will probably never write WSDL contracts by hand—it's just too tedious and error-prone. On the other hand, developers who need to use web services in broader cross-platform scenarios will need to pay attention to the underlying XML representation of their messages and use techniques such as XML serialization attributes (described in the next section) to make sure they adhere to the right schema.

.NET 1.*x* was unashamedly oriented toward remote procedure calls. It significantly restricted the ability of developers to get underneath the web service facade and tinker with the low-level details. .NET 2.0 addresses this limitation with increased support for XML-centric approaches. One example is *contract-first* development.

In the web service scenarios you've seen so far, the web service code is created first. ASP.NET generates a matching WSDL document on demand. However, using .NET 2.0, you can approach the problem from the other end. That means you can take an existing WSDL document and feed it into the wsdl.exe command-line utility to create a basic web service skeleton. All you need is the new /serverInterface command-line switch.

For example, you could use the following command line to create a class definition for the EmployeesService:

```
wsdl /language:VB /serverInterface
        http://localhost/EmployeesService/EmployeesService.asmx?WSDL
```

You'll end up with an interface like this:

```
Public Interface IEmployeesServiceSoap
    <WebMethod()> _
    Function GetEmployees() As DataSet
End Interface
```

You can then implement the interface in another class to add the web service code for the GetEmployees() method. By starting with the WSDL control first, you ensure that your web service implementation matches it exactly.

■ **Note** The interface isn't quite this simple. To make sure your interface *exactly* matches the WSDL, .NET adds a number of attributes that specifically set details such as namespaces, SOAP encoding, and XML element names. This clutters the interface, but the basic structure is as shown here.

You could also use this trick with a third-party web service. For example, you might want to create your own version of the stock-picking web service on XMethods. You want to ensure that clients can call your web method without needing to get a new WSDL document or be recompiled. To ensure this, you can generate and implement an exact interface match:

```
wsdl /serverInterface
 http://services.xmethods.net/soap/urn:xmethods-delayed-quotes.wsdl
```

Of course, for your web service to really be compatible, your code needs to agree to certain assumptions that aren't set out in the WSDL document. These details might include how you parse strings, deal with invalid data, handle exceptions, and so on.

Contract-first development is unlikely to replace the simpler class-first model. However, it's a useful feature for developers who need to adhere to existing WSDL contracts, particularly in a cross-platform scenario.

Customizing SOAP Messages

In many cases, you don't need to worry about the SOAP serialization details. You'll be happy enough to create and consume web services using the infrastructure that .NET provides. However, in other cases you may need to extend your web services to use custom types or serialize your types to a specific XML format (for cross-platform compatibility). In the following sections, you'll see how you can control these details.

Serializing Complex Data Types

As you learned in the previous chapter, the SOAP specification supports all the data types defined by the XML Schema standard. These are considered *simple types*. Additionally, SOAP supports *complex types*, which are structures built out of an arrangement of simple types. You can use complex types for a web method return value or as a parameter. However, if a web method requires complex type parameters, you can interact with it only using SOAP. The simpler HTTP GET and HTTP POST mechanisms won't work, and the browser test page won't allow you to invoke the web method.

You've already used one example of a complex type: the DataSet. When you call the GetEmployees() method in the EmployeesService, .NET returns an XML document that describes the schema of the DataSet and its contents. Here's a partial listening of the SOAP response message:

```
<soap:Envelope xmlns:soap="http://schemas.xmlsoap.org/soap/envelope/" >
  <soap:Body>
    <GetEmployeesResponse xmlns="http://www.apress.com/ProASP.NET/">
      <GetEmployeesResult>
        <xs:schema id="NewDataSet" xmlns=""
         xmlns:xs="http://www.w3.org/2001/XMLSchema"
         xmlns:msdata="urn:schemas-microsoft-com:xml-msdata">
        <!-- Schema omitted. -->
        </xs:schema>
        <diffgr:diffgram xmlns:msdata="urn:schemas-microsoft-com:xml-msdata"
         xmlns:diffgr="urn:schemas-microsoft-com:xml-diffgram-v1">
        <EmployeesDataSet xmlns="">
          <Employees diffgr:id="Employees1" msdata:rowOrder="0">
            <EmployeeID>1</EmployeeID>
            <LastName>Davolio</LastName>
            <FirstName>Nancy</FirstName>
            <Title>Sales Representative</Title>
            <TitleOfCourtesy>Ms.</TitleOfCourtesy>
            <HomePhone>(206) 555-9857</HomePhone>
          </Employees>
          <Employees diffgr:id="Employees2" msdata:rowOrder="1">
            <EmployeeID>2</EmployeeID>
            <LastName>Fuller</LastName>
            <FirstName>Andrew</FirstName>
            <Title>Vice President, Sales</Title>
            <TitleOfCourtesy>Dr.</TitleOfCourtesy>
            <HomePhone>(206) 555-9482</HomePhone>
          </Employees>
          ...
        </EmployeesDataSet></diffgr:diffgram>
      </GetEmployeesResult>
    </GetEmployeesResponse>
  </soap:Body>
</soap:Envelope>
```

You can also use your own custom classes with .NET web services. In this case, when you build the proxy, a copy of the custom class will automatically be added to the client (in the appropriate language of the client).

The process of converting objects to XML is known as *serialization*, and the process of reconstructing the objects from XML is know as *deserialization*. The component that performs the serialization is the System.Xml.Serialization.XmlSerializer class. You shouldn't confuse this class with the serialization classes you learned about in Chapter 13, such as the BinaryFormatter and SoapFormatter. These classes perform .NET-specific serialization that works with proprietary .NET objects, as long as they are marked with the Serializable attribute. Unlike the BinaryFormatter and SoapFormatter, the XmlSerializer works with any class, but it's much more limited than the BinaryFormatter and SoapFormatter and can extract only public data.

To use the XmlSerializer and send your custom objects to and from a web service, you need to be aware of a few restrictions:

Any code you include is ignored in the client: This means the client's copy of the custom class won't include methods, constructor logic, or property procedure logic. Instead, these details will be stripped out automatically.

Your class must have a default zero-argument constructor: This allows .NET to create a new instance of this object when it deserializes a SOAP message that contains the corresponding data.

Read-only properties are not serialized: In other words, if a property has only a get accessor and not a set accessor, it cannot be serialized. Similarly, private properties and private member variables are ignored.

Clearly, the need to serialize a class to a piece of cross-platform XML imposes some strict limitations. If you use custom classes in a web service, it's best to think of them as simple data containers, rather than true participants in object-oriented design.

Creating a Custom Class

To see the XmlSerializer in action, you need to create a custom class and a web method that uses it. In the next example, we'll use the database component first developed in Chapter 8. This database component doesn't use the disconnected DataSet objects. Instead, it returns the results of a query using the custom EmployeeDetails class.

Here's what the EmployeeDetails class looks like currently, without any web service–related enhancements:

```
Public Class EmployeeDetails
    Private m_employeeID As Integer
    Public Property EmployeeID() As Integer
        Get
                Return m_employeeID
        End Get
        Set(ByVal Value as Integer)
                m_employeeID = Value
        End Set
    End Property

    Private m_firstName As String
    Public Property FirstName() As String
        Get
                Return m_firstName
        End Get
        Set(ByVal Value as String)
```

```
                m_firstName = Value
            End Set
        End Property

        Private m_lastName As String
        Public Property LastName() As String
            Get
                Return m_lastName
            End Get
            Set(ByVal Value as String)
                m_lastName = Value
            End Set
        End Property

        Private m_titleOfCourtesy As String
        Public Property TitleOfCourtesy() As String
            Get
                Return m_titleOfCourtesy
            End Get
            Set(ByVal Value as String)
                m_titleOfCourtesy = Value
            End Set
        End Property

        Public Sub New(ByVal p_employeeID As Integer, ByVal p_firstName As String, _
                ByVal p_lastName As String, ByVal p_titleOfCourtesy As String)
            Me.m_employeeID = p_employeeID
            Me.m_firstName = p_firstName
            Me.m_lastName = p_lastName
            Me.m_titleOfCourtesy = p_titleOfCourtesy
        End Sub
    End Class
```

The EmployeeDetails class uses property procedures instead of public member variables. However, you can still use it because the XmlSerializer will perform the conversion automatically. The EmployeeDetails class doesn't have a default zero-parameter constructor, so before you can use it in a web method you need to add one, as shown here:

```
Public Sub New()
End Sub
```

Now the EmployeeDetails class is ready for a web service scenario. To try it, you can create a web method that returns an array of EmployeeDetail objects. The next example shows one such method—a GetEmployees() web method that calls the EmployeeDB.GetEmployees() method in the database component. (For the full code for this method, you can refer to Chapter 8 or consult the downloadable code.)

Here's the web method you need:

```
<WebMethod()> _
Public Function GetEmployees() As EmployeeDetails()
    Dim db As EmployeeDB = New EmployeeDB()
    Return db.GetEmployees()
End Function
```

Generating the Proxy

When you generate the proxy (either using wsdl.exe or adding a web reference), you'll end up with two classes. The first class is the proxy class used to communicate with the web service. The second class is the definition for EmployeeDetails.

It's important to understand that the client's version of EmployeeDetails doesn't match the server-side version. In fact, the client doesn't even have the ability to see the full code of the server-side EmployeeDetails class. Instead, the client reads the WSDL document, which contains the XML schema for the EmployeeDetails class. The schema simply lists all the public properties and fields (without distinguishing between the two) and their data types.

When the client builds a proxy class, .NET uses this WSDL information to generate a client-side EmployeeDetails class. For every public property or field in the server-side definition of EmployeeDetails, .NET adds a matching public property to the client-side EmployeeDetails class.

Here's the code that's generated for the client-side EmployeeDetails class:

```
Public Partial Class EmployeeDetails
    Private employeeIDField As Integer
    Private firstNameField As String
    Private lastNameField As String
    Private titleOfCourtesyField As String

    Public Property EmployeeID() As Integer
        Get
                Return Me.employeeIDField
        End Get
        Set (ByVal Value As Integer)
                Me.employeeIDField = Value
        End Set
    End Property

    Public Property FirstName() As String
        Get
                Return Me.firstNameField
        End Get
        Set (ByVal Value As String)
                Me.firstNameField = Value
        End Set
    End Property

    Public Property LastName() As String
        Get
                Return Me.lastNameField
        End Get
        Set (ByVal Value As String)
                Me.lastNameField = Value
        End Set
    End Property

    Public Property TitleOfCourtesy() As String
        Get
                Return Me.titleOfCourtesyField
        End Get
        Set (ByVal Value As String)
                Me.titleOfCourtesyField = Value
        End Set
    End Property
End Class
```

In this example, the client-side version is quite similar to the server-side version, because the server-side version didn't include much code. The only real difference (other than the renaming of private fields) is the missing nondefault constructor. As a general rule, the client-side version doesn't preserve nondefault constructors, any code in property procedures or constructors, any methods, or any private members.

Note The client-side version of a data class always uses property procedures, even if the original server-side version used public member variables. That gives you the ability to bind collections of client-side EmployeeDetails objects to a grid control. This is a change from .NET 1.*x*.

Testing the Custom Class Web Service

The next step is to write the code that calls the GetEmployees() method. Because the client now has a definition of the EmployeeDetails class, this step is easy:

```
Dim proxy As New EmployeesServiceCustomDataClass()
Dim employees As EmployeeDetails() = proxy.GetEmployees()
```

The response message includes the employee data in the <GetEmployeesResult> element. By default, the XmlSerializer creates a structure of child elements based on the class name (EmployeeDetails) and the public property or variable names (EmployeeID, FirstName, LastName, TitleOfCourtesy, and so on). Interestingly, this default structure looks quite a bit like the XML used to model the DataSet, without the schema information.

Here's a somewhat abbreviated example of the response message:

```
<soap:Envelope xmlns:soap="http://schemas.xmlsoap.org/soap/envelope/" >
  <soap:Body>
    <GetEmployeesResponse xmlns="http://www.apress.com/ProASP.NET/">
      <GetEmployeesResult>
        <EmployeeDetails>
          <EmployeeID>1</EmployeeID>
          <FirstName>Nancy</FirstName>
          <LastName>Davolio</LastName>
          <TitleOfCourtesy>Ms.</TitleOfCourtesy>
        </EmployeeDetails>
        <EmployeeDetails>
          <EmployeeID>2</EmployeeID>
          <FirstName>Andrew</FirstName>
          <LastName>Fuller</LastName>
          <TitleOfCourtesy>Dr.</TitleOfCourtesy>
        </EmployeeDetails>
      </GetEmployeesResult>
      ...
    </GetEmployeesResponse>
  </soap:Body>
</soap:Envelope>
```

When the client receives this message, the XML response is converted into an array of EmployeeDetails objects, using the client-side definition of the EmployeeDetails class.

Customizing XML Serialization with Attributes

Sometimes, you may want to customize the XML representation of a custom class. This approach is most useful in cross-platform programming scenarios when a client expects XML in a certain form. For example, you might have an existing schema that expects EmployeeDetails to use an EmployeeID attribute instead of a nested <EmployeeID> tag. .NET provides an easy way to apply these rules, using attributes. The basic idea is that you apply attributes to your data classes (such as EmployeeDetails). When the XmlSerializer creates a SOAP message, it reads these attributes and uses them to tailor the XML payload it generates.

The System.Xml.Serialization namespace contains a number of attributes that can be used to control the shape of the XML. Two sets of attributes exist: one where the attributes are named Xml*Xxx* and another where the attributes are named Soap*Xxx*. Which attributes you use depends on how the parameters are encoded.

As discussed earlier in this chapter, two types of SOAP serialization exist: literal and SOAP section 5 encoding. The XmlXxx attributes apply when you use literal style parameters. As a result, they apply in the following cases:

- When you use a web service with the default encoding. (In other words, you haven't changed the encoding by adding any attributes.)
- When you use the HTTP GET or HTTP POST protocols to communicate with a web service.
- When you use the SoapDocumentService or SoapDocumentMethod attribute with the Use property set to SoapBindingUse.Literal.
- When you use the XmlSerializer on its own (outside a web service).

The SoapXxx attributes apply when you use encoded-style parameters. That occurs in the following cases:

- When you use the SoapRpcService or SoapRpcMethod attributes
- When you use the SoapDocumentService or SoapDocumentMethod attribute with the Use property set to SoapBindingUse.Encoded

A class member may have both the SoapXxx and the XmlXxx attributes applied at the same time. Which one is used depends on the type of serialization being performed.

Table 32-1 lists most of the available attributes. Most of the attributes contain a number of properties. Some properties are common to most attributes, such as the Namespace property (used to indicate the namespace of the serialized XML) and the DataType property (used to indicate a specific XML Schema data type that might not be the one the XmlSerializer would choose by default). For a complete reference that describes all the attributes and their properties, refer to the MSDN Help.

Table 32-1. *Attributes to Control XML Serialization*

Xml Attribute	SOAP Attribute	Description
XmlAttribute	SoapAttribute	Used to make fields or properties into XML attributes instead of elements.
XmlElement	SoapElement	Used to name the XML elements.
XmlArray		Used to name arrays.
XmlIgnore	SoapIgnore	Used to prevent fields or properties from being serialized.

(Continued)

Table 32-1. *Continued*

Xml Attribute	SOAP Attribute	Description
XmlInclude	SoapInclude	Used in inheritance scenarios. For example, you may have a property or field that's typed as some base class but may actually reference some derived class. In this case, you can use XmlInclude to specify all the derived class types that you may use.
XmlRoot		Used to name the top-level element.
XmlText		Used to serialize fields directly in the XML text without elements.
XmlEnum	SoapEnum	Used to give the members of an enumeration a name different from the name used in the enumeration.
XmlType	SoapType	Used to control the name of types in the WSDL file.

To see how SOAP serialization works, you can apply these attributes to the EmployeeDetails. For example, consider the following modified class declaration that uses several serialization attributes:

```
Public Class EmployeeDetails
    <XmlAttribute("id")> _
    Public Property EmployeeID() As Integer
        Get
                Return employeeIDField
        End Get
        Set (ByVal Value As Integer)
                employeeIDField = Value
        End Set
    End Property

    <XmlElement("First")> _
    Public Property FirstName() As String
        Get
                Return firstNameField
        End Get
        Set (ByVal Value As String)
                firstNameField = Value
        End Set
    End Property

    <XmlElement("Last")> _
    Public Property LastName() As String
        Get
                Return lastNameField
        End Get
        Set (ByVal Value As String)
                lastNameField = Value
        End Set
    End Property

    <XmlIgnore()> _
    Public Property TitleOfCourtesy() As String
        Get
                Return titleOfCourtesyField
        End Get
        Set (ByVal Value As String)
                titleOfCourtesyField = Value
```

```
        End Set
    End Property

    ' (Constructors and private data omitted.)
End Class
```

Here's what a serialized EmployeeDetails will look like in the SOAP message:

```
<soap:Envelope xmlns:soap="http://schemas.xmlsoap.org/soap/envelope/" >
  <soap:Body>
    <GetEmployeesResponse xmlns="http://www.apress.com/ProASP.NET/">
      <GetEmployeesResult>
        <EmployeeDetails id="1">
          <First>Nancy</First>
          <Last>Davolio</Last>
          </EmployeeDetails>
        <EmployeeDetails id="2">
          <First>Andrew</First>
          <Last>Fuller</Last>
        </EmployeeDetails>
        ...
      </GetEmployeesResult>
    </GetEmployeesResponse>
  </soap:Body>
</soap:Envelope>
```

■ **Tip** If you want to experiment with different serialization attributes, you can also use the XmlSerializer class directly. Just create an instance of the XmlSerializer and pass the type of the object you want to serialize as a constructor parameter. You can then use the Serialize() method to convert the object to XML and write the data to a stream or a TextWriter object. You can use Deserialize() to read the XML data from a stream or TextReader and re-create the original object. You can also use a command-line tool called xsd.exe that's included with the .NET Framework to generate class definitions based on XML schema documents. The class declaration will automatically include the appropriate serialization attributes.

This example has only one limitation. Although you can control how the EmployeeDetails object is serialized, you can't use the same attributes to shape the element that wraps the list of employees. To take this step, you have two options. You could create a custom collection class and apply the XML serialization attributes to that class. Or, if you want to continue using an ordinary array, you must add an XML attribute that applies directly to the return value of the web method, like this:

```
Public Function GetEmployees() As <XmlArray("EmployeeList")> EmployeeDetails()
    ...
End Function
```

Now when you call the web method, you'll get this XML:

```
<soap:Envelope xmlns:soap="http://schemas.xmlsoap.org/soap/envelope/" >
  <soap:Body>
    <GetEmployeesResponse xmlns="http://www.apress.com/ProASP.NET/">
      <EmployeeList>
        <EmployeeDetails id="1">
          <First>Nancy</First>
          <Last>Davolio</Last>
          </EmployeeDetails>
```

```
      <EmployeeDetails id="2">
        <First>Andrew</First>
        <Last>Fuller</Last>
      </EmployeeDetails>
      ...
    </EmployeeList>
  </GetEmployeesResponse>
 </soap:Body>
</soap:Envelope>
```

You can do a fair bit more to configure the details. For example, you can insert XML serialization attributes immediately before your parameters to change the required XML of the incoming request message. You can also use the SoapDocument attribute (discussed earlier) to change the name and namespace of the XML element that wraps the return value of your function (in this example, it's named <GetEmployeesReponse>).

Customizing XML Serialization with IXmlSerializable

The XML serialization attributes work well when you can take advantage of a one-to-one mapping between properties and XML elements or attributes. However, in some scenarios developers need more flexibility to create an XML representation of a type that fits a specific schema. For example, you might need to change the representation of your data types, control the order of elements, or add out-of-band information (such as comments or the date the document was serialized). In other cases, it may be technically possible to use the XML serialization attributes, but it may involve creating an unreasonably awkward class model.

Fortunately, .NET 2.0 provides an IXmlSerializable interface that you can implement to get complete control over your XML. The IXmlSerializable attribute has existed in .NET since version 1.0. However, it was used as a proprietary way to customize the serialization of the .NET DataSet, and it wasn't made available for general use. Now it's fully supported. IXmlSerializable mandates the three methods listed in Table 32-2.

Table 32-2. *IXmlSerializable Methods*

Method	Description
WriteXml()	In this method you write the XML representation of an instance of your object using an XmlWriter. You need this method in your web service in order for your web service to serialize an object and send it as a return value.
ReadXml()	In this method you read the XML from an XmlReader and generate the corresponding object. It's quite possible you won't need this method (in which case it's safe to throw a NotImplementedException. However, you will need it if you have to deserialize an object that your web service is accepting as an input parameter or if you decide to deploy this custom class to the client.
GetSchema()	This method is deprecated, and you should return null. If you want the ability to generate the XML schema for your class (which will be incorporated in the WSDL document), you must use the XmlSchemaProvider attribute instead. The XmlSchemaProvider names the method in your class that returns the XML schema document (XSD).

Chapter 12 discussed the XmlReader and XmlWriter classes in detail. Using them is quite straightforward. Here's an example of a custom class that handles its own XML generation:

```
Public Class EmployeeDetailsCustom
    Implements IXmlSerializable
```

```
    Public ID As Integer
    Public FirstName As String
    Public LastName As String

    Private Const ns As String =
        "http://www.apress.com/ProASP.NET/CustomEmployeeDetails"

    Private Sub WriteXml(ByVal w As XmlWriter) Implements IXmlSerializable.WriteXml
        w.WriteStartElement("Employee", ns)

        w.WriteStartElement("Name", ns)
        w.WriteElementString("First", ns, FirstName)
        w.WriteElementString("Last", ns, LastName)
        w.WriteEndElement()

        w.WriteElementString("ID", ns, ID.ToString())
        w.WriteEndElement()
    End Sub

    Private Sub ReadXml(ByVal r As XmlReader) Implements IXmlSerializable.ReadXml
        r.MoveToContent()
        r.ReadStartElement("Employee")
        r.ReadStartElement("Name")
        FirstName = r.ReadElementString("First", ns)
        LastName = r.ReadElementString("Last", ns)
        r.ReadEndElement()
        r.MoveToContent()
        ID = Integer.Parse(r.ReadElementString("ID", ns))
        r.ReadEndElement()
    End Sub

    Private Function GetSchema() As System.Xml.Schema.XmlSchema
     Implements IXmlSerializable.GetSchema
        Return Nothing
    End Function

    ' (Constructors omitted.)
End Class
```

■ Tip Make sure you read the full XML document, including the closing element tags in the ReadXml() method. Otherwise, .NET may throw an exception when you attempt to deserialize the XML.

Now, if you create a web method like this:

```
<WebMethod()> _
Public Function GetCustomEmployee() As EmployeeDetailsCustom
    Return New EmployeeDetailsCustom(101, "Joe", "Dabiak")
End Function
```

here's the XML you'll see:

```
<soap:Envelope xmlns:xsi="http://www.w3.org/2001/XMLSchema-instance"
xmlns:xsd="http://www.w3.org/2001/XMLSchema"
xmlns:soap="http://schemas.xmlsoap.org/soap/envelope/">
  <soap:Body>
```

```
    <GetCustomEmployeeResponse xmlns="http://www.apress.com/ProASP.NET/">
      <GetCustomEmployeeResult>
        <Employee xmlns="http://www.apress.com/ProASP.NET/CustomEmployeeDetails">
          <Name>
            <First>Joe</First>
            <Last>Tester</Last>
          </Name>
          <ID>1</ID>
        </Employee>
      </GetCustomEmployeeResult>
    </GetCustomEmployeeResponse>
  </soap:Body>
</soap:Envelope>
```

■ **Note** When using IXmlSerializable, the only serialization attributes that have any effect are the ones you apply to the method and the class declaration. Attributes on individual properties and fields have no effect. However, you could use .NET reflection to check for your own attributes and then use them to tailor the XML markup you generate.

Schemas for Custom Data Types

The only limitation in this example is that the client has no way to determine what XML to expect. If you look at the <types> section of the WSDL document for this example, you'll see that the schema is left wide open with the <any> element. This allows any valid XML content.

```
<s:element name="GetCustomEmployeeResponse">
  <s:complexType>
    <s:sequence>
      <s:element minOccurs="0" maxOccurs="1" name="GetCustomEmployeeResult">
        <s:complexType>
          <s:sequence>
            <s:element ref="s:schema" />
            <s:any />
          </s:sequence>
        </s:complexType>
      </s:element>
    </s:sequence>
  </s:complexType>
</s:element>
```

On the client side, you could deal with the data as an XML fragment, in which case you need to write the XML parsing code. However, a better idea is to supply an XML schema for your custom XML representation.

To do this, you need to add a Shared method to your class that returns the XML schema document as an XmlQualifiedName object, as shown here:

```
Public Shared Function GetSchemaDocument(
        ByVal xs As XmlSchemaSet) As XmlQualifiedName
    ' Get the path to the schema file.
    Dim schemaPath As String =
        HttpContext.Current.Server.MapPath("EmployeeDetails.xsd")

    ' Retrieve the schema from the file.
    Dim schemaSerializer As XmlSerializer = New XmlSerializer(GetType(XmlSchema))
    Dim s As XmlSchema =
        CType(schemaSerializer.Deserialize(
                New XmlTextReader(schemaPath), XmlSchema))
```

```
    xs.XmlResolver = New XmlUrlResolver()
    xs.Add(s)

    Return New XmlQualifiedName("EmployeeDetails", ns)
End Function
```

Tip This example retrieves the schema document from a file. For best performance, you would cache this document or construct it programmatically.

Now you need to point .NET to the right method using the XmlSchemaProvider attribute:

```
<XmlSchemaProvider("GetSchemaDocument")> _
Public Class EmployeeDetailsCustom
    Implements IXmlSerializable
       Private ...
End Class
```

Now, ASP.NET will call this Shared method when it generates the WSDL document. It will then add the schema information to the WSDL document. However, remember that when you build a client .NET will generate the data class to match the schema, which means the client-side EmployeeDetails will differ quite a bit from the server-side version. (In this example, the client-side EmployeeDetails class will have a nested Name class because of the organization of XML elements, which probably isn't what you want.)

So, what can you do if you want the same version of EmployeeDetails on both the client and server ends? You could manually change the generated proxy code class, although this change will be discarded each time you rebuild the proxy. A more permanent option is to use schema importer extensions, which you'll tackle in the "Schema Importer Extensions" section.

Custom Serialization for Large Data Types

One reason you might use IXmlSerializable is to build web services that send large amounts of data. For example, imagine you want to send a large block of binary data that contains the content from a file. You could use a web service like this:

```
<WebMethod()> _
Public Function DownloadFile(ByVal fileName As String) As Byte()
    ...
End Function
```

The problem is that this approach assumes you'll read the entire data of the file into memory at once, as a byte array. If the file is several gigabytes in size, this will cripple the computer. A better solution is to use IXmlSerializable to implement chunking. That way, you can send an arbitrarily large amount of data over the wire by writing it one chunk at a time.

In the following sections, you'll see an example the uses IXmlSerializable to dramatically reduce the overhead of sending a large file.

The Server Side

The first step is to create the signature for your web method. For this strategy to work, the web method needs to return a class that implements IXmlSerializable. This example uses a class named FileData. Additionally, you need to turn off ASP.NET buffering to allow the response to be streamed across the network.

```
<WebMethod(BufferResponse := False),
    SoapDocumentMethod(ParameterStyle := SoapParameterStyle.Bare)> _
Public Function DownloadFile(ByVal serverFileName As String) As FileData
    ...
End Function
```

The most laborious part is implementing the custom serialization in the FileData class. The basic idea is that when you create a FileData object on the server, you'll simply specify the corresponding filename. When the FileData object is serialized and IXmlSerializable.WriteXml() is called, the FileData object will create a FileStream and start sending binary data one block at a time.

Here's the bare skeleton of the FileData class:

```
<XmlRoot(Namespace:="http://www.apress.com/ProASP.NET/FileData"),
                    XmlSchemaProvider("GetSchemaDocument")> _
Public Class FileData
    Implements IXmlSerializable

    ' Namespace for serialization.
    Private Const ns As String = "http://www.apress.com/ProASP.NET/FileData"

    ' The server-side path.
    Private serverFilePath As String

    ' When the FileData is created, make sure the file exists.
    ' This won't defend against other problems reading the file (such as
    ' insufficient rights, the file being currently locked by another process,
    ' and so on).
    Public Sub New(ByVal serverFilePath As String)
        If (Not File.Exists(serverFilePath)) Then
            Throw New FileNotFoundException("Source file not found.")
        End If
        Me.serverFilePath = serverFilePath
    End Sub

    Private Sub WriteXml(ByVal writer As System.Xml.XmlWriter) _
      Implements IXmlSerializable.WriteXml
        ...
    End Sub

    Private Function GetSchema() As System.Xml.Schema.XmlSchema _
            Implements IXmlSerializable.GetSchema
        Return Nothing
    End Function

    Private Sub ReadXml(ByVal reader As System.Xml.XmlReader) _
          Implements IXmlSerializable.ReadXml
        Throw New NotImplementedException()
    End Sub

    Public Shared Function GetSchemaDocument(ByVal xs As XmlSchemaSet)
            As XmlQualifiedName
        ' Get the path to the schema file.
        Dim schemaPath As String =
          HttpContext.Current.Server.MapPath("FileData.xsd")

        ' Retrieve the schema from the file.
        Dim schemaSerializer As New XmlSerializer(GetType(XmlSchema))
        Dim s As XmlSchema = CType(schemaSerializer.Deserialize
```

```
            (New XmlTextReader(schemaPath), Nothing), XmlSchema)
        xs.XmlResolver = New XmlUrlResolver()
        xs.Add(s)
        Return New XmlQualifiedName("FileData", ns)
    End Function
End Class
```

You'll notice that this class supports writing the file data to XML but not reading it.

In this example, you want to create an XML representation that splits data into separate Base64-encoded chunks. It will look like this:

```
<FileData xmlns="http://www.apress.com/ProASP.NET/FileData">
  <fileName>sampleFile.xls</fileName>
  <size>66048</size>
  <content>
    <chunk>...</chunk>
    <chunk>...</chunk>
    ...
  </content>
</FileData>
```

Here's the WriteXml() implementation that does the job:

```
Private Sub WriteXml(ByVal writer As System.Xml.XmlWriter)
    Implements IXmlSerializable.WriteXml
    ' Open the file (taking care to allow it to be opened by other threads
    ' at the same time).
    Dim fs As New FileStream(
         serverFilePath, FileMode.Open, FileAccess.Read, FileShare.Read)

    ' Write filename.
    writer.WriteElementString("fileName", ns, Path.GetFileName(serverFilePath))

    ' Write file size (useful for determining progress).
    Dim length As Long = fs.Length
    writer.WriteElementString("size", ns, length.ToString())

    ' Start the file content.
    writer.WriteStartElement("content", ns)

    ' Read a 4 KB buffer and write that (in slightly larger Base64-encoded chunks).
    Dim bufferSize As Integer = 4096
    Dim fileBytes As Byte() = New Byte(bufferSize - 1) {}
    Dim readBytes As Integer = bufferSize
    Do While readBytes > 0
        readBytes = fs.Read(fileBytes, 0, bufferSize)
        writer.WriteStartElement("chunk", ns)

        ' This method explicitly encodes the data. If you use another method,
        ' it's possible to add invalid characters to the XML stream.
        writer.WriteBase64(fileBytes, 0, readBytes)
        writer.WriteEndElement()
        writer.Flush()
    Loop
    fs.Close()

    ' End the XML.
    writer.WriteEndElement()
End Sub
```

Now you can complete the web service. The DownloadFile() method shown here looks for a user-specified file in a hard-coded directory. It creates a new FileData object with the full path name and returns it. At this point, the FileData serialization code springs into action to read the file and begin writing it to the response stream.

```
Public Class FileService
    Inherits System.Web.Services.WebService
    ' Only allow downloads in this directory.

    Private folder As String = "c:\Downloads"

    <WebMethod(BufferResponse := False),
          SoapDocumentMethod(ParameterStyle := SoapParameterStyle.Bare)> _
    Public Function DownloadFile(ByVal serverFileName As String) As FileData
        ' Make sure the user only specified a filename (not a full path).
        serverFileName = Path.GetFileName(serverFileName)

        ' Get the full path using the download directory.
        Dim serverFilePath As String = Path.Combine(folder, serverFileName)

        ' Return the file data.
        Return New FileData(serverFilePath)
    End Function
End Class
```

You can try this method using the browser test page and verify that the data is split into chunks.

The Client Side

On the client side, you need a way to retrieve the data one chunk at a time and write it to a file. To provide this functionality, you need to change the proxy class so that it returns a custom IXmlSerializable type. You'll place the deserialization code in this class.

■ **Tip** You can implement both the serialization code and the deserialization code in the same class and distribute that class as a component to the client and the server. However, it's usually better to observe a strict separation between both ends of a web service application. This makes it easier to introduce new clients.

When you create the proxy class, .NET will try to create a suitable copy of the FileData class. However, it won't succeed. Without the schema information, it will simply try to convert the returned value to a DataSet. Even if you add the schema information, all .NET can do is create a class representation that exposes all the details (the name, size, and content) through separate properties. This class won't have the chunking behavior—instead, it will attempt to load everything into memory at once.

To fix this problem, you need to customize the proxy class by hand. If you're creating a web client, you need to first generate the proxy class with wsdl.exe so you have the code available. Here's the change you need to make:

```
Public Function DownloadFile(ByVal serverFileName As String) As FileDataClient
    Dim results As Object() =
         Me.Invoke("DownloadFile", New Object() { serverFileName})
    Return (CType(results(0), FileDataClient))
End Function
```

Obviously, modifying the proxy class is a brittle solution, because every time you refresh the proxy class your change will be wiped out. A better choice is to implement a schema importer extension, as described in the next section.

Here's the basic outline of the FileDataClient class:

```
<XmlRoot(Namespace:="http://www.apress.com/ProASP.NET/FileData")> _
Public Class FileDataClient
    Implements IXmlSerializable

    Private ns As String = "http://www.apress.com/ProASP.NET/FileData"

    ' The location to place the downloaded file.
    Private Shared strClientFolder As String
    Public Shared Property ClientFolder() As String
        Get
                Return strClientFolder
        End Get
        Set(Value as String)
                strClientFolder = Value
        End Set
    End Property

    Private Sub ReadXml(ByVal reader As System.Xml.XmlReader)
         Implements IXmlSerializable.ReadXml
           ...
    End Sub

    Private Function GetSchema() As System.Xml.Schema.XmlSchema
         Implements IXmlSerializable.GetSchema
        Return Nothing
    End Function

    Private Sub WriteXml(ByVal writer As System.Xml.XmlWriter)
         Implements IXmlSerializable.WriteXml
        Throw New NotImplementedException()
    End Sub
End Class
```

One important detail is the Shared property ClientFolder, which keeps track of the location where you want to save all downloaded files. You must set this property before the download begins, because the ReadXml() method uses that information to determine where to create the file. The ClientFolder property must be a Shared property, because the client doesn't get the chance to create and configure the FileDataClient object it wants to use. Instead, .NET creates a FileDataClient instance automatically and uses it to deserialize the data. By using a Shared property, the client can set this piece of information before starting the download, as shown here:

```
FiileDataClient.ClientFolder = "c:\MyFiles"
```

The deserialization code performs the reverse task of the serialization code—it steps through the chunks and writes them to the new file. Here's the complete code:

```
Private Sub ReadXml(ByVal reader As System.Xml.XmlReader)
        Implements IXmlSerializable.ReadXml
    If FileDataClient.ClientFolder = String.Empty Then
        Throw New InvalidOperationException("No target folder specified.")
    End If
    reader.ReadStartElement()
```

```
    ' Get the original filename.
    Dim fileName As String = reader.ReadElementString("fileName", ns)

    ' Get the size (not currently used).
    Dim size As Double = Convert.ToDouble(reader.ReadElementString("size", ns))

    ' Create the file.
    Dim fs As New FileStream(
        Path.Combine(ClientFolder, fileName), FileMode.Create, FileAccess.Write)

    ' Read the XML, and write the file one block at a time.
    Dim fileBytes As Byte()
    reader.ReadStartElement("content", ns)
    Dim totalRead As Double = 0

    Do While True
        If reader.IsStartElement("chunk", ns) Then
            Dim bytesBase64 As String = reader.ReadElementString()
            totalRead += bytesBase64.Length
            fileBytes = Convert.FromBase64String(bytesBase64)
            fs.Write(fileBytes, 0, fileBytes.Length)
            fs.Flush()

            ' You could report progress by raising an event here.
            Console.WriteLine("Received chunk.")
        Else
            Exit Do
        End If
    Loop
    fs.Close()
    reader.ReadEndElement()
    reader.ReadEndElement()
End Sub
```

Here's a complete console application that uses the FileService:

```
Shared Sub Main()
    Console.WriteLine("Downloading to c:\")
    FileDataClient.ClientFolder = "c:\"

    Console.WriteLine("Enter the name of the file to download.")
    Console.WriteLine("This is a file in the server's download directory.")
    Console.WriteLine("The download directory is c:\temp by default.")
    Console.Write("> ")
    Dim file As String = Console.ReadLine()

    Dim proxy As New FileService()
    Console.WriteLine()
    Console.WriteLine("Starting download.")
    proxy.DownloadFile(file)
    Console.WriteLine("Download complete.")
End Sub
```

Figure 32-8 shows the result.

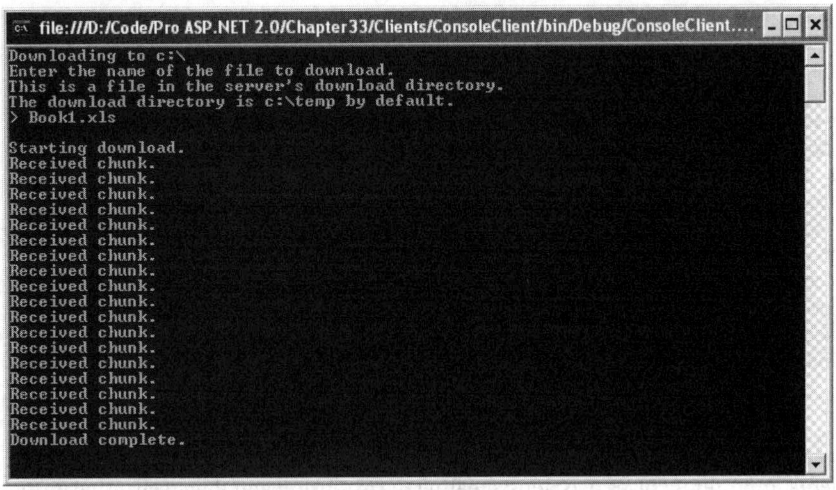

```
file:///D:/Code/Pro ASP.NET 2.0/Chapter33/Clients/ConsoleClient/bin/Debug/ConsoleClient....
Downloading to c:\
Enter the name of the file to download.
This is a file in the server's download directory.
The download directory is c:\temp by default.
> Book1.xls

Starting download.
Received chunk.
Received chunk.
Received chunk.
Received chunk.
Received chunk.
Received chunk.
Received chunk.
Received chunk.
Received chunk.
Received chunk.
Received chunk.
Received chunk.
Received chunk.
Received chunk.
Received chunk.
Received chunk.
Received chunk.
Received chunk.
Received chunk.
Download complete.
```

Figure 32-8. *Downloading a large file with chunking*

You can find this example online, with a few minor changes (for example, the client and server methods for working with the file are combined into one FileData class).

Schema Importer Extensions

One of the key principles of service-oriented design is that the client and the server share contracts, not classes. That level of abstraction allows clients on widely different platforms to interact with the same web service. They send the same serialized XML, but they have the freedom to use different programmatic structures (such as classes) to prepare their messages.

In some cases, you might want to bend these rules to allow your clients to work with rich data types. For example, you might want to take a custom data class, distribute it to both the client and server, and allow them to send or receive instances of this class with a web service. .NET 2.0 makes this possible with a new feature called *schema importer extensions*.

■ **Tip** Think twice about using custom data types. The danger of this approach is that it can easily lead you to develop a proprietary web service. Although your web service will still use XML (which can always be read on any platform), once you start tailoring your XML to fit platform-specific types, it might be prohibitively difficult for other clients to parse that XML or do anything practical with it. For example, most non-.NET clients don't have an easy way to consume the XML generated for the DataSet.

Before developing a schema importer extension, make sure your service is using the XmlSchemaProvider attribute to designate a method that returns schema information. Without the schema information, the proxy generation tool won't have the information it needs to identify your custom data types, so any schema importers you create will be useless.

For the FileData class, the schema is drawn from this schema file:

```
<xs:schema id="FileData" targetNamespace=http://www.apress.com/ProASP.NET/FileData
 elementFormDefault="qualified" xmlns:xs="http://www.w3.org/2001/XMLSchema">
```

```
  <xs:complexType name="FileData" >
    <xs:sequence>
      <xs:element name="fileName" type="xs:string" />
      <xs:element name="size" type="xs:int" />
      <xs:element name="content" >
        <xs:complexType >
          <xs:sequence>
            <xs:element name="chunk" type="xs:base64Binary"
             maxOccurs="unbounded"/>
          </xs:sequence>
        </xs:complexType>
      </xs:element>
    </xs:sequence>
  </xs:complexType>

</xs:schema>
```

Now you're ready to develop the schema importer that allows the client to recognize this data type.

Using a schema importer involves two steps: creating the extension and then registering it. To create the extension, you need to create a new class library component (DLL assembly). In this assembly, add a class that derives from SchemaImporterExtension.

When the proxy generator comes across a complex type (as it generates a proxy class), it calls the ImportSchemaType() method of every schema importer extension defined in the machine.config file. Each schema importer can check the namespace and schema of the type and then decide to handle it by mapping the XML type to a known .NET type.

Here's an example with a FileDataSchemaImporter that configures the proxy to use the FileDataClient class:

```
Public Class FileDataSchemaImporter
    Inherits SchemaImporterExtension
    Public Overrides Function ImportSchemaType(ByVal name As String,
       ByVal ns As String, ByVal context As XmlSchemaObject,
       ByVal schemas As XmlSchemas, ByVal importer As XmlSchemaImporter,
       ByVal compileUnit As CodeCompileUnit,
       ByVal mainNamespace As CodeNamespace,
       ByVal options As CodeGenerationOptions,
       ByVal codeProvider As CodeDomProvider) As String
        If name.Equals("FileData")
            AndAlso ns.Equals("http://www.apress.com/ProASP.NET/FileData") Then
            mainNamespace.Imports.Add(New CodeNamespaceImport("FileDataComponent"))
            Return "FileDataClient"
        Else
            ' Chose not to handle the type.
            Return Nothing
        End If
    End Function
End Class
```

This is an extremely simple schema importer. It does two things:

- It instructs the proxy class to use the class named FileDataClient for this type. That means the proxy class will use your existing class and refrain from generating a client-side FileData class automatically (the standard behavior).
- It instructs the proxy class generator to add a namespace import for the FileDataComponent namespace. It's still up to you to make sure the assembly with the FileDataComponent.FileData class is available in your project.

Once you've created the schema importer, you need to install it in the global assembly cache. Give it a strong name (use the Signing tab in the project properties) and then drag and drop it into the c:\[WinDir]\Assembly directory, or use the gacutil.exe command-line utility.

Once your schema importer is safely installed in the cache, use Windows Explorer to find out its public key token. Armed with that information, you can register your schema importer in the machine.config file using settings like these:

```
<configuration>
...
  <system.xml.serialization>
    <schemaImporterExtensions>
      <add name="FileDataSchemaImporter" type=
"SchemaImporter.FileDataSchemaImporter, SchemaImporter, Version=1.0.0.0,
Culture=neutral, PublicKeyToken=6c8e0bfd71c11c40" />
    </schemaImporterExtensions>
  </system.xml.serialization>
</configuration>
```

The type attribute is the important part. Make sure you use this format on a single line:

```
<Namespace-qualified class name>, <Assembly name without the extension>,
<Version>, <Culture>, <Public key token>
```

Now you're ready to use your schema importer. Try running wsdl.exe on the FileService:

```
http://localhost/WebServices2/FileService.asmx
```

The generated code proxy code will use the type name you specified and include the new namespace import. However, it won't create the FileData class—instead, you'll use the custom version you created in the FileData component.

Finally, add this generated proxy class to your client project. You can now download files with the chunk-by-chunk streaming support that's provided by the FileData class.

■ **Note** Currently, only the wsdl.exe uses schema importers. Schema importers don't come into play when you generate a web reference with Visual Studio. Expect this to change in later releases.

Summary

In this chapter, you took an in-depth look at the two most important web service protocols: SOAP and WSDL. SOAP is an incredibly lightweight protocol for messaging. WSDL is a flexible, extensible protocol for describing web services. Together, they ensure that web services can be created and consumed on virtually any programming platform for years to come. This chapter also discussed in detail how you can tailor the XML returned by your web service.

CHAPTER 33

Advanced Web Services

In the past two chapters, you took a close look at how web services work with ASP.NET. Using the techniques you've learned already, you can create web services that expose data to other applications and organizations, and you can consume .NET and non-.NET web services on the Internet.

However, the story doesn't end there. In this chapter, you'll learn how to extend your web service skills with specific techniques that are often important in real-world web service scenarios. You'll focus on three topic areas:

Calling web services asynchronously: Web service calls take time, especially if the web server is located across the globe and connected by a slow network connection. By using asynchronous calls, you can keep working while you wait for a response.

Securing web services: In Part 4 you learned how you can secure web pages to prevent anonymous users. You can apply some of the same techniques to protect your web services.

Using SOAP extensions: The web services infrastructure is remarkably extensible, thanks to a SOAP extension model that allows you to create components that plug into the SOAP serialization and deserialization process. In this chapter, you'll see a basic SOAP extension and briefly consider the WSE (Web Services Enhancements) toolkit that uses SOAP extensions to provide support for new and emerging standards.

All of these topics build on the concepts you learned in the past two chapters.

Note Although .NET 2.0 uses the same asynchronous programming model as .NET 1.*x*, the asynchronous support in the proxy class has changed, as you'll see in this chapter. The techniques you use for securing web services and using SOAP extensions haven't changed, although web service standards continue to evolve and are provided in new versions of the separate WSE toolkit.

Asynchronous Calls

As you learned in Chapter 31, the .NET Framework shields the programmer from the complexities of calling a web service by providing your applications with a proxy class. The code that uses the proxy class looks the same whether the web service is on the same computer, on a local network, or across the Internet.

Despite superficial similarities, the underlying plumbing used to invoke a web service is very different from an in-process function call. Not only must the call be packaged into a SOAP message, but it also needs to be transmitted across the network using HTTP. Because of the inherent nature of the Internet, the time it takes to call a web service can vary greatly from one call to the next.

Although your client can't speed up a web method invocation, it can choose not to sit idle while waiting for the response. Instead, it can continue to perform calculations, read from the file system or a database, and even call additional web services. This asynchronous design pattern is more difficult to implement, but in certain situations it can reap significant benefits.

In general, asynchronous processing makes sense in two cases:

- If you're creating a Windows application. In this case, an asynchronous call allows the user interface to remain responsive.
- If you have other computationally expensive work to do, or you have to access other resources that have a high degree of latency. By performing the web service call asynchronously, you can carry out this work while waiting for the response. A special case is when you need to call several independent web services. In this situation, you can call them all asynchronously, collapsing your total waiting time.

It's just as important that you realize when you should *not* use the asynchronous pattern. Asynchronous calls won't speed up the time taken to receive a response. In other words, in most web applications that use web services, you'll have no reason to call the web service asynchronously, because your code still needs to wait for the response to be received before it can render the final page and send it back to the client. However, if you need to call a number of web services at once, or you can perform other tasks while waiting, you may shave a few milliseconds off the total request processing time.

In the following sections, you'll see how asynchronous calls can save time with a web client and provide a more responsive user interface with a Windows client.

■ **Note** Asynchronous calls work a little differently in ASP.NET 2.0. The proxy class no longer has built-in BeginXxx() and EndXxx() methods. However, you can use an alternate approach for event-based notification of asynchronous operations that is built into the proxy class and makes sense for long-running clients such as Windows applications.

Asynchronous Delegates

You can use asynchronous threads in .NET in several ways. All delegates provide BeginInvoke() and EndInvoke() methods that allow you to trigger them on one of the threads in the CLR thread pool. This technique, which is convenient and scales well, is the one you'll consider in this section. Alternatively, you could use the System.Threading.Thread class to explicitly create a new thread, with complete control over its priority and lifetime.

As you already know, delegates are type-safe function pointers that form the basis for .NET events. You create a delegate that references a specific method, and then you can call that method through the delegate.

The first step is to define the delegate at the namespace level (if it's not already present in the .NET class library). For example, here's a delegate that can point to any method that accepts a single integer parameter and returns an integer:

```
Public Delegate Function DoSomethingDelegate(ByVal input As Integer) As Integer
```

Now consider a class that has a method that matches this delegate:

```
Public Class TheClass
    Public Function DoubleNumber(ByVal input As Integer) As Integer
        Return input * 2
    End Function
End Class
```

You can create a delegate variable that points to a method with the same signature. Here's the code:

```
Dim myObj As New TheClass()

' Create a delegate that points to the myObj.DoubleNumber() method.
Dim doSomething As New DoSomethingDelegate(myObj.DoubleNumber)

' Call the myObj.DoubleNumber() method through the delegate.
Dim doubleValue As Integer = doSomething(12)
```

What you may not realize is that delegates also have built-in threading smarts. Every time you define a delegate (such as DoSomethingDelegate in the previous example), a custom delegate class is generated and added to your assembly. (A custom delegate class is needed because the code for each delegate is different, depending on the signature of the method you've defined.) When you call a method through the delegate, you are actually relying on the Invoke() method of the delegate class.

The Invoke() method executes the linked method synchronously. However, the delegate class also includes methods for asynchronous invocation—BeginInvoke() and EndInvoke(). When you use BeginInvoke(), the call returns immediately, but it doesn't provide the return value. Instead, the method is simply queued to start on another thread. When calling BeginInvoke(), you supply all the parameters of the original method, plus two additional parameters for an optional callback and state object. If you don't need these details (described later in this section), simply pass a null reference.

```
Dim async As IAsyncResult = doSomething.BeginInvoke(12, Nothing, Nothing)
```

BeginInvoke() doesn't provide the return value of the underlying method. Instead, it returns an IAsyncResult object, which you can examine to determine when the asynchronous operation is complete. To pick up the results later, you submit the IAsyncResult object to the matching EndInvoke() method of the delegate. EndInvoke() waits for the operation to complete if it hasn't already finished and then provides the real return value. If any unhandled errors occurred in the method that you executed asynchronously, they'll bubble up to the rest of your code when you call EndInvoke().

Here's the previous example rewritten to call the delegate asynchronously:

```
Dim myObj As New TheClass()

' Create a delegate that points to the myObj.DoubleNumber() method.
Dim doSomething As New DoSomethingDelegate(myObj.DoubleNumber)

' Start the myObj.DoubleNumber() method on another thread.
Dim handle As IAsyncResult =
        doSomething.BeginInvoke(originalValue, Nothing, Nothing)

' (Do something else here while myObj.DoubleNumber() is executing.)

' Retrieve the results, and wait (synchronously) if they're still not ready.
Dim doubleValue As Integer = doSomething.EndInvoke(handle)
```

To gain some of the benefits of multithreading with this technique, you could call several methods asynchronously with BeginInvoke(). You could then call EndInvoke() on all of them before continuing.

A Simple Asynchronous Call

The following example demonstrates the difference between synchronous and asynchronous code. To test the example, you need to slow down your code artificially to simulate heavy load conditions or time-consuming tasks. First, add this line to the GetEmployees() method in the web service to add a delay of four seconds:

```
System.Threading.Thread.Sleep(4000)
```

Next, create a web page that uses the web service. This web page also defines a private method that simulates a time-consuming task, again using the Thread.Sleep() method. Here's the code you need to add to the web page:

```
Private Sub DoSomethingSlow()
    System.Threading.Thread.Sleep(3000)
End Sub
```

In your page, you need to execute both methods. Using a simple piece of timing code, you can compare the synchronous approach with the asynchronous approach. Depending on which button the user clicks, you will perform the two operations synchronously (one after the other) or asynchronously at the same time.

Here's how you would execute the two tasks synchronously:

```
Protected Sub cmdSynchronous_Click(ByVal sender As Object,
        ByVal e As System.EventArgs)
    ' Record the start time.
    Dim startTime As DateTime = DateTime.Now

    ' Get the web service data.
    Dim theProxy As New EmployeesService()
    Try
        GridView1.DataSource = theProxy.GetEmployees()
    Catch err As Exception
        lblInfo.Text = "Problem contacting web service."
        Return
    End Try

    GridView1.DataBind()

    ' Perform some other time-consuming tasks.
    DoSomethingSlow()

    ' Determine the total time taken.
    Dim timeTaken As TimeSpan = DateTime.Now.Subtract(startTime)
    lblInfo.Text = "Synchronous operations took " _
        & timeTaken.TotalSeconds & " seconds."
End Sub
```

To use asynchronous delegates, you need to define a delegate that matches the signature of the method you want to call asynchronously. In this case, it's the GetEmployees() method:

```
Public Delegate Function GetEmployeesDelegate() As DataSet
```

And here's how you could start the web service first so that the operations overlap:

```
Protected Sub cmdAsynchronous_Click(ByVal sender As Object,
        ByVal e As System.EventArgs)
    ' Record the start time.
    Dim startTime As DateTime = DateTime.Now

    ' Start the web service on another thread.
    Dim theProxy As New EmployeesService()
    Dim myAsync As New GetEmployeesDelegate(theProxy.GetEmployees)
    Dim theHandle As IAsyncResult = myAsync.BeginInvoke(Nothing, Nothing)
```

```
    ' Perform some other time-consuming tasks.
    DoSomethingSlow()

    ' Retrieve the result. If it isn't ready, wait.
    Try
        GridView1.DataSource = async.EndInvoke(handle)
    Catch err As Exception
        lblInfo.Text = "Problem contacting web service."
        Return
    End Try
    GridView1.DataBind()

    ' Determine the total time taken.
    Dim timeTaken As TimeSpan = DateTime.Now.Subtract(startTime)
    lblInfo.Text = "Asynchronous operations took " _
        & timeTaken.TotalSeconds & " seconds."
End Sub
```

Notice that the exception handler wraps the EndInvoke() method but not the BeginInvoke() method. That's because if any errors occur while processing the request (whether because of a network problem or a server-side exception), your code won't receive it until you call the EndInvoke() method.

When you run these two examples, you'll find that the synchronous code takes between 7 and 8 seconds, while the asynchronous code takes only between 4 and 5 seconds. Figure 33-1 shows the web page with the time reading at the bottom.

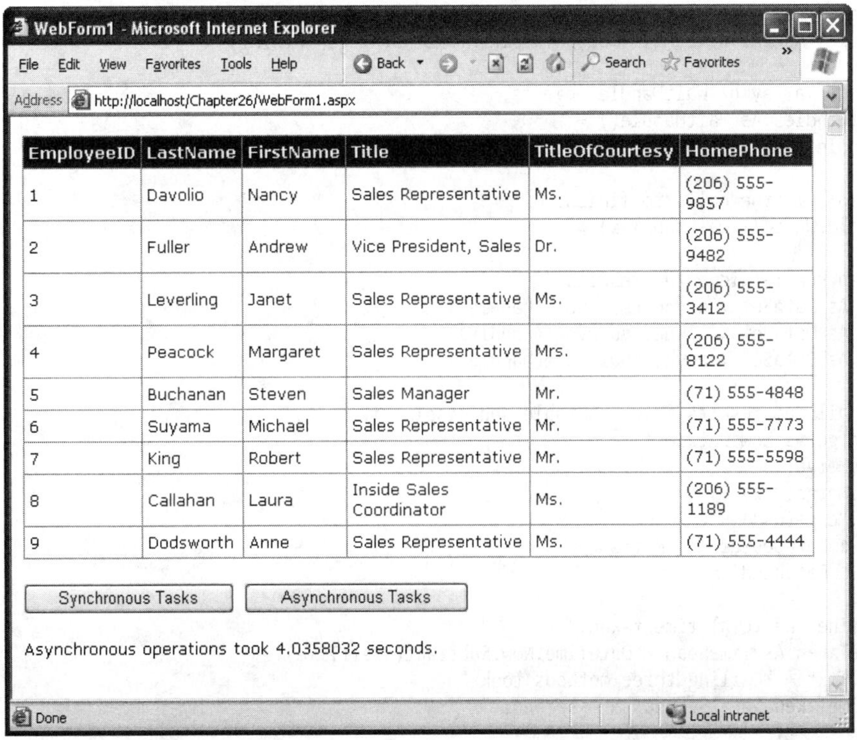

WebForm1 - Microsoft Internet Explorer

File Edit View Favorites Tools Help Back Search Favorites

Address http://localhost/Chapter26/WebForm1.aspx

EmployeeID	LastName	FirstName	Title	TitleOfCourtesy	HomePhone
1	Davolio	Nancy	Sales Representative	Ms.	(206) 555-9857
2	Fuller	Andrew	Vice President, Sales	Dr.	(206) 555-9482
3	Leverling	Janet	Sales Representative	Ms.	(206) 555-3412
4	Peacock	Margaret	Sales Representative	Mrs.	(206) 555-8122
5	Buchanan	Steven	Sales Manager	Mr.	(71) 555-4848
6	Suyama	Michael	Sales Representative	Mr.	(71) 555-7773
7	King	Robert	Sales Representative	Mr.	(71) 555-5598
8	Callahan	Laura	Inside Sales Coordinator	Ms.	(206) 555-1189
9	Dodsworth	Anne	Sales Representative	Ms.	(71) 555-4444

Synchronous Tasks Asynchronous Tasks

Asynchronous operations took 4.0358032 seconds.

Done Local intranet

Figure 33-1. *Testing an asynchronous method call*

■ **Tip** Remember, the advantage of threading depends on the type of operations. In this example, the full benefit of threading is realized because the operations aren't CPU bound—they are simply waiting idly. This is similar to the behavior you'll experience contacting external web services or databases. However, if you try to use threading to simultaneously run two tasks that use the CPU on the *same* computer (and that computer has only one CPU), you won't see any advantage, because both tasks will get about half the CPU resources and will take about twice as long to execute. That's why threading is ideal for web services but not nearly as useful for the rest of your business code.

Concurrent Asynchronous Calls

The IAsyncState object gives you a few other options that are useful when calling multiple web methods at once. The key is the IAsyncState.WaitHandle object, which returns a System.Threading.WaitHandle object. Using this object, you can call WaitAll() to wait until all your asynchronous operations are complete. The following example uses this technique to call the GetEmployees() method three times at once:

```
Protected Sub cmdMultiple_Click(ByVal sender As Object, ByVal e As System.EventArgs)
    ' Record the start time.
    Dim startTime As DateTime = DateTime.Now

    Dim theProxy As New EmployeesService()
    Dim myAsync As New GetEmployeesDelegate(theProxy.GetEmployees)

    ' Call three methods asynchronously.
    Dim handle1 As IAsyncResult = async.BeginInvoke(Nothing, Nothing)
    Dim handle2 As IAsyncResult = async.BeginInvoke(Nothing, Nothing)
    Dim handle3 As IAsyncResult = async.BeginInvoke(Nothing, Nothing)

    ' Create an array of WaitHandle objects.
    Dim waitHandles As WaitHandle() =
        {handle1.AsyncWaitHandle, handle2.AsyncWaitHandle, handle3.AsyncWaitHandle}

    ' Wait for all the calls to finish.
    WaitHandle.WaitAll(waitHandles)

    ' You can now retrieve the results.
    Dim ds1 As DataSet = async.EndInvoke(handle1)
    Dim ds2 As DataSet = async.EndInvoke(handle2)
    Dim ds3 As DataSet = async.EndInvoke(handle3)

    ' Merge all the results into one table and display it.
    Dim dsMerge As New DataSet()
    dsMerge.Merge(ds1)
    dsMerge.Merge(ds2)
    dsMerge.Merge(ds3)
    GridView1.DataSource = dsMerge
    GridView1.DataBind()

    ' Determine the total time taken.
    Dim timeTaken As TimeSpan = DateTime.Now.Subtract(startTime)
    lblInfo.Text = "Calling three methods took " _
        & timeTaken.TotalSeconds & " seconds."
End Sub
```

Instead of using a wait handle, you could launch the three asynchronous calls by calling BeginInvoke() three times and then call the three EndInvoke() methods immediately after that. In this case, your code would wait if required. However, using a wait handle clarifies your code.

You can also use one of the overloaded versions of the WaitAll() method that accepts a timeout value. If this amount of time passes without the calls completing, an exception will be thrown. However, it's usually best to rely on the Timeout property of the proxy instead, which will end the call if a response isn't received in the designated amount of time.

You can also instruct a wait handle to block the thread until any one of the method calls has finished using the Shared WaitHandle.WaitAny() method with an array of WaitHandle objects. The WaitAny() method returns as soon as at least one of the asynchronous calls completes. This can be a useful technique if you need to process a batch of data from different sources and the order that you process it is not important. It allows you to begin processing the results from one method before the others are complete. However, it also complicates your code, because you'll need to test the IsCompleted property of each IAsyncResult object and call WaitAny() multiple times (usually in a loop) until all the methods have finished.

■ **Note** Remember, .NET gives you even more threading options with the Thread class. For example, if you need to call a series of web services in a specific order as part of a long-running background service in a Windows application, the Thread class offers the best solution. For more information about multithreading, consult a book that explores advanced Windows programming techniques.

Responsive Windows Clients

In a Windows client, the threading code you use is a little different. Typically, you'll want to allow the application to continue unhindered while the operation is taking place. When the call is complete, you might simply want to refresh the display with updated information.

Support for this pattern is built into the proxy class. To understand how it works, it helps to look at the proxy class code. For every web method in your web service, the proxy class actually includes two methods—the synchronous version you've seen so far and an asynchronous version that adds the suffix *Async* to the method.

Here's the code for the synchronous version of the GetEmployees() method. The attributes for XML serialization have been omitted.

```
<SoapDocumentMethod(...)> _
Public Function GetEmployees() As DataSet
    Dim results As Object() = Me.Invoke("GetEmployees", New Object(){})
    Return (CType(results(0), DataSet))
End Function
```

And here's the asynchronous version of the same method. Notice that the code actually contains two versions of the GetEmployeesAsync() method. The only difference is that one accepts an additional userState parameter, which can be any object you use to identify the call. When the call is completed later, you'll receive this object in the callback. The userState parameter is particularly useful if you have several asynchronous web methods underway at the same time.

```
Public Sub GetEmployeesAsync()
    Me.GetEmployeesAsync(Nothing)
End Sub

Public Sub GetEmployeesAsync(ByVal userState As Object)
    If (Me.GetEmployeesOperationCompleted Is Nothing) Then
        Me.GetEmployeesOperationCompleted
```

```
            = New System.Threading.SendOrPostCallback(
                Me.OnGetEmployeesOperationCompleted)
    End If
    Me.InvokeAsync("DownloadFile", New Object(){},
        Me.GetEmployeesOperationCompleted, userState)
End Sub
```

The idea is that you can call GetEmployeesAsync() to launch the request. This method returns immediately, before the request is even sent over the network, and the proxy class waits on a free thread (just as with the asynchronous delegate example) until it receives the response. As soon as the response is received and deserialized, .NET fires an event to notify your application. You can then retrieve the results.

For this system to work, the proxy class also adds an event for each web method. This event is fired when the asynchronous method is finished. Here's the completion event for the GetEmployees() method:

```
Public Event GetEmployeesCompleted As GetEmployeesCompletedEventHandler
```

The proxy class code is quite smart here—it simplifies your life by creating a custom EventArgs object for every web method. This EventArgs object exposes the result from the method as a Result property. The class is declared with the partial keyword so that you can add code to it in another (nonautomatically generated) file.

```
' Defines the signature of the completion event.
Public Delegate Sub GetEmployeesCompletedEventHandler(ByVal sender As Object,
      ByVal e As GetEmployeesCompletedEventArgs)

Public Partial Class GetEmployeesCompletedEventArgs
    Inherits System.ComponentModel.AsyncCompletedEventArgs

    Private results As Object()

    ' The constructor is internal, prevent other assemblies from instantiating
    ' this class.
    Friend Sub New(results As Object(),
                   ByVal exception As Exception, ByVal cancelled As Boolean,
                   ByVal userState As Object) As Friend
        MyBase.New(exception, cancelled, userState)
        Me.results = results
    End Sub

    Public ReadOnly Property Result() As System.Data.DataSet
        Get
            Me.RaiseExceptionIfNecessary()
            Return (CType(Me.results(0), System.Data.DataSet))
        End Get
    End Property
End Class
```

Notice that if an error occurred on the server side, it won't be thrown until you attempt to retrieve the Result property, at which point the SoapException is wrapped in a TargetInvocationException.

■ **Note** Result isn't the only property you might find in the custom EventArgs object. If your web method accepts ByRef or <Out()> ByRef parameters, these will also be added. That way, you can receive the modified values of all ByRef or <Out()> ByRef parameters when the call is complete.

Along with the Result property, you can also use a few properties that are declared in the base AsyncCompletedEventArgs class, including Cancelled (returns True if the operation was cancelled before it was completed, a feature you'll see shortly), Error (returns an exception object if an unhandled exception occurred during the request), and UserState (returns the state object you supplied when you called the method).

To try this pattern, you can modify the Windows client developed in Chapter 31 to use an asynchronous call. The first step is to create an event handler for the completion event in the form class:

```
Private Sub GetEmployeesCompleted(ByVal sender As Object,
      ByVal e As GetEmployeesCompletedEventArgs)
      ...
End Sub
```

When the user clicks the Get Employees button, the code will use the GetEmployeesAsync() method to start the process. But first, it needs to attach an event handler to the GetEmployeesCompleted event. Here's the code you need:

```
Private Sub cmdGetEmployees_Click(ByVal sender As Object,
      ByVal e As System.EventArgs)
    ' Disable the button so that only one asynchronous
    ' call will be permitted at a time.
    cmdGetEmployees.Enabled = False

    ' Create the proxy.
    Dim theProxy As New EmployeesService()

    ' Create the callback delegate.
    AddHandler theProxy.GetEmployeesCompleted, AddressOf GetEmployeesCompleted

    ' Call the web service asynchronously.
    theProxy.GetEmployeesAsync()
End Sub
```

When the operation is finished, the proxy class fires the event. When you handle the event, you can bind the result directly to the grid. You don't need to worry about marshaling your call to the user interface thread, because that's handled automatically by the proxy class before the event is raised, which is a significant convenience.

```
Private Sub GetEmployeesCompleted(ByVal sender As Object,
      ByVal e As GetEmployeesCompletedEventArgs)
    ' Get the result.
    Try
        dataGridView1.DataSource = e.Result
    Catch err As System.Reflection.TargetInvocationException
        MessageBox.Show("An error occurred.")
    End Try
End Sub
```

If you run this example and click the Get Employees button, the button will become disabled, but the application will remain responsive. You can drag and resize the window, click other buttons to execute more code, and so on. Finally, when the results have been received, the callback will be triggered, and the DataGridView will be refreshed automatically.

You can use one other trick. The proxy class has built-in support for cancellation. To use it, you need to supply a state object when you call the asynchronous version of the proxy class method. Then, simply call the CancelAsync() method of the proxy class and supply the same state object. The rest of the process is taken care of automatically.

To implement the cancellation model with the existing application, you first need to declare the proxy class at the form level so it's available to all your event handlers:

```
Dim theProxy As New EmployeesService()
```

Next, attach the event handler when the form loads so it's hooked up only once:

```
Private Sub Form1_Load(ByVal sender As Object, ByVal e As EventArgs)
        AddHandler proxy.GetEmployeesCompleted, AddressOf GetEmployeesCompleted
End Sub
```

In this example, the state object that you use isn't important, because you will have only a single operation taking place at once. If you're performing multiple operations at once, it makes sense to generate a new GUID to track each one.

First, declare it in the form class:

```
Dim requestID As Guid
```

Then, generate it, and supply it to the asynchronous web method call:

```
requestID = Guid.NewGuid()
theProxy.GetEmployeesAsync(requestID)
```

Now, all you need to do is use the same GUID when calling the CancelAsync() method. Here's the code for a cancel button:

```
Private Sub cmdCancel_Click(ByVal sender As Object, ByVal e As EventArgs)
    theProxy.CancelAsync(requestID)
    MessageBox.Show("Operation cancelled.")
End Sub
```

This has one important consideration. As soon as you call CancelAsync(), the completed event fires. This makes sense, because the long-running operation has finished (albeit because of programmatic intervention) and you may need to update the user interface. However, you obviously can't access the method result in the completion event because the code was interrupted. To prevent an error, you need to explicitly test for cancellation, as shown here:

```
Private Sub GetEmployeesCompleted(ByVal sender As Object,
              ByVal e As GetEmployeesCompletedEventArgs)
    If (Not e.Cancelled) Then
        Try
            dataGridView1.DataSource = e.Result
        Catch err As System.Reflection.TargetInvocationException
            MessageBox.Show("An error occurred.")
        End Try
    End If
End Sub
```

Asynchronous Services

So far, you've seen several examples that allow clients to call web services asynchronously. But in all these examples, the web method still runs synchronously from start to finish. What if you want a different behavior that allows the client to trigger a long-running process and then connect later to pick up the results?

Unfortunately, .NET doesn't directly support this model. Part of the problem is that all web service communication must be initiated by the client. Currently, the web server has no way to initiate a callback to the client to tell them when a task is complete. And even if standards evolve to fill this gap, it's unlikely that this solution will gain widespread use because of the nature of the architecture of the Web. Many clients connect from behind proxy servers or firewalls that don't allow incoming connections or hide location information such as the IP address. As a result, the client needs to initiate every connection.

Of course, certain innovative solutions can provide some of the functionality you want. For example, a client could reconnect periodically to poll the server and see if a task is complete. You could use this design if a web server needs to perform extremely time-consuming tasks, such as rendering complex graphics. However, one ingredient is still missing. In these situations, you need a way for a client to start a web method without waiting for the web method to finish executing. ASP.NET makes this behavior possible with *one-way methods*.

With one-way methods (also known as *fire-and-forget methods*), the client sends a request message, but the web service never responds. This means the web method returns immediately and closes the connection. The client doesn't need to spend any time waiting. However, one-way methods have a few drawbacks. Namely, the web method can't provide a return value or use a ref or out parameter. Similarly, if the web method throws an unhandled exception, it won't be propagated back to the client.

To create a fire-and-forget XML web service method, you need to apply a SoapDocumentMethod attribute to the appropriate web method and set the OneWay property to True, as shown here:

```
<SoapDocumentMethod(OneWay := True), WebMethod()> _
Public Function GetEmployees() As DataSet
    ...
End Function
```

The client doesn't need to take any special steps to call a one-way method asynchronously. Instead, the method always returns immediately.

Of course, you might not want to use one-way methods. The most important limitation is that you can't return any information. For example, a common asynchronous server-side pattern is for the server to return some sort of unique, automatically generated ticket to the client when the client submits a request. The client can then submit this ticket to other methods to check the status or retrieve the results. With a one-way method, there's no way to return a ticket to the client or notify the client if an error occurs. Another problem is that one-way methods still use ASP.NET worker threads. If the task is extremely long and there are many ongoing tasks, other clients might not be able to submit new requests, which is far from ideal.

The only practical way to deal with long-running, asynchronous tasks in a heavily trafficked website is to combine web services with another .NET technology—*remoting*. For example, you could create an ordinary, synchronous web method that returns a ticket and then calls a method in a server-side component using remoting. The remoting component could then begin its processing task asynchronously. This technique of using a web service as a front-end to a full-fledged, continuously running server-side component is a more complex hallmark of distributed design. To learn more, you may want to consult a dedicated book about distributed programming, such as *Microsoft .NET Distributed Applications* (Microsoft Press, 2003) or a book about .NET remoting, such as *Advanced .NET Remoting* (Apress, 2002). Of course, if you don't need this flexibility, you're better off avoiding it completely, because it introduces significant complexity and extra work.

Securing Web Services

In an ideal world, you could treat a web service as a class library of functionality and not worry about coding user authentication or security logic. However, to create subscription-based or micropayment web services, you need to determine who is using it. And even if you aren't selling your logic to an audience of eager web developers, you may still need to use authentication to protect sensitive data and lock out malicious users, especially if your web service is exposed over the Internet.

You can use some of the same techniques you use to protect web pages to defend your web services. For example, you can use IIS to enforce SSL (just direct your clients to a web service URL starting with `https://`). You can also use IIS to apply Windows authentication, although you need to apply a few additional steps, as you'll learn in the next section. Finally, you can create your own custom authentication system using SOAP headers.

Windows Authentication

Windows authentication works with a web service in much the same way that it works with a web page. The difference is that a web service is executed by another application, not directly by the browser. For that reason, there's no built-in way to prompt the user for a user name and password. Instead, the application that's using the web service needs to supply this information. The application might read this information from a configuration file or database, or it might prompt the user for this information before contacting the web service.

For example, consider the following web service, which provides a single TestAuthenticated() method. This method checks whether the user is authenticated. If the user is authenticated, it returns the user name (which will be a string in the form DomainName\UserName or ComputerName\UserName).

```
Public Class SecureService
    Inherits WebService

    <WebMethod()> _
    Public Function TestAuthenticated() As String
        If (Not User.Identity.IsAuthenticated) Then
            Return "Not authenticated."
        Else
            Return "Authenticated as: " & User.Identity.Name
        End If
    End Function
End Class
```

The web service can also examine role membership, although this web service doesn't take this step.

To submit user credentials to this service, the client needs to modify the NetworkCredential property of the proxy class. You have two options:

- You can create a new NetworkCredential object and attach this to the NetworkCredential property of the proxy object. When you create the NetworkCredential object, you'll need to specify the user name and password you want to use. This approach works with all forms of Windows authentication.
- If the web service is using Integrated Windows authentication, you can automatically submit the credentials of the current user by using the Shared DefaultCredentials property of the CredentialCache class and applying that to the NetworkCredential property of the proxy object.

Both the CredentialCache and NetworkCredential classes are found in the System.Net namespace. Thus, before continuing, you should import this namespace:

```
Imports System.Net
```

The following code shows a web page with two text boxes and two buttons (see Figure 33-2). One button performs an unauthenticated call, while the other submits the user name and password that have been entered in the text boxes.

The unauthenticated call will fail if you've disabled anonymous users. Otherwise, the unauthenticated call will succeed, but the TestAuthenticated() method will return a string informing you that authentication wasn't performed. The authenticated call will always succeed as long as you submit credentials that correspond to a valid user on the web server.

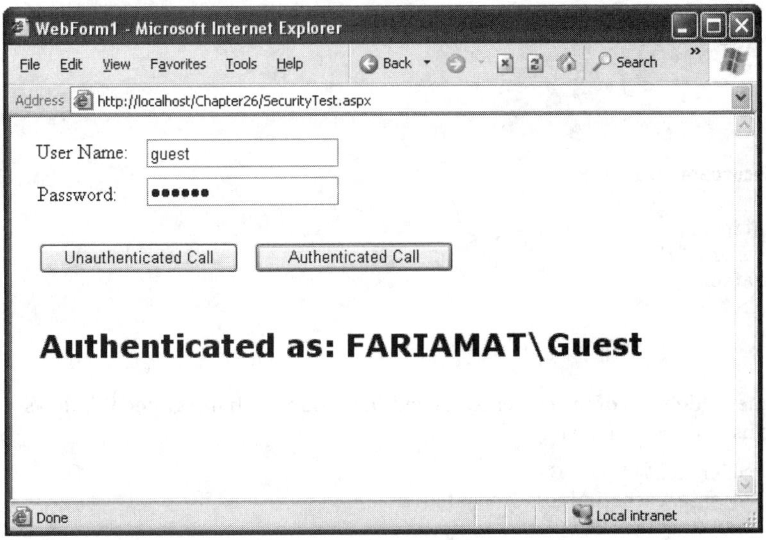

Figure 33-2. *Successful authentication through a web service*

Here's the complete web-page code:

```
Public partial Class WindowsAuthenticationSecurityTest
    Inherits Page

    Protected Sub cmdUnauthenticated_Click(ByVal sender As Object,
                ByVal e As EventArgs)
        Dim proxy As New SecureService()
        Try
            lblInfo.Text = proxy.TestAuthenticated()
        Catch err As Exception
            lblInfo.Text = err.Message
        End Try
    End Sub

    Protected Sub cmdAuthenticated_Click(ByVal sender As Object,
                ByVal e As EventArgs)
        Dim proxy As New SecureService()

        ' Supply some user credentials for the web service.
        Dim credentials As New NetworkCredential(txtUserName.Text, txtPassword.Text)
        proxy.Credentials = credentials

        lblInfo.Text = proxy.TestAuthenticated()
    End Sub
End Class
```

To try this, you can add the following <location> tag to the web.config file to restrict access to the SecureService.asmx web service:

```
<configuration>
    <system.web>
```

```
        <authorization>
            <allow users="*" />
        </authorization>
        ...
    </system.web>

    <location path="SecureService.asmx">
        <system.web>
            <authorization>
                <deny users="?" />
            </authorization>
        </system.web>
    </location>
</configuration>
```

If you want to use the credentials of the currently logged-in account with Integrated Windows authentication, you can use this code instead:

```
Dim proxy As New SecuredService()
proxy.Credentials = CredentialCache.DefaultCredentials
lblInfo.Text = proxy.TestAuthenticated()
```

In this example (as in all web pages), the current user account will be the account that ASP.NET is using, not the user account of the remote user who is requesting the web page. If you use the same technique in a Windows application, you'll submit the account information of the user who is running the application.

Custom Ticket-Based Authentication

Windows authentication is a good solution for web services when you have a small set of users who have existing Windows accounts. However, it doesn't work as well for large-scale public web services. When working with ASP.NET web pages, you usually turn to forms authentication to fill the gaps. However, forms authentication won't work with a web service because a web service has no way to direct the user to a web page. In fact, the web service might not even be accessed through a browser—it might be used by a Windows application or even an automated Windows service. Forms authentication is also cookie-based, which is an unnecessary restriction to place on web services, which might use protocols that don't support cookies or clients that don't expect them.

A common solution is to roll your own authentication system. In this model, users will call a specific web method in the web service to log in, at which point they will supply credentials (such as a user name and password combination). The login method will register the user session and create a new, unique ticket. From this point on, the user can reconnect to the web service by supplying the ticket to every other method.

A properly designed ticket system has a number of benefits. As with forms authentication, it provides complete flexibility. It also optimizes performance and ensures scalability, because you can cache the ticket in memory. On subsequent requests, you can verify the ticket rather than authenticating the user against the database. Finally, it allows you to take advantage of SOAP headers, which make the ticket management and authorization process transparent to the client.

With ASP.NET 2.0, it becomes possible to simplify custom authentication in a web service. Although it's still up to you to transfer the user credentials and keep track of who has logged in by issuing and verifying tickets, you can use the membership and role manager features discussed in Chapter 21 and Chapter 23 to handle the authentication and authorization. In the following sections, you'll see how to create a custom ticket-based authentication system that leverages membership and role management in this way.

Tracking the User Identity

To use custom security, the first step is to decide what user-specific information you want to cache in memory. You need to create a custom class that represents this information. This class can include information about the user (name, e-mail address, and so on) and the user's permissions. It should also include the ticket.

Here's a basic example that stores a user name and ticket:

```
Public Class TicketIdentity
    Private m_userName As String
    Public ReadOnly Property UserName() As String
        Get
                Return m_userName
        End Get
    End Property

    Private m_ticket As String
    Public ReadOnly Property Ticket() As String
        Get
                Return m_ticket
        End Get
    End Property

    Public Sub New(ByVal p_userName As String)
        Me.m_userName = p_userName

        ' Create the ticket GUID.
        Me.m_ticket = Guid.NewGuid().ToString()
    End Sub
End Class
```

■ **Note** You've probably noticed that this identity class doesn't implement IIdentity. That's because this approach doesn't allow you to plug into the .NET security model in the same way you could with custom web-page authentication. Essentially, the problem is that you need to perform the authentication *after* the User object has already been created. And you can't get around this problem using the global.asax class, because the application event handlers won't have access to the web method parameters and SOAP header you need in order to perform the authentication and authorization.

Once you have the user identity class, you need to create a SOAP header. This header tracks a single piece of information—the user ticket. Because the ticket is a randomly generated GUID, it's not practically possible for a malicious user to "guess" what ticket value another user has been issued.

```
Public Class TicketHeader
    Inherits SoapHeader
    Public m_ticket As String

    Public Sub New(ByVal ticket As String)
        m_ticket = ticket
    End Sub

    Public Sub New()
    End Sub
End Class
```

You must then add a member variable for the TicketHeader to your web service:

```
Public Class SoapSecurityService
    Inherits WebService

   Public m_TicketHeader  As TicketHeader
   ...
End Class
```

Authenticating the User

The next step is to create a dedicated web method that logs the user in. The user needs to submit user credentials to this method (such as a login and password). Then, the method will retrieve the user information, create the TicketIdentity object, and issue the ticket.

In this example, a Login() web method checks the user credentials using the Shared Membership.ValidateUser() method. A new ticket is constructed with the user information and stored in a user-specific slot in the Application collection. At the same time, a new SOAP header is issued with the ticket so that the user can access other methods.

Here's the complete code for the Login() method:

```
<WebMethod(), SoapHeader("Ticket", Direction := SoapHeaderDirection.Out)> _
Public Sub Login(ByVal userName As String, ByVal password As String)
    If Membership.ValidateUser(username, password) Then
        ' Create a new ticket.
        Dim idtTicket As New TicketIdentity(username)

        ' Add this ticket to Application state.
        Application(idtTicket.Ticket) = idt_Ticket
        ' Create the SOAP header.
        Ticket = New TicketHeader(idtTicket.Ticket)
    Else
        Throw New SecurityException("Invalid credentials.")
    End If
End Sub
```

Note that in this example, the TicketIdentity object is stored in the Application collection, which is global to all users. However, you don't need to worry about one user's ticket overwriting another. That's because the tickets are indexed using the GUID. Every user has a separate ticket GUID and hence a separate slot in the Application collection.

The Application collection has certain limitations, including no support for web farms and poor scalability to large numbers of users. The tickets will also be lost if the web application restarts. To improve this solution, you could store the information in two places: in the Cache object and in a back-end database. That way, your code can check the Cache first, and if a matching TicketIdentity is found, no database call is required. But if the TicketIdentity isn't present, the information can still be retrieved from the database. It's important to understand that this enhancement still uses the same SOAP header with the ticket and the same TicketIdentity object. The only difference is how the TicketIdentity is stored and retrieved between requests.

Authorizing the User

Once you have the Login() method in place, it makes sense to create a private method that can be called to verify that a user is present. You can then call this method from other web methods in your web service.

The following AuthorizeUser() method checks for a matching ticket and returns the TicketIdentity if it's found. If not, an exception is thrown, which will be returned to the client.

```
Private Function AuthorizeUser(ByVal MyTicket As String) As TicketIdentity
    Dim idtTicket As TicketIdentity = CType(Application(MyTicket), TicketIdentity)
    If MyTicket IsNot Nothing Then
        Return idtTIcket
    Else
        Throw New SecurityException("Invalid ticket.")
    End If
End Function
```

In addition, this overloaded version of AuthorizeUser() verifies that the user has a ticket and is a member of a specific role. The ASP.NET role management provider handles the role-checking work.

```
Private Function AuthorizeUser(ByVal MyTicket As String,
            ByVal role As String) As TicketIdentity
    Dim idtTicket As TicketIdentity = AuthorizeUser(MyTicket)
    If Roles.IsUserInRole(idtTicket.UserName, role) Then
        Throw New SecurityException("Insufficient permissions.")
    Else
        Return idtTicket
    End If
End Function
```

Using these two helper methods, you can build other web service methods that test a user's permissions before performing certain tasks or returning privileged information.

Testing the SOAP Authentication System

Now you simply need to create a test web method that uses the AuthorizeUser() method to check that the user has the required permissions. Here's an example that checks that the client is an administrator before allowing the client to retrieve the DataSet with the employee list:

```
<WebMethod(), SoapHeader("Ticket", Direction := SoapHeaderDirection.In)> _
Public Function GetEmployees() As DataSet
    AuthorizeUser(Ticket.Ticket, "Administrator")
   ...
End Function
```

To make the test even easier to set up, the sample code for this chapter includes a CreateTestUser() web method that generates a specific user and makes that user part of the Administrators role:

```
<WebMethod()> _
Public Sub CreateTestUser(ByVal username As String, ByVal password As String)
    ' Delete the user if the user already exists.
    If Membership.GetUser(username) IsNot Nothing Then
        Membership.DeleteUser(username)
    End If
    ' Create the user.
    Membership.CreateUser(username, password)

    ' Make this user an administrator
    ' and create the role if it doesn't exist.
    Dim role As String = "Administrator"
    If (Not Roles.RoleExists(role)) Then
        Roles.CreateRole(role)
```

```
    End If
    Roles.AddUserToRole(username, role)
End Sub
```

Now you can create a client that tests this. In this case, a web page provides two text boxes for the user to supply a user name and password (see Figure 33-3). This information is passed to the Login() method, and then the GetEmployees() method is called to retrieve the data. This method succeeds for a user with the Administrator role but fails for everyone else.

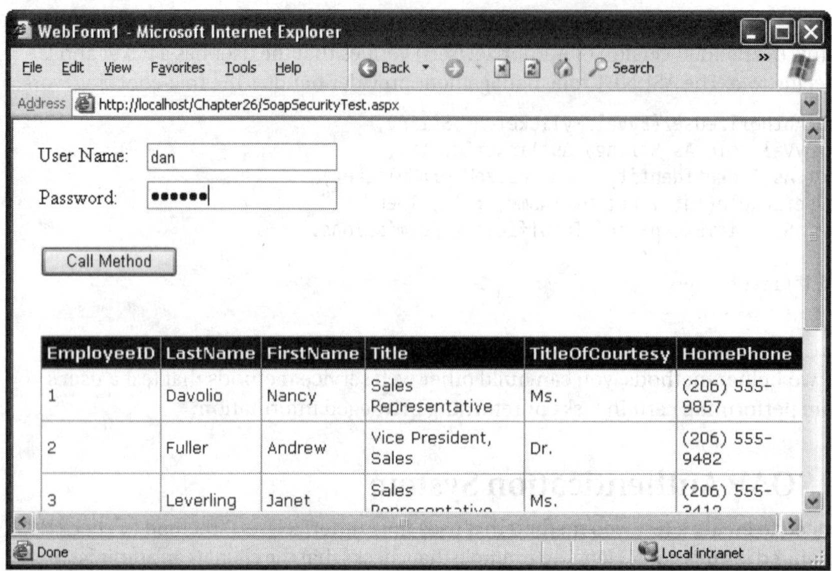

Figure 33-3. *Testing a web method that uses ticket-based authorization*

Here's the web-page code:

```
Protected Sub cmdCall_Click(ByVal sender As Object, ByVal e As System.EventArgs)
    Dim proxy As New SoapSecurityService()

    Try
        proxy.Login(txtUserName.Text, txtPassword.Text)
        GridView1.DataSource = proxy.GetEmployees()
        GridView1.DataBind()
    Catch err As Exception
        lblInfo.Text = err.Message
    End Try
End Sub
```

The best part is that the client doesn't need to be aware of the ticket management. That's because the Login() method issues the ticket, and the proxy class maintains it. As long as the client uses the same instance of the proxy class, the same ticket value will be submitted automatically, and the user will be authenticated.

You can do quite a bit to enhance this authentication system. For example, you might want to record additional details with the TicketIdentity, including the time the ticket was created and last accessed and the network address of the user who owns the ticket. This way, you can incorporate additional checks into the AuthorizeUser() method. You could have tickets time out after a long period of disuse, or you could reject a ticket if the IP address of the client has changed.

SOAP Extensions

ASP.NET web services provide high-level access to SOAP. As you've seen, you don't need to know much about SOAP in order to create and call web services. If, however, you are a developer with a good understanding of SOAP and you want to get your hands dirty with low-level access to SOAP messages, the .NET Framework allows that too. In this section, you'll see how to intercept SOAP messages and manipulate them.

Note Even if you don't want to manipulate SOAP messages directly, it's worth learning about SOAP extensions because they are part of the infrastructure that supports the WSE, which you'll learn about later in the section "The Web Services Enhancements."

SOAP extensions are an extensibility mechanism. They allow third-party developers to create components that plug into the web service model and provide other services. For example, you could create a SOAP extension to selectively encrypt or compress portions of a SOAP message before it is sent from the client. Of course, you would also need to run a matching SOAP extension on the server to decrypt or decompress the message after it has been received but before it's deserialized.

To create a SOAP extension, you need to create a class that derives from the System.Web.Services.Protocols.SoapExtension class. The SoapExtension class includes a ProcessMessage() method that's triggered automatically as the SOAP message passes through several stages. For example, if you run a SOAP extension on a web server, the following four stages will occur:

SoapMessageStage.BeforeDeserialize: Occurs immediately after the web server receives the SOAP request message.

SoapMessageStage.AfterDeserialize: Occurs after the raw SOAP message is translated to .NET data types but just before the web method code runs.

SoapMessageStage.BeforeSerialize: Occurs after the web method code runs but before the return value is translated into a SOAP message.

SoapMessageStage.AfterSerialize: Occurs after the return data is serialized into a SOAP response message but before it is sent to the client application.

At each stage, you can retrieve various bits of information about the SOAP message. In the BeforeDeserialize or AfterSerialize stage, you can retrieve the full SOAP message text.

You can also implement a SOAP extension on the client. In this case, the same four stages occur. Except now, the message is being received, deserialized, and acted upon by the proxy class, not the web service. Figure 33-4 shows the full process.

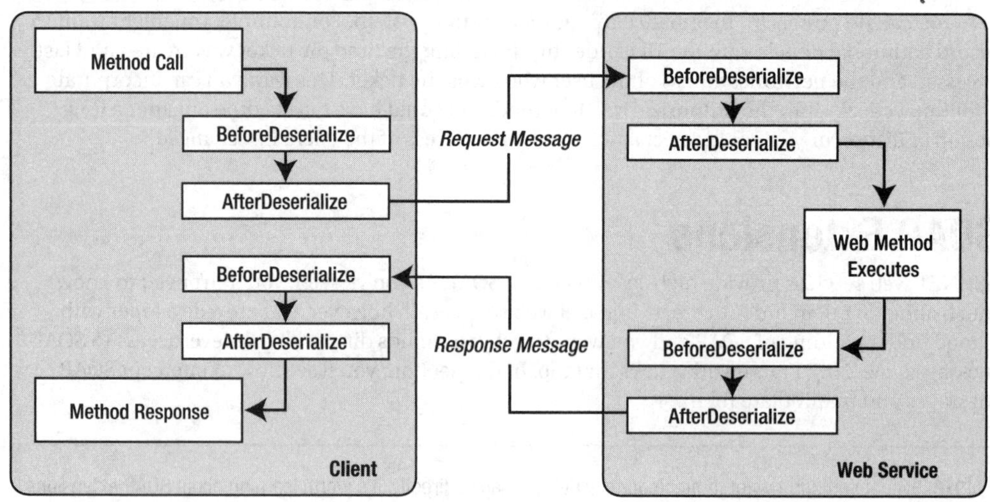

Figure 33-4. *SOAP processing on the client and server*

Creating production-level SOAP extensions is not easy. This has a number of serious challenges:

- SOAP extensions often need to be executed on both the server and client. That means you need to worry about distributing and managing another component, which can be exceedingly complex in a large distributed system.
- SOAP extensions make your web services less compatible. Third-party clients may not realize they need to install and run a SOAP extension to use your service, as this information isn't included in the WSDL document. If the clients are running non-.NET platforms, they won't be able to use the SoapExtension class you've created, and you may need to find another way to extend the SOAP processing pipeline, which can range from difficult to impossible depending on the environment.
- The Internet abounds with examples of SOAP extensions that apply encryption in a poor, insecure fashion. The flaws include insecure key management, no ability to perform a key exchange, and slow performance because of a reliance on asymmetric encryption instead of symmetric encryption. A much better choice is to use a SSL through IIS, which is bulletproof.

In most cases, creating SOAP extensions is a task that's best left to the architects at Microsoft, who are focused on the issues and challenges of developing enterprise-level plumbing. In fact, Microsoft implements several newer, less mature web service standards using SOAP extensions in the freely downloadable WSE component you'll learn about later in the section "The Web Services Enhancements."

■ **Note** SOAP extensions work only over SOAP. When you test a web method through the browser test page, they won't be invoked. Also, SOAP messages won't work if you set the BufferResponse attribute of the WebMethod attribute to False. In this case, the SOAP extension can't act on the SOAP data, because ASP.NET begins sending it immediately, before it has been completely generated.

Creating a SOAP Extension

In the following example, you'll see a sample SOAP extension that logs SOAP messages to the Windows event log. SOAP faults will be logged as errors in the event log.

■ **Tip** Some developers use SOAP extensions for tracing purposes. However, as you already learned in Chapter 32, that's not necessary—the trace utility included with the Microsoft SOAP Toolkit is far more convenient. However, one advantage of the SOAP logger you'll see in this example is that you could use it to capture and store SOAP messages permanently, even if the trace utility isn't running. You also don't need to change the port in the client code to route messages through the trace utility.

All SOAP extensions consist of two ingredients: a custom class that derives from System.Web.Services.Protocols.SoapExtension and a custom attribute that you apply to a web method to indicate that your SOAP extension should be used. The custom attribute is the simpler of the two ingredients.

The SoapExtension Attribute

The SoapExtension attribute allows you to link specific SOAP extensions to the methods in a web class. When you create your SoapExtension attribute, you derive from the System.Web.Services.Protocols.SoapExtensionAttribute, as shown here:

```
<AttributeUsage(AttributeTargets.Method)> _
Public Class SoapLogAttribute
    Inherits System.Web.Services.Protocols.SoapExtensionAttribute
        ...
End Class
```

Note that the attribute class bears another attribute—the AttributeUsage attribute. It indicates where you can use your custom attribute. SOAP extension attributes are always applied to individual method declarations, much like the SoapHeader and WebMethod attributes. Thus, you should use AttributeTargets.Method to prevent the user from applying it to some other code construct (such as a class declaration). You should use AttributeUsage anytime you need to create a custom attribute—it isn't limited to web service scenarios.

Every SoapExtension attribute needs to override two abstract properties: Priority and ExtensionType. Priority sets the order that SOAP extensions work if you have multiple extensions configured. However, it's not needed in simpler extensions such as the one in this example. The ExtensionType property returns a Type object that represents your custom SoapExtension class, and it allows .NET to attach your SOAP extension to the method. In this example, the class name of the SOAP Extension is SoapLog, although we haven't explained the code yet.

```
Private m_priority As Integer
Public Overrides Property Priority() As Integer
    Get
        Return m_priority
    End Get
    Set (ByVal Value As Integer)
        m_priority = Value
    End Set
End Property
```

```
Public Overrides ReadOnly Property ExtensionType() As Type
    Get
        Return GetType(SoapLog)
    End Get
End Property
```

In addition, you can add properties that will supply extra bits of initialization information to your SOAP extension. The following example adds a Name property, which stores the source string that will be used when writing event log entries, and a Level property, which configures what types of messages will be logged. If the level is 1, the SoapLog extension will log only error messages. If the level is 2 or greater, the SoapLog extension will write all types of messages. If the level is 3 or greater, the SoapLog extension will add an extra piece of information to each message that records the stage when the log entry was written.

```
Private m_name As String = "SoapLog"
Public Property Name() As String
    Get
        Return m_name
    End Get
    Set (ByVal Value As String)
        m_name = Value
    End Set
End Property

Private m_level As Integer = 1
Public Property Level() As Integer
    Get
        Return m_level
    End Get
    Set (ByVal Value As Integer)
        m_level = Value
    End Set
End Property
```

You can now apply this custom attribute to a web method and set the Name and Level properties. Here's an example that uses the log source name EmployeesService.GetEmployeesCount and a log level of 3:

```
<SoapLog(Name:="EmployeesService.GetEmployeesCount", Level:=3), WebMethod()> _
Public Function GetEmployeesCount() As Integer
    ...
End Function
```

Now, whenever the GetEmployeesCount() method is called with a SOAP message, the SoapLog class is created, initialized, and executed. It has the chance to process the SOAP request message before the GetEmployeesCount() method receives it, and it has the chance to process the SOAP response message after the GetEmployeesCount() method returns a result.

The SoapExtension

The SoapExtension class we'll use to log messages is fairly long, although much of the code is basic boilerplate that every SOAP extension uses. We'll examine it piece by piece.

The first detail to notice is that the class derives from the abstract base class SoapExtension. This is a requirement. The SoapExtension class provides many of the methods you need to override, including the following:

GetInitializer() and Initialize(): These methods pass initial information to the SOAP extension when it's first created.

ProcessMessage(): This is where the actual processing takes place, allowing your extension to take a look at (and modify) the raw SOAP.

ChainStream(): This method is a basic piece of infrastructure that every web service should provide. It allows you to gain access to the SOAP stream without disrupting other extensions.

Here's the class definition:

```
Public Class SoapLog : Inherits System.Web.Services.Protocols.SoapExtension
    ...
End Class
```

ASP.NET calls the GetInitializer() method the first time your extension is used for a particular web method. It gives you the chance to initialize and store some data that will be used when processing SOAP messages. You store this information by passing it back as the return value from the GetInitializer() method.

When the GetInitializer() method is called, you receive one important piece of information—the custom attribute that was applied to the corresponding web method. In the case of the SoapLog, this is an instance of the SoapLogAttribute class, which provides the Name and Level property. To store this information for future use, you can return this attribute from the GetInitializer() method, as shown here:

```
Public Overrides Function GetInitializer(
          ByVal methodInfo As LogicalMethodInfo,
          ByVal attribute As SoapExtensionAttribute) As Object
    Return attribute
End Function
```

Actually, the GetInitializer() method has two versions. Only one is invoked, and it depends on whether the SOAP extension is configured through an attribute (as in this example) or through a configuration file. If applied through a configuration file, the SOAP extension automatically runs for every method of every web service.

Even if you don't plan to use the configuration file to initialize a SOAP extension, you still need to implement the other version of GetInitializer(). In this case, it makes sense to return a new SoapLogAttribute instance so that the default Name and Level settings are available later:

```
Public Overrides Function GetInitializer(ByVal obj As Type) As Object
    Return New SoapLogAttribute()
End Function
```

GetInitializer() is called only the first time your SOAP extension is executed for a method. However, every time the method is invoked, the Initialize() method is triggered. If you returned an object from the GetInitializer() method, ASP.NET provides this object to the Initialize() method every time it's called. In the SoapLog extension, this is a good place to extract the Name and Level information and store it in member variables so it will be available for the remainder of the SOAP processing work. (You couldn't store this information in the GetInitialize() method, because that method won't be called every time the SOAP extension is executed.)

```
Private level As Integer
Private name As String

Public Overrides Sub Initialize(ByVal initializer As Object)
    name = (CType(initializer, SoapLogAttribute)).Name
    level = (CType(initializer, SoapLogAttribute)).Level
End Sub
```

The workhorse of the extension is the ProcessMessage() method, which ASP.NET calls at various stages of the serialization process. A SoapMessage object is passed to the ProcessMessage() method, and you can examine this method to retrieve information about the message, such as its stage and the message text. The SoapLog extension reads the full message only in the AfterSerialize and BeforeDeserialize stages, because these are the only stages when you can retrieve the full XML of the SOAP message. However, if the level is 3 or greater, a basic log entry will be created in the BeforeSerialize and AfterDeserialize stages that simply records the name of the stage.

Here's the full ProcessMessage() code:

```
Public Overrides Sub ProcessMessage(ByVal message As SoapMessage)
    Select Case message.Stage
        Case SoapMessageStage.BeforeSerialize
            If level > 2 Then
               WriteToLog(message.Stage.ToString(), EventLogEntryType.Information)
            End If
        Case SoapMessageStage.AfterSerialize
            LogOutputMessage(message)
        Case SoapMessageStage.BeforeDeserialize
            LogInputMessage(message)
        Case SoapMessageStage.AfterDeserialize
            If level > 2 Then
               WriteToLog(message.Stage.ToString(), EventLogEntryType.Information)
            End If
     End Select
End Sub
```

The ProcessMessage() method doesn't contain the actual logging code. Instead, it calls other private methods such as WriteLogLog(), LogOutputMessage(), and LogInputMessage(). The WriteToLog() is the final point at which the log entry is created using the System.Diagnostics.EventLog class. If needed, this code creates a new event log and a new log source using the name that was set in the Name property of the custom extension attribute.

Here's the complete code for the WriteToLog() method:

```
Private Sub WriteToLog(ByVal message As String, ByVal type As EventLogEntryType)
    ' Create a new log named Web Service Log, with the event source
    ' specified in the attribute.
    Dim log As EventLog
    If (Not EventLog.SourceExists(name)) Then
      EventLog.CreateEventSource(name, "Web Service Log")
    End If

    log = New EventLog()
    log.Source = name
    log.WriteEntry(message, type)
End Sub
```

When the SOAP message is in the BeforeSerialize or AfterDeserialize stage, the WriteToLog() method is called directly, and the name of the stage is written. When the SOAP message is in the AfterSerialize or BeforeDeserialize stage, you need to perform a little more work to retrieve the SOAP message.

Before you can build these methods, you need another ingredient—the CopyStream() method. That's because the XML in the SOAP message is contained in a stream. The stream has a pointer that indicates the current position in the stream. The problem is that as you read the message data from the stream (for example, to log it), you move the pointer. This means that if the log extension reads a stream that is about to be deserialized, it will move the pointer to the end of the stream. For ASP.NET to property deserialize the SOAP message, the pointer must be set back to the beginning of the stream. If you don't take this step, a deserialization error will occur.

To make this process easier, you can use a private CopyStream() method. This method copies the contents of one stream to another stream. After this method is executed, both streams will be positioned at the end.

```
Private Sub CopyStream(ByVal fromstream As Stream, ByVal tostream As Stream)
    Dim reader As New StreamReader(fromstream)
    Dim writer As New StreamWriter(tostream)
    writer.WriteLine(reader.ReadToEnd())
    writer.Flush()
End Sub
```

Another ingredient you need is the ChainStream() method, which the ASP.NET plumbing calls before serialization or deserialization takes place. Your SOAP extension can override the ChainStream() method to insert itself into the processing pipeline. At this point, the extension can cache a reference to the original stream and create a new in-memory stream, which is then returned to the next extension in the chain.

```
Private oldStream As Stream
Private newStream As Stream

Public Overrides Function ChainStream(ByVal stream As Stream) As Stream
    oldStream = stream
    newStream = New MemoryStream()
    Return newStream
End Function
```

Of course, this is only part of the story. It's up to the other methods to either read data out of the old stream or write data into the new stream, depending on what stage the message is in. You do this by calling the CopyStream() method. Once you've implemented this somewhat confusing design, the end result is that every SOAP extension has a chance to modify the SOAP stream without overwriting each other's changes. For the most part, the ChainStream() and CopyStream() methods are basic pieces of SOAP extension architecture that are identical in every SOAP extension you'll see.

The LogInputMessage() and LogOutputMessage() methods have the task of extracting the message information and logging it. Both methods use the CopyStream() method. When deserializing, the input stream contains the XML to deserialize, and the pointer is at the beginning of the stream. The LogInputMessage() method copies the input stream into the memory stream buffer and logs the contents of the stream. It sets the pointer to the beginning of the memory stream buffer so that the next extension can get access to the stream.

```
Private Sub LogInputMessage(ByVal message As SoapMessage)
    CopyStream(oldStream, newStream)
    message.Stream.Seek(0, SeekOrigin.Begin)
    LogMessage(message, newStream)
    message.Stream.Seek(0, SeekOrigin.Begin)
End Sub
```

When serializing, the serializer writes to the memory stream created in ChainStream(). When the LogOutputMessage() function is called after serializing, the pointer is at the end of the stream. The LogOutputMessage() function sets the pointer to the beginning of the stream so that the extension can log the contents of the stream. Before returning, the content of the memory stream is copied to the outgoing stream, and the pointer is then back at the end of both streams.

```
Private Sub LogOutputMessage(ByVal message As SoapMessage)
    message.Stream.Seek(0, SeekOrigin.Begin)
    LogMessage(message, newStream)
    message.Stream.Seek(0, SeekOrigin.Begin)
    CopyStream(newStream, oldStream)
End Sub
```

Once they've moved the stream to the right position, both LogInputMessage() and LogOutputMessage() extract the message data from the SOAP stream and write a log message entry with that information. The function also checks whether the SOAP message contains a fault. In that case, the message is logged in the event log as an error.

```
Private Sub LogMessage(ByVal message As SoapMessage, ByVal stream As Stream)
    Dim reader New StreamReader(stream)
    eventMessage = reader.ReadToEnd()

    Dim eventMessage As String
    If level > 2 Then
        eventMessage = message.Stage.ToString() +Constants.vbLf & eventMessage
    End If
    If eventMessage.IndexOf("<soap:Fault>") > 0 Then
        ' The SOAP body contains a fault.
        If level > 0 Then
            WriteToLog(eventMessage, EventLogEntryType.Error)
        End If
    Else
        ' The SOAP body contains a message.
        If level > 1 Then
            WriteToLog(eventMessage, EventLogEntryType.Information)
        End If
    End If
End Sub
```

This completes the code for the SoapLog extension.

Using the SoapLog Extension

To test the SoapLog extension, you need to apply the SoapLogAttribute to a web method, as shown here:

```
<SoapLog(Name:="EmployeesService.GetEmployeesLogged", Level:=3), WebMethod()> _
Public Function GetEmployeesLogged() As Integer
    ...
End Function
```

You then need to create a client application that calls that method. When you run the client and call the method, the SoapLog extension will run and create the event log entries.

■ **Note** For the SoapLog extension to successfully write to the event log, the ASP.NET worker process (typically, the account ASPNET) must have permission to access the Windows event log. Otherwise, no entries will be written. Note that if a SOAP extension fails and generates an exception at any point, it will simply be ignored. Your client code and web service methods will not be notified.

To verify that the entries appear, run the Event Viewer (choose Programs ➤ Administrative Tools ➤ Event Viewer from the Start menu). Look for the log named Web Service Log. Figure 33-5 shows the event log entries that you'll see after calling GetEmployeesCount() twice with a log level of 3.

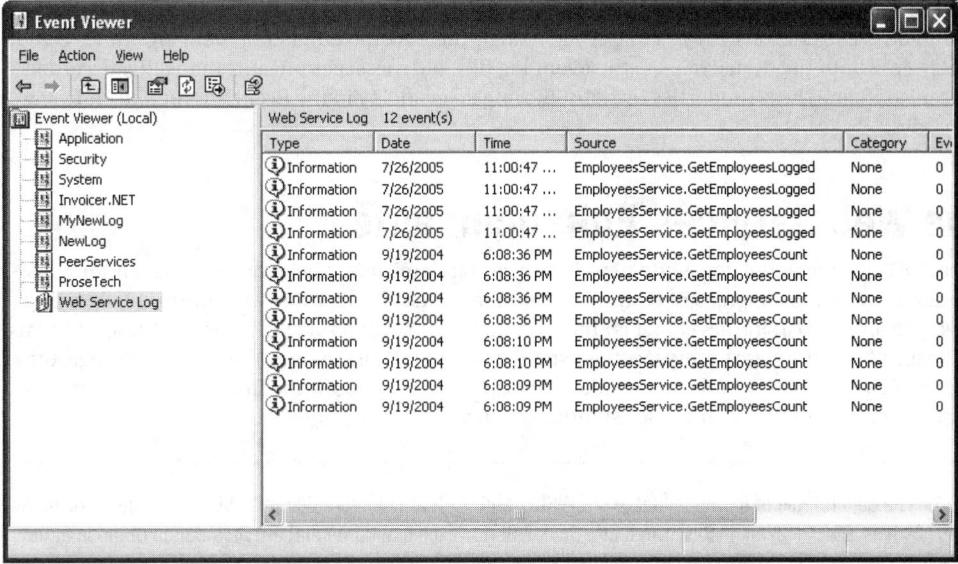

Figure 33-5. *The event log entries for the SOAP extension*

You can look at individual entries by double-clicking them. The Description field shows the full event log message, with the XML data from the SOAP message, as shown in Figure 33-6.

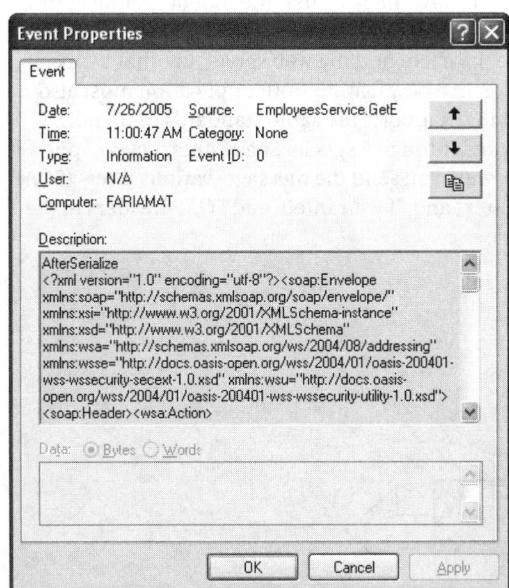

Figure 33-6. *A SOAP message in an event log entry*

The SoapLog extension is a useful tool when developing or monitoring web services. However, you should use it judiciously. If you track even a single method, the number of event log entries could quickly grow into the thousands. As the event log fills, old messages are automatically discarded. You can configure these properties by right-clicking an event log in the Event Viewer and choosing Properties.

The Web Services Enhancements

Since .NET first appeared, the world of web service standards hasn't been quiet. In fact, numerous standards, in various degrees of testing, revision, and standardization, are continuously being developed and used in the developer community. In future versions of .NET, many of these additions will be fused into the class library. As these standards are still fairly new and subject to change, they aren't ready yet. However, you can download another Microsoft tool—the free WSE toolkit—to gain support for a slew of new web service standards today.

■ **Note** The general rule of thumb is that SOAP, WSDL, and UDDI are incorporated into .NET, and recent enhancements (such as SOAP 1.2) are incorporated into .NET 2.0. However, standards that are built on top of these three basics (such as those for SOAP-based encryption, security, and so on) are not yet part of .NET and are the exclusive territory of the WSE.

To install the WSE (or just read about it), browse to `http://msdn.microsoft.com/webservices/building/wse`. The WSE provides a class library assembly with a set of useful .NET classes. Behind the scenes, the WSE uses SOAP extensions to adjust the web service messages. This means your code interacts with a set of helper objects, and behind the scenes the WSE implements the appropriate SOAP standards. Using the WSE has two key disadvantages. First, the toolkit is subject to change. The version that works with Visual Studio 2005 (version 3.0) is not compatible with earlier versions. Second, you need to use the WSE on both the client and the web server. In other words, if you want to use a web service that uses the WSE to gain a new feature, your application must also use the WSE (if it's a .NET client) or another toolkit that supports the same standards (if it's not).

Many of the features in the WSE are implemented through a special SoapContext class. Your code interacts with the SoapContext object. Then, when you send the message, various filters (SOAP extensions) examine the properties of the SoapContext and, if warranted, add SOAP headers to the outgoing message. Figure 33-7 illustrates this process.

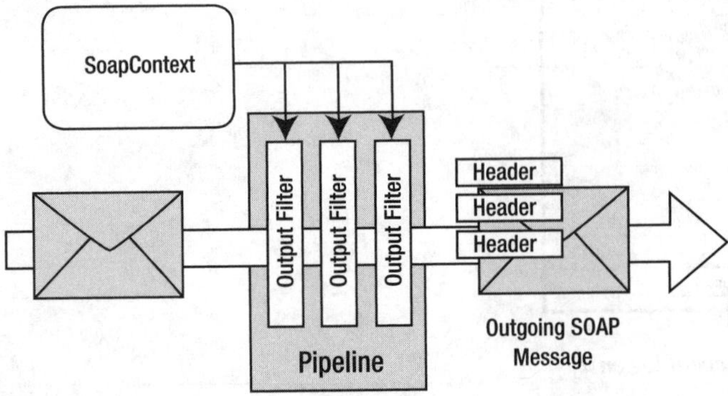

Figure 33-7. *Processing an outgoing SOAP message*

The idea behind the filters is that they can be plugged in only when they are needed. For example, if you don't need a security header, then you can leave the security header filter out of the processing pipeline by tweaking the configuration settings. Additionally, because each filter works by adding a distinct SOAP header, you have the freedom to combine as many (or as few) extensions as you need at once.

When a SOAP message is received, the same process happens in reverse. In this case, the filters look for specific SOAP headers and use the information in them to configure the SoapContext object. Figure 33-8 shows this processing model.

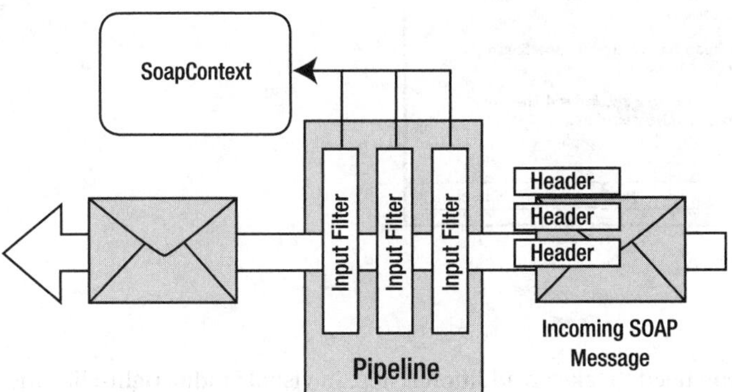

Figure 33-8. *Processing an incoming SOAP message*

So, what are the standards supported by the WSE? The full list is available with the WSE documentation, but it includes support for authentication and message encryption, establishing trust, message routing, and interoperability. The WSE also allows you to use SOAP messages for direct communication over a TCP connection (no HTTP required). In the following sections, you'll take a look at using the WSE for a simple security scenario. For a complete examination of the WSE, refer to Jeffrey Hasan's book *Expert Service-Oriented Architecture in C#: Using the Web Services Enhancements 2.0* (Apress, 2004) or the online documentation included with the WSE toolkit.

Installing the WSE

Before you can go any further, you need to download and install the WSE. When you run the setup program, choose Visual Studio Developer if you have Visual Studio 2003 installed, as this enables project support (see Figure 33-9).

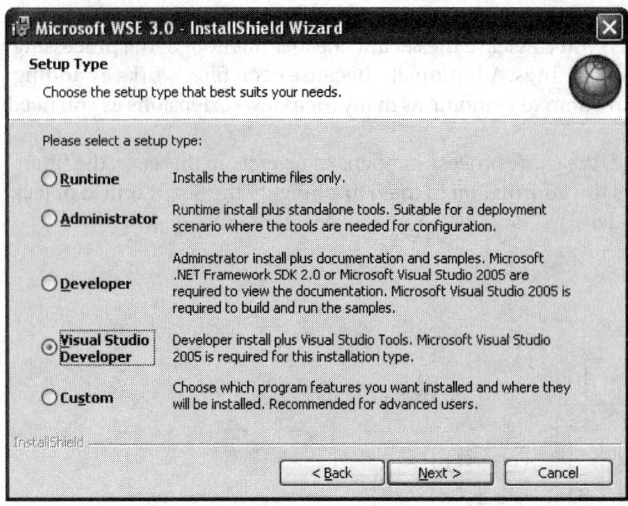

Figure 33-9. *Installing the WSE*

To use the WSE in a project, you need to take an additional step. In Visual Studio, right-click the project name in the Solution Explorer, and select WSE Settings from the bottom of the menu. You'll see two check boxes. If you're creating a web service, select both settings, as shown in Figure 33-10. If you're creating a client application, select only the first setting, Enable This Project for Web Services Enhancements.

When you select the first option, Enable This Project for Web Services Enhancements, Visual Studio automatically adds a reference to the Microsoft.Web.Services2.dll assembly and modifies the web.config for the application to add support for the WSE configuration handler. In addition, any web references that are created from this point on will include WSE support in the proxy class. However, the web references you've already created won't have WSE support until you update them.

When you enable the second option, Enable Microsoft Web Services Enhancements SOAP Extensions, Visual Studio modifies the web.config file to register the SOAP extension that adds support for your web services. This option is required only for ASP.NET web services that use the WSE.

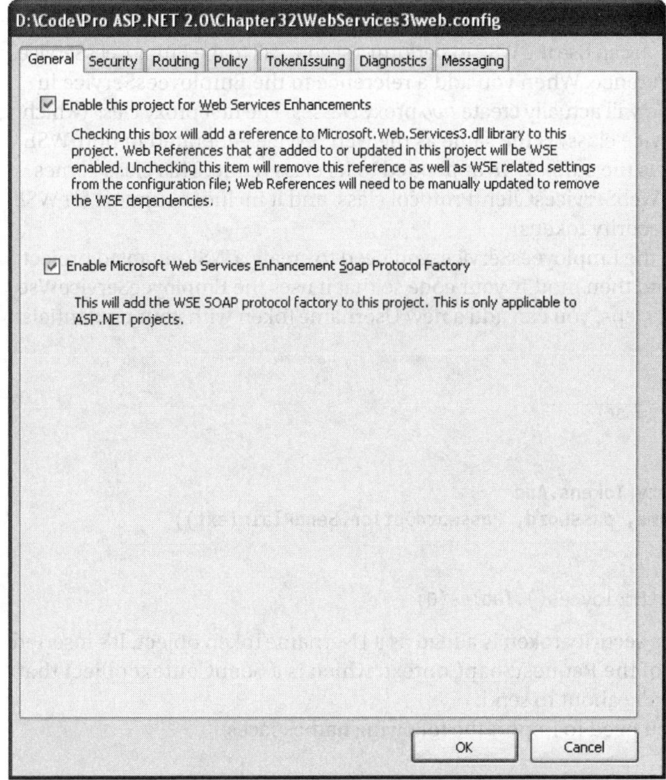

Figure 33-10. *Enabling the WSE for a project*

Performing Authentication with the WSE

Many of the WSE classes support security standards. One of the most simple and straightforward of these classes is the UsernameToken class, which represents user credentials.

The UsernameToken information is added to the message as a SOAP header. However, it's added in a way that conforms to the WS-Security standard, which would be quite laborious to implement on your own. The benefit is that by implementing this general security model, you can add authentication without developing a proprietary approach, which could make it more difficult for third-party and cross-platform use of your web service. Also, it's likely that ASP.NET and WS-Security can provide a more secure, robust approach than one an individual developer or organization could develop (without investing considerable time and effort).

Currently, the security infrastructure in the WSE has a few holes and doesn't fully deliver on its promise. However, it's easy to use and extend. To see how it works, it's helpful to consider a simple example.

Setting Credentials in the Client

In the next example, you'll see how you can use the WSE to perform a secure call to the EmployeesService. The first step is to add the web reference. When you add a reference to the EmployeesService in a WSE-enabled project, Visual Studio will actually create *two* proxy classes. The first proxy class (which has the same name as the web service class) is the same as the web service generated in non-WSE projects. The second proxy class has the suffix *WSE* appended to its class name. This class comes from the Microsoft.Web.Services3.WebServicesClientProtocol class, and it includes support for WSE features (in this case, adding WS-Security tokens).

Thus, to use WS-Security with the EmployeesService, you need to create a WSE-enabled project, add or refresh the web reference, and then modify your code so that it uses the EmployeeServiceWse proxy. Provided you've taken those steps, you can add a new UsernameToken with your credentials using a single code statement:

```
' Create the proxy.
Dim proxy As New EmployeesServiceWse()

' Add the WS-Security token.
proxy.RequestSoapContext.Security.Tokens.Add
    (New UsernameToken(userName, password, PasswordOption.SendPlainText))

' Bind the results.
GridView1.DataSource = proxy.GetEmployees().Tables(0)
```

As this code demonstrates, the security token is added as a UsernameToken object. It's inserted in the Security.Tokens collection of the RequestSoapContext, which is a SoapContext object that represents the request message you're about to send.

To use this code as written, you need to import the following namespaces:

```
Imports Microsoft.Web.Services3
Imports Microsoft.Web.Services3.Security
Imports Microsoft.Web.Services3.Security.Tokens
```

■ **Note** Notice that the WSE namespaces incorporate the number 3, which indicates the third version of the WSE toolkit. This is because the third version is not backward compatible with the first two. To prevent a conflict with partially upgraded applications, the WSE classes are separated into distinct namespaces by version. This is part of the messy reality of working with emerging web service standards.

The constructor for the UsernameToken class accepts three parameters: a string with the user name, a string with the password, and the hashing option you would like to use. Unfortunately, if you want to use the default authentication provider in the WSE (which uses Windows authentication), you *must* choose PasswordOption.SendPlainText. As a result, this code is extremely insecure and subject to network spying unless you send the request over an SSL connection.

Although this example adds only two extra details to the request, the SOAP message actually becomes much more complex because of the way the WS-Security standard is structured. It defines additional details such as an expiration date (used to prevent replay attacks) and a *nonce* (a random value that can be incorporated in the hash to increase security). Here's a slightly shortened example of the SOAP request message:

```
<soap:Envelope xmlns:soap="http://schemas.xmlsoap.org/soap/envelope/"
 xmlns:wsa="http://schemas.xmlsoap.org/ws/2004/03/addressing"
 mlns:wsse="http://docs.oasis-open.org/wss/2004/01/..."
 xmlns:wsu="http://docs.oasis-open.org/wss/2004/01/...">
```

```
  <soap:Header>
    <wsa:Action>http://www.apress.com/ProASP.NET/GetEmployees</wsa:Action>
    <wsa:MessageID>uuid:5b1bc235-7f81-40c4-ac1e-e4ea81ade319</wsa:MessageID>
      <wsa:ReplyTo>
        <wsa:Address>http://schemas.xmlsoap.org/ws/2004/03/...</wsa:Address>
      </wsa:ReplyTo>
      <wsa:To>http://localhost:8080/WebServices3/EmployeesService.asmx</wsa:To>
      <wsse:Security soap:mustUnderstand="1">
      <wsu:Timestamp wsu:Id="Timestamp-dc0d8d9a-e385-438f-9ff1-2cb0b699c90f">
        <wsu:Created>2004-09-21T01:49:33Z</wsu:Created>
        <wsu:Expires>2004-09-21T01:54:33Z</wsu:Expires>
      </wsu:Timestamp>
      <wsse:UsernameToken xmlns:wsu="http://docs.oasis-open.org/wss/2004/01/..."
       wsu:Id="SecurityToken-8b663245-30ac-4178-b2c8-724f43fc27be">
        <wsse:Username>guest</wsse:Username>
        <wsse:Password
         Type="http://docs.oasis-open.org/wss/2004/01/...">secret</wsse:Password>
        <wsse:Nonce>9m8UofSBhw+XWIqf083NiQ==</wsse:Nonce>
        <wsu:Created>2004-09-21T01:49:33Z</wsu:Created>
      </wsse:UsernameToken>
    </wsse:Security>
  </soap:Header>
  <soap:Body>
    <GetEmployees xmlns="http://www.apress.com/ProASP.NET/" />
  </soap:Body>
</soap:Envelope>
```

Reading Credentials in the Web Service

The WSE-enabled service examines the supplied token and validates it immediately. The default authentication provider that's included with the WSE uses Windows authentication, which means it extracts the user name and password from the SOAP header and uses it to log the user in under a Windows account. If the token doesn't map to a valid Windows account, an error message is returned to the client. However, if no token is supplied, no error occurs. It's up to you to check for this condition on the web server in order to restrict access to specific web methods.

Unfortunately, the WSE isn't integrated in such a way that it can use the User object. Instead, you need to retrieve the tokens from the current context. The WSE provides a RequestSoapContext. Using the RequestSoapContext.Current property, you can retrieve an instance of the SoapContext class that represents the last received message. You can then examine the SoapContext.Security.Tokens collection.

To simplify this task, it helps to create a private method like the one shown here. It checks that a token exists and throws an exception if it doesn't. Otherwise, it returns the user name.

```
Private Function GetUsernameToken() As String
    ' Although there may be many tokens, only one of these
    ' will be a UsernameToken.
    For Each token As UsernameToken In RequestSoapContext.Current.Security.Tokens
        Return token.Username
    Next token
    Throw New SecurityException("Missing security token")
End Function
```

You could call the GetUsernameToken() method at the beginning of a web method to ensure that security is in effect. Overall, this is a good approach to enforce security. However, it's important to keep its limitations in mind. First, it doesn't support hashing or encrypting the user credentials.

Also, it doesn't support more advanced Windows authentication protocols such as Digest authentication and Integrated Windows authentication. That's because the authentication is implemented by the WSE extensions, not by IIS. Similarly, the client always needs to submit a password and user name. The client has no way to automatically submit the credentials of the current user, as demonstrated earlier in this chapter with the CredentialCache object. In fact, the Credentials property of the proxy is ignored completely.

Fortunately, you aren't limited to the scaled-down form of Windows authentication provided by the default WSE authentication service. You can also create your own authentication logic, as described in the next section.

Custom Authentication

By creating your own authentication class, you can perform authentication against any data source, including an XML file or a database. To create your own authenticator, you simply need to create a class that derives from UsernameTokenManager and overrides the AuthenticateToken() method. In this method, your code needs to look up the user who is trying to become authenticated and return the password for that user. ASP.NET will then compare this password against the user credentials and decide whether authentication fails or succeeds.

Creating this class is quite straightforward. Here's an example that simply returns hard-coded passwords for two users. This provides a quick-and-easy test, although a real-world example would probably use ADO.NET code to get the same information.

```
Public Class CustomAuthenticator
    Inherits UsernameTokenManager

    Protected Overrides Function AuthenticateToken(
            ByVal token As UsernameToken) As String
        Dim username As String = token.Username

        If username = "dan" Then
            Return "secret"
        ElseIf username = "jenny" Then
            Return "opensesame"
        Else
            Return String.Empty
        End If
    End Function
End Class
```

The reason you don't perform the password test on your own is because the type of comparison depends on how the credentials are encoded. For example, if they are passed in clear text, you need to perform a simple string comparison. If they are hashed, you need to create a new password hash using the same standardized algorithm, which must take the same data into account (including the random nonce from the client message). However, the WSE can perform this comparison task for you automatically, which dramatically simplifies your logic. The only potential problem is that you need to have the user's password stored in a retrievable form on the web server. If you're storing only password hashes in a back-end database, you won't be able to pass the original password to ASP.NET, and it won't be able to re-create the credential hash it needs to authenticate the user.

Once you've created your authentication class, you still need to tell the WSE to use it for authenticating user tokens by registering your class in the web.config file. To accomplish this, right-click the project name in the Solution Explorer, and select WSE Settings. Next, select the Security tab (shown in Figure 33-11).

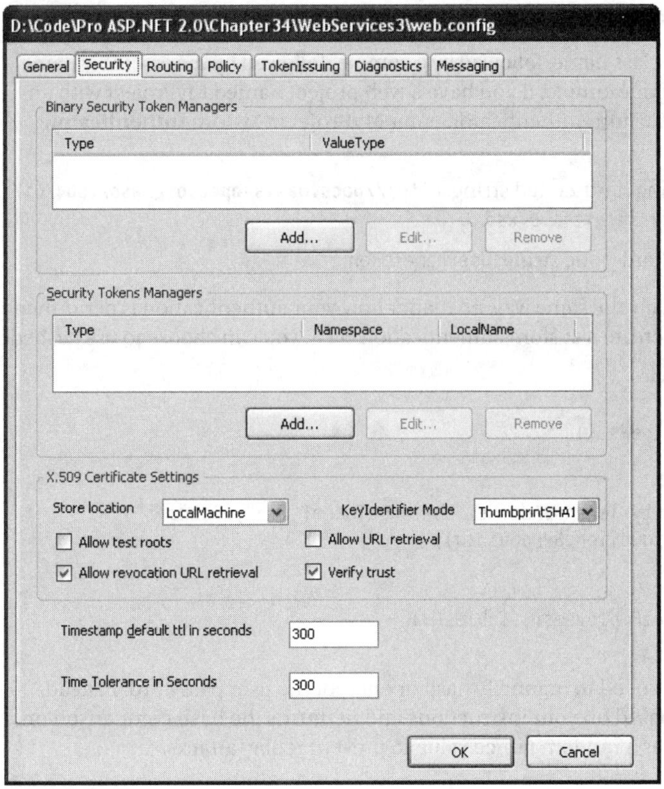

Figure 33-11. *Security settings*

In the Security Tokens Managers section, click the Add button. This displays the SecurityToken Manager dialog box (see Figure 33-12).

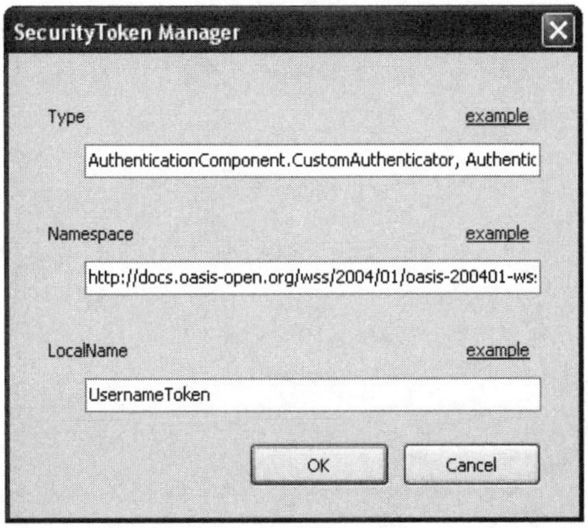

Figure 33-12. *Configuring a new UsernameTokenManager*

In the SecurityToken Manager dialog box, you need to specify three pieces of information:

Type: Enter the fully qualified class name, followed by a comma, followed by the assembly name (without the .dll extension). For example, if you have a web project named MyProject with an authentication class named CustomAuthenticator, enter **MyProject.CustomAuthenticator, MyProject**.

Namespace: Enter the following hard-coded string: **`http://docs.oasis-open.org/wss/2004/01/oasis-200401-wss-wssecurity-secext-1.0.xsd`**.

QName: Enter the following hard-code string: **`UsernameToken`**.

You build the client in essentially the same way, no matter how your authentication is performed on the server. However, when you create a custom authentication class, you can choose to use hashed passwords, as shown here:

```
' Create the proxy.
Dim proxy As New EmployeesServiceWse()

' Add the WS-Security token.
proxy.RequestSoapContext.Security.Tokens.Add(New UsernameToken("dan", "secret",
                         PasswordOption.SendHashed))

' Bind the results.
GridView1.DataSource = proxy.GetEmployees().Tables(0)
GridView1.DataBind()
```

The best part is that you don't need to manually hash or encrypt the user password. Instead, the WSE hashes it automatically based on your instructions and performs the hash comparison on the server side. It even incorporates a random nonce value to prevent replay attacks.

Summary

In this chapter, you learned a variety of advanced SOAP techniques, including how to call web services asynchronously, how to enforce security, and how to use SOAP extensions. The world of web services is sure to continue to evolve, so look for new standards and increasingly powerful capabilities to appear in future versions of the .NET Framework.

PART 7

Client-Side Programming

CHAPTER 34

JavaScript and Ajax

ASP.NET provides a rich server-based programming model. The postback architecture allows you to perform all your work with object-oriented programming languages on the server, which ensures that your code is secure and compatible with all browsers. However, the postback architecture has its weaknesses. Because posting back the page always includes some small but noticeable overhead, it's impossible to react efficiently to mouse movements and key presses. Additionally, certain tasks—such as showing pop-up windows, providing a real-time status message, and communicating between frames—need browser interaction and just aren't possible with server-side programming.

To compensate for these problems, experienced ASP.NET developers sometimes use client-side programming to supplement their server-side web-page code. This client-side script allows you to make more-responsive pages and accomplish some feats that wouldn't otherwise be possible. Often, these considerations occur when creating custom controls that render rich user interfaces (such as pop-up menus or rollover buttons). For the greatest browser compatibility, the client-side script language of choice is JavaScript.

In this chapter, you'll learn some tried-and-true techniques for integrating JavaScript with ASP.NET. You'll even build a few JavaScript-fortified controls and learn how to strengthen your pages with Ajax, a particularly savvy style of JavaScript coding.

JavaScript Essentials

JavaScript is an embedded language. This means that JavaScript code is inserted directly into another document—typically, an HTML web page. The code is downloaded to the client computer and executed by the browser.

You have two ways to embed JavaScript code in a web page:

- You can embed the code directly in an event attribute for an HTML element. This is the most straightforward approach for small amounts of code.
- You can add a <script> tag that contains the JavaScript code. You can choose to run this code automatically when the page loads, or you can create a JavaScript function that will be called in response to a client-side event.

In many cases, you'll use both of these techniques at the same time. For example, you might define a function in a <script> block and then wire this function up to a client-side event using an event attribute. ASP.NET follows this pattern when it performs automatic postbacks. The __doPost-Back() function includes the code needed to trigger a postback and send the event information for every control. It's rendered inside a <script> block. The __doPostBack() function is then connected to different controls using JavaScript event attributes, such as onChange, so that a client-side change causes a postback to the server.

It's important to realize that whether you use <script> blocks, event attributes, or both, you still have two choices about how you create your JavaScript code. Your first option is to embed fixed JavaScript code in the .aspx portion of your page. This is the simplest approach. Your second option is to add JavaScript code dynamically by using the methods of the Page class. This gives you the greatest flexibility, including the ability to tweak the JavaScript code on the fly and decide what you want to render at runtime. For example, you could tailor the JavaScript code to suit different browsers or different property settings. When you create custom controls, the controls render the JavaScript code they need in this way.

The followings sections explore the basic techniques for using JavaScript. You'll learn how to interact with the objects in your web page, handle events, set properties, and move your script into a separate file.

■**Note** You can also use VBScript if your web application exists on a company intranet where Internet Explorer is the standard. However, JavaScript is the only standard supported by a wide range of browsers.

The HTML Document Object Model

As a server-side programmer, you're used to interacting with your web pages as a collection of control objects. As a client-side programmer, you'll work with a similar abstraction. The difference is that each object you work with maps directly to individual HTML tag. This means there aren't any higher-level controls, such as ASP.NET's Calendar and GridView. Instead, almost everything boils down to paragraphs, headings, images, form controls, and tables. For example, if you create a page with an <h1> tag for a heading, two <p> tags for paragraphs, and an <input> tag for a text box, you'll wind up with four controls that you can manipulate individually on the client side. It makes no difference whether you created these tags by writing raw HTML in the .aspx file or whether they were rendered by server controls.

The ability to interact with your web page as a tree of objects is called the HTML DOM (Document Object Model). The combination of JavaScript and the HTML DOM is called DHTML (Dynamic HTML).

■**Note** In other words, DHTML isn't a separate technology. Instead, it's a name that encompasses a specific way to use JavaScript. You'll see the same distinction when you learn about Ajax later in this chapter. Ajax isn't a new technology—it's small set of client-side programming techniques.

As is common in the world of the Web, not all browsers support the same level of JavaScript and the HTML DOM. However, in this chapter, you'll focus on techniques that are known to work on the majority of modern browsers (including Firefox). As usual, if you are creating a web application for a large number of users, you should perform extensive testing.

■**Tip** You can find event compatibility tables on the Internet (see, for example, `www.quirksmode.org/js/events_compinfo.html`). For a comprehensive introduction to DHTML, you can refer to the MSDN website at `http://msdn.microsoft.com/workshop/author/dhtml/dhtml.asp`. You can find a full JavaScript reference at `http://devedge.netscape.com/library/manuals`.

Client-Side Events

JavaScript supports a rich set of client-side events, which are listed in Table 34-1.

Table 34-1. *Common Events of HTML Objects*

Event	Description	Applies To
onChange	Occurs when the user changes value in an input control. In text controls, this event f ires after the user changes focus to another control.	select, text, text area
onClick	Occurs when the user clicks a control.	button, check box, radio, link, area
onMouseOver	Occurs when the user moves the mouse pointer over a control.	link, area
onMouseOut	Occurs when the user moves the mouse pointer away from a control.	link, area
onKeyUp	Occurs when the user presses a key.	text, text area
onKeyDown	Occurs when the user releases a pressed key.	text, text area
onSelect	Occurs when the user selects a portion of text in an input control.	text, text area
onFocus	Occurs when a control receives focus.	select, text, text area
onBlur	Occurs when focus leaves a control.	select, text, text area
onAbort	Occurs when the user cancels an image download.	image
onError	Occurs when an image can't be downloaded (probably because of an incorrect URL).	image
onLoad	Occurs when a new page finishes downloading.	window, location
onUnload	Occurs when a page is unloaded. (This typically occurs after a new URL has been entered or a link has been clicked. It fires just before the new page is downloaded.)	window

■ **Note** If you're coding your pages in XHTML, you must write the JavaScript names in all lowercase, as in onmouseover. We don't use the XHTML convention in this chapter, because it's more difficult to read.

Using the event attributes listed in Table 34-1, you can insert JavaScript code that will be triggered when a specific action occurs. For example, the following web page adds the onMouseOver attribute to two TextBox controls:

```
Public Sub Page_Load(ByVal sender As Object, ByVal e As System.EventArgs)
    TextBox1.Attributes.Add("onMouseOver", _
        "alert('Your mouse is hovering on TextBox1.');")
    TextBox2.Attributes.Add("onMouseOver", _
        "alert('Your mouse is hovering on TextBox2.');")
End Sub
```

When the user moves the mouse over the appropriate text box, the event occurs and the JavaScript alert() function is called, which shows a message box (as shown in Figure 34-1).

Figure 34-1. *Responding to a JavaScript event*

■ **Note** Keep in mind that ASP.NET already uses the onChange event to support the automatic postback feature. If add the onChange attribute and set the AutoPostBack property to true, ASP.NET is intelligent enough to add both your JavaScript and the __doPostBack() function call to the attribute. Your client-side JavaScript code will be executed first, followed by the __doPostBack() function.

Adding JavaScript Attributes Declaratively

This example adds the JavaScript code programmatically, by manipulating the Attributes collection that's provided by every server control. Another option is to add your event attributes declaratively to the control tag, like so:

```
<asp:TextBox id="TextBox1" runat="server"
  onMouseOver="alert('Your mouse is hovering on TextBox1.');" />
```

In this example, ASP.NET is unable to match the onMouseOver attribute to a control property or server-side event, so it simply passes it along to the rendered tag (although Visual Studio IntelliSense will flag this as an error). This technique obviously won't work if the JavaScript event name matches a VB event, like the onClick attribute on a button.

The OnClientClick Property

Usually, you need to insert JavaScript by adding attributes to an HTML tag. However, one exception exists. If you want to handle button clicks with JavaScript code, you can use the OnClientClick property. Here's an example that gets confirmation before a page is posted back:

```
<asp:button id="btnClick" runat="server"
 OnClientClick="return confirm('Post back to the server?');"
 text="Click Me"/>
```

The button click still posts back the page and raises server-side events. The difference is that the OnClientClick client-side logic fires first and *then* triggers the server-side postback.

Tip You can use the OnClientClick attribute to cancel a postback. The basic pattern is to call a JavaScript method. If this method returns false, the postback is canceled.

Script Blocks

It's impractical to place a large amount of JavaScript code in an attribute, particularly if you need to use the same code for several controls. A more common approach is to place a JavaScript function in a <script> block and then call that function using an event attribute.

The <script> tag can appear anywhere in the header or the body of an HTML document, and a single document can have any number of <script> tags in it. However, everything in the document is processed in the order in which it appears in the file, from top to bottom. In other words, if you need to call a function, that function must be defined in a <script> block before the event attribute that calls it.

The <script> tag takes a type attribute that specifies the script language. Browsers will ignore <script> blocks for languages they don't support.

A typical inline script looks like this:

```
<script type="text/javascript">
  <!--
  window.alert('This window displayed through JavaScript.');
  // -->
</script>
```

In this case, the HTML comment markers (<!-- and -->) hide the content from browsers that don't understand script. Additionally, the closing HTML comment marker (-->) is preceded by a JavaScript comment (//). This is because extremely old versions of Netscape will throw a JavaScript parsing exception when encountering the closing HTML comment marker. Modern browsers don't suffer from these problems, and most browsers now recognize the <script> tag (even if they don't support JavaScript).

In this example, the script code is processed as soon as the browser encounters it while rendering the page. If you want your code to occur later, when a specific event occurs, it makes more sense to wrap it inside a function in the script block, like so:

```
<script type="text/javascript">
  function ShowAlert()
  {
      window.alert('This window displayed through JavaScript.');
  }
</script>
```

Now you can hook it up to one or more HTML elements using an event attribute:

```
<asp:TextBox ID="TextBox1" runat="server" onMouseOver="ShowAlert();" />
```

A script block can contain any number of functions. You can also declare page-level variables that you can access in any function:

```
<script type="text/javascript">
  var counter = 0;
  ...
</script>
```

■ **Note** Although JavaScript code has a superficial similarity to C#, it's a much looser language. When declaring variables, you don't need to specify their data types. Similarly, when defining a function, you don't indicate its return type.

If you have too much JavaScript to fit neatly in a page or if you need to reuse the same set of functions in more than one page, it makes sense to move your code to another file. Once you make the transition, you can create a <script> block that points to your external file. The trick is to set the src attribute to point to the file, as shown here:

```
<script type="text/javascript" src="ExternalJavaScript.js">
</script>
```

This technique is often used with complex JavaScript routines. You can also embed a JavaScript resource in a DLL assembly when you build a custom control using the WebResource attribute (as discussed in Chapter 28).

■ **Note** Placing JavaScript in a separate file or even embedding it in an assembly doesn't prevent users from retrieving it and examining it (and even modifying their local copy of the web page to use a tampered version of the script file). Therefore, you should never include any secret algorithms or sensitive information in your JavaScript code. You should also make sure you repeat any JavaScript validation steps on the server, because the user can circumvent client-side code.

Manipulating HTML Elements

Reacting to events is only half the story. Most JavaScript-enabled pages also need the ability to change the content in the page. For example, you might want to refresh a label with up-to-date text or inject entirely new content somewhere on a page. The HTML DOM makes this easy—all you need to do is find the element you want and manipulate its innerHTML property..

■ **Note** The innerHTML property represents the content between the start and end tag of an HTML element. Some web pages use the innerText property instead, which automatically escapes HTML tags (for example, it converts <b> to <b>). However, innerText is discouraged because it isn't supported on Mozilla-based browsers such as Firefox.

Unlike in your server-side code, JavaScript doesn't provide member variables that give you access to the HTML elements on your page. Instead, you need to look up the element you need using the document.GetElementById() method. Here's an example:

```
var paragraph = document.getElementById("textParagraph1");
```

This task is exceedingly common in JavaScript code. The only consideration is that you need to make sure the elements you want to manipulate have unique identifiers (as set in the id attribute).

Once you've retrieved the object that represents the HTML tag you want to change, you read and set its properties. All HTML objects have a wide range of basic properties, as well as a number of tag-specific properties. Table 34-2 lists just a few that you may want to manipulate.

Table 34-2. *Common Properties of HTML Objects*

Event	Description
innerHTML	The HTML content between the start and end tag. May include other elements.
style	Returns a style object that exposes all the CSS style properties for your element. For example, you could use myObject.style.fontSize to change the font size of an element. You can use the style object to set colors, borders, fonts, and even positioning.
value	In HTML form controls, the value attribute indicates the current state of the control. For example, in a check box it indicates whether the check box is checked, in a text box it indicates the text inside the box, and so on.
tagName	Provides the name of the HTML tag for this object (without the angle brackets).
parentElement	The HTML object for the tag that contains this tag. For example, if the current element is a <b> tag in a paragraph, this gets the object for the <p> tag. You can use this property (and other related properties) to move from one element to another.

DEBUGGING JAVASCRIPT

When an error occurs on the client side, you need a whole new approach to diagnose what went wrong. Depending on the browser, you may have some rudimentary script-debugging features. For example, Firefox includes a JavaScript console. Internet Explorer doesn't. Instead, when a script fails on a page, you'll see an error icon in the bottom-right corner of the status bar. You can double-click this error icon to see all the script errors that occurred while processing the page. For a better debugging experience, you may want to use a browser plug-in that's designed specifically for script debugging. One good choice is the ASP.NET Development Helper, an add-in that's created by a member of the ASP.NET team (and was first described in Chapter 2).

Visual Studio 2005 also provides its own little-known but immensely helpful JavaScript debugging service. To try it, choose Tools ➤ Internet Options in Internet Explorer, and select the Advanced tab to see a list of settings. Under the Browsing category, clear the Disable Script Debugging option, which is set by default. Now, when you launch a page from Visual Studio and an error occurs in your script code, Visual Studio will switch into break mode and highlight the offending line. You can then check values by hovering over variables and single-stepping through your script code, just like you can with server-side C# code.

If you want to break into the Visual Studio debugger before an error occurs, simply add this line to your script code wherever you want to pause execution:

```
debugger;
```

Basic JavaScript Examples

Now that you've learned the key points of JavaScript, it's easy to enhance your pages with a dash of client-side code. In the following sections, you'll use JavaScript to put a pretty face on pages and pictures that take a long time to download.

Creating a JavaScript Page Processor

How many times have you clicked a web page just to watch the Internet Explorer globe spin for what seems like an eternity? Did your Internet connection go down? Was there any error connecting to a back-end system? Or is the system just that slow? These issues often complicate new web-based solutions, particularly if you're replacing a more responsive rich client application (such as a Windows application). In this situation, the easiest way to reassure your application users is to provide them with progress messages that let them know the system is currently working on their request.

One common way to give a status message is to use JavaScript to create a standard page processor. When the user navigates to a page that takes a long time to process, the page processor appears immediately and shows a standard message (perhaps with scrolling text). At the same time, the requested page is downloaded in the background. Once the results are available, the page processor message is replaced by the requested page.

You can't solve the processing delay problem by adding JavaScript code to the target page, because this code won't be processed until the page has finished processing and the rendered HTML is returned to the user. However, you *can* create a generic page processor that handles requests for any time-consuming page in your site.

To create a page processor, you need to react to the onLoad and onUnload events. Here's a page that defines a table with the message text "Loading Page - Please Wait." The <body> element is wired up to two functions, which aren't shown here.

```
<html>
  <head>
    <title>LoadPage</title>
    <script type="text/javascript" >
      <!-- JavaScript functions go here. -->
    </script>
  </head>

  <body onLoad="javascript:BeginPageLoad();"
        onUnload="javascript:EndPageLoad();">
    <form id="frmPageLoader"
          method="post" runat="server">
      <table border="0" cellpadding="0"
             cellspacing="0"
       width="99%" height="99%" align="center">
        <tr>
          <td align="center" vAlign="center">
            <span id="MessageText">
              Loading Page - Please Wait
            </span>
            <span id="ProgressMeter"></span>
          </td>
        </tr>
      </table>
    </form>
  </body>

</html>
```

This page is named PageProcessor.aspx. To use the page processor, you request this page and pass the desired page as a query string argument. For example, if you want to load TimeConsumingPage.aspx in the background, you would use this URL:

```
PageProcessor.aspx?Page=TimeConsumingPage.aspx
```

The page processor needs very little server-side code. In fact, all it does is retrieve the originally requested page from the query string and store it in a protected page class variable. You can then access this variable by data binding expressions in the .aspx file. Here's the complete page code:

```
Partial Class PageProcessor
    Inherits System.Web.UI.Page

    Protected PageToLoad As String

    Protected Sub Page_Load(
      ByVal sender As Object,
      ByVal e As System.EventArgs)

        PageToLoad = Request.QueryString("Page1")
    End Sub
End Class
```

The page is then rendered and sent to the client. The rest of the work is performed with client-side JavaScript. When the page processor first loads, the onLoad event fires, which calls the client-side BeginPageLoad() function. The BeginPageLoad() function keeps the current window open and begins retrieving the page that the user requested. To accomplish this, it uses the window.setInterval() method, which sets a timer that calls the custom UpdateProgressMeter() function periodically.

Here's the code for the BeginPageLoad() JavaScript function:

```
var iLoopCounter = 1;
var iMaxLoop = 6;
var iIntervalId;

function BeginPageLoad()
{
    // Redirect the browser to
    // another page while keeping focus.
    location.href = "<%=PageToLoad %>";

    // Update progress meter every 1/2 second.
    iIntervalId = window.setInterval
      ("iLoopCounter=UpdateProgressMeter
        (iLoopCounter,iMaxLoop);", 500);
}
```

The first code statement points the page to its new URL. Notice that the page you want to download isn't hard-coded in the JavaScript code. Instead, it's set with the data binding expression <%=PageToLoad %>. When the page is rendered on the server, ASP.NET automatically inserts the value of the PageToLoad variable in its place.

The last code statement starts a timer using the window.serInterval() method. Every 500 milliseconds, this timer fires and executes the line of code that's specified. This line of code calls another JavaScript function, which is named UpdateProgressMeter(), and keeps track of the current loop counter.

The UpdateProgressMeter() method simply changes the status message periodically to make it look more like an animated progress meter. The status message cycles repeatedly from 0 to 5 periods. Here's the JavaScript code that makes it work:

```
function UpdateProgressMeter(iCurrentLoopCounter, iMaximumLoops)
{
    // Find the object for the <span>
    // element with the progress text.
```

```
    var progressMeter =
      document.getElementById("ProgressMeter")
    iCurrentLoopCounter += 1;
    if(iCurrentLoopCounter <= iMaximumLoops)
    {
        progressMeter.innerText += ".";
        return iCurrentLoopCounter;
    }
    else
    {
        // Reset the progress meter.
        ProgressMeter.innerText = "";
        return 1;
    }
}
```

Finally, when the page is fully loaded, the client-side onUnload event fires. In this example, the onUnload event is hooked up to a function named EndPageLoad().. This function clears the progress message and sets a temporary transfer message that disappears as soon as the new page is rendered in the browser. Here's the code:

```
function EndPageLoad()
{
    window.clearInterval(iIntervalId);

    var progressMeter =
      document.getElementById("ProgressMeter")
    progressMeter.innerText =
      "Page Loaded - Now Transferring";
}
```

No postbacks are made through the whole process. The end result is a progress message (see Figure 34-2) that remains until the target page is fully processed and loaded.

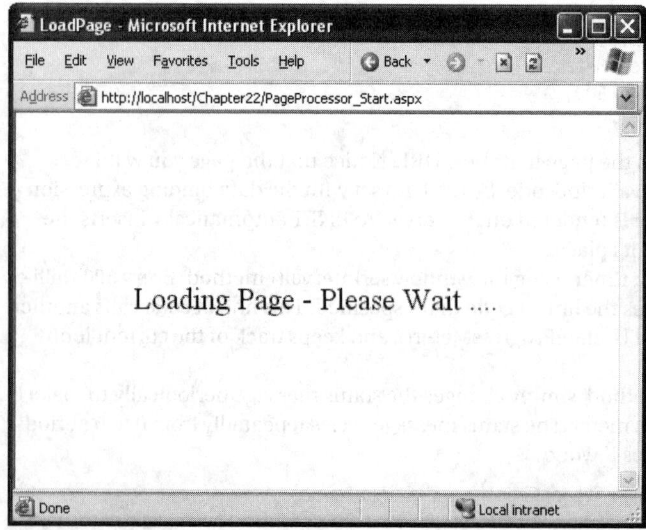

Figure 34-2. *An automated progress meter*

To test the page processor, you simply need to use a target page that takes a long time to execute on the server (because of the work performed by the code) or to be downloaded in the client (because of the size of the page). You can simulate a slow page by placing the following time delay code in the target page, like this:

```
Protected Sub Page_Load(

  ByVal sender As Object,
        ByVal e As System.EventArgs)
    ' Simulate a slow page
       ' loading (wait ten seconds).
    System.Threading.Thread.Sleep(10000)
End Sub
```

Now when you request this page through the page processor, you'll have ten seconds to study the progress message.

■ **Note** To try this with the sample code included for this chapter, request the PageProcessor_Start.aspx , which includes a button that takes you to the time-consuming PageProcessor_Target.aspx using the page processor.

As you can see, with just a small amount of client-side JavaScript code, you can keep the user informed that a page is processing. By keeping users informed, the level of perceived performance increases.

Using JavaScript to Download Images Asynchronously

The previous example demonstrated how JavaScript can help you create a more responsive interface. This advantage isn't limited to page processors. You can also use JavaScript to download time-consuming portions of a page in the background. Often, this requires a little more work, but it can provide a much better user experience.

For example, consider a case where you're displaying a list of records in a GridView. One of the fields displays a small image. This technique, which was demonstrated in Chapter 10, requires a dedicated page to retrieve the image, and, depending on your design, it may require a separate trip to the file system or database for each record. In many cases, you can optimize this design (for example, by preloading images in the cache before you bind the grid), but this isn't possible if the images are retrieved from a third-party source. This is the case in the next example, which displays a list of books and retrieves the associated images from the Amazon website.

Rendering the full table can take a significant amount of time, especially if it has a large number of records. You can deal with this situation more effectively by using placeholder images that appear immediately. The actual images can be retrieved in the background and displayed once they're available. The time required to display the complete grid with all its pictures won't change, but the user will be able to start reading and scrolling through the data before the images have been downloaded, which makes the slowdown easier to bear.

The first step in this example is to create the page that displays the GridView. For the purposes of this example, the code fills a DataSet with a static list of books from an XML file.

```
Protected Sub Page_Load(
  ByVal sender As Object,
  ByVal e As System.EventArgs)
    If Not Page.IsPostBack Then
        Dim ds As New DataSet
        ds.ReadXml(Server.MapPath("Books.xml"))
        GridView1.DataSource = ds.Tables("Book")
```

```
        GridView1.DataBind()
    End If
End Sub
```

Here's the content of the XML file:

```
<?xml version="1.0" encoding="utf-8" ?>
<Books>
    <Book Title="Expert C# Business Objects" isbn="1590593448"
     Publisher="Apress"></Book>
    <Book Title="C# and the .NET Platform" isbn="1590590554"
     Publisher="Apress"></Book>
    <Book Title="Beginning XSLT" isbn="1590592603"
     Publisher="Apress"></Book>
    <Book Title="SQL Server Security Distilled" isbn="1590592190"
     Publisher="Apress"></Book>
</Books>
```

As you can see, the XML data doesn't include any picture information. Instead, these details need to be retrieved from the Amazon website. The GridView binds directly to the columns that are available (Title, isbn, and Publisher) and then uses another page (named GetBookImage.aspx) to find the corresponding image for this ISBN.

Here's the GridView control tag without the style information:

```
<asp:GridView id="GridView1" runat="server" AutoGenerateColumns="False">
  <Columns>
    <asp:BoundField DataField="Title" HeaderText="Title"/>
    <asp:BoundField DataField="isbn" HeaderText="ISBN"/>
    <asp:BoundField DataField="Publisher" HeaderText="Publisher"/>
    <asp:TemplateField>
      <HeaderTemplate>
        Book Cover
      </HeaderTemplate>
      <ItemTemplate>
        <img src="UnknownBook.gif"
         onError="this.src='Unknownbook.gif';"
         onLoad="GetBookImage(this,
           '<%# DataBinder.Eval(Container.DataItem,
           "isbn") %>');"
      </ItemTemplate>
    </asp:TemplateField>
  </Columns>
</asp:GridView>
```

The innovative part is the last column, which contains an <img> tag. Rather than pointing this tag directly to GetBookImage.aspx, the src attribute is set to a local image file (UnknownBook.gif), which can be quickly downloaded and displayed. Then the onLoad event (which occurs as soon as the UnknownBook.gif image is first displayed) begins downloading real image in the background. When the real image is retrieved, it's displayed, unless an error occurs during the download process. The onError event is handled in order to ensure that if an error occurs, the UnknownBook.gif image remains (rather than the red X error icon).

The onLoad event completes its work with the help of a custom JavaScript function named GetBookImage(). When the page calls GetBookImage(), it passes a reference to the current image control (the one that needs the new picture) and the ISBN for the book, which is extracted through a data-binding expression. The GetBookImage() function calls another page, named GetBook-Image.aspx, to get the picture for the book. It indicates the picture it wants by passing the ISBN as a query string argument.

```
<script language="javascript" type="text/javascript">
  function GetBookImage(img, url)
  {
      // Detach the event handler (the code makes just one attempt
      // to get the picture).
      img.onLoad = null;

      // Try to get the picture from the GetBookImage.aspx page.
      img.src = 'GetBookImage.aspx?isbn=' + url;
  }
</script>
```

The GetBookImage page performs the time-consuming task of retrieving the image you want, which might involve contacting a web service or connecting to a database. In this case, the GetBookImage page simply hands the work off to a dedicated class named FindBook that does the work. Once the URL is retrieved, it redirects the page:

```
Protected Sub Page_Load(
  ByVal sender As Object,
  ByVal e As System.EventArgs)
    Dim myFindBook As New FindBook
    Dim imageUrl As String =
      myFindBook.GetImageUrl(Request.QueryString("isbn"))
    Response.Redirect(imageUrl)
End Sub
```

The FindBook class is more complex. It uses screen scraping to find the <img> tag for the picture on the Amazon website. Unfortunately, Amazon's image thumbnails don't have a clear naming convention that would allow you to retrieve the URL directly. However, based on the ISBN you can find the book detail page, and you can look through the HTML of the book detail page to find the image URL. That's the task the FindBook class performs.

Two methods are at work in the FindBook class. The GetWebPageAsString() method requests a URL, retrieves the HTML content, and converts it to a string, as shown here:

```
Public Function GetWebPageAsString(ByVal url As String) As String
    ' Create the request
    Dim requestHtml As WebRequest = WebRequest.Create(url)
    ' Get the response
    Dim responseHtml As WebResponse = requestHtml.GetResponse()
    ' Read the Response Stream
    Dim r As New StreamReader(responseHtml.GetResponseStream())
    Dim htmlContent As String = r.ReadToEnd()
    r.Close()
    Return htmlContent
End Function
```

The GetImageUrl() method uses GetWebPageAsString() and a little regular expression wizardry. Amazon image URLs take the form shown here:

```
http://images.amazon.com/images/P/ + [ISBN] + [some character sequence]
```

Using the regular expression, the code matches the full URL (with the ending character sequence) and returns it. Here's the complete code:

```
Public Function GetImageUrl(ByVal isbn As String) As String
    Try
      ' Find the pointer to the book cover image
      ' Amazon.com has the most cover images
      ' so fo there to look for it
```

```
        ' start with the book details page
        isbn = isbn.Replace("-", "")
        Dim bookUrl As String =
          "http://www.amazon.com/exec/obidos/ASIN/" + isbn
        ' Now retrieve the HTML content of the book details page
        Dim bookHtml As String = GetWebPageAsString(bookUrl)
        ' Search the page for an image tag with the requested ISBN
        Dim imgTagPattern As String
        imgTagPattern =
           "<img src=\"(http://images.amazon.com/images/P/" + _
           isbn + "[^\"]+)\"";
          Dim imgTagMatch As Match =
            Regex.Match(bookHtml, imgTagPattern)
          Return imgTagMatch.Groups(1).Value
      Catch ex As Exception
          Return ""
      End Try

  End Function
```

■Note Using the dedicated Amazon web service would obviously be a more flexible and robust approach, although it wouldn't change this example, which demonstrates the performance enhancements of a little JavaScript. Web services are dealt with in Part 6, and you can get information about Amazon's offerings at `http://www.amazon.com/gp/aws/landing.html`.

The end result is a page that initially loads with default images, as shown in Figure 34-3.

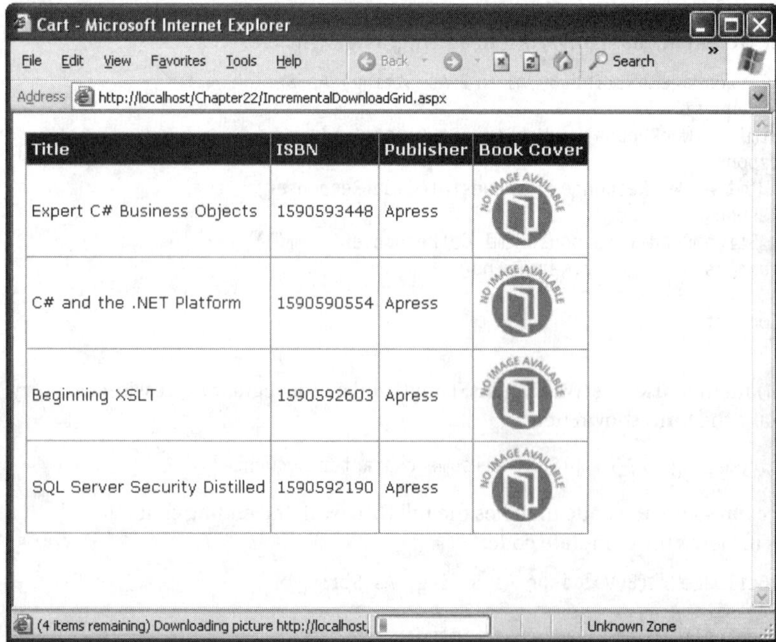

Figure 34-3. *The initial view of the page*

After a short delay, the images will begin to appear, as shown in Figure 34-4.

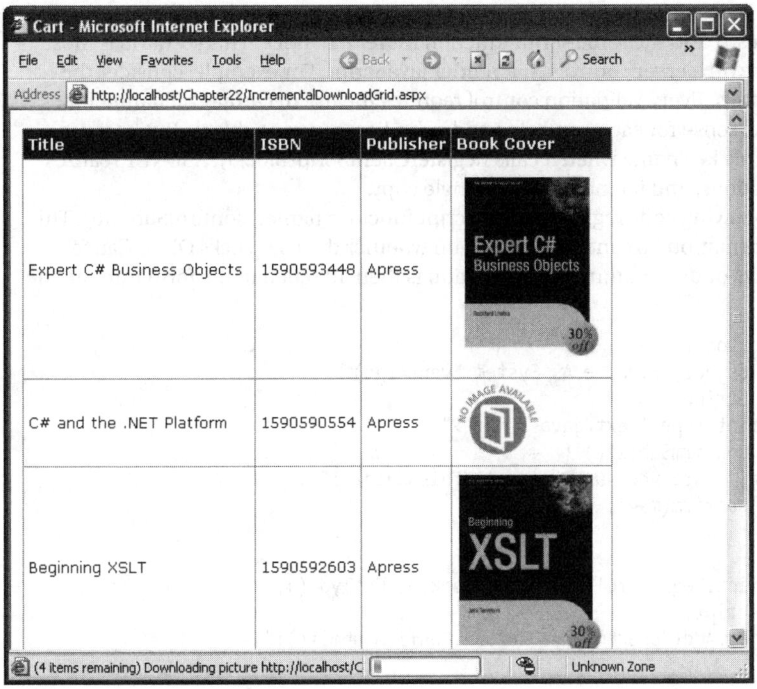

Figure 34-4. *The page with image thumbnails*

Once loaded, the real book images will load in the background, but the user can begin using the page immediately.

Rendering Script Blocks

So far the examples you've seen have used static <script> blocks that are inserted directly in the .aspx portion of your page. However, it's often more flexible to render the script using the Page.ClientScript property, which exposes a ClientScriptManager object that provides several useful methods for managing script blocks. Two of the most useful are as follows:

RegisterClientScriptBlock(): Writes a script block at the beginning of the web form, right after the <form runat="server"> tag.

RegisterStartupScript(): Writes a script block at the beginning of the web form, right before the closing </form> tag.

These two methods perform the same task—they take a string input with the <script> block and add it to the rendered HTML. RegisterClientScriptBlock() is designed for functions that are called in response to JavaScript events. You can place these <script> blocks anywhere in the HTML document. Placing them at the beginning of the web form is just a matter of convention and makes them easy to find. The RegisterStartupScript() is meant to add JavaScript code that will be executed immediately when the page loads. This code might manipulate other controls on the page, so to be safe you should place it at the end of the web form. Otherwise, it might try to access elements that haven't been created yet.

When you use RegisterClientScriptBlock() and RegisterStartupScript(), you also specify a key name for the script block. For example, if your function opens a pop-up window, you might use the key name ShowPopUp. The actual key name isn't important as long as it's unique. The purpose is to ensure that ASP.NET doesn't add the same script function more than once. This scenario is most important when dealing with server controls that render JavaScript. For example, consider the ASP.NET validation controls. Every validation control requires the use of certain validation functions, but it doesn't make sense for each control to add a duplicate <script> block. But because each control uses the same key name when it calls RegisterClientScriptBlock(), ASP.NET realizes they are duplicate definitions, and it renders only a single copy.

For example, the following code registers a JavaScript function named confirmSubmit(). This function displays a confirmation box and, depending on whether the user clicks OK or Cancel, either posts back the page or does nothing. This function is then attached to the form through the onSubmit attribute.

```
Protected Sub Page_Load(
  ByVal sender As Object, ByVal e As System.EventArgs)
    Dim script As String
    script = "<script type='text/javascript'>" + _
      "  function ConfirmSubmit() {" + _
      "    var msg = 'Are you sure you want this data?';" + _
      "    return confirm(msg); " + _
      "   }" + _
      "</script>"
    Page.ClientScript.RegisterClientScriptBlock(Me.GetType(),
      "Confirm", script)
    form1.Attributes.Add("onSubmit", "return ConfirmSubmit();")

End Sub
```

Note To make it easier to define a JavaScript function over multiple lines, you can precede the string with the @ symbol. That way, all the characters are treated as string literals, and you can span multiple lines.

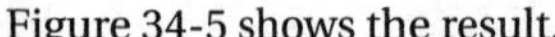

Figure 34-5 shows the result.

Figure 34-5. *Using a JavaScript confirmation message*

Later in this chapter, you'll see a control that uses the RegisterStartupScript() to show a pop-up window.

■ **Note** In previous versions of ASP.NET, developers often used startup scripts to set the control that should get the focus when the page first displays. However, ASP.NET 2.0 encapsulates this functionality with the Control.Focus() method, so you don't have to code your own solution any longer.

Script Injection Attacks

Often, developers aren't aware of the security vulnerabilities they introduce in a page. That's because many common dangers—including script injection and SQL injection—are surprisingly easy to stumble into. To minimize these risks, technology vendors such as Microsoft strive to find ways to integrate safety checks into the programming framework itself, thereby insulating application programmers.

One attack to which web pages are commonly vulnerable is a *script injection* attack. A script injection attack occurs when malicious tags or script code are submitted by a user (usually through a simple control such as a TextBox control) and then rendered into an HTML page later. Although this rendering process is intended to *display* the user-supplied data, it actually *executes* the script. A script injection attack can have any of a number of different effects from trivial to significant. If the user-supplied data is stored in a database and inserted later into pages used by other people, the attack may affect the operation of the website for all users.

The basic technique for a script injection attack is for the client to submit content with embedded scripting tags. These scripting tags can include <script>, <object>, <applet>, and <embed>. Although the application can specifically check for these tags and use HTML encoding to replace the tags with harmless HTML entities, that basic validation often isn't performed.

Request Validation

Script injection attacks are a concern of all web developers, whether they are using ASP.NET, ASP, or other web development technologies. ASP.NET includes a feature designed to automatically combat script injection attacks, called *request validation*. Request validation checks the posted form input and raises an error if any potentially malicious tags (such as <script>) are found. In fact, request validation disallows any nonnumeric tags, including HTML tags (such as <b> and <img>), and tags that don't correspond to anything (such as <abcd>).

To test the script validation features, you can create a simple web page like the one shown in Figure 34-6. This simple example contains a text box and a button.

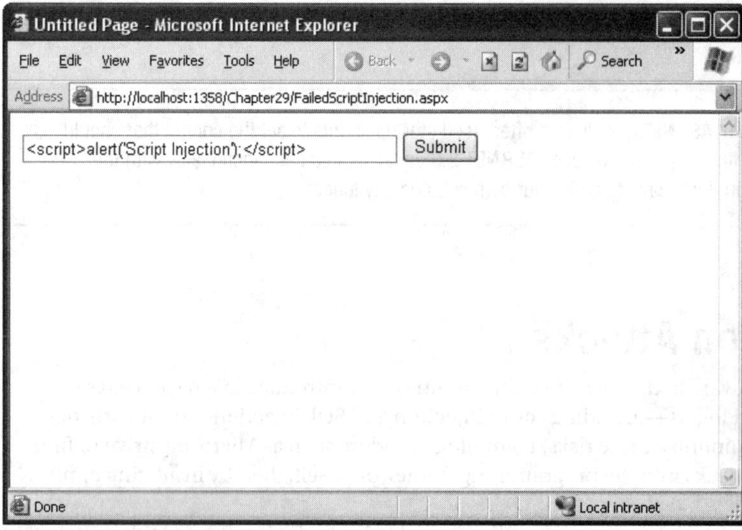

Figure 34-6. *Testing a script injection attack*

Now, try to enter a block of content with a script tag and then click the button. ASP.NET will detect the potentially dangerous value and generate an error. If you're running the code locally, you'll see the rich error page with detailed information, as shown in Figure 34-7. (If you're requesting the page remotely, you'll see only a generic error page.)

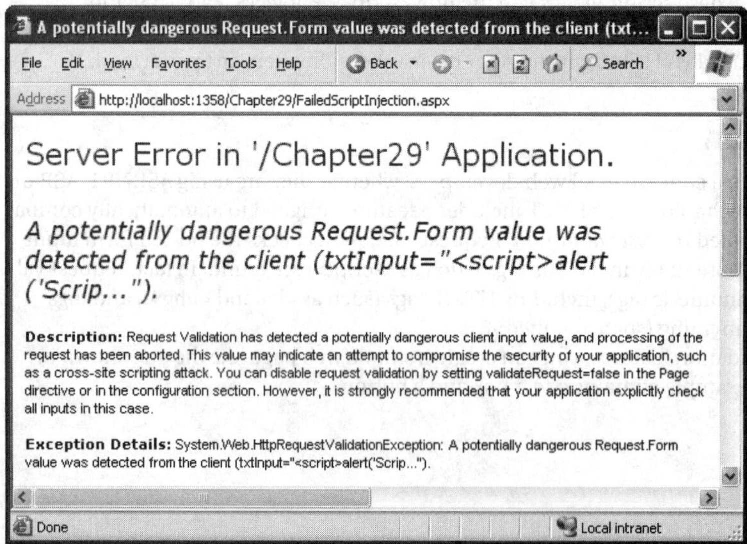

Figure 34-7. *A failed script injection attack*

Disabling Request Validation

Of course, in some situations, the request validation rules are just too restrictive. For example, you might have an application where users have a genuine need to specify HTML tags (for example, when they enter an auction listing or a for-sale advertisement) or a block of XML data. In these situations, you need to specifically disable script validation using the ValidateRequest Page directive, as shown here:

```
<%@ Page ValidateRequest="false" ... %>
```

You can also disable request validation for an entire web application by modifying the web.config file. Add or set the validateRequest attribute of the <pages> element, as shown here:

```
<configuration>
  <system.web>
    <!-- Other settings omitted. -->
    <pages validateRequest="false" />
  </system.web>
</configuration>
```

Now, consider what happens if you attempt to display the user-supplied value in a label with this code:

```
Protected Sub cmdSubmit_Click(ByVal sender As Object,
  ByVal e As System.EventArgs)
  Handles cmdSubmit.Click
    lblInfo.Text = "You entered: " + txtInput.Text
End Sub
```

If a malicious user enters the text <script>alert('Script Injection');</script>, the returned web page will execute the script, as shown in Figure 34-8.

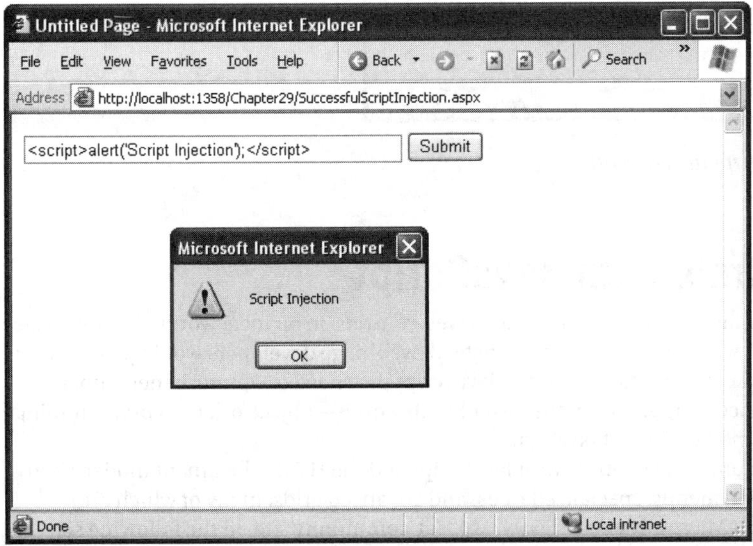

Figure 34-8. *A successful script injection attack*

Keep in mind that the script in a script injection attack is always executed on the client end. However, this doesn't mean it's limited to a single user. In many situations, user-supplied data is stored in a location such as a database and can be viewed by other users. For example, if a user supplies a script block for a business name when adding a business to a registry, another user who requests a full list of all businesses in the registry will be affected.

To prevent a script injection attack from happening when request validation is turned off, you need to explicitly encode the content before you display it using the Server object, as described earlier in this chapter.

Here's a rewritten version of the Button.Click event handler that isn't susceptible to script injection attacks:

```
Protected Sub cmdSubmit_Click(ByVal sender As Object,
  ByVal e As System.EventArgs)
  Handles cmdSubmit.Click
    lblInfo.Text = "You entered: " +
      Server.HtmlEncode(txtInput.Text)
End Sub
```

Figure 34-9 shows the result of an attempted script injection attack on this page.

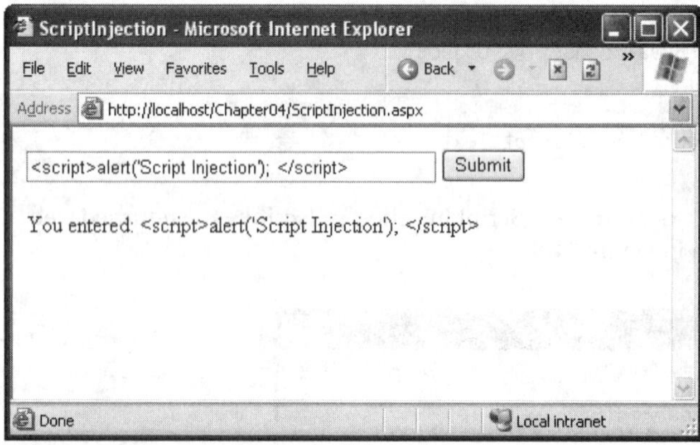

Figure 34-9. *A disarmed script injection attack*

Custom Controls with JavaScript

JavaScript plays an important role in many advanced web controls. In an ideal world, the web-page developer never needs to worry about JavaScript. Instead, web-page developers would program with neat object-oriented controls that render the JavaScript they need to optimize their appearance and their performance. This gives you the best of both worlds—object-oriented programming on the server and the client-side frills of JavaScript.

You can create any number of controls with JavaScript and the HTML document model. Common examples include rich menus, specialized trees, and advanced grids, many of which are available (some for free) at Microsoft's `http://www.asp.net` community site. In the following sections, you'll consider two custom controls that use JavaScript—a pop-up window generator and a rollover button.

Pop-Up Windows

For most people, pop-up windows are one of the Web's most annoying characteristics. Usually, they deliver advertisements, but sometimes they serve the more valid purpose of providing helpful information or inviting the user to participate in a survey or promotional offer. A related variant is the pop-under window, which displays the new window underneath the current window. This way, the advertisement doesn't distract the user until the original browser window is closed.

It's fairly easy to show a pop-up window by using the window.open() function in a JavaScript block. Here's an example:

```
<script type="text/javascript">
  window.open('http://www.apress.com', 'myWindow',
      toolbar=0, height=500,
      width=800, resizable=1, scrollbars=1');
  window.focus();
</script>
```

The window.open() function accepts several parameters. They include the link for the new page and the frame name of the window (which is important if you want to load a new document into that frame later, through another link). The third parameter is a comma-separated string of attributes that configure the style and size of the pop-up window. These attributes can include any of the following:

- height and width, which are set to pixel values
- toolbar and menuBar, which can be set to 1 or 0 (or yes or no) depending on whether you want to display these elements
- resizable, which can be set to 1 or 0 depending on whether you want a fixed or resizable window border
- scrollbars, which can be set to 1 or 0 depending on whether you want to show scrollbars in the pop-up window

As with any other JavaScript code, you can add a <script> block that uses the window.open() function, or you can use the window.open() function directly with a JavaScript event attribute.

You may want to use the same pop-up functionality for several pages and tailor the pop-up URL based on user-specific information. For example, you might want to check whether the user has already seen an advertisement before showing it, or you might want to pass the user name to the new window as a query string argument so that it can be incorporated in the pop-up message. In these scenarios, you need some level of programmatic control over the pop-up, so it makes sense to create a component that wraps all these details. The next example develops a PopUp control to fill this role.

Here's the definition for the PopUp control:

```
Public Class PopUp
    Inherits Control
End Class
```

By deriving this component from Control, you gain the ability to add your pop-up to the Toolbox and drop it on a web form at design time.

To ensure that the PopUp control is as reusable as possible, it provides properties such as Scrollbars, Height, Width, Resizable, Pop, and Url, which allow you to configure the JavaScript that it generates. Here's the code for the PopUp properties:

```
Public Property PopUnder As Boolean
        Get
            Return CType(ViewState("PopUnder"),Boolean)
        End Get
        Set
            ViewState("PopUnder") = value
        End Set
    End Property

    Public Property Url As String
        Get
            Return CType(ViewState("Url"),String)
        End Get
        Set
            ViewState("Url") = value
        End Set
    End Property

    Public Property WindowHeight As Integer
        Get
            Return CType(ViewState("WindowHeight"),Integer)
        End Get
        Set
            If (value < 1) Then
                Throw New ArgumentException("WindowHeight must be
                    greater than 0")
            End If
            ViewState("WindowHeight") = value
        End Set
    End Property

    Public Property WindowWidth As Integer
        Get
            Return CType(ViewState("WindowWidth"),Integer)
        End Get
        Set
            If (value < 1) Then
                Throw New ArgumentException("WindowWidth must be
                    greater than 0")
            End If
            ViewState("WindowWidth") = value
        End Set
    End Property

    Public Property Resizable As Boolean
        Get
            Return CType(ViewState("Resizable"),Boolean)
        End Get
        Set
            ViewState("Resizable") = value
        End Set
    End Property
```

```
Public Property Scrollbars As Boolean
    Get
        Return CType(ViewState("Scrollbars"),Boolean)
    End Get
    Set
        ViewState("Scrollbars") = value
    End Set
End Property
```

Now that the control has defined these properties, it's time to put them to work in the Render() method, which writes the JavaScript code to the page. The first step is to make sure the browser supports JavaScript. You can examine the Page.Request.Browser.JavaScript property, which returns true or false, but this approach is considered obsolete (because it doesn't give you the flexibility to distinguish between different levels of JavaScript and HTML DOM support). The recommended solution is to check that the Page.Request.Browser.EcmaScriptVersion is greater than or equal to 1, which implies JavaScript support.

If JavaScript is supported, the code uses a StringBuilder to build the script block. This code is fairly straightforward—the only unusual detail is that the Boolean Scrollbars and Resizable values need to be converted to integers and *then* to strings. That's because the required syntax is scrollbars=1 rather than scrollbars=true (which is the text you end up with if you convert a Boolean value directly to a string).

Here's the complete rendering code:

```
Protected Overrides Sub Render(ByVal writer As HtmlTextWriter)
        If (Page.Request.Browser.EcmaScriptVersion.Major >= 1) Then
            Dim javaScriptString As StringBuilder = New StringBuilder
            javaScriptString.Append("<script type='text/javascript'>")
            javaScriptString.Append("" & vbLf & "<!-- ")
            javaScriptString.Append("" & vbLf & "window.open('")
            javaScriptString.Append((Url + ("', '" + ID)))
            javaScriptString.Append("','toolbar=0,")
            javaScriptString.Append(("height=" _
                + (WindowHeight + ",")))
            javaScriptString.Append(("width=" _
                + (WindowWidth + ",")))
            javaScriptString.Append(("resizable=" _
                + (Convert.ToInt16(Resizable).ToString + ",")))
            javaScriptString.Append(("scrollbars="
                + Convert.ToInt16(Scrollbars).ToString))
            javaScriptString.Append("');" & vbLf)
            If PopUnder Then
                javaScriptString.Append("window.focus();")
            End If
            javaScriptString.Append("" & vbLf & "-->" & vbLf)
            javaScriptString.Append("</script>" & vbLf)
            writer.Write(javaScriptString.ToString)
        Else
            writer.Write("<!-- This browser does not support
                JavaScript -->")
        End If
    End Sub
```

Figure 34-10 shows the PopUp control in action.

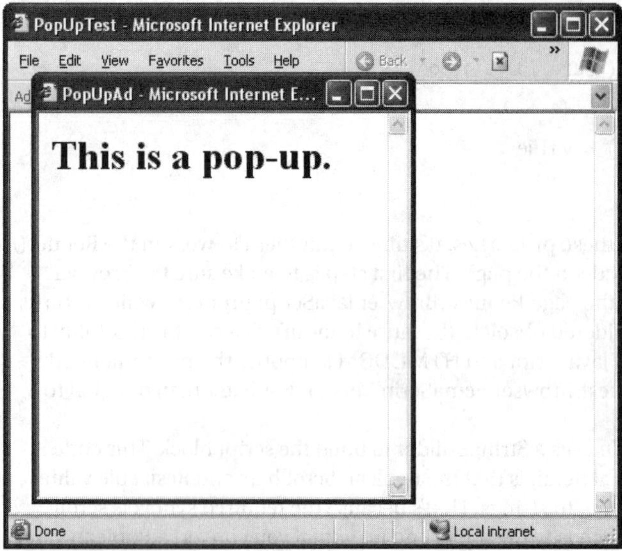

Figure 34-10. *Showing a pop-up window*

■ **Tip** Usually, custom controls register JavaScript blocks in the OnPreRender() method, rather than writing it directly in the Render() method. However, the PopUp control bypasses this approach and takes direct control of writing the script block. That's because you don't want the usual behavior, which is to create one script block regardless of how many PopUp controls you place on the page. Instead, if you add more than one PopUp control, you want the page to include a separate script block for each control. This gives you the ability to create pages that display multiple pop-up windows.

If you want to enhance the PopUp component, you can add more properties. For example, you could add properties that allow you to specify the position where the window will be displayed. Some websites use advertisements that don't appear for several seconds. You could use this technique with this component by adding a JavaScript timer (and wrapping it with a control property that allows you to specify the number of seconds to wait). Once again, the basic idea is to give the page developer a neat object to program with and the ability to use the rendering methods to generate the required JavaScript in the page.

Rollover Buttons

Rollover buttons are another useful JavaScript trick that has no equivalent in the ASP.NET world. A rollover button displays one image when it first appears and another image when the mouse hovers over it (and sometimes a third image when the image is clicked).

To provide the rollover effect, a rollover button usually consists of an <img> tag that handles the onClick, onMouseOver, and onMouseOut JavaScript events. These events will call a function that swaps images for the current button, like this:

```
<script language='JavaScript'>
  function swapImg(id, url)
  {
    var elm = document.getElementById(id);
    elm.src = url;
  }
</script>
```

A configured <img> tag would then look like this:

```
<img src="buttonOriginal.jpg"
 onMouseOver="swapImg('RollOverButton1', 'buttonMouseOver.jpg');"
 onMouseOut="swapImg('RollOverButton1', 'buttonOriginal.jpg');" />
```

Rollover buttons are a mainstay on the Web, and it's fairly easy to fill the gap in ASP.NET with a custom control. The easiest way to create this control is to derive from the WebControl class and use <img> as the base tag. You also need to implement the IPostBackEventHandler to allow the button to trigger a server-side event when clicked.

Here's the declaration for the RollOverButton and its constructor:

```
Imports Microsoft.VisualBasic

Public Class RollOverButton
    Inherits WebControl
    Implements IPostBackEventHandler

    Public Sub New()
        MyBase.New(HtmlTextWriterTag.Img)

    End Sub
End Class
```

The RollOverButton class provides two properties—one URL for the original image and another URL for the image that should be shown when the user moves the mouse over the button. Here are the property definitions:

```
Public Property ImageUrl() As String
        Get
            Return CType(ViewState("ImageUrl"), String)
        End Get
        Set(ByVal value As String)
            ViewState("ImageUrl") = value
        End Set
    End Property

    Public Property MouseOverImageUrl() As String
        Get
            Return CType(ViewState("MouseOverImageUrl"), String)
        End Get
        Set(ByVal value As String)
            ViewState("MouseOverImageUrl") = value
        End Set
    End Property
```

The next step is to have the control emit the client-side JavaScript that can swap between the two pictures. In this case, it's quite likely that there will be multiple RollOverButton instances on the same page. That means you need to register the script block with a control-specific key so that no matter how many buttons you add there's only a single instance of the function. By convention, this script block is registered by overriding the OnPreRender() method, which is called just before the rendering process starts, as shown here:

```
Protected Overrides Sub OnPreRender(ByVal e As EventArgs)
    If Not
      Page.ClientScript.IsClientScriptBlockRegistered("swapImg")
    Then
        Dim script As String = ("<script type='text/javascript'> " _
               + ("function swapImg(id, url) { " + _
               ("var elm = document.getElementById(id); " + _
               ("elm.src = url; }" + _
               "</script> "))))
        Page.ClientScript.RegisterClientScriptBlock(
          Me.GetType, "swapImg", script)
    End If
    MyBase.OnPreRender(e)
End Sub
```

This code explicitly checks whether the script block has been registered using the IsClientScriptBlockRegistered() method. You don't actually need to test this property; as long as you use the same key, ASP.NET will render only a single instance of the script block. However, you can use the IsClientScriptBlockRegistered() and IsStartupScriptRegistered() methods to avoid performing potentially time-consuming work. In this example, it saves the minor overhead of constructing the script block string if you don't need it.

■ **Tip** To really streamline your custom control code, put all your JavaScript code into a separate file, embed that file into your compiled control assembly, and then expose it through a URL using the WebResource attribute, as discussed in Chapter 28. This is the approach that ASP.NET uses with its validation controls, for example.

Remember that because RollOverButton derives from WebControl and uses <img> as the base tag, it already has the rendering smarts to output an <img> tag. The only parts you need to supply are the attributes, such as name and src. Additionally, you need to handle the onClick event (to post back the page) and the onMouseOver and onMouseOut events to swap the image. You can do this by overriding the AddAttributesToRender() method, as follows:

```
Protected Overrides Sub AddAttributesToRender(
  ByVal output As HtmlTextWriter)
    output.AddAttribute("id", ClientID)
    output.AddAttribute("src", ImageUrl)
    output.AddAttribute("onClick",
        Page.ClientScript.GetPostBackEventReference(
          New PostBackOptions(Me)))
    output.AddAttribute("onMouseOver", ("swapImg('" _
                    + (Me.ClientID + ("', '" _
                    + (MouseOverImageUrl + "');")))))
    output.AddAttribute("onMouseOut", ("swapImg('" _
                    + (Me.ClientID + ("', '" _
                    + (ImageUrl + "');")))))
End Sub
```

The last ingredient is to create the RaisePostBackEvent() method, as required by the IPostBack-EventHandler interface, and use it to raise a server-side event, as shown here:

```
Public Event ImageClicked As EventHandler

    Public Sub RaisePostBackEvent(ByVal eventArgument As String)
        OnImageClicked(New EventArgs)
    End Sub

    Protected Overridable Sub OnImageClicked(ByVal e As EventArgs)
        ' Check for at least one listener and then raise the event.
        If (Not (ImageClicked) Is Nothing) Then
            ImageClicked(Me, e)
        End If
    End Sub
```

Figure 34-11 shows a page with two rollover buttons.

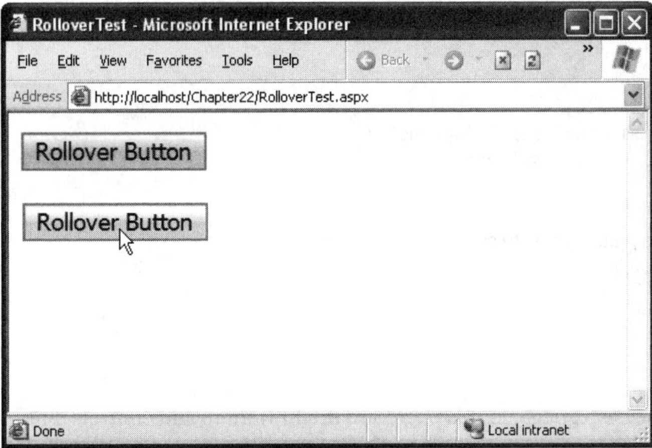

Figure 34-11. *Using a rollover button*

Frames

Another well-established feature of the Web is frames. *Frames* allow you to display more than one HTML document in the same browser window. Frames are commonly used to provide navigational controls (such as a menu with links) that remain visible on every page. You could simulate the same effect by creating a user control for navigation and including it on every page. However, only by using frames can you ensure that the placement is exactly the same. Frames also give you the ability to independently scroll the content frame while keeping the navigational controls fixed in place.

Tip For more information about frames, refer to the tutorial `http://www.w3schools.com/html/_html_frames.asp` or the FAQ at `http://www.htmlhelp.com/faq/html/frames.html`. Frames, like JavaScript, are completely independent of ASP.NET. They are simply a part of the HTML standard.

Unfortunately, frames aren't always that easy to integrate into an ASP.NET page. Showing separate frames is easy—you simply need to create an HTML frames page that references the ASP.NET pages you want to show and defines their positioning. However, developers often want an action in one frame to have a result in another frame, and this interaction is not as straightforward. The problem is that each frame loads a different page, and from the point of view of the web server these pages are completely separate. That means the only way one frame can interact with another is through the browser, using client-side script.

Frame Navigation

When you use frames for navigation, the user needs to be able to click a link in one frame and load a new page in the other frame. You can more easily accomplish this task on the client than on the server.

For example, consider the following HTML page, which defines a frameset with two frames (a navigation frame on the left and a content frame on the right):

```
<html>
  <head>
    <title>Frame Test</title>
  </head>
  <frameset framespacing="1" cols="200,*">
    <frame name="menu" src="Frame1.aspx" scrolling="no" />
    <frame name="content" src="" scrolling="auto" />
    <noframes>
      <body>
        <p>This page uses frames, but your browser
           doesn't support them.</p>
      </body>
    </noframes>
  </frameset>
</html>
```

The left frame shows the Frame1.aspx page. In this page, you might want to add controls that set the content in the other frame. This is easy to do using static HTML, such as an anchor tag. For example, if a user clicks the following hyperlink, it will automatically load the target NewPage.aspx in the frame on the right, which is named content:

```
<a href="NewPage.aspx" target="content">Click here</a>
```

You can also perform the same feat when a JavaScript event occurs by setting the parent.[FrameName].location property. For example, you could add an <img> tag on the left frame and use it to set the content on the right frame, as shown here:

```
<img src="ImgFile.gif" onClick="parent.content.location='NewPage.aspx'">
```

However, navigation becomes more complicated if you want to perform programmatic frame navigation in response to a server-side event. For example, you might want to log the user's action, examine security credentials, or commit data to a database and then perform the frame navigation. The only way to accomplish frame navigation from the server side is to write a snippet of JavaScript that instructs the browser to change the location of the other frame when the page first loads on the client.

For example, imagine you add a button to the leftmost frame, as shown in Figure 34-12. When this button is clicked, the following server-side code runs. It defines the <script> block and then registers it in the page. When the page is posted back, the script executes and redirects the rightmost frame to the requested page.

```
Protected Sub Button1_Click(
  ByVal sender As Object, ByVal e As System.EventArgs)
      Dim url As String = "http://www.google.com"
      Dim frameScript As String =
       ("<script type='text/javascript'>" +
       ("window.parent.content.location='" _+
       (url + "';</script>")))

      Page.ClientScript.RegisterStartupScript("FrameScript",
        frameScript)
    End Sub
```

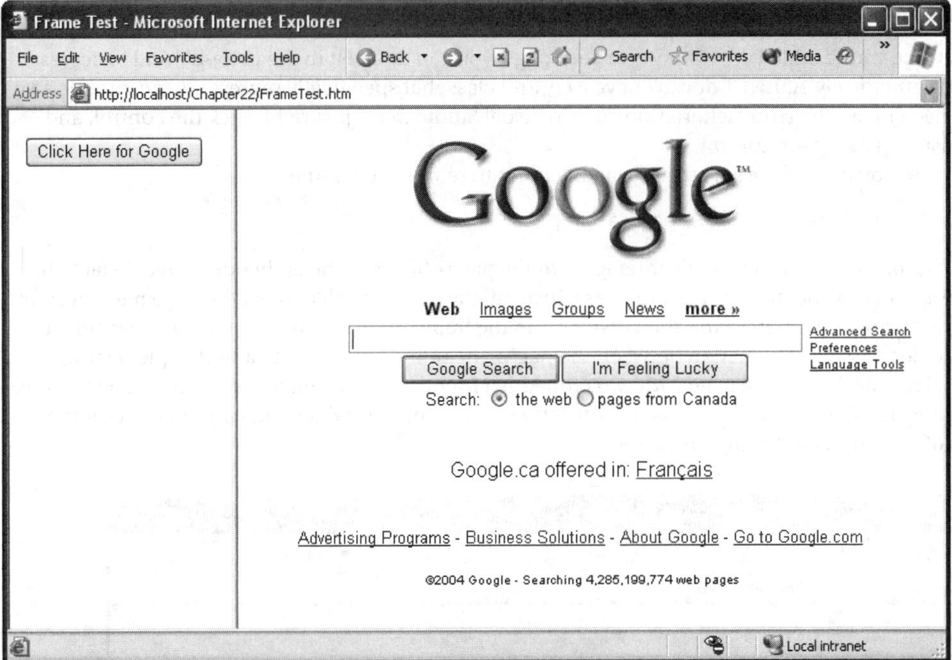

Figure 34-12. *Using server-side code to control frame navigation*

Tip Oddly enough, in this example the RegisterClientScriptBlock() method probably works slightly better than the RegisterStartupScript() block method. No matter how you implement this approach, you will get a slight delay before the new frame is refreshed. Because the script block doesn't depend on any of the controls on the page, you can render it immediately after the opening <form> tag using RegisterClientScriptBlock(), rather than at the end. This ensures that the JavaScript code that triggers the navigation is executed immediately, rather than after all the other content in the page has been downloaded.

Inline Frames

One solution that combines server-side programming with framelike functionality is the <iframe> tag (which is defined as part of the HTML 4.0 standard). The <iframe> in an inline, or embedded, frame that you can position anywhere inside an HTML document. Both the main document and the embedded page are treated as complete, separate documents.

Here's an example of an <iframe> tag:

```
<iframe src="page.aspx" width="40%" height="80" align="right">
</iframe>
```

The key problem with the <iframe> tag is that support is not universal across all browsers. Internet Explorer has supported it since version 3, but Netscape added it only in version 6. However, you can define static text that will be displayed in browsers that don't recognize the tag, as shown here:

```
<iframe src="page.aspx" width="40%" height="80" align="right">
  <p>See the content at <a href="page.aspx">page.aspx</a>.</p>
</iframe>
```

Once you've added an <iframe> to your page, you can define it in the code-behind to access it programmatically. ASP.NET doesn't have a control class that specifically represents the <iframe>, so you need to use the HtmlGenericControl. (In Visual Studio .NET, just right-click the control, and choose Run As Server Control).

Now you can set the src attribute at any point to redirect the frame:

```
IFrame1.Attributes["src"] = "page.aspx";
```

Of course, you can't actually interact with the page objects of the embedded page. In fact, the page isn't even generated in the same pass. Instead, the browser will request the page referenced by the src attribute separately and then display it in the frame. However, you can use a variety of techniques for passing information between the pages, including session state and the query string.

Figure 34-13 shows a page with two embedded frames, one of which has a border. The topmost <iframe> is using the page processor from earlier in this chapter, which indicates to the user that a part of the page is still being processed.

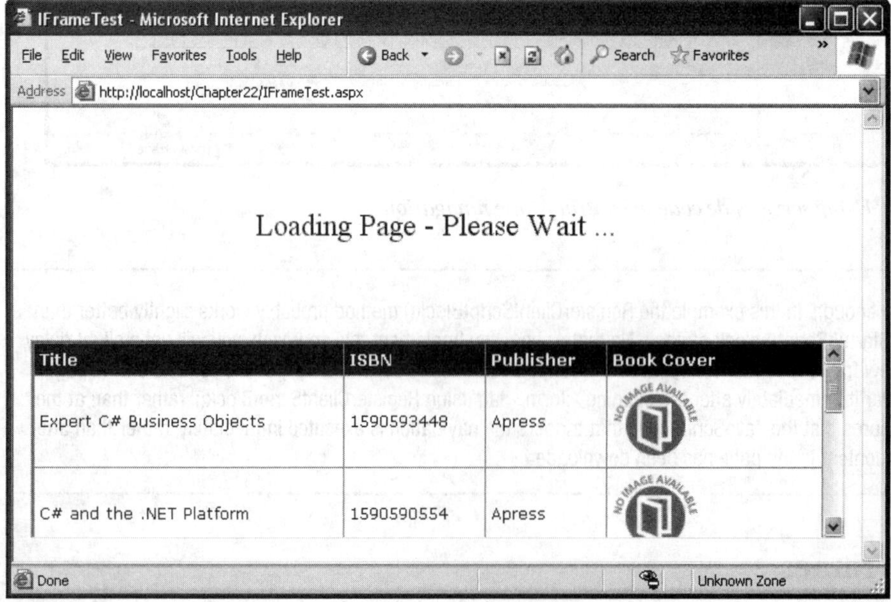

Figure 34-13. *Using inline frames*

Understanding Ajax

One of the main reasons developers use JavaScript code is to avoid a postback. For example, consider the TreeView control, which lets users expand and collapse nodes at will. When you expand a node, the TreeView uses JavaScript to fetch the child node information from the server, and then it quietly inserts the new nodes. Without JavaScript, the page would need to be posted back so the TreeView could be rebuilt. The user would notice a sluggish delay, and the page would flicker and possibly scroll back to the beginning. On the server side, a considerable amount of effort would be wasted serializing and deserializing the view state information in each pass.

You've already seen how you can avoid this overhead and create smoother, more streamlined pages with a little JavaScript. However, most of the JavaScript examples you've seen so far have been self-contained—in other words, they've implemented a distinct task that doesn't require interaction with the rest of the page model. This approach is great when it suits your need. For example, if all you need to do is show a pop-up message or a scrolling status display, you don't need to interact with the server-side code. However, what happens if you want to make a truly dynamic page like in the TreeView example, one that can call a server-side method, wait for a response, and insert the new information dynamically, without triggering a postback? To design this solution, you need to think of a way for your client-side script to communicate with your server-side code.

Recently, a new buzzword has appeared in web programming circles. It's *Ajax* (which was originally shorthand for Asynchronous JavaScript and XML), and it's an application of JavaScript that's distinguished by one special characteristic. Namely, Ajax-style pages communicate with the server to request additional information. When the client-side code receives this information (which is transmitted as an XML package), it carries out additional actions. For example, a page that uses Ajax techniques might grab a live stock quote and refresh a portion of the page, all without triggering a complete postback. The advantages are greater responsiveness and a seamless browsing experience that's free of page refreshes.

■Note Conceptually, these examples are similar to the asynchronous image–downloading example you saw earlier, which fetched additional information (the images) asynchronously and then updated the page. However, the image grid worked because images are really separate resources, not part of the page. You can't use the same technique to insert dynamic text or arbitrary HTML. Instead, you need to use Ajax techniques.

Programming Ajax pages can be complicated, not because the JavaScript techniques are particularly difficult (they aren't), but because you sometimes need messy workarounds to ensure browser compatibility. In an ideal world, ASP.NET programmers wouldn't need to worry about writing Ajax-style pages at all. Instead, you would use a higher-level framework on the server that could emit the JavaScript code you need. ASP.NET is heading in this direction, but it's moving slowly—after all, Microsoft needs time to carefully consider the different ways these client-side features can be integrated into ASP.NET's server-side model. Later in this chapter, you'll learn about *client callbacks*, which are the first rudimentary example of Ajax in ASP.NET.

■Note In the next chapter, you'll learn about the Microsoft Atlas toolkit, which offers much more powerful features for building Ajax-style pages. Atlas is a separate component that's currently still in development.

The XMLHttpRequest Object

The cornerstone of Ajax is the XMLHttpRequest object. XMLHttpRequest is both incredibly useful and deceptively simple. Essentially, it allows you to send requests to the server and retrieve the results as text. It's up to you to decide what you request, how you handle the request on the server side, and what you return to the client.

Although there is wide support for the XMLHttpRequest object in modern browsers, there's a subtle difference in how you access the object. In some browsers, including Internet Explorer 7, Firefox, Safari, and Opera, the XMLHttpRequest object is implemented as a native JavaScript object. In versions of Internet Explorer before version 7, it's implemented as an ActiveX object. Because of these differences, your JavaScript code needs to be intelligent enough to use the correct approach when creating an instance of XMLHttpRequest. Here's the code that Microsoft uses to perform this task for the client callback feature you'll consider later in this chapter:

```
var xmlRequest;
try
{
    // This works if XMLHttpRequest is part of JavaScript.
    xmlRequest = new XMLHttpRequest();
}
catch(err)
{
    // Otherwise, the ActiveX object is required.
    xmlRequest = new ActiveXObject("Microsoft.XMLHTTP");
}
// Either way, by this point xmlRequest should refer to a live instance.
```

■ **Note** This code fails if the browser doesn't provide the native or ActiveX version of the XMLHttpRequest object. This problem occurs with really old browsers, such as Internet Explorer 4 and Safari 1. If you need to support old clients like these, Ajax programming is not suitable. Pages that rely heavily on Ajax also fail if JavaScript is not enabled in the browser.

Sending a Request

You'll use two key methods to send a request with the XMLHttpRequest: open() and send().

The open() method sets up your call—it defines the request you want to send to the server. It has two required parameters: the type of HTTP command (GET, POST, or PUT) and the URL. Here's an example:

```
xmlRequest.open("GET" , myURL);
```

Additionally, you can supply a third parameter to indicate whether the request should be performed asynchronously and two more parameters to supply user name and password information for authentication. It's unlikely you'll use the user name and password parameters, because this information can't be safely hard-coded in your JavaScript code. Client-side code is never the right place to implement security.

■ **Note** By default, all requests you make with the XmlHttpRequest object are asynchronous. There is almost never a reason to change this behavior. If you choose to make the call synchronously, you may as well force a postback—after all, the user will be unable to do anything while the page is stalled waiting for a response. If it's not asynchronous, it's not Ajax.

The send() method fires off the request. Assuming your request is asynchronous, it returns immediately.

```
xmlRequest.send(null);
```

Optionally, the send() method takes a single string parameter. You can use this to supply additional information that's sent with the request, like the values that are sent with a POST request.

■ **Note** On Internet Explorer browsers, it's acceptable to leave out the parameter for the send() method. However, in Firefox you must supply a null reference, or the callback will behave erratically. This is one of the many quirks you'll find in cross-browser compatibility when writing client-side script.

Handling the Response

Clearly, one detail is missing here. You've learned how to send a request, but how do you handle the response? The secret is to attach an event handler using the onreadystatechange property. This function is called when the request is finished and the data is available:

```
xmlRequest.onreadystatechange = UpdatePage;
```

Of course, you need to attach the event handler *before* you call the send() method to start the request.

When the request is finished and your function is triggered, you can extract the information you need from the xmlRequest object using the responseText and responseXML properties. The responseText property gives you all the content in a single long string. The responseXML returns it as a tree of node objects.

■ **Note** Even though the name Ajax implies XML content, you can also return something else from the server, including plain text. For example, if the server is returning a single piece of data, there's no reason to wrap it up in a complete XML document.

An Ajax Example

Now that you've taken a quick tour of the XmlHttpRequest object, you're ready to use it in a simple page. To build an Ajax-style page in ASP.NET, you need two pieces:

- The Ajax-enabled web page, which includes the client-side code for making the request through the XmlHttpRequest object
- Another page or resource that can handle the requests from the first page and send the appropriate response

The first ingredient is obviously an .aspx web page. The second ingredient could be another .aspx web page, or it could be a custom HTTP handler. The HTTP handler is a more lightweight option, because it doesn't use the full-page model.

■ **Tip** For a quick refresher about custom HTTP handlers, refer to Chapter 5.

The following example implements the server-side functionality as an HTTP handler. The HTTP handler accepts information through the query string (in this case, it checks for two parameters) and then returns two pieces of information. The first piece of information is the sum of the two arguments that were passed in through the query string. The second piece of information is the current time on the web server. The information is *not* a legitimate XML document—instead, the two values are simply separated by a comma.

Here's the complete code for the HTTP handler:

```
Imports Microsoft.VisualBasic

Public Class CalculatorCallbackHandler
    Inherits IHttpHandler

    Public ReadOnly Property IsReusable() As Boolean
        Get
            Return True
        End Get
    End Property

    Public Sub ProcessRequest(ByVal context As HttpContext)
        Dim response As HttpResponse = context.Response
        ' Write ordinary text.
        response.ContentType = "text/plain"
        ' Get the query string arguments.
        Dim value2 As Single
        Dim value1 As Single
        If (Single.TryParse(context.Request.QueryString("value1"),
          value1)
            And
            Single.TryParse(context.Request.QueryString("value2"),
          value2))
            Then
            ' Calculate the total.
            response.Write((value1 + value2))
            response.Write(",")
            ' Return the current time.
            Dim now As DateTime = DateTime.Now
            response.Write(now.ToLongTimeString)
        Else
            ' The values weren't supplied or they weren't numbers.
            ' Indicate an error.
            response.Write("-")
        End If
    End Sub
End Class
```

■ **Note** In this example, the HTTP handler has an unrealistically easy job. After all, if you were simply interested in adding two numbers, your client-side code could accomplish the task without the Ajax request. This pattern becomes more important when the server-side code needs to do something the client can't, such as look up information in a server-side resource (a file or database), use sensitive information (such as secret numbers), or perform complex operations using classes that are available only in the .NET Framework.

Now that you have the HTTP handler in place, you can call it at any time using the XMLHttpRequest object. Figure 34-14 shows a sample page that fires off a request every time the user presses a key in either text box. The request supplies the values from the two text boxes, and the result is displayed in the shaded box at the bottom of the page. Just to prove that Ajax is at work, an animated GIF appears at the top of the page. You'll notice that the lava lamp keeps flowing without a pause while the callback takes place.

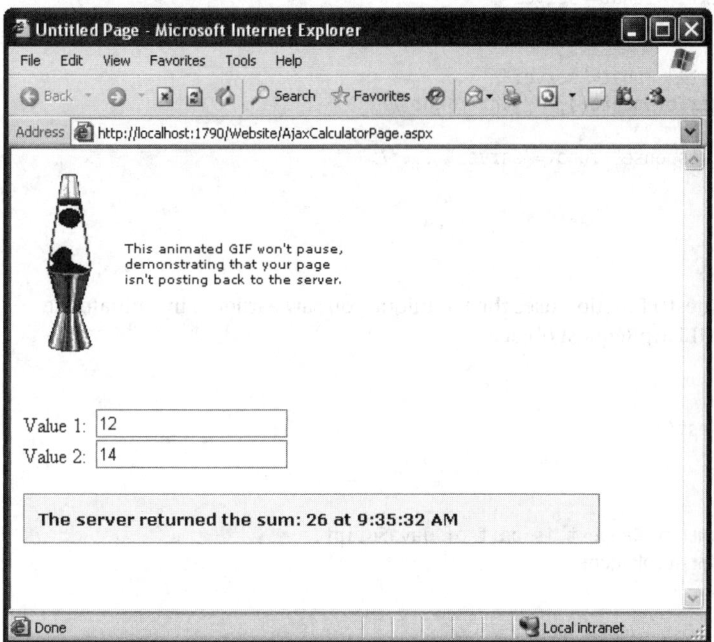

Figure 34-14. *An Ajax-style page*

Here's the basic outline of the page, without the JavaScript code. You'll notice that the page plugs into the client-side JavaScript in two ways. First, the onLoad event in the <body> tag launches the CreateXMLHttpRequest() function, which creates the XMLHttpRequest object. Second, the two text boxes use the onKeyUp event to trigger the CallServerForUpdate() function.

```
<%@ Page Language="VB" AutoEventWireup="true"
  CodeFile="AjaxCalculatorPage.aspx.cs" Inherits="AjaxCalculatorPage" %>

<html>
  <head runat="server">
    <title>Ajax Page</title>
      <script type="text/javascript">
        <!-- JavaScript functions go here. -->
    </script>
  </head>
  <body onLoad="CreateXMLHttpRequest();">
    <form id="form1" runat="server">
      <div>
        <table style="width: 296px">
          <tr>
            <td><img src="lava_lamp.gif" /></td>
```

```
        <td>This animated GIF won't pause, demonstrating that
         your page isn't posting back to the server.</td>
      </tr>
    </table>
    <br /><br />

    Value 1: 
    <asp:TextBox ID="txt1" runat="server"
     onKeyUp="CallServerForUpdate();" /><br />
    Value 2: 
    <asp:TextBox ID="txt2" runat="server"
     onKeyUp="CallServerForUpdate();" /><br /><br />

    <asp:Label ID="lblResponse" runat="server" ... />
   </div>
  </form>
 </body>
</html>
```

The CreateXMLHttpRequest() function uses the technique you saw earlier to instantiate the appropriate version of the XMLHttpRequest object:

```
var XmlRequest;

function CreateXMLHttpRequest()
{
    try
    {
        // This works if XMLHttpRequest is part of JavaScript.
        xmlRequest = new XMLHttpRequest();
    }
    catch(err)
    {
        // Otherwise, the ActiveX object is required.
        xmlRequest = new ActiveXObject("Microsoft.XMLHTTP");
    }
}
```

The CallServerForUpdate() function finds the text box objects, grabs their current values, and uses them to build a URL that points to the HTTP handler. The code then sends an asynchronous GET request to the HTTP handler.

```
function CallServerForUpdate()
{
    var txt1 = document.getElementById("txt1");
    var txt2 = document.getElementById("txt2");

    var url = "CalculatorCallbackHandler.ashx?value1=" +
      txt1.value + "&value2=" + txt2.value;
    xmlRequest.open("GET", url);
    xmlRequest.onreadystatechange = ApplyUpdate;
    xmlRequest.send();
}
```

Finally, the ApplyUpdate() function runs when the response is received. Assuming no error occurred, the new information is parsed out of the returned text and used to create a message that's displayed in the label:

```
function ApplyUpdate()
{
    // Check that the response was received successfully.
    if (xmlRequest.readyState == 4)
    {
        var lbl = document.getElementById("lblResponse");

        var response = xmlRequest.responseText;
        if (response == "-")
        {
            lbl.innerHTML = "You've entered invalid numbers.";
        }
        else
        {
            var responseStrings = response.split(",");
            lbl.innerHTML = "The server returned the sum: " +
              responseStrings[0] + " at " + responseStrings[1];
        }
    }
}
```

■ **Note** It's worth pointing out that Ajax doesn't save you from any server round-trips, and it rarely reduces the server processing time. The real difference is that round-trips occur silently in the background, which gives the application a more responsive feel.

Using Ajax with Client Callbacks

Using the Ajax approach, you can create impressive, highly responsive web pages. However, writing the client-side script is time-consuming. Visual Studio can't provide the same rich design experience you get when writing server-side code, and it doesn't provide debugging tools to help you track down the inevitable errors that crop up in the loosely typed JavaScript language. And even when you've successfully completed your task, you'll need to test on a wide range of other browsers, unless you're intimately familiar with the minor variations in JavaScript support on different browsers.

For these reasons, many developers don't write their client-side script by hand, even when designing an Ajax-style page. Instead, they prefer to deal with a higher-level component that can generate the script code they need. One example is the free third-party Ajax.NET library, which is available at `http://ajax.schwarz-interactive.de/csharpsample`. Ajax.NET uses attributes to flag methods, which then become remotely callable through a client callback. Another example is Atlas, the more comprehensive Microsoft framework for Ajax applications that's still in development (and discussed in the next chapter).

Although both Atlas and Ajax.NET are good choices, you can perform the most essential Ajax task—sending an asynchronous request to the server—using the new *client callback* feature that appears in ASP.NET. Client callbacks give you a way to refresh a portion of data in a web page without triggering a full postback. Best of all, you don't need the script code that uses the XmlHTTPRequest object. However, you *do* still need to write the client-side script that processes the server response.

Creating a Client Callback

To create a client callback in ASP.NET, you first need to plan how the communication will work. Here's the basic model:

1. At some point, a JavaScript event fires, triggering the callback.
2. At this point, the normal page life cycle occurs, which means all the normal server-side events fire, such as Page.Load.
3. When this process is complete (and the page is properly initialized), ASP.NET executes the server-side callback method. This method must have a fixed signature—it accepts a single string parameter and returns a single string.
4. Once the page receives the response from the server-side method, it uses JavaScript code to modify the web page accordingly.

The ASP.NET architecture is designed to abstract away the communication process, so you can build a page that uses callbacks without worrying about this lower level, in much the same way you can take advantage of view state and the page life cycle.

In the next example, you'll see a page with two drop-down lists boxes. The first list is populated with a list of regions from the Northwind database. This happens when the page first loads. The second list is left empty until the user makes a selection from the first list. At this point, the content for the second list is retrieved by a callback and inserted into the list (see Figure 34-15).

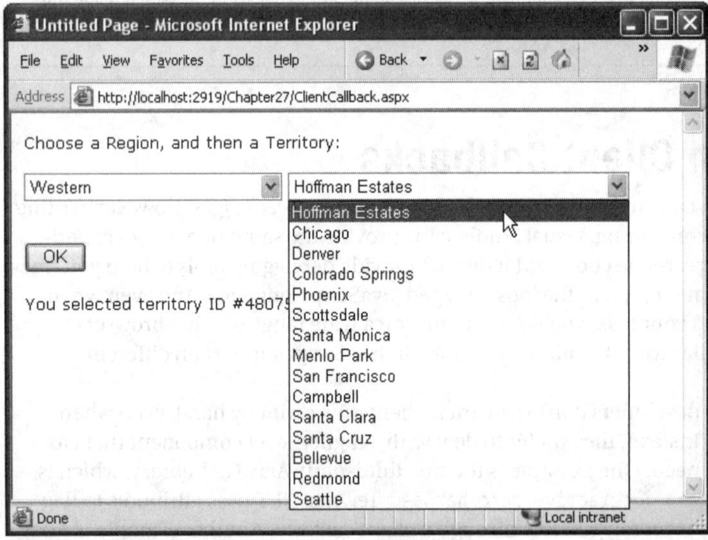

Figure 34-15. *Filling in a list with a callback*

Figure 34-16 diagrams how this process unfolds.

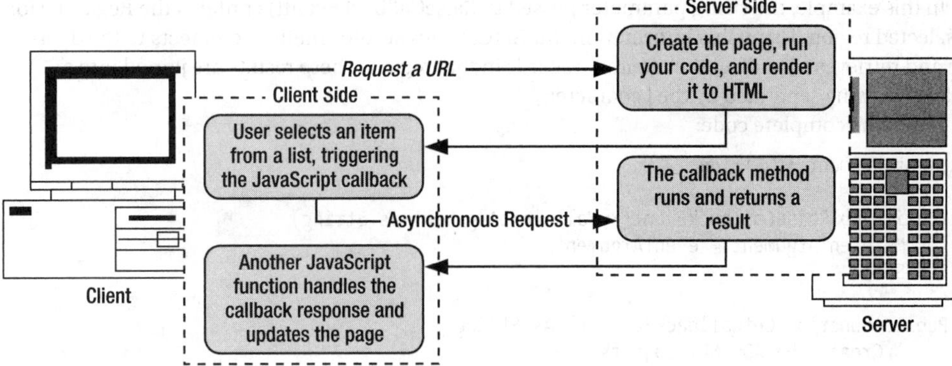

Figure 34-16. *The stages of a callback*

Building the Basic Page

The first step is to create the basic page, with two lists. It's easy enough to fill the first list—you can tackle this task by binding the list declaratively to a data source control. In this example, the following SqlDataSource is used:

```
<asp:SqlDataSource ID="sourceRegions" runat="server"
 ProviderName="System.Data.SqlClient"
 ConnectionString="<%$ ConnectionStrings:Northwind %>"
 SelectCommand="SELECT * FROM Region" />
```

And here's the list that binds to the data source:

```
<asp:DropDownList ID="lstRegions" Runat="server" DataSourceID="sourceRegions"
 DataTextField="RegionDescription" DataValueField="RegionID"/>
```

Implementing the Callback

To receive a callback, you need a class that implements the ICallbackEventHandler interface. If you know your callback will be used in several pages, it makes sense to create a dedicated class (much like the custom HTTP handler used in the previous Ajax example). However, if you want to define functionality that's intended for a single page, you can implement ICallbackEventHandler in your web page, as shown here:

```
Public Class ClientCallback
    Inherits System.Web.UI.Page
    Implements ICallbackEventHandler
End Class
```

The ICallbackEventHandler interface defines two methods. RaiseCallbackEvent() receives event data from the browser as a string parameter. It's triggered first. GetCallbackResult() is triggered next, and it returns the result back to the page.

Note The key limitation of ASP.NET client callbacks is that they force you to transmit data as single strings. If you need to pass more complex information (such as the result set with territory information, as in this example), you need to design a way to serialize your information into a string and deserialize it on the other side.

In this example, the string parameter passed to RaiseCallbackEvent() contains the RegionID for the selected region. Using this information, theGetCallbackResult() method connects to the database and retrieves a list of all the territory records in that region. These results are joined into a single long string separated by the | character.

Here's the complete code:

```
Dim eventArgument As String

    Public Sub RaiseCallbackEvent(ByVal eventArgument As String)
        Me.eventArgument = eventArgument
    End Sub

    Public Function GetCallbackResult() As String
        ' Create the ADO.NET objects.
        Dim con As SqlConnection =
         New SqlConnection(
            WebConfigurationManager.ConnectionStrings("Northwind").
            ConnectionString)
        Dim cmd As SqlCommand =
             New SqlCommand("SELECT * FROM Territories WHERE
                             RegionID=@RegionID", con)
        cmd.Parameters.Add(
           New SqlParameter("@RegionID", SqlDbType.Int, 4))
        cmd.Parameters("@RegionID").Value = Int32.Parse(eventArgument)

        ' Create a StringBuilder that contains the response string.
        Dim results As StringBuilder = New StringBuilder
        Try
            con.Open
            Dim reader As SqlDataReader = cmd.ExecuteReader
            ' Build the response string.

            While reader.Read
                results.Append(reader("TerritoryDescription"))
                results.Append("|")
                results.Append(reader("TerritoryID"))
                results.Append("||")

            End While
            reader.Close
        Finally
            con.Close
        End Try
        Return results.ToString
    End Function
```

You can't use declarative data binding in this example, because the callback method can't directly access the controls on the page. Unlike in a postback scenario, when RaiseCallbackEvent() is called, the page isn't in the process of being rebuilt. Instead, the RaiseCallbackEvent() method is called out-of-band to request some additional information. It's up to your callback method to perform all the heavy lifting on its own.

Because the results need to be returned as a single string (and seeing as this string has to be reverse-engineered in JavaScript code), the code is a little awkward. A single pipe (|) separates the TerritoryDescription field from the TerritoryID field. Two pipes in a row (||) denote the start of a new row. For example, if you request RegionID 1, you might get a response like this:

```
Westboro|01581||Bedford|01730||Georgetow|01833|| ...
```

Clearly, this approach is somewhat fragile—if any of the territory records contain the pipe character, this will cause significant problems.

Writing the Client-Side Script

Client-side scripts involve an exchange between the server and the client. Just as the server needs a method to prepare the results, the client needs a method to process them. The method that handles the server response can take any name, but it needs to accept two parameters, as shown here:

```
function ClientCallback(result, context)
{ ... }
```

The result parameter has the serialized string. In this example, it's up to the client-side script to parse this string and fill the appropriate list box.

Here's the complete client script code that you need for this task:

```
<script type="text/javascript">
function ClientCallback(result, context)
{
    // Find the list box.
    var lstTerritories = document.getElementById("lstTerritories");

    // Clear out any content in the list.
    lstTerritories.innerHTML= "";

    // Get an array with a list of territory records.
    var rows = result.split("||");

    for (var i = 0; i < rows.length - 1; ++i)
    {
       // Split each record into two fields.
       var fields = rows[i].split("|");
       var territoryDesc = fields[0];
       var territoryID = fields[1];

       // Create the list item.
       var option = document.createElement("option");

       // Store the ID in the value attribute.
       option.value = territoryID;

       // Show the description in the text of the list item.
       option.innerHTML = territoryDesc;
       lstTerritories.appendChild(option);
    }
}
</script>
```

One detail is missing. Although you've defined both sides of the message exchange, you haven't actually hooked it up yet. What you need is a client-side trigger that calls the callback. In this case, you want to react to the onChange event of the region list:

```
lstRegions.Attributes["onChange"] = callbackRef;
```

The callbackRef is the JavaScript code that calls the callback. But how exactly do you need to write this line of code? Fortunately, ASP.NET gives you a handy GetCallbackEventReference() method that can construct the callback reference you need. Here's how you use it in this example:

```
string callbackRef = Page.ClientScript.GetCallbackEventReference(
  this, "document.getElementById('lstRegions').value",
  "ClientCallback", "null", true);
```

The first parameter is a reference to the ICallbackEventHandler object that will handle the callback—in this case, the containing page. The second parameter is the information that the client will pass to the server. In this example, a snippet of JavaScript is required to look up the appropriate control (lstRegions) and extract the currently selected value.

■Tip Many client callback samples use the JavaScript collection document.all to retrieve control objects. This is not recommended, because document.all is an extension to JavaScript supported in Internet Explorer but not in other browsers (such as Firefox). Instead, use the document.getElementById() method shown previously.

The third parameter is the name of the client-side JavaScript function that will receive the results from the server callback. The fourth parameter includes any context information that you want to pass to the client-side function. This is helpful if you handle several callbacks with the same JavaScript function and you need to distinguish which response is which. Finally, the last parameter indicates whether you want to perform the callback asynchronously. This should always be true to prevent locking up the page in the event of a network problem.

Here's the complete code for registering the callback when the page loads:

```
Protected Sub Page_Load(
  ByVal sender As Object, ByVal e As EventArgs)
    Dim callbackRef As String =
      Page.ClientScript.GetCallbackEventReference(Me,
        "document.getElementById('lstRegions').value",
        "ClientCallback", "null", true)
    lstRegions.Attributes("onChange") = callbackRef
End Sub
```

This completes the solution.

■Note Clearly, client callbacks represent a powerful feature that lets you build more seamless, dynamic pages. But remember, client callbacks rely on the XMLHttpRequest functionality, which limits them to modern browsers. Some browsers may support JavaScript but not client callbacks. If in doubt, you can check whether a browser appears to support Ajax callbacks using the Request.Browser.SupportsCallback property.

Client Callbacks "Under the Hood"

It's worth noting that when the callback is performed, the target page actually starts executing a trimmed-down life cycle. Most control events won't execute, but the Page.Load and Page.Init event handlers *will*. The Page.IsPostBack property will return true, but you can distinguish this callback from a genuine postback by testing the Page.IsCallback property, which will also be true. The page rendering process is bypassed completely. View state information is retrieved and made available to your callback method, but any changes you make are not sent back to the page. Figure 34-17 shows the life-cycle events.

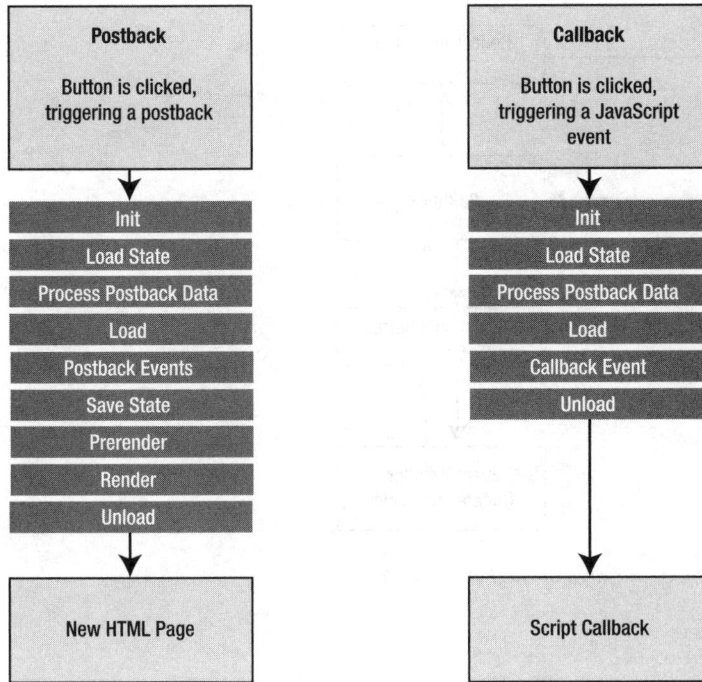

Figure 34-17. *Comparing postbacks and callbacks*

The only problem with the current implementation of client callbacks is that the programming interface is still fairly primitive, especially in its requirement that you exchange only strings. The current trend in ASP.NET is to use the callback features to build dynamic features into dynamic controls, rather than consuming them directly in the page. You'll see an example of this technique in the next section.

Client Callbacks in Custom Controls

Integrating client callbacks into a page is a fair bit of work. However, a much better option is to use them to build rich controls. You can then use these controls in as many pages as you want. Best of all, you'll get the Windows-style responsiveness without having to delve into the lower-level callback infrastructure.

Although there's no limit to the type of controls you might build with dynamic callbacks, many controls use callbacks to simply refresh a portion of their user interface (such as the TreeView). With a little ingenuity, you can create a container control that provides this functionality for free.

The basic idea is to create a new control that derives from Panel. This panel contains content that you want to refresh. At some point, a client-side JavaScript will occur, causing the panel to perform a callback. At this point, the panel will fire a server-side event to notify your code. You can handle this event and tweak any of the controls inside the panel. When the event finishes, the panel gets the new HTML for its contents and returns it. A client-side script replaces the current panel contents with the new HTML using a little DHTML

Figure 34-18 shows the process.

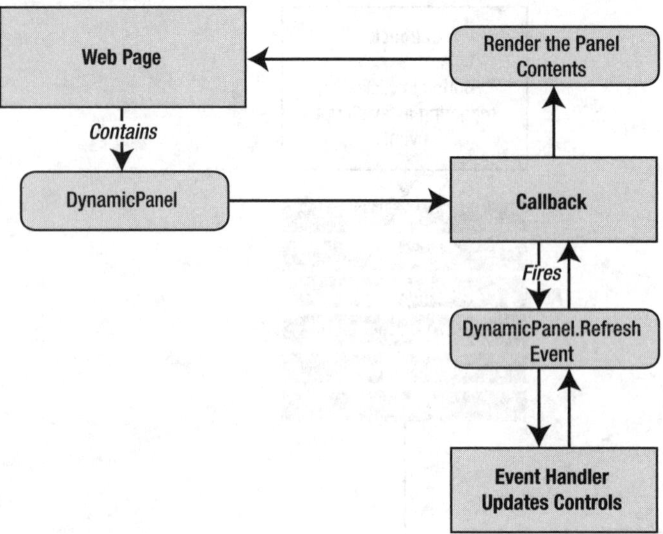

Figure 34-18. *Refreshing a portion of the page through a callback*

The DynamicPanel

The first step is to derive a class from Panel and implement ICallbackEventHandler:

```
Public Class DynamicPanel
    Inherits Panel
    Implements ICallbackEventHandler
End Class
```

As part of the ICallbackEventHandler, the DynamicPanel needs to implement the Raise-_Callback-Event() and GetCallbackResult() method. At this point it's a two-step process. First, the Dynamic-Panel needs to fire an event to notify your page. Your page can handle this event and perform the appropriate modifications. Next, the DynamicPanel needs to render the HTML for its contents. It can then return that information (along with its client ID) to the client-side web page.

```
    Public Event Refresh As EventHandler

    Public Sub RaiseCallbackEvent(ByVal eventArgument As String)
        ' Fire an event to notify the client
        ' a refresh has been requested.
        If (Not (Refresh) Is Nothing) Then
            Refresh(Me, EventArgs.Empty)
        End If
    End Sub

    Public Function GetCallbackResult() As String
        ' Prepare the text response that
        ' will be sent back to the page.
        EnsureChildControls
        Dim w As StringWriter = New StringWriter
        Dim writer As HtmlTextWriter = New HtmlTextWriter(sw)
        ' Add the id that identifies this panel.
```

```
        writer.Write((Me.ClientID + "_"))
        ' Render just the part of the page inside the panel.
        Me.RenderContents(writer)
        Return w.ToString
    End Function
```

If you've programmed DHTML scripts before, you know that all you need to manipulate an HTML element is its unique ID and the getElementById() method. Here's the client-side script code that finds the panel on the page and then replaces its content with new HTML:

```
<script type="text/javascript">
  function RefreshPanel(result, context)
  {
    if (result != '')
    {
      // Split the string back into two pieces of information:
      // the panel ID and the HTML content.
      var separator = result.indexOf('_');
      var elementName = result.substr(0, separator);
      // Look up the panel.
      var panel = document.getElementById(elementName);
      // Replace its content.
      panel.innerHTML = result.substr(separator+1);
    }
  }
</script>
```

Rather than hard-code this script into every page in which you use the panel, it makes sense to register it programmatically in the DynamicPanel.OnInit() method:

```
    Protected Overrides Sub OnInit(ByVal e As EventArgs)
        MyBase.OnInit(e)
        Dim script As String = "..."
        Page.ClientScript.RegisterClientScriptBlock(
          Me.GetType, "RefreshPanel", script)
    End Sub
```

This completes the basics of the DynamicPanel. However, this example still has a significant limitation—the page has no way to trigger the callback and cause the panel to refresh. That means it's up to your page code to retrieve the callback reference and insert it into your page.

Fortunately, you can simplify this process by creating other controls that work with the DynamicPanel. For example, you could create a DynamicPanelRefreshLink that, when clicked, automatically triggers a refresh in the associated panel.

The first step in implementing this solution is to revisit the DynamicPanel and implement the ICallbackContainer interface.

```
Public Class DynamicPanel
    Inherits Panel
    Implements ICallbackEventHandler, ICallbackContainer
End Class
```

This interface allows the DynamicPanel to provide the callback reference, rather than forcing you to go through the page.

To implement ICallbackContainer, you need to provide a GetCallbackScript() method that returns the reference. Here the Panel can rely on the page, making sure to specify itself as the callback target, and on RefreshPanel() as the client-side script that will handle the response.

```
Public Function GetCallbackScript(
  ByVal buttonControl As IButtonControl,
  ByVal argument As String) As String

    Return Page.ClientScript.GetCallbackEventReference(Me, "",
      "RefreshPanel", "null", true)
End Function
```

The DynamicPanelRefreshLink

Now you're ready to implement the much simpler refresh button. This control, named Dynamic-PanelRefreshLink, derives from LinkButton.

```
Public Class DynamicPanelRefreshLink
    Inherits LinkButton
End Class
```

You specify the panel that it should work with by setting a PanelID property:

```
Public Property PanelID As String
    Get
        Return CType(ViewState("DynamicPanelID"),String)
    End Get
    Set
        ViewState("DynamicPanelID") = value
    End Set
End Property
```

Finally, when it's time to render itself, the DynamicPanelRefreshLink finds the associated DynamicPanel control using FindControl() and then adds the callback script reference to the onclick attribute.

```
Protected Overrides Sub AddAttributesToRender(
  ByVal writer As HtmlTextWriter)

    Dim pnl As DynamicPanel =
      CType(Page.FindControl(PanelID),DynamicPanel)
    If (Not (pnl) Is Nothing) Then
     writer.AddAttribute("onclick", pnl.GetCallbackScript(Me, ""))
    End If
End Sub
```

The Client Page

To complete this example, create a simple text page, and add a DynamicPanel and a DynamicPanel-RefreshLink underneath it. Set the DynamicPanelRefreshLink.PanelID property to create the link.

Next, place some content and controls in the panel. Finally, add an event handler for the DynamicPanel.Refresh event and use it to change the content or formatting of the controls in the panel.

```
Protected Sub Panel1_Refresh(ByVal sender As Object,
  ByVal e As EventArgs)
    Label1.Text = ("This was refreshed without a postback at " +
      DateTime.Now.ToString)
End Sub
```

Now when you run the page, you'll see that you can click the DynamicPanelRefreshLink to refresh the panel without posting back the page (see Figure 34-19).

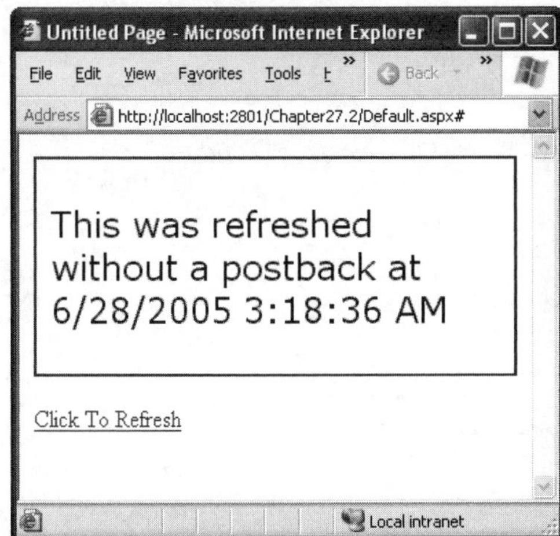

Figure 34-19. *The DynamicPanel*

■ **Note** This example is extremely practical. However, before you start using the DynamicPanel in your applications, you might want to consider a more mature sample by Bertrand Le Roy that uses the same technique but adds a fair bit of extra frills (and a lot more code). To check it out, surf to `http://www.gotdotnet.com/workspaces/directory.aspx`, and search for *RefreshPanel*.

Summary

In this chapter, you saw how a bit of carefully chosen JavaScript code can extend your ASP.NET web pages with more responsive interfaces and more dynamic effects. Along the way, you saw how to develop .NET solutions for some traditional HTML and JavaScript techniques, such as page processors, pop-up windows, rollover buttons, and frames. You also explored Ajax and the new client callback feature that helps you implement seamless page updates. You can do a lot more by creatively applying a little JavaScript. For more ideas, check out some of the custom controls available at Microsoft's `http://www.asp.net` community website, or continue to the next chapter where you'll dip into Atlas, a server-side programming framework for developing Ajax-style pages.

CHAPTER 35

■ ■ ■

Atlas

In the previous chapter, you entered the world of client-side programming. You learned a few essential techniques for using JavaScript, and you considered how to create more responsive pages with Ajax techniques, either on your own or through the client callback feature in ASP.NET.

These examples presented a fairly well-rounded foundation that you can use to build a variety of advanced pages. Unfortunately, the programming model leaves a lot to be desired. If you rely on pure JavaScript, it's up to you to bridge the gap between ASP.NET's server-side abstraction and the more limited HTML DOM. Sadly, it's not easy. Without the benefit of Visual Studio's IntelliSense and its debugging tools, it's difficult to write error-free code and diagnose problems. It's also a challenge to create script code that works on all modern browsers, because minor quirks and implementation differences abound.

The new ASP.NET client callback feature begins to address these problems by giving you a server-side model that you can use to generate some of the client-side code you need (namely, the code that performs asynchronous requests using the XMLHttpRequest object). However, the client callback model is far from perfect. The interfaces feel a bit clunky, the integration into the page model is a bit awkward, and data typing is nonexistent. It's up to you to devise a way to serialize the information you need to transmit into a single string, and it's up to you to write the JavaScript code that receives the callback, deserializes the string, and updates the page. All in all, the client callback feature is an excellent tool for building Ajax-enabled controls but a less appealing way to design complete web pages.

The end result is that ASP.NET developers have several approaches they can use to build responsive, dynamic pages. However, each one of these approaches has its own gaps, quirks, and idiosyncrasies. What ASP.NET needs is a more comprehensive platform that tackles the higher-level features you want to provide in an Ajax-style page—details such as partial-page refreshes, mouse events, and intelligent controls. Microsoft is already well on its way to creating just this sort of framework, which it calls *Atlas*.

Currently, Atlas is a separately downloadable component that gives you the tools for using Ajax-style features. Atlas supports all modern browsers and uses a multilayered architecture that lets you use high-level features (such as prebuilt controls that have Ajax smarts) or much lower-level ones (such as a script library that extends the JavaScript language with support for inheritance and interfaces). As you'll see in this chapter, Atlas can help you perform simple tasks, such as implementing a basic server-side callback, and it allows you to implement completely new effects, such as draggable panels and autocompletion. It's no exaggeration to say that Atlas is the start of a new direction in ASP.NET programming, one that promises the richest set of client-side features that web developers have seen so far.

■ **Note** At the time of this writing, Atlas is still in an evolving beta form. However, it's slated for eventual inclusion in the .NET Framework as a core part of ASP.NET. This chapter is based on the July Community Technical preview (CTP) of Atlas.

The Architecture of Atlas

Many JavaScript libraries aim to make Ajax programming easier. Usually, these libraries add convenience features (such as quick ways to find and update controls) and provide a compatibility layer (by wrapping operations that need different code for different browsers in higher-level functions). The Atlas framework includes its own script library, but it also goes far beyond this by adding a whole server-side object library that plugs into ASP.NET.

This richness allows you to choose exactly how you want to add Ajax support. If you're a die-hard JavaScript expert, you can use the Atlas script libraries directly in your client-side JavaScript code. However, most developers prefer to use Atlas at a higher level by using the server-side components. Here's where Atlas becomes a little tricky, because it provides several different layers of server-side functionality that you can use to achieve the same result.

For example, imagine you want to create a basic callback that gets new information from the server and refreshes a portion of the page. In Atlas, you can create the callback using server-side code and add a small snippet of JavaScript code to handle the callback response and update the page (much as you did in Chapter 34). But if you don't want to touch a single line of JavaScript, you can use a higher-level abstraction: a declarative markup called *Atlas script.* Using Atlas script, you can define how the callback response should be processed and what part of the page should be modified, all without typing a line of JavaScript. Atlas script is the foundation for many more complex features that would be extremely tedious to implement with hand-coded JavaScript.

Figure 35-1 provides a simplified overview of the Atlas architecture. It divides Atlas into three pieces: the script libraries that do most of the client-side work, the extensions that let you write Atlas-enabled web pages, and the web services that let you easily provide data to an Atlas page during a callback.

■ **Note** The division between these three components is somewhat arbitrary, because they all have deep interrelationships. For example, Atlas server controls use the client-side Atlas script libraries and can plug into Atlas services to support features such as data binding.

Atlas on the Client

The client-side script libraries represent the most fundamental building block in Atlas. They provide the glue that holds all the other features together. The Atlas script library is a detailed, surprisingly complex set of JavaScript functions that provides several services:

Script core: This includes JavaScript code that extends the JavaScript language with a few key object-oriented patterns. For example, it allows you to simulate namespaces, interfaces, inheritance, enumerations, and delegates in your JavaScript code. The script core library also introduces a few features that make JavaScript objects a little more like full-fledged .NET objects.

■ **Note** No matter what clever workarounds the Microsoft architects create, the JavaScript language will always be far from a true typesafe, object-oriented language such as C#. For that reason, we won't focus on the script core enhancements in this chapter. Instead, we'll cover the higher-level Atlas features built on top of them.

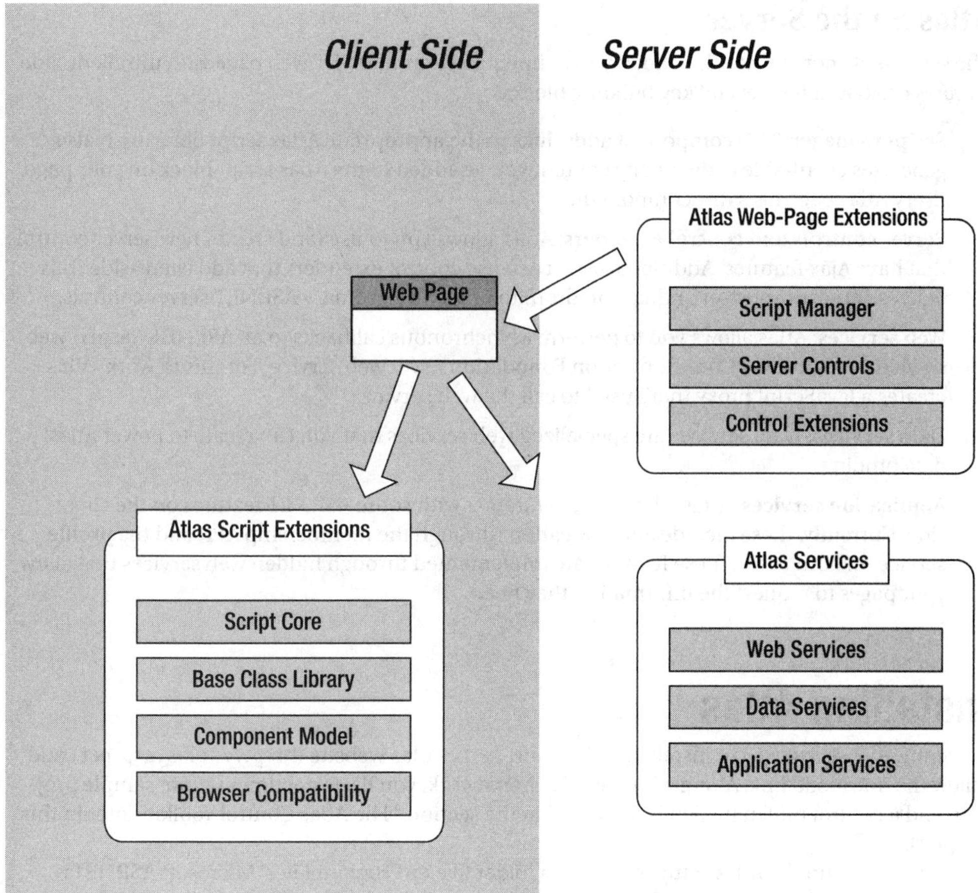

Figure 35-1. *The Atlas architecture*

Base class library: This library is inspired by the base class library in .NET. Although it's not nearly as comprehensive, it includes a few useful types such as StringBuilder, Debug, Event, and IDisposable, all of which you can use in your JavaScript code. It also wraps the XML-HttpRequest object with two more objects—WebRequest and WebResponse—that resemble their .NET equivalents in the System.Net namespace.

Component model: Atlas has its own client-side object model, which uses the HTML DOM but extends it to support more advanced features, such as data binding and validation. The component model is a key building block in Atlas, because it allows you to work with full-featured objects instead of ordinary HTML elements, whether you're programming on the server or on the client. However, the component model also complicates the design of a web page, because every Atlas-enabled web page requires two component abstractions—one that lets you write server-side ASP.NET code and one that lets you add client-side Atlas features.

Browser compatibility: As you'd expect, the Atlas libraries are designed to support all modern browsers seamlessly. This means you don't need to write conditional statements based on the browser version. Instead, all the features you use generate the right script code automatically.

Atlas on the Server

The server-side portion of Atlas allows you to integrate your ASP.NET web page with the client-side features of Atlas. It has several key building blocks:

Script manager: This component adds links to the appropriate Atlas script libraries. It also generates client-side code for any content you've added to the Atlas script block on your page. Every Atlas page uses this component.

Server controls and control extenders: Atlas allows you to use (and create) new server controls that have Ajax features. Additionally, you can use control extenders that add client-side frills (such as autocompletion or drag and drop) to otherwise ordinary ASP.NET server controls.

Web services: Atlas allows you to perform asynchronous callbacks to an ASP.NET (.asmx) web service or a Windows Communication Foundation (.svc) web service. For this to work, Atlas creates a JavaScript proxy that's used to call the web service.

Data services: Data services are specialized web services that you can create to power Atlas data binding.

Application services: Atlas allows you to interact with some ASP.NET features on the client side. Currently, these include authentication (through the membership API) and the profile service. In both cases, these features are implemented through hidden web services that allow your pages to request the information they need.

Installing Atlas

Currently, the easiest way to install Atlas is to surf to the Atlas website (`http://atlas.asp.net`) and follow the download link. Along with the Atlas framework, you'll see documentation, sample projects, and a control toolkit (which is discussed in the section "The Atlas Control Toolkit" later in this chapter).

When you run the Atlas setup, it creates a folder like c:\Program Files\Microsoft ASP.NET\Atlas\[Version]\Atlas, where [Version] is the version of Atlas you've installed. Inside this folder, you'll find the assembly that allows you to build Atlas pages, which is named Microsoft.Web.Atlas.dll. You'll also find a ScriptLibrary subfolder that contains the complete Atlas JavaScript libraries. They include the following files:

Atlas.js: This file contains the full Atlas feature set. It's the most commonly used Atlas script library.

AtlasRuntime.js: This file contains a minimal subset of Atlas features. It's a subset of Atlas.js that supports asynchronous callbacks to web services and supports the JavaScript language extensions. If you don't need to use Atlas controls and additional features, you can use this script instead of Atlas.js to reduce the amount of information the browser needs to download.

AtlasCompat.js and AtlasCompat2.js: These files provide cross-browser compatibility for Atlas features.

AtlasFX.js: This file contains the same content as Atlas.js but without the AtlasRuntime.js code. This is for use with gadgets in hosted scenarios.

AtlasUIDragDrop.js: This file includes code for the drag-and-drop feature.

AtlasUIGlitz.js: This file includes code for a variety of specialized UI effects such as transparency, fading, and animations.

AtlasUIMap.js: This file provides a virtual mapping feature.

AtlasWebParts.js: This file includes code for Atlas features that work with ASP.NET web parts controls.

GadgetRuntime.js: This file includes code for the Atlas gadget feature. A *gadget* is a small, self-contained component that includes user interface and code. You can build entire pages from a combination of gadgets, and gadgets can be easily shared between websites.

■ **Tip** The size of the Atlas script library is a factor you may want to consider when designing an Atlas website. Because the Atlas library is stored in a separate file (rather than placed in every web page), browsers will cache it. This means the user will experience a one-time download cost after which the browser won't need to retrieve the file from the server again. The Atlas libraries you use depend to some extent on the features you use (for example, the mapping script is about 100KB) and the browser you use. Currently, the full Atlas.js library requires 240KB, and the slimmed-down AtlasRuntime.js, which is sufficient when you're just using callbacks, at most other times, weighs in at 56KB.

Creating an Atlas Project

The Atlas setup creates a Visual Studio template that allows you to quickly create Atlas-enabled websites. To use it, select File ➤ New Web Site from the Visual Studio menu, and choose "Atlas" Web Site (as shown in Figure 35-2).

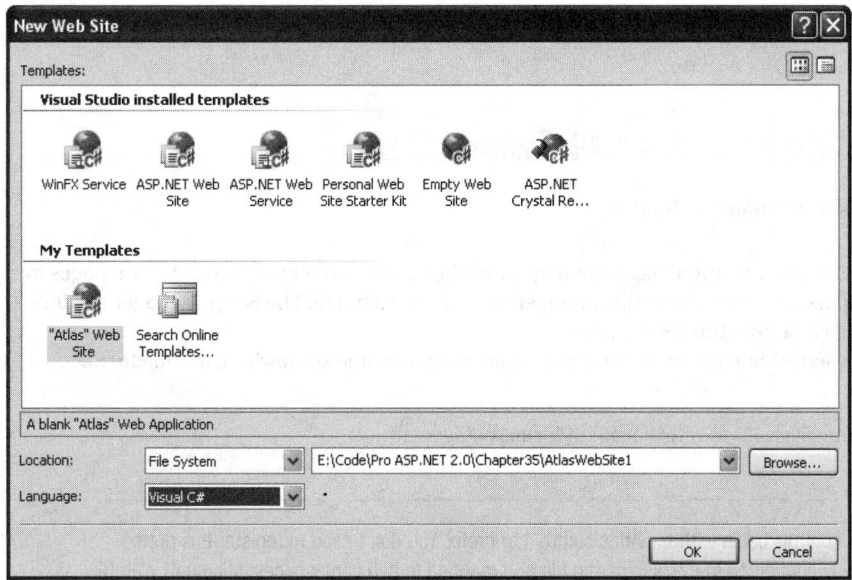

Figure 35-2. *Creating an Atlas project*

Your new Atlas website has a few differences from an ordinary ASP.NET website:

- The Bin folder has a copy of the Microsoft.Web.Atlas.dll assembly.
- The web.config file includes the settings needed to configure Atlas. For example, these settings register HTTP handlers that support some Atlas features and provide support for calling a web service through a JavaScript proxy.
- Two files (readme.txt and eula.rtf) spell out the licensing terms. In the community tech previews for Atlas, these files warn you that Atlas is unsupported prerelease software that shouldn't be incorporated into production web servers.
- The default.aspx page begins has a ScriptManager control placed on it (see Figure 35-3), and the .aspx markup defines the XML script section that allows you to use Atlas declaratively.

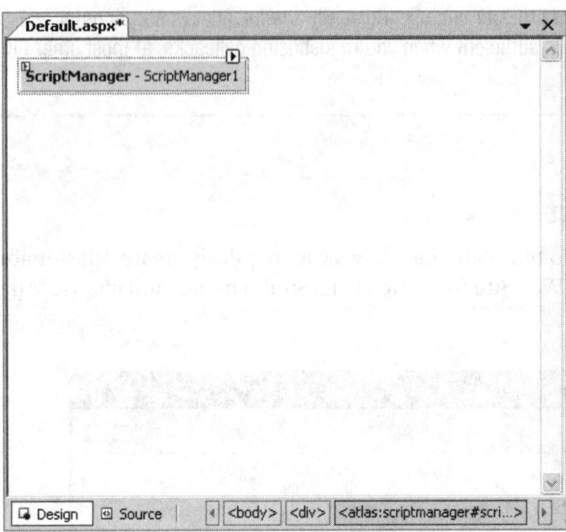

Figure 35-3. *An Atlas-ready page*

Figure 35-3 shows the initial page you begin with in an Atlas project. If you add more pages to your site, you'll need to place the ScriptManager control on each one. The ScriptManager renders the links to the JavaScript libraries for Atlas.

To add the ScriptManager to another page, just insert this line somewhere in the <form> section:

```
<atlas:ScriptManager ID="ScriptManager1" runat="server"  />
```

■ **Note** All Atlas controls begin with the Atlas control tag prefix. You don't need to register this prefix, because it's already configured in the web.config file and mapped to two namespaces: Microsoft.Web.UI and Microsoft.Web.UI.Controls.

Using the Atlas Server Controls

The Atlas framework includes several server controls, but these controls aren't added to the Visual Studio Toolbox. This means if you want to use controls such as the ScriptManager, it's up to you to type the tags into the .aspx markup.

Fortunately, you have an easier option—you can customize the Visual Studio Toolbox so it shows all the Atlas controls. Just follow these steps:

1. Begin by creating a new Toolbox tab to hold your controls. Right-click the Toolbox, choose Add Tab, and type **Atlas** as your tab name.
2. Right-click the new Atlas tab, and select Choose Items. The Choose Toolbox Items dialog box will appear.
3. Click Browse, and find the Microsoft.Web.Atlas.dll assembly in the c:\Program Files\ Microsoft ASP.NET\Atlas\[Version]\Atlas directory. Select it. This adds the Atlas controls to the list of options in the Choose Toolbox Items dialog box.
4. Now, click the Assembly Name column to sort the list based on the assembly where the control is defined. You should now be able to scroll through the list and find the section of controls from the Microsoft.Web.Atlas.dll namespace (see Figure 35-4).

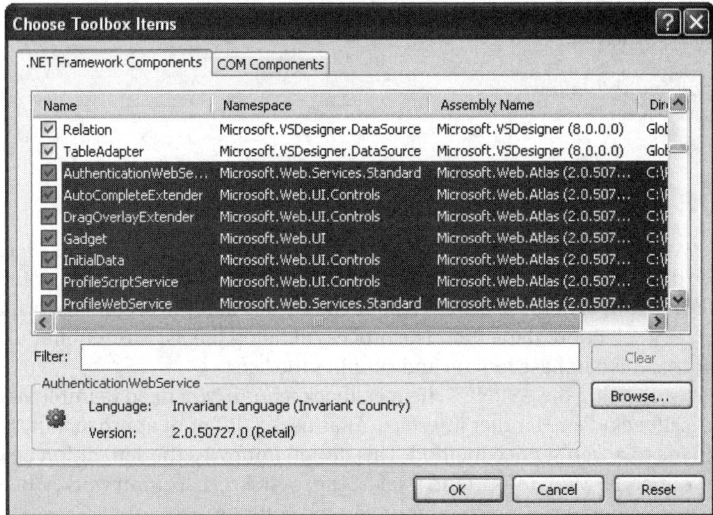

Figure 35-4. *Adding Atlas controls*

5. Make sure all the controls in the Microsoft.Web.Atlas.dll namespace are checked, and then click OK. Visual Studio adds the controls to your Toolbox so they're just a click away (see Figure 35-5).

Figure 35-5. *Atlas controls in the Toolbox*

Web Service Callbacks

The first Atlas example you'll consider is a revised version of the client callback page from Chapter 34. This page includes two drop-down list boxes (see Figure 35-6). The first shows a list of regions, and the second displays the territories in the selected region. The trick is that the second list is filled each time the user makes a selection in the first. The process of filling the list box requires a call to the server, which performs the database lookup and supplies the list.

To make this page work using the ASP.NET client callback feature, you need to implement the slightly cumbersome ICallbackEventHandler interface. Atlas uses a different approach. In Atlas, callbacks are always made to a web service method. This design improves the separation of logic, helping you organize your code. More important, it takes care of the serialization work, which means you no longer need to devise your own method to send complex data.

In the following sections, you'll see how to build the web service you need, and you'll consider several options for consuming it.

Creating the Atlas Web Service

Atlas web services are identical to ordinary ASP.NET web services. In fact, any web service you've created before can be called from the client using Atlas, provided your website has the Atlas extensions enabled in the web.config file. Two key portions are automatically inserted when you create a new Atlas application in Visual Studio.

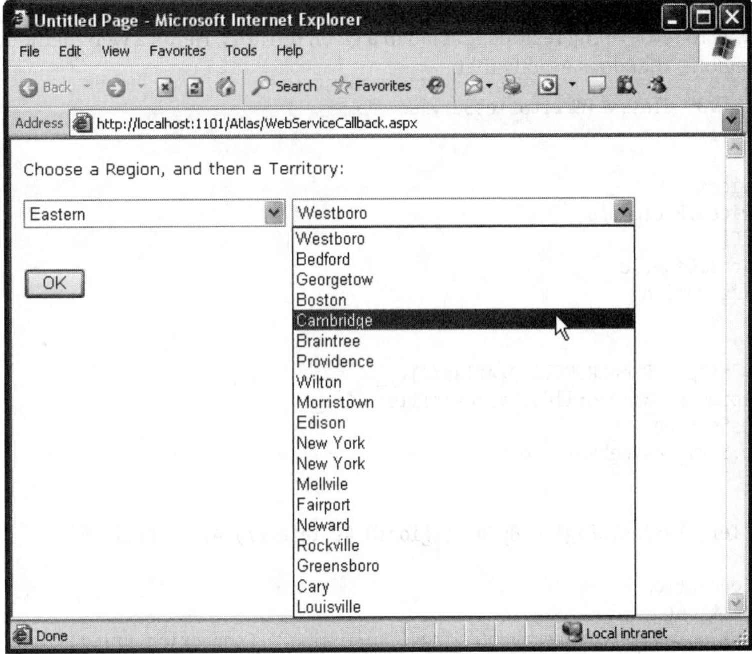

Figure 35-6. *The dynamic list example revisited*

First, the new <webServices> section explicitly allows web browser clients to access your web services:

```
<microsoft.web>
  <webServices enableBrowserAccess="true" />
</microsoft.web>
```

Second, Atlas maps a new HTTP handler to handle web service requests. That way, it can add a new feature—the ability to generate JavaScript proxy code:

```
<httpHandlers>
  <!-- Remove the standard HTTP handler for web requests. -->
  <remove verb="*" path="*.asmx"/>

  <!-- Add a new one with JavaScript proxy support. -->
  <add verb="*" path="*.asmx"
    type="Microsoft.Web.Services.ScriptHandlerFactory"
    validate="false"/>
  ...

</httpHandlers>
```

■ **Note** Unlike the web service examples you saw in Part 6, you don't need to host this web service in an IIS virtual directory in order to use it. Instead, you can test it using the integrated web server in Visual Studio. This works because the script code that calls your web service automatically uses a relative path. As a result, no matter what port the Visual Studio web server chooses, the web page will be able to construct the right URL.

With these details in place, you're ready to create the web service you need. For the drop-down list example, you need a way to retrieve the regions that fall in a given territory. Here's a web method named GetTerritoriesInRegion() that does exactly that:

```
<%@ WebService Language="VB" Class="TerritoriesService" %>

Imports System.Web
Imports System.Web.Services
Imports System.Web.Services.Protocols
Imports System.Data.SqlClient
Imports System.Collections.Generic
Imports System.Web.Configuration
Imports System.Data

<WebService(Namespace:="http://ProASP.NET2.0/Atlas/"), _
 WebServiceBinding(ConformsTo:=WsiProfiles.BasicProfile1_1)> _
Public Class TerritoriesService
    Inherits System.Web.Services.WebService

    <WebMethod()> _
    Public Function GetTerritoriesInRegion(ByVal regionID As Integer) As List(Of
Territory)
        Dim con As SqlConnection =
            New SqlConnection(
            WebConfigurationManager.ConnectionStrings("Northwind").ConnectionString)
        Dim cmd As SqlCommand =
            New SqlCommand(
            "SELECT * FROM Territories WHERE RegionID=@RegionID", con)
        cmd.Parameters.Add(New SqlParameter("@RegionID", SqlDbType.Int, 4))
        cmd.Parameters("@RegionID").Value = regionID
        Dim territories As New List(Of Territory)
        Try
            con.Open()
            Dim reader As SqlDataReader = cmd.ExecuteReader

            While reader.Read
                territories.Add(New Territory(reader("TerritoryID").ToString,
                      reader("TerritoryDescription").ToString))

            End While
            reader.Close()
        Catch err As SqlException
            ' Mask errors.
            Throw New ApplicationException("Data error.")
        Finally
            con.Close()
        End Try
        Return territories
    End Function
End Class
```

The code in the GetTerritoriesInRegion() method is similar to the code you used in Chapter 34 to serve the client callback. However, this code has a key difference—instead of returning a single long string with the results, the information is returned using a dedicated Territory class. This is a much tidier approach that prevents casual errors.

The Territory class wraps two pieces of string information. It uses public member variables rather than properties because it's intended solely as a data package that transports information over the wire:

```
Imports Microsoft.VisualBasic

Public Class Territory
    Public ID As String
    Public Description As String

    Public Sub New(ByVal id As String, ByVal description As String)
        Me.ID = id
        Me.Description = description
    End Sub

    Public Sub New()
    End Sub
End Class
```

If you're curious, you can look at the JavaScript proxy that Atlas creates. To do so, request your web service but tack on /js at the end (as in TerritoriesService.asmx/js). When you do, you'll see the following code (with line breaks added for legibility):

```
var TerritoriesService = new function() {
  this.path = "http://localhost:1101/Atlas/TerritoriesService.asmx";
  this.appPath = "http://localhost:1101/Atlas/";
  var cm = Sys.Net.ServiceMethod.createProxyMethod;
  cm(this,"GetTerritoriesInRegion","regionID");
}
var gtc = Sys.Net.WebMethod.generateTypedConstructor;
var Territory=gtc("Territory");
```

In JavaScript, you define a class by creating a no-parameter constructor. Essentially, the TerritoriesService class stores the location of your web service and uses a few magic bits from the Atlas script library to allow you to call it. If you create a page that uses this web service, Atlas adds a link that imports this JavaScript code so you can use the TerritoriesService variable as a web service proxy.

It's worth pointing out that Atlas web service calls do not use SOAP, because SOAP support is not present in JavaScript (at least not without a separate component). Instead, Atlas web service calls use JavaScript Object Notation (JSON), a lightweight text-based data exchange format that's easier to construct on the client. JSON does not use XML, but it does support arrays (as lists of values) and structures (using name/value pairs). However, JSON obviously won't support SOAP-based features, such as SOAP headers or SOAP extensions. The need to use JSON is another reason why Atlas web services must use a different HTTP handler than ordinary .asmx web services.

■ **Note** When you enable the HTTP handler for Atlas web services, you gain the ability to use JSON calls. However, you don't remove the ability to use other protocols. In other words, SOAP-based clients can still interact with your web service.

Calling a Web Service with JavaScript

Now that you've created the web service you need, the next step is to configure your page so it knows about TerritoriesService. That way, the ScriptManager will automatically generate a JavaScript proxy, which you can use to make your calls.

To configure your page to use TerritoriesService, you simply add the <Services> section in the tag for the ScriptManager control. This section lists all the services your page uses and their locations:

```
<atlas:ScriptManager ID="ScriptManager1" runat="server" >
  <Services>
    <atlas:ServiceReference Path="~/TerritoriesService.asmx" />
  </Services>
</atlas:ScriptManager>
```

Now you can call the TerritoriesService proxy at any time using the fully qualified web service class name. Here's a line of JavaScript code that calls the GetTerritoriesInRegion() method:

```
TerritoriesService.GetTerritoriesInRegion(regionID, OnRequestComplete);
```

Client-side web service calls are asynchronous, so you always need to supply the original web method parameters along with one extra parameter, which identifies the function that should be called when the result is received. Optionally, you can add two more references that point out the functions to use in the case of a client-side timeout or a server-side error:

```
TerritoriesService.GetTerritoriesInRegion(regionID,
  OnRequestComplete, OnTimeout, OnError);
```

The final step that's needed to complete the list box example is to add the JavaScript code that calls the web service and handles the result. In this case, you need at least two functions: one to start the callback and one to receive the result. Here's the JavaScript function that starts the process:

```
function GetTerritories(regionID)
{
    TerritoriesService.GetTerritoriesInRegion(regionID,
      OnRequestComplete, OnTimeout, OnError);
}
```

Changing the selection in the first list box triggers the JavaScript function that performs the callback and passes the regionID value from the current selection:

```
<asp:DropDownList ID="lstRegions" Runat="server" ...
  onChange="GetTerritories(this.value);" />
```

■ **Tip** Technically, you could place all the code from the GetTerritories() function directly in the onChange attribute and reduce the number of JavaScript functions you need to write. However, separating the code that calls the web service improves the readability of your code and makes it easier to maintain.

The OnRequestComplete() method is triggered when the response arrives. It receives the return value through its single parameter and then adds the information to the second list:

```
function OnRequestComplete(result)
{
    var lstTerritories = document.getElementById("lstTerritories");
    lstTerritories.innerHTML = "";

    for (var n = 0; n < result.length; n++)
    {
        var option = document.createElement("option");
        option.value = result[n].ID;
        option.innerHTML = result[n].Description;
```

```
        lstTerritories.appendChild(option);
    }
}
```

The remarkable feature of this code is that it's able to work with the result returned from the web method without any extra deserialization work. That's all the more impressive considering that the web method returns a generic list of Territory objects, which obviously has no equivalent in JavaScript code. Instead, Atlas creates a definition for the Territory object and returns the full list in an array. This allows your JavaScript code to loop over the array and examine the ID and Description properties of each item.

Now this example works exactly as the client callback version in Chapter 34. The difference is that this version uses a strongly typed web method, with no messy string serialization code. Also, you don't need to add any server-side code to retrieve the callback reference and insert it dynamically. Instead, you can use a straightforward proxy that provides access to your web service.

As a finishing touch, you can add timeout and error-handling functions, as shown here:

```
function OnTimeout(result)
{
    var lbl = document.getElementById("lblInfo");
    lbl.innerHTML = "<b>Request timed out.</b>";
}

function OnError(result)
{
    var lbl = document.getElementById("lblInfo");
    lbl.innerHTML = "<b>" + result.get_message() + "</b>";
}
```

The OnError() function receives an error object, complete with a get_message() method that retrieves the error text and a get_stacktrace() method that returns a detailed call stack showing where the error occurred. Figure 35-7 shows what happens when the web method fails to connect to the database and throws a standard ApplicationException.

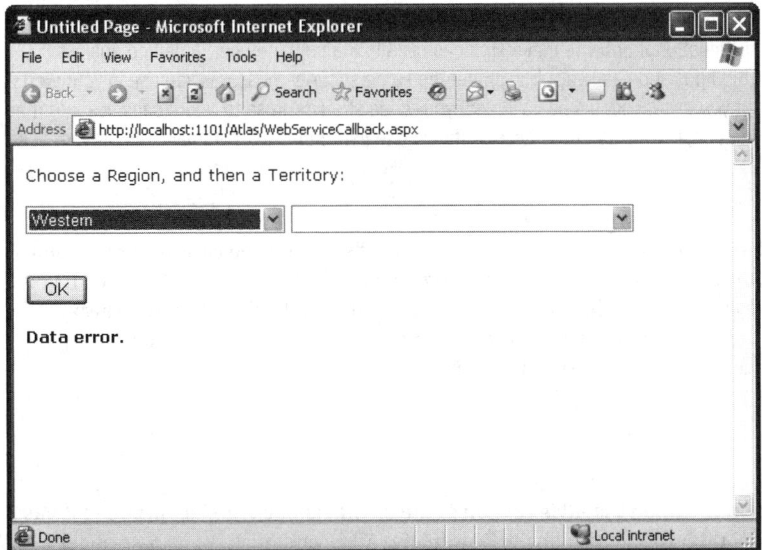

Figure 35-7. *Dealing with server-side errors on the client*

■ **Tip** So far, this example uses the most basic Atlas feature: web service callbacks. As a result, you can save a little download time by using the AtlasRuntime.js library instead of the full Atlas.js library. To do so, set the EnableScriptComponents property of the ScriptManager control to false.

Placing a Web Method in a Page

In most cases, it makes sense to create a separate web service to handle your Atlas callbacks. This approach generally results in clearer pages and makes it easier to debug and refine your code. However, in some situations you may decide you have one or more web methods that are designed explicitly for use on a single page and that really shouldn't be reused in other parts of the application. In this case, you may choose to create a dedicated web service for each page (just take the page name and add the word *Service* or *Callbacks* to the end), or you might choose to move the web service code into the page.

Placing the web method code in the page is easy—in fact, all you need is a simple bit of cut and paste. First, copy your web method (complete with the <WebMethod()> attribute) into your page. Next, remove the reference in the <Services> section of the ScriptManager tag. Finally, change your JavaScript code so it calls the method through the PageMethods object, as shown here:

```
PageMethods.GetTerritoriesInRegion(regionID, OnRequestComplete);
```

The PageMethods object exposes all the web methods you've added to the current web page.

One advantage of placing a web method in a page is that the method is no longer exposed through an .asmx file. As a result, it's not considered part of a public web service, and it's not as easy for someone else to discover. This is appealing if you're trying to hide your web services from curious users.

■ **Note** It makes no difference to the security of your application whether you place your web methods in a page or a dedicated web service. Placing your web method in the page may hide it from casual users, but a real attacker will start by looking at the HTML of your page, which includes a reference to the JavaScript proxy. Malicious users can easily use the JavaScript proxy to make spurious calls to the web method. To defend against threats like these, your web methods should always implement the same security measures you use in your web pages. For example, any input you accept should be validated, your code should refuse to return sensitive information to users who aren't authenticated, and database access should use parameterized commands to prevent SQL injection attacks.

Another reason you might choose to code your web methods in the page class is to read values from view state or the controls on the page. When you trigger a page method, a stripped-down version of the page life cycle executes, just like with the ASP.NET client callback feature you saw in Chapter 34. Of course, there's no point in trying to modify page details because the page isn't being rerendered, so any changes you make will simply be discarded.

Atlas Script

The previous example demonstrated the Atlas version of the client callback model. Although it has the same plumbing as the ASP.NET client callback feature, the Atlas version provides a stronger foundation that's built on web services. However, both approaches have one feature in common. No matter which technique you use, you still need to write your own JavaScript.

This won't always be the case. As you'll see throughout this chapter, Atlas has the ability to generate JavaScript code for a wide range of scenarios. But to tell Atlas what script to generate, you need to master a new standard called *Atlas script*.

Understanding Atlas Script

Atlas script is a chunk of markup you place in a script block inside the .aspx portion of your page. Unlike a block of JavaScript code, this script block has its type set to text/xml-script, as shown here:

```
<script type="text/xml-script">
  ...
</script>
```

The Atlas script block declares the controls you want to use with various Atlas features. It can also define actions that took place in response to certain events, bindings that manage the flow of information from one source to another, behaviors that extend the way controls work, and templates that format complex information.

It's important to understand that the content in the Atlas script block is XML-based markup that describes your page and hooks up various features. The Atlas script block can't contain executable code statements (such as a JavaScript function).

To understand how Atlas script works, consider this simple example:

```
<script type="text/xml-script">
  <page xmlns:script="http://schemas.microsoft.com/xml-script/2005">
    <components>
      <textBox id="text1" />
    </components>
  </page>
</script>
```

Every Atlas script block starts with a root <page> element, which contains a <components> element. The <components> section contains elements for every control you want to use with Atlas. This example declares a single text box. This doesn't necessarily mean the page has only one text box—it may have many other controls—but it does indicate that the text box is the only one you want to use with Atlas.

You can place the Atlas script block in the <head> or <body> portion of the page, but by convention it's usually added just after the </form> tag that closes the <form> section of the page where you declare all the server controls.

■ **Note** Along with controls, the <components> section can also include elements that represent other nonvisual components (such as timers, web services, and so on).

With the addition of the new Atlas script block, an .aspx web page can contain three types of content:

- Server control tags, which are converted to objects on the server and render themselves to HTML at the end of the page life cycle.
- Ordinary HTML content and JavaScript code, which isn't processed by ASP.NET. This content is rendered into the final HTML as is.
- The Atlas script block, which is used by the JavaScript-powered Atlas libraries.

In other words, the Atlas script block plays a similar role to ASP.NET's control tags. The difference is that the control tags are processed by the server-side ASP.NET engine, while the Atlas script block is processed by the Atlas libraries, which run primarily on the client.

■Note Because the Atlas script block is processed on the client, it isn't changed into anything else on the server. This might seem like a fairly obvious point, but it's easy to forget this if you're used to the server-side world of ASP.NET, where web controls are serialized into ordinary HTML. When rendering the page, the browser ignores the Atlas script block, because it doesn't recognize the text/xml-script type.

In many ways, the Atlas script block is the heart of the Atlas framework. It provides a gateway that allows you to access all the other client-side features beyond simple web service callbacks.

The Atlas Life Cycle

When you first learned about web server controls, you considered their life cycle—in other words, when they're created, how long they live, and when they're destroyed. The Atlas life cycle is quite a bit different, because it executes on the client side. It begins when the client receives the fully rendered HTML. At this point, the following tasks take place:

1. **Load the browser compatibility layer (for non-IE browsers)**: Atlas uses certain parts of the HTML DOM that aren't supported on all browsers, such as the attachEvent() and detachEvent() methods. On non-IE browsers, Atlas loads a compatibility layer.

■Note The Atlas team decided to use the compatibility layer for non-IE browsers for two reasons. First, IE is the most widely used browser by far. Second, because of the occasionally poor standards support in IE, it's easier to design a solution that fills the gaps on non-IE browsers rather than the other way around.

---

2. **Load the Atlas core**: This is the base functionality described earlier that makes JavaScript behave a little more like C# and .NET.
3. **Load the second browser compatibility layer**: Currently, a second layer is required only for Safari, which has a quirk of converting tag names to uppercase when they're parsed in the DOM.
4. **Process the Atlas markup**: The window.onload event is raised in the browser. Atlas handles this event and parses the Atlas script block at this point.
5. **Initialize all Atlas components**: After the Atlas markup has been read and all the Atlas controls are instantiated, they're given the chance to initialize themselves. For example, if you've set a property in an Atlas control tag, it's at this point that the property is rendered to the corresponding HTML.

As you interact with the page, various bits of Atlas client-side code may be executed. If the page is posted back, it's rerendered from scratch, and this whole process starts again when the browser receives the new page.

Defining Controls

Before you can do anything with Atlas script, you need to define the controls you want to use. If you're new to Atlas, this step will seem a little odd, because every control you define *already exists on the page.* You define it in the Atlas script block simply so you can use it with other Atlas features. If you don't need to use a given page element, you don't need to include it in the Atlas script block.

To make matters a little more confusing, the mapping between controls in the Atlas script block at the HTML of your page isn't exact. Essentially, Atlas provides a client-side abstraction layer—a set of classes that wraps the underlying HTML of your page. You can think of this layer as a much more powerful version of the HTML DOM. To interact with a page element using an Atlas control, you need to pair the element you want to use with the appropriate Atlas control class.

■ **Note** You can use Atlas to manipulate the HTML that's rendered by ASP.NET server controls, or you can use it to modify otherwise static HTML elements. The only requirement is that the element you want to interact with has an id attribute that gives it a unique name. That way Atlas can find the appropriate element using the document.getElementById() method, just as you do in handwritten JavaScript code.

Currently, Atlas uses a relatively small set of basic classes, all of which are placed in the Sys.UI namespace and derive from the base Control class. Table 35-1 lists them.

Table 35-1. *Atlas Client Controls*

Class	Description
Button	Wraps buttons and other elements that can be clicked to trigger an action.
CheckBox	Wraps the check box input element.
HyperLink	Wraps the <a> anchor tag, which represents a hyperlink.
Image	Wraps the <img> image tag.
Label	Wraps a <div> or <span> element, both of which are used to wrap arbitrary content. The <div> element groups other block elements (such as paragraphs and headings), and <span> is an inline element that often wraps small sections of text inside another block element.
Select	Wraps the <select> element, which represents a list box or drop-down list.
TextBox	Wraps all the text input elements.

For example, consider an ASP.NET page that has the following markup:

```
<html>
<head runat="server">
  <title>Atlas Test</title>
</head>
<body>
  <form id="form1" runat="server">
    <div id="pnlNames">
      <table>
      <tr>
        <td>First Name:  </td>
        <td><asp:TextBox ID="txtFirst" runat="server"></asp:TextBox></td>
      </tr>
      <tr>
        <td>Last Name:</td>
        <td><asp:TextBox ID="txtLast" runat="server"></asp:TextBox></td>
      </tr>
    </table>
    <br />
```

```
    <input type="button" id="cmdOK" style="width: 88px" value="OK" />
    <p><span id="spanResult"></span></p>
    </div>

    <atlas:ScriptManager ID="ScriptManager1" runat="server">
    </atlas:ScriptManager>
  </form>

  <script type="text/xml-script"></script>
</body>
</html>
```

This page includes two TextBox web controls, a button that *isn't* defined as a server control (because you want to handle its button clicks on the client), and a <span> tag that you will use to insert additional text. The page also features the requisite ScriptManager control and an empty Atlas script block. Figure 35-8 shows the page.

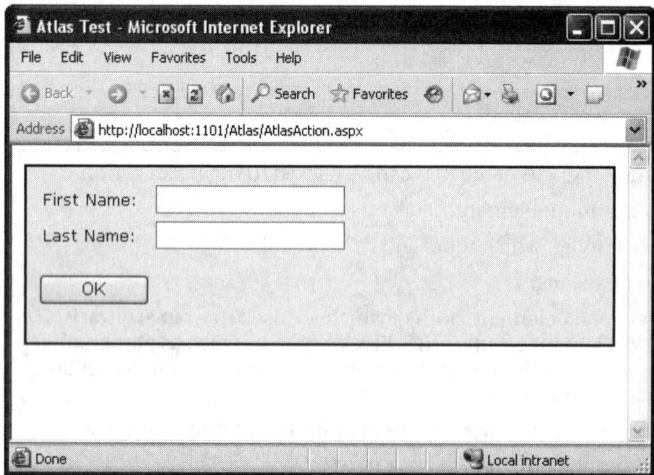

Figure 35-8. *An Atlas-ready web form*

You can fill in the Atlas script block to gain access to the TextBox controls, the button, and the <span> element. Here's the script block you need:

```
<page xmlns:script="http://schemas.microsoft.com/xml-script/2005">
   <components>
     <textBox id="txtFirst" />
     <textBox id="txtLast" />
     <button id="cmdOK" />
     <label id="spanResult" />
   </components>
 </page>
</script>
```

Notice that the Atlas script block doesn't contain any style or layout information. That's because these details are already coded in the HTML portion of the page.

■Note Although the control class names use Pascal case (as in *TextBox*), the XML elements you use to define these controls must use camel case (as in *textBox*). This is the same rule that applies with web.config settings.

In this example, the Atlas controls appear in the same order as the HTML elements on the page. However, this isn't a requirement. It's perfectly fine to place them in any order, as long as you use the correct control IDs. If you're defining Atlas controls that map to ASP.NET controls, you should remember the following quirks:

- Many controls generate more than one element. Usually in this case, the containing element will have the ID. For example, if you use the Calendar control, it renders itself as an HTML table, and the root <table> tag has the id attribute.
- If you place a control inside a naming container, its ID will change. You'll notice this effect if you place a control into a template for a rich data control (such as the GridView) or if you place a control in a master page. You can get the correct ID from the ClientID property.

If in doubt, just take a look at the rendered HTML of your page to find out the exact ID value and to see where they're applied.

The Atlas script block is just a starting point. To actually do anything with these controls, you'll need to add actions, behaviors, or bindings. In the following sections, you'll learn how to create a simple Atlas script block for several sample pages, and you'll see what it allows you to do.

■Note In the future, Atlas script won't be handwritten. Instead, you'll be able to use a tool such as Visual Studio to quickly flag the controls you want to use with Atlas, and the Atlas markup you need will be generated automatically. Unfortunately, Atlas doesn't yet include these design-time features.

Actions

You use actions to perform small tasks. Once you bind an action to a client-side event in an Atlas control, that action will take place automatically when the event occurs.

Currently, Atlas includes three actions, although it's likely that more will be added and you can use JavaScript to define your own. Table 35-2 lists the basic actions.

Table 35-2. *Actions*

Class	Description
SetPropertyAction	Modifies a control by changing a property value.
InvokeMethodAction	Calls a JavaScript method. Using the web service proxy, this action allows you to call a web method.
PostBackAction	Posts the page to the server.

Typically, you'll perform an action in response to an event from an Atlas control. All controls include a propertyChanged event that fires when any property value is modified. Most controls also provide a click event, and the Select control adds a selectionChanged event. (Oddly enough, the TextBox control doesn't provide a textChanged event, but you can respond to the propertyChanged event instead or use the behaviors described in the "Behaviors" section.)

To see how an action works, you can take the "Atlasified" page shown in Figure 35-8 and add a click event to the button. To define an event, you simply add a nested element with the event name, as shown here:

```
<button id="cmdOK">
  <click>
  </click>
</button>
```

■ **Note** To use the click event of a button, you must make sure you're using an ordinary button, *not* the ASP.NET Button server control. That's because the Button server control always renders as a submit button, so clicking it always posts back the page. If you're using Atlas, this isn't the behavior you want—instead, you'd like to handle the event on the client.

Inside the <click> section, you place the element that defines the action you want to use. The following action sets the property of another Atlas control—the spanResult label:

```
<button id="cmdOK">
  <click>
    <setProperty
      target="spanResult"
      property="text"
      value="You clicked the button." />
  </click>
</button>
```

The <setProperty> element takes several attributes. This example uses only the required ones: a target that identifies the control that will be affected by the action, the property of the control you want to change, and the value you want to supply for that property. Figure 35-9 shows the rather underwhelming result.

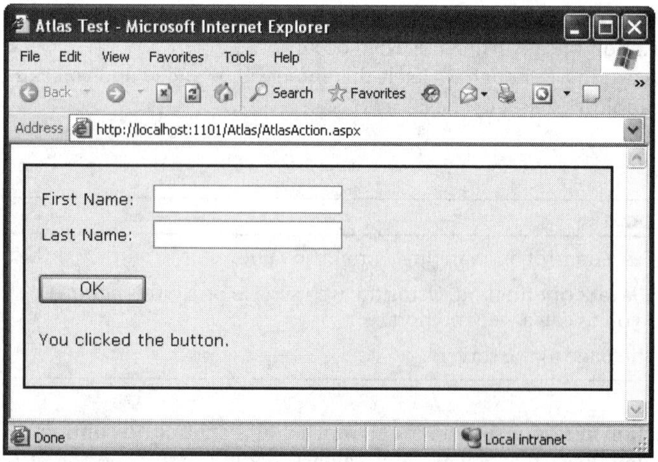

Figure 35-9. *Showing a client-side message*

More commonly, you can use the SetPropertyAction to disable and enable controls or to dynamically hide and show entire panels. For example, consider the revised version of this page shown in Figure 35-10. It provides two links that, when clicked, collapse the panel with all the controls or pop it back into view.

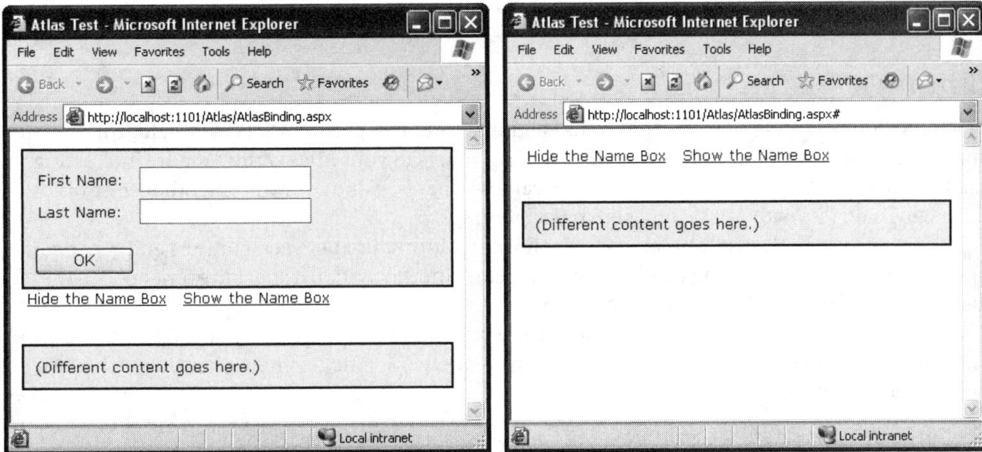

Figure 35-10. *Dynamically hiding and showing panels*

To create this example, you need to start by adding the hyperlinks. The URL is unimportant, because you'll be handling the click event on the client. However, if you leave it blank, you'll need to manually add the formatting you want. (Typically, links display in blue, underlined lettering.) A quicker option is to supply # for the URL, which creates a link that points to the current page:

```
<a href="#" id="lnkHide">Hide the Name Box</a>  
<a href="#" id="lnkShow">Show the Name Box</a>
```

Now, you need to add these two hyperlinks and the <div> that represents the box of controls to your Atlas script. Here's the complete markup:

```
<label id="pnlNames" />

<hyperLink id="lnkHide">
  <click>
    <setProperty target="pnlNames" property="visibilityMode"
     value="Collapse" />
    <setProperty target="pnlNames" property="visible"
     value="false" />
  </click>
</hyperLink>

<hyperLink id="lnkShow">
  <click>
    <setProperty target="pnlNames" property="visible" value="true" />
  </click>
</hyperLink>
```

You'll notice that the lnkHide hyperlink actually performs two actions—first it makes sure the visibilityMode property is set correctly, and then it hides the panel. All controls support two visibility modes: Collapse (which removes the content from the page entirely) and Hide (which replaces the content with blank space). If you want the rest of the page to reflow to fill the space that's vacated by the hidden control, you must use the Collapse mode.

To extend this example, you can add more collapsible controls. You can then allow the user to hide and show each panel individually or choose one panel at a time. The result is similar to what you can achieve with the Panel and MultiView server controls, except Atlas allows all the collapsing to take place without a server postback.

Bindings

In the previous example, you saw how to use actions to change properties. However, for this approach to work, you must hardcode the property values in your Atlas script. A more interesting example is to set the property using dynamic values—that is, values drawn from other controls on the page. To do this with Atlas, you need to use *bindings*.

Bindings are a solution for managing the flow of information between controls and other components. Essentially, a binding connects one object to another. When a specific event occurs, the data is copied from the first object to the second.

For example, imagine you want to modify the previous example so the first and last names you enter appear in the label. One way to do this is to create two <span> elements, one for each piece of bound information:

```
<p><span id="spanFirst"></span> <span id="spanLast"></span></p>
```

Now you can fill the two <span> elements by binding them to the text values in the two text boxes. Here's the Atlas script you need:

```
<label id="spanFirst">
  <bindings>
    <binding dataContext="txtFirst" dataPath="text" property="text" />
  </bindings>
</label>

<label id="spanLast">
  <bindings>
    <binding dataContext="txtLast" dataPath="text" property="text" />
  </bindings>
</label>
```

The minimum information you need to supply for a binding includes the source object (dataContext), the property of the source object that has the data you want (dataPath), and the property in the target object where you want to copy the value (text). By default, the target object is the parent element—in this case, the label.

This binding is known as an *in* binding, because information is copied into the control that's designated by the parent element. However, you could also apply an *out* binding in the text box. The following Atlas markup is equivalent to the previous example:

```
<textBox id="txtFirst">
  <bindings>
    <binding dataContext="spanFirst" dataPath="text" property="text"
     direction="Out" />
  </bindings>
</textBox>

<textBox id="txtLast">
  <bindings>
    <binding dataContext="spanLast" dataPath="text" property="text"
     direction="Out" />
  </bindings>
</textBox>
```

In all these examples, the bound values are updated as soon as you tab out of the text box after modifying its text (in other words, when the JavaScript onchange event occurs).

Finally, Atlas also introduces the concept of *transformers*, which extend data binding. Essentially, a transformer takes the data you're binding and reformats it. For example, you can use a transformer to add or multiply numbers, to invert a Boolean value, or to add text. More usefully, you can create custom transformers using JavaScript code.

The following example uses the ToString transformer to place the text values into a full sentence:

```
<label id="spanFirst">
  <bindings>
    <binding dataContext="txtFirst" dataPath="text" property="text"
     transform="ToString" transformerArgument="Your full name is {0}" />
  </bindings>
</label>

<label id="spanLast">
  <bindings>
    <binding dataContext="txtLast" dataPath="text" property="text"
     transform="ToString" transformerArgument="{0}." />
  </bindings>
</label>
```

Figure 35-11 shows the result.

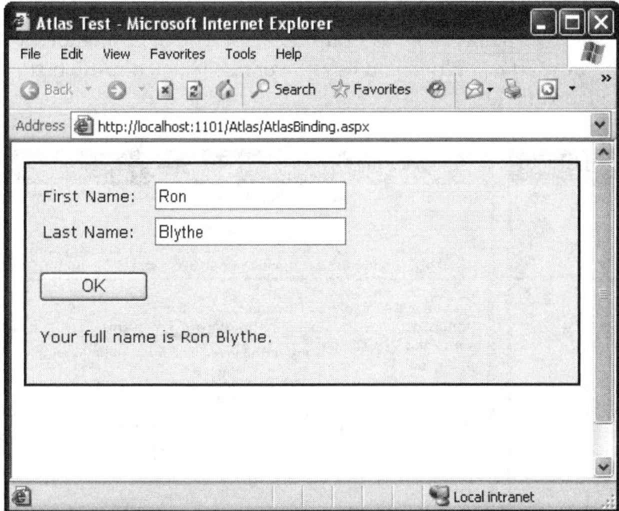

Figure 35-11. *Formatting bound data*

■ **Note** In this example, it's hard to see the benefit of Atlas script. It hardly seems worthwhile to write a whole chunk of tags to deal with updating an ordinary label, especially when the alternative is to use a few concise lines of JavaScript. However, you'll see the real advantage of Atlas script when you begin considering features that would be more difficult to implement in JavaScript. One example is data binding. Using Atlas script, you can quickly define a data binding relationship that tells Atlas how to fill a grid and handle operations such as record deletions, inserts, and updates. Once you define this relationship, Atlas will call the required server code automatically. Trying to design the same solution with pure JavaScript would take much more work.

Behaviors

The ingredient you can use with Atlas controls is behaviors, which are predefined bits of functionality you can attach to other HTML elements. Behaviors are triggered by client-side events and then can update properties, call methods, or provide complex functionality such as autocompletion in text boxes. Of course, you can also create your own behaviors but because they tend to be quite complex, the chief benefit is reusing the prebuilt behaviors that Microsoft and other third parties develop. Table 35-3 lists the behaviors that Atlas includes.

Table 35-3. *Behaviors*

Class	Description
AutoCompleteBehavior	Allows you to show a drop-down list of suggestions under a text control as the user types
ClickBehavior	Performs an action when the user clicks the element to which the behavior is attached
HoverBehavior	Performs an action when the mouse pointer enters or leaves the bounding box of the element to which the behavior is attached
PopupBehavior	Displays a pop-up element overtop of a portion of the page
ProgressBehavior	Provides a busy indicator for long-running operations and disables all controls while the operation is underway

The following example demonstrates HoverBehavior and PopupBehavior. The page includes a piece of underlined text (in this case, the word *Atlas*). When you hover over this text, a pop-up box with several links appears, as shown in Figure 35-12.

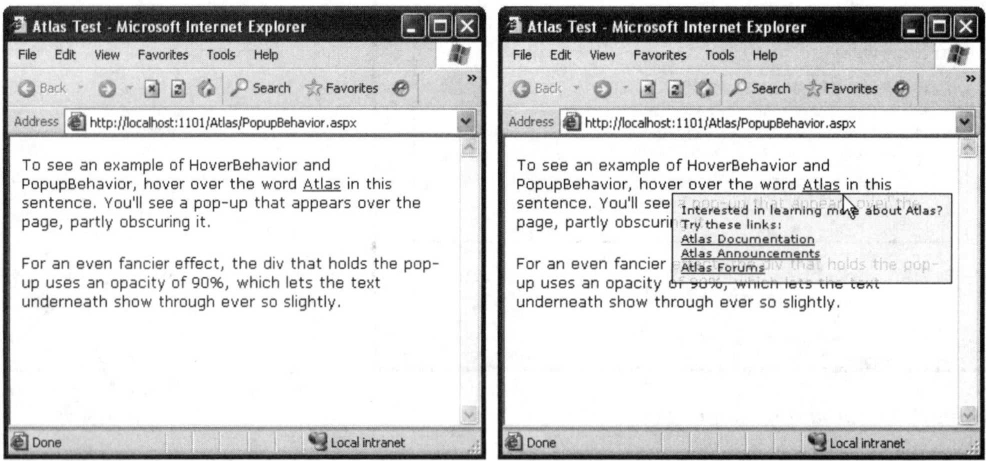

Figure 35-12. *A dynamic pop-up panel*

To create this page, you need to place the content for the pop-up box into a <div> element. Here's the content of the page:

```
<p>
  To see an example of HoverBehavior and PopupBehavior, hover over the
  word <a id="lnkAtlas" class="Link">Atlas</a> in this sentence.
  You'll see a pop-up that appears over the page, partly obscuring it.
</p>
<p>
  For an even fancier effect, the div that holds the pop-up uses an
  opacity of 90%, which lets the text underneath show through ever so
  slightly.
</p>
<div id="popup" style="...">
  Interested in learning more about Atlas?<br />
  Try these links:<br />
  <a href="http://atlas.asp.net/docs/">Atlas Documentation</a><br />
  <a href="http://weblogs.asp.net/atlas/">Atlas Announcements</a><br />
  <a href="http://forums.asp.net/default.aspx?ForumGroupID=34">Atlas Forums</a>
</div>

<atlas:ScriptManager ID="ScriptManager1" runat="server">
</atlas:ScriptManager>
```

Next, you need to define two items—the <a> link and the <div> for the pop-up—in your Atlas script. The pop-up is hidden initially, and given the pop-up behavior, it will appear superimposed over the page, with its top-left corner placed at the bottom-left corner of the link above it:

```
<script type="text/xml-script">
  <page xmlns:script="http://schemas.microsoft.com/xml-script/2005">
    <components>
      <label id="popup" visible="false">
        <behaviors>
          <popupBehavior id="popupBehavior" parentElement="lnkAtlas"
           positioningMode="BottomLeft"/>
        </behaviors>
      </label>
      ...
```

This creates the pop-up, but it doesn't show it. To display the pop-up, you need to use the show() method of the PopupBehavior class. You can call this method when an event occurs using the InvokeMethodAction, as you learned earlier. However, for a fancier effect you can add HoverBehavior to the mix, which handles the mouse events for you. Using HoverBehavior, you can react when the mouse hovers over the link by showing the pop-up, and you can hide it when the mouse moves away. Here's the Atlas script that does the trick:

```
      ...
      <hyperLink id="lnkAtlas">
        <behaviors>
          <hoverBehavior unhoverDelay="1000" hoverElement="popup">
            <hover>
              <invokeMethod target="popupBehavior" method="show"/>
            </hover>
            <unhover>
              <invokeMethod target="popupBehavior" method="hide"/>
            </unhover>
          </hoverBehavior>
        </behaviors>
      </hyperLink>
    </components>
  </page>
</script>
```

This example shows some of the real promise of Atlas. Using prebuilt behaviors, you're able to quickly create a dynamic page with a pop-up panel. Best of all, you don't need to write a line of JavaScript.

Dealing with Data on the Client

One of the goals of Atlas is to allow you to use client-side data functionality. When the Microsoft developers finish these features, you'll be able to use the client-side equivalent of a control such as the GridView or DetailsView control. The difference is that when you perform a record operation (such as deleting, inserting, or updating a record), the page won't post back. Instead, the client-side data control will perform a callback to a web method that performs the task. Ideally, you'll even be able to perform sorting, paging, and editing on the client side.

The data features are some of the fastest-changing parts of the Atlas framework, so they may not stay the same in future builds. However, the platform is mature enough that it's worth considering two examples. In the following sections, you'll see how to use a client-side data list that fetches (and displays) information asynchronously for a smoother and more responsive user experience. You'll also consider a client-side record editor that lets you step from one record to the next and commit your changes without a postback.

Building a Data Service

Before you use either of the client-side data controls you'll consider next, you need to implement the data logic on the server. This means you need to write the code that's responsible for retrieving and updating records. You need to present this code in such a way that it's available to the client-side controls so they can call on it when needed, without forcing you to write additional JavaScript code to manage the process.

The obvious solution is to build a set of web methods that the client-side controls can call to perform the different data tasks. To make this even easier, Atlas supports a new *data service* pattern. The idea is that you create a specialized web service that's expressly designed for use with the client-side data controls. It inherits from a different base class—Microsoft.Web.Services.DataService—and it uses the DataObjectMethod attribute to flag the methods that will be used for different data operations.

The following example presents a complete data service that works with the Employees table from the Northwind database. It doesn't actually contain any data access code—instead, that work is farmed out to the EmployeeDB class in a separate component, which is a pattern you first considered in Chapter 8. However, this data source *does* have everything you need to expose your data logic to the Atlas controls.

```
<%@ WebService Language="VB" Class="EmployeesDataService" %>

Imports System.Web
Imports System.Web.Services
Imports System.Web.Services.Protocols
Imports System.Data
Imports System.ComponentModel
Imports System.Collections.Generic


<WebService(Namespace:="http://tempuri.org/")> _
<WebServiceBinding(ConformsTo:=WsiProfiles.BasicProfile1_1)> _
Public Class EmployeesDataService
    Inherits Microsoft.Web.Services.DataService
```

```
    Public employeeDB As New EmployeeDB

    <DataObjectMethod(DataObjectMethodType.Select)> _
    Public Function GetEmployees() As List(Of EmployeeDetails)
        Return employeeDB.GetEmployees
    End Function

    <DataObjectMethod(DataObjectMethodType.Delete)> _
    Public Sub DeleteEmployee(ByVal employeeID As Integer)
        employeeDB.DeleteEmployee(employeeID)
    End Sub

    <DataObjectMethod(DataObjectMethodType.Insert)> _
    Public Sub InsertEmployee(ByVal emp As EmployeeDetails)
        employeeDB.InsertEmployee(emp)
    End Sub

    <DataObjectMethod(DataObjectMethodType.Update)> _
    Public Sub UpdateEmployee(ByVal emp As EmployeeDetails)
        employeeDB.UpdateEmployee(emp)
    End Sub
End Class
```

The key ingredient here is the DataObjectMethod attribute, which you must use instead of WebMethod to flag the methods that perform data operations.

At a minimum, every data service requires a select method that retrieves the records. This method can return a DataTable, an array, or a strongly typed collection. Additionally, you can use up to three more methods to take care of delete, insert, and update operations. These methods can take the data object you returned (in a collection) from the GetEmployees() method, or they can take a combination of parameters with matching names. For example, if you returned a DataTable in your select method, you can accept a DataRow in your update method. Or, if you used a collection with instances of some custom class (such as the EmployeeDetails class in this example), your update method can accept an EmployeeDetails object. Or, you can create an update method that accepts a list of parameters that have the same names as the DataRow fields or the EmployeeDetails properties. All in all, this is similar to the way the ObjectDataSource works for server-side binding.

Interestingly, the Atlas framework uses these attributes to build two higher-level web methods—one for requesting data and one for updating it. You can see these two methods by requesting the page for your data service. Figure 35-13 shows the page for the EmployeesDataService.

■ Note If you apply the DataObjectMethod attribute *and* the WebMethod attribute to the methods in your data service, you'll also see the individual methods appear in the list. For example, in the EmployeesDataService, you'd see the automatically generated GetData() and SetData() methods along with the GetEmployees(), DeleteEmployee(), UpdateEmployee(), and InsertEmployee() methods. This is a useful technique if you need to call these methods directly in your own code.

If you dig deeper into these methods, you'll discover that the GetData() method is fairly predictable—it returns your data by calling the select method—but the SetData() method is more interesting. It accepts a change list that has separate sections identifying new rows, deleted rows, and modified rows. The server then steps through the list, calling the appropriate method in your data service to handle each item.

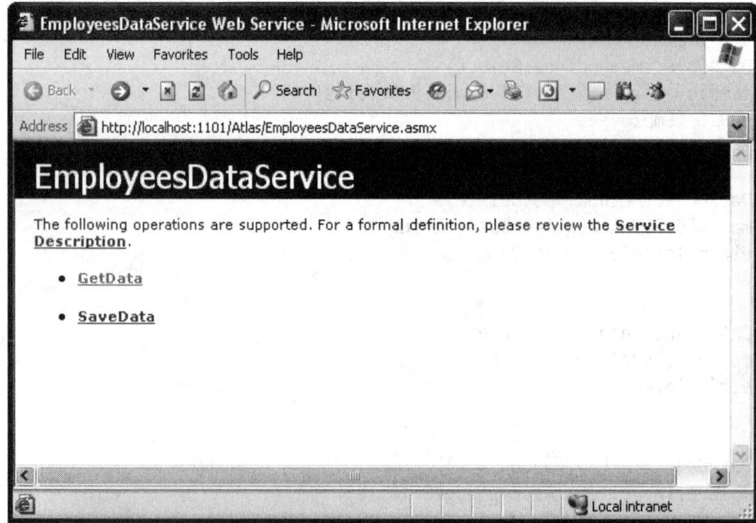

Figure 35-13. *Higher-level data service methods*

Now that you've created the data service, you still need to make one last change. Namely, you need to ensure that your data object will work with your data service. As with all web service objects, this means your data object must have a default no-argument constructor, and all its properties must be readable and writable. In addition, you need to use the DataObjectField attribute on every property. This indicates the property is available for client-side data binding. Here's an example:

```
<DataObjectField(false)> _
    Public Property FirstName As String
        Get
            Return firstName
        End Get
        Set
            firstName = value
        End Set
    End Property
```

The constructor argument identifies whether your field corresponds to the primary key. For example, when defining the EmployeeID property, you'll use true to indicate that the EmployeeID value is the unique, identifying value for each row.

Additionally, it's a good idea to use the DefaultValue attribute to supply the information that will initially appear when the user creates a new record. If you don't set the default value, you'll see the text *(null)* appear in your controls when you create a new record.

```
    <DataObjectField(false), _
     DefaultValue("")> _
    Public Property FirstName As String
        Get
            Return firstName
        End Get
        Set
            firstName = value
        End Set
    End Property
```

Now you're ready to use your data service with two client-side Atlas controls. First, you'll try a read-only example with the ListView. Next, you'll consider a more powerful record editor with the ItemView.

The Client-Side ListView

The ListView is a client-side control that allows you to show multiples records of information on a single page. The ListView works by repeating a template for each record (much as the GridView server control works when using templates). The advantage of the client-side ListView is that it maintains the data on the client and formats it for display in the browser. This means the ListView can use Ajax-style features, such as querying the data asynchronously and providing sorting and paging features that work without postbacks.

Figure 35-14 shows a straightforward ListView with a list of employees, both before and after it has loaded the data.

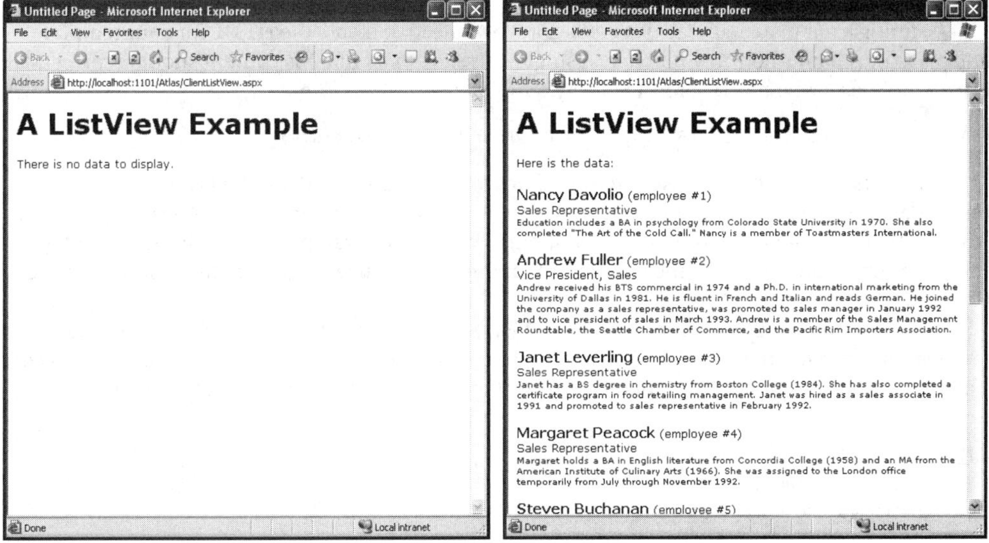

Figure 35-14. *A ListView that loads data asynchronously*

To create a ListView, the first step is to add a <div> element where you want to place the ListView in your page. Initially, this <div> element is empty. When the page is processed on the client, Atlas springs into action, fetches your data, formats it, and inserts it into the <div> element.

```
<h1>A ListView Example</h1>
<div id="listView"></div>
```

To create the ListView, you need to define a template that tells Atlas how to format your record data. (In this case, that means telling Atlas how to arrange the values of the EmployeeDetails object.) Every ListView requires at least two templates: the layout template and the item template. However, you can supply up to four templates. Table 35-4 has the full list.

Table 35-4. *ListView Templates*

Element Name	Description
<layoutTemplate>	This top-level container wraps the entire list. If you're creating a table, this template would contain the opening <table> tag, column headings, and any footer. Inside the <layoutTemplate> is the <itemTemplate> and (optionally) a <separatorTemplate>.
<itemTemplate>	This template renders each item in the list. If you're using a table for your list, the item template would represent a single row (with the <tr> tag).
<separatorTemplate>	This optional template renders a separator between items in the ListView. It must be contained in the <layoutTemplate>.
<emptyTemplate>	This optional template renders alternate content if there's no data to display. It's also used while the ListView is in the process of fetching data from the server.

Defining a template requires two steps. First, you need to create the HTML for your template and place that somewhere in your page. A single <div> tag that contains content should represent each template. For example, here's an empty template:

```
<div id="masterNoDataTemplate">There is no data to display.</div>
```

The Atlas libraries need to use your templates to render the HTML for the ListView, which is inserted in the ListView's <div> tag. However, you don't want your templates to appear on their own where you declare them. For that reason, you must wrap all your templates in a hidden <div> tag. That way, the section can store the templates that the ListView needs but not affect the appearance of the page.

The following are all the templates for the ListView shown in Figure 35-14. You'll find a parent template, an item template, and a no-data template that's used before any information is retrieved. The item template includes five <span> controls that can be used to insert values from the EmployeeDetails class.

```
<div style="visibility:hidden;display:none">
  <div id="layoutTemplate">
    <p>Here is the data:</p>

    <div id="itemTemplate">
      <big><b>
        <span id="firstName"></span>
        <span id="lastName"></span>
      </b></big>
      (employee #<span id="employeeID"></span>)
      <br />
      <span id="title"></span><br />
      <small><span id="notes"></span></small>
      <br /><br />
    </div>
  </div>

  <div id="noDataTemplate">There is no data to display.</div>

</div>
```

Now that you've completed the HTML portion of your page, you need to define the ListView in the Atlas script block. You also need to map the <div> sections you've created to the appropriate templates in the ListView.

But before you can define the ListView, you need to add a link that points to your data service. To do this, you need to add the <dataSource> element to the Atlas script block. The <dataSource> element is an object you haven't seen yet—it's a noncontrol component that allows your page to bind to a data source. Technically, it creates a client-side Sys.Data.DataSource object, which plays the same role as the ObjectDataSource in server-side ASP.NET data binding.

```
<script type="text/xml-script">
  <page xmlns:script="http://schemas.microsoft.com/xml-script/2005">
    <components>

      <dataSource id="dataSource" serviceURL="EmployeesDataService.asmx"
       autoLoad="true"/>
      ...
```

Notice that the <dataSource> element includes an autoLoad attribute. When this is set to true, the data source will fetch the data you need when the page is first rendered. When this is false, you need to trigger this action manually (for example, in response to a client-side event).

Now that the data source is in place, you need to define the ListView. The first step is to link the ListView to the empty <div> section where you want Atlas to render the ListView content, by setting the id attribute:

```
      ...
      <listView id="listView" itemTemplateParentElementId="layoutTemplate">
      ...
```

Using data binding, you can link the data from the data source to the ListView:

```
      ...
        <bindings>
          <binding dataContext="dataSource" dataPath="data" property="data"/>
        </bindings>
      ...
```

Next, you also need to identify the <div> tag that has the parent template and the empty data template:

```
      ...
      <layoutTemplate>
        <template layoutElement="parentTemplate"/>
      </layoutTemplate>

      <emptyTemplate>
        <template layoutElement="noDataTemplate"/>
      </emptyTemplate>
      ...
```

The last, and lengthiest, part of your Atlas script defines the item template. It needs to bind each property from the data object (in this case, EmployeeDetails) to an element in the template. For example, the FirstName property is mapped to the <span> tag with the ID of firstName. This is conceptually quite simple, but it needs a fair bit of markup.

Here's the complete item template:

```
    ...
    <itemTemplate>
      <template layoutElement="itemTemplate">
        <label id="firstName">
          <bindings>
            <binding dataPath="FirstName" property="text"/>
          </bindings>
        </label>
        <label id="lastName">
          <bindings>
            <binding dataPath="LastName" property="text"/>
          </bindings>
        </label>
        <label id="employeeID">
          <bindings>
            <binding dataPath="EmployeeID" property="text"/>
          </bindings>
        </label>
        <label id="title">
          <bindings>
            <binding dataPath="Title" property="text"/>
          </bindings>
        </label>
        <label id="notes">
          <bindings>
            <binding dataPath="Notes" property="text"/>
          </bindings>
        </label>
      </template>
    </itemTemplate>
  </listView>

   </components>
  </page>
</script>
```

This completes the example. To try it, add the following line to the beginning of the Get-Employees() method:

```
System.Threading.Thread.Sleep(2000);
```

This adds a noticeable delay before the data appears in the control. When the page first appears, you'll see the empty data template. The records will be added to the list as they are received from the server.

■ **Tip** The ListView also has properties that allow you to apply styles to your templates. The only caveat is that you need to define these styles separately in an inline or external CSS file. Use itemCssClass to specify the CSS class to format every item, use alternatingItemCssClass to specify the CSS class for alternating items, use selectedItemCssClass to specify the CSS class for selected items, and use separatorCssClass to specify the CSS class for the separator section.

The Client-Side ItemView

The ListView allows you to show all your records at once (or, if you're using paging, in small groups). Atlas also includes a client-side control that's ideal for showing individual records and letting you step through a result set one row at a time. It's the ItemView.

In the next example, you'll see how to create an ItemView and how you can use it with your data source to perform client-side editing. Figure 35-15 shows the record browser you'll build. At the top are navigation buttons that let you move from one record to the next. Underneath is the main section, which presents the fields for the entire record in text boxes. Finally, the bottom of the page includes buttons for deleting the current record, creating a new record, and saving changes to the data source.

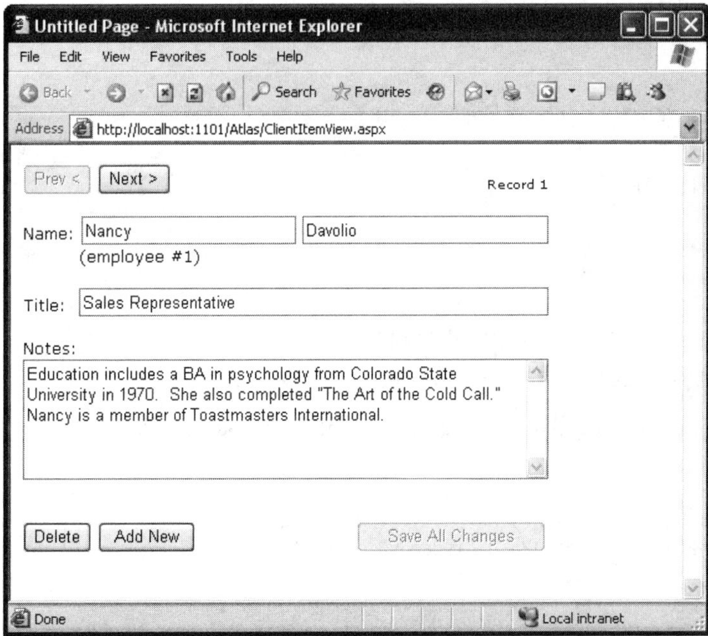

Figure 35-15. *The record browser*

Thanks to the client-side features of the ItemView and the DataSource, you can edit as many records as you want, add new ones, and delete others completely on the client side, without calling the server at all. Finally, when you want to apply the batch of changes, you can use the Save Changes button to call the SetData() method in the EmployeesDataService, which will then perform a sequence of updates, inserts, and deletes.

■ **Note** Obviously, the ability to batch changes increases the likelihood of concurrency issues. If multiple users are changing the same records at once, updates may fail or wipe out other recent changes, depending on how you've written your update logic. As the Atlas platform matures, it will include more tools to help manage problems like these. Currently, the ItemView is not well suited to a professional website that needs ironclad reliability. The server-side data controls (such as the GridView, DetailsView, and FormView) are a better choice, because they restrict edits to one record at a time, which makes it easier to catch errors and handle them gracefully. (See Chapter 10 for an example that shows how to use templates to deal with conflicting edits in the GridView.)

To create the ItemView example, you need to begin by defining the templates you need. The ItemView works in a similar fashion to the ListView. It requires an empty tag where Atlas will insert the HTML for the ItemView:

```
<div id="itemView"></div>
```

And it needs at least one template in a hidden section of the page. The key difference is that this template uses edit controls instead of static elements such as <span> tags, because the example supports editing:

```
<div style="visibility:hidden;display:none">
  <div id="itemTemplate">
    Name: <input type="text" id="firstName" />
    <input type="text" id="lastName" /><br />
    (employee #<span id="employeeID"></span>)
    <br /><br />
    Title:
    <input id="title" style="width: 371px" /><br />
    <br />
    Notes:<br />
    <textarea id="notes"></textarea>
    <br /><br />
  </div>
  <br />
</div>
```

In the Atlas script section, you need to define the data service:

```
<dataSource id="dataSource" serviceURL="EmployeesDataService.asmx" autoLoad="true"/>
```

and you need to define the ItemView with all its bindings to the controls in your template:

```
<itemView id="itemView">
  <bindings>
    <binding dataContext="dataSource" dataPath="data" property="data"/>
    <binding dataContext="dataSource" dataPath="isReady" property="enabled"/>
  </bindings>

  <itemTemplate>
    <template layoutElement="itemTemplate">
      <textBox id="firstName">
        <bindings>
          <binding dataPath="FirstName" property="text" direction="InOut"/>
        </bindings>
      </textBox>
      <textBox id="lastName">
        <bindings>
          <binding dataPath="LastName" property="text" direction="InOut"/>
        </bindings>
      </textBox>
      <label id="employeeID">
        <bindings>
          <binding dataPath="EmployeeID" property="text"/>
        </bindings>
      </label>
      <textBox id="title">
        <bindings>
```

```
            <binding dataPath="Title" property="text" direction="InOut"/>
          </bindings>
        </textBox>
        <textBox id="notes">
          <bindings>
            <binding dataPath="Notes" property="text" direction="InOut"/>
          </bindings>
        </textBox>
      </template>
    </itemTemplate>
</itemView>
```

The ListView here has two noticeable differences from the ItemView example. First, the ItemView maps the DataSource.IsReady property to the ListView.Enabled property, ensuring that the user can't continue to make changes while an update is in progress:

```
<binding dataContext="dataSource" dataPath="isReady" property="enabled"/>
```

Second, all control bindings are declared with the direction InOut (instead of just In), which allows you to take the edited values and apply them to the data source when you save changes.

So far, you've created an ItemView that shows your records, but you've left out an important detail: the handy buttons that appear above and below the ItemView. The buttons that are placed above the ItemView allow you to move from one record to the next:

```
<input type="button" id="previousButton" value="Prev <" />
<input type="button" id="nextButton" value="Next >" />
<small>Record <span id="rowIndexLabel"></span></small>
```

■ **Note** You can place this HTML anywhere on your page. It isn't part of the ItemView template. In this example, the buttons are inserted just above the <div> tag that represents the ItemView.

To make this work, you need to define these controls in the Atlas script and bind them to various methods and properties in the data source. For example, the following declaration for the previous button ensures that it will be disabled when the ItemView.CanMovePrevious property is false and reacts when the button is clicked to invoke the ItemView.MovePrevious() method:

```
<button id="previousButton">
  <bindings>
    <binding dataContext="itemView" dataPath="canMovePrevious" property="enabled"/>
  </bindings>
  <click>
    <invokeMethod target="itemView" method="movePrevious" />
  </click>
</button>
```

Similar logic powers the next button and the label that displays the record number position:

```
<button id="nextButton">
  <bindings>
    <binding dataContext="itemView" dataPath="canMoveNext" property="enabled"/>
  </bindings>
  <click>
    <invokeMethod target="itemView" method="moveNext" />
  </click>
```

```
</button>
<label id="rowIndexLabel">
  <bindings>
    <binding dataContext="itemView" dataPath="dataIndex" property="text" />
  </bindings>
</label>
```

Obviously, you don't need to implement the previous and next functionality using buttons. You could use links instead, or something completely different, as long as you adjust the binding accordingly. You could even interact with the DataSource programmatically by adding a block of JavaScript code to your page.

The controls that appear below the ItemView allow you to delete a record, create a new record (which you can then fill with information), and apply all the changes you've made so far. Here's the HTML you need:

```
<input type="button" id="delButton" value="Delete" />
<input type="button" id="addButton" value="Add New" />
<input type="button" id="saveButton" value="Save All Changes" />
```

Here's how you define these controls in the Atlas script:

```
<button id="addButton">
  <bindings>
    <binding dataContext="dataSource" dataPath="isReady" property="enabled"/>
  </bindings>
  <click>
    <invokeMethod target="itemView" method="addItem" />
  </click>
</button>
<button id="delButton">
  <bindings>
    <binding dataContext="dataSource" dataPath="isReady" property="enabled"/>
  </bindings>
  <click>
    <invokeMethod target="itemView" method="deleteCurrentItem" />
  </click>
</button>
<button id="saveButton">
  <bindings>
    <binding dataContext="dataSource" dataPath="isDirtyAndReady"
     property="enabled"/>
  </bindings>
  <click>
    <invokeMethod target="dataSource" method="save" />
  </click>
</button>
```

Notice that the add and delete buttons trigger methods in the ItemView, but the save button triggers the DataSource.Save() method, which actually starts the callback to the server.

This completes the example. To see it in action, place breakpoints on the UpdateEmployee(), AddEmployee(), and DeleteEmployee() methods of the data service. Then make a few additions, deletions, and changes, and click the Save Changes method to start the update.

Atlas Server Controls

So far, you've focused on examples that use all-out Atlas programming. In fact, the pages you've seen don't have any server-side code at all. Instead, they implement the functionality entirely on the client side.

■ **Note** Interestingly, some Microsoft architects have mused about Atlas becoming a platform for client-side web development, *even without* ASP.NET. In other words, you could create ordinary HTML pages and equip them with Atlas features without any server-side code. Of course, this won't appeal to professional users who need to create applications that use server resources (such as databases) and have bulletproof security.

Most applications that use Atlas features won't be completely client oriented. Instead, you're likely to want to combine existing web forms that use server-side code with a dash of Atlas script in order to present a more responsive interface. Unfortunately, creating pages that have both server-side and client-side features is more complex than creating ordinary ASP.NET web forms. If this is the situation you're in, you might find that Atlas server controls provide a better solution.

Using Atlas server controls, you can work entirely with server-side code. The Atlas controls will emit the Atlas script they need, and they'll use the Atlas script libraries behind the scenes. The drawback of this approach is reduced flexibility. Although server-side controls are more productive, they also limit what you can do. For example, it becomes more difficult to use Atlas effects that require more than one control to interact.

The debate over the different approaches to Atlas coding is still ongoing. However, Microsoft has developed some remarkably imaginative server controls that encapsulate common patterns (such as the related drop-down lists you saw in the first example of this chapter) and offer some cutting-edge visual styling (such as maps and animations). Many of these details are still changing rapidly, but you can take a look at a dedicated book on Atlas such as *Foundations of Atlas* (Apress, 2006) or the Atlas site at `http://atlas.asp.net` for more information.

All in all, it's likely that Atlas server-side controls will be the preferred way to use Atlas—at least in the short term while developers take existing pages and extend them with a little Atlas magic. In the following sections, you'll see how to use the most important Atlas server controls.

Partial Rendering and the UpdatePanel

The UpdatePanel is a handy control that lets you take an ordinary page with server-side logic and make sure it refreshes itself in flicker-free Ajax style.

The basic idea is that you divide your web page into one or more distinct regions, each of which is wrapped inside an invisible UpdatePanel. When an event occurs in an UpdatePanel that would normally trigger a postback, the UpdatePanel intercepts the event and performs an asynchronous callback instead. Here's how it happens:

1. The user clicks a button inside an UpdatePanel.
2. Atlas performs a callback to the server.
3. On the server, your normal page life cycle executes, with all the usual events. Finally, the page is rendered to HTML and returned to the browser.
4. Atlas receives the full HTML and updates every UpdatePanel on the page by replacing its current HTML with the new content. (If a change has occurred to content that's not inside an UpdatePanel, it's ignored.)

■ **Note** The Atlas UpdatePanel serves a similar purpose to the DynamicPanel custom control that was developed using ASP.NET's client callback feature in Chapter 34. Both controls use an asynchronous call to fetch new content and update part of the page without a postback. However, the DynamicPanel in Chapter 34 is more limited, because you must use it with the DynamicPanelRefreshLink in order to trigger the asynchronous update. The UpdatePanel can intercept a postback that's triggered by any control inside the panel. Also, UpdatePanels work in concert—by default, every UpdatePanel is updated after every postback, although you can change this behavior.

The UpdatePanel control works in conjunction with the ScriptManager control. Before you can use an UpdatePanel, you need to set the ScriptManager.EnablePartialRendering property to true. You can then add one or more UpdatePanel controls to your page.

■ **Note** Unlike the standard ASP.NET Panel, an UpdatePanel has no visual appearance and doesn't support style settings. If you want to display a border around your UpdatePanel or change the background color, you'll need to place an ordinary Panel (or just a static <div> tag) in your UpdatePanel.

As you drag and drop controls in an UpdatePanel, the content appears in the <ContentTemplate> section. Here's an example of an UpdatePanel that contains a label and a button:

```
<atlas:UpdatePanel ID="UpdatePanel1" runat="server">
  <ContentTemplate>
    <asp:Label ID="Label1" runat="server" Text="Label"></asp:Label>
    <asp:Button ID="Button3" runat="server" Text="Button" />
  </ContentTemplate>
</atlas:UpdatePanel>
```

On the page, UpdatePanel renders itself as a <div> tag. However, you can configure the UpdatePanel so it renders itself as an inline element by changing the RenderMode property from Block to Inline. For example, you could take this step when you want to create an UpdatePanel that wraps text inside a paragraph or some other block element.

Figure 35-16 shows a sample web page that consists of three UpdatePanel controls (which have been highlighted using a off-white background color). Each UpdatePanel features the same content: a Label control and a Button control. Every time the page is posted to the server, the Page.Load event fills all three labels with the current time:

```
Protected Sub Page_Load(ByVal sender As Object, ByVal e As EventArgs)
    Label1.Text = DateTime.Now.ToLongTimeString
    Label2.Text = DateTime.Now.ToLongTimeString
    Label3.Text = DateTime.Now.ToLongTimeString
End Sub
```

This page demonstrates the flicker-free refreshing of an asynchronous callback. Click any button, and all three labels will be quietly updated.

If you have more than one UpdatePanel and each is completely self-contained, you can save a little work. Change the UpdatePanel.Mode property from Always to Conditional. Now, the UpdatePanel will refresh itself only if you cause a postback by clicking a control in that UpdatePanel. So if you use this with the example in Figure 35-16, when you click a button, the label in that panel will be updated; however, the other panels will remain untouched.

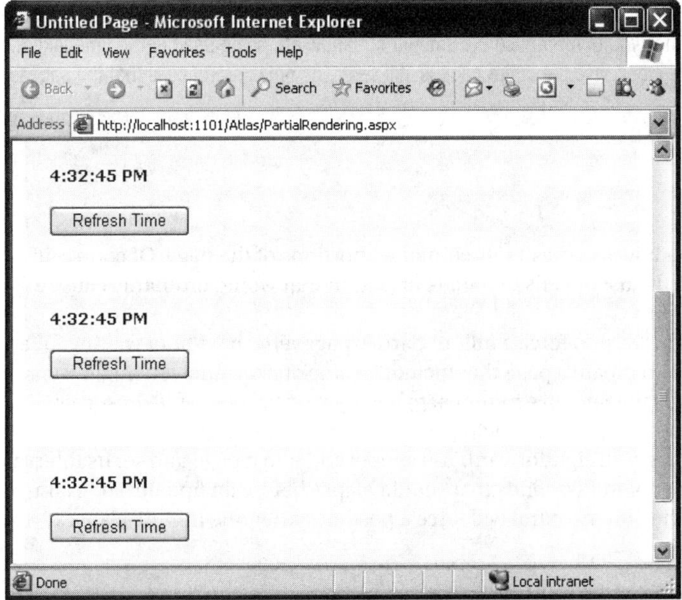

Figure 35-16. *Using the UpdatePanel to avoid postbacks*

■ **Tip** You can force a conditional UpdatePanel to refresh itself in one other way. When your server-side code runs, call the UpdatePanel.Update() method. This forces a panel refresh even if it wouldn't otherwise happen.

You have one other option—you can tell an UpdatePanel to render itself when an event is raised or a property is changed in another control on the page. To set up this relationship, you need to add a trigger to the UpdatePanel.

The following UpdatePanel is conditional and includes a trigger that's linked to the TextChanged event in another text box:

```
<atlas:UpdatePanel ID="UpdatePanel1" runat="server" Mode="Conditional">
  <ContentTemplate>
    <asp:Label ID="Label1" runat="server" Font-Bold="True"></asp:Label>
    <br />
    <br />
    <asp:Button ID="Button1" runat="server" Text="Refresh Time" />
  </ContentTemplate>
  <Triggers>
    <atlas:ControlEventTrigger ControlID="TextBox1" EventName="TextChanged" />
  </Triggers>
</atlas:UpdatePanel>
```

The content in this UpdatePanel will be refreshed in two situations: if you initiate a postback by clicking the button in this UpdatePanel or if you change the text in the text box and then click a button in another UpdatePanel.

■ **Note** When you use the UpdatePanel, you don't reduce the amount of bandwidth being used or the time taken to receive the response from the server, because the entire page is still sent. The only difference is that the page is updated without a distracting flicker.

Timed Refreshes

The previous section showed you how to refresh self-contained portions of the page. Of course, in order for this technique to work, the user needs to initiate an action that would ordinarily cause a postback, such as clicking a button.

In some situations, you might want to force a full- or partial-page refresh without waiting for a user action. For example, you might create a page that includes a stock ticker, and you might want to refresh this ticker periodically (say, every five minutes) to ensure it doesn't become drastically outdated. Atlas includes a TimerControl that can help you implement this design.

The TimerControl is refreshingly straightforward. You simply add it to a page and set its Interval property to the maximum number of milliseconds that should elapse before an update. For example, if you set Interval to 60000, the TimerControl will force a postback after one minute elapses.

```
<atlas:TimerControl ID="TimerControl1" runat="server" Interval="6000" />
```

■ **Note** Obviously, the TimerControl has the potential to greatly increase the overhead of your web application and reduce its scalability. Think carefully before introducing an automatic postback feature, and make the intervals long rather than short.

The TimerControl also raises a server-side Tick event, which you can handle to update your page. However, you don't necessarily need to use the Tick event, because the full-page life cycle executes when the timer fires. This means you can respond to other page and control events, such as Page.Load.

The TimerControl is particularly well suited to pages that use partial rendering, as discussed in the previous section. That's because a refresh in a partially rendered page might just need to change a single portion of the page. Furthermore, partial rendering makes sure your refreshes are much less intrusive. Unlike a full postback, a callback with partial rendering won't cause flicker and won't interrupt the user in the middle of a task.

To use the TimerControl with partial rendering, make sure the EnablePartialRendering property of the ScriptManager is set to true. Wrap the updateable portions of the page in UpdatePanel controls with the Mode set to Conditional, and add a trigger that forces an update whenever the timer fires:

```
<atlas:UpdatePanel ID="UpdatePanel1" runat="server" Mode="Conditional">
  <ContentTemplate>
    ...
  </ContentTemplate>
  <Triggers>
    <atlas:ControlEventTrigger ControlID="TimerControl1" EventName="Tick" />
  </Triggers>
</atlas:UpdatePanel>
```

All the other portions of the page can be left as is, or you can wrap them in conditional UpdatePanel controls with different triggers if you need to update them in response to other actions.

■ **Note** The current version of the TimerControl doesn't include a stop feature. This means the postbacks will continue endlessly while the page remains open. Several workarounds exist, which are discussed in the ASP.NET Atlas forums, but it's highly likely that future builds of Atlas will correct this problem.

Showing an Indicator During Time-Consuming Updates

Atlas also includes an UpdateProgress control that works in conjunction with partial rendering at the UpdatePanel. Essentially, the UpdatePanel allows you to show a message while a time-consuming update is underway.

■ **Note** The UpdatePanel is slightly misnamed. It doesn't actually indicate progress; instead, it provides a wait message that reassures the user that the page is still working and the last request is still being processed. You saw one implementation of this technique with a JavaScript page processor in Chapter 34.

When you use partial rendering and a callback is triggered, the callback happens asynchronously. That means the page remains active. The user can still type into input controls but can't trigger another postback. (For example, clicking the same Submit button twice in a row won't have any effect.) If the server-side processing happens quickly, the page may be refreshed before the user notices any delay. But if the server-side processing takes a more significant amount of time, the user needs to wait—and wonder if the page is working correctly.

When you add the UpdateProgress control, you get the ability to specify some content that will appear as soon as a callback is started and will disappear as soon as the callback is finished. This content can include a static message, but most people prefer to use an animated GIF. Often, this animated GIF simulates a progress bar, as shown in Figure 35-17.

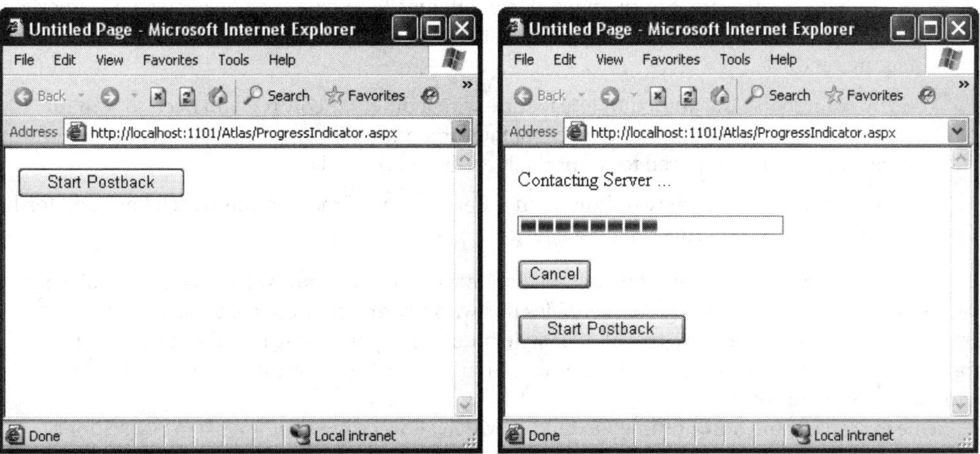

Figure 35-17. *A wait indicator*

The UpdateProgress control supports one other detail: a cancel button. If you add a button tag with the ID value abortButton, the user can click this button to cancel the asynchronous request. Here's the complete markup for the UpdateProgress control shown in Figure 35-17:

```
<atlas:UpdateProgress runat="server" id="updateProgress1">
  <ProgressTemplate>
    Contacting Server ... <br /><br />
    <img src="wait.gif" /><br /><br />
    <button id="abortButton" runat="server" type="button">Cancel</button>
    <br />
  </ProgressTemplate>
</atlas:UpdateProgress>
```

You can use additional JavaScript code to hide controls that shouldn't be used while the callback is underway.

■ **Tip** It makes sense to use an abort button for tasks that can be safely canceled because they don't affect external state. For example, users should be able to cancel time-consuming queries. However, it's not a good idea to add cancellation to an update operation, because the server will continue until it finishes the update, even if the client has stopped listening for the response.

Control Extenders

The Atlas team has been careful to avoid duplicating existing controls with Atlas variants. For example, it might seem tempting to create an AutoCompleteTextBox server control. However, this design introduces several problems:

- You need to replace your existing TextBox controls with AutoCompleteTextBox controls to use this functionality. This is a major (and potentially disruptive) change to make in an established page.
- If you have already extended the TextBox control or are using a third-party component that extends the TextBox control, you need to sacrifice these features.
- If another Atlas feature is implemented in a different TextBox-derived class (say, a NumericOnlyTextBox that discards any keypress that isn't a digit), you won't be able to use both features at once.
- If you want to use the autocomplete feature with a different control, you need to wait for someone to create a control that encapsulates that functionality. A significant amount of duplicated work is required to support all text-based controls.
- Developers need to learn two similar but different control models and switch back and forth between them depending on the scenario.

A better solution would allow you to add dynamic features to your website without replacing the controls you're already using. Atlas enables this with another new concept, called *control extenders*. Control extenders are bits of Ajax-style functionality that plug into ordinary server controls. To use a specific feature, you simply need to add the right control extender and attach it to the appropriate control.

One example is the AutoCompleteExtender, which allows you to show a list of suggestions while a user types in another control (such as a text box). Figure 35-18 shows the AutoCompleteExtender at work on an ordinary TextBox server control. As the user types, the drop-down list offers suggestions. If the user clicks one of these items in the list, the corresponding text is copied to the text box.

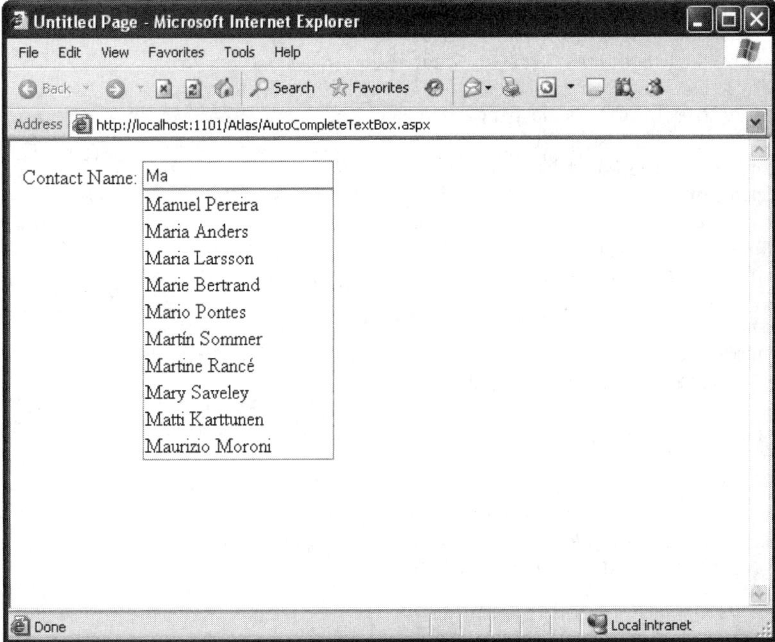

Figure 35-18. *Providing an autocomplete list of names*

Creating this example is fairly easy. First, you need an ordinary text box, like this:

```
Contact Name:<asp:TextBox ID="txtName" runat="server"></asp:TextBox>
```

Next, you need to add an AutoCompleteExtender control that extends the text box with the autocomplete feature. The trick is that the list of suggestions needs to be retrieved from a web method, which you need to create. Assuming you've created a web service named AutoComplete-Service with a method named GetNames() that provides the list of suggestions, this is the tag you need:

```
<atlas:AutoCompleteExtender runat="server"
 ID="autoComplete1">
  <atlas:AutoCompleteProperties TargetControlID="txtName"
   Enabled="True" ServicePath="AutoCompleteService.asmx"
   ServiceMethod="GetNames"
   MinimumPrefixLength="1"  />
</atlas:AutoCompleteExtender>
```

You'll notice that the AutoCompleteExtender links to the corresponding server control through the AutoCompleteProperties.TargetControlID property. It also uses a MinimumPrefixLength property, which allows you to wait until the user has entered a specific number of letters before using the list of suggestions. This is a handy feature if the list is so long that a single character won't provide a useful list of suggestions.

The most time-consuming part of this example is creating the GetNames() web method. It accepts two parameters, which indicate the text the user has typed so far and the desired number of matches (which is ten by default).

```
<WebMethod()> _
Public Function GetNames(ByVal prefixText As String,
         ByVal count As Integer) As List(Of String)

    If Context.Cache("NameList") Is Nothing Then
        Context.Cache.Insert("NameList", QueryNames(),
            Nothing, DateTime.Now.AddMinutes(60),
            TimeSpan.Zero)
    End If
    Dim names As List(Of String) =
         CType(Context.Cache("NameList"), List(Of String))
    Dim index As Integer = -1
    Dim i As Integer = 0
    Do While i < names.Count
        If names(i).StartsWith(prefixText) Then
            index = i
            Exit Do
        End If

        ' Give up if the search has passed to the next letter.
        ' (This improves performance.)
        If String.Compare(names(i), prefixText) = 1 Then
            Exit Do
        End If
        i += 1
    Loop

    ' Give up if there isn't a match.
    If index = -1 Then
        Return New List(Of String)()
    End If
    Dim wordList As List(Of String) = New List(Of String)()
    i = index
    Do While i < (index + count)
        ' Stop when the end of the list is reached.
        If i >= names.Count Then
            Exit Do
        End If

        ' Stop if the names stop matching.
        If (Not names(i).StartsWith(prefixText)) Then
            Exit Do
        End If

        wordList.Add(names(i))
        i += 1
    Loop
    Return wordList
End Function
```

Currently, Atlas provides only two control extenders: the AutoCompleteExtender shown in this example and a DragOverlayExtender that allows you to drag other elements (such as a panel) around the page. However, many more are possible, and the Atlas control toolkit provides a wide range of additional extenders.

The Atlas Control Toolkit

Even though the Atlas framework is still new and hasn't been finalized, developers have already started using it to build innovative controls and components. The best example is Microsoft's Atlas Control Toolkit, which is a remarkable collection of controls and control extenders that use Atlas features but can be dropped onto your web page like any ordinary server control. The Atlas Control Toolkit also provides an API you can use to develop your own Atlas-based controls.

The most remarkable part of the Atlas toolkit is that it's being developed using a collaborative, open source model that allows community participation. (You can suggest enhancements to existing controls or propose your own at `http://www.codeplex.com/Wiki/View.aspx?ProjectName=➥AtlasControlToolkit`.) When the toolkit is complete, it's expected to contain 50 to 100 controls, all with complete source code.

Currently, beta versions of the toolkit include the following components:

CascadingDropDown: This control lets you link drop-down lists without coding the solution by hand as shown in the first example of this chapter.

CollapsiblePanelExtender: This extender lets you collapse and expand panels on your page. The rest of the page content reflows around them automatically. You saw an example of collapsible content in this chapter, with the name box. The difference is that the name box relied on Atlas actions that you created and mapped by hand. The CollapsiblePanelExtender takes seconds to drop into a web page.

ConfirmButtonExtender: This extender adds a confirm dialog box that springs into action when you click a Button, LinkButton, or ImageButton control.

DragPanelExtender: This extender allows you to drag a panel around the page.

HoverMenuExtender: This extender allows content to pop up next to a control when the user hovers over it. This control uses a similar technique to the hover behavior you learned about earlier with the pop-up link box.

PopupControlExtender: This extender turns any panel into a pop-up box.

TextBoxWatermark: This extender allows you to automatically change the background color and supply specific text when a TextBox control is empty. For example, your text box might include the text *Enter Value* in light gray writing on a pale blue background. This text disappears while the cursor is positioned in the text box or once you've entered a value.

ToggleButtonExtender: This extender turns the ordinary ASP.NET CheckBox into an image check box.

AlwaysVisibleControlExtender: This extender allows you to dock a panel to a corner of the browser window and keep it in the same position, even when the user scrolls through the page.

DropShadowExtender: This extender adds attractive drop shadows to any control on the page.

ModalPopupExtender: This extender allows you to create the illusion of a modal dialog box by darkening the page, disabling controls, and showing a superimposed panel overtop.

RoundedCornersExtender: This extender rounds the corners of any control for a clean, professional look.

To use any of these controls, you simply need to drop it onto a form, set the appropriate properties, and run your page. Figure 35-19 shows the collapsible panel in both expanded and collapsed states. Figure 35-20 shows a draggable panel, both before and after dragging.

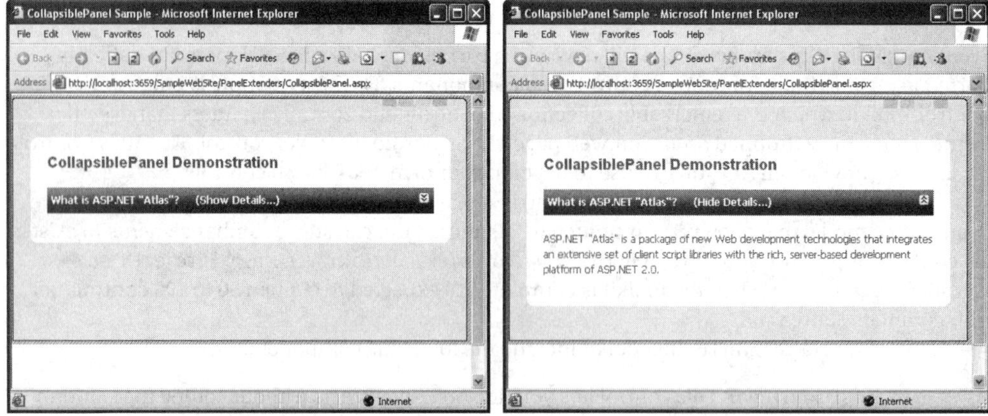

Figure 35-19. *A collapsible panel*

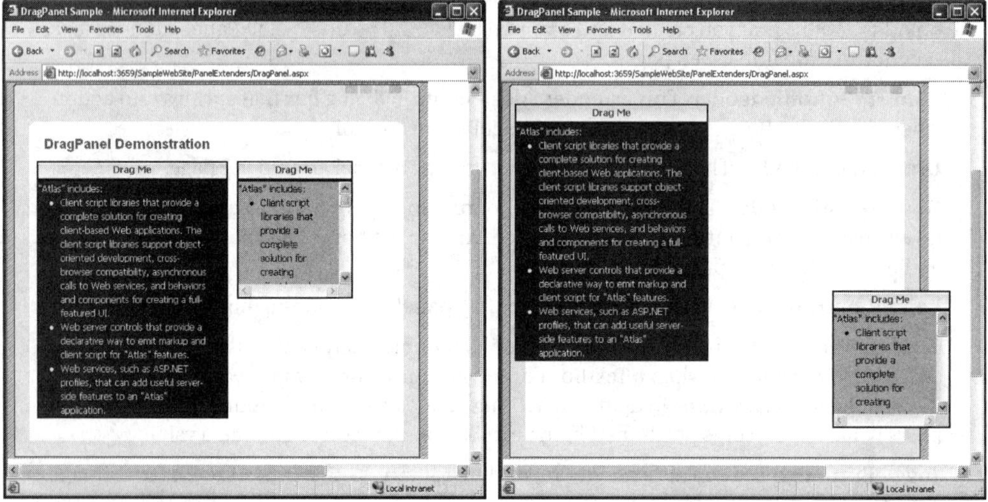

Figure 35-20. *A draggable panel*

Summary

In this chapter, you learned about Atlas, Microsoft's newest innovation in web programming. The most exciting feature of Atlas is that it isn't just another JavaScript library or a simple .NET component that simplifies callbacks. Instead, it's a multilayered platform that allows you to build more responsive and more dynamic pages—and, ultimately, an altogether different type of web application.

As you saw in this chapter, you can plug into the Atlas framework in three separate levels:

- You can write your own JavaScript code that calls server-side functionality. In this case, you expose the web methods you need and use automatically generated JSON proxies to call them.
- You can use a new standard—declarative Atlas script—to set up actions, bindings, and behaviors. You can even use client-side Atlas controls that have rich data-processing capabilities.
- You can keep using ordinary ASP.NET server controls but extend them with Atlas-fortified ingredients such as the UpdatePanel or use snazzy new controls and control extenders.

Remember, the Atlas platform is still evolving rapidly. To keep up with the latest developments, be sure to visit `http://atlas.asp.net`. In the future, you may also want to consult a dedicated book (such as *Foundations of Atlas* from Apress, ISBN 1-59059-647-1) that delves deeper into more specialized Atlas features (such as mapping and animation).

Index

Find it faster at http://superindex.apress.com/

Find it faster at http://superindex.apress.com/

Find it faster at http://superindex.apress.com/

Find it faster at http://superindex.apress.com/

Find it faster at http://superindex.apress.com/

D

Find it faster at http://superindex.apress.com/

Find it faster at http://superindex.apress.com/

E

Find it faster at http://superindex.apress.com/

F

Find it faster at http://superindex.apress.com/

G

Find it faster at http://superindex.apress.com/

H

Find it faster at http://superindex.apress.com/

I

Find it faster at http://superindex.apress.com/

Find it faster at http://superindex.apress.com/

M

Find it faster at http://superindex.apress.com/

Find it faster at http://superindex.apress.com/

Find it faster at http://superindex.apress.com/

Q

Find it faster at http://superindex.apress.com/

Find it faster at http://superindex.apress.com/

Find it faster at http://superindex.apress.com/

Find it faster at http://superindex.apress.com/

Find it faster at http://superindex.apress.com/

Find it faster at http://superindex.apress.com/

U

Find it faster at http://superindex.apress.com/

V

Find it faster at http://superindex.apress.com/

W

Find it faster at http://superindex.apress.com/

Find it faster at http://superindex.apress.com/

X

Z

Find it faster at http://superindex.apress.com/

Quickly Find Out What the Experts Know

Leading by innovation, Apress now offers you its ***SuperIndex***™, a turbocharged companion to the fine index in this book. The Apress ***SuperIndex***™ is a keyword and phrase-enabled search tool that lets you search through the entire Apress library. Powered by dtSearch™, it delivers results instantly.

Instead of paging through a book or a PDF, you can electronically access the topic of your choice from a vast array of Apress titles. The Apress ***SuperIndex***™ is the perfect tool to find critical snippets of code or an obscure reference. The Apress ***SuperIndex***™ enables all users to harness essential information and data from the best minds in technology.

No registration is required, and the Apress ***SuperIndex***™ is free to use.

1. Thorough and comprehensive searches of over 300 titles
2. No registration required
3. Instantaneous results
4. A single destination to find what you need
5. Engineered for speed and accuracy
6. Will spare your time, application, and anxiety level

Search now: ***http://superindex.apress.com***

forums.apress.com

FOR PROFESSIONALS BY PROFESSIONALS™

JOIN THE APRESS FORUMS AND BE PART OF OUR COMMUNITY. You'll find discussions that cover topics of interest to IT professionals, programmers, and enthusiasts just like you. If you post a query to one of our forums, you can expect that some of the best minds in the business—especially Apress authors, who all write with *The Expert's Voice*™—will chime in to help you. Why not aim to become one of our most valuable participants (MVPs) and win cool stuff? Here's a sampling of what you'll find:

DATABASES

Data drives everything.

Share information, exchange ideas, and discuss any database programming or administration issues.

INTERNET TECHNOLOGIES AND NETWORKING

Try living without plumbing (and eventually IPv6).

Talk about networking topics including protocols, design, administration, wireless, wired, storage, backup, certifications, trends, and new technologies.

JAVA

We've come a long way from the old Oak tree.

Hang out and discuss Java in whatever flavor you choose: J2SE, J2EE, J2ME, Jakarta, and so on.

MAC OS X

All about the Zen of OS X.

OS X is both the present and the future for Mac apps. Make suggestions, offer up ideas, or boast about your new hardware.

OPEN SOURCE

Source code is good; understanding (open) source is better.

Discuss open source technologies and related topics such as PHP, MySQL, Linux, Perl, Apache, Python, and more.

PROGRAMMING/BUSINESS

Unfortunately, it is.

Talk about the Apress line of books that cover software methodology, best practices, and how programmers interact with the "suits."

WEB DEVELOPMENT/DESIGN

Ugly doesn't cut it anymore, and CGI is absurd.

Help is in sight for your site. Find design solutions for your projects and get ideas for building an interactive Web site.

SECURITY

Lots of bad guys out there—the good guys need help.

Discuss computer and network security issues here. Just don't let anyone else know the answers!

TECHNOLOGY IN ACTION

Cool things. Fun things.

It's after hours. It's time to play. Whether you're into LEGO® MINDSTORMS™ or turning an old PC into a DVR, this is where technology turns into fun.

WINDOWS

No defenestration here.

Ask questions about all aspects of Windows programming, get help on Microsoft technologies covered in Apress books, or provide feedback on any Apress Windows book.

HOW TO PARTICIPATE:

Go to the Apress Forums site at **http://forums.apress.com/**.

Click the New User link.

Apress®

Apress License Agreement (Single-User Products)

THIS IS A LEGAL AGREEMENT BETWEEN YOU, THE END USER, AND APRESS. BY OPENING THE SEALED CD PACKAGE, YOU ARE AGREEING TO BE BOUND BY THE TERMS OF THIS AGREEMENT. IF YOU DO NOT AGREE TO THE TERMS OF THIS AGREEMENT, PROMPTLY RETURN THE UNOPENED DISK PACKAGE AND THE ACCOMPANYING ITEMS (INCLUDING WRITTEN MATERIALS AND BINDERS AND OTHER CONTAINERS) TO THE PLACE YOU OBTAINED THEM FOR A FULL REFUND.

APRESS SOFTWARE LICENSE

1. GRANT OF LICENSE. Apress grants you the right to use one copy of the enclosed Apress software programs collectively (the "SOFTWARE") on a single terminal connected to a single computer (e.g., with a single CPU). You may not network the SOFTWARE or otherwise use it on more than one computer or computer terminal at the same time.
2. COPYRIGHT. The SOFTWARE copyright is owned by Apress and is protected by United States copyright laws and international treaty provisions. The SOFTWARE contains licensed software programs, the use of which are governed by English language end user license agreements inside the licensed software programs. Therefore, you must treat each of the SOFTWARE programs like any other copyrighted material (e.g., a book or musical recording) except that you may either (a) make one copy of the SOFTWARE solely for backup or archival purposes, or (b) transfer the SOFTWARE to a single hard disk, provided you keep the original solely for backup or archival purposes. You may not copy the written material accompanying the SOFTWARE.
3. OTHER RESTRICTIONS. You may not rent or lease the SOFTWARE, but you may transfer the SOFTWARE and accompanying written materials on a permanent basis provided you retain no copies and the recipient agrees to the terms of this Agreement. You may not reverse engineer, decompile, or disassemble the SOFTWARE. If SOFTWARE is an update, any transfer must include the update and all prior versions. Distributors, dealers, and other resellers are prohibited from altering or opening the licensed SOFTWARE package.
4. By breaking the seal on the disc package, you agree to the terms and conditions printed in the Apress License Agreement. If you do not agree with the terms, simply return this book with the still-sealed CD package to the place of purchase for a refund.

DISCLAIMER OF WARRANTY

NO WARRANTIES. Apress disclaims all warranties, either express or implied, including, but not limited to, implied warranties of merchantability and fitness for a particular purpose, with respect to the SOFTWARE and the accompanying written materials. The software and any related documentation is provided "as is." You may have other rights, which vary from state to state.

NO LIABILITIES FOR CONSEQUENTIAL DAMAGES. In no event shall Apress be liable for any damages whatsoever (including, without limitation, damages from loss of business profits, business interruption, loss of business information, or other pecuniary loss) arising out of the use or inability to use this product, even if Apress has been advised of the possibility of such damages. Because some states do not allow the exclusion or limitation of liability for consequential or incidental damages, the above limitation may not apply to you.

U.S. GOVERNMENT RESTRICTED RIGHTS

The SOFTWARE and documentation are provided with RESTRICTED RIGHTS. Use, duplication, or disclosure by the Government is subject to restriction as set forth in subparagraph (c) (1) (ii) of The Rights in Technical Data and Computer Software clause at 52.227-7013. Contractor/manufacturer is Apress, 2560 Ninth Street, Suite 219, Berkeley, California, 94710.

This Agreement is governed by the laws of the State of California.

Should you have any questions concerning this Agreement, or if you wish to contact Apress for any reason, please write to Apress, 2560 Ninth Street, Suite 219, Berkeley, California, 94710.